# New
## Complete Book
### of the

# AMERICAN MUSICAL
# THEATER

*New*
*Complete Book*
*of the*

# AMERICAN MUSICAL

# THEATER

★

*David Ewen*

*Holt, Rinehart and Winston · New York · Chicago · San Francisco*

*Once again—*
## TO DICK RODGERS—
*whose half-century in the American
musical theater is such a salient
part of its history*

∞∞∞∞∞∞∞∞∞∞∞∞∞∞∞∞∞∞∞∞∞∞∞∞∞∞∞∞∞∞∞∞∞∞∞∞∞∞∞∞∞∞∞∞∞∞∞∞∞∞∞∞∞∞

Acknowledgment is made to the Theatre Collection,
New York Public Library at
Lincoln Center, Astor, Lenox, and Tilden Foundations,
for permission to reproduce
the photographs from The Vandamm Collection.

# CONTENTS

## ERRATA

Illustrations follow pages 228, 388, and 580 *not* pages 202, 394, and 586 as indicated in the list of illustrations.

# ILLUSTRATIONS

○○○○○○○○○○○○○○○○○○○○○○○○○○○○○○○○○○○○○○○○○○○○○○○○○○○○○○○○○○○○

ix

# PREFACE

ooooooooooooooooooooooooooooooooooooooooooooooooooooooooooo

Possibly the most significant development in the American stage of the past
dozen years has been the growth in originality, vitality, and especially popularity of the musical theater. This is the reason why in that time the musical
has reached out to a far larger ticket-buying public than the serious theater.
Since 1960, for example, only three nonmusicals achieved runs of a thousand
or more performances, while there were nine musicals to do so. Not one
nonmusical survived two thousand performances; four musicals did, and
one of them even went beyond the three-thousand figure.

Nor should there be much doubt that a far greater interest has been
generated in the musical theater these last twelve years than in any similar
time span before this. This interest is reflected in the fact that since 1958
twenty-eight musicals had initial runs of five hundred or more performances
(something no other twelve-year period before this could duplicate), with
nine of these productions exceeding one thousand performances; in the fact

that Off Broadway has made such valuable contributions to the musical theater, with five productions since 1958 each exceeding seven hundred performances, several of them unquestioned stage masterpieces; in the fact that there has been such a proliferation throughout the country of touring companies, stock companies, companies performing in summer tents, and semiprofessional companies presenting a rich and varied repertory of musical comedies, including many from past seasons; in the fact that since 1958 so many Broadway musicals have been transformed into multimillion-dollar screen productions (*Funny Girl, Finian's Rainbow, Hello, Dolly!, The Music Man, Paint Your Wagon, Flower Drum Song, Bye Bye Birdie, Li'l Abner, Gypsy, West Side Story, Can-Can, A Funny Thing Happened on the Way to the Forum, How to Succeed in Business Without Really Trying, Song of Norway, Camelot, The Sound of Music, My Fair Lady, Sweet Charity,* and so on); that musicals have even been made into highly successful television specials (*Roberta,* not once but twice; *Kiss Me, Kate; Brigadoon,* which had to be repeated; *Annie Get Your Gun; The Fantasticks;* et cetera). This ever-mounting interest in musicals has also been reflected in the way in which the musical theater has been adopted by the rest of the world. In 1958, an American musical presented abroad, whether in English or in a translation, was a comparative rarity. Today the presentation of American musicals in foreign translations in distant capitals has become so commonplace that a Japanese-language production of *Fiddler on the Roof,* for example, arouses little surprise.

Such growth of interest in our musical theater, both at home and abroad, makes necessary a totally new approach to a source book on the subject. What was serviceable in 1958—in my own *Complete Book of the American Musical Theater,* published that year—is no longer so today. A whole generation of brilliant young librettists, lyricists, and composers dominate the current theater. Their biographies and their work must be included. A new genre of the musical theater has sprung into existence, a child of our disturbed times: those unconventional rock musicals with very little plot and a good deal of controversial procedures, routines, and vocabulary. They must be discussed.

In addition, audiences seem far more sophisticated today than they were a decade back; they have a far greater curiosity in past musicals that had been excluded from my earlier book—for example, some of the less familiar works of masters like Gershwin, Rodgers, Porter, and Berlin. And then, musicals previously treated cursorily must now be written about in depth —audiences today wanting to know so much *more* than ever before.

All these facts were taken into account when the plan to bring out a revised edition of my older book was permanently shelved in favor of a newly conceived project, with a new format and greatly expanded material.

I estimate that about ten percent of the material of the older book has been retained. It has been retained because no additional data on some musicals of the distant past were available to me; also because I felt that no further elaboration or revision of a handful of musicals, or a handful of biographies, was required. But the rest of this book contains altogether new material, presented in a new way.

In the present volume, I have adopted what I feel is a more functional, less cumbersome format than the earlier book showed. The book now offers a panorama of musical productions since 1866 to the present time alphabetically, the way an encyclopedia would. Biographies of leading composers, as well as of leading librettists and lyricists, then follow. At the end of each biography is a cross-reference to those musicals by the composer, librettist, or lyricist under discussion to be found in the book proper. (This cross-reference appears in two ways; alphabetically—the way in which the musicals can be found in the book; and chronologically—for those interested in tracing the development of any given composer, lyricist, or librettist.) An appendix comprises a chronology of the musical theater: that is, from 1866 on, of the musicals with which this book is concerned. This is done for those aficionados who like a bird's-eye view of the changing musical theater. A second section in the Appendix lists the outstanding songs from the musical already discussed, together with the productions in which these songs can be found and the performers who introduced them.

This book has been expanded to embrace not three hundred and ten musicals (as in the former book) but almost five hundred. The biographical section has also been amplified to include over one hundred and sixty composers, librettists, and lyricists—more than doubling the number that had appeared previously. More information about production history, plot, the stars, the songs, and other relevant data put the new emphasis on comprehensiveness; in the earlier book it had been on compactness and succinctness.

Nevertheless, the basic aim of the book has not changed. To emphasize this, I would like to repeat a paragraph from the earlier book: "All the veins of the American musical theater have been tapped: extravaganzas, spectacles and burlesques; operettas and comic operas; revues, both the lavish kind and the intimate variety; musical comedies and musical plays. Material about musicals not only of a bygone era but even some of the recent past is not easily available except to those ready to wade laboriously through clipping files in libraries. This volume hopes to fill this hiatus in the literature of the American musical stage. . . . The book has a dual purpose: to satisfy curiosity in regard to productions of the past about which much still is said but little remembered, and to revive in theatergoers memories of enchanted evenings."

I would also like to summarize here, as before, the considerations guiding my selection of musicals.

1. Only the work of American composers is considered. However, the term "American" is used in its broadest possible conception: anyone born in this country; anyone naturalized as a citizen; and anyone who has established permanent residence in the United States and used Broadway, rather than the foreign stage, as the point of origin for his work. Significant foreign musicals, imported to the Broadway theater, are considered only if an American composer has served as a collaborator or if the music of an important American composer was interpolated into the score. All other foreign importations, however successful they may have proved in New York—say, *Florodora* in the past, or *Oliver!, La Plume de Ma Tante,* or *Oh! Calcutta!* more recently, the comic operas of Gilbert and Sullivan, the opéras bouffes of Offenbach, or the sophisticated musicals of Noël Coward—must be ignored.

2. Since this volume is devoted to the popular musical theater, opera—even those by Gian Carlo Menotti, many of which originated in the Broadway theater rather than in the opera house—cannot come within its scope. A few exceptions, however, had to be made. Marc Blitzstein's *The Cradle Will Rock* and *Regina* are designated as operas, indeed have been presented in opera houses, even though they were first heard in Broadway theaters; but they are discussed in this book because, in my opinion, they are essentially Broadway musical plays in the same way Leonard Bernstein's *West Side Story* and Frank Loesser's *The Most Happy Fella* are musical plays. George Gershwin's *Porgy and Bess* has roots so deeply embedded in the popular musical theater that, though indubitably a folk opera, its omission from this book would have created a deplorable gap.

3. All major box-office successes have been included, indeed, all musical productions with an initial run of more than five hundred performances.

For the sake of clarification, it should be pointed out that the number of consecutive performances enjoyed by any production is not always an accurate barometer of its success. Of course, any musical, past or present, that has lasted for, say, 750 or 800 performances, has yielded handsome profits to all concerned, while a run of over a thousand performances has always proved a bonanza. But in years past a very short run did not necessarily imply failure. In fact, there have been many musicals with comparatively negligible runs on

Broadway that were immensely successful. In the first decade of the twentieth century there were numerous productions with an initial run of less than a hundred performances (George M. Cohan's *Little Johnny Jones,* for example), yet they made a good deal of money. This was due to the fact that the Broadway run was just the starting point for extended tours, where highly impressive revenues were gathered by the producers. Low production costs, low salaries (except for the stars), and the fact that so many musicals were being written by staff composers and staff librettists who drew a modest weekly salary in place of royalties made it possible for a musical produced between 1910 and 1920 to achieve hit status with a run of two hundred performances. In the 1920's and 1930's a run of between two and three hundred performances, and in the 1940's a run of three to four hundred performances, were considered highly profitable ventures.

Take, for example, the 1930's—a very good decade for musicals. It brought us the first musical to win the Pulitzer Prize, *Of Thee I Sing,* and with it such unforgettable names as *Flying High, Fine and Dandy, Girl Crazy, Three's a Crowd, The Band Wagon,* George White's *Scandals of 1931, Cat and the Fiddle, Music in the Air, The Gay Divorce, As Thousands Cheer, Roberta, Anything Goes, On Your Toes, Babes in Arms, Pins and Needles, Hellzapoppin', Leave It to Me, Du Barry Was a Lady*—surely as distinguished a gathering of stage musicals as any decade before or since could provide. All were box-office successes. Except for two musicals—*Pins and Needles* and *Hellzapoppin'*—which became phenomena in musical-theater history by achieving then unprecedented runs of over one thousand performances, not one of the above musicals had a run of five hundred performances. Only three equaled or passed the four-hundred mark; only five others went over the three-hundred mark. Not one of the splendiferous revues mounted by Ziegfeld, George White, Earl Carroll, Irving Berlin, and their competitors ever achieved five hundred performances.

For a long time five hundred performances represented a healthy state of affairs for a musical. No longer so! Today, with production costs skyrocketing, there have been quite a number of musicals that lasted on Broadway over five hundred performances and yet lost a good deal of money: *Golden Boy,* despite its 569 performances, lost $120,000; *What Makes Sammy Run?,* despite its 540 performances, lost $285,000; *Milk and Honey* ran for 543 performances but lost $79,000.

4. These and other so-called failures are not ignored in this book. Throughout the years there have appeared musicals that for one reason or another were failures when first given and were rarely, if ever, revived. Yet a good many of these plays have considerable historic, dramatic, or mu-

sical interest—enough to have them still remembered and spoken of. Some
are of importance in the evolution and development of the musical theater,
particularly those of the distant past; some had provocative, exciting texts;
some were the springboard from which famous stars and songs leaped to
fame; some had unusual routines and procedures; some were thoroughly exciting novelties. Since a knowledgeable theatergoer might from time to time
wish to refer to such plays, these musicals have been included; in most cases
there exists no other book where ample material about them can be found.
To this category of box-office failures belong Vincent Youmans' *Rainbow*
(which was years ahead of its time in musical-play writing); *Allegro* by
Rodgers and Hammerstein (which Hammerstein long dreamed of revising
and reviving); *Paint Your Wagon* by Lerner and Loewe (which suddenly
and inexplicably became a multimillion-dollar motion picture directed by
Joshua Logan eighteen years after it had failed on Broadway); Kurt Weill's
bitter satire on war, *Johnny Johnson; Regina,* Marc Blitzstein's remarkable
musical adaptation of Lillian Hellman's *The Little Foxes;* Leonard Bernstein's *Candide,* a gem through and through; and such other delights as *From
the Second City,* and the rock musical *Celebration.* These and many others
like them—however dismal their fiscal ledgers may read—are the kind of
shows which, it seems to me, a reference book on the musical theater aiming
at comprehensiveness cannot afford to ignore.

DAVID EWEN

*Miami, Florida*
*January, 1970*

# INTRODUCTION

○○○○○○○○○○○○○○○○○○○○○○○○○○○○○○○○○○○○○○○○○○○○○○○○○○○○○○○○○○○○

Since *The Black Crook* (1866) was the first American musical production in which there could be detected some of the ritual that the American musical theater would subsequently pursue, it is often singled out as our first musical comedy. But musical productions of other varieties had existed in this country long before *The Black Crook.* What is generally conceded to be the first musical performance on our stage took place during the Colonial period: *Flora,* a ballad opera, given in a courtroom in Charleston, South Carolina, on February 8, 1735. The English ballad opera subsequently became almost as popular in the Colonies as it was in the mother country. Through its interpolation of popular songs (to which new lyrics were adapted) within the context of a spoken play, the ballad opera was the first suggestion, however faint, of musical comedy.

Other kinds of musical-stage performances besides the ballad opera became popular in this country after the Revolution. Early in the 1800's a native theatrical product, designated as "burlesque," sprang to popularity. The burlesque of this period should not be confused with that of a later era. Its emphasis in the early 1800's was not on sex but on parody and caricature. The first such successful performance came in 1828 with a burlesque on *Hamlet* by John Poole. After that, burlesques of other famous plays, and of performers, became standard operating procedure on the New York stage. Perhaps the best of these was *La Mosquita* (1838), in which William Mitchell satirized the celebrated Viennese dancer Fanny Elssler.

Burlesque left its mark on the American stage for years to come. Travesties like *Evangeline* (1874) and *Adonis* (1884) were burlesques in the style and format crystallized a half-century earlier. The extravaganzas of Weber and Fields, the burlesques of Harrigan and Hart, and outstanding productions like Charley Hoyt's *A Trip to Chinatown* (1891) were all legitimate offspring of early burlesque. Even in a much later era the influence of caricature could be detected: in the rowdy and uninhibited horseplay of Olsen and Johnson in their revues *Hellzapoppin'* and *Sons o' Fun* in 1938 and 1940; and in the more subtle take-offs on current plays and performers found both in lush and intimate revues after 1910.

Burlesque could also be found in the minstrel show, which blossomed on the American stage just before the Civil War, to become another significant genre of our musical theater. The minstrel show, as finally crystallized by Ed Christy, was in a three-part format, the last being a burlesque on all previous activity. The first part of the traditional minstrel show was the olio, made up of variety entertainment; the second was a fantasia, or free-for-all, in which individual performers were featured in their specialties. The revue of a later era generally was a partial development and outgrowth of the first two sections of the minstrel show. The revue also profited from styles, techniques, and formats devised and perfected in the variety show, or vaudeville, which displaced the minstrel show in public favor in the latter part of the nineteenth century.

Some of the elements of ballad opera, burlesque, and the minstrel show were subsequently absorbed by the later-day musical theater. But any resemblance between these early stage plays and musical productions of a later period is, at best, remote. Such resemblance becomes somewhat less remote when we begin to consider the extravaganza, which flourished after the end of the Civil War.

A favorable climate for public acceptance of the extravaganza had been created by the so-called pantomime, which enjoyed a vogue on the New York stage several years before the extravaganza. Usually deriving its plots and characters from fairy tales or *Mother Goose,* the pantomime exploited not only song, dance, and comedy but also spectacular stage effects. The heyday of the pantomime came with such productions as *Humpty Dumpty,* which starred the foremost pantomimist of his day, George L. Fox.

It is but a short step from the pantomime to the extravaganza. The term "extravaganza" makes its first appearance in the American theater with *Novelty, with the Laying of the Atlantic Cable,* produced in New York in 1857 by the Ronzani troupe, a European ballet company. *Novelty* was not a success, but the extravaganza was here to stay. It was the foundation upon which the structure of our musical theater was to be erected.

*The Black Crook* was not only the most successful of these extravaganzas but also the most successful musical production of any genre seen in this country up to 1866. Its significance, however, rests not merely on its box-office appeal but more specifically on the fact that it was the first musical in America to indicate some of the procedures of later stage productions. In its strong emphasis on chorus girls in pink tights or diaphanous costumes, in its concern for stunning stage effects and spectacle, in its dedication to large dance sequences, *The Black Crook* created a tradition that such later showmen as Florenz Ziegfeld would carry on, that was to prosper for about a decade at the Winter Garden in plays starring Al Jolson and for about twenty years at the Hippodrome Theater, and that was suddenly to crop up again in the middle 1930's in *Jumbo.*

If extravaganza still is not musical comedy, the latter is not far off. In 1879 Nate Salsbury presented a "burlesque-extravaganza," *The Brook,* which—through the plot device of a picnic—made a first tentative effort to integrate text, comedy, song, and dance. Primitive and naïve though it was, *The Brook* is so much in the overall pattern of later musical comedies that it comes as no surprise to learn that the term "musical comedy" is used in conjunction with this play—a description by its producer. The first time the term "musical comedy" was used was in 1874 for *Evangeline.*

A powerful influence was now exerted on the American musical theater: European operettas, comic operas, and opéras bouffes dominated the American stage in the 1880's and 1890's. America became enchanted with the glamor world of make-believe and the gay spirit evoked by the theater of Offenbach, Suppé, Johann Strauss II, and, most of all, by Gilbert and Sullivan. *Pinafore,* particularly, was a rage. Introduced to America at the Boston Museum on November 15, 1878, it achieved a triumph equaled by few productions of that era. In one season ninety different companies presented *Pinafore* throughout the country—five different companies running simultaneously in New York alone. There were performances by children's groups, colored groups, and religious groups. There were numerous parodies. Its catch phrases ("What, never? No, never!" and, "For he himself has said it") entered the nation's speech. A success of such proportions affected the theater of the day profoundly, and in more ways than one.

Through *Pinafore,* the musical theater acquired a large, new clientele—women and children. It must be remembered that before *Pinafore,* the stage was looked upon with suspicion by the respectable American family, glorifying as it often did females in various stages of deshabille. *The Black Crook,* for example, was violently denounced in press and pulpit as devil's brew. Consequently, women and children rarely went to the theater—that is, not until *Pinafore* proved that a stage presentation could be wholesome and refined entertainment.

Besides winning for the theater a large and formerly untapped reservoir of theatergoers, *Pinafore* was largely responsible for encouraging American librettists and composers to emulate Gilbert and Sullivan. Two of the earliest American comic operas were obvious and undisguised imitations of *The Mikado:* Willard Spencer's *The Little Tycoon* and Reginald de Koven's *The Begum.*

*The Little Tycoon,* with its 500 performances in Philadelphia before appearing in New York, had the longest run of any American stage production up to that time. This success was decisive proof that an American-made operetta could prove as popular with audiences as a foreign importation. The inevitable result was that other American composers and writers were stirred to emulation. Thus was ushered in a golden age of American comic operas and operettas, first with Reginald de Koven's *Robin Hood,* and after that with the beloved operettas of Victor Herbert, the first great composer for the American stage. Up until about 1930 the American operetta was in its glory, and with such varied composers as Gustav Luders, Ludwig Englander, Gustave Kerker, Karl Hoschna, Rudolf Friml, and Sigmund Romberg. The era of operetta ended with Romberg; but by then the operetta had succeeded in establishing in the American theater a single package labeled "entertainment," coordinating song, dance, comedy, spectacle, burlesque, and large production numbers.

The problem was now to endow such entertainment with contemporary interest and an American identity. Most of the American-written operettas and comic operas were patterned after European models and had a decided European personality. Such a contemporary immediacy and American identity were first realized by George M. Cohan in the early 1900's, with brash, breezy, energetic musicals like *Little Johnny Jones, George Washington, Jr.,* and *Forty-five Minutes from Broadway*. Here the characterization, dialogue, situations, songs, and frequently locale were American to the very core; so were the tempo, spirit, drive, and raciness with which each play was imbued. This was something new and vital for the American stage—something soon also to be found in the work of other composers, notably A. Baldwin Sloane in *Hen Pecks* and *Summer Widowers* and Irving Berlin in *Watch Your Step*. This, at last, was American musical comedy, with some of the clichés, formulas, and stereotypes to which it would henceforth cling.

While American musical comedy was finally coming into existence, another important branch of the musical theater was beginning to flower. It was the revue. The revue, as we have already suggested briefly, was merely an extension of the fantasia section of the minstrel show (in which individual performers did their pet routines) and of the variety show, or vaudeville, entertainment that was prospering in the 1880's in show places like the Tony Pastor Music Hall. To the varied song-and-dance, comedy, and novelty features of minstrel show and vaudeville were added the stage embellishments of the extravaganza (spectacular sets and costumes, stunning stage effects, attractive females in provocative dress and poses, impressive production numbers) and the main attractions of old-time burlesque (satire, travesty, horseplay).

The revue was a conception of George W. Lederer, who rented the Casino Theater in 1894 to present his *Passing Show*. Its success was so immediate and substantial that as early as 1895 similar revues began to sprout on the New York stage. Then in 1907 Florenz Ziegfeld produced the first of his *Follies;* in 1912 J. J. Shubert, the first of his *Passing Shows* (not to be confused with the 1894 *Passing Show* presented by Lederer); in 1919 George White, the first of his *Scandals;* in 1921 Irving Berlin, the first of his *Music Box Revues*. The lush revue was now in its heyday. It passed that heyday in the late 1940's, then seemed to lose caste completely, probably a victim of television, now providing similarly opulent entertainment on a giant scale.

With the passage of time and the accumulation of experience, production techniques grew more ambitious, stage techniques slicker, and techniques in writing music, lyrics, and dialogue more subtle and sophisticated. The revue and the musical comedy prospered in the 1920's and 1930's as more and more they began to tap the talent of creative and imaginative composers, lyricists, librettists, stage directors, scenic and costume designers, and dance directors.

But, in most instances, the revue and the musical comedy of this period adhered to a set pattern and time-tried methods. In the revue one producer tried to outdo another in extravagance of sets and costumes, complexity of stage effects, and in the display of female pulchritude, while skits, sketches, blackouts, songs, dances, and production numbers followed a consistent program. In musical comedy, too, tradition was slavishly adhered to. Plot, characters, and setting were all just a convenient hook on which to hang song, dance, and comedy. The relevancy of such routines within the text was not important; what was important was the interest of these individual routines.

Yet such arbitrary and undeviating procedures were able to yield rich results in productions filled with the magic of wonderful songs, dances, comedy, and the performances of lustrous stars—musicals like Jerome Kern's *Sally; Good News* of De Sylva, Brown, and Henderson; Cole Porter's *Anything Goes;* George Gershwin's *Oh, Kay!;* or *A Connecticut Yankee* of Rodgers and Hart. And that these rigid formulas and patterns can still yield inexhaustible riches in terms of stage entertainment is proved by such more recent productions as Irving Berlin's *Annie Get Your Gun;* Cole Porter's *Kiss Me, Kate;* Frank Loesser's *Guys and Dolls;* Leonard Bernstein's *Wonderful Town; The Pajama Game* by Richard Adler and Jerry Ross; Frank Loesser's *How to Succeed in Business Without Really Trying;* Jerry Herman's *Hello, Dolly!;* and *Funny Girl* by Jule Styne and Bob Merrill.

But from time to time—and increasingly so in recent years—there have been bold attempts to revolutionize the techniques and concepts of the musical theater. One such effort took place as early as 1915, when the so-called "Princess Theater Shows" of Kern-Bolton-Wodehouse represented a reaction against the plush, elaborately designed comedies and operettas then in vogue. These little musicals helped to introduce a new note of intimacy, economy, and informality, a welcome change from the ostentation and display then current on the stage.

A reaction of a similar kind took place with the revue in the 1920's. In 1922 a modest affair called *The Grand Street Follies* was put on in downtown New York. Equipped with more talent and imagination than finances, these *Follies* had to emphasize wit, sophistication, satire, and freshness of ideas over the star system and elaborate staging. Simplicity and a lack of pretension entered the revue. Thus the "intimate" revue came into being. It flourished within the next two decades or so with productions such as *The Garrick Gaieties, The Little Shows, Pins and Needles,* and their numerous contemporaries, successors, and imitators.

An even more radical departure from accepted values in the musical theater came with several writers making a conscious effort to bring to musical comedy originality of subject matter, authenticity of characterization and background, dramatic truth, and freshness of viewpoint. This was a studied effort to make of musical comedy an integrated artistic creation. These writers and composers searched for a more intimate relationship between all the elements of the musical theater. Their aim was to have each song, dance sequence, comedy routine, and production number rise naturally, perhaps inevitably, from the context of the play. Among those who progressed along these lines most boldly were Rodgers and Hart in plays such as *On Your Toes* and *Pal Joey,* Jerome Kern with *Show Boat, Music in the Air,* and *The Cat and the Fiddle,* Gershwin's *Of Thee I Sing,* and Vincent Youmans' *Rainbow.*

And so, slowly, the musical play came into existence—with Rodgers and Hammerstein, Kurt Weill, and productions such as Frank Loesser's *The Most Happy Fella,* Leonard Bernstein's *West Side Story, My Fair Lady* by Frederick Loewe and Alan Jay Lerner, *Fiddler on the Roof* by Jerry Bock and Sheldon Harnick, *Man of La Mancha* by Mitch Leigh and Joe Darion. Dramatic text, musical score, and ballet now acquired new scope and breadth and achieved a singleness of thought and spirit heretofore found only in opera and music drama. Sometimes realism, profound human values—even tragedy—were permitted to intrude into a world previously dedicated only to escapism; sometimes American folklore was accentuated.

In her autobiography Mary Garden has remarked that in her opinion native American opera of the future will probably resemble *South Pacific* and *The King and I.* Perhaps these two plays of Rodgers and Hammerstein or Kurt Weill's *Lost in the Stars* or Bernstein's *West Side Story* are not American operas in the strict sense of the term. But there can be no question that they are vital, dynamic, living theater.

The American musical has traveled a long way since *The Black Crook,* and tortuous has been the road. Today, as yesterday, its goal is entertainment. But today it is also sometimes deeply moving, unforgettable art.

*Part One*

# MUSICAL SHOWS

ADONIS (1884), *a burlesque-extravaganza with book and lyrics by William F. Gill and Henry E. Dixey. Music by Edward E. Rice. Presented by William Gill at the Bijoux Theater on September 4. Cast included Henry E. Dixey, Amelia Summerville, and George Howard (603 performances).*

*Adonis* was the first Broadway musical to have a consecutive Broadway run of over five hundred performances. (Not for another decade would this happen, and when it did, with *A Trip to Chinatown,* the run was even longer.) Before *Adonis* came to New York it had enjoyed a successful engagement in Chicago, and after it left New York it toured the United States and even played in London.

It was Henry E. Dixey's show from beginning to end; he played the leading role more than one thousand times. The play burlesqued the theme of Pygmalion and Galatea: a statue becomes human and gets enmeshed in all kinds of unusual and frequently amusing situations. Within such a context,

3

Henry E. Dixey was given ample opportunities to dance, sing, be funny, indulge in his inimitable gift at improvisation, and look strikingly handsome, particularly when he wore tightly fitting silk tights. He did everything required of him so admirably that he became the matinee idol of his time. Largely because of his performance, people kept coming to see *Adonis* again and again—a fact of which the authors took cognizance by continually introducing new lines, situations, and songs (some of timely interest), while Dixey himself was perpetually improvising new material for himself at the whim of the moment. As the New York *Dramatic Mirror* reported at the time, *Adonis* was "an institution to be regularly patronized like the El railways or the Eden Musee."

The leading songs included "I'm a Merry Little Mountain Maid," "Most Romantic Meeting," and "The Blushing Bride."

ALARUMS AND EXCURSIONS. *See* FROM THE SECOND CITY.

ALLEGRO (1947), *a musical play with book and lyrics by Oscar Hammerstein II. Music by Richard Rodgers. Presented by the Theater Guild at the Majestic Theater on October 10. Stage production supervised by Lawrence Langner and Theresa Helburn. Directed and with dances by Agnes de Mille. Cast included John Battles, Roberta Jonay, William Ching, Annamary Dickey, and (in a minor role) Lisa Kirk (315 performances).*

This was the first Rodgers and Hammerstein musical play for which Hammerstein provided an original text rather than an adaptation. He chose a subject close to his (and Rodgers') heart: the struggle between materialism and idealism, between success and self-fulfillment as a human being and a member of society. It was a significant theme—particularly unusual and fresh for the musical theater at that time—and it was developed without compromise, often with profound insight, and sometimes with satirical overtones. But, regrettably, both Rodgers and Hammerstein (undoubtedly made bolder by the fantastic success of their first two musicals, *Oklahoma!* and *Carousel*) soon became more intrigued with experiment, innovation, and unorthodox procedures than in the subject they were developing. They were like children more fascinated by the inner mechanism of a complicated toy than by what the toy is meant to do. This passion for seeking out new methods and techniques may very well be the reason why *Allegro* was a failure with the general public. But it was a noble failure, one that must command the respect of all true lovers of the musical theater.

The plot traces the biography of a physician—Dr. Joseph Taylor, Jr. (John Battles), son of a small town doctor, Joseph Taylor, Sr. (William

Ching). The son is born in 1905 and raised in his home town. He completes his out-of-town education, weathers the Depression, and returns home to join his father in the general practice of medicine. But after Joe marries his childhood sweetheart, Jennie Brinker (Roberta Jonay), she becomes an ambitious woman, smothered by the narrowness of life in her home town. She persuades Joe to move on to Chicago. There he acquires a large practice of wealthy neurotics and hypochondriacs, becomes rich, and moves with the social elite. When he learns that Jennie has been unfaithful to him, Joe suddenly realizes how empty his life in Chicago has been. Idealism now conquers over materialism. He returns at last to his small town and his comparatively humble practice, the point at which the play ends.

The story is told not only through action and dialogue but also through song, dance, lights, and colors. The score contributed two Rodgers and Hammerstein "standards." One was a touching number about the quiet joys of a happy marriage, "A Fellow Needs a Girl," the duet of father and mother Taylor, sung by William Ching and Annamary Dickey. The other was "The Gentleman Is a Dope," a torch song of an intelligent girl in love with a none too intelligent employer. The latter number, assigned to a comparatively minor character (Emily) helped make Lisa Kirk's Broadway debut successful. (Rodgers and Hammerstein had discovered her in the chorus line of a nightclub.) Several other musical numbers contributed a good measure of stinging satire. "'Yatata, Yatata, Yatata" was a delightful takeoff on cocktail parties (delivered by John Conte, who played the part of Charlie, and chorus); "Money Isn't Ev'rything" pokes fun at the housewife's concern over her pocketbook (presented by a female quartet); and the title number, assigned to Emily, Joe, Charlie, and chorus, emphasizes the frenetic existence of most people in society who make such a fetish of success and fame. An interesting musical curiosity is the inclusion of a quotation from the Rodgers and Hart tune "Mountain Greenery," from *The Garrick Gaieties of 1926,* in "Freshman Dance" to re-create the period of the 1920's.

But the score is also made up of numerous orchestral episodes and choral numbers. A kind of Greek chorus is used to comment (sometimes in speech, sometimes in song) on what is taking place. Episodes in Joe's life are treated in large musical designs—for example, Joe's birth and marriage are extended cantatas for solo voices, chorus, and orchestra. Other biographical incidents unfold in ballets—as in Joe's schooldays.

Agnes de Mille (who had previously served as the choreographer for both *Oklahoma!* and *Carousel*) directed the entire production—the first of many unusual procedures pursued by Rodgers and Hammerstein, since never before had a choreographer been called upon to take directorial charge of an entire musical show. Another innovation consisted in making lighting, rather than sets or costumes, an essential element in the staging. As the action often takes place on a bare stage, not only were lights used to point up an emotion or state of mind; colors were also thrown on a large backstage screen to emphasize a certain mood. Jo Mielziner was responsible for the lights and color effects, as well as for the simple and functional scenery (whenever a scenic background was necessary), which could be easily moved about. The problem of rapidly changing scenes was solved by dividing the stage into several levels.

If the public rejected *Allegro,* the critics embraced it. Brooks Atkinson said it had "the lyric rapture of a musical masterpiece." To Robert Coleman it was a "stunning blending of beauty, integrity, imagination, taste and skill." It received three Donaldson awards—for book, lyrics, and musical score. But in spite of all this, *Allegro* was incapable of surviving a single year.

Both Hammerstein and Rodgers held *Allegro* in high regard; Hammerstein often spoke of revising the text. "I wanted to write a large, universal story, and I think I overestimated the ability of the audience to identify with the leading character." (On this point, Rodgers disagreed: "The comments we made on the compromises demanded by success, as well as some of the satiric asides—hypochondria, the empty cocktail party—still hold.") But both were of one mind that the play deserved reviving, and if it were to be revived, deserved reworking, placing less emphasis on stage techniques and more on the play and the music. When *Allegro* was finally revived (in East Haddam, Connecticut, on July 22, 1968, by the National Lyrics Arts Theater Foundation), some of Hammerstein's ideas for revision were incorporated, but not many. *Allegro* remained in 1968 what it had been twenty years earlier—a musical more interesting for its novel procedures than for its basic dramatic content. As a critic for *Variety* said: "On the basis of this so-called new edition . . . it would have been better to have left it in the archives. . . . Perhaps the times have changed too much for an updating of the show, but a more likely conclusion may be simply that the musical lacks inherent quality."

ALMANAC. *See* JOHN MURRAY ANDERSON'S ALMANAC.

AMERICA. *See* HIPPODROME EXTRAVAGANZAS.

AMERICANA (1926), *a revue with book and lyrics by J. P. McEvoy. Music by Con Conrad and Henry Souvaine, with interpolations by other composers and lyricists. Presented by Richard Herndon at the Belmont Theater on July 26. Directed by Allen Dinehart and Larry Ceballos. Cast included Roy Atwell,*

*Lew Brice, Charles Butterworth, Betty Compton, and Helen Morgan (128 performances). In 1932 a revue entitled* New Americana *with book by J. P. McEvoy. Lyrics by E. Y. Harburg. Music by Jay Gorney, Harold Arlen, Herman Hupfeld, and Richard Meyers. Produced by Lee Shubert at the Shubert Theater on October 5. Directed by Harold Johnsrud. Cast included George Givot, Rex Weber, Albert Carroll, and Georgie Tapps (77 performances).*

Though it went through three editions, *Americana* cannot be numbered among the better or the more successful revues of the 1920's and 1930's. The first edition did moderately well; the other two were failures. None of these productions would merit attention but for the fact that in two of the three editions a number of its parts were superior to the whole, and those parts deserve comment. Two performers in the first edition went on from their then obscurity to considerable fame. One was a wan, lean, lugubrious-looking young man with slicked-down hair, who somehow helped to make even the most ordinary lines and situations funny. He was Charles Butterworth, who initiated a highly successful motion-picture career in the early 1930's, usually in the part of a shy, lonely bachelor. In Max Gordon's picturesque description, Butterworth "could give the appearance of a man always in need of someone to help him across the street, whose grasp of any subject could be as feeble and confused as an American tourist in a five o'clock Paris traffic jam." The other performer was a dark tousle-haired girl with dewy eyes and a quivering throb in her voice. She had a style of her own in singing torch songs. She sang them sitting on a piano, a position that became her trademark. She was, to be sure, Helen Morgan. Jerome Kern heard her sing a blues (with music by Henry Souvaine and lyrics by Morrie Ryskind), "Nobody Wants Me," in *Americana* and immediately knew he had found the actress to play the part of Julie in *Show Boat,* which he was then projecting, thus launching her well on her way to stardom.

Another significant fact about the first edition of *Americana* is that it featured two Gershwin songs. One represented one of the rare times when lyricist Ira Gershwin worked with a composer other than his brother before George's death. The song was "Sunny Disposish," with music by Phil Charig. The other number was the work of both Ira and George Gershwin, "That Lost Barber Shop Chord," sung by Louis Lazarin and the Pan-American Quartet in a barber-shop setting and in costumes re-creating the barber-shop-quartet singing of the late 1890's and early 1900's. "Sunny Disposish" was a modest hit, but "That Lost Barber Shop Chord" was a total failure, even though Charles Pike Sawyer of the New York *Evening Post* called it "Gershwin at his best, which is saying a lot. Full of beautiful melody and swinging rhythm, it is a perfect joy." After *Americana* closed,

"That Lost Barber Shop Chord" became what Ira Gershwin called "a six-page sheet-music nonentity."

The second edition (produced on October 30, 1928) was a disaster, it lasted only twelve performances. About the only thing of even passing interest about it is that the cast included a young girl, Frances Gershwin, the younger sister of George and Ira. Her marriage to Leopold Godowsky, Jr., in 1930 ended her theatrical career.

The third edition (this time produced by J. P. McEvoy for Lee Shubert and named *New Americana*) proved a pioneer among revues in that it included in its program formal ballet with performances by the Weidman and Humphrey Dancers. Into this edition there was interpolated a song called "Satan's Li'l Lamb," whose significance rests in the fact that it marked the first time that Harold Arlen wrote music to lyrics by Johnny Mercer—Mercer collaborating with E. Y. Harburg. But the song remembered most often is "Brother, Can You Spare a Dime?" (words by E. Y. Harburg and music by Jay Gorney), a major hit in 1932–33, and a kind of theme song for the Depression. As presented by Rex Weber and a male chorus in front of the curtain, it was undoubtedly the main attraction of a none too attractive production—but good enough to have been a stand-out in any revue. The third edition also included two other songs worth noting: "Let Me Match My Private Life with Yours" (words by E. Y. Harburg, music by Vernon Duke) and a lighter piece sung by Peggy Cartwright and Gordon Smith, "Wouldja for a Big Red Apple?" (words by Johnny Mercer, music by Henry Souvaine).

AMERICA'S SWEETHEART (1931), *a musical comedy with book by Herbert Fields. Lyrics by Lorenz Hart. Music by Richard Rodgers. Presented by Laurence Schwab and Frank Mandel at the Broadhurst Theater on February 10. Directed by Monty Woolley and Bobby Connolly. Cast included Jack Whiting, Harriet Lake (subsequently known as Ann Sothern), Inez Courtney, and Virginia Bruce (135 performances).*

In 1930 Rodgers, Hart, and Herbert Fields went to Hollywood for the first time to work for the movies. Their contact with the motion-picture industry sparked them into writing a satire on movie stars, movie moguls, and Hollywood in general. Their entire play (except for a brief excursion to the Tennessee hills) was set on the movie lot of Premier Pictures. Two innocents, in love with each other, hitchhike from St. Paul to make their fortune in the movies. The girl, Geraldine March (Harriet Lake) becomes a big star in silent films. Her head turned by the adoration she encounters, she loses all interest in her home-town boy, Michael Perry (Jack Whiting), who has been unable to make any headway whatsoever in the movies. But the talkies create a major upheaval in which Michael Perry suddenly comes to the top of the heap, and Geraldine is unceremoniously dumped to the bottom. More level-headed than his girl friend, Michael is willing to forgive and forget.

The travesties of the life and mores in Hollywood give the play much of its wit and wisdom; and some of the spice is found in the songs. "Sweet Geraldine" pokes fun at movie magazines in hillbilly style, appropriately enough sung by the Forman Sisters, who hailed from the Tennessee hills. "I Want a Man," a lament of a foreign movie star (Denise Torel, played by Jeanne Aubert), is a commentary on the Hollywood sex mania, and "Innocent Chorus Girls of Yesterday," sung by a chorus of movie stars, is a lament of Hollywood "has-beens." "There is a rush about the music and a mocking touch in the lyrics," wrote Brooks Atkinson, "that make the score more deftly satirical than the production."

The most important song was none of those already mentioned but a number soon to become one of the theme songs of the Depression in the early 1930's: "I've Got Five Dollars," a duet by Geraldine and Michael in which they confess that all they possess is five dollars, six shorts, two coats and collars, and debts beyond endurance.

With remarkable appropriateness in a musical show about Hollywood and Hollywood stars, there appeared two young actresses later destined to reach the heights in the movie industry. One was Harriet Lake, who played the heroine, and later became known as Ann Sothern; the other was Virginia Bruce, seen in a minor role as secretary.

ANIMAL CRACKERS (1928), *a musical comedy with book by George S. Kaufman and Morrie Ryskind. Lyrics by Bert Kalmar. Music by Harry Ruby. Presented by Sam H. Harris at the 44th Street Theater on October 23. Cast included the Four Marx Brothers (191 performances).*

*Animal Crackers* was a characteristic Marx Brothers field day. Here they invade and bring chaos to the ritzy Long Island establishment of Mrs. Rittenhouse (Margaret Dumont). Groucho is a famous African explorer, Captain Spaulding, dressed appropriately in sun helmet. Harpo is a professor (category unknown), wearing a full-dress suit that insists on falling down to his knees to reveal him in his underwear. Chico, in immigrant attire, is Emanuel Ravelli, and Zeppo is Jamison, Captain Spaulding's secretary.

The plot involved a stolen painting, which Chico and Groucho try to retrieve. They find a simple solution: The thief must be in the house.

Why not ask everyone there if he is the thief? But, inquires Captain Spaulding, what if the thief is not in the house? Then, explains Ravelli, he must be outside the house, and they will go next door and ask everybody there if he is the thief. Still insistent, Captain Spaulding inquires: "What if there is no house next door?" "Then," replies Ravelli firmly, "we'll build a house."

So it went—in typical Four Marx Brothers fashion. Groucho spoke "asides" in a style made popular in 1928 by Eugene O'Neill's drama *Strange Interlude;* he was quick with a pun (to a South American he says, "you go Uruguay and I'll go my way," and to two female suitors he comments, "it's big of me to commit bigamy"). Chico plays a trick piano. Harpo chases the girls, steals everything in sight, and then in a more placid moment plays a sentimental tune on the harp. Zeppo sings the romantic songs, the best being "Watching the Clouds Roll By" and "Who's Been Listening to My Heart?" The song that has survived is "Hooray for Captain Spaulding" (introduced by Groucho Marx, Robert Grieg, Margaret Dumont, and ensemble); it became Groucho's theme song on his TV quiz program, and thus received national exposure for many years. It was also sung in the movie adaptation of the musical, in which Lillian Roth starred with the Marx Brothers (Paramount, 1930), a production that used two other songs from the stage version, including "Watching the Clouds Roll By."

The funniest single episode in the stage farce had the four brothers playing the "Three Musketeers" ("We're Four of the Three Musketeers," they sing). Groucho becomes King Louis the 57th, frantically trying to make some headway with Mme. Du Barry, while he is consistently being interrupted by the Three Musketeers.

ANNIE GET YOUR GUN (1946), *a musical comedy with book by Herbert and Dorothey Fields. Lyrics and music by Irving Berlin. Presented by Rodgers and Hammerstein at the Imperial Theater on May 16. Directed by Joshua Logan. Dances by Helen Tamiris. Cast included Ethel Merman and Ray Middleton (1,147 performances).*

In 1944 Rodgers and Hammerstein organized a producing firm to put on shows not necessarily of their own writing. Their second project as producers was a musical comedy based on the fabled exploits of Annie Oakley, a rough-and-tumble backwoods girl who was handier with a rifle than with men and who achieved fame as a sharpshooter in wild-west shows. Rodgers and Hammerstein interested Jerome Kern in writing the music, but with Kern's sudden death another composer had to be found. Rodgers and Hammerstein went to the top of the songwriting profession for a replacement —Irving Berlin. Berlin requested a few days to reach a decision. But just three days later he came to Rodgers and Hammerstein with five completed songs, each a little gem. The outpouring of enthusiasm on the part of both Rodgers and Hammerstein convinced Berlin that he should take on a project which was destined to become his greatest box-office success and yield his richest and most varied score.

This is perhaps the only time in stage history that one of America's greatest songwriters was acting as the producer of a musical comedy for which another all-time great in American popular music was writing the score. Rodgers never ventured into Berlin's domain by making suggestions on the kind of songs that were needed (no more than Berlin would tell Rodgers how to run the production). This unusual association may have been the reason why Berlin achieved a miracle of a score. He was probably writing his songs with one eye on his future public and the other on his present producer, whose music he greatly admired.

In any event, *Annie Get Your Gun* became Berlin's only musical to reach the magic circle of one thousand or more performances on Broadway. It sold many record albums; and has had numerous revivals, including a distinguished one in 1966 at the Music Theater of Lincoln Center, of which Richard Rodgers was president and producing director. This production was made into a splendid television special. *Annie Get Your Gun* was adapted successfully for the movies, starring Howard Keel and Betty Hutton and utilizing virtually the complete score (MGM, 1950).

The title role was tailor-made for the gusty, boisterous, and magnetizing Ethel Merman, who here gave one of her most memorable performances. The plot finds Annie Oakley—the star of Buffalo Bill's Wild West Show—at a summer hotel on the outskirts of Cincinnati. She is a girl without learnin', but to whom things must come naturally, as she reveals in "Doin' What Comes Natur'lly," a song to which Miss Merman brought provocative sex insinuations. Annie meets and becomes attracted to the tall and handsome Frank Buttler (Ray Middleton), a performer at the Pawnee Bill Show, rival to Buffalo Bill's troupe. Unfortunately, Frank is the kind of fellow who favors pert and petite and well-bred girls ("The Girl That I Marry"). And Annie is the kind of gal who knows only too well that it takes more than skill with a gun to capture a man ("You Can't Get a Man with a Gun"). But one bond they have in common: their pride in their profession. And, joined by Buffalo Bill, they sing a hymn in what has since become something of an unofficial anthem for all show business: "There's No Business Like Show Business."

After a few weeks, Frank has begun to find Annie so appealing that they can now hint about love ("They Say It's Wonderful"). In fact, Frank goes so far as to confess to Annie, in the Arena, that she has won him over ("My Defenses Are Down"). Within the Arena, a wild-west show is taking place—a spectacle that includes a Drum Dance, and a Ceremonial Chant, with Annie appearing as an Indian squaw singing "I'm an Indian, Too."

One obstacle stands between Frank and Annie: they belong to rival shows. After voicing her regrets at having been so foolish as to fall for Frank ("I Got Lost in His Arms"), Annie hopelessly tries to assuage her wound by finding many things in life for which she could be grateful ("I Got the Sun in the Morning"). Then, miraculously, the obstacle in the way of their love affair is removed when the wild-west shows merge, and Annie and Frank become members of the same company. Frank and Annie are still competitors ("Anything You Can Do"), but there can no longer be any doubt that for both Annie and Frank there lies a happy future together.

Any musical score boasting two or three songs that become standards may regard itself as exceptional. *Annie Get Your Gun* has about half a dozen numbers representing Irving Berlin gold, and another handful that do not have to depend upon the context for which they were planned in order to appeal to ear and heart. Yet, despite the fact that *Annie Get Your Gun* is such a cornucopia of song riches, Irving Berlin felt impelled to contribute a new number to his score when the show was revived so successfully—and so opulently—at the Lincoln Center for the Performing Arts in 1966 (Ethel Merman returning to her original role). The new song was the contrapuntal "Old Fashioned Wedding," which Miss Merman shared with Brune Yarnell (now playing Frank). This song, too, turned out to be eighteen-carat. It stopped the show nightly.

> ANYTHING GOES (1934), *a musical comedy with book by Guy Bolton and P. G. Wodehouse, revised by Howard Lindsay and Russel Crouse. Lyrics and music by Cole Porter. Presented by Vinton Freedley at the Alvin Theater on November 21. Directed by Howard Lindsay. Dances by Robert Alton. Cast included Ethel Merman, William Gaxton, Victor Moore, and Bettina Hall (420 performances).*

*Anything Goes* started out as a brainchild of Vinton Freedley, the producer— a musical built around some of the outlandish developments among a collection of screwball characters after a gambling ship is wrecked on the high seas. Freedley called on P. G. Wodehouse and Guy Bolton to develop this into a musical-comedy text, for which Cole Porter had promised to do the music. Wodehouse and Bolton submitted a script called *Hard to Get.* Soon after that, a major sea disaster took place on September 8, 1934: the *Morro Castle* went up in flames off the coast of New Jersey, costing 134 lives.

Shipwrecks could no longer serve as musical-comedy humor. Freedley now went to Howard Lindsay and Russel Crouse to write a new text based loosely on the discarded one. Bringing together Lindsay and Crouse as collaborators for the first time had consequences even greater than the writing of a successful musical with a wonderful Cole Porter score, and boasting one of Ethel Merman's superlative performances. It created a writing team that would in the future produce many significant musical-comedy texts as well as nonmusical plays that in one way or another would make Broadway history.

Though the names of Wodehouse and Bolton continue to appear in the credits, very little of their work was retained when Crouse and Lindsay completed their own libretto, now named *Anything Goes*. The musical opens in a New York bar, where Reno Sweeney (Ethel Merman), a nightclub entertainer, reveals her emotional interest in Billy Crocker (William Gaxton). She is on the eve of leaving for Europe on a luxury liner, on which Billy happens to become an unlisted passenger. He had come to bid his former fiancée, Hope Harcourt (Bettina Hall), farewell, but discovering he still loved her, stayed on the ship, sans tickets, sans passport. Both ticket and passport were acquired from a round-faced, mild-mannered, and broken-voiced little man—Public Enemy No. 13, who is fleeing the arm of the law disguised as the Reverend Dr. Moon (Victor Moore). One of his confederates had been booked to sail for him and had failed to show up— consequently, if Billy disguised himself as that confederate, he could use the man's passport and ticket. The fact that both Hope and Reno are on the same ship complicates matters for Billy, who—now in his disguise, and now as himself—manages, somehow, to keep things from getting out of hand. When the ship's captain receives word of the presence of Public Enemy No. 13, he puts the criminal in the brig. Then (though the reason for this is not altogether clarified) the captain convokes a kind of revival meeting for some of the passengers to confess their sins.

After the ship has docked in England, Hope is about to marry Sir Evelyn Oakleigh (Leslie Barrie)—a marriage of convenience to save a floundering business. When that establishment is sold for several million dollars, Hope is free to pursue her romance with Billy (and vice versa). At the same time, Sir Evelyn finds Reno very much to his liking. As for Public Enemy No. 13, the FBI has sent in a report from Washington that he is as harmless as a sponge—a development that upsets the little man no end, since he was aspiring to become Public Enemy No. 1. "I can't understand this administration," he whines in his piping, broken voice.

Russel Crouse later reported the impression made upon him when he first heard Cole Porter's score: "All I can say is that no doubt Ludwig van

Beethoven, Johann Sebastian Bach, Wolfgang Amadeus Mozart, Richard Wagner . . . Joseph Haydn, and Francis Scott Key could have marched into the room and I wouldn't have looked up." One can well understand the reason for such enthusiasm. This was Cole Porter's best score up to that time, and second only in importance to that for *Kiss Me, Kate*. It begins with best foot forward—in the opening nightclub scene, where Reno reveals her interest in Billy in "I Get a Kick Out of You," a song as famous for its lyrics as for its dynamic melody (in one place in the chorus there are five consecutive lines that rhyme). It is most unusual for a musical comedy to place so strong a number so early in the play. But Ethel Merman carried this innovation off most successfully, giving the song additional impact by splitting the word "terrifically" in the chorus by pausing a moment after the syllable "rif" and holding on to it longer than the music called for. "She knocked the audience, totally unprepared, for a loop," recalled Russel Crouse. "After she finished 'I Get a Kick Out of You,' she just couldn't do anything wrong for that audience."

Several other numbers which Ethel Merman put over with all her customary verve were "Blow, Gabriel, Blow" (her contribution to the revivalist meeting aboard ship); the title song; and "You're the Top," in which Billy and Reno exchange compliments comparing each other to the best in many fields of endeavor. The idea for "You're the Top" was hatched long before Porter wrote the score for *Anything Goes*—at the Boeuf sur le Toit in Paris, where, during dinner, Cole Porter and Mrs. Alastair Mackintosh competed with each other in finding slick rhymes for a list of superlatives ranging from a Bendel bonnet to a Shakespeare sonnet and from Mahatma Gandhi to Napoleon's brandy. "All Through the Night," with its haunting descending chromatic line in the chorus, was Billy's love song to Hope. A simulated sailor chantey ("There'll Always Be a Lady Fair," sung by the Foursome) was an additional musical bonus.

The music inspired Walter Winchell (among others) to write a rhapsody in praise of "King Cole Porter." The lyrics also gathered accolades—perhaps even more so than the music. The New York *Sun-Record* considered "You're the Top" as "the most exciting lyric ever composed for a song," and *Time* reported that "so popular are composer Porter's lyrics that it is now considered the smart thing to know them all by heart, to rattle them off loudly."

Two screen versions were made of *Anything Goes*. The first came in 1936, with Ethel Merman and Bing Crosby (Paramount), in which six numbers from the score were used with some interpolations by other composers and lyricists. The second came twenty years later. Donald O'Connor, Mitzi Gaynor, and Bing Crosby starred in this Paramount production, which used basic numbers from the stage score, including a Cole Porter song from another of his musicals ("It's De-Lovely"), and three new songs by Sammy Cahn and James Van Heusen. As a stage production, *Anything Goes* returned to New York in 1962 in an Off Broadway presentation which received the Outer Circle Award as the best revival of the season.

APPLAUSE (1970), *a musical comedy with book by Betty Comden and Adolph Green based on the motion picture* All About Eve, *from the original story by Mary Orr. Lyrics by Lee Adams. Music by Charles Strouse. Presented by Joseph Kipness and Lawrence Kasha at the Palace Theater on March 30. Directed and with choreography by Ron Field. Cast included Lauren Bacall, Penny Fuller, Len Cariou, and Bonnie Franklin.*

There is no business like show business; and there is perhaps no musical about show business as good as *Applause. Applause* is old-fashioned musical comedy in that it leans heavily on big production numbers for visual excitement, glorifies the star system, includes a score that makes no pretense at reaching for new sounds or exploiting rock rhythms. But *Applause* is done with such majestic style, such concern for text and characterization, boasts such infectious dance sequences, and so neatly ties up all of its delightful elements into a single attractive package that while it adheres to the traditions of yesterday's musical comedies, it remains very much of today in its overall sophistication and brilliance of execution.

*Applause* has proud ancestry: the motion picture, *All About Eve,* which was written and directed by Joseph Mankiewicz (based on Mary Orr's short story) and which captured the Academy Award in 1951. In the motion picture, Bette Davis was starred as the middle-aged idol of the stage who takes under her wing a young, adoring, seemingly innocent-hearted girl who turns out to be a viper. Behind the façade of her sweet face and honeyed words lurks an overwhelming, irresistible ambition to achieve stardom in the theater—a stardom which she realizes through ruthlessness, opportunism, and willingness to destroy anybody who stands in her way. This, then, is a story about the less glamorous and uglier realism of show business, a behind-the-scenes story with bite and sting.

Thus *Applause*, as a musical comedy, started out with excellent material. Except for totally negligible changes (such as eliminating the character of the drama critic, brilliantly portrayed in the film by George Sanders, a critic whose brilliance of mind is matched by his cynicism and cruelty) and some welcome interpolations (a place called "The Village Bar," the setting of some of the most effective production numbers in the show, and devastating one-liners by Comden and Green that attack the victim with the dead accuracy of a well-aimed gun shot); the adaptors decided wisely to leave well enough alone. They stuck quite faithfully to the essentials in the story line and characters to produce as fine a musical-comedy text as our musical theater has known since *My Fair Lady*. So good is the book that Walter Kerr felt it played "like a solid play; firm, ample, straightforward, hard-hearted, and could probably do without its music if it had to." No small contribution to so solid a libretto was made by Ron Field's remarkable staging and choreography. The songs and production numbers evolve naturally from the text and flow smoothly into and out of the many scenes, in which the plot and the characters are developed, with no seams visible in the overall fabric; the musical is all of one piece. Finally, there is the performance not only of Lauren Bacall (who in her musical-theater debut turns out to be a bombshell), but also of the other principals.

The musical opens with the presentation of the Antoinette Perry Awards. But before that happens, over the strains of the overture, we see on two television screens, placed on opposite sides of the stage, actual Antoinette Perry Award broadcasts with some of the razzle-dazzle accompanying such events. A few moments of this broadcast, and the curtain rises on a fictional "Tony" Award event in which the established star, Margo Channing (Lauren Bacall) opens the envelope for the best female performance of the season and calls out the name of Eve Harrington (Penny Fuller) for her part in *Somewhere to Love*. Eve utters the usual platitudes of grateful acknowledgment, not forgetting to give most of the credit for her success to the friendship, generosity, and inspiration of Margo Channing. The icy cold stare that Margo directs toward the winner would by itself reveal her inmost reaction even if a loudspeaker did not do this for us.

And then, as in the motion picture, we get a flashback: the story of the relationship between Margo Channing and Eve Harrington. It is the evening of the opening night of Margo's new play, *The Friendly Arrangement*, in which she is a triumph. Her dressing room is bedlam, into which is conducted a young, timid angel-faced girl who was found loitering outside with the hope of catching a glimpse of the great star. She is Eve Harrington (Penny Fuller) who—once she is brought to Margo—pours out her adoration for the stage star, her own passion for the theater, and a poignant autobiographical revelation that her husband had recently been killed in Vietnam. Margo is won over completely to this poor, adorable innocent. Instead of going to an opening-night party planned in her honor, Margo decides to take Eve to "The Village Bar" where most of the waiters and waitresses are young theatrical hopefuls working for a living while waiting for a "break." Here Margo lets herself go in song and dance ("But Alive") that sets the place whirling. Eve watches entranced; as she explains in her first song, this is "The Best Night of My Life."

And so, the relationship between Margo and Eve has begun. The sweet-innocent manages to become Margo's efficient secretary, then her understudy. It is not long before Margo begins to sense that Eve carries within her bosom the poison of a cobra. Eve connives with Karen Richards (Ann Williams)—who is the wife of the author of *The Friendly Arrangement*—to get Margo stranded in the country with both Richardses so that Eve might step into Margo's role and prove her ability. (The Richardses cooperate since, now fired with the hatred of Eve, Margo has become intolerably temperamental and volatile to a point where she needs a lesson in humility.) Eve makes her successful debut, but her true personality comes strongly to the fore. Ruthlessly, she tries to get the love of Margo's sweetheart Bill Sampson who rejects her in no uncertain terms. She then becomes the mistress of the producer—an arrangement into which she is more or less blackmailed when the producer has uncovered the unsavory truth that the pathetic tale Eve had concocted about herself and her dead husband was pure fiction. Eve wins the author of *The Friendly Arrangement* away from his wife so that she— not Margo—will get the lead in his next play. That play is *Somewhere to Love* in which Eve captures the "Tony." For Margo there is not only total disenchantment with Eve but also the forceful realization that in the theater the recognized star must accept the competition of talented young newcomers. But her bitterness is sweetened by the fact that, after a turbulent affair that has almost come to the breaking point, she has not lost the man she loves. The musical, therefore, ends on an upbeat, not only with the reconciliation of Margo and the author—and the implied peace of mind and heart Margo has finally found both as a woman and as an actress—but also with the return of the title song, presented by Margo and the company after the curtain calls. The implication left with the audience is that in spite of the ugly double-dealings and the bitter heartaches involved in a stage career, there's really no business like show business, and no reward like an audience's applause.

Miss Bacall's performance is that of a virtuoso with few if any parallels in her long and eventful career both on the stage and screen. Clive Barnes went all out by saying: "Whatever it is Miss Lauren Bacall possesses she throws it around beautifully, most exquisitely." He called her "a sensation" adding: "She sings with all the misty beauty of an on-tune foghorn. She never misses a note—she is not one of your all-talking musical· dramatics—and though her voice is not pretty, it does have the true beauty of unforgettability. Her dancing is more conventional—she is averagely if beautifully groovy. Her acting is her own thing." In "But Alive" she is an uncontrollable force capable of singing and dancing throughout an entire scene without a moment to catch her breath. In "Fasten Your Seat Belts" she lets down her hair and releases her inhibitions; and she can turn riot in a party at her apartment. She can be warm and wistful in her love duet with Bill (Len Cariou), and she is razor-edged in her satirical overtones in singing about the less glamorous aspects of show business in "Welcome to the Theater." She can be tender and sentimental when in "Hurry Back" she entreats her beloved by telephone to return from Rome as soon as possible, and she is good-humored and warmhearted in "Good Friends." Few can deliver a line coated with acid the way she can, or suggest such sensuality with a mere passing inflection. And when she gives way to jealousy and hate—as she discovers Eve's true evil nature— she is a veritable demon. The role gives her an opportunity to go through the entire gamut of human emotions, and she makes the most of it. That her electrifying, magnetizing stage presence—whatever her mood may be at the moment—does not throw into a shade the performance of her colleagues speaks volumes for the insight, subtlety, and personal dynamism that Penny Fuller brings to the role of Eve Harrington, Len Cariou to that of Bill Sampson, and Bonnie Franklin to the comparatively minor role of Bonnie, a waitress at "The Village Bar." Indeed, Bonnie Franklin (formerly seen in New York in *Your Own Thing* and *Dames at Sea*) is an explosive force in her own right. It is to her that the authors assigned the best musical number of the show, the title song, before it leads into a frenetic production number. "When Bonnie Franklin, five foot three, eyes of green, hair like a ripe persimmon, struts her wide-open smile and whippy hip-huggers across the Palace stage as a chorus gypsy," wrote Robert Berkvist in *The New York Times,* "you nearly lose sight of the fact the unquestioned star of the new hit musical is Lauren Bacall. . . . And when, wearing a slithery leathery black jumpsuit, she throws herself into a quick reprise of the title song . . . well, you nearly." So successful was her Broadway debut that she earned a nomination for an Antoinette Perry Award, though she did not win it. The musical comedy itself and Miss Bacall proved more fortunate—capturing "Tonys" as the best musical and the best actress of the season.

The score as a whole is unlikely to yield a single number that will sell a million records or perhaps even be remembered outside the theater. But within the context of the musical, each song is contributory to the overall impact of the production. And that impact, more often than not, is overpowering, leaving the audience limp with exhaustion by the time the curtain descends upon Margo and Bill walking off arm-in-arm.

APPLE BLOSSOMS (1919), *an operetta with book and lyrics by William Le Baron, based on Dumas's* A Marriage of Convenience. *Music by Fritz Kreisler and Victor Jacobi. Presented by Charles Dillingham at the Globe Theater on October 7. Cast included Wilda Bennett, Roy Atwell, Percival Knight, and Fred and Adele Astaire (256 performances).*

Fritz Kreisler (possibly the greatest violinist of his generation) belonged to the world of serious music. But he was also Viennese, which means that he loved Viennese operettas and waltzes. For a long time he nursed the ambition to write an operetta for Broadway, but his worldwide commitments as virtuoso made this impossible. Then came World War I, when he had to go into temporary retirement in America due to the hostility of the public, press, and patriotic groups to his Austrian citizenship and allegiance. He now had the time to think of writing operetta music, and when Dillingham made him an offer, he seized it. "I admit," he has said, "that I wrote it quite as much for my own sake as for the public. Torn and weary with the sorrow of war, I fought my own depression in the work of composition. It was the only thing that saved me. In seeking to write songs that should amuse people and make them happy, if only for a moment, I found I could forget myself."

To safeguard himself against having Kreisler provide a possibly highbrow score, Charles Dillingham contracted Victor Jacobi (an old hand at writing light tunes for the American theater) to write part of the score. Of the nineteen numbers in the operetta, eight were Jacobi's, nine were Kreisler's, and two represented the combined efforts of the two men.

Though Kreisler wrote a good deal of the music during the war, the production of the operetta was postponed until almost a year after the armistice—after the intense feelings against Kreisler had a chance to die down and be forgotten. When *Apple Blossoms* was finally produced, it was described as "a musical comedy of supreme elegance and old-time musical dignity" by the New York *American*. *Apple Blossoms* had much more than a good score to recommend it. It boasted gay comedy, with Percival Knight playing an amiable philanderer, Roy Atwell as a philosophic valet, and Florence Shirley as a flirtatious widow. It boasted two outstanding dance numbers by Fred and Adele Astaire and some highly agreeable singing by John Charles Thomas. Fred and Adele Astaire (despite their previous successes in vaudeville) achieved their initial musical-comedy fame here, and John Charles Thomas received here his first accolades in a career that eventually led him to the concert hall and opera house.

The plot takes place at Castle Hall School, in Clifton-on-the Hudson. Dickie Stewart (Percival Knight) visits the school to propose to Nancy

(Wilda Bennett), whose uncle wants her to marry Philip Campbell (John Charles Thomas). Both Nancy and Philip are indifferent to their marriage, since Philip is interested in a gay, young widow. When the marriage ceremony ends, Nancy reveals to her groom that she is in love with Dickie, while Philip confesses to his bride that he is interested in the widow. But after Dickie and the widow appear on the scene, following the honeymoon of the newly married pair, Nancy and Philip come to the realization that they are really in love with each other and prefer to stay married.

The same charm, grace, and freshness that Kreisler brought to his famous violin pieces can be found in his melodies for this operetta. The opening number, "Who Can Tell?", is a lilting Viennese waltz sung by Nancy. Nancy also presents another infectious Kreisler tune, "Star of Love." It is perhaps to be expected that one of the big musical numbers involves the violin: the duet, "Second Violin," utilizes a background of chorus girls playing violins in pantomime. Victor Jacobi's best numbers were "Little Girls, Good-Bye," sung by Philip, and "You are Free," a duet by Nancy and Philip. "It is good music," said Heywood Broun in the *Tribune*, "pleasant to hear, melodious, and interpretative of the lyrics. Some of it is exciting."

Fred and Adele Astaire had no speaking or singing roles. Their contribution consisted of two dances. One was a routine, "The Sacred Cow," which they had previously used in vaudeville with enormous success. They adapted this dance to the strains of Kreisler's *Tambourin Chinois*—one of the composer's famous concert pieces for the violin. (With lyrics, this same melody was sung elsewhere in the show by Wilda Bennett.) Their second dance (this time to Victor Jacobi's music) began with Adele knitting under a tree and dropping her ball of yarn; Fred jumps over the wall to retrieve it. Then they go into a dance routine.

Fritz Kreisler so enjoyed being involved in the show that he rarely missed a rehearsal. As Victor Jacobi reported in *The New York Times:* "It was no uncommon sight to see the famous violinist with a dozen of the beauties of the chorus clustered around him as he hummed a bit of refrain, marking time with the nervous right hand which has thrilled thousands as it wields a violin bow. Or, again, to see him sweep aside the man on the piano stool with an impatient gesture and seat himself, to swing into a dashing accompaniment for a pair of little dancers who remained quite unmoved at the extraordinary spectacle of a world genius willingly accepting suggestions as to tempo, while they went through their steps without a quiver."

THE APPLE TREE (1966), *three one-act musicals with book by Sheldon Harnick and Jerry Bock, based on Mark Twain's* The Diary of Adam and Eve,

*Frank R. Stockton's* The Lady or the Tiger?, *and Jules Feiffer's* Passionella. *Additional book material by Jerome Coopersmith. Lyrics by Sheldon Harnick. Music by Jerry Bock. Presented by Stuart Ostrow at the Shubert Theater on October 18. Directed by Mike Nichols. Choreography by Lee Theodore and Herbert Ross. Cast included Barbara Harris, Larry Blyden, and Alan Alda (463 performances).*

This musical comprises three one-act productions, each providing a different facet of a woman's personality. The first, "The Diary of Adam and Eve," takes place in the Garden of Eden. Adam, awakened by a voice ordering him to take possession of the garden, begins to concoct names for everything he sees—even for Eve, the only other human being there. Eve begins to experience strange feelings about Adam, which she reveals in the song "Feelings Are Tumbling Over Feelings"; her womanly intuition guides her in different ways and means of attracting Adam's interest. It is not long before Adams asks her to share his hut, where, like any present-day couple, they begin to get enmeshed in marital problems. A snake entices Eve to take a bite of the forbidden apple, and Eve, in turn, nags Adam into doing the same. Suddenly they become aware of their nudity, cover themselves as best they can, then seek shelter in the new hut Adam had built for her. Here she begins to age, grow fat, and give birth to a child, to whom she sings a poignant lullaby, "Go to Sleep Whatever You Are." Somewhat later, Eve is warning her two sons, Cain and Abel (for a second child has meanwhile come into being), to stay out of the garden. Fading lights introduce an ominous atmosphere. Cain kills Abel and has run away. Adam and Eve are once again alone. Eve wonders why she still loves Adam and comes to the conclusion it is because "he is a good man" and "he's mine." With the passing of more time, Adam appears haggard and wan; Eve has just died. Because of his devotion to her, he goes to water the flowers she so loved.

The second one-act musical is entitled "The Lady or the Tiger?" It takes place in a semibarbaric kingdom, long ago. In the opening and the closing, a balladeer (Larry Blyden), strumming on a guitar, provides commentary. Within an arena there are two doors, exactly alike. Behind one is a hungry tiger; behind the other, a ravishing young girl. Prisoners are brought here and made to choose which door to enter. Captain Sanjar and Princess Barbara are involved in a forbidden love affair, because of which the king has ordered him to be arrested and put to trial. Convicted, he must choose one of the doors. Princess Barbara knows behind which door the ravenous tiger is concealed. But she also knows that behind the other door there awaits the glamorous Nadjira, beautifully gowned, a delectable delight for any man. When Sanjar is brought into the arena, Barbara points out to him which door to select. The balladeer now asks the inevitable question: "Which will it be, the lady or the tiger?" He comments further that the deeper one searches into Barbara's heart, the more doubtful does the answer become. Then he asks the audience: "If you were in Barbara's shoes, which would you choose for him—the lady or the tiger?"

The third musical playlet, "Passionella," takes place in our own time and is a devastating satire on the female sex symbol of the movies. Ella is a chimney sweep who loses her job, to be placed by an automaton. Her life's dream had always been to become a movie star, but now she is on the brink of starvation without even a menial occupation to support her. Suddenly from her TV set comes a voice announcing itself as her friendly neighborhood grandmother ready to answer her most cherished dream. Naturally, Ella chooses to become a movie queen. Suddenly and mysteriously she becomes a glamorous blond with oversized bosom, radiant in a stunning evening gown. The TV voice, however, warns her that she can remain La Passionella only during the period between the Huntley-Brinkley newscast and the late-late show; after that she reverts to Ella. Taking full advantage of the period of hours allotted to her, Ella—as La Passionella—becomes a star of stars, worshiped by all those who catch a glimpse of her, the winner of an Academy Award. She falls in love with Flip, the famous recording rock-'n'- roll star, who rejects her because she is too glamorous, while he can fall in love only with a girl who looks as sloppy as he does. When, late one night, La Passionella is changed back to the impoverished and shabby Ella, Flip finds her to be the girl of his heart. Ella is no longer interested in her screen career. As she and Flip embrace, the orchestra strikes up the national anthem, and colorful flags begin to wave.

Having previously only hinted at her potential as an actress, Barbara Harris—playing the leading female role in all three musicals—emerged as a full-fledged star. To Walter Kerr, writing in *The New York Times,* she was "exquisite, appetizing, alarming, seductive, out of her mind, irresistible, and from now on unavoidable. . . . 'Whatever I am, I'm certainly a beautiful one' is practically the first remark out of her face in the opening musical playlet . . . and whoever you are, you're going to agree."

Two of the best songs are found in the first playlet. They are "Eve," sung by Adam (Alan Alda), and Eve's poignant ballad, "What Makes Me Love Him?" "I've Got What You Want," which Passionella presents in the third playlet, has sardonic overtones and a good measure of sex appeal.

To the critic of *Variety,* "the most effective aspect of this production is the inclusion of an animation film sequence by Richard Williams. A screen is lowered and the heroine's antics are traced with a giant montage of stills and footage. This brief section containing the magic lantern's stop-and-go action and exploding colors inflates the on-stage comedy." This takes place in the third musical.

AROUND THE WORLD. *See* HIPPODROME EXTRAVAGANZAS.

ARTISTS AND MODELS (1923), *a revue with book and lyrics by Harold Atteridge. Music by Jean Schwartz. Presented by the Shuberts at the Shubert Theater on August 20. Directed by Harry Wagstaff Gribble and Francis Weldon. Cast included Frank Fay, Grace Hamilton, Harry Kelly, and Bob Nelson (312 performances).*

(1924), *a revue with book by Harry Wagstaff Gribble. Lyrics by Sam Coslow and Clifford Grey. Music by J. Fred Coots and Sigmund Romberg. Presented by the Shuberts at the Winter Garden on October 15. Directed by J. J. Shubert. Cast included Trini, Frank Gaby, and Mabel Wither (261 performances).*

(1925), *a revue with book by Harold Atteridge and Harry Wagstaff Gribble. Lyrics by Clifford Grey. Music by J. Fred Coots, Alfred Goodman, and Maurice Rubens. Presented by the Shuberts at the Winter Garden on June 24. Directed by J. J. Shubert. Cast included the Gertrude Hoffman Girls, Lulu McConnell, Billy B. Van, and Phil Baker (411 performances).*

This revue was evolved from an intimate, sophisticated show staged in Greenwich Village by the Illustrators Society of New York in which many eminent artists participated, including James Montgomery Flagg, Rube Goldberg, H. T. Webster, and Harry Hirschfield. A scout from the Shubert office recommended strongly that the Shuberts buy the material for Broadway production. J. J. Shubert liked the idea, not because the revue had smart, fresh ideas but because it involved artists. A show involving artists must also include models, and who did not know that artists' models habitually posed in the nude? And so, in the hands of the Shuberts, the revue changed character to glorify female nudity. The story goes that at the first rehearsal, J. J. Shubert told the chorus girls: "No broad who won't show her breasts can work in this show, and that's final!"—only Shubert's vocabulary was too earthy to use the word "breasts." Then and there some of the girls withdrew; but replacements were not hard to come by. And so, probably with the hope that it might become the *Folies Bergères* of New York, J. J. Shubert brought nudity to the Broadway theater with *Artists and Models.* In one of the scenes, models parade with a minimum of clothes in an artist's studio; in another, the entire stage was dominated by a palette across which were placed a dozen seminude girls in various poses; a third scene had them in a Grecian scene, once again bare-breasted, and in a variety of poses. In all these and other scenes, the rest of the anatomy of the models was plainly visible through transparent costumes.

*Artists and Models* caused a sensation. The newspapers denounced the introduction of nudity to the stage. The leading editorial in *Variety* described the show as vulgar and maintained that the Broadway theater would be far better off without such displays of nudity. But the public flocked to the box office. *Artists and Models* played to sold-out houses. By February, 1924, it had earned almost one hundred thousand dollars.

Of course, there was more than just female nudity in that first edition. Indeed, there was a good deal of excellent comedy: Frank Fay's highly amusing—and often provocatively suggestive—monologues; a satire on Somerset Maugham's *Rain,* starring Harry Kelly; a satirical skit on drama critics; and a travesty on Presidential cabinet meetings. A dynamic South Sea Island dance was performed by Kura. Jean Schwartz's songs included "Music of Love" and "Somehow."

The 1924 edition was even more daring in its display of nudity and salacious humor. Local color was injected with numbers like "Off to Greenwich Village" and "What a Village Girl Should Know"; there was spectacle in "Mediterranean Nights" and ear-caressing songs in "Who's the Lucky Fellow?" and "I Love to Dance When I Hear a March," both by J. Fred Coots.

The best spectacles in the 1925 edition, once again greatly enhanced by the presence of undraped females, included "Oriental Memories" and "The Magic Garden of Love," while the best of Coots's songs were "Follow Your Stars" and "Take a Little Baby Home with You."

THE ART OF MARYLAND. *See* WEBER AND FIELDS EXTRAVAGANZAS.

AS THE GIRLS GO (1948), *a musical comedy with book by William Roos. Lyrics by Harold Adamson. Music by Jimmy McHugh. Presented by Michael Todd at the Winter Garden on November 13. Directed by Howard Bay. Dances by Hermes Pan. Cast included Irene Rich, Bobby Clark, Betty Jane Watson, and Bill Callahan (420 performances).*

Mike Todd, the colorful producer who made and lost millions on his varied ventures in the world of entertainment, was in a bad way when *As the Girls Go* was being prepared for Broadway. He had not had a stage success for a number of years and was now knee-deep in bankruptcy proceedings. But Todd had confidence in his show. He liked the theme, a stinging political satire about the first woman President of the United States. In Irene Rich he had an ideal performer for that part, and in Bobby Clark (playing her husband, Waldo Wellington) one of the funniest men in the business. How could he miss? But even his supreme faith in his own judgment had to wilt after the Boston tryout. The show received devastating criticisms. One of them advised Todd to close the show permanently. The odds of its coming to Broadway made it a long shot. Backers were withdrawing in droves. There was hardly enough money to pay the hotel bills.

But Todd was not the man to accept defeat. He would have the text completely redone, changing it from a political satire into a rowdy show filled with a kind of lusty, rough-and-tumble humor for which Bobby Clark was so famous, and gorgeous girls. He had new sets constructed, and new skits and songs written. He was now out to put over *entertainment* on a grand scale. To point up his confidence, he took Broadway's largest theater (the Winter Garden), decorating it with a huge outdoor sign painted by Arthur Szyk, the noted artist, in which Bobby Clark ran after the girls and the critics ran after Bobby Clark. He also charged the highest price yet for the best seats in the house ($7.20 a ticket). And he came up with a resounding winner. Brooks Atkinson wrote: "It is a beautiful and uproarious show, gay and rowdy entertainment, with a full cornucopia of music-hall pretties." Robert Coleman reported: "Mike Todd has a smash hit. . . . Bobby Clark is the funniest man in the world." Ward Morehouse described it as "a strident and opulent extravaganza." The wise men of Broadway shook their heads with incredulity at this man Todd, a miracle worker who, in short order, could transform an obvious dud into a live bomb.

The question posed in the first unfortunate version of the text remained: What would happen to the United States if a woman became President? *As the Girls Go* provided the answer. Lucille Thompson Wellington (Irene Rich, making her Broadway-stage debut) is elected the first lady President. As First Gentleman, her husband, Weldo (Bobby Clark), must fulfill the social functions previously assumed by First Ladies. He uses these functions and his high station and authority at the White House to run after the girls. During these farcical proceedings a more normal and orthodox love interest is consigned to two charming youngsters, Kathy Robinson (Betty Jane Watson) and Kenny Wellington (Bill Callahan).

The musical opens strongly. Having just been elected, the first lady President expresses gratitude to her voters—not live, but on a large screen flashed via NBC-TV newsreel. The opening song, "As the Girls Go," follows, sung by Waldo surrounded by a bevy of beautiful girls. From then on the pace of the comedy is permitted to slacken only to allow the interlude of a tender love song between Kathy and Kenny, "You Say the Nicest Things,

Baby," and their rendition of a lovely ballad, "Nobody's Heart but Mine."
"Lucky in the Rain" was another fetching ballad, while the two best comedy
songs were "I've Got the President's Ear" and "It Takes a Woman to Get a
Man."

> AS THOUSANDS CHEER (1933), *a topical revue with book by Moss Hart
> and Irving Berlin. Lyrics and music by Irving Berlin. Presented by Sam H.
> Harris at the Music Box Theater on September 30. Directed by Hassard Short.
> Dances by Charles Weidman. Cast included Marilyn Miller, Clifton Webb,
> Ethel Waters, and Helen Broderick (400 performances).*

Sketches, dances, and even the curtain design contained satirical allusions to
current events. Helen Broderick stepped into the shoes of Herbert Hoover
and the evangelist Aimee Semple McPherson with devastating results; in a
third sketch she was seen as the Statue of Liberty in a song whose chorus
began "We'll all be in heaven when the dollar goes to hell." Clifton Webb
gave unforgettable impersonations of Douglas Fairbanks, Jr., Gandhi, and
the then ninety-four-year-old John D. Rockefeller receiving Rockefeller Plaza
as a birthday gift. Marilyn Miller did travesties on Barbara Hutton and Joan
Crawford. (The skillfully designed masks by Remo Buffano helped to make
these characterizations more realistic visually.) There were amusing comments
on the change of administration in the White House and the effect of radio
sponsorship on the Metropolitan Opera House.

In short, *As Thousands Cheer* was as topical as the daily newspaper,
and it is for this reason that it patterned itself after a newspaper. The
various scenes were intended to simulate different sections of a paper—news
items, the society column, the comics, the lonelyhearts column, and so forth.
Hassard Short devised a trick lighting to flash newspaper headlines across
the proscenium before each number.

There was an abundance of satire and malicious humor. But there was at
least one deeply moving, sober episode. This happened early in the second
act after the lights on the proscenium flashed the news item: "Unknown
Negro Lynched by Frenzied Mob." What followed was Ethel Waters singing
"Supper Time," a ballad telling of a colored woman getting supper ready for
her husband, who had just been lynched. "In singing it," Ethel Waters wrote
in her autobiography, "I was telling my comfortable, well-fed, well-dressed
listeners about my people. . . . When I was through and that big, heavy
curtain came down, I was called back again and again. I had stopped the
show with a type of song never heard before in a revue, and a number that
until then had been a question mark."

But unquestionably the most famous song to come out of this revue—

and it is one of Berlin's greatest—was "Easter Parade," seen in a production number for the first-act finale. This finale was effectively staged. The people parading in their Easter finery down Fifth Avenue were all in brown (to simulate the color of the rotogravure sections then found in the Sunday papers). They suddenly became motionless, frozen into an immobile position, as Marilyn Miller and Clifton Webb sang "Easter Parade." This was not a new melody. Berlin had used it in 1917 for another lyric, "Smile and Show Your Dimple." It was a failure then, and soon forgotten. But with new lyrics and in an appropriate setting it was the song triumph of the show, and from there it went on to become a Berlin classic and a perennial favorite during the Easter holiday season. (In 1948, MGM released a motion picture called *Easter Parade,* featuring that and other Irving Berlin songs; it starred Fred Astaire and Judy Garland.)

Other outstanding songs in this production were "Heat Wave," torridly sung by Ethel Waters (then danced to by José Limon, Letita Ide, and the Weidman dancers), and, in the show's finale, "Not for All the Rice in China," presented by Marilyn Miller, Clifton Webb, and the ensemble.

For Marilyn Miller, *As Thousands Cheer* represented the end of a glamorous career in the musical theater. Even while the revue was still running, she dropped out from the production to marry Chester O'Brien; her part was taken over by Dorothy Stone.

AT HOME ABROAD (1935), *a revue with book and lyrics by Howard Dietz and others. Music by Arthur Schwartz. Presented by the Shuberts at the Winter Garden on September 19. Directed by Vincente Minnelli and Thomas Mitchell. Dances by Gene Snyder and Harry Losee. Cast included Beatrice Lillie, Ethel Waters, Eleanor Powell, and Reginald Gardiner (198 performances).*

The authors described this joyous escapade as "a musical holiday," and it proved a veritable holiday for the theatergoer. Beatrice Lillie's now celebrated line "It's better with your shoes off" comes out of this show in a sketch in which she appeared as a geisha girl. In another extended sequence she changed her nationality to head a company of Alpine mountain climbers. She also sang a hymn to Paree ("I love zee Right Bank, I love zee Left Bank, zee Place de l'Opéra") and got herself involved in trying to purchase a "dozen double damask dinner napkins" in the song "Dinner Napkins," ending up by asking for some wash rags.

Other delights in this revue include Eleanor Powell's nimble tap-dance routine in "Got a Bran' New Suit," "That's Not Cricket," and in a sequence in which she sent coded messages to the enemy through the rhythms of her tapping toes. Reginald Gardiner did some of his inimitable imitations, notably of wallpaper (of all things!) and trains. Ethel Waters presented a torch song, "Thief in the Night," and "Hottentot Potentate." There were some eye-arresting ballet sequences conceived and danced by Paul Haakon—"Love Is a Dancing Thing" and "Farewell, My Lovely"—but the sketch in which he brought down the house was in "Death in the Afternoon," where he appeared as a matador. The finale, "Pomp and Peculiar Circumstance," was also eye-arresting in that it featured an ornate gilt baroque setting conceived by Minnelli.

THE AUTO RACE. *See* HIPPODROME EXTRAVAGANZAS.

BABES IN ARMS (1937), *a musical comedy with book by Rodgers and Hart. Lyrics by Lorenz Hart. Music by Richard Rodgers. Presented by Dwight Deere Wiman at the Shubert Theater on April 14. Directed by Robert Sinclair. Choreography by George Balanchine. Cast included Mitzi Green, Alfred Drake, Wynn Murray, and Ray Heatherton (289 performances).*

*Babes in Arms* was the first musical for which Rodgers and Hart wrote their own book without outside assistance. The accent of the production was on youth. Two of the principals (Mitzi Green as Billie Smith, and Wynn Murray as Baby Rose) were only sixteen. Most of the others in the cast and chorus were also in their adolescence. Some unknowns in the chorus —or, as it was called in the play, "the gang"—were later destined for fame in the theater; among these were Robert Rounseville and Dan Dailey. Alfred Drake played a lesser role, that of Marshall Blackstone, but made it important; Ray Heatherton was Val Lamar. *Babes in Arms* was, as John Mason Brown reported, "a zestful, tuneful and brilliantly danced affair . . . filled with talented striplings and bubbling over with the freshness and energy of youth."

Children dominated the production; in the story, they were the offspring of touring vaudevillians. Left behind in Eastport, Long Island, by their parents, these children must shift for themselves as best they can. The teen-agers include Val Lamar, Marshall Blackstone, Gus Fielding (Rolly Pickert), Billie Smith, Baby Rose, and Dolores Reynolds (Grace McDonald). The adolescent love interest between Val and Billie is reflected in their song "Where or When," in which they feel as if they had met and known each other long before this—though neither knows where or when. But these and the other youngsters have a serious problem on their hands. The local sheriff threatens to transfer them to a work camp if their parents do not immediately return to take care of them. Since money is the solution to their problem, they put on a show of their own, "Lee Calhoun's Follies," where they reveal that they are loaded with talent. The show is an artistic success but a financial failure. They are, however, saved from the work camp when a French transatlantic flyer, Rene Flambeau, literally drops out of the sky by making a forced landing on their farmyard. He is instrumental in guiding the children in straightening out their affairs so as to keep out of the sheriff's clutches.

Within the framework of this central idea were two self-contained, self-sufficient segments. One was a fanciful ballet, "Peter's Journey," in which Marlene Dietrich, Greta Garbo, and Clark Gable appear as characters. The other was "Lee Calhoun's Follies," the fresh and ebullient amateur show put on by the kids. The conventional musical-comedy format was thus continually "thrust aside," as Robert Coleman noted, "in favor of novelty, surprise, and freshness." The score ("one of the most contagious . . . by Rodgers and Hart," said Brooks Atkinson) had four gems, all belonging with the composer's best. The very first song heard in the production proved an ace: the haunting "Where or When," shared by Billie Smith and Val Lamar. To Billie Smith was assigned two other Rodgers and Hart classics: "My Funny Valentine" (a rare instance in which a less than glamorous subject inspires such poignant musical treatment) and, by contrast, the bold and brazen and vigorous "The Lady Is a Tramp." The explosive "Johnny One Note"—about a musician who is in a class by himself in that he produced a single note that made the critics rave—was introduced by Baby Rose. The score also boasted two fine duets in the wistful and nostalgic "I Wish I Were in Love Again" and "All at Once," the first sung by Dolores and Gus, and the latter by Billie Smith and Val.

A motion picture was made of *Babes in Arms* by MGM in 1939 with Judy Garland and Mickey Rooney utilizing the main hit songs from the stage score.

BABES IN TOYLAND (1903), *a musical extravaganza with book and lyrics by Glen MacDonough. Music by Victor Herbert. Presented by Fred R. Hamlin and Julian Mitchell at the Majestic Theater on October 13. Directed by Julian Mitchell. Cast included William Norris, George W. Denham, Mabel Barrison, and Bessie Wynn (192 performances).*

It was no secret to anybody that *Babes in Toyland* was intended as an imitation of the highly successful and recently produced extravaganza *The Wizard of Oz*. The setting of Oz was transferred to the land of Mother Goose and to Toyland, a convenience for introducing characters from fairy tales, children's story books, and nursery rhymes and for bringing toys to life.

The plot was a loosely knit affair, not always logical, and sometimes not even making much sense. It served merely as the means to present picturesque characters, stunning stage spectacles, and a good deal of fetching music.

Uncle Barnaby is a miserly old man who wants to get rid of his nephew, Alan (William Norris), and his niece, Jane (Mabel Barrison), so that he can inherit their estate. He tries to get them shipwrecked, but the children manage to survive and land in a strange story-book country—that of Mother Goose—where they meet Jack and Jill, Tom Thumb, Bo-Peep, Red Riding Hood, Tommy Tucker, and others. When greedy Barnaby forecloses the mortgage on Mother Hubbard's house, he is thrown into a pond. Bo-Peep now appears, bewailing that her sheep are lost; she is consoled by Tom the Piper's Son and his friends. Now Uncle Barnaby hires two evil characters to get the children lost in the Forest of No Return. But the children are saved by gypsies. Alan and Jane now come to Toyland, a land ruled by Toymaker, a tyrant. Here a magnificent Christmas spectacle is seen, "Christmas Tree Grove," and after that a dazzling pageant, "The Legend of the Castle." Toys step in formation and parade. Through a magic incantation, Toymaker brings his toys to life, which now conspire to take Toymaker's life. There follows a scene in Toyland's Palace of Justice, where Alan is unjustly being tried for having murdered Toymaker. Found guilty, he is condemned to die by hanging. But before long, evidence is uncovered to prove him innocent. The children now decide to go home. There Barnaby plots to poison them, but becomes a victim of his own viciousness by drinking the poison by mistake. The children are now free to pursue a rich and happy life.

The show was a continual feast for the eye. The New York *Dramatic Mirror* reported that it was "a perfect dream of delight to the children and will recall the happy days of childhood to those who are facing the stern realities of life."

For Herbert, *Babes in Toyland* represented his return to the theater after an absence of more than three years (a period in which he had been busy as a symphony conductor in Pittsburgh). It was a happy return; he proved he had not lost his magic touch as a stage composer. His music was full of delights. One was the song "Toyland," sung by the toys as a tribute to their country, and another was the infectious "March of the Toys," to whose strains the toys parade. About the now celebrated "March of the Toys," the critic of the *Tribune* wrote in 1903: "It is a capital piece . . . with just a suggestion of the grotesque. [It] harmonizes charmingly with the scene and with the ballet which follows with its sounds from Toyland."

The score also included a delightful little choral piece, "I Can't Do the Sum," in which the children beat out the rhythm with their chalk on slates; a tender lullaby that Alan sings to Jane in the Forest of No Return,

"Go to Sleep, Slumber Deep"; and the witty "Rock-a-bye Baby," in which Herbert parodied the style of several composers, including Sousa and Donizetti.

In the *Sun,* James Gibbons Huneker—one of America's most penetrating critics of music and the theater—wrote: "The songs, the dances, the processions, the fairies, the toys, the spiders, and the bears! Think of them all, set in the midst of really amazing scenery, ingenious and brilliant, surrounded with light effects which counterfeit all sorts of things from simple lightning to the spinning of a great spider's web, with costumes rich and dazzling as well as tasteful, and all accompanied with music a hundred times better than is customary in shows of this sort. What more could the spirit of mortal desire?"

*Babes in Toyland* was adapted for the screen twice. The first time was in 1934, starring Laurel and Hardy. Seventeen years later, Walt Disney produced a new screen version released by Buena Vista, with Ray Bolger, Ed Wynn, and Tommy Sands in the cast. In both versions the main Herbert musical numbers were used.

> BAKER STREET (1965), *a musical comedy with book by Jerome Coopersmith adapted from stories by Sir Arthur Conan Doyle. Lyrics and music by Marian Grudeff and Raymond Jessel. Presented by Alexander H. Cohen at the Broadway Theater on February 16. Directed by Harold Prince. Choreography by Lee Becker Theodore. Cast included Fritz Weaver, Inga Swenson, and Martin Gabel (311 performances).*

*Baker Street* was described in the program as "a musical adventure of Sherlock Holmes." Supposedly, this musical was an adaptation of several stories by Sir Conan Doyle—three in particular ("Final Problems," "The Adventures of the Empty House," and "A Scandal in Bohemia"). Actually, there was a good deal more in the text representing the invention of Jerome Coopersmith, the librettist, than of Sir Conan Doyle. The synthetic plot combined suspense and melodrama with sardonic or quaint humor that made a mockery of Sherlock Holmes's rare gift at deductive logic in solving crimes. It is understandable why so many Conan Doyle enthusiasts ground their teeth at the way the original conceptions of the English author were distorted or treated with tongue in cheek.

Nevertheless, *Baker Street* had much to recommend it, because it was as strong on characterization and atmosphere as it was weak in text. Fritz Weaver and Peter Sallis were respectful to the characters they were representing— respectively Sherlock Holmes and Dr. Watson. And Harold Prince's staging and Oliver Smith's sets re-created London at the turn of the century—London with its fogs and hansom cabs, its cockney urchins and street buskers, Trafalgar Square and Big Ben. One of the scenes that made the greatest impact on audiences was the parade celebrating Queen Victoria's Diamond Jubilee in which Bil Baird's marionettes were used. *Variety* described this scene as "an automated set of a coronation parade with moving cutout soldiers, figures, Queen's carriage, and the roar of crowds amplified, with not a performer on the stage." That one scene was worth the price of admission.

The play opens with Holmes's attempts to retrieve some letters sent to Irene Adler (in Conan Doyle she was a prima donna; in *Baker Street,* a singing actress). Irene Doyle is in love with Holmes (once again stepping beyond the bounds of Conan Doyle) and becomes his ally in tracking down the diabolical Professor Moriarty (Martin Gabel) and frustrating his plans to steal the jewels sent to Queen Victoria for her Jubilee. There is a build-up of suspense at the close of the first act, with Holmes and Watson on Moriarty's yacht moored on the Thames, with an infernal machine ticking off the minutes they still have to live. Sherlock Holmes and Dr. Watson, of course, not only manage to survive but also to track down their man (with Holmes appearing in various disguises—as a vicar, a mourner, a London underworld character) and thus save the Queen's jewels.

Lee Becker Theodore's choreography helped to deflect the attention of the audience from the greatly contrived plot—particularly in a street-fight scene in the London slums, and in a number called "Leave It to Us, Guv," utilizing the talents of the juvenile dancing Baker Street Irregulars. Inga Swenson, as Irene Adler, delivered two affecting ballads, "Finding Words for Spring" and "I'd Do It Again," while in another noteworthy song, Dr. Watson recalls his marital happiness with his late wife in "A Married Man." To a score basically the work of Marian Grudeff and Raymond Jessel, Jerry Bock and Sheldon Harnick contributed two numbers, neither one of which proved a particular asset: "I'm in London Again" and "I Shall Miss You."

THE BAND WAGON (1931), *a revue with book and lyrics by George S. Kaufman and Howard Dietz. Music by Arthur Schwartz. Presented by Max Gordon at the New Amsterdam Theater on June 3. Directed by Hassard Short. Dances by Albertina Rasch. Cast included Fred and Adele Astaire, Frank Morgan, Helen Broderick, Philip Loeb, and Tilly Losch (260 performances).*

In many ways *The Band Wagon* was not only the best of the Dietz-Schwartz revues, but also as one of the best revues ever produced. This fact became obvious the first time the revue was seen anywhere—at its out-of-town tryout at the Garrick Theater in Philadelphia. Noël Coward kept shouting "bravo" throughout the performance, and after the final curtain Oscar Hammerstein II maintained that this was the best revue in his time. Once *The Band Wagon* came to New York, the critics joined the chorus of praises, headed by Brooks Ackinson, who wrote: "After the appearance of *The Band Wagon* . . . it will be difficult for the old-time musical to hold up its head. . . . It is both funny and lovely; it has wit, gaiety and splendor."

It had sparkling sketches by George S. Kaufman. In one of these, "The Pride of the Claghorns," a travesty on the Southland, Frank Morgan (appearing for the first time in a musical) was seen as a Southern colonel who throws his daughter out of his Southern mansion for good, because he can never have a "virgin darken his doorstep." In another, "For Good Old Nectar," a college cheering section is brought into the classroom to root for the history champion—in the traditional manner of football cheering squads. Helen Broderick proved she could maintain a matronly dignity while shopping for undignified bathroom appliances in a swank shop. When she notes that the salesman had failed to show her a sample of *the* basic fixture in any bathroom, the salesman replies: "Heard melodies are sweet, but those unheard are sweeter." (Max Gordon, the producer, who had a horror of off-color humor, tried to delete this sketch from the show. He was talked out of it—and it turned out to be the show-stopper.) Miss Broderick also revealed a gift for satire in her takeoff on torch singers, in "Where Can He Be?"

*The Band Wagon* had glamour, beauty, grandiose displays for the eye, gaiety, humor, and satire. The closing scene of the first act was a stunning Bavarian number, with Fred and Adele Astaire and the ensemble spinning around on a merry-go-round—all taking place to the polka music of "I Love Louisa." Tilly Losch did a fetching solo dance in "The Flag," then joined Fred Astaire in an elaborate ballet sequence set in old Vienna, "The Beggar's Waltz." Fred and Adele Astaire appeared as two French youngsters playing with large hoops in "Hoops."

For "I Love Louisa," and one or two elaborate spectacles, Hassard Short devised twin revolving stages as part of the action to increase the effect on the eye and contribute additional visual beauty with a quick change of setting. This was the first time in any musical that a revolving stage (let alone two of them) was used for anything except to change the scenery.

The Dietz-Schwartz score contained some of their best songs, and one that is now readily conceded to be their masterpiece, "Dancing in the Dark." During the rehearsals, the director and writers felt that a radical change of pace could be achieved through the inclusion of what Schwartz described as a "dark song, somewhat mystical, yet in slow even rhythm." The next morning he had "Dancing in the Dark" written. John Barker sang it, after which Tilly

Losch and her dancers performed a ballet sequence to its strains with ever-changing colored lights reflected by mirrors on the floor. "New Sun in the Sky," was also a musical highlight. Fred Astaire sang it as he shined his shoes, put on his clothes, and preened in front of a mirror. Another song deserving to become a "standard" (though it failed to do so) was "High and Low," introduced by Roberta Robinson, John Barker, and the chorus girls. So good was Arthur Schwartz's music that it even attracted the interest and enthusiasm of New York's powerful music critic Olin Downes of *The New York Times.* He wrote: "We have a composer whose melodic vein is not only graceful but characterized at its best by refinement and artistic quality. . . . He is able in many places to deliver a quality of musical workmanship, which would command the respect of the most serious composer, and perhaps also the envy."

Of historical importance, as far as the American musical theater was concerned, is the fact that *The Band Wagon* was the last production in which Fred and Adele Astaire appeared as a team. Adele married Charles Cavendish and went into retirement—her last appearance taking place at the Illinois Theater in Chicago on March 5, 1932, during the out-of-town tour of *The Band Wagon.* Vera Marsh replaced her in the revue; in later stage musicals Fred Astaire went solo.

Two motion pictures were adapted from this revue. The first adopted the title of its principal song, "Dancing in the Dark." Produced by 20th Century-Fox, it starred William Powell and Betsy Drake, used three songs from the stage score, and was released in 1949. The second, retaining the original title of *The Band Wagon,* was produced by MGM in 1953 with Fred Astaire and Cyd Charisse. This version used most of the popular numbers from the stage revue together with a new Dietz-Schwartz song, "That's Entertainment."

> BANJO EYES (1941), *a musical comedy with book by Joe Quillan and Izzy Elinson, based on the Broadway stage comedy* Three Men on a Horse, *by John Cecil Holm and George Abbott. Lyrics by John La Touche and Harold Adamson. Music by Vernon Duke. Presented by Albert Lewis at the Hollywood Theater on December 25. Directed by Hassard Short. Dances by Charles Walters. Cast included Eddie Cantor, Lionel Stander, June Clyde, Audrey Christie, and the De Marcos (126 performances).*

In *Banjo Eyes,* Eddie Cantor was returning to the Broadway stage for the first time in about a dozen years. Naturally he wanted his return to be a triumph. Consequently, in the out-of-town tryouts of the show, he insisted on retaining in the production every bit of material that had been written, in order to study audience reaction and delete whatever failed to meet with approval. At the first tryout—in New Haven on November 7, 1941—the final curtain did not come down until 12:45, "with practically no one except the girls' mothers, the backers and their families remaining in their seats," as Vernon Duke revealed. Naturally, in New Haven, and later in Boston, a number of scenes and songs were removed, including a few good ballads, which was responsible for making the Vernon Duke score less varied in style and emotion than it had originally been. But Eddie Cantor was far more interested in having a show-stopper song for himself (another "If You Knew Susie," if possible, he told Duke) than good ballads. He drove Duke to write one for him in Boston: "We're Having a Baby" (lyrics by Harold Adamson). Its risqué lines and provocative innuendoes—accentuated by Eddie's rolling eyes and clapping hands—were sure-fire. As presented by Cantor, with the help of June Clyde, the song became such a favorite that at every performance it had to be repeated several times.

The musical adaptation of *Three Men on a Horse* digresses from the original stage play. In the play Erwin Trowbridge is a meek, mild-mannered writer of greeting-card verses who has a unique gift for doping out horses on paper. After a fight with his wife, he goes off to the nearest bar, gets drunk for the first time in his life, and then becomes involved with gamblers who take full advantage of his rare gift for picking horses. But Erwin can pick winners only so long as he does not profit from his choices. Since he has been compelled to take a percentage of the gamblers' winnings, he can figure winners no more. He extricates himself from the clutches of the gamblers, returns to his wife and to his former placid and uneventful existence as a writer of greeting-card poems.

In the musical, Erwin (Eddie Cantor) gets his horse information in a dream, which leads him to the racing stables, where he talks to the horses and finds out from them who will be the winner.

Corn is generously introduced to provide the musical with audience appeal. There is, for example, a hackneyed horse routine—long a staple of vaudeville and burlesque—in which the horse is played by two actors, one the head, the other the tail. Also, since Pearl Harbor had been a recent disaster when *Banjo Eyes* opened and America was deep in war, an Army drill scene was interpolated both for its humorus potentials and to inject a timely martial note. Here Cantor did a routine in which he came running late to the parade ground still in his long underwear and his pants slung over his shoulder. Having missed breakfast, he surreptitiously removed a hard-boiled egg and a salt cellar from his pocket and gulped down the salted egg, while a general was making an inspection. One matinee, Danny Kaye (already a star) became an impromptu replacement for one of the chorus men in this scene. When Cantor saw Kaye, while performing his eating routine, he pushed the egg in Kaye's mouth; then, with Kaye's mouth wide open, Cantor shook salt into it. After that Eddie removed a banana from his own pocket, took a bite, and pushed *that* into Danny Kaye's mouth. By this time, the audience recognized Danny Kaye and gave him an ovation; the performance of that drill scene ran eight minutes late that day.

This Army drill scene culminated in a stirring World War II song for Eddie Cantor, "We Did It Before, And We Can Do It Again" (not by Vernon Duke, but by Charlie Tobias and Cliff Friend). Cantor had an amusing Vernon Duke number in "Who Started to Rhumba?", which he sang to a racehorse. The De Marcos did a sophisticated dance to Duke's ballad "Not a Nickel to My Name."

*Banjo Eyes* was much more successful than its run of 126 performances might suggest. *Billboard* reported that there was not a single dissenting vote among the critics about its entertainment value, and audiences were equally enthusiastic. The show played to capacity houses during its run. When it closed down it was not for lack of customers but because Cantor had to undergo a serious operation. The show had been tailor-made for his special talents; he had dominated it so completely that using a substitute for him was unthinkable.

THE BELLE OF BOHEMIA (1900), *operetta with book and lyrics by Harry B. Smith. Music by Ludwig Englander and T. MacConnell. Presented by George W. Lederer at the Casino Theater on September 24. Directed by George Lederer. Ballets by Aurelia Coccia. Cast included Sam Bernard, Irene Bentley, Virginia Earle, and Trixie Friganza (55 performances).*

*The Belle of Bohemia* is a comedy of errors. Adolph Klotz, a Coney Island photographer (Sam Bernard), and Rudolph Dinkelhauser, a wealthy brewer (Dick Bernard), look alike. While bathing in Coney Island they are mistaken for each other. When Dinkelhauser is arrested for indiscretions committed by Klotz while drunk, Klotz is taken home by Dinkelhauser's wife and valet, who believe he has gone crazy because he insists he is a photographer. At the Dinkelhauser villa in Newport, a fraudulent lawyer is trying to swindle Dinkelhauser of his fortune and confuses Klotz with the man he is trying to swindle. Klotz saves Dinkelhauser's fortune.

"He Was a Married Man," sung by Adolph Klotz, "When Shall I Find Him?", introduced by Klotz's wife, played by Virginia Earle, and "Plain Kelly McGuire" were the principal musical numbers. As a first-act finale the sextet from Donizetti's *Lucia di Lammermoor* was satirized.

THE BELLE OF NEW YORK (1897), *an operetta with book and lyrics by Hugh Morton. Music by Gustave Kerker. Presented at the Casino Theater on September 28. Directed by George W. Lederer. Cast included Edna May and Harry Davenport (56 performances).*

*The Belle of New York* was only a modest success in New York, but subsequently at the Shaftesbury Theater in London it amassed the formidable run of 697 performances and became one of the best-loved operettas of that period; and its success on the road in the United States was hardly less impressive. The setting was New York, where the escapades of Harry Bronson (Harry Davenport) give his father considerable cause for alarm, since the father is actively engaged in fighting vice as the president of the Young Men's Rescue League. Harry finally sees the error of his ways when he falls in love with sweet and simple Violet Gray, a Salvation Army girl.

As Violet, Edna May became a star overnight—after stepping suddenly into the role on the second night. Petite to the point of being wispish, ash blond, and with a baby-faced innocent expression on her exquisite face, she captured the hearts of the men in her audience with songs like "They All Follow Me" ("Men never proceed to follow the light, but they *always* follow me"), "She Is the Belle of New York," and "Teach Me How to Kiss." Both in New York and in London she was pursued by the rich, the highborn, and the playboy. She apparently was as mentally alert as she was physically appealing. She brought her father, a humble Syracuse mail carrier, to Rector's, the famous New York restaurant. When asked by her rich and powerful admirers about her father's profession, she replied quickly, "He is an American man of letters."

LA BELLE PAREE (1911), *a revue, with book by Edgar Smith. Lyrics by Edward Madden. Music by Frank Tours and Jerome Kern. Presented by the Winter Garden Company at the Winter Garden on March 20. Cast included Harry Fisner, Stella Mayhew, Melville Ellis, George White, Kitty Gordon, and Al Jolson (104 performances).*

On March 20, 1911, the Shuberts (who by 1911 had become a major power in the theatrical industry) opened a new theater which they had built on 52nd Street and Broadway to house musical extravaganzas. They called it the Winter Garden, and themselves, the Winter Garden Company. It was a palatial auditorium seating 1590. Coffee and drinks were served during the performance.

For their opening production, the Shuberts offered a triple bill. One half of the show consisted of a Spanish ballet by Tortajada and sixteen Moorish dancing girls; also *Bow Sing,* a Chinese opera in three scenes with book by

Carroll Fleming and Arthur Voegtlin, with music by Manuel Klein, in which the dancer Mlle. Dazie was starred. The other half of the production was "a jumble of jollity," as the program called it, in two acts. This was *La Belle Paree,* a revue which the program described as a Cook's tour through vaudeville, with a Parisian landscape.

*La Belle Paree* made musical-theater history on two counts other than that it helped to open an important new theater. It was the first production for which Jerome Kern wrote not one or two songs interpolated into somebody else's score, but half the score (seven numbers), the other half being the work of Frank Tours. None of the Kern numbers are remembered, or deserve to be—but nevertheless Kern took an important forward step in his career in the Broadway theater.

The second reason why *La Belle Paree* became important was that it marked the Broadway debut of Al Jolson. Appropriately enough, that debut took place during the opening of a theater where he would achieve his greatest triumphs as perhaps the foremost musical-comedy star of that decade. And it was Jolson who transformed *La Belle Paree*—and the opening Winter Garden attraction—from a fiasco to a success. This happened on the third night. At the premiere and the night after that, the audience was obviously bored by a four-hour production that had little to recommend it, and which the critics had annihilated. On the third night, Al Jolson stepped in front of the footlights and remarked spontaneously to his audience: "Lots of brave folks out there. Either that—or they can't read." The audience snickered. Jolson continued with his impromptu remarks: "Come to think of it, after the reviews we got, there's a lot of brave folks up here on the stage." The audience began to sit up and show interest. Jolson continued: "I've got a few songs to sing, that is, if you want to listen." The audience replied with a burst of applause. Jolson sang, and had the audience in the palm of his hand. His performance was mentioned in the newspapers the next day. From then on the theater became filled with people eager to see who this Al Jolson was. Jolson had made himself a star, and as he was to do again and again in the ensuing years, he made his show into a solid hit. Less than two weeks after *La Belle Paree* opened, the Shuberts initiated Sunday-night concerts at the Winter Garden (first performance on April 2, 1911), with Al Jolson as the principal performer. It was not long before Jolson dominated these Sunday-night concerts so completely that the only reason people flocked to the Winter Garden on Sunday evenings was to hear him sing and make impromptu remarks. When *La Belle Paree* closed, Jolson (who had been receiving $250 a week) signed an exclusive contract with the Shuberts paying him $1,500 a week plus a percentage of the gross receipts.

As for Jolson's career prior to *La Belle Paree:* He had been born in Russia on March 26, 1886, his name at birth being Asa Yoelson. When he was four, he and his family came to the United States and settled in Washington, D.C., where his father was a cantor in the synagogue, and the child, Al, sang in the synagogue choir. Life began for him on the afternoon he saw his first vaudeville show. Eddie Leonard was the headliner. When Eddie Leonard invited the audience to join him in singing "I'd Leave My Happy Home for You," little Al rose in his seat and sang—and everybody listened. Several times after that Al tried to run away from home to find a place for himself in show business; each time, he was caught and brought home. Finally he formed a vaudeville act with his brother Harry and Fred E. Moore, billed as "introducers and promoters of high-class ballads and popular songs." At the Rockaway Theater in Long Island, young Jolson blackened his face for the first time. Discovered by Lew Dockstader, Jolson was ultimately hired by the Lew Dockstader Minstrels at a salary of $75 a week. At first he was just an end man, allowed a solo spot in the "olio" section. Then he was starred as a single just before the closing of each show. Sime Silverman took note of him in *Variety* by writing: "Haven't seen a demonstration for a single act, or any act, for that matter, as was given by Al Jolson when he appeared next to closing in Dockstader's Minstrels."

His next significant advance came at Hammerstein's Victoria in 1909. Here he made it a practice to depart from script and formal routines to improvise. In the middle of his act on his opening-night appearance he called out: "Bring up the house lights." Seating himself at the edge of the stage, he started to chat with the audience. "Ya know, folks," he said, "this is the happiest night of my life. Yes siree. I'm so happy. . . . I want to sing and sing and sing. . . . Ya wanna lissen?" He sang; and the audience was his.

For the next two years he performed extensively in vaudeville, sometimes employed simultaneously by three theaters and earning $500 a week. Ziegfeld took note of him and asked him to audition for a possible spot in the *Follies*. "Jolie doesn't audition," was his reply. "If Ziegfeld wants to see me perform, let him catch my act." Ziegfeld lost interest, but that hardly bothered Jolson. "I'm the best," he would say. "There'll be bigger opportunities." Only three weeks after Ziegfeld asked for and did not get the audition, Jolson was signed by the Shuberts for *La Belle Paree.*

BELLS ARE RINGING (1956), *a musical comedy with book and lyrics by Betty Comden and Adolph Green. Music by Jule Styne. Presented by the Theater Guild at the Shubert Theater on November 29. Directed by Jerome Robbins. Dances by Jerome Robbins and Bob Fosse. Cast included Judy Holliday, Sydney Chaplin, and Eddie Lawrence (924 performances).*

The ringing bells are those of "Susanswerphone," a telephone-answering service in Manhattan run by Sue (Jean Stapleton) with the help of Ella Peterson (Judy Holliday). Ella is the kind of girl who puts on lipstick before answering the phone; whose somewhat scatterbrain conversation is punctuated with high squeaks and nervous laughs; who somehow always manages to meddle and get enmeshed in the private affairs of her clients, whom she knows only by voice. When she discovers that playwright Jeff Moss (Sydney Chaplin) has trouble writing his play and is getting a calling down from his producer, she boldly invades his apartment and proceeds to get involved in his life. She helps him start working again and keeps after him until he actually finishes his play and has it produced. While this is going on, Sue has fallen in love with Sandor (Eddie Lawrence), who heads Titanic Records. Sandor prevails on Sue to let him use her office for his "business affairs"— which in actuality consist of taking bets on the horses, his recording company being only a front for this operation. (Names and numbers of symphonies, opus numbers, and their composers serve as the code for horse, track, race, and so forth.) The police begin to monitor the phones of "Susanswerphone," suspecting it of being involved in some vice racket, and thus discover Sandor's illegal operations.

Ella also becomes interested in the problems of a dentist, Dr. Kitchell (Bernie West), a man who wants to write songs, and in a would-be Marlon Brando whose ambition is to become an actor (Frank Aletter as Blake Barton). Somehow, she manages to get both to achieve their respective goals. While performing these benefactions, she falls in love with, and succeeds in winning, Jeff.

*Bells Are Ringing* became a box-office triumph—the recipient of accolades from all the critics—mainly because of Judy Holliday's performance, her first in a musical comedy. Brooks Atkinson said of her: "She sings, dances, clowns—and also carries on her shoulders one of the most antiquated plots of the season."

Three of the best songs in the score were ballads: "Long Before I Knew You," in which Jeff and Ella come to realize how much they are beginning to mean to each other; and the hit songs of the production, "Just in Time," which Jeff, Ella, and the ensemble present in Central Park en route to a swank party, and "The Party's Over," sung by Ella.

For Judy Holliday this appearance marked a reunion with Betty Comden and Adolph Green, authors of book and lyrics—for in 1938 all three had appeared in a nightclub act called "The Revuers," for which Comden and Green wrote all the material. Since that time, the gift of Betty Comden and Adolph Green for sophisticated lyrics, nimble dialogue, and vitriolic satire had developed impressively. Many numbers in *Bells Are Ringing* were dressed in bright, amusing, satirical lyrics: "It's a Simple System," a *Schnitzelbank* based on *The Racing Form;* "Drop That Name," a devastating takeoff on the practice of name-dropping at swank parties; and a "going-home song" to end all such songs, "I'm Goin' Back," with which the play comes to a rousing finale.

A bit of homey philosophy on better human relations was introduced in a song by Ella Peterson in a subway scene—"Hello, Hello There!" That subway scene had one of Jerome Robbins' happy choreographic creations, a whirling fandango.

The basic score from the stage production was used when *Bells Are Ringing* was made into a motion picture (MGM, 1960). Judy Holliday was retained as the star, but the leading male role was usurped by Dean Martin.

BEST FOOT FORWARD (1941), *a musical comedy with book by John Cecil Holm. Lyrics and music by Hugh Martin and Ralph Blane. Presented by George Abbott at the Ethel Barrymore Theater on October 1. Directed by George Abbott. Dances by Gene Kelly. Cast included Rosemary Lane, Nancy Walker, June Allyson, and Gil Stratton, Jr. (326 performances).*

*Best Foot Forward* was a young people's frolic. The principals were comparative youngsters—two of them, Nancy Walker and June Allyson, at the beginning of lustrous careers. The whole production was charged with youthful energy and vitality that reminded many playgoers of the Rodgers and Hart carnival of youth, *Babes in Arms* (1937). (It is interesting to point out that though his name does not appear on the billing, Richard Rodgers was one of the producers of *Best Foot Forward*.)

The setting is Winsocki School near Philadelphia. On a lark, young Bud Hooper (Gil Stratton, Jr.) sends an invitation to the Hollywood star Gale Joy (Rosemary Lane), to be his "date" at the Junior Prom. In Hollywood, Gale's press agent, Jack Haggerty (Marty May), recognizes the publicity value of having Gale attend a school prom with a teen-ager and urges her to accept the invitation. Gale's arrival at Winsocki creates a sensation. Bud ditches his own girl, Helen (Maureen Cannon), to take Gale to the prom. At the dance, in a fit of jealousy, Helen tears the sash from Gale's gown. Realizing they can get valuable souvenirs of a movie queen, the other young people proceed to tear off her clothes, until she is stripped down to bare essentials. A scandal ensues at the school, with Bud in danger of being expelled. But the difficulties are straightened out when Gale returns to Hollywood and Bud and Helen are reconciled.

The principal musical number was a semisatirical football song, "Buckle

Down Winsocki," sung by Tommy Dix and Stuart Langley (playing lesser roles), together with the ensemble. June Allyson scored with "Who Do You Think I Am?", Nancy Walker with "Just a Little Joint with a Juke Box," and Rosemary Lane with "That's How I Love the Blues."

When *Best Foot Forward* was made into a motion picture by MGM in 1943, it utilized the basic stage score, and starred Lucille Ball and William Gaxton.

*Best Foot Forward* was revived on April 2, 1963, in an Off Broadway production that had a run of 224 performances. Of special interest was the fact that this presentation marked the first New York appearance of Liza Minnelli, daughter of Judy Garland, and subsequently a star in her own right on stage, screen, and television.

> BILLION DOLLAR BABY (1945), *a musical comedy with book and lyrics by Betty Comden and Adolph Green. Music by Morton Gould. Presented by Paul Feigay and Oliver Smith at the Alvin Theater on December 21. Directed by George Abbott. Choreography by Jerome Robbins. Cast included Joan McCracken, Mitzi Green, William Tabbert, and David Burns (220 performances).*

Since World War II, there have been a number of musicals that based their subject and characters satirically on the decade of the 1920's. *Billion Dollar Baby* was one of the first to do so, describing itself in the program as "a musical play of the Terrific Twenties." Prohibition and speakeasies, gangsters and racketeers, dance marathons, a soaring stock market, the costumes and foibles and catchwords and quips, the social idiosyncrasies, and the frenetic hunt on everybody's part for good times are some of the ingredients which made *Billion Dollar Baby* both a pioneer endeavor in the musical theater and, at its best, a delightful stage escapade.

The musical is a sophisticated treatment of a young girl from Staten Island, Maribelle Jones (Joan McCracken) who, aided and abetted by a domineering mother, makes her way from rags to riches. On her way up (and sometimes down again) she deserts her comfortable and humdrum middle-class home and naïve boyfriend to become involved with disreputable characters. She passes from one romance to another, living the full life. She enters the "Miss America Contest" in Atlantic City and loses. She becomes involved with one of the country's most formidable gangsters, Dapper Welch (David Burns), then falls in love with one of his henchmen, Rocky Barton (William Tabbert) who is on the run not only from the police but from his boss. His boss gets killed, and Maribelle mourns his passing at a lavish gangster funeral. She finds a new lover in a tycoon just as the stock market collapses. The frivolities, gaieties, and reckless living of the 1920's are over—and so is our musical.

Much of the action—and a good deal of the unusual interest in the musical—is carried by Jerome Robbins' inventive ballet sequences, the best of which are the "Charleston," "The Marathoners," the "Miss America Pageant," the "Gangster Funeral and Wake," and the "Love Ballet." All the music for these ballet sequences (as well as for all the songs and interludes) were orchestrated by the composer himself, a practice not usual on Broadway, particularly at that time.

*Billion Dollar Baby* was Morton Gould's first musical-comedy score. (He wrote a second musical, *Arms and the Girl,* an adaptation of the stage play *Pursuit of Happiness;* it opened on February 2, 1950 and had a run of 134 performances.) Like Gershwin, Gould's career in music has consisted in straddling the two worlds of music—the popular and the serious; and like Gershwin, Gould often introduced popular music in his serious works, just as in the dance sequences of *Billion Dollar Baby* he introduced serious-musical methods for popular entertainment. Gould was born in Richmond Hill, Long Island, on December 10, 1913. A child prodigy both as pianist and as composer, who produced his first piece of music (a waltz for piano) when he was six, he received a thoroughly comprehensive musical training. For a while he appeared as pianist in vaudeville. At seventeen he became staff arranger for the Radio City Music Hall in New York, subsequently becoming staff pianist for the National Broadcasting Company. From 1934, for many years, he was a radio favorite as conductor of a weekly sponsored program devoted to popular music in his own intriguing arrangements. His serious works, many making effective use of popular idioms, have been performed by most of the major symphony orchestras. He also wrote the scores for successful ballets, for movies, and for special radio and television productions.

No single number in *Billion Dollar Baby* became popular, but a few deserve mention: "One Track Mind" (infectiously sung by Mitzi Green playing a character named Georgia Motley who reminds us of the celebrated nightclub hostess of the twenties, Texas Guinan); "I'm Sure of Your Love," sung by Rocky Barton; and "Bad Timing" introduced by two minor characters.

BLACKBIRDS OF 1928 (1928), *an all-Negro revue, with book and lyrics by Dorothy Fields. Music by Jimmy McHugh. Presented by Lew Leslie at the Liberty Theater on May 9. Directed by Lew Leslie. Cast included Adelaide Hall, Aida Ward, Bill Robinson, and Tim Moore (518 performances).*

*Blackbirds of 1928* was not the first all-Negro revue to reach Broadway; that distinction goes to *Shuffle Along* in 1921. But it *was* the first all-Negro revue that could stand comparison with the best that the white revues could offer. For it boasted excellent material and remarkable performers who could make this material sound even better than it was. And it had all the dynamism, electricity, and personal magnetism of which Negro performers, at their best, were capable.

There was, for example, "Bojangles" Bill Robinson—here achieving his first Broadway stage success. He did not appear until the second half of the revue. But from the moment he came on the stage to sing and dance in "Doin' the New Low Down," he captured his audience. As he shuffled across the stage, or tapped up and down a double flight of five steps, or beat out the rhythms of a song with his nimble toes, he was a man of rhythm who electrified the theater. "His feet," reported *Time,* "were as quick as a snare drummer's hands."

But the revue had other riches as well. The cream of the comedy came from Tim Moore—a huge, stout, toothy performer—who did old-fashioned burlesques of a prizefight ("Bear Cat Jones' Last Fight") and a poker game ("Playing According to Hoyle") and who appeared in a riotous sketch involving a Harlem wedding. Satire was interpolated through a Negro version of Elinor Glyn's then best-selling romantic and (for 1928) sexy novel, *It.*

Not the least of the significance of *Blackbirds of 1928* is the fact that it represented the first complete score created for the stage by Dorothy Fields (lyricist) and Jimmy McHugh (composer). Before many years would go by they would become ace songwriters in Hollywood, which came as no surprise to those who knew their songs from *Blackbirds of 1928.* The biggest song hit to come out of that show was "I Can't Give You Anything but Love, Baby," sung by Aida Ward (in her Broadway debut), Willard MacLean, and Bill Robinson. The idea for this number was born, one day, when standing outside Tiffany's on Fifth Avenue, the songwriters happened to hear a young man tell his girl, "Gee, honey, I can't give you nothin' but love." Actually, this song was *not* introduced in this revue. It had previously been sung by Patsy Kelly in *Delmar's Revue in 1927,* a show that folded in two weeks. Sensing its potential, the songwriters decided to use it again—for *Blackbirds*—and they had a sure winner. During the run of the revue, Adelaide Hall took over the number.

Another song hit, however, was written expressly for *Blackbirds:* "Diga, Diga, Doo," a wild Zulu number introduced by Adelaide Hall (also making her Broadway debut) and a group of girls bedecked in red sequin costumes and red feathers. A frenetic Zulu dance followed the singing.

The first-act finale was a tribute to the DuBose Heyward novel *Porgy* in which shadows of the performers were reflected on a back screen—dark, magnified figures that produced a fantastic stage effect. It is interesting to remark that when Rouben Mamoulian directed the first production of Gershwin's folk opera *Porgy and Bess* several years later, he imitated this same stage effect with equal impact—though whether he got the idea from *Blackbirds of 1928* it is, of course, impossible to say.

There were later editions of *Blackbirds,* but none were successful. The one in 1930 starred Ethel Waters and Buck and Bubbles and had a basic score by Eubie Blake. Its best number was "Dinah" (words by Sam M. Lewis and Joe Young, and music by Harry Akst), which Ethel Waters had introduced in a nightclub in the summer of 1924, and interpolated in a Broadway revue, *Africana,* which had a short existence in 1927. She brought it back with her to the *Blackbirds of 1930.* Among the new numbers, the most impressive (largely for Miss Waters' delivery) were "My Handy Man Ain't Handy No More" and "Baby Mine." "Memories of You," introduced by Minto Cato, was also on the plus side. But the show as a whole lacked verve, excitement, and humor—and it lasted only 57 performances. The *Blackbirds of 1933–1934* did not stay even that long, surviving just twenty-five performances. About all that it had to recommend it were two appearances by Bill Robinson in the second act—but it was not enough.

THE BLACK CROOK (1866), *a musical extravaganza, with book by Charles M. Barras. Music consisted mostly of adaptations, with some new numbers by Giuseppe Operti. Presented by William Wheatley and Henry C. Jarrett at Niblo's Gardens on September 12 (474 performances).*

*The Black Crook* has often been called the first American musical comedy. It was the first major success of our musical theater; it was the first musical in which undraped females, suggestive dances, and sex insinuations in song were prominently exploited.

The production was largely the result of chance. In the 1860's Henry C. Jarrett and Harry Palmer imported from France a troupe of ballet dancers and some expensive stage sets. They planned to put on a French ballet at the Academy of Music in New York. Before this production could be realized, the Academy burned down. The only other place Jarrett and Palmer could put on their show was at Niblo's Gardens, and they entered into negotiations with William Wheatley, its proprietor. It so happened that during this period Wheatley had acquired the rights to a melodrama by Charles M. Barras called *The Black Crook.* He consummated a deal with Jarrett and Palmer whereby they would join forces in producing *The Black Crook* at Niblo's Gardens, with the imported ballet troupe and sets.

Once this deal was set, Wheatley began planning his production along most elaborate designs. He rebuilt his stage to permit trap doors everywhere, to accommodate the elaborate settings he had in mind, and to house the complex machinery necessary to create the remarkable stage effects he was planning. He outfitted the girls of the ballet in expensive, usually transparent silks and laces. He built up an enormous cast. By the time the curtain went up he had spent the then unprecedented sum of 50,000 dollars.

The play itself was merely an excuse for presenting a continual succession of spectacles, ballets, transformations, enchantments. Hertzog, the Black Crook, makes a pact with the devil to deliver a human soul each year, just before midnight on New Year's Eve. Endowed by the devil with supernatural powers, Hertzog selects for his victim Rudolph, a painter then imprisoned by Count Wolfenstein. Hertzog manages Rudolph's release from his cell, then leads him on a quest for hidden gold. En route, Rudolph saves the life of a dove, which in reality is a fairy queen. She discloses to Rudolph Hertzog's evil design, and thus Rudolph is saved. Hertzog is led away by the devil for failing to fulfill his bargain, and Rudolph finds not only freedom but also his beloved, Amina.

For five and a half hours audiences were held spellbound not only by the play itself, which was often confusing, but by the fantastic stage effects, mammoth production numbers, opulent ballets, and the sensual display of female beauty. Among the stage effects were a hurricane in the Harz Mountains, a demon ritual, a "grand ballet of gems," a carnival, a masquerade, a pageant. The closing scene depicted fairies on silver couches, and angels in gilded chariots, ascending and descending "amid a silver rain."

Never before had New York seen anything on its stage to equal such splendors. But stage spectacle was not the only attraction to entice audiences into Niblo's Gardens. Another lure was the "sinful entertainment" provided by the girls in pink tights in suggestive dance numbers. "The police should arrest all engaged in such a violation of public decency," bellowed James Gordon Bennett in an editorial in the *Herald*. From a platform the Reverend Charles B. Smythe denounced the "immodest dress of the girls" who appeared "with thin gauze-like material allowing the form of the figure to be discernible." He went on to say: "The attitudes were exceedingly indelicate. . . . When a danseuse is assisted by a danseur, the attitudes assumed by both in conjunction suggest to the imagination scenes which one may read, describing the ancient heathen orgies."

*The Black Crook,* then, became the thing to see—even if respectable women had to wear heavy veils to conceal their identity. Many came not once but several times, as new and ever greater stage spectacles were interpolated. (In 1867 a baby ballet of several hundred infants was introduced! A few months later a lavish carnival and masquerade were interpolated.) The run of 474 performances proved the most profitable for an American theater impresario up to that time. The show earned a profit of over one million dollars in its initial run, and this figure was swelled considerably in succeeding years through numerous revivals.

The impact that this spectacle had on its audience can perhaps be measured by its effect on two famous showmen, each of whom was in his early boyhood when he saw *The Black Crook*. One was Charles Frohman (then only eight), who so fell in love with the production that he got himself a job selling programs in the lobby so that he could have an opportunity of seeing the show at every performance. Then and there was born in him the love for theater which subsequently made him one of America's and England's leading theatrical producers. The other was Sam Shubert, also still a boy, who saw *The Black Crook* in its revival in 1885. He later confessed that it was at this performance that he knew with finality that the theater would become his life's work.

Two musical numbers from the original production became popular. One was the "March of the Amazons," by Operti. The other was the song "You Naughty, Naughty Men" (by T. Kennick and G. Bicknell), which Milly Cavendish sang provocatively to the men in the audience from the front of the stage.

The circumstances surrounding the first production of *The Black Crook* were borrowed and embellished upon for the Sigmund Romberg musical comedy *The Girl in Pink Tights*.

BLOOMER GIRL (1944), *a musical comedy, with book by Sig Herzig and Fred Saidy, based on an unproduced play by Lilith and Dan James. Lyrics by E. Y. Harburg. Music by Harold Arlen. Presented by John C. Wilson in association with Nat Goldstone at the Shubert Theater on October 5. Directed by E. Y. Harburg and William Schorr. Choreography by Agnes de Mille. Cast included Celeste Holm, Joan McCracken, and David Brooks (654 performances).*

Before *Bloomer Girl* came to New York, advance publicity and rumor suggested it was another *Oklahoma!*—the Rodgers and Hammerstein musical play that had taken Broadway by storm a year and a half earlier. And there were some similarities: *Bloomer Girl* was an American period piece; Celeste Holm was in a starring role; its choreography was by Agnes de Mille. But here, regrettably, the similarity ended. There was no artistic pretense about *Bloomer Girl,* nor did it tap folklore either in text or music. It was a big, colorful show that made no attempt to depart from the established conventions and formulas of musical comedy. But what it set out to do, it did very well, indeed.

Its setting is the small New York town of Cicero, in 1861. One of its principal characters is Dolly Bloomer (Margaret Douglass), the dynamic feminist who espoused temperance and women's rights, helped escaped Negroes in the underground, and was passionate about the practicability of women wearing bloomers instead of hoop skirts. (Her real name, incidentally, was not Dolly but Amelia.) The issue of bloomers versus hoop skirts becomes a crisis in Dolly's personal life. Her brother-in-law, Horatio Applegate (Matt Briggs), is a wealthy manufacturer of hoop skirts who wins five of his daughters over to his way of life by having them marry salesmen from his establishment. But his sixth daughter, Evelina (Celeste Holm), is a rebel, Dolly Bloomer's ally. She is even able to influence her Southern sweetheart, Jeff Calhoun (David Brooks), to assist her in arranging the escape of Jeff's slave.

Evelina consents to model hoop skirts for her father at a garden party, but to the horror of all those present, she proceeds to remove her skirt to reveal she is wearing bloomers. Meanwhile, Jeff's brother has caught up with his escaped slave, and has brought legal action against Dolly Bloomer. Dolly, Evelina, and the slave are jailed, but are given their freedom so that they can perform *Uncle Tom's Cabin* at the Opera House. When Jeff joins the Confederate Army after that, Evelina loses interest in him. But all complications are neatly resolved. Dolly becomes the manager of the Applegate factory when the governor has taken it over for the production of Army uniforms—*and* bloomers. And Evelina and Jeff, of course, become reconciled.

To Arlen's biographer, Edward Jablonski, the score is "one of his richest and most varied." Jablonski singles out for special attention "The Rakish Young Man with the Whiskers" (which he describes as a "lovely waltz"); "Satin Gown and Silver Shoe" (a lullaby); the ballads "Right as the Rain" and "Evelina"; a slave song, "a hymn to human dignity," called "The Eagle and Me"; "the blues tinctured 'Man for Sale.'" In addition, there are two songs presented by Joan McCracken, "T'morra', T'morra'" and "I Never Was Born." But perhaps the biggest number in the production—and the song that continually brought down the house—was a blues, "I Got a Song," in the dusky style for which Arlen had already become famous. It was sung by Richard Huey, a former redcap, who had so much trouble learning its intricate rhythms that at one rehearsal he walked off the stage and insisted he would not do the number. But Arlen patiently taught Huey how to sing the song correctly, and on opening night Huey was a triumph in it.

The main contribution by Agnes de Mille came in the closing scene. It was a Civil War ballet, the tragedy of women waiting for their lovers or husbands to return from the war. Everyone connected with the show had his doubts about this dance, with its somber overtones; but in the end, they went along with Agnes de Mille and never regretted that decision. A handsome production number was built around the song "Sunday in Cicero Falls," a satiric number opening Act II, whose lyrics commented sardonically on what kind of citizens the people of Cicero were; another was inspired by the auction of slaves and by other parts of *Uncle Tom's Cabin,* to speak eloquently about American unity in time of war.

The consensus among the critics was that *Bloomer Girl* was not only a "hit" but an outstanding musical. "Not to scurry about for exotic phrases," wrote Louis Kronenberger, *"Bloomer Girl* is an unusually good musical."

BLOSSOM TIME (1921), *an operetta, with book and lyrics by Dorothy Donnelly, adapted from a German operetta,* Das Dreimäderlhaus *based on the life of Franz Schubert. Music by Sigmund Romberg, derived from Schubert's works. Presented by the Shuberts at the Ambassador Theater on September 29. Directed by J. C. Huffman. Dances by F. M. Gillespie. Cast included Bertram Peacock, Olga Cook, and Howard Marsh (592 performances).*

The Shuberts had acquired the American rights to a celebrated European operetta about Franz Schubert. Feeling that the European score was not altogether suited for Americans, the Shuberts asked Romberg to prepare a new one. From the storehouse of Schubert's immortal music, Romberg picked some of the master's most familiar or characteristic melodies and provided new settings within the formal pattern of the American popular song. Thus he wrote the "Song of Love," the hit of the show—a duet of Schober and Mitzi—by adapting the beautiful melody for low strings from the first movement of the Unfinished Symphony. Out of the main theme from the second movement of the symphony he made "Tell Me, Daisy" (a duet of Schubert and Mitzi), and from the ballet music from *Rosamunde,* "Three Little Maids." He also used Schubert's famous lied *"Ständchen"* for his "Serenade," and found a place for Schubert's *Marche Militaire.* To George S. Kaufman, then a critic for the *Times,* the "songs of passionate longing . . . illuminate *Blossom Time* like pictures in a Christmas book." But surely it is not without at least a touch of irony to note that while Schubert earned about $500 for an entire life's output of music, Romberg earned well over a million dollars for songs from which all his melodies had been borrowed from Schubert.

The plot was a manufactured yarn, as remote from biographical truth as Timbuctoo is from the Bronx. The composer (Bertram Peacock), in love with Mitzi (Olga Cook), writes the "Song of Love" as an expression of his tenderness. He asks his best friend, Schober (Howard Marsh) to sing the love song to Mitzi, since he himself is too bashful to do so. When Mitzi hears the love song, she falls in love with Schober. Realizing that Schober has won Mitzi away from him and that she will never be his, Schubert writes a symphony and decides to leave it unfinished. At its premiere, Schubert is sick with his last fatal illness; effete and soul-weary, he writes his greatest religious song, "Ave Maria."

*Blossom Time* became one of Romberg's greatest financial successes— and certainly the greatest he had enjoyed up to this time. It ran almost two years on Broadway and within a few months had four road companies. (One of these companies played only a single night at the Ambassador Theater so that on tour it could carry the legend "direct from Broadway.") By February, 1924, the Shuberts could count a profit of three-quarters of a million dollars. Since then there has hardly been a period when it has not been revived somewhere in the United States.

THE BLUE PARADISE (1915), *an operetta, with book by Edgar Smith, based on a Viennese operetta by Leon Stein and Bela Jensbach. Lyrics by Herbert Reynolds. Music by Sigmund Romberg. Additional music by Edmund Eysler. Presented by the Shuberts at the Casino Theater on August 5. Directed by J. H. Benrimo. Dances by Ed Hutchinson. Cast included Vivienne Segal, Cecil Lean, and Cleo Mayfield (356 performances).*

As a staff composer for the Shuberts, Romberg had been producing a mountain of music for the various extravaganzas, revues, and other musicals the Shuberts were continually mounting. Practically everything he wrote was synthetic, proving he could concoct functional music rapidly to meet the demands of each production. Not until he was called upon to produce a score for a Viennese-type operetta did he reveal his true creative potential; and the first opportunity he got to do so came with *The Blue Paradise*.

Blue Paradise is a little Viennese garden restaurant, the principal set of this operetta. Rudolph Stoeger (Cecil Lean) meets his student friends to bid them farewell, since he is off for America to make his career there. He must also part with Mizzi, the flower girl (Vivienne Segal). She knows that their separation is permanent but feigns that it is temporary. In saying good-bye the lovers sing a tender song of farewell, a song with which Romberg achieved his first classic in three-quarter time, "Auf Wiedersehen." (This is the only one of the eight numbers Romberg wrote for this score that has survived.)

A quarter of a century later Rudolph, now a wealthy man, returns to

Vienna with his fiancée, Gladys (Frances Demarest). In remembrance of things past, he revisits the Blue Paradise, no longer a restaurant but the home of one of his old friends. Rudolph's friends decide to revive the garden of the house into the Blue Paradise as Rudolph had once known it, and during this revival Gaby (Cleo Mayfield), daughter of the owner of the house, appears in the same dress Mizzi had worn a quarter of a century earlier, and sings "Auf Wiedersehen." Rudolph then learns that Gaby is the daughter of Mizzi, that Mizzi has married his old-time friend and has become a shrew. Rudolph is now happy to return to America with his fiancée and forget all about Vienna.

As the flower girl Mizzi, Vivienne Segal made her first Broadway stage appearance. Romberg had been searching for a young singing actress to play the lead in his operetta, and his failure to do so almost led him to abandon the project. A voice scout told him of a young student at the Curtis Institute in Philadelphia who might fill the bill. Romberg made a trip to Philadelphia, heard her sing, and exclaimed: "Thank God, you'll do!" In lifting her from the Curtis Institute to the Broadway theater, Romberg was helping create a career that dominated the Broadway musical stage for over thirty years.

BOMBO (1921), *a musical extravaganza, with book and lyrics by Harold Atteridge. Additional lyrics by Buddy De Sylva. Music by Sigmund Romberg, with numerous interpolations of songs by other composers and lyricists. Presented by the Shuberts at the Jolson Theater on October 6. Directed by J. C. Huffman. Cast included Al Jolson and Janet Adair (219 performances).*

*Bombo* is one of those extravaganzas starring Jolson following the methods and procedures he had first established in *Robinson Crusoe, Jr.* in 1916. He appears as a black-faced character by the name of Gus and goes through all kinds of adventures either in exotic lands or in times gone by, with only the slightest thread of a plot to tie the whole thing together. That thread, tenuous as it was, snapped completely when Jolson followed his now firmly established practice of indulging in impromptu remarks to his audience, and most significantly—during the run of the play, whether in New York or on the road—of interpolating songs not originally in the score (none of them by Romberg), even though these songs had little or no relevance in the overall story.

Discussing *Bombo,* a critic of the New York *Dramatic Mirror* remarked that "the concoction is not well named. It should be called Al Jolson. He's the whole show, which is precisely as it should be." The implication, of course, was that the plot made little sense, and the songs and Jolson routines had little association with that plot. But it had Jolson, singing, joking, and zooming all over the stage like an uncontrolled jet-propelled human missile. The plot had something to do with Christopher Columbus, who discovers America with the help of his colored deck hand, Gus. It involves a bunch of crooks and a seer, and is highlighted by an amusing episode in which Gus barters with the Indians for Manhattan Island. "Give us Brooklyn," Gus tells the Indians, "and I'll give you in exchange a pair of rusty scissors."

Perhaps none of his other extravaganzas yielded such a harvest of songs that would henceforth and forever be identified with Jolson as *Bombo*—none, incidentally, by Romberg, the creator of the basic score. There was, first and foremost, "My Mammy" (words by Joe Young and Sam Lewis, music by Walter Donaldson), which the publisher, Saul Bourne, induced Jolson to use. From the first time he interpolated "My Mammy" into *Bombo,* falling on his knees and throwing out his arms to an imaginary mama, he sent his audience into an uproar. It was as a direct result of Jolson's rendition of this ballad that he—and all other performers of songs about mothers—came to be known as "mammy singers."

Then, from time to time, he introduced similar Jolson specialties: "Toot, Toot, Tootsie" (words by Gus Kahn and Ernie Erdman, music by Dan Russo); "I'm Goin' South" (words by Abner Smith and music by Harry Woods); "Who Cares?" (words by Jack Yellen, music by Milton Ager); "April Showers" (words by Buddy De Sylva, music by Lou Silvers); "Yoo Hoo" (words by Buddy De Sylva, music by Al Jolson); and "California, Here I Come" (words by Al Jolson and Buddy De Sylva, music by Joseph Meyer). The last of these was brought into the show by Jolson when *Bombo* was on the road in 1923.

THE BOYS FROM SYRACUSE (1938), *a musical comedy, with book by George Abbott, based on Shakespeare's* The Comedy of Errors. *Lyrics by Lorenz Hart. Music by Richard Rodgers. Presented by George Abbott at the Alvin Theater on November 23. Directed by George Abbott. Choreography by George Balanchine. Cast included Jimmy Savo, Teddy Hart, Eddie Albert, Ronald Graham, Muriel Angelus, and Marcy Wescott (235 performances).*

Ten years before Cole Porter's *Kiss Me, Kate,* Rodgers and Hart had discovered that Shakespeare could provide material for musical comedy. The idea to translate *The Comedy of Errors* into a musical originated with Rodgers. He won Hart over to the idea, and together they invited Abbott to prepare a text. Abbott retained only two lines from Shakespeare: "The venom clamours of a jealous woman/Poisons more deadly than a mad dog's tooth." But the setting, plot, and main characters were more or less recognizably Shakespeare.

In ancient Greece, Antipholus of Syracuse (Eddie Albert) comes to Ephesus with his servant, Dromio (Jimmy Savo). There they are confused with the local Antipholus (Ronald Graham) and Dromio (Teddy Hart). The two Antipholuses happen to be twin brothers separated as babes during a storm at sea. The Ephesus Antipholus is married to Adriana (Muriel Angelus) and has an attractive sister-in-law, Luciana (Marcy Wescott), while his man Dromio is married to Luce (Wynn Murray). The mistaken identity involves both Antipholuses in all kinds of amusing, irreverent, and at times even bawdy situations that even enmesh the two Dromios, who, by coincidence, resemble each other remarkably. The Syracuse Antipholus finds Luciana very much to his liking but is rejected because she mistakes him for her brother-in-law. The wife of the Ephesus Dromio pursues both Dromios. The complications reach a hilarious climax during a dinner in "Sing for Your Supper" (a song involving Adriana, Luciana, and Luce)—where things get completely out of hand. The Ephesus pair get imprisoned, being suspected of being demented, and the Syracuse pair seek a haven in a priory. But the complexities of the situation are neatly straightened out by the father of the two Antipholuses with the help of the Duke of Ephesus.

The casting of Jimmy Savo and Teddy Hart as the two Dromios was one of the delights of the production. Savo and Hart (the latter was the brother of Lorenz Hart, the lyricist) looked alike, and both had about them the same pathetic air and wide-eyed ingenuousness that made them ideal for their roles. The two Antipholuses were also strong points in a cast that included Burl Ives in a minor role as a tailor's apprentice. (Ives's career in folk music would come later.) The acting, George Abbott's witty and at times provocative dialogue and brisk direction, Balanchine's imaginative choreography, and the occasionally plangent and frequently humorous tunes and lyrics of Rodgers and Hart all combined to make a field day of Shakespeare. "I believe," wrote Sidney Whipple, "that The Boys from Syracuse will be regarded as the greatest musical comedy of its time." To Life it was "a fantastically funny and bawdy show in the best musical tradition." Richard Watts, Jr., said: "If you have been wondering all these years just what was wrong with The Comedy of Errors, it is now possible to tell you. It has been waiting for a score by Rodgers and Hart and direction by George Abbott."

Rodgers was at his best in the haunting waltz (one of the best he ever wrote), "Falling in Love with Love," introduced by Adriana. There were other memorable melodies, notably "The Shortest Day of the Year"

(Antipholus of Ephesus; Assistant Courtesan, played by Dolores Anderson; and the ensemble), "You Have Cast Your Shadow on the Sea" (Antipholus of Syracuse and Luciana), and "This Can't Be Love" (Antipholus of Syracuse and Luciana). Lorenz Hart's lyrics were most iridescent in songs like "He and She" (Dromio of Syracuse and Luce) and "What Can You Do with a Man?" (Luce and Dromio of Ephesus).

The film version, produced by Universal in 1940, starred Allan Jones as both Antipholuses and Joe Penner as both Dromios. Four songs from the stage score were retained. An Off Broadway production revived the stage show on April 15, 1963, and proved highly successful with both audiences and critics. In the New York *Post,* Frances Herridge called it "one of the rowdiest and liveliest shows around." Paul Gardner, in *The New York Times,* described it as "the perfect gin-and-tonic entertainment." It received the Vernon Rice Award as the season's outstanding Off Broadway achievement.

BRIGADOON (1947), *a musical play, with book and lyrics by Alan Jay Lerner. Music by Frederick Loewe. Presented by Cheryl Crawford at the Ziegfeld Theater on March 13. Directed by Robert Lewis. Choreography by Agnes de Mille. Cast included David Brooks, Marion Bell, and George Keane (581 performances).*

A casual remark by Frederick Loewe was the original source of *Brigadoon.* He happened to mention to Lerner the cliché that faith could move mountains, which led Lerner to wonder if this aphorism could not be used as a general theme for a musical. He began conceiving all kinds of miracles brought about through faith, and eventually came upon the idea of faith actually moving a town. And so he set to work on a text set in Scotland, producing *Brigadoon,* destined to become the first of the three Lerner and Loewe classics of the musical theater.

They described their play as a "whimsical musical fantasy," since Brigadoon is a Scottish town which disappeared in 1747, then came back to life for a single day every century. Two American tourists are wandering about in the Scottish highlands: Tommy Albright (David Brooks) and Jeff Douglas (George Keane). They hear the strains of a song, "Brigadoon," from a distance. Suddenly a village comes into being before their very eyes. There, at a fair, they come upon Fiona MacLaren (Marion Bell), and her sister, Jean, the latter about to be married to Charlie Dalrymple (Lee Sullivan). Tommy is enchanted with Fiona and insists on helping her gather heather for her sister's wedding. He wins her consent after singing to her a ballad, "The Heather on the Hill" which she repeats.

At the MacLaren home, Charlie reveals the intensity of his feelings for his bride in the ballad "Come to Me, Bend to Me." Tommy is also in love, which he does not hesitate to confess, upon returning from the fields with Fiona, in another eloquent love duet, "Almost Like Being in Love." When the house, the two young men chance upon a family album and are startled to discover that just a hundred years earlier a Fiona MacLaren had been married to a Charlie Dalrymple. Only after the village schoolmaster, Mr. Lundie (William Hansen), explains to them the history of the village can they understand this coincidence.

Following the wedding ceremony of Jean and Charlie, Tommy tells Fiona how much he loves her ("There but for You Go I"), and because of that love he is determined to remain in Brigadoon forever, come what may. But Tommy is more realistic: It is impossible to live in a dream. They must both return to the United States, where Tommy's fiancée is waiting for him. But back in New York, Tommy can forget neither Brigadoon nor Fiona. And so he returns to Scotland in search of a dream world. Out of the Highland mists steps Mr. Lundie, the schoolteacher. Leading Tommy by the hand, he conducts him to Brigadoon, a miracle made possible because "love can do anything."

Any temptation the authors might have felt to make their play a field day for sentimentality was sidestepped. As Brooks Atkinson wrote: "The plot works beautifully. Mr. Lerner organized the story. He does not get down to the details of the fairy story until the audience has already been won by the pleasant characters, the exuberant music, and the prim though fiery dances. After that the incantation is complete and easy."

Much of the evocative charm and stage music evoked by the play was due to Lerner's sensitive writing. Much, too, stemmed from Loewe's music, some of which had a pronounced Scottish identity, while others—most notably "Almost Like Being in Love," which became the big hit song of 1947—unmistakably Broadwayish. But though individual songs were strong in their appeal, the score as a whole was beautifully integrated with the text; it kept the action fluid as the play progressed from speech to song and back again to speech. The spirited and at times deeply moving choreography of Agnes de Mille was also integral to the folk character of the play, and contributory to its overall fascination.

*Brigadoon* became the first musical to receive the Drama Critics Circle Award as the best play of the year.

As a motion picture (an MGM production in 1954 starring Gene Kelly, Van Johnson, and Cyd Charisse) *Brigadoon* left much to be desired. But as a TV special a few years later it regained its capacity to enchant its audiences and won an Emmy Award. *Brigadoon* has shown no signs of aging in its periodic revivals on the stage, notably at the New York City Center, where it was produced four times between 1957 and 1964. As Richard Watts, Jr., wrote after the 1957 revival: "I had forgotten . . . what a delightful score Frederick Loewe composed for his and Alan Jay Lerner's fantasy. . . . It came to me as almost a revelation . . . that *Brigadoon* was filled with enchanting melodies." And in 1964 Lewis Funke remarked in *The New York Times:* "It still is a treat. . . . A musical fantasy —a kind of retreat to never-never-land—it carries you away, out of contemporary problems, cynicism and materialism into a realm of faith and simplicity."

THE BROOK (1879), *a farce, with book and lyrics by Nate Salsbury. The music consisted of adaptations. Adapted by Nate Salsbury in New York on May 12. The cast included the Five Salsbury Troubadours and Nellie Mc-Henry (six weeks).*

This was one of the first American musical comedies to attempt some kind of integration between plot and musical routines. Topical materials and a vaudeville show were logically interpolated into a workable, even if naïve, plot described in the program as "depicting the pleasures of a jolly pic-nic." The principal characters, the Five Salsbury Troubadours, appear as members of a theatrical troupe who go on a boat trip for a picnic. During the picnic everything that can go wrong does go wrong; a basket supposed to contain watermelons actually yields theatrical costumes. The performers accept this bad situation gracefully, don the costumes, and perform songs, dances, and specialty numbers. Then they return home.

Besides its tentative efforts at integration, *The Brook* was also noteworthy for its naturalism of setting, characterization, and humorous episodes. As Nate Salsbury explained in describing his play as "a novelty," his aim was "the natural reproduction of the jollity and funny mishaps that attend the usual pic-nic excursion." One of the critics of the play pointed up Salsbury's success by saying: "*The Brook* appeals to the natural impulses of everybody, and all Nature is held up to the mirror."

Nate Salsbury, who toured with *The Brook* for many years, took it to London, where it became the first American musical production given in the British Isles.

BYE BYE BIRDIE (1960), *a musical comedy, with book by Michael Stewart. Lyrics by Lee Adams. Music by Charles Strouse. Presented by Edward Padula at the Martin Beck Theater on April 14. Directed and with dances by Gower Champion. Cast included Dick Van Dyke, Chita Rivera, Paul Lynde, and Dick Gautier (607 performances).*

The era of rock 'n' roll—and the idolatry for Elvis Presley—were the stimuli for this rollicking, fast-moving, bouncing satire. Conrad Birdie (Dick Gautier) is a crooner adored by teen-agers all over the country. When they learn he is about to be mustered into the United States Army they are thrown into a hysteria which makes them ready to secede from the Union. Another one profoundly affected by Conrad's up-and-coming military career is his songwriting manager Albert Peterson (Dick Van Dyke), who depends on his livelihood from commissions from his client. He hopes to marry Rose Grant (Chita Rivera), despite the obstacles continually put in his way by a doting, oversolicitous mother (Kay Medford), who physically falls apart whenever the mere mention of her boy's marriage is made. Rose, however, evolves a plan whereby Albert can accumulate enough money to get married, if only he can break the silver cord: He is to write a rock-'n'-roll number entitled "One Last Kiss," which Birdie would introduce as he kisses one of his fans farewell before going into the Army. What is more, Rose plans to promote both the song and Birdie's kiss in a big way—on a coast-to-coast television broadcast on Ed Sullivan's program. The teen-ager chosen (by a chance hit-and-miss process) is Kim MacAfee (Susan Watson) of Sweet Apple, Ohio, and it is to this town that Albert, Rose, and Birdie head to make all the necessary preparations.

Once in Sweet Apple, Albert, Rose, and Birdie find the whole town agog, ready to give their favorite rock-'n'-roll singer a hero's welcome. Birdie is housed with the MacAfees, where he proceeds to assume the attitude of the lord of the manor, besides winning Kim's adulation. The latter fact arouses the jealousy of Kim's boyfriend, Hugo (Michael J. Pollard). Trouble also invades the love life of Albert and Rose, since Albert's mother has followed him to Sweet Apple, ready—she tells him—to kill herself if he marries Rose. Wearying of the humdrum existence at the MacAfee home, Birdie sneaks off for fun with Kim and some other teen-agers in an ice house, where they cut up as they sing "A Lot of Livin' to Do." Meanwhile, Kim's parents are in a state of panic with Kim nowhere to be found; they contemptuously express their opinion of the irresponsibility of the younger generation in "Kids." At the same time, Rose and Hugo are in a bar, each trying to forget his or her respective problem. Albert reaches her by phone, begs her to be patient and understanding ("Baby, Talk to Me"), but Rose hangs up on him. Instead, she storms into an adjoining room where a Shriners convention is taking place, and lets herself go completely by performing a frenetic dance.

Albert finds her. It does not take long for a reconciliation to take place, since he promises her he will marry her without further delay, and that they will settle down to a quiet, rural existence in Pumpkin Falls, Iowa. Hugo and Kim also make up. By this time Kim has become bored stiff with Birdie and his superego. Peace returns to Sweet Apple, after Birdie leaves for the Army.

Not often has a musical comedy come to Broadway offering so much entertainment, even though at first very little had been expected of it. To the veteran Broadwayite *Bye Bye Birdie* had all the appearance of an amateur production before its appearance in New York. The producer was unknown, and for the librettist, lyricist, and composer this production represented their first try at a full-length musical. Gower Champion, while recognized as a fine dancer and choreographer, had never before served as a stage director. The leading performers were played by unknowns or comparative unknowns. Dick Gautier, who took the part of Birdie, was making his Broadway debut. Dick Van Dyke had never before played in a musical comedy. Chita Rivera was not yet a box-office attraction. All in all, it appeared that *Bye Bye Birdie* had little to offer—until the first-night audience gave it a resounding ovation, and John Chapman wrote the next morning that it was "the funniest, most captivating and most expert musical comedy one could hope to see in several seasons of showgoing." The time was ripe for a satire on the rock-'n'-roll craze, on teen-agers, and on the Elvis Presley brand of crooner. The text not only was thoroughly spiced with broad humor and satire, but it continually generated excitement and burst forth with youthful energy. The score was professional throughout, with at least one number to become a major hit ("A Lot of Livin' to Do") and two others, minor ones ("Kids," ond "Baby, Talk to Me"). Dick Van Dyke proved to be star material, Chita Rivera was exciting and visually appealing as Rose, and Paul Lynde as Mr. MacAfee introduced his welcome brand of dry humor. And not the least of the assets of the production was Gower Champion's sure-handed direction, which helped maintain a breathless pace throughout, and his often stunning choreographic concepts, particularly Rose's dance for the members of the Shriners convention.

*Bye Bye Birdie* received the Antoinette Perry and the Outer Circle awards as the best musical of the season.

In the motion picture version (Columbia, 1963), Dick Van Dyke retained his stage role, while the rest of the cast included Bobby Rydell, Janet Leigh, and Ann-Margret.

BY JUPITER (1942), *a musical comedy, with book by Rodgers and Hart, based on Julian F. Thompson's* The Warrior's Husband. *Lyrics by Lorenz Hart. Music by Richard Rodgers. Presented by Dwight Deere Wiman and Richard Rodgers in association with Richard Kollmar at the Shubert Theater on June 2. Directed by Joshua Logan. Dances by Robert Alton. Cast included Ray Bolger, Benay Venuta, Vera-Ellen, Ronald Graham, and Constance Moore (427 performances).*

*By Jupiter* was the last of the Rodgers and Hart musicals—the end of an era. It climaxed almost a quarter of a century of stage collaboration by composer and lyricist by becoming their musical having the longest first-run. Indeed, its impressive total of 427 performances would have been much greater if it had not had to close down at a time when it was still doing capacity business to allow its star, Ray Bolger, to make a secret flight to the South Seas to entertain American troops, this being the period of World War II.

*The Warrior's Husband,* upon which this musical was based, originated as a one-act play produced in 1921. In 1932 its author, Julian F. Thompson, expanded it into a three-act comedy, and in this vehicle Katharine Hepburn first became a star. The setting is Asia Minor in mythological times. In Pontus the sexes are reversed. The women, headed by their Queen, Hippolyta (Benay Venuta), are the warriors. The timid men stay at home to primp and cook—and the most timorous of the lot is Hippolyta's husband, Sapiens (Ray Bolger). This power of distaff stems from the girdle of Diana worn by the Queen. As long as she wears it, the women continue to dominate the men. Theseus (Ronald Graham), Hercules (Ralph Dumke), and a band of Greeks invade the island to wrest the girdle from the Queen. They conquer the Amazon women not with their weapons but with their sex wiles. Once the Greeks are victorious over the Amazon women, Sapiens can assume his full authority as king. And the Greek, Theseus, can find love with Antiope (Constance Moore), Hippolyta's sister.

*By Jupiter* was, in the words of *Variety,* a "lush and lavish musical comedy, extravagant, adult, and betimes amusing." Its rich spice included the condiments of *double entendres* and sex implications. The production profited from two outstanding songs: "Wait Till You See Her," in which Theseus tells his friends of his love for Antiope, and "Careless Rhapsody," a duet of those two lovers. Also of interest was "Nobody's Heart," Antiope's attempt to make light of the fact that nobody loves her, before Theseus finds her so desirable; and "Ev'rything I've Got," a duet of Hippolyta and Sapiens.

By Jupiter was revived on January 19, 1967, in an Off Broadway production, with additional material supplied by Fred Ebb. "The Rodgers and Hart click," said *Variety*, "is still a melodious laughrouser. . . . Laughs are plentiful all the way."

BY THE BEAUTIFUL SEA (1954), *a musical comedy, with book by Herbert and Dorothy Fields. Lyrics by Dorothy Fields. Music by Arthur Schwartz. Presented by Robert Fryer and Lawrence Carr at the Majestic Theater on April 8. Directed by Marshall Jamison. Choreography by Helen Tamiris. Cast included Shirley Booth and Wilbur Evans (270 performances).*

Nostalgia and sentiment, combined with the performance of Shirley Booth, were the redeeming features of *By the Beautiful Sea*. Once again, as in Arthur Schwartz' preceding *A Tree Grows in Brooklyn* (1951), the setting is Brooklyn, at the turn of the century. Shirley Booth appeared as Lottie Gibson, a vaudeville trouper who has invested her savings in a boardinghouse in Coney Island, "By the Beautiful Sea." Her clientele is mostly show people. During one of her tours through the vaudeville circuit, she falls in love with Dennis Emery (Wilbur Evans), a Shakespearean actor. When Emery is booked to appear in the Brighton Theater, Lottie prevails on him to stay at her boardinghouse. Their romance develops against the background of Coney Island attractions: Steeplechase, the scenic railway, the Tunnel of Love. Emery's divorced wife and daughter are also boarders at "By the Beautiful Sea." The child does her best to break up the romance of Lottie and Emery. With the cooperation of some of the boarders, Lottie succeeds in winning the affection of the child and in getting her man.

On the credit side of the ledger was Helen Tamiris' choreography, particularly a devastating takeoff on a moving-picture machine in a penny arcade. The best musical numbers were Dennis' song "Alone Too Long" and "More Love than Your Love" and Lottie's number, "I'd Rather Wake Up by Myself."

CABARET (1966), *a musical play, with book by Joe Masteroff based on the play by John van Druten and stories by Christopher Isherwood. Lyrics by Fred Ebb. Music by John Kander. Presented by Harold Prince (in conjunction with Ruth Mitchell) at the Broadhurst Theater on November 20. Directed by Harold Prince. Dances and cabaret numbers by Ronald Field. Cast included Lotte Lenya, Jill Haworth, Jack Gilford, Joel Grey, and Bert Convy (1,166 performances).*

In *Cabaret* we get a picture of decadent Germany in the years just before the rise of Hitler—the Germany that glorified *Zeitkunst* ("contemporary art") and American jazz; where morality was decaying as rapidly as was the democratic system; a country edging ever closer to the brink of Nazism, of "Deutschland über alles," and war. The musical play was based on John van Druten's Broadway play *I Am a Camera* produced on November 28, 1951, recipient of the New York Drama Critics Award.

The time is 1929–30; the place, Berlin. In the opening scene the Master of Ceremonies (Joel Gray) greets the clients of the Kit Kat Club in Berlin with "Willkommen," pointing out that here life is carefree. The other employees soon join him in the greeting. The scene shifts to a train en route to Berlin on which an American writer and teacher, Clifford Bradshaw (Bert Convy) helps Ernst Ludwig (Edward Winter) through the customs; in gratitude, Ernst promises to be helpful to Clifford in Berlin. There Ernst finds a room for Clifford at a roominghouse run by Fräulein Schneider (Lotte Lenya). They are soon joined by another tenant, Herr Schultz (Jack Gilford), bearing the gift of a bottle of schnapps. Soon afterward, Clifford visits the Kit Kat Club, where he meets one of its performers, Sally Bowles (Jill Haworth), who—after she has delivered a number called "Don't Tell Mama"—joins him at his table. Later on, Sally visits Clifford at his room and suggests, in the song "Perfectly Marvelous," how nice it would be for her to move in with him. Meanwhile, Ernst has been trying to bribe Clifford to make some smuggling trips for him to Paris for "political reasons."

Though Fräulein Schneider berates one of her female tenants for having entertained sailors in her room, she herself is not beyond permitting Herr Schultz to visit and stay with her. An interlude follows in which the Master of Ceremonies and a group of waiters sing "Tomorrow Belongs to Me"—a warning that the morrow will belong to the Fatherland.

Sally, quietly contented with life with Clifford in his room, calmly informs him she is pregnant. Clifford is delighted; he is now determined to get the money to support a baby. This is the reason why Clifford is ready to accept Ernst's bribe to go to Paris for him on a mission.

Fräulein Schneider and Herr Schultz are considering getting married. Ernst warns them to consider this decision most carefully. He reminds Fräulein Schneider that Schultz is a Jew and that in the new Germany it might be dangerous for her to be married to him. At the same time, Clifford—back from Paris, where he had been a messenger for the "party"—tries to convince Ernst that the author of *Mein Kampf* is a madman.

Like a messenger of doom, the Master of Ceremonies crosses the stage of the Kit Kat Club as the scenery vanishes and the curtain descends on the first act.

An opening interlude in the second act has the chorus line of the club break out from a dance into a goose-step routine to the accompaniment of rolling drums. Fräulein Schneider has decided not to marry Schultz, since she fears losing her rooming license should the Nazis come to power. Clifford has come to the decision to return to America, but before this he engages Ernst in a fight at the club and is badly beaten by Ernst's bodyguard. Sally is once again an entertainer at the club, where she now introduces the title song (the only musical number from the production to become popular). Later on, Sally confesses to Clifford, she had been to a doctor and, in return for her fur coat, has had an abortion. She bids Cliff farewell. Aboard the Berlin-Paris express, Clifford begins jotting down his memories of Berlin. As he does so, the people he writes about come to view—and, as in the opening scene, the Master of Ceremonies assures the guests that at the cabaret life is carefree and gay. But there is an ominous cloud hanging over these proceedings; and the music that accompanies them is discordant. Sally is heard in one more chorus of the title song before she and all the other characters disappear. Only the Master of Ceremonies is left on the stage. His last words are "Auf Wiedersehen. A bientot." Then, with a wave of the hand, he bids his audience good-bye.

*Cabaret* is outstanding musical theater—often poignant, often bitter, often penetrating in giving what Walter Kerr described as "a marionette's-eye view of a time and place in our lives that was brassy, wanton, carefree, and doomed to crumble." To the critic of *Variety* the show has "everything." . . . "It has bright music, magnificent production numbers, touches of comedy and tragedy, and four different stories vying for audience attention." Apparently many others agreed with such evaluations. *Cabaret* was the "hottest ticket" on Broadway in 1966. It received the New York Drama Critics and the Antoinette Perry awards as the best musical of the year. Not long after *Cabaret* celebrated its first anniversary on Broadway, it could boast a national company that began an extensive several-year tour in New Haven on December 26, 1967, with other productions (all successful) in London, Iceland, Holland, Switzerland, Germany, Denmark, Austria, Finland, and Sweden.

Casting Lotte Lenya as Fräulein Schneider was sheer inspiration—not only because her personality and her piping, poignant voice suited her role so well. For it was Lotte Lenya who in 1928 had starred in the Bertolt Brecht-Kurt Weill masterpiece *The Three-Penny Opera,* which had pointed up the dry rot eating away at Germany at the time, and satirized the corruption and cynicism that had infected the German people. *Cabaret* had flavors reminiscent of the spicy stew that had been *The Three-Penny Opera*—and it was wise, indeed, to use in the 1966 production one of the basic ingredients of the 1928 recipe.

But it was Joel Grey, as Master of Ceremonies, who emerged as the leading star of *Cabaret*. As often happens, he became a star "overnight"—after being twenty-four years a highly talented performer in practically every medium of show business without achieving the full recognition he so well deserved.

Ronald Field's choreography (that "spins with the vibrant spirit of pre-Hitler Germany," as *Variety* put it); Jean Rosenthal's ingenious lighting effects; and Harold Prince's unusual staging, in which the transition from the cabaret to various other scenes was achieved with remarkable fluidity—all were powerful contributors to the overall success of the production.

As for the John Kander-Fred Ebb score: besides the title number, it boasted several other highly effective numbers. These included "If You Could See Her" (introduced by the Master of Ceremonies); "It Couldn't Please Me More" (a duet by Fräulein Schneider and Herr Schultz); "Why Should I Wake Up?" (a duet by Sally and Clifford) and two numbers that have an almost Kurt Weillish identity, both (appropriately enough) sung by Fräulein Schultz, "What Would You Do?" and "So What?"

CABIN IN THE SKY (1940), *a musical fantasy, with book by Lynn Root. Lyrics by John La Touche. Music by Vernon Duke. Presented by Albert Lewis in conjunction with Vinton Freedley at the Martin Beck Theater on October 25. Directed and with dances by George Balanchine. Cast included Ethel Waters, Todd Duncan, Rex Ingram, and Katherine Dunham (156 performances).*

*Cabin in the Sky* is one of the most poignant and sensitive portraits of Negro life and psychology presented by the Broadway musical theater in the 1940's. The story has the simplicity and at times the ingenuousness of folklore. A tug-of-war ensues between Lucifer, Jr. (Rex Ingram), and the Lawd's General (Todd Duncan) for the poor soul of a humble Negro, Little Joe (Dooley Wilson). Little Joe, though well-meaning, simply cannot keep out of trouble. Petunia (Ethel Waters) tries to help Joe win the battle for the forces of good; and there are the primitive and lustful wiles of Georgia Brown (Katherine Dunham in her first appearance on Broadway) to weaken Little Joe's resistance to evil and arouse his flesh. Joe shoots Petunia in a dance hall, but Petunia is all-forgiving and makes it possible for Joe to slip into heaven.

The folk character of the play was rarely permitted to degenerate into vaudeville humor, gaudy spectacle, or outright caricature. Every element in the production maintained the quiet dignity and integrity of the Lynn Root play, particularly the simple and earthy lyrics of John La Touche, the choreography of George Balanchine, and the exciting dancing of Katherine Dunham.

Duke's music tapped a creative vein hitherto reserved for his more serious efforts for the concert stage. One of his most famous "standards" is found in this score: "Taking a Chance on Love" (lyrics by John La Touche, with the collaboration of Ted Fetter), sung first by Petunia and then reprised by Petunia and Little Joe; George Jean Nathan considered this the best musical-comedy song of the year. Other distinguished numbers were the title number (Petunia and Little Joe), "Honey in the Honeycomb" (Georgia Brown), and "Love Me Tomorrow" (Georgia Brown and Little Joe)—all with the overtones of Negro folk songs.

In the motion-picture version (MGM, 1943), "Taking a Chance on Love" and the title number were sung by Ethel Waters and Eddie "Rochester" Anderson; "Honey in the Honeycomb" by Lena Horne and Ethel Waters. The movie interpolated a significant song not by Vernon Duke: "Happiness Is a Thing Called Joe," lyrics by E. Y. Harburg, music by Harold Arlen, introduced by Ethel Waters.

*Cabin in the Sky* was revived in New York in an Off Broadway production in January, 1964. This production included some new songs "Living It Up," words and music by Vernon Duke, written expressly for the revival; "We'll Live All Over Again" and "My Old Virginia Home on the River," both created for the original 1940 production but never used there; and "Not a Care in the World," which Duke lifted out of his score from another of his shows, *Banjo Eyes.* The revival of *Cabin in the Sky* was a failure. Said Howard Taubman in *The New York Times:* "Even Off Broadway a musical remembered fondly for its cornucopia of songs and the earthy vitality of Ethel Waters must have some measure of style. The revival . . . has been pieced together with so heavy a hand that it has lost most of its verve and charm." Mr. Taubman also felt that what had proved eloquent in 1940 had become somewhat dated and shopworn a quarter of a century later. "For the climate has changed radically. A fantasy in which the Negro is treated like a simple child of nature, moving and talking and sinning and shouting in ways that have become annoying stereotypes, is not so palatable as it was in the seemingly more innocent year of 1940 when this musical was new."

CALL ME MADAM (1950), *a musical comedy, with book by Russel Crouse and Howard Lindsay. Lyrics and music by Irving Berlin. Presented by Leland*

*Heyward at the Imperial Theater on October 12. Directed by George Abbott. Dances by Jerome Robbins. Cast included Ethel Merman, Russell Nype, Galina Talva, and Paul Lukas (644 performances).*

A note in the program explained: "The play is laid in two mythical countries. One is called Lichtenburg, the other is the United States of America."

Lichtenburg of course, is the little duchy of Luxembourg under a fictitious name; and the heroine, Mrs. Sally Adams (Ethel Merman), the American ambassador to Lichtenburg, is Mrs. Perle Mesta, renowned Washington, D.C. party giver whom President Truman appointed as ambassador to Luxembourg. The idea to get Ethel Merman to play Perle Mesta originated in Colorado, where both Howard Lindsay and Ethel Merman happened to be vacationing at the same time. Lindsay, watching Merman in one of her many boisterous and gusty moods, remarked: "She ought to be put in a show that makes her appear as the *most* American American you can think of." What could be more American than an American ambassador to some foreign land? Perle Mesta immediately leaped to Lindsay's mind, and he knew he had the character for Merman to portray. He had quite a time selling the idea to Miss Merman, since at that time she wanted to make her next appearance in a dramatic vehicle. Eventually he won her over. With Crouse as his collaborator, Lindsay completed a book, then got Irving Berlin to do the score, and George Abbott to direct. With such an array of talent, how could a show miss? *Call Me Madam* most certainly did not.

The play moves swiftly from Washington (where Mrs. Adams, like her prototype, is a society woman famous for her parties) to Lichtenburg and back. All the while it embroils its central characters in foreign intrigue, diplomatic red tape, international incidents, and love conflicts. For in Lichtenburg, Mrs. Adams is attracted to its suave and Continental Prime Minister, Cosmo Constantin (Paul Lukas), whom she tries to win over to herself by gaining for his country a Washington loan of one hundred million dollars. Her attempts prove unsuccessful, and she is recalled to Washington. But in the end she emerges triumphant both as a woman and ambassador. A secondary love interest engages the ambassador's assistant, Kenneth Gibson (Russell Nype), and Princess Maria (Galina Talva).

As the American ambassador, Ethel Merman gets entangled in the long train of her impressive gown, fluctuates between diplomatic dignity and earthy American slang, and all in all manages to create confusion and consternation with her brash personality, swagger, and lack of inhibitions. Particularly amusing were her highly informal telephone conversations with President Truman, whom she calls Harry, and from whom she inquires about Bess's bridge games and Margaret's singing. (President Truman's voice is not heard.) It was certainly too much to maintain, as George Jean Nathan did, that Miss Merman was "Miss Atlas of 1950, who carries the show on her powerful shoulders"—since there was a good deal more to *Call Me Madam* than its star. More accurate, surely, was the estimate of Brooks Atkinson when he said of the production: "It is genuine comedy because the character grows and develops in the course of the play and because Ethel Merman puts into it good will as well as swaggering self-confidence. . . . What she does to the likable central character of *Call Me Madam* is further proof of the fact that she can imitate people as fantastic as she is."

When the show tried out out-of-town, George Abbott felt the need of a new song with popular appeal for the second act. He decided that what was needed was one of those songs in which there are two choruses each with its own set of lyrics. First one chorus is sung by one of the leading characters, then the other by the second character, after which both sing together contrapuntally. Irving Berlin spent two days in his hotel room working on such a number and emerged triumphantly with "You're Just in Love." Berlin had planned it as a sentimental number in which Mrs. Adams tells young Kenneth Gibson that the only reason he is victimized by all kinds of hallucinations—such as hearing music when there is none—is that he's in love. But during rehearsals Ethel Merman and Russell Nype concocted all sorts of amusing stage business to accompany each encore, with the result that a sentimental song suddenly acquired comic overtones. "You're Just in Love" became the major hit song of the show. But there were other Irving Berlin delights in his score. Ethel Merman's brassy delivery was heard to good advantage in "The Hostess with the Mostes' on the Ball" and "The Best Thing for You," the latter a duet with Cosmo Constantin in which she tries to convince him that what he most needs is her. A trio of congressmen deliver a paean to Dwight D. Eisenhower, "They Like Ike," which may have had more than a casual influence in carrying him into the White House, since it was used both frequently and effectively as a campaign song for General Eisenhower during his first Presidential campaign. Another delightful number was the duet of Kenneth Gibson and Princess Maria, "It's a Lovely Day Today."

Ethel Merman starred in the motion-picture adaptation (20th Century-Fox, 1953), in which the basic stage score was used with an interpolation of an old Berlin classic, "International Rag."

CALL ME MISTER (1946), *a revue with book by Arnold Auerbach and*

*Arnold Horwitt. Lyrics and music by Harold Rome. Presented by Melvyn Douglas and Herman Levin at the National Theater on April 18. Directed by Robert H. Gordon. Dances by John Wray. Cast included Jules Munshin, Betty Garrett, and Lawrence Winters (734 performances).*

While Harold Rome was serving in the United States Army (in the Special Services division) during World War II, he began thinking of what would happen to all the GI's once peace came. One thought led to another, until he began to crystallize in his mind a musical production that would be the peacetime equivalent of Irving Berlin's wartime all-soldiers' revue, *This Is the Army*. Once Rome was separated from the armed forces he went to work with Auerbach and Horwitt in writing material for such a show. *Call Me Mister* was the result—and it became the last of the successful social and political revues that had been flourishing on Broadway in the 1930's.

The problems of readjustment from military to civilian status, and nostalgic or humorous recollections of life in the Army, provided rich and varied material for a revue, and *Call Me Mister* exploited this material to the full.

The sentiment of the GI's return was effectively highlighted by "Goin' Home Train," poignantly sung by Lawrence Winters, making his Broadway stage debut. Various aspects of Army life were mocked in numbers like "Little Surplus Me" and "Military Life"—particularly in the latter, which maintained that despite the discipline and the physical benefits of a military life, a man who was a jerk in civilian life remains a jerk even after his military experiences. The "Red Ball Express" described the difficulties of a Negro GI become civilian: In the Army he had served with uncommon distinction in the Transportation Corps, while as a civilian he is incapable of getting a job as a truck driver because he is colored.

But though the emphasis in *Call Me Mister* was basically on the GI, both before and after his separation from the armed forces, political and social consciousness was not forgotten—a field in which Harold Rome had earned such distinction in the revues of the late 1920's and the 1930's. *Call Me Mister* included a caricature of three reactionary Southern Senators in "The Senators' Song," while a Negro's poignant tribute to the memory of President Roosevelt was given in "The Face on the Dime." The most successful number of the revue—and the biggest song hit of Rome's score—had, however, no relation whatsoever either to the Army, social problems, or politics. It was a travesty on the craze for South American song and dance— "South America, Take It Away," projected with such devastating effect by Betty Garrett that this one song helped make her a star. "South America, Take It Away" had been written long before *Call Me Mister* was projected— at a time when the craze for Latin-American dances and rhythms was at its height in America. Failing at the time to find a place for it, Harold Rome put it aside and forgot about it until *Call Me Mister* was in rehearsals and a feature number for Betty Garrett was required. Since the song did not fit into the overall context of a show about ex-GI's, Rome was not enthusiastic about its inclusion, but the producer felt it would contribute a change of mood and pace and convinced Rome to use it. He did—and never regretted the decision—since it was destined to be one of his most successful songs, especially after it had been recorded by Bing Crosby and the Andrews Sisters in a Decca release that sold over a million disks.

*Call Me Mister* received the Newspaper Guild of New York Page One Award for outstanding achievement in the theater.

"South America, Take It Away" was—to be sure—retained when *Call Me Mister* was made into a movie by 20th Century-Fox in 1951, starring Betty Grable and Dan Dailey; so were two other numbers from the stage score ("The Face on the Dime" and "Military Life").

CAMELOT (1960), *a musical play, with book and lyrics by Alan Jay Lerner. Music by Frederick Loewe. Presented by Lerner, Loewe, and Moss Hart at the Majestic Theater on December 3. Directed by Moss Hart. Choreography by Hanya Holm. Cast included Richard Burton, Julie Andrews, Roddy McDowell, and Robert Goulet (873 performances).*

As the immediate successor of one of the most triumphant and one of the most glorious musicals ever produced (*My Fair Lady*)—and with many of those who had been involved in the earlier production collaborating again—*Camelot* inevitably aroused enormous anticipation. So much so, indeed, that before it came to Broadway it boasted the then unprecedented advance sale of three and a half million dollars. *Camelot* was, to be sure, no *My Fair Lady;* it could hardly be expected that even the most highly gifted creators could possibly write and produce the equal of *My Fair Lady* so soon. As it turned out, *Camelot* was a grandiose (though somewhat diffuse) production, dressed up in the most stunning sets and costumes. It was beautifully acted, for Richard Burton had been one of the London Old Vic's distinguished actors for over a decade and Julie Andrews (who had previously been the female lead in *My Fair Lady*) was a performer of surpassing charm and talent. In addition to such riches, there was a new shining star in Robert Goulet, as attractive physically as he was vocally. Finally, there were some highly appealing numbers in the Lerner-Loewe score. All this was calculated to make for a solid box-office attraction, which *Camelot* certainly became. But *Camelot* had serious shortcomings. The text was not cohesive, and the succession of scenes did not always make the plot line straight and clear.

It lacked humor. It was weak in providing contrasts of of mood and atmosphere. *Camelot* had for the most part very much the appearance of a show all dressed up in the most expensive finery—but with no place to go. Richard Watts, Jr., put it this way in his review: "It turned out to be a very handsome musical play with many lovely and imaginative things in it. But there is also a curious air of heaviness hanging over it, and it has an unfortunate way of getting lost from time to time between its fantasy, its satirical humor and its romantic wistfulness, with the result that it isn't merely the terrifying but inevitable comparison to *My Fair Lady* which causes me to receive it with somewhat modified rapture. . . . Its moods, ranging from grave to gay, rarely seemed to merge into a pattern, leaving the impression of ponderousness."

It was perfectly obvious that all those connected with *Camelot* were trying to use the mixture as before—in the hopes that a miracle can be repeated twice. In both *My Fair Lady* and *Camelot,* Julie Andrews (as we have already noted) played the female lead, and Robert Coote a secondary role. In both shows, Moss Hart did the stage directing, Oliver Smith the scenery, Hanya Holm the choreography, Robert Russell Bennett the orchestrations, and Franz Allers the conducting. The recipe of *My Fair Lady* was being meticulously followed but for one salient fact: a basic ingredient had been omitted. In *My Fair Lady* the text was derived from a satiric masterwork by George Bernard Shaw. And while *Camelot* came from a respectable source —T. H. White's *The Once and Future King*—White was no Shaw, and *The Once and Future King* was certainly no *Pygmalion*. The theme of King Arthur, Guenevere, and Lancelot was not the most gratifying of subjects to begin with. And the compounding of problems, disputes, and misfortunes that befell *Camelot* before it finally staggered toward Broadway did not help matters either. During the writing of the score, violent friction made both the composer and the lyricist highly flammable. (As it turned out, they were never again to work together after *Camelot*.) But other disasters followed when the show was being tried out in Toronto. Moss Hart suffered a heart attack, and Alan Jay Lerner was confined for a while to a hospital for bleeding ulcers. (For Moss Hart, *Camelot* was to be his farewell to the theater; he died in 1962.)

Misunderstandings, hard feelings, and serious illnesses notwithstanding, *Camelot* arrived on Broadway, where its audience appeal proved sufficiently potent to keep it there for about two years, to make its original-cast recording a best seller, and then to bring it a price tag of some three million dollars in its sale to the movies.

The rise of the first-act curtain finds Guenevere (Julie Andrews) come to Camelot to marry King Arthur (Richard Burton). She wanders about in the neighboring woods, where the shy king is hiding. When they meet, they are instantly attracted to one another without either one realizing who the other is. Upon revealing their identities, at last, they are overjoyed at the thought that they would soon become man and wife.

After this marriage takes place, King Arthur establishes the Round Table to promote peace and brotherhood. Young Lancelot (Robert Goulet) comes from France hoping to become a knight, and is introduced to Guenevere, who regards him as an arrogant fellow. She challenges him to engage three knights of the Round Table in a jousting match—a dare Lancelot accepts, and a contest from which he emerges victorious. Since Lancelot soon falls in love with Guenevere, he decides to leave Camelot because of his loyalty to the king. But he is back in Camelot two years later, is made knight of the Round Table, and wins Guenevere's love—a romantic interest of which King Arthur is not altogether unaware.

At this point, King Arthur's illegitimate son, Mordred (Roddy McDowell), has come to Camelot to try to get his father's throne. He takes advantage of the fact that during the king's absence from the palace, Lancelot is found in Guenevere's boudoir. Mordred orders some of the Round Table knights to imprison Lancelot for treachery, while Guenevere is to be punished by being burned at the stake. But Lancelot manages to escape from prison and to flee with Guenevere to France. This situation brings on a war with France. When King Arthur comes upon Lancelot and Guenevere on the field of battle, he forgives both. Then he knights a young stowaway who had expressed a burning desire to join the Round Table, and sends him back to Camelot to carry on for him the ideals and the traditions he had originally established there.

The title song, which the king sings to Guenevere in describing his country when they first meet in the forest, became one of the two leading musical numbers emerging from a frequently charming and sometimes varied score. The other successful hit number helped make a star of Robert Goulet in his first Broadway appearance—"If Ever I Would Leave You"—Lancelot's love song to Guenevere, and the one song above all others with which Goulet is now identified. "The Lusty Month of May" (which intentionally caught the spirit of an old English madrigal, sung by Guenevere and ensemble); "How to Handle a Woman," with which King Arthur expresses his puzzlement over the opposite sex; Guenevere's uncertainty about herself and her future in the opening scene, "The Simple Joys of Maidenhood"; and the duet of King Arthur and Guenevere, "What Do the Simple Folk Do?", in

their curiosity of the life and diversions of those who are not of royal blood—
these are some of the other pleasing numbers, many of them particularly
appealing because of Lerner's nimble, witty lyrics.

The motion picture (Warner Brothers, 1967) starred Richard Harris
and Vanessa Redgrave as King Arthur and Guenevere, with Franco Nero as
Lancelot. The screenplay followed the lead of the stage production in emphasizing spectacular scenes. But under Joshua Logan's direction, the motion
picture boasted a stronger dramatic action, more vivid characterizations, and
an intensification of romantic interest not found in the stage play.

Inga Swenson (later a musical-comedy star in her own right) was Julie
Andrews' standby in the stage production.

CAN-CAN (1953), *a musical comedy, with book by Abe Burrows. Lyrics
and music by Cole Porter. Presented by Feuer and Martin at the Shubert
Theater on May 7. Directed by Abe Burrows. Dances by Michael Kidd. Cast
included Lilo, Peter Cookson, Hans Conried, Erik Rhodes, and Gwen Verdon
(892 performances).*

Cole Porter's love affair with the city of Paris remained passionate as long
as he lived. This had been his home for many years during the feverish 1920's,
when perhaps no place in the world could equal it as a setting for the kind
of gay and abandoned life Porter enjoyed in those years. A young man of
immense wealth as well as talent, and married to one of the most beautiful
women in the world, Cole Porter knew how to appreciate the good things
of life to the full; and Paris was the place where he appreciated them the
most. Time and again he wrote rhapsodic hymns to his beloved city. It is,
then, poetic justice that the first two musicals with which he and success
crossed paths (*Paris* and *Fifty Million Frenchmen*) should have Parisian
backgrounds; and that his career on Broadway should have ended exactly
as it had begun, with two successful musicals, once again with a Paris setting (*Can-Can* and *Silk Stockings*).

*Can-Can* differs from the other three musicals in that the Paris of a
former generation is our background, rather than the Paris of Porter's own
time. For *Can-Can* was a nostalgic excursion into bohemian Paris of 1893,
a period piece of the city of Toulouse-Lautrec, the can-can, and Moulin
Rouge. Paris of the 1890's was evoked in the eye-filling beauty of the scenery
and costuming—particularly in Jo Mielziner's opening curtain picture of the
city and in his set atop Paris rooftops; in some of the brilliant dances—an
apache dance, for example, and the exciting can-can that closes the play; in
magnetizing performances by two Broadway newcomers, Lilo and Gwen

Verdon. (The former has passed from the Broadway spotlight; but the latter has become one of the most dynamic performers of the American musical theater.)

The story revolves around an investigation of the scandalous dancing (the can-can) seen at a Montmartre café owned by La Mome Pistache (Lilo). An upright judge, Aristide Forestier (Peter Cookson), is dispatched to make an investigation. Much to his own surprise, he finds both the café and its owner a source of delight, which he freely confesses in a duet with Lilo, "C'est Magnifique." Pistache uses all her female wiles on the judge to capture his heart, which she succeeds in doing. The judge now is determined to use his legal skill to clear the names of the nightclub and the owner. Pistache is so overjoyed that not only does she find the judge very much to her liking, but she also sings an exultant and rhapsodic hymn of praise to her city in "I Love Paris." The can-can becomes as legal as the future relationship of the judge and Pistache.

A subsidiary plot involves the amatory complications of a soubrette, Claudine (Gwen Verdon), who is torn between her interest in a Bulgarian sculptor, Boris (Hans Conried), and an art critic, Hilaire (Erik Rhodes). Comic relief comes in the amusing caricature of the sculptor, in an evaluation of his work by the critic, in a brilliant burlesque of a duel atop a Parisian rooftop, in a travesty on an apache dance, and in a comic ballet in the Garden of Eden.

Though Lilo was billed as the star, it was Gwen Verdon, also new to Broadway, who stopped the show. Before *Can-Can* she had made some inauspicious appearances as a dancer in light opera, in a musical that closed out of town, in nightclubs, and with the Jack Cole dancers. Her work and personality went unnoticed by all except Michael Kidd, who thought of her when he cast his dances for *Can-Can*. Her dynamic personality, as flaming as her touseled red hair, won the audience completely. She brought down the house with her wild, uninhibited apache dancing in "The Apaches" and particularly with a strip-tease routine in "The Garden of Eden."

In his score, Cole Porter tried to capture something of the spirit, if not the essence, of the kind of songs Paris sang in 1893, of which he had made an intensive study. It was a source of painful disappointment to him that the critics failed to realize what he was trying to do, and how well he had done it. (Another source of disappointment was that the French government had failed to give him any kind of recognition for having caught and fixed the heart and soul of a bygone Paris in his melodies and lyrics, and for having written "I Love Paris.") Besides numbers already mentioned, those also deserving attention include the title song (shared by Pistache and Claudine),

"Allez-vous en," introduced by Pistache, and "It's All Right with Me," sung by Judge Aristide.

The motion-picture adaptation (20th Century-Fox, 1960) gathered a galaxy of stars: Frank Sinatra, Shirley MacLaine, Maurice Chevalier, and Louis Jourdan. Not only were the principal songs from the stage production used here, but also some Cole Porter standards from other musicals ("Just One of Those Things," "Let's Do It," and "You Do Something to Me").

An unpleasant episode during the rehearsal of Can-Can provides an amusing footnote to the history of the "cold war" of the 1950's. Nikita Khrushchev, then the Premier of the Soviet Union, was paying his first visit to the United States in 1959. In Hollywood, he was invited to attend a rehearsal of Can-Can. The number chosen for his entertainment was the closing can-can, a dance that so shocked the Premier that he hurled a violent denunciation against a state of morals that could permit a scene like this to get filmed.

> CANDIDE (1956), a musical play, with book by Lillian Hellman, based on Voltaire's satirical novel of the same name. Lyrics by Richard Wilbur. Additional lyrics by John La Touche and Dorothy Parker. Music by Leonard Bernstein. Presented by Ethel Linder Reiner in association with Lester Osterman, Jr., at the Martin Beck Theater on December 1. Directed by Tyrone Guthrie, with the assistance of Tom Brown. Cast included Max Adrian, Robert Rounseville, Barbara Cook, and Irra Petina (73 performances).

Lillian Hellman was more or less faithful to Voltaire's famous satire on optimism. Taught by Dr. Pangloss (Max Adrian) that all is for the best in this best of possible worlds, Candide (Robert Rounseville) stoically accepts the unfounded news that his intended bride, Cunegonde (Barbara Cook), has been killed in a war between Westphalia and Hesse. He also decides to set forth on a journey away from Westphalia with Dr. Pangloss. His first stop is Lisbon, where he almost becomes the victim of the Inquisition and where Dr. Pangloss is killed during an earthquake. His next stop is Paris. He is now disturbed by the tragedies he has encountered but soon comes to believe that the fault lies with the philosophy of optimism rather than with him. Much to his amazement, Candide comes upon Cunegonde in Paris, arrayed in finery and jewels, living as a demimondaine in a house shared by a marquis and a sultan. Candide kills both of them in a duel and flees with his beloved. They encounter a band of devout pilgrims en route to the New World and decide to sail with them. They come to Buenos Aires. Cunegonde finds a home at the palace of the governor, who has become interested in her, while Candide is compelled to leave her behind and try to find his fortune elsewhere. He returns from Eldorado, laden with gold, seeking Cunegonde, who, he is told, has set sail for America. Candide, determined to follow her, purchases a decrepit old ship that sinks off the coast. Rescued, Candide now decides to go to Venice, where he is overjoyed to find Dr. Pangloss, apparently saved during the earthquake in Lisbon. Cunegonde is also in Venice, but this time she appears as a scrubwoman. Candide, involved in drink and gambling, gets swindled of all his gold. He is now friendless, penniless, and bereft of all hope—a sadly disillusioned man. But a ray of optimism returns when, back in Westphalia, he finds both Pangloss and Cunegonde. Nevertheless, the philosophy of Dr. Pangloss no longer holds any truth for him. He has become convinced that the only way to live is to make one's own garden grow.

It was rather to the spirit of Voltaire, than to the letter, that Lillian Hellman was not altogether true. As *Time* remarked: "Where Voltaire is ironic and bland, she is explicit and vigorous. Where he makes lightning rapier thrusts she provides body blows. Where he is diabolical, she is humanitarian." This may partially explain why *Candide* was a box-office failure, or it may have been that, as Brooks Atkinson noted, "the eighteenth-century philosophical tale is not ideal material for a theater show." But despite shortcomings of the text, *Candide* was a "distinguished musical," as Robert Coleman described it. "It towers head and shoulders above most of the song-and-dancers you'll get this or any other season. It has wry humor, mannered grace, and marvelous music."

Especially "marvelous music." Bernstein's score alone should have won for *Candide* a far longer run than it enjoyed, the best that Bernstein had written for the popular theater up to that time. The scintillating overture, with its mockery and laughter, immediately sets the proper tone for everything that follows. Bernstein wrote three excellent, rich-sounding melodies in Cunegonde's "Glitter and Be Gay" and Candide's "Eldorado" and "It Must Be So." The parody, satire, and wit were like rapier thrusts: "You Were Dead, You Know" (Candide and Cunegonde); "The Best of All Possible Worlds" (Cunegonde, Candide, Dr. Pangloss, and chorus); and "I Am Easily Assimilated" (sung by Irra Petina, playing the role of the Old Lady). The last three revealed a different and no less delightful facet of Bernstein's creativity. The spacious score further embraced duets, trios, quartets, choral numbers; a mazurka, waltz, serenade, ballad, gavotte, and tango; operatic music, music-hall ditties, folk music, jazz. "None of his previous theater music," said Brooks Atkinson, "has had the joyous variety, humor, and richness of the score." The gay overture (more in the style of opéra bouffe than Broadway musical theater) has become a concert favorite.

CARMEN JONES (1943), *a musical play, a modern Negro adaptation of Georges Bizet's opera* Carmen, *with music entirely by Bizet. Book and lyrics by Oscar Hammerstein II. Presented by Billy Rose at the Broadway Theater on December 2. Directed by Hassard Short. Choreography by Eugene Loring. Cast included Muriel Smith and Muriel Rahn (alternating as Carmen), Luther Saxon and Napoleon Reed (alternating as Joe), Carlotta Franzell and Elton J. Warren (alternating as Cindy Lou), and Glenn Bryant (502 performances).*

In the difficult years just before he began to work with Richard Rodgers, and when successes seemed to have eluded him permanently, Oscar Hammerstein found an idea in a recording of the Bizet opera *Carmen.* Listening to this vital, throbbing music, Hammerstein conceived the notion of modernizing the operatic text. The months he spent on libretto and lyrics represented a labor of love; this was the first time he was writing something for the stage without the stimulus of a signed contract. When he finished, he let his manuscript lie on his desk for about a year, hoping to produce the play himself. One day he happened to show his script to Billy Rose, who was so delighted with it he offered to be its producer.

The critics were unqualified in their praises. Lewis Nichols called it "wonderful, quite wonderful"; Robert Garland said it was "a memorable milestone in the upward and onward course of the great American showshop"; Robert Coleman considered it "superb . . . enchantingly beautiful . . . musically exciting and visually stirring." It stayed on Broadway almost two years, winning the Donaldson Award as the season's best musical, and then went on a transcontinental tour.

In bringing Bizet's opera up to date, Hammerstein transferred its locale from early-nineteenth-century Seville to a Southern town during World War II; from a cigarette to a parachute factory. Don José of the opera becomes Joe, a Negro corporal; Escamillo, the toreador, was transformed into Husky Miller, a heavyweight fighter (Glenn Bryant). The seductive Carmen Jones manages to steal Joe from Cindy Lou. Joe goes AWOL, and the lovers flee to Chicago, where Carmen soon falls in love with Husky Miller and abandons Joe. Joe begs Carmen to return to him. When she refuses, he kills her outside the fighting arena on the night of Husky's championship bout.

The specific details of the plot follow the libretto of *Carmen,* often literally—though always remaining in twentieth-century America by superimposing American scenes, mores, attitudes, and speech on the opera text. Hammerstein remained even truer to the *Carmen* music. In using the opera score for his text and lyrics, Hammerstein made no additions, and only the most negligible deletions. One or two numbers were taken out of their order in the opera; the recitatives were displaced by spoken dialogue (incidentally, as Bizet originally had intended). As Hammerstein explained in the program: "Believing *Carmen* to be a perfect wedding of story and music, we have adhered as closely as possible to the original form. . . . The small deviations we have made were only those which seemed honestly demanded by a transference of *Carmen* to a modern *American* background."

In the modernized score, the celebrated "Habanera" became "Dat's Love" (Carmen Jones with chorus); the "Seguidilla," "Dere's a Café on De Corner" (Carmen Jones and Napoleon Reed); "Gypsy Song," "Beat Out Dat Rhythm on a Drum" (June Hawkins, playing the part of Frankie, and chorus); the "Toreador Song," "Stan' Up and Fight" (Husky Miller); the "Flower Song," "Dis Flower" (Napoleon Reed); "Micaëla's Air," "My Joe" (Cindy Lou); and the opening chorus of Act IV, "Dat's Our Man" (Carmen Jones and chorus).

Dorothy Dandridge, Harry Belafonte, and Diahann Carroll were the stars in the motion-picture adaptation (20th Century-Fox, 1954). The stage score was used.

CARNIVAL (1961), *a musical play, with book by Michael Stewart, based on material by Helen Deutsch. Lyrics and music by Bob Merrill. Presented by David Merrick at the Imperial Theater on April 13. Directed and with dances by Gower Champion. Cast included Anna Maria Alberghetti, James Mitchell, Jerry Orbach, and Kaye Ballard (719 performances).*

Without denigrating the contribution of all the others who made *Carnival* such a stage delight from beginning to end, the lion's share of the honors must go to Gower Champion for his direction and choreography. It was his decision to make the audience participants in the production; to have them feel, see, and experience Lili's enchantment with what, in actuality, is a drab, run-down traveling-circus troupe set up for performances in the outskirts of a south European town.

Gower Champion immediately created a rapport between those on the stage and those in the audience by eliminating the curtain. When the audience arrived into the theater they saw an open stage, a tree in the foreground, and on the horizon a stretch of countryside. The lights go down for the show to begin, but there is no formal overture as such. Instead, a youngster, Jacquot (Pierre Olaf), dressed in carnival clothes, strolls informally in front of the proscenium and plays a tune on his concertina while prognosticating a glowing future for his company in Paris. Then roustabouts appear. They set up a tent. Show wagons and booths are put in place. The circus performers arrive casually. Only then does the orchestra in the pit strike up the strains of an overture. The owner of the circus, Schliegel (Henry Lascoe), and a performer join in singing "Direct from Vienna." And now the show is on, come to life before the very eyes of the audience without any artificial preliminaries.

The informal relationship between audience and show continues throughout the production. Sometimes the performers use the aisles for their entrances and exits. In one of the more telling scenes—between Lili (Anna Marie Alberghetti) and Marco the Magnificent (James Mitchell), with whom she believes she is in love—Marco is in the aisle, while Lili sits on the apron over the orchestra. Hawkers flow through the aisles throwing souvenirs at the customers. From the rear of the auditorium, a Pygmy-sized trumpeter and a huge drummer march to the stage. All the while the audience is a spectator to performances by jugglers, a dog act, strong men, acrobats, dancers—even as if they were a part of that south European audience that had paid the price of admission for the circus show.

Through these means, the motion picture *Lili,* on which *Carnival* was based, acquired a new identity, even while adhering quite closely to the basic plot. One major difference between the movie and the stage musical is that in the former, as enacted by Leslie Caron, Lili is a dancing role, while in the latter, because of Miss Alberghetti's vocal talent, it is a singing part. The plot begins when Lili makes her appearance. She is dressed in an ill-fitting suit and black stockings. She carries a lopsided valise in her hand. She is a skinny, gawky youngster—an orphan come to the carnival to seek out a friend of her late father. The carnival becomes for her a place of wonder and magic. Its magician, Marco the Magnificent, becomes a Romeo to her wide-open eyes, on whom she soon lavishes her adoration. The puppets (created and supervised by Tom Tichenor) almost at once become her most precious friends.

The puppeteer, Paul Berthalet (Jerry Orbach), is a lame, ill-tempered, and frequently offensive fellow who reveals the warmer side of his nature only when he speaks through his puppets. He falls in love with Lili, but his pride and ornery ways make it impossible for him to reveal his feelings. Through Lili's attachment to the puppets, however, she begins to understand the puppeteer and to become interested in him. Romance comes to fulfillment. Then, with the show over, the roustabouts begin to remove booths and tent; the performers drift off the stage; the lights grow dim. There is no descending curtain to announce the end of the musical.

For Anna Maria Alberghetti, *Carnival* represented her Broadway debut. There was no doubt that she came through with flying colors. "She is completely captivating as the childlike young woman who has to grow up," said

Robert Coleman. "Miss Alberghetti proves a sensitive actress and one of the finest assets Broadway has acquired in a long time," reported a critic for the United Press International.

Bob Merrill, as composer-lyricist, was faced with a major problem in writing his score. The movie had produced a highly successful song in "Hi-Lili, Hi Lo," which had become a standard. To compete with it represented a challenge which Merrill met by writing "The Theme from *Carnival*," which became popular as "Love Makes the World Go Round"—a melody that recurs throughout the musical but is given its first full formal presentation by Lili and the puppets. To Lili, too, is assigned another touching number, "Mira." Marco the Magnificent, and his assistant, Rosalie (played by Kaye Ballard), share a fine duet in "Always, Always You," which gets a unique treatment: Rosalie is in a basket, and as they sing, Marco pierces the basket with huge swords, though how this trick is performed is never revealed. "Candy" served as an admirable background for a production number (sung by Lili, the puppets, and the people of the carnival). Another impressive production number comes when the cast of the troupe express their joy on learning they are going to Paris by setting into motion a dance that begins slowly but builds up into a veritable Corybantic.

As for the musical as a whole, the critics left no doubts about their reaction. In *The New York Times,* Howard Taubman said it "mixes sentiment and show business razzle-dazzle into a flashy, eye-filling and occasionally touching entertainment." Paul Aston in the *World-Telegram* came right out and called it "the best musical of the season." Robert Coleman insisted that "it belongs on everyone's must-see list." And Richard Watts, Jr., said: "There is no getting away from the fact that *Carnival* is rich in enchantment." It was selected by the New York Drama Critics Circle as the best musical of the season.

> CAROUSEL (1945), *a musical play, with book and lyrics by Oscar Hammerstein II, based on Ferenc Molnár's* Liliom *as adapted by Benjamin F. Glazer. Music by Richard Rodgers. Presented by the Theater Guild at the Majestic Theater on April 19. Directed by Rouben Mamoulian. Dances by Agnes de Mille. Cast included Jan Clayton, John Raitt, Christine Johnson, Bambi Linn, and Jean Darling (890 performances).*

Hardly had their first musical play, *Oklahoma!,* settled down comfortably in the St. James Theater for its phenomenal run—with the rhapsodies of the critics still ringing in their ears and the line-up at the box office of the St. James Theater presenting a joyous picture to their eyes—when Rodgers and Hammerstein began planning their second collaborative effort: to make

Molnár's *Liliom* into a musical play, a plan that had actually originated with Theresa Helburn of the Theater Guild. The Guild had successfully produced the Molnár play in 1921. Helburn felt that its Hungarian background, carnival setting, and excursions into fantasy made it ideal for musical adaptation. But when she first suggested the project to Rodgers and Hammerstein, they were skeptical, feeling that the setting of Hungary was not feasible for musical-play treatment when America was at war with Nazi Germany and Japan, and Hungary was an ally of the enemy. Not until Rodgers suggested the transfer of the locale to America's New England were he and Hammerstein sparked into action. New England provided ensembles germane to the play—fishermen, mill girls, sailors. Its thoroughly American background and New England geography made it possible to exploit picturesque local speech, customs, diversions, and even local food dishes. All this helped make the subject suitable for the special creative gifts of both the composer and the librettist-lyricist. After discussing the way the adaptation should be made, Rodgers and Hammerstein completed their first musical number—it was the now famous "Soliloquy"—and then, as Rodgers recalls, "we knew we had the play licked." Only then did they sign a contract with the Theater Guild.

Some basic changes had to be made in the Molnár play. The title now became *Carousel*. The leading character was named Billy Bigelow (instead of Liliom). The time of the play was shifted to 1873. In the Molnár play the heroine, Julie, becomes Liliom's mistress and bears him a child; in the musical Billy and Julie get married. But in both versions the principal male character remains a handsome and tough amusement-park barker, a rough-and-ready bully, incapable of meeting his wife's material or emotional needs.

When the play opens, we hear the infectious strains of the "Carousel Waltz" and see an amusement park crowded with New Englanders in a holiday mood. We also see a carousel, and its barker, Billy Bigelow (John Raitt), urging the crowds to buy tickets for this attraction. When the owner of the carousel insults two mill girls—Carrie Pepperidge (Jean Darling) and Julie Jordan (Jan Clayton)—Billy comes to their defense, for which he is summarily fired from his job. Billy invites Julie to share a drink of beer with him, but first goes off to change his clothes. During his absence, Carrie becomes inquisitive why Julie should find Billy attractive, in the song "You're a Queer One, Julie Jordan," and then, in "When I Marry Mr. Snow," confides that she, too, has a lover. Upon Billy's return, their attraction for each other becomes apparent. Billy wants to know if Julie would ever marry an irresponsible and happy-go-lucky fellow like himself, to which Julie replies in the most popular love ballad in the musical (and now recognized as one of Rodgers' choicest love songs), "If I Loved You," a ballad which Billy sings back to Julie.

Romance leads to marriage. It is spring, and the people of New England express their delight in the wonders of the season with the joyous refrains of "June Is Bustin' Out All Over," which then becomes the background music for a ballet sequence. The vernal season has its impact also on Carrie and Enoch Snow (Eric Mattson), who begin dreaming of getting married and raising a family ("When the Children Are Asleep"). For Billy, there is also much to think about. Julie has just told him she is pregnant, which fills him with not only parental pride but also tenderness for both his wife and coming child. He allows his imagination to soar. In the celebrated seven-minute "Soliloquy" he muses about his coming child and its future. This reverie fires him with the determination to get a lot of money soon.

Meanwhile, the New Englanders are enjoying a festive clambake. They are all high-spirited and gay, with the exception of Julie, who cannot help worrying if Billy can become sufficiently responsible and dependable to be a good father to their coming child. Nevertheless, she knows she loves him, and in the end she comes to the conclusion that this is all that counts ("What's the Use of Wond'rin' "). What she does not know, however, is that in his impatience to put his hands on money quickly he gets involved in a hold-up, is caught by the police, and commits suicide to avoid arrest. Once this terrible news reaches Julie, she is overwhelmed, and can find little solace in the efforts of her friend Nettie (Christine Johnson) to console her in "You'll Never Walk Alone."

At this point *Liliom* and *Carousel* differ. In the Molnár play, Liliom defiantly tells two of heaven's policemen that he does not regret his actions. For this he is doomed to purgatory for fifteen years. After that period he must return to earth for a single day to expiate his sins. Liliom appears on earth disguised as a beggar, in his hand a star he has stolen from the heavens, which he is bringing as a gift to his daughter. When she sends him away abruptly, he slaps her face. He is then led away. The play ends on the tragic note of utter frustration.

But in the musical Billy follows his purgatory stay with a visit to the Starkeeper in Heaven, who informs him that he can gain admission only after the redemption of his soul. To achieve redemption, Billy is allowed a day on earth. Stealing a star, he returns to earth and tries to present it as a gift to his unhappy, maladjusted daughter. When she turns it down, he slaps her. But the girl feels no hurt, since the slap is given with love and not hate. His tenderness now helps the child overcome her personal misery, and by this one achievement Billy's soul is redeemed. As he witnesses the exercises of her graduation from school, he realizes joyfully that she can enter upon life with head high and singing heart. And his widow knows again what she had always known when Billy was alive: having been married to him had been worth the pain it had cost. The tragedy of Molnár's play becomes dispelled in the musical by love and forgiveness.

*Carousel* was acclaimed when it reached Broadway. To John Chapman it was "one of the finest musical plays I have ever seen, and I shall remember it always." Robert Coleman called it "beautiful, bountiful, beguiling . . . plays a tune called success—because it is the product of taste, imagination and skill. It will bewitch your senses and race your pulses." Louis Kronenberger regarded it as "an occasion in the theater." It received the New York Drama Critics Award as the best musical of the season, and Donaldson awards in eight categories including that of best musical.

*Carousel* has lost none of its original magic in its frequent revivals. In short, it has become a stage classic. "This is the most glorious of the Rodgers and Hammerstein works," wrote Brooks Atkinson when *Carousel* returned to Broadway in 1954. "When the highest judge of all hands down the ultimate verdict, it is this column's opinion that *Carousel* will turn out to be the finest of their creations. . . . *Carousel* is a masterpiece that grows in stature through the years." Its status as a classic was confirmed in 1958 when it was presented and acclaimed at the United States Pavilion at the Brussels World Fair (a production in which Jan Clayton returned to her original role of Julie). And it was reconfirmed in the winter of 1966 when, presented anew at the New York City Center, it continued to inspire rhapsodic reactions from the critics and the public.

However remarkable had been Rodgers' score to *Oklahoma!*, the one for *Carousel* represented new heights of creativity. His musical writing acquired breadth and spaciousness—for example, the symphonic waltz prelude played under the opening scene, which has since become such a favorite of "pop" and summer concerts, or the extended "Soliloquy," in which the usual musical-comedy song (sixteen measures to the verse, thirty-two to the chorus) is expanded into a seven-minute musical episode, made up of eight different melodic fragments. Now for the first time Rodgers begins to make the orchestra a commentator on what is occurring on the stage, to produce extended orchestral sequences and interludes, at times played under the dialogue, at times connecting one scene to the next one. In addition, a new dramatic expressiveness and a new spirituality begin to penetrate some of his musical thinking, as in "You'll Never Walk Alone," while at other times he proves capable of endowing some of his melodies with an encompassing humanity and tenderness not often encountered before this in his music (as in "When the Children Are Asleep" or when, in "Soliloquy," Billy thinks about the possibility of having a daughter). In short, in *Carousel* Rodgers is no longer merely a writer of wonderful melodies. He has finally become a musical dramatist.

In the motion picture (20th Century-Fox, 1956) Gordon MacRae and Shirley Jones shared the leads. An original TV adaptation was telecast on the Armstrong Circle Theater in 1967 with Robert Goulet, Mary Grover, and Charles Ruggles.

THE CASINO GIRL (1900), *an operetta, with book and lyrics by Harry B. Smith. Music by Ludwig Englander and others. Presented by George V. Lederer at the Casino Theater on March 19. Cast included Virginia Earle, Albert Hart, Sam Bernard, Mabelle Gilman, and Lotta Faust (91 performances).*

The Casino Theater—an ornate structure with Moorish turrets—opened on the southeast corner of Broadway and 39th Street on October 22, 1882, with a presentation of a Viennese operetta. From then on, and for the next two decades, it became the most significant theater in New York for the production of lavish musicals, operettas, and extravaganzas. Across its stage passed some of the most beautiful show girls of the era preceding Florenz Ziegfeld. A "Casino girl," then, became for the late 1800's and the first few years of of the 1900's the equivalent of the "Ziegfeld girl" of a slightly later day— the essence of glamour and pulchritude.

It was inevitable, then, that a Casino Theater production be built around the personality of one of these girls. She is Laura Lee (Mabelle Gilman), who is loved by Percy (Virginia Earle), seventh son of the Earl of Doughmore. Because of Percy's infatuation with a show girl, his father sends him off to faraway Egypt. But Laura grows weary of night life in New York and herself goes off to Cairo to open a millinery shop there. She meets Percy again, falls in love with him, and they finally marry. But before that happens they go through various adventures. Laura must elude the clutches of the Khedive (Sam Bernard), who wants her for his harem, and Percy must extricate himself from the grip of two slick crooks, Fromage and Potage.

The plot was enlivened by sparkling performances—by Sam Bernard, who brought an amusingly incongruous Dutch accent to the character of the Khedive; by Virginia Earle, vivacious in her impersonation of the male character of Percy and who (as one critic noted) "sang and danced like a dream"; by the malapropisms of a minor character played by Carrie E. Perkins. Englander's best songs included an Oriental-type number, "Slave Dealer's Song"; the title song; "Mam'selle"; and a nostalgic tribute, "New

York." But the hit song of the show came from another pen, that of John H. Flynn: "Sweet Annie Moore," whose lyrics (also by Flynn) contained an amusing succession of puns.

The Casino Girl was originally in three acts, but when it reopened at the Casino Theater on August 6, 1900, it was condensed into two acts.

CASTLES IN THE AIR (1890), *an operetta, with book and lyrics by C. A. Byrne, adapted partly from Meitter's text for Offenbach's* Les Bayards *and partly from a one-act intermezzo by Cervantes,* Los Habladores. *Music by Gustave Kerker. Presented by the De Wolf Hopper Opera Bouffe Company at the Broadway Theater on May 5. Cast included De Wolf Hopper, Della Fox, and Marion Manola (160 performances).*

In *Castles in the Air,* De Wolf Hopper had his first starring role. The show was his from beginning to end. His clowning as Judge Pilacoudre stole the thunder from all the other performers, although in one instance Della Fox shared the limelight by joining him in a song duèt about a pantomime game of billiards. Other delightful Kerker numbers were "What in the World Could Compare to This?", "Is it a Dream?", and the title song.

The plot had Bul-Bul (Marion Manola) flee from his creditors in a costume furnished by Cabolastro (Thomas Q. Seabrooke). Cabolastro is willing to provide the costume free of charge if Bul-Bul is successful in bettering Cabolastro's garrulous wife in a battle of words. Bul-Bul consents and is successful. Since Bul-Bul is in love with Cabolastro's daughter, Blanche (Della Fox), the prospective father-in-law is willing to pay all of the young man's debts.

THE CAT AND THE FIDDLE (1931), *a musical comedy, with book and lyrics by Otto Harbach. Music by Jerome Kern. Presented by Max Gordon at the Globe Theater on October 15. Directed by José Ruben. Dances by Albertina Rasch. Cast included Odette Myrtil, George Meader, Georges Metaxa, and Bettina Hall (395 performances).*

Having broken with the past in *Show Boat* in 1927, Kern was emboldened once more to help create an unusual musical comedy with unorthodox ideas and material. As he told Max Gordon, who aspired to be the producer: "I am thinking in terms of another musical which, like *Show Boat,* would attempt to explore new paths. Otto Harbach has an idea for a musical that I think lends itself to serious treatment. You should know that we have been talking about eliminating chorus girls, production numbers, and formal comedy routines. We are striving to make certain that there will be a strong motivation for the music throughout." To all of which Gordon's reaction was: "It sounded fascinating, adventurous."

Harbach's setting was twentieth-century Brussels. Shirley Sheridan (Bettina Hall) is an American popular composer come to Brussels for music study. Along the banks of the city's river she meets an impressive-looking young man. He is a serious Romanian composer, Victor Florescu (Georges Metaxa). They become interested in each other. What they do not know is that they occupy adjoining rooms in the same apartment house. In his studio, Florescu is deep at work on an opera, *The Passionate Pilgrim,* but he is disturbed by the loud sound of American popular music next door. When his brother, Daudet, comes to Florescu's studio to listen to the opera score, he overhears one of Shirley's popular songs and insists that the inclusion of such music could make Florescu's opera more popular. This only tends to anger Florescu further. Nevertheless, when his opera gets performed it proves highly successful, even though its prima donna, Odette (Odette Myrtil), has introduced all sorts of temperamental problems. Florescut and Shirley become more tolerant of each other's music, which permits their romance to progress more smoothly than had been possible up to now.

Convinced he was involved in an important project that might open new avenues for the musical theater, Kern was a demon of energy and dedication at rehearsals. As Max Gordon recalls: "He was tireless in his drive for perfection. It seemed that he hardly needed any sleep at all. No detail escaped him. The slightest misplacement of the tiniest prop was enough to send him screaming down an aisle shouting invective left and right."

Yet, for all his seriousness of purpose, Kern was not beyond perpetrating pranks (for which he always had a weakness), even while a major musical stage production was being rehearsed. Knowing of Gordon's contempt of anything illicit or off-color, Kern concocted a lewd sketch which, with the help of several performers, he skillfully inserted into the show one day in Philadelphia during rehearsals. When Gordon heard the sketch, he became frantic with rage; he shouted that under no circumstance would he allow such material to appear in one of his shows. Then he noticed that everybody around him was doubled up with laughter—and realized with amusement that he had just been a victim of one of Kern's mischievous pranks.

As had been the case with *Show Boat,* old and tried routines were avoided. *The Cat and the Fiddle* had no chorus-girl line, no synthetic comedy scenes, no set production numbers, no spectacle. The characters were believable human beings. The music progressed gracefully out of the context. Kern's score (which at one point was sufficiently adventurous to interpolate a fugal episode) had three outstanding songs: "The Night Was Made for Love," a canzonetta that courses throughout the production, and which was sung by George Meader, playing a subsidiary role; Shirley's song, "She Didn't Say 'Yes' ''; and Victor's serenade, "One Moment Alone." In addition, there were two numbers that still have not received the recognition they deserve, "Poor Pierrot" and "The Breeze That Kissed Your Hair."

It did not take Hollywood long to make a movie out of *The Cat and the Fiddle.* This was done by MGM in 1934, with Ramon Novarro and Jeanette MacDonald in the leads.

CELEBRATION (1969), *a musical comedy, with book and lyrics by Tom Jones. Music by Harvey Schmidt. Presented by Cheryl Crawford and Richard Chandler at the Ambassador Theater on January 22. Directed by Tom Jones. Dances by Vernon Lusby. Cast included Michael Glenn-Smith, Susan Watson, and the Revelers (109 performances).*

In *Celebration,* Tom Jones and Harvey Schmidt created a fable, as the program explained, "about the time and life cycle passing through the cold winter season of disillusionment and satiation to the inevitable spring of rebirth, renewal and love." In actuality it is a fable about hope and optimism, on the one hand, and false illusions and disenchantment, on the other. This was offbeat theater (just as had been *The Fantasticks,* with which Jones and Schmidt had made their sensational theatrical debut). Unfortunately, audiences refused to respond to *Celebration* as they have been doing for years to *The Fantasticks. Celebration* was a failure—but only a box-office failure, not an artistic one. The critics, generally, turned in highly favorable reports, and one or two critics were thoroughly enchanted. *Time* magazine called it a "charmer for sophisticates who have never quite forsaken the magic realm of childhood . . . one of those good things that come in small packages." And Otis L. Guernsey, Jr., thought well enough of *Celebration*—in spite of its brief run—to select it as one of the ten best plays of 1968–69 in his theater yearbook.

The play takes place on New Year's Eve. First we encounter Potemkin (Keith Charles), a cynic who thinks that the only thing that matters in the world is to survive, and who later gets involved in the main action of the musical fable. With the Revelers (a chorus of twelve, wearing masks), he initiates a ritual ("Celebration"). Other characters are symbolic of youth and old age, innocence and corruption, optimism and utter futility. The fable itself (which Clive Barnes said was "as beguiling as a cherubic face advertising baby food") has for its main character an orphan (Michael Glenn-Smith). He is a youth who escapes from his orphanage to find a garden ("My Garden"). All he takes with him are a Bible and a roll of lavatory paper.

He appeals for help to "Mr. Somebody in the Sky." As he wanders, he meets Potemkin disguised as a hobo, who inquires what he is carrying; the boy replies, "the sun" and "the eye of God," the latter stolen from the face of God from the stained-glass window of the orphanage chapel. Potemkin brings the orphan to the world of social climbers, where they crash the party of Mr. Rich (Ted Thurston), a crusty old gentleman in despair because his years have robbed him of his sexual potency; his frustrations are expressed in a singularly effective number, "Where Did It Go?" There, too, Potemkin and the orphan meet an angel (Susan Watson), who in actuality is an entertainer for Mr. Rich's party. She aspires to become an actress because (as she explains in her song "Somebody") she does not want to be a *nobody*. At Potemkin's suggestion, the orphan and angel try to cheer up Mr. Rich with a love song ("Love Song"). Mr. Rich joins in, and when the singing is over the angel rushes into Mr. Rich's arms, much to the old man's delight. But he does not know that Potemkin has come to the angel with a message to meet the orphan in the garden. The scene shifts to the orphan's garden, where the angel and the orphan meet. Each is happy, for the girl is wealthy (thanks to Mr. Rich), and the orphan has his garden. Then Mr. Rich arrives with artificial flowers with which to create a Garden of Eden in which he and the angel would enact the parts of Adam and Eve. The orphan insists that the garden is his, much to Mr. Rich's amusement, since he can tear the whole garden apart with machines. The orphan, however, stops the machines in their tracks with his eye of God. He has fought Mr. Rich successfully, and now the angel joins him, which gives the orphan something to fight for—the girl ("Fifty Million Years Ago").

The pageant Mr. Rich had planned in the garden takes place nevertheless—with the orphan, in disguise, making love to the angel, playing Eve. He then seduces her while Mr. Rich, as Adam, is a spectactor. Before Mr. Rich can respond, Potemkin calls for a battle between winter and summer, in which summer emerges victorious. At the same time, Mr. Rich—who has begun to delude himself into believing he is a young man—sees himself as he really is, in his dotage, a truth that destroys him. The orphan has lost his garden; the angel, the wealth that had made her a somebody. The orphan and angel are ready to enter the real world together. Potemkin blesses them as they take their leave. Joined by the Revelers (who discard their masks and now carry pictures of the sun), they close the fable with a repetition of "Celebration."

Clive Barnes found that the use of the masks by the Revelers is "like the use of color, sometimes subdued, sometimes intentionally garish, far more sophisticated than we are accustomed to in Broadway musicals."

The orchestra comprised nine players, all percussionists. They were placed not in the pit, but upstage behind the backdrop.

THE CENTURY GIRL (1916), *a revue, with book and lyrics by unidentified authors. Additional lyrics by Irving Berlin. Music by Victor Herbert and Irving Berlin. Presented by Charles Dillingham and Florenz Ziegfeld at the Century Theater on November 6. Cast included Leon Errol, Elsie Janis, Harland Dixon, Hazel Dawn, May Leslie, Van and Schenck, and Frank Tinney (200 performances).*

No expense was spared by the producers in their aim to make this one of the most splendiferous revues ever produced. To Edward N. Waters, Victor Herbert's biographer, this show "set new standards of opulent luxury and scenic display." In addition, one of the most glamorous casts ever assembled in one production was gathered for the production—many of them already major stars in the musical theater.

As a revue, *The Century Girl* comprised a seemingly endless parade of sumptuous pageantry, ballet, and production numbers, together with comedy sketches, songs, and the specialties for which each of the stars was famous. Herbert was called upon to write the music for the lavish sequences: "The Birth of the Century Girl" and "The Toy Soldiers" in Act I; "The Stone Age" and "Uncle Sam's Children" in Act II; and "Under the Sea" in Act III. He also contributed "You Belong to Me" and an ear-arresting march, "When Uncle Sam Is Ruler of the Sea." Irving Berlin's musical contribution comprised "The Chicken Walk," "Alice in Wonderland," and "It Takes an Irishman to Make Love," among other numbers.

One of effective sketches, called "The Music Lesson," portrayed Victor Herbert and Irving Berlin, impersonated by Arthur Cunningham and John Slavin, for which Berlin concocted an intriguing countermelody for Victor Herbert's already famous waltz "Kiss Me Again" (lifted, of course, from his operetta *Mlle. Modiste*). One of the most rousing and visually stunning production numbers came as the finale to the second act—a patriotic scene, "Uncle Sam's Children," devised by Ned Wayburn.

CHIN-CHIN (1914), *a musical fantasy, with book by Anne Caldwell and R. H. Burnside. Lyrics by Anne Caldwell and James O'Dea. Music by Ivan Caryll. Presented by Charles Dillingham at the Globe Theater on October 20. Directed by R. H. Burnside. The cast included David Montgomery, Fred Stone, Helen Falconer, and Douglas Stevenson (295 performances).*

This Oriental extravaganza was a modernization of the Aladdin story that ranged from musical comedy to broad burlesque. As the advertisements took pains to publicize, the fantasy was filled with "caravans of pretty girls; car-loads of novelties; tingling-jingling numbers; gorgeous costumes; wonderful scenes; startling situations; quaint toy bazaar; teddy bear dances . . . and so on."

Two Chinese, Chin Hop Lo (David Montgomery) and Chin Hop Hi (Fred Stone), search for the precious lamp of Aladdin. They come to the toy bazaar of Abanazar, where they find a rich American who wants to buy Aladdin's lamp for his daughter Violet (Helen Falconer). Abanazar (Charles T. Aldrich) knows that the precious lamp is owned by a poor widow who does not know its value, and he contrives to defraud her of it. But two Chinese manikins in his store come to life, and they assist the shop's clerk (whose name also happens to be Aladdin) to frustrate the swindle. Violet then falls in love with the clerk.

As Chin Hop Hi, Fred Stone is given ample opportunity to demonstrate his versatility. He assumes the roles of a ventriloquist, lady horseback rider, eccentric dancer, and "Paderiski," who deserts a mechanical piano to dance with Violet.

The hit song was Chin Hop Hi's "Good-bye, Girls, I'm Through" (lyrics by John Golden). Aladdin delivers several attractive numbers: "Violet," "The Mulberry Tree," and "Love Moon," the last two being duets with Violet. During the run of the play an English song was interpolated, soon to become a favorite of World War I: "It's a Long, Long Way to Tipperary," by Harry Williams and Jack Judge.

One of the reasons "Good-bye, Girls, I'm Through" became so popular both in the show and away from it was that it took advantage of the popularity of "good-bye" songs in general—and the bachelor-type good-bye songs in particular—so popular at that time. This number was written while the show was still rehearsing, since some number was needed to give the performers time to change their costumes. "In less than thirty minutes," John Golden, its lyricist, recalled many years later, "I had the first verse and chorus complete. . . . Ivan Caryll was called in hurriedly to set the lyric. The play opened in Philadelphia, and the next day I had a wire that the song was the hit of the piece—everybody was singing it." John Golden also confessed that this song proved a turning point in his career. "Because of it I said good-bye forever to songwriting and, with one of the royalty checks it brought in, I launched into the business of producing plays."

A CHINESE HONEYMOON (1902), *a musical comedy, with book and lyrics by George Dance. Music by Gustave Kerker and Howard Talbot. Presented by Sam S. Shubert at the Casino Theater on June 2. Directed by Gerald*

*Coventry. Cast included Thomas Q. Seabrooke, Adele Ritchie, William Pruette, and Annie Yeamans (376 performances).*

In May, 1902, the Shuberts gained control of the Casino Theater and inaugurated their regime with a major success—*A Chinese Honeymoon,* a London operetta, rewritten for the American public with many new songs by Kerker. Samuel Pineapple (Thomas Q. Seabrooke) is an English stockbroker who marries his typist and takes her off on a honeymoon to Yiang Yiang, a mythical section of China. While Mrs. Pineapple (Adele Ritchie) is herself very much of a flirt, she is intensely jealous of her husband. In Yiang Yiang, Pineapple discovers a long-lost nephew; the young man is about to marry a native princess. When Pineapple kisses her he learns to his horror that by local law he is now the legal husband of the girl. Then, to complicate matters further, Mrs. Pineapple kisses the Emperor, and by this means becomes his wife. The law must now be revised, to the complete satisfaction of all concerned.

As part of the musical score imported from London, there were two charming cockney songs, both of them delightfully presented by Katie Barry, appearing in the role of Fi-Gi, a lovelorn English slavey: "I Want to Be a Loidy" and "Twiddley Bits." But Kerker's contribution was equally notable, highlighted by "À la Girl," and the title song. "Mister Dooley," by Jean Schwartz (a number inspired by Finley Peter Dunn's Irish sketches), was a significant interpolation, sung by Thomas Q. Seabrooke. This was Jean Schwartz's first hit song.

What with its long Broadway engagement (a run of 376 performances in those years represented a success of the first magnitude) and with its numerous road companies, *A Chinese Honeymoon* was responsible for establishing the Shubert brothers for the first time as a power in show business.

COCO (1969), *a musical play, with book and lyrics by Alan Jay Lerner. Music by André Previn. Presented by Frederick Brisson at the Mark Hellinger Theater on December 18. Directed by Michael Benthall. Dances by Michael Bennett. Cast included Katharine Hepburn, George Rose, Gale Dixon, and David Holliday.*

No musical during the 1969–70 season—possibly none since *My Fair Lady* —was preceded by so much word-of-mouth, printed publicity, and such advance fanfare as *Coco.*

Making a musical based on the life of the celebrated Parisian dress designer Gabrielle Chanel (known to all as "Coco," her grandfather's nickname for her when she was a child), was something that had been talked about for years. Frederick Brisson, the producer, was sold on the idea a dozen years before this project was finally realized. Lerner came into the picture in or about 1961, when he got from Mlle. Chanel exclusive rights to her life story after extended negotiations that also involved the House of Chanel. At first, *Coco* had been planned as a project for Lerner and Loewe. But that team split up, and for a brief period it seemed it might become a Rodgers and Lerner musical. That, too, came to naught. Finally, André Previn became Lerner's composer.

The feverish anticipation preceding the opening night of *Coco* sprang from facts other than that its central character was such a celebrated and picturesque character—a crusty, sharp-tongued, fiercely individual and inconoclastic lady—or that the score was the first musical-stage collaboration of Lerner and Previn. The excitement attending *Coco* sprang from the knowledge that (a) it was probably the most expensive musical ever to come to Broadway, costing close to a million dollars—all of it financed by Paramount Pictures; and (b) that the heroine was played by Katharine Hepburn in her first return to Broadway since 1952, and in the first musical of her entire career.

So great was the pre-performance interest in *Coco* that by the time opening night came, the advance sale had passed the two-million mark. The day the box office opened, the line stretched twice around the block, and the first-day sale of tickets established a record. In its first week of previews *Coco* grossed $128,196 (its break-even point was $80,000 a week).

Except for Miss Hepburn, the significance of whose electrifying presence there was no doubt in anybody's mind, *Coco* did not live up to expectations. It was, to be sure, a big show—glamorous, sumptuously mounted and costumed, a veritable feast for the eye (especially the feminine eye, with its virtually uninterrupted procession of gowns designed by Cecil Beaton, culminating in a splendiferous fashion show). But it was, for the most part, slow-paced, with very little plot or variety of material. How little genuine wit the text possessed can possibly be measured by the fact that the biggest laugh in the show came when Coco spluttered out a four-letter word synonymous for excrement. But for the fact that Miss Hepburn was on the stage practically the whole time (she was absent only twelve minutes), the production might have become a bore. Yet Hepburn managed to carry to the stage dynamism, excitement, verve, and a kind of awesome majesty even when the action lagged and the visual display began to pall. "Miss Hepburn is wonderful," wrote Richard Watts, Jr. "She never convinces you that she is Coco Chanel, and I don't think she tries very hard. The important matter is that she is one of the most fascinating and attractive women in the world and everything she does is fascinating. She can be humorous despite a paucity of amusing lines to speak, she is moving when the story calls for it, and while I suppose she hasn't much of a singing voice, she can put over a song." She had seven numbers—which she recited rather than sang, in the way that Rex Harrison had done in *My Fair Lady* most of the time.

*Coco* was, in short, Hepburn's show (in recognition of which she received probably the highest income ever earned by a performer on Broadway—something in the neighborhood of $15,000 a week, combining a guaranteed weekly salary of about $5,000 and a percentage of the gross). Nobody else in the cast was given too much to do. The dozen beautiful girls performing as mannequins were required to parade around in fashionable dress—they had nothing to say, nothing to sing, no routines to perform. Subsidiary roles were reduced to unimportance. Even the love interest that was grafted upon the Coco biography—involving Georges (David Holliday) and the young girl, Noelle who was Coco's protégée (Gale Dixon)—made small demands on the talents of the performers and was all too obviously injected to provide some romantic interest to a slim story.

When all is said and done, *Coco* remains a continuous parade of fashions, to which all other elements are totally subservient. The same thing was said years ago about Jerome Kern's *Roberta* (1933), whose central character was a fictitious Parisian designer and whose story is set in her dress salon. But *Roberta* had more to it than fashions. It had songs like "Smoke Gets in Your Eyes" and "Yesterdays." It had a bright new comic by the name of Bob Hope, as well as Fay Templeton and Tamara.

Discussing *Coco* from the point of view of a fashion critic, Marilyn Bender, writing in *The New York Times,* found much to deplore, even though the costuming had cost well over $160,000. "Broadway has seen more lavish and brilliant extravaganzas . . . [and] buyers and press periodically catch less dated and more professional presentations in showrooms on and off Seventh Avenue. . . . The fashions in *Coco* seldom convey the nonchalant high style and chic functionalism that are the essence of Chanel's genius. . . . Beaton's Chanels are as much Chanel's Chanel as a jar of gefilte fish on a supermarket shelf is to quenelles de brochet at Grand Vefour. There's a circus pink sequin Chanel worn by Noelle, the model, that must have been copied line for line on Division Street."

Actually, the ornateness and the opulence of Beaton's costumes were in direct contradiction to Mlle. Chanel's concept of high fashion. In pre-World War I days, she revolutionized dress styles by introducing simplicity, understated smartness, practicality—at a time when women were more partial to elaborately decorated gowns over stays and bustles. "Elegance in dress," she said, "means freedom to move. Clothes must be natural." And so she created the "Chanel Look": tailored suits, slacks, costume jewelry in place of gems, closely bobbed hair. While completely changing the way women should look and dress, she managed to find the time to involve herself in a long string of romances with the great and near-great; to move with the foremost cultural figures of her time, some of whom she supported, promoted, subsidized, or championed.

In his text, Lerner allowed us only casual glimpses into Coco's past, related by her father and various lovers projected on the screen—perhaps the most fascinating part of her life story. He preferred to concentrate on her later life—in 1954 when, at the age of seventy-one, she was trying to make a comeback. (The House of Chanel had shut down just before World War II, when Coco went into retirement.) Some suspense is built up as to whether this former great lady of design can make the grade again. She gives her first "show" and is turned down by the French press in no uncertain terms. Then buyers from the leading American department stores buy her designs, and Coco is again on the top. That's about all that happens (except for that minor love interest)—a story only intermittently brightened by Lerner's gift with a smart line, a well-turned aphorism (Coco was addicted to spouting aphorisms), and some shining lyrics.

Previn's music revealed a skilled, experienced hand. The best songs included the title number (assigned to Miss Hepburn); "Ohrbach's, Bloomingdale's, Best and Saks" sung by the American buyers responsible for Coco's comeback; "Fiasco" (the closest Previn came to a show-stopper), and "When Your Lover Says Goodbye." Georges had two strong numbers in "Let's Go Home" and "A Woman Is How She Loves."

Though this was Previn's debut in the Broadway theater, he was, of course, no novice. (In fact, this was not even the first time he worked with Lerner; he also wrote music to Lerner's lyrics for several new songs interpolated into the motion-picture adaptation of the Lerner and Loewe musical *Paint Your Wagon*, released in 1969.) Born in Berlin on April 6, 1929, Previn attended the Berlin Conservatory for two years before coming to the United States in 1938. In Los Angeles, his music study continued with Joseph Achron and Mario Castelnuovo-Tedesco. While still attending high school, Previn got his first movie assignment: to arrange the score for the musical *Holiday in Mexico*. Between 1948 and 1960 he was employed by MGM as composer-conductor, and after 1960 he was a freelance composer. He became one of Hollywood's most prolific and most gifted music directors, with a long list of motion-picture credits for which he did the background scoring or contributed original music and random songs (in the last of which his lyricist was his then wife, Dory Langdon Previn). He received Academy awards for his scoring of *Gigi, Porgy and Bess,* and *Irma la Douce,* and was nominated several other times. In addition he was given the Screen Composers Association Award for *Invitation to the Dance,* and the Berlin Film Festival Award for *Bad Day at Black Rock.*

Besides his prolific and highly fruitful contributions to the Hollywood screen, Previn distinguished himself as pianist (both in concert and in jazz performances), and as a symphony conductor of international renown (as musical director and principal conductor of the Houston Symphony and the London Symphony Orchestra—at one time holding both posts simultaneously, until he resigned from the Houston Symphony).

THE COCOANUTS (1925), *a musical comedy, with book by George S. Kaufman. Lyrics and music by Irving Berlin. Presented by Sam H. Harris at the Lyric Theater on December 8. Directed by Oscar Eagle. Dances by Sammy Lee. Cast included the Four Marx Brothers, with Frances Williams and Janet Velie (276 performances).*

Fresh from *I'll Say She Is,* in which they had made their transition from vaudeville to Broadway musical comedy in 1924, the four zany Marx Brothers went through the Kaufman text and the Berlin score with the devastating impact of a bulldozer, leaving behind them only ruin and havoc. The story, such as it finally developed, had Florida for a setting, during its early real-estate boom. Henry W. Schlemmer (Groucho Marx) is in charge of a hotel and real-estate development as phony as its proprietor. (The property is only a stone's throw from the station; throw enough stones and he'll build a station.) Between rapid-fire puns and wisecracks he manages to mishandle haughty Mrs. Potter (Margaret Dumont). Silent Sam (Harpo Marx) tears up the guests' mail, steals the silver, eats telephones as if they were delicacies, and runs pell-mell after every girl in sight; somewhat incongruously, he also manages to produce a sentimental tune or two on his harp. Willie the Wop (Chico Marx) contributes an Italian accent to his own brand of wisecracks and also does digital tricks on the piano keyboard. Jamison (Zeppo Marx) is the normal member of the family who speaks his lines straight, makes love to the heroine, and sings the principal love songs. By the time the brothers are finished with their shenanigans—some of them contrived spontaneously— any resemblance of dialogue and plot to the original concept of the authors is purely coincidental. The story goes that at one point during the run of the show George S. Kaufman turned with dazed amazement to a friend and said, "Say, I really think Groucho just spoke one of my lines as I wrote it."

Irving Berlin's main songs were "A Little Bungalow," "We Should Care," "Lucky Boy," and "Florida by the Sea," the ballads assigned to Frances Williams and/or Zeppo Marx. The Brox Sisters (then recently so successful in Irving Berlin's *The Music Box Revues*) presented an effective close-harmony number in "Monkey Doodle Doo."

In the motion-picture version (Paramount, 1929) Oscar Shaw and Mary Eaton were starred with the Marx Brothers. The stage score was eliminated to make room for one new Irving Berlin song, "When My Dreams Come True."

COHAN REVUES OF 1916 and 1918, THE. *See* HELLO, BROADWAY!

COMPANY (1970), *a musical comedy with book by George Furth. Lyrics and music by Stephen Sondheim. Presented by Harold Prince in association with Ruth Mitchell at the Alvin Theater on April 26. Directed by Harold Prince. Choreography by Michael Bennett. Cast included Dean Jones, Elaine Stritch, Charles Kimbrough, and Beth Howland.*

Despite the formidable competition offered by *Applause, Company* carried off the Drama Critics Award as the best musical of the 1969–70 season. There can be little question that this is a musical with much to recommend it. The text, a kind of sociological commentary on marriage, is consistently amusing, at times ironical, at times even penetrating—a theme not in the tradition of conventional musical comedy by any means. But in addition to the basic subject, this musical also boasted a sharp profile of the background for characters and plot: New York. To Clive Barnes, *Company* was a "very New York show [which] will be particularly popular with tourists. . . . who will get the kind of insight into New York's jungle." Henry Hewes of the *Saturday Review* was also impressed by the way New York was vividly portrayed. "From the moment Boris Aronson's inspired steel and Plexiglas gymnasium setting and the sophisticated babble of New York's swinging couples begins to bounce around the theater, we sense how completely book writer George Furth and lyricist-composer Stephen Sondheim have caught the tone of casual, impersonal Gotham. . . . So accurately does *Company* reflect New York life that the young in heart may want to rise up and scream out their anguish at the supercomfortable, superimpersonal environment our affluent fortyish swingers so unresistingly accept. . . . As a work of art it has remarkably distilled the essence of today's middle-generation New York life."

The central character is a New York bachelor, Robert or Bobby (Dean Jones) who, when the play opens, is celebrating his thirty-fifth birthday. The first musical number belongs to him: the title song wherein he comments on the fact that both love and life is company. Robert has well-meaning married friends who want him to find a wife—not that Robert lacks for female companionship or sex fulfillment. In "Sorry-Grateful" one of Robert's married friends sings of the pros and cons of married life, and in "Poor Bobby" some of them lament that their friend is fated to live alone—completely oblivious to the fact that Bobby has three succulent young ladies with whom he is involved, and with one of whom he engages in an athletic sexual engagement that is vividly and sensuously interpreted in a frenetic dance performed by Donna McKechnie. In time (a year or so separates the two acts), Robert visits five of his married friends and finds much in the activities and relationships of each husband and wife about which to raise a skeptical eyebrow. One couple indulges in pot; another is a sorry duo, what with the husband having to deny himself the pleasures of alcohol while his wife (incidentally an expert at karate) is suffering because she is on a diet; another couple seems to find excitement only in discotheques. Still another couple finds the girl desirous of reneging on marriage, afraid that she and her husband will lose their identities—only to change her mind once more, as the first act ends, and marry him. The efforts of these well-meaning friends to get Robert married notwithstanding, he remains a bachelor at the final curtain—but not without considerable doubts about the wisdom and practicability of failing to share his life and love with a wife instead of relying on the companionship of his girl friends and his married friends.

Top-flight performances are given not only by Dean Jones as our hero (probably the least colorful character in the play) but also by each of the married couples: by Elaine Stritch and Charles Braswell as Joanne and Larry; Barbara Barrie and Charles Kimbrough as Sarah and Harry; Merle Louise and John Cunningham as Susan and Peter; Teri Ralston and George Coe as Jenny and David; and Beth Howland and Steve Elmore as Amy and Paul. The three girls who provide Robert with female companionship are Marta (Pamela Myers), Kathy (Donna McKechnie), and April (Susan Browning).

"The singing and what little dance there is melt into one integrated continuity of action," comments Mr. Hewes. Especially the singing, since Stephen Sondheim has provided an exceptionally meritorious score for which he wrote both the lyrics and the music. The most dynamic single number is "Another Hundred People" in which Pamela Myers as Marta describes the plight of single girls in New York. She carries off this assignment with banners flying as does Susan Browning, in the role of an airline stewardess, performing a number completely different in mood and character: "Barcelona," in which (after a night of lovemaking with Robert) she tells him of her next destination. Elaine Stritch has highly effective satirical numbers in "The

Ladies Who Lunch" and "Drinking Song," each a denunciation of wives in particular, and women in general. Our bachelor has two numbers which serve him well: "Someone Is Waiting" and "Happily Ever After."

"To dress the songs and to drive them in hike-shoulder sidesteps across the stage," said Walter Kerr, "choreographer Michael Bennett has applied endlessly inventive high-pressure patterns; often he uses entire traditional devices, say straw hats and canes, in provocative new ways, letting the hats slash the air and the canes slap the floor to stress the harshness of what is being stomped out." This is found in the outstanding dance routine of the entire production, "Side by Side by Side."

As for the musical as a whole, to Walter Kerr "it gets right down to brass tacks and brass knuckles without a moment's hesitating, staring contemporary society in the eye before spitting in it." To Henry Hewes it "evokes plenty of humor to balance its underlying sadness. . . . Without the slightest hesitation one can appraise *Company* as the season's best and most refreshingly original musical."

> A CONNECTICUT YANKEE (1927), *a musical comedy, with book by Herbert Fields, based on Mark Twain's* A Connecticut Yankee At King Arthur's Court. *Lyrics by Lorenz Hart. Music by Richard Rodgers. Presented by Lew Fields and Lyle D. Andrews at the Vanderbilt Theater on November 3. Directed by Alexander Leftwich. Dances by Busby Berkeley. Cast included William Gaxton, Constance Carpenter, William Norris, and June Cochrane (418 performances).*

The idea of making Mark Twain's story into a musical comedy occurred to Rodgers, Hart, and Fields several years before they achieved success. In 1921, after seeing a silent-movie version of the story, they acquired an option, but at the time were unable to gain a hearing from producers, and the option was dropped. Six years later they were in a position to realize their ambition, and they sold Lew Fields on producing the play.

In his text Herbert Fields prefaced the adventures of the Yankee in sixth-century Camelot with a modern-day prologue. Alice Carter (Constance Carpenter) is so enraged at her fiancé, Martin (William Gaxton), who flirts with another girl at a party, that she hits him over the head with a champagne bottle. Martin loses consciousness and lapses into dreams. He finds himself a captive in King Arthur's court, doomed to be burned at the stake. He suddenly remembers that an eclipse of the sun is about due, and by ordering the sun to go black he so endears himself to King Arthur's men that they make him "Sir Boss." Now assuming the management of the kingdom (on a percentage basis), Martin proceeds to introduce the refinements of twentieth-century civilization into Camelot, including telephones, efficiency experts, radio, billboards, and so forth. King Arthur's men get into the spirit of things by beginning to talk in slang ("Methinks yon damsel is a lovely broad").

With gay dialogue and some of the wittiest, breeziest lyrics of Hart's career, *A Connecticut Yankee* proved "a novel amusement in the best of taste," as Brooks Atkinson said. But according to Alexander Woollcott, "it was Richard Rodgers, with his head full of tunes, who made the most valuable contribution . . . [with] so many fetching songs."

The most "fetching" song, however, was not written directly for this play. It was "My Heart Stood Still," which Alice and Martin introduced in the prologue and repeated in the first act. The idea for the lyric came to Rodgers and Hart in Paris when, in a near-accident in a taxi, one of their girl friends remarked, "my heart stood still." Lyric and melody were written soon afterward in London and introduced in the London revue produced by Charles Cochran in 1927, *One Dam Thing After Another* (sung by Jessie Matthews and Sonny Hale). At first it did not catch on. One evening, at the Café de Paris in London, the Prince of Wales asked the band to play the song for him. When the bandleader confessed he didn't know it, the Prince whistled the melody and the band picked it up. This incident was widely publicized and helped to make the song popular, indeed such a hit that Rodgers and Hart bought it back from Cochran for $5,000 and interpolated it into *A Connecticut Yankee*.

A second song favorite from the score, "Thou Swell," was almost removed from the production before it reached New York. The reaction to it in Philadelphia had been so frigid that the producers insisted that Rodgers take it out. Rodgers said he would agree, but only if the New York public proved equally apathetic. New York loved the song, and it stayed in.

Other outstanding numbers were "On a Desert Island with Thee" and "I Feel at Home with You," both perhaps more remarkable for their sprightly, sophisticated lyrics than for the melodies.

A revival of *A Connecticut Yankee,* on November 17, 1943, was the last production on which Rodgers and Hart were destined to collaborate. Hart died only a few days after the show opened in New York. Six songs were added to the revival. One of them (in a rousing rendition by Vivienne Segal as Morgan Le Fay) was "To Keep My Love Alive," in one of Larry Hart's happiest tongue-in-cheek styles—a running commentary by Morgan Le Fay on the ways and means of demolishing her various husbands. The revival of *A Connecticut Yankee* also brought the text up to date, giving it greater immediacy with a war-conscious audience of 1943; one of the scenes was laid in a munitions factory, and the two principals·wore the uniforms of the United States Navy in the prologue.

The most important songs from the stage score were used in the motion-picture adaptation made by Fox in 1931, starring Will Rogers and Maureen O'Sullivan.

CORDELIA'S ASPIRATIONS. *See* HARRIGAN AND HART EXTRAVAGANZAS.

THE CRADLE WILL ROCK (1938), *a musical drama, with book, lyrics, and music by Marc Blitzstein. Presented by Sam H. Grisman as a Mercury Theater Production at the Windsor Theater on January 3. Directed by Blitzstein. Cast included Howard da Silva, Will Geer, and Marc Blitzstein. Blitzstein played the musical score at the piano while providing a verbal commentary (108 performances).*

One day in December, 1935, Bertolt Brecht, the distinguished left-wing German dramatist, visited Blitzstein and his wife at their apartment in Greenwich Village. Blitzstein performed for Brecht a song he had recently completed, "The Nickel Under the Foot." The subjects treated in the song—poverty, exploitation, prostitution—impressed Brecht. But Brecht also felt that Blitzstein should extend the idea into a complete musical-stage work which would touch upon prostitution in all its forms—not only in sex but also in the press, clergy, business, and so forth. This gave Blitzstein the idea to write *The Cradle Will Rock,* which he worked on in 1936 as an escape from his grief at the death of his wife.

With *The Cradle Will Rock,* Blitzstein emerged as one of the most provocative and exciting new writers for the musical theater in several years (whether or not one agreed with his politics). Virgil Thomson called the play "the most appealing operatic socialism since *Louise,*" and George Jean Nathan described it as a "miscegenation of a Union Square soap box with a talented juke box."

Its premier was as dramatic a page as can be found in the history of the contemporary theater. As a production of the WPA Theater (John Houseman as producer and Orson Welles as director), *The Cradle Will Rock* reached dress rehearsal on June 15, 1937. Pressure was brought to bear on the Federal Theater by government officials and agencies objecting to its left-wing propaganda, and the decision was finally reached in Washington to cancel the production. Notification of this cancellation reached the members of the cast just before curtain time on opening night. The audience already was beginning to file into the Maxine Elliott Theater. While various members of the cast entertained the waiting audience, the neighborhood was scouted for some empty auditorium in which the play could be presented without the financial help of the government. The nearby Venice Theater was available, and performers and audience were shifted there. Since all the scenery and costumes belonged to the Federal Theater, and since there was no money to pay for an orchestra, *The Cradle Will Rock* was given in oratorio style: actors and the chorus stood on a bare stage in everyday dress. Blitzstein performed the score at the piano and between scenes succinctly explained to the audience what was going on.

The curious and unexpected result of this makeshift arrangement was that the play gained in dramatic power. Much that previously had seemed specious and contrived was eliminated by Blitzstein's rambling and charming commentary. Even the music itself profited from the piano rendition and within these informal proceedings. Brooks Atkinson called it "the most versatile triumph of the politically insurgent theater." To the amazement of all concerned, the play was a box-office attraction. Sam Grisman now financed a regular Broadway run. Still played without scenery, costumes, or orchestra —this time by design rather than necessity—*The Cradle Will Rock* moved to the Windsor Theater, where it stayed on for four months and proved a profitable venture.

The setting is a night court; the principal action gravitates around the efforts of steel workers to create a union in Steeltown. Methods fair and foul were adopted by the powerful men of the community to frustrate these efforts. Mr. Mister (Will Geer), symbol of capitalism, who has the entire town under his thumb, compels leading members of each group and organization to join a "Liberty Committee," whose sole aim is to destroy the incipient union. The power of united workers proves more potent than wealth and influence, and the union emerges triumphant.

*The Cradle Will Rock* is sometimes described as an opera—a glaring euphemism. Blitzstein's music—especially numbers like "Junior's Gonna Go to Honolulu," "Croon-Spoon," or "The Nickel Under the Foot"—are popular songs for the popular stage; there is no point in assigning them a status in which they are a decided misfit. Blitzstein's rich score includes ditties, patter songs, tap dances, torch songs, parodies, blues, ballads—most of them in designs and styles completely acceptable to musical comedy. The composer's skill in making his music an active part in projecting dramatic action, however, must be noted. The music becomes commentator and protagonist. Now it points up a personal trait in one of the characters; now it makes a satirical aside; now it emphasizes the conflict. Rhythm, harmony, counterpoint—all serve the play well. But this hardly makes a political musical play into an opera.

A decade following its premiere, *The Cradle Will Rock* was revived by the New York City Symphony under Leonard Bernstein, the first time with orchestra. Audience and critics once again proved enthusiastic. A second attempt was made to bring it in this form to Broadway, on December 27, 1947, with Howard da Silva, Will Geer, Muriel Smith, and Shirley Booth. But the intervening years had dulled its emotional and psychological impact. The play, with its stock characters, contrived situations, unrelieved blackness of villainy and unrelieved whiteness of those who sided with the angels, the unashamed and undisguised propaganda—all this completely lacked conviction, and it died an early death after only thirteen performances. Nevertheless, on February 11, 1960, *The Cradle Will Rock* was once again revived, this time in the kind of production Blitzstein had originally planned—with orchestra, scenery, and costumes. This was done by the New York City Opera. The text, as Howard Taubman noted in *The New York Times,* was "dated and corny," but he also felt that in spite of this it remained "a theater with excitement rare in an era when labor and capital argue their differences in comfortable hotels with high government officials to whisper impartial sweet talk in their ears." When *The Cradle Will Rock* was once again revived— this time in an Off Broadway production in 1964—Lewis Funke felt in *The New York Times* that Blitzstein's music was "stirring . . . laden with that undercurrent of bite, disillusion and pathos."

> CRISS CROSS (1926), *a musical comedy, with book and lyrics by Anne Caldwell and Otto Harbach. Music by Jerome Kern. Presented by Charles Dillingham at the Globe Theater on October 12. Directed by R. H. Burnside. Dances by David Bennett and Mary Read. Cast included Fred Stone, Allene Stone, Dorothy Stone, and Oscar "Rags" Ragland (206 performances).*

The promise shown by Dorothy Stone in her first major stage appearance three years earlier (in *Stepping Stones*) was so completely fulfilled in *Criss Cross* that a few critics ventured the opinion that she threw her eminent father into the shade. This was by no means an easy thing to do. In *Criss Cross*, Fred Stone was at his comic best—appearing with a trick camel, Susie, and singing the droll "I Love My Little Susie"; doing a burlesque of a harem dance; weeping profusely over the poignancy of his music as he plays a cello; serving as a member of a troupe of Algerian tumblers.

Dorothy Stone appeared as Dolly Day, an heiress compelled to attend a French academy. Plotters from Algeria hope to swindle her of her fortune by getting her married to a scoundrel. Christopher Cross, an aviator (Fred Stone) swoops down on a trapeze and saves her. Dolly can now marry the man she really loves, Captain Carleton (Roy Hoyer).

As Dolly, Dorothy participates in the two best songs in *Criss Cross:* "You Will, Won't You?" and "In Araby with You," the latter with lyrics by Harbach and Oscar Hammerstein II.

> DAMES AT SEA (1968), *a "new-30's musical," with book and lyrics by George Haimson and Robin Miller. Music by Jim Wise. Presented by Jordan Hott and Jack Millstein at the Bouwerie Lane Theater on December 20. Directed and with dances by Neal Kenyon. Cast included Tamara Long, David Christmas, and Bernadette Peters.*

*Dames at Sea* was a "sleeper" musical comedy of 1968. Nothing was known about it, and little was expected, when it slipped so unobtrusively into the Bouwerie Lane Theater in the Bowery (seating capacity 188). Its title was hardly something to attract curiosity. Its theme—a lampoon on the movies of the 1930's—did not promise much, particularly when it was being presented by a cast comprising only six members (all unknowns), supplemented by a three-piece orchestra (two pianos and a percussionist). Nor did its past history offer encouraging hopes for its potential audience appeal. It started out seven years earlier as a sketch which its authors were unable to sell and had to shelve for a few years until the owner of an Off Broadway coffee house decided to use it in his place. There the patrons liked it well enough to keep the sketch running thirteen weeks. There was some talk of bringing the sketch to an Off Broadway theater, but all this came to naught. Meanwhile, the authors kept expanding the show to full-length proportions. In the summer of 1967, the new musical played for three weeks in summer stock in Middletown, Virginia. At last, a backer was found ready to gamble on its chances, Off Broadway, on a minimal budget, and with a negligible investment. On opening night and for a few nights thereafter the critics took the trip downtown reluctantly; but they came out cheering. *"Dames at Sea* is a real winner, a little gem of a musical," reported Clive Barnes. In the New York *Post,* Jerry Tallmer called it "indisputably the best musical of the year, or maybe several years." "One of the happiest entertainments in years," reported Norman Nadel. The show became a hit; the producers found the courage to raise the top price for seats to ten dollars.

No holds were barred in this spoof of the big movie musicals of the early 1930's that used to star Dick Powell and Ruby Keeler and boasted those lavish dance routines conceived by Busby Berkeley. (Our heroine is, naturally enough, named Ruby, and our hero Dick.) The old familiar patterns were followed, with mockery and malice of course: the familiar plot where a chorus girl becomes a star at the zero hour by substituting for an ailing performer, in the process getting the man she has set her heart on; those elaborate dance spectacles with the stage overcrowded with chorines doing routines while the camera lens was focused on them from every possible angle; those cliché-ridden songs, as obvious in words and titles as in melodies; and the dialogue that carried over the same bromides from one production to the next.

Much of this could inspire satire and parody, and *Dames at Sea* took full advantage of this choice material. The plot reduced the stories of the 1930 movies to the ridiculous. Ruby (Bernadette Peters)—a wide-eyed innocent from the sticks—has come from Centerville, Utah, to New York, arriving early in the morning. Her sole possession is a pair of tap shoes; her only ambition is to make good on the stage. She is hardly off the bus when she meets Dick, a sailor (David Christmas), whose hobby is writing songs. Typical of those 1930 movies, they knew at once they were meant for each other and expressed their obvious sentiments in a typical song, "It's You." Dick learns that Ruby wants a job in a Broadway musical. She proceeds to show him what she is capable of by doing a complicated tap routine. The musical in which she tries to find a job that same day has for its star a hard-hearted, ruthless, go-getter, Mona Kent (Tamara Long). It occurs to Mona that since this musical has a nautical subject, it would be a good idea to stage it on opening night aboard ship. Mona knows the captain of a battleship, and whatever Mona wants, Mona gets, even if she has to entice the captain with a beguine number, "The Beguine," in which the captain joins and which brought down the house. She gets the battleship for her show. She also tries to steal Dick from Ruby, and even to rob him of one of the songs he has written. But for all of Mona's manipulations, she comes out the loser. She gets seasick, cannot appear in the show, and Ruby is called upon to take her place. Can she do it? "I'll try," she replies bravely. She goes on the stage and naturally brings the house down. What is more, she gets Dick—in a grand wedding finale.

Detail is compounded upon detail to remind us of what the movies of those 1930's were like: those banal lyrics (one so much like another that, in one of the scenes, when Dick sings for Mona the line of one of his songs, she continues with all the rest of the lines without looking at the manusscript); those tricks of staging that utilize twirling transparent umbrellas, opening and shutting, while Ruby sings "Raining in My Heart" (a reminder of "Singin' in the Rain" of the 1930's); those lines that had become so integral to backstage stories that they sprang up on cue ("your name is gonna go up in lights"; "this cold canyon of steel and concrete can't scare me"; "you'll go on that stage a chorus girl but you'll come back a star"); those production gimmicks, as in "The Echo Waltz" where two wall panels turn around to become mirrors, thus multiplying the number of dancers; those tap dances up and down stairways, as in "Star Tar"; those corny songs that saw the silver lining behind the clouds—"Good Times Are Here to Stay." Parody was the meat of the musical score. "Choo Choo Honeymoon" reminded us of "Shuffle Off to Buffalo"; "There's Something About You" paid more than a passing gesture to Cole Porter's "You're the Top"; "That Mister Man of Mine" was a torch song parodying Jerome Kern's "Bill." Other songs borrowed recognized phrases from standards such as Gershwin's "The Man I Love" and Porter's "Begin the Beguine." There is also a brief quotation from "You Are My Lucky Star"—the hit song from one of the screen musicals of the 1930's—while the lyrics in the number "Let's Have a Simple Wedding," which closes the production, unhesitatingly quote a famous Ira Gershwin phrase, "Who could ask for anything more?"

In short, those with nostalgic memories of the *Gold Diggers of Broadway* (and those *Gold Digger* successors in 1933, 1935, and 1937), or the *Hollywood Revue* could find in *Dames at Sea* much to remember, something to scoff at, and—strange as it may sound—even one or two things to suggest why those movies were so popular. For as Richard Watts, Jr., pointed out in his review: "The finest thing about it [*Dames at Sea*] is that it never patronizes or shows contempt for the popular entertainment of the prewar period. It realizes that those musical comedy movies were pretty simple-minded and fairly silly, but it recognizes that they were likewise good, lively fun with fine tunes and attractive performers, and it has due respect for their virtues. Indeed, *Dames at Sea* hews so close to the line of the original product that it is . . . an affectionate pastiche. . . . I wonder how many films I reviewed in which the ingenue said, 'I've been such a fool!' It made for nostalgia."

DAMN YANKEES (1955), *a musical comedy, with book by Douglas Wallop and George Abbott, based on Wallop's novel* The Year the Yankees Lost the Pennant. *Lyrics and music by Richard Adler and Jerry Ross. Presented by Frederick Brisson, Robert E. Griffith, and Harold Prince at the 46th Street Theater on May 5. Directed by George Abbott. Dances by Bob Fosse. The cast included Stephen Douglass, Gwen Verdon, and Ray Walston (1,019 performances).*

This is the first successful musical comedy about baseball. The Faust theme is combined with baseball. Joe Boyd is a middle-aged baseball fan who suffers because his favorite team, the Washington Senators, never seem able to make any progress in the pennant race. We first find him in front of his television set watching his team, and distraught at the fact that they are losing the game. Suddenly the devil—personified by Applegate (Ray Walston)—visits

Joe to make a deal with him: to trade Joe's soul for the Washington Senators winning not only the pennant but also the World Series. Joe is all too willing to accept the bargain. All at once Joe becomes young again (Stephen Douglass); what is more, he is endowed with supernatural abilities at playing baseball. As Joe Hardy he tries out for and becomes a member of the Washington Senators team. Its manager, Van Buren, tries his best to raise the morale of his disgruntled team, who are in the doldrums because of their continual defeats; they can hardly be expected to realize that a mere rookie, Joe Hardy, will change their dismal situation dramatically.

But Joe Hardy is no ordinary player. Through his talent, defeats are transformed into victories. But this does not make Joe happy, since he is homesick for his wife, Meg, whom he had to abandon so suddenly and so mysteriously. Just to be near her, he rents a room in her house—unrecognized by his wife because he is young. The temptation to tell her who he is and why he had deserted her so precipitously becomes overpowering. The devil, Mr. Applegate, realizes that he must act quickly and decisively if he is not to lose Joe and eventually Joe's soul. To help woo Joe from his wife, Applegate calls on a beautiful witch, Lola (Gwen Verdon). She looks upon this luring business as just another job, insisting she always gets what she wants, and then proceeding to try to seduce him by performing a seductive tango. In spite of Lola's sex appeal, in spite of the fact that because of him the Senators have captured the pennant, Joe still wants to go back home to his wife. It suddenly occurs to him that if he refuses to play with the team it cannot possibly win the pennant; and if the Senators do not win the pennant, his bargain with the devil is once and for all negated. Thus he is able to save his soul, forget all about Lola, revert to his former status as a middle-aged baseball fan rooting for a losing team, and return to his wife.

Abbott's direction was one element that helped make *Damn Yankees* a winner. The raciness and excitement he always brought to a production provided this musical with a breathless pace that proceeded unhaltingly from the first to final curtain. As Maurice Zolotow wrote in *Theatre Arts:* "When Abbott is at his best—and he is at his best in *Damn Yankees* . . . there is a feeling of perpetual motion created by the adroit multiplication of hundreds of large and small movements. Everything is fluid. Everything moves. When one character has to divulge a bit of information to another, they do it either strolling, or jumping, or running. A show like *Damn Yankees* has about it the fascination of a fine Byzantine mosaic. At a distance it is a gaudy pageant. Regarded closely, it becomes an artfully assembled design in which many small pieces have been fitted together by a master craftsman."

As the siren Lola, Gwen Verdon (fresh from her recent recognition in

*Can-Can* and now appearing in her first starring role) stole the limelight with a seductive tango, "Whatever Lola Wants," suggesting to Joe that once she has set her heart on something she is sure to get it. She was no less intriguing in the comic mambo, "Who's Got the Pain?", with which she tries out her seductive wiles on Joe. "Whatever Lola Wants" became a hit song, and so did "You've Got to Have Heart," the number in which the manager of the Senators, played by Russ Brown, tries to instill courage into his effete team. The play opens with an amusing chorus, "Six Months Out of Every Year," the lament of wives on the way in which baseball disrupts a normal domestic existence. A soft-shoe routine, reminiscent of vaudeville ("Those Were the Good Old Days"), a hoedown ("Shoeless Joe from Hannibal, Mo."), and the plaintive "Two Lost Souls " (the two lost souls being Lola and Joe Hardy) were three more infectious additions to a superior score.

*Damn Yankees*—which received the Antoinette Perry Award as the season's best musical—was the second stage collaboration of the songwriting team of Adler and Ross, which had previously been responsible for another musical-comedy stage triumph, *Pajama Game.* It was also their last opus; Jerry Ross died in 1955 of a lung ailment.

Even in Hollywood, where casting rarely follows the laws of logic, *Damn Yankees* without Gwen Verdon was unthinkable. And so, in the screen version, produced by Warner Brothers in 1958, Gwen Verdon once again was Lola, while Tab Hunter assumed the role of Joe.

THE DAY BEFORE SPRING (1945), *a musical comedy, with book and lyrics by Alan Jay Lerner. Music by Frederick Loewe. Presented by John C. Wilson at the National Theater on November 22. Directed by John C. Wilson and Edward Padula. Dances by Antony Tudor. Cast included Irene Manning, Bill Johnson, and John Archer (165 performances).*

The first time Lerner and Loewe were heard on Broadway was in a comedy called *What's Up,* produced on November 11, 1943. Though it starred Jimmy Savo, one of the stage's truly great comic performers, *What's Up* was a disaster from whatever perspective one wished to view it: whether as a financial, commercial, or humorous undertaking. Just about two years later, Lerner and Loewe returned to Broadway, apparently having learned much about the stage in the interim. *The Day Before Spring* was not good box office by any means (the only real money Lerner and Loewe made from it was by selling the screen rights to MGM, who had financed the stage production, for $200,000, a production that apparently was never realized). But *The Day Before Spring* was a *succès d'estime.* Walter Winchell described it as "a delight," and Burton Rascoe called it a "brilliant new addition to American operettas." This was a musical comedy—*not* an operetta as Mr. Rascoe referred to it—sufficiently imaginative in text and arresting in music to point up what *What's Up* had completely failed to do: that in Lerner and Loewe the theater had discovered a pair of writers worth watching. Those who did watch were not disappointed, for *Brigadoon,* the very next Lerner and Loewe production, followed *The Day Before Spring* in a year and a half.

A few traits distinguishing *Brigadoon* were already discernible in *The Day Before Spring*: notably the deft way in which the script hovered between reality and fantasy; the capacity of the composer to produce delightful melodies that were basic to the story line but also to introduce musical interludes freed of song lyrics that enhanced the mood and atmosphere; the graceful hand of Lerner in writing a witty lyric or indulging in a dramatically effective monologue.

The play opens in the New York apartment of Katherine Townsend (Irene Manning). She is reading a novel by Alex Maitland (Bill Johnson), an author whom she had known and loved when they both had attended Harrison University. In fact, in their senior year, they planned to elope. En route their car broke down, and they were helped out by a fellow student, Peter Townsend (John Archer). The romance of Katherine and Alex cooled off after that, while that of Katherine and Peter developed into marriage.

Maitland's novel, which Katherine is reading, is actually the story of her romance with Alex—but developing the theme of what would have happened had the car *not* broken down. Sadly, Katherine puts down the book and sings the title song. The novel has brought her face to face with the fact that her life with her husband, Peter, has become humdrum. This more than anything else finally convinces her to do something she had long refused: to go with her husband to Harrison University to celebrate the tenth reunion of their class.

At Harrison University, Maitland, the novelist—who has also come for the reunion—is besieged by young admirers seeking his autograph. He gives them a bit of his optimistic homespun philosophy of life in one of the score's best numbers, "God's Green World." It is not long before Alex is being pursued by the pretty young daughter of the dean—a girl called Christopher Randolph (Patricia Marshall), who in turn is loved by Gerald (Tom Helmore). Another fine Lerner-Loewe song, "My Love Is a Married Man," reflects Christopher's feelings about this situation.

When the Townsends arrive, Katherine is delighted to discover that Alex is present. In fact they are not long together before their old romance flares up again. They go off to the woods for a stroll the way they used to do as students. Suddenly, impetuously, Alex prevails on Katherine to escape with him in his car and find love in some romantic inn. Katherine consents only after, upon return to the university, she finds her husband aloof and cold to her—Peter having meanwhile made a date with Christopher to take her off for a drive and a drink.

Once again, the car that Katherine and Alex use breaks down and frustrates their plans. Peter, in Christopher's car, comes to their help again. He induces Katherine to return to him and to forget about her prospective escapade, which he is willing to forgive and forget. He also convinces Alex that the novelist has been living in a dream world that has no place in everyday reality. Katherine returns to Peter. Alex decides to go off to China to write a new novel. And Gerald tries harder than ever to win Christopher's love.

DEAREST ENEMY (1925), *a musical comedy, with book by Herbert Fields. Lyrics by Lorenz Hart. Music by Richard Rodgers. Presented by George Ford at the Knickerbocker Theater on September 18. Directed by John Murray Anderson. Dances by Carl Hemmer. Cast included Helen Ford, Charles Purcell, and Flavia Arcaro (286 performances).*

Before Rodgers and Hart had had their first taste of success with *The Garrick Gaieties,* they were strolling on Madison Avenue, New York, with Herbert Fields, discussing possible subjects for musical comedies. They lingered momentarily in front of a building on 37th Street that bore the following plaque:

> *Howe, with Clinton, Tryon, and a few others, went to the house of Robert Murray, on Murray Hill, for refreshment and rest. With pleasant conversations and a profusion of cake and wine, the good Whig lady detained the gallant Britons almost two hours. Quite long enough for the bulk of Putnam's division of four thousand men to leave the city and escape to the heights of Harlem by Bloomingdale Road, with the loss of only a few soldiers.*

Hart recognized in this episode from American history the makings of a good musical-comedy plot, and won over his collaborators. Herbert Fields expanded the Murray Hill incident into a full-blown plot. On instructions from George Washington, Mrs. Robert Murray (Flavia Arcaro) detains British officers "by every means at your discretion," as Washington had suggested, long enough to permit the Continental Army to make a strategic withdrawal. A secondary plot involved a romance between the Irish niece of Mrs. Murray, Betsy Burke (Helen Ford), and the redcoat Captain Sir John Copeland (Charles Purcell).

The story permitted Fields to engage in some discreet pornography, and much of the humor of the play stemmed from such risqué remarks and situations. Betsy Burke makes her first-act entrance protecting her nudity with a barrel: While swimming in Kipp's Bay a dog had stolen her clothing. *Double entendres* spiced the dialogue which followed between herself and Captain Henry Tryon (John Seymour). "At first glance," says John, "I thought you were a boy." Betsy replies demurely: "Well, you should have taken a second look." Later on in the play, the Continental ladies learn that British troops are on their way. "Hooray, we are gonna be compromised," they sing, and add philosophically, "war is war."

Notwithstanding this gay and at times impudent text, *Dearest Enemy* found few takers among the producers. Not even Herbert's father, Lew, was sympathetic to it, insisting, "the public just won't buy it, for who ever heard of a musical comedy based on American history?" Eventually, an ally was found in the musical-comedy star Helen Ford, who wanted to play Betsy. Helen Ford interested her husband, George, and after that John Murray Anderson. Then it was produced—but only after the first *Garrick Gaieties* had made Rodgers and Hart songwriters of consequence.

The handsome production provided the play with some of its attraction. Reginald Marsh designed a striking intermission curtain, a map of old New York. For the play itself such attractive sets and costumes had been designed that, as Alexander Woollcott reported, the play presented an "endlessly lovely picture," which alone was "worth the price of admission."

Rodgers' score was such an ambitious collation of songs, duets, trios, choral numbers (also a delightful gavotte evoking the eighteenth century) that Percy Hammond described the play as a "baby grand opera." The hit song was "Here in My Arms," presented just before the first-act finale by Betsy Burke and Sir John. Another song appealed for its sly wit and sex insinuation, "Old Enough to Love"; and to "Cheerio," Sir John and his officers brought a winning martial spirit.

THE DESERT SONG (1926), *an operetta, with book by Otto Harbach, Oscar Hammerstein II, and Frank Mandel. Lyrics by Harbach and Hammerstein. Music by Sigmund Romberg. Presented by Schwab and Mandel at the Casino Theater on November 30. Directed by Arthur Hurley. Dances by Bobby Connolly. Cast included Vivienne Segal, Robert Halliday, Eddie Buzzell, and William O'Neal (465 performances).*

During the 1925–26 revolt of the Riffs, under the leadership of Abdel Drim, against the French protectorate in Morocco, the news was blazed across the front pages of American newspapers. This timely item provided Harbach,

Hammerstein, and Mandel with ideal material for an operetta, since it was a subject readily lending itself to pageantry, an exotic background, colorful personalities (including alluring harem girls and dashing French officers).

The Riffs—Moroccan fighters against the French protectorate rule—are in their secret stronghold with their masked chief, the Red Shadow. They express their defiance of the French Legionnaires in the rousing "The Riff Song." In town, the wives of the Legionnaires are dissatisfied with their lives, what with their men always away in battle. Margot (Vivienne Segal) tries to cheer them up by having them do an imitation of martial routines in the light and gay "French Military Marching Song." But she, too, suffers keenly from the continual absence of Pierre Birabeau (Robert Halliday), the son of the governor, the man with whom she is in love. Pierre, in reality, is the Red Shadow, who has assumed that identity (together with leadership) to right some of the wrongs perpetrated against the Riffs. As the Red Shadow he returns to Margot and tries to lure her into the desert by describing the idyllic life they can have together—in the most famous love ballad in the operetta, the title song (sometimes also known as "Blue Heaven"). In spite of herself, Margot is attracted to this dashing Riff leader who sweeps her in his arms and abducts her to the palace of Ali ben Ali. There he tries to win her love, but Margot insists that her heart belongs to another man. The Red Shadow leaves in an air of mock disappointment, then returns as Pierre, maintaining that he, too, is a prisoner of the Riffs. Coming face to face with Pierre convinces Margot that she is really in love with the Red Shadow— which she first discloses when she sees and lifts up his saber and sings "The Saber Song." When Pierre reassumes the identity of the Red Shadow, he and Margot do not hesitate to reveal to each other that they are in love. With the arrival of the French troops, headed by the governor, the latter challenges the Red Shadow to a life-and-death battle—a challenge which the Red Shadow turns down. At this seeming display of weakness, the Riffs are horrified. They deprive him of leadership and send him off into exile. The French officers follow him into the desert. Finding Pierre, and not the Red Shadow, they are convinced that the governor's son has killed his enemy. Margot is heartbroken at the news that the Red Shadow has been murdered by Pierre, and turns away from her former lover with revulsion. But as her back is turned he puts on the costume of the Red Shadow, thus reveals to all the truth about his double life. Margot is overjoyed—for she is now in the enviable position of finding that her lover and his most serious rival are really one and the same man.

Besides songs already mentioned in the above summation, the Romberg score contains three deeply moving ballads: "One Alone," the Red Shadow's love song for the woman he loves; "Farewell," also sung by the Red Shadow; and Margot's tender "Romance" as she dreams about her absent lover, Pierre, early in the play.

*The Desert Song* was made into a movie on three different occasions, all produced by Warner Brothers. The first, in 1929, starred John Boles and Carlotta King and used the basic stage score. In 1943, Dennis Morgan, Irene Manning, and Bruce Cabot were starred, with only five of the stage numbers being used (together with interpolations of several new numbers). The last adaptation—made in 1953—had Kathryn Grayson and Gordon MacRae in the leading roles and used most of the original stage music.

DESTRY RIDES AGAIN (1959), *a musical comedy, with book by Leonard Gersche, based on a story by Max Brand. Lyrics and music by Harold Rome. Presented by David Merrick in association with Max Brown at the Imperial Theater on April 23. Directed and with dances by Michael Kidd. Cast included Andy Griffith and Dolores Gray (473 performances).*

*Destry Rides Again* is a typical Western made into a musical—the kind of Western the movies and television have so long exploited. In fact, the source from which this musical comes—the novel by Max Brand—was made into a movie several times. (It was in one of these adaptations that Marlene Dietrich sang one of her great successes, "See What the Boys in the Back Room Will Have").

The action in the musical takes place in the cattletown of Bottleneck at the turn of the century. Its citizens are gathered in the Last Chance Saloon, aware that their town needs a wholesale cleaning: corruption and graft are running riot while the gambler Kent (Scott Brady) and his gang hold the town and its people in his grip. One of Kent's maneuvers is to usurp the land of Claggart, a rancher. When the sheriff tries to interfere in this shady deal, Kent has one of his gang kill him. Wash (Jack Prince) is called up to take over the sheriff's office. Caught in the spirit of reform, he calls for Thomas Jefferson Destry, Jr.—son of a famous lawman and gunfighter—to come to town and set things right. The town, of course, expects Destry to be a strong-armed man, fast with a gun. But the townspeople are instantly disenchanted when Destry arrives. He is a mild, meek-mannered, shy young man who hates to use a gun. Kent calls upon his girl friend, Frenchy (Dolores Gray)—one of the leading entertainers at the saloon—to win Destry over with her sex appeal and thus remove him as a potential block to Kent's ambition and greed. She tries, with a beguiling song, "I Know Your Kind," but though Destry temporarily weakens, he resists, a fact that inspires Frenchy's contempt. Destry knows he must get the killer of the sheriff if there is to be any hope for Bottleneck—but he must get him in a lawful, orderly way. He must find where Kent has the body hidden. Destry finds it, thereby providing the evidence he needs to pinpoint the killer—Gyp Watson—and to get him jailed. Kent, however, has no intention of allowing Destry to try Gyp; he plans to kill Destry first. Now becoming increasingly interested in Destry, Frenchy suggests he try Gyp in the Last Chance Saloon, with Gyp's own cronies as judge and jury. But Destry suspects he is being double-crossed. At long last, he slings a pair of guns on his hips and rides off. Upon returning, he brings with him a federal judge to try Gyp Watson lawfully and thus ensure that justice is done. Kent now plans a jailbreak for his crony. Wash the sheriff, trying to stop this, is killed. Destry now realizes that violence must be met with violence. In the ensuing gun battle—in which the badmen are wiped out in a crossfire—Destry's life is saved by Frenchy. They are ready to confess that they love each other. Guided by Destry's example, the citizens of Bottleneck drop their gunbelts. Law and order have finally come to Bottleneck.

Two scenes staged and choreographed by Michael Kidd have special distinction. One is a dance number performed by three of the badmen with bullwhips lashing as they dance; another is set in the saloon, where the revelers give way to their high spirits ("Every Once in a While"). Rome's mocking dirge that opens the second act, "Are You Ready, Gyp Watson?"—sung by the citizens of Bottleneck outside the prison in which Gyp is incarcerated, about to be hanged for murder—and a hymn to prostitution, "Paradise Alley," are the spices to a score that includes more formal numbers. The best of these profit from the electrifying rendition given them by Frenchy; besides "I Know Your Kind," which has already been mentioned, there is "Fair Warning," "I Say Hello," and "Anyone Would Love You," the last a duet with Destry in which for the first time each reveals a growing interest in the other. Destry has an effective number of his own, "Once Knew a Fella," the confession of what it is like for a lonely man to experience love.

DO I HEAR A WALTZ? (1965), *a musical comedy, with book by Arthur Laurents, based on his play* The Time of the Cuckoo. *Lyrics by Stephen Sondheim. Music by Richard Rodgers. Presented by Richard Rodgers at the 46th Street Theater on March 18. Directed by John Dexter. Dances by Herbert Ross. Cast included Elizabeth Allen, Sergio Franchi, and Carol Bruce (220 performances).*

This was the second and the less successful of the Richard Rodgers musicals of his post-Hammerstein era. Not that there is any lack of the kind of charm, entertainment, and skillful production which can almost always be expected of any musical in which Richard Rodgers is involved. It boasted talented performers in the three principals; a handsome representation of Venice and one of its pensions, the retreat of several American tourists; and several delectable songs. But the production as a whole was pitched *sotto voce,* the pace lagged, and very little happens in the text to sustain interest.

Leona Smith (Elizabeth Allen), on her first visit to Venice, is brought by a ten-year-old guide, Mauro, to a pension run by Signora Fioria (Carol Bruce), which is overrun with Americans. On a shopping expedition, Leona meets Renato di Rossi (Sergio Franchi), a handsome shop owner with typically suave and winning ways. In Leona, Renato sees the possibility of an intriguing affair, while in Renato, Leona finds a man she feels she could love. But Leona is of the belief that when she meets the right man she will hear waltz music, and she did not hear any in his presence. They nevertheless arrange a meeting, to which Renato arrives bearing the gift of a garnet necklace. Suddenly Leona hears a waltz: Renato is her man. But the gift of the necklace has not been paid for, and Leona must make good with the payment; to make matters still worse in her eyes, she sees someone bringing Rossi a commission for having made the sale. Leona's disenchantment becomes complete on discovering he is married—and not all of Renato's Italian charm can dispel her anger.

The title song—which carries the slow plot to its climax—was the big Richard Rodgers number of the show. But some of the humorous songs were equally appealing, the best of them profiting from some very deft lyric writing by Stephen Sondheim. One of the most amusing of those was "What Do We Do? We Fly!", an appraisal of the horrors of plane travel. Another was "This Week Americans," in which Signora Fioria describes the follies and foibles of her guests. A third, "Bargaining," tells of the experiences of a shopkeeper with his client, in a one-man duet for Renato. "Moon in My Window," where Signora Fioria regards romance with a practical eye, and Renato's plea to Leona to enjoy life and love to the full while she can in "Take the Moment" are additional song assets.

"Much talent and good intention have arrived at only a modest result and at a disappointingly low amount of emotion-involving interchange in such a highly romantic city," was Henry Hewes reaction in the *Saturday Review.* The public apparently agreed, for *Do I Hear a Waltz?*—like Leona's love affair—promised much but, in the end, reneged on those promises. *Do I Hear a Waltz?* had the shortest Broadway run of any Richard Rodgers show in a quarter of a century.

DO, RE, MI (1960), *a musical comedy, with book by Garson Kanin, based on his short story of the same name. Lyrics by Betty Comden and Adolph*

*Green. Music by Jule Styne. Presented by David Merrick in association with Jones Harris at the St. James Theater on December 26. Directed by Garson Kanin. Dances by Marc Breaux and Deedee Wood. Cast included Phil Silvers and Nancy Walker (400 performances).*

The jukebox business and the attempts of racketeers to take it over—with hilarious insights into the recording business in general—is the subject of a musical that is developed with broad humor and which continually appears to be bursting at the seams with energy and dynamism. The principal character is Hubie Cram (Phil Silvers)—"a small-timer always aiming big and ending up with little," as Robert Coleman described him so well. "He is the well-meaning shnook whose grandiose ideas crash around his ears." We encounter him first getting the kind of rebuff to which he should long ago have become accustomed. Having come to a nightclub in order to feel like a big shot, he suffers the humiliation of getting the worst table in the place—a spot that becomes increasingly less desirable as the arrival of newcomers necessitates the placing of more and more tables between him and the performers. Thus the musical opens on a note of satire—laughing up its sleeve at nightclubs, and nightclub habitués willing to pay such fancy prices to get pushed around. This humiliation at the nightclub is the last straw for Hubie. He is determined more than ever to become a big man. The field he chooses to conquer is the jukebox world. He induces three ex-mobsters to emerge from retirement and join him in the business. In a highly amusing song-and-dance sequence, "It's Legitimate"—Phil Silvers' big number in the show—Hubie gives voice to his joy in at last finding an operation that remains in the law and yet brings him success. But he soon discovers that to control the jukebox industry he must find new talent, make records, plug tunes to success. Before long he also finds himself drawn by his mobster associates deep into graft and corruption. In the process, he has ample opportunity to uncover many different facets of comedy. Now he is the exuberant master of ceremonies who holds a hilarious audition for new talent; now he teaches musicians how to perform on their instruments, though he can hardly draw a belch from a trombone or a squeak from a clarinet ("You hang around, you learn," he informs the musicians). Through it all, his wife, Kay (Nancy Walker), is the devoted mate who tries to maintain patience, equilibrium, and loyalty despite the shenanigans in which her husband gets involved. The way she shuffles across the stage and the weariness of her voice suggest that she has come to terms with herself and her husband. But not entirely—as she admits in a zestful comic number called "Adventure," in which she looks back nostalgically to her one-time middle-class ways. Then she realizes that, after all, her husband is involved in a racket. At the swank Café Imperial she tells him so. When Hubie reminds her that the magnificent gown she is wearing has come from this racket, she proceeds to take it off and return it to him. But Hubie is a man destined to wallow in mediocrity and remain a nonentity. His victory in business is short-lived.

Tilda Mullen (Nancy Dussault), a waitress whom Hubie discovers and makes into a singing star, delivers a folk-song-like lament in "Cry Like the Wind" and a whimsical item, "What's New at the Zoo?" with equal effect. The man she loves, John Henry Wheeler (John Reardon) vigorously puts over a Pollyana-type of homespun philosophy in a song that became a hit, "Make Someone Happy"; also two appealing ballads, "Asking for You" and "I Know About Love." "Fireworks," which starts out as a duet for Tilda and John, ends up as an impressive production number. And in "The Late Late Show" Hubie mimics the absurdities of the gangland world and activities as reproduced on the television screen.

> DU BARRY WAS A LADY (1939), *a musical comedy, with book by Buddy de Sylva and Herbert Fields. Lyrics and music by Cole Porter. Presented by De Sylva at the 46th Street Theater on December 6. Directed by Edgar MacGregor. Dances by Robert Alton. Cast included Ethel Merman, Bert Lahr, Ronald Graham, Betty Grable, and Benny Baker (408 performances).*

In the strange roundabout ways in which some musicals come into being, *Du Barry Was a Lady* started out as a Herbert Fields scenario written for and rejected by Paramount. It seemed to Louis Shurr, the agent, that it was a good stage property for Bert Lahr, then deserting Hollywood. Buddy de Sylva was available to help Herbert Fields rewrite the scenario to suit Bert Lahr's unique personality, comic delivery, guttural sounds, and burlesque-type humor. When they discussed candidates for a possible leading lady, Shurr suggested Ethel Merman, adding that if Miss Merman would be available, then Cole Porter could be counted upon to write the songs. Everything worked out as planned.

The text takes a long step back into history—to the Petit Trianon in France and the epoch of Louis XV; and it carries back in time a hapless nightclub washroom attendant, Louis Blore (Bert Lahr). Louis works for the Club Petite, where he is in love with its vital entertainer May Daley (Ethel Merman). When he wins 75,000 dollars in the sweepstakes, Louis Blore buys the club, hoping thereby to win May's heart. (One of the funniest episodes in the play comes at this point, with Louis instructing his successor in the subtleties, refinements, and art of handling a washroom.) But he has a formidable rival in Alex Barton (Ronald Graham), with whom May is in love. In pique Louis tries to slip Alex a Mickey Finn, but drinks it himself and goes into a deep slumber.

He dreams he is back in the days of Louis XV, indeed that he is the king himself. His would-be regal attitudes jar incongruously with Brooklynese jargon and smoke-room smut, as he brings to the role of the king a lusty peasant quality and an ingenuous formality. "He plays," Richard Watts, Jr., said of Lahr, "with the sort of spluttering, indignant violence and leering impudence that makes him one of the best comedians in the world."

As Louis XV he is passionately pursuing Mme. Du Barry, who looks and acts exactly like May Daley. Just as he is making excellent progress and manages to extract from her a promise to spend the night with him, he is wounded in a most delicate and vulnerable spot by an arrow shot by the half-moronic dauphin (Benny Baker). The indiscreet involvements of king and mistress in and out of the bedroom make up the bulk of his idyllic dreams.

When Louis wakes up, he generously presents Alex with ten thousand dollars so that he can marry May. Since the rest of Louis' money is eaten up by taxes, he must return to the washroom of the Club Petite as attendant.

During the casting, an attractive, sexy performer, then recently released from Paramount, was recommended to Cole Porter to play the second female lead. The moment Cole Porter put eyes on her he knew she would not only be ideal for the part but also would give a sensational performance. She was Betty Grable. Her partnership with Chuck Walters in the songs "Ev'ry Day a Holiday" and "Well, Did You Evah!", and her dance routines with Walters, particularly in an old-world gavotte and a gypsy dance, marked the beginnings of a career that would soon bring her back to Hollywood in triumph and keep her there as a star of stars.

At the suggestion of Buddy de Sylva, who felt that the show needed a song with a "low level sentimental appeal," Porter produced "Friendship" —but with tongue square in cheek. ("If you ever lose your teeth, when you're out to dine, borrow mine, that's friendship!") As delivered by Ethel Merman and Bert Lahr, it stopped the show regularly. Second in popularity to "Friendship" was "Katie Went to Haiti," in Ethel Merman's torrid rendition. (It is believed that Porter got his inspiration for this song by watching a performance of a native band in Haiti.) May and Alex have a melodious duet in "Do I Love You?"

EARL CARROLL'S SKETCH BOOK. *See* SKETCH BOOK.

EARL CARROLL'S VANITIES (1923), *a revue, with book, lyrics, and music by Earl Carroll. Presented by Earl Carroll at the Earl Carroll Theater on July 5. Directed by Earl Carroll. Cast included Joe Cook, Dorothy Knapp, and Peggy Joyce Hopkins (204 performances).*

(1924), *a revue with book and music by Earl Carroll. Presented by Earl Carroll at the Music Box Theater on September 10. Directed by Earl Carroll. Cast included Joe Cook and Sophie Tucker (133 performances).*

(1925), *a revue, with sketches, dialogue, and lyrics by Jimmy Duffy, Arthur "Bugs" Baer, William A. Grew, and others. Music by Clarence Gaskill, Jay Gorney, and others. Presented by Earl Carroll at the Earl Carroll Theater on July 6. Directed by Earl Carroll. Cast included Julius Tannen, Ted Healy, and Felicia Sorel (390 performances).*

(1926), *a revue, with sketches by Stanley, Ruth and William A. Grew. Lyrics and music by Grace Henry and Morris Hamilton. Presented by Earl Carroll at the Earl Carroll Theater on August 24. Directed by Earl Carroll. Dances by David Bennett. Cast included Julius Tannen, Harry Delf, Moran and Mack, Yvette Rugel, and Dorothy Knapp (303 performances).*

(1928), *a revue, assembled by Earl Carroll. Lyrics and music by Grace Harvey, Morris Hamilton, and others. Presented by Earl Carroll at the Earl Carroll Theater on August 6. Directed by Earl Carroll. Cast included W. C. Fields, Joe Frisco, Vincent Lopez and his orchestra, Dorothy Knapp, Lillian Roth, and Ray Dooley (203 performances).*

(1930), *a revue, assembled by Earl Carroll. Dialogue by Eddie Welch and Eugene Conrad. Lyrics by E. Y. Harburg and Ted Koehler. Music by Harold Arlen, Burton Lane, and Jay Gorney. Presented by Earl Carroll at the New Amsterdam Theater on July 1. Directed by Earl Carroll, Priestley Morrison, and Leroy Prinz. Cast included Jimmy Savo, Jack Benny, Dorothy Britton, and Patsy Kelly (215 performances).*

(1931), *a revue, with sketches and dialogue by Ralph Spence and Eddie Welch. Lyrics by Harold Adamson. Music by Burton Lane. Additional songs by various lyricists and composers. Presented by Earl Carroll at the Earl Carroll Theater on August 27. Directed by Earl Carroll. Cast included Will Mahoney, William Demarest, the Slade Brothers, and Lillian Roth (278 performances).*

(1932), *a revue, with sketches and dialogue by Jack McGowan and others. Lyrics by Ted Koehler and Ed Heyman. Music by Harold Arlen and Richard Myers. Presented by Earl Carroll at the Broadway Theater on September 27. Directed by Earl Carroll. Cast included Will Fyffe, Milton Berle, Helen Broderick, and Harriet Hoctor (87 performances).*

(1940), *a revue, assembled by Earl Carroll. Sketches and dialogue by various writers. Lyrics by Dorcas Cochran and Mitchell Parrish. Music by Charles Rosoff and Peter de Rose. Presented by Earl Carroll at the St. James Theater on January 13. Directed by Earl Carroll. Dances by Eddie Prinz. Cast comprised Hollywood starlets (25 performances).*

When Earl Carroll, former songwriter and subsequently to become a producer, decided to compete in the world of lavish revues, he planned to stress that which he felt brought the audiences into the theater—girls. At the stage door he placed the sign: "Through these portals pass the most beautiful girls in the world." This, of course, was intended as a challenge to Ziegfeld. *The Ziegfeld Follies* was by now an institution, and the Ziegfeld girl considered the ultimate in female pulchritude. Carroll was determined to outdo Ziegfeld by making the *Vanities* girl even more glamorous than Ziegfeld's. And so, planning to strum on a single string, he had no hesitancy in becoming another George M. Cohan by taking over every department of his production. Originally, at least, he wrote all his own material, including the songs, did the producing and staging, and used the theater bearing his name. For the time being, at least, he had little interest in first-rank songs or performing stars. What he wanted was the most beautiful girls he could find. And he made his revue a feast for the male eye. He devised the "living curtain"—curtains made up now of silks, now of feathers, now of velvet, but always draped with females in various stages of undress. He concocted spectacular tableaux as luscious settings for his girls wearing transparent costumes, or suggestions of costumes.

He called his first edition simply *Vanities.* It opened with "The Birth of a New Revue." The girls paraded across the stage, each representing one of Broadway's famous revues. The last one was Alice Weaver, and—setting the keynote for the seminudity Carroll would henceforth exploit—she represented the *Vanities* by exposing as much of her anatomy as the law would permit. That first edition ended with a spectacular finale, "Furs," prefaced by the song "When the Snowflakes Fall." Each girl was draped in a different kind of fur. Between these two production numbers, Joe Cook did a one-man vaudeville routine (the best humor to be found in this production) and Bernard Granville sang "My Cretonne Girl," one of the many undistinguished songs Carroll had written. But the star of this edition was Dorothy Knapp, billed as "the most beautiful girl in the world." (Ziegfeld lured her away to the *Follies* a year later, but Carroll got her back again.) Her great talent lay in her body and dazzlingly beautiful face, rather than in any singing or dancing.

The editions of 1924 and 1925 continued the pattern Carroll had established with his first revue. Only the title was changed, in 1924, to *Earl Carroll's Vanities,* which it would retain for all subsequent editions. Once again living curtains and elaborate tableaux were devised for the exhibition of female beauty; once again comedy was the property of Joe Cook. The singing of the principal numbers was assigned to Sophie Tucker, but regrettably she was given nothing that could do justice to her talent or style.

With the 1926 edition Carroll had come to the conclusion that living curtains and tableaux were not enough. He abandoned the idea of making the *Vanities* a one-man show by using the work of many contributors for sketches and songs and strengthening the cast with some stars. The mediocrity of material that prevailed in the first two editions was only temporarily dispelled, for example when the black-faced comedians, Moran and Mack, went through one of their famous routines with their slow, lazy drawl, or when Julius Tannen did a comic bit.

Actually, the *Vanities* never did rise high above the mediocrity it had established in its first editions. But from time to time there were moments of distinction. In the 1930 edition, Jimmy Savo contributed his Chaplinesque pantomime, wearing a bathrobe and huge shoes. He appeared as a property man in "The Noted Chinese Actor, Satunmon," where he was supported admirably by Patsy Kelly; in a skit, "Information Please"; and as Don Juan in a hilarious sketch, "Station YRU," in which Jack Benny was the announcer. Jack Benny (who spelled his name at that time "Bennie") further contributed his droll and suave delivery of wisecracks. Other skits included a travesty on Prohibition. The songs included "Hittin' the Bottle," sung by Betty Veronica, and a number by Harold Arlen to words by Ted Koehler, "The March of Time."

That 1930 edition made front-page news when it ran afoul of the law for being "obscene." The main culprits seemed to be Faith Bacon, who performed a provocative fan dance with a miniature fan; Jimmy Savo, who appeared in a skit as a department-store window-dresser required to remove certain items of feminine clothing from a dummy; and an undersea number in which nymphs were being pursued by a male, all wearing tights and thus seeming to be nude. Robert Benchley called it a "dirty show" full of nudity.

The 1931 revue found a new home—the sumptuous theater that Carroll had built on the site of his old one (50th Street and Broadway). The theater inspired many more "ohs" and "ahs" than the show itself. Trick lighting was used to produce unusual effects as the audience entered the theater. The ushers were dressed as Swiss guards; young men in full-dress suits attended to the comforts and wants of the audience. There were no footlights. A control console was placed behind the musical director, and, controlled by a light director, provided the stage with its lighting effects. The stage entrance had a receptionist in place of a doorman. In the powder rooms, girls could be sprayed with perfume. Between the acts, water wagons served refreshments. As for the show, the emphasis again was on spectacle—in such lavish numbers as Ravel's *Bolero,* or "Chromium," "Ladies of the Veil," "Parasols on Parade," or "Two Hundred Million Years Ago," each a vehicle for the parade of undraped females. This edition, incidentally, was the first to introduce a song that became an outstanding hit, "Good Night, Sweetheart" (words and music by Ray Noble, James Campbell, and Reginald Connelly); Rudy Vallee later made it popular.

The 1932 edition had girls decorating a Maypole, and representing a garden of gardenias and a railway locomotive. But it had other attractions, too. A new young comic revealed his full potential for the first time—Milton Berle. This edition also boasted two fine songs. One was "I Gotta Right to Sing the Blues," by Harold Arlen, to Ted Koehler's words—one of the few songs by Arlen in an authentic blues style. It was introduced by Lillian Shade. The other was "My Darling," words by Edward Heyman and music by Richard Myers, sung by John Hale and Josephine Houston.

Feeling the need for a change of pace and material, Earl Carroll did not produce editions of the *Vanities* in 1933 and 1935. Instead, in 1933 he presented *Murder at the Vanities,* and in 1935 the *Sketch Book.* The first, which had a slight thread of a murder-mystery plot as well as girls, was made into a movie by Paramount in 1934 (where the hit song "Cocktails for Two"—words by Arthur Johnston and music by Sam Coslow—was introduced by Carl Brisson). The latter was an attempt at sophistication, for which Carroll had little taste and less aptitude.

In 1934 Carroll deserted Broadway for Hollywood, where he opened a theater restaurant which prospered for ten years. When he returned to Broadway, in 1940, it was to offer a new—and his last—edition of the *Vanities,* which was really made up of specialties he had featured in his Hollywood restaurant, and whose cast was made up of Hollywood starlets. It survived only three weeks.

Among the performers who first gained Broadway prominence through the *Vanities* besides Milton Berle were Lillian Roth, Patsy Kelly, and Jack Benny. Otherwise the contributions made by the *Vanities* to show business were negligible, when compared to *The Ziegfeld Follies,* George White's *Scandals,* or Irving Berlin's *Music Box Revues.*

Earl Carroll was killed in a plane crash on June 17, 1947, while flying from Los Angeles to New York.

EL CAPITAN (1896), *a comic opera, with book by Charles Klein. Lyrics by Tom Frost and John Philip Sousa. Music by John Philip Sousa. Presented at the Broadway Theater on April 20. Directed by H. A. Cripps. Cast included De Wolf Hopper, Edna Wallace Hopper, John Parr, and Alfred Klein (112 performances).*

*El Capitan* has several points of interest. It was one of the earliest American comic operas; its score was by America's celebrated march king; of Sousa's ten comic operas, this was the most successful; and, finally, a male chorus of the second act became one of Sousa's famous marches, also entitled "El Capitan."

The setting is sixteenth-century Peru, and the story centers around the political struggles of its viceroy, Don Erico Medniga (De Wolf Hopper). A weak ruler, the viceroy transacts all his business through his chamberlain, Pozzo (Alfred Klein). When threatened by overthrow, the viceroy assumes the identity of the bandit El Capitan (who is actually dead, although this fact is known only to the viceroy). As El Capitan, the viceroy comes upon the conspirators, wins them over, and becomes a leader in the conspiracy against himself. He also wins the love of Estrelda (Edna Wallace Hopper). After the revelation that El Capitan and the viceroy are one, the latter must give up Estrelda, since he is a married man, and Estrelda must find solace with the soldier with whom she had previously been in love.

Besides the second-act male chorus, "Behold El Capitan," the score included a topical song in "A Typical Tune of Zanzibar" and a lyrical duet in "Sweetheart, I'm Waiting."

EVANGELINE (1874), *an American extravaganza, with book by Edward E. Rice and J. Cheever Goodwin. Lyrics by J. Cheever Goodwin. Music by E. E. Rice. Presented by Goodwin and Rice at Niblo's Gardens on July 27. Cast included Ione Burke, W. H. Crane, and J. W. Thoman (two weeks).*

*Evangeline* has historical importance for the American theater for several reasons. A travesty on Longfellow's poem of the same name, it was one of the most successful examples of "burlesque," a genre of American musical theater long popular. (The term "burlesque" is here used in its original meaning as travesty or parody or caricature, rather than in its later connotation.) It was also with this extravaganza that the term "musical comedy" was used for the first time. In speaking of *Evangeline,* Rice said he hoped it would "foster a taste for musical comedy relieved of the characteristic and objectionable features of opéra bouffe." Finally, *Evangeline* was one of the earliest musicals in which the entire score was written directly for its production, rather than comprising adaptations and interpolations. Rice's score embraced a waltz, march, topical songs, comedy numbers, ballads, duets, trios, and choral numbers.

Though intended as a burlesque on Longfellow, there was little in the play to identify it with the poem. Most of the locales were far removed from Nova Scotia, as far as Arizona and Africa. Evangeline became, as Rice said of her, "a creature of impulse pursued through love's impatient prompting by Gabriel, and with a view to audacious contingencies—by a whale."

A trick cow (one man in front, another in the rear) performing an eccentric dance and staggering all over the stage was a main attraction; another was a spouting whale; a third was a silent character called "The Lone Fisherman" (played in New York by J. W. Thoman) who seemed to have no relation to anything taking place but who floated in and out at will with half-serious, half-comic routines. To add further to the oddities, the leading male role of Gabriel was played by a woman in tights, while one of the lady characters was played by George K. Fortesque.

*Evangeline* had a long and sustained success—though it is not possible to compute its run. It played only two weeks at first, not because it lacked an audience but because it was used to fill in a lull in the Niblo's Garden season and had to depart to make room for another previously scheduled production. But in the years that followed, it returned to New York frequently and deserves to be placed in the hit class of *The Black Crook* and *Humpty Dumpty*.

FACE THE MUSIC (1932), *a musical comedy, with book by Moss Hart. Lyrics and music by Irving Berlin. Presented by Sam H. Harris at the New Amsterdam Theater on February 17. Directed by Hassard Short and George S. Kaufman. Dances by Albertina Rasch. Cast included Mary Boland, J. Harold Murray, and Katherine Carrington (165 performances).*

The text was peppered throughout with satirical jibes at corrupt politicians, bribable policemen, speakeasies, show business—and most of all at the Depression, which was at its height in 1932. A slender plot serves as a convenient frame for laughter, wit, and malicious comments on the American way of life during those tragic times. Martin Van Buren Meshbesher (Hugh O'Connell) is a police sergeant who has a cache of illicit funds in a tin box. With an investigation of the police under way he must get rid of his money in the fastest possible way. What way could be faster than an investment in a Broadway musical? He becomes the angel for a lavish production put on by Hal Reisman (Andrew Tombes), since Reisman's past association with the musical stage seemed to be a guarantee of financial failure. During out-of-town tryouts the projected Reisman show, *The Rhinestone Girl,* proves to be the kind of dud for which Reisman has become famous. When Meshbesher's fortune is wiped out—not by the show but by the investigation which finds him guilty—he must depend upon Reisman's show to extricate him from his financial woes. *The Rhinestone Girl* is now spiced with sex appeal, becomes a hit, and yields a fortune to all involved.

A good deal of the comedy rested on the shoulders of Mary Boland, who played the part of Mrs. Meshbesher, a lady who wore so many diamonds that "on clear days they can see me way up in Yonkers." One of the hilarious episodes finds her in an outlandish costume astride a papier-mâché elephant— with all the dignity a great lady can summon. But most of the humor sprang from the many allusions to the Depression and its impact on Americans: The Roxy Theater in New York is compelled to give four feature films to attract customers (providing at the same time room and bath free), and all this for a dime; the opening scene finds the Junior League meeting in the Automat; Albert Einstein appears at the Palace Theater as one of its attractions, that theater now offering free lunches with its all-star shows.

The Automat scene was the setting for the song "Let's Have Another Cup o' Coffee," introduced by Katherine Carrington and J. Harold Murray. It became something of a theme song for the Depression years—also for Maxwell House Coffee when it produced a weekly series of radio shows. Another outstanding Berlin number was the ballad "Soft Lights and Sweet Music"—once again introduced by Miss Carrington and Mr. Murray—and effectively prefaced by a dazzling mirror scene devised by Hassard Short.

FADE OUT—FADE IN (1964), *a musical comedy, with book and lyrics by Betty Comden and Adolph Green. Music by Jule Styne. Presented by Lester Osterman and Jule Styne at the Mark Hellinger Theater on May 26. Directed by George Abbott. Dances by Ernest Flatt. Cast included Carol Burnett, Jack Cassidy, and Lou Jacobi (271 performances).*

But for the fact that *Fade Out—Fade In* suffered from "star trouble," which necessitated an interruption in its engagement, it would have enjoyed a far greater success than it did. It was, for all the slim trimmings of its plot, a hilarious takeoff on Hollywood and Hollywood stars, with Carol Burnett in top form both as a comedienne and as a deliverer of songs with emotional or humorous impact. Hope Springfield (Carol Burnett) is an ordinary-looking chorus girl who, through blundering in the Hollywood studio, is hired to star in one of its important productions. The head of the studio loses his job when the mistake is uncovered, since everybody is convinced that Hope is a girl without looks, talent, appeal. Meanwhile, the picture is filmed and put into discard. The nephew of the boss, Rudolf Governor (Dick Patterson), becomes interested in Hope, has the picture previewed before the leading executives, who suddenly realize that they have found a star of stars, and a picture certain to reap vast profits.

As in most such stereotyped stories, it is in the details that the production proves most amusing. A bountiful source of merriment is the character of Lionel Z. Governor (Lou Jacobi), the bigwig of the studio. He is, as Richard Watts, Jr., described him, "a much confused man, who travels with his personal psychiatrist, he can't speak the numeral four because he detests his fourth nephew. He also has an understandable partiality for beautiful girls in his films."

Another delectable element is the appearance of some of Hollywood's all-time greats, played by performers with a flair for mimicry (added, no doubt, by George Abbott's skillful direction). Among those thus imitated, and at times ridiculed, were Ginger Rogers, Fred Astaire, Greta Garbo, Shirley Temple, and Jean Harlow.

But it was Carol Burnett who more than anybody else carried the show, with her inimitable gifts at parody, broad humor, and facial grimaces. Plagued by a back ailment, Miss Burnett was compelled to withdraw from the production, which forced the musical to close down temporarily on November 14. Not until February 15, 1965, did the show reopen, with some changes in the book, and four new songs, two of them written for Miss Burnett. But it was no secret that Miss Burnett was not happy with the production and was eager to leave it for good. The show finally closed down on April 17, with talk of legal action against Miss Burnett, which never materialized. One of Miss Burnett's major gripes was that the score was weak, which happened to be true. Only the title song (presented by Hope and Rudolf), "Call Me Savage" (a duet by Hope and Rudolf), and "I'm with You" (sung by Hope and Byron Prong, a Hollywood leading man, played by Jack Cassidy) were of temporary interest.

THE FAIR CO-ED (1909), *an operetta, with book and lyrics by George Ade. Music by Gustav Luders. Presented by Charles Dillingham at the Knickerbocker Theater on February 1. Directed by Fred G. Latham. Dances by William Rock. Cast included Elsie Janis and Arthur Stanford (136 performances).*

George Ade's humorous nonmusical play *The College Widow*, which was used for Jerome Kern's musical comedy *Leave It to Jane* (1917), was set in Atwater College, in Atwater, Indiana. The traditional rival of Atwater College was Bingham College. And it is the latter institution that is the background for *The Fair Co-ed.* There Cynthia Bright (Elsie Janis) is the only co-ed left, and she is adored by the entire faculty and student body. Cynthia's father, just before his death, had ordered her to marry only a Bingham graduate. Cynthia, however, loves Davy Dickerson (Arthur Stanford), who has a difficult time getting through his college courses. Now that he must graduate to win Cynthia, he decides to devote himself more earnestly to his studies. On a lark, Cynthia disguises herself as a naval cadet and goes to a military reception, where she is in danger of a hazing and must escape by jumping through the window. Davy finally succeeds in passing his courses and in graduating, and Cynthia now can marry him.

Much of the exuberance of the text came from the abundance of college songs and yells in the production. Luders' leading musical numbers, however, were in a sentimental vein and included "Here in the Starlight," "I'll Dream of That Sweet Co-ed," and "A Little Girl That's Wise."

FANNY (1954), *a musical play, with book by S. N. Behrman and Joshua Logan, based on a trilogy of plays by Marcel Pagnol. Lyrics and music by Harold Rome. Presented by David Merrick and Joshua Logan at the Majestic Theater on November 4. Directed by Joshua Logan. Dances by Helen Tamiris. Cast included Ezio Pinza, Walter Slezak, William Tabbert, and Florence Henderson (888 performances).*

Marcel Pagnol's trilogy of plays set on the waterfront of Marseille—*Marius, Fanny,* and *César*—are flooded with heart-warming humanity and compassion, which S. N. Behrman skillfully carried over into the musical adaptation up to the point of including the touching death scene of Panisse. (Behrman, long a successful writer of social comedies, was here making his bow as a writer of musical-comedy librettos.)

Marius (William Tabbert) plans to go off on a five-year scientific expedition on the rigger *Malaise,* for he is the victim of an irresistible love of the sea. Two obstacles are in his way. One is his father, César (Ezio Pinza), who expects Marius to take over the operation of his little waterfront café in Marseille; the other is Fanny (Florence Henderson), with whom he is in love. Somebody else is also in love with Fanny and wants to marry her. He is the middle-aged, kindly, and wealthy widower, the proprietor of a sailmaking establishment, Panisse (Walter Slezak). When, late at night, Marius begins to close down the café, Fanny comes to visit him and confides how deeply she loves him. Marius expresses his own sentiments of love but tells her that they can never mean anything to each other, since he is determined to sail the following morning on the *Malaise.*

Marius sails away without ever discovering that Fanny is pregnant with his child; nor does he know that Fanny now plans to marry Panisse to make her unborn child legitimate. Panisse is overjoyed that Fanny will have him, and he becomes even more tender and solicitous to her than before upon discovering she is bearing Marius' child. Panisse had always hoped to have a son. Now that it is being given to him by the woman he loves, his happiness is doubled. Panisse's love for Fanny is boundless, particularly after her son, Cesario, is born. Panisse regards Cesario as his own child. With true parental pride he changes the sign on his establishment to read "Panisse and Son."

In the second act, Cesario's first birthday is being celebrated. Once the party is over, Panisse must go to Paris to transact some business. Hardly has he left when Marius arrives. Marius and Fanny at first exchange polite, formal greetings. But once Marius discovers that Cesario is his own child, he allows his true feelings to come to the surface and confesses that he has never forgotten Fanny, nor has his love for her waned. Fanny also is made aware that her love for Marius is not dead. They embrace passionately, when César appears and roughly separates them. He sternly reminds his daughter that she is married to a good man who loves Marius' child as if he were his own. Sadly realizing that Fanny and Cesario can never really be his again, Marius makes his departure.

Eleven years have gone by. Cesario is twelve. His birthday is being celebrated with a circus hired for the occasion at Panisse's house outside Marseille. Cesario expresses curiosity about Marius, about whom he has heard a good deal through the years. Upon discovering that Marius is employed in a garage in nearby Toulon, he goes off to visit him. There Cesario reveals to Marius his ambition to go off to the sea, but Marius convinces him his place is with his parents. When Cesario comes back home he finds that his father is deathly sick, dictating a letter in which he urges Fanny to marry Marius. "I will rest easier," he explains in his letter, "knowing she has someone to care for her, especially if it's the one she has always loved."

For the distinguished Metropolitan Opera bass Ezio Pinza, *Fanny* represented his first return to the Broadway musical theater following his triumph in the Rodgers and Hammerstein musical *South Pacific*. Once again he proved himself to be a singing actor of outstanding attainments, even in the popular musical theater. *Fanny* was Pinza's last Broadway musical; he died in 1957.

Rome's score was one of his most ambitious—penetrating deeply into the heart of the play and its principal characters and endowing all with a new dimension. Songs like the tender "To My Wife," which Panisse sings about his beloved Fanny; "Restless Heart," sung by Marius; and César's "Welcome Home"—all provide fresh insights into the personalities of the characters who introduce them. Sometimes Rome's background music brings new emotional overtones to a dramatic scene—while his music for the circus, undersea, and wedding ballets have symphonic breadth. Yet though the artistic horizon of his writing had been extended, Rome had by no means lost the gift of writing a good tune. The title song, delivered by Marius, became a hit, and to a lesser extent so did the amusing "Be Kind to Your Parents." Noteworthy, too, are "Love Is a Very Light Thing," sung by César; Marius' "The Thought of You"; and Fanny's "I Have to Tell You."

*Fanny* became the Second American musical staged in Germany after World War II (in Munich on December 16, 1955); the first had been Cole Porter's *Kiss Me, Kate,* mounted in Frankfurt only fourteen days earlier.

Strange to say, in the motion picture *Fanny* (Warner Brothers, 1960)— in which Charles Boyer, Leslie Caron, and Maurice Chevalier were starred— all the songs were dispensed with. However, the melody of "Fanny" was utilized on the soundtrack as a recurring theme in the background music.

FANTANA (1905), *an operetta, with book by Sam S. Shubert and Robert B. Smith. Lyrics by Robert B. Smith. Music by Raymond Hubbell. Presented by the Jefferson de Angelis Company, "offered" by Sam S. Shubert at the Lyric Theater on January 14. Directed by R. H. Burnside. Cast included Jefferson de Angelis, Adele Ritchie, Katie Barry, and in minor roles Julia Sanderson and Douglas Fairbanks, Sr. (298 performances).*

The program described this extravaganza as "a Japanese-American musical." Commodore Everett (Hubert Wilke) takes his pretty daughter, Fanny, nicknamed Fantana (Adele Ritchie) to Japan to save her from an undesirable marriage with a handsome Englishman. The Englishman follows her and thwarts her father's plan to marry her to a French count by producing the count's wife. Meanwhile, the commodore's valet, Hawkins (Jefferson de Angelis), disguises himself as a Japanese minister, a role in which he involves both his employer and himself in endless trouble. Things become hectic, but the commodore, Fantana, and Hawkins manage to escape retribution by fleeing Japan aboard the yacht of a Japanese ambassador; and the valet can fall into the arms of the girl he loves.

The *tour de force* was Jefferson de Angelis' antics as valet and hokum Japanese minister—including his broad takeoffs on a music leader and a strongman, and his effective rendition of two humorous ditties, "That's Art" and "What Would Mrs. Grundy Say?" Two more songs proved popular: "The Farewell Waltz" and "My Word."

The only song to survive to this day from *Fantana* was not by Hubbell but an interpolation, "Tammany," lyrics by Vincent Bryan, music by Gus Edwards. The song was written for a party held by the National Democratic Club of New York, for which Gus Edwards was master of ceremonies. On his way to the party Gus Edwards heard a hand organ in the street play some Indian songs, and the idea came to him to write a number for the party parodying an Indian song. The song went over so big that it was soon interpolated into *Fantana,* then enjoying a successful Broadway run; there it was introduced by Lee Harrison, who played a minor role. Since then "Tammany" has become an official song of New York's Tammany Society.

The basic idea for the plot of *Fantana,* though in very tenuous form, originated with Sam S. Shubert, who turned it over to his librettist, Robert B. Smith, for development. During the final rehearsals of the show, in Chicago, Smith created a furor because Shubert claimed being a collaborator in the writing of the text. Shubert appeased Smith by calling a press conference in which he denied the "rumor that he was the coauthor of the book of *Fantana.*" However, when the show went over big in Chicago, Shubert changed his mind and had his name put on the program as the coauthor of the text. In New York, *Fantana* did equally well. S. S. Shubert was so delighted with the audience response on opening night that he could not resist the temptation of making a curtain speech in gratitude and of giving a party for the entire cast. But much to Smith's chagrin, no further attempt was made by Shubert to disassociate himself from the text.

> THE FANTASTICKS (1960), *a musical comedy, with book and lyrics by Tom Jones, suggested by Edmond Rostand's play* Les Romantiques. *Music by Harvey Schmidt. Presented by Lorenzo ("Lore") Noto at the Sullivan Street Playhouse on May 3. Directed by Word Baker. Cast included Jerry Orbach, Rita Gardner, and Kenneth Nelson.*

*The Fantasticks* is one of the greatest success stories the American musical theater has known. It was produced on a shoestring (total original investment being $16,500, scraped together from fifty-seven investors). It opened modestly and unpretentiously in a small, barnlike auditorium in Greenwich Village, New York (seating capacity 149). The reviews were lukewarm, although one or two perceptive critics sensed something very special about the production. ("While the virtues it possesses are modest and less than exhilarating, it has freshness, youthful charm and a touch of imagination," said Richard Watts, Jr. Only Henry Hewes of the *Saturday Review* had no reservations, calling it "one of the happiest off Broadway events in a season that has been happier off Broadway than on.") For the first three months the theater was half-empty; the loss was in the neighborhood of $2,000. Only the faith of the producer kept the show going. Then a miracle took place. Suddenly business spurted. Before long, capacity houses became the rule. It received the Vernon Rice Award as the outstanding Off Broadway achievement of the season. And from that point on *The Fantasticks* went on to become the longest-running production in American theater history, still playing to capacity houses over ten years after its opening. In that time there were over a thousand other separate productions, not only in America but in such far-off places as Stockholm, Istanbul, Belgrade, Johannesburg, Berlin, Tel Aviv, Helsinki, Khartoum, Mexico City. On October 18, 1964, it was presented on coast-to-coast NBC television on the Hallmark Hall of Fame—the first time that a live presentation of the musical had to compete with its television presentation. By the time the show celebrated its tenth anniversary on May 3, 1970, it had grossed in New York alone over two and a half million dollars, netting its backers a profit of $638,817. The additional returns from road companies, recordings, motion-picture and foreign rights resulted in probably the highest payoff in the history of American show business—in excess of 5,000 percent. And, as the years go by, *The Fantasticks* continues to be a prime favorite with amateur, stock, summer, and college productions throughout the country.

How to explain such a miracle? Schmidt offers the following: "I think the show may mean different things to many different kinds of people. It's the way the plot is told that makes it distinctive, not the story itself." Jones is more expansive, feeling that the audience has "a very personal sense of participation" in the show and is exhilarated by the overall message, "the necessity of Winter to ensure the rebirth of Spring." "I am also certain," continues Mr. Jones, "that the simpler you do something, the better off it's going to be. . . . The proper words and music can evoke a spectacle in the mind that's so much more satisfying than anything the most skillful designer could possibly devise. . . . The thing to do is to take somthing that is around us every day, that we see and touch, and put it in terms that are poetic." To Jones what *The Fantasticks* has accomplished was to "accept the convention of poetry . . . of people singing their emotions. It is through this unreal poetic world that we can more fully understand the pain and beauty of living."

Actually, *The Fantasticks* started its fabulous history not in Greenwich Village, but even more humbly—for a week's run at Barnard College on August 3, 1959, as one of three one-act plays. The show might then and there have passed into total oblivion but for the fact that a young man in that first-night audience fell in love with it. He was Lorenzo Noto, a one-time agent become producer. He suggested to Jones and Schmidt that they expand it into a full evening's entertainment. Nine months later, *The Fantasticks* came to Greenwich Village in a simple and economical presentation calling for nine players, the staging leaving a good deal to the imagination of the spectator. As the stage instructions read: "This play should be played on a platform. There is no scenery, but occasionally a stick may be held up to represent a wall. Or a cardboard moon may be hung upon a pole to indicate that it's night. When the audience enters the auditorium, the platform is clearly in sight, and there is a tattered drape across the front of it upon which is lettered 'THE FANTASTICKS.' "

The text is a variation of the theme of Pierrot and Columbine. It opens with the narrator (Jerry Orbach) singing "Try to Remember," a ballad which, like the production out of which it emerged, slowly worked its way out of obscurity to national popularity. At least one of several explanations for the ultimate surge of business at the Sullivan Street Playhouse lies in the fact that the song was beginning to achieve a hit status; and since that time it has established itself as a solid "standard."

The narrator then explains that the principal characters are a boy, Matt (Kenneth Nelson), and a girl, Luisa (Rita Gardner), who are separated by a wall. They are in love, but the only reason their respective fathers are keeping them apart is because the older folk are convinced that the disapproval of parents is the best way to bring youngsters close together. As further insurance that the two youngsters become increasingly interested in one another, the fathers call upon a bandit, El Gallo (enacted by the narrator), to attempt to rape the girl and to be frustrated by a heroic rescue by Matt. The plan works. Following the "Rape Ballet," the two youngsters are more passionately in love with each other than ever. But the happiness is of short duration once they learn that they were just pawns in a game played by their respective fathers. The youngsters begin to quarrel. Matt decides he wants to see the world; Luisa runs off with El Gallo. Disenchanted with their children, the fathers once again build a wall separating the two families. But, in the end, boy and girl, disillusioned with life, are drawn together closer than ever. The play ends with the narrator's philosophical comment: "Without a hurt the heart is hollow."

The principal songs (of which "Try to Remember" is undoubtedly the most celebrated) convey a good deal of the poignancy, wistfulness, and even whimsy of the text. The best are: "I Can See It," where Matt, at odds with his girl, yearns to see the world; Luisa's ballad "Much More"; and the duet in which Luisa and Matt express their apprehensions about the future in "Soon It's Gonna Rain"—the last two popularized by Barbra Streisand in her recording in 1963.

FIDDLE DE-DEE. *See* WEBER AND FIELDS EXTRAVAGANZAS.

FIDDLER ON THE ROOF (1964), *a musical play, with book by Joseph Stein, based on stories by Sholom Aleichem. Lyrics by Sheldon Harnick. Music by Jerry Bock. Presented by Harold Prince at the Imperial Theater on September 22. Directed and with choreography by Jerome Robbins. Cast included Zero Mostel, Maria Karnilova, and Beatrice Arthur.*

In *Fiddler on the Roof,* the musical theater invaded a strange, esoteric world formerly completely ignored by the popular musical stage. It was the world of the East European Jew, bound to century-old traditions, whose customs, beliefs, superstitions, way of life and thought, ideals, habits, and dress were all as exotic to non-Jews (and even to a great many Jews of American birth) as might be those of a remote African tribe or those of characters in a Kabuki theater. *Fiddler on the Roof* was a bold undertaking rooted in and based solely on the textual subject. Bolder still was the way in which little effort was made to commercialize the product by offering a recognizable American musical with some Jewish trimmings.

Joseph Stein, the librettist, who drew his material from Sholom Aleichem's stories, used these stories as a starting point for his own invention, rather than transfer the tales literally to the stage. The overall plot may be Stein's, but the humor and pathos, the characters, and backgrounds belong recognizably to Sholom Aleichem. As Stein explained: "The structure of the play required the creation of new scenes and new dialogue. Practically none of the dialogue from the original stories was usable, since the original material was not written for the stage, and the dialogue within it had a very special appeal." The main character, Tevye, was a simple, humble, and passive man in Sholom Aleichem. "To make him the moving force in our story, it was necessary to give him more strength, while keeping the shadings of his character intact." Stein aimed to place a good deal of emphasis on the village itself, which meant "the creation of new characters, who would be at home in the community." Most significantly, Stein wanted to have his story carry over a contemporary message to a twentieth-century audience. "We brought to the foreground an element implicit in the Tevye tales . . . the hostility, the violence, the injustice practiced by a ruling majority against a weak minority. We wanted in this to point up the internal strength, the dignity, the humor of the people and, like minorities today, their unique talent for survival."

As for the music, the composer had no intention of creating Yiddish music; he, too, had to make necessary digressions from authentic folk tunes. He created songs that had an Eastern European Jewish flavor without resorting to quotation or direct imitation of Yiddish folk songs. An augmented or a diminished interval used discreetly here and there, a Hebraic turn of phrase (almost the musical equivalent of the sweep of the Hebrew scholar's thumb as he explains a fine point in the Talmud)—these and other subtleties of Yiddish folk songs were superimposed so skillfully on basically solid show tunes that there was never a suggestion of parody; they rang true.

To Jerome Robbins, who staged and choreographed the entire production, goes the lion's share of credit for the authenticity throughout the play. He did intensive research into Old World Jewry; one of his basic sources was a sociological study called *Life Is with People,* in which the life and customs of the so called "shtetl" (or "little Jewish town") are thoroughly described and historically analyzed. The mannerisms of the characters, and the principal scenes—most notably the wedding scene—were authentic in detail as well as in general outline.

The image of a fiddler playing on a roof comes from one of Marc Chagall's paintings. To the authors of *Fiddler on the Roof* this was symbolic of the precarious life of the religious Jew amid a hostile Christian society— as precarious as is the stance of a man fiddling on a roof. And it is the image of a fiddler, astride a hunchbacked roof of a humble Jewish house, that we see first as the curtain rises. We are in the Russian village of Anatevka, in the year of 1905. Tevye (Zero Mostel)—a man as ready to hold communications with God as he is with the audience—explains that everybody in the town is a fiddler on a roof, living a dangerous existence while trying to earn a living. These Jews stay in Anatevka because this is their town, and the thing that binds them together and gives them courage is tradition—the chant "Tradition" soon being taken up by Tevye and his fellow villagers.

All this is but the prologue to the play that follows, which opens in the kitchen in Tevye's house. Tevye and his wife, Golde (Maria Karnilova), have five daughters whom they want to see married soon to respectable young men. Golde, therefore, is delighted that Yente, the matchmaker, is coming with a prospect for one of the daughters, Tzeitel. The prospect, Motel, a diffident and impoverished tailor, is not what Golde is looking for as a prospective son-in-law. She has her eye on Lazar Wolf, a middle-aged butcher, who has a prosperous business. But Tzeitel, Hodel, and Chava—three of the five daughters—are not at all prejudiced at the prospect of being matched up with desirable young men, as they reveal in "Matchmaker, Matchmaker," even though Hodel is interested in the rabbi's son, and Hodel and Chava are too young to contemplate marriage.

When Tevye appears, he begins a one-way conversation with God, asking him why He found it necessary to make him a poor man. This leads him to think of what he would do if he were rich, developing his dreams in the song "If I Were a Rich Man." Tevye now turns to the business of selling his dairy goods to the villagers. Among them is a stranger, Perchik, whose profession is teaching. Perchik offers to teach Tevye's daughters the Bible and other lessons in return for food. Tevye invites Perchik to share with his family the Sabbath meal, during which Motel stammers out the song "Good Sabbath."

The following evening Tevye and Lazar the butcher meet in the village inn to discuss the possibility of a match between Lazar and Tzeitel. They come to an agreement, and toast the decision with wine and song ("L'Chaim —To Life"). When they announce to the other villagers that Lazar and Tzeitel are engaged, everybody joins in a joyous dance.

Having become Hodel's teacher—he even instructs her how to dance the polka—Perchik finds her to be the kind of girl he would like to have as a wife; and Hodel, on her own part, is not altogether indifferent. Meanwhile, when Tzeitel gets the news she is to marry the butcher, she bursts into weeping, and pleads with her father not to force her into a marriage with a man she does not love. The man she wants is Motel, the poor tailor, and though Tevye realizes only too well that Motel is impractical, he gives his daughter his consent. His main problem is to sell the idea to his wife, Golde. He does so by concocting a dream in which he has seen Grandma Tzeitel give her blessings to a marriage between Motel and Tzeitel. Golde is a believer in dreams and cannot go against the wishes of her dead grandmother. And so, Tzeitel and Motel get married in a ceremony that strictly follows orthodox ritual, while Tevya and Golde, in "Sunrise, Sunset," wonder at the rapid flight of time; it was only yesterday that their full-grown girls were just children. During the wedding ceremony Perchik shocks the guests by flouting tradition. He asks Hodel to dance with him—a dance between a man and a woman alone being something unheard of. Nevertheless, they dance, and others soon join them. The celebration becomes frenetic. Just then Russian police burst in, create havoc and destruction, and leave behind them a mess which Tevye and guests quietly and stoically begin to clean up.

Tzeitel and Motel have been married two months, and are blissfully happy. But Hodel is upset, for Perchik, who has come to mean much to her, has plans to leave Anatevka. He promises to send for Hodel as soon as he can; meanwhile, they can regard themselves as engaged. Reluctantly, Tevye and Golde accept the situation, realizing as they do how much the two young people are in love. This situation leads Golde to ask Tevye if he loves her. As they chant "Do You Love Me?" they realize that they have taken their love and devotion for each other for granted.

Hodel, having married Perchik, is leaving Anatevka to join her husband in Siberia, to which he has been committed for revolutionary activities. Tevye is grief-stricken at losing his daughter, but recognizes the wisdom of her belief that her home is with her husband.

And now it is Chava's turn to get a beau: He is a Russian named Fyedka, and to make matters worse, he is a Christian. But their difference in religion bothers the young people little, though Tevye is thoroughly upset. A ballet sequence reenacts the romance of the three daughters, with Chava dancing away with Fyedka. The sequence vanishes. Chava entreats her father to accept Fyedka as a son-in-law, but Tevye is adamant about sticking to tradition. Now that his two youngest daughters have found their prospective mates through the efforts of the matchmaker, Tevye is more determined than ever not to harbor a Christian in his house. But tragic news soon throws such problems into a shade. The Russian constable has come to announce that all Jews must leave Anatevka in three days. And so, Tevye's family sadly pack their belongings and make ready to leave, each going in a different direction. The family is broken up. But Golde's final thought is that she must sweep the floor of the house, since she does not want to leave behind a dirty home. The villagers of Anatevka begin to go their separate ways. Tevye and Golde, and their pots, pans, and bedding, are off to join their Uncle Abram in Chicago. The family of Tevye and Golde, which now includes a grandchild, are now being scattered to the four winds. The villagers make a last bow to each other, as they form a circle, then each departs, going his own way. Only the fiddler is left, playing a tune. At Tevye's call, the fiddler tucks his violin under his arm and follows his fellow Jews out of Anatevka.

When *Fiddler on the Roof* played out of town prior to its arrival on Broadway, the critic of *Variety* expressed the opinion that this was "no smash, no blockbuster; may have a chance for a moderate success." A moderate success was what even Jerry Bock, its composer, had expected, saying: "It wasn't the sort of show where from first blush you knew you had a hit." But a hit—indeed, a blockbuster—is what *Fiddler on the Roof* proved itself from opening night on. Howard Taubman wrote a rave review in *The New York Times,* saying: "It catches the essence of a moment in history with sentiment and radiance. Compounded of the familiar materials of the musical theater . . . it combines and transcends them to arrive at an integrated achievement of uncommon quality." One or two other major critics had reservations, but they were minor ones, and these critics in the end agreed with their colleagues that the show was "a cinch to satisfy almost anyone who enjoys the musical theater," as the New York critic of *Variety* put it. By 1970, it was well on its way to becoming perhaps the longest-running musical in Broadway's history, after having captured nine Antoinette Perry awards (including that of the season's best musical), together with the New York Drama Critics Circle Award. By then it had taken in over twenty million dollars at the Broadway box office, and an additional ten million dollars from its national touring company. The original-cast recording brought in another million dollars, and two million dollars was the price for the sale of the movie rights. It was produced in London, Warsaw, Vienna, Paris, Copenhagen, Antwerp, Madrid, Geneva, Istanbul, Tel Aviv, Finland, New Zealand, Norway, Holland, South Africa, Australia, West and East Germany, Czechoslovakia, Iceland, South America—and even in Japan, where a cabled report to *The New York Times* said "the humor came through and the huge Imperial Theater laughed heartily at the right times." In London it was acclaimed without qualification as the year's best musical. In Vienna (playing at the historic Theater-an-der-Wien, where Beethoven's *Fidelio* had been introduced) it inspired "thunderous applause from an enthusiastic, but obviously self-conscious, Viennese audience," according to a cable to *The New York Times*. Vienna had known the meaning of anti-Semitism for many years. And, ironically, Hamburg gave this musical one of the greatest ovations it received anywhere. Of particular historic significance was the fact that in 1970 it was produced by the Komische Oper in East Berlin, one of Europe's most eminent opera companies, under the personal direction of the distinguished operatic producer-director Walter Felsenstein.

The world was still being victimized by racial and religious prejudices—and as long as this continues, *Fiddler on the Roof,* for all its excursions into exotica and esoterica, will continue to carry a powerful, timely message.

FIFTY MILLION FRENCHMEN (1929), *a musical comedy, with book by Herbert Fields. Lyrics and music by Cole Porter. Presented by E. Ray Goetz at the Lyric Theater on November 27. Directed by Monty Woolley. Dances by Larry Ceballos. Cast included William Gaxton, Genevieve Tobin, Helen Broderick, and Evelyn Hoey (254 performances).*

One year earlier, Porter had written the score for his first successful musical comedy, E. Ray Goetz's production of *Paris. Fifty Million Frenchmen* was even more Parisian than *Paris*. With seven-league boots it covered the wondrous city on the Seine from the Ritz bar to the Longchamps racetrack; from the American Express Company on Rue Scribe to Montmartre; from the Claridge Hotel to Les Halles. En route, it gently spoofed American tourists. Helen Broderick, for example, played the part of Violet Hildegarde, a hard-boiled and bored American ever on the lookout for shocking experiences; she sends risqué picture cards back to her relatives at home and buys up copies of *Ulysses* to give as gifts to kids. "Here is a show that will make you homesick for Paris," wrote Robert Littell, "and it's grand fun."

The principal character is Peter Forbes (William Gaxton), a wealthy playboy who at the Ritz bar meets and falls in love with Looloo Carroll (Genevieve Tobin), fresh from Terre Haute. He is determined to win her love for himself alone, and not for his wealth. Spurred on by a 25,000-dollar bet with a friend, he decides to live in Paris for a month without any funds. He finds a job as a guide, comes upon Looloo, who is now being pursued by a grand duke picked for her by her ambitious mother. He also becomes a gigolo and an Arabian magician as he undergoes one experience after another in different Parisian settings and backgrounds. In the end he wins his bet and gets his girl.

Trouble and misfortune were compounded upon trouble and misfortune before *Fifty Million Frenchmen* became successful. First, Irving Berlin, who had been expected to be a co-producer, withdrew from the venture before the project reached the planning board. Then, when money for the production was made available by Warner Brothers, Herbert Fields and Cole Porter were fined and suspended for six months by the Dramatists Guild, which prohibited its members from making picture deals without its permission. But all this was only the beginning. The book, with its many, varied episodes, had been so poorly integrated that Monty Woolley ran into staggering rehearsal problems, which he solved by splitting up the company into four units and having each rehearse separately in a different theater. The sets, designed by Norman Bel Geddes (incidentally, this was his first venture as a stage designer), were so cumbersome and elaborate that it required seven railroad cars to transport them out of town for the tryouts and back to Broadway. In Boston, the Colonial Theater—where the production was booked—had a stage incapable of handling those huge sets; Bel Geddes had to work night and day to reduce the proportions and sizes to fit the Colonial Theater, causing a two-day delay in the opening night. Rehearsals continued until one hour before curtain time. Nevertheless, completely unaware of the problems that had harassed the production, the audience enjoyed the show immensely, and so did the Boston critics.

But the end of misfortune was still not yet.in sight. *Fifty Million Frenchmen* opened in New York at the height of the stock-market crash. This—and the tepid reaction of the critics—seemed to forebode inevitable doom for the show. To help stimulate sadly needed business, Irving Berlin paid for a full-page newspaper ad on December 19 calling it "the best musical comedy I have seen in years. More laughs than I have heard in a long time. One of the best collection of song numbers I have listened to. It's worth the price of admission to hear Cole Porter's lyrics." This may have helped. Certainly word-of-mouth enthusiasm did. The show lasted 254 performances, which in those days represented a neat profit.

Florenz Ziegfeld, who was a far better judge of female beauty than of music, confided to the producer of *Fifty Million Frenchmen* that it did not have one "singable melody." How wrong he was is proved by the fact that at least two numbers have become standards: "You've Got That Thing," and "You Do Something to Me," both breezily sung by Peter Forbes. Here the identity of Cole Porter as a composer with few rivals for sophistication and freshness of lyricism is fully established; so is his unique gift to fashion a virtuoso lyric. Sparkling words wedded to suave music are also found in "Find Me a Primitive Man," introduced by Evelyn Hoey, playing the part of Mary de Vere. "I Worship You" revealed Porter's ability to treat the mythology of the Greeks, Phoenicians, and Egyptians in a light and breezy manner, and a similar lightness of touch and gaiety was found in "The Tale of an Oyster." "When it comes to lyrics," said George Jean Nathan, "this Cole Porter is so far ahead of the other boys in New York that there just is no race at all." And to Robert Littell, "Find Me a Primitive Man" was "one of the best pieces of popular music I have ever heard."

William Gaxton and Helen Broderick were both called upon to re-create their roles in the motion-picture version of the musical, supported by Olsen and Johnson. This was a Warner Brothers production released in 1931. Six songs were used from the stage show, with an interpolation of George M. Cohan's "You Remind Me of My Mother."

FINE AND DANDY (1930), *a musical comedy, with book by Donald Ogden Stewart. Lyrics by Paul James. Music by Kay Swift. Presented by Morris Green and Lewis E. Gensler at the Erlanger Theater on September 23. Directed by Dave Gould, Morris Green, Frank McCoy, and Tom Nip. Cast included Joe Cook, Alice Boulden, and Nell O'Day (255 performances).*

As in his earlier musical-comedy hit, *Rain or Shine,* Joe Cook monopolized *Fine and Dandy* and single-handedly made it "not just a good show," in the words of John Mason Brown, "but a grand and glorious one." As Joe

Squibb, the benevolent general manager of Fordyce Drop Forge and Tool Factory, he flirts with the widow who owns the establishment, is engaged to lovely Nancy Ellis (Alice Boulden), and ultimately reveals himself to be married and the father of four children. Also as Joe Squibb he lights a bearded man's whiskers, impersonates four German acrobats, plays the saxophone and ukulele, turns handsprings, plays golf with a shovel, eats lunch from a lunchbox the size of an automobile crate, examines the insurance doctor come to examine him, creates a gadget than can puncture balloons while cracking nuts and another for inflating paper bags so than when punctured they can make a resounding noise. In many of these antics he has an able stooge in Dave Chasen—the same Dave Chasen who later established a famous restaurant in Beverly Hills.

An adagio dance by Nell O'Day nightly received an ovation, while Eleanor Powell's tap dancing also regularly met with public acclaim. The most popular song from the score was the title number, a duet by Joe and Nancy. Nancy also presented a second fine song in "Can This Be Love?"

FINIAN'S RAINBOW (1947), *a musical play, with book by E. Y. Harburg and Fred Saidy. Lyrics by E. Y. Harburg. Music by Burton Lane. Presented by Lee Sabinson and William R. Katzell at the 46th Street Theater on January 10. Directed by Bretaigne Windust. Choreography by Michael Kidd. Cast included Ella Logan, David Wayne, and Donald Richards (725 performances).*

This delightful fantasy about a crock of gold, an Irishman and his young daughter, and a leprechaun is neatly combined with social-conscious conflicts in America involving sharecroppers, labor exploitation, race prejudice, the poll tax, right-wing reaction, and the greed for gold that lurks in most men's hearts. It was not an easy feat to accomplish—this marriage of an Irish-like fantasy with stern American political and social realities. Somehow, E. Y. Harburg and Fred Saidy made the whole thing jell into a thoroughly unified concept combining sentiment with satire, tenderness and compassion and humanity with pointed social criticism. It received the Donaldson Award as the best musical of the season.

The setting is the mythical town of Rainbow Valley in the Southern American state of Missitucky. To this place come Finian McLonergan (Albert Sharpe) and his daughter, Sharon (Ella Logan), fresh from Ireland, for which Sharon expresses her nostalgia so poignantly in the ballad "How Are Things in Glocca Morra?" Finian has come to Rainbow Valley with a specific (and to him highly practical) plan in mind. Having stolen a crock of gold from the leprechauns, he wants to bury it in these lands because he is convinced this soil is fertile for growing gold, since the United States has buried its own gold here in nearby Fort Knox. To achieve this aim, Finian purchases a parcel of land from local sharecroppers, one of whom is Woody Mahoney (Donald Richards), who is in constant danger of losing his property because he cannot pay his mortgage. Nevertheless, he has high hopes for the future, for he has invested in an experiment conducted with primitive equipment by Howard, a Negro, to produce home-grown mentholated tobacco. When Billboard Rawkins, a Negro-hating senator, discovers from geologists that there is gold in this land (the gold being nothing other than Finian's crock, of course), he is determined to defraud the people of Missitucky—most of whom are Negroes—of their land. Woody's property is saved when Finian provides him with the necessary funds to pay his mortgage, but the land of the Negroes is in serious danger of confiscation.

Finian's crock has more than gold. It has magic powers to fulfill three wishes. One of these is used up to transform the senator into a Negro evangelist, so that he, too, might discover what it means to be a Negro in America's South. Og, a leprechaun (David Wayne)—mission-bound to retrieve the crock—falls in love with Woody's sister, Susan (Anita Alvarez), a deaf-mute who can speak to people only through dancing. The crock performs its second magic at Og's request. It restores to Susan the power of hearing and speech. The third wish demanded from the crock is for Susan's happiness with Woody, the young man she has come to love. Howard is finally successful in creating home-grown mentholated tobacco—ensuring jobs for all, and wealth to some. The sharecroppers and the Negroes, now safe on their land, voice their gratitude—and their optimism for the future—in the rousing "That Great-Come-and-Get-It Day." Meanwhile our leprechaun, Og, has learned the joys of being human, the best of which is the pleasure of female company. He is finally transformed into a human and thus can woo—and win—Susan. The crock of gold is now worthless. Finian leaves Rainbow Valley, leaving his daughter behind with Woody.

E. Y. Harburg confesses that he first thought of the idea for this unusual text because he could never understand how the gold standard works and why it was necessary for the United States government to keep a stockpile of gold in Fort Knox. He discussed the question one day with his collaborator, Fred Saidy (with whom he had then just written *Bloomer Girl*), only to learn that Saidy was as much puzzled by the problem as was Harburg. "Gold made us think of a pot of gold," Harburg recalls. "The pot of gold reminded us of leprechauns, those mythical shoemakers who repaired only left shoes, and their legendary crock of gold, which was good for three wishes. Then it occurred to us that it would be funny if an ambitious but naïve Irishman imitated America's way to get rich by taking the leprechaun's crock of gold and burying it near Fort Knox under the logical (for him) assumption that it (like the country) would grow. The three wishes gave us our conflict and a chance to kid both the credit system and the social system. It's credit that makes people wealthy, you know. The only question is, who gets the credit?" Thus came about the idea of combining fantasy with reality, romance with social and political satire. In their research, Harburg and Saidy read Gaelic fairy tales and poetry until they, too, almost came to believe in creatures like leprechauns and mythical places like Glocca Morra.

Burton Lane's remarkable score (the best of his career, and one of the best for the Broadway stage in the 1940's) and E. Y. Harburg's extraordinary lyrics were principal assets to this musical play. Beyond "How Are Things in Glocca Morra?"—to become one of the year's hit songs—romance was emphasized in ballads "Look to the Rainbow" (delightfully flavored with Ella Logan's piquant Irish brogue) and the duet of Sharon and Woody, "Old Devil Moon." The social problems were accented in songs like "When the Idle Poor Become the Idle Rich." Two choral numbers ("The Begat" and "Necessity") and Og's charming and amusing revelations of the appeal females have for him in "When I'm Not Near the Girl I Love" and "Something Sort of Grandish" provided further evidence of the rare gifts of composer and lyricist in their respective departments.

It took twenty years to bring *Finian's Rainbow* to the screen. Warner Brothers-Seven Arts did it in 1968, with Fred Astaire, Petula Clark, and Tommy Steele—in a production somewhat a bit too grandiose in staging, and never quite sure whether it wanted to be a romantic tale or a political and social satire.

FIORELLO! (1959), *a musical comedy, with book by Jerome Weidman and George Abbott. Lyrics by Sheldon Harnick. Music by Jerry Bock. Presented by Robert Griffith and Harold Prince at the Broadhurst Theater on November 23. Directed by George Abbott. Dances by Peter Gennaro. Cast included Tom Bosley, Ellen Hanley, and Howard da Silva (795 performances).*

Fiorello, or "Little Flower," is the short, dumpy, gruff-voiced, dynamic, colorful, provocative, and thoroughly honest politician—Fiorello La Guardia —who was elected mayor of New York City on a fusion ticket. This musical is his biography. It is also a portrait of an era and a city. It did both so well in text and song that it received the Pulitzer Prize, the Drama Critics Award, and a handful of Antoinette Perry and Donaldson awards (including those for the season's best musical), besides being a highly profitable venture at the box office.

In the prologue we see Mayor La Guardia (Tom Bosley) reading the comics to the children into a microphone of the city radio station. The newspapers are on strike. The mayor does not want to deprive the children of their favorite comics. (This episode, which is biographically true, at once provides an insight into an unconventional politician.)

In the first act, Fiorello La Guardia is practicing law in a humble office in Greenwich Village. His clients are the poor and the oppressed—anybody, laments his law clerk, Neil (Bob Hilday), except those capable of paying their bills. Fiorello finds the time to interview all these people, whom he promises to help. He also announces to his staff his intention of trying to get the nomination for Congress with the approval of Ben Marino (Howard da Silva), Republican leader of the 14th congressional district. Marie, Fiorello's secretary (Patricia Wilson), is taken aback at this announcement, since she knows that no Republican has ever been elected to Congress in this district. Nevertheless, she and her boss come to the political clubroom, the hangout of Ben and his cronies, who are in the middle of a poker game. While playing, they sing "Politics and Poker," pointing out the many ways in which the two are similar. Their game is temporarily interrupted by Fiorello's arrival and his request to run on the Republican ticket. Since the election of a Republican is an impossibility, Ben is quite willing to go along with Fiorello's request. Fiorello now joins the workers of Nifty Shirtwaists, who are on strike, and convinces them to desert their picket lines and join him at his headquarters to discuss tactics. There he gives a rousing lecture on the deplorable social conditions in the city among the working people— the horror of the sweat shops; the tyranny of ruthless employers; the long hours and little pay of working people. He promises to be on their side all the way, to raise bail for them if they get arrested, and to take their cases to court without asking any fees. One of the working girls appeals to him personally: Thea (Ellen Hanley), with whom he makes a dinner date.

Running for office, Fiorello is pursuing a vigorous campaign by going to the different ethnic groups in the city and speaking to them in their own language. He succeeds in creating an upset, becoming the first Republican this district has ever sent to Washington. While serving in Congress, Fiorello becomes a vigorous proponent of the draft act, this now being the time of World War I. The draft, to him, is the only way to build an army in a democracy. Fiorello's political bosses, headed by Ben, try to make him change his mind, insisting the draft act is unpopular with the people and would lose a good many votes for the party. But Fiorello insists he is interested only in what is good for America. Once the draft act becomes law, Fiorello enlists in the Army. A farewell party is given him at Ben's clubroom, where the guests dance to the strains of a sentimental waltz, " 'Til Tomorrow."

In a series of staged and motion-picture montages, Fiorello's career in the war is rapidly reviewed. Ten years then go by. Fiorello is married to Thea, who is ill. He is still very much the political reformer, and he is running for mayor against James J. Walker in his effort to clean up the city of its grafters and political opportunists. His opponents contrive to get rid of him by having him killed. A false fire alarm is used to distract the people in the street while Fiorello is giving a speech, while from a rooftop some huge rocks are dumped on him. By a miracle, Fiorello is not hurt. But a different kind of disaster has just struck him: Neil comes with the news that Thea has just died suddenly.

Though Fiorello has lost the election, he does not become disillusioned, nor does he desert his efforts to gain reform for the city. He becomes a prime mover in having Tammany Hall investigated by Judge Seabury and his committee. To Ben, and the other political bosses, this is cause for joy, a way to loosen once and for all the stranglehold that Tammany Hall has had on New York City for so many years. In their clubroom, Ben and his political friends perform a hilarious travesty on the Seabury investigation in the satiric song "Little Tin Box," in which Ben impersonates the various witnesses.

But Fiorello finally does win the mayor's office on a fusion ticket. And he is true to his ideals by destroying political chicanery and graft wherever he finds them. One ambition realized, he fulfills a second one, that of achieving personal happiness by marrying his secretary, Marie, who had been secretly in love with him for many years.

The most successful songs were the three mentioned in the above summary: the ballad, " 'Til Tomorrow," introduced by Thea and the chorus; and the two satirical pieces on petty politics and graft, presented by Ben and his cronies, "Politics and Poker" and "Little Tin Box." "When Did I Fall in Love?", Thea's ballad, also deserves attention.

THE FIREFLY (1912), *an operetta, with book and lyrics by Otto Hauerbach (Harbach). Music by Rudolf Friml. Presented by Arthur Hammerstein at the Lyric Theater on December 2. Directed by Fred G. Latham. Cast included Emma Trentini, Roy Atwell, and Audrey Maple (120 performances).*

*The Firefly* was not only Friml's first successful operetta. It was his first operetta—indeed, the first score he ever wrote for the stage. Before this, he had written concert music, including a piano concerto, and some songs which were published. Chance brought him into the theater as composer. Victor Herbert had planned writing the music for *The Firefly* for Emma Trentini, the sensational singing star of his then recently produced operetta *Naughty Marietta*. Herbert and Mme. Trentini, however, became involved in a bitter feud—a clash of personalities intensified by Mme. Trentini's bulging ego and vanity. At a gala presentation of *Naughty Marietta* which Herbert conducted, he gave Mme. Trentini the signal to repeat the chorus of a number that had just inspired an ovation. Mme. Trentini ignored the signal and went on with her performance without repeating the song. Backstage, Herbert's Irish temper exploded. He vowed that never again would he write an operetta for Mme. Trentini, even though he had been contracted to do so for the coming season. Consequently, he bowed out of *The Firefly,* the show he had been signed up to write. A new composer had to be found quickly, what with an early production of *The Firefly* scheduled. On the advice of two publishers, Rudolph Schirmer and Max Dreyfus, the completely inexperienced and unknown Friml was picked to do the job—both publishers feeling that there were ample indications in Friml's art songs proving he was capable of writing beautiful melodies for operettas. That they had not been mistaken was proved with the score Friml handed in—one of the best written in the second decade of the 1900's in New York.

In *The Firefly,* Mme. Trentini appears as Nina, a little Italian street singer in whom Jack Travers (Roy Atwell) is interested. When Jack is invited as Mrs. Vandare's guest on a yachting trip to Bermuda, Nina disguises herself as a boy and, calling herself Tony, gets a job on the ship. She becomes such a favorite that Mrs. Vandare decides to give her permanent employment. Complications enter when Tony is accused of being a notorious pickpocket sought by the police. She is cleared and is adopted by Jack's valet, Pietro. Two years later Mrs. Vandare gives a garden party during which a famous prima donna performs. She is none other than Nina. Jack now realizes he is in love with her and loses no time in winning her. Friml's score was the work of a highly skilled hand, as H. T. Parker, the noted critic of the Boston *Transcript* took pains to point out by saying: "Mr. Friml writes for an orchestra like a musician, setting it to warm, songful, rhythmic and well-colored accompaniments and not like a Broadway jingler picking out his 'toons' with one finger on the piano and leaving the rest to an assistant and the drum sticks." It overflowed with wonderful melodies, the most important, of course, being those assigned to Emma Trentini. Her large voice and warmth of delivery were important factors in making her songs the successes they became. These were "Giannina Mia," "Love Is Like a Firefly," "The Dawn of Love," and "When a Maid Comes Knocking at Your Heart." Another fine number is "Sympathy," introduced by Audrey Maple and Melville Stewart.

*The Firefly* became a motion picture (MGM, 1937), starring Jeanette MacDonald and Allan Jones. Besides using the basic stage score, it had an enormous new hit song of its own, "The Donkey Serenade." The melody came from one of Friml's piano pieces, *Chanson,* which the composer had written in his early manhood. In 1923 the melody became a song called "Chansonette," words by Sigmund Spaeth, which was revised by Bob Wright and George "Chet" Forrest into "The Donkey Serenade" for the movie of *The Firefly.* Since then, there have been few stage revivals of *The Firefly* that have not included "The Donkey Serenade."

FIVE O'CLOCK GIRL (1927), *a musical comedy, with book by Guy Bolton and Fred Thompson. Music by Harry Ruby. Lyrics by Bert Kalmar. Presented by Philip Goodman at the 44th Street Theatre on October 10. Directed by Philip Goodman. Dances by Jack Haskell. Cast included Mary Eaton, Oscar Shaw, Pert Kelton, and Al Shaw and Sam Lee (280 performances).*

The program described this musical as "a fairy tale in modern clothes." The heroine is Patricia Brown (Mary Eaton), who works in a humble cleaning establishment. Each day at teatime she indulges a whim to telephone wealthy Gerald Brooks (Oscar Shaw) and engage him in conversation. Eventually she meets him in person and tries to convince him that she is really a society girl. He, of course, uncovers her true identity and finds that love has made him indifferent to her lowly station. To round out the story, his valet, Hudgins (Louis John Bartels), falls in love with one of Patricia's co-workers at the cleaning establishment—Susan Snow (Pert Kelton).

The comedy of Hudgins and that of the vaudeville team of Al Shaw and Sam Lee (making their Broadway stage debut) and the dancing of Danny Dare were the brightest ornaments of the production, together with the winning performances of Mary Eaton and Oscar Shaw in the lead parts. The two most important songs were "Thinking of You," a duet by Patricia and Gerald, and "Up in the Clouds." Of secondary interest were "Who Did?" and "Happy Go Lucky."

FLOWER DRUM SONG (1958), *a musical comedy, with book by Oscar Hammerstein II and Joseph Fields, based on a novel by C. Y. Lee. Lyrics by Hammerstein. Music by Richard Rodgers. Presented by Rodgers and Hammerstein in association with Joseph Fields at the St. James Theater on December 1. Directed by Gene Kelly. Choreography by Carol Haney. Cast included Pat Suzuki, Miyoshi Umeki, Larry Blyden, Juanita Hall, and Keye Luke (600 performances).*

In *Flower Drum Song* Rodgers and Hammerstein consciously revert to musical-comedy traditions and formats rather than explore further the world of the musical play which they had previously so enriched with *Oklahoma!,*

*Carousel,* and *South Pacific.* And so, we encounter in *Flower Drum Song* routines hardly to be expected in a Rodgers and Hammerstein musical, such as a strip-tease in a nightclub, and a buck-and-wing dance following a number typical of musical comedies, "Don't Marry Me" (ingratiatingly presented by Larry Blyden), together with one or two other songs of musical-comedy identity, such as "I Enjoy Being a Girl" (the hit song of the production, enchantingly sung by Pat Suzuki, in her Broadway debut) and "Sunday," a duet by Larry Blyden and Pat Suzuki.

The setting is San Francisco's Chinatown in the present time. The main theme involves the generation gap between the Old World Chinese still faithful to their ancient ways and rituals, and the New World Chinese who want to assimilate themselves completely into American life and have discarded their ancestral heritage for American ways.

Sammy Fong (Larry Blyden), an Americanized Chinese, is trying to arrange a match between Wang Ta (Ed Kenney) and Mei Li, an adorable girl from the East (Miyoshi Umeki). When Wang Ta's father sees her, and hears her sing a Chinese-type song, "A Hundred Million Miracles," he approves of her wholeheartedly and is more than ready to sign a marriage contract for his son. But the girl's father is determined to have his daughter stick to a former contractual agreement for her to marry none other than Larry himself. Wang Ta sighs with relief, for his heart is set on Linda Low (Pat Suzuki), the attractive, sexually appealing proprietress of the nightclub Thunderbird. He has a date with her there, where her coy femininity (which becomes obvious when she sings "I Enjoy Being a Girl") and her aggressiveness are a contrast to Wang Ta's shyness. Nevertheless, in spite of his diffidence, he manages to blurt out a marriage proposal. Linda is interested, for Wang's father is a rich man but she tells Wang that she must first get the permission of her brother, Frankie.

Although Wang Ta has not yet met Mei Li, preparations are going ahead in the Wang household for his forthcoming marriage to her. Their first meeting turns out better than might have been expected. Mei falls in love with him at first sight, while Wang—seeing her dressed up in a gorgeous gown—finds her thoroughly appealing.

That evening, during a party at Wang's house, Linda's brother, Frankie, informs Wang's father he has been giving the most serious consideration to having his sister marry young Wang. All this puts Sammy in a sorry predicament. If Wang does not marry Mei Li, then he, Sammy, must do so, as per their parental contract. Not only is Sammy not interested in Mei, but he, too, has his eye on Linda. In "Don't Marry Me" he tries to give Mei the reasons why it would be a mistake for her to consider him as a husband. But when this does not work, he evolves a scheme to make sure that Wang's father would disapprove of a union between his son and Linda. Sammy invites Wang's parents to the Thunderbird, where they are shocked to see Linda perform a strip-tease. The parents rush out of the club. Wang seeks refuge in the apartment of his friend, a seamstress, where he spends the night on the couch. Mei, having come to the seamstress to get Wang's jacket mended, jumps to the wrong conclusion upon noticing Wang's dinner jacket there. Horrified, she runs off without seeking an explanation. Had she waited, she would have learned from the seamstress that her relationship with Wang is a thoroughly innocent one. Love has never come her way, the seamstress laments in the tender ballad "Love, Look Away."

When Wang comes home he is ready to agree with his father that Mei and not Linda is the girl for him. But Mei, suspecting Wang of infidelity, refuses to consider marriage. This problem is brought to the Three Family Association for consultation and decision. Sammy bursts in on this meeting with the news that he is the one who is going to marry Linda, something of which the Association disapproves in light of the contract. In fact, plans are being hurriedly contrived for Sammy's marriage to Mei to take place. When Wang arrives to bring Mei a wedding gift, he cannot conceal where his real feelings lie—with Mei—but there is nothing he can do about it now. During a wedding procession down Grant Avenue, the bride, heavily veiled, is carried on a sedan to Sammy. When her veil is removed, the bride turns out to be Linda. Mei Li now announces that all earlier contracts and agreements entered into by the Family Association are null and void since she had entered the country illegally. Mei Li (now convinced of Wang's innocence) and Wang are now free to marry each other.

An amusing number, "The Other Generation," points up the generation gap—sung first by the older folk, then by the younger ones. Songs like "A Hundred Million Miracles," "Grant Street," and "Chop Suey" have an Oriental character in line with the setting and characters of the musical and offer a piquant contrast to the main numbers, listed in the above summation, which are thoroughly Broadway.

"Under Gene Kelly's stage direction," wrote Brooks Atkinson, "*Flower Drum Song* in general is up to the standards of a Rodgers and Hammerstein show. Everything is done with ease, taste and pride in the theater." To Frank Aston, the show was "sumptuous, tuneful, and a dance fan's dream. . . . It was as if some genius of an engineer had arranged a tried-and-true assembly line and was showing right before our very eyes, exactly how a perfect show is built. The parts fit together precisely, shiningly elegant, guaranteed to give satisfaction, resoundingly true to the mechanical ideal. . . . There was true heart to the proceedings."

The motion-picture adaptation (Universal, 1961) starred Nancy Kwan and Miyoshi Umeki and retained all of the principal musical numbers.

FLYING COLORS (1932), *a revue, with book and lyrics by Howard Dietz. Music by Arthur Schwartz. Presented by Max Gordon at the Imperial Theater on September 15. Directed by Howard Dietz. Dances by Albertina Rasch. Cast included Clifton Webb, Charles Butterworth, Tamara Geva, and Patsy Kelly (188 performances).*

Having had such a resounding winner with the revue *The Band Wagon* in 1931, Max Gordon, the producer, decided to try to create another *The Band Wagon* with Howard Dietz and Arthur Schwartz once again providing the songs. Again and again, in *Flying Colors,* this studied attempt to imitate *The Band Wagon* was evident. A sultry song shared by Tamara Geva and Clifton Webb, "Alone Together," was a faint carbon copy of "Dancing in the Dark" from the earlier show; "Meine kleine Akrobat" was supposed to be another "I Love Louisa." And the first-act finale was an effort to simulate the stunning Bavarian carrousel scene that closed the first act of *The Band Wagon:* a trick effect simulating a night ride, with Clifton Webb, Tamara Geva, and the ensemble singing and dancing to "Louisiana Hayride."

But *Flying Colors* was no *The Band Wagon.* Nevertheless, it had a good many attractive features: the comedy of Charles Butterworth and Patsy Kelly, the former in a wry, frozen-faced lecture, "Harvey Woofter Five Point Plan," and the latter in a sketch, "Bon Voyage," in which she turns on the horde of relatives come to bid her farewell but become pretty much of a nuisance. And there were three solid musical numbers. "Alone Together" and "Louisiana Hayride" have already been mentioned. A third was "A Shine on Your Shoes," sung by Vilma and Buddy Ebsen, after which they did a neat tap dance with Monette Moore around a shoeshine stand.

When the show was in rehearsal it was victimized by so many problems, quarrels, and obstacles that Max Gordon suffered a nervous breakdown and had to be hospitalized. Agnes de Mille had been hired to do the choreography —her first such attempt for the popular musical theater. She was at a total loss in handling the dancers or adhering to rehearsal schedules; in addition, she was in a continual fight with Norman Bel Geddes, who designed the sets, insisting that they were not safe for her dancers, while he hotly maintained that her dances had to be planned to fit his sets. Eventually, Agnes de Mille threw up her hands in surrender, quit the show, and was replaced by Albertina

Rasch. The rehearsals of the songs and sketches were going so badly that both Dietz and Schwartz were in a perpetual outburst of temper. The whole show seemed to fall apart by the time the dress rehearsal was scheduled in Philadelphia. And as if all this were not enough to try the tempers of all concerned, there was the problem of the plunging economy in 1932 to keep audiences away from even a good show. Nevertheless, when *Flying Colors* opened in New York, the whole thing jelled, the critics found things to praise— particularly in the performances of the stars—and enough customers were found to enable the show to remain on the boards for almost two hundred performances and bring in a modest profit.

FLYING HIGH (1930), *a musical comedy, with book by Buddy de Sylva and Jack McGowan. Lyrics by De Sylva and Lew Brown. Music by Ray Henderson. Presented by George White at the Apollo Theater on March 3. Directed by Edward Clark Lilley. Dances by Bobby Connolly. Cast included Oscar Shaw, Bert Lahr, Grace Brinkley, and Kate Smith (357 performances).*

This was the last of the De Sylva, Brown, and Henderson musicals for Broadway. It proved to be the biggest musical-comedy hit of 1930—largely because of Bert Lahr's inimitable clowning. The principal male characters are mail-plane pilots. The hero, Tod Addison (Oscar Shaw), engages in a transcontinental race, which he wins from a hated rival; at the same time, he captures the hand and heart of Eileen Cassidy (Grace Brinkley), whom he first met when his plane landed on the roof of her New York apartment house, and she is found pining away for the need of love in the song "I'll Know Him." Rusty Krause (Bert Lahr) is a comic pilot who steals the plane of Tod's rival. Not knowing how to get it down on the ground again, Rusty breaks an all-time record for keeping a plane in the air, and himself becomes something of a hero.

Except for a digression from the tradition that the chorus girls appear in the opening of the show (they were not on the stage until the third scene), *Flying High* was typical musical-comedy material—especially in the songs. Kate Smith, who had made her Broadway stage debut in *Honeymoon Lane* in 1926—but whose formidable reputation as an interpreter of songs was still some years off—was heard in "Red Hot Chicago," a tribute to the home of jazz. She also gave a reprise of a ballad, "Without Love," which was first sung by Eileen. (Her role was Pansy Sparks, Rusty's girl friend.) "Thank Your Father" (introduced by Eileen and Tod) was a love song by innuendo: each thanks the other's parents for meeting up with one another; otherwise each would have nobody to love. In "Good for You, Bad for Me" (introduced by Pearl Osgood and Russ Brown, playing subsidiary roles), the lyricists coyly refer to one of their greatest song hits in one of the lines by maintaining "But some things in life are *not* free." In a more sentimental vein was "Wasn't It Beautiful?", sung by Eileen, supplemented by John Barker, in a minor part.

Lahr's best scene was in a doctor's office where he had come for a physical examination. He also had an effective comedy number in "Mrs. Krause's Blue-Eyed Baby Boy."

The complete score by De Sylva, Brown, and Henderson was dispensed with when *Flying High* became a movie, starring Bert Lahr, with Charlotte Greenwood (MGM, 1931). Instead, entirely new songs were used, the work of Jimmy McHugh and Dorothy Fields.

FOLLOW THE GIRLS (1944), *a musical comedy, with book by Guy Bolton and Eddie Davis. Additional dialogue by Fred Thompson. Lyrics by Dan Shapiro and Milton Pascal. Music by Phil Charig. Presented by Dave Wolper in association with Albert Borde at the Century Theater on April 8. Directed by Harry Delmar. Dances by Catherine Littlefield. Cast included Gertrude Niesen, Jackie Gleason, and Irina Baranova (882 performances).*

Long before 1944, Gertrude Niesen had proved she could sing a sultry song with extraordinary effect. In *Follow the Girls* she showed that she was not only a singer but an outstanding comedienne as well. She was cast as Bubbles La Marr, a strip-tease burlesque queen who has given up the stage to devote herself to her duties in Spotlight, a servicemen's canteen. Goofy Gale (Jackie Gleason) is madly in love with her. Since he has been rejected by the Army, he cannot gain access to the Spotlight. By stealing a uniform from a British sailor, he finally is able to get into the canteen, only to discover that he has a serious rival for Bubbles in a naval petty officer. At the canteen the dancer Anna Viskinova (Irina Baranova) performs a beautiful adagio dance for the boys, hoping thereby to catch the interest of a theatrical booking agent.

Gertrude Niesen was a sensation in a bawdy comedy song, "I Wanna Get Married." "Where Are You?"—a romantic ballad sung by Frank Parker—and "Today Will Be Yesterday's Tomorrow" were also winning to the ear. But none of the songs from this score really caught on.

Jackie Gleason as the fat, lovelorn Goofy supplied most of the comedy—and proved a winner in what thus far was his best comedy role in the theater, a preview of his later flowering comic gifts in television. Brooks Atkinson remarked prophetically: "Someday when he gets the words, he will be wonderful, instead of just very good."

FOLLOW THRU (1929), *a musical comedy, with book by Laurence Schwab and Buddy de Sylva. Lyrics by De Sylva and Lew Brown. Music by*

*Ray Henderson. Presented by Schwab and Mandel at the 46th Street Theater on January 9. Directed by Edgar MacGregor and Donald Oenslager. Dances by Bobby Connolly. Cast included Jack Haley, Zelma O'Neal, John Barker, and Eleanor Powell (403 performances).*

The program described *Follow Thru* as a "musical slice of country life." The plot revolved mainly around a golf match in a country club between Ruth Van Horn (Madeline Cameron) and Lora Moore (Irene Delroy). The latter, daughter of a golf pro, wins not only the match but also the love of the golf champ, Jerry Downs (John Barker).

Jack Haley appears as Jack Martin, the psychopathic son of a chain-store magnate, afraid of women but relentlessly pursued by Angie Howard (Zelma O'Neal). Martin and his friend, J. C. Effingham (John Sheehan), cavort about in the country club. One of their best comedy scenes is a burlesque of a golf game. ("The trouble with your game," Martin tells Effingham, "is that you stand too close to the ball—*after* you've hit it.") Another hilarious scene involved them in a ladies' shower room, which they had invaded disguised as plumbers.

For Eleanor Powell, *Follow Thru* represented her first Broadway success. From childhood on, she had appeared in vaudeville. And one year earlier, on January 29, 1928, she made her first Broadway appearance—in a minor part in *The Opportunists* at the Casino de Paris. *Follow Thru* provided her with an opportunity to win a Broadway audience with her singing, dancing, and personal charm—and she won it completely. Greater successes were around the corner, particularly in motion pictures during the early years of talking pictures.

Commenting on the cast as well as the authors, Gilbert Gabriel said: "They seem dedicated to the task of making youth flame and love shout out, with crisp, crazy, lusty, ankle-loosing, hip-seizing songs, and lyrics that give this whole razzing, jazzing society circus its cue to get gay. Wild-eyed, free-legged kids shouted catch lines across the footlights that fairly roped and yanked the audience onto the stage."

Zelma O'Neal, risen to stardom in *Good News* in 1927, had a big musical number in "I Want to Be Bad"; and with Jack Haley she sang the show's big number, "Button Up Your Overcoat." They also presented the duet "I Could Give Up Anything but You," while the principal love song, "My Lucky Star," was assigned to John Barker.

THE FORTUNE TELLER (1898), *an operetta, with book and lyrics by Harry B. Smith. Music by Victor Herbert. Presented by Fred J. Perley and the Alice Nielsen Opera Company at Wallack's Theater on September 26.*

*Directed by Julian Mitchell. Cast included Alice Nielsen, Eugene Cowles, Frank Rushworth, Joseph Cawthorn, and Joseph Herbert (40 performances).*

*The Fortune Teller* was Victor Herbert's first operetta to become a classic. He had written two moderately successful operettas before this—*The Wizard of the Nile* (1895) and *The Serenade* (1897)—and each had proved that, when he was in his element, he could produce ingratiating operetta tunes, equal to those of any composer of his time. But in *The Fortune Teller,* Herbert's best and most famous melodies are not only outstanding but also prove the composer's unusual ability to adapt his style and idiom to suit the personality of any text he was setting. For here an Irish-born composer, trained in Germany, and receiving his first experiences as a composer for the popular stage in America, had produced music most of which was in a thoroughly Hungarian-gypsy mood. The gypsy songs sound thoroughly authentic, as if fashioned by a Hungarian hand, besides revealing a mastery of technique not often encountered in operetta or musical-comedy music. As an unidentified critic of *The New York Times* said in his review: "He has written a score which is rich in all varieties of delightful operetta music. There are numbers grave and gay, light and serious, catchy in the most popular manner and musicianly in a thoroughly praiseworthy way. Mr. Herbert's command of national coloring is shown in the fine czardas air of the first act and in the serenade medley of the second. The hussar song and chorus and the brilliant march at the end of the second act show his skill in military music, while the finale of the first act is one of the most admirable pieces of writing ever heard in operettas."

Herbert and his librettist fashioned *The Fortune Teller* specifically for Alice Nielsen, a performer Herbert had discovered and had made into a star in *The Serenade.* With her special talent in mind, he and his librettist created a rich role for her—two roles, as a matter of fact, since she was required to play the dual part of Musette, a gypsy fortune teller, and Irma, a ballet student at the Budapest Opera.

The setting, obviously, is Hungary. Irma (who early reveals her naïveté and innocence in the song "Always Do As People Say You Should") is a ballet student without being aware that, in actuality, she is an heiress. When Count Berezowsky (Joseph Herbert), whose title is just about his only possession, discovers that Irma is rich, he is bent on marrying her to get her fortune. The Hungarian hussar, Captain Ladislas (Frank Rushworth), appears on the scene with his men, singing a rousing hussar chorus ("Hungary's Hussars"). He is the man Irma loves and wants to marry, but first she must get rid of the count. To do so, she decides to enlist the aid of Musette, who is her look-alike. Musette is a gypsy fortune teller. She and her gypsy comrades are heard in two piquant Hungarian-gypsy numbers: "Romany Life" and "Czardas." Once Musette has left her companions, she convinces Musette to assume her place when the count is around and make him think she is Irma. Musette and her gypsies visit the count at his estate, where the count is convinced she is Irma and pursues her relentlessly. In fact, he insists that their wedding take place without further delay. But the arrival of a gypsy musician named Sandor (Eugene Cowles) introduces complications. Sandor insists that the girl the count believes to be Irma is actually Musette, the one with whom Sandor is passionately in love, as he reveals in one of Herbert's unforgettable melodies, the serenade "Gypsy Love Song." When Irma steps into Musette's role, everybody becomes thoroughly confused. But before long the count's opportunistic designs on Irma are discovered. Each of the two girls can now reveal her true identity and claim the man she really loves.

Playing the double role of Irma and Musette with the most ingratiating charm, Alice Nielsen completely captured the hearts of her audiences. Said the critic of *The New York Times:* "She does it without any startling display of histrionic ability, yet with a genuinely fascinating manner and with some very pretty touches of stagecraft. She has the invaluable faculty of always looking pretty and always being refined, while she sings her music excellently with a small but pure and true voice."

FORTY-FIVE MINUTES FROM BROADWAY (1906), *a musical comedy, with book, lyrics, and music by George M. Cohan. Presented by Klaw and Erlanger at the New Amsterdam Theater on January 1. Directed by Cohan. Cast included Fay Templeton, Victor Moore, and Donald Brian (90 performances).*

This was Cohan's second full-length original musical comedy for Broadway, following his first success—*Little Johnny Jones*—by almost two years.

The setting is New Rochelle, a New York suburb "forty-five minutes from Broadway." A local miserly millionaire has died, and no will has been found. It had been assumed that his wealth would go to his housemaid, Mary Jane Jenkins (Fay Templeton), but due to the absence of a will the fortune passes to the dead man's only living relative, Tom Bennett (Donald Brian). Tom arrives in New Rochelle to claim his legacy, accompanied by his show-girl sweetheart, Flora Dora Dean (Lois Ewell), her nagging mother, Mrs. David Dean (Julia Ralph), and his secretary, Kid Burns, former loafer and horse player (Victor Moore). Because of Kid Burns's bad manners and outspoken behavior, Tom gets into a fight with his sweetheart and her mother at a party at the Castleon mansion. Meanwhile, Kid Burns falls in love with the housemaid, Mary Jane. In an old suit of clothes Kid Burns finds the dead man's will, in which the fortune goes to Mary Jane. When Kid Burns refuses to marry an heiress, Mary Jane destroys the document.

On the morning of the premier of *Forty-five Minutes from Broadway,* the New Rochelle Chamber of Commerce called an emergency session to pass several resolutions regarding this musical: (1) to institute a boycott; (2) to send out press releases denouncing the play as libelous to their community and its inhabitants. The Chamber of Commerce objected particularly to the title song, which said that the town did not have a single café and which spoke of the males as having "whiskers like hay." After the show opened, the commotion in New Rochelle died down as the town came to realize that the play was succeeding in making New Rochelle famous.

Most of the critics did not like Cohan's new musical. The editor of *Theatre* reflected the prevailing opinion when he called it "rubbish" and added, "Mr. Cohan had little art" and intended only "to catch the unthinking crowd." But like *Little Johnny Jones,* the new musical, despite a comparatively short Broadway run, was a triumph on its road tour and returned to Broadway on November 5, a success.

For Fay Templeton, the starring female role marked her first appearance in a so-called "clean play"—for twenty years before this she had been a burlesque star. She was a hit; and so was Victor Moore in the first of his many Broadway triumphs as a comedian, after many years in vaudeville and stock companies. (Cohan himself assumed the role of Kid Burns when he revived *Forty-five Minutes from Broadway* in 1912.)

The most famous songs, all still remembered, are the title number, sung by Kid Burns and a chorus; and two songs introduced by Tom Bennett, "Mary's a Grand Old Name" and "So Long, Mary."

FROM THE SECOND CITY (1961), *a revue, with scenes and dialogue written by the company. Music by William Mathieu. Presented by Max Lieb-man, Bernhard Sahlins, Howard Alk, and Paul Sills at the Royale Theater on September 26. Directed by Paul Sills. Cast comprised Howard Alk, Alan Arkin, Severn Darden, Andrew Duncan, Barbara Harris, Mina Kolb, Paul Sand, and Eugene Troubnik (87 performances).*

The "second city" is Chicago, the place from which a group of young adventurous performers arrived in New York to try reviving for the 1960's the wit, sophistication, humor, and freshness of materials that had characterized the best intimate revues of the 1920's and 1930's. For the most part, the Chicago visitors succeeded in capturing a good deal of the tongue-in-cheek attitudes of those little irreverent revues of the past. Their forte was wit and parody. But they also contributed something new of their own, a flair for whimsy, and a gift at group improvisation on subjects submitted by the audience.

The first edition, produced in New York in 1961, mocked silent films as compared to those produced by Ingmar Bergman; an interview in Louisiana as compared to one in West Germany; news broadcasts; and so forth. Perhaps the most significant contribution was a new star. She was Barbara Harris, heard singing "Museum Piece" and "I Got the Blues," who also participated in sketches such as "The First Affair," "Caesar's Wife," and "Football Comes to the University of California." It was in this production that Richard Rodgers saw her and signed her for a musical he was then planning, "I Picked a Daisy." (Eventually, the theme of "I Picked a Daisy" was used by Alan Jay Lerner for *On a Clear Day You Can See Forever,* but with music *not* by Rodgers but by Burton Lane, in which Barbara Harris fully proved she was star material.)

There were several more editions of this revue between 1961 and 1969. The one following *From the Second City* was called *Seacoast of Bohemia,* presented by Bernhard Sahlins, Howard Alk, and Paul Sills at the Square East Theater on January 10, 1962. This edition ran for 258 performances. Highlights included satires on the Kennedy-Khrushchev interview, on "Candid Camera," on interviews with celebrities in nightclubs. Two other sketches were also effective: "The Girls in Their Summer Dresses" and "Clothes Make the Man."

*Alarums and Excursions* was the title given to the next edition, at the Square East Theater on May 29, 1962. The Kennedy-Khrushchev interview was repeated, to which were added takeoffs on do-it-yourself playwriting, commercials, and technical assistants in Vietnam.

After that came *To the Water Tower,* at the Square East Theater on April 4, 1963, and *A View from the Bridge* (not to be confused with the play of the same name by Arthur Miller), at the same theater, on August 5, 1964.

When the revue returned to New York five years later, it once again assumed the title of *From the Second City.* Here the little company made sport of urban neuroses and of an inebriated blues singer in "Muddy Puddle"— the two high points of the production—as well as of President Nixon. "The material," reported Clive Barnes (and he might well have been speaking of the earlier editions as well as of the one in 1969), "is bright and generally witty. There are a lot of one-liners, some more pertinent than others, and one or two merely facetious. . . . Throughout the show the humor is more whimsical than biting, more concerned with human foibles than human folly."

FUNNY FACE (1927), *a musical comedy, with book by Paul Gerard Smith and Fred Thompson. Lyrics by Ira Gershwin. Music by George Gershwin. Presented by Aarons and Freedley at the Alvin Theater on November 22. Directed by Edgar MacGregor. Dances by Bobby Connolly. Cast included Fred and Adele Astaire, Victor Moore, and Allen Kearns (244 performances).*

Having arrived at a winning combination in *Lady, Be Good!* in 1924—namely, a musical comedy with score by George and Ira Gershwin, and with Fred and Adele Astaire as stars—the producers, Aarons and Freedley, decided to repeat the formula. The only trouble was that, having contracted the stars and the composer and lyricist, all that Aarons and Freedley had was a title, *Smarty*. No libretto, not even a plot.

Fred Thompson was recruited to write the text. What he submitted was so obviously poor that enlistments had to be called to put it into some usable form. Robert Benchley, the first to be recruited, would have nothing to do with the script. "Gosh," he remarked, "how can I criticize other people's show if I had anything to do with something like this?" Then Paul Gerard Smith was asked, and while his rewrite job represented no masterpiece, at least it was functional. Meanwhile, the cast had rehearsed the original unusable script and was appearing in it in Washington, D.C., tryouts at the same time that they were learning the new lines. Confusion reigned, and total collapse seemed inevitable. "We were on the road six weeks," Ira Gershwin reveals, "and everyone concerned with the show worked day and night, recasting, rewriting, rehearsing, recriminating—of rejoicing there was none." Victor Moore was hastily drafted to appear in the production to strengthen the comedy situations. This happened in Wilmington. A sudden improvement was immediately apparent. A large part was built especially for him as the blundering thug, Herbert, whose hobby was to take pictures of comets. Many of the numbers George and Ira Gershwin had prepared for the old text were replaced by new, strong ones (though a very fine song, "How Long Has This Been Going On?"—and one that later became highly successful—was one of the casualties). The last new number inserted was "The Babbitt and the Bromide." "It went on on a Thursday or Friday night in Wilmington," says Ira Gershwin. "The number was introduced at 10:50 and concluded with Fred and Adele doing their famous 'run around'—to show-stopping applause—and suddenly, with all the other changes, the show looked possible."

*Funny Face* opened a new theater—the Alvin, on 52nd Street, owned by Aarons and Freedley. The theater, as it turned out, had an auspicious beginning rather than a disaster. During its first week the show grossed $40,000 (it was bringing in only $6,000 a week in Wilmington), and with a run of almost two hundred and fifty performances it represented a profitable venture.

The plot remained a routine affair from beginning to end. Jimmy Reeve (Fred Astaire) is the guardian of Frankie (Adele Astaire). He insists upon keeping her pearls in a safe. Frankie gets her boy friend, Peter (Allen Kearns), to try to procure the pearls for her; at the same time the two comic thugs— Dugsie Gibbs (William Kent) and Herbert (Victor Moore)—are also hot on the trail of this treasure. Inevitably, Frankie gets both her man and the pearls.

The two thugs contributed to the play most of its comedy. In one scene, while on the job of trying to steal the pearls, they get drunk, with hilarious consequences; in another, Herbert is about to be shot by his crony, Dugsie, a development that he accepts with almost amazing stoicism.

But it was the songs that put *Funny Face* over—as remarkable a score as any to be found in the musical theater of the 1920's, and one of the best that the Gershwin brothers had produced up to this time—the musical delights of *Lady, Be Good!* in 1924 and *Oh, Kay!* in 1926 notwithstanding. The most important number was the love song " 'S Wonderful," a duet between Frankie and Peter; it has remained a Gershwin classic. Then there was the title number and "Let's Kiss and Make Up," both of them introduced by Jimmy and Frankie Reeves; "He Loves and She Loves," shared by Frankie Reeves and Peter; "My One and Only," sung by Gertrude MacDonald, appearing in a subsidiary role, and danced to by Fred Astaire; and, finally, "The Babbitt and the Bromide" (sung by Frankie), largely outstanding for some of the wittiest lyrics of Ira Gershwin's career, good enough to become the only song lyrics included in Louis Kronenberger's *An Anthology of Light Verse*.

Anybody who remembered the musical comedy would hardly have recognized it when *Funny Face* came to the screen in a Paramount production in 1957 that starred Fred Astaire and Audrey Hepburn. The highly dispensable text of the stage musical was totally discarded for a new story. Only a few of the songs from the stage version had been retained. "How Long Has This Been Going On?"—deleted when the production was trying out of town—was brought back; and several new numbers, not by the Gershwins, were interpolated.

FUNNY GIRL (1964), *a musical comedy, with book by Isobel Lennart, based on the life and career of Fanny Brice. Lyrics by Bob Merrill. Music by Jule Styne. Presented by Ray Stark in association with Seven Arts Productions at the Winter Garden on March 26. Directed by Garson Kanin and Jerome Robbins. Dances by Carol Haney. Cast included Barbra Streisand and Sydney Chaplin (1,348 performances).*

It took ten years for a musical comedy based on Fanny Brice to outgrow a germinal idea in the mind of Ray Stark, a producer who also happened to be Miss Brice's son-in-law, and to come to life in *Funny Girl*. This is almost as if a kindly fate were nursing the show until the right performer could come along to play Fanny. In any event, Ray Stark would be the first to admit that all that waiting had paid off fabulous dividends by bringing him Barbra Streisand. Now it is impossible to conceive of anybody else playing the part. Without abandoning her own puckish, whimsical, and at other times tormented identity—or changing an iota of her own phenomenal gift at song styling—Barbra Streisand *was* Fanny Brice: Fanny Brice, the greatest comedienne of her generation; Fanny Brice, who had broken the hearts of her audience with her rendition of "My Man"; Fanny Brice, who could pass from sentiment and tragedy to burlesque humor in a split second, without anybody able to detect just how the modulation took place; Fanny Brice, who mimicked infantile ways as "Baby Snooks." Barbra Streisand was all of these things. Her performance was a tour de force with few parallels in the American musical theater, and deservedly lifted her to the alpine heights of her profession, achieved by nobody else as far as financial rewards are concerned, and equaled by few in the matter of artistic achievement. "She goes as far as any performer can toward recalling the laughter and the joy of Fanny Brice," wrote Howard Taubman in *The New York Times*. "Miss Streisand, imagining herself in a radiant future in 'I'm the Greatest Star,' an appealingly quirky song, is not only Fanny Brice but all the young performers believing in their destinies. Fanny's personality and style are remarkably evoked by Miss Streisand."

Completely convinced of her talent when she was still in her teens—and refusing to be discouraged by the fact that, by existing motion-picture and Broadway standards, she was no glamour girl—Barbra Streisand accepted poverty, rejection, and often hunger and cold while biding her time. Sometimes she worked as a switchboard operator, and sometimes as a theater usher. Most of the time she kept going by borrowing a few dollars from or accepting the hospitality of friends. More than once she went without food, and many a night her own lodging was a couch in some office she had borrowed. But her confidence in herself was as unshakable as her will. Then, without ever having made a public appearance, she won a talent contest in Greenwich Village which led to an engagement in a local bar, and soon afterward an eleven-week assignment at a Greenwich Village nightclub that paid her $108 a week. On October 21, 1961, she appeared on the stage for the first time, in an Off Broadway production, *Another Evening with Harry Stones,* which closed after the second performance. But it had been on long enough to draw attention to her and bring her an engagement at the renowned Blue Angel nightclub, out of which many an unknown stepped to stardom. Producer David Merrick heard her there, and forthwith signed her to appear in the Broadway musical *I Can Get It for You Wholesale* in 1962. There she practically stole the whole show—not with her singing but with her comedy. Offers now came profusely: appearances on TV; a Columbia recording contract, with her first two albums becoming national best sellers. Her unusual delivery of familiar songs, and her poignant interpretation of new ones, made her a cult. She was invited by President John F. Kennedy to appear at the White House Correspondents Dinner in May of 1963. She was sought after for leading television programs. It did not take Ray Stark long to realize that here was the one to bring Fanny Brice's story to the stage.

*Funny Girl* had planned to open on February 13, 1964. But so many changes were continually being made—not only in the script but by the various collaborators in the different departments of the production—that the opening had to be delayed by over a month. In the interim the only sure thing about the production was Barbra Streisand as Fanny; of that there was never a question. And it was on the strength of Barbra Streisand that almost a million dollars in advance sales had accumulated by the time *Funny Girl* reached its premiere.

Barbra Streisand made no conscious effort whatsoever to be a carbon copy of Fanny Brice. She had never seen Fanny Brice perform in person. She now refused to listen to her recordings, to do any research about her personality, or to analyze Fanny's style from radio tapes and old movies. She would not even allow the inclusion of any song identified with Fanny Brice—though the use of "My Man" had seemed inevitable. She intended to perform Miss Brice as if the star were a fictional character. And yet, though the personality of Barbra Streisand shone through with a blinding light, her performance brought back vivid memories of Fanny in the way Miss Streisand looked, in her facial grimaces and manual gestures, in the Yiddish-type inflection with which some comic lines were delivered, and in the broad burlesque in which some funny scenes were played.

*Funny Girl* was only incidentally concerned with Fanny Brice's rise from total obscurity to stardom. Its principal theme was the romance and tragic marriage with the gangster Nick Arnstein, whom she loved so dearly, and to whom she remained so faithful and devoted even after he had been imprisoned.

The musical opens with Fanny Brice as a star of the *Ziegfeld Follies*. In her dressing room she is worried about her husband, Nick Arnstein, who is about to be released from prison. She wonders what their reunion will be like and what their future can be. And as she wonders, images of her past life come to the surface of her consciousness.

She is the unattractive but stagestruck teen-ager again, determined to make her way in the theater, something of which her mother (Kay Medford) disapproves. But Fanny cannot be discouraged. She auditions for Keeney's Music Hall and is turned down. But a vaudeville hoofer, Eddie Ryan (Danny Meehan), becomes her friend, and to him she confides her unshakable ambition to become an actress ("I'm the Greatest Star"). Eddie becomes her coach and prepares her for Keeney's Music Hall in a ragtime number, "Cornet Man," with which she brings down the house. Backstage, she is congratulated by the gambler Nick Arnstein (Sydney Chaplin), and is the recipient of a telegram from Florenz Ziegfeld offering her a part in the *Follies*. She is on her way. In the *Follies* she transforms a huge production number, "Bridal Finale," into a comedy routine that delights the audience. Once again, backstage, Nick Arnstein is there to offer his congratulations.

Fanny invites Nick to attend a block party on Henry Street that Fanny's mother is giving in her honor. It is there that, for the the first time, they began to realize that they are falling in love. But Nick has to leave for Kentucky to buy a horse farm, and Fanny must tour with the *Follies*. Thus they are separated for several months until their paths finally cross. At a private dining room, Fanny does her best to get Nick to seduce her—a scene in which Barbra Streisand is at her comic best. No longer able to accept separation from Nick, Fanny refuses to go on with her tour. She abandons the *Follies* to remain with Nick.

They get married, and make their home in Long Island, where they are tendered a surprise party by their many friends, and where, in "Sadie, Sadie," Fanny gives a hilarious account of what marriage is like. But what marriage really means to her is proved when she stands ready to turn over her savings for her husband to build a gambling casino in Florida. After a performance of the *Follies,* Nick comes to Fanny with the confession that the casino has collapsed and that they are broke. Fanny tries to assume a devil-may-care attitude, which only hurts Nick that much more. Determined to lift her husband out of his doldrums, Fanny secretly invests in a talent agency in which Nick is a partner. When Nick discovers Fanny's plans, he rejects them vigorously, and, in his desperation to make money, gets involved in a crooked deal. Nick is found guilty of embezzlement and is imprisoned. Fanny continues to star in the *Follies* but cannot forget her husband, betraying her heartbreak in one of her Ziegfeld numbers, "The Music That Makes Me Dance," intended as a substitute for and equivalent of Fanny Brice's performance of "My Man" in the *Follies*.

The reminiscences evaporate. The opening scene, in Fanny's dressing room, returns. Nick arrives; it does not take them long to realize that it is impossible to mend the broken threads of their lives. Sadly they take leave of each other—Fanny to find whatever solace she can in her career as a reigning star of the *Follies*.

Two of the numbers made unforgettable—and successful—through Barbra Streisand's rendition are "People" and "Don't Rain on My Parade." She sings the first at the block party, when she first realizes how much Nick has come to mean to her; the second is heard when she abandons the *Follies* tour for the sake of staying with Nick, her only chance, she feels, at happiness.

If *Funny Girl* was Barbra Streisand's show from beginning to end, this proved even more forcefully the case in the motion-picture adaptation, with which Miss Streisand made her screen debut. A huge and splendiferous production released by Columbia in 1968, and pairing Miss Streisand with Omar Sharif, the movie proved to be, in the opinion of Renata Adler in *The New York Times,* "an elaborate, painstaking launching pad" for Miss Streisand, whose "talent is very poignant and strong." Her performance won her the Academy Award, the coveted "Oscar." For the movie, Jule Styne and Bob Merrill produced four new songs, the strongest of which was the title number, sung by Miss Streisand. In addition—at long last—"My Man" was interpolated.

**A FUNNY THING HAPPENED ON THE WAY TO THE FORUM** (1962), *a musical comedy, with book by Burt Shevelove and Larry Gelbart, based on plays of Plautus. Lyrics and music by Stephen Sondheim. Presented by Harold Prince at the Alvin Theater on May 8. Directed by George Abbott. Dances by Jack Cole. Cast included Zero Mostel, Jack Gilford, David Burns, Raymond Walburn, and John Carradine* (964 *performances*).

Nobody really gets to the Forum in this musical, just as nobody here really intended to achieve a work of art, though the material was drawn from various plays by Plautus. The authors aimed to re-create good, old-fashioned burlesque—with its rough-and-tumble humor, bawdy innuendos, none too subtle gags, girls in transparent and revealing gowns—and place the whole paraphernalia in a Roman setting. Fun, the show proved to be; of merriment —though not of the innocent brand—there was aplenty. The whole thing was contrived to produce laughter for laughter's sake without too much concern where the plot was heading for or if it was going in a straight direction; nor with too much of an attempt to make logical the remarkable situations in which the characters become inextricably enmeshed. The parts add up to an earthy, noisy, riotous low comedy with lechers and courtesans all over the place, and line after line with authentic burlesque-house *double entendres* and innuendos. "Carry my bust with pride," one of the matrons orders her slave—though she is speaking about a piece of sculpture rather than of her anatomy. "Don't you lower your voice at me," exclaims a courtesan at a eunuch. And when Pseudolus is measured for size against a luscious courtesan, back to back, and find they fit each other perfectly, all he can think of to say is: "Yes, but how often will we find ourselves in this position?" Old man Senex sniffs the smell of a mare's sweat that had been sprinkled on him and thinks he himself exudes this peculiar odor. *A Funny Thing Happened on the Way to the Forum* is that kind of show. Since it pretends to be nothing but what it really is—burlesque in Roman dress—it turned out to be a very funny show indeed, and a very popular one.

The plot is not particularly significant and can be reduced to essentials. Pseudolus (Zero Mostel), a slave, wants his freedom from Hero (Brian Davies). In order to gain it he tries to get for Hero a dumb but beautiful courtesan, Philia (Preshy Marker), from a brothel. The only trouble is that the sturdy warrior Milos Gloriosus (Ronald Holgate) had bought her from Lycus (John Carradine), a dealer in courtesans. To complicate matters a bit more, Hero's father, Senex (David Burns), has desires of his own for Philia. To discourage the warrior, who comes storming for his girl, Pseudolus informs him that the courtesan is the carrier of a plague. In fact, she is dead; and Pseudolus arranges to get her buried, with Hysterium (Jack Gilford), dressed as a woman, acting out the part of a corpse. What follows is a typical Mack Sennett-like chase.

As Pseudolus, Zero Mostel "runs through his repertoire of grimaces, anguished sounds, mincing steps and perpetual alarm," as Norman Nadel wrote in the *World-Telegram and Sun*. And Jack Gilford is a strong second in projecting the obvious, broad, and frequently sexy humor. Humor is a strong point in Stephen Sondheim's score, particularly in "Everybody Ought to Have a Maid" (the philosophy of Senex, Pseudolus, Hysterium, and Lycus, which lies on the outer fringes of respectability); also "Lovely," which Pseudolus and Hysterium make into a travesty on the sentimental ballads of traditional musicals. (One critic even suspected that Stephen Sondheim went in for some gentle spoofing on himself in "Lovely," by making it a satire on "Tonight" from *West Side Story,* of which he was the lyricist.) In a more sober mood is Hero's ballad, "Love, I Hear."

*A Funny Thing Happened on the Way to the Forum* received the Antoinette Perry Award as the season's best musical.

The motion picture also proved to be an uninhibited Roman holiday. It was a United Artists release in 1966, bringing Zero Mostel and Jack Gilford back to their stage roles and coupling them with those irrefutable masters of comedy and burlesque, Phil Silvers as Lycus, and the pan-faced genius of the silent-motion-picture days, Buster Keaton, in a minor role.

THE GARRICK GAIETIES (1925), *a revue, with sketches and additional lyrics by Benjamin Kaye, Louis Sorin, Sam Jaffe, Newman Levy, and Morrie Ryskind, among others. Lyrics by Lorenz Hart. Music by Richard Rodgers, among others. Presented by the Theater Guild, sponsoring the Theater Guild Junior Players, at the Garrick Theater on May 17. Directed by Philip Loeb. Dances by Herbert Fields. Cast included Sterling Holloway, Romney Brent, June Cochrane, Betty Starbuck, Philip Loeb, Edith Meiser, and Hildegarde Halliday (211 performances).*

(1926), *a revue, with sketches and additional lyrics by Benjamin Kaye, Newman Levy, Herbert Fields, and Philip Loeb, among others. Lyrics by Lorenz Hart. Music by Richard Rodgers, among others. Presented by the Theater Guild at the Garrick Theater on May 10. Directed by Philip Loeb. Dances by Herbert Fields. Cast included Romney Brent, Hildegarde Halliday, Sterling Holloway, Philip Loeb, Edith Meiser, Betty Starbuck, and Lee Strasberg (174 performances).*

(1930), *a revue, with sketches by Newman Levy, Benjamin Kaye, Sterling Holloway, and others. Lyrics by Ira Gershwin, E. Y. Harburg, Johnny Mercer, and others. Music by Marc Blitzstein, Aaron Copland, Vernon Duke, Kaye Swift, and others. Presented by the Theater Guild at the Guild Theater on June 4. Directed by Philip Loeb. Cast included Albert Carroll, Imogene Coca, Ray Heatherton, Sterling Holloway, Hildegarde Halliday, Philip Loeb, and Edith Meiser (158 performances).*

In the fall of 1924, a group of youngsters associated with the Theater Guild met from time to time to discuss the possibilities of putting on a smart, intimate revue, placing emphasis on satire and parody. These youngsters were supplemented by Benjamin Kaye, a lawyer and a friend of the Rodgers family, who liked writing satirical sketches and lyrics. When their planning became serious—and it first became serious when they decided to use such a production to finance two tapestries for a new theater then being built by the Theater Guild as a permanent home—Kaye brought Rodgers and Hart into the picture.

The revue, called *The Garrick Gaieties,* was informal and intimate, gay and sophisticated, spirited and youthful. As the second number pointed out ("Gilding the Guild," by Rodgers and Hart), what was here being offered was a "mild dish" of things "quaintly childish," or even "Oscar Wildish"— in songs and dance and pantomime. The revue included parodies of current plays: *Fata Morgana,* with Sterling Holloway doing a devastating takeoff on Miss Emily Stevens; Sidney Howard's *They Knew What They Wanted,* re-titled *They Didn't Know What They Were Getting;* Molnár's *The Guards-man,* with Romney Brent impersonating Alfred Lunt, Edith Meiser as Lynn Fontanne, and Philip Loeb as Dudley Digges. Hildegarde Halliday mimicked the celebrated diseuse Ruth Draper in a solo sketch. Eleanor Shaler performed an ingenious scarf dance. Romney Brent, Sterling Holloway, and Philip Loeb made a mockery of the Three Musketeers. There were hilarious episodes about the police force and about manners in the subway. There was a thoroughly delightful number with lyrics by Benjamin Kaye and music by Mana-Zucca that was sung by Harold W. Conklin and given an imaginative staging by Edith Meiser: "Butcher, Baker, Candle-Stick Maker." There were serious numbers, too, such as an American jazz opera, *The Joy Spreader* (libretto by Hart), but this was seen only during the first two performances; and an exoctic musical production number, *Rancho Mexicano,* with music by Tatanacho and settings by Miguel Covarrubias.

The Rodgers and Hart songs (of which there were seven) were just as bright and fresh as the wit and satire of the sketches and parodies. Two became hits: "Manhattan" (still popular), introduced by June Cochrane and Sterling Holloway, and "Sentimental Me" (added to the revue later in June), sung by Miss Cochrane, Holloway, James Norris, and Edith Meiser.

The critics raved. To Alexander Woollcott it was "bright with the brightness of something new minted"; to Robert Garland it was the "most civilized show in town"; Gilbert Gabriel described it as a "witty, boisterous, athletic chowchow." The songs of Rodgers and Hart also gathered praise. "They clicked," reported *Variety,* "like a colonel's heels at attention."

The original plan had been to give only two presentations—matinee and evening of Sunday, May 17. But the praises of the critics and the delight of the audience called for a longer run. Four more performances were scheduled in June (all matinees), all of them sellouts. Finally it was put on a regular run, beginning with June 8, and it remained in town twenty-five weeks. *The Garrick Gaieties* not only carried Rodgers and Hart to their first success—a not inconsiderable achievement when we contemplate their sub-sequent work—but it also made popular the intimate, smart, economically devised revue, a genre that flourished in the Broadway theater for the next decade or so.

The second edition, a year later, once again brought joy and gaiety to the stage. This edition started right off with parodies of six Theater Guild plays, including two by Bernard Shaw (*Arms and the Man* and *Androcles and the Lion*). Eleanor Shaler gave her version of Nijinsky doing Debussy's

*Afternoon of a Faun* in *"L'Après midi d'un papillon."* There was a tennis sketch which changed the sexes around by having Romney Brent appear as Helen Wills, Edith Meiser as William Tilden, and Philip Loeb as Suzanne Lenglen. One of the best sketches was that of Newman Levy on George Washington and the Society Ladies, while one of the most brilliant travesties was Hildegarde Halliday's impression of Queen Elizabeth. Among the new Rodgers and Hart songs was a new hit, "Mountain Greenery," sung by Bobbie Perkins and Sterling Holloway. In a more ambitious vein was a burlesque of musical comedy, *Rose of Arizona,* in which some of the song styles of the day were parodied.

It took four years to bring on the third and last edition; the revue lost none of its shining brightness during this interim. Rodgers and Hart no longer were its songwriters (they were now top men in the Broadway musical theater). But their replacements had found an important hearing for the first time. One of them was Vernon Duke, for whose melody to "I Am Only Human After All" Ira Gershwin, in collaboration with E. Y. Harburg, wrote the lyrics. Another was Johnny Mercer, lyricist of "Out of Breath and Scared to Death of You" (music by Everett Miller). Both Vernon Duke and Johnny Mercer would be heard of in the musical theater in the years to come. (Incidentally, one of the dancers in this edition of *The Garrick Gaieties* was Elizabeth Meehan. Mercer and Elizabeth Meehan met while the show was in rehearsal, and before the show had finished its run they had become man and wife.) Among those who came in for the now familiar *Garrick Gaieties* form of parody and satire were John Wanamaker, King George and Queen Mary, and Grover Whalen.

THE GAY DIVORCE (1932), *a musical comedy, with book by Dwight Taylor, adapted by Kenneth Webb and Samuel Hoffenstein from an unproduced play by J. Hartley Manners. Lyrics and music by Cole Porter. Presented by Dwight Deere Wiman and Tom Weatherly at the Ethel Barrymore Theater on November 29. Directed by Howard Lindsay. Dances by Carl Randall and Barbara Newberry. Cast included Fred Astaire, Luella Gear, Eric Blore, and Claire Luce (248 performances).*

Cole Porter was so taken with the text of *The Gay Divorce* that he began writing songs for it even before he had signed a contract to do so. Actually, the plot is routine stuff—a bedroom farce in which Mimi, an actress (Claire Luce), seeks divorce from a dull husband. To get that divorce she goes to an English seaside resort to be compromised by a correspondent. There she meets Guy (Fred Astaire). Guy had seen her briefly two weeks earlier and had fallen in love with her, but Mimi does not recognize him. Guy manages to get the password by which the correspondent is to identify himself to Mimi, and passes himself off as that man. What had been planned as a staged rendezvous becomes the real thing as Guy relentlessly pursues Mimi and finally wins her.

Fred Astaire here made his first musical-comedy appearance without his lifetime partner, his sister Adele. He had considerable misgivings about going it alone, but when Porter played for him one of the songs for the show ("After You, Who?") Astaire decided to take the plunge. But one song that he introduced—and which Cole Porter had written with the range and quality of his voice in mind—was to become a standout, "Night and Day." Porter got the stimulus for this melody from hearing a Muhammadan priest pray in Morocco—and for a while there were a good many skeptics who felt that Morocco was the place where the melody should have been left. But, as it turned out, it was "Night and Day" that made the show a success. The production had been badly reviewed by the New York critics, one of whom remarked: "One thing is certain, after viewing last night's performance we have come to the conclusion that two Astaires are better than one." Even while the show was being presented, changes were constantly being made, while tickets were being sold at cut-rate prices to help fill the theater. When "Night and Day" caught on, the cut-rate prices could be dispensed with; in fact the musical came to be known as that "Night and Day" show. Luella Gear's comedy helped—particularly in her delivery of a slightly risqué number, "Mister and Missus Fitch," and in "I Still Love the Red, White and Blue" (delivered at a Communist rally). Business was booming at the box office, so a larger theater had to be found to meet the demand for seats—the Shubert.

Two other Porter numbers, both ballads, were of more than passing interest: "I've Got You on My Mind," a duet by Guy and Mimi, and "You're in Love," in which Guy and Mimi were joined by Erik Rhodes, the last appearing in a subsidiary role.

When the musical became a movie the title had an "e" added to it. Now called *The Gay Divorcee* (RKO, 1934), it paired Ginger Rogers with Fred Astaire for the second time (the first had been in *Flying Down to Rio*) and established them solidly as the most appealing and successful song-and-dance partners in motion pictures. Only one song ("Night and Day") was kept from the Cole Porter score, all the other numbers being new creations by other composers and lyricists. One of these intruders was "The Continental" —sung and danced to by Astaire and Rogers—written by Herb Magidson, lyricist, and Con Conrad, composer, the first song ever to win an Academy Award (an award for songs having been instituted in 1934).

THE GEEZER. *See* WEBER AND FIELDS EXTRAVAGANZAS.

GENTLEMEN PREFER BLONDES (1949), *a musical comedy, with book by Anita Loos and Joseph Fields, based on the novel and the Broadway stage comedy of the same name by Anita Loos. Lyrics by Leo Robin. Music by Jule Styne. Presented by Herman Levin and Oliver Smith at the Ziegfeld Theater on December 8. Directed by John C. Wilson. Dances by Agnes de Mille. Cast included Carol Channing, Yvonne Adair, and Jack McCauley (740 performances).*

*Gentlemen Prefer Blondes* was lively stage entertainment. Its greatest strength lay in the sharp lines with which an era was drawn—the raucous, jazz-mad, iconoclastic 1920's. The musical comedy may have lacked some of the split-second timing of dialogue and exciting pace of the action found in the nonmusical stage play that had preceded it. But it did succeed in bringing again to life a decade symbolized by the heroine, Lorelei Lee. With her shrill, baby voice and Dixie accent, this provocative blonde became the personification of the roaring 1920's—her background and experiences succinctly summed up in "A Little Girl from Little Rock" (delivered with appropriate grinds and bumps); and her philosophy of life and her materialistic values expounded in "Diamonds Are a Girl's Best Friend." In these two songs, as Lorelei Lee, Carol Channing proved what one year earlier she had merely suggested in the revue *Lend an Ear:* that here was a new, shining musical-comedy star, a star that would glow even more brilliantly in a much later year, in *Hello, Dolly!*

The musical opens as the French liner *Ile de France* is about to make a midnight sailing for France. The year is 1924. Aboard ship are two dizzy American flappers, on leave from the *Follies:* Dorothy Shaw (Yvonne Adair), whose main aim in going abroad is to get away from Prohibition. With her is Lorelei Lee (Carol Channing). Lorelei's fiancé, Gus Edmond, a button manufacturer, has come to bid her bon voyage, and does so in the third song hit of the show, "Bye Bye Baby." In Paris Dorothy meets and falls in love with Henry Spofford (Erich Brotherson), a wealthy Philadelphia bachelor, whose favorite song is "Just a Kiss Apart." Lorelei, after a mild flirtation with Sir Francis Beekman, manages to borrow $5,000 from him so she can buy a diamond tiara from Sir Francis' wife. The French lawyers are hot on Lorelei's trail when Lady Beekman discovers where she got the money to buy the tiara. Poor Lorelei's troubles are compounded with the sudden arrival of Henry Esmond, for she has been carrying on with a zipper manufacturer, Josephus Gage, and Henry finds them together behaving far too amorously for his taste. Lorelei's complications create a break between herself and Henry—

much to the poor girl's distress. But after Lorelei has made a sensational debut in a Paris nightclub, Henry finds he cannot live without her. They make up; Henry pays Sir Francis back the money Lorelei had borrowed; and the two of them decide to come back home and get married.

A hot American novelty number, "Mamie Is Mimi," presented in the Paris nightspot where Lorelei makes her debut, and the finale, "Keeping Cool with Coolidge," maintained the frenetic spirit of the 1920's.

It took almost thirteen years for *Gentlemen Prefer Blondes* to come to London, and when it finally did, one London critic found that "this brash, often vulgar and visually ugly recreation of the flapper era has an outmoded air. It hasn't the edge of sharp parody. It is a simply old-fashioned musical staged with little style or imagination."

Marilyn Monroe took over the part of Lorelei Lee when 20th Century-Fox released *Gentlemen Prefer Blondes* as a movie in 1953. Her personalized sexy delivery of the show's two big songs—"A Little Girl from Little Rock" and "Diamonds Are a Girl's Best Friend," in each case supported by Jane Russell playing the part of Dorothy Shaw—were the high points of the production.

GEORGE M! (1968), *a musical comedy, with book by Michael Stewart and John and Fran Pascal. Lyrics and music by George M. Cohan. Presented by David Black, Konrald Matthei, and Lorin E. Price at the Palace Theater on April 10. Directed and with dances by Joe Layton. Cast included Joel Grey and Betty Ann Grove (427 performances).*

For those who get nostalgic and sentimental about a bygone era in the theater, *George M!* proved a welcome entry into the Broadway sweepstakes in 1968. This was a production which, as Haskel Frankel noted, was "rich in the flavor of a man and an era of unabashed patriotism, sentimentality and anything-goes showbiz." Mr. Frankel then adds: "Tap dancing is back, and the stage is alive with machine-gun bursts of happy feet at work. Player pianos are back; so is the girl in the mothlike skirt leading a line of boys in a flirtatious dance. Jugglers, comedy violinists, fire batons, living statues, choruses in drill formations with American flags at the head—it's all back and it is just grand."

*George M!*, to be sure, was a musical comedy based on the life of George M. Cohan, as fabulous a character as the American musical theater has produced; but also a man who—for all his unrivaled successes in virtually every area of show business—knew the meaning of frustration and heatbreak. But the many details of Cohan's biography are touched upon ever so fleetingly, in kaleidoscopic fashion, with no effort made to create an integrated story or build a three-dimensional character. The book is a poorly integrated, sprawling collection of eighteen scenes, most of them serving merely as cues for songs and dances. The songs are all by Cohan—thirty-two, no less, including all the big standards ("Give My Regards to Broadway," "Mary's a Grand Old Name," "You're a Grand Old Flag," "Harrigan," "Forty-Five Minutes from Broadway," "So Long, Mary," and "Yankee Doodle Dandy") and a good many songs that have either long since been forgotten or never achieved any measurable degree of popularity (including two that have never even been published). It would have been a much stronger show if it had concentrated on the standards and let the forgotten numbers remain in the obscurity most of them deserve. For those standards, while they make no claim to having changed the destiny of American popular music, are full of an infectious spirit, lilting tunes, honest emotions, wholesome sentiments, with no pretense at sophistication. Somehow they always stir the heart. These songs give a new meaning to the old saw about "this is the kind of a musical you come *into* the auditorium humming its tunes." The audiences did enter the Palace humming the Cohan songs they remembered, and as the show progressed, they burst into applause once the first measures of a familiar number were struck up.

Above and beyond the Cohan songs, *George M!* owed its appeal to the wonderful staging and choreography of Joe Layton, who made some of the less appealing of Cohan's songs a joy to the eye if not to the ear. And then there was the zestful, jaunty, boisterous, cocky performance of Joel Grey as George M. Cohan. He did not try to look like Cohan, nor did he try too obviously to imitate Cohan's well-known stage mannerisms. But he did bring back to life one of the greatest performers of all time. "Sharp as a whiplash," as Clive Barnes described his performance in *The New York Times,* "either with his derby titled down to his nose, or his eyes cast upward sightlessly searching the mid-distance of destiny, with his cane twirling, or his arms thrown out in that supremely egocentric empty embrace of show business, Mr. Grey operated. Mr. Grey operated and operated and operated. He screwed himself into one tight, taut bundle of nerves, threw himself at the show and came out on top and smiling like a tiger. He sang lightly and beltingly, he danced with a frenetic passion and a God-given sense of timing, and when all else failed, he even acted the script they had been inconsiderate enough to give him. Indeed, once in a while, he even made sense of its showbiz platitudes."

A prologue brings us the present generation of youngsters—girls in miniskirts, boys with tight pants and long hair. Joel Grey joins them to inform the audience that these young people never heard about George M. Cohan, nor do they know his songs. The rest of the show is intended to fill in these gaps.

George M. Cohan's father, Jerry, is completing his vaudeville act in Providence, Rhode Island, in 1878, when he gets the news that his wife has just given birth to a son. By the time Jerry Cohan's act reaches Cedar Rapids, little George M. is a member of the act of the Four Cohans (father Jerry, mother Nellie, and sister Josie). Given some more passage of time, George, now fifteen, not only dominates the act but even writes its material. E. F. Albee auditions them, when George M. and his family sing some of George M. Cohan's songs ("Musical Moon," "Oh, You Wonderful Boy," and "All Aboard for Broadway"). Albee wants the act to try out in Poughkeepsie, but George M. turns him down in no uncertain terms: he is thinking of the big time in New York, as he explains to his sister Josie, and like an express train he has no time to make local stops.

The Cohans finally come to New York, though to the humble Adams Street Theater rather than the big time. On the same bill is Ethel Levey (Jamie Donnelly) with whom George M. falls in love, with whom he gains success in vaudeville, and whom he marries. And now the young firebrand is aflame with a new ambition: to graduate from vaudeville to musical comedy. His first such effort is a failure. George M. is then seen building up *Little Johnny Jones* from auditions through rehearsals to its successful opening night. The first act of *George M.* ends on this note of triumph, with the hit song from *Little Johnny Jones,* "Give My Regards to Broadway."

By the time the curtain rises on the second act, George M. is "Mr. Big of Broadway." With Sam H. Harris as his producing partner he tries to induce the star Fay Templeton to appear in his new musical, *Forty-Five Minutes from Broadway.* She resists even after hearing some of its infectious musical numbers. But eventually she gives in as George M. uses every trick, and every influence, he can bring to bear. The show goes over big, especially after Fay Templeton sings "Mary's a Grand Old Name."

George M.'s domestic life, however, is not getting along well. For years he has promised to spend more time with Ethel, only to get continually involved in a new show. At a New Year's Eve party in 1906, George M. receives a wire from Ethel that she is divorcing him. Leaving the party, he comes upon Agnes Nolan (Jill O'Hara), who had appeared in one of his shows. She consoles him; he responds; before long she becomes his second wife.

There follows a panorama of George M.'s later career in the theater, up to the writing of "Over There" during World War I, and the creation of such major hits for various musicals as "Harrigan," "You're a Grand Old Flag," and "Nellie Kelly, I Love You." In spite of his successes he becomes a broken man when, as a theater manager, he is soundly defeated in a strike called by Actors Equity. For a while he threatens to desert the theater forever. But he soon comes back, to become a successful actor in the Rodgers and Hart musical *I'd Rather Be Right*. But Cohan is far from happy. As far as his own plays are concerned—the musical and the nonmusical—and the kind of songs he used to write, all these had become passé in the sophisticated 1920's. We see him for the last time as his beloved wife, Agnes, tries to lift his spirits and to restore his self-confidence. She almost succeeds, as they leave the stage to the strains of "Yankee Doodle Dandy."

In the epilogue, the youngsters from the prologue return to join the rest of the company in a potpourri of unfamiliar Cohan songs ("Dancing Our Worries Away," "The Great Easter Sunday Parade," "Hannah's a Hummer," "Barnum and Bailey Rag," "The Belle of the Barber's Ball," "The American Ragtime," "All in the Wearing," "I Want to Hear a Yankee Doodle Tune"). The musical ends appropriately enough as we hear George M. Cohan himself in a recording, singing in that peculiar nasal twang of his—once again to flood the theater with nostalgia.

> GEORGE WASHINGTON, JR. (1906), *a musical comedy, with book, lyrics, and music by George M. Cohan. Presented by Sam H. Harris at the Herald Square Theater on February 12. Directed by George M. Cohan. Cast included the Four Cohans and Ethel Levey (81 performances).*

The coincidence of alphabetical sequence has placed one of George M. Cohan's famous musicals directly under *George M!*, the musical based on his career in the theater. *George Washington, Jr.* was Cohan's third successful full-length musical comedy, having been preceded by *Little Johnny Jones* and *Forty-five Minutes from Broadway.*

Described as "an American play," it had for its central theme the rivalry of two senators in Washington, D.C.: James Belgrave (Jerry J. Cohan) from Rhode Island, and William Hopkins (Eugene O'Rourke) from the South. When Senator Hopkins makes a determined effort to expose corruption in the Senate, Belgrave decides to go off to England to buy his way into British society by inducing his son, George (George M. Cohan), to marry Lord Rothburt's daughter. But George is in love with Senator Hopkins' lovely niece, Dolly Johnson (Ethel Levey). Disgusted by his father's Anglophile tendencies, young George becomes a superpatriot and assumes the name of the first President of the United States. As it turns out, the lord and his "daughter" are frauds, hired by Senator Hopkins to get the goods on his rival. This fact is uncovered by young George, who sets his father wise. Senator Belgrave now becomes an intense patriot. Since Senator Hopkins is in love with Belgrave's widowed sister, he is ready to forget his hostility and at the same time give his blessings to George and Dolly.

The pace of the play is so swift, the dialogue so amusing, and the songs so effective that the editor of *Theatre*—who had recently referred to *Forty-five Minutes from Broadway* as "rubbish"—said that there was "plenty that is genuinely and legitimately diverting" and called the play "mighty good entertainment."

The outstanding song in *George Washington, Jr.* is "You're a Grand Old Flag," in which Cohan does the routine for which he became so famous and which he would repeat in many plays—draping an American flag around his body and running up and down the stage singing the praises of flag and country. Strange to recall, a scandal followed the first performance of this song in the play. The idea for the song first occurred to Cohan when a GAR veteran told him he had been a color-bearer during Pickett's charge at Gettysburg; pointing to the American flag, the old man said, "she's a grand old *rag*." In writing his song Cohan kept the expression "grand old rag." One day after opening night, several patriotic societies arose to denounce Cohan for insulting the American flag by referring to it as a rag. (Cohan insisted that this protest had been instigated by a New York drama critic who had been denied seats for his show.) When Cohan changed "rag" to "flag" all was forgiven, and the furor died down.

Two other songs became popular in 1906: Dolly Johnson's "I Was Born in Virginia" and "All Aboard for Broadway." A high spot of the production was Cohan's delivery of some homey philosophy in a verse monologue entitled "If Washington Should Come to Life."

GEORGE WHITE'S SCANDALS (1919), *a revue, with book and lyrics by George White and Arthur Jackson. Music by George A. Whiting. Presented by George White at the Liberty Theater on June 2. Directed by George White. Cast included George White, Ann Pennington, Lou Holtz, and Yvette Rugel (128 performances).*

(1920), *a revue, with book by Andy Rice and George White. Lyrics by Arthur Jackson. Music by George Gershwin. Presented by George White at the Globe Theater on June 7. Directed by George White and William Collier. Cast included Ann Pennington, Lou Holtz, George White, Lester Allen, and "Doc" Rockwell (134 performances).*

(1921), *a revue, with book by Bugs Baer and George White. Lyrics by Arthur Jackson. Music by George Gershwin. Presented by George White at the Liberty Theater on July 11. Directed by George White and John Meehan. Cast included Ann Pennington, George White, Charles King, Lou Holtz, and Lester Allen (97 performances).*

(1922), *a revue, with book by George White, W. C. Fields, and Andy Rice. Lyrics by E. Ray Goetz and Buddy de Sylva. Music by George Gershwin. Presented by George White at the Globe Theater on August 28. Directed by George White. Cast included W. C. Fields, Jack McGowan, Lester Allen, and Paul Whiteman and his orchestra (88 performances).*

(1923), *a revue, with book by George White and William K. Wells. Lyrics by E. Ray Goetz, Buddy de Sylva, and Ballard MacDonald. Music by George Gershwin. Presented by George White at the Globe Theater on June 18. Directed by George White. Cast included Johnny Dooley, Winnie Lightner, Tom Patricola, and Lester Allen (168 performances).*

(1924), *a revue, with book by George White and William K. Wells. Lyrics by Buddy de Sylva. Music by George Gershwin. Presented by George White at the Apollo Theater on June 30. Directed by George White. Cast included Tom Patricola, Winnie Lightner, Will Mahoney, and Lester Allen (192 performances).*

(1925), *a revue, with book by George White and William K. Wells. Lyrics and music by Buddy de Sylva, Lew Brown, and Ray Henderson. Presented by George White at the Apollo Theater on June 22. Directed by George White. Dances by Albertina Rasch. Cast included Tom Patricola, Helen Morgan, Harry Fox, and the McCarthy Sisters (171 performances).*

(1926), *a revue, with book by George White and William K. Wells. Lyrics and music by Buddy de Sylva, Lew Brown, and Ray Henderson. Presented by George White at the Apollo Theater on June 14. Directed by George White. Cast included Ann Pennington, Frances Williams, Willie and Eugene Howard, Tom Patricola, and the Fairbanks Twins (424 performaces).*

(1928), *a revue, with book by George White and William K. Wells. Lyrics and music by Buddy de Sylva, Lew Brown, and Ray Henderson. Presented by George White at the Apollo Theater on July 2. Directed by George White. Dances by Russell Markert. Cast included Willie and Eugene Howard, Harry Richman, Tom Patricola, Frances Williams, and Ann Pennington (240 performances).*

(1929), *a revue, with book by George White and William K. Wells. Lyrics and music by Irving Caesar, George White, and Cliff Friend. Presented by George White at the Apollo Theater on September 23. Directed by George White. Abbott Dancers directed by Florence Wilson. Cast included Willie and Eugene Howard and Frances Williams (161 performances).*

(1931), *a revue, with book by George White, Lew Brown, and Irving Caesar. Lyrics by Lew Brown. Music by Ray Henderson. Assembled and presented by George White at the Apollo Theater on September 14. Directed by*

*George White. Cast included Willie and Eugene Howard, Rudy Vallee, Ethel Merman, and Ray Bolger (202 performances).*

*(1935), a revue, with book by George White, William K. Wells, and Howard A. Shiebler. Lyrics by Jack Yellen. Music by Ray Henderson. Presented by George White at the New Amsterdam Theater on December 25. Directed by George White. Dances by Russell Markert. Cast included Willie and Eugene Howard, Rudy Vallee, Bert Lahr, Cliff Edwards, and Gracie Barrie (110 performances).*

*(1939), a revue, with book by Matt Brooks, Eddie Davis, and George White. Lyrics by Jack Yellen. Music by Sammy Fain. Presented by George White at the Alvin Theater on August 28, 1939. Directed by George White. Cast included Willie and Eugene Howard, Ben Blue, Ann Miller, Ella Logan, and the Three Stooges (120 performances).*

George White, who had been born on New York's East Side in 1890, had had a varied career before he finally became a producer of some of the most successful revues of the 1920's—the *Scandals*. As a boy, he earned his living as a messenger, as a dancer in Bowery music halls (for pennies and nickels the patrons threw at him), and even as a jockey. In 1910 he became an actor with a part in *The Echo* at the Globe Theater (a musical with a score by Deems Taylor, long before Taylor's name became known both as a serious composer and as a music critic). From actor, White turned hoofer, soon becoming so successful in various musicals—particularly as a performer of the Turkey Trot, which he helped make famous—that Ziegfeld hired him for the *Follies* of 1915. Realizing that the big money lay in producing, White was impelled to combine his talents as performer with those of producer by putting on a revue (without any financial backing). The first three editions he called simply the *Scandals,* while all editions, beginning that in 1922, came to be named *George White's Scandals.* His aim, he stated simply, was to put on the stage the prettiest girls he could find. But he also studded his revues with stars and frequently with excellent song material and sketches. He made four million dollars from his productions, and he lost more than that, most of it through gambling (especially on horses). Several times he was driven into bankruptcy, the last time being in 1942, when he listed his liabilities as $500,000 and his assets as $500 and a Rolls Royce. In 1946 he served an eight-and-a-half-month prison term for having killed a couple while driving his car. Even in prison he spoke of putting on another edition of the *Scandals,* bigger and better than any before. But all he could do was to present a vest-pocket edition in 1963 at the International Theater Restaurant. He died broke in 1968.

In his bow as producer, with the *Scandals* in 1919, he spared no expense in making his production as lavish as possible; the emphasis here was on huge production numbers, gorgeous sets and costumes, and elaborate dance numbers. The dances, ranging from ballet to the shimmy, highlighted performances by George White himself, and by Ann Pennington, the now acknowledged queen of the shimmy.

This new review was a veritable feast for the eye. What it lacked most of all was fresh comedy, whose main representatives were Lou Holtz (in his debut on the Broadway stage) and a blackface team by the name of Bennett and Richards. "When there was so much money to be spent," lamented Arthur Hornblow in *Theatre* magazine, "Mr. White might have set aside a few dollars for a good scenario writer." The musical score was just as mediocre, the three best numbers—and they were hardly anything to boast about—being "Broadway Belles," "Girls in My Address Book," and "Gimme the Shimmy."

Nevertheless the *Scandals* proved at once a formidable rival to *The Ziegfeld Follies,* and nobody recognized this more quickly than Ziegfeld himself. Immediately after the opening of the *Scandals,* Ziegfeld tried to remove a serious competitor by offering George White and Ann Pennington three thousand dollars a week to appear in the *Follies.* White's reply was immediate. He was ready to offer seven thousand dollars for Ziegfeld and his wife, Billie Burke, to appear in the *Scandals.*

He also had a ready reply to the critics, who unanimously agreed that the *Scandals* had little to offer. (Burns Mantle insisted that "George White's *Scandals* proves that a hoofer should stick to his dancing.") White said: "I made $400,000."

For his second edition, George White engaged as his composer the then young and comparatively inexperienced Gershwin, paying him at first fifty dollars a week for the job. Gershwin remained with the *Scandals* five years, and during this period he developed to maturity as a song composer and gave repeated hints of his future direction as a serious composer.

The 1920 edition showed marked progress over the earlier one, both in text and music. Comedy was strengthened through the interpolation of satire: one sketch mocked Prohibition, its setting an airship three miles up in the air; another jeered at profiteering landlords; others spoofed political conventions and the grim Russian drama. Nevertheless, it was the dancing of Ann Pennington, the "shimmy queen"—and a graduate from *The Ziegfeld Follies*—that was the high point of the production.

Gershwin wrote seven numbers, the best being "Idle Dreams." In 1921, Gershwin had six numbers, among them "South Sea Isles" and "Drifting

Along with the Tide." The 1922 edition—with twelve Gershwin numbers —had the first of his songs from the *Scandals* to be remembered and admired: "Stairway to Paradise," in which the young composer revealed for the first time his original bent for unusual approaches and techniques in rhythm and meter. This song had originated as a lyric by Ira Gershwin called "New Step Everyday." When Buddy de Sylva read the lyric, he suggested to Ira that they collaborate on another, using one of its lines as the title. With George's music it was brought into the *Scandals*. White provided a lavish setting: a huge white stairway with dancers dressed in black, walking up and down as the song was sung by Winnie Lightner, and then danced to by Pearl Regay.

Besides his more formal songs, Gershwin also contributed to this edition a one-act Negro opera, the first testimony of his subsequent evolution as a serious composer. Originally it was called *Blue Monday,* text by Buddy de Sylva, and a cast including Richard Bold, Lester Allen, Jack McGowan, and Colletta Ryan. The setting was a basement on Lenox Avenue in New York's Harlem. Vi is loved by both Joe and Tom. When Joe leaves New York to visit his sick mother, Tom convinces Vi he has really gone off for a rendezvous with a girl. When Joe returns, Vi shoots him but discovers her error just before he dies.

Gershwin's score was his first attempt to write in a design larger than the song. The opera contained a few good individual numbers: "Blue Monday Blues," "Has Anyone Seen Joe?", and the spiritual "I'm Going to See My Mother." But the score was not a coherent entity. Inchoate and immature though it was, however, *Blue Monday* was the embryo out of which Gershwin's opera, *Porgy and Bess,* emerged a decade later. *Blue Monday* appeared only once in the *Scandals,* on opening night. It was removed the following day because White felt that it depressed the audience. However, since then—and under its new title, *135th Street*—it has been revived several times, including once on television.

The 1923 edition of the *Scandals* had a Folies Bergère curtain of living nudes, perhaps its most interesting feature. Gershwin had twelve songs but none of distinction. But for 1924 he produced one of the songs by which he will always be remembered—"Somebody Loves Me," fetchingly sung by Winnie Lightner. This edition also had a delightful social-drama sketch in which not a single word was spoken—but which consisted merely of the sound "ah."

In the cast in 1924 were two sisters, both of them then still unknowns, and both in the chorus. They were Helen and Dolores Costello, daughters of the famous idol of the silent screen, Maurice Costello. Both girls later achieved some measure of recognition on the screen, while Dolores became even more famous by becoming the wife of John Barrymore.

When George Gershwin asked White for a raise in 1925 and was turned down, he withdrew from the *Scandals* and devoted himself to musical comedies. The replacement for Gershwin was the song-writing team of Buddy de Sylva, Lew Brown, and Ray Henderson. Their first effort as Gershwin's replacement was hardly impressive. Their score for their first *Scandals,* in 1925, was second-rate. Songs like "I Want a Lovable Baby," "Lovely Lady," and "What a World This Would Be" hardly gave warning that this team of songwriters would soon become one of the most formidable in the business—with all their best work completed within the next five years.

For that matter, the entire edition lacked distinction, as more than one critic pointed out. There was a pleasing parade of beautiful girls dressed in various furs; a presentation of a melodrama by a Southern stock company with the same emphasis on the dance that many Broadway productions gave in the 1925 era; an amusing takeoff on Irving Berlin (enacted by Gordon Dooley) who sang "All Alone" while a bevy of beautiful girls swarmed all around him; and Tom Patricola doing the Charleston—the dance rage of this period—helped along by sixty dancing chorines. The contributions made by the principal stars were less impressive.

But in 1926 the *Scandals* presented one of its best editions—its finest array of stars, some of the best material it ever offered, and some of the best songs to come out of a George White production. In consequence it had the longest run of any of the *Scandals*. De Sylva, Brown, and Henderson created a remarkable score that had four bull's-eye hits. "Black Bottom" was danced to by Ann Pennington—a new dance routine devised by George White, as some say, while trying to invent effective opening steps for an Ann Pennington dance; or, in the opinion of others, a dance invented by Alberta Hunter, who copyrighted it in 1926. In any event it was through Ann Pennington's performance—and the song to which she danced it in the *Scandals*—that made this dance a social-dance rage throughout the country in 1926.

Harry Richman sang "Lucky Day," and with Frances Williams he shared "The Girl Is You," two significant songs in the production. But undoubtedly the greatest of the De Sylva, Brown, and Henderson songs in this score—and the highlight of the whole edition—was "The Birth of the Blues," a lavish production number. Here White made use of a glittering staircase, flanked by girls dressed as angels. The scene represented a battle between the blues and the classics. Margaret McCarthy sang "The Memphis Blues," and Dorothy McCarthy, "The St. Louis Blues." The Fairbanks Twins were on the side of the classics, each representing a famous classical work, one by

Schumann, the other by Schubert. The climax came with the resolution of the conflict by having the blues merge with the classics as a part of Gershwin's *Rhapsody in Blue* was performed. So popular did "The Birth of the Blues" become that it inspired a motion picture using its title as its own name, starring Bing Crosby, who sang it under the titles, in the movie, and during the climax of the story.

The 1926 *Scandals* deserves attention for two reasons other than its songs. It was here that Helen Morgan made her entry into the Broadway theater. She went unnoticed, was dropped, and in another two months or so was found in *Americana* sitting atop a piano singing a torch song. That's where Jerome Kern found her while he was casting *Show Boat,* and that's how he helped make a star of Helen Morgan as Julie.

Another reason why the 1926 edition was unusual was that an opening-night ticket for a seat in the first ten rows cost the unprecedented sum of $5.50. To justify such extravagance, George White gave an opulent production. Besides "The Birth of the Blues," which all by itself was worth the price of the ticket, the revue had a second remarkable production number in "Triumph of Woman." The cream of the comedy included Willie Howard as a feuding Southern mountaineer, and a Western Union skit burlesqued the then recent marriage of Irving Berlin and Ellin Mackay.

There was no edition of the *Scandals* in 1927. In 1928 it once again boasted a score by De Sylva, Brown, and Henderson. To Harry Richman went one of the best numbers, "I'm on the Crest of a Wave," while one of the most successful dance routines, "Pickin' Cotton," was danced to by Ann Pennington, after it had been sung by Frances Williams. George White had hoped that "Pickin' Cotton" would take the country by storm as a new dance, the way "Black Bottom" had done, but in this he was to be disappointed.

The 1928 edition was the last one with a De Sylva, Brown, and Henderson score. The 1929 edition represented a let-down after 1928 in all departments, though two of the songs presented by Frances Williams were pleasing enough, "Bottoms Up" and "Bigger and Better than Ever." A new comedy team, Mitchell and Durant, supplemented the shenanigans of Willie and Eugene Howard, a *Scandals* staple.

Once again, White skipped producing a *Scandals* for a year. The intermission proved healthful. The 1931 edition was another resounding winner, with a score by Lew Brown, lyricist, and Ray Henderson, composer (Buddy de Sylva having deserted the team), that had no less than six outstanding hit songs. Ethel Merman sang "Life Is Just a Bowl of Cherries" and "Ladies and Gentlemen, That's Love"; Rudy Vallee, "This Is the Missus"; together Miss Merman and Rudy Vallee offered "My Song"; Everett

Marshall introduced "The Thrill Is Gone" and "That's Why Darkies Were Born." Because of this wealth of musical material, Brunswick issued a twelve-inch disc that included all these songs on the two sides, sung by Bing Crosby and the Boswell Sisters—the first time in recording history that the principal songs of a musical show were recorded in a single release.

Of secondary interest, as far as the 1931 edition was concerned, were the fact that here Ethel Barrymore Colt made her debut in the musical theater; Alice Faye—soon to become a star in talking pictures—appeared as a chorus girl; and Eleanor Powell, her stardom also just around the corner, was making her first appearances as a Broadway hoofer.

There were only two more Broadway editions of the *Scandals* after that— in 1935 and 1939. Both were failures, representing the beginning of the decline and fall of the George White theatrical empire. In 1935 Gracie Barrie had a good number in "I've Got to Get Hot" and Rudy Vallee in "The Pied Piper of Harlem." This was also the last Broadway musical in which Helen Morgan appeared as a star. In 1939 Ann Miller emerged as a new dancing star, and Ella Logan was the singing attraction of the production, particularly with the hit song "Are You Having Any Fun?"

Three motion pictures were filmed using the name *George White's Scandals:* (20th Century-Fox, 1934), with Rudy Vallee, Jimmy Durante, and Alice Faye; (20th Century-Fox, 1935), with James Dunn, Alice Faye, and Eleanor Powell; and (RKO, 1945), with Jack Haley and Joan Davis.

THE GINGHAM GIRL (1922), *a musical comedy, with book by Daniel Kussell. Lyrics by Neville Fleeson. Music by Albert von Tilzer. Presented by Schwab and Kussell at the Earl Carroll Theater on August 28. Cast included Eddie Buzzell and Helen Ford (322 performances).*

John Cousins (Eddie Buzzell) and Mary Thompson (Helen Ford) are natives of Crossville Corners, New Hampshire. Besides being in love, both are fired with ambition to get ahead in the world. John comes to New York, where he becomes a success, assumes the attitudes of a city slicker, and has various amatory adventures in Greenwich Village. Mary follows him to the city and is disheartened to see how her beau has changed. She sets herself up in the cookie business and becomes prosperous. Finally John comes to his senses and realizes that Mary is the girl he loves. The eccentric dancing of Helen Coyne and Henri French and the song "As Long as I Have You" were two attractions helping to make *The Gingham Girl* an outstanding hit.

GIRL CRAZY (1930), *a musical comedy, with book by Guy Bolton and John McGowan. Lyrics by Ira Gershwin. Music by George Gershwin. Presented by Aarons and Freedley at the Alvin Theater on October 14. Directed by Alexander Leftwich. Dances by George Hale. Cast included Ethel Merman, Ginger Rogers, Allen Kearns, and Willie Howard (272 performances).*

The plot was not one calculated to bring distinction to the musical stage. Danny Churchill (Allen Kearns) is a Park Avenue playboy. As a cure for his dilatory ways, he is sent by his father to Custerville, Arizona, a town with few temptations and no women. Danny makes the trip in the taxi of Gieber Goldfarb (Willie Howard). It does not take him long to transform Custerville into a fleshpot. He opens a dude ranch studded with Broadway chorus girls and equipped with a gambling room. He manages to get into all kinds of trouble, but then sees the error of his ways when he falls in love with the town postmistress, Molly Gray (Ginger Rogers).

What lifted the play to significance was the earthy, shattering performance of Ethel Merman. In the role of Kate Fothergill, wife of the man who runs the gambling room, she made her Broadway stage debut and was immediately lifted to the summit of her profession.

A former stenographer named Ethel Zimmerman, who had appeared in small nightclubs, at parties and weddings, Merman came to the attention of Vinton Freedley during an appearance in a nightclub and at the Brooklyn Paramount Theater. Freedley, in turn, introduced her to Gershwin, who auditioned her at his apartment and forthwith engaged her for *Girl Crazy*. She did not have looks by Broadway standards; her voice was not the kind that caresses and woos an audience. Yet when she appeared for the first time on that stage, dressed in a tight black satin skirt, slit to the knee, and a low-cut red blouse, and threw her brassy tones across the footlights in "Sam and Delilah"—filling the entire theater with the dynamism of an irresistible personality—the effect of singer on audience was cyclonic. As one unidentified critic said: "She has the magnificent vitality of a steam calliope in red and gold loping down a circus midway playing the 'Entry of the Gladiators.'"

"Sam and Delilah," a parody of the Frankie and Johnny type of ballad, was one of three numbers introduced by Merman in *Girl Crazy*. The other two Gershwin gems are also inevitably associated with her. In "I Got Rhythm" she electrified the theater by holding a high C for sixteen bars while the orchestra proceeded with the melody; the second was a sophisticated ditty called "Boy! What Love Has Done to Me!"

There were other treasures in this score. "Embraceable You"—this was Molly Gray's big song, the role in which Ginger Rogers was making her Broadway starring debut (her triumphs in movies with Fred Astaire soon to follow). This is one of Gershwin's most beautiful love songs. It was written for an earlier show, *East Is West,* which was never completely written and of course never produced. But in *Girl Crazy*—and for Ginger Rogers—it was a "natural." "But Not for Me," also presented by Molly, is also a poignant ballad. (Strange to say, Willie Howard used the latter song to set forth his talent at imitating famous performers of the day, including Rudy Vallee and Maurice Chevalier.) And "Bidin' My Time" was presented by a quartet of rubes who sing it while drifting in and out during the scene changes while accompanying themselves on a harmonica, jew's harp, ocarina, and tin flute; this is a takeoff on hillbilly tunes.

The orchestra that played in the pit for *Girl Crazy* deserves at least a footnote in the history of jazz, for its members included Benny Goodman, Glenn Miller, Red Nichols, Gene Krupa, Jack Teagarden, and Jimmy Dorsey.

*Girl Crazy* was made into three different motion pictures. The first two were called *Girl Crazy:* (RKO, 1932), with Bert Wheeler and Robert Woolsey; and (MGM, 1943), with Judy Garland and Mickey Rooney. Both used the basic stage score and both adhered more or less to the story line. The third (MGM, 1965) was renamed *Where the Boys Meet the Girls* and starred Connie Francis with Harve Presnell. The original stage plot is here no longer recognizable, but five of the stage songs were retained, and were supplemented by several new numbers by other lyricists and composers.

THE GIRL FRIEND (1926), *a musical comedy, with book by Herbert Fields. Lyrics by Lorenz Hart. Music by Richard Rodgers. Presented by Lew Fields at the Vanderbilt Theater on March 17. Directed by John Harwood. Dances by Jack Haskell. Cast included Sam White, Eva Puck, and June Cochrane (301 performances).*

When *The Melody Man,* by Rodgers, Hart, and Herbert Fields, was running on Broadway, its authors promised two stars of that ill-fated show, Sam White and Eva Puck, that they would someday write a musical comedy for them. They kept that promise with *The Girl Friend.* In this play Sam White was cast as a cyclist, Leonard Silver. Silver becomes proficient by training on a wheel attached to a churn on his Long Island dairy farm. Eva Puck was Mollie Farrell, daughter of a professional cyclist, with whom Leonard is in love. An unscrupulous cycling promoter encourages Leonard to enter a fixed six-day race. Despite the devious efforts of corrupt gamblers, Leonard is victorious in the race and wins his girl.

It is not an original or imaginative plot, but it is lent distinction through amusing episodes (a burlesque on grand opera, for example, and another on minstrel shows), through some striking dances (particularly by Dorothy Barbour), and through the music of Rodgers. Two songs were of particular merit; both became outstanding hits in 1926. The first was the title song, with rhythmic interest, and the second, "Blue Room," its melody of surpassing charm; both were sung by Leonard and Mollie.

As a matter of fact, the two hit songs were largely responsible for making *The Girl Friend* a success. Business at first was slow. But when the two songs gained popularity throughout the country, interest in the play was aroused to a point where it attracted enough customers to warrant a run of over 300 performances; *The Girl Friend* also toured the road until February 26, 1927.

THE GIRL FROM UTAH (1914), *a musical comedy, with book and lyrics by Harry B. Smith, James F. Tanner, and others. Music by Paul Rubens, Sydney Jones, and Jerome Kern. Presented by Charles Frohman at the Knickerbocker Theater on August 24. Directed by J. A. E. Malone. Cast included Julia Sanderson, Joseph Cawthorn, and Donald Brian (120 performances).*

*The Girl from Utah* originated in London as an operetta with a score by Rubens and Jones, starring Ina Claire. In its transfer to the American stage it retained some of the musical numbers of the original production (all of them forgotten), and interpolated several new songs by Jerome Kern. Those Kern songs were the first in which he gave indication of his future creative power and are the reason why *The Girl from Utah*—the first Broadway musical to bring Kern a substantial box-office success—will be remembered.

Una Trance (Julia Sanderson) flees from Utah to London rather than be one of the many wives of a Mormon. The Mormon pursues her across the ocean. A taxi accident brings Una to Rumpelmeyer's tea room, where she seeks haven and meets Sandy Blair (Donald Brian), a young actor. The pursuing Mormon also comes to the tea room, and so does Trimpel, proprietor of a ham and beef shop (Joseph Cawthorn). Somehow the Mormon and Trimpel accidentally exchange hats, and Trimpel becomes helplessly involved in difficulties as he is mistaken for the Mormon. The Mormon finally succeeds in carrying Una off to a house in Brixton. But since she leaves a trail of confetti, she is tracked down by Blair and Trimpel, who have joined forces to save her. They finally catch up with her at the Arts Ball, where all difficulties are solved, with Una in Sandy's arms.

The three stars each contributed his or her own special gift to make the play a lively diversion: Julia Sanderson brought her enchanting singing; Donald Brian, his vital dancing; and Cawthorn, his rich comedy, particularly when, while searching for Una, he assumes various disguises. But it is the songs of Kern that are the most rewarding features of the production. Since one of these is Kern's first to sell a million copies of sheet music or more, and is now acknowledged as Kern's first masterpiece, it deserves some special attention. Considering the year it was written, "They Didn't Believe Me" was most remarkable for its technical innovations: the expansion of the melody of the refrain for eight measures in simple quarter notes; the subtle change of key midway in the song; the introduction of a new four-bar musical thought in the recapitulation of the opening section; the way in which rhythm changes from quarter- and half-notes to triplets. The last of these occurs in a phrase that was greatly criticized ("and I'm certainly going to tell them"), one or two of the critics regarding the inclusion of this phrase as banal and as an unnecessary digression from the main thought of the lyric. But it was not the lyricist (Herbert Reynolds) who introduced this phrase into the song, but Kern himself, to permit him to make an important change in the rhythmic pattern.

"They Didn't Believe Me" was written for Julia Sanderson, and her poignant rendition is certainly one of the reasons why the song—for all its technical complexities and novelties—captured the hearts of its audiences, and why it went on from there to become such a resounding commercial success outside the theater.

The other enchanting Kern numbers in this music were "I'd Like to Wander with Alice in Wonderland," sung by Una; "Same Sort of Girl"; and an infectious rhythmic number called "Why Don't They Dance the Polka Any More?"

THE GIRL IN PINK TIGHTS (1954), *a musical comedy, with book by Jerome Chodorov and Joseph Fields. Lyrics by Leo Robin. Music by Sigmund Romberg. Presented by Shepard Traube in association with Anthony B. Farrell at the Mark Hellinger Theater on March 5. Directed by Shepard Traube. Dances by Agnes de Mille. Cast included David Atkinson, Brenda Lewis, Charles Goldner, and Jeanmaire (115 performances).*

This was Romberg's last score, and he did not live to see it reach the stage. About a year before the composer's death, Chodorov and Fields discussed with Romberg the idea for a yet unwritten play: a period piece set in New York immediately after the Civil War and built around the first production of *The Black Crook.* The composer liked the suggestion, and the collaborators went to work. Romberg completed all his music before his death.

The setting was the New York theatrical district just after the end of the Civil War. There is excitement in the air, for a new French ballet company is due at the Academy of Music. Lotta Leslie (Brenda Lewis) regards this event with apprehension. Across the street from the Academy she operates

Niblo's Gardens, which is offering *Dick the Renegade,* a melodrama by Clyde Hallam (David Atkinson), hardly competition for a show featuring French ballet girls wearing pink tights. One of the members of his French company is Lisette Gervais (Jeanmaire), with whom Clyde instantly falls in love, as he reveals in the ballad "Lost in Loveliness." At the same time, the manager of the French company, Maestro Gallo (Charles Goldner), is trying to capture the interest of Lotta.

Clyde and Lisette carry on their romance all over New York. They take a ride on the newly opened elevated railway with Lisette singing of this experience in "Up in the Elevated Railway." They go to Battery Park. They come to the conclusion that love is sweetest of all in Paris, as they explain in "In Paris and in Love." Lisette is so taken with Clyde that she is negligent about rehearsals, for which she is severely taken to task by her manager. During one of those rehearsals, the manager experiments with some new stage innovations involving gunpowder. Its explosion causes the Academy to burn down. Lisette, locked in her dressing room at the time, is rescued by Clyde.

The French company is now in a bad way. It has no theater to play in, no funds with which to return home. Lotta, however, comes up with a solution, with the help of a wealthy man-about-town. Why not combine the ballet with Clyde's melodrama, present it at Niblo's Gardens, and thus offer a totally new kind of production? Naturally, Clyde's melodrama has to be drastically rewritten, something which the author resents; nor does he like the manager's idea that the Faust legend be interpolated into the story. Discussions and arguments even endanger the romance of Lisette and Clyde, since the girl insists that, after all, ballet is more important than the play, and Clyde is of the opposite opinion. But Clyde's professional pride, so deeply wounded up to now, is rejuvenated when he attends the opening night of the rewritten show, named *The Black Crook,* and sees what a formidable success it is—particularly the French girls with their pink tights, and an elaborate finale with skyrockets and American flags, with a ballet of bats, with the suggestion of the Faust legend, and with Lisette (wearing pink tights and a French Civil War cap) all amalgamated into a grandiose production number.

Regrettably, Romberg's valedictory to the stage was a comparative dud. The play had a kind of nostalgic charm, but it lacked pace and sustained interest. As Richard Watts, Jr., said: "The narrative plods along with a strange and uncharacteristic lack of imagination and invention, and there are only a few occasions when it lives up to either its own potentialities or the entirely delightful talents of its heroine."

The heroine referred to by Mr. Watts was played by Jeanmaire, making her American musical-comedy debut. (She had first appeared in the United States in 1949 in the Ballets de Paris, and then was seen on the screen in *Hans Christian Andersen,* the motion picture starring Danny Kaye.) As Lisette she proved herself to be a "Gallic edition of Mary Martin," in Brooks Atkinson's description.

Jeanmaire and several delightful dances conceived by Agnes de Mille ("The Ballet Class," "Pas de Deux," and a French bacchanal) were the assets of the production. The Romberg score contained some fetching moments, the best of which are listed in the summary of the plot. "My Heart Won't Say Goodbye" is Clyde's love ballad to Lisette.

GOING UP (1917), *a musical farce, with book and lyrics by Otto Harbach, based on James Montgomery's* The Aviator. *Music by Louis A. Hirsch. Presented by Cohan and Harris at the Liberty Theater on December 25. Directed by Edward Royce and James Montgomery. Cast included Frank Craven, Edith Day, Ruth Donnelly, and Donald Meek (351 performances).*

The main attraction of *Going Up* was the performance of Frank Craven as Robert Street, author of six best-selling books on aviation. In a summer resort in the Berkshire Mountains, he boasts of his skill at aeronautics until he is coerced into acccepting a challenge in an air race with an actual aviator. His efforts to extricate himself from this disagreeable proposition provide most of the comedy of the play and give Craven many opportunities for his winning characterization. Actually, to win the girl he loves—she is Grace Douglas (Edith Day)—he must go through with the challenge, from which he emerges victorious.

The musical had an outstanding song hit in "Tickle Toe" ("Ev'rybody Ought to Know How to Do the Tickle Toe"), which was introduced by Grace and the ensemble. Three other songs were also of interest: the title song, "Do It for Me," and "If You Look in Her Eyes."

THE GOLDEN APPLE (1954), *a musical play, with book and lyrics by John La Touche. Music by Jerome Moross. Presented by the Phoenix Theater at the Phoenix Theater on March 11, and at the Alvin Theater on April 20. Directed by Norman Lloyd. Choreography by Hanya Holm. Cast included Kaye Ballard, Stephen Douglass, and Jonathan Lucas (125 performances).*

*The Golden Apple* was written with the aid of a Guggenheim Fellowship several years before it was produced. In all that time it was turned down by several producers, who insisted that it was too unorthodox to have public appeal. When finally presented, it was so successful in an Off Broadway production that five weeks later it was transferred to Broadway. To John McClain it was "easily the most satisfactory and original song and dance effort of the past several seasons, and in my opinion can be classed as an American Gilbert and Sullivan." Robert Coleman called it "a magnificent achievement . . . a sensational success . . . quite the most original and imaginative work of its kind to blaze across the theatrical horizon in many a moon."

Sung throughout, *The Golden Apple* is a satire that transfers the Homeric legend of Helen and Ulysses to an American town, Angel's Roost, near the town of Rhododendron, in the state of Washington. Ulysses is an American soldier (Stephen Douglass) returning home from the Spanish-American War. Penelope (Priscilla Gillette) is his wife. Helen (Kaye Ballard), a farmer's daughter, is married to the sheriff, Menelaus. At a county fair, a salesman, Paris (Jonathan Lucas), descends in a balloon which bears the slogan "Paris Notions, Inc." Helen falls in love with Paris, and they decide to run off to Rhododendron. For ten years Ulysses goes to search for Helen to save her from Paris. Finally he comes to Rhododendron, where its mayor, Hector, subjects him to the city's temptations and allurements, including the seductive wiles of Siren and Circe among others. He bests Paris in a boxing match, then finally returns home, to his patient, long-waiting Penelope, content to spend the rest of his years with her.

The story is told briskly in song, lyrics, pantomime, and some beautiful dances conceived by Hanya Holm; of the last, among the most memorable was a hilarious travesty called "By Goona Goona Lagoon." The most significant song is the sentimental and nostalgic "Lazy Afternoon," sung by Helen, followed by an attractive dance by Paris. A duet by Ulysses and Penelope, "It's the Going Home Together," and a comedy number, "The Judgment of Paris," are also worthy of mention.

*The Golden Apple* received the New York Drama Critics and the Donaldson Awards as the best musical of the season.

GOLDEN BOY (1964), *a musical comedy, with book by Clifford Odets and William Gibson, based on Odets' play of the same name. Lyrics by Lee Adams. Music by Charles Strouse. Presented by Hillard Elkins at the Majestic Theater on October 20. Directed by Arthur Penn. Dances by Donald McKayle. Cast included Sammy Davis, Billy Daniels, Paula Wayne, and Kenneth Tobey (569 performances).*

The idea to make a musical production out of Clifford Odets' successful play *Golden Boy* was born with Hillard Elkins, a young man of the theater eager to make a bow as producer. In its original nonmusical form, as produced in 1938, the hero of the Odets play was an Italian boy who played the violin well, but who turns to boxing out of the necessity to make money and the inner compulsion to achieve fame and power. When, in a match, Joe kills his opponent, he loses control of himself, goes off for a wild drive in his car with his girl, Lorna, and is killed in an accident.

Hillard Elkins did not want to let the play stand as it was and then dress it up with music. He had an idea that if the principal character was a Negro—this business of the hero playing the violin can be dispensed with—and if this Negro were impelled to become a boxer out of his hunger for the self-esteem, prestige, and wealth his black skin denied him, the musical could have timely significance at a time when the race problem had become such a major issue in the United States. Clifford Odets liked this idea and went to work on a libretto. The job was left unfinished when he died of cancer in 1963. The task of refining and revising what Odets had already written, and finishing the text, went to William Gibson.

The musical opens impressively: in a gymnasium where a workout by boxers is set to music. Joe Wellington (Sammy Davis) is a Negro with ambition for power and wealth in a world of white people who have subjected his race to such humiliation and debasement. He falls in love with a white girl with a disreputable past, Lorna Moon (Paula Wayne), who is attracted to him because she bears tender feelings for the abused and the downtrodden. Despite his father's objections, Joe goes ahead with his boxing career, and almost reaches the top of his profession, when he discovers that Lorna is in love with his spineless manager, Tom Moody (Kenneth Tobey). This so upsets Joe that he almost loses the championship match. But when the match is over, he goes off on a wild car ride, gets into a smashup, and is killed.

To the role of Joe Wellington, Sammy Davis brought his abundantly varied talents as actor, singer, dancer—particularly in a production number called "Don't Forget 127th Street," where, revisiting the scenes of his boyhood poverty, he reminds the black-faced kids not to forget their racial origins. Howard Taubman described this memorable scene in *The New York Times:* "Young chicks and razor-sharp blades, old folks and a couple of kids, join Mr. Davis in intoning the dubious Harlem virtues. As their comments grow more acidulous, the spirits rise. The tempo of the song quickens, and the movement of the dancers become swifter."

Sammy Davis was also heard in a moody ballad, "No More," and in "Night Song," which reflected the high inner tensions of the Negro. With Lorna he shared the love song "I Want to Be with You."

Not the least of the attractions of the production was the choreography—

two ballets particularly. One offered a boxing match translated in terms of the dance, with percussion instruments providing the musical background. "The view from the ringside is breathtaking," wrote Walter Kerr, "as Mr. Rogers takes his last spin and drops; it is as though rhythm had died while you were looking." In this two-man ballet, Jaime Rogers (playing the part of Lopez) shared the spotlight with Sammy Davis. The second impressive dance was performed by Jaime Rogers, Lester Wilson, and Mabel Robinson, after Billy Daniels (appearing as Eddie Satin, a racketeer) has finished singing the ballad "While the City Sleeps."

GOLDEN RAINBOW (1968), *a musical comedy, with book by Ernest Kinoy, based on Arnold Schulman's stage comedy* A Hole in the Head. *Lyrics and music by Walter Marks. Presented by Joseph P. Harris and Ira Bernstein at the Shubert Theater on February 4. Directed by Arthur Storch. Dances by Tom Panko. Cast included Steve Lawrence, Eydie Gorme, and Scott Jacoby (383 performances).*

It was greatly to be regretted that Ernest Kinoy, in making *A Hole in the Head* into a musical renamed *Golden Rainbow,* did not adhere more closely to the original intent of its author, Arnold Schulman. Both in the play and in the motion picture that followed, the central point of interest is the portrayal of the principal character, Larry Davis. He is a happy-go-lucky, shiftless, irresponsible, hustler for a buck, but in many ways a charming and lovable widower who has two major loves in his life: his rundown hotel in Miami and his eleven-year-old son, Ally, whom he raises as a friend and as a companion. Larry is in serious danger of losing both: the hotel because he cannot raise the $5,000 to meet a mortgage payment; the son because Larry's sister-in-law, Judy Harris, is out to rescue the boy from the unsavory background in which he is being reared, into an environment more conducive to the normal life of a boy. Larry's highly personal way of facing life and its problems, and his glib and often amusing comments, gave the play and the movie their focal point of interest.

But in making the transfer to the musical-comedy stage, Kinoy was much less concerned with characterization and wit and touches of humanity than with providing his stars, Steve Lawrence (as Larry) and Eydie Gorme (as Judy Harris), with enough songs to sing, since singing is, of course, their forte. Kinoy is also concerned with lavish production numbers filled with glamorous settings and lovely half-naked girls—and so he changed the setting from Miami to Las Vegas. *Golden Rainbow* opens with one such lavish extravaganza; and it makes an effort at satire in the opening of the second act with "The Fall of Babylon," in which the pretensions of such lavish extravaganzas are mildly burlesqued. The big production numbers are the highlights of the musical. The book fails to allow Steve Lawrence to portray Larry with any kind of depth, while Steve Lawrence's wife and singing partner, Eydie Gorme (here making her musical-comedy debut) is uncomfortable in the role of the sister-in-law who has always loved Larry and who, before the final curtain, gives him the money to pay the mortgage and after that gains him as a husband, thereby saving his son for him as well.

Above and beyond the production numbers there are the songs, fifteen in all. Some are tuneful, such as "I've Got to Be Me"; one or two are amusing, such as "Desert Moon," a takeoff on the operetta type of romantic ballad popularized by Romberg and Friml. "Songs pour upon songs," commented Whitney Bolton, "tunes upon tunes, sets move in and out on wheels and wires, and there is a kind of razzle-dazzle in the frantic spirit of Las Vegas."

In the final analysis, *Golden Rainbow* turned out to be exactly what Kinoy as adapter and Walter Marks as composer-lyricist had intended it to be: a vehicle for Steve Lawrence and Eydie Gorme. As the critic of *Variety* noted, the stars "give absolutely brilliant portrayals of themselves. Since that is virtually all they're required to do and precisely what the audience expects and wants, the effect is presumably adequate for the occasion. They're both enormously accomplished pop singers." But *Golden Rainbow* would have been a far better show—and a far more successful one—if the interest lay less in giving Steve Lawrence and Eydie Gorme so many opportunities to sing within a pretentious setting and more in concentrating on needle-pointed dialogue, penetrating character portrayal, and the human interest involving the singular and at times touching relationship that exists between Larry and his son, Ally (Scott Jacoby.) "Even if you adore them [Steve Lawrence and Eydie Gorme] at the other side of idolatry," commented Clive Barnes, "you should be warned that as a vehicle for its stars *Golden Rainbow* is at best ramshackle."

GOOD BOY (1928), *a musical comedy, with book by Otto Harbach, Oscar Hammerstein II, and Henry Myers. Lyrics by Bert Kalmar. Music by Harry Ruby and Herbert Stothart. Presented by Arthur Hammerstein at the Hammerstein Theater on September 25. Directed by Reginald Hammerstein. Dances by Busby Berkeley. Cast included Eddie Buzzell, Barbara Newberry, Charles Butterworth, and Helen Kane (253 performances).*

Two country bumpkins—Walter Meakin (Eddie Buzzell) and his brother Cicero (Charles Butterworth)—come to the big city from Butlersville, Arkansas. In the city Walter soon forgets the girl he left behind, falls in love with a chorus girl, Betty Mummers (Barbara Newberry), and marries her. Betty manages to get Walter on the stage as a chorus boy. In time she tires of him and he loses her. But he regains her when he makes a fortune by creating a commercially successful doll.

The ingenious staging provided most of the novelty in a hackneyed story: the realistic reproduction of the sights and sounds of the big city upon the first arrival to New York of the two Arkansas hicks; the effective first-act finale, in which a hotel room swings up to reveal Walter and Betty on the balcony, the panorama of New York and Central Park stretching below. (During a visit to Berlin, Oscar Hammerstein II had seen a production of *The Good Soldier Schweik* in which complex and ingenious staging was made possible through the use of treadmills. He made a mental note to experiment someday with these treadmills; and he incorporated them into *Good Boy* with telling effect.)

Otherwise most of the interest in the play lay in the dry, wry humor of Charles Butterworth as Cicero; in the enchanting singing and dancing of Barbara Newberry; and in Helen Kane (the "Boop-de-Boop" Girl), who brought her famous pipsqueak voice and baby talk to the play's foremost song, "I Wanna Be Loved by You." The duet of Walter and Betty, "Some Sweet Someone," and "The Voice of the City" were two other attractive numbers, while "Manhattan Walk" and "Oh, What a Man" profited from the nimble hoofing of Dan Healy.

GOOD MORNING DEARIE (1921), *a musical comedy, with book and lyrics by Anne Caldwell. Music by Jerome Kern. Presented by Charles Dilling-ham at the Globe Theater on November 1. Directed by Edward Royce. Cast included Louise Groody, Oscar Shaw, Harland Dixon, and Ada Lewis (347 performances).*

Billy van Cortland (Oscar Shaw) is a wealthy young man who falls in love with Rose-Marie (Louisa Groody), an employee in a costume shop. She in turn has a boy friend, a crook known as Chesty (Harland Dixon). In China-town, the two rivals exchange blows without solving any problems. Later on, at a ball at the house of Billy's sister, Rose-Marie appears in a disguise to save the family jewels from being stolen by Chesty. Rose-Marie keeps the jewels from Chesty, a fact that helps considerably to bring her and Billy together.

Kern's score is not one of his more distinguished efforts. Its most important song was a Hawaiian number, "Ka-lu-a," sung by Billy. But if "Ka-lu-a" is today remembered, it is mainly because in 1921 it was involved in a historic plagiarism suit. The plaintiff was the composer Fred Fisher, who insisted that Kern had usurped a repetitious rolling bass from the syncopated fox-trot "Dardanella" (which Fisher had published, and of which he was one of the two lyricists). This was the first time that a plagiarism involved not the basic melody but its accompaniment. Many distinguished musicians (including Leopold Stokowski and Victor Herbert) took the stand for Kern, maintaining that many a composer had used a similar rhythmic device in their music long before "Dardanella." When Fisher came to the realization he had no legal leg to stand on, he offered to settle the matter out of court for the price of two suits. Kern turned the offer down hotly. He would have won the case easily, but he proved such a hostile and vociferous witness that he antagonized the court, which compelled him to pay damages of $250.

The special attractions of *Good Morning Dearie* were Harland Dixon's nimble dancing, a farcical performance of Mme. Bompart by Ada Lewis, and an amusing caricature of a detective by William Kent.

> GOOD NEWS (1927), *a musical comedy, with book by Laurence Schwab and Buddy de Sylva. Lyrics by De Sylva and Brown. Music by Ray Henderson. Presented by Schwab and Mandel at the 46th Street Theater on September 6. Directed by Edgar MacGregor. Dances by Bobby Connolly. Cast included John Price Jones, Mary Lawlor, Zelma O'Neal, Inez Courtney, and Gus Shy (557 performances).*

*Good News* was the first musical comedy for the songwriting team of De Sylva, Brown, and Henderson, who had previously worked for, and achieved major successes in, *George White's Scandals,* an annual revue. As it turned out, *Good News* was to be their box-office triumph, catching, as it did, the hyperthyroid spirit of the 1920's. College and college life seemed to hold a particular fascination for the 1920's—not, to be sure, the college life of the classroom and the lecture hall, but the extracurricular college activities of football games, sororities and fraternities, class dances and romances, and the shenanigans of undergraduates. *Good News* was a musical with a college setting, story, and characters. There had been college musicals before this (Jerome Kern's *Leave It to Jane,* for example), but none were so thoroughly and completely collegiate as *Good News.* Ushers wearing college jerseys conducted the patrons to their seats. Just before curtain time, the men of George Olsen's orchestra ran down the aisles, wearing college sweaters, and yelling "rah-rahs" before going into the pit and beginning the rousingly loud overture. Robust tunes, many of them typically collegiate, helped maintain this rah-rah atmosphere throughout the production, which Brooks Atkinson described as a "constantly fast entertainment with furious dancing and catchy tunes played to the last trombone squeal." In collegiate style were songs like "The Girls of Pi Beta Phi," sung by a girl chorus, and "The Varsity Drag," the latter introduced by Zelma O'Neal and George Olsen and his band; so successful did "The Varsity Drag" become that it stimulated the nationwide popularity of a new social dance, successor to the Charleston and the Black Bottom. Similarly, songs like the title number, also sung by Zelma O'Neal, and "Flaming Youth" carried the heartbeat of the 1920's, if not specifically of college life. Paradoxically, the biggest hit to come from this score was neither a child of the twenties nor of college, but a song in which the heroine is reassured by her boyfriend that her lowly social station is not something to be ashamed about, that there were a great many things in life that counted for much more than position and money. The song was "The Best Things in Life Are Free," a duet by Mary Lawlor and John Prince. When in 1956, 20th Century-Fox filmed the screen story of De Sylva, Brown, and Henderson, they called it *The Best Things in Life Are Free.*

Two other songs in the score were of equal sentimental appeal: "Lucky in Love," a duet by Mary Lawlor and John Price Jones, and "Just Imagine," in which Miss Lawlor was supplemented by two of the lesser female characters and an ensemble of girls.

The setting is Tait College, a school where football holds a position of greater importance than the curriculum, the kind of a place that has a college attached to the football stadium. Tom Marlowe (John Price Jones) is captain of the football team. He can play in the season's big game with Colton College only because Constance Lane (Mary Lawlor) has coached him in astronomy well enough for him to pass the exams. During the all-important game he is saved by Bobby Randall (Gus Shy) from making a fumble, and the game is won by Tait. Marlowe, still a hero, can now proceed to the more important business of winning Constance, whom he has loved for a long time.

The production was highly charged with the dynamic, seemingly inexhaustible energy of youth; this was perhaps the show's strongest appeal. Speaking of these youths, Burns Mantle said: "They sway from the hips. They wear their trousers baggy and their panties short. They sing with raucous abandon and dance like all get out. They rah-rah with gusto. They are very collegiate. Oh, very!"

It was the vigor and exuberance of Zelma O'Neal, particularly in the rendition of her musical numbers, that made her a star. But when MGM made *Good News* into a movie in 1930, they avoided Zelma O'Neal, while keeping Mary Lawlor. Another screen adaptation was made by MGM in 1947, with June Allyson and Peter Lawford. In both versions, six principal songs from the stage show were retained.

THE GRAND STREET FOLLIES (1922), *a revue, with book assembled by Agnes Morgan. Music arranged by Lily Hyland. Lyrics and music by various contributors. Presented at the Neighborhood Playhouse. Cast included Albert Carroll and Aline McMahon (148 performances).*

(1924), *a revue, with book and lyrics by Agnes Morgan. Music by Lily Hyland. Presented at the Neighborhood Playhouse on May 20. Staged by Helen Arthur. Dances by Albert Carroll. Cast included Albert Carroll, Joanna .Roos, Helen Arthur, and Agnes Morgan (172 performances).*

(1925), *a revue, with book and lyrics by Agnes Morgan. Music by Lily Hyland. Presented at the Neighborhood Playhouse on June 18. Cast included Albert Carroll, Paula Trueman, Dorothy Sands, and Marc Loebell (166 performances).*

(1926), *a revue, with book and lyrics by Agnes Morgan. Music by Lily Hyland, Arthur Schwartz and Randall Thompson. Presented at the Neighborhood Playhouse on June 15. Directed by Agnes Morgan. Cast included Albert Carroll, Dorothy Sands, and Marc Loebell (174 performances).*

(1927), *a revue, with book and lyrics by Agnes Morgan. Music by Max Ewing. Presented at the Neighborhood Playhouse on May 19. Directed by Agnes Morgan. Cast included Albert Carroll, Dorothy Sands, Marc Loebell, and Agnes Morgan (30 performances).*

(1928), *a revue, with book and lyrics by Agnes Morgan. Music by Max Ewing, Lily Hyland, and Serge Walter. Presented by Actors-Managers, Inc., at the Booth Theater on May 28. Directed by Agnes Morgan. Cast included Albert Carroll, Marc Loebell, James Cagney, Dorothy Sands, and Paula Trueman (144 performances).*

(1929), *a revue, with book and lyrics by Agnes Morgan. Music by Arthur Schwartz, Max Ewing, and others. Presented by the Actors-Managers, Inc., in association with Paul Moss, at the Booth Theater on May 1. Directed by Agnes Morgan. Dances by Dave Gould. Cast included Albert Carroll, Dorothy Sands, Paula Trueman, Marc Loebell, and James Cagney (85 performances).*

This was the parent of the intimate revue that flourished on Broadway in the 1920's, 1930's, and early 1940's with productions like *The Garrick Gaities, The Little Show,* and *Pins and Needles.* Entered into with a spirit of levity—the program described the first edition as a "low-brow show for high-grade morons"—its creators emphasized wit and satire. The first edition mocked Walt Whitman's poetry and stars of stage, ballet, and opera

(Pavlova, Irene Castle, Chaliapin, and so forth); and it ridiculed current dances. Albert Carroll immediately revealed himself a master of caricature and mimicry, equally adept in male and female impersonations—perhaps best in "The Royal Damn Fandango," in which he impersonated a lady with a fan.

The first edition merely suggested the potential of these gifted young iconoclasts. In 1924 these potentials were fully realized. In fact this was probably the best edition of the series, and the one that served as the immediate inspiration for *The Garrick Gaieties* in 1925. Albert Carroll was supplemented by Dorothy Sands, the two dominating this and later productions with their devastating takeoffs on outstanding personalities of stage, ballet, and opera. Albert Carroll mimicked Emily Stevens and John Barrymore; others in the cast re-created with remarkable verisimilitude such varied personalities as Elsie Janis, Beatrice Lillie, Fanny Brice, and Rudolf Valentino. (One of these impersonators was Danton Walker, later to become famous as a columnist.) The sketches covered a wide area for their satirical thrusts, including Joan of Arc; the Algonquin "round table" (then the meeting place of Alexander Woollcott, Heywood Broun, Dorothy Parker, F. P. A., Robert Benchley, and other famous Broadwayites); the Russian Art Theater in a hillbilly sketch; a farcical medieval musical comedy which becomes the recipient of the "Ignoble Prize." These and other brilliant numbers brought the carriage trade to downtown Grand Street, where the Neighborhood Playhouse was situated; and it firmly established the little, intimate, sophisticated revue as a new genre in the musical theater.

Among the high spots of subsequent editions were more irreverent caricatures: for example, Albert Carroll as Ethel Barrymore and Dorothy Sands as a Town Hall recitalist. The best satirical sketches included "The Wild Duck of the 18th Century" (as Ibsen would have written the play had he lived a century earlier); "The South Sea Islands according to Broadway"; "The Siege of Troy" (as David Belasco might have produced it); "Caesar's Invasion of Britain" (with lyrics by Noël Coward). The Ziegfeld girl was lampooned in "Glory, Glory, Glory," and a delightful impression of the zany four Marx Brothers featured Albert Carroll as Harpo.

In the 1926 edition, a young lawyer contributed some of the songs— none of them particularly significant or giving the slightest indication that their creator, Arthur Schwartz, would become in the 1930's perhaps the foremost composer for revues in general and the intimate revue in particular. Another contributor of songs was Randall Thompson, who went on to become one of America's most distinguished composers of serious music, while a young lady, in a bit part—Jessica Dragonette—would within a few years become a singing star on radio. In 1928 James Cagney—another unknown at the time—was seen as a tap dancer.

THE GREAT WALTZ (1934), a "musical romance," with book by Moss Hart, adapted from librettos by A. M. Willner, Heinz Reichert, Ernst Marischka, and Caswell Garth. Lyrics by Desmond Carter. Music by Johann Strauss, father and son. Directed by Hassard Short. Dances by Albertina Rasch. Presented by Max Gordon at the Center Theater on September 22. Cast included Guy Robertson, Marie Burke, and Marion Claire (297 performances).

Waltzes from Vienna was a successful operetta based on the life of Johann Strauss, the son, the composer of The Blue Danube, produced in London in 1931. Hassard Short felt that a similar ambitious musical could do well in New York—a huge spectacle with the background of Johann Strauss music. Naturally, he wanted the libretto rewritten to suit American tastes. He discussed the project with Max Gordon, who was thoroughly intrigued with it, so much so that he said he would house it in one of the largest and most luxurious theaters in New York, the Center Theater in Rockefeller Plaza. Moss Hart, who originally was skeptical about the whole idea, finally consented to write the text; and the Rockefellers helped Gordon to pay the enormous bills such a venture incurred by contributing $50,000 for costumes and new stage machinery. So grandiose were the plans for the staging, costuming, and sets that before the curtain went up $250,000 had been spent—an unheard-of figure in those days. And so lavish were the forces employed that even with a long run it could hardly hope to break even. The singing chorus numbered one hundred voices. The cast comprised forty-two principals and supporting players; there were forty members in the Albertina Rasch ballet and fifty-three musicians conducted by Frank Tours. Backstage a stage crew of ninety had to handle ten tons of scenery. The costumes, designed by Irene Sharaff, employed more than a score of tailors and seamstresses to produce the five hundred costumes needed. Still sparing no expense, Max Gordon brought H. Reeves-Smith from London to play the part of Johann Strauss the father; Marion Claire, who had previously sung with the Chicago Civic Opera, was signed for the feminine lead; the younger Strauss was played by Guy Robertson, who demanded and got a fat weekly check.

Despite the appalling complexities of Hassard Short's staging, the production went off smoothly, even in the spectacular finale that needed complicated machinery to get the entire cast on the stage and a brass band to march across it. For the most part, the critics enjoyed what they saw. Percy Hammond called it "the biggest, the most beautiful, the most tasteful and the most extravagant show of its kind"—which it was. It had a run of 297 performances attended by over one million customers. It could have stayed on for several months more to crowded houses had not Max Gordon underestimated its appeal and before the New York opening booked the show to begin its road tour.

Moss Hart's libretto made no more studied an effort to stick to the biographical truth than did other operettas based on the lives of composers—*Blossom Time,* for example. As the musical opens we find Johann Strauss I (H. Reeves-Smith) the waltz king of Vienna. He is the father of a young man, also named Johann Strauss (Guy Robertson), whose crowning ambition it to write waltzes and conduct them in cafés the way his father did. But his father was violently opposed to his son's making music a career and did everything he could to block the boy's progress in his chosen career. There now appears an influential Russian lady, Countess Olga (Marie Burke)—a character that is a Moss Hart invention—to help young Johann Strauss. On the night that Dommayer's Gardens is to open to the music of the elder Strauss, she evolves a plan whereby the father is waylaid, and the son has to take his place. The son creates a furor in his debut, especially after he has performed *The Blue Danube Waltz.* Now it is the son who is the waltz king of Vienna, and the father who has been dethroned. The younger Strauss falls in love and marries Therese (Marion Claire); besides enjoying fabulous success in his profession, he also knows domestic happiness. But the father has no use for his son's music—bitterness and envy having now added fresh fuel to the fires of his resentment.

All the music came from the works of Johann Strauss, father and son—frequently bearing strange, new titles to fit in with the manufactured story. Of course, *The Blue Danube* was there, and so was the father's *Radetzky March,* both of them bearing their original titles.

THE GREENWICH VILLAGE FOLLIES (1919), *a revue, with book by Philip Bartholomae. Lyrics by Arthur Swanstrom and John Murray Anderson. Music by A. Baldwin Sloane. Presented by the Bohemians at the Greenwich Village Theater on July 15. Directed by John Murray Anderson. Cast included Ted Lewis and his band, Harry Delf, and Bessie McCoy Davis (232 performances).*

(1920), *a revue, with book by Thomas J. Gray. Lyrics by Arthur Swanstrom and John Murray Anderson. Music by A. Baldwin Sloane. Presented by the Bohemians at the Greenwich Village Theater on August 30. Directed by John Murray Anderson. Cast included Frank Crumit, Jay Brennan, Bert Savoy, Howard Marsh, and Harriet Gimble (192 performances).*

(1921), *a revue, with book and lyrics by Arthur Swanstrom and John Murray*

*Anderson. Music by Carey Morgan. Presented by the Bohemians at the Shubert Theater on August 31. Directed by John Murray Anderson. Cast included Irene Franklin, Ted Lewis and his band, Peggy Hope, Donald Kerr, and Brown and Watts (167 performances).*

*(1922), a revue, with book and lyrics by George V. Hobart, John Murray Anderson, and Irving Caesar. Music by Louis A. Hirsch. Presented by the Bohemians at the Shubert Theater on September 12. Directed by John Murray Anderson. Cast included John Hazzard, Savoy and Brennan, Carl Randall, and Yvonne Georges (216 performances).*

*(1923), a revue, with book and lyrics by Irving Caesar and John Murray Anderson. Music by Con Conrad and Louis A. Hirsch. Presented by the Bohemians at the Winter Garden on September 20. Directed by John Murray Anderson. Cast included Tom Howard, Sam White, and Eva Puck (140 performances).*

*(1924), a revue, with book by Irving Caesar and John Murray Anderson. Lyrics by Irving Caesar, Cole Porter, and John Murray Anderson. Music by Cole Porter and Jay Gorney. Presented by the Bohemians, A. J. Jones, and Morris Green at the Shubert Theater on September 16. Directed by John Murray Anderson. Cast included Vincent Lopez and his orchestra, Bobbe Arnst, the Dolly Sisters, and Moran and Mack (127 performances).*

*(1925), a revue, with book by unidentified authors. Lyrics and music by Irving Caesar, Harold Levey, and Owen Murphy. Presented by the Bohemians, A. J. Jones, and Morris Green at the 46th Street Theater on December 24. Directed by Hassard Short. Cast included Tom Howard, Frank McIntyre, Irene Delroy, and Florence Moore (180 performances).*

*(1928), a revue, with sketches by Harold Atteridge. Lyrics by Max and Nathaniel Lief. Music by Ray Perkins and Maurice Rubens. Presented by the Bohemians, Inc., at the Winter Garden on April 9. Directed by J. C. Huffman, Chester Hale, and Ralph Reader. Cast included Doc. Rockwell, Benny Fields, Grace La Rue, Blossom Seeley, and the Chester Hale Girls (158 performances).*

The plan to produce *The Greenwich Village Follies* was born with John Murray Anderson, then just a producer of cabaret revues, and before that a ballroom dancer. His idea was to combine the spirit of Greenwich Village with the elegance of lavish Broadway revues, and to present these productions in their native milieu—Greenwich Village. The original title of the revue was *Greenwich Village Nights,* but before long the word "Nights" was changed to "Follies" in spite of Ziegfeld's protests. In this first edition the atmosphere and life of Greenwich Village were not only evoked but often satirized as well. Very much in the bohemian way of life of that district were songs like

"I'll Sell You a Girl." Chorus girls, some in berets and smocks and others in scanty transparent costumes, burlesqued art life in Greenwich Village, while "I'm the Hostess of a Bum Cabaret" (sung by Bessie McCoy Davis) made fun of prohibition and the three-mile limit in a down-to-earth cabaret number. Ted Lewis and his band gave a medley of his favorites and introduced the number that thenceforth became his theme song, "When My Baby Smiles at Me," and Bessie McCoy Davis did an effective marionette dance, simulating a puppet by having strings attached to arms and legs. Out of this edition came a hit song in Sloane's "I Want a Daddy Who Will Rock Me to Sleep."

With the critics unanimously in favor of the revue, it found new and larger quarters at the Nora Bayes Theater in the heart of Broadway six weeks after it had opened downtown.

The 1920 edition once again opened at the small Greenwich Village Theater, and once again soon had to move to a larger auditorium, this time to the Shubert Theater uptown. Greater stress was placed on sex than in the first edition—the opening scene, "The Naked Truth," revealing artists, models, bohemians, art students—the girls in various stages of undress. Burlesque humor was introduced through the antics of Savoy and Brennan —Savoy particularly hilarious in his impersonations of females. One of their best sketches was "Come to Bohemia," with Savoy appearing as Lady Nicotine and Brennan as an apache. There were several outstanding production numbers. One was called "The Birthday Cake," with chorus girls dressed like birthday candles and dancing on an elaborately decorated table; this scene was introduced by one of the best songs in this edition, "Just Sweet Sixteen," sung by Howard Marsh and a bevy of sweet innocents. Another was a cabaret scene with Russian costumes, folk songs, and dances called "Song of Samovar"; another, "The Krazy Kat's Ball," presented comic-strip characters; and a fourth, "Tsin," had showgirls placed on several tiers made up as bottles of perfume, with Mary Lewis (who subsequently sang at the Metropolitan Opera) singing "Perfume of Love." Frank Crumit delivered two good songs in "Just Snap Your Fingers at Care" and "I'm a Lonesome Little Raindrop."

For burlesque comedy, the 1921 edition offered the rowdy team of Brown and Watts (the Brown being Joe E. Brown, later a comedy star in the movies). They went to town with their slapstick humor in sketches like "A Dying Duck in a Thunderstorm" and "Love's Awakening." For music, the edition had a blockbuster in "Three O'Clock in the Morning," melody by Dorothy Terriss, used in the closing scene, sung by Rosalind Fuller and Richard Bold, and providing the excuse for an elaborately staged waltz for

Margaret Petit and Valodia Vestoff and a dancing ensemble. Ballet was further represented by "Snowflake," using silver-colored sets; its star, Margaret Petit, performed a dance in which she melted into nothingness with the coming out of the sun.

It did not take the 1922 edition long to justify the title of the revue—even though the geographical location of the production had changed to uptown. The overture curtain offered an attractive view of Greenwich Village. Otherwise there was not much in the revue to remind audiences any longer of the downtown bohemian origin of the revue. The edition highlighted a beautiful ballet based on the Oscar Wilde tale "The Nightingale and the Rose," danced by Ura Sharon and Alexander Yakeoff to Chopin's music. (The ballad ballet, as this kind of production was called, came to be a regular feature of *The Greenwich Village Folllies* from this time on.) Other eye-filling production numbers were "Sweetheart Lane," set in Washington Square, and "You Are My Rainbow," an elaborate ballet stunningly colored by ever-changing lighting and vividly hued costuming. Broad comedy was represented by the hilarities of Savoy and Brennan, a travesty on the melancholy plays of Eugene O'Neill, and an effective parody on old ballads by John Hazzard in "Goodbye to Dear Old Alaska." Yvonne Georges, an importation from Paris, sang *"Mon Homme"* (undoubtedly in competition to Fanny Brice, who was singing the same number in English as "My Man" at *The Ziegfeld Follies*). Hirsch's best songs were "A Kiss from a Red-Headed Miss" and "Sixty Seconds Every Minute I Dream of You." A popular interpolation was "Georgette," by Lew Brown and Ray Henderson, one of Henderson's first song hits; it was introduced by Ted Lewis and his band. This edition ended with a travesty called "Greenwich Village Nights," in which Savoy and Brennan were featured. For Savoy, appearances in this finale represented his farewell to the stage, his life being cut short by lightning in Long Beach, New York.

Big production numbers proved to be the staple of the 1923 edition, which moved to the more spacious quarters of the Winter Garden. The ballad ballet of this edition was "The Raven," based on Poe's poem. It proved a bore and had to be removed from the program. Another ballad ballet, and more attractive, was "The Garden of Kama," a fantasy based on Laurence Hope's love lyrics of India, set to music by Amy Finden. One of the dancers in this number was Martha Graham—a novice, her career in modern dance still some years off. Martha Graham was also seen dancing in a Spanish-fiesta scene. "Moonlight Kisses" offered a parade of beauties, each costumed as some character from history or legend. "Barcarolle" was a dream fantasy to add to the production-number riches.

But there was no sacrifice of comedy or nostalgia or sentiment. Eva Puck and Denman Maley presented a burlesque about a quarrelsome married couple. Tom Howard appeared in a howling skit atop a floating raft where he is slowly starving to death. Buster West delighted audiences with his amusing eccentric dancing. Nostalgia was found in several delightful English music-hall songs sung by Daphne Pollard, while sentiment was contributed by Marion Green's romantic singing. Hirsch's best song was "Just a Bit of Heaven in Your Smile."

The 1924 edition was one of the poorer ones of this set. Its main importance lay in the fact that the score was the work of Cole Porter—one of his earliest contributions to the Broadway musical theater. This was still Cole Porter the apprentice, to be sure, who could produce only one number that had any measure of distinction, "I'm in Love Again," which provided Robert Alton with attractive background music for a fetching dance number. Even with the presence in the cast of the Dolly Sisters, Moran and Mack ("The Two Black Crows"), and Vincent Lopez and his orchestra, this edition was definitely substandard, in spite of an attractive ballad ballet "The Happy Prince," inspired by the tale of Oscar Wilde, and sung by George Rasley and Dorothy Neville. To strengthen the production, Fred Allen was brought into the cast to add his droll humor to the proceedings (Portland Hoffa, who later became his wife, was in the chorus), and Toto the Clown to introduce novelty. But the show remained more or less a "dud."

John Murray Anderson left the revue for the 1925 edition, to be replaced by Hassard Short, who evolved some spectacular numbers, including "Lady of the Snow," and made stunning use of lighting effects. Florence Moore was the main comedienne. But like its immediate predecessor, the 1925 edition lacked fresh, new materials, both in the humor and the music departments.

The last edition, in 1928, featured a galaxy of stars and a good deal of fine entertainment—Benny Fields and Blossom Seeley, Grace La Rue, Doc. Rockwell, Bobby Watson, and Grace Brinkley being the main contributors. A newcomer, Sheila Barrett, revealed a gift for mimicry she soon exploited in later productions, and an exciting calypso number used the services of the Chester Hale Girls. As with the two preceding editions, none of the musical numbers deserve mention, and all of the songs from the three productions have long since been forgotten.

GUYS AND DOLLS (1950), *a musical comedy, with book by Jo Swerling and Abe Burrows, based on a story and characters by Damon Runyon. Lyrics and music by Frank Loesser. Presented by Feuer and Martin at the 46th Street*

*Theater on November 24. Directed by George S. Kaufman. Dances by Michael Kidd. Cast included Isabel Bigley, Sam Levene, Robert Alda, Vivian Blaine, and Pat Rooney (1,200 performances).*

*Guys and Dolls* not only belongs with that aristocratic society of musicals that have had a run of over one thousand performances, but it is also one of the very best ever produced. It is wonderful entertainment in which the audience interest is never allowed to relax. It is the model of what an ideal musical comedy should be. Like different parts of a solved jigsaw puzzle, each part is made to fit neatly into the complete picture and is basic to the overall pattern. George S. Kaufman's staging gave the play much of its tingling air of excitement and its breathless pace. The opening scene, for example, is a pantomime of Broadway life and characters which sets the mood for the entire production. Michael Kidd's dances are exciting, with a genuine masterpiece in a large ballet number using for its theme a crap game in a sewer. Jo Mielziner's sets were daringly imaginative. The performances of all principals and subordinates were equally effective—not a weak link in the entire chain. Finally, both the melodies and the lyrics of Frank Loesser were remarkable. No wonder then that John Chapman singled out *Guys and Dolls* as the finest play of 1950 because of its "originality and its avoidance of the usual musical comedy patterns." No wonder, too, that it captured the Antoinette Perry, New York Drama Critics Circle, Donaldson, and Outer Circle awards as the best musical of the season.

Described as a "musical fable of Broadway," *Guys and Dolls* is a vibrant, pulsating, and human portrait of the world of Broadway—of big- and little-shot gamblers and Salvation Army proselytizers, of nightclub entertainers and a variety of jerks and eccentrics. Each routine, song, dance, and bit of humor is germane to the plot and succeeds in giving it additional depth. As Abe Burrows wrote in *Theatre Arts:* "Nothing is in there that doesn't belong. We didn't care about how a single number or scene would go. We didn't concern ourselves with reprising songs for no reason at all. We cared about the whole show and nothing went in unless it fit. . . . Everything fits. That must be what makes it a hit."

The principal source was Damon Runyon's short story,"The Idylls of Sarah Brown," but with characters borrowed from other Runyon tales. (As one of the two adapters, Abe Burrows here makes his bow as a writer for the Broadway musical-comedy stage.) Two love plots are woven into the fabric. The first involves Sky Masterson (Robert Alda), a high-living, happy-go-lucky sport, with the Salvation Army lass, Sarah Brown (Isabel Bigley). The subsidiary love interest is found in gambler Nathan Detroit (Sam

Levene) and the nightclub entertainer Miss Adelaide (Vivian Blaine); they have been engaged for fourteen years but their ever-impending marriage is always frustrated by some crap game or other.

When the curtain rises, Broadway is bustling with activity. It is morning. Nicely-Nicely, Benny, and Rusty Charlie are trying to pick out the horses for the day's races, in a three-voice canonic chant, "Fugue for Tinhorns" (or "I've Got the Horse Right Here"). Sky Masterson, another chronic gambler, meets Sarah Brown, a Salvation Army lass from the nearby Save-a-Soul Mission, run by her father, Abernathy (Pat Rooney). She is, of course, a modest, demure, and virtuous girl. In "I'll Know" she tells Sky in no uncertain terms he is not *her* kind of man; that when the right man comes along she'll recognize him at once. Her contemptuous dismissal of Sky only makes him all the more determined to capture her heart.

The scene shifts to a nightclub, the Hot Spot, where the chorus girls perform their numbers, first "A Bushel and a Peck," and after that "Take Back Your Mink"—the latter the horrified reaction of the girls when they realize what men want when they present them with a gift of a mink coat. Adelaide, a star performer at the nightclub, is an unhappy girl, suffering from a psychosomatic illness (chronic colds) caused by her boyfriend, Nathan Detroit, to whom she had been engaged for fourteen years. In "Adelaide's Lament" (which Moss Hart once said was one of the finest musical-comedy numbers he had ever heard) she speaks about her condition.

Nathan Detroit has no time for Adelaide's misery. He must find a place for a floating crap game, since some big-money men with a weakness for games of chance have come to town—meek sheep ready for the shearing. (He eventually finds the place down in a sewer.) Nathan cannot understand why Adelaide is unable to be sympathetic to his problems. His gambling friends, in the title number, express their contempt for any "slob" who allows himself to get into the grips of a girl friend to the point of losing all sense of values about things that are really important.

Meanwhile, Sky is determined to arouse Sarah's interest in him, something which his friends insist is impossible. Sky is so sure of his powers with females that he makes a bet with one of his friends that Sarah will even go with him to Havana. After a good deal of vacillation, Sarah consents to go—not for an illicit adventure (as Sky hopes) but because her Salvation Army mission is in danger of closing down for lack of customers, and Sky has promised her to seek out ways to save it. In Havana, Sarah reveals that she is more interested in Sky than she had suspected ("If I Were a Bell") just as Sky is rapidly coming to the conclusion he has fallen in love with

Sarah ("I've Never Been in Love Before"). He refuses to take advantage of her even though she has become inebriated with a drink she was told was harmless, and takes her back immediately to Broadway.

When Sarah learns that Sky took her to Havana just to win a bet, she is determined never again to see him. But she needs Sky's help to save the mission. Sky musters his large circle of friends to crowd the mission to the doors. When the Salvation Army authorities arrive they become convinced the mission is really needed in that neighborhood. The mission saved, Sarah's interest in Sky is revived, and their romance takes a serious turn as they talk of marriage. Even Nathan Detroit is now ready to get married to Adelaide.

Loesser's score—most of the principal numbers of which are listed in the summary of the plot—revealed him as a master of ballads and humorous or satirical numbers, both in the music and the lyrics (he wrote both). In the latter category belong such other numbers as "The Oldest Established"—a takeoff on Alma Mater songs, but this one is honor of crap games—and "Sue Me," in a mock-operatic style. A new, touching ballad, "Your Eyes Are the Eyes of a Woman in Love"—as good as any of the ballads in the stage score—was written for the motion-picture adaptation by MGM, in 1955, starring Frank Sinatra, Jean Simmons, Marlon Brando, and Vivian Blaine.

GYPSY (1959), *a musical comedy, with book by Arthur Laurents, based on the autobiography of Gypsy Rose Lee. Lyrics by Stephen Sondheim. Music by Jule Styne. Presented by David Merrick and Leland Hayward at the Broadway Theater on May 21. Directed and with choreography by Jerome Robbins. Cast included Ethel Merman, Sandra Church, and Jack Klugman (702 performances).*

Though *Gypsy* is based on the autobiography of Gypsy Rose Lee (the successful burlesque star)—and despite the title of this musical—it is not the character of Gypsy who dominates the production and endows it with its remarkable force and exciting exhilaration. Rather, it was the performance of Ethel Merman as Rose, mother not only of Gypsy Rose Lee, but also of June Havoc, another little girl who grew up to be a star. A domineering woman of overpowering ambition—a stage mother to end all stage mothers, determined to make stars of her two little girls—Rose, as propelled by Ethel Merman's energy, became a cyclone sweeping relentlessly through the entire musical, laying waste anything or anybody in her way. Rose proved to be one of Miss Merman's most dynamic roles, which is saying a great deal of a lady who had been queen of musical comedy since she had literally burst forth like an explosive time bomb in *Girl Crazy* in 1931, and since then had had many a juicy part in numerous musical-comedy successes, including *Anything Goes* and *Annie Get Your Gun*.

*Gypsy* is a musical about show business—specifically vaudeville—and so it is a Cook's tour of auditions, backstage activities, dingy hotel rooms on one-week stands. The time is the twenties; the place Seattle, Washington. Rose's two wonder children are under her vigilant eye, rehearsing "Let Me Entertain You." Actually they are preparing for a kid's show, but for mother Rose this is just nonsense, since her children are meant for the big time. She now becomes, as Brooks Atkinson described her, "the female juggernaut who drives her two daughters into show business and keeps their noses to the grindstone." They become a vaudeville act known as Baby June and her Newsboys, managed by Herbie (Jack Klugman), who soon finds much in Rose to admire and like. The years go by, and the act of Baby June and her Newsboys continues to travel the Orpheum circuit. But the ascent to success is not made any easier when one of Rose's two girls, June, deserts show business to elope with her sweetheart. Rose is heartbroken—but undaunted. She will now throw all her energies and resourcefulness into making Louise (Sandra Church) a star—a full-time job that makes it impossible for Rose to consider seriously Herbie's marriage proposal. The new act, "Madame Rose's Toreadorables," with Louise as its star, does not get very far—for vaudeville is on its last legs. A strip-teaser in the local burlesque theater instructs Louise in the art of stripping, insisting that Louise's future lies in burlesque. When the stripper gets arrested, Louise takes her place and creates a sensation. Louise becomes the star her mother always dreamed she would become—though the fact that Louise has become a star as a stripper is a source of considerable disappointment to Rose. Mother and daughter quarrel. Bitter, Rose parodies her daughter's act in a rousing number called "Rose's Turn" in the final scene. But a reconciliation between mother and daughter does take place soon, and there is even the prospect that now that Louise is on her own Rose might seriously consider marrying Herbie.

The principal song from this thoroughly catchy score was "Everything's Coming Up Roses," which Rose sings at the end of the first act when the world seems to be crumbling at her feet while she insists that no setbacks or disappointments can smother the fires of her hopes and ambitions. "Together," "Small World," and "You'll Never Get Away from Me" are also musically impressive.

Two of the best humorous episodes in the production occur when Baby June gives a performance utilizing all the nauseating little tricks and gimmicks that characterize baby stars; and when burlesque performers give a demonstration of the art of stripping. But in the last analysis, it is Ethel Merman that was the strong suit of *Gypsy*—a fact sublimely ignored by Warner Brothers when they made their motion-picture adaptation, released in 1962: Merman was sidestepped for Rosalind Russell, who was supplemented by Natalie Wood as Louise and Karl Malden as Herbie. Substituting Miss Russell for Miss Merman—without minimizing Miss Russell's own brand of irresistible energy and talent—was exchanging a tornado for a big wind, as Bosley Crowther put it. "She misses the Merman magic and magnificence in the mama role that is still the big thing in the movie," Crowther added.

> HAIR (1968), *"the American Tribal Love-Rock Musical," with book and lyrics by Gerome Ragni and James Rado. Music by Galt MacDermot. Presented by Michael Butler at the Biltmore Theater on April 29. Directed by Tom O'Horgan. Dances by Julie Arenal. Cast included James Rado, Gerome Ragni, Shelley Plimpton, Sally Eaton, and Ronald Dyson.*

The rock-'n'-roll era of the late 1950's brought us a highly successful musical in *Bye Bye Birdie*. The psychedelic years of the late 1960's had a musical stage spokesman in *Hair*. The authors, Gerome Ragni and James Rado, have revealed that for two years they had been putting down random ideas for a musical about the chaotic world around them, the people they knew and loved, and the people and things they hated and rebelled against, and the various other vagaries and indiscretions of the younger generation in the Vietnam war years. Whenever the authors thought of something appropriate, they jotted it down on scraps of paper. After two years these scraps must have accumulated into quite a mass. One suspects that the authors then threw all the slips of paper high in the air, let them fall pell-mell, and then proceeded to write their text by picking up the pieces of paper at random and following the chain of thought in the same sequence in which those papers were so haphazardly picked up (very much in the way that some aleatory composers write their music).

That's the kind of musical *Hair* is. In its outspoken revolt, it has even rebelled against the musical theater. It has no plot to speak of, no logical sequence of events, no train of thought, no recognizable format, no creative discipline, no shape or design. It's an explosion. Things are allowed to happen, however much some of these doings are unconventional or outright shocking. The dialogue is thick with profanity, and so are some of the song lyrics. The hippies, the love children, protest against war, racism, the draft, patriotism, morality, cleanliness, and most of all against middle-class values—all this and more are to be found in this highly unconventional musical.

As one of the characters, Jeanie, remarks as, looking through her glasses, she inspects the audience: "What's going on in all those little *Daily News* heads?"

The characters wear the recognizable uniform of their clan; and in one scene they wear nothing at all. They run all over the stage, roll over one another, explode out into the audience, and run amok up and down the aisles. They speak in favor of smoking pot, making love indiscriminately, sex perversion—freedom of thought and action. They promote demonstrations, and carry placards, some of which descend to the absurd, as the one that commands in large letters: "See Ethel Merman in Hair." And they sing all kinds of songs in many different styles and idioms, some with a strong rock beat, some primitive and formless (words in kind), some with a swinging and lusty emotion, and some (surprisingly enough) with a good deal of tender feeling to them. The most popular of the strong rhythmed numbers is "Aquarius." The best of the ballads is "Frank Mills," which Crissy (Shelley Plimpton) sings about her hot-rod lover. Another is "Good Morning Starshine." The closing number, "Let the Sunshine In" (or "The Flesh Failures") became a hit song.

There are two versions of *Hair* (both of which were recorded). The first became the initial production of Joseph Papp's New York Shakespeare Festival Public Theater and was given Off Broadway at the Florence Sutro Anspacher Theater on October 29, 1967. It stayed there eight weeks. From there it moved uptown to the former discothèque Cheetah. Then it went through an extensive period of rewriting. Most of the plot was deleted from the original production, a great many songs were added, together with new irrelevant sequences and production novelties. What emerged was an almost entirely new stage adventure. The much-publicized nudity sequence, for example, was one of the new ideas that was born when *Hair* was being thus thoroughly revised. At last, the production moved into the Biltmore Theater to create dismay in some, shock in others, confusion in still others and—most surprising of all—a good deal of honest praise from some of the most reputable critics. The conservative Clive Barnes of *The New York Times* thought it "masterly," "new," "subtle," adding that it was "the first Broadway musical in some time to have the authentic voice of today rather than that of the day before yesterday."

Actually, while it would be euphemistic to call the goings-on a plot—just as it would be a misnomer to call the free-wheeling stage antics choreography—there is some sort of a basic theme running through the production. The musical opens with "Aquarius" (hauntingly introduced musically by electronic sounds), in which Ron (Ronald Dyson) suggests that mankind is progressing into an age when peace will guide the planets and love will steer the stars. From then on, the musical goes on to condemn everything that is wrong with the Establishment and to praise everything that is right with the hippies and the love children. Claude (James Rado), a long-haired hippie, leaves his Flatbush home, pretends he is from Manchester, England, and proceeds to establish a *ménage à trois* at the apartment of his friend Berger (Gerome Ragni) and Berger's girl, Sheila (Lynn Kellogg). Claude is about to be drafted into the Army, much to the despair of Jeanie (Sally Eaton)—though she is pregnant with somebody else's child—and their hippie friends. As for Claude, his main ambition before going into uniform is to seduce the girl who seems to find more pleasure in painting protest posters than in sex. When Claude is eventually drafted, his hippie friends mourn the death of his spirit.

Shock treatment is introduced in the famous "Be-In" scene that comes at the end of the first act, which concludes with cast members appearing totally nude. There is much more within the rest of the show to make the Establishment uncomfortable. There is Woof's song, "Sodomy," which talks about various unsavory sexual practices, and wonders why words identifying them should sound so nasty. There is "I Got Life," where Claude glorifies his body, and the ensemble glorify theirs. There is "White Boys" (a wonderful spoof of the Supremes), in which a trio of girls wearing a single size-60 gown speak of the reaction of the Establishment to interracial sex practices. There is "Colored Spade," where Hud (Lamont Washington) calls the Negro every conceivable name he can think of. More appealing, however—and very much in the tender spirit of "Frank Mills" (whose lyrics, incidentally, are in prose)—is a number poignantly sung by Sheila, a girl who has a good deal of trouble adjusting herself to her environment: "Easy to Be Hard."

While enjoying its long run on Broadway, *Hair* was represented by different companies in Los Angeles, San Francisco, and Chicago. The sensation and triumph enjoyed by all these productions were matched by what happened in Toronto, and particularly in Europe. Performed in London and Paris, *Hair* was given with so many interpolations of local humor and comments of London or Parisian interest that in each instance it became quite a different show from what it was in America. In Paris, *Hair* became the first French-language version of an American musical to become a box-office sellout (and at the unprecedented top price of ten dollars, instead of the more usual one for Paris of six dollars) since *Rose-Marie,* years ago. (The only other two American musicals to have been highly successful in Paris had both been played in English—*West Side Story* and *Porgy and Bess.*) "This French-accented *Hair* . . . not only shows the vitality of the show in the first place," reported Clive Barnes from Paris, "but also emerges as a perfect original in its own right." *Hair* was also mounted in Amsterdam, Lisbon, Tokyo, and other foreign capitals. When *Hair* was mounted in Acapulco, the authorities forced it to close down after the opening night, and the cast had to leave town the following day. Censors closed down the show in Boston pending legal action.

*Hair* celebrated its second anniversary in the Mall of Central Park in New York on April 26, 1970 before an audience of about ten thousand. All the hit numbers of the show were performed, with the huge crowd joining the cast in a rousing rendition of "Let the Sun Shine In." By April of 1970, the show had brought its backers a profit of well over two million dollars, the gross in New York alone having been about seven million dollars.

HALLELUJAH, BABY! (1967), *a musical comedy, with book by Arthur Laurents. Lyrics by Betty Comden and Adolph Green. Music by Jule Styne. Presented by Albert W. Selden, Hal James, Jane C. Nusbaum, and Harry Rigby at the Martin Beck Theater on April 26. Directed by Burt Shevelove. Dances by Kevin Carlisle. Cast included Leslie Uggams, Robert Hooks, and Allen Case (293 performances).*

*Hallelujah, Baby!* brought a shining new star to the musical theater: Leslie Uggams, who had previously proved the stature of her talent in cabarets and television but never on the Broadway stage. When she was in front of the footlights, she made the musical alive, vital, and electrifying. She could have made it a major success instead of a very minor one, particularly since she and her very able colleagues had some immensely effective material to work with—both in songs and dances—had the text (which at first glance sounds fresh and invigorating enough) been able to decide whether it wished to be entertaining or to preach a message about racism.

*Hallelujah, Baby!* is the only musical in 1967 with an original text rather than an adaptation. The text is based on an intriguing idea. Sixty years of life go in review—Negro life, show-business life, life in New York —but during all that time none of the characters gets a day older than when first we confronted them in the early 1900's. As the text passes into the twenties, thirties, forties, fifties, and sixties, the characters retain all their energy and exuberance in presenting the song, dance, and entertainment styles of the various decades. Had the text remained a panorama of the Negro in show business, *Hellelujah, Baby!* might have been an exciting adventure in the musical theater, for it profited from some excellent staging and choreography as well as from performances and songs. But Arthur Laurents also seemed determined to point up the racial problems of the different periods, and in this area he resorts to stock situations of Negroes vis-à-vis the whites, stereotype characters, bromides about race relationships, and stilted and at times cliché-ridden dialogue which might have passed off as effective propaganda in the 1920's but was totally obsolete in the world of 1967. *Hallelujah, Baby!* would have profited no end had all this been avoided.

The play opens simply and unpretentiously to give the feeling that we are on the threshold of a fresh experience in the theater. No big scene; no chorus girls; no songs—just Leslie Uggams, as Georgina, on an empty stage to explain to the audience that though sixty years go by through the course of the play, all characters will never get old. She, for instance, will always be twenty-five, "a nice age for a girl," she explains. Then she tosses off, "See you at the turn of the century," leaving the stage while she twirls her parasol.

We see her next in the period of the early 1900's. She is in a kitchen in the Deep South, driven by Momma (Lillian Hayman) to mop the floor. But Georgina dreams about a happier future in a simple, forthright ballad, "My Own Morning." One of her present dreams, however, is shattered when her boyfriend, Clem (Robert Hooks) has lost the money they had been saving for their dream house in a crap game. She now realizes that whatever future there is for her must be of her own making. She breaks into show business, playing typical Negro stereotypes, but confronts frustration when the law forbids her to appear with whites on the same stage. Now more than ever Georgina is determined to make her way in a white man's world, and through success in the theater gain that dignity and high esteem which the world denies her because her skin is black. As the decades go by, she passes from one stage medium to another—from the nightclub of the twenties into the federal theater of the thirties, and finally in the forties and fifties to the very top of her profession, a star of stars. Her former boyfriend, Clem, now a leader in the civil-rights movement, is disgusted at the way in which Georgina has come to terms with the whites, to the point even of her falling in love with some of them. But Georgina has stardust in her eyes: "I can't believe it! All these people I read about giving a party for me!", while her mother—in one of the most dramatic songs in the production—can't get over the fact that her daughter has become such a success, in "I Don't Know Where She Got It." The shows ends with a rousing production number for the entire company, "Now's the Time," a song boisterously presented by Georgina and followed by a dynamic, electrifying dance finale.

The score includes a vigorous number typical of the twenties in "Feet Do Yo' Stuff," in which Georgina's rendition is followed by an intriguing dance routine performed by Tip and Tap (Winston De Witt Hemsley and Alan Weeks), and a racial song in the spirit of the twenties, "Smile, Smile, Smile," which mocks Uncle Tomism; a vigorous number from the thirties, "Another Day," for a quartet of voices that include Georgina and Clem; a trio for Georgina, Clem and Harvey (Allen Case) in which each soliloquizes about his or her own state of affairs in the forties; and a ballad sung by Harvey, "Not Mine," in which critic John S. Wilson finds a touch of Gershwin.

*Hallelujah, Baby!* received the Antoinette Perry Award as the best musical of the 1967–68 season.

HANKY PANKY. *See* WEBER AND FIELDS EXTRAVAGANZAS.

HAPPY HUNTING (1956), *a musical comedy, with book by Howard Lindsay and Russel Crouse. Lyrics by Matt Dubey. Music by Harold Karr. Presented by Jo Mielziner at the Majestic Theater on December 6. Directed by Abe Burrows. Dances by Alex Romero and Bob Herget. Cast included Ethel Merman, Fernando Lamas, Virginia Gibson, and Gordon Polk (408 performances).*

*Happy Hunting* had an old-fashioned kind of musical-comedy content with stereotyped book, routine situations, and more or less humdrum dialogue. But it counted heavily on its star, Ethel Merman—and it was the star who carried the show on her shoulders to success. Returning to the Broadway stage after a six-year absence, Ethel Merman belted out songs and lines with all her old verve and vigor, and made them sound much better than they really were. Whether she had a confidential chat with a horse, or went to bed wearing all her jewels to avoid being robbed, or questioned with bewilderment, "Is his name Grace *too?*" when she heard Prince Rainier being referred to as "His Grace"—she was her inimitable robust self, a boon to a sagging book. "The thing about Merman is that she doesn't need comedy because she just naturally drips comedy the way some trees drip maple syrup," reported Walter Kerr. "Lines? Who needs lines? Her tone is funny, her attitude . . . is funny, her simple presence in the neighborhood is humor itself. . . . A glorious creature, capable of saying 'What the hell!' in twenty different inflections and making celestial melody out of all of them."

Ethel Merman appears as Liz Livingstone, a rich Philadelphian who resents the fact that she has not been invited to Monaco to attend the wedding of Grace Kelly and Prince Rainier. She is determined to arrange a festive wedding for her own daughter, Beth (Virginia Gibson), which will outdo the Monaco ceremony. However, when she finds and buys for her daughter a Spanish grandee, the Duke of Granada (Fernando Lamas), she falls in love with the man herself. This hardly poses a problem to Beth, since she is in love with a Philadelphia lawyer, Sanford Stewart, Jr. (Gordon Polk).

The duet of mother and daughter, "Mutual Admiration Society," became a hit with disk jockeys and on jukeboxes even before *Happy Hunting* reached Broadway. The mother delivered two more effective musical numbers in the title song and "Mr. Livingstone." During the run of the show Ethel Merman interpolated into the production two new songs by Kay Thompson, "I'm Old Enough to Know Better" and "Just a Moment Ago."

THE HAPPY TIME (1968), *a musical comedy, with book by N. Richard Nash, based on the play by Samuel A. Taylor and the book by Robert L. Fontaine. Lyrics by Fred Ebb. Music by John Kander. Presented by David Merrick at the Broadway Theater on January 18. Directed, filmed, and choreographed by Gower Champion. Cast included Robert Goulet and David Wayne (285 performances).*

Samuel Taylor's nonmusical play *The Happy Time* had a successful run of 614 performances when it was produced on Broadway in 1949–50. It went on to become a charming motion picture, still without songs. Then it became a musical, with a creditable score, remarkable staging and direction, and superlative performances by its two stars, Robert Goulet and David Wayne. The basic plot of the successful stage play and movie were retained, the gentle story of a French-Canadian family. Grandpère Bonnard (David Wayne) is a lecherous but gentle old man whose fourteen-year-old grandson, Bibi (Mike Rupert), with whom he has a touchingly tender relationship, is going through the problems of puberty. Bibi's uncle, Jacques Bonnard (Robert Goulet), helps the boy go through this trying period.

The musical opens without an overture but with Jacques Bonnard singing the title song. By profession, Jacques is a globe-trotting photographer, who is recalling his visit to his family in a small French-Canadian town. As his memories come to mind, pictures are flashed on the screen, slowly bringing into focus Jacques's family sitting at the dinner table. From then on, Jacques steps in and out of the plot as it develops in the home of the Bonnards while serving as an objective commentator when he is not part of the action. Slides and photographs serve to make graceful transitions and to suggest elapses of time. Eventually, besides gently leading Bibi through his problems about sex, Jacques falls in love with Laurie Mannon (Julie Gregg), the local schoolteacher.

The song that brought down the house was "The Life of the Party," in which the grandfather—wearing a red coat and red paper top hat because he thinks it is his birthday—boasts about the kind of a devil he has been with the ladies. In a more tender and sentimental vein is "A Certain Girl," sung by Jacques, Bibi, and the grandfather. "For each of these—the old widower, the lady killer, and the adolescent—the song means something different," wrote Jack Kroll in *Newsweek*. Robert Goulet's best number was the title song.

The first-act finale has an excellent production number, "Without Me," in which Bibi tries to impress his schoolmates with the importance his uncle plays in his life. The most elaborate ballet sequence comes in the second act, once again with Bibi playing a principal role: here he is trying to get back from his schoolfriends the nude pictures he had distributed to them and had stolen from his grandfather. A honky-tonk girls' routine proves to be another effective dance number.

Of the production as a whole, Emory Lewis, writing in *Cue*, found it to be "original, bouncy, charming, melodic, alive. . . . Broadway finally catches up with the electronic age . . . best use of mixed-media in memory . . . photo blow-ups of every kind, in and out of focus, multiple images —all flashed vividly, artfully on stage and all an integral part of N. Richard Nash's book. . . . A stunning visual show, a Marshall McLuhan-ish show . . . a revolution in swinging stage style."

HARRIGAN AND HART EXTRAVAGANZAS. *See* THE MULLIGAN GUARDS' BALL.

HELEN OF TROY, NEW YORK (1923), *a musical comedy, with book by George S. Kaufman and Marc Connelly. Lyrics by Bert Kalmar. Music by Harry Ruby. Presented by Rufus Le Maire at the Selwyn Theater on June 19. Directed by Bertram Harrison and Bert French. Cast included Helen Ford, Queenie Smith, Tom Lewis, and Paul Frawley (191 performances).*

In this, his first musical comedy, George S. Kaufman already demonstrated his gift of satire. The object of his attack was business and advertising; and the Yarrow collar factory in Troy, New York, provided a vulnerable target. This musical spoofs an efficiency expert (enacted by Roy Atwell); a lisping, moronic collar-ad idol (Charles Lawrence); and the head of the collar firm, Mr. Elias Yarrow (Tom Lewis), who can operate an immense establishment but who can never remember the size of his own collar without consulting his memorandum book. Satire was further accented in a Russian-type ballet in which famous trademarks spring to life.

For this plot Kaufman devised a romance between Helen McGuffey, a stenographer at the Yarrow firm (Helen Ford), and David Williams (Paul

Frawley), son of the owner of a rival concern. When Helen is fired, she invents a semisoft collar that becomes a success and puts David's firm on the map.

Two of the best musical numbers were in a comic vein, a patter song, "I Like a Big Town," and "What Makes a Business Man Tired." In a lyrical and more sentimental vein were "Happy Ending," sung by Helen and the duet "It Was Meant to Be." The last number was shared by David Williams and Helen McGuffey's sister, Maribel (Queenie Smith). As Maribel, Queenie Smith sang and danced her way to fame in the musical theater.

HELLO, BROADWAY! (1914), *a revue, with book, lyrics, and music by George M. Cohan. Presented by Cohan and Harris at the Astor Theater on December 25. Directed by Cohan. Dances by New Wayburn. Cast included George M. Cohan, William Collier, Louise Dresser, Peggy Wood, and Lawrence Wheat (123 performances).*

One of the properties of the producing firm of Cohan and Harris was the Astor Theater. It needed a show late in 1914, and since none seemed available, Cohan decided to write one. Up to this time he had tried his hand in every possible branch of the theater except one—the revue. Now that the revue was enjoying such prosperity on Broadway, Cohan could not see why he couldn't present one of his own. With typical Cohan self-assurance, he wrote his own material and featured himself as star. He dubbed his show "a musical crazy quilt patched and threaded together by George M. Cohan."

Actually, unlike the typical revue, there was a thin thread of a plot to tie the whole thing together, but for all that, the production remained a revue. The plot concerned two men-about-town—George Babbitt, millionaire son of a Jersey soap manufacturer (George M. Cohan), and his friend, Bill Shaverham (William Collier)—who tour the sights of New York. The things they do and see contribute the songs, dances, sketches, and production numbers of the revue. Actually, the whole production was a burlesque very much in the style of those made famous by Weber and Fields. Many of the current plays were burlesqued broadly. Louise Dresser appeared as "Patsy Pygmalion," a flower girl (an obvious travesty on Mrs. Patrick Campbell in Shaw's *Pygmalion*), and Peggy Wood impersonated Elsie Ferguson as that star in *Outcast*. George M. Cohan did a takeoff on Leo Dietrichstein; and William Collier, of Pauline Frederick. The first-act finale was called "Those Irving Berlin Songs," and consisted of a medley of Irving Berlin favorites, including "Everybody's Doin' It," "Alexander's Ragtime Band," and "International Rag." Irving Berlin contributed two new songs for this revue, one of which was "Down by the Erie Canal," sung by Louise Dresser.

The rest of the score was by Cohan, and its best songs were "Hello, Broadway," "That Old Fashioned Cakewalk," and for one of his famous flag routines, "My Flag."

George M. Cohan wrote and produced two more revues after *Hello, Broadway!* (but appeared in neither one of them). They were the *Cohan Revue of 1916,* which opened at the Astor Theater on February 9 and had a run of 165 performances. It starred Elizabeth Murray, Harry Delf, Charles Winninger, Fred Santley, and Harry Bulger. Cohan's last revue was the *Cohan Revue of 1918* (which he dubbed "a hit and run play"). It came to the New Amsterdam Theater on December 31, 1917, stayed on for 96 performances, and starred Nora Bayes, Fred Santley, Charles Winninger, and Irving Fisher. Travesty and burlesque were once again emphasized in both these productions. In the first, for example, "Julia, Donald, and Joe" was a parody on Julia Sanderson, Donald Brian, and Joseph Cawthorn, all three then starring on Broadway. Richard Carle sang a pleasing Irish number, "You Can Tell That I'm Irish," and a production number consisted of a medley of Sousa's most famous march tunes, entitled "Those Sousa Melodies." The 1918 edition, besides satirizing a few of the then current productions, had some songs by Irving Berlin and several other composers and lyricists. Nora Bayes sang "Who Do You Love?" (by Ed Moran and James Brocknen) and "Regretful Blues" (by Grant Clarke and Cliff Hess). Irving Berlin had six songs, among them "A Man Is Only a Man" and "King of Broadway"; Cohan also contributed six songs; and Berlin and Cohan collaborated on a seventh for each, "Polly, Pretty Polly with a Past."

HELLO DADDY (1928), *a musical comedy, with book by Herbert Fields, based on a nonmusical German farce,* The High Cost of Living. *Lyrics by Dorothy Fields. Music by Jimmy McHugh. Presented by Lew Fields at the Lew Fields Mansfield Theater on December 26. Directed by Alexander Leftwich and John Murray Anderson. Dances by Busby Berkeley. Cast included Lew Fields, George Hassell, Mary Lawlor, and Allen Kearns (198 performances).*

Having achieved a triumphant debut in the Broadway musical theater with their score for *Blackbirds of 1928,* Dorothy Fields and Jimmy McHugh did not wait long to return to the scene of their victory. Before the year 1928 was over, they were once again represented on Broadway.

*Hello Daddy* was based on a play in which Lew Fields had starred on Broadway a few years earlier. As Henry Block he is one of three middle-aged respectable men, all members of the local Purity League, who through the years have been secretly supporting the illegitimate son of a burlesque queen, each one thinking the son was his. The other two men are Edward Hauser (George Hassell) and Anthony Bennett (Wilfred Clark). They finally discover that none of them was the responsible party. But before they do, Connie Block (Mary Lawlor) and Lawrence Tucker (Allen Kearns) pursue a legitimate romance.

The scene in which Lew Fields as Henry discovers he is not the father of the illegitimate son is one of the high comedy moments of the production. Other outstanding comedy scenes are found with Billy Taylor (Noel Burnham), the nincompoop whose paternity is in so much doubt, and in the girl he pursues, Betty Hauser (Betty Starbuck). Their song, "In a Great Big Way," in which they give a funereal description of the pleasures they are supposed to derive from loving each other, was a show-stopper. Other outstanding musical numbers included a hot serenade, a duet by Mary and Lawrence, "I Want Plenty of You," and "Let's Sit and Talk About Love."

HELLO, DOLLY! (1964), *a musical comedy (original all-white production), with book by Michael Stewart, suggested by Thornton Wilder's play* The Matchmaker. *Lyrics and music by Jerry Herman. Presented by David Merrick at the St. James Theater on January 16. Directed and with dances by Gower Champion. Cast included Carol Channing, David Burns, Eileen Brennan, Sondra Lee, and Charles Nelson Reilly.*

*Hello, Dolly!* was based on the rather old-fashioned concept that people come to the musical theater solely to be entertained—not to be uplifted, not to be preached at, not to be stirred by dramatic or even tragic episodes. The kind of story *Hello, Dolly!* brought us was simply a convenience for the presentation of some songs, dances, production numbers, amusing dialogue, and exciting performers. It had three aces in its hand: the extraordinary choreography and direction of Gower Champion; the devastating presence of Carol Channing as Dolly; and the title song.

Placed under a critical microscope, *Hello, Dolly!* revealed numerous blemishes. Howard Taubman used such a microscope in *The New York Times* and pointed out flaws "like the vulgar accent of a milliner's clerk, like the irritating wail of a teen-ager crying for her beau, like the muddle chases in the midst of a series of tableaux vivants. Mr. Stewart's book has settled for some dull and cheap lines the musical would not have missed." But once Mr. Taubman removed the microscope, what he found was a musical with "qualities of freshness that are rare in the run of our machine-made musicals. It transmutes the broadly stylized mood of the mettlesome farce into the gusto and colors of the musical stage. What was larger and droller than life has been puffed up and gaily tinted without being blown apart."

Richard Watts, Jr., also had a microscope, and yet came up with an affirmative analysis. "The fact that it seems to me short on charm, warmth and the intangible quality of distinction in no way alters my conviction that it will be an enormous success. *Hello, Dolly!* has all the elements of a resounding Broadway hit."

A resounding hit it became—in fact, it became one of the greatest box-office draws in Broadway history. By January, 1969 (with the show still playing to such large houses that the end of the run was nowhere in sight) it had earned a profit of almost eight million dollars on its original investment of $350,000. It had been produced in West Germany, England, Czechoslovakia, Israel, Spain—with presentations in other countries being projected. The original-cast recording had been on the best-seller lists, and the movie rights sold for an astronomical sum. With better than a one-thousand-percent return to its backers by 1969—and the percentage due to rise far higher than that by the time *Hello, Dolly!* had run its course—it turned out to be one of the biggest payoffs in stage history. *Hello, Dolly!* received the Antoinette Perry and the New York Drama Critics Circle awards as the season's best musical.

The text reaches back to New York of 1898. Dolly Levi (Carol Channing) is a widow of a dry-goods merchant; she has since become a marriage broker. She is working on a deal to find a second wife for the wealthy Horace Vandergelder (David Burns) of Yonkers. At the same time, in her heart of hearts, she is aspiring to win him for herself. In Yonkers, Vandergelder reveals why he has decided to get married—in an amusing number with sprightly lyrics, "It Takes a Woman." Dolly has a formidable rival for Vandergelder in Mrs. Molloy (Eileen Brennan), the owner of a New York shop. Mrs. Molloy, also a widow, is bored with living alone, and Horace is very much to her taste. Horace comes down to New York, ostensibly to march in the 14th Street Association Parade, but actually to meet Mrs. Molloy. His two clerks, Cornelius (Charles Nelson Reilly) and Barnaby (Jerry Dodge), also decide to take the day off and enjoy the delights of the city. They come to Mrs. Molloy's shop just as Vandergelder arrives, and have to seek refuge in cupboards and under tables. Vandergelder soon begins to suspect that men are hiding in the shop, a fact that so infuriates him that he decides not to have further traffic with Mrs. Molloy. When Dolly sees that Cornelius, the clerk, is taken with Mrs. Molloy, she arranges for him to take her to the fashionable Harmonia Gardens, with Barnaby escorting Minnie Fay (Sondra Lee). At the restaurant there is a good deal of excitement, for word has spread that Dolly Levi will be a guest there that evening—the first time she has come to the restaurant since her husband's death. She arrives in a splendiferous red gown, elaborate jewels, and a headdress choked with feathers, and causes a sensation. The whole place goes into an uproar as all the employees welcome her with the title song and then march about in the most resplendent production number in the show.

Once Dolly confronts Vandergelder in the restaurant she uses every trick in her book to capture his interest. Distractions come when Vandergelder discovers his two clerks in the restaurant. He fires them on the spot, a development that bothers Cornelius very little, since by now he and Mrs. Molloy have become a harmonious pair. Vandergelder creates such a disturbance in the restaurant that he is arrested. Released from prison and back in his shop, Vandergelder becomes aware of his misfortunes. His shop is without clerks. He thinks he has lost Dolly for good, whom by now he has come to relish. But Dolly has known all the time that her absence would make his heart grow fonder. When she finally appears in his shop, he proposes to her and is accepted. The final curtain descends with the delighted Vandergelder chanting "Hello, Dolly!"

Carol Channing stole the show from the other performers, despite the excellence of David Burns, Eileen Brennan, Sondra Lee, and Charles Nelson Reilly. As Dolly, Miss Channing was at turns naïve and conniving, sexy and as innocent as a baby. She was loud and boisterous when required—a veritable cyclone; she could also be a cooing dove. Said Howard Taubman: "Miss Channing's Dolly is all benevolent guile. . . . She sings the rousing title song with earthy zest and leads a male chorus of waiters and chefs in a joyous promenade around the walk that circles the top of the pit." To Richard Watts, Jr., she was "in her best humorous and dynamic form." To Jack Gaver of UPI, she was a star "that has the quality of always seeming to enjoy what she is doing to such a degree that her enthusiasm can't help but catch up an audience. . . . Miss Channing . . . is a complete delight whether she is dancing, singing in that inimitable voice or just sitting at a table eating." Notwithstanding Miss Channing's triumph—the greatest of her career—not she but Barbra Streisand was chosen to play Dolly when 20th Century-Fox made it into a fabulously successful motion picture, released in 1969.

The title song is the kind of stereotyped tune that causes feet to tap, that can be listened to effortlessly, and which is easily remembered. It was a good number for the purpose for which it had been planned, but it was hardly above ordinary musical-comedy standards. Little had been expected of it even by its author, who dashed it off as a period piece for that gala production number. Unexpectedly, the title song became one of the greatest hits to come out of Broadway in over a decade—in fact, one of the greatest show-tune hits of all time. It was a blockbuster not only in the United States but even in Europe; within a year's time no less than seventy-two versions had been pressed on discs by American companies, while thirty-five other recordings came from various European countries. With appropriate lyrics it became a rousing campaign song for Lyndon B. Johnson's successful Presidential campaign in 1964. It sold sheet music by the hundreds of thousands.

Jerry Herman had written it in a single afternoon as a kind of a "Lillian Russell turn-of-the-century production number . . . very 1890's." It had a functional purpose to serve in the show, and more than that Jerry Herman did not expect. "But," he went on to explain, "Louis Armstrong recorded the song as if it were written for *him*. And it's Mr. Armstrong's version that really knocked everybody out. . . . I went to a cast party where they had the first cut of the recording. Before then I never expected it would have any popular market, but the way the other members of the company loved it, I began to realize that it was going to be something special."

Jerry Herman earned a fortune from the song "Hello, Dolly!" But it also cost him a fortune. Mack David and Paramount-Famous Music Company brought suit against the composer for infringement of copyright, maintaining that the melody had been used by David in 1948 for "Sunflower." The suit was settled out of court, with Herman paying David a sum estimated at about half a million dollars (while retaining the rights to the song), the largest damages ever paid in a song-copyright-infringement case. Since there is nothing monumentally original about "Hello, Dolly!"—being the kind of melody that Jerry Herman can shake out of his sleeve by the dozen whenever he wishes—it can only be surmised that "Sunflower" (which had never been a hit) had somehow clung tenaciously in the background of his memory, and that when he sat down to produce a melody for his lyrics, the old melody came to the surface of the composer's consciousness without his having the slightest realization that somebody else had written it almost twenty years earlier.

A hit tune of the proportions of "Hello, Dolly!" inevitably tends to throw the other songs of the show into the shade—undeservedly so, for there were some highly infectious tunes in that score. Two of these were sung by Dolly, "So Long, Dearie" (also successfully recorded by Louis Armstrong) and "Before the Parade Passes by"; "Put On Your Sunday Clothes," presented by the two clerks; and Irene Molloy's number, "Ribbons Down My Back."

With *Hello, Dolly!* settled down at the St. James Theater for what looked like an endless run, judging by the demand for tickets, its producer,

David Merrick, hit upon the ingenious idea of mounting on Broadway a second production of the same show, without any changes, but with an all-Negro cast headed by Pearl Bailey and Cab Calloway. Mr. Merrick must have felt that *Hello, Dolly!* was such a boisterous, lusty, energetic, and exciting show that a Negro company would charge it with a new powerful electric current. Presented at the St. James Theater on October 11, 1967, it was a daring gamble that paid off. There were many who thought the Negro-cast version even better than the original one. Clive Barnes, in *The New York Times,* confessed that he had never really liked *Hello, Dolly!* when he first saw it, and the idea of a nonintegrated Negro version "offended" his "sensitive white liberal conscience." But after he saw the Negro cast he said: "Believe me, from the first to the last I was overwhelmed. . . . For Miss Bailey this was a Broadway triumph. . . . She took the whole musical in her hands and swung it around her neck as easily as if it were a feather boa. Her timing was exquisite . . . her singing had that deep throaty rumble that is, at least to me, always so oddly stirring. . . . But even apart from Miss Bailey and Mr. Calloway, a great face job has been done on the whole show, which now goes like a rocket in a shower of sparks." The other critics were hardly less rapturous. A new smash hit had come to Broadway, and of such dimensions that it became speculative as to which would in the end make the more money, get the most kudos, enjoy the longest runs, and be the one to be most often remembered.

On opening night of the Negro version, Carol Channing was in the audience. At the end of the performance, which brought forth a thunder of an ovation, Pearl Bailey called Miss Channing to the stage. Together, impromptu, to a piano accompaniment, they sang and danced to the title song, inviting the audience to join in the singing. The improvised routine lasted over fifteen minutes. "It was," said a critic for *Variety,* "a tribute not only to the two stars, but to a show that has become a legend."

When *Hello, Dolly!* had first been conceived (for a white company), the producer and writers hoped to star Ethel Merman. Miss Merman turned down the offer thus allowing Carol Channing to assume the part of Dolly. On March 30, 1970, Ethel Merman finally assumed the role that had been created with her in mind. For this occasion, several songs written originally for her, but discarded when Miss Channing took the part, were reinstated into the score.

HELLZAPOPPIN' (1938), *a free-for-all vaudeville revue, with book mostly by Olsen and Johnson. Lyrics by Irving Kahal, Charles Tobias, and others. Music mainly by Sammy Fain. Presented by Olsen and Johnson at the 46th Street*

*Theater on September 22. Directed by Edward Dowling. Cast included Olsen and Johnson, Barto and Mann, Hal Sherman, the Radio Rogues, Bettymae and Beverly Crane, and the Charioteers (1,404 performances).*

At first, *Hellzapoppin'* was a one-hour burlesque farce put on by Olsen and Johnson in Philadelphia. Lee Shubert, the producer, saw it there and offered to finance its transfer to Broadway if Olsen and Johnson were willing to expand it into a full two-hour show. Olsen and Johnson were more than willing. (Shubert offered one of the writers of the sketches, Tom McKnight, a twenty-percent interest in the show, once it hit Broadway, for $15,000. McKnight turned down the offer, convinced that the zany show did not have a chance with sophisticated Broadway audiences. After *Hellzapoppin'* had been on Broadway several years, McKnight told Bobby Clark: "I had a chance to get twenty percent of that show. That shows you what *I* know about show business." Bobby Clark replied: "No, it just shows what Lee Shubert knows about show business.")

In any event, *Hellzapoppin'* came to Broadway and stayed for over fourteen hundred performances—a veritable gold mine, since it had a comparatively small overhead. The program described it as a "screamlined revue designed for laughing." Except for the "audience-participation" number at the end of the show, the program tried to follow the accepted pattern of the formal revue. There were skits (on English detectives, cabinet meetings of foreign powers, Wall Street, maternity wards); songs ("It's Time to Say 'Aloha,' " for example, beautifully sung by Bettymae and Beverly Crane, and "Strolling Through the Park"); parody and satire (the Radio Rogues gave travesties of celebrities like Walter Winchell, Kate Smith, and Rudy Vallee). What the program did not suggest—and what made this show one of the most successful in Broadway history, with the longest run of any Broadway play up to that time—was the endless parade of improvisations, scatterbrained stunts, unexpected bits of tomfoolery, and schoolboy pranks. These made a shambles of the formal program and sometimes transformed the theater into bedlam.

The revue began in an unorthodox manner, with a motion-picture newsreel showing President Roosevelt, Mayor La Guardia, Mussolini, and Hitler—with unexpected sounds and sentiments coming out of their mouths. (Hitler was made to speak with a Yiddish accent.) Then Olsen and Johnson appeared in an outlandish automobile, and from then on the surprises descended on the audience with profusion. A woman kept running down the aisles calling for "Oscar." A ticket scalper hounded some in the audience to sell them seats for other shows. A lady suddenly left her seat to announce she was going to the lady's room. A stuffed gorilla dragged a lady from her box seat, and a gentleman Godiva rode a horse in the balcony. A cyclist performed on a bicycle with square wheels. The theater suddenly grew black, and through a loud-speaker came the warning that the audience would be afflicted with snakes and spiders—as it was pelted with puffed rice.

The cast included midgets, barkers, clowns, even pigeons. Balloons burst, autos exploded, guns popped. The breathtaking sequence of incongruous events and slapstick created a momentum that was irresistible and made some of the critics—the most vocal being Walter Winchell—say this was the funniest show they had ever seen.

An attempt was made to create a new *Hellzapoppin'* almost thirty years after the old one had opened on Broadway. Called *Hellzapoppin' '67*, it was first staged at Expo '67 in Montreal, Canada, on July 1, 1967. The intention was to bring it to Broadway after that. Though the show went over well in Montreal—with a good deal of fresh new material no less scatterbrained than that of the original production—it never did reach New York.

THE HEN PECKS (1911), *a musical extravaganza, with book by Glen MacDonough. Lyrics by E. Ray Goetz. Music by A. Baldwin Sloane. Presented by Lew Fields at the Broadway Theater on February 4. Directed by Ned Wayburn. Cast included Lew Fields, Lawrence Wheat, Vernon Castle, Gertrude Quinlan, Blossom Seeley, and Ethel Johnson (137 performances).*

The program described this extravaganza as a "musical panorama" to emphasize that it placed more importance on individual sequences than on the text. A slight plot, however, helped to create unity. The entire Peck family makes a trip to New York from their farm in Cranberry Grove. Son Henderson and his bride, Verbena, have come to make New York their permanent home; Father Peck (Lew Fields) is running away from a termagant wife, Henrietta, who pursues him. Each of the Peck daughters has her own reason for coming: Henoria (Gertrude Quinlan) because she is being pursued by Zowie (Vernon Castle); Henolia (Ethel Johnson) because she has eloped with the real-estate promoter Ayer Castle (Lawrence Wheat), and Henelia (Blossom Seeley) to become a Broadway chorus girl.

The production opened well—with a farcical enactment of life on a farm at sunrise. A good deal of the appeal of *The Hen Pecks* was visual, particularly in its effective display of colors: in a sunrise scene; in the garish splashes of vivid colors in a series of pageants; in the bright yellows, blacks, purples, lavenders, and violets of the costumes.

Blossom Seeley (a young actress imported from San Francisco for this production) created the show-stopper. She sang a ragtime tune called

"Toddlin' the Toledo." During this performance she did a toddling dance that proved a sensation. Toddling soon became a favorite form of social dance, very much in the style of the Turkey Trot, and was one more stimulus in creating a nationwide interest in social dancing.

Vernon Castle—who in two years' time or so would become the high priest of this dancing religion that seized the country—took note of Blossom Seeley's toddling number and was impressed by it. He had recently married Irene Foote, a member of New Rochelle high society, and had managed to get her a small part in *The Hen Pecks*—marking the beginnings of a stage partnership that would create dance history. After *The Hen Pecks* closed, Vernon and Irene Castle, remembering the toddling number, did a similar routine at the Café de Paris in Paris, where they achieved their first success. From then on, they progressed from triumph to triumph in New York until they were the idols of the dance-craze age of 1913, had shows written for them, opened up their own nightclubs and schools, and created many of the dances that immediately took the country by storm.

Jerome Kern had one of his songs interpolated in *The Hen Pecks:* "The Manicure Girl." Sloane's best songs were "June," "Little Italy," "White Light Alley," and "It's a Skirt."

HERE'S LOVE (1963), *a musical comedy, with book, music, and lyrics by Meredith Willson, adapted from the motion picture* The Miracle on 34th Street. *Presented by Stuart Ostrow at the Shubert Theater on October 3. Directed by Sam Ostrow. Dances by Michael Todd. Cast included Janis Paige and Laurence Naismith (334 performances).*

Apparently, Meredith Willson neatly spaced his musical-comedy successes by three years. His first musical, and simultaneously his first triumph in the theater, was *The Music Man,* in 1957. *The Unsinkable Molly Brown,* a lesser success but nevertheless still a substantial one, followed in 1960. And in 1963 came *Here's Love,* whose run of 334 might appear picayune compared to figures accumulated by his two earlier productions but which nevertheless represented profits for all concerned.

In his two earlier musicals the texts were exclusively his. In *Here's Love* he resorted to adapting a singularly charming motion picture called *The Miracle on 34th Street,* in which an old gentleman assumes the identity of Santa Claus for the Christmas season, radiating such a glowing holiday spirit that even Macy's and Gimbels—the two competing department stores in New York—became friendly.

In Meredith Willson's musical, the opening takes place during Macy's Thanksgiving Parade. Little Susan Walker (Valerie Lee) confides in Fred

Gaily, a Marine officer (Craig Stevens) that her mother, Doris Walker (Janis Paige), is divorced. To cheer up Susan, Fred buys her a balloon and urges her to join him in the parade. But the parade is in trouble, since the store Santa Claus has gone on a binge and is drunk. Doris Walker, personnel manager at Macy's, hurriedly summons Mr. Kris Kringle (Laurence Naismith) to take Santa's place in the parade. Despite a brief outbreak of thundershowers, the parade goes off well—particularly when Kris proudly rides in his sleigh dressed as Santa.

The Christmas spirit soon begins to make itself felt. R. H. Macy personally suggests that his clientele go to F.A.O. Schwartz for toys his department store does not have in stock. Kris has by now convinced himself that he *really* is Santa Claus, and has even succeeded in making the heartbroken Susan believe that the Christmas spirit is something genuine and indestructible.

Through Doris' influence, Kris is hired by Macy's as its permanent Santa Claus for the holiday season. But the store psychologist is convinced that Kris is mentally unbalanced—believing, as Kris does, that he is a real Santa Claus—and that Kris must be committed to an asylum. After the police have taken him away, Kris is determined to fight in court the insanity charge made against him, strengthened by the faith that Susan has in him. The public creates a furor over the case, siding with Kris; tons of mail descend on Macy's for its cruelty in committing the old man, whose only crime is that he has been promoting the true spirit of Christmas. Fred Gaily turns lawyer to plead Kris's case. He not only wins the case; he also wins the girl—Doris. And Kris is back at his job as Santa at Macy's, much to the delight of the whole neighborhood, who express their delight by repeating the title number.

The radiance of the Yuletide season is found in the title song, sung by Kris Kringle, Fred, and the ensemble to point up the genuineness of the spirit of Santa Claus; and in "Pine Cones and Holly Berries" (Kris Kringle, and Fred Gwynne, playing the part of Shellhammer, a clerk). Other songs worth noting were: "Arm in Arm," which Doris sings to her daughter, Susan, at bedtime; "Look, Little Girl," sung by Fred Gaily to Susan, who then sings it back to him; and "My Wish," a duet by Fred Gaily and Susan.

One of the best production numbers is a fantasy occurring toward the end of the first act in a land which Kris has named "Imagination." The characters appear on a huge birthday cake, each trying to substitute for the absent Daddy when Susan wants to cut the cake. Fred Gaily finally cuts the cake, and the fantasy dissolves.

The musical exuded a good deal of charm, humanity, and a holiday glow. Howard Taubman put it as follows in his review in *The New York*

*Times:* "The product is wholesome, with a scattering of laughs, a hint of tremulous emotion, the triumph of true love, a touch of fantasy, all appearing just where you anticipate them. . . . In years gone by musicals were put together to tickle the tired businessman. Now they aim for the family trade. *Here's Love* is a model in which the family can ride in comfort, even if it will not see any new, exhilarating vistas."

HIGGELDY PIGGELDY. *See* WEBER AND FIELDS EXTRAVAGANZAS.

HIGH BUTTON SHOES (1947), *a musical comedy, with book by Stephen Longstreet, based on his own novel. Lyrics by Sammy Cahn. Music by Jule Styne. Presented by Monte Proser and Joseph Kipness at the New Century Theater on October 9. Directed by George Abbott. Dances by Jerome Robbins. Cast included Phil Silvers, Nanette Fabray, Jack McCauley, and Joey Faye (727 performances).*

*High Button Shoes* was a peppery mixture of burlesque, vaudeville, and musical comedy—with a generous dash of nostalgia. It received the Donaldson Award as the best musical of the season.

In the year 1913 a couple of swindlers—Harrison Floy (Phil Silvers) and Mr. Pontdue (Joey Faye)—arrive in New Brunswick, New Jersey. New Brunswick is Floy's boyhood town. And there he now finds a welcome at the home of the Longstreets, a family comprising Papa (Jack McCauley), Mama (Nanette Fabray), Mama's sister, Fran (Lois Lee), and the Long-street son, Stevie. They are all convinced that Floy and his buddy are the essence of business acumen and are delighted when he offers to sell some of the property which they have long owned. With his hard-sale methods, Floy manages to sell the land at a picnic, intending to make a discreet getaway once the money is in his hands. The picnic is a merry affair. Even Mama and Papa indulge in dancing the polka, "Papa, Won't You Dance With Me?" But the merriment ends abruptly when one of the customers of the land comes storming in with the news that it is just swampland. When the neighbors rush off to verify, Floy induces Fran to elope with him to Atlantic City, taking with them Floy's crony and the money from the land.

In Atlantic City Floy and Pontdue are chased by the cops, get involved with a bunch of crooks, and in the process of chasing and being chased, they now lose the money, and now retrieve it, until finally Pontdue gets hold of it at the point of a gun.

Meanwhile, Fran has returned to New Brunswick, reconciled with her old-time boyfriend, Hubert. Floy makes a sudden reappearance. Repentant of his shady dealings, he promises the Longstreets to return all the money.

Whatever sum he can extract from Pontdue he places as a bet on the Princeton-Rutgers game. In typical Floy fashion, he bets on the wrong side. But Floy is indestructible. He comes up with the idea of marking the mud from the swamplands as beauty clay.

The polka, "Papa, Won't You Dance With Me?"—the hit number of the show—is one of three songs which Jack McCauley shares with Nanette Fabray. Another is a poignant ballad, "I Still Get Jealous" (when Papa suspects that Mama is interested in Floy), while a third is a specialty number, "Security." Through her singing, dancing, and miming, Nanette Fabray (in the second lead role) proved herself an ace performer.

But it was Phil Silvers who dominated the limelight. To the role of a con man he brought much of the bounce, rowdy humor, and boisterousness he had formerly injected for so many years in burlesque theaters (and which, in years to come, he would introduce in his television series as Sergeant Bilko). Only once before had he appeared on the Broadway stage—in 1939 in *Yokel Boy*—but it was first in *High Button Shoes* that he proved his true comic potential. Singlehanded, he tries to annihilate a whole football squad; he delivers a speech to a ladies' bird-watching society; he does a burlesque fight scene with a football player; and with equal vigor and élan he delivers "You're My Girl" and does impersonations in "Can't You Just See Yourself in Love with Me?"

Nostalgia was evoked by the 1913 setting, with its amusing recollections of the feminine fashions of the day, the perverse behavior of a Model-T Ford, and the escapades of Keystone Kops and Mack Sennett Bathing Beauties of silent-film days, re-created in a hilarious ballet conceived by Jerome Robbins ("a masterpiece of controlled pandemonium," in the words of *Time* magazine).

HIGH JINKS (1913), *a musical comedy, with book by Otto Haverbach (Harbach) and Leo Dietrichstein. Music by Rudolf Friml. Presented by Arthur Hammerstein at the Lyric Theater on December 10. Directed by Fred Smithson. Cast included Elizabeth Murray, Tom Lewis, and Elaine Hammerstein (213 performances).*

It was the incidentals to the plot, rather than the plot itself, that made *High Jinks* so attractive. These incidentals included fascinating cartwheel dances by Emilie Lea (in the role of Chi-Chi); the song "All Aboard for Dixie," magnetically sung by Elizabeth Murray; a hilarious after-dinner speech in the last act delivered by Tom Lewis in the part of J. J. Jeffreys (not the boxing champ, but an American who is continually being mistaken for him); and Ignacio Martinetti's amusing caricature of a jealous

Frenchman. The story, such as it is, concerns the effect a certain perfume has in making people feel gay and irresponsible; under its influence a doctor, at a French bathing resort, passes off another lady as his wife with amusingly risqué consequences.

The casting had two points of interest. One was Elaine Hammerstein, daughter of Arthur, who was here making her stage debut and who made a profound impression singing the principal musical number of the show, "Something Seems Tingle-Ingleing" (supported by a female chorus) and "When Sammy Sang the 'Marseillaise.' " The other was Mana-Zucca, seen in a minor role. Mana-Zucca had been a child-prodigy pianist; in subsequent years she would make her mark as a composer ("I Love Life," "Nichevo," and so forth).

HIGH SPIRITS (1964), *"an improbable musical comedy," with book, lyrics, and music by Hugh Martin and Timothy Gray, based on Noël Coward's play* Blithe Spirit. *Presented by Lester Osterman, Robert Fletcher, and Richard Horner at the Alvin Theater on April 7. Directed by Noël Coward. Dances by Danny Daniels. Cast included Beatrice Lillie, Tammy Grimes, and Edward Woodward (375 performances).*

If there was a single person in that first-night audience of *High Spirits* naïve enough to believe that Beatrice Lillie could go through an entire evening without leaving an indelible impress of her pixyish, antic personality on the play as Noël Coward originally wrote it, and as Hugh Martin and Timothy Gray adapted it for the musical stage, he or she was instantly disenchanted with Miss Lillie's first entrance. Wearing an outlandish costume, and burdened by the instruments of her profession, she arrives on a bicycle fixed on a movable ground, a bicycle she seems to be manipulating with curious gyrations of body and arms. As she travels she sings "The Bicycle Song," a number obviously made to order for her type of delivery. Arriving at her destination, she removes the clips that have kept her skirts in place and puts them on her wrists as bracelets. Then, with a haughty, disdainful look at the audience, she enters the house to go about her business of being a spiritualist (or, as she prefers to call herself, a "happy medium"). The audience can make no mistake about it: Beatrice Lillie is being let loose on the stage in a typical Lillie-like rampage, and there is nothing much Noël Coward and his adapters can do about it.

With a number of scenes interpolated either to permit Miss Lillie to have her day on the stage or to make room for some exciting choreography, the musical remains very much like the Noël Coward play, a spoof on spiritualism. Madame Arcati (Beatrice Lillie) is the spiritualist who comes to the home of Charles Condomine (Edward Woodward) to conduct a séance. In the process, she brings back to life Charles's first wife, Elvira (Tammy Grimes), much to the chagrin of his present wife, Ruth (Louise Troy). A delectable creature, Elvira uses her seductive feminine wiles (which she apparently has not lost, even though she is just a spirit) to entice her former husband to take her out on the town. When she does not glide about the stage in flimsy attire, Elvira flies like Peter Pan over a party on a roof of a London hotel—fully enjoying her happy state until nostalgia sets in. In front of a curtain, and alone on the stage, she remembers the good times she had had in the world she had just come from in one of the show's strongest musical numbers, "Home Sweet Heaven." Poignant, too, are the two songs in which Charles and his wife reveal their feelings for one another (the intrusion of Elvira notwithstanding): "Where Is the Man I Married?" and "If I Gave You."

The scene that stood out most prominently, however, belonged exclusively to Miss Lillie, who made the most of it. She is in her boudoir, ready for bed. Her night attire is no less quixotic than the costumes to which she is partial during the day: a flowing bouffant night cap; a long simple old-fashioned nightgown decorated with a yellow flower on her bosom; floppy bedroom slippers with bunnies as decoration. She slips into bed with her Ouija board for a communion, singing "Talking to You." Then she does a takeoff on the classical ballet that is little short of being a Lillie classic. Here is how Howard Taubman described the scene in his review in *The New York Times:* "Overflowing with coziness, she begins to move like a ballerina. Her hands flutter as she takes mincing, little steps, then they wave broadly as the afflatus of Terpsichore possesses her. She does leaps and splits and delicate turns in a perfect Lillie travesty of a great dancer. And when the audience roars for more and won't let the show go on, she flutters through a devastating mockery of curtsies and fond gestures of farewell that should make a prima ballerina assoluta self-conscious for life."

Madame Arcati's spiritualist headquarters becomes the setting for two frenetic production numbers entitled "Go into Your Trance" and "Something Is Coming to Tea."

THE HIGHWAYMAN (1897), *a comic opera, with book and lyrics by Harry B. Smith. Music by Reginald de Koven. Presented by Andrew A. McCormick at the Broadway Theater on December 13. Directed by Max Freeman. Dances by Carl Marwig. Cast included Jerome Sykes, Joseph O'Mara, and Hilda Clarke (144 performances).*

*The Highwayman* is one of De Koven's best scores and, all things considered, one of his best comic operas. The character of Foxy Quiller—performed in the original production by Jerome Sykes—was so well delineated that the term "foxy quiller" entered the argot of the period to describe a shrewd and conniving fellow.

The plot is set in England, where Dick Fitzgerald (Joseph O'Mara), soldier of fortune, has come to ruin at the hands of the gambler, Hawkhurst. He is forced to become "Captain Scarlet," a highwayman who is the terror of the countryside. He is eventually pardoned, but his pardon papers fall into the hands of his arch-enemy. These papers are rescued through a bold and ingenious maneuver by Lady Constance (Hilda Clarke), who, disguised as Captain Scarlet, holds up the stagecoach in which the papers are concealed.

A consistently tuneful score includes such delights as the duet of Dick and Constance, "Do You Remember, Love?" Constance's "Moonlight Song," the "Gypsy Song" of Quiller and his men, and the robust "Highwayman Song" of Dick and his followers.

HIP! HIP! HOORAY. *See* WEBER AND FIELDS EXTRAVAGANZAS.

HIP, HIP, HOORAY. *See* THE HIPPODROME EXTRAVAGANZAS.

THE HIPPODROME EXTRAVAGANZAS (1905), A Society Circus, *an extravaganza, with book by Sydney Rosenfeld. Lyrics by Sydney Rosenfeld and Manuel Klein. Music by Manuel Klein and Gustav Luders. Presented by Thompson and Dundy at the Hippodrome Theater on December 13. Staged by Edward P. Temple and Frederic Thompson (596 performances).*

*(1906), Pioneer Days, an extravaganza, with book by Caroll Fleming. Lyrics and music by Manuel Klein. Presented by Shubert and Anderson at the Hippodrome Theater on November 28. Staged by Edward P. Temple (288 performances).*

*(1907), The Auto Race, an extravaganza, with book and lyrics by Manuel Klein and Edward P. Temple. Music by Manuel Klein. Presented by Shubert and Anderson at the Hippodrome Theater on November 25. Staged by Edward P. Temple (312 performances).*

*(1908), Sporting Days, an extravaganza, with book and lyrics by Manuel Klein and Edward P. Temple. Music by Manuel Klein. Presented by the Shuberts at the Hippodrome Theater on September 4. Staged by R. H. Burnside (477 performances).*

*(1909), A Trip to Japan, an extravaganza, with book by R. H. Burnside. Lyrics and music by Manuel Klein. Presented by the Shuberts at the Hippodrome Theater on September 4. Staged by R. H. Burnside (447 performances).*

(1910), The International Cup and the Ballet of Niagara, *an extravaganza, with book by R. H. Burnside. Lyrics and music by Manuel Klein. Presented by the Shuberts at the Hippodrome Theater on September 3. Staged by R. H. Burnside (333 performances).*

(1911), Around the World, *an extravaganza, with book by Carroll Fleming. Lyrics and music by Manuel Klein. Presented by the Shuberts at the Hippodrome Theater on September 2. Staged by Carroll Fleming (445 performances).*

(1912), Under Many Flags, *an extravaganza, with book by Carroll Fleming. Lyrics and music by Manuel Klein. Presented by the Shuberts at the Hippodrome Theater on August 31. Staged by Carroll Fleming (445 performances).*

(1913), America, *a spectacle, "invented" by Arthur Voegtlin. Book by John P. Wilson. Lyrics and music by Manuel Klein. Presented by the Shuberts at the Hippodrome Theater on August 30. Staged by William J. Wilson (360 performances).*

(1914), Wars of the World, *an "entertainment," "conceived and invented" by Arthur Voegtlin. Lyrics and music by Manuel Klein. Dialogue by John P. Wilson. Presented by the Shuberts at the Hippodrome Theater on September 5. Staged by William J. Wilson (229 performances).*

(1915), Hip, Hip, Hooray, *an extravaganza, with book by R. H. Burnside. Lyrics by John Golden. Music by Raymond Hubbell. Presented by Charles Dillingham at the Hippodrome Theater on September 30. Staged by R. H. Burnside. Cast included Joseph Parsons, Toto, Anna May Roberts, and Sousa and his band (425 performances).*

(1916), The Big Show, *an extravaganza, with book by R. H. Burnside. Lyrics by John L. Golden. Music by Raymond Hubbell. Presented by Charles Dillingham at the Hippodrome Theater on August 31. Staged by R. H. Burnside. Cast included Toto, Anna Pavlova, and the Leighton Brothers (425 performances).*

(1917), Cheer Up, *a musical revue, with book by R. H. Burnside. Lyrics by John L. Golden. Music by Raymond Hubbell. Presented by Charles Dillingham at the Hippodrome Theater on August 23. Staged by R. H. Burnside (456 performances).*

(1918), Everything, *a musical spectacle, with book by R. H. Burnside. Lyrics by John L. Golden. Music by John Philip Sousa, Irving Berlin, and others. Presented by Charles Dillingham at the Hippodrome Theater on August 22. Staged by R. H. Burnside. Cast included De Wolf Hopper (461 performances).*

(1919), Happy Days, *a musical spectacle, with book and lyrics by R. H. Burnside. Music by Raymond Hubbell. Presented by Charles Dillingham at the Hippodrome Theater on August 23. Staged by R. H. Burnside (452 performances).*

(1920), Good Times, *a musical spectacle, with book and lyrics by R. H. Burnside. Music by Raymond Hubbell. Presented by Charles Dillingham at the Hippodrome Theater on August 9. Staged by R. H. Burnside (456 performances).*

(1921), Get Together, *a vaudeville revue. Authors of book and lyrics and the composer not identified. Presented by Charles Dillingham at the Hippodrome Theater on September 3. Staged by R. H. Burnside. Cast included Fokine and Fokina, Marceline, and Bert Levy (397 performances).*

(1922), Better Times, *a musical spectacle, with book and lyrics by R. H. Burnside. Music by Raymond Hubbell. Presented by Charles Dillingham at the Hippodrome Theater on September 2. Staged by R. H. Burnside. Cast included Marceline, the Bell Brothers, the Berlo Sisters (409 performances).*

The Hippodrome Theater first opened on April 12, 1905, under the management of Thompson and Dundy, with a gala program including a circus show and ballet for the first half of the show, and a spectacular war drama in two tableaux entitled *Andersonville* as the second half. Individual performers were not the attraction, the principals in the cast being made up mostly of unknowns. The accent was always on spectacle and more spectacle, the like of which New York had never before seen.

The Hippodrome was advertised as "the largest, safest, and costliest playhouse in the world." Built at a cost of close to two million dollars, it had a seating capacity in excess of five thousand and one of the largest stages in the world, together with the most elaborate trappings and stage equipment of any theater anywhere. The apron of the stage was two hundred feet wide and one hundred feet deep, capable of holding some six hundred performers and 150 animals. The rear stage extended fifty feet. An intricate conglomeration of cranes made it possible to handle the most elaborate scenery efficiently.

The theater had some other unusual features, such as a sideshow and menagerie for the children downstairs, a restaurant and café for the adults, an enormous promenade leading from the box offices to the theater entrance, and—perhaps most unusual of all—a curtain that rose upward from the ground rather than being lowered from the ceiling. The price of admission ranged from twenty-five cents to two dollars. Since the shows were presented twice daily every day, forty weeks a season, each of the productions was capable

# THE
# BIRTH
# OF
# EXTRAVAGANZA

*The Grotto of Stalacta spectacle from* THE BLACK CROOK *(1866)*

# THE
# HEYDAY
# OF
# MUSICAL
# TRAVESTY

*Harrigan and Hart (1879)*

*Weber and Fields in a characteristic scene* (1898)

*Scene from* THE PRINCE OF PILSEN (1903)

*Fred Stone (interpreter) and Dave Montgomery (tourist)
arrive at* THE RED MILL *(1906)*

*Sam Bernard ( Mr. Hoggenheimer )
bids adieu to Georgia Caine ( Flora Fair )
in* THE RICH MR. HOGGENHEIMER *( 1905 )*

*George M. Cohan and Fay Templeton in*
FORTY-FIVE MINUTES FROM BROADWAY *(1906)*

*Fanny Brice (center) and four bathing belles (1910)*

**THE HEYDAY OF THE ZIEGFIELD FOLLIES**

*Leon Errol, Will West, and Ed Wynn (about 1914)*

*"Every little movement has a meaning all its own,"*
*in* MADAME SHERRY *(1910)*

Hazel Dawn sings
"My Beautiful Lady,"
the sentimental waltz hit from
THE PINK LADY (1911)

Emma Trentini (2nd from left) in THE FIREFLY (1912)
(The young man at the extreme right is Sammy Lee,
later famous as a dance director for musical comedies.)

(Culver Service)

*Al Jolson bids his "Toot, Toot, Tootsie, Good-bye" in* BOMBO *(1921)*

*Dennis King and Mary Ellis
in* ROSE MARIE *(1924)*

*Florrie Millership, Janet Velie,
James Marlow, and
Georgia Caine in* MARY *(1920)*

*Joseph Cawthorn, Donald Brian, and*
*Julia Sanderson in*
*Jerome Kern's first Broadway success,*
THE GIRL FROM UTAH *(1914)*

*Ernest Truex and Alice Dovey in*
*the "Princess Theatre Show,"*
VERY GOOD, EDDIE *(1915)*

*Dorothy Walters, Eva Puck, and Gladys Miller in* IRENE *(1919)*

EARLY

RODGERS AND

HART

(Culver Service)

*William Gaxton as*
A CONNECTICUT YANKEE
IN KING ARTHUR'S COURT *(1927)*

*Charles Winninger, Howard Marsh, Norma Terris,*
*and Edna May Oliver in a scene from* SHOW BOAT *(1927)*

of accumulating impressive performance figures—particularly impressive for those years.

The second production threw the limelight on at least one star, the lovable clown Marceline, making his debut. This show was notable for such outstanding production numbers as "Song of the Flowers" (the entire ensemble being made up to look like a bouquet of flowers), "Motoring in Mid-Air," and "The Court of Golden Fountains." Perfume was sprayed throughout the theater. In this presentation, Manuel Klein became affiliated with the Hippodrome for the first time as a composer. He would remain its principal composer, and frequently its lyricist as well, for the next ten years.

Despite a run of 596 performances, Thompson and Dundy lost so much money on their initial presentation, due to the vast expense involved in their lavish production numbers, that they withdrew for the second production, to turn the venture over to the Shuberts in collaboration with Anderson. From 1907 through 1914 the Shuberts were the sole producers of the Hippodrome spectacles. Under their regime, the Hippodrome presented stage miracles to startle, delight, and at times baffle audiences. *Pioneer Days* (1906) opened with a spectacle involving cowboys, Sioux Indians, Mexicans, and even the U.S. Cavalry. A circus act presented the Powers Elephants, Herzog's Performing Stallions, the Eight Flying Jordans, and Little Hip, the smallest elephant in the world. And the production ended with a tank act, "Neptune's Daughters," for which, from then on, the Hippodrome became famous. Bespangled chorus girls marched down a flight of stairs into a forty-foot-deep tank filled with water, never to reappear. During all the years the Hippodrome flourished, the secret was never disclosed how this trick worked. But when the answer was finally revealed, it proved remarkably simple. Behind the scenes there was partly submerged in water an airproof "shed," a kind of diving bell, which because of the pressure of water from underneath retained the air originally in it. The girls had only to hold their breath for two or three seconds, duck under the edge of the bell, and emerge inside it above the water. Having got their breath, they then ducked under the further edge of the bell and walked up a second set of stairs to the safety of the backstage. A telephone operator, sitting at his switchboard, within the bell, reported to a central office upstairs the safe arrival and departure of each girl.

The stage wonders continued during the ensuing years. In 1907 there took place a naval battle in a huge tank, and the Vanderbilt Cup Auto Race was reproduced. "The Four Seasons" featured Margaret Townsend as the "Ice Maid." During the run of this production "The Battle of Port Arthur" replaced "Circus Evens," while "Lady Gay's Garden Party" was substituted for the auto race.

In 1908 *Sporting Days* presented, among other attractions, a bird ballet and an airplane battle. In *Around the World* (1911) the audience was carried off to England, Switzerland, Egypt, and the Sahara Desert amid the most unusual effects of clouds, storms, distances, and depths. In *Under Many Flags* (1912) herds of deer pounded across an Arizona scene. Additional thrills were provided by a reproduction of a tornado and an earthquake. In the opening scene of *America* (1913), American history was traced, from the discovery of the country by Columbus to a rush-hour scene at the Grand Central Station. In this production there was also seen a fire on New York's East Side, finally subdued by the Fire Department. *Wars of the World* (1914) provided a realistic picture of the French Revolution, the Civil War, the Battle of Vera Cruz, and other historic conflicts. And so it went.

Most of the music Klein wrote for these extravaganzas was functional, serving the individual and specific needs of the Hippodrome. Nevertheless—and despite the fact that the huge house was not ideal for presenting ingratiating songs—he did manage to write some numbers that retained their popularity outside the theater. One of Klein's best songs, "Moon Dear," was heard during his first association with the Hippodrome. Other Klein song hits were: "Meet Me When the Lanterns Glow" in *A Trip to Japan;* "Home Is Where the Heart Is" and "Sweetheart" in *Under Many Flags;* "In Siam" in the *Wars of the World;* and "Love Is Like a Rainbow" in *The International Cup and the Ballet of Niagara.*

A new regime was inaugurated in 1915. The management changed from the hands of the Shuberts to those of Dillingham. Manuel Klein was no longer the composer of the score and author of many of the lyrics. He was supplanted by others, mainly John L. Golden as lyricist and Raymond Hubbell as composer. A new policy was instituted where spectacle would not serve as the be-all and end-all of every Hippodrome production, but stars from every possible medium of entertainment would provide much of the entertainment. In the ensuing years, the Hippodrome spectacles would serve to bring to the famous stage such world-famous figures as Houdini, Anna Pavlova, Annette Kellerman, Sousa and his band, Fokine and Fokina and their Russian ballet, the clown Toto, and the opera tenor Orville Harrold, among many others.

*Hip, Hip, Hooray,* the first production under this new scheme of operations, had an international character, what with skaters from Scandinavia, Toto (a clown from Germany), acrobats from England, dancers from Italy, and a native band from Guatemala. America was represented by its famous march king, John Philip Sousa, and his renowned band.

One spectacular scene followed another in breathtaking sequence: one depicted the rooftops of New York, with the Brooklyn Bridge in the distance; cats impersonated by dancers cavorted on the roofs. Another showed Grand Central Station, with tumblers deftly juggling baggage. A third reproduced a fashion parade on Fifth Avenue. A fourth carried the audience to Chinatown, and a fifth to St. Moritz, Switzerland, for a thrilling winter scene as background for a skaters' ballet. "Toyland" featured the wedding of Jack and Jill; a haunting song, "The Ladder of the Roses," was sung within a setting of a bower of roses. The climax was achieved with a background of the "Tower of Jewels" for a performance by Sousa and his band, the concert ending with a potpourri of marches from various states.

The big attraction of *The Big Show,* in 1916, was the world-famous ballerina Anna Pavlova, who was seen in excerpts from Tchaikovsky's *The Sleeping Beauty,* with scenery designed by Leon Bakst. The big song from the same production—indeed, it was the only song from any of the Hippodrome shows to become a formidable hit and to be remembered—was "Poor Butterfly," words by John L. Golden, music by Raymond Hubbell. The curious thing about this number is that it was written through a misunderstanding. When John Golden was told that an Oriental prima donna would appear in *The Big Show,* he jumped to the conclusion that she was Tamaki Miura, who had then recently become famous in *Madama Butterfly.* With Tamaki in mind, he wrote a lyric in which the story of *Madama Butterfly* is suggested, and Hubbell then went on to write the music. But when the song was done, the authors learned that the Oriental star of their show was a Chinese-American, Haru Onuki, and not a Japanese. Nevertheless, the song was assigned to her. It completely failed to make an impression. Sophie Bernard was then asked to sing it in *The Big Show.* It was her performance—supplemented by a well-selling record—that started "Poor Butterfly" on its way to phenomenal success. As John Golden recalled in his autobiography: "Two months later the entire country was Butterfly mad. 'Poor Butterfly' was strummed, hummed, whistled and wept over by as many voices and hands as there are pianos and ukuleles, typewriters and tenors in the land. I think I am safe in saying that T. B. Harms, the publishers, in all their experience, never had a bigger-selling song, and I know I never had one which made more money."

Dillingham continued the successful pattern evolved in *Hip, Hip, Hooray* and *The Big Show* of combining vaudeville (headed by a few stars), circus, musical-comedy sketches, and stupendous scenic effects and production numbers through 1922. The Hippodrome also became famous for its Sunday-evening concerts, which featured some of the most celebrated performers from the concert and opera world. Convinced that the one-time appeal of the Hippodrome spectacle was gone, and the kind of revue spectacles he had been putting on from 1919 on was being done better by the lavish revues produced by Ziegfeld, George White, and others, Charles Dillingham withdrew from the Hippodrome after the 1922 production. And that marked the end of the Hippodrome extravaganza, which had dominated the entertainment field in New York for almost a quarter of a century. In 1925 the Hippodrome temporarily became a home for vaudeville, but that did not last very long. From time to time, major musical productions found a home at the Hippodrome. With the Rodgers and Hart circus spectacle musical comedy, *Jumbo,* in 1935, there was a fleeting reminder of the grandeur that had once been the Hippodrome. The Hippodrome Theater was torn down in 1952 to make room for an office building and garage.

> HIT THE DECK (1927), *a musical comedy, with book by Herbert Fields, based on* Shore Leave, *a play by Hubert Osborne. Lyrics by Leo Robin and Clifford Grey. Music by Vincent Youmans. Presented by Vincent Youmans and Lew Fields at the Belasco Theater on April 25. Directed by Alexander Leftwich. Dances by Seymour Felix. Cast included Louise Groody, Charles King, and Stella Mayhew (352 performances).*

The courage (or the inflation of ego) that came from writing the music for a monumental stage success like *No, No, Nanette* in 1925 impelled Vincent Youmans in *Hit the Deck* to assume the dual role of composer *and* co-producer. Youmans wanted to be in a position to select those actors and singers that would do most justice to his songs and his production, and his co-producer, Lew Fields, stood ready to give him a free hand. With true beginner's luck, Youmans' first producing venture was a winning hand—not of the magnitude of *No, No, Nanette,* but a highly impressive one nevertheless. Following its Broadway run of over 350 performances, it had several companies touring the United States, was produced in several foreign capitals, and was made into a motion picture by RKO in 1930 with Polly Walker and Jack Oakie. As it turned out, *Hit the Deck* was Youmans' last Broadway success. He tried producing his own shows on several more occasions, with disastrous results; and even for those musicals in which he remained solely the composer—and in some instances the composer of song classics—he suffered one failure after another.

*Hit the Deck* was a nautical musical comedy. Loulou (Louise Groody) is the proprietress of a coffee shop in Newport, Rhode Island, frequented by sailors. She falls in love with one of them—Bilge (Charles King). When Bilge sails for distant ports, Loulou—now an heiress—follows him around the world, hoping to convince him to marry her. She finally catches up with him, but he seems reluctant to marry a wealthy woman. Loulou saves the situation by signing away her fortune—to their first-born child.

Percy Hammond found the show to be "clean, pretty, bright, and happy." He also liked the songs, two of which have become classics. Curious to say, neither of these songs had originally been written for the show. One of them, "Hallelujah"—a rousing sailor's chorus—had been written a decade earlier when Youmans served in the Navy, The other, "Sometimes I'm Happy"—a duet of Loulou and Bilge—had started out as "Come on and Pet Me," its melody written for *Mary Jane McKane* but dropped from that show before it came to Broadway (where it was a failure in 1923). Rewritten as "Sometimes I'm Happy," it was put into another show, *A Night Out,* which died out of town. Finally, the right place was found for it in *Hit the Deck.* "If 'Sometimes I'm Happy,' " wrote critic Alan Dale, "isn't sung all over the world until sometimes you'll be unhappy, I'll eat my chapeau."

When *Hit the Deck*—with an updated text and a score amplified by several other composers and lyricists—was revived at the Jones Beach Marine Theater in Long Island on June 23, 1960, it was still capable of providing a good deal of entertainment. As Lewis Funke reported in *The New York Times:* "*Hit the Deck* is a musical in a tradition the theater has left behind. Nevertheless . . . it is recommended; you can hit the road for *Hit the Deck,* a nautical, teeny-weeny bit naughty, and altogether friendly frolic by the beautiful sea."

HOITY TOITY. *See* WEBER AND FIELDS EXTRAVAGANZAS.

HOKEY POKEY. *See* WEBER AND FIELDS EXTRAVAGANZAS.

HOLD EVERYTHING (1928), *a musical comedy, with book by Buddy de Sylva and John McGowan. Lyrics by De Sylva and Lew Brown. Music by Ray Henderson. Presented by Aarons and Freedley at the Broadhurst Theater on October 10. Dances by Jack Haskell and Sam Rose. Cast included Bert Lahr, Jack Whiting, Ona Munson, and Victor Moore (413 performances).*

Though Bert Lahr, after half a lifetime in burlesque and vaudeville, had made his Broadway debut one year earlier in Harry Delmar's *Revels of 1927,* his career as a star of the Broadway musical-comedy stage began in *Hold Everything,* where he appeared as Gink Schiner, a badly mauled pugilist. His boisterous, rough-and-ready comedy (punctuated by exclamations of "gang, gang, gang"), grimaces, and clowning—and a hilarious sparring routine in the dressing room of the boxing champ—inspired rapturous reports from the critics. "He had me rocking," said Gilbert W. Gabriel. St. John Ervine, then guest critic for the New York *World,* wrote: "His resourcefulness is astonishing. He seems never at a loss for a way of making fun. If he cannot think of a facial expression he uses a ludicrous utterance, or a floppy gesture, or the funniest of all, falls silent. . . . This man is funny."

*Hold Everything* spoofs the prizefight game and "clean sportsmanship." Sonny Jim Brooks (Jack Whiting), the welterweight champion, and Sue Burke (Ona Munson) are in love. But society girl Norine Lloyd (Betty Compton) is also after Sonny. Enraged by her jealousy, Sue refuses to have anything to do with Sonny. The champ is so downcast he has lost all interest in the forthcoming welterweight championship match. Sue rallies Sonny by convincing him she still loves him, and arouses him to fight his best match by telling him his opponent had insulted her.

The big song hit was presented by Sonny Jim Brooks: "You're the Cream in My Coffee." Another outstanding number, "Don't Hold Everything," was sung by Alice Boulden, who appeared in the role of Betty Dunn.

HOLD ON TO YOUR HATS (1940), *a musical comedy, with book by Guy Bolton, Matt Brooks, and Eddie Davis. Lyrics by E. Y. Harburg. Music by Burton Lane. Presented by Al Jolson and George Hale at the Shubert Theater on September 11. Directed by Edgar MacGregor. Supervised by George Hale. Dances by Catherine Littlefield. Cast included Al Jolson, Bert Gordon, Eunice Healey, Martha Raye, and Jack Whiting (158 performances).*

Whatever its value as musical-comedy entertainment—and that value was not far above the average—*Hold on to Your Hats* will always provide an important footnote to the history of American musical comedy. It was the last vehicle in which the great Al Jolson appeared on the Broadway stage. This star of stars who so helped to make Broadway glow, and then went on to Hollywood to make screen history with the first motion picture to use sound for song and speech (*The Jazz Singer*), and after that to achieve the heights in several more pictures, had, in the late 1930's, seen a disheartening deterioration of his box-office appeal as a screen performer. He was yearning to get back to Broadway, back to the scene of his greatest triumphs, confident that once he had a live audience before him he would once again be the great Jolson. He talked to Vinton Freedley about doing a musical, but nothing came of that. Then he negotiated with the young and enterprising Michael Todd about a musical satirizing the Ziegfeld era. Todd was interested, but this project also came to nothing. Finally, one of Jolson's friends, George Hale, brought him the script of *Hold on to Your Hats,* which so pleased Jolson that he stood ready to invest eighty percent of the production costs. He would not only be the star of the show, but also a co-producer. He lined up a star-studded cast. He was determined to conquer Broadway again the way he used to do in the good old days at the Winter Garden.

The reviews were good and so was the box-office draw. The public had not forgotten Jolson. Jolson, on the stage before a live audience, felt he was home again, where he belonged. He enjoyed being surrounded by his old-time cronies, being recognized in the streets, and singing his heart out to an adoring public. But the winter climate in New York began to affect him. One week he had to be hospitalized for laryngitis. Then, in February, 1941, he decided he could stand New York no longer. He closed down the show in New York in spite of the fact that business was good, and took it on the road. There the show hit the skids. More often than not, the auditoriums were half-empty. Frequently the box-office receipts did not pay for the basic expenses, let alone yield a profit. Sadly, Jolson had to call it a day and close down the show for good—and with it his own career on the musical stage.

Al Jolson was cast as a radio cowboy, the Lone Rider—a timid, gun-shy singer who allows himself to be convinced by his scriptwriter to go off to Sunshine Alley and try to recapture the Mexican bandit Fernando (Arnold Moss). Out West and in Mexico, the Lone Rider gets involved in madcap developments, and through a series of fortunate accidents actually manages to capture the bandit.

The play was studded with songs written with Jolson in mind and delivered by him with his customary gusto and dynamism. Among these were "Walkin' Along Mindin' My Business," "There's a Great Day Coming Mañana," and "Would You Be So Kindly?" Toward the end of the evening, Jolson abandoned his role and the plot to step in front of the stage to sing a cycle of the songs he had helped to make famous; and in 1940, as in years earlier, he took complete command of his audience.

Besides the Jolson numbers there were several others of interest, including two ballads, "The World Is in My Arms" and "Don't Let It Get You Down," and two boisterous songs presented by Martha Raye, "Life Was Pie for the Pioneer" and "She Came, She Saw, She Can-Canned." Still another song found favor with audiences nightly: "Down the Dude Ranch," introduced by Jolson, Raye, and Bert Gordon, the last of whom ("The Mad Russian" on Eddie Cantor's then popular radio program) contributed an amusingly incongruous Russian accent to his role of Concho, the Indian.

HONEYDEW (1920), *an operetta, with book and lyrics by Joseph Herbert. Music by Efrem Zimbalist. Presented by Joe Weber at the Casino Theater on September 6. Directed by Hassard Short. Cast included Ethelind Terry, Hal Forde, and Mlle. Marguerite (231 performances).*

Efrem Zimbalist was undoubtedly stimulated to invade the popular musical theater by his colleague Fritz Kreisler, who one year earlier had achieved success on the musical-comedy stage with his delightful score for *Apple Blossoms*. Himself a world-famous violin virtuoso, Zimbalist flooded his operetta with a wealth of lovable tunes, topped by "Oh, How I Long for Someone," "The Morals of a Sailorman" (which had the flavor of a Gilbert and Sullivan song), "Drop Me a Line," and "Believe Me, Beloved."

*Honeydew* was a satire on a musician—Henry Honeydew (Hal Forde) —an eccentric who spent his time writing cantatas about insects. His father-in-law, head of an exterminating business, takes one of his ditties, "The June Bug," and gives it as a premium with one of his products. "The June Bug" becomes a hit, and Honeydew is finally a successful composer.

The Spanish dancing of Mlle. Marguerite was a strong point of the production. A beautiful pantomime was enacted in a Chinese interlude in which the figures on a tea-service set—a maid and a mandarin—come to life. In the leading feminine role of Muriel, Ethelind Terry was making her first major Broadway musical-comedy appearance and was scoring her first personal success.

HONEYMOON LANE (1926), *a musical comedy, with book and lyrics by Eddie Dowling. Music by James T. Hanley. Presented by A. L. Erlanger at the Knickerbocker Theater on September 20. Directed by Edgar MacGregor. Dances by Bobby Connolly. Cast included Eddie Dowling, Pauline Mason, and Kate Smith (364 performances).*

Honeymoon Lane is a street in Canningville, Pennsylvania, where Tim Murphy (Eddie Dowling) buys a cottage as a home for his future bride, Mary Brown (Pauline Mason). They both work in the same pickle factory, where the boss' son turns Mary's head until she wants to go to New York to become a stage star. Simpleheated Tim is horrified to learn of the adventures that beset Mary in the big city. But the whole New York excursion turns out to be merely one of Tim's dreams. The final scene finds them embracing in their cottage on Honeymoon Lane.

Before the show reached New York, the producer sent out releases prophesying that an unknown comedienne and singer, Kate Smith, about to make her first Broadway appearance, would steal the limelight. The critics agreed with him when they saw her in the role of Tiny Little. "As a dancer and blues singer," reported *The New York Times*, "she proved unusually adept, and stop the show she did last night."

The hit song was presented by Tim, "The Little White House at the

End of Honeymoon Lane" (lyrics by Irving Caesar). "Dreams for Sale" also proved a strong favorite.

HOORAY FOR WHAT? (1937), *a musical comedy, conceived by E. Y. Harburg, with book by Howard Lindsay and Russel Crouse. Lyrics by E. Y. Harburg. Music by Harold Arlen. Presented by the Shuberts at the Winter Garden on December 1. Production supervised by Vincente Minnelli. Directed by Howard Lindsay. Dances by Robert Alton. Cast included Ed Wynn, Paul Haakon, June Clyde, Vivian Vance, and Jack Whiting (200 performances).*

*Hooray for What?* started out as one kind of a show and ended up on Broadway as a completely different conception. E. Y. Harburg had in mind a stinging satire on war and warmongers. But once the show went beyond the talking stage, and E. Y. Harburg's conception was turned over to Howard Lindsay and Russel Crouse to be made into a workable libretto, a good deal of the original good intentions went into discard. For one thing, the show had to be tailored to fit the lunatic antics of its star, Ed Wynn, so that he could bring to the plot his varied assortment of bizarre costumes and hats, his inexhaustible repertory of screwy inventions and gadgets, his lisp, and the other equipment and routines with which he had by now so long been identified. Thus broad comedy had to replace subtle satire. Other ambitious plans also die stillborn. The show was to include an antiwar ballet (choreographed by Agnes de Mille)—an expressionist-type dance with Stravinsky-like music. But as the show was being whipped into shape, the ballet became such a musical-comedy stereotype (in which girls wore gas masks, guns, and bayonets, and the stage became a battlefield in miniature) that Agnes de Mille forthwith resigned from the production. As time went on, two leading performers also handed in their resignations: Kaye Thompson and her singing ensemble, who were supposed to bring to the production some of the humorous routines she had made famous on the radio, and Hannah Williams (wife of Jack Dempsey). A new cast had to be assembled; with Agnes de Mille gone, a Broadway dance director was brought to devise new dance numbers; and E. Y. Harburg's bitter attack against war became little more than broad comedy with only passing suggestions of satire.

Nevertheless, when the show arrived on Broadway it was well received, with John Mason Brown still capable of perceiving in its greatly watered-down text a highly amusing ribbing of munitions makers, the League of Nations, and the absurdities of war.

Ed Wynn was cast as Chuckles, a horticulturist who seeks a formula for a gas to destroy insects and worms. In the search he comes upon a lethal gas that can destroy human beings and which becomes an important weapon of war. The League of Nations gets hot on its trail. Chuckles manages to elude both international spies and the delegates of the League of Nations; he also saves the world from his awesome discovery. While all this is happening, "Chuckles" gives voice to pearls of wisdom. For example: "The trouble with Europe [and one must recall that the year was 1937] is that Italy'th in Ethiopia, Japan'th in China, Ruthia'th in Thapain—and nobody's home." And again, on the subject of war debts: "Don't you know that if you fellows miss a couple more payments America will own the last war outright!"

"Down with Love" was a song that was used for a stirring first-act finale, sung by Jack Whiting, June Clyde, and Vivian Vance. The score included a typical Harold Arlen blues number in "Moanin' in the Mornin'," particularly as sung by Vivian Vance, while the best love ballad was "I've Gone Romantic on You," sung by Jack Whiting and June Clyde. The score also included "God's Country," a patriotic number that had little impact in the show but did much better when interpolated into the motion picture *Babes in Arms* in 1939.

> HOT CHOCOLATES (1929), *an all-Negro revue, with book and lyrics by Andy Razaf. Music by Thomas "Fats" Waller and Harry Brooks. Presented at the Hudson Theater on June 20. Directed by Leonard Harper. Cast included Jazzlips Richardson, the Jubilee Singers, Baby Cox, Edith Wilson, and Louis Armstrong (219 performances).*

With *Blackbirds* a success of the first order in 1928, it was inevitable that before long another all-Negro revue arrive as competition. The rival to *Blackbirds* was *Hot Chocolates,* whose importance rests on two significant events. One is that it brought Louis Armstrong to the Broadway stage for the first time, Armstrong having then recently arrived in New York from Chicago. (Actually, he was a member of the "pit" orchestra rather than of the cast, even though he was recruited to do a specialty number.) The other significant event in *Hot Chocolates* was the birth of a song classic which, as it turned out, was introduced by Louis Armstrong, lifted from the orchestra pit for the occasion. The song was "Ain't Misbehavin'," words by Razaf, music by Fats Waller. "Satchmo" Armstrong has often claimed that his international fame began with this number, and with his appearance in *Hot Chocolates,* and the song always remained a strong Armstrong favorite. A good deal of the energy and dynamism that had made *Blackbirds* so appealing were caught in *Hot Chocolates* in numbers such as "That Rhythm Man" and "Say It with Your Feet," while additional songs, as well as comedy and dance, were well represented through performances by Eddie Green, Jazzlips Richardson, Edith Wilson, Margaret Simms, and the Jubilee Singers.

HOUSE OF FLOWERS (1954), *a musical comedy, with book and lyrics by Truman Capote. Music by Harold Arlen. Presented by Saint Subber at the Alvin Theater on December 30. Directed by Peter Brook. Dances by Herbert Ross. Cast included Pearl Bailey, Juanita Hall, Ray Walston, and Diahann Carroll (165 performances).*

Truman Capote, author of sensitive short stories and novels, here wrote his first musical-comedy text. And, as Ottilie, Diahann Carroll made here her impressive debut on the Broadway stage. A native of Trinidad, she had first attracted attention in the United States on a TV program, where she was discovered for *House of Flowers.*

The "House of Flowers" is a bordello run by Mme. Fleur (Pearl Bailey), its name derived not only from that of the proprietress but also from the fact that each of its girls was named after a flower. This house is run in competition with another one headed by Mme. Tango (Juanita Hall), as a result of which it comes upon hard times. During an epidemic of mumps brought on by visiting sailors, the House of Flowers is forced to close. In an effort to retrieve her lost fortune Mme. Fleur is ready to turn over her young and innocent protégée, Ottilie (Diahann Carroll) to a wealthy white ship merchant. But Ottilie is in love with Royal, a barefoot boy from the hills (Rawn Spearman). To get him out of the way, Mme. Fleur contrives to get him abducted aboard a ship, from which he manages to escape. At first he is believed to be the victim of sharks. But just as Ottilie is about to give herself up to the wealthy merchant, Royal appears, becomes the town hero, and is reunited with the girl he loves.

The rich atmospheric colors and vivid local background of the West Indies—fully exploited by Oliver Messel in his beautiful sets and costumes—provide much of the interest. But the play itself had an irresistible charm. Its more or less static tempo is accelerated by a frenetic voodoo rite, and by some exciting native dances. Such moments provide a welcome change of pace and mood, but the overall languorous spell remains unbroken, maintained in Capote's poetic dialogue, and in some of Arlen's songs, richly spiced with West Indian flavors. The most popular of the Arlen songs proved to be "Two Ladies in de Shade of de Banana Tree," which was introduced by two of the lesser characters, enacted by Ada Moore and Enid Mosier. One of the most original numbers was "A Sleepin' Bee" (sung by Ottilie and others before it was used for a stunning dance number). The phrase "a sleepin' bee" refers to a Haitian folk belief which Capote talked about in one of his stories; Arlen's melody was one he had previously written for the motion picture *A Star Is Born,* where it was not used. Edward Jablonski described it as "a sensuous, undulating melody that rises a tenth and drops a fifth in a mere four bars. This swelling and lowering give it its characteristic shape, an almost languid personality of great melodic beauty." A third important and highly original number was "I Never Has Seen Snow," sensitively presented by Ottilie. "Gladiola" was the inspiration for a breathtaking dance by Dolores Harper, Carmen de Lavallade, and the ensemble.

A good many critics did not like *House of Flowers,* some of them regarding it as "dull and dirty" and "mediocre." A few responded enthusiastically, and one of those was George Jean Nathan, who called it "the most visually beautiful and in some respects the most exotically exciting evening I have encountered since I was last on the semitropical island where it is laid." Actually, *House of Flowers* was much better than its brief stay on Broadway would suggest, having been victimized from the outset by bitter feuds and dissensions within the company, which—during rehearsals—led George Balanchine to resign from his job as choreographer and turn the assignment over to Herbert Ross, and at one time almost made Truman Capote withdraw from the project because his book had been so badly tampered with.

Convinced that *House of Flowers* deserved another "try" on Broadway, Capote and Arlen revised it and presented it Off Broadway on January 28, 1968. It still failed to make the mark. In *The New York Times* Clive Barnes described Capote's book as "thin and desultory," while the critic for *Variety* remarked that "the show is not bad, but by no means great." The main strength in the revival, as in the original production, lay in a few of Arlen's songs, which had not lost their exotic appeal with the passing of thirteen years.

HOW TO SUCCEED IN BUSINESS WITHOUT REALLY TRYING (1961), *a musical comedy, with book by Abe Burrows, Jack Weinstock, and Willie Gilbert, based on the novel of the same name by Shepherd Mead. Lyrics and music by Frank Loesser. Presented by Feuer and Martin in association with Frank Productions, Inc., at the 46th Street Theater on October 14. Directed by Abe Burrows. Musical staging by Bob Fosse. Dances by Hugh Lambert. Cast included Robert Morse, Virginia Martin, Bonnie Scott, and Rudy Vallee (1,417 performances).*

Having experimented successfully with musical-play writing in *The Most Happy Fella* in 1956, and unsuccessfully with *Greenwillow* in 1960, Frank Loesser returned to the musical-comedy medium that had brought him into the Broadway limelight with such glaring brilliance with *Where's Charley?* in 1948 and particularly with *Guys and Dolls* in 1950. *How to Succeed in*

*Business Without Really Trying* makes no pretense at being anything but what it was—an entertaining show overflowing with humor, pleasant and at times brilliant songs, effective dance numbers, and some stunning performances. And it struck oil. It became the sixth-longest-running show in Broadway history when it closed on March 6, 1965. It captured all of the three major awards: the Pulitzer Prize for drama (the fourth musical to get this honor), the Antoinette Perry Award as the best musical of the season (together with six other "Tonys"), and the award of the New York Drama Critics Circle. It also received the Theater Club Award for the best play of the season by an American, the second musical ever to capture this honor. And in 1967 it became, in a Mirisch Corporation production, a highly successful motion picture starring Robert Morse and Rudy Vallee in their stage roles.

A satire on big business, *How to Succeed* was—both on the stage and on the screen—a frolic from beginning to end, which, as Howard Taubman said of the stage version, "stings mischievously and laughs uproariously . . . as impudent as a competitor who grabs off a fat contract and as cheerful as the tax collector who gets his cut no matter who makes the deal. Its irreverence is as bracing as a growth stock that matures into a nice capital gain." Robert Coleman reported that on opening night of the stage musical "the lucky customers . . . rocked the house's rafters with their cheers."

The musical satirizes the role that ambition, perseverance, self-confidence, brashness, opportunism, and ruthlessness play in making a man a success in big business. All these qualities are found in our young hero, Finch (Robert Morse), a go-getter if ever there was one. We first encounter him as a window-cleaner who is deeply absorbed in studying a success guide. Finch is convinced that he, too, can become a business tycoon if he follows the rules set down in this book. Rule Number One is to find a job with a big firm. Finch gets such a job—a humble one in the mail room—with World Wide Wickets. One of the secretaries employed there is Rosemary (Bonnie Scott), who instantly finds Finch appealing, indeed the ideal kind of man for her as she describes her ideal in the song "Happy to Keep His Dinner Warm."

Finch's immediate boss in the mail room is Mr. Twimble. Twimble explains the methods by which he had become a success in "The Company Way." Upon Twimble's promotion to a higher position, Finch is chosen as his successor, but Finch's success guide had warned him not to remain too long in the first department in which he is employed. He turns down the appointment "for the sake of the team," an act of nobility that attracts the notice of Mr. J. B. Biggley, the president of the company (Rudy Vallee).

Having won the president's favor, Finch rises in the firm step by step. In getting ahead he ignores Rosemary's interest in him. Besides, there is another girl who has her eye on him: Hedy, who had been brought into the firm by Biggley for his own delectation, but whose flaming sex appeal stimulates all the other males in the firm. "A Secretary Is Not a Toy" is an amusing number with which Hedy reminds the predatory male that she is something more than just a plaything. When Hedy becomes Finch's secretary he is not immune to her obvious female attractions. Forgetting himself completely one day, he takes her in his arms and kisses her passionately. It is only then that he realizes for the first time that the girl who interests him most is not this sex animal but gentle and lovable Rosemary.

In order to progress further in his career in World Wide Wickets, Finch manages once again to attract the attention of Biggley, this time by conniving to have Biggley find him at his desk all night, deep at work. Such dedication to duty is not all that impresses Biggley about Finch. Finch also leads Biggley to believe that he is a graduate of Biggley's own alma mater (which inspires them to sing its praises in "Grand Old Ivy") and, more remarkable still, that Finch shares Biggley's passion for knitting. Biggley is now so completely won over by Finch that he appoints him vice-president in charge of advertising. Finch devises a treasure-hunt program for television to advertise World Wide Wickets, with Hedy as star. The program is a fiasco; for the first time Finch has met his Waterloo. But his defeat is soon forgotten when Mr. Womper, chairman of the board of directors, discovers that Finch had once been a window-cleaner, this being the same humble job Mr. Womper had held before he made his own soaring flight to the heights of success. Having thus gained Mr. Womper's interest, Finch convinces him to see that a more liberal policy is instituted in the firm in dealing with its employees, since all men are brothers—a cliché that inspires both of them, and some of the employees, to sing "Brotherhood of Man." Mr. Womper succumbs to Hedy's sex appeal so completely that he takes her as his wife. In order to devote himself to her completely, he resigns from the firm. Finch replaces him as chairman of the board. Thus Finch has come to the top, as he always knew he would, having previously expressed his self-confidence in "I Believe in You." And this is the song that Rosemary sings as an expression of her faith in and love for Finch as the final curtain descends.

As Finch, young Robert Morse was ideally cast. As Norman Nadel wrote in the *World-Telegram and Sun:* "He has the look of rosy innocence. His J. Pierpont Finch can lie more smoothly than most people can tell the truth. To keep you from hating him, he lets you savor his unholy delight at his double-dealing, with side glances as brash and honest as his company face is 'sincere.' He fawns and conforms, plots and parries, and butters up the man at the top."

As "the man on the top," Rudy Vallee was appearing in a book musical for the first time, though he had previously been seen often in revues. About his performance, Nadel was impressed by the way in which he played high comedy "without relinquishing his dignity. . . . He never clowns. Advising his young friend, placating his mistress, enduring his nephew who works for him, he is firmly in character, believable and delightfully impossible, without conflict. He almost stole the show away from Robert Morse."

In his score Loesser was undoubtedly best in his satirical numbers: when he laughs at the practices and policies of big business in "The Company Way" and "Coffee Break"; when he mocks at self-aggrandizement in "I Believe in You" and at the golden rule in "Brotherhood of Man"; when he pokes fun at the career girl in "A Secretary Is Not a Toy" and at illicit relationships in "Love from a Heart of Gold" (the last a duet by Biggley and Hedy).

Thus Loesser's brilliant career in the Broadway musical theater ended on a triumphant note. His score for *How to Succeed* was his last, his career ended by cancer when he was fifty-nine.

HUMPTY DUMPTY (1868), *an extravaganza, with book mostly by George L. Fox. Music by A. Reiff (mostly adaptations). Presented by George L. Fox at the Olympic Theater on March 10. Cast included G. L. Fox, F. Lacy, C. K. Fox, and Emily Rigl (483 performances).*

*Humpty Dumpty* was an attempt to capitalize on the fabulous success of *The Black Crook* (which it followed by about two years) by imitating some of its predecessor's attractions. *Humpty Dumpty* featured transformation scenes, spells, and rituals. The elaborate ballets were more than a casual reminder of those in *The Black Crook,* since one of these used babies headed by a five-year-old premiere danseuse, and another starred Rita Sangalli, a graduate of the earlier extravaganza. The huge stage held not only enormous forces including dancers, circus acts, a bicycle act by two tots, and even a roller-skating routine (the last said to be the first of its kind on the American stage); it also included sumptuous sets displaying a subterranean fairy grotto, a moonlit skating pond featuring champion skaters Carrie A. Moore and John Engle, a dell of ferns, a Neapolitan marketplace, and so forth.

But in one important respect this extravaganza differed from *The Black Crook.* It was the frame for the remarkable pantomime art of its producer-star, George L. Fox. As an unidentified critic of that day said of him: "He was not content to please merely by being knocked down numerous times and jumping over tables and through windows. His muteness and passivity were infinitely more ludicrous than the bustling antics of other clowns, as also was his affectation of ignorant simplicity and credulous innocence."

Like *The Black Crook, Humpty Dumpty* enjoyed many revivals through the years. Its star, George L. Fox, appeared in it 1,128 times.

HURLY BURLY. *See* WEBER AND FIELDS EXTRAVAGANZAS.

I CAN GET IT FOR YOU WHOLESALE (1962), *a musical play, with book by Jerome Weidman, based on his novel of the same name. Lyrics and music by Harold Rome. Presented by David Merrick at the Shubert Theater on March 22. Directed by Arthur Laurents. Dances by Herbert Ross. Cast included Lillian Roth, Elliott Gould, Sheree North, Harold Lang, and Barbra Streisand (300 performances).*

If *I Can Get It for You Wholesale* will be remembered, it is principally for Barbra Streisand's debut on Broadway. She was nineteen years old then, with very little professional experience behind her. Previously she had appeared in an Off Broadway production that had lasted a single evening; had sung in two supper clubs—the Bon Soir and the Blue Angel—where she made a strong impression with her song styling; and several guest shots on the Mike Wallace and the Jack Paar television shows. Casting her in the comedy role of the sadly overworked, harassed, befuddled secretary, Miss Marmelstein, represented an act of courage as well as remarkable perception —for Miss Streisand's talent in comedy had yet to be tested. Yet she emerged from this performance with banners flying, particularly in her delivery of "Miss Marmelstein," the best comedy number in the score. There did not seem to be much question in the minds of any of the critics that even in a minor role she stole the show from the other performers; that here was a potential star of considerable stature (something which she went on to prove in no uncertain terms in her very next musical, *Funny Girl*). "She is just a minor mouse in the story," reported John Chapman. "She is a harried, frantic, put-upon, homely frump of a secretary, and she is hilariously played by a nineteen-year-old newcomer, Barbra Streisand."

The musical was based on Jerome Weidman's successful novel about the garment industry on New York's Seventh Avenue in 1937. The "big mouse" in the musical, as in the novel, is Harry Bogen (Elliott Gould)—an obnoxious, callous, ruthless double-dealer determined to become a success in a business infamous for its dog-eat-dog maneuvers. He puts one foot into the garment business as a strikebreaker by starting a delivery service during a delivery strike. The other foot enters when he opens his own dress business with associates. He goes on to exploit both the talents and weaknesses of his partners to his own advantage, until he achieves the goal he has set for himself. He is even a double-dealer with his next-door girl friend in the Bronx, Ruthie Rivkin (Marilyn Cooper), who loves him in spite of his obvious shortcomings and who dreams of marriage. He does not hesitate to make a strong play for a sexy nightclub performer, Martha Mills (Sheree North), a girl who knows all the answers to suggestive questions. Monster though he is, Harry Bogen is more or less a typical product of an industry where success was invariably bartered for integrity, self-respect, and generosity; where the only measure of importance is the accumulation of money. To Bogan "the sound of money" is the sweetest in the world, as he explains in the song of that name.

The musical, however, is not quite as hardboiled as its main character. A tender, solicitous Jewish mother (Lillian Roth) can interject a good deal of humanity and understanding when dealing with a son like Harry. When he has achieved the apex of success, she tries to reveal to him that his dishonest ways and cruel methods are not to her liking, even while she pleads with him to "eat a little something" as she feeds him a typical Jewish dinner. And one of the best ballads in the score is a love song of husband to wife (and vice versa), "Have I Told You Lately?", sung by Ken Le Roy and Bambi Linn in the subsidiary roles of Meyer and Blanche Bushkin.

A choreographic highlight comes immediately after Harry's song "Momma, Momma, Momma," in which he performs a dance routine while smothering his mother with expensive gifts of furs and gowns. Another highlight in the production is a comedy sequence: a fashion show that goes off elegantly enough front stage while, at the same time, backstage, the girls go through all kinds of mishaps and contortions in changing their costumes.

The musical ends in a mellow mood, after Harry plunges from his heights of prosperity into bankruptcy. He has finally discovered that there is more to life than just the lovely sound of money. There is Ruthie, for example—and, of course, his mother, too.

The undeviating line with which the plot progresses in telling the saga of Harry's rise and fall—always supported and strengthened by the songs and dances—is undoubtedly the main strength of I Can Get It for You Wholesale. As Walter Kerr remarked in the New York Herald Tribune, the show "never cheats in an anxiety to be likable where likable doesn't belong. Its humor grows from inside it. . . . Its language sounds like human speech (told by her son that he got something for peanuts, Miss Roth wants to know where he got the peanuts). Its story-telling moves at a cynical gallop that gives the sightseers out front credit for a little intelligence."

Of incidental interest: Barbra Streisand, who played Miss Marmelstein, and Elliott Gould, who played Harry Bogen, were married after *I Can Get It for You Wholesale* had ended its run.

> I DO! I DO! (1966), *a musical play with book and lyrics by Tom Jones, based on Jan de Hartog's play* The Fourposter. *Music by Harvey Schmidt. Presented by David Merrick at the 46th Street Theater on December 5. Directed by Gower Champion. Cast comprised Mary Martin and Robert Preston (560 performances).*

*I Do! I Do!* requires only two characters and a single set (a balustrade-shaped bedroom whose huge and solid fourposter bed is symbolic of marriage). With such limited means, Jean de Hartog fashioned a successful and penetrating play of married life spanning half a century, produced as *The Fourposter* in 1951, with Hume Cronyn and Jessica Tandy. This was a portrait in depth of two highly sensitive people as they respond to each other's shortcomings and glow at each other's virtues while confronting the ecstasies and agonies of living.

In making a musical out of this play, its adapters took the bare outlines of the portrait and filled it in with decorative embellishments of their own. From a wise, sophisticated, amusing, and often deeply touching play it now became a slight, sentimental, and frequently all too cute escapade that was concerned exclusively with amusing and entertaining its audiences. The fact that this material had been placed in the hands of two performers as skilled, talented, and experienced as Robert Preston and Mary Martin was insurance that this material would be exploited not only to its fullest potential but beyond it. Robert Preston does a barefoot tap dance after confiding on his wedding night how much he loves his wife, in "I Love My Wife." He does a Harry Richman-like routine, wearing a green dressing gown over his full-dress outfit, a high hat, and a walking stick. Mary Martin assumes the air of an abandoned woman in a jazzy number, "Flaming Agnes," or she gives an imitation of how her husband sounds as he chews and mutters in his sleep. The two fool around with a ukulele, a violin, and a saxophone. In short, they never allow the slender plot to collapse into boredom. And since they are masters of their trade, *I Do! I Do!* proved from beginning to end a source of sheer delight. But somewhere along the line the subtler, richer overtones of De Hartog's play got lost. What could have been a musical play of profound and deeply moving emotion and characterization was made into entertainment pure and simple—but at times wonderful entertainment.

The musical begins with the wedding day of Michael ("He"), played by Robert Preston, and Agnes ("She"), portrayed by Mary Martin. They sing about the coming momentous event and of their hopes and fears for their future life together in "All Dearly Beloved," followed by the sentimental "Together Forever." The wedding over, they are back in their bedroom, explaining to each other what marriage means in the title song.

Continually embellished with appropriate songs, the play follows their marital life through the birth of their two children (when, as they explain in the appealing waltz, "My Cup Runneth Over"); they come to realize how much more dependent they are on each other than ever before. But this idyllic relationship can hardly be expected to last forever. As they grow older, they are beset by marital problems. Agnes cannot avoid envy when Michael, now a successful writer, dominates the proceedings at a dinner given in his honor, nor is her mood brightened when he reveals that he has had an extramarital affair, or insists (in the most amusing number in the score, "A Well Known Fact") that a man in his middle age is more appealing and attractive to the opposite sex than before, while a middle-aged woman goes to "pot." If it is true that a middle-aged woman disintegrates, muses Agnes angrily, then she's a "pot whose gonna get hot." She puts on a bird-of-paradise hat she has been saving for years and goes into a jazzy number, "Flaming Agnes," to prove to herself that there is still plenty of hot blood in her veins. All this infuriates Michael; a minor brawl develops into a major confrontation. Agnes threatens to leave him but is finally dissuaded from doing so.

And the years continue to pass. Agnes and Michael are celebrating New Year's Eve by themselves. They reflect on the past in "Where Are the Snows?", are accepting the present, and are speculating on the future. But the future brings further disagreements and conflicts between them. Michael is unhappy over the fact that his daughter has just been married, and thus he becomes harder to live with. Agnes finds her life has become empty. Eventually, however, they come to terms with old age, are grateful that life after all has been kind.

The ending of the musical differs from the play, possibly pointing up better than any other single episode the way an urbane and deeply human study of a married couple in *The Fourposter* was allowed to descend to the obvious. In the play the wife has died. The husband, now at the dusk of life, realizes for the first time in many years what a vital role she has played in his life as man and writer. He will miss her sorely. In *I Do! I Do!* the ending maintains the sentimentality and the amusement the adapters had been dispensing. The closing scene shows husband and wife moving out of their apartment. The new occupants are a pair of recently married young people about to begin their life together just as Michael and Agnes had done so many years before. As they are about to depart, in a mood of levity, they leave behind them on the fourposter the small pillow (on which is embroidered "God Is Love") but make sure to place it behind a bottle of champagne.

A good deal of the strong public appeal of *I Do! I Do!* was due (beyond the performance of the two stars) to Gower Champion's direction. As the critic for *Variety* remarked: "The whole performance has a choreographic pattern that only a dancer-stager of Champion's demonstrated ability could design and carry out. The dancing, in other words, tends to be part of the action and dramatizes the situation and the ideas and emotions of its stars."

After a change of casting—which saw Carol Lawrence and Gordon MacRae replaced by Preston and Martin while the latter pair were on tour with the show—*I Do! I Do!* was twice given, in a period of less than two months, at festive dinner parties at the White House hosted by President and Mrs. Johnson. On both occasions the musical was seen in an abbreviated half-hour version, staged by Mr. Champion. The first time was a dinner honoring both Vice-President Humphrey and Supreme Court Justice Earl Warren; the other time was for the parents of Marine Captain Charles S. Robb on the eve of his wedding to Lynda Johnson.

It might be interesting to note the unusual fact that *I Do! I Do!* represented the third time *The Fourposter* was made into a musical. The first musical, the work of Edward Earl, was to have starred Robert Rounseville and Anne Ayers, and was to have been produced by a summer stock company in 1962. This presentation was canceled due to difficulties over obtaining the rights. The following summer *The Fourposter* once again emerged as a musical, this time adapted by Martin Kalmanoff, starring Gail Manners and Walter Cassell; it was performed in several stock-company theaters in Pennsylvania and New Jersey, but never reached Broadway.

I'D RATHER BE RIGHT (1937), *a musical comedy, with book by George S. Kaufman and Moss Hart. Lyrics by Lorenz Hart. Music by Richard Rodgers. Presented by Sam H. Harris at the Alvin Theater on November 2. Directed by George S. Kaufman. Dances by Charles Weidman. Cast included George M. Cohan, Austin Marshall, Joy Hodges, and Florenz Ames (290 performances).*

Like *Of Thee I Sing,* the Gershwin Pulitzer Prize musical produced in 1931, *I'd Rather Be Right* is a satire on politics in Washington, D.C. But in the Rodgers and Hart musical, the emphasis is on specific timely issues and actual political luminaries rather than on fictitious characters and episodes.

A highly improbable situation sets into motion all ensuing satirical developments. Peggy Jones (Joy Hodges) and Phil Barker (Austin Marshall) find
that they cannot get married until he gets a raise; and he won't get that
raise unless the national budget is balanced. Phil dreams that he and Peggy
meet the President of the United States on a bench in Central Park—the
President bearing a striking resemblance to Franklin D. Roosevelt (George
M. Cohan). When they confide their troubles to him, the President promises
to do all he can to balance the budget. But the political forces inside Washington—and the social and economic forces outside—frustrate his every effort. When, in a fireside chat, he suggests to American women that they
give up cosmetics for a year and donate the money to the national budget,
they rise in vociferous protest. When an effort is made to use the gold in
Fort Knox, there is the threat of a stock-market crash and panic in the business world. The budget goes unbalanced. The President urges the young
people to have faith in themselves and their country by getting married
anyway. Phil awakens and decides to heed the counsel given him in his dream.

The New Deal and New Dealers are satirized. "What did you do with
all the money I gave you last week?" inquires the President peevishly of
the Secretary of the Treasury, when the latter comes for more funds. "Three
hundred millions *ought* to last a week!" James A. Farley comes to the
President seeking an appointment for the chairman of the 4th Assembly
District of Seattle as Collector of the Port of New York. When the President
suggests that New York already has such a collector, Farley replies quickly:
"But not in Seattle!" The rapidity with which laws are created, the federal-
subsidized theater, taxes, Walter Lippmann, the brain trust, labor—these are
some of the other subjects laughed at in song and dialogue.

Song is so completely integrated with text that it often cannot be divorced from it without losing something vital. The only excepion is "Have
You Met Miss Jones?" a first-act duet of Peggy and Phil. The other songs
are dependent for relevance upon the action in the play, and the dialogue
that precedes it; these include such sprightly items as "A Homogeneous
Cabinet," "A Little Bit of Constitutional Fun," "We're Going to Balance
the Budget," "Labor Is the Thing," and the President's off-the-cuff con-
fidences, "Off the Record."

Not the least of the attractions of this witty musical was the performance of George M. Cohan as President Roosevelt. It was a performance with
dimension and depth, a performance touched with warmth and humanity
and wistfulness as well as mockery and gaiety. But to work with Cohan
had not been easy. He was starring in a play and singing songs that he had
not written. Neither the brittle dialogue nor the spicy songs were the kind

with which for many years he had been identified. He took on the role reluctantly, made no effort to conceal the low opinion he had of the Rodgers and Hart songs, and even tried changing some of the lyrics until severely reprimanded after an out-of-town tryout performance.

> I'LL SAY SHE IS (1924), *a revue, with book and lyrics by Will B. Johnstone. Music by Tom Johnstone. Presented by James B. Beury at the Casino Theater on May 19. Directed by Eugene Sanger and Vaughan Godfrey. Cast included the Four Marx Brothers (313 performances).*

This revue marked the first appearance on the Broadway stage of the Four Marx Brothers after their many years of touring the vaudeville circuit. The book was made up mainly of material they had previously used in their vaudeville acts, including such sketches as "Home Again," "Mr. Green's Reception," and "On the Mezzanine." The identities of Groucho, Harpo, Chico, and Zeppo—which they would henceforth assume and make famous in all their musical comedies and motion pictures—were now established: Groucho—in his ill-fitting tails and trousers, painted moustache, and heavy eyebrows continually lifting over his eyeglasses—slouching around the stage as he triggers his puns and wisecracks; Chico, dressed as an impoverished Italian and assuming an Italian dialect, playing the piano with eccentric fingering; Harpo, in red wig under a lopsided top hat, mute throughout the play, running after every girl in sight, stealing everything he can put his hands on, and then sitting down at the harp for a virtuoso performance; Zeppo playing the straight man to whom were assigned the ballads. Their madcap · antics inspired such accolades from Alexander Woollcott, Ben Hecht, and other New York sophisticates that not only did *I'll Say She Is* become a hit, but from this point on the Four Marx Brothers became something of a cult. The score's best songs were "Only You," "I'm Saving for a Rainy Day," and "Give Me a Thrill."

> ILYA DARLING (1967), *a musical play, with book by Jules Dassin, based on the motion picture* Never on Sunday. *Lyrics by Joe Darion. Music by Manos Hadjidakis. Presented by Kermit Bloomgarden in association with United Artists at the Mark Hellinger Theater on April 11. Directed by Jules Dassin. Dances by Onna White. Cast included Melina Mercouri and Orson Bean (318 performances).*

*Never on Sunday* had proved to be a cinematic masterpiece. In the transfer to the Broadway stage as a musical, no effort was spared to be faithful to the original source. Jules Dassin, who had written and directed the movie, adapted the musical play himself and once again filled the role of director; Melina Mercouri, whose performance in the motion picture had been an unforgettable experience, was recruited to repeat her role in the flesh; and then, of course, there was the tune, "Never On Sunday," which, as the theme music of the movie, captured an Academy Award.

But in making the transfer of a motion picture to a musical play, Jules Dassin forgot, perhaps, how much greater flexibility the camera has in capturing a scene than does the stage. The opening is a case in point. In the motion picture, Ilya (her bountiful curves bulging generously and provocatively from the merest suggestion of a bathing suit) jumps into the water for a swim. As far as the eye can see, sailors jump from all types and sizes of boats into the water after her. From vivid illustration on the screen, this amusing scene can only be suggested on the stage, and the effervescent humor becomes as stale as does sparkling water that has been standing too long.

Ilya (Melina Mercouri), is a prostitute in Piraeus, in present-day Greece. She is a generous, gregarious, lovable young woman whose heart is as large as her clientele, all of whom are her friends; for whom love is not only a profession but a way of life. She is happy with her place in society until her path crosses that of a visiting American, Homer Thrace (Orson Bean), come to Greece as a professor-tourist seeking out the ancient glories of that country. He recognizes that Ilya is pure gold, though slightly tarnished, and he is determined to return the gleaming shine to the precious metal. In short, he is out to remake Ilya not only into a lady of virtue but also into a lady of culture. Ilya abandons her profession and submits to an intensive regimen of study, under Horace's guidance, of books, music, Greek drama, and history. At the same time, Horace also aspires to introduce learning into the redlight district of Athens, until he becomes victimized by a procurer who tries to use him as the means to raise the rentals for the girls' rooms. By the time Horace gets ready to go home, he has learned to like the easygoing and free ways of the humble Greek people he has come to accept as friends, and Ilya reverts to her former happy self. In a spirited finale, "Ya Chora," his Greek friends bid him farewell, while urging him to make an early return.

One of the most amusing and at the same time poignant scenes in the motion picture comes across with equal effect in the musical. It is the episode in which an American sailor comes to Ilya to learn the facts of life. It is here that Ilya sings one of her best numbers, "Love, Love, Love"—a song about sex—with a projection that Rex Reed (in *Hifi Stereo Review*) called "mesmerizing." He added: "Never before has the subject seemed so healthy. Melina breathes the first *love* through her nostrils, though she is sniffing Fabèrgé for the first time, purrs the second *love* like an unpredictable, half-tamed cheetah, then hits the third *love* on the head with a satin tuning fork. Goose-pimple time."

As a matter of fact, it was Melina Mercouri who virtually carried the entire musical, electrifying the audience with her dynamism, enchanting it continually with her little mannerisms, gestures, and lively movements of face and body. She delivers a line or a song with devastating impact. What Mr. Reed says about her singing is true about everything she does on the stage (even the way she performs some dance steps, though she is not a dancer). "This warmth and this total reality, coupled with an unattainable out-of-reach quality that has made her a legend in her own time, is the stuff Melina is made of." She is to Rex Reed "a Greek goddess—svelte, fiery, delicious, ethereal—transplanted right into the middle of the twentieth century. Melina throws her golden hair back, offers her butterscotch-tan throat to the spotlights, grins her wall-to-wall grin that could cause a revolution if she so desired, and sings the Greek songs with her heart as well as her lungs, and the result is devastating."

One of her big numbers is—to be sure—"Never on Sunday," in which she is effectively supported by a chorus. Orson Bean has an excellent song in "I Think She Needs Me" (he is, of course, speaking about Ilya); so has a lesser character, Despo, in "I'll Never Lay Down Anymore." Songs like the last two are assets—and so are the vigorous dance routines by an all-male group—when Melina Mercouri is not around to light up the stage.

I MARRIED AN ANGEL (1938), *a musical comedy, with book by Rodgers and Hart, adapted from a play by John Vaszary. Lyrics by Lorenz Hart. Music by Richard Rodgers. Presented by Dwight Deere Wiman at the Shubert Theater on May 11. Directed by Joshua Logan. Choreography by George Balanchine. Cast included Vera Zorina, Dennis King, Vivienne Segal, Audrey Christie, and Walter Slezak (338 performances).*

While working in Hollywood in 1938, Rodgers and Hart became impressed with the possibilities of John Vaszary's play *I Married an Angel* for the musical stage. When they learned that MGM owned the rights, they prepared a scenario, hoping to spur that studio into some action. But the studio felt that the scenario was not screen material and stood ready to sell Rodgers and Hart the musical-comedy and screen rights.

*I Married an Angel* belongs to the world of fantasy in which Rodgers and Hart had long since proved themselves adept. Count Willy Palaffi (Dennis King) is disillusioned with women and vows he will marry only an angel. When an angel (Vera Zorina) flies through the window, he falls in love with her and marries her. But an angel as wife is not quite so ideal an arrangement as the count had expected. She refuses to tell lies or to deceive anybody, the way most human beings do, and thus manages to involve her husband in all kinds of embarrassment. But the angel finally acquires some of the less desirable traits of humans, and the marriage is a success.

As the angel, Vera Zorina achieved her first success in the American musical theater. By profession a ballet dancer, a graduate of the Ballet Russe de Monte Carlo, she had appeared in the London company of *On Your Toes,* and later was starred in the motion-picture adaptation of that play. The original plan had been to cast her in a minor role in *I Married an Angel;* but after Rodgers met her, he wired Wiman, *"Small Part Nothing. Zorina Plays the Angel."* Naturally the ballets of George Balanchine were conceived with her experience and background in mind, the most ambitious being the "Honeymoon Ballet" in the first act.

The stage direction was in the skillful hands of Joshua Logan. This, then, was the first time Logan worked in a Richard Rodgers musical; he would work with Rodgers again in the future, and with epoch-making consequences.

These were the best songs: the title number, presented by Count Palaffi; "Spring Is Here," a duet by the count and the countess (the latter played by Vivienne Segal), which, both in lyrics and melody, poignantly explains that the vernal season has little attraction to people not in love; and "Did You Ever Get Stung?", sung by Count and Countess Palaffi with the support of Charles Walter as Peter Mueller. The score included several interesting musical interludes—"The Modiste" in the first act, and "Angel Without Wings" in the second. These interludes, and the ballet music, revealed Rodgers' enlarged canvas; so did the rhythmic dialogue, a successful experiment in which the conversation preceding a song is provided with a soft musical background.

The best comedy sequence was a hilarious takeoff on the kind of extravaganza stage shows put on by such New York movie palaces as the Radio City Music Hall and the Roxy, in which Audrey Christie (appearing as Anna Murphy) regularly brought down the house with her rendition of "At the Roxy Music Hall."

Song, dance, comedy, and fantasy combined to make *I Married an Angel* stage magic. Brooks Atkinson called it "one of the best musical comedies of many seasons, an imaginative improvisation with a fully orchestrated score and an extraordinarily beautiful production. Musical comedy has met its masters." Regrettably, the motion-picture adaptation (by MGM in 1942, starring Jeanette MacDonald and Nelson Eddy) came off far less successfully than did the stage production, with which it tampered in more ways than by just interpolating some additional and not particularly beneficial songs by other composers.

> INNOCENT EYES (1924), *a revue, with book by Harold Atteridge. Lyrics by Harold Atteridge and Tot Seymour. Music by Sigmund Romberg and Jean Schwartz. Presented by the Shuberts at the Winter Garden on May 20. Directed by Frank Smithson. Dances by Jack Mason and Seymour Felix. Cast included Mistinguette, Cleo Mayfield, Cecil Lean, and Frances Williams (119 performances).*

Mistinguette, the darling of the Casino de Paris, had been brought to the United States by Florenz Ziegfeld, who planned to star her in his *Follies*. Once she arrived and Ziegfeld heard some of her routines, he lost interest in her, dropped her, and turned over one of Mistinguette's Casino de Paris song hits, "My Man" ("Mon Homme") to Fanny Brice.

The Shuberts took her on and built a revue around her, featuring her with Earl Leslie in an apache dance (with which she was so identified in Paris), assigning to her a few nondescript songs, and surrounding her with a chorus line named "The Mistinguette Girls" and chorus boys (one of whom, Jack Oakie, later became famous in the movies). Ziegfeld had been right and the Shuberts wrong: Mistinguette failed to make an impression on New York audiences.

Far more impressive was the comedy of Cecil Lean and Cleo Mayfield; Vanessi's exotic dances; the specialty numbers of singing pianist Edythe Baker; and especially the singing of young Frances Williams, the "diva with the baby-talk," achieving her first Broadway stage success in this production. The undistinguished score included "Day Dreams," "I Love the Boys," and "Love Is like a Pinwheel."

> INSIDE U.S.A. (1948), *a revue, with book by Arnold Auerbach, Moss Hart, and Arnold B. Horwitt. Lyrics by Howard Dietz. Music by Arthur Schwartz. Presented by Arthur Schwartz at the New Century Theater on April 30. Directed by Robert H. Gordon. Dances by Helen Tamiris. Cast included Beatrice Lillie, Jack Haley, Valerie Bettis, and Herb Shriner (339 performances).*

In the 1930's the songwriting team of Howard Dietz (lyricist) and Arthur Schwartz (composer) contributed songs to some of the most successful and memorable revues of that decade, most notably *The Band Wagon,* one of the best revues ever produced. After writing the score for *Stars in Your Eyes* in 1939 (a failure), they went their separate ways. It took them almost a decade to be reunited, and when they finally were—in *Inside U.S.A.*—they once again proved themselves to be among the best songwriters the American revue has produced. Two songs from this production have not been forgotten: "Haunted Heart," introduced by John Tyers and Estelle Loring (a song Dietz and Schwartz had originally written in 1940 but did not use until they found a suitable place for it in *Inside U.S.A.*); the other, "Rhode Island Is Famous for You," sung by Estelle Loring and Jack Haley, cataloguing the products for which each state in the Union is famous.

Early in the revue, Herb Shriner appeared with a copy of John Gunther's *Inside U.S.A.* under his arm. Except for the fact that the scenes skip around all over the American map from Miami Beach to New York and from Rhode Island to San Francisco, this is about the only connection between this production and the Gunther book from which it purchased the title. Perhaps a better title would have been *Inside Comedy,* for comedy was the keynote. Beatrice Lillie appeared as a mermaid and as an Indian squaw; in a Moss Hart sketch she played a fussy, annoying maid whose antics drove a Broadway star mad just before an opening-night performance; in a travesty, "Song to Forget," she was pursued by suitors who included Tchaikovsky, Chopin, and Liszt; as a choir leader she leads a group of singers in a mock madrigal, "Come, Oh Come, to Pittsburgh"; and as a lady not afraid to let her hair down she runs loose in New Orleans during the Mardi Gras. Jack Haley was seen in a Miami Beach hotel, to which he came for a sadly needed rest, only to become involved with a trick bed; he is found in a swank nightclub, where he gives waiters valuable instruction on how best to pursue their profession. Herb Shriner (making his debut on the Broadway stage, after appearing with his harmonica and folksy humor in a one-man show at conventions, vaudeville, fairs, square dances, and so forth) carried off the rest of the comedy with his penetrating impression of Will Rogers and in his own specialty—Hoosier monologues. And there was a fine topical satirical number sung by two Indians, "We Won't Take It Back."

Other departments were also strong. Valerie Bettis starred in two effective ballet sequences, "Tiger Lily" and "Haunted Heart," the latter with a San Francisco background. And John Tyers delivered a good Western number in "My Gal Is Mine No More."

THE INTERNATIONAL CUP and THE BALLET OF NIAGARA. *See* HIPPODROME EXTRAVAGANZAS.

INVESTIGATION. *See* THE MULLIGAN GUARDS' BALL.

IRENE (1919), *a musical comedy, with book by James Montgomery. Lyrics by Joseph McCarthy. Music by Harry Tierney. Presented by Joseph McCarthy at the Vanderbilt Theater on November 18. Cast included Edith Day, Walter Regan, Adele Rowland, and Bobbie Watson (670 performances).*

*Irene* made stage history by having the longest run of any musical on Broadway up to that time—surpassing by thirteen performances the record achieved a quarter of a century earlier by *A Trip to Chinatown*. Besides this long New York run, the play enjoyed seventeen road companies.

Its charm lay in its escapist Cinderella story. Irene O'Dare (Edith Day), a poor girl who lives in the slums on Ninth Avenue, New York, is a shopgirl who must make a delivery to the home of wealthy Donald Marshall (Walter Regan). Donald becomes interested in her and, to advance her career, finds her a job as model at the modiste establishment of Mme. Lucy. At a party on Long Island, Irene sings, dances, and wears the shop's beautiful clothing—winning the hearts of all those present. Through her beauty and charm, Irene helps bring success to Mme. Lucy's shop. She also wins the love of Donald, who now must overcome the prejudice of Mrs. O'Dare to rich young men before he can marry Irene.

In this play we find one of the most popular American waltzes of all time, and its composer's best-known song: "Alice Blue Gown." The color blue had come into fashion in 1919, popularized by Alice Roosevelt Longworth, the daughter of Theodore Roosevelt; and the beguiling waltz took advantage of this fact in its lyrics. In *Irene* it was introduced by Adele Rowland in a subsidiary role. While "Alice Blue Gown" was a standout, there were other appealing numbers in this superior score. These included: the title number, sung by the heroine supplemented by the ensemble; and "Castle of Dreams" (melody borrowed from Chopin's *Minute Waltz*), introduced by Bernice McCabe (in a minor role) and the ensemble.

*Irene* had to wait until 1940 before being made into a motion picture. It starred Anna Neagle and Ray Milland in an RKO production. Most of the score from the original stage musical was used as background music while a new song, written by McCarthy and Tierney especially for the movie, was interpolated, "You've Got Me out on a Limb."

THE ISLE OF CHAMPAGNE (1892), *a comic opera, with book by Charles A. Byrne and Louis Harrison. Music by William Wallace Furst. Presented at the Manhattan Opera House on December 5. Cast included Thomas Q. Seabrook, Walter Allen, Eugene O'Rourke, and Eliva Crox.*

The Isle of Champagne is a happy kingdom where the only known beverages are wine and champagne. It is ruled by King Pommery Sec'nd (Thomas Q. Seabrook), with Appollinaris Frappé as an unscrupulous prime minister (Walter Allen) who has robbed the king of both power and wealth. A schooner from New Bedford is blown toward the island with a cargo of water—a beverage hitherto unknown to the Isle of Champagne. To replenish his empty coffers, the king decrees water to be a beverage superior to wine and champagne; and to gain possession of the water, he must marry the owner of the schooner, the New England spinster Abigail Peck. Water becomes a luxury, and the king becomes rich. The most pleasing numbers in Furst's score were "Fly Sweet Bird," "There's a Land in the Shimmery Silver Moon," and a topical song called "Old King Mumm Could Make Things Hum."

IT HAPPENED IN NORDLAND (1904), *a comic opera, with book and lyrics by Glen MacDonough. Music by Victor Herbert. Presented by Fred R. Hamlin, Julian Mitchell, and Lew Fields at the Lew Fields Theater on December 5. Directed by Julian Mitchell. Cast included Lew Fields, Harry Davenport, Bessie Clayton, Joseph Herbert, and Marie Cahill (154 performances).*

When the comedy team of Weber and Fields split up in 1894, Lew Fields formed the Lew Fields Stock Company with Fred R. Hamlin and Julian Mitchell. They arranged for Victor Herbert to provide music for its productions at the new Lew Fields Theater, opening in the fall of 1904. The comic opera with which the new producing company and the theater made their simultaneous bow was *It Happened in Nordland* (originally called *The American Ambassadress*).

By using as its central character an American ambassadress to the court of Nordland, *It Happened in Nordland* anticipated Irving Berlin's *Call Me Madam* by almost half a century. Katherine Peepfoogle, the ambassadress (Marie Cahill), bears a striking resemblance to the Nordland queen. When the queen disappears to escape an undesirable marriage, the American ambassadress is compelled to impersonate her in order to save the kingdom. The difficulties are straightened out when the queen is permitted to marry the man she loves, Prince Karl (Frank O'Neill). The ambassadress finds happiness in recovering a long-lost brother, Hubert (Lew Fields).

Herbert's biographer, Edward N. Waters, regarded the score as a "lighter work than Herbert usually wrote." He added: "The separate numbers were shorter, there were fewer concerted pieces, and choruses and finales were less massive. Most of the reviews praised the score without emphasizing excerpts, and they all agreed on its sparkling quality and infectious tunefulness."

The most familiar number in this score is "Al Fresco," which opens the second act. Herbert published it originally as a piano piece under an assumed name to see if it could win the public without the benefit of the composer's fame. When it sold well, he decided to adapt it for the carnival scene in this musical. Immediately after the performance of the "Al Fresco" music in the second act comes an infectious waltz, "The Knot of Blue," sung by a girl's chorus. Other numbers included the sophisticated "Absinth Frappé"; "The Woman in the Case," introduced by Harry Davenport, playing the role of Prince George; and the spirited march tune "Commanderess-in-Chief," sung by Katherine.

Marie Cahill, the star of the show, had been severely treated by the critics both during the out-of-town tryout in Harrisburg, Pennsylvania, and in New York. Immediately after the New York run she left the cast impetuously, following a bitter fight with Herbert, who objected to her frequent interpolations of songs by other composers. On October 29—when Herbert was conducting as a substitute for Max Hirschfield, who was ill—she left the stage weeping midway in singing "Any Old Tree" (*not* by Herbert), complaining that Herbert had purposely interpolated two discords to disconcert her. (Herbert insists the discords were the result of her singing off pitch.) When the play went on to Boston, she refused to go along with the company, and her role was assumed by several other performers, including Blanche Ring (who was also prone to interpolate songs by composers other than Herbert) and Pauline Frederick; the latter here began a career that would bring her stardom in the theater and on the silent screen.

In spite of its troubles with its stars (and in spite of the fact that it lacked romantic interest), *It Happened in Nordland* proved highly successful. It played two weeks in Boston following the original New York run of 154 performances, went in to Chicago for ten weeks, and then came back to New York for an additional one hundred performances, at which time Blanche Ring replaced Marie Cahill.

IT'S A BIRD, IT'S A PLANE, IT'S SUPERMAN (1966), *a musical comedy with book by David Newman and Robert Benton based on the comic strip,* Superman. *Lyrics by Lee Adams. Music by Charles Strouse. Presented by Harold Prince in association with Ruth Mitchell at the Alvin Theater on March 29. Directed by Harold Prince. Dances by Ernest Flatt. Cast included Bob Holiday, Jack Cassidy, and Patricia Marand (75 performances).*

Though this production was a box-office fiasco, it nevertheless was such a refreshing departure from the routinized norm of the average musical (even successful ones), and was frequently so delightfully spiced with sardonic humor and absurdity, that Otis L. Guernsey, Jr., selected it as one of the ten best in his annual compendium, *The Best Plays of 1965–1966.* The text was based on that popular comic strip and comic-strip book, *Superman.* "Superman" is the superhuman being who disguises himself as the timid and meek reporter, Clark Kent, on the *Daily Planet.* Whenever trouble brews in the vicinity of Metropolis (the time is the present), Kent removes his daily clothes and becomes an athletic and muscular figure dressed in a blue and red cape, white shirt bearing the letter "S" and clinging tights. He soars like a bird—or is it a plane?—to the scene of disaster to destroy the enemy and rescue the victims.

The musical, notes Mr. Guernsey, "was not camped, but played as straight as possible in a good laugh at our secret longing for a hero who could solve all problems, defeat all enemies. The joke is not on Superman. . . . The joke is right where it should be—on us and our childish instincts." The text covers a number of other areas, as the playwrights themselves reveal in Mr. Guernsey's compendium. The musical deals with "the concept of Loss of Communication" (Clark Kent is unable to reveal in his everyday life as reporter the red letter "S" concealed on his white shirt behind his everyday suit, which puts him in a class by himself). The musical touches on the "loss of identity," is expressed by the symbolic act of having Kent leave his street clothes in a phone booth. It deals with cruelty. And it is not afraid to invade the realm of Absurdity (the lyrics of "Pow! Bam! Zonk!").

The play opens with Superman (Bob Holiday), having overcome a gang of bank robbers, entering a phone booth to put on his Clark Kent suit as he laments the Kent role he is compelled to play ("Doing Good"). Max Mencken (Jack Cassidy), a columnist on the *Daily Planet,* is most assuredly not one of Superman's admirers, but the reporter, Lois Lane (Patricia Marand) expresses her own view and that of the mob in exclaiming "We Need Him." At the newspaper office, Lois confesses who it is she loves in "It's Superman." Just then the evil scientist, Dr. Abner Sedgwick (Michael O'Sullivan) enters. He is distraught, because a dangerous buildup in his nuclear reactor is endangering Metropolis. He does not notice Clark Kent making a discreet exit. At the laboratory, Superman helps Dr. Sedgwick set matters straight in the reactor room. Metropolis is saved. But Dr. Sedgwick is not grateful. Bitter at never having won the Nobel Prize, he had hoped the radiation would destroy Superman and do away with the good in the world. The physicist's all-abiding ambition is, as he reveals in a song, "Revenge."

Dr. Sedgwick phones Lois to inform her he has decided to name a new Physics Hall after Superman. In return, Lois invites him to the newspaper office to witness a movie of Superman's life, material Dr. Sedgwick might use for his dedicatory address. This movie describes a scientist on the planet

Krypton which explodes, but not before one of its babies is saved and brought to earth. That baby becomes Superman. The film over, Superman makes an ingratiating speech to his admiring, adoring youngsters. Dr. Sedgwick now realizes that Superman survives on admiration. Robbed of it, Superman can be destroyed.

Superman flies in to the campus for the dedication ceremonies of Superman Hall. He is enthusiastically received by the crowd in "It's Super Nice." But while this is going on, Dr. Sedgwick has arranged to have the City Hall Tower dynamited. Superman has proved incapable of avoiding this disaster, and thus faces disgrace. His despair is echoed in "The Strongest Man in the World," but he is momentarily cheered by the presence of Lois, whom he now knows he loves.

In the presence of Max Mencken, Dr. Sedgwick uses his computer to disclose the identity of Superman. Thus they discover that Superman is Clark Kent, which sends them into a joyous song and dance ("You've Got What I Need"). They now evolve a complicated, devious plan to destroy Superman. Clark Kent is induced to come to an abandoned power plant where Lois is strapped to a chair connected to a 6,000-volt generator. Any move by Superman will instantly kill Lois. At the same time, Dr. Sedgwick taunts Superman. Why does Superman always save the victims of crimes instead of preventing the crimes? Why does Superman need so pretentious an outfit? Why does Superman feed so hungrily on the adulation of masses? Why does he lead a double life? Such questions cause first confusion, then total despair in Superman. Dr. Sedgwick is besides himself with joy. He is victorious over Superman, at last. More than that, representatives of Red China have come to decorate him and to carry him off to Red China in a helicopter. It is only then that Superman emerges from his desolation and impotency. He attacks and defeats the enemy ("Pow! Bam! Zonk!"). He saves Lois. And then he rescues Metropolis which is being attacked by a missile. As for the evil Dr. Sedgwick, he meets the doom he deserves: electrocution from the 6,000-volt generator.

JAMAICA (1957), *a musical comedy, with book by E. Y. Harburg and Fred Saidy. Lyrics by E. Y. Harburg. Music by Harold Arlen. Presented by David Merrick at the Imperial Theater on October 31. Directed by Robert Lewis. Dances by Jack Cole. Cast included Lena Horne, Ricardo Montalban, Adelaide Hall, Ossie Davis, and Josephine Premice (557 performances).*

In *House of Flowers* (1954), Harold Arlen had written the music for a musical comedy with a Caribbean setting. He returned to the same setting in *Jamaica,* which provided him, and the writers of the text, with ample material for colorful sets, costumes, dances, production numbers, and songs. The specific locale is Pigeon Island, off Kingston, Jamaica. Savannah (Lena Horne) yearns to leave the island for the allurements of New York, about which she has heard from tourists and read in magazines. A humble fisherman, Koli (Ricardo Montalban), loves her, but she refuses to marry him unless he is willing to go off with her to New York. For a while she is beguiled by the slick, oily talk and free spending of Joe Nashua (Joe Adams), a visitor from Harlem come to the island to exploit the shark-ridden pearl bed. But a hurricane reveals Koli to be a hero, when he saves the life of Savannah's little brother, Quico (Augustine Rios). Savannah is now reconciled to find happiness on the island with Koli. Her ambition to see New York has been realized only in a brief "dream" sequence, set in the Persian Room. The secondary love interest engages Cicero (Ossie Davis), whose visions of grandeur to rule the island are momentarily realized by the hurricane, and Ginger (Josephine Premice).

The plot is only incidental to its trimmings and adornments, the most arresting being the performance of Lena Horne, making her first Broadway appearance in a starring role. (The last time she was seen on the stage was long before she became a celebrity of nightclubs and motion pictures—in 1939, when she was a member of the chorus in an edition of the *Blackbirds* revue.) In *Jamaica*—as in motion pictures, nightclubs, and on television—Lena Horne was irresistible. "She shines," reported *Life,* "like a tigress in the night, purring and preening and pouncing into the spotlight." Walter Kerr described her as an "enchantress," adding: "She stands as lithe as a willow at the center of the stage, sucks in her breath as though she were inhaling a windstorm, and coos out the most imperturbable of mating-pigeon sounds."

The authors see to it that she is on the stage most of the time. Of the eighteen numbers in the prolix score, she is heard in five solos (one reprised) and three duets (two reprised). Some of these are Arlen's best: the sensual torch song that she sings in the "dream" sequence, "Take It Slow, Joe"; a glib patter song, "Ain't It de Truth?"; the ballad "Cocoanut Sweet," first introduced by Adelaide Hall playing the role of Grandma and then heard as a duet of Grandma and Savannah; "Push de Button," Savannah's dream picture of life in New York, made blissful by mechanical wonders; the satirical "Napoleon," where she proves that most of the great men and women of the past are now merely trade names for commercial products; and a lovely melody, "Pretty to Walk With."

Nor does the strength of Arlen's music end here. There are several other highly appealing numbers: a haunting lullaby, "Little Biscuit," presented by Cicero and Ginger; Koli's ballad, "Savannah," which opens and closes the play—a hymn to the girl he loves; and two songs whose lyrics reveal Harburg's strong social and political consciousness, "Leave the Atom Alone," a witty treatment of a deadly serious subject, and the calypso "Incompatibility."

In contemplating the absence of an original plot and the wealth of music, Walter Kerr inquired: "The question is: can you make a whole show out of sheet music?" Brooks Atkinson apparently was convinced you could. "*Jamaica*," he wrote, "is a beautiful, jovial old-fashioned musical comedy that has been produced and staged with taste and style." The success of *Jamaica* also proved that it could be done—provided Lena Horne is present to sing continually, and provided the production enjoys the embellishments of Oliver Smith's scenery, Miles White's costuming, Jack Cole's choreography, and Philip Lang's highly original and at times provocative orchestration.

That *Jamaica* could be effective even without the benefit of Lena Horne in the principal female role was proved in Cleveland, in December of 1959, when the production was given without many of the deletions made out of town before the show reached Broadway. Scheduled for a run of a few weeks, it survived several months.

JOHN MURRAY ANDERSON'S ALMANAC (1953), *a revue, with sketches by Jean Kerr, Sumner Locke-Elliott, Arthur MacRae, and others. Lyrics and music by Richard Adler, Jerry Ross, Cy Coleman, and others. Presented by Michael Grace, Stanley Gilkey, and Harry Rigby at the Imperial Theater on December 10. Directed by John Murray Anderson. Dances by Donald Sadler. Cast included Hermione Gingold, Harry Belafonte, Billie De Wolfe, Orson Bean, and Polly Bergen (229 performances).*

John Murray Anderson ended his career in the musical theater in the same way he had begun it: by producing, staging, and devising a successful revue. A man of many talents in the theater—producer and/or creator of circus shows, aquacades, pageants, nightclub productions, movie-house stage shows, as well as thirty-eight major musical comedies and revues (twenty-nine on Broadway and nine in London)—Anderson began life as a showman with a production of *The Greenwich Village Follies,* in 1919. He ended that life almost forty years later with the *John Murray Anderson Almanac.* Though he lived another few years—he died on January 30, 1958—he was never again represented on Broadway.

The *John Murray Anderson Almanac* was the second such show he had devised and produced. The first was called simply *Almanac.* It was presented at the Erlanger Theater on August 14, 1929. Though it had some amusing sketches by Noël Coward and Rube Goldberg, and a well-assembled cast headed by Jimmy Savo, Fred Keating, Roy Atwell, and Trixie Friganza, it was a failure lasting just sixty-nine performances.

His second and last *Almanac*—named *John Murray Anderson's Almanac* this time—followed about a quarter of century later. It was a good revue, and it made money—a worthy exit from the Broadway scene which Anderson had enriched for so many years with his varied talents. Perhaps the most significant contribution of this *Almanac* was its introduction to the American musical theater of several new faces and personalities who would ultimately become stars. There was Polly Bergen, a young singer, giving a poignant rendition of such ballads as "I Dare to Dream" (by Sammy Gallup, Michael Grace, and Carl Tucker) and "My Love Is a Wanderer" (by Bert Howard). There was Hermione Gingold, also making her bow on Broadway, now appearing as a cellist; now, with Billie De Wolfe, as a European tourist; now in her amusing song rendition of "Which Witch" (by Melville and Zwar) and "Fini" (by Ross and Adler). In the writing department, new faces were found in Richard Adler and Jerry Ross, a team of songwriters soon to dominate the musical-comedy limelight with their songs for two successive musical-comedy triumphs, *Pajama Game* and *Damn Yankees*.

Comedy was strengthened by the presence of Orson Bean, starring in "Dan Brown's Body," a travesty on a Mike Hammer mystery, written by Jean Kerr; he was also heard in a hilarious Chinese monologue. There was a second humorous sketch by Jean Kerr, "My Cousin," in which Billie De Wolfe starred. Novel specialty numbers were contributed by Harry Belafonte (another face then completely unknown to the general theater public), singing two of his own songs, "Mark Twain" and a calypso, "Hold 'Em Joe" (the latter became the inspiration for a stunning dance routine).

One of the best production numbers was a carryover from one of the early *Greenwich Village Follies*—a "ballet ballad" based on Oscar Wilde's *The Nightingale and the Rose*.

JOHNNY JOHNSON (1936), *a musical play, with book and lyrics by Paul Green. Music by Kurt Weill. Presented by the Group Theater at the 44th Street Theater on November 19. Directed by Lee Strasberg. Cast included Russell Collins, Art Smith, Morris Carnovsky, and Phoebe Brand, with John Garfield, Elia Kazan, and Lee J. Cobb in minor roles (68 performances).*

This is the music with which Kurt Weill, a refugee from Nazi Germany, made his bow as a Broadway composer. This alone would suffice to bring importance to *Johnny Johnson*. But, in spite of the fact that it was a box-office failure, *Johnny Johnson* had significance as a musical production with a powerful message, though disguised in a text abounding with absurd situations. It was throughout a bitter indictment of war. Described in the program as a "fable"—and by its authors as a "legend"—*Johnny Johnson* was, as Richard Watts, Jr., noted in his review, "a medley of caricature, satire, musical comedy, melodrama, social polemic and parable." The hero, Johnny Johnson, is a character "slapped" by the world with the "ultimate indignity," wrote Brooks Atkinson. "It can no longer find room for a completely honest man, for it has surrendered to charlatans, opportunists, and rogues who are captains and kings of destruction."

The play opens in the village square of a small American town in 1917. Just as a monument to peace, designed by Johnny Johnson (Russell Collins), is being unveiled, there comes the news that America has declared war on Germany. Suddenly, people who just a few moments earlier had been peace-loving were beginning to cry "Kill the Huns." This transformation puzzles Johnny; so does the fact that his girl friend, Minny Belle Tompkins (Phoebe Brand), urges him to enlist in the Army. But eventually Johnny, too, becomes infected with the war virus, convinced that this war *was* different: It was a war to end all wars. His girl friend expresses her pride in "O Heart of Love."

Johnny passes the Army intelligence test so brilliantly that he is suspected by his examiner of being insane. Losing his temper, Johnny fells his accuser with a telling blow—an act that convinces the recruiting officer that Johnny is suitable material for the Army. Johnny leaves for France, where he finds American soldiers war-weary behind the lines. An American cowboy is nostalgically recalling his life on the range in "On the Rio Grande."

Sent on a dangerous mission to capture an enemy sniper, Johnny (equipped with a bread knife as his sole weapon) finds him in a churchyard. He is a young German boy who insists that he never did want to go war. Johnny releases him on the condition he go back to Germany to preach the gospel of peace.

On his way to rejoin his troops, Johnny gets wounded and has to be hospitalized. He escapes by stealing laughing gas and using it on the doctors and nurses who try to stop him. Having uncovered an Allied plan to launch a major battle, Johnny invades a conference of the Allied High Command to convince it to call off the battle. When they ridicule him, he uses his laughing gas on them, the effect of the gas being not only to make them abandon their plan of battle but also to give Johnny a promotion as general. But soon the effect of the gas wears off; the High Command sees to it that Johnny gets arrested. Breaking out of prison, Johnny rejoins his troops, enters the maelstrom of battle, and discovers that the German soldier he had released has been killed. Tenderly, Johnny takes him into his arms, as if the young German soldier were a child, a treasonable act that sends Johnny back to prison. This time he is sent to a psychiatrist, who finds him insane and consigns him to an asylum, where Johnny founds a league to promote peace. At long last, Johnny is realeased from the asylum and permitted to go home. He finds that Minny Belle has married a wealthy man. Johnny is reduced to peddling toys for a living. When a Boy Scout (who turns out to be Minny Belle's son) comes to him to purchase a toy soldier, Johnny turns on him with fury, maintaining that he never sells toy soldiers, only toy animals. Johnny then sings about his continued faith in peace and the fate of humanity.

*Johnny Johnson* was weakest when it mounted a soap box, in its repeated tirades against war; it was strongest when it used propaganda as the starting point for sentiment and comedy. Several of the comedy scenes were so good that Mr. Watts was repeatedly reminded of "the quality of Charlie Chaplin's greatest comedy, *Shoulder Arms.*" One such scene is when Johnny takes his army psychological test; another involves him in the manual-of-arms; a third is his scene with the psychiatrist, who gives voice to a delightfully satirical song about his profession in "Psychiatry."

Songs, musical incidents, and background musical episodes were intended as integral to the story development. The score neatly assimilated many elements of American popular music—including Tin Pan Alley tunes, sentimental ballads, folk songs. The song that stood out most prominently was Johnny Johnson's ballad, "To Love You and to Lose You," which first became a popular song hit under the title of "Johnny's Melody" in a recording by Ray Noble and his orchestra. "Mon Ami, My Friend" is also worthy of attention, even though it was not successful, introduced by Paula Miller in a minor role.

*Johnny Johnson* enjoyed a brief revival in New York in an Off Broadway production on October 21, 1956.

JOY (1970), *with music, lyrics and direction by Oscar Brown, Jr. Presented by Sunbar Productions of High-John production at the New Theater on January 27. Cast included Oscar Brown, Jr., Jean Pace, and Sivuca.*

*Joy* is an Off Broadway curiosity not easy to classify. It is most assuredly neither musical comedy nor musical play since it has no plot nor characterizations. It is not revue, lacking as it does the variety of material with which revues are identified, from humor and songs to production and dance numbers. The program refers to *Joy* as a "musical come-together" while critics have described it as "cabaret" or "night-club entertainment." The truth of the matter is that *Joy* is in a genre all its own.

Whatever it may be, it is good entertainment from beginning to end, suprisingly lacking in monotony considering the fact that it consists of nothing more than songs (sixteen in all), most of them of a Latin-American or an American rock identity. "Difficult to describe, perhaps even difficult to experience," wrote Clive Barnes in *The New York Times,* "it does have a quality of its own. . . ." It exerts its own spell, a spell cast by the musicians and particularly by the singers. The singers are Oscar Brown, Jr. (a performing songwriter from Chicago) and his wife, Jean Pace—both of whom know how to deliver a song whatever the style. The starring musician is a remarkable Brazilian jazz accordionist-pianist-guitarist, Sivuca. Norman Shobey, James Benjamin, and Evaraldo Ferrerra provide background music.

As the title of this unconventional musical suggests, the songs promote the concept of joy, beginning with "Time" which explores "the roots and routes that are traveled from beginning to end, from man to woman, from woman to man" (as Mort Goode has explained). "Time" is dramatically sung by Oscar Brown, Jr. who also offers the closing number, "Funky World." Songs like "Funny Feelin' " and "Wimmen's Ways" inspect womankind— the latter about Adam's discovery of woman through Eve. Both are presented by Jean Pace. Other songs touch on a variety of subjects about life and places and people. The best are "What Is a Friend?", heard from Oscar Brown, Jr., Sivuca, and Norman Shobey; "Nothing But a Fool," offered by Oscar Brown, Jr. and Sivuca; "Afro-Blue" and "Brown Baby," both gaining in excitement through Jean Pace's delivery.

The critic of *Variety* described the "curious" staging—by no means the least of the attractions of *Joy.* "There are giant wildly colored pillows that all but cover the multi-level stage. Now and then a performer stretches out on one or another of the pillows or coyly peeks over the top of a pile of them." Because of the amplification system, the stage is cluttered with wires. The critic of *Variety* found that "the amplification is not only excessive, it is tricky. When Brown moves from one microphone to another, he is a new singer."

*Joy* first came into existence in Chicago in 1966, then was seen in Central Park, New York. After that it passed out of existence for about two years when, revised and with changes in the casting that included the presence of Sivuca, it opened in San Francisco in June of 1969 where it ran for about three months. Another brief hiatus, and it arrived to an Off Broadway theater to contribute both zest and novelty to the 1969–70 musical-stage season.

JUBILEE (1935), *a musical comedy, with book by Moss Hart. Lyrics and music by Cole Porter. Presented by Sam H. Harris and Max Gordon at the Imperial Theater on October 12. Directed by Hassard Short and Monty Woolley. Dances by Albertina Rasch. Cast included Melville Cooper, Mary Boland, and June Knight (169 performances).*

*Jubilee* was written by Moss Hart and Cole Porter while they (and some of their friends) took a cruise around the world aboard the *Franconia*. During the four-and-a-half-month voyage to exotic places, Cole Porter found material for songs for his new musical by watching a native dance in Martinique; by listening to some Balinese music; by getting some tourist information about the kling-kling bird in Kingston, Jamaica; and from a meeting with the Sultan of Zanzibar. The idea for the most significant song in the entire score of *Jubilee*—and one of the most famous songs Porter was destined to write—came from listening to rhythms of a native dance witnessed at Kalabahi in the Dutch East Indies. That song was "Begin the Beguine." When Porter played this number for the first time for Moss Hart, the latter had "reservations about the length," as he himself later confessed. "Indeed, I am somewhat ashamed to record that I thought it had ended when he was only half way through playing it."

Introduced in *Jubilee* by June Knight (playing the part of Karen O'Kane, a nightclub singer), "Begin the Beguine," strange to report, made very little of an impression. Nobody apparently seemed to be aware that here was a masterpiece. After the show closed down, the song was forgotten, and seemed destined for permanent obscurity. Then Artie Shaw recorded it, and it sold two million discs, establishing "Begin the Beguine" as a classic. *Jubilee* would probably have long since been forgotten but for that song.

The setting is a mythical kingdom where the ruling family has grown weary of the restrictions imposed upon their lives by their positions as rulers. The family comprises the king (Melville Cooper), the queen (Mary Boland), Princess Diana (Margaret Adams), and Prince James (Charles Walters). A stone, thrown mischievously by a nephew through the window of the palace, instigates an uprising among the radicals, which sends the royal family into hiding in a distant castle. They escape from it, go into the town incognito, and proceed at once to lose all their inhibitions and let themselves go as human beings. The king can perform all the parlor tricks he wishes. The queen finds diversion in the company of the renowned Mowgli (Mark Plant), the famous apeman of motion pictures. Prince James is enchanted with the charming nightclub singer Karen O'Kane (June Knight). And Princess Diana realizes one of her life's dreams by singing duets with Eric Dare (Derek Williams), a famous novelist and playwright. A few days of such shenanigans, however, are all that the royal family is allowed. They must then return to court to resume their high station.

The character of Mowgli is a takeoff on Johnny Weissmuller, the swimming champion who went on to become so famous in the movies as Tarzan; and one of the minor characters was meant to represent Elsa Maxwell, friend of Cole Porter and celebrated party-giver. Caricatures such as these were readily recognizable to audiences, but there were too many places in the musical where remarks, humorous asides, and satirical allusions held meaning only for the intimate Cole Porter circle and made little sense to others. This may have been one of the reasons why the show was a failure. Another was the fact that Mary Boland (returning to Broadway after three years in Hollywood), who had given such a robust portrayal of the queen—and had been responsible for its best comedy sequences—withdrew from the cast because of "illness." (She wanted to go back to Hollywood.) Once she left, the box office suffered severely, and the show had to close down. Cole Porter lost his investment in the production, which taught him a valuable if somewhat expensive lesson: never again to invest his own money in his shows.

Besides "Begin the Beguine," the score boasted another standard, "Just One of Those Things," a duet by Karen O'Kane and Prince James which Porter included in the show after the Boston tryouts. "The Kling-Kling Bird on the Divi-Divi Tree," introduced by Eric Dare, is a minor but nevertheless delectable Cole Porter song gem.

JUMBO (1935), *a spectacular musical comedy, with book by Ben Hecht and Charles MacArthur. Lyrics by Lorenz Hart. Music by Richard Rodgers. Presented by Billy Rose at the Hippodrome Theater on November 16. Production staged by John Murray Anderson. Directed by George Abbott. Dances by Allan K. Foster. Cast included Jimmy Durante, Gloria Grafton, Donald Novis, and Paul Whiteman and his orchestra (233 performances).*

The ambition to bring back to the Hippodrome Theater in New York the kind of breathtaking spectacles for which it had been famous two decades earlier led Billy Rose to devise a production combining the best features of musical comedy, circus, spectacle, and carnival. He procured financial backing from Jock Whitney, tore out the insides of the theater to put the stage right in the middle and make the place look like a circus ring; engaged Ben Hecht and Charles MacArthur to write a text. The play itself was a routine affair, but elastic enough to permit daredevil acts, stunts of all kinds, and the accouterments of the circus (jugglers, trapeze acts, clowns, contortionists, wire-walkers, bears, horseback riders, and so forth). The story centered around the rivalry of two circus proprietors: John A. Considine (Arthur Sinclair) and Matthew Mulligan (W. J. McCarthy). Their feud is intensified when Matt Mulligan, Jr. (Donald Novis), and Mickey Considine (Gloria Grafton) fall in love. Because of his weakness for liquor, Father Considine allows his circus to run down and become bankrupt, and at one point the revenue people are about to confiscate his property. In an effort to save his boss, Considine's press agent, Claudius B. Bowers (Jimmy Durante), solves the financial problems by burning down his employer's residence and collecting the insurance. In the end the family feud is amicably settled and the lovers can get married.

Billy Rose stirred interest in his production and kept that interest alive during the months of rehearsal. Outside the Hippodrome he posted huge signs reading: "Sh-sh-*Jumbo* Rehearsing." He offered to sell a private preview to a distiller. When rehearsals kept dragging on, he advertised in the papers: "I'll be a dirty name if I'll open *Jumbo* before it's ready." Tickets for the opening-night performance were nine times the usual size.

He also went to town in mounting the production. It boasted a thousand animals. Jimmy Durante made his first entrance clinging to the neck of an elephant named Big Rosie, better known as "Jumbo"; Paul Whiteman entered on a big white horse. Aerial acrobats did stunts dangling on their toes from a speeding plane; one couple balanced themselves on a plank over an open cage of roaring lions; the clown had bananas thrown into his left pocket while he played the violin.

New York had seen nothing like this since the heyday of the Hippodrome, and loved what it saw. Gilbert Gabriel said it was "chockful of so many thrills, musical, scenic, gymnastic, and humanitarian, it deserves an endowment as an institution." The *Literary Digest* wrote of Billy Rose that he had inherited the mantles of Ziegfeld and Barnum.

For Rodgers and Hart, *Jumbo* meant a return to the Broadway theater after an absence of some four years in Hollywood. Apparently refreshed by his absence from the stage, Rodgers produced a score that included three of the best songs of Rodgers and Hart: "The Most Beautiful Girl in the World," which Matt, Jr., and his girl Mickey sing while riding horseback around the ring; Mickey's lovely ballad, "Little Girl Blue"; and one of Rodgers' most beautiful love songs, "My Romance," a duet of Matt, Jr., and Mickey.

*Jumbo* was the first play in which George Abbott collaborated with Rodgers and Hart; it was also the first musical production with which Abbott became involved. Since Abbott was henceforth to work so fruitfully in the musical theater—and at times with Rodgers and Hart—his work as stage director is surely not the least of the significant elements in *Jumbo*.

*Jumbo* waited seventeen years to be made into a motion picture. It was an MGM production, released in 1962, in which Jimmy Durante reassumed his one-time stage role; it also starred Doris Day, Martha Raye, and Stephen Boyd. Besides using the principal numbers from the stage score, the screen adaptation interpolated "This Can't Be Love" from another Rodgers and Hart stage musical (*The Boys from Syracuse*).

KID BOOTS (1923), *a musical comedy, with book by William Anthony McGuire and Otto Harbach. Lyrics by Joseph McCarthy. Music by Harry Tierney. Presented by Florenz Ziegfeld at the Earl Carroll Theater on December 31. Cast included Eddie Cantor, Mary Eaton, Jobyna Howland, and George Olsen and his orchestra (479 performances).*

Florenz Ziegfeld, who had previously starred Eddie Cantor in his *Follies,* was planning to find a musical-comedy vehicle for the comedian. Joseph McCarthy offered an idea that sounded feasible, about a caddie at a country club who is a bootlegger on the side. Ziegfeld had McCarthy work out a libretto and contracted Tierney to do the music. After *Kid Boots* had been rehearsing for about three weeks, Ziegfeld became convinced the show was weak and announced he would cancel the production. Cantor pleaded with Ziegfeld to change his mind; Cantor even went through for Ziegfeld a one-man show with the most comic routines in the production. Only because Cantor proved so insistent did Ziegfeld finally give in. The opening-night tryout, in Detroit, was such a success that after the performance Ziegfeld told Cantor: "From now on you don't have to call me Mr. Ziegfeld, but Flo or Ziggy." *Kid Boots* was making so much money in New York that midway in the run Ziegfeld replaced all the scenery and costumes of the first act and the finale at a cost of twenty thousand dollars. He also convinced Cantor to change his stage outfit. Up to now, Cantor had worn a costume calculated to inspire laughter: oversized knickers and sweater and an absurd-looking cap. Ziegfeld insisted that Cantor did not need an outlandish costume to get laughs. He had him wear a pair of neat cashmere knickers, a well-fitting sweater, and a good-looking cap. The laughs still came just as big and fast.

The play, of course, was a showcase for the dynamic, restless, popeyed comedian. Cast as Kid Boots, Eddie Cantor was caddie master of the Everglades Golf Club in Palm Beach, Florida. For a sideline he sells bootleg liquor. He also gives golf lessons (with crooked balls so that his clients might be convinced of their need for more instruction). He is the general nosybody. Nobody has the nerve to fire him, since he has something on every member of the club. But his heart is in the right place, and he manages to straighten out the love life of Polly (Mary Eaton) and Tom (Harry Fender)—even while one of his crooked balls costs Tom the match in a golf tournament.

In some of the major comedy scenes, Eddie Cantor is handsomely supported by, and is the helpless victim of, Jobyna Howland, appearing as Dr. Josephine Fitch, the club physical-training director. She discovers him in the locker room, where he has been concealing his bottles of bootleg liquor. When Kid Boots tries to divert her suspicions by feigning illness, she gives him an electrical treatment in an electric bath, during which she almost shocks him to death, then handles him mercilessly on an osteopath table during an all too vigorous treatment.

The principal love songs were entrusted either to Polly or to Tom or to both. They were "If Your Heart's in the Game" and "Someone Loves You, After All." The outstanding hit song of this musical, however, was not the work of Tierney, but an interpolation—"Dinah," by Sam M. Lewis and Joe Young (lyricists) and Harry Akst (composer). It was introduced by Kid Boots in the finale of the play, from which time on it became one of Cantor's famous song favorites. Akst, the composer, was then a song plugger for Irving Berlin's publishing house. Before *Kid Boots* opened, he came to Cantor to try to have him use a new Irving Berlin number. Cantor was not interested. A few hours later, when Akst was in Cantor's hotel suite, he started playing a tune he himself had just written. It was "Dinah," Cantor, immediately taken with it, wanted it for *Kid Boots*. It required a good deal of sensitive diplomacy on the part of Akst to explain to his boss, Irving Berlin, that Cantor had preferred a song Akst had written to one by Berlin. But Berlin understood; more than that, he even published it.

THE KING AND I (1951), *a musical play, with book and lyrics by Oscar Hammerstein II, based on Margaret Landon's novel* Anna and the King of Siam. *Music by Richard Rodgers. Presented by Rodgers and Hammerstein at the St. James Theater on March 29. Directed by John van Druten. Choreography by Jerome Robbins. Cast included Gertrude Lawrence, Yul Brynner, Dorothy Sarnoff, and Doretta Morrow (1,246 performances).*

Before Rodgers and Hammerstein made their musical adaptation of Landon's novel, it had been a successful motion picture, starring Rex Harrison and Irene Dunne, released in 1946. Gertrude Lawrence was enchanted with the picture, and, seeing herself as Anna, asked her lawyer to acquire the rights. Once these negotiations were completed, Rodgers and Hammerstein were brought into a project to make the musical-play adaptation and to serve as producers.

It was not an easy adaptation for Rodgers and Hammerstein to make. For the librettist it meant preparing a text with "an Eastern sense of dignity and pageantry, and none of this business of girls dressed in Oriental costumes and dancing out onto the stage and singing 'ching-a-ling-a-ling' with their fingers. in the air," as Hammerstein himself explained. For Rodgers, it meant writing a score with an Oriental flavor. "I never heard the music of the Far East," he said, "and I couldn't write an authentic Far Eastern melody if my life depended on it." Both Hammerstein and Rodgers solved their respective problems—Hammerstein by not treading on Oriental toes and by treating the potentate and his many wives and children with dignity and respect; Rodgers by not attempting to produce Oriental music but by creating a score that suggested to him musically what the Far East was like.

Hammerstein did not change the basic structure of the Landon story. Anna Leonowens, an attractive, dignified, mid-Victorian lady (Gertrude Lawrence) comes to Siam from England to teach the royal princes and princesses the ways of Western culture. A widow, she has come with her little boy, Louis, having been promised a house of her own, as well as a salary in English pounds. When she arrives, she tries to quiet the apprehensions of her son, as well as her own, with an optimistic song, "I Whistle a Happy Tune." In the palace, she discovers that the king (Yul. Brynner) has reneged on his promise; she must live in the palace with the royal wives, children, and servants. Nor is she at all pleased to see Tuptim, a Burmese girl (Doretta Morrow), being handed over as a gift to the king by Lun Tha (Larry Douglas), as though she were a lifeless commodity. The king is not interested in Anna's reactions. He calls for his royal children (all sixty-seven) to meet their new schoolmistress. They march before Anna in a formal procession, accompanied by the music of the "March of the Siamese Children." When the children leave, Anna discovers that Tuptim and Lun Tha are in love; that once Tuptim becomes the king's property, she and Lun Tha will never again see one another. This is something that can arouse Anna's sympathy further, for she too once had a lover she can never forget, and about him she reminisces in one of the most eloquent ballads ever written by Rodgers and Hammerstein, "Hello, Young Lovers."

The king expresses his bewilderment at Western ways, and his doubts about what is right and what is wrong, in the extended narrative, "A Puzzlement." Anna finds him overbearing, unreasonable in his dictatorial attitudes, stubborn, childish, and volatile in mood. But Anna is equally dogmatic and intransigeant in her own Western attitudes and thinking. And she remains insistent on getting a house of her own. The king and Anna demonstrate their obvious lack of understanding and sympathy for each other in no uncertain terms. But between Anna and the children there springs up an affectionate bond once they had become acquainted ("Getting to Know

You"). While all this is going on, Tuptim and Lun Tha are hiding in the shadows, exchanging tender sentiments before separating forever ("We Kiss in a Shadow").

The clash between Eastern and Western cultures is personified in the king and Anna, who, after a while, find themselves drawn to each other. Anna discovers that behind the hard surface of the king's despotism is an endearing charm, warmth, and childlike ingenuousness that cannot fail to appeal to a woman who adores children. And the king cannot altogether suppress his admiration for a woman so unlike any he had heretofore known —fiery in her independence, proud, idealistic. The attachment between them, however, is of the mind and spirit, and not of the heart. Love is out of the question between two people of such different cultures and social stations. Anna describes her admiration for the king in "This Is a Man" and stands ready to help him out as a political crisis begins to develop. The British have come to regard the king of Siam as a barbarian and want to make Siam into a protectorate. They are sending Sir Edward Ramsey and other high-ranking English officials to make an investigation. It is Anna's idea to entertain them in a grand, elegant manner—in European style and dress —to prove that the Siamese are as modern in their ways as the English. A ball is given in honor of the visitors, and with it a ballet, "The Small House of Uncle Thomas." The affair turns out to be a huge success. The visiting Englishmen are now convinced that the Siamese are sensitive, cultured people. This, of course, delights Anna no end, who proceeds to teach the king something of Western social dancing ("Shall We Dance?").

Meanwhile, Tuptim and Lun Tha had laid plans to run away together ("I Have Dreamed"), but are caught. The king orders that Tuptim be whipped, something which Anna helps to prevent; but there is nothing she can do to help Lun Tha, who has been killed.

With the king still adamant about having Anna live in the palace, Anna decides to leave Siam for good. Her plan, however, is aborted when she learns that the king is dying. Anna now gets her house. After the king's death she decides to stay on in Siam as a teacher of the children she has come to love.

Beyond the exotic setting, much else in the play defied convention. The cast was made up mostly of Orientals, with only four Anglo-Saxon characters, none of whom was American. No love interest involves the two principals (they do not even exchange a single kiss), and one of them dies before the final curtain. Convention was also broken in the way music and dance helped to tell the story. In the opening of the play Anna speaks to the Siamese minister through an interpreter; for a while (that is, until the audience gets used to the idea of hearing English come from the mouths of Siamese) the characters remain silent, and their conversation is assumed by several instruments in the orchestra. Music thus becomes a basic part of the plot, and it is henceforth used to point up some important piece of stage action—in orchestral fragments, as background to the dialogue, as a preface to or interlude after a song, to usher in or dismiss a character. The music itself, while not Oriental at all, is delicately flavored with Oriental idioms and instrumentation. The delightful march of the royal Siamese children is characteristic of such Oriental colorations in melody, harmony, and orchestration; and so are Tuptim's monologue, "My Lord and Master" and the king's effective narrative, "A Puzzlement." Other important musical numbers, however, are more characteristically Rodgers than Oriental in their sensitive lyricism, poignant moods, and at times compelling dramatic thrust.

Innovation could also be found in the ballet sequence, "The Small House of Uncle Thomas" (choreography by Jerome Robbins), in which *Uncle Tom's Cabin* is translated in terms of the Siamese dance. The literalness and pictorial beauty of the dance sequences have both an irresistible charm and a delicate humor. For his musical background Rodgers utilizes only percussive effects of woodblock and ancient cymbals, to punctuate commentaries by a spoken chorus. The childlike realism of the dance is thus carried over into the music.

There were some important "firsts" in the production of *The King and I;* also a tragic "last." John van Druten, eminent playwright and director, was here making his first attempt at directing a musical production. And Yul Brynner, as the king, here stepped quickly from obscurity to fame. Brynner had previously appeared on Broadway in one or two failures and had been directing television plays. He auditioned for Rodgers and Hammerstein at the Hotel Plaza, singing gypsy songs to his own guitar accompaniment while sitting cross-legged on the floor. As soon as they heard him, Rodgers and Hammerstein knew they had found their king.

For Gertrude Lawrence, the part of Anna was both one of her most resplendent performances and, sadly, her last anywhere. "She came to the stage," wrote John van Druten in *The New York Times,* "with a new and dazzling quality, as though an extra power had been added to the brilliance of her own stage light. She was radiant and wonderful." "The radiance was there—the star quality, indefinable but intensely vivid, that comes from something other than human or technical talents of the actress," wrote her husband, Richard Stoddard Aldrich, in a biography of his wife, *Mrs. A,* "giving her an iridescence, a power to move not only the audience, but the very boards of the stage as she steps on them."

While *The King and I* was still running at the St. James Theater, Gertrude Lawrence died of hepatitis on September 6, 1952. Her role (at her own request) was taken over by Constance Carpenter.

When *The King and I* opened on Broadway, the critics found a great deal to delight them—not only the charm and beauty of the action, music, and dance, but also the stunning scenery of Jo Mielziner and the dazzling costuming by Irene Sharaff. The whole production was, as Danton Walker said, "a flowering of all the arts of the theater with moments . . . that are pure genius." Other critics spoke of the authenticity and good taste with which the Orient was re-created, "an East of frank and unashamed romance," as Richard Watts, Jr., wrote, "seen through the eyes of . . . theatrical artists of rare taste and creative power."

*The King and I* became the first musical to receive the Theater Club Award as the best play of the season by an American author. It was also given the Antoinette Perry Award as the season's best musical.

Like two or three of the other Rodgers and Hammerstein masterworks, *The King and I* has become a classic of the American musical theater, whose enchantment and beauty never seem to fade, no matter how many times it is revived. This was the musical which Richard Rodgers chose to open the Music Theater of Lincoln Center, of which he was president and producing director, on July 6, 1964. "If you have warm and cheerful recollections of this musical," reported Howard Taubman in *The New York Times* after this eventful revival, "your memory is not playing you false. If you have not seen it before, you should seize the opportunity of this revival so that you, too, may have fragrant memories to recall." In any event, as Mr. Taubman added, inaugurating the Music Theater at New York's Lincoln Center proved a most fortunate choice, since the new venture opened "with a sentimental and charming flourish." Risë Stevens played Anna at this revival, and Darren McGavin the king.

Nor did *The King and I* lose any of its magic when it was given a screen production by 20th Century-Fox in 1956, in a cast headed by Deborah Kerr and Yul Brynner. Practically the entire stage score was used, with Deborah Kerr's singing parts dubbed on the soundtrack by Marni Nixon.

KING DODO (1902), *an operetta, with book and lyrics by Frank Pixley. Music by Gustav Luders. Presented by Henry W. Savage, in arrangement with Daniel Frohman, at Daly's Theater on May 12. Directed by Charles H. Jones. Cast included Raymond Hitchcock, Margaret McKinney, Greta Risley, and Gertrude Quinlan (64 performances).*

In Dodoland, King Dodo (Raymond Hitchcock) seeks youth again, since he wishes to win the love of Angela (Margaret McKinney). Angela, however, is in love with one of the king's soldiers, Piola (Cheridah Simpson). When Piola informs the king that there exists a fountain of youth in far-off Spoojuland, the king and his retinue set forth for that land. Spoojuland is ruled by Queen Lili (Greta Risley), who has a weakness for older men. There, King Dodo drinks from the fountain of youth and becomes a young man again. But, unhappily, the king falls in love with Queen Lili, who has no use for him because of his youth. By falling accidentally into a magic spring he becomes an old man again—much to his delight, since he is now being pursued by the queen. King Dodo renounces his throne in Dodoland and turns it over to Piola, together with his blessings for Piola's marriage with Angela.

Among the brightest songs in a gay score were "The Tale of a Bumble Bee" (one of Luders' best songs), a march called "The Lad Who Leads," and a ballad, "Diana."

KISMET (1953), *a musical extravaganza, with book by Charles Lederer and Luther Davis, based on the play of the same name by Edward Knoblock. Lyrics by Robert Wright and George "Chet" Forrest. Music adapted by Wright and Forrest from the works of Alexander Borodin. Presented by Charles Lederer at the Ziegfeld Theater on December 3. Directed by Albert Marre. Choreography by Jack Cole. Cast included Alfred Drake, Richard Kiley, Doretta Morrow, and Joan Diener (583 performances).*

For several decades the musical extravaganza had been regarded as an obsolete form of the American musical theater, when *Kismet* came along to demonstrate that, treated with imagination and good taste, extravaganza still had the capacity to win the favor of audiences. The authors of *Kismet* remained true to the traditions of extravaganza by utilizing an exotic setting and equally exotic characters; by exploiting lavish scenes, ballet sequences, and ceremonials; by catching and winning the eye with stunning costuming; and by offering a plot whose development and denouement could be predicted after the first thirty minutes. But *Kismet* profited from remarkable performances by the principals, who brought some credibility and even freshness to a stereotype text. And the main strength of this musical lay in a thoroughly enchanting score derived from the works of the Russian master Alexander Borodin. Borodin's haunting, Oriental-like lyricism, and at other times the barbaric force of his rhythms, are transferred into the popular-song medium—or into the background music for ballets and ceremonials—with such dignity and taste that Borodin's own personality is never completely distorted even though drastic revisions and alterations have to be made.

The program described *Kismet* as "a musical Arabian night," and it comes from the Broadway play in which Otis Skinner starred so triumphantly between 1912 and 1914. The public poet of ancient Bagdad, Hajj (Alfred Drake), comes to town with his beautiful daughter, Marsinah (Doretta Morrow). Hajj has plans for her to marry the handsome young caliph (Richard Kiley). He achieves this aim and himself manages to elope to an oasis with the beautiful widow of the police wazir and to compete successfully in the writing of verses with Omar the tentmaker (Philip Coolidge).

The score boasted three hits. "Stranger in Paradise," a duet of Marsinah and the young caliph, came from one of the Polovtsian Dances from *Prince Igor;* Marsinah's ballad, "And This Is My Beloved," is derived from the atmospheric Nocturne of the Quartet in D major; and a third hit, also sung by Marsinah, is "Baubles, Bangles, and Beads," from an unidentified Borodin melody. Other songs, though less popular, were significant contributors to the esoteric charm of the production: notably "Fate" (theme from the Symphony No. 2), a duet by Hajj and Marsinah; "He's in Love" (from the Polovtsian Dances), introduced by Hal Hackett, playing a subsidiary role; "Night of My Nights" (from the piano piece *Serenade*), sung by the caliph; and "Sands of Time" (theme from *In the Steppes of Central Asia*), a number shared by Hajj, Marsinah, and a minor character. The background music for the caliph's ceremonial and the presentation of the princesses were also of interest.

*Kismet* received the Antoinette Perry and the Outer Circle awards as the best musical of the season.

KISS ME, KATE (1948), *a musical play, with book by Bella and Samuel Spewack, based on Shakespeare's* The Taming of the Shrew. *Lyrics and music by Cole Porter. Presented by Saint Subber and Lemuel Ayers at the New Century Theater on December 30. Directed by John C. Wilson. Choreography by Hanya Holm. Cast included Alfred Drake, Patricia Morison, Lisa Kirk, and Harold Lang (1,077 performances).*

As one of the handful of musicals to enter the select circle of a thousand performances or more, *Kiss Me, Kate* is one of the outstanding successes of the American theater. It captured the Antoinette Perry Award as the best musical of the season. Above and beyond this triumph on Broadway, *Kiss Me, Kate* sent a national company on tour for three years; made a recording of the original cast which was a best-seller; contributed at least four songs to the hits of the year; and resulted in a beautifully produced motion picture starring Kathryn Grayson, Howard Keel, and Ann Miller, released by MGM in 1953, a box-office smash.

*Kiss Me, Kate* gathered accolades, as well as currency, outside the United States. Presented at the Volksoper in Vienna on February 14, 1956, in a German translation, it became the greatest box-office draw in the fifty-eight-year history of that opera house, and was retained in the repertory for over a decade. *Kiss Me, Kate* was also heard in seventeen other languages—in Berlin, Turkey, Japan, Czechoslovakia, Budapest, Poland (where it became the first American musical ever to be produced there, and where it played for two hundred sold-out performances), South America, and elsewhere.

The paradox about the fame and fortune of *Kiss Me, Kate*—Cole Porter's greatest success—was that very little had been expected of it when first it came to Broadway. It was a musical derived from Shakespeare, and though Rodgers and Hart had done well with *The Boys from Syracuse* years before, Shakespeare was not the material from which a popular stage success is woven. The producers were novices at the game of putting on a Broadway show and could hardly be expected to cope with the imponderable problems that beset even the most experienced producers. Not one of the principal performers in the cast had box-office appeal. Worst of all was the fact that Cole Porter, who was to write the songs, had not enjoyed a successful production on stage or screen for a number of years; he had not created a durable song hit in over a decade. The general belief prevailed on Broadway that Cole Porter was "through," that the endless suffering and pain of which he had been a victim following a disastrous accident in 1937 had finally vitiated him creatively as well as physically.

But one of those miracles that makes the producing of shows such an exciting adventure somehow took place. *Kiss Me, Kate* turned out to be an integrated masterwork, distinguished in every single department—and with the best score Porter ever wrote, and one of the best ever written for the American musical stage. And it also boasted one of the best texts ever written for the Broadway stage.

The springboard for the Spewack text was Shakespeare's comedy about the taming of Katherine, a shrew. Utilizing the play-within-a-play technique, however, *Kiss Me, Kate* was actually a contemporary musical, set in the present-day United States. Within that context, however, scenes from the Shakespeare comedy are re-created in terms of the Broadway musical theater. The device works neatly.

As the musical opens we find a touring theatrical company in Baltimore, Maryland, about to present *The Taming of the Shrew*. Four principals in this company are Fred Graham (Alfred Drake), his former wife, Lilli (Patricia Morison), Bill Calhoun (Harold Lang), and a girl in whom he is interested, Lois Lane (Lisa Kirk). We early learn that, though now divorced, Fred and Lilli are still interested in each other. This is *their* problem: to put on a face of indifference to each other while inwardly nursing an inextinguishable love. That they have a nostalgia for their past life together as troupers is revealed when they recall the shows they appeared in, particularly a Viennese operetta ("Wunderbar").

Bill's problem is that he is a hopeless gambler who must soon redeem an I.O.U. for $10,000 from professional gamblers. "Why Can't You Behave?" is Lois's poignant lament to Bill.

On opening night, Fred sends flowers to Lois, who is the female star; by mistake the flowers are delivered to Lilli. This further intensifies her latent love for her former husband, which she is now willing to allow to rise to the surface of her consciousness ("So in Love").

The production of *The Taming of the Shrew,* set in old Padua, opens with the lively chorus, "We Open in Venice." The play develops the theme of how Bianca cannot get married until her older sister, Katherine, has found a husband. Necessity being the mother of invention, a candidate is soon found in the form of Petruchio, come to Padua to find himself a rich wife. Hotly, Katherine rejects him, just as he rejects all males ("I Hate Men"). While Petruchio is convinced that Katherine is not for him ("Were Thine That Special Face"), he stands ready to go through with the marriage for the sake of money.

The scene shifts back again to the present and the complications within the theatrical company. Once Lilli discovers that the flowers had been intended for Lois, she goes into a rage and announces her determination to leave the troupe for good. Bill's gambling troubles reach a climax when gangsters come to collect the $10,000.

The second act reverts to *The Taming of the Shrew.* Katherine—now Petruchio's wife—is not a woman easily handled. She is hot-tempered and uncontrollable. She makes Petruchio's life so miserable that he can only look back to his one-time happiness as a single man with nostalgia ("Where Is the Life That Late I Led?"). While all this is going on in front of the footlights, behind the stage Bill upbraids Lois for flirting with other men, an accusation which she takes ever so lightly ("Always True to You in My Fashion").

But just as in *The Taming of the Shrew* Petruchio solves his personal-life difficulties by taming his wild mate, so in the company the seemingly insoluble problems find a neat resolution. A shake-up in the gangster world no longer makes Bill's I.O.U. claimable. Freed of this obligation, he promises to reform; in doing so, he is reconciled with Lois. As for Fred and Lilli, it is not long before they are ready and willing to recognize the basic truth that they cannot live without each other.

For Patricia Morison the part of Lilli was her first successful Broadway starring role; her only previous Broadway appearance had been in 1938 in and inept, ill-fated operetta, *The Two Bouquets,* where she had also appeared with Alfred Drake. After that she played in several minor motion pictures.

The brilliant Spewack book, the felicitous performances of the principals, and Hanya Holm's exciting choreography were some of the elements in this remarkable musical comedy. The Cole Porter score was perhaps the most significant element of all, "one of the loveliest and most lyrical yet composed for the contemporary stage," in the opinion of Walter Kerr. Never before (or subsequently) had he traversed so wide a gamut of styles and emotions in a single score, both in music and lyrics. Never before (or subsequently) had he produced a score that yielded so many standards and in which virtually each and every number is a gem of its kind. He was at turns hauntingly romantic and acidly satiric, nostalgic and witty. "So in Love" and "Were Thine That Special Face" are two ballads in the purple mood that is so characteristically Porter at his best. "Wunderbar" is an amusing takeoff on the Continental type of operetta waltz, another familiar Porter attitude. He tapped a rich satiric vein in two numbers not included in the above summary of the plot: "Brush Up Your Shakespeare," in which the gangsters discover that to "wow" the girls and get them ravin', all you have to do is to quote the Bard of Avon." Or "Too Darn Hot," an acidulous appraisal of Baltimore weather. (He'd like to give his all to his baby tonight, but it's too darn hot!). This last number culminated in an incendiary dance.

KNICKERBOCKER HOLIDAY (1938), *a musical comedy, with book and lyrics by Maxwell Anderson. Music by Kurt Weill. Presented by the Playwrights Company at the Ethel Barrymore Theater on October 19. Directed by Joshua Logan. Dances by Carl Randall and Edwin Denby. Cast included Walter Huston, Ray Middleton, Jeanne Madden, and Clarence Nordstrom (168 performances).*

Maxwell Anderson, one of America's leading playwrights, here turned for the first time to the musical-comedy stage to produce a libretto with a strong political consciousness. He tore a leaf from Washington Irving's *Father Knickerbocker's History of New York* and placed his setting in New Amsterdam, in 1647. The conditions prevailing there then enabled Anderson to point up some of the political problems and misadventures in America in 1938: the threat of invasion of fascism from overseas and the suppression of American liberties. Peter Stuyvesant (Walter Huston), the peg-legged governor general, is a dictator who sets up a semifascist, semi-New Deal state, which antagonizes the good Dutch people, ever resentful of confining orders and systems. He is surrounded by scurrilous councilmen who exploit the people for their own benefit and who, in the end, are exploited by the even more scurrilous governor. A song like "How Can You Tell an American?"—presented by the characters Brom Broeck and Washington Irving—was political propaganda identifying the true American as the one who loves liberty.

Washington Irving (Ray Middleton) is an important character in the musical. He first appears in the prologue, where he has come to the decision to write a satire on the early Dutch settlers at New Amsterdam. The first act carries us to New Amsterdam of 1647, where the town council, of which Mynheer Tienhoven is the head, are discussing the imminent arrival from Holland of their new governor, Peter Stuyvesant. Washington Irving now reappears to introduce the hero of the musical. He is an impoverished young man named Brom Broeck who earns his living sharpening knives and who has a special gift for getting into trouble. Brom loves Tienhoven's daughter, Tina (Jeanne Madden), and for her sake is trying his best to behave himself. But he becomes the innocent victim of the Council. This is hanging day, and with nobody to hang, the Council selects Brom because he has failed to take out a permit for sharpening knives. Brom counters by telling the councilmen that each is a good candidate for hanging, having broken the law repeatedly by selling brandy and firearms to the Indians. Brom's life, however, is saved with the arrival of Peter Stuyvesant, who proceeds to put the community under severe discipline and to issue all kinds of new laws putting himself in sole charge of all illicit operations. Being a practical man, Tienhoven decides that the governor would be an ideal husband for Tina, a development that delights Stuyvesant but throws Tina into consternation. She begs that such a wedding be postponed awhile. Peter Stuyvesant, however, reminds Tina he cannot wait too long, since he is no longer a young man.

Brom soon comes to the governor to object to his despotism, and is imprisoned. Those councilmen who object to Stuyvesant's high-handed methods are forced, at the point of guns, to change their minds and submit meekly to the governor's tyranny.

On commenting on Brom's imprisonment, Washington Irving points out that in times of despotism, all good people are in jail, while only criminals are out of it. He sees Tina come to Brom to plan an escape, and overhears

Tina's father warn her that such an action can lead only to disaster—all of which arouses his sympathy.

Stuyvesant grows increasingly ruthless. Though there is no enemy in sight, he plans to go to war, since it is his philosophy that a nation in peace is a stagnant nation. He also revises the economy to rid it of all free enterprise. Seeing their basic liberties completely destroyed, the councilmen now become restive. But Stuyvesant disregards them. He is thinking of his imminent marriage to lovely young Tina. The wedding ceremony, however, is interrupted with an invasion by Indians. Brom escapes from jail and joins his neighbors in fighting the Indians. Though he proves himself a hero and is responsible for saving the community, Brom must still stand trial for his old offense of having defied the governor. When Brom openly accuses Stuyvesant of illicit dealings with the Indians, the latter orders that Brom be hanged. The Council defies this order. At this point, Washington Irving returns to remind Peter Stuyvesant that if he is to be remembered kindly in history, it would be wise for him to change character and abandon his despotic ways. Stuyvesant becomes convinced to the point where he not only frees Brom but even allows him to marry Tina.

Despite the love interest involving Brom and Tina, which plays only a minor part in the text, the play would have bogged down in the morass of political and social thinking but for two happy factors. One was Walter Huston's earthy, infectious portrayal of the role of Stuyvesant; the other, Weill's score, the most tuneful he had written for the American stage up to this point. Weill's best number was the now famous "September Song," delivered by Stuyvesant in a nasal, half-recitative style when, in refusing to consider a postponement of his marriage to Tina, he reminds her of the great difference in their ages. Weill wrote this song with Huston's nonsinging style in mind, and song and actor became one. "It is the composer Weill with his delightful music and actor Huston, gaily spinning about on his peg leg, who provide the holiday," reported Brooks Atkinson. Several other Weill songs and sequences—though far less familiar now than "September Song"—added brightness and charm to the play. They included the tender duet of Tina and Brom, "It Never Was You"; "There's Nowhere to Go But Up," in which Washington Irving expresses his sympathy for the imprisoned Brom and his plan to escape with Tina; and "Will You Remember Me?", sung by Brom Broeck.

The motion-picture version, produced by United Artists and released in 1944 with Nelson Eddy as star, placed far greater emphasis on romance than on politics. Three Weill songs were used, including, of course, "September

Song." The other numbers were the work of various composers and lyricists, including Sammy Cahn and Jule Styne.

LADIES FIRST (1918), *a musical comedy, with book and lyrics by Harry B. Smith, based on Charles Hoyt's* A Contented Woman. *Music by A. Baldwin Sloane. Presented by H. H. Frazee at the Broadhurst Theater on October 24. Directed by Frank Smithson. Cast included Nora Bayes, William Kent, Irving Fisher, and Clarence Nordstrom (164 performances).*

By 1918, Nora Bayes had been one of the truly great ladies of American show business for over a decade. She had long since become famous for her husky, throbbing delivery of a song that overwhelmed rather than wooed an audience—as she strode up and down the stage, swinging her hips, and usually holding either a delicate lace hankerchief or a fan in her hand. She was first known as the "Wurzburger Girl" because it was she who had introduced Harry von Tilzer's "Down Where the Wurzburger Flows" in vaudeville (at the Orpheum Theater in Brooklyn in 1902), and it was she who made it into an enormous song hit. Later in the same decade she became identified with the song she introduced and made famous in *The Ziegfeld Follies,* "Shine on, Harvest Moon." After that any show starring Nora Bayes was built to order to set off her unique personality and talent. *Ladies First* was such a show. The slender plot concerned the suffragette movement, with Nora Bayes playing Betty Burt and William Kent appearing in a comical role as Uncle Tody. But the story was just the framework on which to display Miss Bayes most effectively. Midway the plot was completely forgotten to allow her to give a recital of her song specialties. One of these was an early George Gershwin song, "Some Wonderful Sort of Someone" (lyrics by Schuyler Greene), written before Gershwin had produced his first song hit ("Swanee") or his first musical-comedy score (*La, La, Lucille*).

When *Ladies First* went on tour, George Gershwin was hired to be her piano accompanist for the song sequence. During this tour, the first George Gershwin song with lyrics by Ira Gershwin to get performed publicly was interpolated by Nora Bayes in her program. It was "The Real American Folk Song." She introduced it at the Trent Theater in Trenton, New Jersey, then kept it on her program for about eight weeks of her tour. She never brought it to New York, however; and Ira never earned anything from it. (The song did not get either published or recorded until some forty years after this premiere.)

It was at a performance of *Ladies First* in Pittsburgh that Oscar Levant became acquainted for the first time with the name of George Gershwin.

Levant was in the audience, having come to enjoy Nora Bayes; but he remained to marvel at young Gershwin's piano playing. "I had never before heard such brisk, unstudied, completely free inventive playing, all within a consistent framework," Levant was to reveal years later in his first book, *A Smattering of Ignorance*. Levant became a Gershwin admirer then and there—but it was still some years before he met Gershwin personally.

Another song interpolated by Miss Bayes in the song sequence in *Ladies First* was "Just Like a Gypsy," by Seymour B. Simons and Nora Bayes. One of Miss Bayes's most successful numbers in the actual show was "Spanish," a satire on a country that had contributed to America outlandish dances, the flu, and Columbus. Other popular songs by Sloane were "What Could Be Sweeter than You?" and "What Men Can Do."

> LADY, BE GOOD! (1924), *a musical comedy, with book by Guy Bolton and Fred Thompson. Lyrics by Ira Gershwin. Music by George Gershwin. Presented by Aarons and Freedley at the Liberty Theater on December 1. Directed by Felix Edwards. Dances by Sammy Lee. Cast included Fred and Adele Astaire, Cliff Edwards, and Walter Catlett (330 performances).*

When Gershwin left the *Scandals* in 1924, after a five-year stint, to advance his own career in musical comedy, he joined up again with Alex A. Aarons, who had produced Gershwin's first Broadway musical, *La, La, Lucille,* in 1919. In 1924 Aarons had just formed a producing partnership with Vinton Freedley. The new producing firm decided to make its bow with George Gershwin's second book musical; for the next half-dozen years Aarons and Freedley would continue to present several outstanding Gershwin musicals. Freedley was not at all enthusiastic about having Gershwin write the music for his first venture as producer, considering Gershwin too sophisticated for popular appeal. But Aarons was adamant about using Gershwin, and Freedley was forced to consent.

The musical, first called *Black Eyed Susan* but soon renamed *Lady, Be Good!,* cast Fred and Adele Astaire as Dick and Susie Trevor, a brother-and-sister dance team. They lose their money, are unable to get engagements, and are reduced to entertaining at private parties and at the homes of friends. A rich girl in love with Dick, but for whom he has little interest, brings about the eviction of the Trevors from their apartment. One of the best scenes in the play follows this eviction early in the first act. The Trevors, homeless and broke, find their furniture in the street. Susie tries to bring a homey atmosphere to her new setting by arranging her furniture neatly around the corner lamppost and hanging a sign on it reading "God Bless Our Home." The Trevors then try to find an answer to their financial problem by having Dick tie up with the rich girl. Susie, however, contrives to rescue her brother from this undesirable marriage by plotting with a shady lawyer, J. Watterson Watkins (Walter Catlett), to impersonate a Mexican widow for the purpose of gaining an inheritance. The scheme falls apart. But even though the Trevors are unable to put their hands on this fortune, they are able to arrive at a happy resolution of their problems.

*Lady, Be Good!* was Gershwin's first hit musical. It established several important precedents which many later Gershwin musical-comedy successes would follow. One—and by far the most important—was having Ira Gershwin write the lyrics for George's music. Ira had provided words to George's melodies for several songs in the past, one of which was "The Real American Folk Song" which Nora Bayes sang in *Ladies First* and which marked Ira Gershwin's debut in the theater. *Lady, Be Good!,* however, was the first musical for which Ira supplied all of George's lyrics, initiating a words-and-music partnership that lasted for over a decade and which found few rivals in the Broadway theater of the 1920's and early 1930's. The freshness and the virtuosity of Ira Gershwin's versification—his often appealingly original ways of expressing himself—played no negligible part in George Gershwin's rapid growth in *Lady, Be Good!* as one of the leading musical-comedy composers.

A second innovation to be repeated in several later Gershwin musicals was the placement of the two-piano team of Ohman and Arden in the orchestra pit—now to play with the orchestra, now to perform by themselves, but always contributing a new sound to the accompaniment of the songs.

And the songs, as a critic for the *Sun* remarked, were consistently "brisk, inventive, gay, and nervous." George Gershwin's forward stride in his creative originality and technical resources from the days of *La, La, Lucille* in 1919 and the five editions of the *Scandals* between 1920 and 1924 inclusive, was of giant proportions. The number that continually brought down the house was "Fascinating Rhythm," remarkable for its ever-changing rhythms and meters. Gershwin had not written this number for *Lady, Be Good!,* but sometime earlier. Alex A. Aarons heard it, and was so delighted with it that he urged Gershwin to hold it for their next show together—which Gershwin did. The number was sung by Dick and Susie Trevor, who followed the vocal rendition with a complicated dance routine. During rehearsals Fred Astaire had considerable difficulty bringing this dance number to a final resolution. The problem, which occupied him for days, seemed insoluble until Gershwin (an agile dancer himself) came forward with a logical exit step, which, as Astaire has revealed in his autobiography, *Steps in Time,* "we didn't think . . . was possible." But it turned out to be the "perfect answer to our problem . . . this suggestion by hoofer Gershwin, and it turned out to be a knockout applause puller."

"Fascinating Rhythm" was only one of many strong musical pieces in this production. Another was "Oh, Lady Be Good!", with its effective repeated triplets in cut time in the chorus. J. Watterson Watkins sang to a chorus line of "flappers." As heard in the show, the music was given slowly and gracefully, since then, however, the number is played or sung in a much brisker tempo. In his autobiography, Astaire confesses that when the musical comedy adopted the title of *Lady, Be Good!* he was not at all enthusiastic until he heard the title number—and then he was completely sold.

"So Am I," introduced by Susie Trevor (and Alan Edwards, in a subsidiary role) proved to be a haunting ballad. "The Half of It, Dearie, Blues," written for Fred Astaire, was, in Astaire's opinion, one of Gershwin's most ingenious contributions. As Dick Trevor, Astaire sang it to one of his romantic interests. What was unusual in Astaire's rendition of this number was that, after he had sung it, he did a solo tap-dance routine—the first time he had ever danced without his sister, Adele.

The score would also have boasted one of Gershwin's song classics—if it had been allowed to remain in the score. "The Man I Love" was written for *Lady, Be Good!,* was tried out in the opening scene by Adele Astaire when the show opened in Philadelphia, and was found wanting. Vinton Freedley said it was too static and convinced Gershwin to drop it from the production.

*Lady, Be Good!* came to London in April of 1926, where it was a huge success; it then toured the English provinces. On July 25, 1968, the musical returned to London and was once again admired, but mostly for the Gershwin songs, which proved ageless.

It took seventeen years after its Broadway premiere for *Lady, Be Good!* to reach the screen. When it did, it had a new story. Produced by MGM in 1941 with Ann Sothern, Robert Young, and Eleanor Powell, the screen *Lady, Be Good!* used only three numbers from the Gershwin score. Interpolated into the movie was "The Last Time I Saw Paris," by Jerome Kern and Oscar Hammerstein II, which won the year's Academy Award as the best song written for motion pictures.

LADY IN ERMINE (1922), *a musical comedy, with book by Frederick Lonsdale and Cyrus Wood, based on a London musical,* The Lady of the Rose, *by Rudolph Schanzer and Ernest Welisch. Lyrics by Harry Graham and Cyrus Wood. Music by Jean Gilbert and Alfred Goodman. Presented by the Shuberts at the Ambassador Theater on October 2. Directed by Charles Sinclair and Allan K. Foster. Cast included Wilda Bennett, Walter Woolf, and Harry Fender (232 performances).*

During the Napoleonic invasion of Italy, Count Adrian Beltrami (Harry Fender) and his sister Mariana (Wilda Bennett) occupy a castle that is forced to quarter a French regiment, headed by Colonel Belovar (Walter Woolf). The colonel thinks Adrian and Mariana are husband and wife. Since he is determined to make love to Mariana, he manufactures a charge accusing Adrian of being a spy, and offers to save his life only if Mariana is ready to surrender to him. Mariana accepts the bargain, then tells the colonel about a "lady in ermine," whose picture hangs on the wall and who had triumphed over a similar predicament some centuries earlier. While awaiting his tryst with Mariana, the colonel gets drunk. Suddenly the "lady in ermine" descends from the picture frame and invites him to dance with her. By the time Mariana comes to pay her debt to the colonel, the "lady in ermine" has returned to the picture and the colonel, now convinced that he loves Mariana, finds he cannot take advantage of her.

The hit song from this musical was the title number, which Count Adrian introduced with two subsidiary characters played by Gladys Walton and Helen Shipman. "When Hearts Are Young"—a secondary hit, which was interpolated into the score—represented the joint melody-writing effort of Alfred Goodman and Sigmund Romberg; this one was Mariana's big number. As Colonel Belovar, Walter Woolf made a successful debut on the Broadway stage with the help of two effective songs, "Land o' Mine" and "Mariana," the latter a duet with Mariana.

LADY IN THE DARK (1941), *a musical play, with book by Moss Hart. Lyrics by Ira Gershwin. Music by Kurt Weill. Presented by Sam H. Harris at the Alvin Theater on January 23. Directed by Hassard Short and Moss Hart. Choreography by Albertina Rasch. Cast included Gertrude Lawrence, Victor Mature, Danny Kaye, and Bert Lytell (388 performances).*

The idea for this play came to Moss Hart from his own experiences with psychoanalytic treatment. Since psychoanalysis was still a comparatively un-cultivated field in the theater of 1941, Hart seized on the subject. Hart recognized that his play would require dream sequences. (*Lady in the Dark*, however, was not the first musical to use dream sequences; Rodgers and Hart had done this a decade earlier in *Peggy-Ann*.) And with an equally sure instinct he felt that music was indispensable in pointing up such sequences and intensifying their moods.

In *Lady in the Dark*, Hart leads his heroine—Liza Elliott (Gertrude Lawrence), editor of *Allure*—through the tortuous labyrinth of an analysis and carries her to its final happy resolution. She complains of physical ailments, of behaving abnormally as a woman, of being a victim of fatigue and melancholia. Consulting a psychiatrist, Dr. Brooks, she describes the first thing that comes to her mind: a song, "My Ship," which she had learned in childhood and which recurs to her whenever she is stricken by fears. As she hums this tune, the first of the dream sequences unfolds. In it she is a glamorous siren whom twelve men, in evening clothes, are serenading with "Oh, Fabulous One." Her chauffeur, Russell Paxton (Danny Kaye)— who, in her real life, is the photographer for *Allure*—drives her in her Duesenberg to Columbus Circle, where she mounts a blue soap box to justify her fantasies; then to an expensive nightclub, where the affable head waiter in her actual life is Kendall Nesbitt (Bert Lytell), her lover, and the publisher of *Allure*. As this dream sequence fades away, the crowd is singing her praises. Dr. Brooks explains that though in her daily appearance she is plain, and in her dress conservative, Liza sees herself in her dream as a seductive and alluring woman.

At *Allure,* Randy Curtis (Victor Mature), a cowboy movie star, is being photographed. This completed, Kendall Nesbitt comes to tell Liza the good news that he will soon be free to marry her, since his wife has consented to give him a divorce. Far from being overjoyed, Liza sinks into one of her depressions. Humming "My Ship," she allows herself to drift into the dream world. First she attends her graduation from Mapleton High. Then she sees Kendall purchasing her a wedding ring, with the jeweler bringing him not a ring but a golden dagger. Suddenly, Randy, the movie star, leaps into the dream sequence to make love to Liza, but is soon enticed away by six highly attractive girls. Still in her dream, Liza sings "The Princess of Pure Delight," about a princess who can be won by any man able to solve a riddle posed him by the king. Two suitors fail this test, but a minstrel passes it. This vision over, another comes into view. Liza and Kendall are in church getting married. A chorus of voices denounces her for marrying a man she does not love, although Liza insists she does. The dream becomes a nightmare.

We next meet up with Liza at the office of Dr. Brooks, where she reveals she has made a date with Randy which she is breaking. The psychiatrist points up the fact that Liza's determination to appear plain—indeed, one of the reasons she is breaking her appointment with Randy—is her inability or refusal to compete with other women.

The following morning at *Allure* Liza informs Kendall she does not love him. Then she dresses up elegantly to keep a dinner appointment with Randy.

A conference the following day at Liza's office over the design of the Easter issue brings up the suggestion of a circus scene. Suddenly the scene comes vividly to life, with Russell Paxton as ringmaster. This shifts gracefully into still another scene in which Liza is being tried for her failure to make up her mind, with Russell Paxton as her defense lawyer. Russell Paxton takes Liza severely to task for a failing to marry Kendall. His accusation is given to the tune of "The Best Years of His Life," which, when Russell discovers that it is a melody by Tchaikovsky, leads him to deliver a patter song about Russian composers ("Tschaikowsky"—Ira Gershwin's spelling of the master's name). Liza now defends herself in "The Saga of Jenny." The jury decides in favor of Liza.

The same evening, Liza has a session with Dr. Brooks, during which she discloses a dream in which she relived the humiliation she had suffered in childhood. As she speaks, she is carried back to her earlier years. She is jealous of her mother's beauty and is unable to rid herself of this feeling until her mother dies. The boys avoid her. Dr. Brooks now tries to show her that, after losing one boy friend after another to other girls, Liza has been seeking refuge in plainness. In short, she has been running away from womanhood.

One week later Randy proposes to Liza. He needs her strength to lean on, for he is weak. But Liza by now has arrived at the truth. The man she really loves, the man she has always secretly loved without confessing it to herself—and the man whose strength she needs so badly—is not Kendall or Randy, but Charley Johnson (MacDonald Carey, one of her editorial associates, with whom she had up to now been so high-handed). When Charley comes into her office with suggestions for a new issue, she makes her feelings known, and is overjoyed that they are reciprocated. Together they begin singing the strains of "My Ship" as the curtain falls.

A consummate writing technique was required to keep the play moving fluidly from the reality of Liza's actual business and love life to the confused world of her subconscious; from her everyday problems and frustrations to the nebulous world of her dreams and the misty memories of her past. Hart possessed that skill. But he also profited from one of the most remarkable virtuoso performances of our contemporary musical stage, that of Gertrude Lawrence. Long a star, Gertrude Lawrence helped make the production the vital and unforgettable experience it proved to be. But *Lady in the Dark* was not only the showcase for an established star; it also helped create a star of its own in Danny Kaye. During the writing of *Lady in the Dark* Moss Hart saw Kaye in a nightclub act in which the young comedian made his first entry to Broadway by way of an adult camp in Pennsylvania. The impact on Hart of Kaye's versatility, and his unique delivery of comedy numbers, was such that Hart decided to write into the play the part of Russell Paxton for Kaye.

Weill's music (so ably supplemented by Ira Gershwin's remarkable lyrics) also made a fruitful contribution to the success of the play. His atmospheric music was so perfectly attuned to the dream situations that it seemed to be an inextricable part of them; and Liza's theme song, "My Ship," was beautifully suited for such dream sequences, with its hauntingly individual melodic structure.

Two other all-important musical numbers come in immediate succession to one another. One is assigned to Russell Paxton, followed by the other, sung by Liza Elliott. Paxton's song was "Tschaikowsky," whose chorus consists of a rapid sequence of the names of forty-nine Russian composers of the past and present. With his athletic tongue Kaye spluttered the chorus in thirty-nine seconds. (Kaye broke his own record once, in Madrid, by delivering this chorus in thirty-one seconds.) It was a show-stopping song, as its authors well knew it would be. There was also a fear among many connected with the production that Danny Kaye's success with it might throw Gertrude Lawrence, the star, into the shade. It was then that the decision was reached to include, immediately after "Tshaikowsky," a number just as strong and as individual for Gertrude Lawrence. That song was "The Saga of Jenny." Actually this was not Gertrude Lawrence's dish, being a lusty burlesque-house type of ditty. But Gertrude Lawrence was convinced she could put it over—and put it over she did, in a way to amaze those who heard her sing it for the first time. After Danny Kaye had received a thunderous ovation for "Tshaikowsky," Gertrude Lawrence went into her act. As Richard Aldrich recalls: "Suddenly, startlingly, the exquisite, glamorous Gertrude Lawrence was transformed into a tough, bawdy dive singer. As a piece of impromptu impersonation it was superb with few parallels. . . . A miracle in showmanship was accomplished that night; two tremendous hits followed each other immediately and with equal effect. The success of the Danny Kaye number did not cut down Gertrude's prestige. Instead it made possible, by its challenge, her triumph with 'Jenny.' " And Ira Gershwin wrote: "She hadn't been singing more than a few lines when I realized an interpretation we'd never seen at rehearsal was materializing. Not only were there new nuances and approaches, but on the top of this she 'bumped' it and 'ground' it to the complete devastation of the audience."

"The Princess of Pure Delight" and "Oh, Fabulous One" were also standouts in the Weill score. Even such numbers (good as they were in themselves, and appealing though they remain outside their context) are so basic to the dramatic pattern that *Lady in the Dark* must be considered a "play with music" (as Moss Hart designated it) rather than a musical comedy or even a musical play.

Curious to say, in view of the importance that the song "My Ship" had in the play, it was completely omitted from the score when *Lady in the Dark* was made into a movie; it was merely referred to in the script. That picture (produced by Paramount in 1944, with Ginger Rogers and Ray Milland) did not think the Weill score, remarkable though it was, could stand on its own feet. Two songs (and they were good ones, and became very popular) by other writers were interpolated: "Suddenly It's Spring," by Johnny Burke and James Van Heusen, and "Dream Lover," by Clifford Grey and Victor Schertzinger.

LAFFING ROOM ONLY (1944), *an extravaganza, with book by Olsen and Johnson and Eugene Conrad. Lyrics and music by Burton Lane. Presented by the Shuberts and Olsen and Johnson at the Winter Garden on December 23. Directed by John Murray Anderson and Edward Cline. Dances by Robert Alton. Cast included Olsen and Johnson, Betty Garrett, Mata and Hari, and the Fred Waring Glee Club (233 performances).*

*Laffing Room Only* was an offspring of the fantastically successful *Hellzapoppin'* (1938) and *Sons o' Fun* (1944), with which Olsen and Johnson had regaled Broadway audiences. But *Laffing Room Only* lacked much of the spontaneity that made its parents such boisterous entertainment. In *Laffing Room Only* guns popped, sausages fell into the laps of the audience, a live bear paraded down the aisles, and the audience was encouraged to dance and sing songs and come on the stage to compete for prizes. But the overall impression was that the show was imitating past achievements rather than contributing something vital and fresh. About the best thing about the production was one of the songs, one of the biggest hits Burton Lane had produced up to this time: "Feudin' and Fightin' " (lyrics by Al Dubin), introduced by Pat Brewster. But this song actually became a success about two years after the show closed when it was reintroduced over the radio by Dorothy Shay (on the Bing Crosby program), whose recording after that became a best seller.

LA, LA, LUCILLE (1919), *a musical comedy, with book by Fred Jackson. Lyrics by Arthur Jackson and Buddy de Sylva. Music by George Gershwin. Presented by Alex A. Aarons at the Henry Miller Theater on May 26. Directed by Herbert Gresham and Julian Alfred. Cast included John Hazzard and Janet Velie (104 performances).*

In 1918 young George Gershwin was contracted for the first time to write a complete score for a musical production. That production was a revue called *Half-Past Eight,* which proved such a disaster out of town that it never reached Broadway. Gershwin never even received the fee of $1,500 that had been promised him for his work.

But one year later Gershwin made his bow on Broadway with his first musical-comedy score; this is the significance of *La, La, Lucille.* It was a routine bedroom farce set in a Philadelphia hotel. John Smith, a dentist (Jack Hazzard), can inherit a fortune from his aunt, but only if he is willing to divorce his wife, Lucille (Janet Velie), a former chorus girl. A shrewd lawyer advises him to divorce his wife, take over the inheritance, then re-marry her. To gain that divorce John Smith goes to a Philadelphia hotel to be compromised by a woman selected for him by Lucille—the hotel scrub-woman. It so happens that at that very time·the hotel was crowded with no less than thirty-eight John Smiths. One of these is a honeymoon couple, whose suite adjoins that of our hero and his corespondent. The difficulties and embarrassments that result from the problem of mistaken identities pro-vide the musical with much of its merriment.

*La, La, Lucille* marked the bow of young Alex A. Aarons as a Broadway producer. It was he who selected Gershwin for the musical score (though wiser and more experienced men advised him to consider Victor Herbert), because he was delighted with the fresh and original approaches he found in Gershwin's songs. A few years later, in partnership with Vinton Freedley, Aarons would produce most of Gershwin's leading Broadway successes.

The most important song to come out of *La, La, Lucille* was "Nobody but You," whose fresh and ingratiating lyricism betrayed the influence that Kern had had on Gershwin at the time; it was introduced by minor characters played by Helen Clark and Orin Baker, together with a chorus. Gershwin had written this number while he was working for the publishing house of Remick's as a piano demonstrator. Two other numbers he had written earlier, and then placed into *La, La, Lucille,* were "The Ten Commandments of Love" and "There's More to the Kiss than the Sound." Of the new numbers the best were "Tee-Oodle Um-Bum-Bo" and "From Now On."

THE LAST SWEET DAYS OF ISAAC (1970), *two one-act musicals with book and lyrics by Gretchen Cryer. Music by Nancy Ford. Presented by Haila Stoddard, Mark Wright, and Duane Wilder at the East Side Playhouse on January 26. Directed by Word Baker. Cast comprised Austin Pendleton, Fredericka Weber, and C. David Colson.*

The first entry into the musical-stage sweepstakes for the new decade proved a winner—though it was a long shot. It was a "rock musical" which, upon its arrival to Off Broadway, was so little known, and so little was expected of it, that by the time the first-night curtain went up it had an advance sale of just two tickets! But the critics, headed by Clive Barnes, liked it—considered it exciting, novel, provocative, and thoroughly amusing. Business picked up perceptibly almost immediately. Our humble newcomer overnight gave the appearance of becoming a highly successful box-office venture. Certainly it was a venture that would be much talked about—pro and con.

*The Last Sweet Days of Isaac,* as this new "rock musical" was entitled, is made up of two one-act musicals, each independent of the other. Both call for just three performers: Austin Pendleton as Isaac, Fredericka Weber as Ingrid and Alice, and C. David Colson as The Cop. The first musical is called "The Elevator," using only two of the three characters; the second musical, "I Want to Walk to San Francisco," calls for all three. In addition the two little musicals boast a rock group called "The Zeitgeist" which provides rock music (placed high above the actors) and serves as a chorus. Accompaniment to the singing is provided by an electric harpsichord.

Unlike other "rock musicals" that usually are a bitter indictment of and rebellion against The Establishment, *The Last Sweet Days of Isaac* is also capable of making a mockery of the rebels themselves—for example, their preoccupation with electronics as well as sex, and their indictment of the abuses suffered by the younger generation in our society. But as Gretchen Cryer and Nancy Ford insist, "it isn't a put-down of the young. . . . We hope audiences will laugh and also that they'll see why young people are doing what they're doing. We kind of understand what the kids are talking about but we're over thirty, so we're really in between. We're not part of The Establishment, but we're not teen-agers. We see both sides."

In the first musical, the two characters are found in a stalled elevator. Isaac, though only thirty-three, believes he is close to death. He is a social outcast who is determined to record everything about his life with a tape recorder and a camera. Ingrid is a young secretary who wears a wig and a chain around her waist (the latter is there not only for appearance sake but also to serve as a chastity belt). The two young people do a good deal of talking. The young man uses his camera and tape recorder to provide posterity with a history of what is taking place. The youngsters discover each other, touch each other, practically fall in love with one another. He undresses her while she sings a plaintive number. Then the stalled elevator begins to move—and the idyll ends. One of the more memorable episodes here is when Isaac sings of his approaching death without resentment or bitterness. Ingrid, as Walter Kerr has written, "put a trumpet to her lips and, with the most earnest eyes that ever crowned a trumpet in an elevator, supports him in his outcry heart and brass and soul. It is a splendid theatrical memory."

The authors consider the second musical as a "metaphor on McLuhanism." Here Isaac is a nineteen-year-old rebel who has been put in jail because he protested against power. Through TV he tells his mother, "if I'm going to stop a war I have to put myself directly down in front of the recruiting center so nobody can get in." Alice is carried into another cell, her crime having been to involve herself in a demonstration. Isaac and Alice communicate with each other by means of television sets, get involved emotionally even though they are cells apart, start kissing each other's image on the television screen. By means of television both Alice and Isaac's mother see him die, strangled by the strap of his movie camera which has photographed his death.

The music is thoroughly integrated into the text, at frequent intervals contributing dramatic or amusing impulses to supplement the spoken word or stage action. One of the most poignant moments in the second musical comes after Isaac's death where all we get is the music—"like a recurring throb in the temple," said Walter Kerr, "to reunite them."

In the way in which text, music, acting, and staging are all beautifully coordinated is where the real strength of this unusual musical production lies. Describing the scene in the first musical where the boy undresses the girl while she sings to his tape recorder, Clive Barnes noted that "the writing . . . like the acting is often gorgeously ridiculous. And the rock music . . . is tuneful and appealing." In saying this, Mr. Barnes might well have been referring to the production as a whole, for in a later paragraph he adds: "The book and lyrics . . . and the music . . . are easily among the best of the present Off Broadway crop, and the staging . . . has great stylishness. . . . Miss Weber . . . is . . . a very lovable image . . . [while Mr. Pendleton] positively glitters with dimness and yet is radiant with understanding. . . . Like he was, well, beautiful, man, just—well—beautiful."

THE LAUGH PARADE (1931), *a revue, with book by Ed Wynn and Ed Preble. Lyrics by Mort Dixon and Joe Young. Music by Harry Warren. Presented by Ed Wynn at the Imperial Theater on November 2. Directed by Ed Wynn. Dances by Albertina Rasch. Cast included Ed Wynn, Jeanne Aubert, and Lawrence Gray (231 performances).*

By the time *The Laugh Parade* came to Broadway, Ed Wynn had long since established his identity on the Broadway musical stage as "the perfect fool," wearing his quixotic assortment of hats, baggy pants, and ill-matched jacket, introducing all sorts of absurd inventions, and punctuating his humorous remarks with interjections in a squeaky, high-pitched voice. He had been a star of *The Ziegfeld Follies* before writing and producing his own revues, in which he could go to town with his own peculiar brand of humor and shenanigans: *Ed Wynn's Carnival* in 1920, *The Perfect Fool* in 1921, *The Grab Bag* in 1924. In *The Laugh Parade* he introduced another Ed Wynn innovation (which, in a few years, would become known and imitated all over the country as a result of Ed Wynn's success on his weekly radio show). That innovation was to squeal out an extended "s-o-o-o." It was an idea he got from his grandmother, who always used it whenever she was being interrupted. At a whim, Ed Wynn interpolated it into his act toward the end of the show. The audience roared, and from then on it became one of his many trademarks.

One of the most amusing scenes in the revue had Ed Wynn as a waiter in a Western saloon. A tough-looking customer ordered some whiskey, then spat it out, insisting he had been given the wrong brand. "I can tell any brand blindfolded," he boasted. Wynn took up the challenge. The tough man was blindfolded, following which Ed Wynn dragged in a gas tank and pumped some gasoline into a liquor glass. The tough man sipped it and yelled: "That's gasoline." Meekly, Wynn inquired: "What brand?"

There were two hit songs in the revue, both of them sung by Lawrence Gray and Jeanne Aubert: "Ooh That Kiss" and "You're My Everything," the latter to become a Harry Warren standard.

*The Laugh Parade* had proved a fiasco during its out-of-town tryouts. With a Broadway advance sale of only $200, it gave every appearance of becoming a box-office disaster. Ed Wynn's ingenuity, however, changed the picture. He bought out all the tickets for the opening night and had them distributed to the employees of Macy's. The critics were impressed when they saw the house sold out, and possibly were influenced by this into writing favorable reviews. Ed Wynn also bought all the tickets for the second night, this time distributing them to the employees of Ludwig Baumann. Word now was spreading throughout Broadway that *The Laugh Parade* was selling out at each performance. Curiosity in the show began to attract paying customers. A certain "flop" had been transformed into a success.

LEAVE IT TO JANE (1917), *a musical comedy, with book by Guy Bolton and P. G. Wodehouse, based on George Abe's play* The College Widow. *Lyrics by P. G. Wodehouse. Music by Jerome Kern. Presented by William Elliott, F. Ray Comstock, and Morris Gest at the Longacre Theater on August 28. Directed by Edward Royce. Cast included Edith Hallor, Robert G. Pitkin, Oscar Shaw, and Georgia O'Ramey (167 performances).*

*Leave It to Jane* represented for Bolton-Wodehouse-Kern a temporary digression from the intimate, sophisticated, little shows they were then writing for the Princess Theater. *Leave It to Jane* is a full-scale musical comedy with all the elaborate trappings of the Broadway musicals of that period. The text was a satire on college life in a Midwestern town. In Atwater College in Indiana, Jane (Edith Hallor), the daughter of the college president and often referred to by the collegiates as "a college widow," uses the wiles of a siren to keep the star halfback, Billy Bolton (Robert G. Pitkin), from going off to a rival college. Her siren's ways are sufficiently alluring not only to keep Billy at Atwater but also to win him for herself.

Most of the comedy was assigned to Georgia O'Ramey as Flora, a waitress. Her brusque and at times grotesque characterization provided the brightest humor of the evening, and for her Kern wrote the best comedy song of the musical, "Cleopatterer." To Jane, Kern assigned two other song winners, the title number and "The Siren's Song," in both of which she was aided by a chorus of girls.

*Leave It to Jane* was revived in an Off Broadway production in 1959, to enjoy a run of several years (928 performances). What had made the show a success in 1917 was also responsible for its success forty-two years later: Kern's songs. Richard Watts, Jr., wrote, in reviewing the revival: "I have remembered the Kern score with delight, recalling five of the songs in particular. And hearing them again last night, I was happy to find that, not only was the score as a whole as charming and freshly tuneful as memory has made it, but my quintet came off easily as the best of a gloriously melodious lot."

LEAVE IT TO ME (1938), *a musical comedy, with book by Bella and Samuel Spewack, based on their own stage comedy,* Clear All Wires. *Lyrics and music by Cole Porter. Presented by Vinton Freedley at the Imperial Theater on November 9. Directed by Samuel Spewack. Dances by Robert Alton. Cast included William Gaxton, Sophie Tucker, Victor Moore, Tamara, and Mary Martin (291 performances).*

*Leave It to Me* was Cole Porter's most successful musical since *Anything Goes* in 1934. It was also the first successful spoof of the Soviet Union on the musical stage. The principal character provides most of the amusement. He is Alonzo P. Goodhue (Victor Moore), the sadly befuddled American ambassador to the Soviet Union. He has no idea why he was chosen for the job. "Somebody in Washington musn't like me," he believes. He is homesick, and even grows nostalgic about the banana splits he used to get back home. What he does not know is that while he was pitching quoits in his backyard in Topeka, Kansas, his domineering and ambitious wife (Sophie Tucker) had contributed $95,000 to the party campaign fund—$5,000 more than a newspaper owner who had aspired to this ambassadorial post—and thus the job went to Goodhue. But Mrs. Goodhue had not counted on going to Russia. Her goal was London, and was just as upset as her husband to be in the Soviet Union, blaming this unexpected development on the fact that she had only five children, whereas Joseph Kennedy had nine.

Buckley Joyce Thomas (William Gaxton), a brash young newspaperman, is sent to Moscow by his employer—the same newspaper owner who had been beaten out for the ambassadorial post by Goodhue. Thomas' mission is to get the goods on Goodhue so that Goodhue will be recalled. Through the machinations of the young journalist, willingly Goodhue gets into all kinds of trouble, hoping thereby to get home soon, but only to discover to his dismay that things always turn out right. He makes provocative speeches which are misinterpreted by the Soviets as favorable to them. He kicks an arrogant Nazi ambassador in the stomach and receives a cable of congratulation from Secretary of State Hull. He shoots a Russian diplomat, managing thereby to destroy a notorious Trotskyite; for this he becomes a hero of a two-week celebration in Red Square. Finally he decides to take his job seriously by making a speech on how to stop the world from going into another war. He now antagonizes both Russia and the American State Department and comes to the end of his diplomatic career. While all this is going on, Buckley Joyce Thomas carries on a romance with Colette (Tamara) and ends up winning her.

Sophie Tucker, William Gaxton, Tamara, and Victor Moore were hardy veterans of the musical stage. Yet it was not one of these but a complete newcomer who attracted the thunder of the audience: Mary Martin, as Dolly Winslow. Shedding her ermines in a simulated strip-tease (in, of all places, a wayside Siberian railroad station)—an episode hurriedly interpolated into the production during rehearsals to allow time for a change of scene—she sang "My Heart Belongs to Daddy." Her innocent, quavering, childlike voice —her baby eyes staring upward at the sky—proved a delightful contradiction to the suggestive *double entendres* of the lyric and the provocative gestures of her pseudo strip-tease. She became at once one of the radiant stars of the American stage. A native of Weatherford, Texas, where she made her first stage appearance at the age of five at a Fireman's Ball, she went to school in Nashville, Tennessee (the Ward-Belmont School), then returned home to open a dancing school. She got her first chance to appear before the public again at the Hotel Roosevelt in Hollywood, California, which was followed by several none too successful appearances in other nightclubs and over the radio. Laurence Schwab heard her sing at the Trocadero in Hollywood and signed her up. When *Leave It to Me* was cast, Schwab lent her to Vinton Freedley for what had been planned as a highly minor role. But since there are no such things as minor roles for great performers, Mary Martin made herself the toast of Broadway; her debut has been described as one of the most sensational in the history of the American musical theater. And "My Heart Belongs to Daddy" became the hit song of the show.

Sophie Tucker, that old "pro," also had a way with a song or two. As Mrs. Goodhue, she made the most of "Most Gentlemen Don't Like Love," "I'm Taking the Steps to Russia" (supported by her five daughters), and "From U.S.A. to U.S.S.R." (in which her husband, Alonzo, provided an "off-to-Buffalo" routine). Colette contributed the purple moods for which Porter had become so famous, in ballads like "Get out of Town" and "From Now On" (the latter in a duet with Buckley).

Mary Martin was not the only unknown in the cast of *Leave It to Me* destined to reach heights. There was one other in the cast, although he had to wait for a later date and other productions for recognition. A careful scrutiny of the program reveals that among those who appeared in the chorus, and doubled as a male secretary, was Gene Kelly.

During the successful run of *Leave It to Me,* the production was harassed by labor strife that for a while threatened to close down the show for good. The actors resented attempts by the stagehands' union to absorb them, and went on strike. Sophie Tucker stood on the side of the stagehand union. The conflict between the rival factions compelled the production to suspend performances for a brief period until the dispute was settled to the satisfaction of all concerned.

> LEND AN EAR (1948), *an intimate revue, with sketches, lyrics, and music by Charles Gaynor. Additional sketches by Joseph Stein and Will Glickman. Presented by William Katzell, Franklin Gilbert, and William Eythe at the National Theater on December 16. Directed by Hal Gerson. Dances by Gower Champion. Cast included Carol Channing, William Eythe, and Yvonne Adair (460 performances).*

Just as it was generally conceded in 1948 that the revue—both the elaborate kind and the more intimate ones—had lost its audiences, *Lend an Ear* came to New York (by way of Pittsburgh, where it had been conceived by Charles Gaynor, and Cohasset, Massachusetts, and Hollywood, California, where it had been developed before being shelved for a number of years). It proved that brightness, vivacity, and fresh entertainment will always have box-office appeal, whatever the medium. Carol Channing and Yvonne Adair were two unknowns in the cast who were here swept to recognition. Miss Channing was particularly effective in a satire on the twenties, "The Gladiola Girl," the first-act finale—a brilliant lampoon of a 1925 road-company musical, laughing at the dress, habits, mores, and indiscretions of the roaring 1920's. Here Yvonne Adair brought down the house regularly with her inimitable renditions of "Doin' the Old Yahoo" and "In Our Teeny Weeny Nest." (This sequence was used several times on television some years later, including on an "Omnibus" program in 1958.) The second-act finale was an opera without music. One outstanding sketch satirized psychiatry by showing the psychiatrist to be sicker than his patient; two other sparkling sketches were devoted to juvenile delinquency and the secret love of a secretary for her boss. The songs ran the gamut from the witty and satirical to the romantic and the sentimental. The best were: "Neurotic You and Psycopathic Me," "Three Little Queens of the Silver Screen," "When Someone You Love Loves You," "Where Is the She for Me?", and "I'm Not in Love."

Gower Champion here proved for the first time his true potential as stage director and choreographer. Another comparative unknown, this time in the cast, later became popular in the movies—Gene Nelson.

*Lend an Ear* was revived Off Broadway on September 24, 1959, when it had a run of 94 performances. With a little bit of updating that proved hardly a valuable contribution, *Lend an Ear* was given several performances at the Equity Theater in October of 1969.

LET 'EM EAT CAKE (1933), *a musical comedy, with book by Morrie Ryskind and George S. Kaufman. Lyrics by Ira Gershwin. Music by George Gershwin. Presented by Sam H. Harris at the Imperial Theater on October 21. Directed by George S. Kaufman. Dances by Eugene von Grona and Ned McGurn. Cast included William Gaxton, Victor Moore, Philip Loeb, and Lois Moran (90 performances).*

*Let 'Em Eat Cake* was an unfortunate attempt to duplicate the success of *Of Thee I Sing* by calling on the same producer, writers, and stars, and narrating the further adventures of Wintergreen (William Gaxton) and Throttlebottom (Victor Moore) as President and Vice-President of the United States. They run for reelection and are defeated. Wintergreen then becomes head of a revolutionary movement to overthrow the government, abetted by the Union Square rabble-rouser Kruger (Philip Loeb). The revolution proves successful, and a dictatorship of the proletariat is set up. A critical international dispute arises, the settlement of which requires a baseball game between the nine members of the Supreme Court and nine foreign representatives of the League of Nations. Throttlebottom, officiating as umpire, makes an unhappy decision that almost brings him doom at the guillotine, imported for this unhappy event from France. Mary Wintergreen (Lois Moran) saves his life through her quick thinking, and when the republic is restored, Wintergreen becomes President.

Like so many sequels, *Let 'Em Eat Cake* was a failure, but an interesting one. It had moments in which the wit and satire sparkled no less brilliantly than in *Of Thee I Sing:* the opening scene, which recalls "Wintergreen for President" from the earlier production, then progresses to "Tweedledee for President"; the Union League scene; "Comes the Revolution"; "Union Square," with its piquant interlude, "Down With Ev'rything That's Up." And it had one outstanding Gershwin song in "Mine," introduced by Wintergreen, in which delightful use is made of an aside by the chorus sung contrapuntally (and with its own set of lyrics) to the main melody. ("Mine" was interpolated into the revival of *Of Thee I Sing* in 1952.)

But the play as a whole touched on too many unsavory subjects to be consistently amusing—a left-wing revolution, dictatorship in America with a blue-shirt army gaining control, the threatened death of a principal at the guillotine. As Brooks Atkinson noted: "Their [the writers'] hatred had triumphed over their sense of humor."

LET'S FACE IT (1941), *a musical comedy, with book by Herbert and Dorothy Fields, based on the stage comedy* The Cradle Snatchers. *Lyrics and music by Cole Porter. Presented by Vinton Freedley at the Imperial Theater on October 29. Directed by Edgar MacGregor. Dances by Charles Walters. Cast included Danny Kaye, Eve Arden, Mary Jane Walsh, and Edith Meiser (547 performances).*

*The Cradle Snatchers* was a Broadway sex comedy in 1925 in which three ladies decide to avenge themselves on their wandering husbands by taking in young gigolos for the weekend. *Let's Face It* borrowed only the bare trimmings of the plot, superimposing upon it timely military trimmings— since this was the period just before Pearl Harbor, when American boys were beginning to be mustered into uniform. The three women in *Let's Face It* are Nancy Collister (Vivian Vance), Cornelia Abigail Pigeon (Edith Meiser), and Maggie Watson (Eve Arden). Since they reside in Southampton, Long Island—only a stone's throw from Camp Roosevelt—they decide to take on three inductees as young gigolo lovers. One is Jerry Walker, played by Danny Kaye in his first starring role since his success earlier the same year in *Lady in the Dark.* The other two are Frankie Burns (Benny Baker) and Eddie Hilliard (Jack Williams). Jerry's adventures in Southampton complicate his own love life, since he is in love with Winnie Potter

(Mary Jane Walsh), who in the end is ready to forgive and forget. Frequent allusions to the vicissitudes of an inductee's life give the book topical interest to an audience concerned over the European war clouds spreading across the Atlantic.

As an Army inductee, Danny Kaye confirmed the powerful impression he had made in *Lady in the Dark* as a comic with few rivals. He delivered a routine that from then on became a staple of his repertory: "Melody in Four F," a tongue-twister relating in double-talk the adventures of being conscripted into the Army. That song, and another routine entitled "A Modern Fairy Tale," were interpolated into the score for Kaye and are not by Cole Porter but by Sylvia Fine (Mrs. Danny Kaye).

There was another comparative newcomer besides Danny Kaye in the cast who would also soon achieve significance in the musical theater. She was Nanette Fabray, who began her stage career in vaudeville at the age of three, then toured the vaudeville circuit as Baby Nanette. After some stage appearances in California she came to New York and made her New York stage debut in 1940 in the revue *Meet the People,* a performance good enough to land her a role the following year in this major Cole Porter musical. She was given a minor role—that of Jean Blanchard—but nevertheless was assigned the two most important songs in the Cole Porter score: "Ace in the Hole," which she sang with Winnie and a minor character named Muriel, played by Sunnie O'Dea; and "You Irritate Me So," a duet with Eddie Hilliard. Danny Kaye had a good duet with Winnie, "Ev'rything I Love."

The motion picture of *Let's Face It,* released by Paramount in 1943, retained only two Cole Porter songs, and included several new ones by Sammy Cahn and Jule Styne. The stars of this production were Bob Hope and Betty Hutton.

LIFE BEGINS AT 8:40 (1934), *a revue, with book by David Freedman and others. Lyrics by Ira Gershwin and E. Y. Harburg. Music by Harold Arlen. Presented by the Shuberts at the Winter Garden on August 27. Directed by John Murray Anderson and Philip Loeb. Dances by Robert Alton and Charles Weidman. Cast included Bert Lahr, Ray Bolger, Brian Donlevy, Luella Gear, and Frances Williams (237 performances).*

*Life Begins at 8:40* had started life as *The Ziegfeld Follies* of 1934, then adopted its new and final title when the rights for the use of the name *Ziegfeld Follies* could not be cleared. Comedy and satire were its strong suits. Bert Lahr was in his element in "Quartet Erotica," where he appeared as Balzac (to a trio of performers impersonating Rabelais, De Maupassant, and Boccaccio). Luella Gear had a choice satirical number in "My Paramount

—Publix—Roxy Rose" and did a devastating impersonation of Mrs. Eleanor Roosevelt (in "Beautifying the City"), which delighted Mrs. Roosevelt no end. The rage for Cuban dance was spoofed at in "Shoein' the Mare." There were memorable sentimental and romantic moods, too. Frances Williams delivered "Fun to Be Fooled"; James Reynolds, "The Love Song"; Josephine Houston and Barlett Simmons, "What Can You Say in a Love Song?"; and John McCauley and Dixie Dunbar, "Let's Take a Walk Around the Block"— all of them strong musical numbers. Ray Bolger had a duet with Dixie Dunbar in "You're a Builder Upper," which he followed with one of his characteristic and incomparable dance routines. All in all, as Gilbert W. Gabriel reported, *"Life Begins at 8:40 is all orchids and laurel."*

> LI'L ABNER (1956), *a musical comedy, with book by Norman Panama and Melvin Frank, based on characters created by Al Capp. Lyrics by Johnny Mercer. Music by Gene de Paul. Presented by Norman Panama, Melvin Frank, and Michael Kidd at the St. James Theater on November 15. Directed and with dances by Michael Kidd. Cast included Edith Adams, Peter Palmer, Stubby Kaye, and Tina Louise (693 performances).*

*Li'l Abner* carries the grotesque characters of Dogpatch, in Al Capp's famous cartoon strip, into the theater. The principals, of course, are Daisy Mae (Edith Adams), who is bent on catching the recalcitrant bachelor Li'l Abner (Peter Palmer); in the final scene Abner drinks a potion that makes him want to marry Daisy Mae. Others in Dogpatch include Appassionata von Climax (Tina Louise), Daisy Mae's rival for Li'l Abner during the Sadie Hawkins sweepstakes, in which the women go racing after the men; Mammy Yokum (Charlotte Rae), with her delusions of grandeur, and Pappy (Joe E. Marks); and the industrialist General Bullmoose, the politician Senator Phogbound, Marryin' Sam, Evil Eye Fleagle, who "gives the whammies," and so forth. These good and kind people, so sound of body and mind, help to point up the follies of civilization on the periphery of their own fantastic world. And the satire that Capp always permits to intrude into his comic strip also penetrates the musical, which finds occasion to mock big business, our atom policy and security program, and can find comfort in the scientific discovery of a formula capable of producing healthy people by depriving them of their minds.

Brooks Atkinson pointed up the fact that "ballet is a more suitable medium for comic-strip theatricalization than the complex form of the musical stage. . . . Motion is a better medium than words for animating this sort of drawing." And it is in the dances, conceived by Michael Kidd, that tective sails aboard the same ship as Johnny's friends, with the hope of uncovering some evidence clearing Johnny. A signal has been prearranged between Johnny and the detective. Should the detective come upon some important information, he will discharge fireworks from the deck of the ship. As Johnny watches the ship sail away, he suddenly sees fireworks discharged from the boat. He now knows that it will not be long before his honesty is proved. He sails home, where he not only uncovers Anstey's role in destroying his reputation but also Anstey's iniquitous activities in San Francisco's Chinatown, were he runs a gambling house. More important still, he is now free to marry Goldie Gates, the girl of his dreams (Ethel Levey).

In his first original full-length Broadway musical comedy, Cohan abandoned many of the little tricks and the absurd costume he had used as his trademark up to now in vaudeville. With his first breezy entrance song, "The Yankee Doodle Boy," the "new Cohan" won the hearts of his audience completely; and he solidified that affection with his equally vivacious rendition of another Cohan classic, "Give My Regards to Broadway," which he sings to his friends as he bids them bon voyage at the Southampton pier.

In this musical Cohan initiated two routines which he would henceforth use frequently in his musicals. One was to deliver monologues with homespun philosophy, a kind of sentimental sermon; in *Little Johnny Jones* he did this in "Life's a Funny Proposition." Another was to drape an American flag around his body and strut up and down the stage doing a flag-waving routine with a patriotic ditty.

Of the remaining numbers in the Cohan score, the best were "Good-Bye Flo," sung by Ethel Levey, and an amusing ditty presented by six coachmen, "'Op in My 'Ansom."

*Little Johnny Jones* marked the bow of a new producing team on Broadway, that of Cohan and Harris, which would contribute numerous successful productions to New York, many of them the works of Cohan himself.

LITTLE MARY SUNSHINE (1959), *a musical comedy, with book, lyrics, and music by Rick Besoyan. Presented by Howard Barker, Cynthia Baer, and Robert Chambers at the Orpheum Theater on November 18. Directed by Rick Besoyan. Dances by Ray Harrison. Cast included Eileen Brennan and William Graham (1,143 performances).*

Of the musicals that sprang into existence Off Broadway, *Little Mary Sunshine* proved to be one of the most refreshing satires ("a merry and sprightly spoof," as Brooks Atkinson described it), and one of the most successful.

*Li'l Abner* has exceptional interest. One of these comes just before the end of the first act, during the Sadie Hawkins Day helter-skelter chase of the women after the men. "All that happens," explains Brooks Atkinson, "is that the girls leg it after the boys at top speed. But Mr. Kidd is the man who can see comic-strip humor in this primitive rite by varying the speed, by introducing low-comedy antics and by giving *Li'l Abner* its most exuberant scene."

The comedy songs were the best, especially "Jubilation T. Cornpone," with which Marryin' Sam (Stubby Kaye) stopped the show. In a broader satirical vein were "The Country's in the Very Best of Hands," "Oh, Happy Day," and "Progress Is the Root of All Evil"; and the sentimental duet of Abner and Daisy Mae, "Namely You," and Abner's homey ditty, "If I Had My Druthers," were more in character with the warm and gentle people who inhabit Dogpatch.

In the motion picture (Paramount, 1959), as in the stage musical, one of the best sequences was the "Jubilation T. Cornpone" number, in which Stubby Kaye repeated his stage performance with the aid of the ensemble. Virtually the entire stage score was used in this adaptation, which starred Leslie Parrish, Peter Palmer, and Stubby Kaye.

LISTEN LESTER (1918), *a musical comedy, with book and lyrics by Harry L. Cort and George E. Stoddard. Music by Harold Orlob. Presented by John Cort at the Knickerbocker Theater on December 23. Cast included Johnny Dooley, Ada Lewis, Clifton Webb, Hansford Wilson, and Eddie Garvie (272 performances).*

Colonel Rufus Dodge (Eddie Garvie) has written indiscreet letters to Arbutus Quilty (Gertrude Vanderbilt). Since he is now in love with Tillie Mumm (Ada Lewis), he must recover and destroy them. Two allies help him get his letters back: William Penn, Jr. (Johnny Dooley), and Lester Lite (Hansford Wilson). During the quest for the letters Jack Griffith (Clifton Webb) pursues and wins Mary Dodge (Ada Mae Weeks); and when the quest is successful, the colonel woos and wins Tillie.

The hit song was a ballad, "Waiting for You." But the main attraction was not so much the music as the dancing, which was virtually continuous throughout the production. One of those who helped these dancing sequences so admirably was Clifton Webb. He had begun his career as a dancer in 1910, then with Bonnie Glass became one of New York's most popular ballroom attractions. In 1917 he appeared on Broadway in *Love o' Mike*, a minor Jerome Kern musical, but it was in *Listen Lester* that he first won a secure place for himself in the musical theater, to become one of its most suave and sophisticated performers as well as dancers during the next two decades.

LITTLE JESSIE JAMES (1923), *a musical farce, with book and lyrics by Harlan Thompson. Music by Harry Archer. Presented by L. Lawrence Weber at the Longacre Theater on August 15. Cast included Nan Halperin, Allen Kearns, and Miriam Hopkins (385 performances).*

The main reason *Little Jessie James* had the highly profitable run of almost four hundred performances—and the only reason it is remembered today—is because of a song. That number was "I Love You," one of the foremost hit songs of the early 1920's. It was sung repeatedly throughout the play, after having been introduced by the heroine, Jessie Jamieson, and the boy she falls in love with, Tommy Tinker. Above and beyond the presence of this song *Little Jessie James* contributed an important footnote to the history of the American musical theater by providing Nan Halperin and (in a very minor part) John Boles with their first roles on the Broadway stage, and Miriam Hopkins her first important role in a musical comedy; Miss Hopkins had previously been seen in a minor dancing part in *The Music Box Revue* of 1921.

Jessie Jamieson (Nan Halperin) is a flapper from Kansas who meets Tommy Tucker (Allen Kearns) in his apartment. With her open, staring eyes and baby voice she wins him away from his girl friend, Juliet (Miriam Hopkins).

Jessie sings three other fetching musical numbers besides "I Love You": "My Home Town in Kansas," "From Broadway to Main Street," and "Suppose I Had Never Met You." The production also boasted a seductive octet of chorus girls and a Paul Whiteman orchestral combination called the James Boys.

The fact that *Little Jessie James* was not only Harry Archer's greatest Broadway success, but his only one—and the overwhelming popularity of its hit song, "I Love You"—obscured a career that produced the scores for numerous Broadway musicals whose main significance rests in the fact that they proved the point of origin for the successful careers of such performers as Joe E. Brown, John Boles, and Allen Kearns, among others. Archer was born Harry Aruacher in Creston, Iowa, on February 21, 1888. He attended military academy, then studied music at Princeton University. His first Broadway musical was *Pearl Maiden* in 1912, which was followed by *Love for Sale, Frivolities of 1920, Peek-a-Boo* (starring Clark and McCullough), and *Paradise Alley,* among others. Among his better-known songs were "White

Sails," "You and I," "I Was Blue," and "I'm Going to Dance with the Guy What Brung Me." For a while Archer was a leader of his own jazz band; then he became a member of the Paul Whiteman orchestra. He died in New York on April 23, 1960.

LITTLE JOHNNY JONES (1904), *a musical comedy, with book, lyrics, and music by George M. Cohan. Presented by Sam H. Harris at the Liberty Theater on November 7. Directed by George M. Cohan. Cast included George M. Cohan, Ethel Levey, Jerry and Helen Cohan, and Donald Brian (52 performances).*

Though *Little Johnny Jones* had an initial Broadway run of only fifty-two performances, it was, nevertheless, a success. And it was a success because after its first appearance on Broadway, it went on the road, where it proved itself to be a sound box-office attraction. This inspired Cohan to bring it back to Broadway on May 8, 1905, when it played up to August 26, 1905, and from November 13, 1905, to December 9, 1905. On April 22, 1907, it was back again in New York for an additional two-week run.

This was George M. Cohan's first successful musical comedy. Two earlier Cohan musicals on Broadway had been expansions of his vaudeville skits, and both were failures. But *Little Johnny Jones* was the first musical he wrote expressly for the Broadway stage, and for it he developed a major role for himself suitable to his personality and talents. The character of Johnny Jones became his first starring vehicle in the musical theater.

The idea for *Little Johnny Jones* came to Cohan during a visit to England. There he decided he must write a musical comedy using two locales that had impressed him particularly: one the pier at Southampton, the other the court of the Cecil Hotel in London. Back in America, he heard about Tod Sloan, an American jockey who had ridden in the Derby for the king of England in 1903. Cohan put two and one together, and in short order came up with his first musical comedy—text, lyrics, and music.

At the turn of the present century, Johnny Jones (George M. Cohan), an American jockey, comes to London to ride in the Derby. There he meets Anthony Anstey (Jerry Cohan), an American gambler who tries to bribe Johnny to throw the race. Failing to do so, Anstey tries to destroy Johnny's reputation by spreading the word that the reason Johnny lost the race in the Derby was because he had been dishonest. This leads an angry mob to follow Johnny to Southampton, where he has come to say good-bye to some of his friends. Johnny, however, refuses to go home, since he first wants to clear his name in England. He hires a detective, who poses throughout the play as a drunkard and who is merely called "The Unknown." This de-

It was the first Off Broadway musical to have its score recorded in its entirety by the original cast (Capitol).

It had the third-longest run of any Off Broadway production. And it brought Rick Besoyan the Vernon Rice Award for outstanding achievement in the Off Broadway theater.

One need only mention that the setting is in the Rocky Mountains in the early part of the twentieth century, that the cast includes a company of forest rangers, and that the principal love duet is "Colorado Love Call," to recognize instantaneously what was being satirized in this musical. The victim of this none too innocent merriment is the kind of operettas for which Friml, particularly, and in some instances Romberg, had become so famous.

*Little Mary Sunshine* opens in typical Friml fashion with the arrival of forest rangers singing a rousing song about their calling in "The Forest Rangers." They come to the little inn—the Colorado Inn in the Rockies—owned by Little Mary Sunshine (Eileen Brennan), whom they greet with their song. Mary is in trouble. Her property, which is government-owned, will be taken from her since she did not make the payment due on her mortgage. But Mary is the kind of girl who can see the silver lining behind the dark clouds, as she reveals in "Look for a Sky of Blue."

The inn soon becomes a beehive of activity. Captain Big Jim Warington, a ranger (William Graham), reveals to Mary he is on a mission to capture renegade Indians. A European opera star nostalgically remembers her past in a romantic European town, in "In Izzenschnooken on the Lovely Essenzook Zee," and soon finds an admirer in General Oscar Fairfax after they discover they both had had gay times in Vienna. Vacationing Eastern girls are flirting with the rangers. And Jim and Mary exchange tender sentiments in "Colorado Love Call."

Looking for Jim in the garden at night, Mary is attacked by Yellow Feather, an Indian, but is rescued by Jim. Her property is also saved. The government has just conceded that Brown Bear, head of a friendly Indian tribe, has a legal claim to most of Colorado. In a gesture of rare nobility, Brown Bear not only gives Mary her land as a gift but presents the rest of his claim to the rangers to be used as a national park. With a reprise of "Colorado Love Call," we know that the romance of Jim and Mary will turn out equally well. The musical ends when Yellow Feather, repentant of his dastardly behavior, comes out waving an American flag.

*Little Mary Sunshine* was Rick Besoyan's first musical. He wrote two others—*The Student Gypsy* in 1963 and *Babes in the Wood* in 1964—neither of which were successful. He died in Sayville, Long Island, on

March 13, 1970. At the time of his death he was working on the lyrics of his new musical, *Mrs. 'Arris Goes to Paris*.

LITTLE ME (1962), *a musical comedy, with book by Neil Simon, based on the novel by Patrick Dennis. Lyrics by Carolyn Leigh. Music by Cy Coleman. Presented by Feuer and Martin at the Lunt-Fontanne Theater on November 17. Directed by Cy Feuer and Bob Fosse. Dances by Bob Fosse. Cast included Sid Caesar, Virginia Martin, and Nancy Andrews (257 performances).*

The last time Sid Caesar had appeared on Broadway before *Little Me* was in 1948 in the revue *Make Mine Manhattan,* in which he proved himself a caricaturist second to none, and a comic of the first order. The years that followed established him as one of television's most original and versatile comics, inimitable in presenting a varied assortment of odd characters, pointing up their unique little foibles, mannerisms, idiosyncrasies, and accents. With Caesar returning to the Broadway stage after an absence of fourteen years—and now a celebrity—he could be expected to be given a vehicle taking full advantage of his talent for portraying unusual characters. *Little Me* did just that. Sid Caesar played the following parts: Noble Eggleston, first a sixteen-year-old snob who considers himself a genius, then a daredevil flyer during World War I, and finally Noble's son; Mr. Pinchery, a parched, old-aged miser; Val du Val, a nightclub singer who regards himself as the world's greatest entertainer; Fred Poitrine, a World War I private, a nincompoop blinking behind the thick lenses of his eyeglasses; Prince Cherney of Rozenzweig, an imperious princeling; Otto Schnitzer, an overbearing German film director.

All these men play a vital role in the life of Belle Poitrine, a little girl born on the wrong side of the tracks to a mother who stood on the wrong side of morality. Young Belle is determined to find wealth, culture, and social position. Belle is played by two performers—one representing Belle in her younger years, the other, Belle late in her life. As the play opens, Belle Poitrine (Nancy Andrews) is a movie queen dictating the memoirs of her picaresque life to Patrick Dennis. She promises to tell all, as she explains in "The Truth." The rest of the musical traces her varied love life as well as her rise to stardom and wealth.

The time reverts to the year of 1916, when Belle was young, poor, ambitious. Noble Eggleston, a wealthy snob living on the Heights in a small town in Illinois, invites young Belle from Drifters Row to his sixteenth birthday party. In "The Other Side of the Tracks," Belle reveals that she has no intention of wallowing forever in poverty. She attends the party and finds Noble a highly desirable and convenient means of fulfilling her ambition. They hold hands, talk about love. But Noble can love a girl without culture and social position only so far and no farther, as he sings in "I Love You as Much as I Am Able." Besides, his mother rejects Belle in no uncertain terms. Belle's path now crosses that of an eighty-year-old banker whom she tries to convince that he has something fine and human deep within him, though his outside is a bit crusty. She ends up killing him, but is acquitted of the murder. Her notoriety brings her a job in vaudeville. After that her life becomes enmeshed with Val du Val, the bumbling sad-sack Fred Poitrine, and a variety of other men—but most frequently her first love, Noble. Show business treats her better than her men and better than she treats them. She eventually becomes a star in the movies. In the end she is found celebrating Christmas Eve with her friends at her mansion in Southampton, Long Island. She has wealth, culture, social position—everything except Noble Eggleston.

Though the acting honors went to Caesar for his various impersonations—some better than others—and to Virginia Martin as the younger Belle and Nancy Andrews as the older one, there was one other performer who attracted the enthusiasm of audience and critics. He was Swen Swenson, playing the part of George Musgrove, Belle's admirer from the time he was a child; he becomes a gambler and tries to seduce her in later years. His way with a dance number and with a song like "I've Got Your Number" was irresistible. One of the best musical numbers was "Real Live Girl," sung by Fred Poitrine, the World War I private. The title number was shared by the two Belles, and a rousing song, "Here's to Us," comes in the last scene at Belle's party in Southampton. This last number, incidentally, was liked so well by Judy Garland, that it was one of the numbers chosen to be played at her funeral.

THE LITTLE MILLIONAIRE (1911), *a musical comedy, with book, lyrics, and music by George M. Cohan. Presented by Cohan and Harris at the Cohan Theater on September 25. Directed by George M. Cohan. Cast included George M. Cohan, Jerry Cohan, Helen Cohan, and (in a minor role) Donald Crisp (192 performances).*

The late Mrs. Spooner has left a will specifying that her fortune can be shared by her husband and son only if they get married. Since Robert Spooner, the son (George M. Cohan), loves Goldie Gray (Lila Rhodes), the demands of the will present no problem to him. However, his friend Bill Costigan (Tom Lewis) is sure that Goldie is interested only in Robert's fortune, and does everything he can to break up the love affair. In this he is unsuccessful, since Goldie loves Robert for himself alone.

To fulfill the requirements of the will, the father—Henry Spooner (Jerry Cohan)—courts and wins Goldie's aunt, Mrs. Prescott (Helen Cohan).

A pattern already established by Cohan in his musicals was here rigidly followed. The play was filled with sentimental recitations, topical songs and ballads, flag numbers, and eccentric dances. One of the leading song hits was a comedy number, "We Do All the Dirty Work"; other popular musical items included "Oh, You Wonderful Girl," "Musical Moon," and "Barnum Had the Right Idea."

THE LITTLE SHOW (1929), *an intimate revue, with book and lyrics by Howard Dietz and others. Music mainly by Arthur Schwartz, with additional songs by Kay Swift, Ralph Rainger, and others. Presented by William A. Brady, Jr., and Dwight Deere Wiman, in association with Tom Weatherly, at the Music Box Theater on April 30. Directed by Dwight Deere Wiman and Alexander Leftwich. Dances by Danny Dare. Cast included Fred Allen, Clifton Webb, Libby Holman, John McCauley, and Romney Brent (321 performances).*

*(1930), an intimate revue, assembled by Dwight Deere Wiman. Book and lyrics by Howard Dietz and others. Music by Arthur Schwartz and others. Presented by William A. Brady, Jr., Dwight Deere Wiman, and Tom Weatherly at the Royale Theater on September 2. Directed by Dwight Deere Wiman and Monty Woolley. Dances by Dave Gould. Cast included Al Trahan, Jay C. Flippen, and Gloria Grafton (63 performances).*

*(1931), an intimate revue, assembled by Dwight Deere Wiman. Lyrics and music by various contributors. Presented by Dwight Deere Wiman, in association with Tom Weatherly, at the Music Box Theater on June 1. Directed by Alexander Leftwich. Cast included Beatrice Lillie, Walter O'Keefe, Ernest Truex, and Constance Cummings (136 performances).*

In the early and middle 1920's, *The Grand Street Follies* and *The Garrick Gaieties* introduced a new approach and format to the revue. Simplicity and economy replaced elaborateness of setting and costuming and the large casts found in such revues as *The Ziegfeld Follies* and *George White's Scandals;* satire and parody were given preference over formal skits and sketches; sophistication and an adult intelligence were introduced into song, lyric, and dance. *The Little Show* became one of the most successful of these intimate revues, and it helped induce a vogue for this kind of entertainment on Broadway.

*The Little Show* developed out of informal Sunday-evening entertainments put on at the Selwyn Theater by James B. Pond and Tom Weatherly.

With the principal musical numbers supplied by Schwartz and most of the book and lyrics by Dietz, *The Little Show* was made into slick entertainment from opening to final curtain. And it helped to lift several unknown performers to recognition in the theater. One of them was Libby Holman. As an unknown chorus girl in *Merry-Go-Round* (1927), she was allowed to sing a featured number, Gorney's "Hogan Alley." A year later she was given a leading role in Vincent Youmans' operetta *Rainbow* (a box-office flop), in which she sang "I Want a Man." But in *The Little Show* she finally came into her own as a striking new torch singer, with her sultry, plangent renditions of blues songs.

Another newcomer was Fred Allen, onetime vaudeville juggler and ventriloquist, whose previous appearance on the Broadway stage, in *Polly* (1928), had done little to advance his career. In *The Little Show* he stopped the show nightly with his deadpan deliveries of wry monologues in a slow, rasping voice; from 1932 on, and for almost two decades, he would be one of the most brilliant and freshest comedians on radio.

Romney Brent (by no means an unknown in the theater when he first appeared in *The Little Show*) here tapped a new vein for himself by becoming a sophisticated comedian, particularly in a wry number satirizing motion-picture title songs, then so much in vogue—in "Hammacher-Schlemmer, I Love You," a hymn of praise to a business establishment in New York. Clifton Webb had long been a celebrity on the stage; but in *The Little Show* he reached new heights in his debonair and suave delivery of "I Guess I'll Have to Change My Plan," and in his sleek dance performance in "Moanin' Low."

"I Guess I'll Have to Change My Plan" was one of Schwartz' best numbers, but he had not written this melody for *The Little Show*. He had conceived it while working as a counselor in a boys' summer camp some years earlier, and Lorenz Hart, then also still unknown, had provided lyrics. At that time the song was called "I Love to Lie Awake in Bed." In *The Little Show* the title and lyrics were changed, but not the melody—to give Arthur Schwartz his biggest hit song up to that time. Two other Dietz-Schwartz numbers were most appealing: "I've Made a Habit of You" and "Little Old New York." But the most successful songs in *The Little Show* were not by Schwartz. "Moanin' Low" was by Ralph Rainger (a pianist in the orchestra pit), lyrics by Dietz. First Libby Holman sang it in its original key, then repeated the chorus in a lower range, to produce an altogether magical effect; that song lifted her to stardom. Once she was finished, Clifton Webb performed his dance wiith her in what Richard Lockridge described as "a mad grotesque." Another song made unforgettable by Libby Holman's rendition was "Can't We Be Friends?", by Kay Swift and Paul James, the latter a pseudonym for James Warburg, Kay's husband at the time.

The revue was studded with bright, sparkling sketches. One of the best was by George S. Kaufman, "The Still Alarm," in which some imperturbable firemen continue to play cards peacefully while the bells clang all around them, announcing a hotel fire nearby. A second sketch satirized advertisements designed to develop hidden personal charms and powers.

There were two more *Little Shows,* but neither managed to catch the verve and spontaneity of the original product, and both did poorly. The *Second Little Show* had an endearing little musical number by Herman Hupfeld, "Sing Something Simple," which was introduced by Ruth Tester. The *Third Little Show* starred Beatrice Lillie. A top attraction of this revue was Lillie's performance of Noël Coward's "Mad Dogs and Englishmen." The most popular song in this revue was "When Yuba Plays the Tuba," by Herman Hupfeld, introduced by Walter O'Keefe. Constance Cummings, supported by Carl Randall and a chorus of girls, sang "You Forgot Your Gloves" (by Edward Eliscu and Ned Lehak), which had some appeal. But it was Beatrice Lillie who had to carry the show virtually single-handed. Though she was at her comic best throughout the revue, she apparently was not enough to keep the revue on the boards for longer than 136 performances.

THE LITTLE TYCOON (1887), *a comic opera, with book, lyrics, and music by Willard Spencer. Presented at the Standard Theater in New York on March 29. Cast included R. E. Graham. Carrie M. Dietrich, and Joseph Mealy.*

Since it had no foreign derivation and since its authorship is exclusively American, *The Little Tycoon* is sometimes spoken of as the first American comic opera. It opened not in New York but in Philadelphia, where it enjoyed a run of five hundred performances before coming to New York's Standard Theater.

Aboard an ocean liner bound for the United States, General Knickerbocker (R. E. Graham) is eager to make a favorable match for his daughter, Violet (Carrie M. Dietrich), and chooses for her Lord Dolphin, one of the passengers. But Violet loves Alvin, an American. Back in America, Alvin comes to the Newport estate of General Knickerbocker, where he is ejected unceremoniously. But when he returns disguised as the Great Tycoon of Japan he is welcomed with pomp and ceremony. He is now able to win the general's consent to his marriage with Violet, who acquires from Alvin the honorary title of "the little tycoon."

The leading musical numbers were the title song, "On the Sea," "Doomed Am I to Marry a Lord," "Love Comes like a Summer Night," and "Sad Heart of Mine."

LOST IN THE STARS (1949), *a musical tragedy, with book and lyrics by Maxwell Anderson, based on Alan Paton's novel* Cry, the Beloved Country. *Music by Kurt Weill. Produced by the Playwrights Company at the Music Box Theater on October 30. Directed by Rouben Mamoulian. Cast included Todd Duncan, Inez Matthew, Leslie Banks, and Herbert Coleman (273 performances).*

*Lost in the Stars* was Kurt Weill's last score for the Broadway theater. He continued here what he had begun doing in his preceding musical, *Street Scene* (1947): to elevate the popular American musical theater to the status of musical drama. Indeed, he gave such dimension and scope to his orchestral, solo vocal, and choral writing that he considered *Lost in the Stars* an opera and not a Broadway musical play. The eminent music critic of *The New York Times* (Olin Downes) agreed with him, and so did the New York City Opera when it presented it in its operatic repertory during the spring season of 1958.

Like the novel from which it was derived, *Lost in the Stars* is stirring dramatic art, touching in its compassion and humanity, and inspiring in its promise of a better life of tolerance and human understanding.

The setting is the village of Ndotsheni in South Africa, of which the Reverend Stephen Kumalo (Todd Duncan) is the Negro preacher. He and his wife are pining for their son, Absalom (Julian Mayfield), from whom they had received no news since he had left for Johannesburg to earn money for his education. Fearful he might be in trouble, the two old people use their life savings to go to Johannesburg to seek Absalom out, but fail to locate him. For Absalom is living in the disreputable part of the town with his sweetheart, Irina, who is pregnant. In his compulsion to find money with which to support his future child, Absalom becomes a partner in a gang robbery, during which he kills a white man. A poignant commentary by the chorus remarks on the terror now seizing South Africa as a result of this crime.

Absalom is captured and imprisoned. He is visited in prison by his father, who in the title song is wondering if God had not abandoned him and his flock and who, in one of the most moving airs in the play ("O Tixo, O Tixo, Help Me"), implores God for assistance.

During the trial, Absalom's accomplices in the crime are acquitted, saved by their lies. Absalom, however, is condemned to die by hanging. The chorus now once again raises its voice in commentary—this time in a deeply moving episode bewailing the loss of a good man ("Cry, the Beloved Country").

Heartbroken, the old preacher Kumalo returns to Ndotsheni, where his flock delivers a poignant chant, "Bird of Passage," describing how man is born in and must die in darkness. Before Absalom is executed, the dead man's father comes to Kumalo to bring him pity and understanding in place of hate and vengeance. Their mutual disaster in losing their sons has made them brothers, even though they are of different races. Tragedy has united white man and black in a mutual bond of sympathy.

Music endows a human, and at times a profound, play with deeper overtones. Perhaps never before or since has the popular American stage boasted such moving choral music. The solo melodies (one is reluctant to refer to them as songs, so fluidly do they rise and then ebb back again into the dramatic situation) are no less expressive. The numbers listed in the above summary are among the most poetic and emotional. But other numbers help define character vividly, that of a honky-tonk entertainer Linda, for example, in "Who'll Buy?", and that of Irina in "Trouble Man."

LOUISIANA PURCHASE (1940), *a musical comedy, with book by Morrie Ryskind, based on a story by Buddy de Sylva. Lyrics and music by Irving Berlin. Produced by Buddy de Sylva at the Imperial Theater on May 28. Directed by Edgar MacGregor. Dances by George Balanchine and Carl Randall. Cast included William Gaxton, Victor Moore, Vera Zorina, and Irene Bordoni (444 performances).*

Senator Oliver P. Logansberry (Victor Moore) is sent down to New Orleans by the United States Senate to investigate the Louisiana Purchase Company and its slick and shady lawyer, Jim Taylor (William Gaxton). It did not require much snooping for the senator to uncover the high-handed deals taking place and the unsavory methods being employed. There was only one way to silence the troublesome senator, and that was by involving him in scandal and then blackmailing him into silence. The dancer Marina van Linden (Vera Zorina) and the vivacious flirt Mme. Bordelaise (Irene Bordoni) become partners in the business of undermining the senator's unimpeachable moral character. First he is wheedled by Marina into partaking of intoxicating drinks. When Marina manages to fall into the senator's lap, planted photographers snap his picture in this compromising·position. But the hapless senator manages to wriggle out of these intrigues and to emerge triumphant over the crooks.

The principal song is a ballad, "It's a Lovely Day Tomorrow," delivered by Mme. Bordelaise, who also contributes an amusing defense of Latin techniques in lovemaking in "Latins Know How." The senator and Marina share another intriguing ballad, "You're Lonely and I'm Lonely." To Carol Bruce, in a subsidiary though not insignificant role, is given two highly appealing numbers—the title song (which she shares with a male chorus) and a spiritual, "The Lord Done Fixed Up My Soul," the latter becoming the preface for an elaborate dance sequence. A delightful comic number, "Sex Marches On," is given by Jim Taylor, and another one by Victor Moore, "What Chance Have I?"

Despite the number of stars in the cast, *Louisiana Purchase* was basically Victor Moore's show—a fact realized by the motion-picture industry when it returned him to his role of the senator (Paramount, 1941). Vera Zorina and Irene Bordoni also repeated their stage roles. Bob Hope replaced William Gaxton as Jim Taylor.

LOVE LIFE (1948), *a musical comedy, with book and lyrics by Alan Jay Lerner. Music by Kurt Weill. Presented by Cheryl Crawford at the 46th Street Theater on October 7. Directed by Elia Kazan. Dances by Michael Kidd. Cast included Ray Middleton and Nanette Fabray (252 performances).*

The provocatively unusual text of *Love Life* carries Sam and Susan Cooper (Ray Middleton and Nanette Fabray) through a marriage that lasts from 1791 to 1948. Sam and Susan never grow a day older. But the marriage does —withered and desiccated and finally destroyed by greed and crass materialism.

*Love Life* is not only a study of marriage and a side glance at social mores. It is also a cavalcade of America from 1791 on. The story of America is told intriguingly through vaudeville acts, madrigal singers, crooners, magicians, vocal quartets. But the overall idea is perhaps more striking than its execution; individual numbers are perhaps more arresting than the play as a whole. This is also true of Weill's music, which is better for its parts than as a unified whole. One of his most famous songs appears here: "Green-Up Time," introduced by Susan. Other notable Weill numbers are "Here I'll Stay" (a duet by Susan and Sam) and "Mr. Right" (a duet by Susan and a minor character, played by Sylvia Stahlman).

THE LOVELY LADY (1927), *a musical comedy, with book by Gladys Unger and Cyrus Wood, based on the French farce* Déjeuner de soleil. *Lyrics by Cyrus Wood. Music by Dave Stamper and Harold Levey. Presented by the Shuberts at the Sam H. Harris Theater on December 29. Directed by J. C. Huffman. Dances by Dave Bennett. Chester Hale Dances arranged by*

*Mr. Hale. Cast included Edna Leedom, Guy Robertson, Frank Greene, Doris Patston, and Jack Sheehan (164 performances).*

The "lovely lady" is Folly Watteau (Edna Leedom), a rich, spoiled American girl on the loose in Paris. She falls in love with a svelte but penniless nobleman, Count Paul de Morlaix (Guy Robertson), and is being pursued by an English nincompoop, Lord Islington (Frank Greene). She finally gets the man she loves.

A dance-studded production was highlighted by the spirited jazz number "At the Barbecue," starring Eloise Bennett. A melodious score included the title song and "Make Believe You're Happy," both presented by Count Paul de Morlaix, together with "Lingerie," "Boy Friends," and "Ain't Love Grand."

MADAME SHERRY (1910), *an operetta, with book and lyrics by Otto Hauerbach (Harbach), adapted from George Edwardes' adaptation of a French vaudeville. Music by Karl Hoschna. Presented by Woods, Frazee, and Lederer at the New Amsterdam Theater on August 30. Directed by George W. Lederer. Cast included Ralph Herz, Lina Abarbanell, and Frances Demarest (231 performances).*

*Madame Sherry* is one of the most famous operettas in the era preceding World War I. Edward Sherry (Jack Gardner) tries to dupe his wealthy Uncle Theophilus (Ralph Herz) by passing off his Irish landlady, Catherine, as Madame Sherry (Elizabeth Murray). Her antics in trying to pass herself off as a grand lady provide a good deal of the comedy in the ensuing developments. At the same time, Edward Sherry presents Lulu (Frances Demarest) and her dancing pupils as his children. Most of the plot now is devoted to Theophilus' successful maneuvers in uncovering this deception through some ingenious detective work. He forgives his nephew, who by now is in love with his charming cousin, Yvonne Sherry (Lina Abarbanell), whom he decides to marry.

Hoschna's music was described by the editor of *Theatre* magazine as "the best native score since *Mlle. Modiste*." The hit song was a charmingly suggestive thing called "Every Little Movement," which was given a provocative treatment by two subsidiary characters, enacted by Florence Mackie and Jack Reinhard. But there were other musical pleasures, among them an "Afro-American" number (as the program described it), "Mr. Johnson, Good Night"; the infectious waltzes "Girl of My Dreams" and "The Birth of Passion"; and a ditty that amusingly disclosed the inebriated condition of

Theophilus, "I'm All Right." Notable dancing sequences were provided by Dorothy Jardonas, particularly in a solo Spanish number.

MADEMOISELLE (MLLE.) MODISTE (1905), *a comic opera, with book and lyrics by Henry Blossom. Music by Victor Herbert. Presented by Charles Dillingham at the Knickerbocker Theater on December 25. Directed by Fred G. Latham. Cast included Fritzi Scheff, William Pruette, Pauline Frederick, and Walter Percival (202 performances).*

The setting is Paris—in Mme. Cecile's hat shop on the Rue de la Paix, where Fifi (Fritzi Scheff) is employed. She and Captain Etienne de Bouvray (Walter Percival) are in love. Since Etienne's family objects, marriage is out of the question. An American millionaire, Hiram Bent (Claude Gillingwater), becomes interested in Fifi, who has a talent for singing. He finances her studies and her career until she becomes a famous prima donna. Under her stage name of Mme. Bellini, Fifi comes to sing at a charity affair at the De Bouvray castle. Her singing makes such a profound impression on Etienne's uncle, Count Henri de Bouvray (William Pruette), that he now allows his nephew to marry Fifi.

As Fifi, Fritzi Scheff soared to the heights in the American musical theater. Previously she had enjoyed only a moderately successful career at the Metropolitan Opera. Victor Herbert recognized her possibilities in the popular theater and lured her away from the Metropolitan by offering her one thousand dollars a week to appear in an operetta he wrote expressly for her—*Babette. Babette* (1903), a failure. But two years later, in her second Victor Herbert operetta—*Mlle. Modiste*—she was a triumph, particularly when she sang "Kiss Me Again," unquestionably the most celebrated single number in the score.

Many legends exist about the origin of that famous waltz. One has it that when Herbert first kissed Fritzi Scheff, after the premiere of *Babette,* she said to him, "Kiss me again," and an idea for a waltz was born. Another legend insisted that one hot summer night, as Herbert strolled in the garden of the Grand Union Hotel in Saratoga Springs, New York, he heard a woman asking her lover to kiss her again. Such stories are manufactured, but it is no legend that Herbert did not write this melody for *Mlle. Modiste.* He had completed it in 1903 and put it aside for future use. In preparing the score for *Mlle. Modiste,* Herbert wrote a first-act number called "If I Were on the Stage," in which Fifi proves her versatility by singing various types of songs—a gavotte, a polonaise, a dreamy waltz, and so forth, each being a caricature of that type of song. For the waltz part, Herbert reached back to the melody he had written in 1903, and intended it as a parody of sentimental waltzes. The audience liked this part so well that Herbert eventually had to write a new verse for the melody and present it as a sentimental waltz.

When Herbert first went through "Kiss Me Again" for Fritzi Scheff, she did not like it, insisting the tonal register was too low for her voice. Herbert was insistent that she sing it, and she finally consented. Her success with the waltz was of such magnitude that from that time on she and the song became inextricably associated.

There are other appealing numbers in this operetta, though they have been somewhat obscured by the enormous popularity of "Kiss Me Again." One is one of the best marches Herbert ever wrote, "The Mascot of the Troop," which contains a brief quotation from the "Marseillaise"; it is rendered by Fifi, assisted by a male chorus. Count Henri de Bouvray has an amusing piece, "I Want What I Want When I Want It"; this number became so thoroughly identified with William Pruette, who introduced it, that whenever he came to Rector's restaurant after the performance he would have to sing it to the restaurant patrons as they thumped their fists or glasses on the table to accentuate the word "Want" each time. No less effective in its humor is "The Time, the Place and the Girl," in which Etienne speaks of his disappointment in being unable to combine all three into a single blessed unity. In "The Nightingale and the Star," Fifi reveals her vocal artistry—and Fritzi Scheff as Fifi her operatic background and experience.

When First National made a movie out of *Mlle. Modiste* in 1931, it used the title of its great waltz hit, "Kiss Me Again." Herbert's score was used practically intact in a production starring Walter Pidgeon, June Collyer, and Bernice Clare.

MAKE MINE MANHATTAN (1948), *an intimate revue, with sketches and lyrics by Arnold Horwitt. Music by Richard Lewine. Presented by Joseph Hyman at the Broadhurst Theater on January 15. Directed by Hassard Short. Dances by Lee Sherman. Cast included Sid Caesar, David Burns, Jack Kilty, Kyle MacDonnell, and Sheila Bond* (429 performances).

The intimate revue was considered passé by 1948. Nevertheless, *Make Mine Manhattan* made the grade because, as *Variety* said of it, it was "a crowded entertainment of bubbling youth." Perhaps its greatest significance lay in the fact that it introduced Sid Caesar as one of the supreme comics of our time. Sid Caesar had previously worked as a musician in various jazz bands. Between 1942 and 1945 he served in the Coast Guard. It was during this period that he changed from a musician into a comedian—in the Coast Guard production *Tars and Spars,* directed by Max Liebman (it was also made into a movie in 1946). *Make Mine Manhattan* was his first appearance in "big time"; he stole the show. In his very first sketch, a satire on the UN, Caesar betrayed his extraordinary gift for caricature by assuming the identities of various UN delegates. In later sketches he appeared as a dentist in a hilarious travesty on the Rodgers and Hammerstein musical play *Allegro;* he narrated the trials and tribulations of a gum machine that grows up to be a quarter slot machine; he appeared as a customer trying to buy a fountain pen; he did a takeoff on critics and Hollywood producers. In the last two routines he was superbly assisted by David Burns.

*Make Mine Manhattan* also featured a beautiful song-and-dance fantasy, "Phil the Fiddler"; an effective production number following a cabbie, milk-man, street cleaner, and newsboy on their daily rounds, "Noises in the Street"; a fine romantic song in "I Don't Know His Name," presented by Jack Kilty and Kyle MacDonnell in a rooftop scene; and a good jitterbug number by Sheila Bond and Danny Daniels.

MAME (1966), *a musical comedy, with book by Jerome Lawrence and Robert E. Lee, based on Patrick Dennis' novel and play* Auntie Mame. *Lyrics and music by Jerry Herman. Presented by Fryer, Carr, and Harris at the Winter Garden on May 24. Directed by Gene Saks. Dances by Onna White. Cast included Angela Lansbury, Frankie Michaels, Beatrice Arthur, Jane Connell, and Willard Waterman (1,508 performances).*

Before *Mame* became one of the most successful musicals of the middle 1960's, it had (under the title of *Auntie Mame*) scored first as a novel, then as a Broadway play adapted by Jerome Lawrence and Robert E. Lee from the novel, and after that as a movie in 1958 starring Rosalind Russell. Em-bellished with songs, dances, beautiful settings, and a stunning performance by Angela Lansbury as Mame, it remained sure-fire entertainment. "It was," said the critic of *Variety,* "the whopping musical-comedy hit that everybody had been waiting for . . . a song and dance blockbuster."

The heroine, Mame, is, of course, that delightfully eccentric and boister-ous lady who suddenly inherits an orphaned nephew, Patrick Dennis. Some-how she must fit him into her own crazy scheme of life. The play traverses the years from 1928 to 1946, beginning with the last strident sounds of the roaring twenties, then carrying Mame and her nephew through the Depression and destitution. Better times come with Mame's marriage to a wealthy South-erner. Meanwhile, Patrick, grown into a young man, gets married to the right girl—after getting involved with the wrong one. By the time the play ends, in 1946, we see Mame beginning to direct her crazy ideas at Patrick's son.

This broad outline was probably familiar to most of those who went to see *Auntie Mame* in its latest reincarnation, the musical comedy *Mame.*

Despite the fact that the story was thus so familiar, the musical surprised most by being so excitingly new in details, so fresh in treatment, so thoroughly engaging in the many new approaches of the adapters. Take, for example, the first part, in which the twenties gets such a vigorous satirical treatment. "There is," as Henry Hewes wrote in *The Saturday Review,* "a delicious parody of the sort of production number that Broadway boasted in those days. In the cheesily celestial charade we are invited to regard the moon more romantically. To syrupy innocuous music, a showgirl reveals one of nature's secrets, singing 'Don't ever offend her, remember her gender, the man in the moon is a miss.' Take, too, the travesty on Southern chivalry both by the amount of manicure torture an enamored Southern gentleman eagerly makes light of and in the first-act cakewalk finale, 'Mame.' "

The musical opens with Patrick Dennis, aged ten (Frankie Michaels) come from Des Moines to New York to live with his aunt, Mame (Angela Lansbury). He arrives while a party is taking place in her penthouse apartment. This sort of wild party life to which Mame is addicted is, of course, not the sort of thing a boy should grow up with. And so, young Dennis is sent off for his schooling to St. Boniface in Massachusetts. When Mame is financially destroyed by the stock market crash, she tries to earn her living by acting in a musical, an effort that turns out disastrous. She takes on one job after another, until she meets the wealthy Southerner, Beauregard Jackson Picket Burnside (Charles Braswell), whose wealth carries to Mame a promise of relief from her problems. Having decided to celebrate Christmas early in December, she has Patrick come home for the weekend to receive his gifts, his first pair of long trousers. Beauregard takes Mame and Patrick out for a festive dinner. He is now deadly serious about marrying Mame, gains the necessary consent of his mother, and takes her off on a honeymoon. The years go by: Patrick has grown into young manhood (Jerry Lanning), Beauregard has been killed in the Alps. Mame, now a wealthy widow, must make a new life for herself in her swank Beekman Place apartment. She resumes her life as a "swinger," which disturbs Patrick. He is in love with Gloria (Diana Walker) a suburbanite with a head as light as the color of her hair. Patrick feels that the disgrace Mame is bringing to their name will ruin his romance. Mame, of course, has already taken full measure of this young lady and realizes that this is no wife for her nephew. She invites Gloria and her parents to dinner, acts up, then quietly announces she has bought the plot next door to build a prospective home for unwed mothers. Gloria's parents leave in a shocked state. Gloria's romance with young Patrick is—as Mame had carefully planned—on the rocks. But young

Patrick finds solace with Pegeen (Diane Coupe), with whom he is soon in love, and whom he ultimately marries.

World War II has come and gone. There is a new young Patrick in the Dennis household—the son of the older Patrick and Pegeen. Mame is planning a trip around the world, and she convinces the parents of the boy Patrick to allow the child to go along with her. The finale carries the following warning to the audience: "And so, if you read tomorrow that a glamorous American widow won a race on a mad water ox, then went on to a party for the Egyptian ambassador, where she served cheese blintzes, it will be Mame."

Angela Lansbury as Mame and Frankie Michaels as the first young Patrick were by no means the least of the strong assets of this musical. "The star vehicle deserves its star, and vice is very much versa," said Stanley Kaufmann in *The New York Times*. "Miss Lansbury is a singing-dancing actress. . . . In this marathon role she has wit, poise, warmth and a very taking coolth. The one visceral test, I suppose, is whether one is jealous of little Patrick growing up with an aunt like that. I was green." As for little Patrick, as played by Frankie Michaels: "I am sure that Miss Lansbury would be the first to assert how difficult her job would be with a lesser nephew."

The big song was, of course, the title number, introduced by Beauregard and the ensemble in the first-act finale (a number strongly reminiscent of the same composer's title song for *Hello, Dolly!*—and as effective as the older number had been within its context). Mame's song "If He Walked into My Life" and the duet of Mame and Patrick, "My Best Girl," had equally potent impact.

*Mame* received the Antoinette Perry Award as the best musical of the season.

MAN OF LA MANCHA (1965), *a musical play, with book by Dale Wasserman. Lyrics by Joe Darion. Music by Mitch Leigh. Presented by Albert W. Selden and Hal James at the Anta Washington Square Theater on November 22. Directed by Albert Marre. Dances by Jack Cole. Cast included Richard Kiley, Ray Middleton, Robert Rounseville, Irving Jacobson, and Joan Diener.*

If there was any kind of a stir when *Man of La Mancha* was first produced— and this performance took place at the Goodspeed Opera House in Connecticut before it came to New York—it was not felt ten yards from the theater. *Man of La Mancha* arrived in New York preceded by no sound of publicity bugles. The advance sale was niggardly. No recording company was interested in signing up the original-cast-album rights. Then came the ecstatic reviews, followed by word of mouth that this was not just another musical, but a masterpiece—the work of young men uncommonly gifted in the art of staging, choreography, and performances; of a librettist with an extraordinary imagination and originality; and of a composer whose talent more than measured up to the demands of his brilliant collaborators. What happened after that is stage history. *Man of La Mancha* received both the New York Drama Critics and the Antoinette Perry awards as the season's best musical. The original-cast recording, released by Kapp, became a best seller. The New York theater sold out for years: with the end of its New York run nowhere in sight, it had earned almost five million dollars by early 1970, returning to its backers a profit of well over 1,000 percent. It had in addition completed a five-million-dollar deal for the sale of the motion-picture and the sound-track-recording rights. Over two million copies of sheet music of its leading hits had been sold, possibly a record for a Broadway musical. All this while, companies were appearing in London, Paris, Mexico City, Belgium, Israel, Japan, and Australia and receiving rave reviews. The stars from each of these productions were eventually invited to take over the leading male role at different performances in New York, all performing in English. *Man of La Mancha* earned the additional rare distinction (for a Broadway musical) of being included into the opera reperatory—at the world-famous Komische Oper in East Berlin.

*Man of La Mancha* is the story of Don Quixote and coincidentally of its author, Cervantes—both become in the musical one and the same man, though in different circumstances. For Dale Wasserman had no intention of making a literal transfer of *Don Quixote* to a musical play. His aim, as he explained, was to capture "the spirit of its creator. I wanted to interweave and merge their identities. . . . Miguel Cervantes was Don Quixote." Wasserman further added that it was only a quotation from Manuel Unamuno that was his initial inspiration: "Only he who attempts the absurd is capable of achieving the impossible." Wasserman concludes: "In that quixotic spirit, the play was written." And, now to quote Howard Taubman's review: "As Dale Wasserman has written him, Albert Marre directed him, and Richard Kiley plays him, he [Don Quixote] is . . . a mad, gallant, affecting figure who has honestly materialized from the pages of Cervantes. . . . At its best it [*Man of La Mancha*] is audacious in its conception and tasteful in execution."

The play is given on a darkened stage without an intermission. (The orchestra players are split up into two sections, one half on either side of the stage.) A single set is used, but the ingenious use of various props manages to change the background in line with the demands of the text. "All the characters in the play," explains the program heading, "are imprisoned in a dungeon in Seville at the end of the sixteenth century. The entire action takes place there and in various other places in the imagination of Miguel de Cervantes."

Cervantes (Richard Kiley) and his manservant (Irving Jacobson) are imprisoned because, as a tax collector, Cervantes had foreclosed on a church for failure to pay taxes. The governor explains that Cervantes, like all others before him in this prison, must be tried by his fellow prisoners, and if found guilty, must surrender all his possessions. But all Cervantes owns is a few theatrical properties and a huge manuscript. Since Cervantes is allowed to speak on his own behalf, he entreats the prisoners to become his audience while he acts out his defense. He tells them he is now a country squire who aspires to be Don Quixote de La Mancha, a knight-errant, while his manservant becomes Sancho Panza. "I, Don Quixote," is the song with which Cervantes identifies himself as the knight-errant. The two jump upon wooden horses to seek adventure. In the distance, Don Quixote espies a windmill, which he takes to be an ogre. He rushes forth, returning tattered and bedraggled, insisting that an enchanter has transformed the ogre into a windmill. Indeed, he is convinced he will always be at the mercy of the enchanter unless he is formally dubbed a knight, a ritual that can be performed by the lord of a castle. And so Don Quixote and Sancho Panza go forth to find a castle. They come to a noisy inn, crowded with muleteers, who make provocative and at times obscene advances to Aldonza, a waitress (Joan Diener). To Don Quixote she is not the strumpet the others consider her, but a fair lady, as he romantically serenades her in "Dulcinea." Later on, he sends Sancho into the kitchen with a love letter to his lady, beseeching her to present him with one of her personal tokens to serve him as a charm in battle. Aldonza throws a dirty dish rag at him, which to Don Quixote becomes a wondrous silken scarf. Don Quixote now entreats a padre to crown him with a golden helmet (actually a brass shaving basin), to which he attaches Aldonza's rag. He then insists that the innkeeper—whom he now looks upon as the lord of a castle—perform the ceremony dubbing him a knight.

Don Quixote is a mystery to Aldonza, since she cannot understand what he is after and what he wants from her. Don Quixote insists that all he wants is to serve her, to fight battles for her, to give up his life for her if need be. When Aldonza is more puzzled than ever, Don Quixote explains that what is most important to him, a knight, is the quest, whether one emerges from it victorious or not. He goes on to explain further what he means in the most memorable song in the production, "The Quest," or "The Impossible Dream." He finishes by telling Aldonza that when he looks at her what he sees is beauty and purity, that she is his Dulcinea.

Without any warning, the muleteers engage in a free-for-all in which Don Quixote gets involved, and from which he emerges limping and wounded —but victorious. Having gained a major victory, Don Quixote feels he now deserves to be knighted. The innkeeper dutifully goes through the mock ceremony, dubbing him Knight of the Woeful Countenance. Aldonza now comes to try to help some of the wounded muleteers. One of them seizes her, then another. In an extraordinary ballet sequence—one of the most gripping episodes in the production—she is seduced by each of the muleteers. To Don Quixote all this represents only an effort on the part of the muleteers to rob his Dulcinea of her magic healing powers. He repeats his vow to dream the impossible dream.

The prison scene finds the men of the Inquisition come to seize and drag away one of the men. Cervantes continues with his story, as he slowly recalls his chant, "I, Don Quixote."

Don Quixote and Sancha Panza are again off for adventure. They come to a gypsy camp. One of the girls tries to seduce him, but to Don Quixote she is the daughter of an African lord, who has been captured and is being held for ransom. Don Quixote gives the girl money to free the lord, after which the gypsies proceed to rob him.

He and his manservant return to the inn destitute. Aldonza, who has been off with a muleteer, is also back—her clothes tattered, her flesh bruised. To Don Quixote she remains his lovely Dulcinea, even though she entreats him to see her as she really is—a slut. With a fanfare of trumpets, a huge knight appears, come to challenge Don Quixote for being a pretender. He is the Knight of the Mirrors; one side of his shield is a mirror which reveals to the person looking into it what he really is. The huge knight orders Don Quixote to look into the mirror and see himself for what he is—a madman, a fool. When Don Quixote falls to the ground weeping, Aldonza rushes to him with pity. Neither of them knows that the knight is Dr. Carrasco in disguise, sent by the squire's niece to effect a cure, to rid the squire of his delusion that he is Don Quixote, a knight.

Within the prison, the captain of the Inquisition warns Cervantes that his time is running out; Cervantes must now finish his defense.

Don Quixote is in a coma, being tended by Sancho Panza, who tries to bring his master back to consciousness with small talk. Recovering from that coma, Don Quixote tells his man that he, Don Quixote, is near death, and must make out his will. Aldonza makes a sudden appearance, but Don Quixote does not recognize her. She reminds him she is his Dulcinea, recalls to him his need to dream the impossible dream. As Aldonza kneels before him, Don Quixote begins to repeat his song, "The Quest." Suddenly he feels momentarily revived. He is Don Quixote, who demands that his sword and armor be given him so that he may set forth for further adventures. But a moment later he collapses and dies. Sancho Panza pronounces him dead, but Aldonza refuses to believe it, just as she now insists that her name is not Aldonza but Dulcinea.

The captain of the Inquisition and his hooded men have come back to the prison to drag Cervantes and his manservant away. As they slowly ascend the steps out of the prison, we hear Aldonza singing "The Quest," in which all the others soon join.

Before *Man of La Mancha,* composer Mitch Leigh had been represented on Broadway with incidental music for two plays, *Too True to Be Good* (1963) and *Never Live over a Pretzel Factory* (1964), both failures. He was born in Brooklyn, New York, on January 30, 1928, and received his Bachelor and Master of Arts degrees from Yale University, where he studied comprosition with Paul Hindemith. He subsequently founded and served as president and creative director of Music Makers, which specialized in singing or musical commercials. It was an exceptionally successful venture, capturing virtually every major award radio and television could offer. Leigh combined this lucrative commercial venture with more serious endeavors at composition, ranging from jazz to opera. *Man of La Mancha* was his first musical, thus launching his career in the profesional theater with a triumph of the first magnitude.

His lyricist, Joe Darion, had previously been heard only once on the Broadway stage. This was when a popular adaptation of his opera *Archy and Mehitabel* was produced in 1957 as *Shinbone Alley,* for which he wrote book and lyrics in collaboration with Mel Brooks. Darion was born in New York City on January 30, 1917, and attended the College of the City of New York. After serving in the armed forces during World War II, he turned to songwriting. In 1953 he produced a number of hits that sold several million records: "Ricochet," with Larry Coleman and Norman Gimbel; "Changing Partners," with Larry Coleman; and "The Ho Ho Song," the TV theme song of Red Buttons, written in collaboration with Buttons and Jack Wolf. It took Darion more than a decade after that to duplicate his Tin Pan Alley successes in the musical theater, which he did so decisively with *Man of La Mancha.*

MARY (1920), *a musical comedy, with book and lyrics by Otto Harbach and Frank Mandel. Music by Louis A. Hirsch. Presented by George M. Cohan at the Knickerbocker Theater on October 18. Directed by Julian Mitchell, George M. Cohan, and Sam Forrest. Cast included Jack McGowan, James Marlowe, Janet Velie, Georgia Caine, and Charles Judels* (219 *performances*).

*Mary* was the kind of sweet, sentimental, and wholesome musical comedy for which George M. Cohan was famous, even though his only association with it was as a producer. Jack Keane (Jack McGowan) hopes to rehabilitate his family fortune in Kansas by building cheap homes known as "love nests." The land which he purchases for this venture has oil. Thus Jack suddenly becomes a wealthy man. He now realizes that he is in love with simple, wholesome Mary Howells (Janet Velie) and not the seductive widow he has thus far been pursuing.

If any single element was responsible for the success of *Mary,* it was neither the story nor any of the performers—but the song "Love Nest," which appeared as a recurrent leitmotif throughout the play. It is first heard as a solo by Jack, then as a duet by Jack and Mary, as a choral number, and in a variety of other guises. The title song, "Anything You Want to Do, Dear," "Every Time I Meet a Lady," and "Waiting" were some of the other numbers. "Love Nest," a quarter of a century later, became the radio and after that the TV theme song of Burns and Allen.

> MAYTIME (1917), *an operetta, with book and lyrics by Rida Johnson Young and Cyrus Wood. Music by Sigmund Romberg. Presented by the Shuberts at the Shubert Theater on August 16. Directed by Edward F. Temple. Dances by Allen K. Foster. Cast included Peggy Wood, Charles Purcell, and William Norris (492 performances).*

After the success of *The Blue Paradise,* Romberg determined to devote himself to writing music for the European kind of operetta in preference to the American revues and extravaganzas assigned him by the Shuberts. In 1916 he decided to part company with the Shuberts and try to find projects more suited to his talents. J. J. Shubert urged him to reconsider, promising to try to find for Romberg a book that would lend itself to operetta treatment. Shubert kept his word and early in 1917 turned over to the composer *Maytime,* a European operetta adapted for the American stage by Rida Johnson Young.

*Maytime* became one of the most successful operettas of the Broadway stage, a triumph that firmly set Romberg's reputation as a composer of operettas. It was such a box-office attraction that within a year a second company opened in a nearby playhouse to accommodate the demand for seats— one of the rare occasions that a musical had two productions running simultaneously on Broadway.

It is quite true that Rida Johnson Young's text used an American setting and American characters. The ingredients may be American, but the overall dish remained an authentic Viennese, or at least European, operetta concoction, both in the sentimentality and romance of the story and in the kind of *gemütlich* music Romberg wrote for it. Its sentimental plot involved the frustrated love affair of Ottilie van Zandt (Peggy Wood) and Richard Wayne (Charles Purcell), carrying them from 1840 to the end of the century. Also involved in the story was a deed to a mansion owned by Richard's father but which he had to turn over to Colonel van Zandt in payment of a long-standing debt. At the old Washington Square home of the Van Zandts, Ottilie and Richard come upon the deed in the garden, blown there through the window of the colonel's study. They bury it in the garden in a box containing a ring, and while doing so pledge eternal love. Fifteen years later Ottilie is compelled to marry Claude, a distant relative and a gambler. He dies, leaving Ottilie penniless. Richard, still in love with her, buys the mansion when it is put up on auction and deeds it to Ottilie without disclosing that he is the benefactor. At the turn of the century the mansion becomes a dress shop managed by Ottilie's granddaughter. Richard's grandson is in love with the girl, and it is the third generation that finds the happiness that had been denied to the grandparents.

Although Peggy Wood had been appearing on the Broadway musical stage since 1910—when she had appeared in the chorus of *Naughty Marietta* —and had been seen since in various operettas either on the road or as a replacement on Broadway, it was only with the role of Ottilie that she became a musical-comedy star. To her was assigned the hit song of *Maytime* —a number tha tran throughout the play as a kind of leitmotif, the waltz, "Will You Remember?", which she first sang as a duet with Richard, and which at the end of the play is repeated for the last time by Richard's and Ottilie's respective grandchildren. Other popular numbers include another romantic duet by Ottilie and Richard, "The Road to Paradise," and two lighter numbers: "Jump Jim Crow," a modernized version of a minstrel-show favorite routine; and "Dancing Will Keep You Young."

Only three numbers from the stage score—including of course the popular "Will You Remember?"—were used when *Maytime* became a motion picture (MGM, 1937) starring Nelson Eddy and Jeanette MacDonald. Otherwise, this production used some new numbers by Robert Wright, George "Chet" Forrest, and Herbert Stothart.

MAY WINE (1935), *a musical play, with book by Frank Mandel, based on* The Happy Alienist, *a novel by Wallace Smith and Erich von Stroheim. Lyrics by Oscar Hammerstein II. Music by Sigmund Romberg. Presented by Laurence Schwab at the St. James Theater on December 5. Directed by José Ruben. Cast included Walter Slezak, Nancy McCord, and Walter Woolf King (213 performances).*

Psychoanalysis is here subjected to musical-comedy treatment. In Vienna the psychiatrist Professor Johann Volk (Walter Slezak) falls in love with Marie, Baroness von Schlewitz (Nancy McCord). The baroness, however, loves a poor but high-born gentleman, Baron Kuno Adelhorst (Walter Woolf King). The psychiatrist marries the baroness, but his assistant soon fills him with doubts about his wife's fidelity. As an escape from his mental torment, Professor Volk turns to drink. In a fit of madness he shoots at a figure he believes to be his wife but which is only a dummy. The professor's fears prove completely groundless, and he and his wife are reconciled.

The authors made a notable effort to integrate music and play. Brooks Atkinson noted that the "excrescences and stock appurtenances" of most operettas were here avoided. Mr. Atkinson added: "To some extent they [the authors] have succeeded. . . . But the operetta has certain plodding mannerisms that dull the fine edge of appreciation." Percy Hammond, however, found it to be a "dignified little grand opera," and Gilbert Gabriel felt it was "one of those fragrant and tasty concoctions which, poured in one ear, warms the affections and tickles the humors considerably before it flies out of the other."

Two notable songs were by Marie, "Dance, My Darlings" and "Somebody Ought to Be Told." "I Built a Dream" and "Just Once Around the Clock" were two delightful vocal trios. Several dance routines by Jack Cole and Alice Dudley added to the charm of the production.

ME AND JULIET (1953), *a musical comedy, with book and lyrics by Oscar Hammerstein II. Music by Richard Rodgers. Presented by Rodgers and Hammerstein at the Majestic Theater on May 28. Directed by George Abbott. Dances by Robert Alton. Cast included Isabel Bigley, Bill Hayes, and Joan McCracken (358 performances).*

In 1952 there had taken place the highly successful revival of the Rodgers and Hart musical *Pal Joey.* Preparing that revival awakened in Rodgers a nostalgia for the musical theater of a bygone day, a theater which he and Hammerstein had helped to change through their musical plays *Oklahoma!, Carousel, South Pacific,* and *The King and I.* He suggested to Hammerstein that, as a change of pace, they try their hand at "musical comedy" rather than a musical play. Rodgers further outlined an idea he had nursed for some time: a musical comedy that would be set in a theater and would reveal the inner mechanism of a musical show and the people it involves.

*Me and Juliet* turned out to be a compromise between old ways and new. It was a musical comedy, not far different from the kind Rodgers used to write with Hart. But it also incorporated some of the new ideas, techniques, and approaches he had explored with Hammerstein in integrating plot, music, and dance.

The text was made up of two love themes running contrapuntally. Two timid people of the theater—Jeanie, a chorus girl (Isabel Bigley), and Larry, an assistant manager (Bill Hayes)—are in love, but they are terrorized by an electrician, Bob (Mark Dawson), who is also in love with Jeanie. At one point Bob tries to murder both Jeanie and Larry. A lighter plot involves a dancer, Betty (Joan McCracken), and a stage manager, Mac (Ray Walston). Mac's principle is never to become emotionally involved with anybody working for him. Jeanie and Larry get married secretly in spite of Bob's heavy-handed attempts to break up their romance. And Mac is able to marry Betty and yet remain true to his principles by joining up with another show.

As the story unfolds, the play shifted swiftly from an electrician's bridge to the orchestra pit; from the dressing room to the smoking room; onstage and backstage; into the company manager's office and to a candy counter during intermission; in a back alley outside the theater during an actual performance or audition. What Rodgers and Hammerstein were trying to do was to infect audiences with their own love and enthusiasm for the theater. But as Walter Kerr pointed out: "Like a lot of lovers bent on declaring their passion, the authors strike a point at which they become tongue-tied. They want to say so much, they want to say it burstingly, they want to be sure that no heartfelt endearment is omitted anywhere, that they wind up gasping for breath, and making slightly disconnected sounds."

Individual parts of the play were fascinating, and the action moved so swiftly that interest never lagged. But all the ingredients never quite added up to a single dish.

Rodgers' score in many instances reverted to the styles of a former era, particularly in the hit song, a tango presented as a duet for Larry and Jeanie, "No Other Love." This song was lifted by Rodgers from his own score for the documentary film *Victory at Sea*. Three vivacious numbers— "Keep It Gay," "We Deserve Each Other," and "It's Me"—were the kind of bright, sophisticated pieces Rodgers used to write so well for Larry Hart's lyrics. On the other hand, an extended narrative about theater audiences, "The Big, Black Giant," delivered by Larry, and an extended sequence about show business called "Intermission Talk" were in the vein of the kind of musical playwriting for which Rodgers and Hammerstein had previously become so famous.

A brief revival of *Me and Juliet* by the Equity Library at the Master Institute in New York in May of 1970 failed to convince the critics that they had underestimated the musical when it was first produced. In 1970 as in 1953, *Me and Juliet* represented to them a minor Rodgers and Hammerstein musical that will never be missed.

MEET THE PEOPLE (1940), *an intimate revue, with book by Henry Myers. Sketches by Edward Eliscu, Milt Gross, and others. Music by Jay Gorney and George Bassman. Presented by the Hollywood Alliance at the Mansfield Theater on December 25. Directed by Danny Dare. Cast included Jack Gilford, Nanette Fabares (Nanette Fabray), Marion Colby, and Joey Faye (160 performances).*

*Meet the People* originated in Hollywood on December 25, 1939, at a modest outlay of 3,600 dollars. It was a "topical revue," so refreshing in its originality and so brash in its satire that it stayed on in California for about a year, passing through three editions. It then came for a short run to Chicago and, a little over a year after its birth in California, reached Broadway.

Its incisive social viewpoints, sardonic commentaries on the political scene, and devastating attacks on current foibles were a delight. "Let's Steal a Tune from Offenbach" laughed gaily at the prevailing Tin Pan Alley practice of stealing melodies from the classics. "It's the Same Old South" was a barbed commentary on Southern bigotry. "Union Label" pointed up social consciousness, and "The Bill of Rights" and "Senate in Session" were gay asides on the facts of life of the political scene. Torch songs were satirized in a flat, deadpan rendtion by Marion Colby.

Besides being a source of not-so-innocent merriment, *Meet the People* proved to be the incubator for future stars for the Broadway stage. The most important of these were Nanette Fabray (still passing under her original name of Nanette Fabares) and Jack Gilford—both unknowns when the revue first hit Broadway.

The two outstanding songs, both by Henry Myers and Jay Gorney, were "The Stars Remain" (introduced by Beryl Carew, Robert Davis, Marie De Forest, and Marion Colby) and "In Chi-Chi-Castenango" (introduced by Josephine Del Mar, Robert Davis, and Doodles Weaver).

MEXICAN HAYRIDE (1944), *a musical comedy, with book by Herbert and Dorothy Fields. Lyrics and music by Cole Porter. Presented by Mike Todd at the Winter Garden on January 28. Directed by Hassard Short and John Kennedy. Dances by Paul Haakon. Cast included June Havoc, Bobby Clark, Wilbur Evans, and George Givot (481 performances).*

When *Mexican Hayride* opened out of town, Cole Porter did not have much hope for its success. In fact, he thought the show simply awful, "with forty-five minutes of unadulterated boredom which we are now trying to eliminate," as he wrote to a friend. "The only really great thing about the opus is the production, which is out of this world. But after all, it would really help us quite a lot if we had the show billed as 'Scenery and Costumes of *Mexican Hayride.*' " Some of those dull moments were deleted, but as Cole Porter put it tersely: "That thing, *Mexican Hayride,* still stinks."

A skillfully contrived publicity campaign created the impression in New York that *Mexican Hayride* was a smash success out of town. As a result, the advance sale at the Winter Garden was several hundreds of thousands of dollars. Much to Cole Porter's amazement, most of the critics liked the musical a good deal—especially the slapstick clowning of Bobby Clark and June Havoc's gift with a comic line and situation as well as her charm and talent with a song or a dance. This combined with Cole Porter's songs—and the sumptuous sets and costuming about which Cole Porter raved—made for good box office. *Mexican Hayride* stayed on for almost five hundred performances—which, for 1944, was a run about which even Cole Porter could be thoroughly contented.

A Mexican setting, a lady bullfighter from the United States, and a screwball American fugitive from justice were the material which Herbert and Dorothy Fields fashioned into a serviceable, though hardly inspired, libretto.

The American fugitive from justice is Joe Bascom, alias Humphrey Fish (Bobby Clark); the American lady bullfighter is Montana (June Havoc). In the Plaza de Toros, after her successful tussle with the bull, Montana is about to throw the bull's ear to David Winthrop, the American *chargé d'affaires.* Mexican tradition dictated that he who catches the ear becomes the government's honored guest for a full week. On suddenly catching a glimpse of Joe (who is her relative), Montana gets so upset that she forgets herself and throws the ear at him. Thus Joe is destined for the honors—honors and adulation he is trying to elude in order not to attract attention to himself. But Joe submits to the inevitable. He will stay out the week and hope for the best. He meets a shady speculator, Lombo Campos (George Givot), with whom he concocts a scheme for an unauthorized lottery. The venture is successful until the Mexican government track down Joe and Lombo. They manage to escape. David Winthrop now falsely accuses Montana not only of being involved in this lottery operation but also of being a member of the crooked gang.

The second act takes place at Xochimilco, where natives and tourists are enjoying the sights. Joe and Campos come here disguised as mariachi performers. Montana, determined to clear herself, joins David in pursuing them. When they catch sight of Joe, he once again manages to flee. Then Joe and Campos come to Taxco disguised as tortilla vendors. They are finally caught and returned to their respective governments to stand trial. By this time David has become convinced that Montana is innocent, and their romance is revived.

Cole Porter's own favorite among his numbers was "Sing to Me, Guitar," music with a strong Mexican flavor, introduced by Corinna Maura, in a subsidiary role. Montana has an effective song in "There Must Be Someone for Me" and she participates with Joe and Campos in a number that usually stopped the show, "Count Your Blessings."

The most significant love ballad was called simply "I Love You," David's love song to Montana. Cole Porter wrote it on a twenty-five-dollar bet with Monty Woolley, who had insisted that Porter was good only with esoteric subjects, but given an everyday title and an everyday theme he would be out of his depth. Porter took on the wager, chose the most obvious title he could think of, and proceeded to write a set of lyrics filled with clichés. Nevertheless, he did manage to produce a soaring melody that made this song a standout hit, one that occupied the top spot of the Hit Parade for several weeks running.

When a movie was made out of *Mexican Hayride*—a Universal production in 1948 starring Abbott and Costello—the entire Cole Porter score was dispensed with, even "I Love You."

MICHAEL TODD'S PEEP SHOW (1950), *a revue, with sketches by Bobby Clark, H. I. Phillips, William Roos, and Billy K. Wells. Lyrics by Bob Hilliard, Herb Magidson, and others. Music by Sammy Fain, Jule Styne, Harold Rome, and others. Presented by Michael Todd at the Winter Garden on June 28. Cast included Lina Romay, Lily Christine, Bozo Snyder, and Peanuts Mann (278 performances).*

In 1942 Michael Todd—an unconventional showman if ever there was one— made a move to revive burlesque in New York by putting it within the context of a Broadway revue. He called his production *Star and Garter*. If the venture had originally been a gamble, it proved one that paid off handsomely—to the tune of more than six hundred performances on Broadway. What he had done once, he felt he could do again. And so, eight years later, Michael Todd put on *Michael Todd's Peep Show,* another attempt to carry burlesque into the Broadway musical theater.

Actually his original plan was to combine vaudeville with burlesque. There were quite a number of good vaudeville routines in his *Peep Show*. One was "Cocktails at Five," a takeoff on T. S. Eliot's sophisticated *The Cocktail Party;* another was Harold Rome's sketch, "I Hate a Parade." Then there was a ballad, "Blue Night," whose interest—and publicity value —rested in the fact that it was the creation of the King of Siam, no less.

But it was the burlesque parts that brought the crowds to the Winter Garden. Seven well-known burlesque comedians were distributed in various suggestive skits, blackouts, and rowdy slapstick episodes—all directed by that hardy veteran of burlesque and musical comedy, Bobby Clark. They were Bozo Snyder, Peanuts Mann, Hi Wilberforce Conley, Red Marshall, Loony Lewis, Spike Hamilton, and Dick (Gabby) Dana. One typical burlesque sketch was "Love Nest," another, "Friendly Neighbors," whose *double entendres* and suggestive gestures brought back vividly memories of the happy time when burlesque was in its heyday.

But Mike Todd was too shrewd a showman not to recognize that the basic ingredient of burlesque, for audiences in 1950, was not slapstick humor— but girls and sex. He went to town on both. From New Orleans he brought in a young lady, Lily Christine, whose slithering body as it went through a strip-tease brought her the billing of "The Cat Girl." Her exhibition was *sui generis*—even more provocative than the genuine article, once the prime exhibit of old burlesque shows. Her strip-tease, and the way in which she performed the bumps and grinds, proved so suggestive that after the opening night of the *Peep Show* a representative from the New York City Commission of Licenses warned Todd he would close down the show if she did not tone down her act. A tone-down Lily Christine was still torrid stuff, not only in her strip-tease routine but also in the finale of the show, where she did a shimmy in a production number called "Gimme the Shimmy," after it had been sung by Lina Romay.

Sex was also exploited in the first-act finale, in which forty-eight chorus girls took a bath on the stage, their nudity covered by soap bubbles. (It cost Michael Todd $36,000 to get the right formula for bubbles that would not irritate the skin of the girls and cause it to itch.) In fact, sex was omnipresent in all the production numbers in which the girls appeared. The costumes they wore consisted of "three strategically placed clusters of rhinestones," as Art Cohn informs us, "a wisp of tulle and a navel stone." One of the best of these numbers was "Violins from Nowhere" (by Herb Magidson and Sammy Fain), introduced by Art Carroll. In another number, they sang "you've never been loved, until you've been loved, below the border." Provocative and tantalizing to sex appetites though all this was, the show would have boasted an even more sizzling act in a dance by Corinne and Tito Valdez, had not the out-of-town censors compelled Todd to remove it from the show before it came to New York.

The critics took note of these burlesque escapades. John Chapman called Mike Todd "a gaudy, bawdy stag smoker." Walter Winchell reported that "the only one in it [the show] who wears clothes is Michael Todd." *Life* talked about the "acres and acres of girls swaying like ripe corn in summer, all with hip bones loose in their sprockets so that they cannot dance or walk or even stand without going in what they call bumps and grinds."

The score was nondescript, with the best number being "Stay with the Happy People" (by Hilliard and Styne), sung by Lina Romay and ensemble.

MILK AND HONEY (1961), *a musical comedy, with book by Don Appell. Lyrics and music by Jerry Herman. Presented by Gerard Oestreicher at the Martin Beck Theater on October 10. Directed by Albert Marre. Dances by Donald Saddler. Cast included Robert Weede, Mimi Benzell, and Molly Picon (543 performances).*

*Milk and Honey* was the first American musical set in present-day Israel—a land overflowing not merely with milk and honey but also with American tourists. Once Don Appell and Jerry Herman hit upon the happy idea of doing a musical about Israel—and once they had found the necessary backing —they spent several months in that country soaking up local color. They met up with such picturesque characters as Hasidim, Israeli Arabs, farmers from kibbutzim, sabras, and absorbed the varied sights offered by modern-day cities and little biblical towns, the Negev, the Galilee district, and so forth. It became obvious that they had plenty of material to work with.

In place of writing a show in which the main characters were Israeli, they worked out a plot involving American tourists. As tourists they help celebrate Independence Day, attend a colorful Yemenite wedding, visit and stay at a kibbutz (collective farm) in the Negev, are witnesses to Israeli folk dances. Actually the writers were more concerned in making their main point of interest the country itself rather than their characters. Israel, with its exciting contrasts, comes into full view, bursing with vitality and energy, quivering with the promise of a new life and exalted with the fulfillment of an age-old ideal.

A slender plot provides the excuse for this stage travelogue. The curtain rises on a morning scene in Jerusalem. Phil (Robert Weede), an American tourist, meets another tourist, Ruth Stein (Mimi Benzell). Unlike Ruth, Phil speaks Hebrew, thus is able to explain to her the full meaning of the Israeli greeting "Shalom." From time to time after that Phil and Ruth keep meeting up with one another. They enjoy the celebration of Independence Day, particularly when the Israelis perform an exciting hora. As the friendship of Phil and Ruth deepens, he becomes troubled by the fact that he is a married man, although separated from his wife for years. His daughter, Barbara (Lanna Saunders), has no such qualms, and does not hesitate to invite her father and Ruth to visit a kibbutz in the Negev, where Barbara has been making her home with David (Tommy Rall). Phil's enthusiasm for Israel grows in the kibbutz to the point where he considers the possibility of remaining in Israel for good, building a home near the kibbutz and spending there the rest of his days with Ruth. A group of American tourists now comes to visit this same kibbutz, one of whom is Clara Weiss (Molly Picon), who hopes to find a husband in Israel.

Barbara insists that her father reveal to Ruth his marital status, which he does reluctantly, while entreating her not to leave him. Ruth is torn by doubts and inner torments. Nevertheless, while attending a Yemenite wedding with Phil, she gives way to her emotions and accepts Phil's love and his proposition to live with him in his new house.

In the spirit of an Israeli pioneer, Phil begins to work his fields, contented with his new life in this new country. But his happiness is short-lived. Tormented by her conscience, Ruth has deserted him and returns to Tel Aviv. Phil follows her there, meets Clara at a café, and is unsuccessful in trying to draw from her the information where Ruth can be found. Clara meanwhile has met an American widower, Mr. Horowitz, in whom she has become interested. Despite Horowitz' hesitation about getting married again, it is not long before Clara's persistence wears down his doubts, and he proposes to her.

Ruth returns to the kibbutz, convinced that her place is with Phil. Now it is Phil who is conscience-stricken, compelled by his inner honesty to advise Ruth to leave him until he is free to marry her. At the airport, Phil bids Ruth a tender farewell, promising to get his divorce as soon as he can. For both of them the experience of separation is heartbreaking as Ruth boards the plane—Ruth left with only the lingering hope that somehow, someday, she and her beloved Phil will be reunited. Clara, however, has found happiness with Sol. And David, convinced that his wife, Barbara, is really homesick, stands ready for her sake to leave Israel for America.

Comic relief is provided by that grand lady who had been the darling of the Yiddish musical theater for half a century—Molly Picon. In her inimitable way she explains that it's nice having a husband because if you wake up in the middle of the night and want a glass of water there's somebody to get it for you. Her performance was described by *Variety* as "a sort of

Jewish combination of Helen Hayes and Ethel Merman" who just about "makes away with the audience in the juicy comedy, singing and dancing the role of a schmaltzy American widow who snares a husband." Nobody could steal the show from her—not even such sturdy professionals as Robert Weede and Mimi Benzell (both of them former stars of the Metropolitan Opera). But one young man almost did. He was Tommy Rall, whose singing, dancing, and infectious personality thoroughly captured the hearts of his audiences.

*Milk and Honey* was Jerry Herman's first completed score for a Broadway show. He proved himself a slick professional. The official greeting in Israel becomes the title of the show's main hit song, "Shalom," heard at the beginning of the musical as a duet between Phil and Ruth, then returning in the finale, repeated by the same characters, supplemented by the entire ensemble. The title number, another song hit, was introduced by David, his friend Adi (played by Juki Arkin), and the company. Other attractive musical numbers included "That Was Yesterday" (Ruth, Phil, Adi, and company); David's song, "I Will Follow You," when he realizes that his wife is homesick for America; and Phil's song, "There's No Reason in the World." "Independence Day Hora" provides a fitting musical background for the best dance sequence.

MINNIE'S BOYS (1970), *a musical comedy with book by Arthur Marx and Robert Fisher. Lyrics by Hal Hackady. Music by Larry Grossman. Presented by Arthur Whitelaw, Max J. Brown, and Byron Goldman at the Imperial Theater on March 26. Directed by Stanley Prager. Dances by Marc Breaux. Production consultant, Groucho Marx. Cast included Shelley Winters, Lewis J. Stadlen, Irwin Pearl, Daniel Fortus, Alvin Kupperman, and Julie Kurnitz.*

*Minnie's Boys* are the four Marx Brothers—Groucho, Chico, Harpo, and Zeppo—whose irreverent, madcap, unpredictable shenanigans on stage and screen have made them something of a cult. (They are represented in this volume in three of their Broadway stage successes—*I'll Say She Is, The Cocoanuts,* and *Animal Crackers.*) And Minnie is their hard-driving, persevering Jewish stage mother who, faced with a brood with no visible talent for anything that might some day earn them a livelihood, was determined to find for them a place in the theater. And *Minnie's Boys* is a musical about the early hectic life of mother and sons (there is a fifth son, Gummo, who never made it on the stage) as they struggle to advance their early careers in show business, progressing from one flea-bitten boarding house to the next (usually skipping out without paying the bill) as they traveled to one-horse towns with broken-down vaudeville houses. The musical ends just at the point where the boys, having finally established their stage personalities and adopted their stage costumes, are about to make the grade.

With Groucho's son Arthur, as a collaborator on the text, and with Groucho himself serving as a production consultant, the text can be expected to have authenticity. More or less authentic it is, if we can use the various biographies of the Marx Brothers as sources. There was no attempt to make this musical another Marx Brothers escapade; no attempt to drag into it any of the lines or idiotic goings-on and mannerisms which the Marx Brothers made so famous. This may very well be the reason why some of the critical reaction was comparatively lukewarm; those critics probably came to the theater expecting a Marx Brothers carnival, which *Minnie's Boys* had no intention of becoming. There are, of course, a number of episodes that give us a clue of things to come: Groucho diverting the landlady while the other Marxes make a strategic withdrawal from their boarding house through the back door with their trunks; the boys making a bonfire in the wastebasket of their hateful employer and then roasting marshmallows over it; a hilarious scene in which Groucho is forced to double for the absent Chico, and still perform his own part, during their act; and an amusing contractual involvement with E. F. Albee, the celebrated vaudeville producer. But Marxisms such as these serve merely as subsidiary diversion to the overall theme the authors are trying to propound: how the Marx Brothers slowly developed the identities, formulas, behavior patterns, and verbal exchanges that later sent the world into guffaws.

At that, it was undoubtedly a wise decision for the authors to avoid trying to write another Marx Brothers extravaganza. Such a musical without the Marx Brothers themselves would have been as fake as counterfeit money, and, of course, one with the Marx Brothers had become impossible. Harpo today is in that heavenly abode where surely his harp playing is finding a receptive audience—though, undoubtedly, he is still creating Bedlam by chasing every blonde in sight, stealing everything in reach, and eating whatever utensils and commodities he cannot steal. Chico is up there too, probably rounding up a crap game or playing the horses. Zeppo, the straight man (who never was very much of an asset in the old days) retired from the screen while his three brothers were still flourishing. And Groucho makes only random guest appearances on television after having served for many years as the quick-witted, sharp-tongued master-of-ceremonies on a television quiz show. Even if the Marx Brothers were still around, their presence in a typical Marx show would have been a sorry mistake. For not even the most rabid Marxophiles would hesitate to confess that in their last motion pictures they were a bore, reduced to imitating themselves.

One critic—Walter Kerr of *The New York Times*—recognized the wisdom in the procedure followed by the authors of *Minnie's Boys*. For this reason he found much in the production to rave about. His remarks are well worth quoting: "Where *Minnie's Boys* was smart, unbelievably bright really, was starting them all out in birch-bark canoes, sans wigs, sans mustaches, sans tricks. . . . Thus it's easy to meet Groucho while he's still leaning against a portal, a couldn't-care-less kid in unaccented spectacles, nose in a book. When he turns toward whatever melee is currently erupting about him to toss off a oneliner, the oneliner is a baby Grouchism all right. . . . He thinks in quick negations, but they haven't begun to expand into world-destroying sassiness." With Harpo, "the wig is never put on . . . until the last two minutes of playing time. . . . Playing an ordinary kid (who can talk) he only teases us, at first, with an up-and-down, then right-and-left, then repeat-both, head shake that is utterly flawless imitation—but only of a detail. The shy, sweet smile crops up as another detail later, and straight. It isn't until deep in the second act that he unobtrusively slips his knee into the astonished E. F. Albee's hand, and that's the last you see of that." As for Chico, "Ditto infinitely amiable in Irwin Pearl's provocative hint at that slightly clockwork, lumbering walk, the cap on his head progressing by stages from a tight green crown to the full Pinocchio flowering."

Shelley Winters, as Minnie, is billed as the star—a part in which she is more often than not uncomfortable, with her singing, dancing, and delivery of biting lines leaving much to be desired. The top acting honors went to Lewis J. Stadlen's portrayal of Groucho, not only because he *is* Groucho Marx ("the walk, the talk, the sneer, the leer, everything from the rasp in the throat to the crick in the back, seem perfect," as Clive Barnes remarked), but also because he can act, sing, and dance with winning, professional grace. Daniel Fortus plays Harpo convincingly, and so does Irwin Pearl the role of Chico. In all Marx Brothers productions there has always been a big, haughty, noble lady who is the butt for abuse, physical as well as verbal. In *Minnie's Boys* she is Mrs. McNish, the landlady, effectively played by Julie Kurnitz.

In *Minnie's Boys*—as in the Marx Brothers extravaganzas—the songs are pleasant adornments interpolated to provide audiences with moments to catch their breath. Those by Hal Hackaday and Larry Grossman provide pleasing interludes. Among the best are "Rich Is?" (which elaborates on the cliché that rich is better than poor), "Mama Is a Rainbow," and "Be Happy."

MISS LIBERTY (1949), *a musical comedy, with book by Robert E. Sherwood. Lyrics and music by Irving Berlin. Presented by Irving Berlin, Robert Sherwood, and Moss Hart at the Imperial Theater on July 15. Directed by*

*Moss Hart. Dances by Jerome Robbins. Cast included Eddie Albert, Mary McCarty, and Allyn McLerie (308 performances).*

Robert E. Sherwood—three times recipient of the Pulitzer Prize for drama— here made his only attempt at writing a musical-comedy book. He chose the setting of New York and Paris in 1885, and involved the great New York editors (James Gordon Bennett of the *Herald* and Joseph Pulitzer of the *World*) in a bitter rivalry for circulation. At first, as the musical opens, it is Pulitzer who seems to have gained the upper hand by promoting a subscription to raise money for the base of the then recently acquired Statue of Liberty. During the ceremonies attending the presentation of the check by Pulitzer to the mayor of New York, Horace Miller (Eddie Albert), a reporter for the *Herald,* pulls a boner in his photography by having taken pictures of the packing cases containing the statue instead of the ceremony. He is fired, and so he decides to go home where he can be a big fish in a little pond, instead of vice versa. But his girl friend, Maisie Dell (Mary McCarty) convinces him to go to Paris instead, there to seek out the original model for the statue, and bring her back to New York—a publicity stunt that would undoubtedly get a good deal of attention and might even give Horace his job back. Arriving in Paris, he comes to the studio of the sculptor Bartholdi, who is interviewing models. One of them is Monique Dupont (Allyn McLerie). At the time of Horace's arrival, Monique is posing as the Statue of Liberty, which leads Horace to believe that she was the original model. Horace sees to it that he and Monique become good friends. They stroll about Paris, explaining their reactions in one of the best songs in the score, "Let's Take an Old-Fashioned Walk." Horace even is led to tell Monique he loves her, in "Just One Way to Say I Love You." Meanwhile, back home, Maisie has sold James Gordon Bennett the idea to promote an American tour for Monique. This compels Horace to bring Monique back with him to New York, where they get a tremendous ovation. This is the first time that Monique discovers that she is being mistaken for the model of the Statue of Liberty; for Horace's sake she is willing to go ahead with the fraud. Maisie is not unaware of the growing romantic interest between Horace and Monique. She visits Monique to have it out with her, but once the two girls meet, they instantly become friends and decide to wash their hands of Horace ("You Can Have Him").

Upon Bartholdi's arrival in America, the fraud is uncovered. Trying to evade Bennett, Horace and Monique find a hiding place at a Policeman's Ball, where Monique completely captures everybody's heart with her exciting dancing. But Bennett soon catches up with them there, determined to get

Horace arrested and Monique deported. Through the efforts of Pulitzer, Horace is not only released from the clutches of the law but even lands a job on the *World*. The musical ends with Monique at the base of the Statue of Liberty, singing to it a deeply moving tribute, "Give Me Your Tired, Your Poor." This last number is a setting to music of the poem by Emma Lazarus inscribed on the base of the statue.

Besides songs already mentioned, standouts in this Irving Berlin score are "Paris Wakes Up and Smiles," a paean to Paris sung by a Paris lamplighter, which inspired Monique to perform a rapturous dance; and the duet of Maisie and Horace, "A Little Fish in a Big Pond."

MISTER (MR.) PRESIDENT (1962), *a musical comedy, with book by Russel Crouse and Howard Lindsay. Lyrics and music by Irving Berlin. Presented by Leland Heyward at the St. James Theater on October 20. Directed by Joshua Logan. Dances by Peter Gennaro. Cast included Nanette Fabray, Robert Ryan, and Anita Gillette (265 performances).*

Over a dozen years separate *Miss Liberty* (discussed above) and *Mr. President*. In that time, Irving Berlin had written music for *Call Me Madam*, whose central character was a female American ambassador to a fictional foreign country. In *Mr. President,* Berlin goes a giant step upward in American politics (though by no means a giant step upward artistically) by taking for his central character the President of the United States. International diplomacy is a theme here, and so is Washington politics, just as they were in *Call Me Madam*. But for the most part, *Mr. President* is concerned with the family life of the President during his last months in the White House.

The book fashioned for Irving Berlin was, as Howard Taubman described it in *The New York Times,* "patched together out of remnants of lame topical allusions, pallid political jokes and stale gags based on White House tribal customs. Its Presidential family, meant to be as American as apple pie, is as tame as the impersonal product rolling off a musical-comedy assembly line." The fabric is throughout synthetic; at times it gives the appearance of falling apart. But it manages somehow to hold together until the rousing finale, with its George M. Cohanesque tribute to flag and country, "This Is a Great Country." (When one critic took Mr. Berlin severely to task for his bad taste in using a flag-waving routine as a finale, Mr. Berlin replied hotly: "Do you know a better flag to wave?").

Just as the authors were not afraid of being so obviously chauvinistic in their finale, so throughout the musical they made no effort to sidestep sentimentality and an old-fashioned and trite kind of love story, for which most critics condemned them in no uncertain terms. But for their obvious attempts to manufacture something with sure audience appeal, the collaborators had no apologies to offer. Leland Heyward said: "For some reason—maybe it's the title and the Kennedys being in the White House—the intellectuals came expecting a cross between *State of the Union* and *Of Thee I Sing.* A satire, with big jokes and 'Wintergreen for President.' Well, we're not doing a satire. We're doing a warm, human simple story of a man who is President, and his family." To which Joshua Logan added: "The sophisticated intellectuals would like to see our man in the White House a sophisticated intellectual, but that's not the story we set out to tell. Somebody said we should call it the 'Hardy Family in the White House,' and there's some truth in that. This is a very simple, nostalgic story, almost a fairy tale."

Unfortunately, *Mr. President* was not a simple, nostalgic story, nor was it warm and human. If it did not fall flat on its face it was only because Nanette Fabray portrayed the First Lady with considerable personal charm; that Robert Ryan made for a highly personable and appealing President; and that the shopworn book was relieved by several pleasant-sounding, though by no means top-drawer, Irving Berlin tunes. Even with these assets, the musical was unable to reach three hundred performances, at a time when appealing and entertaining musicals could be expected to double that figure.

The musical opens with a theater manager, standing in front of a silhouette of the White House, explaining to the audience that the President about to be portrayed is not Mr. Truman, nor Mr. Eisenhower, nor Mr. Kennedy—but a fictional character named Stephen Decatur Henderson (Robert Ryan). The scene shifts to the Oval Room of the White House during a ball. In one of Jerome Robbins' best choreographic concepts in this musical, a "Twist" is being danced. But with the arrival of the President and his wife, Nell (Nanette Fabray), the more stately waltz replaces the Twist.

The core of the plot has international implications: the President's visit to Moscow, an invitation that is revoked by Moscow while he is en route to the Soviet Union because of one of his speeches. The President, however, refuses to turn back. He makes the visit without permission or authorization, meets a few simple workmen at the airport, then returns home. But in America the repercussions are great; this diplomatic fiasco results in a landslide for the opposition party in the next Presidential election. The Hendersons bid the White House and Washington farewell, to return home where they can revert to the simplicities of life. Henderson can serve as a judge at a fair and begin to learn to dance. Nell is back in the kitchen—baking. When a vacant Senate seat is offered to Henderson, he turns it down, since he is totally disillusioned with politics. Eventually, of course, Henderson returns to government service, since he cannot free himself of his concern for his country. And while all this is happening, his daughter, Leslie (Anita Gillette), can pursue her romance with a former Secret Service man, Pat Gregory (Jack Haskell). As for Nell she manages to win a prize for her coconut cake.

The sentimental or romantic numbers were the best of Berlin's songs, such as "Empty Pockets Full of Love," a duet of Leslie and Pat in which Pat laments the fact that empty pockets are all that he can offer to a former President's daughter. Pat and Leslie offer another appealing duet in "Pigtails and Freckles," as Leslie recalls the time when she was a little girl and Pat a little boy. Leslie shares "Is He the Only Man in the World?" with her mother, Nell. In "Meat and Potatoes," Pat realizes that he and Leslie are worlds apart, something, of course, which the authors of the text prove is simply not the case by the time the final curtain descends.

MISTER (MR.) WIX OF WICKHAM (1904), *a musical comedy, with book and lyrics by Herbert Darnley and John H. Wagner. Music by Herbert Darnley, George Everard, and Jerome Kern. Presented by Edward E. Rice at the Bijou Theater on September 19. Directed by Edward E. Rice. Cast included Frank Lalor, Thelma Fair, Harry C. Clarke, and Julian Eltinge (41 performances).*

*Mr. Wix of Wickham* would hardly deserve inclusion in this volume but for one salient fact: it was the first Broadway musical for which Jerome Kern contributed songs, initiating a songwriting career that would, of course, make stage history. As Kern's first American venture into the American musical stage, *Mr. Wix of Wickham* is likely to inspire some curiosity in the theater-goer. It was an American adaptation of an English musical which, truth to tell, had not made too much of an impression in its own country, and far less when transplanted into the United States. The play was a comedy set in Australia, where Mr. Wix of Wickham is a shopkeeper. He is duped into believing that he is the missing heir to a fortune. The real heir turns out to be the hero of the musical, who is in love with the girl working in Mr. Wix's establishment.

When Kern was called in to adapt the English score, he was just a humble employee in Tin Pan Alley, a song plugger for the firm of Shapiro-Remick. Kern contributed four songs of his own. The best was "Waiting for You," lyrics by John H. Wagner, introduced by Harry C. Clarke; the other three were "Angling by the Babbling Brook," "From Saturday 'Til Monday," and "Susan." In addition, Kern freshened up the English numbers with his harmonizations and orchestrations. Kern's work stood out so prominently in an otherwise quite drab undertaking that Alan Dale, the critic, inquired in his review: "Who is this Jerome Kern whose music towers in an Eiffel way above the average primitive hurdy-gurdy accompaniment of the present-day musical comedy?"

MISTER (MR.) WONDERFUL (1956), *a musical comedy, with book by Joseph Stein and Will Glickman. Lyrics and music by Larry Holofcener and George Weiss. Music by Jerry Bock. Presented by Jule Styne and George Gilbert, in association with Lester Osterman, Jr., at the Broadway Theater on March 22. Production conceived by Jule Styne. Directed by Jack Donohue. Cast included Sammy Davis, Jr., Jack Carter, Olga James, and Chita Rivera (383 performances).*

*Mr. Wonderful* brought Sammy Davis, Jr.—the brilliant and versatile night-club dynamo of the Will Mastin Trio—into the Broadway theater. In writing a musical for Sammy Davis, the authors had to find a place for Sammy's famous nightclub routines. They solved the problem simply—by interpolating a nightclub scene into the second act, having the musicians clamber up to the stage from the pit and Sammy and the two other members of his trio do their act. Sammy sings, dances, plays the drums, does impersonations— and with all his restless energy—and as far as *Mr. Wonderful* is concerned, *this* is the show. The frail plot that preceded it was merely a necessary preliminary. In Union City, New Jersey, Charlie Welch (Sammy Davis, Jr.) is an ingratiating song-and-dance man. His girl friend, Ethel Pearson (Olga James), and his friend Fred Campbell (Jack Carter) want him to aspire to Broadway success, but Charlie is diffident about leaving Union City. He is finally convinced to make a try, and the second-act nightclub scene establishes him as a star.

Sammy Davis, Jr., provides all the momentum needed to keep the play moving to its breathtaking nightclub finale. Such comedy as is found in the play appears with Fred Campbell, and his wife, Lil (Pat Marshall), especially in a scene set in Miami. Ethel's beautiful ballad, "Mr. Wonderful," became the show's big song hit, with Charlie's number, "Too Close for Comfort," crowding it for honors. A duet by Fred and Lil Campbell, "Without You I'm Nothing," was also melodically appealing.

THE MOST HAPPY FELLA (1956), *a musical play, with book, lyrics, and music by Frank Loesser, based on Sidney Howard's 1925 Pulitzer Prize play,* They Knew What They Wanted. *Presented by Kermit Bloomgarden and Lynn Loesser at the Imperial Theater on May 3. Directed by Joseph Anthony. Dances by Dania Krupska. Cast included Robert Weede, Jo Sullivan, Mona Paulee, and Art Lund (676 performances).*

Though *The Most Happy Fella* has over thirty basic musical numbers (the program made no effort to list them) and though most of the play is music rather than spoken dialogue, Loesser refused to designate the play as an opera. He considered it an "extended musical comedy"—and with good reason. Its music is steeped in the traditions of Tin Pan Alley and the Broadway stage. There are plenty of excellent show tunes, and some became hits. But the score is far more than just a collection of good musical-comedy songs and routines. It is, rather, an expansive and ambitious frame for recitatives, arias, duets, canons, choral numbers, dances, instrumental interludes, parodies, and folk hymns. It includes such sentimental delights as Joe's tender consolation to Rosabella, "Don't Cry"; the waltz "How Beautiful the Days," which the music critic Harriet Johnson called a "gem of its kind, probably never before equaled on Broadway for subtlety or loveliness of vocal sound"; and two numbers in imitation of Italian folk songs, "Abbondanza" and "Benvenuta." "We're trying to create a form so you can say in music that which might be too emotional for dialogue," explained Don Walker, the orchestrator of the score. "We pass into dialogue only for those developments that are not emotional in content, such as exposition."

The idea to make a musical comedy out of Sidney Howard's play came to Loesser from a playwright friend, Samuel Taylor. "I thought he was crazy," Loesser explained. "But when I reread the play, I knew he was right." Loesser came to realize that, though a tragedy, Howard's play had a good deal of humor to it, and that such humor could lend itself admirably to musical treatment. It took Loesser four years to complete both his musical-comedy adaptation of the Howard play (for the first time he wrote his own text) and the music.

The basic Howard play remained unchanged. On a visit to San Francisco, Tony (Robert Weede), an aging winegrower from Napa, California, sees in a San Francisco restaurant a young waitress, Rosabella (Jo Sullivan). Back in his Napa ranch, Tony begins to correspond with her. The exchange of letters brings Tony Rosabella's picture, which convinces him he is in love with her and wants to marry her. The only trouble is, she wants his picture in return. Being old and unattractive, he is reluctant to comply. The foreman of his ranch, Joe (Art Lund), however, is young and handsome. Tony borrows Joe's photograph and sends it to Rosabella as his own. This convinces Rosabella to come to Napa and marry Tony.

Tony is overjoyed. He throws a huge party to welcome Rosabella, while he himself goes off to the bus depot to pick her up. They miss each other. When Rosabella arrives at the ranch, she sees Joe and rushes to him, regarding him as her future husband. But Joe soon sets her straight, even tells her about Tony's deception in sending her Joe's picture. Rosabella is about to return to San Francisco when word comes winging that Tony, on his way to the bus depot, was in an automobile accident. He is being brought home on a stretcher. When Tony is home and sees Rosabella, he forgets his pain and disability completely. So obvious is his joy that Rosabella is incapable of leaving him.

Once Tony is on his way to recovery, he and Rosabella get married. Hardly is the wedding ceremony over when Rosabella, overwhelmed with disappointment at the man she married, rushes out of the house, where she is consoled and comforted by Joe. Their young, warm blood begins to glow and they fall into each other's arms passionately.

Afraid that his wife might become bored with Napa, Tony has sent for Rosabella's friend Cleo (Susan Johnson) to live with them. Cleo and one of the hired hands, Herman, become interested in each other. Roasbella now reveals to Cleo how Tony's tenderness, generosity, and solicitude have won her over to him completely; that she actually has come to love him. Discovering that Rosabella has said this, Tony celebrates by throwing a lavish party. But, realizing that she is pregnant with Joe's child, Rosabella flees from the party and tries to leave Napa. Tony is incapable of understanding her sudden decision until she confesses the truth. This shatters Tony to the point where he forgets himself, goes into a violent rage, is about to strike Rosabella with his cane, and vows to kill Joe.

Rosabella and Cleo have gone to the bus depot to go back to San Francisco for good. But Tony has a sudden change of heart. He knows that regardless of what Rosabella has done, or why, he cannot live without her. His love has sprouted into forgiveness. He follows Rosabella, catches up with her at the depot, and pleads with her to come home with him. He insists he is proud to become the father of a "bambino"—even if it is not his. Rosabella, now deeply committed to Tony emotionally, is only too ready and willing to yield to his persuasion.

In his play Howard stressed the growth in maturity of Tony when he recognizes that certain compromises must be made for the happiness of all concerned. But in Loesser's adaptation, greater stress is laid upon the theme of the search of lonely people for companionship and happiness. "Frank Loesser," said Robert Coleman, "has taken an aging play and turned it into a timeless musical."

Of the hit songs, the leading one was "Standing on the Corner," a kind of hillbilly number sung by a male quartet after it had commented on how

Tony's love affair by correspondence has made him happy; the four are jealous because all they can do is to stand on the corner of Main Street and watch the girls go by.

Other important show tunes are: "Big D," introduced by Cleo and Herman as a tribute to the city of Dallas, a melody in the style of the popular songs of the 1920's; "Joey, Joey, Joey," sung by the character named in the song; the title song, Tony's expression of the warmth that glows in his heart when he first decides to marry Rosabella, and his later song of love to Rosabella, "My Heart Is So Full of You"; and Rosabella's ballad, "Somebody, Somewhere."

Though Loesser prefers to call *The Most Happy Fella* a musical comedy instead of an opera, it is nevertheless a play in which much of the emotional, dramatic, and humorous impact comes from the music. Brooks Atkinson emphasized this when he wrote in his review: "He has told everything of vital importance in terms of dramatic music." And in a later article Mr. Atkinson added: "His music drama . . . goes so much deeper into the souls of its leading characters than most Broadway shows and it has such an abundant and virtuoso score in it that it has to be taken on the level of theater."

Besides being a resounding box-office success, *The Most Happy Fella* was selected by the Drama Critics Circle as the best musical of the year.

THE MULLIGAN GUARDS' BALL (1879), *a burlesque, by Ed Harrigan and Tony Hart. Lyrics by Ed Harrigan. Music by David Braham. Presented by Harrigan and Hart at the Theater Comique, New York on January 13. Cast included Harrigan and Hart, Annie Yeamans, John Wild, and William Gray.*

On July 15, 1873, at the Academy of Music in Chicago, Ed Harrigan and Tony Hart appeared in a vaudeville sketch in which they sang "The Mulligan Guards," lyrics by Harrigan, music by David Braham. At that period there existed splinter organizations (aftermath of the Civil War) that enjoyed flaunting military uniforms. The Harrigan and Hart sketch, with its song, reduced this practice to absurdity. Both Harrigan and Hart appeared in outlandish military costumes, and in their song they made a mockery of the pretenses that inspired men to keep wearing uniforms.

The song proved a sensation and was heard all over the country. As E. J. Kahn noted in his book *The Merry Partners:* "Newsboys, policemen, hot-corn venders, the oyster sellers at their street-corner stalls, the hokey-pokey men, who sold ice cream, whistled it as they went about their various chores." It was heard from organ grinders and on thousands of parlor pianos. "Throughout America, children, who in other eras might have chanted 'Ten Little

Indians' could be found chanting a variation on that theme called 'Ten Little Mulligan Guards.' "

Nor was the song's popularity confined to America alone. Kipling mentioned it in *Kim* as being sung by a regiment of soldiers; and the Coldstream Guards of London used its melody as march music. A translation in French was sung throughout Paris. The Viennese composer of operettas Karl Milloecker tried to borrow it for the finale of *The Beggar Student* for a New York production, but was dissuaded from indulging in such pilferage.

The sketch and the song were the embryo of the series of New York burlesques, with Braham's music, that made Harrigan and Hart the toast of the city for a decade or so. In these burlesques Harrigan and Hart presented a cross-section of life in New York, particularly in the lower echelons of society, embracing such national and racial groups as the Irish, Germans, and Negroes. Their plays represented one of the first attempts of the American musical theater to identify itself with everyday life (however much that life was satirized); to provide locales, characters, manners, speech, and types indigenous to New York and familiar to all New Yorkers.

Harrigan and Hart complemented each other beautifully. As the Boston *Traveler* had noted in their day, "Hart could play all the parts seven Harrigans could write," adding, "and Harrigan could write what seven Harts could play." Harrigan—described by Kahn as a stocky, serene man who had practically no interests outside of the theater—was more gifted as writer than performer. He was extraordinarily prolific, having completed some thirty-five full-length plays besides some ninety sketches. He acted in them, sang his lyrics to Braham's music, and in addition produced, directed, and financed the productions, and had them play in his own theater. To Nat C. Goodwin, the famous stage comedian of that period, the only word applicable to Hart was "genius." He wrote: "He sang like a nightingale, danced like a fairy, and acted like a master comedian. . . . His magnetism was compelling, his personality charming. He had the face of an Irish Apollo. His eyes were liquid blue, almost feminine in their dovelike expression." Incidentally, Hart, as gifted in playing female roles as he was in male ones, did so frequently.

The first of the full-length burlesques was *The Mulligan Guards' Ball*. It set a pattern for all future Harrigan and Hart "Mulligan" plays. Its overture incorporated the tune of "The Mulligan Guards"—a practice Braham would follow with every Harrigan and Hart production that followed. The principal characters included Dan Mulligan (played by Harrigan); his wife, Cordelia (Annie Yeamans, who became a star in these productions); their son, Tom; their colored maid, Rebecca Allup; and sundry other characters, including two lovable Negroes (played by John Wild and William Gray), a German butcher, his Irish wife, the captain of the Skidmore Guards (the Skidmores being rivals to the Mulligans), and so forth. Tony Hart usually played a leading female part.

Through Harrigan's subtle gift of characterization—though more in his text and lyrics than in his acting—and in his remarkable attention to detail as producer and director, he helped establish for the first time on the American musical stage racial characters. "He has really had more influence in directing the course of the contemporary stage than any personage of his time." So reported the *Illustrated American,* a journal of that period. And Isaac Goldberg wrote: "As playwright, as producer . . . and as actor, Edward Harrigan marks an important epoch in the development of the American song and dance show. His day was a great day for the Irish."

*The Mulligan Guards' Ball* won New York completely. A sequel was inevitable, and after that still another sequel. A whole series of Mulligan Guards' plays followed at the Theater Comique. They were: *The Mulligan Guards' Chowder* (1879); *The Mulligan Guards' Christmas* (1879); *The Skidmore Fancy Ball* (1879); *The Mulligan Guards' Surprise* (1880); *The Mulligan Guards' Picnic* (1880); *The Mulligan Guards' Nominee* (1880); and *The Mulligan Guards' Silver Wedding* (1880). In 1881 Harrigan and Hart opened their new theater, the New Theater Comique, with *The Major,* in which Harrigan abandoned the character of Mulligan to play Major Gilfeather. The Harrigan and Hart extravaganzas that came after that were: *Squatter's Sovereignty* (1882); *Mordecai Lyons* (1882); *McSorley's Inflation* (1882); *The Muddy Day* (1883); *Cordelia's Aspirations* (1883); *Dan's Tribulations* (1884); *McAllister's Legacy* (1885); and *Investigation* (1885). A fire destroyed the New Theater Comique in 1884, and *Investigation* ended permanently the partnership of Harrigan and Hart.

These were spoken plays with interpolations of songs and dances, usually ending up in some kind of variety entertainment. The plots carried the Mulligans, or their later counterparts, to a picnic, chowder party, silver wedding anniversary—usually simple, homey, everyday kind of affairs enjoyed by simple, homey, everyday kind of people. Complications set in through the coincidences, accidents, and mishaps that continually dog these good people. Sometimes the incidents are somewhat beyond the pale of the daily life of simple people. In one of the plays Dan Mulligan runs for alderman and wins through the help of the Negro population. In another, Cordelia makes a mess of her effort to reach high society and tries to commit suicide. She drinks from a bottle marked *Poison,* but which actually contains liquor, and yields not to death spasms but to a hilarious drunken scene.

For Tony Hart, the breakup of Harrigan and Hart meant not only his last days in the theater but also his last days in life. He appeared in two or three plays, then died in 1891. With Dan Collyer taking Hart's place, Ed Harrigan continued the tradition of the Harrigan and Hart era with another long succession of typical extravaganzas with strong racial overtones and emphasis on everyday people in everyday situations. These were: *Old Lavender* (1885); *The Grip* (1885); *The Leather Patch* (1886); *The O'Reagans* (1886); *McNooney's Visit* (1887); *Pete* (1887); *Waddy Googan* (1888); *The Lorgaire* (1889); *Reilly and the Four Hundred* (1890); *The Last of the Hogans* (1891); *The Woolen Stocking* (1893); and *The Merry Malones* (1896). With *Reilly and the Four Hundred,* in 1890, Harrigan opened his new theater. This is the show in which the "sweater girl" invaded the American musical theater—Ada Lewis, allowing the outlines of her ample bosom to become visible behind a tight sweater by abandoning a corset. This was the first time such a costume was worn by a female on the musical stage. Ada Lewis continued to wear sweaters in Harrigan's extravaganzas, always made to represent a tough girl, but a girl with a heart of gold.

Out of these extravaganzas, both before and after the breakup of Harrigan and Hart, came a long chain of popular songs, all by David Braham, which delighted the nation for a decade. These were some of the most famous:

"The Babies on Our Block," from *The Skidmore Fancy Ball* (1879), which quoted some popular Irish tunes and is believed to have inspired James W. Blake and Charles B. Lawlor to write "The Sidewalks of New York" in 1894.

"Danny by My Side," from *The Merry Malones* (1896), a song that was such a favorite with Alfred E. Smith, governor of New York, that he sang it when he helped celebrate the fiftieth anniversary of the opening of the Brooklyn Bridge in 1933.

"The Last of the Hogans," from the extravaganza of the same name (1891), introduced by Harrigan and Hart.

"Locked out After Nine," from *The Mulligan Guards' Picnic* (1880), introduced by Harrigan and Hart.

"Maggie Murphy's Home," introduced by Emma Pollack in *Reilly and the Four Hundred* (1890), and a waltz with which she was henceforth always identified.

"My Dad's Dinner Pail," from *Cordelia's Aspirations* (1883), introduced by Harrigan and Hart.

"Poverty's Tears Ebb and Flow," from *Old Lavender* (1885), one of the most famous sentimental ballads to come out of these extravaganzas.

"The Skidmore Fancy Ball," "The Skidmore Guard," and "The Skidmore Masquerade," the first two (1879, 1884) from extravaganzas of the same names, and the third from *The Mulligan Guards' Nominee* (1880).

THE MUSIC BOX REVUE (1921), *a revue, with book by various writers. Lyrics and music by Irving Berlin. Presented by Sam H. Harris at the Music Box Theater on September 22. Directed by Hassard Short and William Collier. Dances by Bert French. Cast included William Collier, Sam Bernard, Joseph Santley, Ivy Sawyer, the Brox Sisters, and Wilda Bennett (440 performances).*

(1922), *a revue, with book by various writers. Lyrics and music by Irving Berlin. Presented by Sam H. Harris at the Music Box Theater on October 23. Directed by Hassard Short and Sam Forrest. Dances by William Seabury and Stowitts. Cast included Clark and McCullough, Grace La Rue, Charlotte Greenwood, William Gaxton, John Steel, and the Fairbanks Twins (330 performances).*

(1923), *a revue, with book by various writers. Lyrics and music by Irving Berlin. Presented by Sam H. Harris at the Music Box Theater on September 22. Directed by Hassard Short and Sam Forrest. Dances by Sammy Lee and Alex Oumansky. Cast included Frank Tinney, Joseph Santley, Ivy Sawyer, Robert Benchley, John Steel, the Brox Sisters, and Phil Baker (273 performances).*

(1924), *a revue, with book by various writers. Lyrics and music by Irving Berlin. Presented by Sam H. Harris at the Music Box Theater on December 1. Directed by John Murray Anderson. Dances by Carl Randall and Mme. Serova. Cast included Fanny Brice, Clark and McCullough, Oscar Shaw, Grace Moore, and the Brox Sisters (184 performances).*

The annual *Music Box Revue* (of which there were four editions) combined lavishness of production with smartness and sophistication of material. The first edition entailed a production cost of $187,613—a figure unequaled up to then by any revue. No wonder, then, that many skeptics along Broadway insisted that the venture was sure to ruin both Harris and Berlin; that the new theater, the Music Box, they had just built for that production at a cost of close to a million dollars would prove not a monument but a tomb.

"Such ravishingly beautiful tableaux, such gorgeous costumes, such a wealth of comedy and spectacular freshness, such a piling of Pelion on Ossa of everything that is decorative, dazzling, harmonious, intoxicatingly beautiful in the theater—all that and more was handed out in a program that seemed to have no ending." Thus wrote Arthur Hornblow in *Theatre* Magazine. The show was a box-office smash. With a five-dollar top—once again, without precedent—it grossed $28,000 the first week and drew in a profit of over half a million dollars during its run.

A most effective tableau, "Dining Out," presented the girls dressed as various courses of a gala dinner. One of the best production numbers, "The Legend of the Pearls," had a set with a dazzling jewel effect. A novelty called "Eight Notes" presented a girl as each of eight notes of the musical scale (one of those girls was played by the then unknown Miriam Hopkins), with Irving Berlin on the stage with them. Fresh comedy was offered by Sam Bernard and René Riano in "I'm a Dumbbell" and "They Call It Dancing"; also by Willie Collier. Berlin's score of twelve numbers included one of his classics, "Say It with Music." Berlin's original plan had been to use this as a kind of theme song for all subsequent editions of this revue. But before the opening night of the first edition he had a band try it out; it caught on so quickly, and spread like contagion, that Berlin had to prohibit all further performances until the revue opened. There it was sung by Wilda Bennett and Paul Frawley and easily was the principal musical number of the entire show. Indeed, the song became such a hit that year that Berlin felt it was too well known to be used any longer in later editions.

There was another fine Berlin song in "Everybody Step," sung by the Brox Sisters, a dynamic syncopated piece that led into a frenetic dance typical of the Twenties.

The 1922 edition had other Berlin song delights. "Lady of the Evening" was a ballad beautifully sung by John Steel on an empty stage in front of a painted rooftop setting. An exciting syncopated number, "Pack Up Your Sins," was presented by the McCarthy Sisters in an elaborate first-act finale called "Satan's Palace," in which Charlotte Greenwood represented the devil passing in judgment on whether or not characters representing such performers as Ted Lewis, Bee Palmer, Gilda Gray, and Joe Frisco were sinners. Grace La Rue, wearing a huge hoop skirt, introduced a bit of nostalgia in "Crinoline Days." Comedy prospered with the first appearance on a major Broadway stage of Clark and McCullough. Already their identity was established with their outlandish costumes and broad slapstick humor, acquired in burlesque, Bobby Clark—cigar, cane, and painted eyeglasses around his eyes—going around with a perpetual leer.

Another comedy highlight was Charlotte Greenwood singing "I'm Looking for a Daddy Long Legs." Then there was a hilarious takeoff on grand opera. Six characters appeared to the strains of the "Triumphal March" from *Aïda,* then made a burlesque of several famous operatic ensembles. In this sketch Bobby Clark appeared as a character from *Il Trovatore* and William Gaxton (also in his first major Broadway appearance) as Siegfried.

Opera was again the subject in "Diamond Horseshoe," but this time treated with opulent stage settings and costumes—Grace La Rue attired as Thaïs wearing a gown whose train covered the whole stage. In an Oriental fantasy, "The Porcelain Maid," Hassard Short produced one of his most dazzling spectacles.

Berlin's principal songs in the 1923 edition were "Climbing up the Scale" (a delightful tune built on the ascending steps of a major scale) and the sentimental and tender "The Waltz of Long Ago." The latter was sung by Grace Moore, then a young, unknown singer making her Broadway debut (before going on, in later years, to become a world-famous prima donna). She was also heard in a production number, "An Orange Grove in California," the stage filled with oranges, while the scent of oranges was sprayed throughout the theater. Interpolated into this production was one of Berlin's greatest ballads, "What'll I Do?", in an unforgettable rendition by Grace Moore. If any single song can be said to have lifted her to stardom in the musical theater, this was it. (She sang it the same year at a benefit performance for Equity at the Metropolitan Opera House—the first time she ever stepped on the stage where within a few years or so she would be hailed as one of the most glamorous operatic sopranos of the day.) For an injection of rhythm, the Brox Sisters offered the dynamic "Learn to Do the Strut."

Florence O'Denisshawn did a pantomime dance of a starfish in "A Fisherman's Dream," while in another elaborate spectacle, a row of girls and a reflecting mirror appear to be two rows of dancing girls.

The edition was also strong on comedy. It was here that Robert Benchley, the distinguished drama critic and humorist, presented his classic monologue, "The Treasurer's Report." George S. Kaufman contributed a devastating skit in which the title reveals the content: "If Men Played Cards as Women Do"; and, back at the old game of poking fun at opera, six comedians sang "Yes, We Have No Bananas" (the novelty nonsense song hit by Frank Silver and Irving Cohn that was the rage in 1923) in the style of the Sextet from *Lucia di Lammermoor.*

In the 1924 (and last) edition, Grace Moore returned to sing another immortal Berlin ballad (also an interpolation). It was "All Alone," in which she was assisted by Oscar Shaw. They stood at opposite ends of a totally dark stage singing the poignant ballad into lighted telephones. Grace Moore also sang "Call of the South" and "Rock-a-bye Baby." Humor and burlesque were contributed by Bobby Clark as a hapless boxer in "The Kid's First and Last Fight"; by Clark and McCullough as "A Couple of Senseless Censors"; by Fanny Brice as a befuddled Russian immigrant singing "Don't Send Me

Back to Petrograd"; by Fanny Brice with Clark and McCullough in "I Want to Be a Ballet Dancer"; and by Fanny Brice with Bobby Clark in a sketch by Harry Ruby and Bert Kalmar, "Adam and Eve." The principal dance numbers were presented by Ula Sharon and Carl Randall in "Ballet Dancers at Home" and by Tamiris and Margarita in "Tokio Blues," while the principal production numbers included "Little Old New York" and "Alice in Wonderland."

MUSIC IN THE AIR (1932), *a musical comedy, with book and lyrics by Oscar Hammerstein II. Music by Jerome Kern. Presented by Peggy Fears at the Alvin Theater on November 8. Directed by Oscar Hammerstein II and Jerome Kern. Cast included Walter Slezak, Katherine Carrington, Tullio Carminati, and Al Shean (342 performances).*

The program described *Music in the Air* as a "musical adventure." This "adventure" takes place in the little Bavarian mountain town of Edendorff, a setting and atmosphere which the Germans describe as *gemütlich*. Here Dr. Walter Lessing (Al Shean) is a music teacher and conductor of the local choral society. His daughter Sieglinde (Katherine Carrington) and Karl Reder, the local schoolmaster (Walter Slezak), are in love. Dr. Lessing had written a melody for which Karl has provided the lyrics—"I've Told Ev'ry Little Star"—which he wants to get published, the reason why Karl and Sieglinde go off to Munich on foot. In Munich, Karl meets and engages in a mild flirtation with Frieda Hatzfeld, an operetta star (Natalie Hall); at the same time, Sieglinde befriends an operetta librettist, Bruno Mahler (Tullio Carminati), who wants her to appear in his new musical, *Tingle Tangle*. Sieglinde and Karl thus come to the parting of the ways. But Sieglinde is a failure as a performer in operetta, and Frieda Hatzfeld soon finds Karl an utter bore. Sieglinde and Karl come to the realization that the only place they can be happy is in Edendorff—together. And there they return, only too glad to forget about the temptations of the big city and to resume their romance.

Such a plot, such characters, and such a setting are the stuff from which the old-fashioned operettas of the 1920's and earlier used to be made. But *Music in the Air* was not a stilted, synthetic operetta, but a fresh and delightful musical play. Hammerstein's diaglogue, lyrics, and characterizations —as Brooks Atkinson reported—had "sentiment and comedy that are tender and touching without falling back into the clichés of the trade." In fact, he went so far as to exclaim that "at last, musical drama has been emancipated."

The picturesque background of a Bavarian mountain town provides much of the charm of the play, and this charm is enhanced by songs like "Egern on the Tegern See" and the beer-hall tunes rendered by Dr. Lessing's Chorale, which have the personality of German folk songs. There are also songs of the American variety, two of which represent Kern at his best: "I've Told Ev'ry Little Star" (the melody for which came to Kern from listening to the song of a finch at Cape Cod), a duet of Karl and Sieglinde; and Bruno Mahler's love song to Sieglinde, "The Song Is You." This does not mean that the rest of the score was not brimming over with infectious tunes. As Percy Hammond remarked: "Almost every minute . . . is full of . . . mesmeric airs."

After playing for almost a year in New York, *Music in the Air* was produced in Los Angeles, San Francisco, and (in 1933) in London. On October 8, 1951, it was revived on Broadway (the cast including Mitchell Gregg, Charles Winninger, Dennis King, Jane Pickens, and Lillian Murphy). In reviewing the revival, Brooks Atkinson had no reason to regret his enthusiasm when he first had seen the musical. He said in 1951: "Although ours is a graceless world, the lovely Kern score is still full of friendship, patience, cheerfulness and pleasure."

In the motion-picture version (Fox, 1934), the two leading roles were assumed by Gloria Swanson and John Boles, and six songs were used from the stage score.

THE MUSIC MAN (1957), *a musical comedy, with book, lyrics, and music by Meredith Willson, based on a story by Meredith Willson and Franklin Lacey. Presented by Kermit Bloomgarden and Herbert Greene in association with Frank Productions, Inc., at the Majestic Theater on December 19. Directed by Morton da Costa. Dances by Onna White. Cast included Robert Preston, Barbara Cook, and David Burns (1,375 performances).*

Unlike most outstandingly successful musicals, *The Music Man* slipped in rather unobtrusively and quietly to Broadway. Few in that first-night audience had any reason to suspect that something special was being presented. They were, then, caught completely by surprise by the irresistible charm of a play that wore its heart so openly on its sleeve, and sought to woo and win its audience with sentiment that often turned to sentimentality, with comedy that sometimes became corn, with nostalgia for an American past that was more old-fashioned than homey, and for excitement which sometimes was mere razzle-dazzle. "Not in recent memory," said *Variety*, "has a Broadway audience been so spectacularly carried away. Something happened in that theater on opening night which was without precedent: In the touching finale, the audience broke out spontaneously into applause to the even rhythm of the music. Nothing like it has ever been seen on Broadway."

*The Music Man* did not delay longer than the rise of the first curtain to cast its spell on the audience. The opening scene was a moving railroad coach, in which the dialogue of a traveling salesman and the music were beautifully integrated with the bouncy rhythm of the moving train. The infectious mood thus established is not dissipated until the equally fresh and exciting final scene.

The "music man" is a swindler named Harold Hill (Robert Preston) who goes from town to town selling the idea of forming a local boys' band. He says he is ready to outfit and train the boys if the town buys all the necessary equipment. However, since Hill cannot read a note of music and knows nothing about training a band—and since he is just a "con" man— he absconds with the money as soon as he had made the deal.

He comes to the town of River City, Iowa; the year is 1912. There he meets one of his old associates, who insists that River City is not the place for Harold's racket, since the town librarian and music teacher, Marian Paroo (Barbara Cook), is just too bright and perceptive not to see through Harold's shenanigans. But Harold refuses to be discouraged. He gathers the local townspeople together and in a long spiel (in a song called "Trouble," which Robert Preston delivered with breathless vitality) convinces the good people that the only way to keep their children out of trouble (such as going to the pool parlor) is to have them play an instrument in a band. Harold next tries to work his powers of persuasion and charm on Marian, who brushes him off rudely.

At a patriotic tableau at Madison High School, Harold thoroughly infects the people again with the idea of a boys' band. But there is still the skeptical Marian to convince. Harold goes to the library to impress her with the fact that he is a professor of music, a graduate of Gary (Indiana) University, class of 1905. Marian is still not convinced. Harold tries another maneuver. He tells her he is in love with her, which begins to soften Marian somewhat and to make Harold appear more attractive to her.

Marian notwithstanding, the applications for joining the boys' band come in like a deluge upon Harold. Marian has no hesistancy in calling Harold a fraud (her personal interest in him notwithstanding), since, having consulted the Indiana State Educational Journal, she has discovered that the Gary University had not even been founded in 1905. She feels that it is her duty to warn her neighbors and friends. But with the arrival into town of the musical instruments and the uniforms, there is so much excitement and enthusiasm that Marian does not have the heart to deflate her towns-people. Besides, much to her amazement, Harold has failed to abscond with the money, and apparently has now every intention of forming a band. This increases her interest in him, an interest that soon blossoms into love. Harold vindicates himself completely when the boys march through the town in full regalia, puffing away at their instruments and doing their best to make a concord of sound half as harmonious as the tender relationship that now exists between Harold and Marian.

Every element in the production was beautifully coordinated to create a consistent picture of life in a small American town in 1912. The staging of Morton da Costa had a keen eye for detail. The costumes of Raoul Pene du Bois and the settings of Howard Bay were evocative of the Midwest of yesteryear. The choreography of Onna White had a folksy character, to the point of including a soft-shoe dance. The performance of principals and supporting cast was completely in tune with story and background. For Robert Preston, a stage veteran, the role of music man was his first invasion of the musical theater. "It took his current vehicle," said Robert Coleman, "to bring home . . . just how versatile our boy really is. He paces the piece dynamically, acts ingratiatingly, sings as if he'd been doing it all his life, and offers steps that would score on the cards of dance judges. A triumphant performance in a triumphant musical!"

Recognition of the fact that it was the best musical of the season came with the winning of the Antoinette Perry, the New York Drama Critics Circle, and the Outer Circle awards.

Though Meredith Willson was a veteran as a serious composer, as a creator of song hits, and as a performer on radio, *The Music Man* represented his maiden effort in the musical theater. He was courageous enough to make his stage debut not only as a composer, but also as a lyricist and librettist—and in all three departments he proved himself at once to be a slick professional. His score was filled with delectable numbers, of which the most popular, and the most infectious, was the march, "Seventy-Six Trombones," which twice carried the plot to a stirring climax, each time sung by Harold Hill and the boys and girls of River City: when they first become enthusiastic about joining the band, and in the end of the musical play when they parade in their colorful costumes as a fully formed band. Willson also had a skilled hand at tender ballads, as he proved in "Goodnight, My Someone," sung by Marian as she gazes at the stars (into her tender melody she interpolates strains of "Seventy-Six Trombones," for Harold was beginning to invade her thoughts and emotions), and the love duet of Marian and Harold, "Till There Was You."

With Robert Preston returning to his role as Harold Hill (but with Shirley Jones replacing Barbara Cook as Marian), *The Music Man* became a big, bountiful, and highly successful motion picture when released by Warner Brothers in 1962. "The munificence of the big, booming sentimental show," reported Bosley Crowther in *The New York Times,* "has been enhanced and expanded. . . . Let all those who were sadly disappointed that they never got to see *The Music Man* with Robert Preston . . . be assured that they are going to miss nothing of its quality and character in the film."

MY FAIR LADY (1956), *a musical play, with book and lyrics by Allan Jay Lerner, adapted from George Bernard Shaw's* Pygmalion. *Music by Frederick Loewe. Presented by Herman Levin at the Mark Hellinger Theater on March 15. Directed by Moss Hart. Choreography by Hanya Holm. Cast included Rex Harrison, Julie Andrews, and Stanley Holloway (2,717 performances).*

This musical, which has so firmly established itself as one of the most successful productions in the history of the American musical theater (artistically as well as financially), took a long time to reach the stage and had to overcome many formidable obstacles. A good many producers had been interested in making *Pygmalion* into a musical but were all firmly turned down by Shaw. As he wrote to Theresa Helburn of the Theater Guild when she had suggested turning another of his plays into a musical: "After my experience with *The Chocolate Soldier,* nothing will ever induce me to allow any other play of mine to be degraded into an operetta and set to any music except my own. . . . Hands off!" Meanwhile, Gabriel Pascal, the motion-picture producer, transferred *Pygmalion* to the screen (without songs, of course), for which Shaw wrote the elaborate embassy-ball scene which was the climax of that screen production. Now—even if Shaw could be made to change his mind about making a musical out of *Pygmalion*—Gabriel Pascal would have to be part of the undertaking; for in any musical, as in the movie itself, the ball scene was indispensable.

After Shaw's death in 1950, Pascal asked Rodgers and Hammerstein if they would be interested in a musical *Pygmalion.* Their reply was in the negative. Pascal then came to Theresa Helburn, who was delighted with the idea. A good many composers, lyricists, and librettists were then contacted, among them Cole Porter, Leonard Bernstein, Gian Carlo Menotti, Betty Comden and Adolph Green—and Lerner and Loewe. Meanwhile, highly complex and prolonged negotiations were going on with the Shaw estate, which, at long last, were satisfactorily completed in 1952. Then Pascal died in 1954, and the whole project seemed to have collapsed. But late in 1954 Lerner and Loewe tried to see if they could do anything with Shaw's play. As Lerner said: "We have decided that *Pygmalion* could not be made into a musical because we just didn't know how to enlarge the play into a big musical without hurting the content. But when we went through the play again . . . we had a great surprise. We realized we didn't have to enlarge the plot at all. We just had to add what Shaw had happening offstage." And they had to include the ball scene.

Now completely convinced of the practicability of this project, Lerner and Loewe found their enthusiasm mounting. They decided to work on the adaptation. They acquired the rights from the Shaw estate (the Theater Guild now bowing out of the picture) and brought in Herman Levin as producer and Moss Hart as director. Rex Harrison was signed for the starring role of Higgins, though he long hesitated in accepting the part because of his limitations as a singer. Lerner was burning to cast Mary Martin as Eliza, but Miss Martin felt herself obligated to do the next Rodgers and Hammerstein play and therefore was not available. A comparative unknown, Julie Andrews (who had made her stage debut in a revue at the London Hippodrome in 1947 and eventually made her American bow on September 30, 1954, in *The Boy Friend*, a musical imported from London) was chosen as Eliza, but only after a number of other candidates had been seriously considered and rejected. By July of 1955, all papers were signed. A single backer had been found in the Columbia Broadcasting System (thanks to the foresight and acumen of Goddard Lieberson, president of Columbia Records), which put up all the money, $400,000. Because of the necessity of using the ball scene used in the Pascal movie, the Pascal estate had to be given a percentage in the show.

When, at long last, *My Fair Lady* came to the Mark Hellinger Theater on March 15, 1956, it was received with a delight inspired by few musicals. Brooks Atkinson went all out and called it "one of the best musicals of the century. . . . It gets close to the genius of creation. . . . In taste, intelligence, skill and delight, *My Fair Lady* is the finest musical in years." William Hawkins wrote: "This is a legendary evening. . . . It has everything. *My Fair Lady* takes grip on your heart, then makes you exult with laughter." *My Fair Lady* captured the Antoinette Perry, the New York Drama Critics Circle, and the Outer Circle awards as the best musical of the season.

Alan Jay Lerner had enough taste and intelligence in his adaptation to allow as much of Shaw's play as possible to remain. A few additions had to be made—but these, and Lerner's consistently scintillating lyrics, were so Shavian in spirit and style that it is often difficult to tell where Shaw left off and Lerner began. If a new note of humanity, or sentimentality, was introduced into the play to offset Shaw's irony and malice, this was all to the good, as far as the musical theater was concerned.

For the most part, the Shaw play never loses its original bite or sting or its penetrating social viewpoints; in the musical, as in the play, there is laughter at false class distinctions and at the so-called "high society" in England.

Except for the ending, Shaw's plot remains unaltered. Outside Covent Garden, in London, in 1912—just before the evening's performance at the opera—Eliza Doolittle (Julie Andrews) is selling flowers. She is a somewhat bedraggled cockney girl, with an appearance as inelegant as her accent. Her flowers are upset by Freddy Eynsford-Hill (John Michael King), a rich man-about-town, much to Eliza's highly vocal chagrin. Near at hand is the phonetician Professor Henry Higgins (Rex Harrison), who is making notes in a notebook. He insists that by a man's dialect he can place him within five miles of his home. He becomes interested in Eliza's uncouth cockney speech and manages to win her confidence, though at first she suspects him of being a policeman. After lamenting the failure of the English people to speak their own language correctly in "Why Can't the English?", he is goaded on to make a bet with Colonel Pickering (Robert Coote). Higgins is to change not only Eliza's speech but also her manners and dress so that she will be mistaken for a duchess. To Eliza, a duchess is of little consequence, and in "Wouldn't It Be Loverly?" she explains her own concept of the good life.

Her father, Alfred P. Doolittle (Stanley Holloway), a widower, is in Tottenham Court Road enjoying rounds of drinks with his friends. He explains in "With a Little Bit of Luck" that all a man needs to get the best out of life, including remaining unmarried, was luck.

Professor Higgins has convinced Eliza to come to live in his house so that he can work on his experiment. Other than this scientific project, he has no further interest in her—as he takes pains to explain to both Eliza and her father. He, Higgins, is a bachelor, too happy in his single blessedness to allow himself to get interested in a woman, a philosophy he expounds in "I'm an Ordinary Man."

The exercises Professor Higgins compels Eliza to perform finally yield results. In "The Rain in Spain" she proves she has lost her cockney accent completely—an achievement that so delights both Higgins and Pickering that, with irrepressible good spirits, they go into a fandango dance.

Eliza's first appearance in public as a lady of breeding takes place at Ascot. Fine ladies and gentlemen are watching the races—their behavior and reactions beautifully caught in one of the best ballet sequences in the musical, to the music of "Ascot Gavotte." Then the elegantly gowned Eliza appears with Higgins. Freddy Eynsford-Hill falls in love with her at sight— as he later proves by watching outside Higgins' house with the hope of catching a glimpse of her ("On the Street Where You Live").

And now the night has come when Eliza is to be put to the decisive test—the embassy ball. In dress, manner, poise, and sophistication she is a lady to the manner born. With great elegance she dances a waltz with Higgins ("The Embassy Waltz"). Everybody at the ball is captivated with her, convinced she is of Hungarian nobility. Eliza has carried off her assignment with flying colors—and Higgins has emerged from his experiment victorious.

Back at Higgins' home both Higgins and Pickering are gloating over what has happened. Eliza is in a world of her own, unable to forget her evening, and the dancing ("I Could Have Danced All Night"). But her pleasure soon turns to rage as she suddenly realizes that now she has had a taste of what it means to be a fine lady, it is difficult if not impossible for her to return to her former status as an impoverished cockney flower girl. Angrily, she inquires from Higgins what will now become of her, to which Higgins replies lightly that undoubtedly she will find a gentleman to marry. This only further enrages Eliza, who packs her bags and leaves Higgins' home in a huff. Outside she stumbles across Freddy, who protests he loves her. Unconvinced ("Show Me"), Eliza brushes him aside. She returns to Covent Garden, where none of the flower girls recognize her. It even takes her father a while to know that she is his daughter, and when he does he reveals that he is about to get married ("Get Me to the Church on Time").

Puzzled by Eliza's strange behavior, Higgins, at home, wonders why women cannot possibly behave as sensibly as men do ("A Hymn to Him"). At his mother's house later he learns that Freddy has proposed marriage to Eliza. Without quite understanding why, this piece of news angers Higgins. He calls her a fool, to which Eliza responds hotly that she is a free agent, can marry anybody she wishes, and most of all can get along very well indeed without the assistance of Professor Higgins ("Without You").

It is a sad Higgins who is sprawling in his comfortable chair at home at dusk. He cannot get Eliza out of his mind ("I've Grown Accustomed to Her Face"). He does not notice that Eliza has quietly slipped into the house. When he does he feigns indifference, takes her presence for granted, and asks her to get him his slippers.

Many helped to bring magic to the production of *My Fair Lady:* Oliver Smith with felicitous sets, particularly a black-and-white background for the "Ascot Gavotte"; Cecil Beaton's costuming in pre-World War I style; Hanya Holm's imaginative staging of songs and dances; masterful direction by Moss Hart, the celebrated "Rain in Spain" episode being merely one example of his inventiveness; remarkable performances by the three principals.

Loewe's music, in its graceful Continental manner and air—especially the "Ascot Gavotte" and "Embassy Waltz"—is beautifully attuned to the atmosphere and background of London in 1912. There are two major song hits, and both had become popular on radio, television, and records even before the first curtain went up: "I Could Have Danced All Night," Eliza's expression of exhilaration in her transformation; and Freddy's ballad, "On the Street Where You Live." Touching sentiment is found in both these songs, but also in Professor Higgins' "I've Grown Accustomed to Her Face," with which the play closes. But Loewe's music, at other times, is also touched with a coating of Shavian satire in two of Higgins' patter songs, "Why Can't the English?" and "A Hymn to Him"; and it is also filled with Shavian mockery at middle-class morality in Doolittle's two cockney songs, "With a Little Bit of Luck" and "Get Me to the Church on Time."

*My Fair Lady* captured more than one-third of the awards in the seventeen categories embraced by the annual Antoinette Perry awards, equaling a record held previously by *South Pacific* and *Damn Yankees*. Both in New York and in London it enjoyed the longest original run of any musical production in either city. Beyond London, *My Fair Lady* was produced in twenty-one countries in eleven translations—even in Japan, Israel, and the Soviet Union. A national company in the United States toured for several years. From its various productions the world over, *My Fair Lady* grossed over eighty million dollars—again something without parallel in American musical-stage history. But all this by no means was the end of its fabulous financial return. The original-cast album, released by Columbia, sold over five million copies, and there were fifty other recordings of the score in many different languages. When the motion-picture rights were sold, the price paid was the highest ever given—five and a half million dollars plus a percentage of the gross. That motion picture, produced by Warner Brothers and released in 1964, also proved a giant box-office draw after winning eight Academy Awards, including that of the best picture of the year. Once again Rex Harrison played Professor Higgins, but Julie Andrews (who had proved so radiant in the stage production) had been replaced by Audrey Hepburn.

NAUGHTY MARIETTA (1910), *a comic opera, with book and lyrics by Rida Johnson Young. Music by Victor Herbert. Presented by Oscar Hammerstein at the New York Theater on November 7. Directed by Jacques Coini. Cast included Emma Trentini and Orville Harrold (136 performances).*

In April, 1910, the first Oscar Hammerstein sold his interests in the Manhattan Opera Company to the Metropolitan Opera. One month later he decided to enter the Broadway musical theater. He contracted Victor Herbert and Rida Johnson Young to write an operetta, and for its leads Hammerstein selected two alumni from his opera house—Emma Trentini and Orville Harrold. The Manhattan Opera also contributed a few of the lesser singers, the members of the chorus, a large part of the orchestra, and the conductor.

Herbert's operetta used New Orleans of 1780 as a setting, a period when Louisiana was under Spanish rule. The opening scene takes place in the Place d'Armes, into which come marching Captain Richard Warrington (Orville Harrold) and his men, singing "Tramp! Tramp! Tramp!" They have come to capture the pirate Bras-Pique. In the square, Captain Richard meets Marietta (Emma Trentini), a Neapolitan lady of noble birth who had fled from an undesirable marriage in Naples by joining a group of *casquette* girls enroute to Louisiana to marry planters. Marietta is a mischievous, somewhat frivolous, girl who is part bad and part good, as she herself admits in the title number. Though Captain Richard finds her attractive, he convinces himself he is interested in her only platonically. Adah (Marie Duchene), a quadroon slave of Etienne Grandet (Edward Martindel), son of the lieutenant governor, now appears. She loves Etienne, but realizes that he is beyond her reach (" 'Neath the Southern Moon") and diverts her thoughts from Etienne by recalling her early years in Naples in the nostalgic "Italian Street Song."

At a ball at the Jeunesse Dorée Club, attended by the elite of the city, Etienne realizes he is deeply in love with Marietta. In order to be free to marry her, he auctions off Adah, who is purchased by Captain Richard, but only so that he may free her. Marietta, however, does not understand Captain Richard's noble motive. Though she is now thoroughly in love with Captain Richard, she decides to marry Etienne out of pique and vengeance. By this time Captain Richard knows that his interest in Marietta is highly serious— expressing his feelings in the operetta's leading love ballad, "I'm Falling in Love with Someone." Adah provides him with information he needs to prevent Marietta from marrying Etienne: the latter is Bras-Pique, the pirate. Etienne escapes before he can be caught and imprisoned. Earlier, Marietta had disclosed that she had heard in her dreams the fragment of a most haunting melody. She had promised to marry any man who can finish that melody for her. Captain Richard does so with "Ah! Sweet Mystery of Life," and thus wins Marietta.

Possibly inspired by the fact that he was here working with a famous opera impresario, and with so many graduates from opera, Herbert produced his most ambitious score. Some of his songs have the spaciousness of arias, while some of the instrumental numbers have symphonic breadth. The opening scene, with interpolations of street cries, and the chorus of flower girls are two excerpts demonstrating the amplitude of Herbert's style. Among the many varied songs in the score are three which must be numbered with the best Herbert ever wrote. Story has it that one of these—"Ah! Sweet Mystery of Life"—originated as an instrumental number, but that Orville Harrold, aware of its commercial appeal, convinced Herbert to have words added to it. This is not true, since the song was in the operetta from the very beginning. "I'm Falling in Love with Someone" is remarkable for its chromaticisms in the opening measures and in the unusual leap of a ninth in the refrain. " 'Neath the Southern Moon" is in Herbert's most winning lyrical vein. In addition, "Tramp! Tramp! Tramp!" is one of his best marches, and "Italian Street Song" one of his most evocative and atmospheric ballads.

During the run of the operetta Herbert and Trentini became so hostile to each other that they vowed never again to work together. Herbert was antagonized by Trentini's artistic temperament and whims, her tendency to stay away from a performance when she felt like it, and her refusal to give encores. Trentini considered Herbert a tyrant. An operetta that Herbert had been contracted to write for Mme. Trentini as a successor to *Naughty Marietta,* therefore, had to be assigned to another composer. The composer was Rudolf Friml, and the operetta, *The Firefly.*

NEW AMERICANA. *See* AMERICANA.

NEW FACES (1934), *a revue, conceived and assembled by Leonard Sillman. Sketches, lyrics, and music by various writers. Presented by Charles Dillingham at the Fulton Theater on March 5. Directed by Elsie Janis. Cast included Imogene Coca, Hildegarde Halliday, and Henry Fonda (149 performances).*

(1936), *a revue, conceived and assembled by Leonard Sillman. Sketches, lyrics, and music by various writers. Presented by Leonard Sillman at the Vanderbilt Theater on May 19. Directed by Leonard Sillman and Anton Budsmann. Dances by Ned McGurn. Cast included Imogene Coca, Jack Smart, and Tom Rutherford (193 performances).*

(1952), *a revue, with book, lyrics, and music by various writers. Presented by Leonard Sillman at the Royale Theater on May 16. Directed by John Murray Anderson. Dances by Richard Barstow. Cast included Eartha Kitt, Alice Ghostley, Ronny Graham, and June Carroll (365 performances).*

(1956), *a revue, conceived by Leonard Sillman. Sketches mostly by Paul Lynde, Richard Murray, and Louis Botto. Music and lyrics by various writers. Presented by Leonard Sillman and John Roberts, in association with Yvette Schumer, at the Ethel Barrymore Theater on June 14. Directed by Leonard*

*Sillman and David Tihmar. Cast included T. C. Jones, Inga Swenson, and Maggie Smith (220 performances).*

In *New Faces,* Leonard Sillman attempted to revive the spontaneity and youthful freshness of the first *Garrick Gaieties* and other of the famous intimate and sophisticated revues of the 1920's. He tried to do this by tapping the resources of young, unknown writers and performers. Consequently, the title *New Faces* is most appropriate—particularly when we remember that it was in the various editions of these revues that were uncovered such later stars as Henry Fonda, Imogene Coca, Van Johnson, Alice Ghostley, Ronny Graham, Eartha Kitt, and Carol Lawrence, among others.

In the first edition, in 1934, the discoveries included Henry Fonda (featured in several sketches and one solo, "Little Accident"); also Imogene Coca, whose obviously natural gift for zany comedy did not require the accouterment of an oversized camel-hair coat which she wore throughout the production. Another newcomer was Nancy Hamilton, who not only did a wonderful takeoff of Katharine Hepburn in *Little Women,* but who also contributed some sparkling lyrics ("People of Taste," "So Low") and some of the better sketches ("The Disney Influence"). James Shelton sang "Lamplight" and "The Gutter Song," both of which he wrote.

The 1936 edition introduced Van Johnson (he was a last-minute addition to the show, a kind of afterthought) and brought back Imogene Coca for some more of her pixyish comedy. It boasted two fine songs in "My Last Affair," by Haven Jones, introduced by Billie Haywood, and "You Better Go Now" (words by Rickley Reichner, music by Irvin Graham), sung by Nancy Nolan and Tom Rutherford. The better satirical sketches poked into the ribs of Mrs. Eleanor Roosevelt, Mrs. Herbert Hoover, and the Girl Scouts. When the revue, on tour, came to Philadelphia, its mayor walked out of the theater in protest against these sketches. The walk-out stirred a good deal of newspaper publicity, which led Mrs. Roosevelt to insist that she enjoyed the sketch about herself heartily and had found nothing offensive in it.

The 1952 edition was the best of the lot, the one that came closest to achieving Sillman's ideal to revive the sparkling little revue of the 1920's and to uncover bright new faces. The major discovery this time was Eartha Kitt. Singing "Bal Petit Bal" and "Monotonous," she became instantly one of the most provocative new singers to appear on Broadway in some years. Of her performance of "Monotonous," Leonard Silman wrote: "She sang the song sullenly . . . hissing most of it in an absolute paralysis of boredom until the very end, when she really let loose—and killed the customers." Another find was Alice Ghostley, a fresh new comedienne—outstanding in sketches like "Time for Two," "Of Fathers and Sons," and "The Great American Opera" and in the song "Boston Beguine." Paul Lynde did a monologue on an African adventure; Ronny Graham performed a travesty on Truman Capote and appeared in a parody of a Menotti opera. It was no wonder that Brooks Atkinson regarded this edition as "one of the pleasantest events of the year," and that it did so well at the box office. After a year's run on Broadway it toured the United States for another year and then was made into a motion picture by 20th Century-Fox—a motion picture that remained basically true to the spirit and material of the stage production. (An earlier movie, released in 1937, just used the title *New Faces of 1937,* and nothing more—concocting a backstage story about a musical comedy that was produced by a crook and saved through the efforts of a young author and a girl dancer.)

The 1956 edition was almost as good as the one in 1952. The later revue had an international character, what with Amru Sani from Bombay, Inga Swenson from Sweden, Maggie Smith from London, Franca Baldwin from Italy, and Suzanne Bernard from Paris. But the one who literally stole the show was an American—T. C. Jones, who proved himself inimitable as a female impersonator in "Stars in the Rough" (a sketch by Paul Lynde), "Isn't She Lovely" (where he played the part of the "moth of desire"), and "The Broken Kimono" (where he was the broken kimono). Inga Swenson sang "Boy Most Likely to Succeed," and Amru Sani was heard in "Mustapha." One of the funniest sketches was a satire on the motion picture *The Blackboard Jungle* called "Twenty Years in Blackboard Jungle." Of historic importance is the fact that one of the "new faces" among the writers was a young man named Neil Simon, who, in collaboration with his brother Danny, contributed a sketch. Without the help of his brother, Neil Simon would soon rise from such humble beginnings to the top echelon of writers for the Broadway stage—musical and nonmusical.

It took Leonard Sillman a dozen years to bring out another *New Faces.* He did so in 1968, and it was a failure (though it had some delectable moments, the most memorable being Madeline Kahn's imitation of Lotte Lenya singing a Kurt Weill song, in "Das Chicago Song"). The cards were stacked against the *New Faces* in 1968. Television had by now made the revue totally obsolete, and the tube was daily bringing new faces into the home. There was no longer any place for Leonard Sillman and his *New Faces* on Broadway. But they had made a notable contribution through the years—and in that time had brought a good deal of solid entertainment.

NEW GIRL IN TOWN (1957), *a musical play, with book by George Abbott, based on Eugene O'Neill's 1922 Pulitzer Prize play,* Anna Christie. *Lyrics and music by Bob Merrill. Presented by Frederick Brisson, Robert E. Griffith, and Harold S. Prince at the 46th Street Theater on May 14. Directed by George Abbott. Dances by Bob Fosse. Cast included Gwen Verdon, Thelma Ritter, Cameron Prud'homme, and George Wallace (431 performances).*

In fashioning a musical play out of Eugene O'Neill's *Anna Christie,* George Abbott made only minor alterations, none in the basic plot. In the musical, as in the play, Anna Christie (Gwen Verdon) remains a prostitute from the Midwest who, recovering from tuberculosis, returns to New York to find shelter with her father, Chris (Cameron Prud'homme), whom she has not seen in twenty years. The father, of course, knows nothing of his daughter's sordid past and welcomes her tenderly, determined to be a worthy father to a wonderful daughter. In New York, Anna falls in love with Mat (George Wallace), an Irish seaman. Anna's past becomes known to Mat, who denounces her and then goes off to sea to forget her. But he returns and, convinced that love has purified Anna, is ready to forget and forgive.

One of the changes in the adaptation came in shifting the time of the play from 1921 to 1900 because, as Abbott explained, "clothes were prettier then." *New Girl in Town,* then, becomes a decorative period piece, bright and colorful with custumes, sets, and dances of the period. At times it is a nostalgic backward look into the era of 1900, and at times it burlesques that era. The play loses no time in setting forth its purpose. It opens with a rousing routine called "Roll Yer Socks Up," set against a picturesque waterfront backdrop in which sailors and girls do a fandango. Later in the play a picturesque ballroom ballet is once again evocative of the early 1900's.

Another important change came through bolstering and building up the role of Marthy—Chris's middle-aged and blowsy mistress and companion. As played by Thelma Ritter, in her first appearance in the musical theater, the character of Marthy is one of the brightest ornaments of the production. Indeed, Thelma Ritter would undoubtedly have stolen the show from the rest of the performers if Gwen Verdon, as Anna, did not prove so sensational. In *Can-Can* and *Damn Yankees,* Gwen Verdon had proved that she was an exciting dancer. In *New Girl in Town* she was given ample opportunities to demonstrate that talent, particularly in a ballet revealing her disgust at men's carnal appetite for sex. But in portraying Anna she also proved herself to be an outstanding actress. As Brooks Atkinson wrote: "She gives a complete characterization from the slut to the woman—common in manner, but full of pride, disillusioned, but willing to believe, a woman of silence and mysteries. It would be an affecting job on any stage. Amid the familiar diversions of a Broadway musical jamboree, it is sobering and admirable."

With *New Girl in Town,* a new composer appeared on the Broadway scene—young Bob Merrill, a man who proved himself at once as apt with a bright and catchy lyric as with a pleasing melody. His gift for affecting lyricism was revealed perhaps most forcefully in the ballad "Sunshine Girl," introduced by Del Anderson, Eddie Phillips, and Mike Dawson, appearing in subsidiary roles; also in the tender duet of Anna and Mat, "Did You Close Your Eyes?", and Mat's song, "Look at 'Er." Merrill's strength with lyrics is found in Marthy's amusing ditty, "Flings," about the rewards two older people can find in love ("Flings is wonderful things—but they gotta be flung by the young"). And his fine gift for writing atmospheric music was displayed in effective background music for several scenes between Chris and Marthy.

THE NEW MOON (1928), *a "romantic musical comedy," with book and lyrics by Oscar Hammerstein II, Frank Mandel, and Laurence Schwab. Music by Sigmund Romberg. Presented by Schwab and Mandel at the Imperial Theater on September 19. Dances by Bobby Connolly. Cast included Evelyn Herbert, Robert Halliday, and William O'Neal (509 performances).*

*The New Moon* had one of the longest runs of any operetta; later on, when it was first bought for the screen, it brought the highest price paid up to then for a Broadway musical. (It was produced by MGM in 1930 with Grace Moore and Lawrence Tibbett. A second adaptation was made by MGM ten years later with Jeanette MacDonald and Nelson Eddy.) Yet in out-of-town tryouts it gave every indication of being a failure. The audiences were so apathetic that the producers were convinced they had a failure. Extensive revisions then took place, with happy consequences. When the play came to New York it was acclaimed. St. John Ervine, then serving as guest critic for the New York *World,* called it "the most charming and fragrant entertainment of its sort that I have seen in a long time."

The text was based on the life of Robert Mission, the French aristocrat turned revolutionary. The setting is New Orleans in 1792, where, a political refugee from France, Robert Mission (Robert Halliday), is hiding under the identity of a bondservant to Monsieur Beaunoir, a wealthy New Orleans shipowner. *The New Moon* is a ship just come to New Orleans from France bringing Ribaud (Max Figman), an emissary with secret orders from the king to capture Robert Mission and bring him back to France. Robert is in love with Beaunoir's daughter, Marianne (Evelyn Herbert), and before long so is Paul Duval, captain of *The New Moon.* At a tavern, Robert's friend Philippe (William O'Neal) warns him that love brings danger. But Robert is undaunted in his pursuit not only of love but also of liberty. He spurs the sailors on to fight for liberty, then goes off to a masked ball for the purpose of stealing a kiss from Marianne. There Marianne confides to her friends that her one kiss is being saved for the right man. She knows who that right man is once she sees Robert, and a tender love scene follows. They are interrupted with the appearance of Duval, who seizes Robert and drags him away. After this has happened, Ribaud convinces Robert that it was through Marianne that his true identity had been revealed.

Robert is brought aboard *The New Moon* to be shipped to France for trial. Marianne manages to steal aboard ship by creating the fiction that she loves Captain Duval and must see him. Aboard ship Marianne dispatches a tender note to Robert, entreating him to return her love. En route to France, a mutiny, instigated by Robert, breaks out, with the crew gaining control of the ship. They make for an island, where they establish a new free government. Marianne is there too, and though she had opposed the mutiny, she finds she cannot leave Robert, with whom she is head over heels in love. Stormy incidents follow when Ribaud tries to arouse the captives to revolt. Their hopes are raised with the arrival of two French ships, but those hopes are soon dashed. The admiral brings the news of the revolution that had just made France into a republic, and that Ribaud is to be brought back to Paris to face the guillotine. Robert Mission's ideal to create a new free society on his island can now be realized without interference, and his romance with Marianne can follow an untroubled course.

The outstanding love song (and it is one of Romberg's most famous melodies) is Marianne's "Lover Come Back to Me" (its middle section borrowed from a Tchaikovsky piano piece). This is the song Marianne sings as she writes her letter to Robert aboard *The New Moon*. Marianne's song "One Kiss" (the one kiss she is saving for the man she loves) and the love duet of Marianne and Robert, "Wanting You," are also in a romantic vein. Philippe's warning to Robert of love's dangers in "Softly, as in a Morning Sunrise," and the virile "Stout-Hearted Men," sung by Robert and a male chorus, are also famous.

> A NIGHT IN PARIS (1926), *a revue, with book and dialogue by Harold Atteridge. Lyrics by Clifford Grey and McElbert Moore. Music by J. Fred Coots and Maurice Rubens. Presented by the Shuberts at the Casino de Paris on January 5. Directed by J. C. Huffman. Cast included Jack Osterman, Jack Pearl, and Norma Terris (335 performances).*

*A Night in Paris* opened the reconstructed Casino de Paris atop the Century Theater. While the emphasis was on beautiful sets and costumes and huge production numbers—of the last, one of the best being "In Chinatown, in 'Frisco"—there was also considerable comedy in the capable hands and suave personality of Jack Osterman (who almost made a shambles of rehearsals when he punched Jake Shubert in the mouth during one of their many violent altercations); also in the rowdy burlesque humor of Jack Pearl. Even satire was well represented, principally in burlesques on two stage plays then recently successful on Broadway, Noël Coward's *Vortex* and Michael Arlen's *The Green Hat.* Nostalgia for Paris was expressed in a song called "Paris," rendered by Yvonne George.

NOBODY HOME. *See* THE PRINCESS THEATER SHOWS.

NO, NO, NANETTE (1925), *a musical comedy, with book by Otto Harbach and Frank Mandel. Lyrics by Irving Caesar and Otto Harbach. Music by Vincent Youmans. Presented by H. H. Frazee at the Globe Theater on September 16. Directed by H. H. Frazee. Dances by Sammy Lee. Cast included Louise Groody, Charles Winninger, Wellington Cross, Mary Lawlor, and John Barker (321 performances).*

*No, No, Nanette* started out as a disaster and ended up as one of the most profitable musicals of the 1920's, with one of Vincent Youmans' best scores, and two songs that are today classics.

Its history began in Detroit in 1924, where the reaction was so negative that the producer had to have the entire show overhauled from the bottom up, with a totally new libretto, some new lyrics, and four new Youmans songs replacing five that were discarded. The addition of those new Youmans songs—perhaps more than any other single factor—changed this musical from a fiasco to a triumph, and with good reason: Two of those songs were "Tea for Two" and "I Want to Be Happy."

Thoroughly revamped, *No, No, Nanette* continued on the road, gaining strength as it went—so that by the time it reached Chicago it proved such a draw that it remained in that city for a year. Only after that did it come to New York to begin its run of over three hundred performances. It went on to score the impressive total of 665 performances in London. Seventeen companies played it in Europe, South America, New Zealand, the Philippines, and China. It brought in a profit of over two million dollars.

The text, however, though revamped, remained a trifle. Billy Early (Wellington Cross), the wealthy publisher of Bibles, is the father of a young, vivacious, fun-loving girl, Nanette (Louise Groody). Her fiancé, Tom (John Barker), is not pleased with her happy-go-lucky ways, but is willing to bide his time until she settles down. Billy Early, who is married to Sue, a domineering wife, also possesses a good deal of *joie de vivre*—that and a weakness for young girls, particularly those who need protection. During a holiday in Atlantic City, New Jersey, Billy finds three young, charming, helpless girls who need his help: Betty from Boston (Beatrice Lee), Flora from San Francisco (Edna Whistler), and Winnie from Washington (Mary Lawlor). He makes the most of this happy situation, while his lawyer, Jimmy Smith (Charles Winninger), pursues Nanette. When Nanette is away from her hotel for a whole night, Tom becomes increasingly concerned; nevertheless he expresses his faith and belief in her purity. Sue, Billy's wife, makes a sudden appearance in Atlantic City, tracks down her husband, and pays off the girls handsomely to maintain a discreet silence about what has happened. The wife forgives her wandering husband, but warns him that since he finds such enjoyment in spending money on girls she plans to make his life happy henceforth with excessive extravagance.

It was in the deft handling of this rather slight and hackneyed material that the play won its distinction. Comic episodes were so generously sprinkled throughout that the merriment was never relaxed. And then there was Vincent Youmans' score, his best up to that time. A deceptive simplicity and a remarkable economy of means concealed the skill with which the two main songs—"Tea for Two" and "I Want to Be Happy"—were fashioned.

"Tea for Two" was written late one night. Youmans played his melody for Caesar, who liked it and said he would write the lyric the next morning. But Youmans insisted that Caesar do the words then and there, late as it was. Weary and sleepy, Caesar produced a dummy lyric, hoping to appease Youmans for the time being, until he could write the actual lyric the following morning. But the dummy lyric proved ideal, and it was retained. In the musical it was sung by Nanette and Tom when the latter expresses his faith in his girl.

"I Want to Be Happy" was the duet of Nanette and Jimmy during their mild flirtation in Atlantic City. The score possessed a third strong number, the title song, a sprightly piece of music.

Three motion pictures were made from this musical. The first was a First National production in 1930 (with Alexander Gray and Bernice Claire), which, amazing to say, dispensed completely with Youmans' songs and used new ones written by Grant Clarke and Harry Akst, among others. An RKO production in 1940, with Anna Neagle, used the three principal Youmans songs. The third adaptation was renamed *Tea for Two,* its plot a far cry from the original. Once again Youmans' principal songs were used, though other numbers were interpolated by other composers and lyricists, including George and Ira Gershwin and Harry Warren and Al Dubin. This last was a Warner

Brothers production, in 1950, with a cast headed by Doris Day, Gordon MacRae, and Gene Nelson.

> NO STRINGS (1962), *a musical play, with book by Samuel Taylor. Lyrics and music by Richard Rodgers. Presented by Richard Rodgers, in association with Samuel Taylor, at the 54th Street Theater on March 15. Directed and with dances by Joe Layton. Cast included Richard Kiley and Diahann Carroll (580 performances).*

*No Strings* was the first musical of Richard Rodgers following the death of Oscar Hammerstein II. Since an Oscar Hammerstein was not so easily replaced, Richard Rodgers decided to write his own lyrics. He succeeded in doing a thoroughly professional job. "His lines," wrote Howard Taubman in his review in *The New York Times,* "have a touch of the wholesome ease of a Hammerstein and a soupçon of the peppery impertinence of Lorenz Hart." Rodgers' skill with words should have surprised nobody. A man of keen intelligence and thorough verbal articulateness could not have worked for forty years with two of the greatest lyricists the American song has known without learning a good deal about their craft. Besides, Rodgers had then recently written words for his own music, in the remake of the motion picture *State Fair.* And many years before that, when Lorenz Hart was indisposed and was unavailable at rehearsals, Rodgers was often called upon to prepare lyrics for melodies that were being hastily interpolated.

The idea for *No Strings* originated with Rodgers. The writing of the text, however, was left to an experienced playwright, Samuel Taylor. It was unusual in theme only in that it treated the romance of a Negro girl and a white man with undemonstrative tolerance, accepting their relationship naturally, without apologies or preaching, as a love affair between two beautiful people; only in the denouement of the plot did the racial issue emerge.

The girl in the play is Barbara Woodruff, a Negro model in Paris (Diahann Carroll); the young man, David Jordan, a white American in Paris, onetime winner of the Pulitzer Prize. Without the preliminaries of an overture, but only with the pipings of a flute, Barbara makes her appearance singing "The Sweetest Sounds." The sound of a clarinet then brings David Jordan (Richard Kiley) to the stage singing the same number. They are at opposite ends of the stage; they have not yet met. David Jordan has for a number of years been wasting his time in France, enjoying its delights, and supporting himself by exploiting the hospitality and generosity of rich American tourists; it is eight years since he has done any writing. When David and Barbara meet first it is at a photographer's studio. They fall in love at first sight, then go off to wander about the streets of Paris together.

Louis De Pourtal (Mitchell Gregg) is also interested in Barbara. Since he is wealthy, he hopes to win her through expensive gifts.

When returning from a brief visit to Nice David finds Louis with Barbara, he reveals his jealousy by demanding she drop the Frenchman for good. In a spirit of fiery independence she refuses to do so. David leaves in a huff, but is soon back, as reconciliation takes place. They once again freely acknowledge their love for each other.

Barbara is determined to get David back at his writing. When he invites her to go off with him to Honfleur she consents not only to be with him at that seashore resort but also because she feels she might be able to get him to work again. But David finds it impossible to start a new novel. His conscience troubled, he accuses Barbara of meddling in his life and goes off without her, first to Deauville, then to St. Tropez to enjoy carefree living. Finally, he comes face to face with the reality that his life is wasting away. He comes back to Paris and to Barbara, but only because he has by now come to the conclusion he must leave them both. If he is ever to write another novel it will have to be at home in Maine. In view of her color, Barbara, of course, will not go back with him to America. David promises Barbara he will someday return. Meanwhile she must forget they have ever met. As they walk off in different directions, the curtain descends slowly.

Innovation and experiment made *No Strings* a consistently exciting stage experience. In line with the title of his musical, Rodgers used no strings in his orchestra—only wind instruments and a string bass. Specific instruments are used to identify specific characters. There is no overture, only that piping of a flute for Barbara and of a clarinet for David; even more daring is the fact that the musical begins with its most important song, "The Sweetest Sounds," instead of assigning it to a place somewhere in the middle of the production where so significant a number belongs according to tradition. Equally iconoclastic was the fact that throughout the play, one, two, or more musicians would saunter onto the stage, stand behind the characters, and provide an instrumental commentary to what was being said or sung. "In short," remarked Walter Kerr, "the composer's hirelings are used to support rather than to intercept the principals and . . . Mr. Rodgers' impudent resettlement works." For the first time in the history of the American musical theater, the artificial barrier separating the orchestra (in the pit) from the performers (on the stage) had been broken down.

Another innovation was to use as little scenery as possible and often to let the characters, as part of the stage action, move the props around to suggest a new setting. As Rodgers himself said, he was trying "to push the walls of the theater out."

The score was made up of several exceptional songs, and filled with musical sounds that float in and out of the play so often and so effectively that they almost become a kind of tonal dialogue supplementing the actual stage dialogue. The hit song was the opening number, "The Sweetest Sounds." Two duets by Barbara and David—"Nobody Told Me" and the title song— are equally pleasing. Barbara's "Loads of Love" is another strong addition. "He is still a magician of the musical theater," said Howard Taubman. "Approaching sixty, he has written enchanted music like a youngster who had discovered the unimaginable wonders of the notes in the tempered scale."

*No Strings* received the Antoinette Perry Award as the best musical score of the season. The original-cast recording was given a Grammy (the recording industry equivalent of an Oscar) as the best show album of the year.

OF THEE I SING (1931), *a musical comedy, with book by Morrie Ryskind and George S. Kaufman. Lyrics by Ira Gershwin. Music by George Gershwin. Presented by Sam H. Harris at the Music Box Theater on December 26. Directed by George S. Kaufman. Dances by George Hale. Cast included William Gaxton, Victor Moore, Lois Moran, Grace Brinkley, June O'Dea, and George Murphy (441 performances).*

*Of Thee I Sing* made stage history by becoming the first musical comedy to win the Pulitzer Prize for drama. The prize went to the librettists and to the lyricist (Ira Gershwin thus becoming the first song lyricist to earn this honor), but not to George Gershwin, whose music played so important a role in making this production so epoch-making. The Pulitzer committee explained that it had no authority to give a prize for stage music, a specious argument it dropped when next it awarded a Pulitzer Prize to a musical.

In breaking fresh ground, the Pulitzer Prize citation explained: "This award may seem unusual, but the play is unusual. . . . Its effect on the stage promises to be considerable, because musical plays are always popular and by injecting satire and point into them, a very large public is reached."

The citation was right on both counts. The play was "unusual" in that it avoided the trite boy-meets-girl theme so prevalent on the musical stage at the time; in that it sidestepped the stilted trappings of formal musical comedy; in that through dialogue, lyrics, and music it introduced a devastating wit and needle-pointed satire in musical comedy while considering the political scene in Washington, D.C. And its "effect on the stage" *did* prove considerable—it encouraged other and later musical comedy writers (and particularly composers) to adopt fresh and unorthodox subjects, treatments, and manner.

In the year 1931, Washington, D.C., was a stuffy place filled with sometimes dull, sometimes self-righteous politicians and a musty legislature that failed to cope wiith the grim realities of a major economic depression. The times were ripe for dissection by a satirical scalpel. Kaufman, Ryskind, and the Gershwins handled that scalpel with the skill and sensitivity of a master surgeon.

The main thread of the story was a Presidential campaign. The musical opens with best foot forward, with a five-minute political torchlight parade. The illuminated signs read: "A Vote for Wintergreen Is a Vote for Wintergreen," and "Even Your Dog Loves Wintergreen," and so forth, while the music, "Wintergreen for President," carries sly references to such old chestnuts as "Hail, Hail, the Gang's All Here," "A Hot Time in the Old Town Tonight," "Tammany," and "The Stars and Stripes Forever"; there are even melodic references to Jews and the Irish, for our Presidential candidate loves them equally. (Oscar Hammerstein II once wrote that the phrase "Wintergreen for President" represented *the* perfect mating of words and music, since it was impossible to think of the words without remembering the music, and vice versa.)

The torchlight parade over, the scene shifts to a smoke-filled hotel room, where Wintergreen (William Gaxton), the candidate for the Presidency, and the politicians are gathered to discuss campaign tactics. Wintergreen is a blustery, brash kind of fellow. A timid little man enters. He is Alexander Throttlebottom (Victor Moore)—a meek, sad man with a high-pitched voice that is always breaking, and a spirit that is always broken. Nobody recognizes him, until diffidently, and not without a suggestion of shame, he reveals that he is the candidate they have chosen to run as Vice-President. (In the 1920's and early 1930's, the Vice-President was invariably the forgotten man in Washington.) He further discloses he has come to withdraw from the campaign: He simply cannot summon the courage to tell his mother that he is running for the Vice-Presidency. The politicians calm his fears: His mother would never find out. This problem overcome, the politicians devote themselves to the campaign issue. They decide that since "love" is the most important thing in life, then, surely, love is the best of all possible campaign issues. And since Wintergreen is a bachelor, what better way to promote a love issue than by having him fall in love and marry? An Atlantic City beauty contest would pick the "Miss White House" after the election, who would become First Lady.

The Atlantic City contest finds a winner in Diana Devereux, a Southern belle. But Wintergreen suddenly gets ideas of his own. He finds his campaign secretary, Mary Turner (Lois Moran), more to his liking because she can make corn muffins. After the judges get a sample of those muffins, they agree.

Mary Turner and not Diana is to become Miss White House, and after that First Lady.

The love issue catches fire. The whole country is backing Wintergreen. Outside Madison Square Garden in New York (a political rally is taking place inside), the impact of the campaign issue is brought forcefully home with the singing of "Love Is Sweeping the Country." Within the Garden, as part of the political campaign program, a wrestling match is taking place. Then Wintergreen comes to the platform to deliver his campaign song, "Of Thee I Sing."

Having been elected by a landslide, Wintergreen and Throttlebottom are sworn in. The nine Supreme Court judges arrive singing a jingle. Wintergreen bids farewell to his bachelor days. Suddenly, Diana Devereux creates a furor by accusing Wintergreen of breach of promise. *She* had been chosen in Atlantic City, and *she* is the one the President must marry. But Wintergreen turns a deaf ear, and Mary Turner becomes his wife.

An international incident develops when it is discovered that the spurned Diana Devereux is of French descent, being "the illegitimate daughter of the illegitimate son of an illegitimate nephew of Napoleon." The French ambassador arrives to deliver a sharp protest for his country. The possibility of war is not to be discounted. The more discreet and timid of politicians begin talking about asking for the President's resignation; the more belligerent ones demand impeachment. To all these incendiary developments, Wintergreen remains calm, as he reveals in the song "Who Cares?" He has Mary Turner as his wife—and that is all that matters.

On the Senate floor, the Southern bloc plans to push through a vote on the impeachment of the President. But another piece of business must first be dispensed with: the government had negligently forgotten to bestow a pension on Paul Revere's horse, Jenny. Informed that Jenny has long been dead, the members of the Senate rise in homage, and for a few moments stand with heads bowed. And now the time has come to vote on the President's impeachment. As the Vice-President calls the roll for votes, impeachment seems inevitable until Mary bursts into the Senate with the startling news that the President is in a "delicate condition," since she is about to become a mother. In its entire history, the United States has never yet impeached a President who is an expectant father, and the Senate has no intention of breaking with precedent. The tide turns sympathetically toward Wintergreen. Hurriedly the members of the Supreme Court are summoned to decide the sex of the baby. With the sounding of a fanfare the verdict is "boy"; with the sounding of a second fanfare, the second verdict is "girl." Mary, it has been learned, has given birth to twins. Everybody is jubilant, with the exception of the French ambassador. He still feels his country has been insulted through the slighting of Diana Devereux, and insists that the newborn infants rightfully belong to France. But he is soon appeased by a compromise that meets with general approval. Since the Vice-President is required by the Constitution to assume duties the President is unable to fulfill, Throttlebottom must marry Diana Devereux. With the appearance of Mary on a gold-canopied bed—one child in each arm—the curtain falls.

Stimulated by his text, Ira Gershwin produced some of his most brilliant lyrics with a Gilbertian virtuosity. George Gershwin prepared a spacious score which included two hit songs (the title number and "Love Is Sweeping the Country"), together with extended sequences combining melodies with recitatives, solo numbers with choruses. Innumerable subtle details translated into musical terms nuances of the text. The mock pomp of the Senate is pointed up with the "vamp till ready" chords that usher in the scene; the recitatives are a tongue-in-cheek takeoff on grand opera. The music laughs gaily at maternity with a sentimental Viennese-type waltz ("I'm About to Be a Mother"), at France and the French ("Garçon, s'il vous plaît," the lyrics in gibberish French), at political campaigns ("Wintergreen for President").

No wonder, then, that the critics raved. George Jean Nathan called it a "landmark in American satirical musical comedy"; H. T. Parker of Boston considered it "one of the drollest musical operettas of all time"; Brooks Atkinson thought it was "funnier than the government, and not nearly so dangerous."

Besides winning the Pulitzer Prize, Of Thee I Sing broke a second precedent. It became the first musical-comedy text to be published in book form. Other earned distinctions included the longest run of any Gershwin musical on Broadway, with a second company on tour (the only Gershwin musical ever to have two simultaneous productions). The national company included Oscar Shaw, Donald Meek, and Harriet Lake—the last now better known as Ann Sothern.

Two years after the production of Of Thee I Sing, its authors (Kaufman, Ryskind, the Gershwins) wrote a sequel that was rejected by the critics and audiences—Let 'Em Eat Cake.

An attempt to revive Of Thee I Sing in 1952 (with Jack Carson and Paul Hartmann) also proved a failure. A startling innovation in 1931, Of Thee I Sing had had so many imitators since then that, in 1952, it provided neither shock nor surprise; it is also possible that after four terms of the Roosevelt administration and a world war, a satire on Washington politics no longer held appeal for the general public.

A second attempt to revive this musical satire—this time Off Broadway in 1968—proved an even greater failure. Clive Barnes of *The New York Times* called the text "not just weak" but "tottering . . . not just bad, it is terrible." But he did find the George Gershwin music and the Ira Gershwin lyrics timeless and dateless. "They don't write musical scores like that anymore," he added.

OH BOY! *See* THE PRINCESS THEATER SHOWS.

> OH, KAY! (1926), *a musical comedy, with book by Guy Bolton and P. G. Wodehouse. Lyrics by Ira Gershwin. Music by George Gershwin. Presented by Aarons and Freedley at the Imperial Theater on November 8. Directed by John Harwood. Dances by Sammy Lee. Cast included Gertrude Lawrence, Victor Moore, Oscar Shaw, and Harland Dixon* (256 *performances*).

Aarons and Freedley discussed with Gertrude Lawrence the possibility of starring her in her first Broadway musical comedy. (She had previously made her American debut in 1924 as one of the stars in the visiting *Charlot's Revue* from London, but she had never appeared in an American production.) She told them she was considering a similar offer from Florenz Ziegfeld. Only when Aarons revealed he had George Gershwin under contract for the music did she decide to hitch her wagon to his star.

The writing of the songs for *Oh, Kay!* was complicated by the fact that before they got written Ira Gershwin became a victim of appendicitis. Those were the years when an appendectomy required a few weeks of hospitalization, and several more weeks of regular treatment by a physician. Under those conditions, completing his lyrics for George's music would have been difficult if not impossible had not Howard Dietz (a close friend of the Gershwins, and a highly gifted lyricist) come to Ira's help by assisting him in the writing of some of the lyrics, making suggestions for several others, and contributing the title "Someone to Watch over Me" to the main love ballad.

In the text, Gertrude Lawrence appears as Kay, sister of an English duke (Gerald Oliver Smith), come to the United States on their yacht. The duke, in financial distress, is plying the trade of a bootlegger, assisted not only by Kay but also by Shorty McGee (Victor Moore). The duke and Kay use the Long Island estate of Jimmy Winter, a wealthy playboy (Oscar Shaw), as the scene of their operations, storing their liquor there under the watchful eye of Shorty McGee, who poses as a butler. All goes well as long as Jimmy Winter is out of town. But, as the musical opens, he is about to come home (much to the delight of the bevy of girls who anticipate the return of good times). Back at his estate, Jimmy toasts the girls. But Jimmy is the kind of man who is always getting into difficulties with women. He is a married man; he is engaged to a judge's daughter; and when he meets Kay (whom he recognizes as the girl who had once saved him from drowning in Long Island Sound) and finds her most attractive, he proposes to *her*. The arrival of a revenue agent almost brings disaster to Kay, her brother, and Shorty. But Jimmy comes to their aid and helps them outwit the agent. This problem out of the way, Jimmy can proceed to untangle his marital and love life so that he can pursue his romance with Kay, the girl he *really* loves.

To cast Gertrude Lawrence as Kay was a happy event for Broadway. Kay was the first of several unforgettable performances she would contribute to the American theater. But no less felicitous was placing Victor Moore in the role of hapless Shorty McGee, the pseudo-butler. Since he achieved in this part one of the triumphs of his long and active career in the theater, it is amusing to note that at first the producers thought he was miscast. When the play tried out in Philadelphia, Vinton Freedley planned paying Victor Moore $10,000 to step out of the play and allow Johnny Dooley to take over the part. As it turned out, Victor Moore brought down the house in Philadelphia, and he remained in the cast. A large measure of the play's success was due to his poignant characterization, his unique gift of blending humor with wistfulness—with his sad face and high-pitched, broken voice.

*Oh, Kay!* was one of Gershwin's best scores up to this time—a veritable storehouse of musical richness, which Percy Hammond described as "a marvel of its kind." The love song, "Someone to Watch over Me," introduced by Kay, is a Gershwin classic. Kay also presented "Do, Do, Do," which probably would have become far more popular than it did had it not been boycotted by the radio; this was because many female singers, through their vocal inflections, suggested sex implications in the song that neither Ira nor George Gershwin had intended. In a more rhythmic and dynamic vein were "Clap Yo' Hands" and "Fidgety Feet," both of them introduced and danced by Harland Dixon, playing a subsidiary role. "Maybe" was a delectable duet by Kay and Jimmy.

OH, LADY! LADY! *See* THE PRINCESS THEATER SHOWS.

OH! MY DEAR. *See* THE PRINCESS THEATER SHOWS.

OH! OH! DELPHINE (1912), *a musical comedy, with book and lyrics by C. M. S. McLellan (Henry Morton), based on* Villa Primrose, *a French farce by George Barr and Marcel Guillemaud. Music by Ivan Caryll. Presented by Klaw and Erlanger at the Knickerbocker Theater on September 30. Directed by Herbert Gresham. Cast included Octavia Broske, Frank McIntyre, Frank Doane, and Grace Edmond (248 performances).*

*Oh! Oh! Delphine* reveals its French origin by being a frothy sex comedy. Alphonse Bouchette (Frank McIntyre) and Victor Jolibeau (Scott Welsh) decide to bring a new filip to their lives by exchanging wives. Thus Simone Bouchette (Stella Hoban) marries Victor, and Delphine Jolibeau (Grace Edmond) becomes Alphonse's wife. Victor's rich uncle would disinherit his nephew if he ever knew of this arrangement. Consequently, when uncle and nephew cross paths, Victor must convince Delphine to come back and live with him as wife, even though they are divorced. The problems and situations that crop up as a result of this arrangement provide most of the humor of the play; other amusing episodes are contributed by Frank Doane as a lady-killing colonel, and Octavia Broske as a Persian-carpet salesman. By the time the uncle and nephew separate, Victor and Delphine are convinced they are, after all, made for each other; and Alphonse and Simone must console each other.

The principal musical numbers were the title song, a duet by Delphine and Alphonse, and the charming "Venus Waltz," sung by Octavia Broske, dressed in flimsy Turkish dress. Alphonse delivers two comic numbers, "Why Shouldn't You Tell Me That?" and "Everything's at Home Except Your Wife," the latter a decided favorite with audiences.

OKLAHOMA! (1943), *a musical play, with book and lyrics by Oscar Hammerstein II, based on Lynn Riggs' play* Green Grow the Lilacs. *Music by Richard Rodgers. Presented by the Theater Guild at the St. James Theater on March 31. Directed by Rouben Mamoulian. Dances by Agnes de Mille. Cast included Alfred Drake, Joan Roberts, Celeste Holm, Betty Garde, Joan Mc-Cracken, Bambi Linn, Howard da Silva, and Joseph Buloff (2,212 performances).*

By 1942 the Theater Guild of New York had come upon unhappy days. It had suffered a series of failures which had brought it to the threshold of insolvency. To extricate themselves from this difficulty, Lawrence Langner and Theresa Helburn conceived the idea of producing a musical, their first since Gershwin's *Porgy and Bess.* Helburn had long been convinced that Riggs' folk play, *Green Grow the Lilacs,* produced by the Guild in 1931, would make a charming musical. She approached Rodgers and Hart with the idea of making the adaptation. Rodgers was willing, but Hart was tired and ill and could summon neither the energy nor the enthusiasm for the project. When Hart left for Mexico for a prolonged vacation, urging Rodgers to seek out a new collaborator, Rodgers asked Oscar Hammerstein II to work with him.

By a curious coincidence, Hammerstein himself had been interested in making a musical out of *Green Grow the Lilacs*. He tried to sell the idea to Jerome Kern, but Kern was not enthusiastic. When Hammerstein offered to buy the rights from the Theater Guild, hoping to find some composer for it, he was informed that Rodgers and Hart were being considered for the adaptation and that the rights were not on the market.

In discussing the nature of their adaptation, Rodgers and Hammerstein came to an early decision: to abandon old methods. They realized that a play with folk character demanded fresh and original points of view. Consequently, a great deal in their play defied tradition. The play had to open, not with a stage crowded with chorus girls and men, but simply, with a woman churning butter while the hero sings offstage. In fact, there were no chorus girls on the stage until midway in the act. In place of formal dances there were American ballets, fully in character with the setting; for this purpose a leading personality of the ballet world, Agnes de Mille, was recruited for the choreography. And not only the dances, but also every bit of music and comedy, had to be germane to the plot. Hammerstein explained: "Such a course was experimental, amounting almost to a breach of implied contract with a musical-comedy audience. . . . Once we had made the decision, everything seemed to work right, and we had the inner confidence people feel when they have adopted the direct and honest approach to a problem."

And so, having decided upon the course to follow—a course that would not diverge from the path previously beaten out by Lynn Riggs in his folk play—Rodgers and Hammerstein proceeded to break down most of the shopworn concepts, clichés, and rituals of musical comedy to produce a musical play that was a single artistic whole, a musical play in which the text would always dictate their methods and procedures, however iconoclastic.

The simplicity of the opening scene was a clue that something fresh and new was going to take place on the stage. As the woman is churning butter on an otherwise empty stage, we hear Curly (Alfred Drake) singing offstage, "Oh, What a Beautiful Mornin'." In words and music this number had all of the lack of pretension, all the simplicity and charm of an American folk song—a style a world removed from the kind of song that might be expected to open a musical.

We are in the western Indian country (now known as Oklahoma) at the turn of the century. Eller (Betty Garde) is the woman churning the butter; she is the aunt of Laurey (Joan Roberts), whom Curly is coming to visit and with whom he is in love. Curly is inviting Laurey to be his girl at the "box social" taking place that night, and in order to convince her to come with him, he picturesquely describes how he plans to get her there in "The

Surrey with the Fringe on Top." Laurey pretends to be indifferent to Curly, though in truth she is interested in him. But when Curly has to confess that going in a surrey was just fiction, she becomes outraged. At this point, Will Parker (Lee Dixon) enters. He has just come from Kansas City, whose wonders he describes in the song of the same name. He won there fifty dollars in a steer-roping contest. With that fifty dollars he hopes to be able to marry Ado Annie (Celeste Holm), whose father, Judge Andrew Carnes had previously set down that amount as the sum Will must have before he can marry her.

Piqued at Curly, and determined to arouse his jealousy, Laurey decided to go to the box social with Jud Fry (Howard da Silva), a hired hand. He is a lecherous fellow with a strong appetite for liquor. Upon learning that Curly was planning to go to the affair with another girl, Laurey feigns indifference in "Many a New Day." The romance of Will and Ado Annie is also complicated. Ado Annie decides that her partner to the social will be a Persian peddler, Ali Hakim (Joseph Buloff), and freely confesses that she can deny men nothing ("I Caint Say No"). Besides, Will has foolishly spent his fifty dollars on extravagant gifts—and so to Judge Andrew Carnes, Ali Hakim and not Will seems to be the proper man to marry his daughter.

A reconciliation between Curly and Laurey finally takes place. They decide to go to the social after all, but in order that their friends and neighbors might not mistake the seriousness of their relationship, they decide to be polite and discreet ("People Will Say We're in Love"). To Curly goes the job of informing Jud Fry that he has lost his date. To get him in a good humor, Curly tries to convince Jud that he is really well liked and that his death would be widely mourned ("Pore Jud").

In an extended ballet sequence, Laurey dreams what it would be like to be married to Curly. In that dream Jud Fry becomes an ugly, evil, disruptive force. The dream sequence ended, fantasy turns partly to reality with the appearance of Jud, come to demand that Laurey keep her promise and go with him to the social. Apprehensive that her dream might be a prognostication of the future, Laurey agrees to go with him—much to the confusion of Curly, who is unable to understand her sudden change of plan and heart.

The second act opens with the box social, attended by farmers and cowmen, who discuss their rivalry good-humoredly in "The Farmer and the Cowman," and by all the young men and women of the vicinity. One of the attractions is the auctioning off of the box lunches. Whoever buys the box lunch can share it with the girl who had brought it. Jud and Curly become competitors in the bidding for Laurey's box lunch, with Curly emerging the winner by paying $41.35. They go off to partake of their repast, happy to be together. Will and Ado Annie have also come together again. Since Akim has no intention in the world of marrying Ado Annie, he wisely decides to eliminate himself as a prospective husband by purchasing Will's presents for fifty dollars and thereby making Will a candidate once again for Ado Annie's hand. This development pleases everybody concerned; Ado Annie and Will begin to talk about their future relationship in "All er Nothin'."

The romance of Curly and Laurey now develops quickly. Three weeks after the social, they get married. The festivities are interrupted with the appearance of Jud, who is dead drunk. He rushes toward Curly with knife in hand. In the struggle that ensues, Jud falls on his knife and is killed. A court is hurriedly improvised by Judge Carnes to absolve Curly of the crime so that the young couple can proceed on their honeymoon to a land soon to became known as Oklahoma ("Oklahoma").

In both his lyrics and his text, Hammerstein used the simplest possible vocabulary, and phrases that belong to everyday speech; he was partial to dialect and colloquialism; his imagery was drawn from subjects indigenous to the play; he avoided unusual techniques and tricky rhymes. His verses were so direct and simple that at times they appear almost threadbare, yet they manage to retain the lyric quality of poetry.

In writing his music Rodgers revealed new grains in his style and texture. He caught the spirit and flavor of American folk character beautifully not only in "Oh, What a Beautiful Mornin'," but in three other songs that have the freshness and the personality of autochthonous Western music: "The Surrey with the Fringe on Top," "The Farmer and the Cowman," and "Kansas City." The mock tragedy of "Pore Jud," the virility of "Oklahoma," the irresistible enchantment of "Out of My Dreams," and the beguiling seductiveness of the rippling triplets that begin each phrase of "Many a New Day" all demonstrate his rapidly growing creative powers.

The complete score has thirteen basic numbers. These are used in several different ways. They appear, of course, as self-sufficient numbers, growing out of the text as naturally as flowers out of rich soil. But they recur in the play, sometimes in fleeting quotations, sometimes in slightly altered shapes, sometimes as background to the dialogue—thereby more closely knitting text and music (a technique that Rodgers would develop to a highly sophisticated degree in his subsequent musical plays). Six of these numbers provide the threads to make up the warp and woof of the dream-ballet music of the first act, "Laurey Makes Up Her Mind."

It took Hammerstein three weeks to write the lyrics of "Oh, What a Beautiful Mornin'." Rodgers wrote the waltz melody to these words in less than ten minutes. Writing the main love song, "People Will Say We're in Love," posed a more difficult problem for Rodgers. After all, though the two main characters were in love with each other, they covered their true feelings with a superficial coating of hostility. A formal type love song would have been out of order. Rodgers and Hammerstein finally decided that the only kind of love song that would do was one in which Curly and Laurey cautioned each other against any outward demonstrations of love. Yet beneath such warnings there had to be a strong undercurrent of real tenderness. It took quite a while for Rodgers to evolve the proper mood and feeling for his melody. Once he succeeded, Hammerstein was given the clue he needed for the type of lyric that was needed. This, incidentally, was the only song in which the melody was written before the lyric.

Except for a few mildly amusing lines in "Kansas City," the score lacked a humorous number. To fill in the gap, Rodgers and Hammerstein wrote "Pore Jud," a duet for Jud and Curly. Curly is describing to Jud what kind of funeral Jud would have should he die, and how he would be mourned. "Unwelcome as the idea seems at first," Hammerstein explained, "Jud finds some features not unattractive to speculate on—the excitement he would cause by the gesture of suicide, the people who would come from miles around to weep and moan." Thus Jud suddenly becomes not a sinister but a comic figure, and the song becomes a highly amusing diversion.

It is now history how virtually everyone connected with the production —except Rodgers—suspected that while *Oklahoma!* might well become an artistic triumph it would surely be a disaster at the box office; how long and painful was the process of gathering the 83,000 dollars needed for production costs. Everything about *Oklahoma!* seemed to smell of failure. It had no stars; it had very little humor; its ballets and extended musical sequences were too high-brow for popular consumption; it had no traditional chorus-girl numbers. It was based on a stage play that had been a failure (with only sixty-four performances); the director, Mamoulian, had had little experience with the musical theater, his only past effort in this direction having been Gershwin's *Porgy and Bess,* a financial deficit to all concerned; the librettist-lyricist, Oscar Hammerstein, came to *Oklahoma!* with a recent distressing succession of flops; and the composer, Rodgers, was here working for the first time in a quarter of a century with a new collaborator.

All the odds, then, seemed to be against *Oklahoma!* being a success. It would have required a fool or a dreamer—or possibly a combination of both —to dare prophesy for it the magnitude of its ultimate triumph. But the accolades of all the critics worked in its behalf. Lewis Nichols called it a "folk opera"; Burns Mantle described it as "different—beautifully different";

Woollcott Gibbs said his "gratitude is practically-boundless"; John Anderson described it as "beautiful . . . delightful . . . fresh . . . imaginative." Given such a handsome send-off, *Oklahoma!* went on to create history. Its Broadway run of five years and nine weeks was the longest of any musical production and its New York gross of seven million dollars broke all known box-office records up to that time. After the end of the New York engagement the company went on tour, covering seventy cities in fifty-one weeks. Then there was a national company traveling for ten years, appearing in about 250 cities before an audience estimated at ten million and grossing about twenty million dollars. There were companies throughout Europe, South Africa, Sweden, Denmark, Australia, and other far-off places (including a unit dispatched to every Pacific area to perform for American troops, this being the period of World War II). In London it had the longest run of any play in the 287-year history of the Drury Lane Theater. In addition, it sold about a million albums of the original-cast recording—the first time in the recording industry that an original-cast reproduction of an entire musical had been tried. And the magnificent motion picture, filmed in the-then new Todd-A-O process (produced by Magna Theater Pictures in 1955, starring Gordon MacRae and Shirley Jones), grossed about ten million dollars in the United States alone. In all, *Oklahoma!* earned about a hundred million dollars, a sum that is destined to keep growing, since the musical is being revived all the time, and always with outstanding success. (At the Music Theater of Lincoln Center, at its 1969 revival, it brought into the box office almost $100,000 during the first week of its run.) The profit for investors was in the neighborhood of ten million dollars. Each one earned in excess of five thousand percent on his original investment. The Theater Guild made over five million dollars' profit, and Rodgers and Hammerstein earned over a million dollars each.

*Oklahoma!* received a special award from the Pulitzer committee. The various companies that performed it served as an incubator of stars, many of these performers having been unknowns when they first stepped into the play, including Celeste Holm, Shelley Winters, Alfred Drake, Joan McCracken, Bambi Linn, and Howard Keel. When the show first reached the state after which it was named, the governor proclaimed a national holiday. In 1955 an "*Oklahoma!* Song Fest" took place in Central Park, attracting fifteen thousand admirers, including Governor Harriman and Mayor Wagner. And in 1968, on the occasion of its twenty-fifth anniversary, it was given in a concert version, with spoken documentary, at Philharmonic Hall at the Lincoln Center for the Performing Arts.

But most significant of all, *Oklahoma!* opened altogether new vistas for the musical theater which would make possible the writing and production of such later masterworks as *Carousel, South Pacific,* and *The King and I,* all three by Rodgers and Hammerstein; Frank Loesser's *The Most Happy Fella;* Leonard Bernstein's *West Side Story;* and many other treasurable works that now form the repertory of the musical play, as distinguished from musical comedy. Olin Downes, the music critic, went so far as to suggest that "the sum of the piece indicates a direction that American opera of native cast might take in the period before us."

ON A CLEAR DAY YOU CAN SEE FOREVER (1965), *a musical comedy, with book and lyrics by Alan Jay Lerner. Music by Burton Lane. Presented by Alan Jay Lerner, in association with Rogo Productions, at the Mark Hellinger Theater on October 17. Directed by Robert Lewis. Dances by Herbert Ross. Cast included Barbara Harris and John Cullum (280 performances).*

After having written the lyrics and music for *No Strings* (his first musical after the death of his collaborator, Oscar Hammerstein II), Richard Rodgers conceived the idea for a musical in which the central character was a young girl who was clairvoyant and possessed extrasensory perception. He asked Alan Jay Lerner to work on the book and lyrics, and since the idea intrigued Lerner, he consented. Their progress went well enough for them to contract Barbara Harris to play the lead, to choose a title (*I Picked a Daisy*), and to make arrangements for a New York opening the following spring. But as the work of collaboration began to reach depths—Lerner had been compelled to discard his first draft completely and write a new one from the beginning—sharp differences arose between Lerner and Rodgers about the way the play should progress. Then Rodgers bowed out of the picture, permitting Lerner to develop his text along whatever lines he wished. Once Lerner was satisfied with the text, Burton Lane came into the picture as composer.

The basic theme remained, though a good deal of change took place in details. The main character, Daisy Gamble (Barbara Harris) reveals to Dr. Mark Buckner, a psychiatrist (John Cullum), that she has the power of extrasensory perception; she even has the power to make flowers grow. She decides to become the doctor's patient to cure herself of her craving for cigarettes. Mark consents to accept her, but only on the condition that, when under hypnosis, she reveal to him how she makes flowers grow. During her hypnotic state, Daisy discloses that in the eighteenth century she had been Melinda Wells, married to a Sir Edward Moncrief. Emerging from her hypnosis, Daisy further amazes Mark by anticipating when his phone will ring and knowing precisely where he has misplaced his car keys.

Though she has a boyfriend, Warren (William Daniels), Barbara becomes attracted to and interested in her physician. In her next session she once again becomes Melinda of the eighteenth century, and the whole era—as well as Melinda's personality—suddenly comes to life. Melinda, infatuated with Sir Edward, comes to his house to persuade him to marry her. He makes advances which she does not resist.

By now Mark is convinced of the validity of Daisy's past life, so much so that he feels he has fallen in love with this eighteenth-century Melinda. He writes a medical report about the case, which his colleagues ridicule. Then a Greek magnate reveals to him that from research he has discovered that there actually existed a painter by the name of Sir Edward Moncrief, who had had a wife named Melinda. This revelation serves not merely to substantiate Mark's findings but also to make him more involved emotionally with Melinda than ever—a fact revealed to Daisy when she accidentally comes upon and hears a tape recording of one of her sessions and begins to suspect that Mark is using her merely to bring Melinda back to life.

Determined to lead a normal existence, Daisy returns to Warren. Mark follows her, but Daisy rejects him. Returning to his office, Mark tries to use extrasensory control to bring Daisy back to him. He does. Daisy now knows that Mark is *her* man, just as Mark realizes that it is Daisy he loves truly and not some amorphous character from the eighteenth century.

Whatever appeal this musical had for audiences came not from its text, which was humdrum, nor from its score, which had its good moments, but from Barbara Harris' performances as Daisy. To Howard Taubman she combined "something of the brash wistfulness of the late Judy Holliday and a freshness and versatility of her own. She is a blithe spirit and a living doll." William Glover of the Associated Press said: "As a gawky kook of 1955 with a Betty Boop squeal in her voice who can become a genteel belle of 1794 while in hypnotic trance, Miss Harris is merry and marvelous." Gary Paul Gates in *Holiday* called her "a comic actress of the first magnitude; her handling of the extremely offbeat role is governed by a remarkable subtlety and discipline that somehow enable her to rush headlong into clownish antics without sacrificing one shred of feminine charm."

As for the musical comedy, William Glover considered it "droopy," Taubman called it "labored and creaky," and the critic of *Variety* thought it "disappointing."

The title song, introduced by Mark, achieved hit status (particularly after Robert Goulet helped to popularize it over television and in his recording). Mark had two more strong numbers in "Come Back to Me" and "Melinda," while "What Did I Have That I Don't Have Now?" as presented by Barbara Harris as Daisy, proved totally enchanting.

The motion-picture adaptation stars Barbra Streisand.

ONCE UPON A MATTRESS (1959), *a musical comedy, with book by Jay Thompson, Marshall Barer, and Dean Fuller. Lyrics by Marshall Barer. Music by Mary Rodgers. Presented by T. Edward Hambleton, Norris Houghton, and William and Jean Eckart at the Phoenix Theater on May 11. Directed by George Abbott. Dances by Joe Layton. Cast included Carol Burnett, Joe Bova, and Jack Gilford (460 performances).*

Even in an amateur production (when it was tried out at Camp Tamiment, in the Pocono Mountains in Pennsylvania, under the title of *Princess and the Pea*) *Once Upon a Mattress* proved itself a highly diverting evening at the theater. But in New York it could not fail to come out as a winner—aided as it now was by the magic hand of George Abbott as stage director; profiting from the polish and gloss of professional performers; embellished with some intriguing dance sequences conceived by Joe Layton; and most of all featuring Carol Burnett in the principal role of Princess Winnifred, a total newcomer to the stage who then and there emerged as a comedienne of the first rank (and subsequently grew into one of the funniest ladies since Fanny Brice, both on stage and on television).

The old fairy tale by Grimm of the princess who reveals her royal lineage by being incapable of sleeping in a bed in which a pea had been placed under a mattress, is here retold with zest, verve, and a good dose of unobjectionable burlesque humor. The lyrics have sparkle, and the melodies are effective. And then there is Carol Burnett, though a total novice, performing "with the assurance of a trooper," as Brooks Atkinson noted. "Miss Burnett is a funny scatterbrain who can sing loud and destroy decorum with a leer, a shrug, or a deprecating gesture, and she makes a lively character of a storybook part." Called upon to sing "Shy" or "The Swamps of Home," she "discharges" them, says Mr. Atkinson, "as though she were firing a field mortar . . . a lean, earthy young lady with a metallic voice, an ironic gleam and an unfailing sense of the comic gesture."

Queen Agravain (Jane White) has decreed that nobody can wed her beloved son, Prince Dauntless (Joe Bova), unless she be a princess. Actually, the queen is as overprotective as she is garrulous; she would like her son to remain single. Prospective candidates are rejected one after another. The last one to be judged and passed on is Princess Winnifred (Carol Burnett), who arrives soaked to the skin, having "swum the moat." She is gawky, graceless, raucous-voiced—and painfully shy. In fact, she is at first mistaken for a chambermaid and compelled to mop the floor. Her true identity, however, is soon discovered. Prince Dauntless is taken with her after he hears her sing "The Swamps of Home." But the queen wishes to put her to the final test. A single pea is to be placed under twenty mattresses—and if Winnifred is disturbed by its presence, her royalty can be unquestioned. At a ball given in her honor, the princess proves indefatigable; she even insists that all present learn a new dance, "The Spanish Panic."

Twenty mattresses are now being carried ceremoniously into Winnifred's boudoir. Meanwhile, through miming the king (Jack Gilford), who is doomed to silence, reveals to his son the facts of life.

In bed, Winnifred is incapable of sleeping. She counts sheep until morning. This horrifies the queen, but the prince is now so thoroughly taken with Winnifred he refuses to lose her. Only then is the discovery made that foul play has been at work: a minstrel has placed not only a pea but also a considerable amount of hardware under the mattresses. Now that Winnifred has proved herself a princess, and marriage to Prince Dauntless is an accepted fact, she can go into a blissful slumber.

Mary Rodgers, who wrote the music, is the daughter of Richard Rodgers. The older of two children (the other also being a daughter), Mary was born in New York City on January 11, 1931, and received her education at Wellesley College and the David Mannes College of Music. She made numerous musical contributions to revues, nightclubs, television, and theater concerts (including a marionette production, *Davy Jones' Locker,* and the Mary Martin television special, both in 1959) before she became famous for *Once Upon a Mattress,* her first complete stage score. Her second musical comedy, *Hot Spot* (1963), was a failure. Between 1957 and 1963 she was script editor and assistant producer of Leonard Bernstein's young people's concerts over television, and in 1963 she wrote the music for a television special, *Feathertop.*

As the daughter of one of the greatest composers the American musical theater has known, Mary Rodgers was not in an enviable position in this her first appearance as composer in the professional theater. Comparisons between father and daughter were to be expected. But as Brooks Atkinson said: "Nothing she has written sounds like his portfolio. She has a style of her own, an inventive mind and a fund of cheerful melodies; and *Once Upon a Mattress* is full of good music." Besides the numbers that Carol Burnett made so effective, there was "Song of Love," Winnifred's duet with Prince Dauntless, and a charming little song-and-dance routine called "Very Soft Shoes" that recalls the old days of vaudeville and the soft-shoe dance.

*Eddie Cantor makes* WHOOPEE *(1928)*

*Victor Moore as Vice-President Throttlebottom and William Gaxton as President Wintergreen in the first musical to win the Pulitzer Prize,* OF THEE I SING *(1931)*

*(Theatre Collection, New York Public Library at Lincoln Center)*

*Ethel Waters starts a "Heat Wave"*
*in* AS THOUSANDS CHEER *(1933)*

*Fred and Adele Astaire in*
THE BAND WAGON *(1931)*
*their last appearance as a team*

red Allen in
is first Broadway success,
HE LITTLE SHOW *(1929)*

*There's* MUSIC IN THE AIR
*in the little Bavarian town
of Edendorff (1932)*

THE

HEYDAY

OF

RODGERS AND

HART

*A scene from* ON YOUR TOES *(1936)*
*(The two gentlemen in the center are*
*Monty Woolley and Ray Bolger.)*

*Mitzi Green*
*and two young men in*
BABES IN ARMS *(1937)*

*Gene Kelly is "Bewitched, Bothered, and Bewildered"*
*by Vivienne Segal in* PAL JOEY *(1940)*

*A scene from* ROBERTA *(1933). The man seated at the piano is*
*a young and still unknown comedian named Bob Hope.*
*Standing near him is young George Murphy.*
*Tamara is standing behind Fay Templeton.*

*Todd Duncan and Anne Brown in* PORGY AND BESS *(1935)*

*Todd Duncan, Ethel Waters,*
*and Dooley Wilson*
*in* CABIN IN THE SKY *(1940)*

*Luther Saxon and*
*Muriel Smith in*
CARMEN JONES *(1943)*

EARLY RODGERS

AND

HAMMERSTEIN

*(Theatre Collection, New York Public Library at Lincoln Center)*

OKLAHOMA! *(1943)*

CAROUSEL *(1945)*

*Danny Kaye and Eve Arden in* LET'S FACE IT *(1941)*

*A scene from Irving Berlin's* THIS IS THE ARMY *(1942)*

*A scene from* BRIGADOON *(1947)*

**MEET MISS TURNSTILES**

*Exotic IVY SMITH*     for the Month

Ivy is a home-loving type who loves to go out night-clubbing.
Her heart belongs to the Navy, but she loves the army.
She's not a Career Girl, but she's studying singing and ballet at Carnegie Hall and painting at the Museums. She is a frail and flower-like girl—who's a champion at polo, tennis and shotput.

*Exotic IVY SMITH*

*Sono Osato as exotic Ivy Smith in* ON THE TOWN *(1944)*

*Ezio Pinza and Mary Martin find an "enchanted evening"
in* SOUTH PACIFIC *(1949)*

*Yul Brynner and Gertrude Lawrence in*
THE KING AND I *(1951)*

*Carol Haney and Reta Shaw*
*as employees of the Sleep-Tite pajama factory*
*in* THE PAJAMA GAME *(1954)*

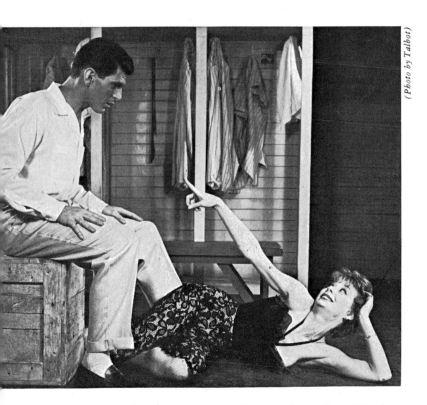

*Stephen Douglass discovers from Gwen Verdon*
*"Whatever Lola Wants," in* DAMN YANKEES *(1955)*

*Ethel Merman discovers that "You Can't Get a Man with a Gun"*
*in* ANNIE GET YOUR GUN *(1946)*

*Jo Sullivan makes Robert Weede*
THE MOST HAPPY FELLA *(1956)*

*Teen-age street gangs meet at a dance in* WEST SIDE STORY *(1957)*

*(Photo by Fred Fehl)*

*Iggie Wolfington and Robert Preston do a buck and wing in* THE MUSIC MAN *(1957)*

*(Friedman-Abeles)*

*Julie Andrews and Rex Harrison in* MY FAIR LADY *(1956)*

Though it opened Off Broadway, *Once Upon a Mattress* soon proved such a draw that it had to be moved uptown to the Broadway sector, where it remained over a year. A highly successful national tour followed.

110 IN THE SHADE (1963), *a musical play, with book by N. Richard Nash, based on his play* The Rainmaker. *Lyrics by Tom Jones. Music by Harvey Schmidt. Presented by David Merrick at the Broadhurst Theater on October 24. Directed by Joseph Anthony. Dances by Agnes de Mille. Cast included Inga Swenson, Robert Horton, and Stephen Douglass (330 performances).*

As the program explained: "This play takes place in a Western state from dawn to midnight of a summer day in a time of drought." Lizzie (Inga Swenson) is coming home—a place singed by heat and continuous dry weather. Her father (Will Geer) and her two brothers are, however, for the moment more concerned about Lizzie than about the heat. Lizzie, a plain-looking girl, had left town hoping to find a husband but has failed. She seems doomed to be an old maid. Into this situation invades a stranger, Fabulous Starbuck (Robert Horton). He is a man with a glib tongue, suave manner, and winning ways. He insists he is a "rainmaker" and for the modest price of one hundred dollars he can make the rains fall. To Lizzie he has all the earmarks of a fraud, and she tells him so. But Lizzie's family is taken in by him and enters into a deal. At a picnic, Starbuck tries his charm on Lizzie. He is eloquently propounding the theme that she has a beauty all her own, and he urges her to dream only marvelous dreams. Lizzie, however, insists that it is the simple little things that interest her. It does not take long for Lizzie to become a victim to Starbuck's winning ways and to be in his arms. Starbuck, softened by affection, is led to confess that, indeed, he is a fake. The sheriff, File (Stephen Douglass), is also convinced of this fact, for he has come to arrest Starbuck. Lizzie, however, talks File out of it; and since File is interested in her personally, he cannot deny her wish. Recently avoided by men, Lizzie suddenly finds herself being sought after by two attractive men, Starbuck and File, each of whom begs her to go off with him. Meanwhile, Lizzie's family beat on huge bass drums in order to disturb the skies and help bring on the rain. *Mirabile dictu!*—the rains do come, and so does love to Lizzie and File.

For Inga Swenson, *110 in the Shade* meant a Broadway debut. She proved irresistibly poignant when she sings of her loneliness in "Love, Don't Turn Away" and just as irresistibly comic in a number she delivers with her father in which she mocks at sex, though it is perfectly obvious she is fascinated by it ("Raunchy"). One of her finest moments comes in the presentation of "Is It Really Me?" (which she shares with Starbuck), in which, having found love, she is shocked to discover herself free of fears and doubts. These numbers, and one or two others—"Everything Beautiful Happens at Night," for example, or File's "Another Hot Day," which he sings with a chorus of townspeople—reveal lyricist Tom Jones and composer Harvey Schmidt fully capable of writing songs that "sustain the simplicity and tenderness of the story," in Henry Hewes' words in *The Saturday Review.* As for the musical play, Mr. Hewes by no means found it "overpowering," and he felt it lacked "complexity and sophistication." But he added: "Its integrity, its simplicity, and its tenderness are endearing without being the least bit sentimental."

ONE TOUCH OF VENUS (1943), *a musical comedy, with book by S. J. Perelman and Ogden Nash, suggested by F. Anstey's* The Tinted Venus. *Lyrics by Ogden Nash. Music by Kurt Weill. Presented by Cheryl Crawford, in conjunction with John Wildberg, at the Imperial Theater on October 7. Directed by Elia Kazan. Choreography by Agnes de Mille. Cast included Kenny Baker, Mary Martin, John Boles, and Paula Laurence (567 performances).*

In his previous musical, *Lady in the Dark* (1941), Kurt Weill had provided the score for a musical play. Possibly as a change of pace, in *One Touch of Venus* he reverts to formal musical comedy.

A lovelorn barber, Rodney Hatch (Kenny Baker), is in love with Gloria (Ruth Bond). Upon paying a visit to the Whitelaw Savory Foundation of Modern Art, he sees a statue of Venus. Though he is convinced his girl Gloria is more beautiful than Venus, he is led by an inexplicable impulse to place an engagement ring he has purchased for Gloria on the finger of Venus. Suddenly Venus (Mary Martin) comes alive. She falls in love with Rodney at sight, follows him to his apartment, where he keeps insisting that his love is reserved for Gloria and Gloria alone ("How Much I Love You"). This does not discourage Venus, who continues to follow him wherever he goes. Rodney, in an attempt to avoid attention, takes Venus to Rockefeller Plaza to outfit her in modern clothes. The noonday hubbub there is re-created in a ballet sequence. Venus is incapable of understanding why Rodney is immune to her charms and rejects her love. Could it be, she wonders, that during the long period she was frozen in clay as a statue that love had become outmoded? ("I'm a Stranger Here Myself"). Impetuously, she enters a dress shop, removes the clothes from a dummy in the window, and proceeds to put them on. The police are about to arrest her, but she is rescued by Whitelaw Savory (John Boles), the owner of the museum, who falls instantly in love with Venus. Venus protests in "Foolish Heart" that she can love one man alone—Rodney.

When Gloria comes in from New Jersey to visit Rodney, she asks for the engagement ring and is taken aback to be told that it has been stolen by a statue. Both she and her mother are convinced that Rodney has another woman. Upon recognizing Gloria as her rival, Venus uses her magical powers to have Gloria wafted off to the North Pole. By now matters have become highly complicated, for Rodney is being suspected of having stolen the statue of Venus, and Rodney and the live Venus are accused of having murdered Gloria. Rodney and Venus are carted off to jail, where Venus, after repeating how much she loves Rodney, once again employs her necromantic powers, this time to open the cell doors. They flee to a hotel, where Rodney can no longer resist Venus. He begins to dream what it would be like to be married to her and spend the rest of his life in a suburban development—the inspiration for another ambitious ballet sequence, which ends with the return of Venus to her own land.

Venus is a statue again, and is again on exhibit at the Whitelaw Savory Foundation of Modern Art. Gloria, magically recalled from the North Pole, will have no further traffic with Rodney. Unable to forget Venus, Rodney visits the museum and looks at the statue adoringly. Just then a young girl comes to Rodney for some information. He is amazed to find how much she resembles Venus. Rodney answers her, then escorts her out of the museum.

The principal songs were assigned to Rodney and Venus: "Speak Low" (in which Venus comforts Rodney for having lost Gloria) and "How Much I Love You?". One of Venus' best numbers was "Foolish Heart," while Paula Laurence, who plays the part of Whitelaw's acidulous secretary, has an amusing piece in "Very, Very, Very." The principal comedy in the play comes from her performance and that of Teddy Hart as a private detective.

THE ONLY GIRL (1914), *a musical, with book by Henry Blossom adapted from Frank Mandel's comedy* Our Wives. *Lyrics by Henry Blossom. Music by Victor Herbert. Presented by Joe Weber at the 39th Street Theater on November 2. Directed by Fred G. Latham. Cast included Wilda Bennett, Thurston Hall, and Adele Rowland (240 performances).*

*The Only Girl* is a compromise between operetta and musical comedy, but it comes closer to being the latter than the former. Its history goes back to 1897, when a comedy by Ludwig Fulda, *Jugendfreunde,* was produced in Germany with outstanding success. (The emperor considered it the funniest show he had ever seen.) In 1912 the play was Americanized by Frank Mandel and as *Our Wives* was presented on Broadway, where it proved a failure. Henry

Blossom thought it had the makings of a good musical, and apparently convinced Herbert, for Herbert completed his score in a week.

In its musical setting, the background is New York, and the time is "the present." Alan Kimbrough (Thurston Hall) is a librettist in search of a composer for his new show. The one he finally selects is Ruth Wilson (Wilda Bennett). Once they decide to collaborate, Kimbrough makes it perfectly plain that theirs must remain purely an artistic relationship, first because work and play do not mix, and more importantly because he has made a vow with three other bachelors to avoid the state of matrimony at all costs. While their musical is getting written, the three other bachelors forget their vows, and having found girls of their choice, get married. Kimbrough is the last holdout, until he comes to the realization that he is in love with Ruth, that she is the only girl for him, and that he, too, now wants to get married.

In his biography of Herbert, Edward N. Waters explains that *The Only Girl* "is a play with music, but the music is more than incidental to the action." He points out that there are "no dramatic scenes with musical emphasis, no passages of recitative or declamation, no passionate ariosos, no choruses in the accepted sense." Herbert's score is "predominantly a series of solos and part songs which are utterly charming and characteristic of the moods expressed." One of the best of these numbers is Ruth's waltz, "When You're Away," while the main love duet (naturally that of Ruth and Kimbrough) is "You're the Only Girl for Me." The trio of bachelors is given a mildly amusing tidbit in "When You're Wearing the Ball and Chain," to which their wives respond with "Why Should We Stay Home and Sew?"

*The Only Girl* was one of the few musicals by Victor Herbert to be produced in London. This happened in the spring of 1915, when it had a three-month run at the Apollo Theater.

ON THE TOWN (1944), *a musical comedy, with book and lyrics by Betty Comden and Adolph Green, based on an idea by Jerome Robbins. Music by Leonard Bernstein. Presented by Oliver Smith and Paul Feigay at the Adelphi Theater on December 28. Directed by George Abbott. Choreography by Jerome Robbins. Cast included Sono Osato, Betty Comden, Adolph Green, and Nancy Walker (463 performances).*

Stage history was made with *On the Town.* It marked the debut of Leonard Bernstein (then already having proved himself as a conductor and a serious composer) in the popular musical theater. As was customary with Bernstein throughout his incredible career, here, as elsewhere, he started on the top. *On the Town* was a smash success on Broadway. The Newspaper Guild of New York presented it with its Page One Award as the outstanding achievement in the theater in 1945. It was a major success as a movie musical, starring Frank Sinatra, Gene Kelly, and Ann Miller (MGM, 1949). The stage musical was revived simultaneously in two Off Broadway productions in 1959, when Walter Kerr said, "it still stands as one of the most original, inventive and irresistibly charming of all American musicals." When, belatedly, it came to London in 1963, it inspired an ovation on opening night and lines at the box office the next morning.

This musical was an adaptation of the ballet *Fancy Free,* choreography by Jerome Robbins, and music by Bernstein, in which three sailors on leave are in pursuit of girls.

In the musical the three sailors are on shore leave for twenty-four hours. They are Gabey (John Battles), Ozzie (Adolph Green), and Chip (Chris Alexander). Gabey is the romantic of this trio; Ozzie is carefree and irresponsible; Chip is the serious-minded member. They are out for adventure— which means they want to find girls. In the subway Gabey sees a picture of Ivy Smith (Sono Osato), the month's "Miss Turnstiles," and is determined to find her and date her. Chip and Ozzie offer their help in this blind and seemingly hopeless pursuit, each going in a different direction. Chip meets Claire (Betty Comden), a woman taxi driver who interests him, a woman of irrepressible enthusiasms and a lusty appetite for males, as she readily confesses in "I Get Carried Away." Ozzie, on a visit to the Museum of Natural History, comes upon an anthropology student, Hildy (Nancy Walker), a girl with more talents than one ("I Can Cook, Too"). Gabey finds himself at a music studio in Carnegie Hall, and it is there that he finds "Miss Turnstiles"—taking singing lessons.

*On the Town* was a young people's frolic. The average age of producers, co-authors (the co-authors appeared in the cast), stars, and composer was in the neighborhood of twenty-five. And it was the energy, breeziness and ebullience of youth— aided not a little by George Abbott's skill in keeping the production moving at a breathless pace—that proved so exhilarating. These and the highly imaginative choreographic sequences conceived by Jerome Robbins. "It shoves dullness off the curbstone," remarked *Time* magazine. Lewis Nichols called it one "of the freshest of musicals to come to town in a long time."

The production gave Bernstein opportunities to demonstrate his serious musical background with episodes requiring spacious orchestral design, such as the breezy opening scene, "New York, New York" (a song since become almost as frequently identified with the city as "East Side, West Side"), the subway-ride fantasy, and the ballet music for two of Robbins' outstanding choreographic conceptions, "Miss Turnstiles" and "Gabey in the Playground of the Rich." But Bernstein also revealed a strong hand in the writing of haunting ballads, in "Lucky to Be Me" and "Lonely Town," both introduced by Gabey, the latter with chorus.

ON YOUR TOES (1936), *a musical comedy, with book by Lorenz Hart, Richard Rodgers, and George Abbott. Lyrics by Lorenz Hart. Music by Richard Rodgers. Presented by Dwight Deere Wiman at the Imperial Theater on April 11. Directed by Worthington Miner. Choreography by George Balanchine. Cast included Ray Bolger, Tamara Geva, Doris Carson, Luella Gear, and Monty Woolley (315 performances).*

While working in Hollywood in the early 1930's, Rodgers and Hart prepared an outline of a motion-picture script about a vaudeville hoofer involved with the Russian ballet. They hoped to induce Pandro Berman to buy it for Fred Astaire. The project was turned down. Sometime later, after returning to New York, Rodgers and Hart sold the idea to Shubert for Ray Bolger. Enlisting the aid of George Abbott, Rodgers and Hart whipped together a completed musical-comedy book. But by then Shubert bowed out of the picture and turned the entire project over to Dwight Deere Wiman.

*On Your Toes,* as the musical was finally titled, drew its background from the world of ballet—a subject then comparatively esoteric for American musical comedy.

Before the ballet theme is presented, we are introduced to a pair of vaudeville hoofers—Phil Dolan II and Lil, who offer a typical vaudeville routine in "Two-a-Day for Keith." For their son, Phil Dolan III (Ray Bolger), they have lofty ambitions that transcend vaudeville. They want him to engage in some cultural activity. And so young Phil becomes a music instructor interested in "The Three B's," a delightful musical number of the same name expressing his outlook. He also becomes a devotee of ballet. He soon meets up with a serious young lady, Frankie Frayne (Doris Carson), who writes songs for diversion. That they are one of a kind they soon discover, and they voice the wish of going to a simple hideaway with nobody around them in the most important song in the score, a song that proved a hit in the 1930's and became a standard—"There's a Small Hotel." But Phil is actually in love with Vera Baranova (Tamara Geva), a member of the Russian ballet. In order to be near her, he joins the company and becomes involved in a ballet production that is a total fiasco—an elaborate spectacle called *La Princesse Zenobia,* derived from the subject of Scheherazade. Just as it seems that the Russian ballet would have to close down (its patron, Peggy Portenfeld, has threatened to end her support), a friend of Phil's brings him the scenario of a modern jazzy ballet, "Slaughter on Tenth Avenue." The Russian ballet had repeatedly turned it down, but Phil is convinced it would be the saving of the company. Out of sheer desperation, the company decides to mount that ballet, with Phil taking over as Vera's partner. The jazz ballet is a tremendous success. The Russian ballet is back in business. And, at long last, Phil comes to realize that it is not Vera he loves, but Frankie.

Since the plot concerned itself with ballet and ballet dancers, *On Your Toes* placed considerable emphasis on the dance, perhaps the earliest musical to do so. It enlisted the services of a noted choreographer, George Balanchine (onetime ballet master of the Diaghilev Ballet and the Ballet Russe de Monte Carlo), the first time he engaged in the American popular theater. Balanchine created two large ballet sequences. The first, *La Princesse Zenobia*, was intended as a satire on the classic dance traditions. The second, "Slaughter on Tenth Avenue," was a jazz ballet—a satire on gangster stories—and it became the high point of the production. The latter described the flight of a hoofer and his girl from gangsters. They are caught in a Tenth Avenue café, and the girl is shot; but the hoofer is saved by the police. For "Slaughter on Tenth Avenue," Rodgers created his most ambitious orchestral score up to that time, the heart of which was a beautiful lament for strings in the blues style, with a saucy little jazz theme serving as a secondary subject. "Slaughter on Tenth Avenue," with which the plot of *On Your Toes* comes to a climax, always drew thunderous approval from audiences. When *On Your Toes* was revived on Broadway in 1954, it was this one episode in the play that had not aged at all, but continued to exert an inescapable spell. Richard Watts, Jr., said: "A sizable number of jazz ballets have passed this way since it first appeared, but it still is something of a classic in its field, and the music Mr. Rodgers wrote for it continues to seem one of the major achievements of his career." And in 1968 George Balanchine and the New York City Ballet presented an evening of serious ballet at the New York State Theater at the Lincoln Center for the Performing Arts, featuring only two works on the program. One was "Slaughter on Tenth Avenue"; the other, Stravinsky's *Requiem Canticles*.

Besides "There's a Small Hotel" and "The Three B's," which we have already mentioned above, the Rodgers and Hart score included a plangent blues number, "Quiet Night," and an amusing ditty, "Too Good for the Average Man."

Vera Zorina and Eddie Albert were starred in the motion-picture adaptation made by Warner Brothers and released in 1939. Three songs and "Slaughter on Tenth Avenue" were used from the stage score.

PAINT YOUR WAGON (1951), *a musical comedy, with book and lyrics by Alan Jay Lerner. Music by Frederick Loewe. Presented by Cheryl Crawford at the Shubert Theater on November 12. Directed by Daniel Mann. Dances by Agnes de Mille. Cast included James Barton, Olga San Juan, and Tony Bavaar (289 performances).*

In the progress of the writing team of Lerner and Loewe, *Paint Your Wagon* came after *Brigadoon* and before *My Fair Lady*. A good many of the people who had worked on *Brigadoon* returned to do *Paint Your Wagon:* Agnes de Mille as choreographer, Oliver Smith as designer, Cheryl Crawford as producer, and Franz Allers as musical director. But good as it was, *Paint Your Wagon* could not repeat the success of *Brigadoon*. It failed at the box office, and it inspired more carping criticism than praise from the critics. It took over fifteen years for the motion-picture industry to become interested in it—a sumptuous Paramount production starring Lee Marvin, Clint Eastwood, and Jean Seberg, released in 1969, at a cost of about twenty million dollars. The most important songs, of course, came from the original stage score, but several new numbers were written for the screen adaptation, with lyrics by Lerner and music by André Previn.

The stage musical deserved a far better and more enthusiastic response than it received. It was most delightful in its colorful exploitation of American tradition, lore, and geography; a realistic, earthy representation of the Old West. Both Lerner and Loewe had done considerable research, and a good deal of text incorporated actual episodes from history, just as much of the dialogue absorbed the vernacular favored by the miners of the 1850's. And the music had a geinuine American folk-music character—one of Loewe's best and least appreciated scores. "They have eschewed the caricature of routine musical comedy," wrote Walter Kerr, one of the few critics who found the musical at least in part appealing, "and they have avoided almost entirely the interpolation of random vaudeville." But even Kerr had reservations. "Writing an *integrated* musical comedy—where people are believable and the songs are logically introduced—is no excuse for not being funny from time to time. But the librettist of *Paint Your Wagon* seems to be more interested in the authenticity of his background than in the joy of his audience."

The setting was northern California in 1853 during the Gold Rush, and the play traces the history of a mining camp from its beginnings through its development into a boom town, down to its disintegration into a ghost town when the lode peters out. (The play, however, ends optimistically: the town is revivified through irrigation and agriculture.)

The town in California is named after the central character who had founded it, Ben Rumson (James Barton). He tries to fill the varied roles of town sheriff, mayor, judge. He and his daughter, Jennifer (Olga San Juan), had come here to find gold. While bringing water from a stream, Jennifer comes upon a gold nugget. Word spreads like contagion that gold has been found, attracting prospectors to the town in droves. As the only girl in town, Jennifer is overwhelmed by the attentions showered upon her by men lonely for women. Her father, recognizing the danger inherent in such a situation, sends her East for schooling, but not before she has fallen in love and carried on a romance with Julio Valveras (Tony Bavaar), a Mexican of noble birth. The lack of women in Rumson is remedied with the arrival of ladies by stage-coach, infecting the air with exhilaration and bringing to the men a new spurt of desire and ambition. Ben Rumson gets a woman of his own, by purchasing her from a Mormon at an auction.

While Jennifer is in the East, the gold in Rumson has petered out; the town has become desolate. Ben Rumson is reduced to poverty and afflicted with disenchantment. Jennifer comes back to Rumson in time to be with him before his lonely death. Her romance with Julio is resumed. But the town itself, which had once promised to grow into a great city, was, like its founder, facing death, until the promise of irrigation and agricultural development brings hopes of survival.

The play is filled with scenes rich in local color—in a saloon, a mine, a miner's cabin, the town square. The action is filled with exciting incidents and episodes—free-for-all saloon fights, can-can dancing, a treasure hunt, and so forth. It was not strong on humor, but some mild amusement was contributed when Ben, after buying his wife, tries to sell her again because he must raise cash. The background and atmosphere were enriched through the folk choreography of Agnes de Mille, and particularly the exciting dances of James Mitchell and Gemze de Lappe. The two best ballet sequences were "Hand Me Down That Can o' Beans" and "Whoop-Ti-Ay."

Ben Rumson's ballad, "Wand'rin' Star," which he sings both at the beginning and at the end of the play, has the personality of authentic Western folk song and is one of the musical highlights of Loewe's score. But the song above all others to survive from the production was "They Call the Wind Maria," which is sung by Rufus Smith (in a subsidiary role) and male chorus, before being danced to by James Mitchell. This number has come close to becoming a "standard," thanks mainly to its revival in the early 1960's by Robert Goulet over TV, in a recording, and in nightclubs. (It was with this song that Robert Goulet auditioned for the role of Lancelot in *Camelot* for Lerner and Loewe and captured the desirable role.) Other distinguished songs, including Julio's haunting "Another Autumn," the poignant duet of

Julio and Jennifer, "I Talk to the Trees," Ben Rumson's ballad, "I Still See Elisa," and the choral episode, "There's a Coach Comin' In."

> THE PAJAMA GAME (1954), *a musical comedy, with book by George Abbott and Richard Bissell, based on Bissell's novel 7½¢. Lyrics and music by Richard Adler and Jerry Ross. Presented by Frederick Brisson, Robert Griffith, and Harold Prince at the St. James Theater on May 13. Directed by George Abbott and Jerome Robbins. Dances by Bob Fosse. Cast included John Raitt, Eddie Foy, Jr., Carol Haney, and Janis Paige (1,063 performances).*

A great deal of new, fresh talent was gathered for this musical, with which the 1953–54 theatrical season in New York came to its culmination. Adler and Ross were writing their first complete musical-comedy score. Two of the producers (Griffith and Prince), the choreographer (Bob Fosse), and one of the stars (Carol Haney) were unknowns making their Broadway bows. In the chorus line was a young lady named Shirley MacLaine, about whom practically nothing was known, because up to then she had accomplished nothing. (Bob Fosse picked her out of the chorus to take over for Carol Haney when the latter became indisposed for one of the performances; the movie producer Hal Wallis was in the audience that night, was impressed, and signed her to a contract that lifted her to movie stardom.)

Besides drawing so heavily on new people, *The Pajama Game* challenged Broadway tradition on other counts. It opened in May, just before the summer months, which usually spelled disaster for any production with an as yet unestablished popularity. And it used for much of its setting such drab surroundings as a pajama factory and union headquarters, while much of its plot was motivated by labor strife between employer and the union—not material calculated to excite a musical-comedy audience.

Yet *The Pajama Game* not only weathered the summer heat of 1954, but several summer heats thereafter. It became the eighth musical in Broadway history to exceed a run of over one thousand performances. It captured the Antoinette Perry and Donaldson awards as the best musical of the season. It was made into an outstandingly successful motion picture by Warner Brothers in 1957, with Doris Day as its star, but with most of the other performers recruited from the stage production. As for the stage presentation, William Hawkins described it as "about the best-natured musical you may have ever seen . . . young and funny and earthy and fast," while Robert Coleman called it a "royal flush and grand slam all rolled into one."

The musical opens at the Sleep-Time Pajama Factory in Cedar Rapids, Iowa. Hines (Eddie Foy, Jr.), the factory manager and efficiency expert, explains to the audience that a "problem play" is about to be presented. Assuming his identity in the play, he speeds up the operation in the plant, and with stopwatch in hand, drives the girls to increase the quantity of their production at their machines. But trouble is brewing. The union is demanding from Mr. Hasler, the boss, a raise of 7½ cents an hour. Babe Williams (Janis Paige), head of the union grievance committee, comes to Sid Sorokin (John Raitt), the new factory superintendent, with this demand. Since both these people are attractive and possess more than the natural allotment of sex appeal, they are instantly drawn to each other. In fact, Sid tries to date Babe, only to be reminded that they are on opposite sides in a labor-management dispute. But Sid cannot get Babe out of his mind, and in the song "Hey, There" confides his feelings into his dictaphone.

Labor problems notwithstanding, the workers are attending their annual picnic. Everybody is in good spirits. During the many activities, with everybody in holiday mood, Sid manages to steal a kiss from Babe, who offers no protest. Several days after the picnic, Sid visits Babe at her home, where he tries to get her interested in him. But all that Babe has on her mind is the union demand for a raise; she insists that her personal feelings for Sid will not interfere with her determination to gain this victory for the union. Nevertheless, a romantic interest between Babe and Sid is rapidly developing. The only thing that stands between them, as Babe informs Sid in song, is seven and a half cents ("7½¢"). But this proves a formidable obstacle indeed, since Mr. Hasler is determined not to give in. In rebuttal, the workers plan to sabotage production. There is a marked slow-down in their work, which is also so careless that the buttons from the pajamas keep falling off. Infuriated, Sid threatens to fire the whole factory if the women cannot deliver an honest day's work. This causes Babe to kick the machinery with such vigor that the entire plant breaks down. For this, Sid fires her.

But later on Sid tries in vain to convince Babe that his heart is in the right place—on the side of the workers—that he was only doing his duty in threatening to fire them. Babe, however, closes her ears to his arguments. Sid now becomes determined to find some way of squaring himself with the girl he loves. By now Sid has become convinced that Mr. Hasler has been earning a far greater profit on his product than he had claimed; that, therefore, the raise demanded by the workers was not unreasonable. What he needs is evidence. To get access to the company's books, Sid must first ingratiate himself with the bookkeeper, Gladys (Carol Haney), who also happens to be Hines's girl friend. When Sid asks to date her, she suggests that they go off to an intriguing night spot called Hernando's Hideaway ("Hernando's Hideaway"). There Sid plies her with drinks until it becomes a simple task for him to get from Gladys the key to the safe where the ledgers are kept. Studying them, Sid discovers that for months now Mr. Hasler has been adding the cost of the anticipated seven-and-a-half-cent-an-hour wage increase to his product. It is not difficult now for Sid to get Mr. Hasler to agree to give the workers their raise, which causes a good deal of jubilation in the union headquarters—and, to be sure, a permanent reconciliation between Babe and Sid.

The score had two substantial hits. One was the principal love song, "Hey, There," introduced by Sid Sorokin into his dictaphone machine when he first discovers he loves Babe; it then becomes a delightful one-man duet when the dictaphone plays the song back to him while he makes pointed comments. (The popularity of this number was enormously enhanced in 1954 through Rosemary Clooney's recording for Columbia, which sold about two and a half million disks.) The other hit was the tango (or, to be more accurate, a takeoff on traditional tangos) "Hernando's Hideaway."

Other numbers were good enough not to be completely thrown into the shade by these two substantial successes: the love duet of Sid and Babe, "There Once Was a Man"; "Once a Year Day," presenting Sid and the union members in a jubilant mood during their annual picnic; Hines's song of reassurance of his faith in Gladys after having repeatedly accused her of infidelity, "I'll Never Be Jealous Again."

In two amusing, show-stopping dance numbers, Carol Haney proved herself a star, novice though she then was on Broadway. She had been a dance teacher, a dancer with Jack Cole, and for five years assistant to Gene Kelly. For several years she hung around the MGM studios waiting for the "break" that never came, though she did do a short dance number with Bob Fosse in the screen adaptation of Cole Porter's *Kiss Me, Kate*. Bob Fosse remembered that dance when he was preparing the choreography for *The Pajama Game* and brought Carol to Broadway.

One of her dance numbers was a travesty on a strip-tease, performed during the union picnic festivities. The other, and the triumph of the production, was "Steam Heat." Dressed as a gamin, but in derby and black tight-fitting suit—and flanked by two men similarly dressed—she performs a routine accompanied by hissing and other vocal sounds. Miss Haney also appeared with Eddie Foy, Jr., in a slapstick bedroom-closet episode, "Jealousy Ballet," in which Eddie Foy as Hines imagines what it would be like to be married to a girl as faithless as Gladys.

Eddie Foy, Jr., provided much of the comedy. He participated in one of the score's best comedy numbers—the song "I'll Never Be Jealous Again"—in which he proved himself adept not only in the delivery of a humorous song but also in a most ingratiating soft-shoe dance with Reta Shaw as his partner. He was also heard in a second appealingly amusing number, "Think of the Time I Save," in which he details his many time-saving devices. He was the central figure in the show's two most farcical scenes. One involved him with a zipper, and in the other he models pajamas whose trousers insist on falling down.

Less than six months after its long run, *The Pajama Game* was revived on Broadway—at the New York City Center on May 15, 1957. In 1969 George Abbott announced plans to revive *The Pajama Game* in an "integrated production" starring Nipsey Russell as Hines, Gerri Granger as Babe Williams, and Paula Kelley as Gladys.

A unique experiment was tried by Richard Bissell, the author of the novel from which *The Pajama Game* was derived and one of the collaborators of the musical-comedy text. This was (with the assistance of Abe Burrows and Marian Bissell) to concoct a musical comedy on how *The Pajama Game* came to be written and produced. The musical was called *Say, Darling;* lyrics were by Betty Comden and Adolph Green; music was by Jule Styne; Abe Burrows was the director. David Wayne appeared as Bissell, Robert Morse as the young producer Harold Prince, Jerome Cowan as George Abbott, and Johnny Desmond as a songwriter representing Adler and Ross. Vivian Blaine appeared as a glamorous star. The show opened at the Anta Theater on April 3, 1958. It proved for the most part an undistinguished effort both as to text and songs.

> PAL JOEY (1940), *a musical comedy, with book by John O'Hara, based on his stories. Lyrics by Lorenz Hart. Music by Richard Rodgers. Presented by George Abbott at the Ethel Barrymore Theater on December 25. Directed by George Abbott. Dances by Robert Alton. Cast included Gene Kelly, June Havoc, Vivienne Segal, and Leila Ernst (374 performances).*

Rodgers and Hart never lacked courage to do the unusual and the unexpected on the musical stage. They did not lack such courage in bringing O'Hara's stories about Joey into the Broadway theater. In 1940 a musical like *Pal Joey* represented iconoclasm. Nobody else would have dared to populate the stage with such disreputable characters; to point up so realistically the seamy side of life—blackmail, illicit love affairs, hypocrisy, skulduggery, and crass opportunism. This was adult musical theater, mature in approach and concept —a far distance from the sugar-and-spice-and-all-that's-nice that characterized musical comedies up to this time.

*Pal Joey* originated as a series of letters in story form by John O'Hara, published in *The New Yorker*—Joey being a "heel" who started out as a nightclub entertainer and developed into a nightclub operator. O'Hara himself suggested to Rodgers and Hart that they make these stories into a musical, and the pair was delighted with the idea. O'Hara wrote his own text.

The setting is Chicago's South Side. Joey Evans (Gene Kelly) is a nightclub hoofer—a cheap opportunist who never misses a chance, however discreditable, to advance himself either professionally or with girls. His winning, engaging ways land him a job with a small Chicago night spot, and also the interest of two girls: Gladys (June Havoc), a member of the night spot's chorus line, and Linda (Leila Ernst), a simple, forthright lass who works as a salesgirl in a pet shop. The latter soon becomes convinced that Joey is in love with her. When she comes to the night spot to see Joey perform, Linda finds herself snubbed by Joey because one of the patrons that evening is the wealthy, hard-boiled, pleasure-loving matron Vera Simpson (Vivienne Segal). Joey realizes that Vera has the wherewithal to advance his career and his personal fortunes. Yet, in spite of this knowledge, he manages to insult her with his brash and brazen ways, so that she leaves the club in a huff. When the nightclub owner threatens to fire Joey, the latter is fully confident that Vera will soon be back. He is not wrong—for Vera, unaccustomed to the kind of treatment Joey has given her, has become fascinated by him. It is not long before a torrid affair develops between them. Joey becomes the recipient of Vera's generous gifts and bounties, since she has become wild over him. She sets him up in a luxurious apartment. She even buys him a nightclub—*Chez Joey*—which becomes successful.

Linda has overheard a plot between an agent and a singer to blackmail Vera. The blackmailers intend to disclose to Vera's husband her affair with Joey if Vera fails to pay them a handsome price. That Linda should thus be willing to warn her intrigues Vera no end. But Linda assures Vera her own romantic interest in Joey has long since died and that as far as her own heart is concerned, Joey can be Vera's for good. At this point the black-mailers come to carry out their threat. To their amazement, they find that Vera is no pushover; in fact, she has called for the police. This sends the blackmailers into retreat. Vera is no longer a pushover for Joey, either. In no uncertain terms she informs him she is tired of his antics and sends him on his way. Thus Joey has lost Vera, Linda, and his nightclub—and must leave town to try his luck and charm elsewhere.

Long before the final plans were crystallized to bring *Pal Joey* to Broadway, Rodgers and Hart knew who their leading performers would be. Hart had long since promised Vivienne Segal he would put her in a play that would do justice to her vital talent, and he knew that the part of Vera was just right for her. Rodgers had seen Gene Kelly in Saroyan's *The Time of Your Life* and recalled that performance when he began thinking about Joey. Though Rodgers and Hart did not know it at the time, when they cast June Havoc in the minor role of Gladys they were also making an act of discovery; for June Havoc, who had never before appeared on the Broadway stage, was able to use *Pal Joey* as the springboard from which to jump into a rich career on stage and screen.

*Pal Joey* inspired sharply divided reactions when finally produced. Some loved it, considered it fresh, original, daring, exciting. In this group belonged Louis Kronenberger, who thought it was the most unhackneyed musical he had ever seen. Many others were repelled by its vivid realism. "If it is possible to make an entertaining musical comedy out of an odious story, *Pal Joey* is it," wrote Brooks Atkinson. "Although *Pal Joey* is expertly done, can you draw sweet water from a foul well?" The "nays" had it. *Pal Joey* did not do too well at the box office; the public simply could not take to it.

But one decade later *Pal Joey* was revived—on January 3, 1952—with Harold Lang, Helen Gallagher, Vivienne Segal, and Pat Northrop. It was now a triumph. The critics were unanimous in their praises. Brooks Atkinson wrote: "No one is likely to be impervious to the tight organization of the production, the terseness of the writing, the liveliness and versatility of the score, the easy perfection of the lyrics. Brimming over with good music and fast on its toes, it renews confidence in the professionalism of the theater." Critics Richard Watts, Jr., and Robert Coleman did not hesitate to label it a work of art, a masterpiece. The audience was also enchanted. The play's run of 542 performances was the longest of any musical revival in the history of the American theater. The New York Drama Critics Circle chose it as the best musical of the year; and it received eleven of the sixteen Donaldson awards, the first time in the then nine-year history of these awards that one play received so many honors. The original shock may have gone from *Pal Joey* since it was first produced; but the excitement was still there.

When *Pal Joey* was subsequently revived at the New York City Center in 1961 and 1963, the role of Joey was assumed by Bob Fosse. When *Pal Joey* became a movie in 1957 (Columbia), it starred Rita Hayworth, Frank Sinatra, and Kim Novak, and used songs from several other Rodgers and Hart productions besides the basic stage score.

The haunting love duet of Joey and Linda in the first act, "I Could Write a Book," was one of two main songs in the production. The other—which boasted a most felicitous set of lyrics by Hart—was Vera's lusty and lustful reactions to Joey in "Bewitched, Bothered and Bewildered." This song became a major hit in Paris before it did so in New York, under the title *"Perdu dans un rêve immense d'amour."* This was because in 1940 ASCAP, in a dispute with the radio networks, had banned from the airwaves all music by its members—and "Bewitched, Bothered and Bewildered" suffered for lack of radio circulation. But in the late 1940's the song began to gain attention in nightclubs, on records, and on radio (the ASCAP dispute by this time having long since been resolved). In 1950 it climbed to the top place in radio's Hit Parade. Its fame developed further in 1951 when Columbia issued a recording of the entire *Pal Joey* score and when in 1952 *Pal Joey* had its triumphant revival.

Vera had a couple of other vigorous numbers that gave insight into a personality of which Vivienne Segal gave a three-dimensional portrayal: "What Is a Man?" and her duet with Joey after she had set him up in his swank apartment, "In Our Little Den of Iniquity." She shared an amusing duet with Linda in "Take Him," when both come to the final decision that neither is any longer interested in Joey. Other numbers of special interest included "That Terrific Rainbow," which was in a torrid jazz style, and "Zip," the reflections of a strip-tease artist—the latter distinguished particularly for Hart's vivacious, suggestive, and scintillating lyrics.

PANAMA HATTIE (1940), *a musical comedy, with book by Buddy de Sylva and Herbert Fields. Lyrics and music by Cole Porter. Presented by Buddy de Sylva at the 46th Street Theater on October 30. Directed by Edgar MacGregor. Dances by Robert Alton. Cast included Ethel Merman, Rags Ragland, James Dunn, Joan Carroll, Betty Hutton, and Arthur Treacher (501 performances).*

*Panama Hattie* was not only the first Cole Porter show to achieve a run of five hundred performances, but the first musical to do so in twelve years.

"Panama Hattie" is Hattie Maloney (Ethel Merman), who runs the Tropical Shore Bar in the Panama Canal Zone. She is a loud, brassy lady who is partial to garish attire and earthy manners and mannerisms. She decides to reform and acquire social polish, since she is in love with Nick Bullett (James Dunn), a Philadelphia socialite serving as an official of the United States. Nick is divorced and has custody of an eight-year-old daughter, Geraldine (Joan Carroll), whom he has left behind in Philadelphia. When Nick and Hattie fall in love and decide to get married, Hattie insists that Geraldine come down to the Canal Zone and give her approval. Little Geraldine, brought up in genteel society, is at first repelled by Hattie's vulgar ways and dress. The marriage is now in serious danger. Then Hattie overhears a plot by some spies to blow up the canal. With the help of three gobs she thwarts the enemy.

This endears her again to Nick, and since Geraldine has come to be fond of Hattie, the marriage can now take place.

There was a great deal of rowdy, and at times ribald, humor here; a great deal of burlesque, particularly when Rags Ragland, as a gob, was on the stage with his buddies (Ragland making his first successful appearance in the legitimate theater after years in burlesque); a good deal of hard-boiled theater. Ethel Merman, supplemented by Betty Hutton as Florry, added considerably to the vigor and vitality of the proceedings. But some engaging tomfoolery frequently lightened the atmosphere, as in the whacky duet "You Said It"; and even cloying sentimentality—such as one would hardly expect from Cole Porter—crept into the production: in a song like "My Mother Would Love You," a duet by Hattie and Nick, and especially in "Let's Be Buddies," sung by Geraldine and Hattie. The last-named was the hit of the show, and invariably inspired an ovation. Cole Porter revealed to an interviewer why he wrote "Let's Be Buddies" the way he did: "There was a spot where Joan Carroll, who is eight years old, and Ethel Merman, who is more than sixteen, had to sing and dance a duet. The spot required it. The law forbade it. The spot also stipulated that the song—as Ethel sang it—must be boozily sentimental, in, of course, a ladylike way. So I wrote it that way, boozily sentimental . . . and in rhythm that can be walked to, in order to compensate for Joan having been prevented by law from dancing, and with a patter in between so that Joan could recite instead of court jail by singing. Also, I put in an A-natural for Ethel, because while all her notes are extraordinarily good, A-natural is her best and the C above is a good finish for her." Here is what Brooks Atkinson said of this routine: "Gruff old codgers are going to choke a little this winter when tot and temptress sing 'Let's Be Buddies' and bring down the house."

*Panama Hattie* was the first musical in which Ethel Merman occupied the only starring role. Though supported by an excellent cast, she was the dynamo of the production. She was in her finest form, "than which there is none finer," as John Mason Brown put it. "Ethel Merman sweeps triumphantly through *Panama Hattie*. . . . The evening she dominates with all the strident precision which is hers is a happy example of our professional theater when it is functioning at its professional best." Her best songs, besides the two already mentioned, were "I've Still Got My Health" and "I'm Throwing a Ball Tonight."

It is not generally known that it was at a performance of *Panama Hattie* that June Allyson made her first important step toward stardom. She was a member of the chorus when, in 1941, she was called upon to substitute for Betty Hutton, stricken with measles. "June Allyson did a perfect job," Ethel

Merman recalls. "I'd never seen an understudy take over with such confidence." It was as a result of this performance that Allyson won from George Abbott a starring role in her next stage appearance, *Best Foot Forward*.

In spite of the fact that Ethel Merman was practically the whole show— so much so that when she was replaced by another performer during the road tour the musical was a failure—she was sidestepped when *Panama Hattie* was made into a movie by MGM in 1942. Ann Sothern took her place. Only two songs were used here from the stage production, supplemented by numerous new numbers by E. Y. Harburg and Burton Lane, and E. Y. Harburg and Walter Donaldson.

A PARISIAN MODEL (1906), *a musical comedy, with book and lyrics by Harry B. Smith. Music by Max Hoffmann, with additional songs by Will D. Cobb and Gus Edwards. Presented by Frank McKee at the Broadway Theater on November 27. Directed by Julian Mitchell. Cast included Anna Held, Henry Leoni, and Truly Shattuck (179 performances)*.

*A Parisian Model* was one of the most luxurious frames created by Florenz Ziegfeld for his wife, Anna Held; and as Anna, a model in a dress establishment, Anna Held scored one of the oustanding personal triumphs of her career. She had made her American debut a decade earlier in a revival of Charles Hoyt's *A Parlour Match,* presented by Florenz Ziegfeld in his initial venture as producer on September 21, 1896. When she sang "Won't You Come and Play with Me?" with a piquant French accent, while rolling her eyes, she instantly became a beloved of New York theatergoers. A year later she married Ziegfeld, who presented her in the next few years in a series of musicals built around her winning personality. These appearances—and the publicity about her baths in milk—made her one of the most glamorous singing and dancing stars on Broadway in the early 1900's. *A Parisian Model* was the best of these plays. Once again she rolled her eyes roguishly; in a saucy, captivating French accent sang provocative songs like "I Just Can't Make My Eyes Behave" (by Will D. Cobb and Gus Edwards); wore in one scene six alluring gowns while a chorus of girls chanted "A Gown for Each Hour of the Day"; with Gertrude Hoffmann danced a sexy number imported from Paris which shocked some of the critics.

Ziegfeld surrounded Anna Held with some of the most beautiful girls he had thus far brought before the footlights. They appeared in an eye-filling "pony ballet"; and they sang "I'd Like to See a Little More of You" (by Cobb and Edwards) while undressing—a trick stage effect making them appear completely nude.

*A Parisian Model* had all this—and a story too. Anna falls heir to a fortune and has her portrait painted by Julien de Marsay (Henry Leoni), with whom she falls in love. She must compete for his love with Violette (Truly Shattuck), over whom she is finally victorious. Comedy scenes featured Charles Bigelow as Silas Goldfinch, an American trying desperately to spend some of his money, and who is forced to appear throughout the play in various disguises—as Paderewski, a Mexican, and an old woman.

THE PASSING SHOW (1894), *a revue, with book and lyrics by Sydney Rosenberg. Music by Ludwig Englander. Presented by George W. Lederer at the Casino Theater on May 12. Cast included Jefferson de Angelis, Adele Ritchie, Johnny Henshaw, and Paul Arthur.*

*The Passing Show* created a new genus in the American musical theater—the revue. Consequently, it was the forerunner of *The Ziegfeld Follies, George White's Scandals, The Earl Carroll Vanities,* Irving Berlin's *Music Box Revues,* and all the other elaborate or intimate revues that brightened the Broadway theater for half a century. (This 1894 production should not be confused with the annual editions of *The Passing Show* which the Shuberts presented in the Winter Garden from 1912 on and which is discussed in the next section.)

The revue as a medium of the musical theater was a conception of George W. Lederer, who was convinced that if vaudeville were dressed up with the splendor of a Broadway extravaganza and presented in a Broadway theater it could command a far higher price of admission than such variety entertainment could draw at a place like Tony Pastor's Music Hall in Union Square. In carrying out his ambition, Lederer rented the Broadway theater most celebrated for musical productions—the Casino. He digressed from the prevailing practices in vaudeville by having text, lyrics, and music expressly written for his production—whereas in vaudeville these were the work of many different people, each act bringing in its own material. But in other respects, as this writer said elsewhere, *"The Passing Show* was vaudeville in coat tails, top hat and white tie." It was much more than that, too. It also embraced burlesque and extravaganza, ballet and female pulchritude. It boasted comedy in skits and routines by the Tamale Brothers; acrobatics in stunts by the Amazons; comedy in imitations of popular actors of the day and satires of current plays; female pulchritude in a series of "living pictures"; spectacle in a sumptuously mounted "divertissement" on *L'Enfant prodigue;* dancer Lucy Daley, who contributed a novel plantation dance with a group of young colored men.

So popular was *The Passing Show* that other producers rushed in with similar productions. In 1895 came *The Merry Whirl;* in 1896, *In Gay New*

*York;* in 1897, *All of the Town;* in 1899, *In Gay Paree.* By the time a new century was at hand, the revue had become an institution in the American musical theater—an institution whose most flourishing years came between 1907, when the first edition of *The Ziegfeld Follies* was produced, and the period preceding World War II.

THE PASSING SHOW (1912), *a revue, with book by George Bronson Howard. Lyrics by Harold Atteridge. Music by Louis A. Hirsch. Presented by the Winter Garden Company (the Shuberts) at the Winter Garden on July 22. Directed and with dances by Ned Wayburn. Cast included Willie and Eugene Howard, Jobyna Howland, and Harry Fox (136 performances).*

*(1913), a revue, with book and lyrics mainly by Harold Atteridge. Music mainly by Jean Schwartz and A. W. Brown. Presented by the Shuberts at the Winter Garden on July 24. Directed and with dances by Ned Wayburn. Cast included Charles and Mollie King, Bessie Clayton, Charlotte Greenwood, and Wellington Cross (116 performances).*

*(1914), a revue, with book and lyrics mainly by Harold Atteridge. Music mainly by Sigmund Romberg. Presented by the Shuberts at the Winter Garden on June 10. Directed by J. C. Huffman. Dances by Jack Mason. Cast included Marilyn Miller, Jose Collins, Bernard Granville, and Lew Brice (133 performances).*

*(1915), a revue, with book and lyrics mainly by Harold Atteridge. Music mainly by Leo Edwards and W. F. Peters. Presented by the Shuberts at the Winter Garden on May 29. Directed by J. C. Huffman. Dances by Jack Mason. Ballets by Theodor Kosloff. Cast included Marilyn Miller, John Charles Thomas, Willie and Eugene Howard, and Harry Fisher (145 performances).*

*(1916), a revue, with book and lyrics mainly by Harold Atteridge. Music mainly by Sigmund Romberg and Otto Motzan. Presented by the Shuberts at the Winter Garden on June 22. Directed by J. C. Huffman and Allen K. Foster. Cast included Ed Wynn, Frances Demarest, Herman Timberg, and the Ford Sisters (140 performances).*

*(1917), a revue, with book and lyrics mainly by Harold Atteridge. Music mainly by Sigmund Romberg and Otto Motzan. Presented by the Shuberts at the Winter Garden on April 26. Directed by J. C. Huffman. Cast included De Wolf Hopper, Jefferson de Angelis, Johnny Dooley, and Irene Franklin (196 performances).*

*(1918), a revue, with book and lyrics, mainly by Harold Atteridge. Music mainly by Sigmund Romberg and Jean Schwartz. Presented by the Shuberts*

*at the Winter Garden on July 25. Directed by J. J. Schubert and J. C. Huffman. Musical numbers and ballets staged by Jack Mason. Cast included Marilyn Miller, Fred and Adele Astaire, Eugene and Willie Howard, Charles Ruggles, and Frank Fay (124 performances).*

*(1919), a revue, with book and lyrics mainly by Harold Atteridge. Music mainly by Sigmund Romberg and Jean Schwartz. Presented by the Shuberts at the Winter Garden on October 23. Directed by J. C. Huffman. Cast included Charles Winninger, Blanche Ring, James Barton, the Avon Comedy Four, Olga Cook, and Reginald Denny (280 performances).*

*(1921), a revue, with book and lyrics mainly by Harold Atteridge. Music mainly by Jean Schwartz. Presented by the Shuberts at the Winter Garden on December 29, 1920. Directed by J. C. Huffman. Cast included Eugene and Willie Howard, Marie Dressler, Janet Adair, and Harry Watson (200 performances).*

*(1922), a revue, with book and lyrics mainly by Harold Atteridge and Jack Santley. Music mainly by Alfred Goodman. Presented by the Shuberts at the Winter Garden on September 20. Directed by J. C. Huffman. Cast included Eugene and Willie Howard, George Hassell, Janet Adair, and Fred Allen (95 performances).*

*(1923), a revue, with book and lyrics mainly by Harold Atteridge. Music mainly by Sigmund Romberg and Jean Schwartz. Presented by the Shuberts at the Winter Garden on June 14. Directed by J. C. Huffman. Cast included Walter Woolf, George Hassell, George Jessel, and Helen Shipman (118 performances).*

*(1924), a revue, with book and lyrics mainly by Harold Atteridge. Music mainly by Sigmund Romberg and Jean Schwartz. Presented by the Shuberts at the Winter Garden on September 3. Cast included James Barton, George Hassell, Lulu McConnell, Olga Cook, and Harry McNaughton (104 performances).*

This annual series of revues should not be confused with *The Passing Show*, in 1894, with which the modern revue came into being, and which was discussed in the preceding section. The 1912 *Passing Show* was the first edition of a new revue put on annually by the Shuberts at the Winter Garden until 1924.

*The Passing Show* came into existence because J. J. Shubert detested and envied Ziegfeld. For several years Shubert had watched the growing popularity and importance of *The Ziegfeld Follies*, until he was driven to imitation. What Ziegfeld had accomplished, Shubert was convinced he could equal if not surpass. He became a man driven with the passionate determination to put on an annual splendiferous revue of his own.

His first production, in 1912, was divided into two sections. The first comprised a "mime dramatic ballet"—*The Ballet of 1830,* imported from the Alhambra Theater in London. Spectacle was here apotheosized. The second part of the production was an "almanac in seven scenes"—*The Passing Show.* Here beautiful chorus girls (eighty, no less), stupendous costumes and sets, and spectacular production numbers were combined with song, dance, humor, and particularly satire. The audience was carried from a steamship pier to a harem, from Greeley Square in New York to a hotel roof garden. En route, the current happenings in the theatrical, social, and political world were touched upon, and most frequently laughed at. Personalities (many of them long since forgotten) were burlesqued by Jobyna Howland, Anna Wheaton, Trixie Friganza, and so forth; Eugene Howard, for example, appeared as David Belasco, and Clarence Harvey as Andrew Carnegie. The two most famous cartoon characters of the day, Mutt and Jeff, were brought to life by Daniel Morris and George Moon. Adelaide Hughes did some striking dances (particularly in the harem scene); Clarence Harvey did a lively dance to the song "Handy Andy."

It was in this edition that Willie and Eugene Howard made their first step from vaudeville to the Broadway theater. They would remain the comic mainstay of many an edition of *The Passing Show,* wherein they graduated from obscurity to success. Another performer to enjoy her first stage success here was Charlotte Greenwood, with her eccentric dancing and her flair for comic facial expressions. The best songs by Louise A. Hirsch were "Always Together" and "The Wedding Glide." Irving Berlin had a number interpolated into the score—"The Ragtime Jockey Man," introduced by Willie Howard.

The two-part format was abandoned in 1913. From this year on the production became a revue in the style of the "almanac" in the second part of the 1912 edition—but with a slight difference. In 1913—and only then—a slight thread of a plot bound the production into a single package. Peg o' My Heart (Mollie King) came to the United States to be taught the Turkey Trot under the direction of Mrs. Potiphar (May Boley) and Joseph Asche Kayton (Herbert Corthill). In America, Peg falls in love with Broadway Jones (Charles King). Other characters borrowed from various Broadway productions of that period were burlesqued—from *Within the Law, Oh! Oh! Delphine, Peg o' My Heart,* and *Broadway Jones.*

The plot idea was an innovation for a revue. Much more significant, however, in the 1913 edition was the use of a runway, which J. J. Shubert had built so that the public could get a closer glimpse of his dazzlingly attractive, half-draped chorus girls. Shubert got the idea for the runway from the famous German producer Max Reinhardt, who had then recently come to Broadway for a Shubert-sponsored production and extended the stage into the first few rows of the auditorium in order to bring the audience closer to the performers. Planning his 1913 edition, Shubert decided to outdo Reinhardt by building not a stage extension but a runway through the middle of the auditorium and right across the entire theater. The runway helped to bring into existence a *new* type of chorus girl (which is perhaps the greatest single contribution made to the Broadway musical theater by *The Passing Show*). Cecil Smith in *Musical Comedy in America* places the beginnings of this modern chorus girl in the 1914 edition, but the building of the runway in 1913 was the motivating force for the change. Here is how Cecil Smith described this change:

"Gone forever were the gigantic chorus ladies with their Amazonian marches and drill. . . . The choral Amazon had been on the way out for some years. But with *The Passing Show of 1914* the metamorphosis was complete. . . . The girls' legs, which had been emerging from their tights inch by inch for several seasons, were now presented unadorned and *au nature*. . . . Skirts were short and arms were bare, and at one point the glittering spangles were dispensed with, revealing bare midriffs on the upper-class New York stage for the first time. The 'winsome witches' gave a new and piquant meaning to the runway."

In the 1913 edition Charlotte Greenwood was back with her unique type of comic acrobatics and to assume the role of a character named Molly Turner, "a woiking goil." Mlle. Dancrey was imported from France to inject a Gallic flavor, and Bessie Clayton to do some of her effective specialties. Famous show people (Gabys Delys and Billie Burke) and famous shows of the time (*The Sunshine Girl* and *Peg o' My Heart*) were burlesqued. Two particular highlights were a big production number reviving the cakewalk, and a striking scene in which the huge staircase of the Capitol in Washington, D.C., leads a bevy of beautiful showgirls to heaven. In addition, there was a striking "Silhouette Dance" performed by Wellington Cross and Lois Josephine, and Ned Wayburn's conception of the tango and the Turkey Trot. The comedy included allusions to the political events of the day and an irreverent burlesque of President Wilson. Jean Schwartz replaced Louis A. Hirsch as songwriter. Schwartz' best songs were "If You Don't Love Me, Why Do You Hang Around?", "I'm Looking for a Sweetheart," and "My Cinderella Girl." Some of these numbers profited from the beautiful baritone voice of John Charles Thomas (later so famous in concert hall and opera house), making here his Broadway stage debut.

*The Passing Show of 1914* was the first edition for which Sigmund Romberg provided the music. He would contribute scores to most of the other editions, though sometimes in collaboration with Jean Schwartz, and sometimes with Otto Motzan. The 1914 edition was one of the most lavish, the most eye-catching, the most entertaining, and the most varied of these spectacular revues. It set a standard that subsequent editions found hard to match. It signaled the Broadway stage debut of Marilyn Miller (then only in her teens) after an apprenticeship in vaudeville. This alone would give this edition historic importance. She appeared as a Dresden doll; she impersonated notable actresses of the day (Bessie McCoy, Sophie Tucker, Fritzi Scheff, and the female impersonator Julian Eltinge); and she danced. And whatever she did, she proved herself at once to be of star material. Bernard Granville and Lew Brice contributed burlesque dancing and brought down the house with a pantomime interlude entitled "The Grape Dance." The singing was assigned to Lillian Lorraine, who was particularly effective in "Smother Me with Kisses," and to Jose Collins, who was heard in "You're Just a Little Bit Better" and "Dreams of the Past"; Miss Collins also appeared as a princess in one of the most sumptuously mounted sketches of the production, a scene in a Persian garden. Another breathtaking stage effect was achieved in the finale, with a view of San Francisco from an altitude. One of the best comic sequences was a takeoff on silent movies, with George Monroe impersonating Mary Pickford.

In the 1915 edition Marilyn Miller proved further that she was *sui generis*—as singer, dancer, and impersonator. Willie and Eugene Howard performed their comic routines as Hamlet, Macbeth, and Trilby. Elsie Ferguson, Ethel Barrymore, and Ruth Chatterton were some of the stars of the day to be burlesqued. A "Spring Ballet" was one of the best production numbers; another, "The Hula Maid," took cognizance of the craze for the Hawaiian hula dance then seizing America.

The first hit song to emerge from *The Passing Show* came in 1916. It was an interpolation: "Pretty Baby" (words by Gus Kahn, music by Tony Jackson and Egbert van Alstyne), sung by Dolly Hackett. Another song interpolation was "Making of a Girl," whose sole importance rests in the fact that this was the first time that young George Gershwin was being heard on a Broadway stage. Otherwise, the greatest importance of the 1916 revue came with the comic presence of Ed Wynn, who had made his Broadway stage debut in *The Ziegfeld Follies of 1914* but who here became a star for the first time. During one of the performances of this 1916 edition Wynn stopped the show to inform the audience that his wife had just given birth to a boy— Keenan Wynn (who would make quite a name for himself in the movies)— at which the orchestra struck up the strains of "Pretty Baby." One of the comedy classics in which Ed Wynn was involved in this production was "A Modern Garage," in which he tried to fix an inner tube with saw and hammer. Charlie Chaplin, Teddy Roosevelt, President Wilson, and Pancho Villa were some of the celebrities who were burlesqued; and one of the most impressive spectacles saw the United States Cavalry charge in a Mexican scene.

The 1917 edition boasted two hardy veterans of the musical stage—De Wolf Hopper and Jefferson de Angelis—and a newcomer named Chic Sale who did some of the humorous monologues with which he would subsequently become famous. Two outstanding production numbers were "The Wanderer" and "Under the Willow Tree," and a third one was a college number, "College Boys, Dear," ending in a fracas between the boys of Yale and Harvard (on the runway). An interpolated song caught the martial spirit of the times (this was the period of World War I) and became a hit, "Good-bye Broadway, Hello France!" (words by C. Francis Reisner and Benny Davis, music by Billy Baskette); it sold about four million copies of sheet music. This patriotic spirit was carried over further into a spectacular finale entitled "Ring Out Liberty."

In 1918 the production was dominated by the war. There was a skit on War Saving Stamps (chorus girls went down the aisle to sell stamps to the audience); a takeoff on Salome, in which Salome danced with the head of the Kaiser on a tray; and a reproduction of an aerial raid. The best comedy was contributed by Eugene and Willie Howard: in their entrance lines, in which Willie explained to Eugene that he was holding dead geese under his arms because he was going to make himself a pair of white duck pants; in their takeoff on the Metropolitan Opera in the "Galli-Curci Rag."

The outstanding dance numbers in the 1918 edition came from Fred and Adele Astaire, who now came into their own for the first time. For many years barred from the Broadway stage because they were underage, Fred and Adele Astaire had for years been hoofing up and down the country in vaudeville theaters. As early as 1906 (when Fred was only seven) the act of Fred and Adele Astaire was billed as "Juvenile Artists Presenting an Electric Musical Toe-Dancing Novelty." They were vaudeville headliners when, in 1917, the Shuberts brought them for the first time into the legitimate theater in a wartime revue called *Over the Top,* presented at the 44th Street Roof on December 1 (score by Romberg). The entire production had been built around the dynamic personality of its star, Justine Johnson. Yet each time the Astaires went through their suave and sophisticated dance-routines the stage was theirs. *Over the Top* was a failure, but the Astaires survived the wreckage. A year later Shubert placed them in *The Passing Show of 1918,* presenting them for the first time as stars. They did a bird number, in which they wore bird plumage, supported by a dance group similarly attired. Fred Astaire joined Sammy White and Lou Clayton, all portraying waiters in a Childs' restaurant, and doing amusing turns by sliding all over the tables, by serving pancakes sloppily, and so forth. "In an evening in which there was an abundance of good dancing," wrote Heywood Broun in his review, "Fred Astaire stood out. He and his partner, Adele Astaire, made the show pause early in the evening with a beautiful loose-limbed dance. It almost seemed as if the two young persons had been poured into the dance."

Romberg's best songs were "My Baby Talking Girl," sung by Frank Fay; "My Holiday Girl," introduced by a juvenile comic yet to make his mark—Charles Ruggles; and "I Can't Make My Feet Behave." But the real musical standouts were interpolations which have since become standards: "Smiles" (by J. Will Callahan and Lee G. Roberts), introduced by Neil Carrington and chorus (a three-million-copy sheet-music sale) and "I'm Forever Blowing Bubbles" (by Jean Kenbrovin and John W. Kellette), sung by June Caprice (a two-and-a-half-million-copy sheet-music sale).

A lot of new, unknown names appeared in the cast of the 1919 edition; they would not remain unknown for long, for they included Walter Woolf (soon to become famous in operettas as Walter Woolf King), Olga Cook, Reginald Denny, James Barton, and Charles Winninger. One of the members of the chorus was Mary Eaton—also eventually destined for stardom. Charles Winninger and Blanche Ring joined in a travesty on *The Jest,* a famous Broadway stage play for that period starring John and Lionel Barrymore; Charles Winninger played Lionel with almost incredible similitude, and Blanche strutted around as John. Even broader humor appeared in several skits starring the Avon Comedy Four, one of which was "King Solomon's Kitchen" and the other of which became their classic, "The Doctor's Office." Reginald Denny appeared as a genial master of ceremonies. James Barton (making his first Broadway appearance after a career in vaudeville, stock, and repertory companies) scored heavily in specialty dances; and the singing of Blanche Ring was as arresting as her comedy.

There was no separate edition of *The Passing Show* in 1920—the first clue that this historic series of revues was beginning to limp toward its last mile.

The 1921 edition was notable mostly for burlesques of current plays and the Metropolitan Opera. Willie Howard did a takeoff of Frank Bacon in

*Lightnin'*, while with his brother Eugene he helped make a shambles of *Rigoletto*. Marie Dressler appeared in a travesty on the mystery play *The Bat*. One of the best comedy routines was a skit, "Spanish Love," starring Marie Dressler as a much-sought-after señorita; one of the best dance numbers was an exotic performance by Cleveland Bronner; and one of the best production numbers was a ballet, "Dream Fantasies." The Schwartz score included "In Little Old New York," "When There's No One to Love," "Let's Have a Rattling Good Time," and "Charm School."

A new comic emerged into the limelight in the 1922 edition, young Fred Allen (formerly a juggler in vaudeville), whose dry humor and deadpan face made "The Old Joke Cemetery" a comic highlight of the production. Lloyd George and the Prince of Wales came in for ribbing; Ethel Shutta delivered a number inspired by (of all things) Eugene O'Neill's drama *The Hairy Ape;* and Willie and Eugene Howard sang "My Coal Black Mammy" and the hit song of the revue, "Carolina in the Morning" (words by Gus Kahn, music by Walter Donaldson).

Apparently the Shuberts had become convinced that the now dwindling audiences had become tired of the humor of Willie and Eugene Howard. In the 1923 edition they were replaced by George Jessel. But it was a weak production, as proved by the fact that one of its features was a demonstration of trick golf shots by Alex Morrison, a golf champion. Production numbers included a pageant about the French Revolution and a scene at an English royal wedding.

The 1924 edition was worse still, despite the noble efforts of George Hassell and James Barton to give it a life-saving infusion of some humor. It had a run of only 104 performances—an unmistakable signal to the Shuberts that critics and audiences had grown tired of this revue and that the time had finally come to call a halt. The only single point of theatrical importance in this, the last edition of a historic revue, was the appearance of a young performer name Lucille Le Sueur in a living curtain and as "Labor Day" in a "Holiday Revue." As Joan Crawford, Lucille Le Sueur would ultimately develop as one of the most glamorous stars in the history of motion pictures.

PEEP SHOW. *See* MICHAEL TODD'S PEEP SHOW.

PEGGY-ANN (1926), *a musical comedy, with book by Herbert Fields, based on Edgar Smith's* Tillie's Nightmare. *Lyrics by Lorenz Hart. Music by Richard Rodgers. Presented by Lew Fields and Lyle D. Andrews at the Vanderbilt Theater on December 27. Directed by Robert Milton. Dances by Seymour Felix. Cast included Helen Ford, Lester Cole, Lulu McConnell, and Betty Starbuck (333 performances).*

The dream fantasies of the heroine, Peggy-Ann, provide the startlingly un-orthodox material that makes up the plot of this musical play, one of the earliest attempts on the American musical stage to exploit Freudian psychology.

The story itself is not unusual. Peggy-Ann (Helen Ford) is the niece of a boardinghouse proprietress, Mrs. Frost (Lulu McConnell), in Glens Falls, New York. For three years she is the fiancée of a local boy, Guy Pendleton (Lester Cole). Swallowed in the morass of a humdrum existence, she can find escape only in dreams and fantasies. There she sees herself in New York, the wealthy heroine of many adventures, including a love idyll aboard a yacht, and marriage. Her dreams must finally be crushed by reality, which dictates that she reconcile herself to both Glens Falls and Guy Pendleton.

It is in the treatment of this plot that the musical becomes a daring, and at times a brilliant, adventure. Fantasy becomes inextricably intertwined with reality; the absurd, the impossible, the grotesque acquire plausibility. When Peggy-Ann makes her trip to New York, accompanied by a chorus of girls, the scene shifts from Glens Falls to the metropolis while the girls change from country to city dress. What follows in New York acquires a kind of surrealistic quality, as chaos is projected through undisciplined lighting and disordered dancing; absurdities mount, the confusions grow. Pills become as large as golf balls; fish speak with an English accent; the New York City police wear pink moustaches; race horses are interviewed. At her wedding Peggy-Ann appears only in step-ins, and the ceremony calls for the use of a telephone book in place of a Bible. A yacht, in which Peggy-Ann takes a cruise with her lover, becomes the scene of a mutiny when the crew discovers the pair is not married.

The authors were equally bold in their use of musical-comedy techniques. There was no singing or dancing for the first fifteen minutes of the produc-tion; and the play ended on a darkened stage with a slow comedy dance. All this meant the shattering of existing musical-comedy procedures—and so did the ballet character of the dancing and the integration of the musical numbers with the action. Though Rodgers' score often caught the strange and nebulous character of the stage action through a considerable amount of atmos-pheric music, it also had some hit songs: "A Tree in the Park" and "Maybe It's Me," both duets of Peggy-Ann and Guy; and "Where's That Rainbow?", by Peggy-Ann. A gay Cuban number, "Havana," was also effective.

THE PERFECT FOOL (1921), *a revue, with book, lyrics, and music by Ed Wynn. Presented by A. L. Erlanger at the George M. Cohan Theater on November 7. Directed by B. C. Whitney and Julian Mitchell. Cast included Ed Wynn (256 performances).*

Of the seventeen scenes, Ed Wynn expropriated seven. He appeared in his various bizarre costumes and hats, introduced some of his newer inventions—including a typewriterlike machine for eating corn on a cob, a non-eye-destroying spoon for iced tea, and a shield to prevent a knife from cutting the mouth. In his first curtain routine Ed Wynn explained that his show had some kind of a plot: A young fellow and a girl get married, and three months later he gets stuck on another girl. But the plot is forgotten even before it is allowed to develop, to make room for Ed Wynn's clowning, routines, and rambling and aimless monologues. When he was off the stage, it was able to present several beautiful production numbers: a dueling dance, with rapiers, by chorus girls; a huge typewriter in which the key bars are girls' legs. Janet Velie and Guy Robertson either shared or joined in the leading songs: "Girls, Pretty Girls," "She Loves Me, She Loves Me Not," "Days of Romance," and "My Garden of Perfume."

> PIFF, PAFF, POUF (1904), *a musical comedy, with book by Stanislaus Stange. Lyrics by William Jerome. Music by Jean Schwartz. Presented by F. C. Whitney at the Casino Theater on April 2. Directed by Gerard Coventry. Cast included Joseph Miron, Alice Fischer, Eddie Foy, and Mabel Hollins (264 performances).*

August Melon (Joseph Miron) can inherit his share of the fortune left him by his deceased wife only if each of his four daughters gets married successively according to their ages. Since August is bent on marrying the widow Mrs. Lillian Montague (Alice Fischer), he is determined to see his daughters marry quickly. But three of them have eccentric ideas on the kind of husbands they want. One wants a man who has never been kissed; another, a man who is a paragon of virtue; the third, a man who has posed for a patent-medicine ad. The fourth daughter is not capricious at all, but being the youngest, she cannot marry until the others do. After numerous amusing trials, the three girls find their men in Poufle, Piffle, and Paffle; and the fourth selects Dick Daily, a newspaper reporter.

Eddie Foy appeared as Peter Poufle, a "Scarecrow" character similar to the one in which he had achieved a triumph a year earlier in *The Wizard of Oz,* as a replacement for Fred Stone, who created the role. His song, "The Ghost That Never Walked," was one reason for the success of *Piff, Paff, Pouf.* Other Schwartz tunes included a ballad, "Good Night, My Own True Love," and a lilting melody, "Love, Love, Love." "The Radium Dance" was an outstanding production number in which chorus girls appeared on a darkened stage, their phosphorescent costumes gleaming in the darkness.

THE PINK LADY (1911), *a musical comedy, with book and lyrics by C. M. S. McLellan (Harry Morton), adapted from* Le Satyre, *a French farce by Georges Berr and Marcel Guillemaud. Music by Ivan Caryll. Presented by Klaw and Erlanger at the New Amsterdam Theater on March 13. Directed by Herbert Gresham and Julian Mitchell. Cast included Hazel Dawn, William Elliott, Alma Francis, and Alice Dovey (312 performances).*

*The Pink Lady* shattered the existing attendance record for the New Amsterdam Theater; it also enjoyed a triumphant national tour equaled by few other musicals of that period; and it was responsible for making pink the fashionable color in lady's clothes throughout 1911. "Everyone should see *The Pink Lady*," wrote Earl Derr Biggers. Philip Hale reported that "here we have . . . an amusing book, pleasing music, a rare combination. Here we have a musical comedy that does not depend upon the antics of an acrobatic comedian, or the independent display of brazen-faced showgirls."

The plot was of modest proportions. Lucien (William Elliott) takes his onetime girl friend Claudine, the "Pink Lady" (Hazel Dawn), to a restaurant. When by chance they meet Lucien's current fiancée, Angele (Alice Dovey), he introduces Claudine as Mme Dondidier, wife of a furniture dealer. The ensuing entanglements take up the rest of the evening, but as one critic pointed out, "the fun develops logically out of the situations."

Some of the interest stemmed from the effective scenery, particularly the settings for the forest of Compiègne, a furniture shop on the Rue Ste.-Honoré, the Ball of Nymphs and Satyrs. But most of the interest rested in the infectious score, the highlight being a sentimental waltz, "My Beautiful Lady," sung by the Pink Lady as she seems to be playing her own accompaniment on the violin. In the "Kiss Waltz," the Pink Lady tries teaching a male the art of kissing. A breezy comic song, "Donny Did, Donny Don't," usually stopped the show—presented by the cast as it filed down a sweeping double stairway. Another pleasing number was a duet, "By the Saskatchewan," sung by John E. Long, Ida Lewis, and chorus.

PINS AND NEEDLES (1937), *an amateur political revue, with book by Arthur Arent, Marc Blitzstein, Emanuel Eisenberg, and others. Lyrics and music by Harold Rome. Presented by the International Ladies Garment Workers' Union at the Labor Stage Theater on November 27. Directed by Charles Friedman. Dances by Gluck Sandor. Cast was made up of union members (1,108 performances).*

*Pins and Needles* had the longest run of any revue up to its time. It created a vogue for political and social-conscious revues, which populated the Broadway stage during the 1930's and early 1940's—a reflection of the aroused consciousness of America during the Depression years in working conditions, politics, and the international scene; and it brought to Broadway for the first time a composer-lyricist of no small consequence—Harold Rome.

Harold Rome had long been dabbling with songwriting when Louis Schaeffer, head of the International Ladies Garment Workers' Union, came to him with a proposition. The union was planning a show with a cast of union members, though outside help would be recruited for various technical and creative departments. The production was to be a modest affair, intended exclusively for the delectation of union members. Would Rome write the songs? With assignments nonexistent, Harold Rome accepted with alacrity, though the possibility of a show like this advancing his songwriting career appeared slight indeed. With some of his collaborators, Rome worked out songs, sketches, and other bits of topical routines which were tried out before a union committee in a studio on June 14, 1936. The committee liked what they heard and approved the project. It took a year to train union members to sing, dance, art, and deliver funny lines and situations—even though nobody concerned had any intention of making the show anything but an amateur production to be shown over several weekends, in a theater seating only three hundred, and with the price of admission only one dollar. (The theater, incidentally, was the Princess—the same place where the famous Princess Theater Shows had been produced; but its name had been changed to Labor Stage.)

The sparkling scene reviewed the economic, political, social, and international scene with a discerning eye. It discussed labor, domestic politics, and the international situation with sprightly sketches, songs, and dances; with sentiment and laughter. Described by the New York *Post* as a "Puckish proletarian romp," *Pins and Needles* was an amateur production by a labor union, and as such identified itself unequivocally with a progressive point of view. This viewpoint was expressed in one of its principal songs, "Sing Me a Song with Social Significance," and in such numbers as "Big Union for Two," and "It's Better with a Union Man." Capitalism was ridiculed in "Doin' the Reactionary." Park Avenue etiquette and social viewpoints were lampooned in "It's Not Cricket to Picket." European fascism was scored in "Three Little Angels of Peace Are We." The simple pleasures of the working man were sentimentalized in the hit song, "Sunday in the Park" (which received the ASCAP Award in 1937).

Planned merely as a weekend diversion, *Pins and Needles* turned out to be a money-making plant. The praises of the critics and the delight of audiences soon induced its sponsors to put it on a regular run. It remained at the Labor

Stage for three years, then moved to larger quarters—to the Windsor Theater uptown, which sold out regularly. "It clicked so solidly," remarked *Variety*, "that the very people it mocked and ridiculed—the carriage trade—came in droves."

During its extended run the name of the revue was changed to *New Pins and Needles* and *Pins and Needles of 1939*—but its basic concept remained unaltered. New items, however, were continually interpolated to reflect the rapidly changing headlines. After Munich, Prime Minister Chamberlain of England was ridiculed in "Britannia Waives the Rules." After the Soviet-Nazi pact, Stalin was mocked in "The Red Mikado." As mounting national consciousness swept the country, a stirring tribute to the American way of life was introduced in 1940 in "We Sing America."

Besides songs already mentioned, two others deserve mention: "Mene, Mene, Tekel," introduced in the second edition of the revue, a popular treatment of the story of the handwriting on the wall from the book of Daniel; and "Nobody Makes a Pass at Me," the complaint of a plain girl who, having tried all the advertised beauty cosmetics, discovers they have done her little good.

PIONEER DAYS. *See* HIPPODROME EXTRAVAGANZAS.

PIPE DREAM (1955), *a musical play, with book and lyrics by Oscar Hammerstein II, based on John Steinbeck's novel* Sweet Thursday. *Music by Richard Rodgers. Presented by Rodgers and Hammerstein at the Shubert Theater on November 30. Directed by Harold Clurman. Dances by Boris Runanin. Cast included Helen Traubel, William Johnson, and Judy Tyler (246 performances).*

The plan to transform Steinbeck's novel *Sweet Thursday* into a musical was born in the producing offices of Feuer and Martin, who hoped to interest Frank Loesser in writing the score. When this project fell through, Feuer and Martin turned the idea over to Rodgers and Hammerstein, who expressed immediate interest because of the story's unusual setting, and the human and sympathetic treatment it gave to a strange assortment of social misfits.

The love interest is provided by "Doc" (William Johnson), an indigent scientist who studies marine life in his laboratory in Cannery Row, and a vagrant, Suzy (Judy Tyler). Suzy is picked up for breaking into a grocery store where she tries to steal some food. But she is saved from prison when Fauna, a softhearted madame of the local brothel (Helen Traubel), offers her a home. "Doc" and Suzy are attracted to each other but are separated by a quarrel at a masquerade party. They are finally reunited with the unasked-for assistance of Hazel (Mike Kellin), deeply concerned over the Doc's romantic troubles.

But the love complications of Doc and Suzy are only of secondary interest to the misfits who envelop them with their love and unselfish devotion, and who inhabit a sorry place called "The Palace Flophouse." Their concern for Doc and their attachment for Suzy flood the play with heart-warming humanity. They raffle off their house to raise money for a microscope Doc needs badly for his work, then they fix it so that Doc himself is the winner of the raffle. Hazel connives to bring him and Suzy together again by breaking Doc's arm in his sleep; Suzy had previously said that she would come to Doc only if he was in trouble, and with his broken arm he was in need of Suzy's ministrations. These people contribute to the play all of its sentiment and some of its pathos. They also enliven the proceedings with a hilarious episode called "The Bum's Opera" and with several amusing songs, among them "A Lopsided Bus," "The Happiest House on the Block," and Hazel's confession of his mental inadequacy in "Think."

In a more lyrical and sentimental vein are two fine Rodgers songs: Suzy's poignant lament, touched with a kind of radiance Rodgers often brings to his inspiring melodies, "Ev'rybody's Got a Home but Me," and the love duet of Doc and Suzy, "All at Once You Love Her." Doc's ballad, "The Man I Used to Be" (supplemented by a dance fantasy by Don Weissmuller), and Fauna's infectious cakewalk, "Sweet Thursday," are also assets.

The casting of Helen Traubel (for many years the leading Wagnerian Soprano of the Metropolitan Opera) as the madame of a brothel—her bow in musical comedy after a lifetime in the opera house—lacked conviction, and her efforts at earthiness and vigor were at times embarrassing to those who recalled her as Isolde and Brünnhilde. Much more rewarding was the performance of Judy Tyler as Suzy, making a successful Broadway debut and launching what at the time seemed to be the beginning of a rich career. But Judy's life and career came to a tragic ending in 1957 in an automobile accident.

PLAIN AND FANCY (1955), *a musical comedy, with book by Joseph Stein and William Glickman, suggested by an original play by Marion Weaver. Lyrics by Arnold B. Horwitt. Music by Albert Hague. Presented by Richard Kollmar and James W. Gardiner, in association with Yvette Schumer, at the Mark Hellinger Theater on January 27. Directed by Morton da Costa. Dances by Helen Tamiris. Cast included Richard Derr, Shirl Conway, Stefan Schnabel, and David Daniels (461 performances).*

The authors found their characters and setting with the Amish sect, which inhabits parts of Pennsylvania and which has clung tenaciously to its time-honored customs, speech, dress, and morality.

Ruth Winters (Shirl Conway) and Dan King, a magazine writer (Richard Derr), come down to the Amish town of Bird in Hand, in Lancaster County, Pennsylvania, to sell a farm Dan had just inherited. The couple soon fall under the spell of the people and their way of life. A potential customer for Dan's farm is Papa Yoder (Stefan Schnabel), whose daughter, Katie (Gloria Marlowe), is to marry the farmer Ezra. Just as the marriage preparations are being completed. Ezra's brother, Peter (David Daniels), comes home after two years' absence. Peter and Katie had once been in love. Despite the passage of time—and the fact that Peter always was and obviously still is a shiftless and irresponsible fellow—they discover they still love one another. Nostalgically, they remember all the foolish things they used to do together—in the most important and successful song in the score, "Young and Foolish." It also soon becomes apparent that Katie is not in love with Ezra, that she had consented to marry him only because her father has ordered her to do so. Nor is Ezra particularly eager to take Katie as a wife. When Dan inquires from Papa Yoder why he is so insistent on having two people marry who do not love each other, the old man gives him some Amish philosophy. The Amish are simple, moral, good people to whom the presence of love is of far lesser importance than the existence of respect and the pursuit of a useful life ("Plain We Live").

Complications arise when Papa Yoder's farm burns down. Since Peter is convinced he is a curse on his family, he is determined to leave his folk again; this time he urges Katie to come along with him, expressing his plea in the tender song "Follow Your Heart." When Ezra gets drunk (through the guile of Ruth Winters), he disgraces himself with his family and neighbors. He would have become involved in serious trouble at a carnival had not his brother, Peter, come to help him. This act convinces Papa Yoder that Peter is not such a bad person after all, that he might even make a good husband for Katie. Dan sells his farm to Peter, where he and his future bride can settle down. With Katie's marital problem solved, Dan must disentangle himself from Hilda Miller, an Amish girl who had fallen in love with him. He convinces her that she can find happiness only by marrying somebody in her own sect. This argument having proved fruitful, Dan must now convince Ruth that he loves her—which is not difficult to do, since Ruth has all the while been in love with him.

The song "It Wonders Me," sung by Katie, provides a picture of the Amish people much in the same way as does the already mentioned number (with chorus) of Papa Yoder, "Plain We Live." These possess a decided folk character. An attractive carnival ballet and the hit song "Young and Foolish," however, are more typical of musical-comedy material.

POPPY (1923), *a musical comedy, with book and lyrics by Dorothy Donnelly. Music by Stephen Jones and Arthur Samuels. Presented by Philip Goodman at the Apollo Theater on September 3. Directed by Julian Alfred and Dorothy Donnelly. Cast included W. C. Fields, Madge Kennedy, Luella Gear, and Robert Woolsey (328 performances).*

W. C. Fields had been a star of *The Ziegfeld Follies* for a number of years, and of *George White's Scandals* for one, when he was suddenly struck with the ambition to appear in musical comedy. Philip Goodman, a producer, came forward with a role he felt was ideally suited for Fields's personality and brand of comedy: an out-and-out "con" man named Eustace McGargle who milked gullible people of their money at carnivals through any quack operation he could think of. It was an unpalatable role, but Fields seized it. One of his friends remarked: "I think what sold him was the name of the character— Eustace McGargle." Closer to the truth is what Robert Lewis Taylor said in his biography of Fields: "He found all his instincts attuned to the grandiose humbug of his part; thereafter he seldom strayed far from his character in *Poppy.*"

Professor Eustace McGargle is the foster father of Poppy (Madge Kennedy). The time is 1874. During their trips in which the professor earns a dishonest "buck" as gambler and medicine man—and Poppy assists him as a fortune-teller—they arrive at Meadowbrook, Connecticut, Poppy's home town and the scene of a county fair. There Poppy meets and falls in love with the wealthy William van Wyck (Alan Edwards). Learning of an unclaimed inheritance, the professor presents Poppy as the lost heiress, but Poppy balks at the idea of entering into such a swindle. But it turns out that Poppy really is the heiress, a development that brings about a happy culmination to her love affair with William.

Though the text did not call for it, Fields—among his other shenanigans —did a good deal of juggling (always a basic part of his act), some of it of the humorous variety, and in one instance called for the help of mucilage to assist him in his manipulations. Both as a comedian and as a juggler, W. C. Fields now proved himself beyond doubt one of the greatest comics the American musical theater has produced. Said Heywood Broun: "Mr. Fields is so good a juggler that recognition of his ability as an actor was delayed until last night. Not only does he handle lines just as deftly as cigar boxes, but he creates an authentic and appealing character. At the moment we can't remember anybody who ever made us laugh more. It is first-rate clowning, but that is only the beginning of the job Fields has done. In addition to his familiar but nonetheless hilarious stunts, he gives us a real and complete portrait of as merry a rascal as the stage has seen in years."

One of the funniest episodes was a poker game—a situation in which Fields was in his element. "His hands, graceful and expressive, are carefully shielding his cards from any possible snooping by the man on the left," wrote Robert Lewis Taylor, "while his own furtive, suspicious gaze is plainly directed into the hand of the player on the right. His attitude is so frankly dishonest that the other players seem to sense the inevitability of their financial downfall. Their stunned faces pay homage to a situation, and a character which defy all the known rules regarding cheats." The reviewer of the *Herald* said: "The stud game in which he manages to deal himself four fours and to win a thousand-dollar pot without having undergone the burdensome necessity of putting up any money himself is the most hilarious minor episode of the new season."

As Poppy, Madge Kennedy was making her Broadway stage debut—and an impressive debut it was, Heywood Broun calling her "one of the two or three best light-comedy actresses in America and the best *farceuse* of them all."

The two best songs were presented by Luella Gear, in a subsidiary role: "Mary" (lyrics by Irving Caesar) and "Alibi Baby" (lyrics by Howard Dietz, his first published song).

PORGY AND BESS (1935), *an opera, with libretto by DuBose Heyward, based on the play* Porgy, *by Dorothy and DuBose Heyward. Lyrics by DuBose Heyward and Ira Gershwin. Music by George Gershwin. Presented by the Theater Guild at the Alvin Theater on October 10. Directed by Rouben Mamoulian. Cast included Todd Duncan, Anne Brown, John W. Bubbles, J. Rosamond Johnson, and the Eva Jessye Choir. Alexander Smallens conducted (124 performances).*

Since *Porgy and Bess* is an opera (by any definition at all), it would hardly seem to require a place among Broadway musical comedies, revues, and plays. Yet its composer came from the Broadway musical stage, and a great many of the finest pages in the opera had their artistic roots embedded deeply in the soil of that stage; moreover, it was on the Broadway stage—and not in an opera house—that *Porgy and Bess* was first performed; and it was in the popular musical theater that it has been revived in America through the years. Actually, *Porgy and Bess,* while an opera, is popular musical theater elevated to the status of a powerful and moving native art; and the arbitrary fact that it has recitatives in place of spoken dialogue should not exclude it from consideration in any panorama of the American musical theater.

The idea of writing *Porgy and Bess* came to Gershwin several years before he actually sat down to work—when he first read DuBose Heyward's novel *Porgy* and wrote to the author expressing his enthusiasm. Then and there he and DuBose Heyward decided to collaborate on an opera based on the novel, but pressing commitments compelled both men to postpone the project continually; for one thing, DuBose Heyward was busy working with his wife on a play adaptation of the novel for the Theater Guild.

Then, one day in 1933, Heyward informed Gershwin that the Theater Guild was interested in adapting the Dorothy and DuBose Heyward play, *Porgy,* into a Jerome Kern musical comedy starring Al Jolson. "I want you to tell me if you're really going to write our opera," Heyward told him. "If you are, I'm going to turn the Guild down definitely." Gershwin promised DuBose Heyward to begin work immediately—and he did.

It took Gershwin about twenty months to write and orchestrate the opera. Some of that time was spent in South Carolina, where Gershwin steeped himself in the life and folk music of the Negroes there, and acquired a first-hand acquaintance with the locale of his opera. The actual date of completion appears at the end of the manuscript—September 2, 1935—but Gershwin continued to revise and edit, up to the time that the cast was being assembled by the Theater Guild and first rehearsals began.

The cast was mostly Negro, and the principals were all new to the stage. Todd Duncan, Porgy, was a teacher of music at Howard University in Washington, D.C. Anne Brown, Bess, was a then unknown young singer without much professional experience. Both auditioned for Gershwin (together with many others); Gershwin recognized their talent and accepted them; both, then, may well be said to have been Gershwin's discoveries. For that matter, so was John W. Bubbles, Sportin' Life, even though he had previously had a long career in vaudeville. Bubbles could not read a note of music and seemed completely incapable of mastering his role. Yet Gershwin was convinced he was the ideal Sportin' Life, and exerted infinite patience in training him in the intricate score (at times the rhythm of a song had to be tapped out for Bubbles in a dance before he could understand it). The effort expended by Gershwin on Bubbles brought rich reward, for his performance was one of the shining lights of the production.

The setting of *Porgy and Bess* is a Negro tenement, Catfish Row, in Charleston, South Carolina. As the curtain rises, a crap game is taking place in one corner of the court, while in another part a few people are dancing.

Clara (Abbie Mitchell) is sitting in a third corner, lulling her baby to sleep with one of the most beautiful and popular songs from the entire opera, "Summertime." When the child fails to fall asleep, Clara's husband, Jake (Edward Matthews), seizes the child and sings to it a ditty of his own, "A Woman Is a Sometime Thing." As the heat and the fever of the gamblers rise in the crap game, a quarrel erupts between Robbins (Henry Davis) and Crown (Warren Coleman), in which the former gets killed. Crown goes into hiding, leaving behind his girl, Bess, who is now being enticed by Sportin' Life (John Bubbles) to go off with him to New York. Bess, however, prefers the protection of the cripple, Porgy, who loves her selflessly and devotedly.

The scene shifts to Robbins' room, where the mourners are lamenting Robbins' death, and neighbors drop in to put coins in the saucer for burial money. The widow, Serena (Ruby Elzy), distraught with grief, gives voice to her tragedy in "My Man's Gone Now," and the religious atmosphere is heightened with Bess's spiritual, "Oh, the Train Is at the Station."

The second act returns to Catfish Row. Bess is happy with her new life with Porgy and has come to love him. Porgy speaks of his newfound joy in an exultant refrain, "I Got Plenty o' Nuttin'," while the lovers exchange tender sentiments in the duet "Bess, You Is My Woman Now." Since the people of Catfish Row are about to leave for a lodge picnic on Kittiwah Island, Porgy insists that Bess go along with them.

The lodge picnic on Kittiwah Island is a gay affair, marked by riotous singing and dancing. Sportin' Life entertains his friends with a recital of his cynical philosophy, "It Ain't Necessarily So." When the picnic is over and the merrymakers proceed back to the boat, Crown—who has been in hiding on the island—accosts Bess, breaks down her resistance, and drags her off into the woods.

A few days later, in Catfish Row, the fishermen are off to sea. While they are gone, Bess returns, sick and feverish, to be gently nursed by a forgiving and solicitous Porgy. In "I Loves You, Porgy," they repeat their avowal of love. Suddenly hurricane bells sound an ominous warning. The hurricane sweeps across the skies, and the womenfolk huddle in Serena's room to pray for the safe return of their husbands. Suddenly Crown bursts in, searching for Bess. He injects a mocking, sacrilegious note into the terrified atmosphere by singing "A Red-Headed Woman Makes a Choochoo Jump Its Track." From her seat at the window, Clara sees her husband, Jake, fall out of his boat. Crown taunts Porgy for being a cripple and unable to give any help to anyone. Then Crown runs out into the storm to save Jake. When he returns to Catfish Row for Bess, he is murdered by Porgy.

Porgy is taken to prison for questioning. Sportin' Life arrives to tempt

Bess to go off with him to New York in "There's a Boat Dat's Leavin' Soon for New York." When she spurns him, he uses a package of "happy dust" to break down her resistance.

Now back from prison, and free, since no one will provide any testimony against him, Porgy searches for Bess. When he learns she has gone off to New York with Sportin' Life, he steps into his goat cart to follow her, chanting "Oh, Lawd, I'm on My Way to a Heavenly Land."

When *Porgy and Bess* tried out in Boston it was received rapturously by audience and critics. But there was mixed reaction in New York two weeks later, with most music critics bringing in negative reports. When, therefore, the opera closed after only 124 performances—and piled up a considerable deficit—it seemed that American opera had once again chalked up a failure. Gershwin, who never wavered in his conviction that he had produced an important work, did not live to see his faith justified.

A revival in New York on January 22, 1942 (almost five years after Gershwin's death), marked the beginning of the resuscitation of the opera. It proved so successful that it stayed on eight months and achieved the longest run up to then of any revival in New York stage history. The music critics now reversed themselves by unequivocally calling it a masterwork—"a beautiful piece of music and a deeply moving play for the lyric theater," as Virgil Thomson said of it. A decade later the triumph of *Porgy and Bess* was complete. In a production by Blevins Davis and Robert Breen, an American Negro company toured for several years through Europe, the Near East, the Soviet Union, other countries behind the Iron Curtain, South America, and Mexico—to arouse unparalleled excitement and enthusiasm wherever the opera was given. One Viennese critic said that no new foreign opera had been so well received in Vienna since the Austrian premier of *Cavalleria Rusticana* in 1902. The *Daily Herald* of London announced in a headline that "it was worth waiting 17 years for *Porgy*." An Israeli newspaper described the performance of the opera in Tel Aviv as "an artistic event of first-class importance." When *Porgy and Bess* came to the historic La Scala opera house in Milan (the first time an opera by an American-born composer was performed there), *L'Unità* placed the work "among the masterworks of the lyric theater." Since then, foreign opera companies have mounted their own productions, including Vienna (the Volksoper), Bulgaria, Turkey, and France, and Germany. The German production—at the world-renowned Komische Oper in East Berlin on January 24, 1970—had particular significance. This was the first time that *Porgy and Bess* entered the regular repertory of a major German opera company, and it was the first time that *Porgy and Bess* had ever been produced in Germany in that country's native language. In East Berlin, as elsewhere in Europe, the production was a triumph of the first magnitude.

*Porgy and Bess* is a folk opera, an epic of the Negro people told with humanity and compassion. Gershwin made extended use of musical materials basic to the Negro. His recitatives were modeled after Negro speech; his songs and choral numbers were derived from the folk and religious music of the Negro and the street cries of vendors in Charleston. So completely did Gershwin assimilate all the elements of Negro song and dance into his own writing that, without quoting a single melody, he produced authentic Negro folk music.

As this writer said in his biography *George Gershwin: His Journey to Greatness:* "*Porgy and Bess* was Gershwin's inevitable achievement . . . for it represents, at last, the meeting point for the two divergent paths he had all his life been pursuing—those of serious and popular music. The serious music is found at its best in the musically distinguished tone-speech, in the powerful antiphonal choruses, in the expressive dissonances and chromaticisms, in the brilliant orchestration, in the effective atmospheric writing, in the skillful use of counterpoint in the duets and particularly in the last-scene trio. The popular composer emerges in the jazz background of several choruses, like that in 'Woman to Lady'; in the two songs of Sportin' Life, 'It Ain't Necessarily So' and 'There's a Boat Dat's Leavin' Soon for New York'; and in Crown's blues ditty, 'A Red-Headed Woman Makes a Choochoo Jump Its Track.' Yet there is no feeling of contradiction, no sense of incongruity, in this mingling of the serious and the popular, for the popular is as basic to Gershwin's design as the serious, with its own specific artistic function."

POUSSE CAFE. *See* WEBER AND FIELDS EXTRAVAGANZAS.

PRESENT ARMS (1928), *a musical comedy, with book by Herbert Fields. Lyrics by Lorenz Hart. Music by Richard Rodgers. Presented by Lew Fields at the Lew Fields Mansfield Theater on April 26. Directed by Alexander Leftwich. Dances by Busby Berkeley. Cast included Charles King, Flora Le Breton, and Busby Berkeley (155 performances).*

Herbert Fields had in 1927 collaborated with Vincent Youmans on a successful musical comedy about the Navy called *Hit the Deck*. Having found the Navy a lucrative source for musical-comedy material, Fields convinced Rodgers and Hart to consider the Marines. Fields now prepared a book with a Hawaiian setting in which Chick Evans (Charles King), a Brooklyn hick serving in Pearl Harbor, as buck private in the Marines, flirts with Lady Delphine (Flora Le Breton), daughter of an English peer. She in turn is being sought after by a German, Ludwig von Richter (Anthony Knilling), who is spending his time in Hawaii raising pineapples. In order to make an impression on Lady Delphine, Chick passes himself off as a captain. He is discovered and dismissed from the service. He also loses the esteem of Lady Delphine, particularly after she learns he is only a plumber's son. By proving his heroism in a yacht wreck, Chick manages to win Lady Delphine's love.

One of the most effective moments in the production came after the shipwreck scene through some ingenious staging. A raft, floating on the sea, is holding three persons. As it floats, a tropical island is sighted in the distance and, without lowering the curtain, a dense forest appears.

Rodgers' music won critical approval. To Brooks Atkinson it was "the most beautiful element in the production." The best songs were "You Took Advantage of Me," introduced as a duet between a tourist and a Marine sergeant, played respectively by Joyce Barbour and Busby Berkeley. " 'You Took Advantage of Me,' " wrote Alison Smith, "will alone keep the music of *Present Arms* echoing over the roof gardens far into another summer"— and it did. "A Kiss for Cinderella," a burlesque of the Cinderella theme, sung by a male quartet, was an amusing episode; and two pseudo-Hawaiian numbers in the last scene contributed local color.

THE PRINCE OF PILSEN (1903), *an operetta, with book and lyrics by Frank Pixley. Music by Gustav Luders. Presented by Henry W. Savage at the Broadway Theater on March 17. Directed by George W. Marion. Cast included John W. Ransone, Arthur Donaldson, Lillian Coleman, Anna Lichter, and Albert Paar (143 performances).*

*The Prince of Pilsen* was a far greater success than its initial New York run of 143 performances might indicate. For five consecutive seasons it played to capacity houses on the road, and on three of those seasons it returned to New York for additional runs. It had many revivals throughout the country in the early 1900's: Jess Dandy, who took over the role of Hans Wagner from John Ransone, played the part over 5,000 times.

Hans Wagner (John W. Ransone) is a brewer and alderman from Cincinnati who goes to Europe with his daughter Nellie (Lillian Coleman) to visit his son Tom (Albert Paar), an American Navy man stationed near Nice, France. Upon his arrival in Nice, Hans is mistaken for a prince who was expected at the hotel. Despite all his protests, Wagner becomes the center of many festivities and is showered with favors. The real prince, Carl Otto (Arthur Donaldson), arrives, sizes up the situation, and decides that he can have more fun by going about incognito and letting Hans act the part of a prince. Incognito, the prince flirts with Nellie; before long they fall in love.

Hans Wagner, meanwhile, has an amatory adventure of his own—with a rich American widow, Mrs. Madison Crocker, while Tom is squiring Edith, a girl from Vassar (Anna Lichter). Hans comes into possession of a map of secret fortifications. When it is found on his person, he is accused of being a spy. But Carl Otto steps out of his anonymity to straighten out all difficulties and to reveal that he will marry Nellie.

*The Prince of Pilsen* was Luders' greatest hit and his best score. The music included the duet of Tom and Edith (the hit song), "The Message of the Violet," and a second duet—by Otto, Nellie, and a hidden female chorus —"Pictures in the Smoke." Two stirring choruses—"The Heidelberg Stein Song" and "The Tale of the Seashell"—and an amusing topical song by Hans, "He Didn't Know Exactly What to Do," provided contrast.

PRINCESS BONNIE (1895), *a comic opera, with book, lyrics, and music by Willard Spencer. Presented at the Broadway Theater on September 2. Directed by Richard Barker. Cast included Fred Lennox, Jr., William M. Armstrong, George O'Donnell, and Hilda Clark (40 performances).*

The figure of forty performances credited to *Princess Bonnie* is highly deceptive. The comic opera had a run of 1,039 performances in Philadelphia before it came to New York; and after its brief initial New York run it remained a favorite for a long time through periodic revivals and extended road tours. *Princess Bonnie* was undoubtedly one of the most successful American comic operas produced before 1900.

Its heroine, Bonnie (Hilda Clark), had been rescued from a shipwreck by Captain Tarpaulin (George O'Donnell), a Maine lighthouse-keeper who has raised her. She falls in love with Roy Stirling (Will M. Armstrong), but their romance is shattered when a Spanish admiral comes to claim her as his niece and proves she is really a princess. He carries her back to Spain, where she is followed by both the captain and Roy. They save her from an impending disagreeable marriage, and Princess Bonnie finds happiness with Roy.

THE PRINCESS PAT (1915), *a comic opera, with book and lyrics by Henry Blossom. Music by Victor Herbert. Presented by John Cort at the Cort Theater on September 29. Directed by Fred G. Latham. Cast included Eleanor Painter, Joseph R. Lertora, and Al Shean (158 performances).*

Certainly the opening night of no Herbert musical had a more dramatic preface than did *The Princess Pat*. Three nights before the opening, Pearl Palmer, who was cast in the second feminine lead, was murdered by her fiancé, who felt he had lost her love; the murder was followed by his suicide.

Naturally, the newspapers had a field day. Naturally, too, there was not much of the holiday spirit invariably attending openings when *The Princess Pat* came to the Cort Theater with a substitute (Eva Fallon) called in to replace a murdered performer.

Nevertheless, *The Princess Pat* went over well. The setting is Long Island in 1915. Price Antonio, better known as Toto (Joseph R. Lertora), has become cool to his wife, Pat (Eleanor Painter). At the same time, young Tony Schmalz, son of a millionaire, is enamored of Grace Holbrook (Eva Fallon), whose family is in serious financial trouble. A friendship develops between Grace and Pat, in which each helps the other to resolve her respective problem. By making her husband jealous, Pat wins back Toto's love, and by marrying young Tony Schmalz, Grace's money problems are over.

The outstanding number is the "Neapolitan Love Song," in which Toto, the Italian prince, pines for the woman of his life. The score also boasts a fine duet for Pat and Toto in "All for You," a comedy number sung by Mr. Schmalz, "I Wish I Was on an Island in an Ocean of Girls," and a mazurka-like number for Pat, "Love Is the Best of All."

This comic opera saw the elevation to stardom of two performers who would henceforth enrich the musical theater with their respective talents: Eleanor Painter, with her singing and performances of ingenue parts, and Al Shean, as a comedian.

THE PRINCESS THEATER SHOWS (1915), Nobody Home, *an intimate musical comedy, with book by Guy Bolton and Paul Rubens. Lyrics by Schuyler Green. Music by Jerome Kern. Presented by F. Ray Comstock and Elizabeth Marbury at the Princess Theater on April 20. Directed by J. H. Benrimo. Dances by David Bennett. Cast included Lawrence Grossmith, Adele Rowland, Alice Dovey, and Charles Judels (135 performances).*

(1915), Very Good, Eddie, *an intimate musical comedy, with book by Philip Bartholomae and Guy Bolton, based on Bartholomae's* Over Night. *Lyrics by Schuyler Green. Music by Jerome Kern. Presented by the Marbury-Comstock Company at the Princess Theater on December 23. Cast included Ernest Truex, Alice Dovey, Oscar Shaw, Ada Lewis, and Helen Raymond (341 performances).*

(1917), Oh Boy! *an intimate musical comedy, with book by Guy Bolton and P. G. Wodehouse. Lyrics by P. G. Wodehouse. Music by Jerome Kern. Presented by William Elliott and F. Ray Comstock at the Princess Theater on February 20. Directed by Edward Royce and Robert Milton. Cast included Tom Powers, Anna Wheaton, Edna May Oliver, and Marion Davies (463 performances).*

(1918), Oh, Lady! Lady!, *an intimate musical comedy, with book by Guy Bolton and P. G. Wodehouse. Lyrics by P. G. Wodehouse. Music by Jerome Kern. Presented by F. Ray Comstock and William Elliott at the Princess Theater on February 1. Directed by Robert Milton and Edward Royce. Cast included Carl Randall, Vivienne Segal, Janet Velie, and Florence Shirley (219 performances).*

(1918), Oh, My Dear!, *an intimate musical comedy, with book and lyrics by Guy Bolton and P. G. Wodehouse. Music by Louis A. Hirsch. Presented by William Elliott and F. Ray Comstock at the Princess Theater on November 27. Directed by Robert Milton and Edward Royce. Cast included Roy Atwell, Joseph Stanley, Ivy Sawyer, and Georgia Caine (189 performances).*

*Nobody Home* was the first of the Princess Theater Shows, named after the theater in which it was housed. These shows helped to introduce a new kind of musical theater to Broadway, consisting of intimate entertainment, small casts and orchestra, economical scenery and costuming, an intimate tone, an informal manner, and a bright, sophisticated air. All this was a radical departure from the sumptuous musical entertainment then being presented by producers like Ziegfeld and the Shuberts.

The idea for a compact and intimate kind of musical show was born with Elizabeth Marbury. She was the first woman ever to become a play agent. She also ran the Princess Theater in New York in conjunction with Ray Comstock. The theater had only 299 seats, and it was suffering financially because there were not enough productions around willing to use such a small house; the last venture there, a series of one-act plays, had been a box-office disaster. To turn defect into virtue Elizabeth Marbury thought up the idea of a miniature musical with no more than two sets, an orchestra of about ten, eight to twelve girls in the chorus, and a similarly small cast of principals—the whole to be budgeted for about $7,500. Guy Bolton was one of Miss Marbury's clients. She introduced him one day in 1914 to Jerome Kern, then already the proud composer of a successful musical, *The Girl from Utah*. She suggested that the two men team up to adapt for the Princess Theater a London operetta with music by Paul Rubens, *Mr. Popple of Ippleton*. Guy Bolton would get five hundred dollars for his text; Jerome Kern would be entitled to royalties. Her only specification: that the show be conceived along the most economical lines possible.

Before Bolton and Kern got around to this assignment, they wrote a musical, *90 in the Shade,* which opened on January 15, 1915, and was a failure. With this out of the way, they went to work on the adaptation of *Mr. Popple of Ippleton*. Its central character was Freddy Popple of Ippleton, England (amusingly portrayed by Lawrence Grossmith). He comes to the

United States—fully equipped with the accouterments of a hunter, trapper, and fisher—to find his brother, Vernon (George Anderson), a New York society dancer. Freddy's escapades in America—and more specifically in the apartment of Tony Miller (Adele Rowland), a Winter Garden prima donna —provide much of the hilarity of the evening. The text was not much to speak of, but the contributions of Jerome Kern included two gems. One was "The Magic Melody," introduced by Adele Rowland as Tony, which the distinguished musicologist Carl Engel said "was the opening chorus of an epoch. . . . It was a relief, a liberation." The other song was "You Know and I Know," sung by Alice Dovey and George Anderson in subsidiary roles.

*Nobody Home* had a run of over one hundred performances, not enough to make much money in a house as small as the Princess Theater, yet enough to encourage Elizabeth Marbury to proceed further with this new kind of entertainment. Once again Kern and Bolton were hired. This time they achieved a major success—*Very Good, Eddie*—with which the Princess Theater Show became a vogue in New York, besides creating a revolution in the American musical theater.

The title came from a pet phrase used by Fred Stone in one of his extravaganzas. The text concerned two honeymoon couples about to take a trip on the *Catskill,* a Hudson River Dayline boat. One couple is Eddie Kettle (Ernest Truex) and Georgina (Helen Raymond); the other, Percy Darling (John Willard) and Elsie (Alice Dovey). The two men had been onetime acquaintances and they are delighted to see each other at the boat pier and to introduce their respective wives. Somehow the couples become separated, and Eddie sails with Percy's wife, Elsie, while Percy remains behind with Georgina. The principal action now involves Eddie and Elsie, two innocents who—to avoid attention and comment—must put up a pretense of being husband and wife. Eventually the other couple catches up with them at the Rip Van Winkle Inn, but not before Eddie and Elsie undergo many embarrassing developments.

Everything about the production was so intimate and informal that the audience was made to feel that the performers were playing in its own living room. One unidentified critic described the musical as a "kitchenette production"; another referred to it as "parlor entertainment." To Cecil Smith in *Musical Comedy in America,* "scarcely any previous musical comedy had been favored with a plot and dialogue so coherent, so neatly related to those of well-written musical plays. . . . The intimate musical comedy has become established as a suitable and successful genre."

Kern's score now began to reveal the scope of his versatility. His personal way with a soft, sensitive melody—and an enchanting mood—was demonstrated in "Babes in the Wood"; in "Nodding Roses," introduced by Oscar Shaw and Ann Orr in minor roles; and in "Some Sort of Somebody." The last of these, once again sung by Oscar Shaw and Ann Orr, was an interpolation: Kern had written it for *Miss Information,* an unsuccessful musical produced earlier the same year. And Kern's gift with a comic song was just as forcefully evident in "When You Wear a Thirteen Collar," which Ernest Truex delivered with more charm and histrionic skill than voice.

*Oh Boy!,* which followed *Very Good, Eddie* by a little over a year, was an even greater hit. Guy Bolton tried to point out the qualities that set *Oh Boy!* apart from other musicals of the same period. "It was straight, consistent comedy with the addition of music. Every song and lyric contributed to the action. The humor was based on the situation, not interjected by comedians." Then Bolton went on to say that "realism and Americanism" were other distinguishing traits."

Perhaps *Oh Boy!* did not do everything Bolton said. Nevertheless, it was a gay adventure. The setting was a college town, and the rah-rah spirit of college life gave the play much of its vitality. Lou Ellen (Marie Carroll), a bride, must suddenly leave her husband, George Budd (Tom Powers), to attend and ailing mother. While she is away, Tom attends a party at the local college inn. A rumpus ensues, in which Jackie Simpson (Anna Wheaton) becomes involved. To save her from the police, Tom must secrete her in his apartment. The play now becomes a boudoir farce in which the young lady must go through various impersonations to give plausibility to her presence in the young man's apartment, and in which a pair of lace-trimmed blue pajamas becomes a vital piece of stage property. The sudden return of Lou Ellen does not help matters. The whole entanglement becomes unraveled when Lou Ellen's father explains that he had been Jackie's escort at the party and that Tom's involvement with the lady was entirely innocent.

Not a little of the gaiety came from the effervescent song lyrics of P. G. Wodehouse, who can justifiably be called the first significant American lyricist, and one whose influence on such later lyricists as Lorenz Hart and Ira Gershwin was frequently conceded by both these men. Though Wodehouse had previously worked with Bolton and Kern, *Oh Boy!* was their first Princess Theater Show, and the first in which he revealed the full scope of his gift with verses. Both in *Oh Boy!* and in its successor, *Oh, Lady! Lady!,* the team of Bolton, Wodehouse, and Kern worked together so harmoniously that one unnamed New York drama critic was led to write:

> *This is the trio of musical fame:*
> *Bolton and Wodehouse and Kern;*

*Better than anyone else you can name.*
    *Bolton and Wodehouse and Kern.*
*Nobody knows what on earth they've been bitten by*
*All I can say is I mean to get lit an' buy*
*Orchestra seats for the next one that's written by*
    *Bolton and Wodehouse and Kern.*

Kern's score for *Oh Boy!* was outstanding for two ballads: "Till the Clouds Roll By" (sung by Jackie with the assistance of Lynn Overman in a minor role), a song so distinguished that many years later it was used as the title of Kern's screen biography; and "An Old-Fashioned Wife," in which Lou Ellen gives voice to her life's ambition. An excellent comedy number was "Nesting Time," a parody on the then and still popular "When It's Apple Blossom Time in Normandy"—but with Flatbush, Brooklyn, as the setting.

*Oh, Lady! Lady!* (a phrase popularized by the celebrated Negro comic star of *The Ziegfeld Follies,* Bert Williams) was set in Long Island. As a bridegroom, Willoughby Fitch (Carl Randall) is confronted at his bride's house by an old girl friend, Mollie Farringham (Vivienne Segal). He thinks she has come to make trouble for him, and contrives all kinds of situations to prove to her that he is really a bounder and a cad, unworthy of her. Actually, Mollie is not interested in him at all; she has come merely to help prepare the bride's trousseau. Further hilarity is contributed by Edward Abeles as a reformed crook who has become the bridegroom's valet, and his fiancée, played by Florence Shirley, who has a weakness for shoplifting.

Kern's score included three lilting tunes: a duet by Mollie and Willoughby, "Before I Met You"; the title song, introduced by Willoughby and a girls' chorus; and "You Found Me, and I Found You." All three songs would have been obscured by the tremendous shadow of a fourth, had it been allowed to stay in the production. For it was for *Oh, Lady! Lady!* that Kern and Wodehouse wrote the song classic "Bill." Vivienne Segal, for whom it was intended, felt it did not suit her voice, and it had to be dropped. Eventually "Bill" came into its own—in *Show Boat.*

Dorothy Parker, then a drama reviewer, had this to say of *Oh, Lady! Lady!:* "Well, Bolton and Wodehouse have done it again. If you ask me I will look you fearlessly in the eye and tell you in low throbbing tones that it has it over any other musical in town. . . . I like the way the action slides casually into the songs. I like the deft rhyming of the song that is always sung in the last act by the two comedians and the comedienne. And oh, how I do like Jerome Kern's music!"

Only one more Princess Theater Show was mounted—*Oh, My Dear!.* The music was written not by Kern but by Louis A. Hirsch. The absence of

Kern's talent was strongly felt not only in the music department but in the stimulation it had provided to Wodehouse and Bolton, both of whom revealed a stodgy hand in *Oh, My Dear!*.

But with the Princess Theater productions that had preceded *Oh, My Dear!* theatrical history was made. The methods, techniques, nuances, subtleties, sophistication, and originality of the Princess Theater Shows helped bring into existence not only the bright and sparkling intimate revues of the 1920's, beginning with *The Grand Street Follies,* but also the unconventional musical comedies of Rodgers and Hart, as Rodgers himself has confessed.

PROMENADE (1969), *a musical, with book and lyrics by Maria Irene Fornes. Music by Al Carmines. Presented by Edgar Lansbury and Joseph Beruh at the Promenade Theater on June 4. Directed by Lawrence Kornfeld. Cast comprised Margot Albert, Marc Allen III, Shannon Bolin, Michael Davis, Pierre Epstein, Edmund Gaynes, George S. Irving, Madeline Kahn, Glenn Kezer, Ty McConnell, Art Ostrin, Alice Playten, Gilbert Price, Florence Tarlow, and Carrie Wilson (259 performances).*

It is difficult, indeed impossible, to categorize *Promenade*. It is *sui generis*. It is part musical comedy and part revue—but it is a lot of other things as well, including circus, carnival, vaudeville, social satire. It is part Bertolt Brecht, part Gertrude Stein, and part Edith Sitwell (the Sitwell who wrote the dadaistic verses for *Façade*). Deftly directed by Lawrence Kornfeld, with a cast of fifteen performers, each of whom is so important that nobody gets special billing on the program, it is an unconventional romp compounded of wisdom and nonsense and occasionally a touch of sheer madness.

The plot that ties all this together is slight indeed. Two likable prisoners dig their way out of their cells, to come face to face with the hard realities of the outside world. It is a hard-boiled world they face, as they learn soon enough—the world of the sophisticated rich and the less sophisticated powerful, all ruled by a mayor who is an out-and-out idiot. The prisoners come to realize what life really is: "an almost dreamlike world of parties, war and disillusion," as William A. Raidy wrote. "From cell to banquet room to battlefield, to drawing room and back to cell."

To the critic of *Variety,* "most of the comedy is in the lyrics." He adds: "Miss Fornes' brand of absurdity must be taken on its own terms, and she's a persuasive exponent of ordered daffiness. Her lyrics are refreshingly free of clichés, but they're also incomprehensible. One of the delights of the show is the fervor with which the players deliver the loonier lyrics, as if they were crystal clear."

Walter Kerr's enthusiasm was spent on some of the details of the text.

"Gilbert Price, whose eyes have opened on nothing but holocaust since he was a lad, sings warmly and movingly of how wonderful it is with your eyes closed. Madeline Kahn announces, with jazz bravura, that she has just discovered what life is all about. It's all about the glory of walking down the street with a mean look on your face, a cigarette in your right hand, a toothpick in your left. Miss Kahn is contented, gay, nearly ecstatic as she alternates cigarette and toothpick, right foot and left, syncopated bass notes and riffed treble. Shannon Bolin could not be more confident as she sings 'I Know everything—half of it I'm sure of, the rest I make up.' Alice Playten could not be more scorching as she dresses down a love between plaintive cries of 'Come, come, come.' There is an enormously funny number . . . in which one soldier gives another a letter to be mailed in case of his death. The letter is to a Mr. Phelps, manager of the dining car on the Colonial Boston run, and it informs him that he served the deceased the worst hamburgers he ever had in his life."

This, then, is a thoroughly zany, offbeat show with a point of view all its own. If it has a social message to propound (and it has), this is not done with strident voice but through innuendo and suggestion. The whole production is disjointed and rambling—as its creators had carefully intended.

Composer and the librettist-lyricist work in perfect harmony with one another. Rouben Ter-Artunian in his designing and expressionist set and Willa Kim in her costuming, in turn, work in perfect harmony with the authors. Speaking of the set, Clive Barnes said that it is "a maze of bicycle wheels and lights. It means nothing, but it contributes a lot." Miss Kim's costumes are "high-camp boutique style, elegantly unexpected, and calmly facetious." In short, "the designers give the show the ideal inconsequential background for its mixture of heartbroken insincerity and heartfelt honesty."

The score is made up of thirty-three numbers, each so good that it is difficult to single out any one or two that stand out most prominently. If, however, one were compelled to do so, one might select "I Saw a Man," sung by Madeline Kahn; or "Capricious and Fickle," presented by Alice Playten.

It is not generally known that when *Promenade* opened in 1969 it was not, a new musical. It had been produced Off Broadway four years earlier, when it went totally unnoticed. The times then were too soon for a show as unconventional as a hippie, as irate as a draft-card burner, and as loony and at times as meaningless as some of the lyrics found in rock-'n'-roll. But in 1969 it was well received. It is altogether possible that *Promenade* has pointed an altogether new way in the musical theater which other writers undoubtedly will pursue.

PROMISES, PROMISES (1968), *a musical comedy, with book by Neil Simon, based on the motion picture* The Apartment, *by Billy Wilder and I. A. L. Diamond. Lyrics by Hal David. Music by Burt Bacharach. Presented by David Merrick at the Shubert Theater on December 1. Directed by Robert Moore. Dances by Michael Bennett. Cast included Jerry Orbach and Jill O'Hara.*

The motion picture *The Apartment,* in which Jack Lemmon and Shirley Mac-Laine starred, proved a hilarious satire on the morals, or lack of them, among men in big business. The comic lines and the farcical situations came thick and fast. Then the happy idea was born to make the movie into a musical. As *Promises, Promises* it was still an uproarious commentary on immorality. But since Neil Simon was the one called upon to make the adaptation (and surely nobody is quicker with a shatteringly funny line, a totally unexpected exchange of words, an unconventional piece of stage business, or a masterfully built up comic climax than he), the musical became even funnier than the movie. And, as if this were not enough of a blessing, the musical was embellished with a score by Burt Bacharach, which must be ranked with one of the best heard on Broadway in some years. Neither text nor music tries to usurp the audience interest. The songs fit in neatly, snugly, unobtrusively at times—never interfering with or impeding Neil Simon's inventions, just as Neil Simon's frothy, effervescent text never tries to push a song into the background.

*Promises, Promises* received (as it deserved) an enormous bear hug from the critics. "Neil Simon has produced one of the wittiest books a musical has possessed in years," said Clive Barnes. "The Burt Bacharach music excitingly reflects today. . . . The whole piece has a sad and wry humanity to it, to which the waspishly accurate wisecracks are only a background." Martin Gottfried of *Women's Wear Daily* considered it "easily the most satisfying and successful musical in a very long time," and Leo Mishkin of the *Daily Telegraph* exclaimed, "it delivers, it delivers!"

Except for a few minor deviations, the story line in the musical adheres closely to the one in the movie. Chuck (Jerry Orbach) is a young fellow, as likable as he is ingenuous—a charming, inoffensive "shnook." He lives in a bachelor apartment, and is employed at the Consolidated Life Insurance Company, whose top executives conspire to use his apartment for their extra-curricular amatory pursuits. In order to bribe him to turn over the key to his apartment, now to one executive, now to another, for an evening, Chuck is promised continual and rapid promotions in the firm. Being ambitious, Chuck goes along with this arrangement, however much personal hardship it may cost him on the nights he has no home to go to. Then Fran Kubelik (Jill

O'Hara), a waitress in the company restaurant, and a girl whom Chuck has admired from a distance, uses the apartment with the personnel director of the insurance company, J. D. Sheldrake (Edward Winter). When Fran learns she has been discarded by Sheldrake, she tries to commit suicide in Chuck's bed. A Jewish doctor who lives next door, Dr. Dreyfuss (A. Larry Haines), saves her life. Dr. Dreyfuss is a man as quick with a humorous or quixotic comment as he is with a hypodermic needle. A good deal of the humor comes from his lips. When Fran tries to thank him for rescuing her, he is quick on the draw: "You want sympathy? Go see a specialist. I'm a general practitioner." Or, to quote him on another occasion: "I once took a trip for an experiment on LSD. Believe me, it's better to spend two weeks in Miami Beach in the rain!"

Much in the same way that Jack Lemmon dominated the motion picture, Jerry Orbach's performance helped keep *Promises, Promises* entertaining. A graduate from *The Fantasticks,* where he created the role of El Gallo and introduced the hit song "Try to Remember," Jerry Orbach was called by the critic of *Variety* "the show's most spectacular element. . . . His characterization . . . is superb from beginning to end; half slickie, half schlemiel, but always endearing—especially in a funny series of audience asides Simon has created for him." One of those asides occurs at the rise of the second-act curtain. The first act ends with his heartbreak in discovering that Mr. Sheldrake has been entertaining Fran at his apartment. The second-act curtain rises with the crisp line he hurls at the audience: "I don't wanna talk about it."

There were several solid numbers in the Bacharach score, of which the most notable were "Whoever You Are," sung by Fran; the duet of Fran and Chuck, "I'll Never Fall in Love Again"; and the title song, assigned to Chuck. Perhaps even more significant than any individual number is the *new* sound Bacharach helped to evolve for the musical theater with his score—the result of considerable experimentation and innovation. As he explained to an interviewer: "I tried to get the right musicians who could play my kind of pop music, instead of the usual pit orchestra. . . . I put in an electronic booth to control the choral voices I used with the music. I inserted fiberglass panels to separate the sound from mike to mike and tried to achieve the same conditions you get in a recording session without the isolated sound of music coming through speakers. It's a very complicated electronic system, with echo chambers and equalizers and technical equipment."

Burt Bacharach here makes his highly auspicious debut as a composer for the Broadway theater; but he was no novice by any means. He had previously distinguished himself as a composer for motion pictures (receiving

Academy Award nominations three times). He had also produced a long string of hit songs, all with lyrics by Hal David, including "Magic Moments," "The Story of My Life," "Wives and Lovers," "Walk on By," "What the World Needs Now," "I Say a Little Prayer." He was born in Kansas City, Missouri, on May 12, 1928, and received a thorough training in music both at conservatories and privately with such eminent composers as Milhaud and Martinu. After serving in the army for two years, he received his professional apprenticeship in popular music as accompanist to Vic Damone, Polly Bergen, and the Ames Brothers, and as conductor and arranger for Marlene Dietrich. When the New York drama critics were polled for their favorites in many different categories for the 1968–69 season, they selected Burt Bacharach as the best composer and Hal David as the best lyricist for their work in *Promises, Promises.* In 1970 he received two Academy Awards, one for the song "Raindrops Keep Falling on My Head" (lyrics by Hal David), and the other for the best score for a nonmusical. Both were for the motion picture, *Butch Cassidy and the Sundance Kid.*

> PURLIE (1970), *a musical comedy with book by Ossie Davis, Philip Rose, and Peter Udell based on the play* Purlie Victorious *by Ossie Davis. Lyrics by Peter Udell. Music by Gary Geld. Presented by Philip Rose at the Broadway Theater on March 15. Directed by Philip Rose. Choreography by Louis Johnson. Cast included Cleavon Little, Melba Moore, and John Heffernan.*

At a time when racial strife and tensions in the United States have brought to the surface so much ugliness, bitterness, terror, and death, a musical like *Purlie* is as refreshing and as cleansing as a Spring breeze.

This musical is based on the stage play, *Purlie Victorious,* produced in 1961 when it was warmly received by most of the critics, enjoyed the longest run of any non-musical production of the 1961–62 season (even though the run was not particularly spectacular), and was rumored to have been the runner-up for the Pulitzer Prize. It was then made into a motion picture whose major fault was that it was virtually a filmed staged play instead of being translated into cinematic terms; this was released in 1963.

The play was the work of Ossie Davis, who played the leading role in both the stage and the screen productions. He is a distinguished Negro actor whose active sympathy for the rising tide of the Negro struggle for equality cannot be questioned. But in writing his play, Mr. Davis cleansed his heart of hate. In writing about the racial struggle in the bigoted South he had laughter rather than vituperation in his pen. His Negro characters are not even above laughing at themselves. When he creates stereotypes—an "Uncle Tom" character in Gitlow (Sherman Hemsley), for example, or a white-exploiting bigot in Ol' Cap'n (John Heffernan)—Davis does so consciously, to add touches of mockery to his comedy. And when he brings his play to a happy resolution he does so to introduce hope and optimism rather than frustration and despair.

This frequently light or comic treatment of a deadly serious subject is carried over into a musical comedy which profits from a remarkably good text, outstanding song material, effective settings, and exceptional performances by Cleavon Little as Purlie and Melba Moore as Lutiebelle. Indeed, Miss Moore—who had been the only black leading lady in *Hair*—proved herself to be a luminous star, about whom much undoubtedly will be heard in the years to come. She captured the Antoinette Perry Award for the best supporting musical role. Richard Watts, Jr. maintained that she "walks off with the evening. . . . She is a darling-looking girl, and at a quick opening glance, she seems so shy and retiring that she appeals to one's sympathy immediately. But she is also deceptive. You soon discover that she has a splendid voice, a gift for skillful humorous acting, and a glowing stage personality. You emphatically don't forget her."

The story of the musical (as in the play and movie that had preceded it) takes place in "cotton plantation country in the old south [Georgia], in the recent past." Its theme: the success of illiterate cotton pickers, headed by their preacher, Purlie, in triumphing over Ol' Cap'n, the bigot. The tongue-in-cheek humor balanced by moments of poignancy, the spice that endows the dialogue, the depth of some of the characterizations help the author to avoid clichés, bromides, and platitudes to which the none too original plot might readily have succumbed. "The musical," said Clive Barnes, "is a fine mixture of humor and passion. . . . This is by far the most successful and richest of all black musicals . . . that . . . should have you calling out 'Hallelujah!' "

The principal character, of course, is the Negro preacher, Purlie. He is a garrulous, amusing, conniving braggart who basically is something of a phony but whose heart is where it should be: with his oppressed people, the cotton pickers of Cotchipee who are so ruthlessly exploited and oppressed by Ol' Cap'n. Purlie wants to free his people from the grip of this white tyrant. He also dreams of having a church built. The play concerns itself with how he achieves both aims.

The play opens with a stirring prologue, the dedication ceremonies of a new church, Big Bethel. Purlie preaches about the newly won freedom of his congregation, come about through the death of Ol' Cap'n. A mighty gospel hymn, "Walk Him Up the Stairs" is then sung by the congregation which, compassionately, prays for the saving of the soul of Ol' Cap'n.

What follows in the two acts is a flashback to events leading up to this dedication ceremony. Purlie has devised a scheme to regain from Ol' Cap'n an inheritance the bigot has been holding from Purlie's dead mother and which he refuses to give up. Purlie wants that money—for then he can bring to life his dream of purchasing Big Bethel, a church in which he can become "A New Fangled Preacher Man," as he explains in his dynamic song. Purlie's plan is to pass off Luitebelle as a long lost cousin to whom that inheritance is due. Lutiebelle is secretly in love with Purlie, a confession she makes in the striking title number, one of the two songs that helped elevate Melba Moore to stardom. But Purlie also has an ally in the camp of the enemy—no less than Ol' Cap'n's son, Charlie (C. David Colson), a guitar-playing troubadour whose hobby is writing folk songs.

Purlie brings Lutiebelle to the commisary owned by Ol' Cap'n where the bigot has been fleecing the cotton pickers. Ol' Cap'n is not there. After Purlie leaves to find Ol' Cap'n, Lutiebelle brings down the house with a number in which she betrays the depths of her feelings for Purlie, "I Got Love." Ol' Cap'n is found—and is just about being deceived into giving up the inheritance when he discovers that Lutiebelle has signed the wrong name to the receipt. Purlie's well-laid plans collapsing, he expresses his disappointment in the deeply moving song, "Down Home." Meanwhile, Ol' Cap'n has induced Lutiebelle to visit him at the Big House where he becomes amorous and kisses her. When Purlie learns about this he is determined to seek revenge.

At the rise of the second-act curtain, we find the cotton pickers sleepily getting out of bed before dawn to begin their day of hard work. But in "First Thing Monday Mornin' " they insist that they will see to it that their conditions change for the better.

Purlie, back from the Big House, brings Lutiebelle the tall tale that he has avenged her, that Ol' Cap'n is dead, and that he, Purlie, has killed him. What really had happened, however, was that the Ol' Cap'n died "standing up" upon discovering that his own son, Charlie, in buying Big Bethel, had registered it in Purlie's name. Purlie and the cotton pickers are jubilant, raising their voices loud and clear in one of Charlie's folk songs, "The World Is Coming to a Start."

The action now shifts back to the setting of the prologue—Big Bethel. Purlie has finished the dedication of his church. An exultant gospel by his congregation—filled with optimism and hope—brings the musical to its end, "Walk Him Up the Stairs."

A good deal of the score has a soft "rock" quality (electrified guitars are used in the orchestration). Some of it is in the style of gospel music. Some numbers with their sentiment and melodic appeal are ripe fruits from the soil of the popular Broadway theater. But whatever the style, the score is top-drawer, and its creators prove themselves true song professionals, even though they are here writing their first Broadway musical. "The score," said John S. Wilson in *The New York Times,* "draws on the root forms of American music—both black and white. . . . The pulsating mixture of melody and rhythm that flows all through the show is established in the opening gospel song . . . and it is amplified in Cleavon Little's singing of 'New Fangled Preacher Man,' a song developed over a series of rocking rhythmic breaks. One song after another, right down the line . . . erupts with spirit, with vehemence and joy."

QUEEN HIGH (1926), *a musical comedy, with book and lyrics by Buddy de Sylva and Laurence Schwab. Music by Lewis E. Gensler and others. Presented by Laurence Schwab at the Ambassador Theater on September 8. Directed by Edgar MacGregor. Dances by Sammy Lee. Cast included Charles Ruggles, Frank McIntyre, Luella Gear, and Mary Lawlor (378 performances).*

T. Boggs Johns (Charles Ruggles) and George Nettleton (Frank McIntyre) are partners in a garter and novelty business. Embroiled in squabbles, they decide to play a game of poker—the winner to become the boss, the loser to act as his butler. Nettleton wins, and the comedy that follows results from Johns's efforts to serve as a butler. The romantic interest is centered on their two offspring, Richard Johns and Polly Nettleton, played by Clarence Nordstrom and Mary Lawlor. Gaile Beverly scored a personal hit in the part of an amorous housemaid whose activity is extracurricular, divided between loving and dancing. Richard and Polly have the most important song, "Cross Your Heart." Another delightful number is "You'll Never Know."

RAINBOW (1928), *a romantic musical play, with book by Laurence Stallings and Oscar Hammerstein II. Lyrics by Hammerstein. Music by Vincent Youmans. Presented by Philip Goodman at the Gallo Theater on November 21. Directed by Hammerstein. Dances by Busby Berkeley. Cast included Brian Donlevy, Allan Prior, Charles Ruggles, Louise Brown, and Libby Holman (29 performances).*

There was no mistake about it—*Rainbow* was a financial disaster. But this may very well have been because it was years ahead of its time. Had it been produced a quarter of a century later, audiences might have found it to be a play whose adjustment of spoken text and music was almost operatic; whose atmosphere, local color, and dramatic truth were all in the best traditions of the legitimate theater. Here was a romantic play almost in the folk style later made so popular by Rodgers and Hammerstein in *Oklahoma!* Had *Rainbow* came in the 1940's it might have enjoyed a far greater audience response than it did in 1928, when it could not survive even a single month.

Many critics, however, recognized its originality and beauty—even if they failed to convince audiences. Howard Barnes described it as "a prodigal, bright-hued entertainment . . . with absorbing melodramatic overtones which burst through the thin veil of a graceful score and pretty dances." To Robert Littell, "the best of *Rainbow* is wonderfully good and also brand new . . . so gorgeously different in its high spots that the weaker spots don't matter." Gilbert Gabriel regarded it as "a stirring treat . . . a lusty, happy, often handsome show, picturesque . . . and somehow full of . . . simple and effective fervor."

The play was set mostly in California, the time the era of the 1849 gold rush. Harry Stanton (Allan Prior), a young scout at Fort Independence, kills Major Davolo (Rupert Lucas) in self-defense. Escaping from prison, he sets out for the West and settles in California, where the fever for gold prospecting was then at its height. He meets and falls in love with Virginia Brown (Louise Brown) and wins her.

Despite strong performances of the principals, two minor stars stole the limelight. As Nasty Howell, the muleteer, Charles Ruggles scored a personal triumph singing "The Bride Was Dressed in White," in the style of the period. And when she sang "I Want a Man," the then unknown Libby Holman—appearing as Lotta—for the first time gave full measure to her ample talent as a singer of ballads and torch songs. Some of the choral numbers (such as "On the Golden Trail," with which the play opens and closes) and the dances had an American folk character that at the time was something vital and fresh and new for the American stage.

RAIN OR SHINE (1928), *a musical comedy, with book by James Gleason and Maurice Marks. Lyrics by Jack Yellen. Music by Milton Ager and Owen Murphy. Presented by A. L. Jones and Morris Green at the George M. Cohan Theater on February 9. Directed by Alexander Leftwich. Cast included Joe Cook, Tom Howard, and Janet Velie (356 performances).*

*Time* magazine said: "It is a wretched show. But for those who like Joe Cook it is heavenly." For Joe Cook was the whole show. He is Smiley Johnson, proprietor of a bankrupt circus. When the troupe goes on strike, Smiley takes over and does the performance himself. He juggles twenty Indian clubs; balances himself on a wire and shoots out rows of lighted candles; balances himself atop a twelve-foot pole swinging hoops on his heels; walks a huge ball up a steep incline; whirls with his foot a pole with a man dangling at each end; catches lighted matches in his mouth. He also sings, dances, and tells long, disconnected stories, many of them without endings. And he fills the stage with a mammoth crazy Rube Goldberg-like contraption.

Additional comedy was provided by the dry, brittle humor of Smiley's partner, Amos K. Shrewsberry (Tom Howard). The love interest involved Jack Wayne (Warren Hull) and Mary Wheeler (Nancy Welford), owner of the Wheeler Circus.

The principal musical numbers were the title song, "So Would I," "Falling Star," and "Forever and Ever."

THE RAMBLERS (1926), *a musical comedy, with book by Guy Bolton and Bert Kalmar. Lyrics by Bert Kalmar. Music by Harry Ruby. Presented by Philip Goodman at the Lyric Theater on September 20. Directed by Philip Goodman. Cast included Clark and McCullough and Marie Saxon (289 performances).*

Clark and McCullough, who had previously scored successes in various revues, were here appearing in their first full-length musical comedy—and it was written for them with their special talents in mind. Clark was cast as Professor Cunningham, a spiritualistic medium; McCullough, as his servant, Sparrow. They are wandering along the Mexican border when they come upon a movie company filming a picture. They begin to mingle freely with the actors and before long become involved in their affairs, even to tracking down the star of the company, Ruth Chester (Marie Saxon), after she had been kidnapped by Black Pedro.

All the equipment by which Clark and McCullough had long since become familiar in revues was carried over into *The Ramblers:* the bouncing cane, trick cigar, painted glasses, raccoon coat, and most of all their own brand of loud, boisterous, burlesque comedy. Besides Clark and McCullough, the big asset of the production was Marie Saxon. She sang the show's hit number, "All Alone Monday," and performed an electrifying "aeroplane Charleston dance"—and regularly drew ovations for both achievements. An acrobatic dance performed by Norma Gallo also won favor, as did two additional Ruby songs, "You Smiled at Me" and "Any Little Tune."

REDHEAD (1959), *a musical comedy, with book by Herbert Fields, Sidney Sheldon, and David Shaw. Lyrics by Dorothy Fields. Music by Albert Hague. Presented by Robert Fryer and Lawrence Carr at the 46th Street Theater on February 5. Directed and with dances by Bob Fosse. Cast included Gwen Verdon and Richard Kiley (452 performances).*

*Redhead* was planned as a murder mystery set to music. What really made it a success (the winner of six Antoinette Perry awards, including that of best musical of the season) was not a plot to keep the audience balanced on the edge of the seat; its denouement becomes a foregone conclusion once the story gets under way. The appeal of *Redhead* rested in Bob Fosse's versatile and imaginative choreography and in the performance of a young lady who stole the show—Gwen Verdon, fresh from her triumphs in *Damn Yankees* in 1955 and *New Girl in Town* in 1957. Brooks Atkinson said the show really began fifteen minutes after the curtain went up, when Miss Verdon appeared dressed as a man, wearing a hard hat, swinging a cane, flaunting a flower in her lapel, and breaking into a routine that her father used to do. "A slender and supple lady," is the way Mr. Atkinson described her, "with pointed features, an amiable grin and a red top-knot, she does everything that anyone could expect of a musical performer. She can portray a character like a fully licensed dramatic actress. She can sing in a russet-colored voice that is mighty pleasant to hear. . . . And Miss Verdon can dance with so much grace and gaiety that her other accomplishments seem to be frosting on the cake." Some of her best dances, which Mr. Atkinson described as "comic explosions," included the following, as singled out by that critic: "Miss Verdon dreaming of glamorous success as the leading lady in various shows and demonstrating her successes in sweeping movement; Miss Verdon in a Spanish number or dancing in a brawl." And when she is asked to sing—as in "Just for Once" (with Richard Kiley and Leonard Stone) or "Look Who's in Love" (with Kiley)—she somehow manages to make the songs more infectious and appetizing than they really are. As for Bob Fosse's choreography, it ranges all the way from a simple music-hall strut to such elaborate production numbers as "The Uncle Sam Rag" (a music-hall number set to ragtime music—a delicious takeoff on the "Ascot Gavotte" from *My Fair Lady*) and "Pick-Pocket Tango."

The plot, such as it is, finds Gwen Verdon in the early twentieth century, cast as a simple, wistful little redhead named Essie Whimple, who works in her aunt's wax museum in London. She is a girl full of fancies and dreams, whose favorite flight into fantasy involves the meeting of some big handsome man. He turns out to be Tom Baxter (Richard Kiley), a strong-man performer at the Odeon Theater, whose partner has been murdered by a fiend. The same fiend threatens Essie as well. The rest of the musical concerns the efforts of Tom and Essie to catch the murderer and fall in love, both of which they succeed in doing—a story line strung out long enough to allow for the always welcome choreographic interpolations and inventions by Bob Fosse for his star. (This harmonious collaboration of Bob Fosse and Gwen Verdon became more personal when, during the run of the show, in 1960, they became man and wife.)

"Two Faces in the Dark," sung by Bob Dixon (playing the role of the Tenor) and chorus, and "The Right Finger of My Left Hand" are two numbers, other than those already mentioned, that were of more than passing interest.

THE RED MILL (1906), *a comic opera, with book and lyrics by Henry Blossom. Music by Victor Herbert. Presented by Charles Dillingham at the Knickerbocker Theater on September 24. Directed by Fred G. Latham. Cast included Fred Stone, David Montgomery, and Augusta Greenleaf (274 performances).*

The success of Fred Stone and David Montgomery in *The Wizard of Oz* (1903) led Henry Blossom and Victor Herbert to fashion an operetta for the comic talent of these two performers. *The Red Mill*—ambitiously designated in the program as a "musical play," and just as ambitiously promoted outside the theater with the first moving electric sign used on Broadway—had Holland for a setting, specifically the little Dutch port of Katwyck-aan-Zee. Two Americans are stranded penniless in the little inn, "The Sign of the Red Mill." They are Con Kidder (Fred Stone) and Kid Conner (David Montgomery). Trying to evade paying their bill at the inn, they sneak out of their window, but are caught red-handed by Jan Van Borkem, the burgomaster, and unceremoniously thrown into jail. Willem, the innkeeper, pitying their plight, gets their release by having them work in the inn until their bill is paid off, Con as an interpreter and Kid as a waiter. The innkeeper and the burgomaster have "daughter trouble," what with neither girl willing to accept as husband the men their fathers had selected for them, about which the two men complain in the song "You Can Never Tell About a Woman." Gretchen (Augusta Greenleaf), daughter of the burgomaster, loves Captain Doris Van Damm (Joseph W. Ratliff), while her father prefers the governor of Zeeland (Neal McCay). Con and Kid become the allies in Gretchen's efforts to marry the captain, and by the same token they become the enemies of the governor of Zeeland. They are only too willing to help the lovers when Doris and Gretchen plot to run off to some remote island. But Willem has overheard the lovers' plot and relays the news to the burgomaster. He then locks Gretchen in the mill, where she pines away for the man she loves in her solitary confinement. Kid Conner and Con Kidder contrive to rescue her by taking her through the window and bringing her to safety on the arm of a revolving windmill. All this, however, is of little help to the unhappy lovers, for the burgomaster has made all the arrangements for the marriage of his daughter to the governor, much to the governor's delight. These wedding festivities are enlivened by the intermittent appearance of our two Americans in various disguises (as Italian organ grinders, Sherlock Holmes and Dr. Watson, and so forth), an attempt to delay the official ceremony. When the discovery is made that Captain Van Damm is heir to a large fortune, all resistance to him collapses. The lovers are reunited, and the two Americans can go home to New York.

"*The Red Mill,*" wrote one New York critic prophetically in 1906, "will grind its grist of mirth, music and melody for a long time to come." The comic opera had the longest run of any Victor Herbert musical while the composer was still alive. And when it is revived—and it is done periodically— it is always well received: in a return to New York on October 16, 1945, with the text revised and modernized but the score left untouched, it amassed the impressive run of 531 performances.

However much the text may be changed, it remains a sadly dated period piece. But Herbert's music is, today as yesterday, fresh and winning to the ear. One of the most beguiling songs is the duet in which Gretchen and the captain plot to flee to some island where they can be together forever and ever—"The Isle of Our Dreams." No less poignant is the haunting refrain "Moonbeams," with which Gretchen pines for her love during her solitary imprisonment in the mill, mood music that casts an inescapable spell. As a change of pace Herbert included in his score a delightful comedy song in "Every Day Is Ladies' Day," with which the governor anticipates his delight in marrying Gretchen; and the spirited "The Streets of New York," with which the operetta ends, sung by Con and Kid and the ensemble.

A mystery that has not been solved to the present day involves a number called "Good-a-bye, John," which Con and Kid sing at the wedding when they invade it disguised as Italian street musicians. A year before *The Red Mill* opened, a song was written by Egbert van Alstyne in which the words of the first stanza and of the refrain, and the melody of the refrain, were all exactly the same as Herbert's "Good-a-bye, John." It would be ridiculous to conceive of Herbert stealing a song so recently published and performed in a Broadway musical (*The Belle of Avenue A*). Besides, neither Williams nor Van Alstyne ever challenged Herbert over the rights to the song. The only possible explanation may lie in the fact that the stars of the show, one day while it was still in rehearsal, demonstrated to Herbert the kind of song they would like to have for their Italian number, and patterned their demonstration number after the Van Alstyne song just published and just performed. Herbert, agreeing, went ahead and wrote such a number, in turn patterning his own number after the one the stars had demonstrated, without realizing that the material was the work of established songwriters rather than the improvisation of two performers.

REGINA (1949), *a musical drama, with book, lyrics, and music by Marc Blitzstein, based on Lillian Hellman's play* The Little Foxes. *Presented by Cheryl Crawford, in association with Clinton Wilder, at the 46th Street Theater on October 31. Directed by Robert Lewis. Dances by Anna Sokolow. Cast included Jane Pickens, William Warfield, and Brenda Lewis (56 performances).*

Lillian Hellman's vitriolic play about a decaying Southern family had been a bitter account of the way deceit, avarice, ruthlessness, and hate annihilate all its members, until only a single one is left, Regina Giddens (Jane Pickens). Having destroyed all those around her, including her invalid husband, whom she refuses to help during a fatal heart attack, Regina is now in a position to control a lucrative cotton mill built up by the family. But her victory is hollow. She is lonely and afraid and hated by her own daughter.

If there is an indictment of society in this play, it is not thundered from a soapbox but lies implicit in the tragedy of a family consumed by its own vices. This is also the basic strength of Blitzstein's musical. It is a human drama on a large design, a drama underscored and emphasized through music varied in style and idiom. When a colored band appears on the stage in the party scene, the music has the pulse of ragtime; and when a group of servants raise their voices in song, we hear a spiritual. There are lilting tunes, and other songs that are tortured and anguished, like Birdie's "scena" in the third act. There are also some songs touched with mysticism, as in Addie's "Night Could Be the Time to Sleep." Blitzstein employed Handelian recitatives and others that resemble the *Sprechstimme* (song-speech) of Alban Berg. He presents some remarkable ensemble numbers, notably in the quartet, "Listen to the Sound of Rain." "With *Regina,*" wrote Leonard Bernstein, "we have a kind of apex, a summation of what Blitzstein was trying to do. The words sing themselves, so to speak. The result is true song—a long, flexible, pragmatic, dramatic song."

*Regina* was effective theater when originally introduced at the 46th Street Theater, even if it failed to attract customers. It was also effective opera when the New York City Opera Company incorporated it into its repertory on April 2, 1953. Regardless of its official genre—musical play or opera—*Regina* provided proof of how far Blitzstein was able to progress in the theater when he abandoned the soapbox and became concerned with the forces motivating the lives and actions of his characters.

THE RICH MR. HOGGENHEIMER (1906), *a musical comedy, with book and lyrics by Harry B. Smith. Music by Ludwig Englander and others. Presented by Charles Frohman at Wallack's Theater on October 22. Directed by*

*Ben Teal. Cast included Sam Bernard, Marion Garson, and Georgia Caine (187 performances).*

In 1903 a musical comedy by Ivan Caryll called *The Girl from Kay's* was imported from London and presented on Broadway with Sam Bernard in the role of a rich, overbearing Jew named Mr. Hoggenheimer. Bernard's success in that part led him to appear as Mr. Hoggenheimer in several subsequent Broadway musicals. *The Rich Mr. Hoggenheimer* was not only his greatest triumph in a Hoggenheimer role but also in any role up to 1913, when he joined Alexander Carr to star in the nonmusical *Potash and Perlmutter.*

Mr. Hoggenheimer (Sam Bernard) of London learns that his son Guy (Edwin Nicander), while visiting the United States, was planning to marry Amy Leigh (Marion Garson), a poor, untitled American girl. Hoggenheimer decides to make a secret trip to America to prevent his son from making such an undesirable match. Since he is a friend of the actress Flora Fair (Georgia Caine), and since she is aboard the same ship as he, Hoggenheimer's wife is convinced that the only reason he is going to America is for a love escapade. She follows him and catches up with him at a charity bazaar in Great Neck, where Hoggenheimer is toasting Flora. When Hoggenheimer arranges for Flora to marry the man she actually loves—Percy Vere (Percy Ames)—Mrs. Hoggenheimer becomes aware of his innocence. Meanwhile Hoggenheimer has become reconciled to Guy's forthcoming marriage to Amy.

As Flora Fair, Georgia Caine completely won over her audiences, particularly when she gave her charming rendition of songs like "Don't You Want a Paper, Dearie?" and "This World Is a Toy Shop." But the hit song of the play, the love duet of Guy and Amy, "Any Old Time at All," was not by Englander but by Jean Schwartz, to William Jerome's lyrics. Another interpolation in the Englander score was one of Jerome Kern's earliest songs, "Bagpipe Serenade," sung by Flora Fair and a bevy of young girls dressed in fetching Scottish kilts.

> RIO RITA (1927), *a musical comedy, with book by Guy Bolton and Fred Thompson. Lyrics by Joe McCarthy. Music by Harry Tierney. Presented by Florenz Ziegfeld at the Ziegfeld Theater on February 2. Directed by John Harwood. Cast included Ethelind Terry, J. Harold Murray, Bert Wheeler, Robert Woolsey, and Ada May (494 performances).*

On February 2, 1927, Ziegfeld opened his new palatial theater on Sixth Avenue—the Ziegfeld. And as befitted the occasion, he put on one of his most lavish productions. The Mexican setting of *Rio Rita* gave scenic designer Joseph Urban and costume designer John Harkrider an opportunity to conceive some of their most colorful and exotic designs; and the production was endowed with handsome ballets and spectacles, the best of which was called "Black and White."

The play itself seemed just a convenience for the display of handsome scenes and glamorous costumes. Jim, a Texas Ranger captain (J. Harold Murray), is with his men hunting along the Rio Grande for a notorious Mexican bandit. After crossing into Mexico he falls in love with Rio Rita (Ethelind Terry). Their love affair is complicated by the fact that Rio Rita is loved by General Esteban (Vincent Serrano), and also by the suspicion that the bandit is her brother. In trying to win Rio Rita's love, General Esteban entreats her to pretend he is Jim. But Rio Rita is incapable of such pretense. When she and Jim come together, there is no doubt where her heart lies. The persistent general now succeeds in convincing her that Jim's only interest in her is to capture her brother, the bandit, which causes a break between the lovers. But then when the bandit is finally captured, the truth that he is not Rio Rita's brother is uncovered. Rio Rita and Jim become lovers again. The play ends with their wedding, upon which even the general bestows his blessings.

Comic relief is generously contributed by Wheeler and Woolsey, playing the roles of Ed Lovett and Chick Bean, two American visitors to Mexico. One of the amusing songs in the score is sung by Ed Lovett, "I Can Speak Espagnol." Sentiment comes from the title number, which serves as the love duet of Jim and Rio Rita; with "Sweetheart," which Rio Rita sings as a further token of her love for him; and with Jim's lament at losing Rio Rita's love, "Following the Sun Around." With the stirring march tune, "The March of the Rangers," vigor replaces sentiment.

*Rio Rita* was made into a motion picture twice, the first time by RKO in 1929 with John Boles and Wheeler and Woolsey, when the basic stage score was used; the other time by MGM, in 1942, with Abbott and Costello, a version that used only two of the stage songs, supplemented by several new numbers by E. Y. Harburg and Harold Arlen.

ROBERTA (1933), *a musical comedy, with book and lyrics by Otto Harbach, based on the novel* Gowns by Roberta, *by Alice Duer Miller. Music by Jerome Kern. Presented by Max Gordon at the New Amsterdam Theater on November 18. Directed by Hassard Short. Dances by José Limón. Cast included Tamara, Raymond E. (Ray) Middleton, Fay Templeton, George Murphy, Bob Hope, and Fred MacMurray in a minor role (295 performances).*

It was Kern's idea to make Alice Duer Miller's *Gowns by Roberta* into a musical, feeling as he did that it provided the excuse for a colorful background, effective production numbers, and most of all a lavish display of beautiful gowns. The show opened in Philadelphia under the title *Gowns by Roberta*. It was so badly received that the producer, Max Gordon, called in Hassard Short to restage the whole production and dumped all the costumes and sets to order new and more splendiferous ones. The show did hardly better when it first opened in New York. Most critics thought it a colossal bore, little more than a glorified fashion show. But once one of its songs, "Smoke Gets in Your Eyes," began to be heard on the radio and turned into a tremendous hit, business improved perceptibly.

But the critics were right. *Roberta* was hardly more than an attractive showcase for a fashion parade. The musical was particularly disappointing to some of Kern's admirers, who felt that he was satisfied to return to the clichés and stereotypes of traditional musical comedy after he had been involved in such bold stage innovations as *Show Boat, The Cat and the Fiddle,* and *Music in the Air.*

The story and love interest were incidental, the humor perfunctory. An All-American fullback, John Kent (Ray Middleton), is jilted by his girl, a debutante, Sophie Teale (Lyda Roberti). To escape from heartbreak, John comes to Paris—in the company of his friend Huckleberry Haines, a crooner (Bob Hope)—to visit his Aunt Minnie, known as "Roberta" (Fay Templeton), proprietress of a modiste shop. Together with the shop's chief designer, Stephanie, a Russian expatriate (Tamara), John takes over the management of the establishment. A romantic interest, of course, soon involves John and Stephanie, an affair complicated for a while by the unexpected appearance in Paris of Sophie Teale, who has had a change of heart where John is concerned. The establishment—once the parade of fashions has been dispensed with—becomes a huge success. And so does the romance of John and Stephanie, the latter turning out to be a Russian princess.

In writing his music, Kern may have abandoned some of the more unusual methods adopted in earlier musical plays, but his melodic touch had lost none of its magic. It was Kern's music that was responsible for making *Roberta* successful on the stage—and after that twice on the screen and in two different television Specials starring Bob Hope, the first produced in 1958 and the second in 1969. For out of this score come three masterpieces: "Smoke Gets in Your Eyes," with which Tamara created a storm in the second act each time she sang it. Actually, Kern had not written this melody for *Roberta,* but as signature music for a radio series that failed to materialize. When *Roberta* was being planned and the need for a second-act song for Stephanie recalling her childhood was needed, Kern had Harbach write lyrics for his discarded radio melody. It did not impress anybody at first because it was in strict march time. Then Kern used a slower tempo and a more sentimental mood—and the right song had come along to make Tamara a star and *Roberta* a success. "Smoke Gets in Your Eyes" became one of Kern's greatest hits from the point of view of sheet music and record sales, and it is now accepted as one of his unqualified classics.

Then there was the poignantly nostalgic "Yesterdays," introduced by Aunt Minnie, and "The Touch of Your Hand," which Stephanie sang with William Hain, appearing in a minor role. Bob Hope also had a song winner—"You're Devastating."

As Roberta, Fay Templeton made her farewell to the stage after years of stardom. (In fact, she had already been in total retirement when she was induced to take this role.) By 1933 she had developed into a formidable woman of two hundred and fifty pounds. In considering the problem of a performer carrying that much weight, the librettist, Harbach, considerately wrote her part so that she could perform much of it in a seated position.

With Miss Templeton on her way out of the theater in *Roberta,* two new performers were on their way in by way of compensation. One was Tamara, who had been discovered at the Kretchma, a Russian restaurant on 14th Street in New York. Then there was Bob Hope, making his Broadway stage debut. The producer found him in the Palace Theater doing a vaudeville monologue. When the producer first suggested to Kern casting Bob Hope as Huckleberry Haines, Kern replied tartly: "What are you trying to do, palm off one of your old vaudevillians on me?"

Sprinkled generously throughout the production were several other unknowns later to make their mark in show business. Sidney Greenstreet played the small part of Lord Delves, one of Roberta's friends. The production used a jazz band, "The California Collegians," one of whose members was Fred MacMurray. And such a negligible part was assigned to a young man named George Murphy that he passed completely unnoticed. Who would have then prophesied for him a career as song-and-dance man of outstanding screen musicals, let alone the exalted office of United States senator?

*Roberta* emerged twice on the screen. The first production starred Fred Astaire and Ginger Rogers, an RKO production in 1935. Their song-and-dance rendition of "Smoke Gets in Your Eyes" remained one of their finest achievements. For this production Kern wrote two new numbers, a rhythmic piece for Astaire, "I Won't Dance" (but he did, of course), and a ballad, "Lovely to Look At." The latter became such a hit that when *Roberta* was remade by MGM in 1952 for Kathryn Grayson and Howard Keel, it was named after the song.

ROBIN HOOD (1890), *a comic opera, with book and lyrics by Harry B. Smith. Music by Reginald de Koven. Presented by the Bostonians at the Chicago Opera House on June 9 (and at the Standard Theater, New York, on September 22, 1891). Cast included Eugene Cowles, George Frothingham, Edwin Hoff, Jessie Bartlett Davis, and Caroline Hamilton.*

*Robin Hood* was the most successful comic opera written in the United States before Victor Herbert; and it is the only pre-Herbert operetta that is remembered and sometimes revived. The story, to be sure, is based on the exploits of Robin Hood during the reign of Richard I of England. The operetta opens with the celebration of May Day in the town of Nottingham (" 'Tis the Morning of the Fair"). Robin Hood (Edwin Hoff)—an earl deprived of title and lands who has turned into a notorious outlaw—comes to the celebration. He is greeted ceremoniously, for to the good people of Nottingham he is a hero. Robin Hood meets and falls in love with Maid Marian (Marie Stone), ward of the sheriff of Nottingham, who wants her to marry Guy of Gisborne (Peter Lang), and together they sing "Though It Was Within This Houre We Met." When the sheriff comes on the scene, Robin Hood demands that his lands and title be restored to him. Rejected, Robin Hood vows to continue leading the life of an outlaw ("An Outlaw's Life, the Life for Me").

In Sherwood Forest Robin Hood and his men are making merry with a song in praise of the outdoor life. Will Scarlet (Eugene Cowles) contributes an amusing ditty in "The Tailor and the Crow," and Little John (W. H. McDonald) follows with a lusty drinking song, "Brown October Ale." Maid Marian comes to the forest in search of Robin Hood to promise him she will never leave him. Their tender love scene is rudely interrupted with the arrival of the sheriff and his men, who capture some of Robin Hood's followers, although Robin Hood himself manages to escape.

The sheriff is now more determined than ever to have Marian marry Guy as soon as possible. During the wedding ceremony, Alan-a-Dale (Jessie Bartlett Davis) sings the tender and romantic idyll which has immortalized this comic opera, "Oh, Promise Me." Before the marriage ceremony can be consummated, Robin Hood and his men burst in, bearing the news that Robin Hood has received a royal pardon from the king, and is once again a prosperous earl. Robin Hood is now in the position to claim Marian as his own bride.

Were it not for "Oh, Promise Me" (which has become something of a permanent fixture at American weddings) it is doubtful if *Robin Hood* would ever be revived. In view of its importance in the comic opera, and in

American popular music in general, it is interesting to note that the song was not originally intended for *Robin Hood*. Isidore Witmark tells the story in his autobiography, *From Ragtime to Swingtime:* "It was not part of the original score; and the lyric had been written not by Harry B. Smith but by Clement Scott, the English critic. The song had been published independently. It had been found that *Robin Hood* needed another song; De Koven for some reason did not relish composing a new tune, so he brought this old one to rehearsal. He could not interest any of the singers in the song! Finally, it was offered to Jessie Bartlett Davis, the contralto, playing the role of Alan-a-Dale. Miss Davis, annoyed because she had not been offered the song at first, hummed it over, then disdained it. Something in the melody, however, remained. She found herself singing it an octave lower. MacDonald (the producer) happened to pass her dressing room; all who heard Jessie sing will understand why he stopped. He could not contain himself until the song was finished. 'Jessie!' he cried, bursting into her room, 'if you ever sing that song as you're singing it now, on the low octave, it will make your reputation.' She sang it, and the prophecy came true."

While "Oh, Promise Me" has thrown into obscurity the other musical numbers of the opera, a few are not without merit. The best are the two songs of Little John "Brown October Ale" and "The Armourer's Song"; and "The Tailor and the Crow," with its delightful background of humming voices.

ROBINSON CRUSOE, JR. (1916), *an extravaganza, with book by Harold Atteridge. Lyrics by Atteridge and others. Music by Sigmund Romberg and others. Presented by the Shuberts at the Winter Garden on February 17. Directed by J. C. Huffman. Dances by Allen K. Foster. Cast included Al Jolson, Kitty Doner, Claude Flemming, and Lawrence D'Orsay (139 performances).*

*Robinson Crusoe, Jr.* set a pattern for the Winter Garden extravaganzas that starred Al Jolson; they were continued for the next few years and were completely dominated by his dynamic personality. They would have him fill various colorful roles (usually named Gus) in fantasies that carried him from the present to another age and to far-off exotic places. The plot would generally be diffuse and amorphous, always elastic enough to permit Jolson to seize the limelight and strut his wares.

In *Robinson Crusoe, Jr.* he first appears as Gus, the chauffeur of Hiram Westbury (Claude Flemming). Weary after permitting a movie company to take film shots of his estate, Hiram falls asleep and dreams he is Robinson Crusoe, dressed in skins. His chauffeur, Gus (Al Jolson), becomes his man

Friday. However, they are not confined to any single island. They pass from one exotic scene to another: from a Spanish castle to a beautifully staged pirate ship, and from there to a forest in which trees come alive and become chorus girls swaying to the lilting rhythm of "My Voodoo Lady." About a half-hour before the ending of the play, background, time, and story are forgotten as Al Jolson takes over—singing (often songs interpolated during the run of the show), ad-libbing, telling stories, clowning. His best comic number was "Where Did Robinson Crusoe Go with Friday on Saturday Night?", and his biggest hit was a Hawaiian song, "Yacka Hula Hickey Dula." (Both these songs were not by Romberg but by E. Ray Goetz, Joe Young, and Pete Wendling.) Jolson also presented "Where the Black-Eyed Susans Grow" (by Dave Radford and Richard Whiting).

ROB ROY (1894), *a comic opera, with book and lyrics by Harry B. Smith. Music by Reginald de Koven. Presented by Fred C. Whitney at the Herald Square Theater on October 29. Directed by Max Freeman. Cast included William Pruette, Lizzie Machnicol, Juliette Cordon, and Joseph Herbert (168 performances).*

The setting is Perth, Scotland, during the uprisings attending the attempt to restore the Stuarts to the throne of England. Rob Roy (William Pruette) is a Highland chief secretly married to Janet (Juliette Cordon), daughter of the mayor of Perth. Rob Roy's men pledge allegiance to the cause of Prince Charles Edward Stuart, "the young pretender" to the English throne (Barron Berthald), but the mayor of Perth, always an opportunist, betrays the prince for a reward. One of the prince's adherents, Flora MacDonald (Lizzie Machnicol), disguises herself as the "pretender" and is imprisoned, but is saved from death by the prince. Flora is once again captured, and in an attempt to save her life, the prince surrenders himself. The Highlanders, however, are able to obstruct the advance of the English troops until the prince and Flora can effect their escape to France.

No single number stands out as prominently in this score as "Oh, Promise Me" does in *Robin Hood*. But the music for *Rob Roy* is more consistently notable. Of special interest is Janet's haunting ballad, "My Home Is Where the Heather Blooms"; the rousing song of Rob Roy and his men, "Come, Lads of the Highlands"; Flora's tender love song, "Dearest Heart of My Heart"; "Rustic Song," a duet of Rob Roy and Janet; and the "Lay of the Cavalier" by the prince and his men.

THE ROGERS BROTHERS IN WALL STREET (1899), *a vaudeville farce, with book by John J. McNally. Lyrics by J. Cheever Goodwin. Music by Maurice Levi. Produced at the Victoria Theater on September 18. Cast included Max and Gus Rogers, Ada Lewis, and Georgia Caine (108 performances).*

Max and Gus Rogers—the former a comedian, the latter a straight man—were an acting partnership like that of Weber and Fields. In a series of vaudeville farces from 1899 on, beginning with *The Rogers Brothers in Wall Street,* they imitated not only the dialect and low comedy of Weber and Fields but even the kind of burlesque then being presented at the Weber and Fields Music Hall. In later productions the Rogers Brothers carried their burlesques, horseplay, and rowdy humor into Central Park (1900), Washington, D.C. (1901), Harvard (1902), London (1903), Paris (1904), Ireland (1905), and Panama (1907). The death of Gus Rogers on October 19, 1908, brought this series of "vaudeville farces" to an end.

In *The Rogers Brothers in Central Park,* Della Fox initiated a hairdo that became a national fad: the spit curl in the middle of the forehead. The *Rogers Brothers in Washington* initiated the successful Broadway stage career of that inimitable songstress Nora Bayes. Born in Chicago as Leonora Goldberg, Miss Bayes had received her start in amateur shows in Chicago, following which she appeared in vaudeville as a child performer. The Rogers Brothers production gave her her first real chance on Broadway. (This was one year before her fame was solidly established in vaudeville with the singing of "Down Where the Wurzburger Flows," through which she came to be known as "the Wurzburger Girl," as well as "queen of coon shouters"). In this same production Pat Rooney (himself the son of a famous vaudevillian) appeared as a dapper song-and-dance man, and most especially as a hoofer. He would continue to appear in Rogers extravaganzas for a number of years, and in 1907 he would direct the dances for *The Rogers Brothers in Panama.* In *The Rogers Brothers in Harvard,* Pauline Frederick made her first stage appearance. Here she was just a chorine; in due time she would be a star of stars in the silent films.

Until 1903, all the music for the Rogers Brothers farces was written by Maurice Levi, who was also the conductor. Beginning with *The Rogers Brothers in London,* the music was by Max Hoffman. Levi's most popular songs from these productions included: "The Belle of Murray Hill," from *The Rogers Brothers in Wall Street;* "When Reuben Comes to Town," from *The Rogers Brothers in Central Park;* "The Girl of Greater New York," from *The Rogers Brothers in Washington;* and "Troubles of Reuben and the Maid," from *The Rogers Brothers in Harvard.* Hoffman also produced several distinctive numbers in his scores, among which were "By the Sycamore Tree," from *The Rogers Brothers in London;* "My Irish Maid," from *The Rogers Brothers in Ireland;* and "Smile, Smile, Smile," from *The Rogers Brothers in Panama.*

ROSALIE (1928), *an operetta, with book by Guy Bolton and William Anthony McGuire. Lyrics by Ira Gershwin and P. G. Wodehouse. Music by George Gershwin and Sigmund Romberg. Presented by Florenz Ziegfeld at the New Amsterdam Theater on January 10. Directed by William McGuire. Dances by Seymour Felix. Cast included Marilyn Miller, Bobbe Arnst, Frank Morgan, and Jack Donahue (327 performances).*

Gershwin wrote music for two Ziegfeld productions. *Rosalie* was the first (the second being *Show Girl*). Sigmund Romberg had originally been signed to do the music. But Ziegfeld demanded the full score in three weeks, a deadline Romberg could not meet; Romberg suggested that George Gershwin be recruited for half the score. As it turned out, Romberg wrote eight numbers and Gershwin contributed seven. Of Gershwin's seven, unquestionably the top number was "How Long Has This Been Going On?", which Bobbe Arnst introduced. It is still popular. Actually, this one was a discard from an earlier Gershwin musical, *Funny Face,* and so were three other Gershwin songs: "Show Me the Town," from *Oh, Kay!;* "Beautiful Gypsy," from the English production *Primrose,* where it had been called "Wait a Bit"; and "Yankee Doodle Rhythm," from *Strike Up the Band.* Of the new songs Gershwin created expressly for *Rosalie* were "Oh Gee! Oh Joy!" and "Say So!" (both to lyrics by P. G. Wodehouse). But, truthfully, this was not a score of which either Gershwin or Romberg could be proud. For Romberg's mediocrity of musical production there is perhaps less excuse than for Gershwin's, since operetta was Romberg's meat, while Gershwin's powerful and original creative talent was unsuited for this medium, as he had demonstrated earlier in *Song of the Flame.*

*Rosalie* was a typical operetta in that it involved a princess from a mythical kingdom. She is Rosalie of Romanza (Marilyn Miller), who falls in love with an American lieutenant from West Point, Richard Fay (Jack Donahue). When the royal family of Romanza visits the United States, Richard becomes the leader of its color guard and thus can pursue his love affair; and when Rosalie's father, King Cyril (Frank Morgan), is forced to abdicate, Richard can seek Rosalie's hand in marriage.

There is no relationship whatsoever between this stage musical and the Cole Porter screen musical *Rosalie,* produced by MGM in 1937.

ROSE-MARIE (1924), *an operetta, with book and lyrics by Otto Harbach and Oscar Hammerstein II. Music by Rudolf Friml and Herbert Stothart. Pre-*

*sented by Arthur Hammerstein at the Imperial Theater on September 2. Directed by Paul Dickey. Dances by David Bennett. Cast included Dennis King, Mary Ellis, William Kent, and Arthur Deagon (557 performances).*

It occurred to Arthur Hammerstein one day that of all the settings already exploited by operettas, the one that had never yet been used was the Canadian Rockies. This thought brought on another: the Canadian Mounted Police would provide an operetta with colorful characters. Once these ideas were crystallized, Arthur Hammerstein asked Harbach to work out a libretto using this setting and these characters, and Harbach in turn invited Oscar Hammerstein II to collaborate with him. A serviceable libretto was easily fashioned, and one which handsomely lent itself to the kind of music for which Rudolf Friml had already long been famous.

To this day, *Rose-Marie* is the only successful operetta with a Canadian Rockies background. There, Rose-Marie La Flamme (Mary Ellis) is a singer at Lady Jane's hotel in Saskatchewan, a favorite of the hotel's clientele, comprising Mounties and fur trappers. Ed Hawley, a wealthy trader, is in love with Rose-Marie, who, in turn, favors Jim Kenyon (Dennis King), a young man come to Canada to make his fortune. Ed Hawley (Frank Greene) contrives to throw on Jim the suspicion that he murdered the Indian Black Eagle (who, in actuality, had been killed by an Indian maid in love with Hawley). Rose-Marie is fully aware that Ed Hawley has the proof to clear Jim. She therefore offers herself to Ed if, in return, he sees to it that Jim is cleared of the murder charge. The Canadian Mounted Police, headed by Sergeant Malone (Arthur Deagon), get into the act and uncover the facts proving that the Indian girl and not Jim is guilty of the murder. With Jim vindicated, and Ed Hawley discredited, the lovers can pursue their romance without further interference. "Its plot," reported the New York *Telegram,* "clings together sufficiently to sustain interest." But in the New York *Tribune,* Charles Belmont Davis went further to call the production: "A bon-voyage basket of musical shows. . . . There is drama and melodrama, musical comedy, grand opera, and opéra-comique. . . . A beautiful . . . composite photograph of a three-ring circus . . . [with] the most entrancing music it has long been our privilege to hear."

Mary Ellis, formerly of the Metropolitan Opera Company, here made her bow on the Broadway stage. "She establishes herself," said Arthur Hornblow in *Theatre,* "as the peer of any musical-show star in the country."

A program note had this to say about the Friml score: "The musical numbers of this play are such an integral part of the action that we do not think we should list them as separate episodes." Nevertheless, several numbers did stand out prominently. Two are among Friml's best songs: the duet of

Jim and Rose-Marie, "Indian Love Call," and the title song, a duet by Jim and Sergeant Malone. Others are Rose-Marie's haunting ballad with chorus, "The Door of My Dreams"; the stirring march tune with which the Mounties make their initial appearance, "The Mounties"; and "Totem Tom-Tom," which profited from the ingenious bit of staging in which the girls were costumed to resemble totem poles. Several attractive instrumental episodes included the Empire March and Gavotte and the Bridal Procession.

Besides its run of one year and four months at the Imperial Theater, *Rose-Marie* had four touring companies, one of which brought the production back to Broadway in 1927. In addition, there were two motion-picture adaptations: one by MGM in 1936 with Jeanette MacDonald and Nelson Eddy; the other by MGM in 1954 with Howard Keel and Ann Blyth. In both, the principal numbers from the stage score were used.

THE RUNAWAYS (1903), *an extravaganza, with book and lyrics by Addison Burkhardt. Music by Raymond Hubbell. Presented by Sam S. Shubert, Nixon and Zimmerman at the Casino Theater on May 11. Cast included Alexander Clark, Edna Goodright, Dorothy Dorr, Arthur Dunn, and William Gould (167 performances).*

The producers made a great to-do of the fact that they had expended 75,000 dollars before the curtain went up on *The Runaways*. It was a sumptuously mounted production. Much less distinguished was the plot. General Hardtack (Alexander Clark) is an ex-waiter who rises to his high military station through political pull. At a racetrack he meets and is captivated by Josey May, comic-opera prima donna (Dorothy Dorr). The general, a dyspeptic, is delighted to learn from Josey that there exists an island in the South Seas where dyspepsia does not exist. When the general wins a fortune on a horse race, he decides to marry Josey and settle on that island. There he becomes king. But uneasy rests his crown: He discovers that by the law of the land he must either marry the widow of the preceding king or commit suicide. At a critical moment he and Josey are saved by American warships.

The strength of the play—apart from the sets and costumes—lay in the comedy of William Gould as a racetrack tout and Al Fields as a patent-medicine faker; in a brilliant clog dance by Walter Stanton, Jr., dressed up as a giant rooster; and in several Hubbell songs, the best being "If I Were a Bright Little Star" and "A Kiss for Each Day in the Week."

ST. LOUIS WOMAN (1946), *a musical play, with book by Arna Bontemps and Countee Cullen, based on Bontemps' novel* God Sends Sunday. *Lyrics by Johnny Mercer. Music by Harold Arlen. Presented by Edward Gross at the*

*Martin Beck Theater on March 30. Directed by Rouben Mamoulian. Dances by Charles Walters. The all-Negro cast included Pearl Bailey, Ruby Hill, Rex Ingram, and the Nicholas Brothers (113 performances).*

The authors had originally intended creating an authentic Negro folk play, set in the colored section of St. Louis in 1898. But somewhere in the writing, the artistic direction was completely lost. Folk drama was often sidestepped for straight musical comedy, with the result that *St. Louis Woman* was at times a folk musical and at times a formalistic musical comedy. The authors were not even quite sure whether to make the play funny or serious. There were numerous excursions into levity, yet the story as a whole remained pretty somber. The final scene of the second act took place in a funeral parlor; from then on, the audience found it hard to find the show amusing, even though the musical had a happy ending.

During out-of-town tryouts, *St. Louis Woman* became a child of misfortune. Countee Cullen, one of two authors of the text, died, making it impossible to make significant alterations in what was obviously a disjointed, rambling, and thoroughly unconvincing text. Lena Horne, who had been selected to star, quit the show cold, and so did the choreographer, Antony Tudor. Rouben Mamoulian was rushed in to help pull the show together. He did the best he could, but he was working with a text that did not give him much cooperation. And so, limping badly on the legs of a bad book and a poorly organized production, *St. Louis Woman* came to New York, and departed after only a little more than a hundred performances.

The story involves the turbulent love affair of jockey Little Augie (Harold Nicholas) and his St. Louis woman, Della Green (Ruby Hill). That love leads Augie to kill his rival, Brown (Rex Ingram). The dying man utters a deathbed curse that throws a jinx on all the horses Augie henceforth rides. But the jinx does not prevent the love of Augie and Della to disintegrate.

As long as the story line was adhered to, the text could past muster, particularly when the situation was emotionally charged with songs like the sexy and at times comic "Legalize My Name" and "A Woman's Prerogative," both torridly sung by Pearl Bailey; or the duet of Della and Augie, "Come Rain or Come Shine"; or the lyrical "I Had Myself a True Love," beautifully presented by a young performer named June Hawkins, onetime schoolteacher; or the eloquent "Any Place I Hang My Hat Is Home," introduced by Robert Pope. In fact, when there were songs to be heard, *St. Louis Woman* proved an exciting emotional and aesthetic experience—for in this score both Harold Arlen, as composer, and Johnny Mercer, as lyricist, proved themselves creative masters.

But when the play digressed into a cakewalk routine with which the first act ends—however beautifully executed in deadpan by Enid Williams—or into a big carnival scene, it was folk drama no more. "There are moments of exciting theatrical alchemy in the production," wrote Howard Barnes, "but they are random and infrequent. . . . Unfortunately it has inspired little more than colorful tableaux, which have some vitality as nicely done picture postcards." That—and one of the best musical scores heard on the Broadway stage in many a season.

Fully aware of the limitations of this production—and of its inherent strength—Arlen rewrote it entirely and renamed it first *Blues Opera,* and after that *Free and Easy.* The score was enriched with songs previously written by Arlen for other productions: "Blues in the Night," for example, and "That Old Black Magic." An extended five-minute sequence in pantomime was also interpolated into the first act. The entire structure was extended to make the work more of an opera than a popular musical production. Under the title of *Free and Easy* it opened in Amsterdam, Holland, in December of 1959 with the intention of bringing it to Broadway. But little had been done to improve the book, with the inevitable result that *Free and Easy* once again proved a failure and closed down after a few days. It never came to New York.

For a long time the original-cast recording made by Capitol was a collector's item, until the company re-released it in 1967.

SALLY (1920), *a musical comedy, with book by Guy Bolton. Lyrics by Clif-ford Grey and Buddy de Sylva. Music by Jerome Kern. Additional ballet music by Victor Herbert. Presented by Florenz Ziegfeld at the New Amsterdam Theater on December 21. Directed by Edward Royce. Cast included Marilyn Miller, Walter Catlett, Leon Errol, and Stanley Ridges (570 performances).*

Ziegfeld was planning three different musicals, each to star one of the following: Marilyn Miller, Leon Errol, and Walter Catlett. When Bolton and Kern brought him the text and score of *Sally,* Ziegfeld decided to roll the three projects into one. The Bolton text had a part for Errol—as Connie the waiter, formerly a Balkan grand duke thrown out of his country during a revolution. Its starring role of Sally was ideal for Marilyn Miller. All that remained was for Bolton to write into the play a special part for Walter Catlett, that of Otis Hooper.

As Sally, the dishwashing waif at the Elm Tree Inn, Marilyn Miller dominated the production. Through the strategy of her waiter-friend, Connie (Leon Errol), Sally is able to invade a millionaire's Long Island estate during a garden party, where she poses as a Russian dancer. Her dancing wins the hearts of everyone present and starts Sally off on a dancing career that carries her into the *Ziegfeld Follies.* At the party she also meets and falls in love with the wealthy Blair Farquar (Irving Fisher). The love affair progresses through various vicissitudes until it ends in marriage.

*Sally* was one of Ziegfeld's most bountiful productions, and it had a great deal with which to woo audiences: Joseph Urban's elaborate settings and costuming; the grotesque dances and the droll comedy of Leon Errol; the buffoonery of Walter Catlett. But the brightest attraction was Marilyn Miller, as Ziegfeld well knew she would be when for the first time in his career he offered her in place of a salary a percentage of the box-office gross. (She drew about $3,000 a week, becoming the highest-paid musical-comedy star up to that time.) "*Sally* is Marilyn Miller—from her head to her toes," wrote Louis R. Reid in the New York *Dramatic Mirror.* "She danced divinely. . . . Her performance is one of the daintiest things of this unusual season." Even the perspective of many years was unable to dim Guy Bolton's recollection of Miss Miller. In *Bring on the Girls,* written collaboratively with P. G. Wodehouse, Bolton recalled: "It was Marilyn who really mattered. . . . Marilyn who gave to the play a curious enchantment that no reproduction in other lands or other mediums ever captured." She brought a radiance to whatever she said and did; while merely standing on the stage she flooded it with glamour. But she was particularly unforgettable in one of the most beautiful songs Kern ever wrote, sung as a duet with Blair: "Look for the Silver Lining." Kern had not written this classic for *Sally,* though it was there that it first became famous. He had previously intended it for *Brewster's Millions,* which was never produced; after that it was interpolated into his musical *Good Morning, Dearie* (1919). But it was Marilyn Miller who catapulted the song to the heights of public acceptance. So thoroughly did she become identified with this number that when the screen biography of Marilyn Miller was filmed, released in 1949, it was named *Look for the Silver Lining.*

Another number was thunderously received by audiences each evening, "The Church 'Round the Corner," introduced by Mary Hay and Walter Catlett in the finale. The title song (shared by Blair and chorus), "Whip-poor-Will" (a duet for Sally and Blair), and "Wild Rose," sung by Sally, were also of outstanding interest.

Marilyn Miller starred in the motion-picture adaptation produced by First National and released in 1929.

SALLY, IRENE AND MARY (1922), *a musical comedy with book by Eddie Dowling and Cyrus Wood. Lyrics by Raymond Klages. Music by J.*

*Fred Coots. Presented by the Shuberts at the Casino Theater on September 4. Directed by Frank Smithson. Cast included Eddie Dowling, Jean Brown, Kitty Flynn, and Edna Morn (318 performances).*

J. Fred Coots was a comparatively unknown and inexperienced composer when one day, early in 1922, he met Eddie Dowling at the Friars Club in New York. Dowling by then was a famous song-and-dance man who had made his reputation first in vaudeville, then in several editions of the *Ziegfeld Follies.* Deciding to expand his activities, Dowling had then recently collaborated in writing the text for a musical in which he planned to star. He was looking for a composer. Coots, somehow, managed to sell himself to Dowling, even though the latter was on the hunt for a famous name. The several musical samples Coots played for Dowling had apparently convinced the veteran he could take a chance on this unknown. The gamble paid off. The show, with which Coots made his Broadway debut and forthwith established his reputation as a songwriter, was *Sally, Irene and Mary,* one of the leading musical comedy hits of its year.

Eddie Dowling played the part of a small-town plumber, Jimmie Dugan, in love with Mary (Edna Morn), who had been the girl next door. Mary was now occupying an apartment in New York with two other young ladies, Irene (Kitty Flynn) and Sally (Jean Brown)—all three had ambitions to become actresses. They gain the interest of a producer who gives them an opportunity in one of his shows. Within a year, all three girls become stars, live in luxury, are surrounded by adulation, and sought after by some of the most desirable millionaire bachelors in town. One of these rich men pursues Mary and wants to marry her. But Mary comes to a sensible decision. Jimmie Dugan, having saved up some money and bought himself a Ford, comes to New York and manages to win Mary away from her affluent admirer.

Handsomely mounted, aided by one or two show-stopping dance numbers, and filled with beguiling tunes, *Sally, Irene and Mary* had such potent box-office appeal that following its then long run on Broadway at the Casino Theater, it went on an extensive national tour, and returned to New York for a second brief run on March 23, 1925.

Coots' melodious score included a duet by Jimmie and Mary, "Time Will Tell," its best and most successful number. But two other songs pointed strongly to Coots' gift for ingratiating melodies, "I Wonder Why" and "Do You Remember the Days?." It was on the strength of his work in this production that Coots signed a lucrative contract with the Shuberts to provide music for some of their lavish musical productions.

Beyond the similarity in title, there is no relationship between this musical, and the motion picture, *Sally, Irene and Mary*, which starred Alice Faye in 1938, a 20th Century-Fox production.

SALVATION (1969), *a rock musical, with book, music, and lyrics by Peter Link and C. C. Courtney. Presented by David Black at the Jan Hus Theater on September 24. Directed by Paul Aaron. Dances by Kathryn Prosyn. Cast included Peter Link, C. C. Courtney, Yolande Bavan, and Boni Enten.*

*Salvation* had a truly humble beginning in a Greenwich Village nightclub, where it was seen and admired by David Black. He acquired producing rights and tried to place it with the Repertory Theater at the Lincoln Center for the Performing Arts, but without success. He then interested Capitol Records, who financed it for an Off Broadway production and released the original-cast recording. Salvation proved a profitable investment. Mounted at a cost of only $37,682, it earned a profit of over $40,000 before 1969 had ended, not counting the income from the recording. Thus it was already in the black before its success was beginning to achieve its full momentum. With various productions in the stage of preparation—one for Los Angeles, for example, and another for London—and with numerous other companies planned for America and Europe (not to mention the possibility of a motion-picture sale), *Salvation* turned out to be the most successful Off Broadway musical production of the season.

While *Salvation* was unquestionably stimulated by *Hair* (1968), it did not yield to the temptation of imitation. *Salvation* had its own personal gospel to preach, and its own individual method. In belonging to a new genre of the musical theater, *Salvation,* like *Hair,* populates the stage with young iconoclasts who allow their energies to spring forth like an uncontrolled geyser eruption; it makes very little use of scenery or costumes; makes a minimal demand on plot, in fact almost none at all; is preoccupied with drugs and sex. But *Salvation* has its own format and its own theme. It is in a single act, and is virtually operatic in that the nineteen musical numbers (vigorously accompanied by a rock group calling itself "Nobody Else") follow one another so rapidly that there is little opportunity for dialogue to intrude. The message comes through in song rather than in spoken word or even stage action. And the message is an attack against organized religion, which *Salvation* feels has no place in present-day society. The production is a travesty on a revival meeting, with no holds barred in its mockery of Christianity. "The sentiment of the piece," said Clive Barnes, "varies from the irony of a boy suffering, strangely, disconsolately, from Portnoy's complaint to the joyousness of kids who find Sunday more conducive to the sins of the flesh than the food of the soul." Barnes's overall estimate of *Salvation* was that it was "loud, daring, adventurous, and even outspoken . . . a zany, zippy, disarmingly frank show."

Among the musical numbers, two might be singled out for special attention: "If You Let Me Make Love to You Then Why Can't I Touch You?" and a rock spiritual, "There Ain't No Flesh on Jesus."

SAY, DARLING. *See* THE PAJAMA GAME (last paragraph).

SCANDALS. *See* GEORGE WHITE'S SCANDALS.

SEACOAST OF BOHEMIA. *See* FROM THE SECOND CITY.

THE SECOND LITTLE SHOW. *See* THE LITTLE SHOW.

THE SERENADE (1897), *a comic opera, with book and lyrics by Harry B. Smith. Music by Victor Herbert. Presented by Henry Clay Barnabee and William H. MacDonald (the Bostonians) at the Knickerbocker Theater on March 16. Directed by W. H. Fitzgerald. Cast included Eugene Cowles, Jessie Bartlett Davis, Henry Clay Barnabee, and Alice Nielsen (79 performances).*

Harry B. Smith long insisted that this play was derived from an interlude by Carlo Goldoni, but this was finally proved a hoax; no such Goldoni interlude exists. Smith's text (it is his own) concerned Alvarado (W. H. MacDonald) a handsome opera singer who wins the heart of Dolores (Jessie Bartlett Davis) with a beautiful serenade. For her he is ready to jilt his former sweetheart, Yvonne (Alice Nielsen). Alvarado and Dolores come into the hands of the brigand chief Romero (Eugene Cowles). The Duke of Santa Cruz (Henry Clay Barnabee) brings Dolores into a monastery to keep her from Alvarado, but Alvarado finally wins Dolores, and Yvonne finds consolation with another man.

It has been said that the real hero of the play is not a character but the serenade "I Love Thee, I Adore Thee," which first appears as the second half of a duet between Alvarado and Dolores and then courses throughout the entire operetta. The serenade reappears in many different forms: as a parody on grand opera; a monk's chant; a parrot's call; a rousing song of brigands. It makes a final appearance in its original sentimental version—as love conquers all.

Though Yvonne is not the heroine of the play, Alice Neilsen first became a star in that role. She had not originally been intended for the part when the operetta was first contemplated. One day, just before *The Serenade* went into rehearsal, Victor Herbert's wife heard the then unknown Neilsen at the Murray Hill Theater and became convinced she was the actress to play Yvonne. Herbert concurred. Though Hilda Clark had been engaged for the part, Neilsen was contracted, and they shared the role at alternate performances.

While the serenade was the leading vocal number in the score, there were several others that caught on: a humorous parody on the serenade, "The Singing Lesson"; a gay waltz sung by Yvonne, "Cupid and I"; "The Monk and the Maid," a lusty idyll of the pleasures of the flesh; and Alvarado's rousing postilion song, "With Cracking of Whip." Also in the score were some fine concerted and dramatic numbers, including such appealing choruses as the opening brigands' hymn and the chant of the monks, "In Our Quiet Cloister."

1776 (1969), *a musical play, with book by Peter Stone, based on a conception of Sherman Edwards. Lyrics and music by Sherman Edwards. Presented by Stuart Ostrow at the 46th Street Theater on March 16. Directed by Peter Hunt. Dances by Onna White. Cast included William Daniels, Paul Hecht, Clifford David, Roy Poole, and Howard Da Silva.*

In 1925 *Dearest Enemy,* with a score by Rodgers and Hart, had torn a leaf out of the American history book (the Revolutionary War) to create a musical comedy—something which the cognoscenti of the musical theater insisted at the time was sheer box-office poison. *Dearest Enemy,* however, was a success. Since then there have not been many other successful musicals based on authentic American historical events. When, therefore, it was discovered that *1776* had for its theme the Continental Congress of 1776 and contained the arguments propounded by those favoring revolution and those opposed to it, with the suspense built upon whether or not America would gain its freedom, the climax of the show being the signing of the Declaration of Independence, a good deal of healthy skepticism was expressed about the financial potential of this newcomer. This skepticism was increased by the fact that the production had an uncommercial title; that the cast did not boast a single outstanding star, a single spectacular scene, a chorus, or dancing (except for a brief waltz performed spontaneously by Benjamin Franklin and John Adams with Martha Jefferson), and no sex appeal (there were only two women in the cast, one married to Jefferson, the other married to John Adams but existing only within the reaches of his imagination). Yet, wonder of wonders, *1776* became the "sleeper" of the 1969 theatrical season, a show that inspired such eloquent rhapsodies from the critics that overnight it became a box-office attraction of formidable proportions. It went on to win three Antoinette Perry awards, including the one for the best musical of the season.

There were a dozen songs in the show, not the kind of tunes you are likely to hum once you leave the theater, but nevertheless tunes that are important as background material for a powerful and frequently charming text. There is a strong opening number, "Sit Down, John," in which John Adams complains about the lackadaisical way in which the Continental Congress is going about its business, followed by his low estimate of his colleagues in "Piddle, Twiddle and Resolve." There is an excellent antiwar song, "Momma Look Sharp," sung by a mock Continental Congress comprising a courier, a congressional custodian, and Leather Apron. There is a song about slavery which Edward Rutledge of South Carolina directs toward the Northern businessmen, "Molasses and Rum." There is a moving tribute to a venerable family by Lee, Franklin, and Adams in "The Lees of Old Virginia." There is a song by the leaders of freedom, "But, Mr. Adams" (a humorous explanation of how Jefferson was inveigled into accepting a job nobody else wanted). And there was a song Dickinson and the conservative group give in reply, "Cool, Considerate Men." None was calculated to sell a million records or to get frequent hearings over television and in nightclubs. But each plays a basic role in the telling of the enthralling story of America's birth.

But the text is most important—a tightly developed drama with such vivid characterizations that the famous personalities of the Revolutionary period emerge with all their foibles and idiosyncrasies. It is the text and the characterizations that led Clive Barnes to say that the music was full of "style, humanity, wit and passion." He called it "most striking, most gripping . . . [which] makes even an Englishman's heart beat faster." *1776* is a history lesson the way it should be taught in schools and never is. "You find yourself grasping without effort the relative possibilities of all thirteen colonies," said Walter Kerr, adding: "The show makes you feel smarter than you used to be . . . and smarter without having to slave for it."

Sherman Edwards, a former history teacher who conceived the idea for this musical, had no "special pleading in mind when I set out to create this show," as he told an interviewer. "I didn't set out to answer anyone. My concept simply was to show what men and events of the time were, with honesty and respect for reportage of the facts. I wanted to show these man at their outermost limits. These men were the cream of their colonies. Some were very erudite and others were simple, honest men. They were moved by self-interest, of course. But they were non-neurotic, the kind of people I've always liked. They form a diverse group. They disagreed and fought with each other.

But they understood commitment, and though they fought, they fought affirmatively. They didn't fight negatively and leave it at that. They were struggling toward a goal, though each had his own ideas of what that should be. And they came up with something that never was perfect. But it was as good as they could make it at the time."

The action, of course, takes place in Philadelphia, during a three-month period in 1776, ending on the fourth of July. There is no intermission, the entire play being performed in uninterrupted continuity. John Adams (William Daniels) is upset at the easygoing and uninterested way in which the Continental Congress is going about the business of creating independence for the colonies. He comes to Benjamin Franklin (Howard Da Silva) with his frustrations. Franklin points out that never in history has a colony broken from its parent country. What is more, Franklin stresses the fact that Adams is not the kind of likable and ingratiating fellow who can sell an idea; that perhaps a gentleman like Richard Henry Lee might be more successful. In any event, the Congress is just making no progress. Dispatches from General Washington bring discouraging news from the war front.

At long last, Lee becomes the spokesman for independence, to inspire a vigorous exchange of arguments, pro and con. Most favor freedom but are hesitant to vote for it. A motion is passed that a unanimous vote will be required for any decision; also that a committee will be formed to draw up the Declaration of Independence. A long harangue follows as to who should draw up this Declaration. Though Jefferson (Ken Howard) insists he does not possess the literary qualities required for the job, he is chosen—a task that progresses rather slowly, since he prefers spending as much of his time as possible with his young, attractive, but neglected bride. At the Congress, things continue to move slowly, and the reports from George Washington continue to be pessimistic. There are rumors that the American Colonials are spending a good deal of their time carousing with women and drink—a state of affairs that a committee, headed by Franklin, is sent to investigate.

With Franklin and the rebels away, the conservatives could sit back and relax—especially John Dickinson of Pennsylvania (Paul Hecht), whose sympathy lay strongly with remaining with Great Britain. But Franklin, Jefferson, and the rebels are soon back with reports that the morale among the Colonials was not quite so bad as had been rumored. And now the original draft of the Declaration of Independence is read, and severely criticized. And a discussion begins over the bird to be used as a national symbol, with Jefferson favoring the dove, and Adams the eagle.

Slowly, the Declaration is being whipped into shape, with numerous changes and deletions made. A main objection is raised by Edward Rutledge of South Carolina (Clifford David) : the Declaration speaks of freeing the slaves, something that would ruin the South. To this, Adams can only be bitter, remarking sarcastically that all the gentlemen seem to worry about is the economy. Rutledge replies with equal bitterness that economy had been the first consideration with the New England shipowners when the famous Triangle Trade was devised. Reluctantly, Benjamin Franklin insists that the antislavery provision be deleted in order to save the Declaration from defeat. One by one the representatives of the different colonies sign the Declaration, with the exception of John Dickinson, who prefers leaving the Congress and joining the Continental Army. A report from the front tells of further defeats: George Washington must evacuate Manhattan; and he is forced to face a well-trained army of twenty-five thousand soldiers with only five thousand poorly equipped, poorly trained men. But the victory of the Declaration of Independence brings hope for the future. The colonies have voted for freedom. In spite of the military odds against it, a new country has come to birth.

1776 became the first musical ever produced in its entirety at the White House. This took place on February 22, 1970 (exactly one year after the show had opened in New York) at a special command performance for President and Mrs. Nixon and their guests.

SHE LOVES ME (1963), *a musical comedy, with book by Joe Masteroff, based on Miklos Laszlo's play* Parfumerie. *Lyrics by Sheldon Harnick. Music by Jerry Bock. Presented by Harold S. Prince, in association with Lawrence Kaska and Philip C. McKenna, at the Eugene O'Neill Theater on April 23. Directed by Harold Prince. Dances by Carol Haney. Cast included Barbara Cook, Daniel Massey, and Jack Cassidy (301 performances).*

*She Loves Me* had started out in life as a thoroughly delightful and frothy stage play set in glamorous prewar Budapest. This in turn became an equally appealing and nostalgic motion picture, *The Shop Around the Corner,* starring Margaret Sullavan. (Just for the record: the motion picture *The Shop Around the Corner* was made into a screen musical for Judy Garland and Van Johnson, an MGM production in 1949 called *In the Good Old Summertime.* Any relation between this movie and the earlier one, or the stage play from which both had sprung, was purely coincidental.) In its third reincarnation, as a musical comedy, the play retained what Howard Taubman called "the Hungarian gift for laughter and love and make believe, none of which are too deep and serious in so many of their factions . . . and by an odd creative filip has also taken on an American dash and sheen. . . . The humors . . . are gentle rather than robust. The characters are the familiar figures of happily bittersweet fairy tales; yet they have individuality and charm. You keep thinking that you cannot digest an array of desserts, no matter how attractive and tasty they are, but you find yourself relishing nearly all of them in *She Loves Me.*"

The time is 1933, the place an unidentified middle-European city strongly suggestive of Budapest. The main setting is a shop, "Parfumerie," owned by Mr. Maraczek (Ludwig Donath). Business is bad. Mr. Maraczek is in an evil humor, which gets worse when a recent delivery of music boxes fails to interest customers. Amelia Balash (Barbara Cook) comes into the store looking for a job. She proves her ability by selling a music box, and is instantly hired. Another employee, George Nowack (Daniel Massey) has been carrying on a romantic correspondence with a female he has never met. Amelia and George soon prove they cannot get along with each other; continually they quarrel over trifles. What neither, however, knows—but what the audience is soon made to discover—is that they are the correspondents in this exchange of love letters. In his most recent letter, George has finally arranged a personal meeting the following Tuesday.

As Christmas is drawing near, the staff is ordered on Tuesday to work late to decorate the store. This upsets both George and Amelia, both of whom are looking forward with considerable anticipation to their rendezvous. When George arrives for the appointment at the Café Imperiale, Amelia is waiting for him at a table; her identification is a book with a rose placed nearby. Timid about meeting the girl at last, George sends his friend into the café to have a look at her. The friend recognizes Amelia and blurts out the truth to George, who enters the café and comes to Amelia's table. She explains she is waiting for somebody and begs him to leave her alone; George, however, insists on sitting down with her for a while. The more Amelia entreats him to leave, the more insistent does George become to stay on. Amelia calls him a pompous, smug tyrant who will never amount to anything. And now comes the closing time for the café—and Amelia is heartbroken that her dear friend of the letters has failed to show up.

The next day, the failure of Amelia to show up for work gives George concern, particularly when he learns that she is ill. He visits her at her apartment, but being of suspicious mind, Amelia is sure that George has come to spy on her and learn whether she is really sick. Gently, George orders her to go back to bed. He feeds her some ice cream he has brought her. Slowly, as she eats her ice cream, Amelia begins to react favorably to George. She now reveals to him why she had been at the café the other night. To console her, George creates the fiction that he actually had seen a man outside the café looking for a girl but, failing to find her, had left. This so delights Amelia that impulsively she kisses George. When George leaves, Amelia begins to realize that she really likes George a good deal.

The following evening, George (now elevated to the post of store manager) accompanies Amelia to her bus stop. En route he invites her to join him in a café for coffee, an invitation she gladly accepts. Carolers are singing Christmas hymns, for Christmas is just around the corner.

Holiday business has been booming at the shop. Mr. Maraczek (despite troubles with a faithless wife) is in good spirits. He treats his help to champagne. Amelia and George spend Christmas Eve together, going off to a café, where they are to meet not only Amelia's mother but also her dear friend of the letters. As they leave the shop, Amelia takes along a music box as a gift to her friend of the letters. George insists that he has always liked music boxes and would enjoy possessing one, especially since it would be a permanent reminder to him of the day Amelia first put foot into the store. Amelia and George now break down and confess that they liked each other from their first meeting; that all their squabbles had been a disguise concealing their true feelings. It is only then that Amelia discovers that George is the man of her letters—and the man of her life.

The principal songs are "Dear Friend," introduced by Amelia; "Days Gone By," a nostalgic number sung by Mr. Maraczek as he advises George to marry a nice girl; "She Loves Me," George's realization he is love with Amelia; "Ice Cream," a song in pseudo-operatic style sung by Amelia as for the first time she begins to look with favor on George; and the ironic "Grand Knowing You," sung by Jack Cassidy in the role of Mr. Kodaly, after he gets fired as manager of the store, to be replaced by George. An amusing dance number is a mock-romantic tango danced to the tune "Come With Me, Ilona" —one of several pleasing choreographic inventions by Carol Haney, all in modest dimension. In a similar economical vein is the absence of a chorus. One of the best comic scenes involves a waiter and a café-house violinist, enacted respectively by Wood Romoff and Gino Conforti.

THE SHO-GUN (1904), *an operetta, with book and lyrics by George Ade. Music by Gustav Luders. Presented by Harry W. Savage at Wallack's Theater on October 10. Directed by George F. Marion. Cast included Edward Martindel, Georgia Caine, and Charles Evans (125 performances).*

Spoofing American ways, manners, and behavior is nothing new for the musical stage. George Ade did it at the turn of the century in *The Sho-Gun*, which he called "a playful treatise upon the gentle arts of promoting and trust-building." *The Sho-Gun* pokes fun at the American go-getter, advertising, politics, big business, and the American love of high-sounding titles.

The setting is an imaginary island, Ka Choo, which lies between Japan and Korea, ruled by the Sho-Gun. William Henry Spangle (Charles Evans), manufacturer of chewing gum, comes to the island. There he hires as lawyer, Hanki-Pank (Thomas C. Leary), the island astrologer, and teaches him the subtleties of American law the better to circumvent that of Ka Choo. By forming trusts and fomenting strikes—and through the far-reaching influence of Hanki-Pank—Spangle becomes the island's new Sho-Gun. Then he marries Omee-Omi (Georgia Caine), the widow of a former Sho-Gun. In office, Spangle wastes no time in reorganizing the island along American ideas, by introducing high-pressure promotion and advertising, together with American political ideas and methods. The islanders do not take kindly to this revolution, and Spangle must finally escape to safety through the help of the U.S. Marines.

The principal songs are: "Little Moozoo May," "I Am Yours Truly," "Flutter Little Bird," and "I'll Live for You."

SHOW BOAT (1927), *a musical comedy, with book and lyrics by Oscar Hammerstein II, based on the novel of the same name by Edna Ferber. Music by Jerome Kern. Presented by Florenz Ziegfeld at the Ziegfeld Theater on December 27. Directed by Zeke Colvan. Dances by Sammy Lee. Cast included Helen Morgan, Howard Marsh, Charles Winninger, Edna May Oliver, Jules Bledsoe, and Norma Terris (572 performances).*

With *Show Boat,* the musical theater in America acquired new dimensions. This was musical comedy no more (though it was thus designated by its authors). This was a musical play with an artistic entity, dramatic truth, authentic characterizations, effective atmosphere, a logical story line. This, too, was a musical in which music, dance, and comedy were basic to the stage action.

When Kern first approached Edna Ferber with the plan to adapt her novel *Show Boat* into a musical, she thought he had gone mad. She could hardly envision her atmospheric story of life on a Mississippi showboat, in the closing 1800's, as a "girlie" show crammed with conventional musical-comedy attractions. Only when Kern explained he was thinking in terms of a new kind of musical theater, in which old methods would be bypassed in favor of more imaginative approaches, was she willing to assign to Kern the musical-comedy rights.

Friends of Kern insisted that this project was not commercially sound. People attending musical comedies, they argued, were concerned with diversion, not art. They tried to dissuade Kern from such a quixotic project. Only Oscar Hammerstein was quickly convinced (it took only a single telephone call to win him over). He, too, had definite ideas on the direction musical comedy should take, and a quick reading of the Ferber novel convinced him that this material could carry the musical theater toward goals he had in mind. Neither Kern nor Hammerstein allowed themselves to be discouraged by their well-intentioned colleagues and friends—and went to work with a will. "We had fallen in love with it," Hammerstein explained. "We couldn't keep our hands off it. We acted out scenes together and planned the actual direction. We sang to each other. We had ourselves swooning."

Their enthusiasm apparently infected Florenz Ziegfeld, who consented to be the producer, even though *Show Boat* was not actually his meat. But there were agonizing delays. When *Show Boat* was not ready for the recently constructed Ziegfeld Theater, Ziegfeld opened his new house with *Rio Rita;* and *Rio Rita* was so successful that *Show Boat* had to wait a full year before the Ziegfeld Theater was again available. Then, before it was finally produced, *Show Boat* had to undergo extensive alterations and deletions. This accomplished, Florenz Ziegfeld suddenly lost heart in the whole venture and had to be won back all over again.

But despite his recalcitrance and doubts, Ziegfeld spared no expense in making his production as handsome as possible; that is the only way Ziegfeld worked. Practically an all-star cast had been assembled. Joseph Urban designed remarkable nostalgic sets. John Harkrider prepared the striking costumes.

*Show Boat* was both an artistic and box-office triumph. It grossed about $50,000 a week for almost two solid years in New York. After that it played to sold-out houses on a national tour, beginning in Boston on May 6, 1929, and continuing across the country until March, 1930. The original company returned for a New York run of 180 performances in 1932. Meanwhile, in 1928 it played at the Drury Lane in London and soon after that in Paris in a French translation. In 1929 the first of several motion-picture adaptations was released, a Universal production starring Joseph Schildkraut, Laura La Plante, and Alma Rubens, in what was only partly a sound picture, with only the songs and a synchronized musical score heard.

The critical acclaim for *Show Boat* was impressive. Robert Garland called it an "American masterpiece," and Richard Watts, Jr., described it as a "beautiful example of musical comedy." Alan Dale wrote: "*Show Boat* is going to have a wonderful sail—no storms—no adverse winds—nothing to keep it from making port—goodness knows when."

The play opens with the arrival of the showboat *Cotton Blossom* into Natchez in the 1880's. The festive crowds gathered at the levee are jubilantly welcoming it with the song "Cotton Blossom." Cap'n Andy, owner of the boat (Charles Winninger), invites the people to see his show, starring the glamorous Julie La Verne (Helen Morgan). With Cap'n Andy are his wife, Parthy Ann (Edna May Oliver), and their lovely daughter, Magnolia (Norma Terris). When the crowds disperse, Gaylord Ravenal (Howard Marsh)—a handsome riverboat gambler—lingers on. He has caught a glimpse of Magnolia and is attracted to her; nor has Magnolia failed to notice or be impressed by Gaylord. Meeting up with each other, they express their mutual interest in "Make Believe." After Ravenal leaves Magnolia, the stevedore, Joe (Jules Bledsoe), appears on the levee. Magnolia tries to find out from him his opinion of Gaylord, but the stevedore refuses to give a positive response. Instead, he asks Magnolia to direct her questions to the Mississippi River. In singing about the Mississippi, "Ol' Man River," Joe unburdens his heart of his own problems as a sweating stevedore and as a Negro, while the Mississippi just keeps rolling along.

In the kitchen pantry of the *Cotton Blossom,* Julie La Verne and her friend Queenie are complaining about their respective men. Nevertheless, they realize fully that come what may they cannot stop loving their men ("Can't Help Lovin' Dat Man"). Magnolia now confides to Julie that she, too, is in love, and is warned by Julie to be careful to choose a man worthy of her.

Meanwhile, the sheriff has received the information that Julie is Negro and that her husband, Steven, is half-white. Miscegenation being forbidden by local law, the sheriff insists that Julie and Steve must leave the ship. Since replacements are needed for the parts they play in the show, Magnolia and Ravenal are recruited. Thus brought together by circumstance, they fall in love, as they reveal on the night after their premiere performance in "You Are Love." Gaylord proposes marriage, and Magnolia accepts ecstatically.

Years go by. A daughter, Kim, has been born to Gaylord and Magnolia. Cap'n Andy, his wife, Magnolia, and Gaylord are in Chicago for the 1893 World's Fair. All is not well with Magnolia and Gaylord, as the latter reveals to her father. He has resumed his gambling ways and his irresponsible way of life; in fact, he has deserted his family. Nevertheless, she still loves him deeply. Magnolia is forced to seek a job at the Trocadero Music Hall, whose star is Julie La Verne, entertaining her audience with her poignant rendition of "Bill." Learning that Magnolia needs a job, Julie magnanimously resigns so that Magnolia can take her place. At first Magnolia's performance fails to generate much heat. Then Cap'n Andy gets her to sing a popular sentimental ballad of the day—Charles K. Harris' "After the Ball"—and whips up the audience into joining the singing. Magnolia goes over big. But Cap'n Andy convinces her that the Trocadero is no place for her, and the life of the stage not the way to bring up Kim. And so he convinces Magnolia to return to the *Cotton Blossom* (a new *Cotton Blossom*). A repentant Gaylord Ravenal is waiting for her there, ready to resume his marital responsibilities. And Kim becomes the star of the showboat.

Without sacrificing entertainment values—as the response at the box office proved—Kern and Hammerstein succeeded in producing a musical with bold, new concepts, a show that was both a revelation and a revolution. Here was a production totally unique for the 1920's, which re-created faithfully a chapter from America's past and gave its story credibility and its characters dimension. Here were atmosphere and background that rang true. Here was a story that dared to touch on the provocative subject of miscegenation, and a musical that dared to dispense with chorus girls and the kind of synthetic humor and production numbers which in the 1920's were so basic to the musical theater. Here were dialogue and lyrics that, while frequently remaining in the vernacular, reached heights of poetry and dramatic eloquence. And, finally, here was a score with few if any rivals in the American musical theater of that period. Long before 1927 Kern had proved himself to be one of Broadway's leading melodists. But to his score for *Show Boat* he brought a range and variety of style—and tapped veins of tenderness and compassion —new even for him. One of the reasons *Show Boat* proved as successful as it was in 1927—and why it has become such a classic—is that Kern's score is a veritable cornucopia of riches, a score consistently inspired and consistently revealing the hand of a consummate craftsman.

Perhaps most famous of all the songs—and few musicals have so many songs that have become so famous—is Joe's immortal hymn to the Mississippi, "Ol' Man River." It is so remarkable in catching the personality and overtones of the Negro spiritual that it is now sometimes described as an American folk song. "Here," Hammerstein has explained, "is a song sung by a character who is a rugged and untutored philosopher. It is a song of resignation with a protest implied." When Kern first played "Ol' Man River" for Edna Ferber, "the music mounted, mounted, and I give you my word my hair stood on end, the tears came to my eyes, and I breathed like a heroine in a melodrama," she has written. "This was great music. This was music that would outlast Jerome Kern's day and mine."

"After the Ball" was the only song in the score whose music was not the work of Kern and the lyrics not the creation of Hammerstein. "Bill"—the song that made Helen Morgan into a star, after only one year earlier she had been only a minor ballad singer in the revue *Americana*—had music by Kern, but the lyrics were the work of P. G. Wodehouse and not of Hammerstein. This is because this song had originally been meant for the "Princess Theater

Show" *Oh, Lady! Lady!* in 1918. But the ballad's unusual intervallic construction, together with its somber mood, made it seem out of place in a gay show, and it was removed in 1918. When Kern heard Helen Morgan sing in *Americana,* he realized at once that his forgotten song had found its singer, and it was not difficult for him to find a place for it in the play.

*Show Boat* has often been revived, and each return is more welcome than the last. Ziegfeld brought it back to Broadway in 1932, with Irene Dunne replacing Norma Terris (Miss Dunne had been her understudy in 1927, and in later years would become a top movie star), and Dennis King and Paul Robeson taking over the roles of Gaylord Ravenal and Joe. A new, revitalized production came to the Ziegfeld Theater on January 4, 1946 (this time with a cast including Carol Bruce, Jan Clayton, Charles Fredericks, and Kenneth Spencer). It had a run of 418 performances and received the Donaldson Award. For this revival Kern wrote a new song, "No One but Me"—the last song he was destined to produce, as it turned out, since he died suddenly before the revival opened. Two years after that the producing firm of Rodgers and Hammerstein once again lit up the skies of Broadway with a run of *Show Boat.* And in 1966 *Show Boat* sailed proudly into the New York State Theater at the Lincoln Center for the Performing Arts, to gross almost $100,000 a week. And all these Broadway revivals do not take into account the number of times *Show Boat* has been played all over the United States through the years.

In 1952 Oscar Hammerstein prepared a special concert version of the play, with narrative, for performance at the Lewisohn Stadium in New York. Kern himself developed the principal music from his score into a symphonic work, *Scenario,* introduced by the Cleveland Orchestra under Artur Rodzinski in 1941. And on April 8, 1954, *Show Boat* made its first appearance in a regular opera repertory, when it was performed by the New York City Opera.

After the 1929 motion-picture adaptation, *Show Boat* was transferred to the talking screen twice more: in 1936, with Allan Jones, Helen Morgan, and Irene Dunne (Universal); in 1951 with Kathryn Grayson, Howard Keel, and Ava Gardner (MGM).

Like the Mississippi in "Ol' Man River," *Show Boat* just keeps rolling along. What Brooks Atkinson said after one of the revivals, Americans have been saying through the years: "Can't help loving that treasure house of melodies and legends."

SHOW GIRL (1929), *a musical comedy, with book by William Anthony McGuire, based on J. P. McEvoy's novel of the same name. Music by George*

*Gershwin, with additional songs by Jimmy Durante. Lyrics by Gus Kahn. Presented by Florenz Ziegfeld at the Ziegfeld Theater on July 2. Directed by McGuire. Dances by Bobby Connolly and Albertina Rasch. Cast included Ruby Keeler, Clayton Jackson and Durante, Joseph MacCaulay, Harriet Hoctor, and Duke Ellington (111 performances).*

*Show Girl* was Gershwin's second and last job for Ziegfeld. (His first had been *Rosalie,* a score in collaboration with Sigmund Romberg.) The text traced the history of Dixie Dugan (Ruby Keeler) in her rise to stardom on the musical stage. Ziegfeld himself becomes involved in her career. Dixie crashes an interview with him, wins him over completely, and becomes the star of the *Follies.* En route to fame Dixie becomes involved in several love affairs.

Dixie (accompanied by Duke Ellington and his orchestra) sang and danced to the leading musical number in the Gershwin score, "Liza" (a song to which Gershwin himself was always partial). During the first few nights of the run of *Show Girl* both out-of-town and in New York, Dixie found an unexpected and unpaid-for collaborator in her performance of "Liza"; in Ruby Keeler's recently married husband, Al Jolson, who, since he was then making a motion picture in Hollywood, had hired a plane to bring him to these performances. Uninvited and unexpectedly, Jolson would rise from his seat in the audience and run up and down the aisle singing the song with and to his wife. "So Are You!" was another outstanding Gershwin song, presented by Eddie Foy, Jr., and Kathryn Hereford in subsidiary roles. Gershwin's tone poem *An American in Paris* (it had been recently introduced at Carnegie Hall by the New York Philharmonic under Walter Damrosch) was used as background music for a stunning ballet by Harriet Hoctor and the Albertina Rasch girls.

Jimmy Durante, appearing as a property man, interpolated three songs, which he had formerly featured in nightclubs and which remained in his permanent song repertory: "So I Ups to Him," "I Can Do Without Broadway," and "Who Will Be with You When I'm Far Away?" (none of them, to be sure, by the Gershwins).

Despite the winning performances of Jimmy Durante and Ruby Keeler, the spectacular production by Ziegfeld, and two outstanding Gershwin songs, *Show Girl* was a box-office failure. It was too slow-moving to be dramatically effective, and the plot, such as it was, was crushed under the weight of Ziegfeld's massive production numbers. Gershwin had to threaten a lawsuit before he could collect the royalties Ziegfeld owed him—money that Ziegfeld had lost not only in the ill-fated production but also in the stock-market crash.

THE SHOW IS ON (1936), *a revue, with sketches by David Freedman, Moss Hart, and others. Lyrics and music by numerous writers and composers. Presented by the Shuberts at the Winter Garden on December 25. Entire program conceived, directed, and designed by Vincente Minnelli. Dances by Harry Losee. Cast included Beatrice Lillie, Bert Lahr, and Reginald Gardiner (237 performances).*

Three routines—one by each of the three principals—alone would have made *The Show Is On* outstanding. Beatrice Lillie, sitting on a sickle moon, swings out in the audience, distributing garters while singing a satirical version of a Tin Pan Alley ballad (Herman Hupfeld's "Buy Yourself a Balloon"). Bert Lahr delivers a number that remained a staple in his repertory, "Song of the Woodman," by E. Y. Harburg and Harold Arlen—a hymn in praise of wood (as Lahr hacks away at a tree), wood that can be made into all sorts of things, including "seats all shapes and classes, for little lads and little lasses." And Reginald Gardiner (in his first Broadway appearance) presents a devastating impersonation of a prima donna conductor (undoubtedly Leopold Stokowski) leading his orchestra.

But there were other high spots. Lillie mimicked Josephine Baker, appeared as an amorous French actress, made a shambles of all female singers of rhythm songs in "Rhythm," proved herself a first-night nuisance, and served as a garrulous ticket saleslady at the Theater "Geeld." Bert Lahr was a much-harassed taxpayer being examined by the Internal Revenue Service, spoofed jazz in "Woof," and appeared as a Republican working in the home of Democrats in a travesty on the sad plight of Republicans in 1936. Lillie and Lahr did a burlesque on burlesque—Lillie as a strip-tease artist ogled by putty-nosed Lahr—and Reginald Gardiner starred in a Moss Hart sketch lampooning John Gielgud in *Hamlet*.

George and Ira Gershwin had a song interpolated into this score, "By Strauss." In New York, at a party, Vincente Minnelli heard George Gershwin (in one of Gershwin's playful moods at the piano) poke fun at schmaltzy Viennese waltzes. In planning *The Show Is On,* Minnelli felt such a number would fit in nicely with his plans, and he wired the Gershwins (then in Hollywood to write music for the movies) to provide him with one. They complied with "By Strauss," which Gracie Barrie gave a delectable presentation. Hoagy Carmichael was also represented—with the sentimental "Little Old Lady" (lyrics by Stanely Adams), sung and danced to by Mitzi Mayfair and Charles Walters. A third outstanding number was "Now" (lyrics by Ted Fetter, music by Vernon Duke), sung by Gracie Barrie and Robert Shafer and danced to by Paul Haakon and Evelyn Thawl. "The Casanova Ballet," starring Paul Haakon, was one of the most ambitious dance sequences in the production.

SHUFFLE ALONG (1921), *an all-Negro revue, with book by Miller and Lyle. Lyrics and music by Noble Sissle and Eubie Blake. Presented by the Nikko Company at the 63rd Street Music Hall on May 23. Directed by Walter Brooks. Cast included Noble Sissle and Florence Mills (504 performances).*

*Shuffle Along* was the parent of all those all-Negro revues that sprouted out with such fertility on Broadway throughout the 1920's. It was planned originally only for Negro audiences, played two weeks at the Howard Theater in Washington, D.C., and one week in Philadelphia before finally coming to New York to occupy a humble auditorium far from the glitter of Broadway's lights, up at 63rd Street. The show became so popular, and the traffic became so jammed on 63rd Street, that the police had to make it a one-way street. Whirlwind dancing and spectacular choral singing were the strong suits in a production that was vital and energetic from first to final curtain. A slender plot held the whole thing together: a mayoralty race in Jim Town between Steven Jackson (F. E. Miller) and Sam Peck (Aubrey Lyle). The hit song was "I'm Just Wild About Harry," which helped make Florence Mills (a replacement for Gertrude Saunders) a star. Other appealing numbers were "Bandana Days," sung by Arthur Porter and chorus; the blues, "He May Be Your Man but He Comes to See Me Sometime," sung by Trixie Smith; and "Love Will Find a Way." One of the members in the chorus was Josephine Baker, soon to become the toast of Paris. Two of the members in the pit orchestra became famous musicians: William Grant Still as a serious composer, and Hall Johnson as conductor of a Negro chorus.

SILK STOCKINGS (1955), *a musical comedy, with book by George S. Kaufman, Leueen McGrath, and Abe Burrows, suggested by the motion picture* Ninotchka. *Presented by Feuer and Martin at the Imperial Theater on February 24. Directed by Cy Feuer. Dances by Eugene Loring. Cast included Don Ameche, Hildegarde Neff, and Gretchen Wyler (478 performances).*

*Silk Stockings* was Cole Porter's twenty-fifth score for Broadway, and during its run his fortieth anniversary as composer for the theater was celebrated. *Silk Stockings* proved a happy event for such celebration, for, as Brooks Atkinson said of it, it was "one of Gotham's memorable shows on the level with *Guys and Dolls*" and with some of the "wittiest dialogue in years." To John Chapman it was "everything a musical should be . . . handsome, slick, brisk, intelligent, witty and delightfully acted, and whenever the plot shows the merest sign of trying to take over more than its share, Cole Porter shoulders it aside with some of his best melodies, lyrics and rhythms."

If *Silk Stockings* gave cause for celebration as Porter's twenty-fifth musical and his fortieth anniversary on Broadway, it also provided good reason for sorrow. As it turned out, this was the last score he was destined to write for the Broadway stage. Perhaps that is the way it should have been—bringing his career on Broadway to a full circle. He had made his first strong impressions on Broadway with two successive shows set in Paris: *Paris* and *Fifty Million Frenchmen*. And he ended his Broadway career with two successive shows also set in Paris: *Can-Can* and *Silk Stockings*.

*Silk Stockings* was Cole Porter's second musical to poke malicious fun at the Soviet Union, the first having been *Leave It to Me*. But in *Silk Stockings* the satire cuts deeper. Americans are still the butt of malicious humor, as they had been in the earlier musical; particularly devastating in *Silk Stockings* were the portraits of a high-powered artist's agent and a loud and vulgar movie star. But in *Silk Stockings* the main ammunition is reserved for Soviet officialdom (in the broad caricatures of the Soviet agents, Ivanov, Brankov, and Bibinski, for example; of Soviet red tape; and of the tyranny of Red dictatorship). The commissar of art asks for a copy of "Who's Still Who." When a Soviet agent is informed that the great Soviet composer Prokofiev is dead, he remarks sadly: "I didn't even know he was arrested." Passing the buck of authority from top to bottom, with each in turn shrugging off the responsibility for decisive action and decisions, becomes an indoor sport. And all this satire is not confined exclusively to the text. There are travesties on Russian songs to which slick, suave Porter lyrics are wedded with delightful incongruity to pseudo-Russian music in antiphonal choruses combining asides on dialectical materialism with romantic balladry, as in "Siberia" or "Too Bad."

The original source of *Silk Stockings* was *Ninotchka,* a motion picture in which Greta Garbo had starred in 1939. In the musical, as in the movie, Ninotchka is a hard-boiled, frozen-faced Soviet agent (Hildegarde Neff).

The setting is Paris, where a Soviet composer, Peter Boroff (Philip Sterling), has come to write the score for a motion-picture adaptation of *War and Peace*. In Paris he comes under the influence of the slick and persuasive American theatrical agent Steve Canfield (Don Ameche), who is doing his best to induce Peter to stay on in Paris for more assignments, something Peter is not at all reluctant to do. Peter keeps dallying in Paris so long that the Soviets send the inflexible, stern, and disciplined Ninotchka to bring Peter back to the Soviet Union. Ninotchka now comes in contact not only with luxury, jazz, freedom, and good living—but also the charm and personal attraction of Steve. And she enjoys them all, in spite of her loyalty to her own country. While all this is going on, a Hollywood film star, Janice Dayton (Gretchen Wyler), arrives in Paris to produce a "nonwater picture": She had been forced in Hollywood to appear in so many aquatic productions that her ears have gone bad and now she is determined to work only in "dry" films. She becomes the producer of *War and Peace,* then goes on in "Josephine" to demonstrate how a strip-tease can be introduced into the classic. She also gives newsmen a hilarious account of the developments in Hollywood movies in "Stereophonic Sound."

Ninotchka grows increasingly feminine in Paris, and at the same time her romance with Steve develops. Now it is the duty of the three Russian agents (Ivanov, Brankov, and Bibinski) to keep track of her and to convince her to return to the Soviet Union. She does return to her native land, but Steve follows her there and effects her escape to a world Ninotchka can never forget.

The romance of Ninotchka and Steve provides a mellow antidote to the humor and satire. Broad comedy is injected through the antics of Ivanov, Brankov, and Bibinski in Paris. It is also introduced through the performance of Gretchen Wyler as the noisy, exuberant, sexy Hollywood movie star. Gretchen Wyler was here making her first Broadway appearance, and her voluptuous personality and uninhibited ways won the audience completely, particularly in her hilarious strip-tease number.

The main love song was Steve Canfield's geographical survey of Ninotchka in "All of You." An effective ballad, "As on Through the Seasons We Sail," was shared by Canfield and Ninotchka, and a great deal of nostalgia for Paris was created with still another duet of Canfield and Ninotchka, "Paris Loves Lovers."

In the motion-picture version (MGM, 1957) the two principal parts were assumed by Fred Astaire and Cyd Charisse in a production that utilized virtually the entire stage score.

SIMPLE SIMON (1930), *a musical comedy, with book by Ed Wynn and Guy Bolton. Lyrics by Lorenz Hart. Music by Richard Rodgers. Presented by Florenz Ziegfeld at the Ziegfeld Theater on February 18. Directed by Zeke Colvan. Dances by Seymour Felix. Cast included Ed Wynn and Ruth Etting (135 performances).*

*Simple Simon* was created by Florenz Ziegfeld for Ed Wynn, who brought his lisp, peculiar hats, absurd giggle, individual facial mannerisms, and manual gestures—these and his uncommon gift to find comedy in the ways of a simpleton—to the role of Simon, "the keeper of Information and Newspaper Shop." He is truly a simpleminded man, who delights in daydreams that bring him into the world of nursery rhymes and Mother Goose fairy tales, in which some of the people he meets in everyday life become storybook characters. The whole is a synthetic concoction to give its star ample opportunities to hold the limelight, which he does. As Brooks Atkinson said: "It is Ed Wynn's field day."

For Ed Wynn, *Simple Simon* proved one of his more delectable characterizations. But for songwriters Rodgers and Hart, the show was anything but a happy experience. Working with Ziegfeld was not easy (as Rodgers and Hart had previously discovered with a fiasco called *Betsy*). Ziegfeld always had the last word, even where the music was concerned. And so, one of the songs which Rodgers and Hart rightly felt was one of their best in the score—"Dancing on the Ceiling"—was summarily thrown out of the show by the dictatorial producer. (It found a place in an English musical, *Ever Green,* became a tremendous hit in both England and America, and grew into an all-time Rodgers and Hart classic.) Another fine number, "I Can Do Wonders with You," was also discarded upon Ziegfeld's orders. And Ziegfeld not only dictated what songs should stay out, but also on how the songs that were retained should best be presented; and his own ideas did not always jibe with those of the songwriters.

Rodgers and Hart also had trouble with the leading lady playing the role of Sal. She was a star whose weakness for alcoholic beverages was notorious. During a final tryout of the show at the Colonial Theater in Boston, she was so drunk she fell off the stage. Then and there, Ziegfeld fired her and telephoned to New York for Ruth Etting, already famous as a torch singer. With only a few days to learn her part, Ruth Etting stepped into the role in Boston like a veteran. Then, with the Broadway opening only a day away, Ziegfeld insisted that Rodgers and Hart write a new number expressly for Miss Etting. They spent all night working, and came up with "Ten Cents a Dance," the lament of a "taxi-dancer" with which Miss Etting regularly brought down the house (though the song had little relevancy within the text). Because of Miss Etting's presence, a song—not by Rodgers and Hart— was interpolated into the show, a song with which by now she had become firmly identified: "Love Me or Leave Me," by Gus Kahn and Walter Donaldson.

Another Rodgers and Hart song, besides "Ten Cents a Dance," stood out prominently. It was "Send for Me," introduced by Doree Leslie (playing the part of Elaine King and Cinderella and Alan Edwards (appearing as Tony and Prince Charming). This was a melody Rodgers had previously written for one of their unsuccessful musicals, *Chee-Chee*—but dressed up with new Hart lyrics.

The most prominent dance sequence was a Hunting Ballet, featuring Harriet Hoctor and a company of ballet dancers.

SINBAD (1918), *a musical extravaganza, with book by Harold Atteridge. Lyrics by Atteridge and others. Music by Sigmund Romberg and others. Presented by the Shuberts at the Winter Garden on February 14. Directed by J. C. Huffman. Dances by Alexis Kosoff and Jack Mason. Cast included Al Jolson, Kitty Doner, Forrest Huff, and Mabel Withee (164 performances).*

*Sinbad,* like other Al Jolson extravaganzas, had little rhyme or reason in its plot, but it provided ample room for his contagious personality to unfold. The scene shifts from the North Shore Country Club on Long Island to Sinbad's palace in Bagdad and back again to Long Island. In a series of flashbacks, Inbad, a porter (Al Jolson), finds himself in old Bagdad, where he confronts characters out of the *Arabian Nights,* including Sinbad himself (Forrest Huff). He is then carried to "The Perfumed East," "Cabin of the Good Ship Whale," "Grotto of the Valley of the Diamonds," "Island of Eternal Youth," and on a "Raft on the Briny Deep." What transpires is not particularly significant beyond providing a means of introducing elegant sets and stage effects and several routines ranging from a dog act in the opening scene to an exotic Hindu snake dance performed by Roshanara. Significance came when Jolson appeared on the stage. As was customary, he carried the whole show with his infectious singing, ribbing, and ad-libbing.

Though Romberg wrote ten numbers for this Jolson show, the hit songs came from other composers. By now Jolson had established the practice of interpolating during the run of a play any song that struck his fancy, without much regard for its relevance. His cogent delivery made them hits; a few were ever after identified with him: "Rock-a-bye Your Baby with a Dixie Melody," "Hello, Central, Give Me No Man's Land," and "Why Do They All Take the Night Boat to Albany?"—all three by Joe Young, Sam M. Lewis, and Jean Schwartz; "My Mammy," by Joe Young, Sam Lewis, and Walter Donaldson; "Chloe," by Buddy de Sylva and Al Jolson; "I'll Say She Does," by Buddy de Sylva, Gus Kahn, and Al Jolson; and "Swanee," by Irving Caesar and George Gershwin. Gershwin had not written "Swanee" for Jolson but for a stage show at the Capitol Theater in New York, where it failed to attract attention. One day, at a party, Gershwin played the song for Jolson, who was so delighted with it that he decided to introduce it at one of his Sunday-evening "concerts" at the Winter Garden. Soon after that, Jolson interpolated it into *Sinbad,* where the song became so successful that in a year's time it sold over two million records and one million copies of sheet music—not only Gershwin's first hit song, but also the greatest of his entire career.

THE SKETCH BOOK (1929), *a revue, with book by Eddie Cantor and others. Lyrics by E. Y. Harburg and others. Music by Jay Gorney and others. Presented by Earl Carroll at the Earl Carroll Theater on July 1. Directed by Edgar MacGregor and Leroy Prinz. Cast included Will Mahoney, William Demarest, Patsy Kelly, and George Givot (400 performances).*

(1935), *a revue, with book by Eugene Conrad, Charles Sherman, and Royal Foster. Lyrics and music by Charles Tobias, Murray Mencher, and Charles Newman. Presented by Earl Carroll at the Winter Garden on June 4. Directed by Earl Carroll. Cast included Ken Murray and Jack Haley (207 performances).*

The best parts of the 1929 *Sketch Book* were those written by Eddie Cantor. There was a filmed sequence in which Earl Carroll negotiates with Cantor for the writing of this material; when Cantor explains how generous Ziegfeld has been to him (showing Carroll a gold watch Ziegfeld had presented him), Carroll proves even more generous: he gives Cantor a grandfather clock. The opening scene was called "Legs, Legs, Legs": The curtain is only partially raised, to reveal a row of shapely legs, to which a chorus of female voices sings a hymn of praise; but when the curtain rises, the legs are attached to phonographs. The best comedy sketch was a bathroom scene in which Patsy Kelly (who here revealed for the first time her gifts at comedy) takes a bath while Will Mahoney, her husband, is shaving. A plumber comes to fix a leak. "My wife is taking a bath," Mahoney shouts. "So what?" inquires the plumber. "Didn't I take off my hat?" He proceeds to work on the pipes with no further concern. Before Patsy can finish her bath, the room becomes crowded with policemen; with supreme nonchalance Patsy emerges from the tub to serve them tea.

Gorney's best songs were "Like Me Less, Love Me More" and "Kinda Cute." Harry and Charles Tobias, in collaboration with Vincent Rose, contributed two other fine numbers, "Song of the Moonbeams" and "Fascinating You."

The program described the 1935 edition of *The Sketch Book* as "a new hysterical historical revue." It was hardly hysterical; and if it was historical, it was because of episodes like that involving President McKinley remarking he liked Hawaiian music and thus encouraging a huge Hawaiian production number called "Silhouettes Under the Stars." It was the kind of show in which an acrobatic dog, named Red Dust, could steal the thunder from the stars. Whatever comedy there was was contributed by two veterans who made their slight material seem funnier than it really was—Jack Haley and Ken Murray.

SKYSCRAPER (1965), *a musical comedy, with book by Peter Stone, based on Elmer Rice's play* Dream Girl. *Lyrics by Sammy Cahn. Music by James Van Heusen. Presented by Feuer and Martin at the Lunt-Fontanne Theater on November 13. Directed by Cy Feuer. Dances by Michael Kidd. Cast included Julie Harris, Peter L. Marshall, and Charles Nelson Reilly (241 performances).*

When Elmer Rice's play *Dream Girl* became the musical comedy *Skyscraper,* very little of Elmer Rice was left, and a good deal of Peter Stone and Michael Kidd were put in. The basic theme remained the same, that of a sensitive young girl who escapes from reality in romantic daydreams. In the musical, this young girl, Georgina (Julie Harris), owns an antique shop in her old family brick house, which she stubbornly refuses to sell to the Bushman Construction Company, which is building a skyscraper right next to her house. Georgina is not only a daydreamer, but something of an idealist as well, with firm ideas about the evil of removing New York's picturesque landmarks and architectural attractions to make way for modernity, convenience, and big business. She keeps on spending her time in her little shop daydreaming. And in those dreams, her assistant, Roger Somerhill (Charles Nelson Reilly), is transformed romantically into a distinguished Southern gentleman, an English officer, an FBI agent, and a toreador—each of whom woos her passionately. The one, however, who is genuinely interested in her is Timothy Bushman (Peter L. Marshall), a young architect, who provides one of the comic highlights of the production when he takes Georgina to the Gaiety, a delicatessen in the Broadway setting that can accommodate a handful and usually has to cater to a truckful. (Another feast of hilarity is provided by an Italian movie with absurdly unnecessary English subtitles, into which Georgina's face suddenly intrudes.) Roger turns out to be a rascal scheming to sell her property behind her back while pretending to love her. Timothy, of course, sees to it that this does not happen. Georgina in time comes to realize that Timothy, in the flesh, is worth a carload of romantic heroes in her dreams.

Early in the musical there comes one of Michael Kidd's most striking dance sequences, performed by a chorus of males dressed as construction workers, and chorus ladies. "The number illustrates in dance language," explained Gary Paul Gates in *Holiday,* "that the girls simultaneously resent and enjoy the whistling and propositioning that erupt whenever they stroll by a building construction site. Even the rather pointed symbolism of the jackhammer is choreographically exploited." Another of Michael Kidd's happy choreographic inventions is the battle of men of long ago for the honor of our dream-prone heroine.

For Julie Harris, *Skyscraper* represented her debut in musical comedy. That she can act with the best of them is something she had long since proved. In *Skyscraper,* however, her acting talent was hardly matched by her ability at singing (she spoke most of her lines rather than sang them) or dancing. Nevertheless, she gave a most endearing, heart-warming performance throughout.

Sammy Cahn and James Van Heusen were here making their Broadway debut as songwriters. In Hollywood, separately and together they had produced enough song hits to pave the distance from New York to Hollywood, not to mention the closetful of Oscars and Oscar nominations they had been gathering all the while. Hollywood's ace songwriters were not quite so fruitful on Broadway as they had been in the movie capital. Their score yielded "Everybody Has a Right to Be Wrong," introduced by Timothy Bushman. It became a hit song. To Tim were also assigned two other successful ballads, "I'll Only Miss Her When I Think of Her" and "More Than One May." Beyond this, their score was hardly more than just functional.

In his review in *The New York Times* Howard Taubman singled out some of the imperfections in this musical. "It punches too hard; some of its jokes are strained. Not all of the songs have wit and melodic grace to equal their opportunities." But the strong points outweighed the weak ones. At its best, *Skyscraper* proved to be "a bright, amusing, and imaginative entertainment," as Richard Watts, Jr., noted, "with freshness and humor, an attractive production, brilliantly hilarious choreography by Michael Kidd, and delightful performances by Julie Harris and Charles Nelson Reilly."

THE SOCIAL WHIRL (1908), *a musical comedy, with book by Charles Doty and Joseph Herbert. Lyrics by Joseph Herbert. Music by Gustave A. Kerker and others. Presented by the Shuberts at the Casino Theater on April 9. Directed by R. H. Burnside. Cast included Charles J. Ross, Adele Ritchie, and Elizabeth Brice (195 performances).*

A certain gadfly, identified only as "J.E.," is accused by *The Social Whirl,* a society paper, of having gone off on an auto ride with the Broadway actress Viola Dare (Adele Ritchie) and then stopping off at a roadside inn for champagne. Since there are four gentlemen in the play whose initials are "J.E.," and since three of them are married, and, finally, since each uses every means to throw suspicion on the others, the complications are numerous, involving even attempted blackmail; and they are amusing. Two of the suspects are elderly gentlemen, still susceptible to the allure of feminine charm.

What actually happened is that Viola took both of them in her car—but only because she wanted to persuade James Ellingham (Frederick Bond) to consent to her marriage with his son, Jack (Willard Curtiss). At the Hunt Club everything is finally explained, and the suspicions that have beclouded the four men are completely dispelled.

The best musical numbers were "You're Just the One I'm Looking For," "Old Man Manhattan," and a specialty number, "Just Kids," performed by Frederick Bond. All three songs were by Kerker.

A SOCIETY CIRCUS. *See* HIPPODROME EXTRAVAGANZAS.

SOMEBODY'S SWEETHEART (1918), *a musical comedy, with book and lyrics by Alonzo Price. Music by Anthony Bafunno. Presented by Arthur Hammerstein at the Central Park Theater on December 23. Cast included Nonette, William Kent, and Louise Allen (224 performances).*

In Seville, Spain, Henry Edwards (Walter Scanlan) is about to be married to Helen (Eva Fallon), daughter of the U.S. consul. The natives of Seville arrange a festival in his honor, at which the seductive gypsy violinist, Zaida (Nonette), is principal performer. Harry's shady past included an affair with Zaida. To avoid embarrassment at the party, Harry arranges for his friend Sam Benton (William Kent) to occupy Zaida's time and interest when she is not performing. Since Sam is in love with the bride's sister, he must do some tall explaining before his sweetheart realizes that his attentions to Zaida are innocent.

The score has several delightful melodies, the best being "Spain Girl of My Heart," "Then I'll Marry You," "It Gets Them All," and "In the Old-Fashioned Way" (the last two by Arthur Hammerstein and Herbert Stothart). A great deal of the appeal of this musical came from the dancing of Louise Allen and the comedy of William Kent.

SOMETHING FOR THE BOYS (1943), *a musical comedy, with book by Herbert and Dorothy Fields. Lyrics and music by Cole Porter. Presented by Michael Todd at the Alvin Theater on January 7. Directed by Hassard Short and Herbert Fields. Dances by Jack Cole. Cast included Ethel Merman, Paula Laurence, Bill Johnson, and Allen Jenkins (422 performances).*

Two news items provided Herbert and Dorothy Fields with a theme for *Something for the Boys* (which they originally called *Jenny Get Your Gun*). One was about three cousins, each a stranger to the others, inheriting a ranch. The other was about a person becoming the instrument for radio transmission because of Carborundum filling in a tooth. The Fieldses described their ideas to Cole Porter, who liked them. Since Vinton Freedley, who usually produced Porter's shows, did not share their enthusiasm, the young and dynamic Michael Todd (who had recently scored on Broadway with *The Hot Mikado*) stepped in as producer. Todd did not even bother to inquire what the show was all about. The fact that Porter was its composer and that Porter planned using Ethel Merman as star was enough insurance to Todd that he was investing his money wisely.

As Louis Kronenberger noted in *PM, Something for the Boys* was "the third time that Mr. Porter and Miss Merman have teamed up for success, and *Something for the Boys* more than sustains the level of *Du Barry Was a Lady* and *Panama Hattie*." Actually, Kronenberger was somewhat overenthusiastic. *Something for the Boys* was inferior to its two predecessors both in text and in music. In fact, Porter's score was one of his weakest in several years. Only Ethel Merman upheld the expected standards, and one suspects that it was Miss Merman's dynamic presence that kept the show running as long as it did. "Ethel Merman," wrote Lewis Nichols in *The New York Times*, "gives a performance that suggests all her performances before last night were simply practice."

With America at war in 1943, Herbert and Dorothy Fields fashioned a timely text involving military personnel. The main characters are three cousins located by the Court of Missing Heirs and brought together to San Antonio to learn that they have inherited a four-hundred-acre ranch in Texas. They are Blossom Hart, a former chorus girl recently become a defense worker (Ethel Merman); Chiquita Hart, a nightclub singer from Kansas (Paula Laurence); and a New York sidewalk hawker of dolls and buttons, Harry Hart (Allen Jenkins). They meet for the first time in San Antonio and take an instantaneous dislike to each other. But for the sake of the inheritance, they decide to bury the hatchet.

The ranch turns out to be a broken-down building located near the Keeley Field Air Base. During maneuvers, some of the men from the base have occupied the ranch. Their officer is Staff Sergeant Rocky Fulton (Bill Johnson), who had been a bandleader in civilian life. Blossom Hart finds Rocky very much to her liking, first because she just adores bandleaders, and secondly because he happens to be tall and handsome. Unfortunately for Blossom, she has competition in Melanie Walker (Frances Mercer).

An industrious and ambitious girl, Blossom decides to turn the ramshackle building into a boardinghouse for flyers' wives and to organize a defense plant in some of the lower-story rooms. Melanie, fearful of Blossom's designs on Rocky, tries to ruin her rival by hinting to the commanding officer of Keeley Field that Blossom's house is actually a house of ill repute. The commanding officer comes to investigate. What he sees is soldiers coming in and out of the house (they are using one of the rooms for a crap game), and, inside the house, girls dressed in towels (having finished their day's work, they are taking showers). This convinces the officer that Melanie's accusation is based on fact. He immediately orders the house off limits to the soldiers.

With the world tumbling around her ears, Blossom makes the fantastic discovery that she is a human radio, thanks to the Carborundum fillings in her bridgework. Revealing this information to the commanding officer makes her a heroine, since every soldier now can be his own radio. She also saves a plane and its flyers by serving as a radio when the one in the plane breaks down. Winning the interest of the commanding officer, she can now straighten him out about the nature of her establishment. The house is reopened, and Blossom and Rocky are reunited.

Ethel Merman's biggest numbers were "Hey, Good Lookin' " (her estimate of Rocky) and a comedy number delivered with Paula Laurence, "By the Mississinewah." In the latter the two appeared as Indian maids from Indiana ("the funniest in a musical show this year," said Brooks Atkinson). The three cousins have an amusing takeoff on cowboys songs in "When We're Home on the Range."

During a full week, when Ethel Merman was sick, a young understudy, new to Broadway, stepped into the star's formidable shoes without stumbling. She was Betty Garrett, selected to replace Miss Merman by the shrewd Mike Todd, who felt she was a potential star. She was—as she was to prove decisively during her one-week stand-in for Miss Merman and in such subsequent productions as *Call Me Mister,* in 1946.

SOMETIME (1918), *an operetta, with book and lyrics by Rida Johnson Young. Music by Rudolf Friml. Presented by Arthur Hammerstein at the Shubert Theater on October 4. Directed by Oscar Eagle. Dances by Allan K. Foster. Cast included Francine Larrimore, Ed Wynn, and Mae West (283 performances).*

The play opens in the dressing room of a famous stage star, Enid Vaughn (Francine Larrimore), who for five years has been separated from the man she loves, Henry. A flashback carries us back five years, explaining the cause of the separation. Finding her lover in a compromising position with a vampire, Mayme Dean (Mae West), Enid refuses to see him any longer or allow him to explain. But in a return to the opening scene, five years later, Mayme Dean confesses to Enid that she had planned to compromise Henry and that he had been innocent of any wrongdoing. The play ends on a sentimental note with the long-delayed reconciliation.

Whatever humor the operetta had rested solidly on the capable shoulders of Ed Wynn, who had long since proved his unique gift at comic characterizations and strange get-ups and routines. Sex appeal came from the performance of Mae West, then a graduate from vaudeville, who was here making her first successful appearance on the Broadway stage. As a provocative sex symbol her greatest successes would, of course, come in later years, both on the stage and in the movies. Francine Larrimore, onetime child star who, one year earlier, had appeared in *Fair and Warmer* but who now was a recognized star, was being seen in her first musical-comedy role. She here proved herself, as she had previously done in nonmusical stage plays, a skillful performer. Mildred La Gue, in a minor part, was acclaimed for a striking Argentine dance. A none too notable Friml score had three songs that were above average, the title number, "Keep on Smiling," and "The Tune You Can't Forget."

SONG OF NORWAY (1944), *an operetta, with book by Milton Lazarus, based on a play by Homer Curran. Lyrics by Robert Wright and George "Chet" Forrest. Music by Wright and Forrest, adapted from the works of Edvard Grieg. Presented by Edwin Lester at the Imperial Theater on August 21. Directed by Charles K. Freeman. Choreography by George Balanchine. Cast included Lawrence Brooks, Irra Petina, Helena Bliss, and Sig Arno (860 performances).*

Operetta had appeared to be a dead-and-buried musical-stage form hardly likely for resurrection when along came *Song of Norway* (with most of the clichés and stereotypes that characterized the operettas of Romberg or Friml) to become one of the longest-running productions of its kind in American musical-theater history. This did not mean that operetta had ceased to be as dated as a horse-drawn tramcar. What it did mean was that *Song of Norway* had enough vitality, entertainment value, charm, nostalgia—and a good deal of infectious music—to prove the exception to the rule that sophisticated audiences of the 1940's could no longer respond to this form of entertainment.

The story is supposedly the life of Edvard Grieg (Lawrence Brooks), Norway's greatest composer, with accent on his love affair with and marriage to Nina Hagerup (Helena Bliss).

When the musical opens, the town of Bergen is celebrating the Midsummer Eve Festival of St. John. Rikard Nordraak, a young poet and composer (who played a highly significant role in Grieg's early development as a national composer), prophesies that "Norway will find her voice and sing again. She waits for the song of one man." Nordraak is thinking of one man in particular, his young friend Grieg, whose ambition is to become the musical spokesman for his country, to write the kind of music that reflects and interprets his land and its people. Young Grieg, however, is not only looking forward with optimistic anticipation to his future as a musician but also as a human being. Since childhood he has been in love with Nina Hagerup, a gifted singer. So far, the operetta has been faithful to biographical truth. At this point, the imagination of the librettists begin to take over. Louisa Giovanni, a sexy prima donna (Irra Petina), uses her beauty and magnetism to win Grieg away from Nina. They go off together to Rome. But once the excitement of this idyll has begun to wear off, Grieg begins to pine away for Nina. The sudden and unexpected death of young Nordraak brings Grieg back to his senses. He leaves Louisa and returns to Norway to marry Nina and to fulfill his destiny as a composer of Norwegian music.

The entire score represents adaptations of Grieg's music, its best songs being generally a tasteful version of Grieg's most familiar melodies, and some of its music being presented with alteration. The most famous song (and it proved a resounding hit in the middle 1940's) was "Strange Music," a popular-song transformation of "Wedding Day in Troldhaugen," from *Lyric Pieces* for piano, and from "Nocturne"; it is heard as a duet by Grieg and Nina. The love song, "I Love You," was a popularization of Grieg's famous lied "Ich liebe Dich," which he did actually write to Nina, but which in the operetta is introduced by Nina and a chorus. "Freddy and His Fiddle" comes from *Norwegian Dance No. 2;* "Now," from the Second Violin Sonata and the Waltz, Op. 12; and "Midsummer Eve" from the Scherzo in E minor and the art song " 'Twas on a Lovely Eve in June." Grieg's music was also used as an eloquent tonal background for a sumptuously mounted ballet, "Song of Norway," starring Alexandra Danilova and Frederic Franklin of the Ballet Russe de Monte Carlo.

It was a quarter of a century before *Song of Norway* was filmed. It was shot in Norway and England with a cast including Edward G. Robinson, Florence Henderson, and Robert Morley—produced by ABC Pictures and released in 1970.

SONG OF THE FLAME (1925), *an operetta, with book and lyrics by Otto Harbach and Oscar Hammerstein II. Music by George Gershwin and Herbert Stothart. Presented by Arthur Hammerstein at the 44th Street Theater on December 30. Directed by Frank Reicher. Dances by Jack Haskell. Cast included Tessa Kosta, Greek Evans, Guy Robertson, Dorothy MacKaye, and Hugh Cameron (219 performances).*

In *Song of the Flame* George Gershwin temporarily parted company with his brother Ira (with whom he had started such a successful words-and-music stage partnership in 1924 in *Lady, Be Good!* and would continue it for the rest of his life). This may have been one of the reasons why this Gershwin score is below par; Ira Gershwin had always proved a powerful stimulant to George Gershwin's creativity. Another reason may be because Gershwin was writing music in collaboration with Herbert Stothart. Stothart was a disciplined and experienced writer of show tunes—but a Gershwin he most certainly was not—and working with an inferior creator can only bring inferior results. The most important reason, however, for Geshwin's inferior creativity was that in *Song of the Flame* he was involved in an operetta—and writing operettas was just not his dish (as he would prove again later in *Rosalie*).

*Song of the Flame* was a "romantic opera" with a Russian setting. A peasant uprising takes place under the leadership of Anuita (Tessa Kosta), a rebel of noble birth who came to be known as "the Flame." She falls in love with Prince Volodya (Guy Robertson). Each succeeds in modifying the other's political beliefs, and they end up together in Paris.

Colorful sets and costumes, big scenes, songs with a pseudo-Russian identity, frenetic folk dances, and poignant choral music were combined in a lavish spectacle that did not always come off successfully. As Percy Hammond wrote: "There were mobs, riots, balls, and carnivals, both in Paris and Moscow. Picture trod on picture as fast as they came . . . yet the play lacked what used to be known as 'that something.'" Brooks Atkinson called it a "romantic spectacle," but complained that "the size of the production makes the opera generally heavy."

Gershwin produced two numbers with a recognizable Slavic personality. They were the cream of a poor crop. One was the title song, presented by Anuita and the Russian Art Choir; and the other was the main love song, "Cossack Love Song" (also known as "Don't Forget Me"), a duet of Anuita and Volodya.

SONS O' FUN (1941), *a vaudeville revue, with book by Olsen and Johnson and Hal Block. Lyrics by Jack Yellen and Irving Kahal. Music by Sammy Fain and Will Irwin. Presented by the Shuberts at the Winter Garden on December 1. Directed by Edward Dowling. Dances by Robert Alton. Cast included Olsen and Johnson, Carmen Miranda, Ella Logan, and Frank Libuse (742 performances).*

Madcap improvisations and interpolations made *Sons o' Fun* as riotously funny—and almost as successful—as *Hellzapoppin',* which in 1938 had also been a vaudeville revue starring Olsen and Johnson. When the audience entered it was warned by a policeman not to smoke—but he himself was puffing on a huge lighted cigar. Frank Libuse conducted some of the patrons to their seats—the wrong ones. Other patrons had to reach their seats in the boxes on ladders. During the performance, members of the audience were invited on the stage, where they jumped hurdles, and where women's skirts were blown over their heads. Chorus girls came down to the audience to dance in the aisles with celebrities. During the intermission an Indian family in full regalia created havoc in the lobby.

And so it went—from the unexpected to the absurd. The woman who had been running down the aisles in *Hellzapoppin'* calling for "Oscar" was still looking for her man. A stork flying overhead neatly deposited a child in a lady's lap. A fellow atop a telegraph pole was listening to the radio. When Chic Johnson appeared on the stage dressed in panties, a man rose haughtily in his seat in the audience and proceeded to undress as a protest; and so did his wife.

Amid all these shenanigans there was a show—a revue hewn along more traditional lines. Ella Logan sang "Happy in Love," one of two outstanding songs; the other was "It's a New Kind of Thing." Rosario and Antonio performed exciting Spanish dances, and Carmen Miranda went through her frenetic South American ways. The skits included burlesques on *Panama Hattie* and *Charlie's Aunt,* a farcical Army-training sketch with Joe Besser, and another with Chic Johnson spending a "quiet night in the country."

SONS O' GUNS (1929), *a musical comedy, with book by Fred Thompson and Jack Donahue. Lyrics by Arthur Swanstrom and Benny Davis. Music by J. Fred Coots. Presented by Connolly and Swanstrom at the Imperial Theater on November 26. Directed by Bobby Connolly. Dances by Albertina Rasch. Cast included Jack Donahue, Lily Damita, and William Frawley (295 performances).*

*Sons o' Guns* had an Army background and threw nostalgic glances back to the days of World War I. Jimmy Canfield (Jack Donahue) is a wealthy, happy-go-lucky, irresponsible young man who has to go to war. In camp he finds that his former valet, Hobson (William Frawley), is his top sergeant. Jimmy's unhappy adventures at the hands of his onetime employee, who takes full advantage of his august military position, and his tribulations with a vivacious French girl, Yvonne (Lily Damita), provide the basic materials for much of the comedy. Aggravating Jimmy's complications is the further fact that he is falsely accused of being a spy. He manages to clear himself and even to become a hero—particularly to Yvonne.

A vivacious tune, "Cross Your Fingers," introduced by Milton Watson and Shirley Vernon playing subsidiary roles was the leading song in the score. Additional musical interest was provided by "May I Say I Love You," "Why?" (sung by Yvonne and Jimmy), "Sentimental Melody," and Yvonne's "It's You I Love."

THE SOUND OF MUSIC (1959), *a musical play, with book by Howard Lindsay and Russel Crouse, suggested by Maria Augusta Trapp's* The Trapp Family Singers. *Lyrics by Oscar Hammerstein II. Music by Richard Rodgers. Presented by Leland Hayward, Richard Halliday, and Rodgers and Hammerstein at the Lunt-Fontanne Theater on November 16. Directed by Vincent J. Donehue. Dances by Joe Layton. Cast included Mary Martin, Patricia Neway, Kurt Kaznar, and Theodore Bikel (1,443 performances).*

The golden age of Rodgers and Hammerstein ended with *The Sound of Music*. And, with eloquent appropriateness, it ended on a note of triumph. It is quite true that *The Sound of Music* was not accepted with the unqualified enthusiasm which the critics had bestowed on *Oklahoma!, Carousel, South Pacific,* and *The King and I.* Between words of praise, some critics remarked that *The Sound of Music* was too much like an old-fashioned operetta, and too little like the kind of musical play with which Rodgers and Hammerstein had revolutionized the theater. Some felt the inclusion of the Nazi invasion of Austria into the plot contributed a disturbingly jarring note. Some insisted that this musical was sentimental (which led Oscar Hammerstein to inquire: "What's wrong with being sentimental?"). But such negative comments notwithstanding, *The Sound of Music* was found by a good many other critics to be a glowing and radiant production that lit up the theater like a sudden burst of sunshine; whose charm and sweetness suffused the hearts of audiences with warmth and well-being; and which had about it more than just a passing touch of theatrical fireworks. To Brooks Atkinson (he was one of the critics who objected to the operetta-like personality of the show), *The Sound of Music* was "moving" and "occasionally . . . glorious." Richard Watts, Jr., said it had a "warm-hearted, unashamedly sentimental and strangely gentle charm that is wonderfully endearing." Frank Aston said it brought Rodgers and Hammerstein "back in top form." John McClain went so far as to call it "the most mature product of the Rodgers and Hammerstein team. It has style, distinction, grace and persuasion . . . the full ripening of these two extraordinary talents."

*The Sound of Music* proved more than just a substantial hit show. It was a blockbuster. Its Broadway run almost touched the 1,500-performance mark, while gathering six Antoinette Perry awards, including that of the best musical of the season. The touring company, which opened in Detroit on February 27, 1961, kept moving for two and a half years, closing in Toronto on November 23, 1963—to a capacity house, just as it had opened to one. The original-cast album sold over three million copies. In London the show had a several-year run. When, in 1965, 20th Century-Fox released the motion-picture adaptation (with Julie Andrews and Christopher Plummer), screen history was made when more people paid more money in more places throughout the civilized world than had ever before happened for a movie. The soundtrack recording sold eight million discs, the largest in recording history, and the picture captured the Academy Award as the best of the year. And when *The Sound of Music* returned for a brief visit to Broadway in 1967, it was still found to be, by a critic for *Variety,* "one of the select list of about a dozen durable giants of the musical stage repertoire . . . a beautiful work."

As everybody must know by now, *The Sound of Music* was inspired by the history of the famous Trapp Family Singers, who started singing as a family hobby in Salzburg, Austria, and ended up by touring concert halls. The true story had been made into a German movie which Mary Martin saw and fell in love with. Then and there she decided that this must become a Broadway musical, and she must appear as Baroness von Trapp. It took eight months to find the baroness, who was finally located in a hospital in Innsbruck, Austria, recovering from malaria. It took hours upon hours of argument to persuade her to agree to allow a musical to be made out of her life story, which she herself had already described in an autobiography. Only when she was told that the huge sums she would earn from the stage rights could be used for missionary work (with which she was then deeply involved in New Guinea) did she give her reluctant consent. After that came the trying business of clearing the rights with all the Trapp children, who seemed to be scattered all over the face of the earth. Once these matters were finally settled, Howard Lindsay and Russel Crouse wrote the text, and Rodgers and Hammerstein completed the songs.

In writing the text, Crouse and Lindsay were fully aware that they were standing at the edge of a precipice, falling from which would land them straight in the valley of operetta. "We're in operetta country with this show," Lindsay explained. "The minute you say Vienna, everyone thinks of a chorus of boys in short pants, and the minute you have a waltz, you're sunk. We had to work to keep the story convincing and believable, not letting it get into the never-never-land operetta lives in." They were also conscious of the fact that bringing Nazis into their plot would, on the other hand, introduce an unwelcome melodramatic development. They solved this latter problem, without changing their basic story, by not allowing a single Nazi in uniform to appear on the stage—although the audience was thoroughly made conscious that the Trapps were being pursued by the brownshirts in making their escape from Austria.

The year in which the musical is placed is 1938. We find Maria (Mary Martin), a postulant at the Nonnberg Abbey in Austria, drinking in the beauty of nature on a hammock atop a mountain peak, while giving vent to her emotions in the title song. She has lost all sense of time, forgotten the duties awaiting her at the abbey. There the mother abbess (Patricia Neway) and her assistants worry about her. They are convinced that Maria is not ready to renounce the world for the life of a nun, as they reflect on her volatile personality in "Maria," a delightful song characterization of the heroine. It is quite true that the mother abbess enjoys some of the delights Maria favors, as she confesses in a duet with Maria in "My Favorite Things." But Maria is not the kind of girl ready to surrender those delights. The abbess, therefore, decides to send Maria away for a while, to work as a governess to the seven children of Captain Georg von Trapp (Theodore Bikel), a widower.

Timidly, Maria arrives at the baronial home of Captain von Trapp, to find him a stern ruler of his household, and a disciplinarian who has his children follow inflexible rules. This kind of treatment for these lovable children Maria finds intolerable. She surrounds them with her warmth and gentleness, and they come to love her. She teaches them the delights of singing ("Do-Re-Mi") and proves a solace to them during a thunderstorm, as all of them bundle into Maria's bed while she sings to them a folk-like tune, "The Loney Goatherd." She is a sympathetic ally to the love affair going on between the oldest of the children, Liesel (Lauri Peters), and the village boy, Rolf Guber (Brian Davies), who give voice to their innocent romance in "Sixteen Going on Seventeen."

The captain takes a trip to Vienna and returns, bringing with him his fiancée, Elsa Schraeder (Marion Marlowe), and a friend, Max Detweeler (Kurt Kaznar). When the captain hears his children sing, he is delighted, caught by their enthusiasm as well as their new-found talent. Elsa encourages the captain to throw a huge party. At bedtime, the children bid the guests good night in "So Long, Farewell." It was during this party that Maria first comes to the realization that she loves the captain. This discovery so disturbs her that she escapes from the household and returns to the abbey. There the abbess encourages her to meet life squarely, to overcome its obstacles, and to look upon love as something holy ("Climb Ev'ry Mountain").

The ominous cloud of Nazism and Anschluss hangs over the head of Austria. The captain and his fiancée quarrel over the issues involved, the captain being violently anti-Nazi. Their engagement is terminated. There is now nothing to stand in the way of a romance developing between Maria and the captain, particularly since by now he has come to recognize how much she has come to mean to him. They get married in an impressive ceremony at the abbey. Upon their return from their honeymoon (the Anschluss, meanwhile, having become a reality), the captain receives orders from the Nazis to return to his naval duties, which he refuses to do. Buying time, Max Detweeler suggests that Maria and her children appear at a music festival nearby; meanwhile, they can think of some plan of operation. At the concert, the children enchant their audience with an Austrian-type folk melody, "Edelweiss." The concert over, the captain discovers that an escort is awaiting to take him to Berlin. The entire family manages to elude the escort, as Max keeps him occupied with conversation. First the entire family finds a hiding place in the garden of the abbey, where they are pursued by Nazi brownshirts. Then the Von Trapps decide to try gaining their freedom by climbing over the mountains into neutral Switzerland. The nuns send them off with the encouraging strains of "Climb Ev'ry Mountain."

One can readily understand why, whether on stage or screen, *The Sound of Music* had such universal appeal. Here there was something for everybody: for the religious; for the romantics; for those who adore children (the scenes with the seven children could melt a heart of stone); those who doted on Mary Martin (as Maria she had a role tailor-made for her inimitable personality and talent); and those who admired Rodgers and Hammerstein (who here produced their best score since *The King and I,* and one of the most varied and imaginative one of their entire careers).

Rodgers' unique talent in catching the mood, atmosphere, and background of whatever text he was setting—and his courage always to try something new—was nowhere made more obvious than in this score. Look at the way he begins his play musically. There is no orchestral overture, only a "Preludium" for unaccompanied voices, in the style of old church music, evoking at once a religious spirit that dominates so much of the first act, set in the Nonnberg Abbey. In the spirit of the country which served as the setting of the play, Rodgers was able to produce numbers which, while original, had the identity of Austrian folk songs—"Edelweiss," for example, and "The Lonely Goatherd." On the one hand he could be inspirational, as in "Climb Ev'ry Mountain," and on the other hand simple and direct in his emotions, as in "My Favorite Things" or "Sixteen Going on Seventeen." The soaring flights of lyricism for which he was famous could be found in the title song, particularly in the expansive release in the chorus. And rarely has he proved more disarmingly charming than in his songs for the children, "So Long,

Farewell," for example, and especially "Do-Re-Mi." The latter number became the major song hit of the score. This is a melody built for the most part on the framework of the rising and descending steps of a diatonic scale, with which Maria teaches her children to sing. A thoroughly enchanting effect is then produced by having the children sing this melody, while Maria launches off contrapuntally on a melody of her own, with its own lyrics.

SOUTH PACIFIC (1949), *a musical play, with book by Oscar Hammerstein II and Joshua Logan, based on James A. Michener's* Tales of the South Pacific. *Music by Richard Rodgers. Presented by Rodgers and Hammerstein, in association with Leland Hayward and Joshua Logan, at the Majestic Theater on April 7. Directed by Joshua Logan. Cast included Mary Martin, Ezio Pinza, William Tabbert, Juanita Hall, and Betta St. John (1,925 performances).*

Having already written and triumphed with *Oklahoma!* and *Carousel,* it hardly seemed likely that Rodgers and Hammerstein could be capable of outdoing themselves by creating an even greater stage-musical work of art than the two earlier productions. But outdo themselves they certainly did in *South Pacific,* one of the greatest musicals to come out the American musical theater, or out of any musical theater, for that matter.

One evening at a dinner party early in 1947, Kenneth MacKenna, story editor of MGM, mentioned to Jo Mielziner and Joshua Logan that he had recently read and turned down for his studio a volume of World War II stories by James Michener. MacKenna felt the book might be suitable for stage dramatization and encouraged Logan to consider the project. Logan read the book and immediately decided to bring it to the stage. Since at the time he was co-producer with Leland Hayward of *Mister Roberts,* he interested Hayward in joining him in procuring the stage rights. As they discussed ways and means in which the stories could be adapted for the stage, Logan suggested the necessity of music creating the proper mood and atmosphere. This matter was further explored by Joshua Logan with Richard Rodgers, who, in turn, won over the approval of his collaborator, Oscar Hammerstein. The decision was finally reached to have Hammerstein collaborate with Logan in making the stage adaptation and for Rodgers to produce the score. Since Rodgers and Hammerstein had recently agreed to produce their own plays, they acquired the dramatic rights, Logan was engaged as stage director, and Logan and Hayward joined as co-producers. Not long after these complicated negotiations were completed, the faith of all concerned in Michener's book of stories was fully justified when *Tales of the South Pacific* received the Pulitzer Prize in fiction.

In making their adaptation, Hammerstein and Logan used only two of the stories from Michener's book. One was "Our Heroine," telling of the love of Emile de Becque, a local planter of French origin, and the American nurse Nellie Forbush. The other was "Fo' Dolla," describing the romance of the American Marine lieutenant Joseph Cable and the native girl Liat. To consolidate the two stories, an episode of their own invention was introduced—dispatching Cable and De Becque on a hazardous war mission.

In the final version of the text, the setting remains the French-run islands of the South Pacific during World War II, captured from the Japanese. Emile de Becque (Ezio Pinza) is a wealthy middle-aged owner of a large plantation. He and his two Eurasian children are dancing around and singing a little French tune, "Dites-moi." De Becque has been on the island several years before the outbreak of the war. This evening he is to be the dinner host to Ensign Nellie Forbush, an American nurse (Mary Martin). They enjoy each other's company immensely. In "A Cockeyed Optimist," she reveals to Emile the optimistic side of her personality, and in "Some Enchanted Evening" he discloses that he has fallen for this charming young American. In fact, before Nellie leaves for the evening, he begs her to consider seriously becoming his wife.

Across the bay is the island of Bali Ha'i, which is off limits to the American forces, suspected of being a hiding place for French women as protection from the Americans. One of the inhabitants of this mysterous island is Bloody Mary, a Tonkinese (Juanita Hall), whose praises the Americans sing in "Bloody Mary." Girls are something very much on their minds. They complain that the absence of females in their lives represents a very serious gap, for—as they complain in "There Is Nothin' Like a Dame"—there just is no substitute for the opposite sex.

Bloody Mary is interested in promoting a marriage between her lovely seventeen-year-old daughter, Liat (Betta St. John), and Lieutenant Joseph Cable (William Tabbert). She stimulates his interest in the mysterious island across the bay in an effort to get him there to meet Liat. But Cable is for the moment more concerned about the military mission to which he has just been assigned: to establish a coast watch on a nearby Japanese-held island, for which he would like to enlist the help of Emile, since the Frenchman is so familiar with this terrain. To make sure that Emile is the right man for this job, the commanding officers visit Nellie to get from her as much information about the Frenchman as she can supply.

Nellie has been giving considerable thought about Emile's marriage proposal. First she decides that their differences in age, experience, and background would dictate a refusal on her part. As she goes through the routine of washing her hair, she announces her decision in "I'm Gonna Wash That Man Right Outa My Hair." But when she sees Emile again, all her good intentions evaporate. Emile's charm is as irresistible as his arguments are persuasive. Nellie's doubts about their future are reduced to dust. In "I'm in Love with a Wonderful Guy" she makes her true feelings known.

Delighted he has won Nellie's consent for marriage, Emile refuses the request by the American forces that he go with Cable on his highly dangerous mission. Thus, for the time being, the mission is shelved. This allows Cable the time to visit Bali Ha'i, where he meets Liat and falls in love with her (even though she can speak only French, and he only English). But Liat has no doubts about Cable's feelings, which he makes known eloquently in "Younger than Springtime."

While Cable and Liat are thus discovering love, the romance of Nellie and Emile encounters serious complications. Nellie has discovered that Emile has had a Polynesian girl as mistress for several years; that the Eurasian children in his home are the fruits of this illicit relationship. This fact so shocks Nellie she vows never again to set eyes on him.

Bloody Mary brings Liat from Bali Ha'i to Cable to convince him to accept her as his wife. In "Happy Talk," Bloody Mary speaks of the happy life these two young people can have on this island; Bloody Mary is even ready to give as a dowry the money she has saved through a lifetime. All this so touches Cable that he presents Liat with a gold watch he had inherited from his grandfather. But with all the tenderness he can muster he tries to explain to Bloody Mary that marriage is unthinkable between two people of different races. This explanation so infuriates Bloody Mary that she smashes the watch to smithereens and drags Liat away, muttering she will find another husband for the girl.

Emile comes to Nellie pleading that his former relationship with a Polynesian, and his Eurasian children, must not stand in the way of their marriage. This scene, which is being witnessed by Cable, brings home to the younger man how much he, too (like Nellie), has been the victim of race prejudice. Now he knows—and says so eloquently in "Carefully Taught"—that man is not born with hate in his heart but has been taught to hate people with different-colored skins by society and environment. Having come face to face with this truth, Cable is now determined to make this island his permanent home after the war. Emile, however, now sees the island in a different light. It is his paradise lost, now that he can no longer have the woman he loves. He has even lost interest in living, and is ready to go with Cable on his hazardous mission.

Their mission is successful. The information they relay back makes it possible for the Americans to launch an attack and destroy twenty Japanese ships, and thus facilitate the invasion of fourteen Japanese-occupied islands. But the price paid for this victory is high: Cable has been killed. Emile manages to stay alive. He makes his way back to his plantation where he finds Nellie waiting for him with a heart full of love, and with tolerance in her heart; for Emile finds her playing with his Eurasian children.

It took courage for the authors to make a middle-aged, gray-haired man the hero of a musical play; and it took courage to cast Ezio Pinza in that role, since the celebrated opera singer had never before appeared on the Broadway stage. But even greater independence of thought and action was required to make the secondary love plot of Cable and Liat a plea for racial tolerance, to write a song on the subject, and, after having built up a favorable atmosphere for this love affair, to have Cable killed. All this inconoclasm paid off. Ezio Pinza became a matinee idol; the secondary love plot brought to the play strength and beauty; and the song "Carefully Taught" gave it a new dimension.

For the part of Nellie Forbush, Rodgers and Hammerstein engaged Mary Martin, already a star in the musical theater by virtue of her then recent success in *One Touch of Venus*. (Hammerstein had seen her in *One Touch of Venus,* during the planning of *South Pacific,* and he told his wife: "This is the real Mary Martin, a corn-fed girl from Texas—and that's the kind of part she should play.") As Nellie Forbush she scaled to the heights which she would henceforth occupy.

In preparing his score, Rodgers made a conscious effort to make each of his songs reflect the innermost currents of the characters who sang them. As he said: "I tried to weave De Becque's character into his songs—romantic, rather powerful, but not too involved—and so I wrote for him 'Some Enchanted Evening' and 'This Nearly Was Mine.' Nellie Forbush is a nurse out of Arkansas, a kid whose musical background probably had been limited to the movies, radio, and maybe a touring musical comedy. She talks in the vernacular, so her songs had to be in the vernacular. It gave me a chance for a change of pace, and the music I wrote for her is light, contemporary, rhythmic 'A Cockeyed Optimist,' 'I'm Gonna Wash That Man Right Outa My Hair,' 'I'm in Love with a Wonderful Guy.' Cable's songs—'Younger than Springtime' and 'Carefully Taught'—are like the man, deeply sincere, while Bloody Mary's songs, 'Bali Ha'i' and 'Happy Talk,' try to convey some of the languor and mystery of the race."

Rodgers wrote "Bali Ha'i" in about five minutes; "Happy Talk" in about twenty. "Younger than Springtime" had been written for an earlier Rodgers and Hammerstein musical, *Allegro,* but had not been used there and was found thoroughly suitable for *South Pacific*. In "I'm in Love with a Wonderful Guy," it was Rodgers' suggestion to repeat the phrase "I'm in love" five times in the closing line of the chorus. The first time Mary Martin tried out this song was at Joshua Logan's apartment, at two o'clock in the morning. "I almost passed out," she confesses, "I was so excited. After the repeats I fell off the piano bench, and I remember that the management had to call up to complain of the noise."

Long before *South Pacific* opened on Broadway, word had begun to circulate that here was a musical to challenge *Oklahoma!* in beauty and originality. *South Pacific* fulfilled all such promises. Not only was it as good as rumor had indicated, it was even better. It was, as Howard Barnes said, a "show of rare enchantment, novel in texture and treatment, rich in dramatic substance, and eloquent in song." Brooks Atkinson described it as "a magnificent musical frame."

*South Pacific* went on to create stage history, even as *Oklahoma!* had done earlier. It had the second-longest run of any musical in Broadway history (only 323 performances less than *Oklahoma!*), was seen in New York by 3,500,000 theatergoers who paid nine million dollars at the box office. A national company toured several years. The financial returns were astronomic, a profit of five million dollars, not counting the revenue from the sale to motion pictures. The sheet music sold over two million copies, the long-playing recording of the original cast over one million discs. The name "South Pacific" was licensed for dolls, cosmetics, dresses, lingerie, and so on.

In addition, *South Pacific* absorbed virtually every prize in sight, including the 1950 Pulitzer Prize for drama (the second musical thus honored), and the Drama Critics, Antoinette Perry, and Donaldson awards as the year's best musical.

*South Pacific* has been produced in the major capitals of Europe. Through the years it has often been revived in the United States—most significantly in 1967 at the Music Theater of Lincoln Center in New York, when the two principal roles were assumed by Florence Henderson and Giorgio Tozzi. It was made into a triumphant motion picture by 20th Century-Fox, released in 1958, starring Mitzi Gaynor and Rossano Brazzi; this film established an all-time box-office record in England, with a first run extending for 230 weeks and grossing almost four million dollars.

By 1969 *South Pacific* had earned a net profit of more than seven million dollars, on an original investment of $225,000, bringing each of its backers a return of 1,569 percent on his original investment.

SPORTING DAYS. *See* HIPPODROME EXTRAVAGANZAS.

STAR AND GARTER (1942), *a revue, with book, lyrics, and music by various writers and composers. Presented by Michael Todd at the Music Box Theater on June 24. Directed by Hassard Short. Dances by Al White, Jr. Cast included Bobby Clark, Gypsy Rose Lee, Georgia Sothern, and Professor Lamberti (609 performances).*

Burlesque became illegal in New York in a decision handed down by Supreme Court Judge Aaron J. Levy, in which he described this form of entertainment as "artistic filth." A renewal of a license to the Minsky Brothers for the presentation of burlesque was therefore denied. Michael Todd, then still young at the hand of producing, decided to bring burlesque into the Broadway musical theater by the simple expedient of labeling it a "revue." Burlesque by any other name, he felt, remained burlesque—and would always find an audience. His "revue" would star such burlesque stars as Gypsy Rose Lee and Bobby Clark and would charge customers the top Broadway price of $4.50 rather than the more modest one previously asked for by burlesque theaters. He found some backers, and *Star and Garter* was rapidly whipped into shape.

Lacking sufficient funds for an out-of-town tryout, Michael Todd decided that a single preview in New York would be enough to prepare the show for its regular run. He proved wrong; the preview was a disaster. One of the larger backers demanded his investment back. At this point, Gpysy Rose Lee came to the rescue of the show by offering enough money (about $50,000) to help finance it, thus permitting a week's time in which to revamp the production. New sets and costumes were ordered; new material was introduced. When the week ended, *Star and Garter* opened and, miraculously, proved a delight. Louis Kronenberger of *PM* wrote: "Burlesque, the fast and fallen woman of the theater, swept into the Music Box all done up in silks and ermine. A leg-and-laugh show with considerable lure and good filthy fun, it is fleshed with style rather than suggestiveness and offers an entertaining evening."

If Michael Todd had intended to make a lady out of burlesque by calling it a "revue," the lady still remained a tramp. The main attractions of burlesque had been retained: strip-tease acts, bumps and grinds, undraped females, songs and skits with *double entendres* and broad slapstick. One comedy scene found Bobby Clark in a saloon asking for the "powder room." The bartender pointed outside the saloon, where a snowstorm was raging. Clark remarked: "It's too cold. I'll wait till spring." He also appeared as a roué from Pennsylvania; a judge at a murder trial who busies himself by throwing spitballs; and a lover caught redhanded by an irate husband in "That Merry Wife of Windsor."

Georgia Sothern did a hot strip-tease routine. Gypsy Rose Lee did a sedate and leisurely one; she also lamented on how hard it is to do a strip-tease to classical music. Also in the tradition of burlesque was an amusing routine by Professor Lamberti (a seedy-looking musician), who played the xylophone and was delighted with joy at the loud enthusiasm of his audience; what he did not know was that a luscious wench was standing behind him doing a strip-tease. Professor Lamberti's act and several other skits were interpolated from other, earlier musical productions. So were some of the best songs, including Irving Berlin's "The Girl on the Police Gazette" (serving as a first-act-finale production number) and Harold Arlen's "Blues in the Night."

STEPPING STONES (1923), *a musical comedy, with book by Anne Cald-well and R. H. Burnside. Lyrics by Anne Caldwell. Music by Jerome Kern. Presented by Charles Dillingham at the Globe Theater on November 6. Directed by R. H. Burnside. Dances by John Tiller and Mary Read. Cast in-cluded Fred Stone, Allene Stone, Dorothy Stone, Jack Whiting, Oscar "Rags" Ragland, and Roy Hoyer (241 performances).*

The pun in the title points up the fact that *Stepping Stones* was written for the three performing Stones—Fred, the father; Allene, his wife; and Dorothy, their seventeen-year-old daughter. Fred and Allene were veterans of the musical-comedy stage, but Dorothy was here making her bow in an important stage role. The text—hardly more than an excuse to permit the various Stones to demonstrate their respective gifts—was a modernization of the Red Riding Hood fairy tale. Dorothy played Roughette Hood, who meets adventure with Prince Silvio (Roy Hoyer) and becomes involved with a trio of conspirators, one of whom is a villain named Otto de Wolfe (Oscar "Rags" Ragland). Allene Stone is her widowed mother. In the end Roughette Hood is saved by a plumber, Peter Plug (Fred Stone).

The story was sufficiently elastic to enable Fred Stone to go through many of the routines for which he became famous. Always certain of doing the unexpected, he made his first entrance from the ceiling by parachute and ended the first act with tricks on a horizontal bar. However, the limelight was not his, but Dorothy's. She sang, danced, and acted enchantingly, all the while flooding the stage with the sunshine of her personality. Kern had two important songs in this score: "Once in a Blue Moon" (introduced by John Lambert and Lilyan and Ruth White, playing minor roles, supplemented by a female chorus) and "Raggedy Ann," introduced by Fred and Dorothy Stone and the Tiller Sunshine Girls.

STOP! LOOK! LISTEN! (1915), *a musical comedy, with book by Harry B.*

*Smith. Lyrics and music by Irving Berlin. Presented by Charles Dilling-*
*ham at the Globe Theater on December 25. Directed by R. H. Burnside.*
*Cast included Gaby Deslys, Harland Dixon, Harry Fox, and Harry Pilcer*
*(105 performances).*

This was Irving Berlin's second score for the Broadway stage, the first having been *Watch Your Step* in 1914. Though called a musical comedy, *Stop! Look! Listen!* was more of a revue. Only the slightest thread of a romantic plot was used to bring the characters, routines, and songs to various locales in the United States, Europe, Hawaii, and so forth. Gaby Deslys, the female star, played the role of a chorus girl, and her partner was Harry Pilcer. Though Miss Deslys, an import from France, had previously appeared in Winter Garden productions, it was in this musical that she assumed the status of a star. "Wearing outlandish costumes—fantastic color schemes, and towering hats of plumes, ropes of pearls and satin gingerbread—she made headlines with quips like 'I can't sing, I can't dance, but I can do It,'" wrote Roger Baral. Her principal song was "Everything in America Is Ragtime," used in the finale.

The stage was crowded with beautiful chorines who were seen in a stunning production number in which each girl represented a magazine cover girl. (Marion Davies, later the motion-picture star of silent film days, was one of these chorines.) Harland Dixon did some of his dancing routines, and Harry Fox contributed comedy and song. One of his vocal numbers was the best song in the score, "I Love a Piano." Another good Berlin tune was "When I Get Back to the U.S.A."

STREET SCENE (1947), *a musical play, with book by Elmer Rice, based on his 1929 Pulitzer Prize play of the same name. Lyrics by Langston Hughes. Music by Kurt Weill. Presented by Dwight Deere Wiman and the Playwrights Company at the Adelphi Theater on January 9. Directed by Charles Friedman. Dances by Anna Sokolow. Cast included Norman Cordon, Anne Jeffreys, Hope Emerson, Polyna Stoska, and Brian Sullivan (148 performances).*

*Street Scene* is a drama in which the music brings new dimensions to a compelling stage play. The elemental passions, frustrated ideals, tortured hopes, and poetic dreams that seize and activate the lives of a group of people in a New York City tenement make for realism; and realism rarely profits from musical adaptation. Yet in *Street Scene* the febrile atmosphere and the mounting tragedy gain in momentum, power, and intensity through Weill's evocative background music. Rosamond Gilder said in *Theatre Arts:* "Kurt Weill turned *Street Scene* into a symphony of the city with its strands of love and yearning and violence woven into the pattern of daily drudgery. His music reflects the hot night, the chatter and gossiping housewives, the sound of children at play, the ebb and flow of anonymous existence."

While Weill's score had several numbers to haunt the memory—principally Sol Kaplan's number "Lonely House"; Mrs. Maurrants' "Somehow I Never Could Believe" and her song to her little son, "A Boy Like You"; and the duet of Rose and Sam, "We'll Go Away Together"—it is no single number that gives the play its emotional urge, but the integrated musical texture. In fact, so ambitious is Weill's musical writing (the second-act trio and septet, for example) and so major a role does the music perform in the overall artistic context that *Street Scene* has been presented by the New York City Opera in its regular operatic repertory. Indeed, it comes closer to being an opera than a Broadway musical play.

*Street Scene* may be described as a white man's *Porgy and Bess*—a slice of everyday life carved from the New York City slums in the same way that *Porgy and Bess* portrayed Negro life in Catfish Row in Charleston, South Carolina.

Mrs. Anna Maurrant (Polyna Stoska), hungry for love, which her husband, Frank (Norman Cordon), denies her, is carrying on an affair with the milkman. Love also complicates the life of their daughter, Rose (Anne Jeffreys), and her neighbor, the college student Sam Kaplan (Brian Sullivan). Sam is only too willing to give up his studies to marry Rose, but she is reluctant to have him make this sacrifice. When Frank Maurrant returns home unexpectedly one day to find his wife with the milkman, he shoots them and is led off by the police. This tragedy convinces Rose that she must not destroy Sam's life by marrying him before he has made his way in the world. She flees with her younger brother to find a new life elsewhere.

THE STREETS OF PARIS (1939), *a revue, with book by various writers. Lyrics by Al Dubin and others. Music by Jimmy McHugh and others. Presented by the Shuberts, in association with Olsen and Johnson, at the Broadhurst Theater on June 19. Dances by Robert Alton. Cast included Bobby Clark, Luella Gear, and Carmen Miranda (274 performances).*

This is the show in which Carmen Miranda came from Brazil to rock the walls and shake every timber of the Broadhurst Theater with her cyclonic personality. Her explosive manner with song and dance first erupted in a production number called "South American Way," a song introduced by Ramon Vinay (before he became famous in opera) and the Hylton Sisters, then danced to frenetically by an energetic dancing group, and finally brought to a climax with the appearance of Carmen Miranda, wearing one of those fruit-basket hats for which she became so famous. She tore the house apart with her rendition; a star was born.

Every once in a while the show tried desperately to remember its title by contributing Parisian scenes and episodes. Abbott and Costello—madmen new to the Broadway musical-comedy scene—were featured in a zany sketch called "On Zee Boulevard." Bobby Clark enacted the part of "Robert le Roué" (from Reading, Pennsylvania). Luella Gear contributed further hilarity as a "grand cocotte." And the then still unknown Jean Sablon, brought in from Paris, sang "Rendezvous Time in Paree." But to the critic of the *Tribune* the show was "about as French as Canarsie, but it is a strutting lusty show with a cockeyed leer in its eye, a battery of inspired comedians, herds of girls, good songs."

Gower Champion, with Jeanne Tyler as partner (this was before he had teamed up with Marge), was featured in an ambitious dance number with timely political overtones, "Doin' the Chamberlain," a song first presented by Luella Gear as a preface to the dancing.

STRIKE UP THE BAND (1930), *a musical play, with book by George S. Kaufman and Morrie Ryskind. Lyrics by Ira Gershwin. Music by George Gershwin. Presented by Edgar Selwyn at the Times Square Theater on January 14. Directed by Alexander Leftwich. Dances by George Hale. Cast included Clark and McCullough, Blanche Ring, and Doris Carson (191 performances).*

Four years before they wrote and had produced their epoch-making musical satire on the American political scene, *Of Thee I Sing,* the Gershwin brothers and George S. Kaufman wrote a devastating satire on war in the vein of Gilbert and Sullivan—with no holds barred. All the customary paraphernalia of musical comedy was abandoned while the writers concentrated on a theme that lashed out savagely at international diplomacy, war, and war profiteers with all the stinging irony, and the partiality for absurdity and the ridiculous for which Gilbert and Sullivan had become so famous. Called *Strike Up the Band*—and starring Jimmy Savo and Vivienne Hart—the show first tried out in 1927 in Long Branch, New Jersey, and then in Philadelphia. The critics were as one in expressing their delight. The reaction of audiences was something else again: They just stayed away. During the final days of the second week in Philadelphia (where the show planned to stay six weeks) the theater was so empty that the decision had to be reached to close the show down for good.

Then, late in 1929, the producer decided to take one more chance with the long neglected *Strike Up the Band*—but only on the condition that Morrie Ryskind be brought in to revise the Kaufman text to make it less highbrow and consequently more commercial. Naturally a revised text demanded elaborate changes in the songs the Gershwins had written and a good deal of the instrumental passages George Gershwin had created. Also a radical change of cast was required.

*Strike Up the Band,* a far different commodity from what it had been in 1927, finally showed up in New York on January 14, 1930. In spite of the obvious concessions made to pander to public taste, it still remained one of the most original and provocative musical satires to reach Broadway in some years. With Clark and McCullough now selected as the stars to bolster the comic elements in the text—and to make the show so much more marketable —*Strike Up the Band* was still acclaimed by the critics for its adult intelligence, bite, and sting. "Here," wrote William Bolitho, "is a bitter . . . satirical attack on war, genuine propaganda at times, sung and danced on Broadway."

It might be illuminating to compare the plots of the original script, as conceived by Kaufman, and the one that was finally used, in which Ryskind was collaborator. The first version raised the issue of an American tariff against Swiss cheese. This brings such a violent response from Switzerland that Horace J. Fletcher, proprietor of the American Cheese Company, uses his influence to get the United States to declare war. (Fletcher is even ready to foot the whole war bill if the struggle gets called the Horace J. Fletcher Memorial War.) Jim Townsend, a newspaperman in love with Fletcher's daughter, uncovers the fact that Fletcher has been using Grade B milk in his cheese. This makes Townsend into a vocal pacifist, a development upsetting American patriots determined upon pursuing the war. Learning that Townsend owns a Swiss watch only confirms the belief of these patriots that he is a traitor. Then the war breaks out—much to the delight of the American warmongers and the Swiss hotel keepers. The latter can raise the prices of their hotel rooms exorbitantly, since the American soldiers need housing. But apparently there's not much fighting going on. The American soldiers sit in their hotels knitting sweaters and socks for the folks back home. They regard the war as "simply charming," since it "keeps them in the open," allows them to sleep in "downy feathery beds," provides them (by contract) with ice-cream sodas "when the weather's hot" and brings them "a helluva lot of publicity" if any of them ever gets shot.

By discovering that the yodel is the secret signal of the Swiss Army, Townsend manages to get the whole Swiss force captured. A Swiss spy now confesses it was he who was responsible for making Fletcher's cheese with Grade B milk. The American Army returns home in triumph. But they are heroes only for a day; they soon find they can't even find menial jobs. They are, therefore, none too miserable when the Soviet Union sends in a protest

against the rise in tariff on caviar. The war fever rises once again in America
—and it becomes thoroughly obvious which way America is heading when
the final curtain descends.

Even commercialized in its revision, *Strike Up the Band* managed to heap
ridicule on American big business, international relations, secret diplomacy,
international treaties, Babbittry. Horace J. Fletcher (Dudley Clements) is a
manufacturer of chocolates who harbors a grievance against Washington,
D.C., for its refusal to raise the tariff on Swiss chocolates. A sedative ad-
ministered to him by his doctor induces sleep and dreams. He soon sees himself at the head of an American Army that goes to war with Switzerland over
the issue of chocolates. Accidentally, the enemy's secret call to arms is discovered—a yodel—and the American troops are able to corner and rout the
Swiss Army. Fletcher becomes a national hero, but not for long. The American
newspapers uncover the unsavory fact that Fletcher's chocolates use Grade B
milk—a fact that shocks the nation. The love interest still involves Fletcher's
daughter, Joan (Margaret Schilling), and Jim (Jerry Goff), who is suspicious
about Fletcher almost from the beginning. Bobby Clark played the role of
Colonel Holmes, the unofficial spokesman of the United States President
(obviously inspired by Colonel House, President Wilson's personal adviser).
McCullough was the leader of the enemy army. In addition, Victor Moore
appeared as the President of the United States, and Blanche Ring in the part
of a famous Washington hostess.

Up to 1930 Gershwin had produced music only for formal musical
comedies. Now he was inspired by an unusual text—and by the incisive,
biting lyrics of Ira Gershwin—to create songs that had mockery and malice,
which caught every subtle nuance of the play and the characters. "A Typical
Self-Made American" laughingly detailed the ways and means by which a
man becomes successful, a recipe clearly outlined by Fletcher, Jim, and chorus.
The now celebrated title song deflated military pomp and circumstance. "The
Unofficial Spokesman" was Colonel Holmes's formula for getting ahead in
politics. A delightful little march called "Entrance of the Swiss Army" was a
tongue-in-cheek commentary on a bogus army. There was more spacious writing (a hint of Gershwin's later powers at producing stage music) in the
brilliant finale, where the chorus reviews all that has occurred, in a series of
sprightly lyrics, while the music itself is a recollection of some previously
heard melodies in a skillful tonal synthesis.

There were some prominent songs, too. "Soon," introduced by Joan
Fletcher, is one of Gershwin's most poignant ballads; this song was built
from an eight-bar sequence previously used for the first-act finale of the
first version of the play. "I've Got a Crush on You" had actually been written

for an earlier musical (*Treasure Girl*) but had been deleted from that production; it now became a hit. Gershwin's famous "The Man I Love," omitted from *Lady, Be Good!* in 1924, was once again tried out in the first version of *Strike Up the Band,* once again was found wanting, and once again had to be abandoned.

The famous march music provided the title for and was heard in a movie produced by MGM in 1940, starring Judy Garland and Mickey Rooney; otherwise no relationship exists between the stage play and the movie.

THE STROLLERS (1901), *an operetta, with book and lyrics by Harry B. Smith, based on* Die Landesstreicher, *by L. Kremm and C. Lindau. Music by Ludwig Englander presented by George W. Lederer at the Knickerbocker Theater on June 24. Directed by Messrs. Nixon and Zimmerman. Cast included Francis Wilson, Irene Bentley, Harry Gilfoil, and Eddie Foy (70 performances).*

The word "strollers" is a euphemism for "tramps." The tramps in this operetta are August Lump (Francis Wilson) and his wife, Bertha (Irene Bentley). When, in a small Austrian town, they find a thousand-mark note and try to cash it, they are arrested as suspicious characters. They manage to escape and stay free when a prince (Harry Gilfoil) and his girl friend are mistaken for them and are herded into prison. Meanwhile, the strollers go through varied adventures in different towns and in high society. They attend a swank garden party and elude detection through the assumption of numerous disguises.

At one of the society parties they manage to crash, the strollers witness an elaborate spectacle, "The Ballet of the Fans," the production highlight of the play; and during their incarceration they are attended by a drunken jailer (Edwin Fay), who contributes some of the big comic moments. Otherwise the play was most notable for the following numbers by Englander: "Gossip Chorus"; Bertha's "A Lesson in Flirtation"; and a song that courses throughout the play, a duet of Lump and Bertha, "Strollers We."

THE STUDENT PRINCE IN HEIDELBERG (1924), *an operetta, with book and lyrics by Dorothy Donnelly. Music by Sigmund Romberg. Presented by the Shuberts at the Jolson Theater on December 2. Directed by J. C. Huffman. Dances by Max Scheck. Cast included Ilse Marvenga, Howard Marsh, George Hassell, and Greek Evans (608 performances).*

Three years went by before Romberg was able to enjoy another Broadway success of the dimensions of *Blossom Time* (1921). Meanwhile, he had completed scores for fourteen musical comedies, extravaganzas, and revues produced by the Shuberts—most of whose music was synthetic, perfunctory, and is mercifully forgotten. When Romberg came into his own again as a major composer for Broadway, it was only when once again he was asked to prepare music for the medium for which he was so uniquely suited: the operetta, with a colorful European setting and characters and a sentimental plot. This happened to him when the Shuberts called on him to write a score for an American adaptation of a popular European operetta, *Old Heidelberg,* the rights to which they had held for quite a while. In fact, they had already produced versions (nonmusical) of the play twice on Broadway, once as *Heidelberg,* and another time as *Prince Karl,* starring Richard Mansfield, and both had been dismal failures. Nevertheless, the Shuberts were not yet ready to call it quits on their property. They now felt that perhaps *Old Heidelberg* could be sold to the theatergoers better with music than as a straight play. And so they called on Dorothy Donnelly to prepare a text to which their staff composer, Romberg, might contribute the music.

It was the kind of text that could make Romberg's creative juices flow (and flow they did). The setting is the old German university town of Heidelberg, in 1860. In his mythical kingdom of Karlsberg, Prince Karl Franz (Howard Marsh) is bored with life. He is yearning to go to Heidelberg with his tutor, Doctor Engel (Greek Evans), who recalls his own happy romantic days in that picturesque town in "Golden Days." They come to Heidelberg incognito, at a time when Heidelberg was at its loveliest, the springtime. The prince joins up with the students, who regale themselves with the student's song, "Students' Marching Song," then go off to their favorite meeting place, "Golden Apple Inn," where they raise their mugs of beer in toast to life and romance in the famous "Drinking Song." The waitress, Kathie (Ilse Marvenga), sings for the prince a sentimental tune about Heidelberg, to which the students respond with the song favored by university students the world over, "Gaudeamus igitur."

A romance develops between Kathie and the prince. They exchange tender sentiments in a love duet, "Deep in My Heart," and the prince sings the "Serenade" to her as a token of his love. (These two are among the most famous love songs ever written by Romberg. This may very well be because when he wrote them he was in love himself—with Lillian Harris, whom he married three and a half months after *The Student Prince* had opened in New York.)

But though they are genuinely in love, the future of Kathie and the prince is clouded, particularly after the arrival of the news that the king of Karlsberg has just died and that the prince must come home to ascend the throne and marry Princess Margaret for reasons of state. Tearfully, the prince and Kathie bid each other good-bye. But in his own land as king—and as husband to

Margaret—he cannot stop thinking of Kathie. One more visit he must make to that German city where he had been so happy. The reunion of Kathie and the prince is an ecstatic one—but both of them realize that this happiness is ephemeral. Once they leave each other again—and it must be soon—they must part forever. They finally take leave of each other, promising to keep alive the memory of their romance.

There were a great many things about this text, and the music that Romberg wrote for it, that distressed the Shuberts. They regarded Romberg's music as too highbrow. ("Who goes to the theater for opera?" asked Lee Shubert. "If a man wants opera he goes to the Metropolitan! Do you call this music music?") They were horrified that the operetta ended on a sad note, instead of with the hero and heroine kissing each other, and the stage full of singing and dancing—following the tradition of operetta. ("People don't like sad ends in musicals," was Lee Shubert's comment.) They were shocked to learn that the text would not call for a line of attractive chorus girls, and in their place demanded a male chorus of forty voices. ("You mean pretty girls can't sing?" inquired Shubert. And then he added: "Forty men singing that crap? Who needs it? Twenty men is enough, and that's final.") But Romberg was intransigent; he would make no compromises. At one time the Shuberts threatened to throw him out of the theater. At another point they said they would have the whole operetta rewritten. Romberg had to threaten legal action before the Shuberts finally gave in and produced the operetta as Donnelly and Romberg had written it—the Shuberts convinced that their poor property, *Old Heidelberg,* would suffer a fiasco for a third time.

But the Shuberts were proved wrong, and Romberg right. *The Student Prince* played to a capacity house for years, and had nine different companies touring the country. So large was the sale of the sheet music that Witmark, who published the score and was then in such financial difficulties that they were on the verge of bankruptcy, once again became a major power in Tin Pan Alley.

Since that time, *The Student Prince* has become one of the most beloved operettas ever written. There is hardly a season when it is not revived somewhere. And when it was made into a motion picture by MGM, in 1954—with Edmund Purdom and Ann Blyth (but Mario Lanza singing those wonderful Romberg melodies on the soundtrack for Purdom)—it proved the greatest box-office success of any movie using Romberg's music.

THE SUMMER WIDOWERS (1901), *a musical extravaganza, with book and lyrics by Glen MacDonough. Music by A. Baldwin Sloane. Presented by*

*Lew Fields at the Broadway Theater on June 4. Directed by Ned Wayburn. Cast included Irene Franklin, Ada Lewis, Ada Dovey, Willis P. Sweatnam, and Vernon Castle (140 performances).*

*The Summer Widowers* was described in the program as "a musical panorama." It was vaudeville entertainment rather than musical comedy, consisting more of self-sufficient sequences than of an integrated plot. It had scenes in Atlantic City, New Jersey (an opening episode on the boardwalk; a closing number realistically reproducing girls bathing in the surf); an extended sketch in a delicatessen store of which Lew Fields was proprietor; an apartment-house scene presenting a cross-section of a typical New York apartment with its tenants; a roof-garden act in which dancing routines and acrobatic specialties were given.

Lew Fields provided the principal comedy with his familiar German Jewish dialect. Other leading performers included Willis P. Sweatnam, a Negro comedian appearing as a janitor; Ada Lewis as a flirtatious widow; Irene Franklin as an eccentric detective; and an eight-year-old girl, Helen Hayes, who had made her stage debut two years earlier in *Old Dutch,* a Victor Herbert musical starring Lew Fields. Sloane's major songs were "On the Boardwalk," "I'd Like to Furnish a Flat for You," and "Those Were the Happy Days."

SUNNY (1925), *a musical comedy, with book and lyrics by Otto Harbach and Oscar Hammerstein II. Music by Jerome Kern. Presented by Charles Dillingham at the New Amsterdam Theater on September 22. Directed by Hassard Short. Dances by Julian Mitchell, David Bennett, and others. Cast included Marilyn Miller, Jack Donahue, Mary Hay, Clifton Webb, Joseph Cawthorn, and George Olsen and his orchestra (517 performances).*

This was the first musical in which Kern teamed up with librettist-lyricist Oscar Hammerstein II. Their job, as Hammerstein explained, was: "One of those tailor-made affairs in which [we] . . . contrived to fit a collection of important theatrical talents. Our job was to tell a story with a cast that had been assembled as if for a revue. Charles Dillingham, the producer, had signed Cliff Edwards, who sang songs and played the ukulele and was known as Ukulele Ike. His contract required that he do his specialty between ten o'clock and ten fifteen! So we had to construct our story in such a way that Ukulele Ike could come out and perform during that time and still not interfere with the continuity. In addition to Marilyn Miller, the star, there was Jack Donahue, a famous dancing comedian, and there was Clifton Webb and Mary Hay, who were a leading dance team of the time, Joseph Cawthorn, a star comedian, Esther Howard, another, Paul Frawley, the leading juvenile. In addition to the orchestra in the pit we had also to take care of George Olsen's Dance Band on the stage. Well, we put it all together and it was a hit."

Hammerstein might also have added that the writers had still another mission to perform—to duplicate the success won earlier by Marilyn Miller in *Sally* (1920). The plot—inevitably complicated, in view of all the demands it had to meet—remained essentially a showcase for Marilyn Miller, for her personal glamour, for her remarkable gifts at song and dance. She now played the part of Sunny Peters, a horseback rider in a circus in Southampton, England. There, a New York regiment of World War I pays tribute to her in the spirited title song, in the singing of which Tom Warren (Paul Frawley) joins lustily, since Sunny had often entertained them during the war. A love interest quickly develops between Sunny and Tom. Love's path never being smooth (particularly in the musical theater), Sunny can return to America— to which Tom is now heading—by remarrying Jim Deming, the circus owner (Jack Donahue), she had divorced a few years earlier. This Sunny will not do. She prefers to stow away aboard the ship that is carrying Tom home.

The most important song from this Kern score, together with the title number, is "Who?"—the love duet of Sunny and Tom. The writing of this lyric presented a formidable problem to Oscar Hammerstein II, since the refrain began with a single note held for two and a quarter measures (or nine beats). It was impossible to use a phrase for such an extended melodic phrase, and if a single word were used it had to be a word strong enough to sustain interest through five repetitions. Hammerstein solved the problem with the word "who," and Kern always maintained that it was the selection of this word for the opening measures of his song that was responsible for the great success the song enjoyed. Another good reason for its success lay in Marilyn Miller's performance. As Kern himself once remarked, she was the song's "editor, critic, handicapper, clocker, tout, and winner." Infectious, too, was the way Sunny sang still another delectable Kern number, "D'ye Love Me?"

*Sunny* was made into two motion pictures. The first—a First National production in 1930—starred Marilyn Miller; the second was produced by RKO in 1941 with Anna Neagle. The leading hit songs from the stage score were used in both productions.

SWEET ADELINE (1929), *a musical comedy, with book and lyrics by Oscar Hammerstein II. Music by Jerome Kern. Presented by Arthur Hammerstein at the Hammerstein Theater on September 3. Directed by Reginald Hammerstein. Dances by Danny Dare. Cast included Helen Morgan, Charles Butterworth, Irene Franklin, and Robert Chisholm (234 performances).*

*Sweet Adeline* is a period piece described by its creators as a "musical romance of the Gay Nineties." Its heroine is Addie (Helen Morgan), a singer at her father's beer garden, where she falls in love with Tom Martin (Max Hoffman, Jr.), first mate of the SS *St. Paul.* Tom goes off to fight in the Spanish-American War. Addie enters the professional musical-comedy stage and becomes a star. She then gets involved with the backer of her show, but falls in love with its star, James Day (Robert Chisholm), whom she marries.

It was a play heavy with sentiment and nostalgia; a play filled with fresh comedy (in the hands of Irene Franklin and Charles Butterworth). Most of all it was a play overflowing with heart-warming melodies which in their sweetness and sentiment captured the spirit of the times. The play opened with a gay song and dance, "Play the Polka Dot." Two teary ballads, sung as only Helen Morgan could sing them, became from then on inextricably associated with her name, "Why Was I Born?" and "Here Am I." As Addie, Helen Morgan also introduced " 'Twas Not So Long Ago," which had an American folk-song identity (and which was reprised by the chorus at the end of the show), and "Don't Ever Leave Me."

All in all, *Sweet Adeline* was the kind of entertainment that spelled business at the box office. The critics were virtually unanimous in their praises. Robert Littell said it was "a grand and gorgeous show"; Percy Hammond called it a "gentle opera"; John Mason Brown felt it rose to "its moments of complete enjoyment." So brisk was the demand at the box office that sold-out performances became the rule. But less than two months after *Sweet Adeline* opened, the stock market crashed—and the Great Depression was just around the corner. Suddenly the kind of sweetness, nostalgia, and humor engendered by *Sweet Adeline* had lost its appeal. *Sweet Adeline* managed to last 234 performances—placing it in those days in the hit class—only because the advance sale had been so heavy; but once that advance was tapped, the play was doomed.

Irene Dunne replaced Helen Morgan when *Sweet Adeline* was filmed, a Warner Brothers release in 1935, in which she was costarred with Donald Woods.

SWEET AND LOW (1930), *a revue, with sketches by David Freedman and others. Lyrics by Ira Gershwin, Billy Rose, and others. Music by Harry Warren, Louis Alter, and others. Presented by Billy Rose at the 46th Street Theater on November 17. Directed by Alexander Leftwich. Cast included Fanny Brice, Hannah Williams, James Barton, and George Jessel (184 performances).*

It is with this revue that Billy Rose made his bow as a Broadway producer. He did not have to look far for a star—no further than his own apartment—

for at that time he was Fanny Brice's husband. She and George Jessel carried the burden of the comedy—particularly in a sketch called "Strictly Unbearable," in which Miss Brice played a Southern gal being wooed by an Italian count, a role assumed by George Jessel. Sometimes the humor descended into questionable taste, as when Jessel sang "When a Pansy Was a Flower" and Paula Trueman sang "Ten Minutes in Bed."

The best things to come out of this revue were two songs by Harry Warren, both of them sung by Hannah Williams (who in 1933 became Mrs. Jack Dempsey): "Cheerful Little Earful," words by Ira Gershwin and Billy Rose, which Miss Williams shared with Jerry Norris; and "Would You Like to Take a Walk?", words by Mort Dixon and Billy Rose, with Miss Williams supplemented by Hal Thompson and a female chorus. When Billy Rose made his second try at producing shows—the revue *Crazy Quilt* in 1931, once again starring his wife, Fanny Brice—he interpolated into it "Would You Like to Take a Walk?"

SWEET CHARITY (1966), *a musical comedy, with book by Neil Simon, based on* Nights of Cabiria, *an Italian motion picture with screenplay by Federico Fellini, Tullio Pinelli, and Ennio Flaiano. Lyrics by Dorothy Fields. Music by Cy Coleman. Presented by Fryer, Carr, and Harris at the Palace Theater on January 30. Directed and with dances by Bob Fosse. Cast included Gwen Verdon, John McMartin, and Helen Gallagher* (608 performances.)

In 1965 Bob Fosse, the choreographer, and his wife, Gwen Verdon, saw a revival of the Federico Fellini motion picture *Nights of Cabiria,* which had originally been released eight years earlier. Fosse immediately recognized its possibilities as a stage musical for his wife, and became increasingly convinced of this judgement when he had sketched out a rough musical-stage version. Once this project passed the dreaming stage, Neil Simon was called in to prepare the text. Simon changed the main character of the Italian movie from a lusty and lustful streetwalker in Rome into an ingenuous American dance-hall hostess who has about her an air of the most ingratiating innocence. He used her as a symbol of womankind searching for love. He departed from his usual method of filling his dialogue with rapierlike thrusts of wisecracks in rapid succession. Comic lines and asides, rather than being a part of the dialogue, were flashed on an overhead electric signboard while scene shifts were being made. Simon placed more emphasis on sentiment than on comedy. Nevertheless, he did not abandon his partiality for drawing humor by placing his main characters in unusual situations: the heroine and a young man suffering from claustrophobia in a stuck elevator; the heroine, hiding in a closet, from which vantage point she is forced to spend the night watching a bedroom scene between the man who had invited her to his apartment and his girl friend; the heroine and her boy friend stuck in midair in a parachute-jump ride in Coney Island.

As *Sweet Charity,* the musical opened the newly redecorated and re-opened Palace Theater—once the shrine of vaudeville, later a movie house. The overhauling had transformed the theater, long grown somewhat shabby, into a glamorous auditorium; and appropriately that handsome auditorium was opened with a musical that was a solid winner.

There was not much hesitation by the critics to give the credit for the success of *Sweet Charity* where it belonged: to Gwen Verdon for her perform-ance and to Bob Fosse for his choreography and staging. Between them they *made* the show—though some of Neil Simon's funnier scenes, and a very respectable musical score, should not be underrated. From the moment Miss Verdon slipped onto the stage dancing, in silhouette (while the overhead electric sign read: "The Story of a Girl Who Wanted to Be Loved"), she remained in front of the footlights practically throughout the entire produc-tion (without a change of costume): singing, dancing, and projecting a galvanic personality that left the audience breathless not only for her per-formance but also for her sustained energy and dynamism. Bob Fosse's best contributions included "Rich Man's Frug" (a hilarious takeoff on modern social dancing); "Rhythm of Life" (a religious revival meeting by a cult performing the ritual in jazz); and "Big Spender" (in which the dance hostesses freeze into seductive positions as they are lined up waiting for customers).

Charity Hope Valentine (Gwen Verdon) is a simple, goodhearted girl who never loses the hope that she will find the romance of her life. She is continually searching for it. She is a dance hostess at the Fandango Ballroom ("a musical snakepit," as one of the girls describes it), the kind of a place where the girls "have to defend themselves to music." In the opening scene Charity meets a man in Central Park, only to have him steal her purse and throw her in the lake. For the moment she is disenchanted with men, but not for long. Accidentally, she meets up with the Italian movie idol Vittorio Vidal (James Luisi), who has just had a quarrel with his "date" outside a fashionable nightclub. Left dateless when his girl leaves him in a huff, he stumbles across Charity, who has maneuvered herself into the position of having him invite her first into the nightclub and then to his apartment. There she begs for and gets souvenirs to prove to her ballroom friends that she really had spent that evening with the movie idol: his top hat, his cane, his photograph. Proudly she struts across the floor of his apartment—the top hat at a rakish angle, the cane jauntily poised under her arm—singing "If My Friends Could See Me Now," one of the most delectable numbers in the score. But just then the date of the movie idol storms into the apartment. She has had a change of heart and is willing to forgive Vittorio and to make love to him. Poor Charity must spend the night hiding in the bedroom closet, while a passionate love scene transpires in the room. Once again frustrated in love, Charity is now fired with the ambition to improve her mind. She goes to the YMHA on 92nd Street to attend a lecture. There she meets Oscar (John McMartin), an accountant who is a victim of claustrophobia, and with whom she gets stuck in an elevator. Poor Oscar sprawls on the floor, then almost climbs the walls and ceiling, in his fright ("I'd be all right," he whines, "if I could just get out for a few minutes"). Charity does what she can to soothe him. By the time the elevator gets working, they are good friends. They go off to Coney Island, where this time they get stuck in midair on a parachute-jump ride. Now it is Charity's turn to be panicky, and Oscar's turn to be encouraging, sympathetic, and soothing until they reach safety. Things between Oscar and Charity seem to be growing serious. Oscar is even beginning to talk of marriage. Afraid of losing him, Charity had told him she worked in a bank, only to discover, much to her relief, that Oscar knew about her occupation all the time. Oscar insists he can forgive and forget—but apparently both do not come easily. In the end, Oscar leaves Charity for good, saying a happy marriage for him is impossible with a girl that has led the kind of life Charity has. And so, once again, poor Charity meets up with utter frustration, but not without the hope that someday she will meet a man who will love her.

"If My Friends Could See Me Now" was Gwen Verdon's big song-and-dance number. But she was certainly no less effective voicing her frustrations in "Where Am I Going?" or giving an electrifying song-and-dance presentation of "I'm a Brass Band." From her sister-employees at the ballroom—Nickie (Helen Gallagher) and Helen (Thelma Oliver)—she gets noble support in the presentation of "There's Gotta Be Something Better Than This" —their optimism that fate still holds for them some promise of a good life; and without the benefit of Miss Verdon's collaboration Nickie and Helen do very well for themselves in "Big Spender" and "Baby, Dream Your Dream."

In 1969 *Sweet Charity* emerged from the studios of Universal as one of the best screen musicals of the year—with Shirley MacLaine replacing Gwen Verdon and giving one of the most versatile performances of her career.

SWEETHEARTS (1913), *a romantic operetta, with book by Harry B. Smith and Fred de Gresac. Lyrics by Robert B. Smith. Music by Victor Herbert. Pre-*

*sented by Werba and Luescher at the New Amsterdam Theater on September 8. Directed by Frederick G. Latham. Dances by Charles S. Morgan, Jr. Cast included Christie MacDonald, Tom McNaughton, and Thomas Conkey (136 performances).*

A program note explained: "The story of the opera is founded on the adventures of Princess Jeanne, daughter of King René of Naples, who reigned in the 15th century. Time has been changed to the present, the locale to the ancient city of Bruges, to which the little princess is carried for safety in time of war and is given the name of Sylvie."

Sylvie (Christine MacDonald) is a foundling, raised as a daughter by Paula, proprietress of the Laundry of White Geese. When Prince Franz of Zilania (Thomas Conkey) meets and falls in love with her, Sylvie rejects him, for she realizes she can never marry one of so high a station. The rival of Franz for Sylvie's love is Lieutenant Karl (Edwin Wilson). Sylvie is repelled by Karl's fickle nature, and when it turns out that Sylvie is really the crown princess of Zilania—abducted from her native land in childhood—she is all too willing to accept Prince Franz.

Herbert F. Peyser, later a noted music critic, said this of Herbert's score: "From first to last this music is utterly free from any suggestions of triviality. The abundant melodic flow is invariably marked by distinction, individuality, and a quality of superlative charm." This charm was most apparent in the duet of Franz and Sylvie, permeated with a radiant glow, "The Angelus." No less enchanting is Sylvie's popular waltz, "Sweethearts," a spacious two-octave melody with an intriguing rhythmic pulse. "Sweethearts" was written long before the production of the operetta itself, a sketch having been found in Herbert's notebook dated 1896. "Pretty as a Picture," in which women's use of cosmetics is deplored, was intended by Herbert as a comedy number, but in the play, sung by the chorus, it was changed into a sweet, sentimental song.

In a more ambitious vein was the effective entr'acte, built from the thematic material of the opening chorus; the burlesque of religious music in "Pilgrims of Love"; and the elaborate finale, made up of recitatives, choral ejaculations, orchestral interludes, and a recurrence of the main love song.

The motion picture (MGM, 1938) starred Nelson Eddy and Jeanette MacDonald.

TAKE A CHANCE (1932), *a musical comedy, with book and lyrics by Buddy de Sylva and Laurence Schwab, and additional dialogue by Sid Silvers. Music by Richard A. Whiting, Herb Brown Nacio (Nacio Herb Brown), and Vincent Youmans. Presented by Laurence Schwab and Buddy de Sylva at the Apollo Theater on November 26. Directed by Edgar MacGregor. Dances by*

*Bobby Connolly. Cast included Ethel Merman, Jack Haley, Jack Whiting, Sid Silvers, and June Knight (243 performances).*

Before it came to Broadway as *Take a Chance,* this musical was a dud called *Humpty Dumpty,* which gave every appearance of falling flat on its face and staying that way in its out-of-town tryouts. As *Humpty Dumpty,* the music was the work of Richard A. Whiting and Herb Nacio Brown (soon to become better known as Nacio Herb Brown), while the book and lyrics were written by Buddy de Sylva. Radical changes had to be made, including the complete rewriting of the text, radical changes in costuming and scenery, and in strengthening the music. It was at this juncture that Vincent Youmans was called in to supply some new numbers for the revamped show. He contributed several. One became a Youmans classic, "Rise 'n Shine," with its revivalist fervor intensified by Ethel Merman's rendition. Other significant Youmans songs included two duets for Ethel Merman and Jack Haley—"Oh, How I Long to Belong to You" and "So Do I"—and "Should I Be Sweet?", sung by June Knight. These were the last pieces of music that Youmans was destined to write for the Broadway stage.

But the song that regularly stopped the show was not by Youmans, but by Whiting and Brown (with lyrics by Buddy de Sylva, and additional lyrics by Roger Edens): "Eadie Was a Lady," another song that owed some of its tremendous impact to Miss Merman's delivery. As Percy Hammond wrote: "She sings it in an ante-Prohibition New Orleans supper club where, surrounded by chorus girls disguised as amorous sailors from the U.S. battleship *Tampico,* she mourns the death of Eadie, a sister in sin. Ere she is through with the jocular threnody, her audience is clapping its hands and waving its handkerchiefs in deserved approval." "You're an Old Smoothie" was another outstanding Whiting and Brown number, this one serving as a duet for Miss Merman and Jack Haley.

The music is talked about first in this discussion of *Take a Chance* because here lay the main strength of the revised production—here, and in the way Ethel Merman put over its principal numbers. As for the altered text, it remained a sorry stereotype. Kenneth Raleigh (Jack Whiting) is a rich young man from Harvard who gets a taste of show business through the Hasty Pudding Shows. He decides to go professional by putting on a Broadway musical. Two confidence men—Duke Stanley (Jack Haley) and Louie Webb (Sid Silvers)—are trying to promote the stage career of Toni Ray (June Knight). They become involved with Kenneth, who, in turn, becomes involved with Toni. Much of the interest of *Take a Chance* comes from backstage glimpses into the trials and tribulations of producing a musical show. Much of its comedy came from the mad antics of Sid Silvers (formerly the stooge of Phil Baker) and Jack Haley—especially in the scene where, recuperating from a hangover, they inexplicably find themselves in the same bed.

> TAKE ME ALONG (1959), *a musical comedy, with book by Joseph Stein and Robert Russell, based on Eugene O'Neill's comedy* Ah Wilderness! *Lyrics and music by Bob Merrill. Presented by David Merrick at the Shubert Theater on October 22. Directed by Peter Glenville. Dances by Onna White. Cast included Jackie Gleason, Walter Pidgeon, Una Merkel, Eileen Herlie, and Robert Morse* (448 *performances*).

*Take Me Along* was Jackie Gleason's most successful Broadway show before he became so potent a monarch of the television airwaves via Miami Beach; and this Broadway musical gave him ample opportunities to prove not only his gift at comedy but also his ability to delineate a character in depth. These opportunities were afforded him because *Take Me Along* is more a play embellished with songs than a musical comedy. Since its source is one of the most lovable plays by America's greatest playwright, Eugene O'Neill, it had more penetrating insight into character than generally encountered in musical productions.

Here is what Richard Watts, Jr., said about Mr. Gleason's performance: "Playing with charm, in addition to skill, he offered a real, humorous and appealing characterization of Sid Davis. . . . It is an attractive performance, artful and unexpectedly modest." And surrounded as Mr. Gleason was by such hardy stage veterans as Walter Pidgeon, Una Merkel, and Eileen Herlie —and such a brilliant young newcomer as Robert Morse—characterization, more than any single element, stood out vividly from all the other facets of this production. "Good scripts make good actors, of course," commented Brooks Atkinson. The reverse is frequently true too. Good actors often make good scripts. And one of the main reasons why Brooks Atkinson found that "the innocence and sweetness of Eugene O'Neill's *Ah, Wilderness!* triumphed over the razzle-dazzle of a Broadway musical show" was because each of the major characters was beautifully unfolded into a three-dimensional structure by its performer.

Brooks Atkinson found Robert Morse, in the role of the innocent and love-stricken adolescent, particularly appealing. "He describes the bumptious innocence of a youth struggling with literary ideas that are beyond him. And he does not forget that in addition to being comic, Richard is honest and lovable. Mr. Morse does not sentimentalize a very real character. . . . He plays young Richard without a false note."

The story is set at a time when America was young, when the only problems besetting Americans were those springing up in their own backyards rather than from far-off lands. The time is in the early 1900's, the place an imaginary small town named Centerville, Connecticut. Nat Miller (Walter Pidgeon), a newspaper editor, could enjoy the good life, since he is highly esteemed by his townspeople (especially after he has acquired a fire engine for the town), likes his work, and is proud of his family. But he has problems. One of them is his brother-in-law, Sid Davis (Jackie Gleason), a reporter from Waterbury, who is so partial to alcohol that it keeps him from marrying Lily (Eileen Herlie), a woman totally devoted to him and of whom he is actually very fond. Then Nat Miller has concern over his adolescent son, Richard (Robert Morse). The boy is passing through the stage where he is writing love poetry, reading books by such "iconoclasts" as Wilde and Shaw, and is madly in love with his neighbor, Muriel Macomber (Susan Luckey). And the thing that most concerns Nat about his son is the fact that Muriel's father has stormed into Nat's house in fury, calling Richard's poetry "dirty." Muriel is quarantined in her house, and her father has threatened to withdraw all his advertisements from Nat's paper if Robert does not keep clear of Muriel. All this Nat can accept with equanimity, but when Muriel's father insists that Nat punish Robert severely, Nat throws the man out of his house.

Nor can matters at Nat's home be expected to improve with the arrival of Sid for a visit. Nat's wife, Essie (Una Merkel), insists to Lily that this is the time to snare Sid into marrying her and gives her instructions on how to go about the business of getting a proposal. Sid's arrival introduces further disturbances into the Miller household, since he is not inclined to remain aloof from the bottle. Nevertheless, he docs propose to Lily, who accepts him on the condition that he remain sober. But Sid fails to keep his promise; he even breaks a date with Lily.

Richard, on his part, is in the depths of despair. His girl, Muriel, has written him that their "engagement" is broken for good. This, combined with the encouragement of his friends, sends him to the nearby brothel to pursue a life of sin. There he gets drunk for the first time in his life. When a prostitute approaches him, he sends her off, but not before he pays her far more than the price for her services. In his alcoholic stupor he has a confused dream, which becomes the most ambitious ballet sequence in the production— done in black and white à la Aubrey Beardsley's drawings. In it people from books Richard has read come to life to puruse him like demons: Salome (carrying the head of John the Baptist on a platter), Camille, George Sand, Chopin, Hedda Gabler, Shaw.

When Richard comes home from this escapade—an escapade which, of course, has upset his parents no end—he learns to his delight that Muriel had been compelled to write the letter breaking their engagement. She has secretly sent him another note suggesting a meeting on the beach. There they vow eternal love but also agree that first it is Richard's duty to go for four years to Yale for his education.

Richard's problem apparently solved, repentant Sid goes home meekly to Waterbury, promising Lily he will make every effort to reform so that he might be worthy of her.

The title song, shared by Nat Miller and Sid, became one of the leading hit numbers in 1959. Other songs were equally effective: the frantic duet of young Richard and Muriel describing their feelings were they fated to stay apart, "I Would Die"; Sid's song with chorus, "Sid, Ol' Kid," in which the townspeople of Centerville welcome him; the duet of Sid and Lily when Sid promises never again to touch a drink, "Promise Me a Rose"; and Nat's self-appraisal in "Staying Young."

> TAKE THE AIR (1927), *a musical comedy with book by Anne Caldwell. Lyrics by Gene Buck. Music by Dave Stamper. Presented by Gene Buck at the Waldorf Theater on November 22. Directed by Alexander Leftwitch and Gene Buck. Dances by Ralph Reader. Cast included Will Mahoney, Kitty O'Connor, Dorothy Dilley, and Trini (206 performances).*

*Take the Air* was the first musical comedy starring Will Mahoney (he had previously appeared only in revues), and he dominated the production. In his eccentric dancing he fell all over his tangled legs; his gift at travesty revealed itself in a takeoff on a ventriloquist and on a prima donna delivering a curtain speech. He mimed and mugged and mimicked his way through a complicated plot that featured him as Happy Hokum, a Broadway hoofer stranded in Texas near an air base. With the help of Señorita Carmela Cortez (Trini), a visitor from Spain, he manages to foil a smuggling plot, and in the process wins the heart of Lillian Bond (Dorothy Dilley), daughter of a Long Island banker. The play ends as Hokum makes off in a plane for the Long Island estate of Lillian's father, to ask him for her hand.

Kitty O'Connor's throbbing, low-register singing of "We'll Have a New Home in the Morning" was a musical high spot; another was the song "All I Want Is a Lullaby."

> TANGERINE (1921), *a musical comedy, with book by Philip Bartholomae and Guy Bolton. Lyrics by Howard Johnson. Music by Carlo Sanders. Presented by Carle Carleton at the Casino Theater on August 9. Directed by George Marion and Bert French. Cast included Julia Sanderson, Shirley Dalton, and Frank Crumit (337 performances).*

Fred Allen (Joseph Herbert, Jr.), Jack Floyd (Harry Puck), and Lee Loring (Jack Kearns) are confined to Ludlow Street Jail for failing to pay alimony. Their friend Dick Owens (Frank Crumit) arranges for their release and suggests that they go off to a South Sea island where man is king and women do his bidding. The three Americans set forth for this island. There they luxuriate at home while their women do all the work. But they soon get tired of this arrangement and are only too happy to return home—and to their ex-wives. Romantic interest is confined to Dick Owens and Shirley Dalton, the latter played by Julia Sanderson, to whom the hit song of the play is assigned, "Sweet Lady" (lyrics by Howard Johnson, music by Frank Crumit and David Zoob).

> TENDERLOIN (1960), *a musical comedy, with book by George Abbott and Jerome Weidman, based on the novel of the same name by Samuel Hopkins Adams. Lyrics by Sheldon Harnick. Music by Jerry Bock. Presented by Robert Griffith and Harold Prince at the 46th Street Theater on October 17. Directed by George Abbott. Dances by Joe Layton. Cast included Maurice Evans, Ron Hussmann, and Eileen Rodgers (216 performances).*

"Tenderloin" was a district in New York in or around 23rd Street west of Broadway in the 1880's and 1890's, notorious for corruption and vice—a veritable beehive of brothels, dives, and gambling places, populated by the lowest strata of New York City. This was the district which, in the 1880's, a Presbyterian minister named Parkhurst tried to clean up.

Librettists Jerome Weidman and George Abbott, and songwriters Sheldon Harnick and Jerry Bock—having reaped such a harvest with their previous musical, *Fiorello!* (1959), which had used New York of yesteryear as a nostalgic setting, and a historical New York personality as the principal character—tried to repeat a proved formula in *Tenderloin.* For in *Tenderloin* they once again had the setting of New York's yesterday, and a central character (though fictionalized) who represented somebody from New York's past history. In *Tenderloin,* Parkhurst becomes Reverend Brock (Maurice Evans), whose mission it is to cleanse the Tenderloin district of its corruption. The scene shifts back and forth from Brock's church to a bawdy house. Salacious dialogue alternates with moral preachings. The musical becomes lively and vivid when it roams on the other side of the tracks. Perhaps the finest dance sequence is the one that transpires in a bordello. And one of the liveliest musical numbers comes when one of the girls of ill repute sings "Little Old New York"—a description of life in the Tenderloin district.

Involved in Brock's clean-up campaign are Nita (Eileen Rodgers), reputed to be "the highest-priced girl in Tenderloin"; the corrupt police officer

Lieutenant Schmidt (Ralph Dunn); and Tommy (Ron Hussmann), who works as a reporter on a scandal sheet and also sings at Clark's, a house of ill repute. Tommy makes a pretense of helping Brock's crusade while, on the side, he works with the corrupt Schmidt. When, disguised, Brock comes to Clark's to see for himself what goes on in that den of iniquity, he finds Schmidt, who warns him to drop his crusade. Brock firmly refuses to do so. He is then framed through faked photographs. At a trial, Schmidt accuses Brock of being a lecher. But Tommy comes forward to tell the truth, having been converted through his love affair with Laura (Wynn Miller), a society girl who sings in the church choir. Clark's is closed down; the girls must leave town. Brock also leaves New York—to find a new area of sin to cleanse, in Detroit.

*Tenderloin* was no *Fiorello!*, first because its central character, Brock, is much less arresting a personality than was the dynamic Fiorello La Guardia; also because *Tenderloin* (unlike *Fiorello!*) lacked a consistent point of view and mood. As Richard Watts, Jr., complained: "At first they [the authors] are gaily satirical about it, pretending to look on the activities of the vice set as a spendid example of the blessings of free enterprise, and this is when *Tenderloin* is at its best. But they have on their hands the matter of the framing of the pompous but noble-minded clergyman and the reformation of a dubious young man of the underworld, who comes under the influence of true love and Dr. Brock, and then they become sentimental and dull."

Sentimental is "Artificial Flowers," as sung by Tommy, but Tommy also has a way with a cynical number, too, as he proved with "The Picture of Happiness." Tommy, as played by Ron Hussmann, almost stole the limelight from Maurice Evans'—who here stepped from Shaw and Shakespeare into the lower regions of musical comedy without losing dignity. (This was not Mr. Evans' first appearance in musical comedy; he had appeared in a musical in London a quarter of a century earlier.)

There were several more things to recommend in *Tenderloin:* the briskly paced, vital direction of George Abbott; the choreography of Joe Layton; and the sets and costumes of Cecil Beaton. About the last, Howard Taubman said in *The New York Times:* "For freshness of invention and consistency of viewpoint there is no contribution more valuable than Cecil Beaton's sets and costumes. In their brightness and garishness they make clear what *Tenderloin* might have been."

THE THIRD LITTLE SHOW. *See* THE LITTLE SHOW.

THIS IS THE ARMY (1942), *an all-soldier revue, assembled by Irving*

*Berlin, with his own book, lyrics, and music. Additional dialogue by James McColl. Presented for the benefit of Army Emergency Relief Fund by Irving Berlin at the Broadway Theater on July 4. Directed by Ezra Stone. Dances by Robert Sidney and Nelson Barclift. Cast included Ezra Stone, William Horne, Gary Merrill, Jules Oshins, and Irving Berlin (113 performances).*

The idea to produce an all-soldier show—like *Yip, Yip Yaphank,* the one he had previously given during World War I—occurred to Berlin soon after Pearl Harbor, when he recognized the acute need of American soldiers for entertainment. Army officials, faced with the grim business of transforming civilians into seasoned troops quickly, frowned on his suggestion. But he persevered until he won the grudging consent of the Pentagon.

Assigned to a small room in the barracks at Camp Upton (the same camp where he had been stationed during World War I), Berlin gained firsthand experiences of life in a modern Army camp. He found material for songs, sketches, and dances on the training field, in the service club, the mess hall, the PX, and so on. Getting seasoned performers was something else again, involving as it did Army red tape and the cumbersome machinery of transferring men from one unit to another. It also meant working mainly with amateurs (though there were a few professionals around); of the final cast, sixty percent had never before appeared on any stage. "It wasn't long before I realized I had taken on more than I could handle, but it was too late," Berlin later told an interviewer. "I had the tiger by the tail, and I just couldn't let go."

With the help of Dan Healy (who had trained dancers in the 1917 *Yip, Yip, Yaphank*) and Ezra Stone, a veteran of theater and radio, Berlin selected about 300 candidates for his show. Since the Army insisted that this be no "goldbrick" assignment, rehearsals could take place only after regular Army details had been completed. But by fits and starts, and usually late into the night, the show was gradually whipped into shape. Starring Ezra Stone, Philip Truex, Jules Oshins, and Irving Berlin (of whom only the last was a civilian), *This Is the Army* finally came to Broadway on July 4.

The revue passed from sentiment to humor, burlesque, and satire, from song and dance to large production numbers. There were rousing tributes to other branches of the service: to the Air Force in "American Eagles" and to the Navy in "How About a Cheer for the Navy?" There was humor in the opening chorus, "This Is the Army, Mr. Jones," in which a group of inductees in long underwear are being warned what their new life will be like; in the overoptimistic belief expressed by Ezra Stone, Philip Truex, and Jules Oshins in "The Army's Made a Man out of Me"; in the delightful takeoffs on Vera Zorina, Alfred Lunt and Lynn Fontanne, and Gypsy Rose Lee in the Stage

Door Canteen scene. There was abundant sentiment in two beautiful ballads: "I'm Getting Tired So I Can Sleep," delivered by Stuart Churchill in the barracks scene and in "I Left My Heart at the Stage Door Canteen," sung by Earl Oxford in the Stage Door Canteen number. There were eye-filling sequences, too: "What the Well-Dressed Man in Harlem Will Wear," vital with Negro song and dance; and an anti-Hitler dirge called "That Russian Winter." Finally there were poignant bits of nostalgia. One scene was dedicated entirely to veterans of *Yip, Yip, Yaphank,* all of them wearing the Army uniform of that period. Berlin's song "Mandy" was revived from the 1917 Army show. And the number that always stopped *This Is the Army* was "Oh, How I Hate to Get Up in the Morning," from *Yip, Yip, Yaphank,* delivered in a rasping, broken voice by Irving Berlin, wearing his 1917 uniform. (The chorus that supported him included six alumnae from *Yip, Yip, Yaphank.*)

*This Is the Army,* in short, had everything that made for effective musical theater, and *The New York Times* described it as "the best show of a generation."

So great was the demand at the box office of the Broadway Theater that a four-week engagement had to be extended to twelve weeks. A nationwide tour followed, culminating in Hollywood, where the production was filmed by Warner Brothers and released in 1943, the all-soldier cast supplemented by Joan Leslie, George Murphy, Kate Smith (the last singing Berlin's "God Bless America," an interpolation), and others. The tour then swung back East, across the ocean to England, Scotland, and Ireland. By special permission, it was then dispatched to the combat areas of Europe, the Near East, and the Pacific. *This Is the Army* gave its last performance in Honolulu on October 22, 1945. It earned almost ten million dollars for Army Emergency Relief and another $350,000 for British relief agencies. It was seen by two and one-half million American soldiers in all parts of the world. For this epic achievement Berlin was decorated with the Medal of Merit by General George C. Marshall.

On July 5, 1967, one hundred members of the cast of *This Is the Army* gathered for a sentimental reunion at Sardi's Belasco Room in New York to commemorate the twenty-fifth anniversary of the show. Irving Berlin could not attend because he was expecting the imminent arrival from London and Paris of his two daughters in his Catskill Mountains retreat. He was, however, the chief topic of conversation. The group sang some of the principal numbers of the show, then paid silent tribute to thirty members of the production who had died.

THE THREE MUSKETEERS (1928), *an operetta, with book by William Anthony McGuire, based on the romance of the same name by Alexander Dumas. Lyrics by Clifford Grey and P. G. Wodehouse. Music by Rudolf Friml. Presented by Florenz Ziegfeld at the Lyric Theater on March 13. Directed by William Anthony McGuire and Richard Boleslavsky. Choreography by Albertina Rasch. Cast included Dennis King, Vivienne Segal, Lester Allen, and Harriet Hoctor (319 performances).*

In this musical adaptation of the famous Dumas romance, D'Artagnan (Dennis King) comes to Paris, where he becomes friendly with the king's guards and falls in love with Constance Bonacieux (Vivienne Segal). He then joins the musketeers Athos, Porthos, and Aramis. He proceeds to London to recover the queen's jewels, which had come into the possession of the duke of Buckingham. Swordplay and the heroics of D'Artagnan and his musketeers glamorize this mission and bring to it a successful resolution. D'Artagnan, now back in Paris, is able to avert a major scandal at the king's sumptuous ball.

This was Friml's last successful stage production, and for it he produced an opulent score that included a stirring choral number, "March of the Musketeers," and the equally virile "With Red Wine," introduced by Detmar Poppen, playing a subsidiary role, and a chorus. In a more sentimental vein were D'Artagnan's love ballad, "Ma Belle," and "Heart of Mine" and "Queen of My Heart."

The extreme length of the production—which did not bring the final curtain down until about midnight—inspired the following comment from Alexander Woollcott: "I did greatly enjoy the first few years of Act I."

THREE'S A CROWD (1930), *an intimate revue, with book by Howard Dietz and others. Lyrics by Howard Dietz and others. Music by Arthur Schwartz and others. Presented by Max Gordon at the Selwyn Theater on October 15. Directed by Hassard Short. Dances by Albertina Rasch. Cast included Fred Allen, Libby Holman, Clifton Webb, and Tamara Geva, with Fred MacMurray in a minor role (272 performances).*

*Three's a Crowd* was planned as a successor to the first *Little Show* (1929) and strictly followed the informal, intimate pattern of the earlier highly acclaimed production. The idea to put on another *Little Show* came to Max Gordon (making his bow as a producer) when he saw that the three principals that had made the first *Little Show* such an innovation had not been used in the two subsequent editions of that show. Starring those principals again, Gordon felt, would be sound insurance for box-office success. Through one of his friends, Gordon interested Fred Allen in such a project (Allen consenting on the condition that Howard Dietz do most of the book and lyrics and Arthur Schwartz most of the music), and Allen in turn brought Clifton Webb and Libby Holman into the picture. All three were enthusiastic about once again putting on a smart show with sophisticated material—something that the second and third editions of *The Little Show* had failed to do.

Libby Holman had two new blues numbers to add to her permanent repertoire: Schwartz' "Something to Remember You By" and John Green's "Body and Soul." The first of these had not been written for this revue; it had originated as a comedy number called "I Have No Words" for a London revue, *Little Tommy Tucker*. When Dietz and Schwartz decided to use the melody with new lyrics for *Three's a Crowd,* they were still thinking in terms of a comedy song. Libby Holman, however, convinced them to allow her to sing it in a slow tempo and sultry mood and transform it into a sentimental ballad.

"Body and Soul" was also something not originally planned for this revue. Green had written it as special material for Gertrude Lawrence, who introduced it in England, where it soon became a big hit. Max Gordon liked it and acquired the rights for his show, where it was planned as one of its biggest numbers—first sung by Libby Holman and then danced to by Clifton Webb. Somehow, during out-of-town tryouts of the revue, the song failed to make an impression. Then a new orchestration was prepared, and a new ending was created to build up a stirring climax. With these revisions, and with her effective rendition, Libby Holman regularly stopped the show.

Fred Allen had a new selection of drawling monologues, one of the best being his lecture with lantern slides about his recent polar expedition—Allen, wearing a motheaten fur coat, enacting the role of Admiral Byrd. Allen contributed most of the comedy, but in addition there was a hilarious sketch, "The Event," written by Groucho Marx in collaboration with Arthur Sheekman.

Clifton Webb's aristocratic air and subtle sense of timing again personalized his songs and dances. But he, too, had his lighter moments, such as giving an impersonation of Rudy Vallee and imitating the grand-manner style of an usher in a movie palace.

Other performers included Portland Hoffa (later to become Mrs. Fred Allen), Tamara Geva, and the California Collegians (one of whose members was Fred MacMurray, a stage neophyte at the time). Albertina Rasch choreographed several stunning dance sequences.

Of stage-technical interest was the fact that the traditional footlights were eliminated—for the first time in the musical theater; the stage was lit with lights flooded from the balcony.

Arthur Pollack wrote: *"Three's a Crowd* has beauty and grace without effort, and a high polish and a civilized sophistication and a little good, clean-cut gentlemanly dirt unmarred by vulgarity and exhibitionism.'' Characteristic of the "gentlemanly dirt" is a bathroom sketch in which a young lady intrudes upon a young man taking a bath. They are strangers—and then the lady accidentally stumbles near the bathtub, catches a glimpse of the young man's anatomy, and suddenly recognizes him as an old-time acquaintance.

THE THREE TWINS (1908), *an operetta, with book by Charles Dickson, adapted from a farce by R. Pancheco,* Incog. *Lyrics by Otto Hauerbach (Harbach.) Music by Karl Hoschna. Presented by Joseph M. Gaites at the Herald Square Theater on June 15. Directed by Gus Sohlke. Cast included Bessie McCoy, Clifton Crawford, and Willard Curtiss (288 performances).*

One day in 1908 the actor-playwright Charles Dickson stepped into the office of Witmark, the music publisher. He arrived to discuss the possibility of adapting *Incog* into an operetta. Witmark thought the idea sound, and suggested as composer his arranger, Karl Hoschna. Hoschna in turn brought his friend and collaborator Otto Harbach into the picture. Witmark signed Harbach by paying him a flat fee of one hundred dollars and a royalty of one cent a copy for the sheet-music sale; Hoschna was engaged on a royalty basis.

The operetta, named *The Three Twins,* was Hoschna's first success for the stage and the making of the team of Hoschna and Harbach. The "three twins" in the play were the brothers Harry and Dick Winters (Willard Curtiss and Joseph Kaufman) and Tom Stanhope (Clifton Crawford), who decides to disguise himself as Harry. The reason for this deception is that Tom is in love with Kate Armitage (Alice Yorke). Since his rich, dyspeptic father, General Stanhope (Joseph Allen), threatens to disinherit him if he pursues Kate, Tom finally decides to look and act like Harry Winters in carrying on his affair with Kate. What Tom does not know is that Harry has a twin brother who is half-insane. In the role of Harry, Tom finds himself in all kinds of amusing complications. Finally his father is willing to let him marry the girl of his choice, and the two real twins are left in peace to pursue their own respective love affairs.

One of the salient reasons—if not *the* reason—why *The Three Twins* was a triumph was the performance of Bessie McCoy as Molly Sommers, Harry Winters' girl friend. Bessie McCoy was then only eighteen and un-known (one year earlier she had appeared in *The Echo,* music by Deems Taylor, a failure). Dressed in a cone-shaped cap and white-pomponed black velvet trouser suit—and singing her songs with a tiny pouting mouth while performing a dance step—she became a sensation, particularly in the song "Yama-Yama Man" (lyrics not by Harbach but by Collin Davis). So completely was Bessie McCoy identified with the song that from then on, as one of Broadway's luminous stars, she was known as the "Yama-Yama Girl."

A second song hit was Kate Armitage's song, "Cuddle Up a Little Closer," sung against a setting representing the seven stages of lovers from infancy to old age.

Strange to say, neither "Cuddle Up a Little Closer" nor "Yama-Yama Man" was originally intended for *The Three Twins*. Hoschna wrote the music for the first song for a vaudeville sketch, and only much later decided to interpolate it into his operetta score. "Yama-Yama Man" was written while the operetta was already in rehearsal, and was put into the score in Chicago before the New York premiere.

Tom Stanhope delivered two other pleasing numbers, "Over There" and "Good Night, Sweetheart," and most of the comedy sprang from a riotous performance by W. J. McCarthy as a sanatorium doctor.

> THUMBS UP (1934), *a revue, with book and lyrics by H. I. Phillips, Harold Atteridge, and others. Music by James Hanley and Henry Sullivan. Presented by Eddie Dowling at the St. James Theater on December 27. Directed by John Murray Anderson. Dances by Robert Alton. Cast included Eddie Dowling, Clark and McCullough, Hal LeRoy, J. Harold Murray, and the Pickens Sisters (156 performances).*

Perhaps the most significant thing about *Thumbs Up* was the fact that it was the birthplace of two important songs. One was the Vernon Duke classic "Autumn in New York," introduced by J. Harold Murray and the ensemble in the highly effective finale. The other was "Zing Went the Strings of My Heart" (by James F. Hanley), presented by Hal LeRoy and Eunice Healey in song and dance.

Comedy was represented by the wild antics of Clark and McCullough in their last Broadway appearance as a team, the break-up of this inimitable comedy pair brought about by McCullough's death; by Sheila Barrett's mimicry; and by Ray Dooley (Mrs. Edward Dowling), onetime Ziegfeld star, here making a welcome return to the Broadway musical stage, and particularly effective in an acrobatic number entitled "My Arab Complex."

Spectacle was a particularly strong suit, beginning with an opening number in the style of Currier and Ives, and including a sumptuous presentation of an Irish fantasy, "Eileen Avoureen." A novel feature devised by John Murray Anderson was the use of mobile screens showing views of New

York in the "Autumn in New York" finale and in a lavish number entitled "Color Blind."

TICKLE ME (1920), *a musical comedy, with book and lyrics by Otto Harbach, Oscar Hammerstein II, and Frank Mandel. Music by Herbert Stothart. Presented by Arthur Hammerstein at the Selwyn Theater on August 17. Directed by William Collier. Dances by Bert French. Cast included Frank Tinney, Louise Allen, and Marguerite Zander (207 performances).*

Herbert Stothart was a Broadway composer whose best work was done in collaboration with other composers, as was the case in *Rose-Marie* (1924) and *Wildflower* (1923), in which he worked with Rudolf Friml and Vincent Youmans respectively. *Tickle Me* was one of the less frequent instances in which he successfully wrote a complete score without outside assistance. (A half-year earlier he had also written a complete stage score—*Always You*, in which Oscar Hammerstein II made his bow as a musical-comedy librettist and lyricist; but *Always You* had been a failure.)

*Tickle Me* was a production conceived for and dominated by Frank Tinney, who appeared as himself. He is seen as a man-of-all-trades in a movie studio, where he writes a scenario that is accepted and hailed as a masterpiece. When the "angel" arrives to finance the film production, he calls in Tinney for a conference. Spurred on by his love of travel, Tinney suggests location shots in Tibet. The company, headed by the star Mary Fairbanks (Louise Allen) and accompanied by Tinney, make for Tibet, where they confront innumerable complications and where Tinney is given frequent opportunity to engage in all kinds of ad-libs, songs, dances, buffoonery, and eccentric whirligigs. "Frank Tinney," reported the New York *Globe,* "had never before been so entertaining. . . . *Tickle Me* is a joyous, romping absurdity." The principal songs in a score which the *Globe* described as "uniformly excellent," included two duets introduced by Marguerite Zander and Allen Kearns ("If a Wish Could Make It So" and "Until You Say Goodbye") and "We've Got Something," sung by Marietta O'Brien and chorus.

TIP-TOES (1925), *a musical comedy, with book by Guy Bolton and Fred Thompson. Lyrics by Ira Gershwin. Music by George Gershwin. Presented by Aarons and Freedley at the Liberty Theater on December 28. Directed by John Harwood. Dances by Sammy Lee. Cast included Queenie Smith, Allen Kearns, Robert Halliday, Andrew Tombes, and Jeanette MacDonald in a minor role (194 performances).*

Though *Tip-Toes* had less of a run than several other Gershwin musicals produced by Aarons and Freedley, it was nevertheless a box-office success and earned more money for the producers than did some other productions with longer runs. Queenie Smith played the heroine—Tip-Toes Kaye, a young and attractive dancer. She is brought to Palm Beach by two conniving brothers, Al and Hen (Andrew Tombes and Harry Watson, Jr.), who fit her out in style and put her on the marriage market. She succeeds in winning the heart of wealthy Steve Burton (Allen Kearns) and is able to convince him she loves him for himself alone and not for his money.

The Gershwin score was studded with gems: "That Certain Feeling," a duet of Tip-Toes and Steve; "Sweet and Low-Down," "sung, kazooed, tromboned and danced to" (as Ira Gershwin explained in his book *Lyrics on Several Occasions*) by Al Kaye, supplemented by Gertrude McDonald playing a subsidiary role, and an ensemble at a party in Palm Beach; and Tip-Toes' haunting refrain, "Looking for a Boy." Gershwin's music was certainly the strong point of the show, as Alexander Woollcott pointed out. "Tip-Toes," he wrote, "was a Gershwin evening, so sweet and sassy are the melodies he has poured out . . . so fresh and unstinted the gay, young blood of his invention."

Another strong point was Ira Gershwin's lyrics, representing an important advance in technique and sophistication over his previous work in *Lady, Be Good!* (1924), the first musical in which he had served as his brother's lyricist for the entire production. Ira Gershwin was particularly proud of his work in the comedy trio, "These Charming People," which the three Kayes introduced. Lorenz Hart was so impressed by the high quality of Ira Gershwin's lyric writing in *Tip-Toes* that he wrote him a fan letter saying: "Your lyrics . . . gave me as much pleasure as Mr. George Gershwin's music, and the utterly charming performance of Miss Queenie Smith. I have heard none so good this many a day. . . . It is a great pleasure to live at a time when light amusement in this country is at last losing its brutally cretin aspect. Such delicacies as your jingles prove that songs can be both popular and intelligent."

> TOP BANANA (1951), *a musical comedy, with book by Hy Kraft. Lyrics and music by Johnny Mercer. Presented by Paula Stone and Mike Sloane at the Winter Garden on November 1. Directed by Jack Donahue. Dances by Ron Fletcher. Cast included Phil Silvers, Joey and Herbie Faye, Rose Marie, and Jack Albertson (350 performances).*

In 1951 Milton Berle was "top banana" of the television industry, "Mr. Television." The character of Jerry Biffle (Phil Silvers), comic star of the Blendo Soap Program, may not have been Berle, but there was little doubt

that the writers had Berle in mind when they created him. The febrile, frenetic, even hysterical activity surrounding the preparation of a weekly television
program is largely of Jerry's making. For he is loud, brash, bossy, a dynamo
of energy. He must always be in motion, always functioning at top speed,
always occupying the center of attention. Surrounded by a retinue of gag
writers, cronies, and other hangers-on, he is a man convinced of the infalli-
bility of his judgment and genius, a man so in love with himself that he
continually blows kisses to his image in the mirror.

A slim plot unfolds as the sponsor insists that Jerry's TV program needs
love interest to gain a larger public. Jerry brings Sally Peters (Judy Lynn)
into his show, gets the idea that he is in love with her, then is ready to help
her elope with the singer Cliff Lane (Lindy Doherty) when he discovers that
Cliff is the man she really loves.

The play was charged with the electricity of Phil Silvers' performance
as a TV comic. Two episodes in which he was involved had particular impact. In one, Jerry and his cronies sing the title song, which inspires Jerry
to reminisce on his old days in burlesque—the gags, the slapstick, the color,
and the atmosphere of burlesque entertainment. In another, Jerry gets tangled up with Walter Dare Wahl's old vaudeville routine, a hectic elopement
scene.

Rose Marie, as Betty Dillon, discharged the main comedy songs zest-
fully. The best were a duet with Jerry, "A Word a Day," filled with choice
malapropisms; "I Fought Every Step of the Way," describing romance in
terms of a prizefight; and "Sans Souci." "Only if You're in Love" was the
love duet of Sally and Cliff.

A TREE GROWS IN BROOKLYN (1951), *a musical play, with book by
Betty Smith and George Abbott, based on Betty Smith's novel of the same
name. Lyrics by Dorothy Fields. Music by Arthur Schwartz. Presented by George
Abbott, in association with Robert Fryer, at the Alvin Theater on April 19.
Directed by George Abbott. Dances by Herbert Ross. Cast included Shirley
Booth, Johnny Johnston, Marcia Van Dyke, and Dody Heath (270 per-
formances).*

It cannot be said that the musical-play adaptation caught all the nostalgic
charm and heart-warming sentiment of the novel from which it was derived.
But when Shirley Booth was on the stage as the earthy Cissie, it did possess
an endearing quality. The basic story was retained, though with slightly
changed emphasis. Where the main interest in the novel had been largely
focused on little Francie and on the tragic love of Katie and Johnny Nolan,
the musical concentrated on the amoral, rowdy character of Cissie, the chil-

dren's aunt, with her long string of common-law husbands—a part built up for clowning and hilarity but with a deep undercurrent of tragedy.

Otherwise, the musical, like the novel, concerned itself with the vicissitudes of the Nolan family in the Williamsburg section of Brooklyn at the turn of the century. Johnny Nolan (Johnny Johnston) is a singing waiter who finds refuge from a world he cannot understand in dreams and in drink. He has an appointment to meet his girl, Hildy O'Dair (Dody Heath), but comes across Katie (Marcia Van Dyke), with whom he instantly falls in love. Katie lives with her sister, Cissie (Shirley Booth), and Cissie's common-law husband at that time, Oscar (whom she always calls Harry in honor of her first common-law husband). Johnny comes to their home, proposes to Katie, and is accepted. After the birth of their daughter, Francie (Nomi Mitty), Johnny seeks the solace of hard drink and daydreams more than ever. He is a genuinely kind and gentle fellow—drunk or sober—and between him and his daughter there develops a close bond. But he is also irresponsible, and he loses one job after another. Working as a sandhog, he gets killed when a tunnel collapses—leaving behind just enough money with which to buy for his daughter Francie flowers for her graduation. Grief-stricken at the loss of a husband she both loved and pitied, Katie finds solace in the fact that her daughter is receiving her diploma.

The atmospheric settings by Jo Mielziner helped to establish the mood and settings of the play. So did the songs, the best of which were two sung by Cissie ("He Had Refinement" and "Love Is the Reason"), one by Johnny ("I'll Buy You a Star"), the love duet of Johnny and Katie ("Make the Man Love Me"), and a duet by Katie and Cissie ("Look Who's Dancing").

A TRIP TO CHINATOWN (1893), *a musical farce, by Charles Hoyt. Music by Percy Gaunt, with interpolated numbers. Presented by Charles Hoyt at the Madison Square Theater on November 9. Cast included J. Aldrich Libby, Harry Conor, and Loie Fuller (657 performances).*

*A Trip to Chinatown* toured for over a year before finally settling down at the Madison Square Theater for the longest run achieved up to then by any stage production in New York. Even while the farce was drawing the crowds into the Madison Square Theater, several different road companies were on tour; and on one occasion, one of these road companies was playing in New York in competition to the original production.

Taking his cue from Harrigan and Hart, Charles Hoyt filled his play with recognizable American types and realistic everyday scenes. The plot was a silly one, and thoroughly contrived as a convenience for the songs and comedy. Rasleigh Gay and his friends want to go to the Riche Restaurant in San Francisco for a gay time—especially since an attractive widow, Mrs. Guyer, had sent him a note asking him to meet her there. Rasleigh knows his uncle, Ben, would never allow him to go to the restaurant, so he asks for permission to go to Chinatown, which the uncle also turns down. By mistake, the note from the widow intended for Rasleigh comes to Ben, who is delighted to have a rendezvous with so appealing a woman. To divert suspicion from his escapade, he now allows his nephew and his friends to go to Chinatown. However, they all wind up at the restaurant, which has several dining rooms. In one is poor Ben, waiting for a woman who will never come; in another are Gay, his friends, and the delightful widow having the time of their lives. The attempts of the young people to remain hidden from Uncle Ben, the continual mistakes of the waiters in bringing the orders to the wrong room, the inability of Ben to pay his bill because he has forgotten his wallet at home, until his friend, Mr. Strogg, lends him the money—all this provides the material for the broad humor. All the characters meet up finally. Ben proves understanding and forgiving. He even invites them all to dine with him.

What gave the trivial play its main appeal, apart from the characterizations, were the numerous satirical allusions to topical subjects, such as women's suffrage and the temperance crusade. But the adornments of the musical stage—dance and song—were not slighted either. Loie Fuller enchanted audiences with a butterfly dance in which she used her skirt as the wings of a butterfly. And some of Percy Gaunt's songs were among the most popular in America in the 1890's. Indeed, *A Trip to Chinatown* has a special place in the history of American popular music by becoming the first musical production to discover what a bountiful source of revenue could be derived from sheet-music publication. Three of Gaunt's songs sold hundreds of thousands of copies of sheet music, and the first two of these songs named here are still remembered: "The Bowery," "Reuben, Reuben" (sometimes also known as "Reuben and Cynthia"), and "Push the Clouds Away."

"The Bowery" is, of course, a popular-song classic—one of the most famous songs ever written about New York or one of its districts. It was not in the production when it first opened out of town before coming to New York. The show started out doing so badly that Charlie Hoyt immediately realized a strong musical number was needed to strengthen the show. He and Gaunt wrote "The Bowery" and placed it in the show, even though it had no possible relevance in a San Francisco setting. It was sung by Harry Conor, impersonating a rube from the sticks who finds himself on the Bowery surrounded by drunks and thieves. When introduced, the song created such a furor after Conor had delivered the six verses to the chorus that he had to repeat the song from the beginning.

Equally popular is a sentimental ballad interpolated into the show before its arrival in New York, Charles K. Harris' "After the Ball." That song had been a failure when first introduced in vaudeville. Then (in one of the earliest examples of "payola"), Charles K. Harris induced J. Aldrich Libby to sing it in *A Trip to Chinatown,* using as inducement a flat payment of $500 in addition to a share in royalties from the publication of the song. Libby, dressed in evening suit and white tie, sang it in the second act, even though the song had no relation to story or background. When he had completed the first verse and chorus, there was not a sound in the theater, and Harris was convinced that once again his number had encountered failure. Then Libby sang the second verse and chorus. Once again—silence. Let Charles K. Harris tell the rest of the story: "I was making ready to bolt, but my friends . . . held me tightly by the arm. Then came the third verse and chorus. For a full minute the audience once again remained quiet, and then broke loose with applause. . . . The entire audience arose and, standing, applauded wildly for five minutes."

The publishing house of Witmark immediately offered Harris $10,000 for the song, which Harris wisely turned down. A few days after he himself published the ballad, the Boston music shop Oliver Ditson sent Harris an order for 75,000 copies of sheet music, setting into motion a sale throughout the country that eventually reached the five-million mark (the first American popular song to do so) and earned for Harris several million dollars.

A TRIP TO JAPAN. *See* HIPPODROME EXTRAVAGANZAS.

TWIDDLE TWADDLE. *See* WEBER AND FIELDS.

TWIRLY WHIRLY. *See* WEBER AND FIELDS.

TWO LITTLE GIRLS IN BLUE (1921), *a musical comedy, with book by Fred Jackson. Lyrics by Arthur Francis (pseudonym for Ira Gershwin). Music by Vincent Youmans and Paul Lannin. Presented by A. L. Erlanger at the Cohan Theater on May 3. Directed by Ned Wayburn. Cast included the Fairbanks Twins, Oscar Shaw, and Fred Santley (135 performances).*

There are two reasons why *Two Little Girls in Blue* has importance. It is the first musical to which Vincent Youmans contributed the songs (even if with the collaboration of Lannin). And it was the first musical for which Ira Gershwin (using the pen name of Arthur Francis) wrote all the lyrics—

this being two years before he entered into a permanent working arrangement with his brother George.

It was George Gershwin who made both these developments possible. Gershwin, impressed by young Youmans' talent, induced the producer Alex A. Aarons to use the composer for a musical Aarons was then projecting. Aarons finally consented, but as insurance called in Paul Lannin, an experienced hand at writing music for shows, to work with Youmans. Once this was decided upon, George also managed to sell his brother Ira to Aarons— though up to this time Ira Gershwin, like Youmans, had never written a show.

Alex A. Aarons did not produce *Two Little Girls in Blue,* selling out to A. L. Erlanger. Ned Wayburn, who did the directing, gave the two composers and their lyricist slips of paper instructing them on what kind of songs and dances were needed, with no mention of subject matter or the mood of melody required. The only instructions Wayburn gave were the time values and such indications as "opening" or "finale." Says Ira Gershwin: "Obviously to Wayburn neither the play nor the numbers were the thing— only tempo mattered."

The plot revolved around the efforts of the Sartoris twins, Dolly and Polly (the Fairbanks Twins), to get to India to claim an inheritance. Since they have only the price for a single steamship ticket, they try to fool the ship's captain by taking turns in the dining room, on the deck, in the ballroom, and in the stateroom. They manage well enough until each meets the young man of her heart's desire—Robert Baker (Oscar Shaw) and Jerry Lloyd (Fred Santley). The two men, not knowing they are involved with twins, get confused in their pursuit now of one girl, and now of another, until the two girls can finally disclose that they are really different people. From then on their love affairs can achieve a happy resolution.

The two best songs came from Youmans: "Oh Dolly," a haunting melody with a Jerome Kern-like personality; and the duet of Robert and Dolly, "Oh Me, Oh My, Oh You." The title of the latter was a hurried concoction by Gershwin until he could think of something better. Youmans liked it, and it was retained.

TWO ON THE AISLE (1951), *a revue, with book and lyrics by Betty Comden and Adolph Green and others. Music by Jule Styne. Presented by Arthur Lesser at the Mark Hellinger Theater on July 19. Directed by Abe Burrows. Dances by Ted Cappy. Cast included Bert Lahr, Dolores Gray, Elliott Reid, and Colette Marchand (281 performances).*

Sketches involving Bert Lahr, and several songs sung by Dolores Gray, were the high spots of this revue. One of the sketches, "Space Brigade," had Bert

Lahr playing Captain Universe in a farcical satire on such popular television serials of the 1950's as "Captain Video"; a second sketch was a Wagnerian travesty, "At the Met," which cast Bert Lahr as Siegfried and Dolores Gray as Brünnhilde; and the third sketch became a Bert Lahr classic, "Schneider's Miracle," with Lahr as a street cleaner in Central Park proud of his achievements in gathering refuse and faced with disaster when a competitive go-getter street cleaner proves more diligent than he. A fourth sketch, "Triangle," presents a husband, a wife, and her lover first in the manner of a burlesque skit, then in the style of T. S. Eliot, and finally as Cole Porter might have conceived it. In addition to these, Bert Lahr appeared solo as a clown, and with Dolores Gray as a pair of vaudevillians.

The three outstanding songs of the revue, all sung by Dolores Gray, were "If You Hadn't But You Did" (particularly memorable for the sparkling lyrics of Comden and Green), "Give a Little, Get a Little Love," and "Hold Me, Hold Me, Hold Me."

UNDER MANY FLAGS. *See* HIPPODROME EXTRAVAGANZAS.

THE UNSINKABLE MOLLY BROWN (1960), *a musical comedy, with book by Richard Morris. Lyrics and music by Meredith Willson. Presented by the Theater Guild and Dore Schary at the Winter Garden on November 3. Directed by Dore Schary. Dances by Peter Gennaro. Cast included Tammy Grimes and Harve Presnell (532 performances).*

Meredith Willson's first musical, *The Music Man,* had been a happy and choice bit of Americana. So was his second musical, *The Unsinkable Molly Brown.*

After *The Music Man,* Willson had been looking around for another suitable American subject for musical-stage treatment, and kept rejecting one project after another—including *Take Me Along,* the musical version of Eugene O'Neill's *Ah, Wilderness!,* which starred Jackie Gleason in 1959. Then Morton da Costa (who had directed *The Music Man*) and Dore Schary came to him with a libretto by Richard Morris. While vacationing in Denver, Morris had heard tales about a fabulous female named Molly Brown who had become something of a legend in the mining towns of Colorado because of her unconquerable spirit, and because throughout her life she had proved more than a match against an unkindly Fate. At first Morris thought of writing a novel about her, then decided the material was better suited for the musical-comedy stage. The Theater Guild, together with Dore Schary, became interested in the idea and started hunting for a composer who could do justice to this kind of American saga. Morton da Costa suggested Meredith Willson. Willson took to the libretto at once. "I saw in it things I believed fit my kind of interest—period Americana," he later explained, "and the love story of two characters I could like." He was particularly taken with the heroine—a human cyclone. And the setting and the period enchanted him.

It is at the turn of the present century that the musical begins, and we are in the town of Hannibal, Missouri. Molly Tobin (Tammy Grimes) is a tomboy who is frolicking around in a rough-and-tumble battle with her brothers. She may lack schooling or refinement, and she may belong to a poverty-stricken family, but she does not lack ambition. She insists that someday she will be a rich and powerful grand lady, a statement that inspires only derision from her brothers. But Molly is a girl determined to get what she wants, even if she has to walk all the way to Leadville, Colorado. There she finds employment as a singer in the Saddle Rock saloon (a hangout for miners), where she meets and becomes friendly with a young miner, Johnny Brown (Harve Presnell). Romance develops, Johnny proposes marriage, and even though Molly had been looking for a millionaire—and Johnny seems to be anything but that—she accepts. On their wedding night, Johnny disappears, much to Molly's bewilderment. But he returns one week later to bring her $300,000, which he has made by selling a claim. Molly is rich, at last—but not for long. She accidentally burns the money, reducing the wealth to mere ashes. This does not overwhelm Johnny. With quiet confidence he insists he will go out and find himself another claim. He leaves, and, true to his word, becomes one of Colorado's richest miners.

Johnny and Molly make their home in Denver, in a lavish mansion. But, for all their wealth, they are not accepted by Denver's high society. They are snubbed at a swank affair. In retaliation, Molly decides to give the swankiest party Denver has ever seen—but, unfortunately, nobody comes to it. Molly and Johnny feel it is time for them to get a touch of social poise and culture. For this purpose they go off to Europe.

A few years go by. Molly has become the darling of European royalty and the social elite. Her salon in Paris is overcrowded with celebrities. But Molly cannot forget how Denver snubbed her; she is bent on revenge. She invites many of her distinguished European friends to come back with her to Denver, where she throws another gala party. This time she finds the "who's who" of Denver falling all over themselves to get an invitation to come into contact with distinguished titled Europeans. Things progress swimmingly until several of Leadville's less creditable citizens break into this shindig. A rowdy brawl ensues. The party disintegrates into a total fiasco. Once again frustrated, Molly decides to return to Europe with Prince de Long

(Mitchell Gregg). Johnny, weary of foreign travel, prefers going back to Leadville.

In Monte Carlo, the prince tries to convince Molly to divorce Johnny and marry him. The temptation to accept is great, but Molly misses Johnny sorely. In the end she decides to go home. She books passages on the *Titanic*'s ill-fated maiden voyage. The *Titanic* sinks after colliding with an iceberg, fifteen hundred passengers meeting their death. But Molly is unsinkable. She takes command of a lifeboat and with her strength of will and spirit manages to survive. (Two of the best-staged scenes are those that show the *Titanic* colliding with the iceberg and Molly in her lifeboat tossed about by the waves). Molly finally comes home. Johnny is waiting for her in Colorado. Back with the man she has always loved, she knows (and so does her audience) that whatever else may lay in store for her in the future, she is unconquerable.

Howard Taubman called the character of Molly "an original"—which was the case. As Molly, Tammy Grimes was an "original" in her own right. There was no facet of Molly's unique personality that Miss Grimes did not uncover with her ebullient, spirited, boisterous, earthy performance. To her irresistible dynamism, Harve Presnell provided a welcome contrast with his undertoned characterization—and some appealing singing.

Impressive, too, were the costumes devised by Miles White, which, as Henry Hewes has said, "culminate in an effusion of gaily feathered hats bobbing up and down in Peter Gennaro's staging of a frenzied burlesque of a 1912 high society dance." Mr. Hewes also had reason to praise "the occasional well-timed piece of comic pantomime that pops up"—a product of Dore Schary's skillful direction.

And, finally, there were the songs of Meredith Willson. He could always be depended upon to produce at least one rousing march tune that clings tenaciously to the memory and refuses to let go. He had done this in *The Music Man* with "Seventy-Six Trombones," and he did it again in *The Unsinkable Molly Brown* in "I Ain't Down Yet." We hear it first in the very beginning of the musical, when Molly confidently foresees for herself a prosperous and influential future; and we hear it again at the end of the musical, as her friends and neighbors in Colorado hail her for her courage. Willson can also be counted upon to produce a haunting ballad. The best one in *The Unsinkable Molly Brown* is "Dolce far Niente," a duet of Molly and Prince de Long. There are other catchy tunes, such as "My Own Brass Bed," "The Beautiful People of Denver," and "Belly Up to the Bar, Boys," to all three of which Tammy Grimes does full justice. But whether he is writing a melody full of bounce and swing or a sentimental one, Willson "writes

Americana into his music the way Betsy Ross sewed a flag," as Whitney Bolton wrote. His songs are "dyed, dunked, dimpled and dappled with the true and genuine richness of Americana. . . . It is star-spangled, Yankee Doodle music, home-brewed and home-bottled."

Tammy Grimes did not appear in the motion picture MGM released in 1964. Her part was taken over by Debbie Reynolds, whose performance was a veritable *tour de force* in its own right. Harve Presnell, however, once again filled the shoes of Johnny Brown—making his screen debut.

> UP IN CENTRAL PARK (1945), *a musical comedy with book by Herbert and Dorothy Fields. Lyrics by Dorothy Fields. Music by Sigmund Romberg. Presented by Michael Todd at the Century Theater on January 27. Directed by John Kennedy. Dances by Tamiris. Cast included Wilbur Evans, Betty Bruce, and Maureen Cannon (504 performances).*

This was the last musical Romberg lived to see produced, and its great success was a source of considerable personal satisfaction. For years before *Up in Central Park* appeared, there had been rumors circulated that Romberg was through as a composer for the stage; that Romberg was incapable of adapting his Continental style of writing to the new demands of the Broadway theater since the mid-1930's, away from the old-fashioned operetta and toward the more briskly paced and more Americanized musical comedy and revue. Romberg defied these critics by achieving one of his biggest box-office attractions (the third greatest of his entire career) with a thoroughly American play, a play that in every sense was a musical comedy and not an old-fashioned operetta. And he produced a score that, at its best, was a pure delight, and which yielded at least two song hits.

The idea to make a musical comedy about Boss Tweed, the power behind Tammany Hall and the cause of much of the corruption in New York in the 1870's, came to Michael Todd after reading Dennis Lynch's book *Boss Tweed and His Gang.* He discussed the idea with Herbert and Dorothy Fields and suggested using Central Park as a principal background. He told the Fields pair that he stood ready to produce such a show if they would write the book and lyrics; and the two Fieldses called in Romberg for the music.

When *Up in Central Park,* as the musical was finally named, tried out in Philadelphia, its critics were outspoken in their low opinion of the show. Nevertheless, Michael Todd was so sure of its appeal that before the show came to New York he bought out the interests of his backers and gave them a handsome profit. With his customary flair for the grand gesture, Michael Todd saw to it that the opening night become a truly festive affair. The leaders of New York's political and social life attended. After the performance, the celebrities were brought by horse-drawn carriages to a caviar-and-champagne party at the Tavern-on-the-Green in Central Park. However, Michael Todd did not require such ceremonies to publicize his show. The critics did it for him the next day. Otis Guernsey called it a "flawless production." Lewis Nichols said that it was "about as big as its namesake and just as pretty to look at." Ward Morehouse wrote: "The overall effect is one of beauty and charm." Stimulated by such and similar accolades, the musical proved a highly profitable investment for Todd. In its first six weeks the box-office intake exceeded $300,000. During its long New York run the show grossed four million dollars, netting its producer a weekly profit of some $20,000. Then there was the income from the road companies—and, to be sure, from the movie rights, which were sold to Universal, who released the motion-picture adaptation in 1948 with Deanna Durbin and Dick Haymes playing the leads.

The setting is New York of the 1870's, during the rule of the "Tweed Ring." Rosie Moore (Maureen Cannon), daughter of one of Tweed's wards, has ambitions to become a star in the theater. She loves wandering about Central Park and enjoys not only its natural beauties but its attractions—rhapsodizing, for example, over the "Carousel in the Park," one of Romberg's most attractive songs. Rosie meets and falls in love with John Matthews (Wilbur Evans), a reporter for *The New York Times* who is investigating the crooked political machine of Boss Tweed, particularly its fraudulent deals connected with the building of Central Park. Boss Tweed and his henchmen are hardly upset by this. They-have bought themselves out of difficult situations before, and they are certain they can do so again. But when Boss Tweed comes to the office of the *Times,* he discovers that the paper, and John, cannot be bribed. The power of Boss Tweed and his "ring" is smashed—and Rosie's father is ruined. Upset with John for having been instrumental in destroying her father financially, Rosie deserts him for Richard Connolly, the city comptroller, who promises to use his influence to further her career in the theater. They get married. But when Connolly turns out to be a bigamist, the marriage is annulled. Rosie meets John in Central Park at the bandstand—and their old romance is revived.

Three songs are perfectly attuned to the style and mood of the time and the setting, not only "Carousel in the Park," but also two romantic duets by Rosie and John, "Close as Pages in a Book" and "It Doesn't Cost You Anything to Dream." Powerful contributors to the atmospheric charm and appeal of the play were a delightful ice-skating ballet in a Currier and Ives manner and a Maypole Dance, both creations of Tamiris; and the settings and costumes, all patterned after famous Currier and Ives lithographs.

UP SHE GOES (1922), *a musical comedy, with book by Frank Craven, based on his own comedy* Too Many Cooks. *Lyrics by Joseph McCarthy. Music by Harry Tierney. Presented by William A. Brady at the Playhouse on November 6. Directed by Frank Craven. Dances by Bert French. Cast included Donald Brian and Gloria Foy (256 performances).*

Albert Bennett (Donald Brian) and Alice Cook (Gloria Foy) are planning to get married. Albert is having a bungalow built in Pleasantville, New York, for that happy day. But the Cook family, which numbers ten members, insists on making so many suggestions about the construction of the house that they finally succeed in embroiling the lovers in a fight that separates them. They are reconciled when Alice comes to the bungalow to get a look at it, and while there confronts Albert.

This sweet and sentimental play had a score to match, its leading numbers including Albert's song, "Lady Luck, Smile on Me," and the duets of Albert and Alice, "Journey's End" and "Let's Kiss and Make Up."

THE VAGABOND KING (1925), *a musical play, with book and lyrics by Brian Hooker and W. H. Post, based on J. H. McCarthy's romance* If I Were King. *Music by Rudolf Friml. Presented by Russell Janney at the Casino Theater on September 21. Directed by Max Figman. Dances by Julian Alfred. Cast included Dennis King and Carolyn Thomson (511 performances).*

*The Vagabond King* is one of a handful of operettas for which Rudolf Friml will always be remembered, and one of the most successful operettas of the 1920's. It followed the Rudolf Friml triumph *Rose-Marie* by one year. Its central character is François Villon, the fifteenth-century French vagabond-poet, played by Dennis King in one of his most celebrated roles. Villon is the leader of a group of vagabonds who in the musical is made to play a vital as well as romantic role in French history. For King Louis XI, in one of his lighter moments, decides to make Villon king for a day for the purpose of humbling the pride of beautiful Katherine de Vaucelles (Carolyn Thomson), one of the ladies of the court. It is Villon's mission to win the love and hand of lovely Katherine within that day or else forfeit his head. Villon—though loved by Huguette, a peasant girl—goes about this task with relish. Villon and Katherine fall in love with each other. While this romantic episode is going on, the duke of Burgundy has been plotting to overthrow Louis XI. He sends his troops to Paris, where they defeat the king's troops. Villon now gathers the forces of his rabble friends to fight for the king. In the heat of battle, Huguette (Jane Carroll) loses her life saving Villon. Villon and his men help to defeat the Burgundians, after which, by royal decree, Villon is permitted to marry Katherine.

The picaresque character of the play is admirably reflected in the rousing chorus of Villon's followers, "Song of the Vagabonds," about which Alexander Woollcott said, "It cut loose magnificently." Other songs were in a more lyric or romantic vein, the best being Villon's love ballad to Katherine, "Only a Rose"; Katherine's romantic song, "Some Day"; Huguette's lilting "Waltz Huguette"; and the love duet of Villon and Katherine, "Love Me Tonight."

*The Vagabond King* was filmed twice: in 1930 by Paramount with Jeanette MacDonald and Dennis King; and again in 1956, by Paramount, with Kathryn Grayson and Oreste. Two new Friml songs were added to the latter version, "Bon Jour" and "This Same Heart," words by Johnny Burke.

VANITIES. *See* EARL CARROLL'S VANITIES.

VERA VIOLETTA (1911), *an extravaganza, with book by Harold Atteridge and Leonard Liebling, adapted from a German play by Leo Stein. Music by Louis A. Hirsch, Edmund Eysler, and others. Presented by the Winter Garden Company (the Shuberts) at the Winter Garden on November 20. Cast included Al Jolson, Gaby Deslys, Harry Pilcer, and Jose Collins (112 performances).*

When Al Jolson had helped open the Winter Garden for the Shuberts in March of 1911 with *La Belle Paree,* he had subsidiary billing earning $500 a week. In *Vera Violetta,* later the same year—and with his very next Winter Garden show—he was its reigning star, drawing $1,500 a week.

*Vera Violetta* was just a part of a triple attraction that began with some vaudeville entertainment (one of whose performers was Belle Baker, later a vaudeville headliner). It continued with *Undine,* a spectacular starring Annette Kellerman wearing a one-piece tutu that made the eyes of the male audience pop. (In January of 1912 the vaudeville part was displaced by a ballet troupe headed by Michael Mordkin.) Then, and only then, came *Vera Violetta*—and Jolson. As a character named Claude, he wandered in and out of what was essentially a revue with a tenuous story line, to tell jokes, make impromptu remarks, and sing numbers like George M. Cohan's "That Haunting Song" and Jean Schwartz' "Rum Tum Tiddle." The audience was in the palms of his hands. He was—there was no question about it—a star of stars. After the run of *Vera Violetta,* Jolson inaugurated his famous Sunday-evening concerts at the Winter Garden for show people. In 1913 the Shuberts gave him a bonus of $10,000 to sign a seven-year contract, guaranteeing him $1,000 a week for a thirty-five-week period; he toured the vaudeville circuit the rest of the time for $2,500 a week. He remained the brightest light of the Winter Garden for the next decade.

Yet there were other worthwhile attractions in *Vera Violetta*, and they would have made a much stronger impression had not the luster of Jolson's personality shoved them to secondary importance. There was, for example, Gaby Desyls. She had been imported from France by the Shuberts and had made a rather unimpressive debut in September of 1911 in the Winter Garden production *Revue of Revues*. She had a piquant French accent (which frequently made the English lyrics she sang incomprehensible) and a none too impressive voice. But she was loaded with sex appeal. In *Vera Violetta* she delivered (with Harry Pilcer) a number written expressly for her—a tantalizing ragtime number called "The Gaby Glide" that finally won her over to American audiences, more for her dancing than for her singing.

Besides Gaby Desyls, there was Jose Collins to give a dynamic rendition of the rowdy 1890 classic "Ta-ra-ra-bom-de-re" (a welcome interpolation). Miss Collins sang other far less dynamic numbers appealingly: songs like the title number and "Olga from the Volga" (both by Edmund Eysler) and "Come and Dance with Me" and "When You Hear Love's Hello" (by Hirsch). Another sexpot in the cast was eighteen-year-old Mae West. She had been appearing on the stage since she was five and had made her Broadway debut in 1911 in *A la Broadway*. But neither there nor, a few months later, in *Vera Violetta*, was she given much attention. Her own peculiar brand of sex appeal was something which would make its potency felt a number of years later.

VERY GOOD, EDDIE. *See* THE PRINCESS THEATER SHOWS.

WALK A LITTLE FASTER (1932), *a revue, with sketches by S. J. Perelman and Robert MacGuingle. Lyrics by E. Y. Harburg. Music by Vernon Duke. Presented by Courtney Burr at the St. James Theater on December 7. Directed by Monty Woolley. Dances by Albertina Rasch. Cast included Beatrice Lillie, Clark and McCullough, and Evelyn Hoey (119 performances).*

*Walk a Little Faster* was Vernon Duke's first complete score for the Broadway theater. It was not a success, but it deserves to be remembered because it was the showcase for the most popular song Duke ever wrote, "April in Paris." Writing that song was almost an afterthought, and it was interpolated into the revue after the latter had gone into rehearsal. One day, during the rehearsal period, Duke and some of his collaborators discussed the necessity of including a romantic number. During the course of the conversation somebody happened to remark wistfully, "Oh, to be in Paris now that April's here." Though Paris is not particularly lovely in April, as Vernon Duke well knew, this remark served as a cue for the romantic song he needed, and Harburg provided a lyric. The song was introduced into the revue during Boston tryouts in a scene re-creating the Left Bank, setting by Boris Aronson; it was sung by Evelyn Hoey. H. T. Parker, renowned Boston drama and music critic, singled out the song for special praise. " 'April in Paris,' " he wrote, "is worthy, in place and kind, of that city in spring. There's a catch in the throat from it—if one has too many memories." But, strange to say, the song was a failure when the show hit New York. One reason may have been that, a victim of laryngitis, Evelyn Hoey sang it almost in a whisper. Most of the critics ignored the song entirely, while Robert Garland even considered it an "unnecessary item." This neglect infuriated the Boston writer Isaac Goldberg, who wrote to Duke: " 'April in Paris' is one of the finest musical compositions that ever graced an American production. If I had my way, I'd make the study of it compulsory in all harmony courses." But in time the song caught on (long after *Walk a Little Faster* was gone and forgotten), particularly after it was sung in intimate nightclubs, where it charmed the sophisticated, and was successfully recorded for Liberty by the society chanteuse Marian Chase.

"April in Paris" was unquestionably the best song in the Duke score, but there were two other numbers worthy of mention: "Speaking of Love," introduced by Donald Burr and Dave and Dorothy Fitzgibbon; and "Where Have We Met Before?", sung by a quartet comprising John Hundley, Sue Hicks, Donald Burr, and Patricia Dorn.

Beatrice Lillie and Bobby Clark were the standout performers in the revue. Indeed, one of the best sketches was a takeoff on the then recent musical *Flying Colors,* in which Bobby Clark impersonated the suave Clifton Webb, and Beatrice Lillie the elegant Tamara Geva. Miss Lillie also appeared as a 1906 college girl; as Frisco Fanny, a belle of the Yukon; as a radio songstress; and as a French diseuse who provides commentary on the songs she sings. Her comedy was supplemented by that of Clark and McCullough, who appeared in their familiar outfits and equipment. Clark was at his best as a dictator of Russia, as a member of the secret police, and as a miner.

WALL STREET GIRL (1912), *an operetta, with book by Margaret Mayo and Edgar Selwyn. Lyrics by Hapgood Burt. Music by Karl Hoschna. Presented by Frederick McKay at the George M. Cohan Theater on April 15. Directed by*

*Charles Winninger and Gus Sohike. Cast. included William P. Carleton, Harry Gilfoil, Charles Winninger, Will Rogers, and Blanche Ring (56 performances).*

Though *Wall Street Girl* had had a far less prosperous Broadway career than several other Hoschna operettas, it nevertheless deserves special attention for a number of reasons. In it Blanche Ring, as the heroine, gave her first winning performance in New York, and Charles Winninger, in a secondary role, scored his first stage hit in what was his second musical-comedy appearance, the first having taken place in 1910 in *The Yankee Girl.* Then, too, Will Rogers stole some of the limelight with his extraordinary lariat feats, thus achieving his first major Broadway victory. (His next step, a year later, would be the *Ziegfeld Follies.*) Finally, Hoschna's score contained an outstanding number in "I Want a Regular Man," which profited from Blanche Ring's presentation.

Blanche Ring appeared as Jemina Greene, a young lady who likes men, money, and ostentatious clothes. She comes to Wall Street, there to create something of an upheaval. She meets Dexter Barton, a Westerner (William P. Carleton) who induces her—despite the advice of her well-intentioned friends—to join him in a mining investment in Goldenrod, Nevada. They hit the jackpot. Jemina becomes rich and can now indulge her passion for men and clothes. She is also able to rescue her father, James (Harry Gilfoil), from financial ruin.

WANG (1891), *a comic opera, with book and lyrics by J. Cheever Goodwin. Music by Woolson Morse. Presented at the Broadway Theater on May 4. Cast included De Wolf Hopper and Della Fox (151 performances).*

*Wang* was described by its authors as an "operatic burletta." The "operatic" half of this description referred to its debt to Gilbert and Sullivan's *Mikado,* in which the star of *Wang*—De Wolf Hopper—had enjoyed outstanding success in the 1880's. The "burletta," part justified the appearance of the female star, Della Fox, in tights—in the male role of Mataya. Comic opera or "burletta," *Wang* was one of the most popular extravaganzas of the period, justifying its advertising slogan, *"Wang* goes with a bang!" After a successful stay in New York, the company went on a nationwide tour, traveling in elegant George Wagner Palace Cars—a trip that was described in a pamphlet entitled "De Wolf Hopper's Wagner Tour."

Much of the popularity of *Wang* was due to the comical portrayal of the title role by De Wolf Hopper. Wang is the regent of Siam, beset by financial problems, partly through his own extravagance (one of his indulgences is the purchase of a sacred elephant) and largely because his empire is poverty-stricken. Uncle and guardian of Mataya, Wang learns that Mataya's dead father had left a fortune to the boy in the custody of the widow of the late French consul. To gain this fortune, Wang marries the widow and assumes parental control over her large retinue of daughters, one of whom falls in love with Mataya. When the treasure chest is brought to Wang, it proves to be empty. But Wang's despair is soon dissipated when he learns where the treasure actually is concealed. Mataya, eager only to marry the girl he loves, turns over the fortune to Wang and renounces his right to the throne.

The Woolson Morse score was nondescript, best in some Oriental-type marches (Wang's first entrance on an elephant, and the wedding and coronation marches), in Wang's amusing topical song, "The Man with the Elephant," and in the ballads "A Pretty Girl" and "Ask the Man in the Moon."

WARS OF THE WORLD. *See* HIPPODROME EXTRAVAGANZAS.

WATCH YOUR STEP (1914), *a revue, with book by Harry B. Smith. Lyrics and music by Irving Berlin. Presented by Charles Dillingham at the New Amsterdam Theater on December 8. Directed by R. H. Burnside. Cast included Vernon and Irene Castle, Charles King, Frank Tinney, and Elizabeth Brice (175 performances).*

Having been crowned "king of ragtime" by virtue of "Alexander's Ragtime Band" in 1911 and the other ragtime hit numbers that followed immediately in its footsteps, Irving Berlin became the inevitable choice for Charles Dillingham, the producer, to write all the songs for a "syncopated revue" he was planning to star Vernon and Irene Castle, the ace dancing team of the world. Berlin had previously had a good many of his songs interpolated into various successful shows, including the *Ziegfeld Follies*. But *Watch Your Step* was the first time he had a show all to himself as composer-lyricist, and he made the most of the opportunity. One unidentified critic wrote: "More than anyone else, *Watch Your Step* belongs to Irving Berlin. He is the young master of syncopation, the gifted and industrious writer of words and music for songs that have made him rich and envied. This is the first time the author of 'Alexander's Ragtime Band' and the like has turned his attention to providing the music for an entire evening's entertainment. For it, he has written a score of his mad melodies, nearly all of them of the tickling sort, born to be caught up and whistled at every street corner, and warranted to set any roomful a-dancing."

Actually, not all of Berlin's songs for the revue—not even the best ones —were of the syncopated variety. In ragtime there was "Syncopated Walk," for which Vernon and Irene Castle did a catchy ragtime dance. But the best number in the score, and the one that is still remembered, was a ballad, "Play a Simple Melody," introduced by Sallie Fisher and Charles King. This was one of Berlin's earliest numbers in which the chorus was sung contrapuntally to a patter melody with its own lyrics after that chorus was introduced. Another good Berlin ballad was "When I Discovered You."

Vernon Castle was the star of the show. With his wife, Irene, he not only danced enchantingly the tango, polka, and fox-trot, but also played the tap drums, sang a delightful satirical number about his success as a dance teacher, and filled the stage with his charm and personality. The Castles were already an institution before the first-night curtain had risen on *Watch Your Step*. They had first attracted success in 1911 (coincidentally enough, the same year that Berlin himself had become a ragtime institution with "Alexander's Ragtime Band") in the French supper club Café de Paris. Back in America, they starred in their first Broadway show—*The Sunshine Girl* —in 1913. By the time *Watch Your Step* was written for them, they had become the dancing rage of the country, starting one dancing vogue after another (the Turkey Trot, the Castle Walk, the Maxixe, the Hesitation Waltz). In vaudeville they did one-night stands that brought them $30,000 a week. In time they would be the founders of dancing schools, dancing palaces, nightclubs. Irene Castle would change the social habits of her times and the physical appearance of her sex by bobbing her hair, wearing a loose flowing gown in place of the accepted hobble skirt (she wore one for the first time in *Watch Your Step*), favoring Dutch bonnets, and making her sylphlike, boyish figure the standard of female beauty to replace the more buxom variety that had been favored up to now.

In *Watch Your Step*, Frank Tinney appeared (in blackface) as a carriage caller at the opera, as a Pullman porter, and as a coatroom boy—and indulged in his famous practice of engaging the orchestra leader in the pit in informal conversation. Elizabeth Murray brought a charming brogue to the delivery of "Minstrel Parade," and Charles King and Elizabeth Brice sang sentimental numbers. Harry Kelly did a comedy routine with a dog. A production highlight came in the second act, when the master of opera, Giuseppe Verdi, appeared to protest about the irreverent manner in which his tunes were being syncopated, and was silenced into submission when he was convinced that syncopation gave his music a new "zip."

WEBER AND FIELDS EXTRAVAGANZAS (1896), The Art of Maryland, *with book and lyrics by Joseph Herbert. Music by John Stromberg. Presented by Weber and Fields at their Music Hall on September 5. Cast included Weber and Fields, Lottie Gilson, Sam Bernard, John T. Kelly, and the Beaumont Sisters.*

(1898), Hurly Burly, *with book and lyrics by Edgar and Harry B. Smith. Music by John Stromberg. Presented by Weber and Fields at their Music Hall on September 8. Cast included Weber and Fields and Fay Templeton.*

(1899), Whirl-i-Gig, *with book by Edgar Smith. Lyrics by Harry B. Smith. Music by John Stromberg. Presented by Weber and Fields at their Music Hall on September 21. Cast included Weber and Fields, Peter F. Dailey, David Warfield, and Lillian Russell* (264 *performances*).

(1900), Fiddle-De-Dee, *with book by Edgard Smith. Lyrics by Harry B. Smith. Music by John Stromberg. Presented by Weber and Fields at their Music Hall on September 21. Cast included De Wolf Hopper, David Warfield, Fay Templeton, and Lillian Russell* (262 *performances*).

(1901), Hoity Toity, *with book by Edgar Smith. Lyrics by Harry B. Smith. Music by John Stromberg. Presented by Weber and Fields at their Music Hall on September 15. Directed by Julian Mitchell. Cast included De Wolf Hopper, Sam Bernard, Lillian Russell, Fay Templeton, and Bessie Clayton* (225 *performances*).

(1902), Twirly Whirly, *with book by Edgar Smith. Lyrics by Edgar and Harry B. Smith. Music by Joseph Stromberg and W. T. Francis. Presented by Weber and Fields at their Music Hall on September 11. Directed by Julian Mitchell. Cast included Weber and Fields, William Collier, Peter F. Dailey, Lillian Russell, Mabel Barrison, and Bessie Clayton* (244 *performances*).

(1903), Whoop-De-Do, *with book and lyrics by Edgar Smith. Music by W. T. Francis. Presented by Weber and Fields at their Music Hall on September 24. Directed by Ben Teal. Cast included Weber and Fields, Peter F. Dailey, Louis Mann, Carter De Haven, and Lillian Russell* (151 *performances*).

(1904), Higgeldy Piggeldy, *with book and lyrics by Edgar Smith. Music by Maurice Levi. Presented by Joseph M. Weber and Florenz Ziegfeld, Jr., at the Music Hall on October 20. Directed by George F. Marion. Dances by Sam Marion. Cast included Joseph Weber, Anna Held, and Marie Dressler* (185 *performances*).

(1906), Twiddle Twaddle, *with book and lyrics by Edgar Smith. Music by Maurice Levi. Presented by Joseph M. Weber at the Music Hall on January 1. Directed by Al M. Holbrook. Cast included Joe Weber, Marie Dressler, and Trixie Friganza* (137 *performances*).

(1907), Hip! Hip! Hooray, *book and lyrics by Edgar Smith. Music by Gus Edwards. Presented by Joseph M. Weber at Weber's Theater on October 10. Directed by Julian Mitchell. Cast included Joe Weber, Velaska Suratt, and Bessie Clayton* (64 *performances*).

(1912), Hokey Pokey, *with book and lyrics by Edgar Smith and E. Ray Goetz. Music by John Stromberg, A. Baldwin Sloane, and W. T. Francis. Presented by Weber and Fields at the Broadway Theater on February 8. Directed by Gus Sohike. Cast included Weber and Fields, William Collier, Lillian Russell, Fay Templeton, Ada Lewis, and Bessie Clayton (108 performances).*

Joe Weber and Lew Fields inaugurated their acting partnerships as boys on New York's East Side in 1877, when they formed an Irish song, dance, and comedy act that appeared in variety theaters and at Duffy's Pavilion in Coney Island. In 1884 they were hired for Ada Richmond's burlesque shows at Miner's Bowery Theater. It was there that they evolved their own personal brand of broad and rowdy humor and horseplay, and created their caricatures of Dutchmen for which they later became famous.

With a loan of 1,500 dollars from Fields' brother-in-law added to their own capital (300 dollars), Weber and Fields acquired in 1895 a theater just off Broadway and Twenty-ninth Street, henceforth known as the Weber and Fields Music Hall. It opened in September, 1896, with *The Art of Maryland.* For a while Weber and Fields had to supplement their activity in New York by taking their troupe on extensive road trips in order to make ends meet. But their burlesques caught on and became a vogue in New York. By 1898 they were operating such a financially successful venture that they could afford to pay their stars some of the highest salaries in the trade.

Like the burlesques of Harrigan and Hart, those of Weber and Fields followed a pattern. The first half of each production consisted of broad satires on nonmusical plays of current New York interest. *The Art of Maryland* was a travesty on *The Heart of Maryland,* in which Mrs. Leslie Carter had then recently starred in New York. The second half of the production was a variety show with various leading performers offering their song-and/or-dance specialties, either singly or in groups. It was in this part that Weber and Fields performed their well-known routines and exchanged ridiculous repartee in their thick German accent. Each wore clothes too large for him, usually checked suits or evening clothes, as well as ludicrous-looking derbies. Each had foolish-looking little tufts of hair as beards. Weber, always called Mike, was the little fat man (his stomach padded out with pillows). Fields, called Myer, was the tall bully who always abused poor Mike by choking him, or gouging out his eye, or kicking him in his stomach, or hitting him over his derby. They invariably made their first appearance with Weber yelling: "Don't poosh me, Myer!" Weber would come out first, pursued by Fields brandishing a threatening cane at him. They would then have their corny exchanges in their personalized vocabulary as well as dialect. Weber might say to Fields: "I am delightfulness to meet you," to which Fields would reply: "Der disgust is all mine." Fields might shout: "Didn't I telling you, watch your etiquette," to which Weber would reply defensively: "Who says I et a cat?" It is not often remembered that perhaps the most famous joke to come out of show business was a Weber and Fields invention. For it was out of their lips that there first emerged·the celebrated query and answer: "Who vass dat lady I seen you with last night?" "That was no lady, she vass my wife!"

Of course, they were also involved in the burlesques on plays and in all types of skits. In *The Art of Maryland* Weber and Fields introduced their famous pool-table skit. Somehow, in some way, there was a time and place for other acts and performers. Lottie Gilson—known as "The Little Magnet" because she was such a box-office magnet—sang several numbers. A novelty was provided by something called an Animatograph, described as "a new kind of motion picture."

From out of the Weber and Fields shows came some of the foremost stars of the New York stage of the 1890's and early 1900's—in many cases their first important step toward greatness. And not only great stars were born in the Weber and Fields Music Hall, but frequently great popular songs, all by John Stromberg until the time of his death in 1902.

The formula of the first burlesque-extravaganza, *The Art of Maryland,* was adhered to for about a decade. Always there were the travesties on the current plays—in later productions on William Gillette's *Secret Service,* J. M. Barrie's *The Little Minister,* Rostand's *Cyrano de Bergerac, The Geisha, Quo Vadis, Sappho, Barbara Frietchie. Quo Vadis* became *Quo Vass Iss?; Cyrano de Bergerac, Cyranose de Bric-a-Brack; Barbara Frietchie, Barbara Fidgety; Sappho, Sapolio* (a famous soap product at the time). These travesties did so much to publicize the plays which they parodied that Broadway shows began using whatever influence they could summon in order to get Weber and Fields to satirize their productions. In fact, the producer of *Cyrano de Bergerac* had Weber and Fields see his show before it came to New York so that the production—and the Weber and Fields travesty—might run simultaneously.

Always after the travesties were Weber and Fields with their broad slapstick humor in German dialect and outrageous English, their peculiar verbal exchanges, their low burlesque humor—and with poor Weber always a helpless victim at the hands of the tyrant Fields. To their comedy was added the horseplay of other comedians, including the pie-in-the-face routine which in another decade would become a staple of comedy on two-reel "flickers." And always there were the specialties of the stars—with more and more stars gathered into the fold as the years went by, and some of them of the first magnitude.

In *Hurly Burly,* David Warfield made his first appearance in New York as a mimic and a comedian in Jewish dialect (a strange beginning for an actor who would develop with David Belasco as a tragedian). Fay Templeton here became the first star to be hired by Weber and Fields, at a salary of $400 a week. *Hurly Burly* yielded the first two hit songs to come out of these Weber and Fields extravaganzas: "Keep Away from Emmaline," sung by Miss Templeton, and "Kiss Me Honey, Do" (sometimes also known as "Dinah"), sung to Miss Templeton by Peter F. Dailey.

An even greater star was to be seen and heard in *Whirl-i-Gig:* the fabulous Lillian Russell. She was already an idol of the New York theater by virtue of appearances at Tony Pastor's Music Hall and, in Union Square, in operettas and various musicals. She was not easy to get. Weber and Fields had to pay her $1,250 a week with a guarantee of thirty-five weeks of appearances. She was worth the price. Though she had a small, piping voice (the eminent music critic James Gibbons Huneker once compared it to a teakettle), she was a ravishing sight on the stage—and men flocked to see the one whom many regarded as the most beautiful woman on the stage at the time. For her debut in a Weber and Fields extravaganza, Miss Russell sang her first "coon" song—"When Chloe Sings a Song" (described in the sheet music as a "southern plantation song"). Peter F. Dailey sang "Say You Love Me, Sue," a traditional love ballad. It was in this production that *Sappho* became *Sapolio,* one of the better of the travesties.

*Fiddle-De-Dee* marked the Weber and Fields debut of De Wolf Hopper, already the grand homme of the American musical theater. Perhaps the most famous song ever to come out of the Weber and Fields Music Hall is found in this production: "Ma Blushin' Rosie," sung by Miss Templeton. (In later years it became an Al Jolson specialty.) Two other songs were of special interest, "Tell Us, Pretty Ladies" and "Come Back, My Honey Boy, to Me" (the latter sung at John Stromberg's funeral in 1902).

In *Hoity Toity* Miss Templeton sang "I'm a Respectable Working Girl." She did not like this number and was reluctant to use it. Nevertheless, it proved so popular with the audiences that she had to repeat it three or four times at each performance. Fritz Williams, in his first appearance as a regular of the Weber and Fields company, introduced another hit, "De Pullman Porter's Ball."

Before the curtain rose on *Twirly Whirly,* John Stromberg—who had written all the music for these extravaganzas up to this time—committed suicide. In his pocket was the manuscript of his last song, and probably his greatest, "Come Down Ma Evenin' Star." Lillian Russell sang it on opening night—and broke down in the middle of the rendition. From that time on, that song became inextricably identified with Miss Russell. Since Stromberg's death left much of the score for the production yet to be written, the task was taken over by William T. Francis, who succeeded Stromberg not only as composer but also as the conductor. In *Twirly Whirly* William Collier and Louise Allen made their Music Hall debuts. Second in importance to "Come Down Ma Evenin' Star" in this score was "Dream on, Dream of Me," also by Stromberg.

*Whoop-De-Do* was the first of the shows for which William T. Francis created the entire score. He never measured up to Stromberg. No more hit songs came from these productions. But *Whoop-De-Do* was strong on satire and travesty and such routines as "Looney Park" and "Waffles."

*Higgeldy Piggeldy* saw the tragic breaking up of the inimitable team of Weber and Fields. Fields would go on to become a producer, and from this time on Weber would have to go it alone in his rowdy burlesque scenes. Weber's partner as producer was young Florenz Ziegfeld, Jr., then comparatively new to the business; in three years' time he would begin to make history with his *Follies*. And the production marked the first appearance at the Music Hall of Anna Held, whom Ziegfeld had imported from France to New York for his first Broadway production—*A Parlor Match* in 1896. One year after that she became Mrs. Florenz Ziegfeld. Here, as earlier, she was— as Marjorie Farnsworth described her—"the epitome of Gallic spice and naughtiness," what with her dark, luminous eyes, baby face, eighteen-inch waist, and piquant French accent.

*Twiddle Twaddle* had a rousing burlesque of *The Girl of the Golden West* (retitled *The Squaman's Girl of the Golden West*); and *Hip! Hip! Hooray,* had one of a popular play of the time, *The Thief.* Among the newcomers to the cast were Trixie Friganza in the former, and Velaska Suratt in the latter—each destined to become stars later on.

Then there was a long hiatus before another such extravaganza was produced. This took place in 1912 in *Hokey Pokey,* a sentimental occasion indeed, for it marked the first time Weber and Fields were reunited. This show was a valiant attempt to revive the brilliance and the abandon of the old Weber and Fields burlesques. The overture consisted of all the John Stromberg favorites. The production included a travesty in the old Weber and Fields style. And the cast included such old Music Hall favorites as Lillian Russell, Fay Templeton, and Bessie Clayton, among others. Inevitably, Lillian Russell sang "Come Down Ma Evenin' Star" and sent many in the audience into tears. *Hokey Pokey* did quite well at the box office, but it was apparent that the glorious day of the Weber and Fields shows was over for good.

The only other time Weber and Fields were on the same platform was in 1932, when they were honored by the theater world on the occasion of the golden jubilee of their partnership. Lew Fields died in 1941; his partner, Weber, died a year later.

The shows commented on above represent the cream of the crop, but there were many other productions during the years that Weber and Fields worked together so fruitfully. Those that have been omitted from comment were: *The Geezer* (1896); *Under the Red Globe* (1897); *The Glad Hand* (1897); *Pousse Café* (1897); *The Con-Currers* (1898); *Cyranose de Bric-a-Brack* (1898); *Catherine* (1899); and *Helter Skelter* (1899). John Stromberg was the composer for all these productions, from which came one important song, "How I Love My Lou," first introduced in *The Glad Hand,* where it proved so popular that it was repeated in *Pousse Café*.

WEST SIDE STORY (1957), *a musical play, with book by Arthur Laurents, based on a conception of Jerome Robbins. Lyrics by Stephen Sondheim. Music by Leonard Bernstein. Presented by Robert E. Griffith and Harold S. Prince at the Winter Garden on September 26. Directed and with choreography by Jerome Robbins. Cast included Carol Lawrence, Larry Kert, and Chita Rivera (734 performances).*

*West Side Story* is one of the crowning masterworks of the American musical theater—both on the stage and on the screen. In spite of this, plans to produce it at the World's Fair in Brussels and in the Soviet Union collapsed because of opposition from some high American government quarters to present to foreign audiences so sordid and realistic a portrait of American life. But wherever else *West Side Story* played in Europe it was welcomed not so much as a criticism of America as a unified stage concept of which any country could be proud. One of the highest accolades a popular American musical production can receive came to *West Side Story* in 1968 when it entered the regular repertory of Vienna's distinguished opera house, the Volksoper.

It took many years for the idea to be fertilized into a musical play. The idea was born in 1949 with Jerome Robbins, who discussed it with Leonard Bernstein. They wanted to write a musical with depth, perception, and a social point of view—a view which would rise far above the level of mediocrity to which so many Broadway musicals succumbed. The first idea was something to be called *East Side Story,* pointing up the poison of racial prejudice by treating a love story between a Jewish girl and a Catholic boy on New York's East Side. But as Robbins and Bernstein analyzed this theme in depth, they recognized that an interracial subject was "old hat." The project then remained stillborn, or so it seemed. Then, about six years later, Robbins and Bernstein returned to their idea because of an exciting subject. A huge migration of Puerto Ricans into New York had taken place, creating intense hostility between New Yorkers and the islanders, a hostility that affected the young even more than it did the old. *East Side Story* now became *West Side Story* (Puerto Ricans settled, for the most part, on the extreme West Side of New York); the Jewish-Catholic theme was changed into the American-Puerto Rican problem. Arthur Laurents became interested in developing this idea into a text, and Stephen Sondheim, a writer for television who never before had contributed anything to the theater, became Leonard Bernstein's lyricist.

From the very beginning, Robbins and Bernstein had planned to make their musical a contemporary treatment of Shakespeare's *Romeo and Juliet*. They considered this idea even more serviceable for their Puerto Rican theme. And so, Italy's Verona became present-day Manhattan. The feuding Capulets and Montagues are re-created in two teen-age gangs, the "Jets" and the "Sharks." Romeo is a city boy named Tony; Juliet is a Puerto Rican girl, Maria. The balcony scene becomes an idyll on the fire escape of a Puerto Rican tenement, and, as in Shakespeare, the love affair has a tragic ending for the lovers.

The entire action takes place in two days, but within this brief period of time there is uncovered all the ugliness, bitterness, neuroticism, savagery, hate, and turbulence in the lives of young people of the city street. But there are also flashes of beauty, love, and hope that also sometimes—however fleetingly—touch them.

The Jets are a teen-age gang of American boys determined not only to check but to destroy the growth of Puerto Rican population and influence on their block. Riff, the leader of the Jets, speaks in "Jet Song" in no uncertain terms of this determination. They are opposed by a Puerto Rican gang, the Sharks, led by Bernardo (Ken Le Roy). Riff gets the support of Tony (Larry Kert), who was the founder and leader of the Jets before turning over the job to Riff. Both gangs meet at a dance in the neighborhood gym, where in song ("Dance at the Gym") and in choreography their violent hostility to each other is reflected. At the dance Tony meets the lovely Maria (Carol Lawrence). She is Bernardo's sister who has just arrived from Puerto Rico to marry Chino. With Tony and Maria it is a case of love at first sight, as they realize at once. They pledge eternal love on the tenement fire escape, in what is surely the most famous single musical number to come from Bernstein's score, the love ballad "Tonight." Then they plan to meet in the bridal shop where Maria is employed when the place is closed to customers to improvise a mock marriage—with dress dummies as wedding attendants.

Meanwhile, the two gangs leave for a nearby drugstore to name the place, time, and weapons for a big "rumble," deciding which one of the two gangs will be dominant in the neighborhood. Through Tony's influence, an agreement is reached to have a boy represent each of the two gangs, and have them fight it out to a finish the following day. Having learned that his sister is interested in Tony, Bernardo comes to him with dire threats. This inspires a fight, which develops into a giant "rumble" between the two gangs. Riff is killed. Blinded by anger and bitterness at the death of his friend, Tony murders Bernardo with Riff's knife. And this in turn inspires Chino—Maria's intended husband—to shoot and kill Tony.

Bernstein once confessed that the writing of *West Side Story* was like walking a tightrope between too much realism and too much poetry and symbolism. What he said about the problem of choreographing the "Rumble" ballet applied to every phase of the production. "If it had been too balletic, we would have fallen off on one side—all you'd have is just another ballet. And if it had been too realistic, we would have fallen off on the other side—and there would have been no poetry to it, no art." To solve this problem, the authors had to create a new form of musical theater in which the drama is projected not only through music but even more forcefully through the dance. From the very opening scene—when, against the bleak background of warehouse windows, the two gangs drift into view in a sinister dance movement—the bitter story unfolds with what Walter Kerr described as a "catastrophic roar." The dance carries the action forward up to the shattering climax of "Rumble," savage teen-age warfare interpreted in ballet terms. In "Cool," on the other hand, dance reveals the deceptive facade of relaxation behind which these teen-age gangsters reveal their inner frenzy, while "Somewhere" is a dream ballet that introduces a touch of softness and tenderness. In short, the theatrical substance of *West Side Story* is realized, as John Martin pointed out, "not in talked plot but in moving bodies. The muscles of trained dancers are tensed and untensed and tensed again, stimulated by emotional tensions and stimulating them still further in return. These tensions are transferred automatically, across the footlights and into the musculature of every spectator in the house, willy nilly. The cast acts and reacts in terms of movement, and that is the most direct medium that exists for the conveying of inner states of feeling."

But though the choreography was as basic to the overall structure as it was remarkable for its originality of concept, *West Side Story* would hardly have become the enduring stage masterwork it is if it were not all "of one piece," as the critic of *Theatre Arts* reported. "Nearly everything is economical, streamlined and vital. . . . This not only results in a sense of immediacy, but actually pushes the American musical theater several steps closer to that ultimate goal of integration of component parts. . . . The dance is fully as

important here as the spoken word in carrying the taut story line; and . . .
the exciting musical score complements both extremely well."

There could be no question that that musical score—the best that Leonard
Bernstein has done for the musical theater—is one of the powerful assets
to this grim tragedy. The excitable music of the overture, with its mood of
grim foreboding, is vivid and dramatic tone-painting. Much of the rest of the
score is similarly high-tensioned, but a great deal of it is painted in lighter
hues. The wonderful love ballad of Tony and Maria, "Tonight," has already
been mentioned. But there are other unforgettable lyrical episodes: Tony's
hymn of love, "Maria"; Maria's sudden consciousness of her attractiveness in
"I Feel Pretty"; the ballad "Somewhere," sung off stage. While neither the
play nor the choreography has an element of humor—all is stark tragedy—
Bernstein's musical numbers include two excellent comic songs. In "America"
the Shark girls speak of the joyous life encountered by Puerto Ricans in their
new country, while "Gee, Officer Krupke!" is a satirical commentary by several
members of the Jets on the problem of juvenile delinquency.

After *West Side Story* ended its run of 734 performances in New York,
it went on an extended tour of the United States. It returned to New York on
April 27, 1960, to begin a new run—this time of 249 performances. An
excellent revival was given at the Music Theater of the Lincoln Center for
the Performing Arts in New York in 1968. The motion-picture adaptation—
which made no compromise with the high standards set by the stage presentation—proved cinematic art of the first order. Produced by Robert Wise for
Mirisch Pictures, in association with Seven Arts Productions—and starring
Natalie Wood and Richard Beymer—it was released in 1961, to become one
of the greatest box-office successes in the history of American screen musicals,
and captured ten Academy Awards, including one as the best motion picture
of the year.

> WHAT MAKES SAMMY RUN? (1964), *a musical comedy, with book by
> Budd and Stuart Schulberg, based on Budd Schulberg's novel of the same
> name. Lyrics and music by Ervin Drake. Presented by Joseph Cates at the
> 44th Street Theater on February 27. Directed by Abe Burrows. Dances by
> Matt Mattox. Cast included Steve Lawrence, Sally Ann Howes, and Robert
> Alda (540 performances).*

In 1941, Budd Schulberg published a devastating novel about a Hollywood
tycoon entitled *What Makes Sammy Run?* Young Schulberg knew what he
was writing about. Besides himself being a screen writer—and therefore
having had a firsthand knowledge of what makes a top man of a Hollywood
studio "tick"—he was also the son of one of the industry's giant producers,

B. P. Schulberg. The novel led to a good deal of speculation as to which single producer he had in mind in presenting the life of a ruthless go-getter who allows nobody and nothing to stand in the way of his success. Actually this was not the story of any one man but a composite of many men—all those tycoons who did not hesitate to destroy and devastate everything and everyone near them as they climbed the rough mountainside of the Hollywood industry.

Twenty-three years after this novel became a best-seller, it was finally made into a Broadway musical. Once again the central interest lay in the principal character, Sammy Glick, who rises from the lower depths of his social and economic environment to the uppermost echelon of the Hollywood industry—only, in the end, to have the taste of victory turn sour in his mouth. He is a man whose passion is success, whose driving force is ambition; a man who, without the slightest twinge of conscience, exploits everybody who can help him reach his goal. He is a thorough superegotist, and what makes him run is the lust for power.

He is, of course, also the center of interest in the musical comedy. Sammy Glick (Steve Lawrence) starts out as a copy boy in the city room of a New York newspaper, where his questionable integrity makes its presence felt immediately when he steals copy for a radio column, and then explains to his boss, Al Mannheim (Robert Alda), that his only motive was to improve the quality of the newspaper. From copy boy, Sammy maneuvers and connives to get the best agent in town to market one of his scripts. It is not long before he has found himself a job as a writer of scripts in Hollywood for World Wide Pictures, which is filming *The Queen of Sheba*. At the studio he meets Kit, a secretary (Sally Ann Howes)—a quiet, decent girl whose main interest is to solve the problems of the men she meets. She becomes interested in Sammy, who finds her attractive—and useful. Sammy's first concern, however, is not romance, but to get ahead in the business—no matter what. He manages to reach the main producer, Sidney Fineman (Arny Freeman), to whom he sells the idea of filming *Monsoon,* a South Sea Island story, stolen straight from Maugham's *Rain.* At a private screen showing, *Monsoon* makes a profound impression on the studio head, H. L. Harrington (Walter Klavun); Sammy is now looked upon as movietown's new genius and is elevated to the rank of producer by Fineman. Sammy now finds that Harrington's daughter, Laurette (Bernice Massi), is a sultry and seductive young lady who can not only provide him with sexual stimulation but become an important ally in Sammy's upward climb in his profession. Al Mannheim, whom Sammy now regards as a friend, warns Kit about Sammy's hypocrisy and double-dealings; he entreats her not to trust Sammy. Sammy overhears this and annihilates his friend with stinging words, which brings about an immediate rupture in their friendship. Then Sammy invites Kit to spend a weekend with him in Tijuana —a token of the sincerity of his love. Kit is willing, but just then Laurette telephones Sammy to come to her room. He finds a pretext to leave Kit suddenly. On arriving for his rendezvous with Laurette, he discovers that, quixotically, she no longer is interested in him but prefers to go off with a friend.

Several years pass. Sammy is Hollywood's genius, the boy who has produced one screen triumph after another. He is attending a gala premiere of one of his pictures at Grauman's Chinese Theater. This production also proves a winner. With mock humility, Sammy insists that all the credit for his great success really belongs to the man who helped him become a producer —Sidney Fineman.

Al Mannheim, back in New York, is busy writing a play about Sammy. In spite of all of Sammy's telephone calls urging him to come back to Hollywood, Al remains deaf. He has had enough of Sammy. Sammy now pays a visit to New York to give a grand party. When his brother, Seymour, crashes in to beg him to visit their mother on her birthday, he strikes him and throws him out. Sammy forgets all about his mother to devote his concentrated interest on selling himself to Laurette, who is rather fascinated by Sammy's cold-blooded ruthlessness. Sammy also uses his party to convince Laurette's father to fire Sidney Fineman, who, Sammy insists, has outlived his usefulness to the studio. All this endears Sammy to Laurette further, to the point where she consents to marry him.

Back in Hollywood, Sammy is told that Fineman has committed suicide; also that Al and Kit have left Hollywood for good and are planning to get married. Sammy shrugs off such developments. After all, has he not reached the top, at last, even to the point of capturing the boss's daughter as his wife? He even assumes a stoic air when he finds his bride in bed with a French movie star, by singing "Some Days Everything Goes Wrong," as the final curtain descends. For even now, Sammy has no intention of stopping to run.

Steve Lawrence's thoroughly engaging performance as the contemptible Sammy came as a surprise—the New York Drama Critics poll picked him out as the best male performer in a musical for that season. Steve Lawrence up to now had established his reputation as a singer, had built himself into a star in nightclubs, over television, and on records solely through his voice and personal charm. *What Makes Sammy Run?* was his first attempt to invade the Broadway stage. He proved himself thoroughly capable in projecting character, in delivering lines effectively, and of course in making the most of the two best songs in the score: "My Hometown," and his duet with Kit, "A Room Without Windows." Kit's song, "Something to Live For" (when she first becomes aware of her attachment to Al), is another strong musical number. In a satirical vein—and it is one of the best episodes in the entire production—is "Lites—Camera—Platitude," in which, through a series of improvised parodies, Sammy, Kit, and Al make a mockery of the kind of clichés to which most movie plots succumb. Beyond this sequence, most of the humor in the play came from Abe Burrows' astute sense of timing in his direction, and in some scintillating dialogue with the accent on Hollywood; while a good deal of additional interest was created in the production of effective dances staged by Matt Mattox, and in the thoroughly polished performances of Robert Alda and Sally Ann Howes.

*What Makes Sammy Run?* had enough strong points of audience interest to warrant a much longer run than it enjoyed—though 540 performances is certainly a figure not to be taken lightly. Unfortunately for the production, Steve Lawrence—the main attraction in the show—began to acquire the habit of missing performances (in four months he missed twenty-four performances), and after several months it became obvious that his heart was no longer in his work. Sally Ann Howes left the show, and her role was turned over to Bernice Massi who, though she had proved excellent as Laurette, was not suited to play the less sophisticated Kit. Budd Schulberg complained that too much ad-libbing was being introduced in the play. On one occasion Lawrence tried to delete one of the songs. There was a continual threat of legal action—now by one party, now by another. All this played havoc with a production that might very well have doubled the number of performances it was capable of surviving. And though a run of over five hundred performances usually brings in a very decent profit, *What Makes Sammy Run?* closed down with a deficit of almost $300,000 on a $400,000 investment—so badly had the audience interest in the show deteriorated during the run.

*What Makes Sammy Run?* represented Ervin Drake's initiation into the Broadway theater. Born in New York City on April 3, 1919, he was educated at the College of the City of New York, where he wrote some of its varsity shows and edited one of its magazines. His musical training took place privately with Tibor Serly and Jacob Drucman at the Juilliard School of Music. His first successes came by way of television, where he sometimes served as producer but most often as writer, composer, and lyricist for innumerable attractions. In 1943, he wrote words and music for the hit song, "The Rickety Rickshaw Man" and the lyrics for "Tico-Tico" to a Brazilian melody, which was introduced in the Walt Disney motion picture *Saludos Amigos* and popularized by Xavier Cugat. He also contributed lyrics and music to other motion pictures. Among his greatest hit songs were "I Believe" (which he wrote with Irvin Graham, Jimmy Shirl, and Al Stillman), a leader in 1953; in 1961, "It Was a Very Good Year," made famous in 1965 by Frank Sinatra; and in 1968, "Father of the Girls," introduced and popularized by Perry Como.

WHERE'S CHARLEY? (1948), *a musical comedy, with book by George Abbott, based on Brandon Thomas' farce* Charley's Aunt. *Lyrics and music by Frank Loesser. Presented by Feuer and Martin, in association with Gwen Rickard (Mrs. Ray Bolger), at the St. James Theater on October 11. Directed by George Abbott. Dances by George Balanchine. Cast included Ray Bolger, Allyn McLerie, Doretta Morrow, and Byron Palmer (792 performances).*

Frank Loesser had long established a solid footing as one of the ace songwriters in Hollywood when he made his first step into the Broadway musical theater with *Where's Charley?* Cy Feuer, head of the music division at the Republic studios in Hollywood, was the one responsible for encouraging Loesser to take that step. Feuer, in conjunction with Ernest Martin, had acquired the rights to Brandon Thomas' 1893 farce, *Charley's Aunt,* for musical-comedy treatment, and in their first venture at Broadway producing, they planned to star Ray Bolger in it. Feuer had the highest esteem for Loesser's gift at writing lyrics and music. But it took a good deal of plodding on his part to get him to win over Loesser's interest in a vehicle which had been such a sturdy war horse of the professional, amateur, and even public-school stage for half a century. (It had also been made into motion pictures several times, once starring Jack Benny.) Loesser was convinced that this play was so tired that nothing could put new life into it. But Feuer was Loesser's very close friend, and Feuer was persuasive—and Loesser eventually yielded. Nor did Loesser come to regret this decision. His entry into the Broadway musical theater came with a production that had a run of almost eight hundred performances.

George Abbott made the musical-comedy adaptation with only some minor changes in the all too familiar plot. The setting is Oxford, England. Two of the university students—Charles Wykeham (Ray Bolger) and Jack Chesney (Byron Palmer)—are planning to invite their girls, Amy Spettigue (Allyn McLerie) and Kitty Verdun (Doretta Morrow), to the university. The young men's intentions are thoroughly honorable, for they plan to propose marriage. But Stephen Spettigue (Horace Cooper), the guardian of the girls, refuses to give them permission to visit their boyfriends unless they go accompanied by a chaperon. Charley's aunt, Donna Lucia D'Alvadorez, a wealthy widow, is due soon from Brazil; she is chosen to fill the role of chaperon. But Jack is suddenly faced with a major disaster: his father has become so burdened with debts that Jack must leave school and marry the wealthy Donna Lucia. Fortunately for him, Donna Lucia is delayed in Brazil, a development about which his father is completely unaware. In order to have the freedom to see their girls, the two students contrive to have one of them, Charley, impersonate the aunt and act as chaperon—at the same time allowing him to do his own wooing at those convenient moments when he can dispense with his female disguise. Dressed up as the wealthy aunt—in black dress, gray wig, and lace gloves—Charley is being hunted by the fathers of the two students. As if matters were not sufficiently complex, the wealthy Brazilian widow does make an appearance at last. But she is wise enough to size up the situation at first glance and to assume a false identity. Through her efforts, she gets the two fathers to consent to their sons marrying the girls of their choice—while she herself lands a husband in Jack's father, who is thus relieved of his financial problems.

George Abbott's musical-comedy version was a bountiful source of entertainment, even though the sight of a man cavorting in woman's dress and assuming woman's mannerisms was not calculated to amuse a sophisticated audience. One of the main reasons for the success of this musical was Ray Bolger's ingratiating performance as Charley and as the "aunt." In a ladies' room, in an athletic love scene with a vigorous man, while fussing around with an affected feminine air, Bolger always succeeded in being amusing without stooping to Varsity Show vulgarity or offending good taste. His adept tap dancing added still another dimension to his performance. And he had a charm uniquely his in putting over a song, as in "Once in Love with Amy" (his amatory tribute to his girl friend), in which he had the audience participate in singing the chorus.

This business of having the audience join in the singing of "Once in Love with Amy"—a routine that stopped the show regularly, sometimes for as much as twenty minutes—was not in George Abbott's script but was the result of pure chance. At one of the first matinees, Cy Feuer's seven-year-old son was sitting in the front row. The boy knew everything about the show, including all its songs, having witnessed rehearsals and having watched them performed at his home. At this matinee, Ray Bolger momentarily forgot some of the lines of "Once in Love with Amy." Without any self-consciousness, he asked: "What were those lyrics, anyway?" At this point, Feuer's son got up from his seat and sang the words. The audience was delighted. Ray Bolger, veteran trouper that he was, decided then and there to ask the audience to join him in singing the song, teaching the number line by line. The audience was even more delighted. Ray Bolger decided to keep this business in the show.

As good and as popular as "Once in Love with Amy" was, it was not the hit song from the Loesser score. That honor went to the love duet of Jack Chesney and Kitty Verdun, "My Darling, My Darling," which for several weeks' running usurped the number-one position on the Hit Parade. Other fetching Loesser tunes included a vigorous march number, "The New Ashmolean Marching Society and Student Conservatory Band," and "Make a Miracle," the latter in Amy Spettigue's and Charley's sprightly rendition. Abe Laufe points out in *Broadway's Greatest Musicals* that "Make a Miracle" was one of the first songs in a Broadway show in which Loesser resorted to a pet technique of "using one vocalist to begin a chorus and then have the second vocalist cut into the song before the chorus had ended, starting on a new set of lyrics." Laufe went on to explain: "For example, as Bolger sang, he kept trying to gain Amy's attention; Amy's lyrics, however, showed that her mind was elsewhere, and the humor of the song increased with each new chorus and each new interruption of one singer by the other."

Despite the fact that there had been a number of motion pictures based on *Charley's Aunt,* Hollywood did not hesitate to film the musical comedy. It was done by Warner Brothers, released in 1952, and brought both Ray Bolger and Allyn McLerie from Broadway to the screen to fill their stage roles.

**WHIRL-I-GIG.** *See* WEBER AND FIELDS EXTRAVAGANZAS.

**WHOOP-DE-DO.** *See* WEBER AND FIELDS EXTRAVAGANZAS.

**WHOOPEE** (1928), *a musical comedy, with book by William Anthony Mc-Guire, based on Owen Davis' Broadway comedy* The Nervous Wreck. *Lyrics by Gus Kahn. Music by Walter Donaldson. Presented by Florenz Zieg-feld at the New Amsterdam Theater on December 4. Directed by William Anthony McGuire. Dances by Seymour Felix. Cast included Eddie Cantor, Ruth Etting, and Tamara Geva (379 performances).*

Henry Williams, a hypochondriac (Eddie Cantor), leaves for California to recover his health, accompanied by a valiseful of pills. Out West, at the Bar M Ranch at Mission Rest, Henry gets involved with a girl and Indians. Wanenis, believed to be a half-breed (Paul Gregory), and Sally Morgan (Frances Upton) are in love. When she is compelled to marry the local sheriff, Bob Wells (Jack Rutherfold), she tries to elude this disaster by inducing Henry to elope with her. They are pursued by the sheriff to an Indian reservation, where it is discovered that Wanenis is no Indian at all. Henry loses the girl, and so does the sheriff.

Ziegfeld originally intended to cast Ruby Keeler in the principal female role opposite Eddie Cantor; in fact, the contracts had been signed. Since Miss Keeler up to now had concentrated only on nightclubs, this starring appearance with Eddie Cantor represented a significant development in her career. But Al Jolson, who had then recently married Ruby Keeler, and who was forced to remain in Hollywood to do a picture, pleaded with his wife not to take on the musical, but to come out to the Coast and join him. Ruby allowed herself to be swayed. She abandoned *Whoopee* and was replaced by Ruth Etting, a comparative newcomer then among singers. *Whoopee* placed her solidly in the star category—especially when she sang "Love Me or Leave Me," which she made so famous (and vice versa) that henceforth it became inextricably identified with her. When her screen biography was filmed, it was titled after this song. Ruth Etting also sang "I'm Bringing a Red, Red Rose."

As for Cantor's numbers, they included a song destined to grow into one of his all-time favorites: "Makin' Whoopee," made up of half a dozen amusing verses of topical interest.

Florenz Ziegfeld went all out for his favorite star to give him a lavish production. Two scenes were particularly eye-arresting: one set in the Grand Canyon; and the other on an Indian reservation, with the Ziegfeld girls wearing feather headdresses.

While *Whoopee* had a successful Broadway run of about a year, it would have lasted much longer, since even the last performances played to crowded theaters. What happened was that Ziegfeld went broke and had to sell the movie rights to Samuel Goldwyn; he also had to close down the show to allow Eddie Cantor to act as consultant for and star in the movie adaptation (Cantor's first appearance on the screen). The picture was released by United Artists in 1930. Eddie Cantor, of course, sang "Makin' Whoopee." But he also introduced a new Eddie Cantor favorite which had been written especially for the movie by Gus Kahn and Walter Donaldson, "My Baby Just Cares for Me." This number was done at the insistence of Samuel Goldwyn, who demanded from the songwriters that it be completed in a single day. They delivered the song in time. When they brought it to Goldwyn, the motion-picture producer inquired if the song were suitable for dancing. Gus Kahn replied by humming the melody, grabbing Goldwyn, and beginning to dance with him around his office.

WILDCAT (1960), *a musical comedy, with book by N. Richard Nash. Lyrics by Carolyn Leigh. Music by Cy Coleman. Presented by Michael Kidd and N. Richard Nash at the Alvin Theater on December 16. Directed by Michael Kidd. Cast included Lucille Ball, Paula Stewart, and Keith Andes (171 performances).*

Lucille Ball—onetime stenographer, soda-fountain girl, and fashion model—had had a long career in the musical theater before she was starred in *Wildcat*. Her first stage appearance had been as a chorus girl in the Jerome Kern musical *Stepping Stones* in 1923, in its pre-Broadway tryouts. She continued to occupy a humble place in the musical theater for the next decade. Then she went to Hollywood in 1933 to appear in her first movie, *Roman Scandals*, starring Eddie Cantor. Her innumerable appearances on the screen after that hardly gave any indication of star quality. It was not until she came to television in the series "I Love Lucy" that she proved herself one of the foremost co-mediennes of our time, and television's number-one attraction for several consecutive years. Now a box-office attraction to be reckoned with, she returned to Broadway after her long absence to assume the principal role in a musical fashioned for her. As long as she stayed in the show, it was a sellout. But when the fatigue of eight performances a week became too oppressive—and when the novelty of appearing on a Broadway stage had worn off—Miss Ball decided to call it a day and withdrew from the production. Since *Wildcat* was not a very good musical to begin with, it had virtually no audience appeal whatsoever without its star; and so it had to close down.

Lucille Ball deserved a better vehicle for her Broadway return. The writers concocted for her a rough-and-tumble part that contributed no glamour to the production. (Her costume for most of the time was a blue shirt and a dirty pair of dungarees.) Her remarkable gifts at mimicry and comedy were rarely touched upon. There was some amusing business of her trying to get her Stutz Bearcat to run and finally frightening it into movement by the thunder-ous sound she produced on a drum. And there was some hilarity in the fiesta scene, where, finally discarding her work clothes, she was seen in an out-landishly ornamented gown, and with feathers all over her head. This is about the height to which the comedy aspired.

When she had something effective to work with—as she had in the vigorous and catchy tune she sang with her sister, Jane, "Hey, Look Me Over"—*Wildcat* seized the attention of the audience. At moments here and there she showed how effectively she could deliver a funny line, that she could dance, and that her very presence was electrifying. But the opportuni-ties offered her were regrettably lean pickings.

There were one or two good production numbers choreographed by Michael Kidd, the best being toward the end of the first act, following Lucille Ball's rendition of "Give a Little Whistle." And there was a piece of stage business which Howard Taubman in *The New York Times* called "the most stirring event of the evening." He wrote: "As Joe and the company sang

'Corduroy Road,' a wood hut was dismantled. Part of it was used to make a road, and another part went into the construction of a grand-looking derrick with drilling apparatus in action. It was like watching a Christmas stunt for the kiddies."

The action takes place in Centavo City in 1912, where oil has been discovered. When Wildcat Jackson (Lucille Ball) comes to town with her lame sister, Jane (Paula Stewart), she wants some of the action. She uses her powers of persuasion to convince the townspeople she owns some oil leases and manages to get Joe Dynamite (Keith Andes) to become her foreman. Then she acquires some oil leases from a local hermit, Sookie. Her foreman, Joe, becomes convinced that those leases are worthless. When he tries to leave his job, Wildcat convinces the sheriff that Joe is a fugitive from justice. He is arrested, but then released in Wildcat's custody. Drilling begins. But it is not long before Joe and his men leave their jobs in disgust, convinced that the land will yield no oil. Thoroughly depressed, Wildcat throws a stick of dynamite into the well hole to blow up the whole works once and for all. The explosion produces an oil gusher. And it brings Wildcat into Joe's arms.

*Wildcat* brought the songwriting team of Carolyn Leigh and Cy Coleman to Broadway for the first time—and with a serviceable score. "Hey, Look Me Over" would have been a sure-fire hit, even without the lusty presentation of Lucille Ball and Paula Stewart. In a more subdued and poignant vein, Wildcat had another effective number in "That's What I Want for Janie." Also of more than evanescent appeal in this score were Wildcat's "Give a Little Whistle" and Joe Dynamite's "You've Come Home."

WILDFLOWER (1923), *a musical comedy, with book and lyrics by Otto Harbach and Oscar Hammerstein II. Music by Vincent Youmans and Herbert Stothart. Presented by Arthur Hammerstein at the Casino Theater on February 7. Directed by Oscar Eagle. Dances by David Bennett. Cast included Edith Day, Guy Robertson, and Evelyn Cavanaugh (477 performances).*

Certainly the major significance of *Wildflower* springs from the fact that it represented the first major Broadway musical success for two giant figures of the American musical stage: Oscar Hammerstein II and Vincent Youmans. It was a charming play, rich with atmospheric interest, and enlivened by the delightful characterization of the fiery, hot-tempered little peasant maid Nina Benedetto (Edith Day). The death of a distant uncle brings her a legacy, but only if she can control her temper and act like a lady for a six-month period. Failing to fulfill this provision meant that Nina must let the fortune pass on to her detestable cousin Bianca (Evelyn Cavanaugh)—a thought so distasteful to Nina that she finds the discipline to carry out the demands of the legacy, even to the point of temporarily deserting her lover, Guido (Guy Robertson).

The New York *World* described *Wildflower* as "a musical comedy of delightful manner and really gorgeous melodies," adding that "these song numbers not only are prepared with taste and understanding, but they seem a most essential part in the make-up of the whole. . . . Its music and tempo are extraordinary." The two main songs are still remembered: the title number, introduced by Guido, and "Bambalina," first presented by Nina and an ensemble. The latter described an eccentric country fiddler who enjoyed confusing dancers by stopping midway in his rendition of a dance number.

WISH YOU WERE HERE (1952), *a musical comedy, with book by Arthur Kober and Joshua Logan, based on Kober's Broadway comedy* Having a Wonderful Time. *Lyrics and music by Harold Rome. Presented by Leland Hayward and Joshua Logan at the Imperial Theater on June 25. Directed and with dances by Joshua Logan. Cast included Patricia Marand, Sheila Bond, and Jack Cassidy (598 performances).*

This was Harold Rome's first musical comedy, all his previous associations with the Broadway stage being in revues. *Wish You Were Here* was a musical adaptation of an amusing and at times touching play about adult summer camps and the romances they inspire; and the main love interest of the original production was carried over into the musical, whose characters are all obviously Jewish. At Camp Karefree, in the Berkshires, Teddy Stern (Patricia Marand), from the Bronx, meets and falls in love with the camp waiter, Chick Miller (Jack Cassidy), a young law student earning summer money in order to pay for his winter's tuition at law school. For Chick, Teddy throws over her old beau, Herman Fabricant (Harry Clark), a prosperous businessman. What follows is a warmly appealing and sympathetic account of two young people in love, their problems and dreams. All this is placed against the setting of a summer camp where the pursuit of happiness and love is relentless and around the clock, stimulated by the ready wisecracks and the indefatigable activity of Itchy, the social director (Sidney Armus), and the untiring quest of females by the camp Romeo, Pinky Harris (Paul Valentine). Pinky Harris is responsible for a misunderstanding between Teddy and Chick, when the latter is led to believe by circumstantial evidence that Teddy has spent the night in Pinky's cabin. But when the matter is cleared up, the romance between Teddy and Chick can continue without further disturbance.

One of the more striking attractions of the production was a large and permanent swimming pool, built at a cost of $15,000, to serve for the first-act finale.

Chick Miller's song "Wish You Were Here" was the hit song of the production and one of Rome's must successful musical numbers up to that time. It appeared on the Hit Parade for twenty weeks, while Eddie Fisher's recording for RCA Victor sold over a million discs. A secondary hit was "Where Did the Night Go?", a duet by Teddy and Chick (supplemented by the ensemble). This was a difficult number for Rome to write. He could not come up with a serviceable idea for a place in the show when the evening's dancing in the social hall had ended and a spot number was needed for his two principal characters. One evening, after entertaining his friends at his home, Rome heard one of his guests remark: "Where did the night go?" Rome immediately knew that this was precisely the subject he needed for his song, and he completed the number that same night. The score also included some amusing sidelights on adult camp life in "Ballad of a Social Director" and "Don José of Far Rockaway."

THE WIZARD OF OZ (1903), *a musical fantasy, with book and lyrics by L. Frank Baum, adapted from Baum's novel of the same name. Music by A. Baldwin Sloane and Paul Tietjens. Presented by Fred R. Hamlin at the Majestic Theater on January 21. Directed by Julian Mitchell. Cast included Fred Stone, David Montgomery, Grace Kimball, and Bessie Wynn (293 performances).*

*The Wizard of Oz* began its fabled career in 1900 when a child's novel by L. Frank Baum entitled *The Wonderful Wizard of Oz* was published. It sold about 100,000 copies in its first year of publication, and has since become a classic in children's literature. It might be interesting to note where the author got the name of "Oz." He owned a filing cabinet with three drawers, the top one covering the letters from "A" to "G," the second from "H" to "N," and the third from "O" to "Z." Seeking a name for his mythical land, he noticed the identifying letters on the bottom drawer of his cabinet and accepted "Oz" as the name he was looking for. In time Baum wrote fourteen books about Oz, but it is his first one that has remained the most famous.

Only three years after the book was published it was adapted by its author into a musical fantasy, at which time its name was shortened to *The Wizard of Oz* (a title which was henceforth used in all subsequent publications of Baum's novel).

With this musical fantasy a new theater opened in New York, the Majestic. This was certainly an auspicious beginning for a theater, since few productions of the early 1900's were so handsomely acclaimed and so widely imitated. Made up of a series of unforgettable stage pictures, numerous specialties and production numbers, and lavish sets and costumes—and touched with the storybook magic of a child's world of fantasy—*The Wizard of Oz* completely won the hearts of young and old.

Dorothy Dale (Anna Laughlin) and her pet cow, Imogene, are lifted by a cyclone from their Kansas farm and carried into the fairy garden, Oz. Her Kansas homestead crashes from the sky to kill the cruel witch who has ruled the Munchkins, inhabitants of Oz, and set them free from her spell. The good witch of Oz, in gratitude, presents Dorothy with a ring capable of fulfilling two wishes. Dorothy wastes the first wish on a triviality, but with the second she brings to life Scarecrow (Fred Stone). The Scarecrow has lost his brains, and the only one able to restore them is the Wizard of Oz. Dorothy accompanies the Scarecrow in the search for the Wizard, and they are soon joined by Tim Woodman (David C. Montgomery), who seeks his heart, which had been taken away from him when he fell in love with Cynthia. After numerous vicissitudes and adventures, they manage to find the Wizard (Bobby Gaylor), who magnanimously returns the Scarecrow's brains and Tim Woodman's heart.

As the Scarecrow and Tim Woodman, Fred Stone and David Montgomery became Broadway stage stars, though they had been around the theater a long time. Stone had appeared as a boy actor in Kansas in 1884 when he was eleven, and two years after that he became a member of a traveling circus. In 1895 he started an acting partnership with David Montgomery that lasted twenty-two years. For several years they appeared in vaudeville both in the United States and in England before scoring personal triumphs in *The Wizard of Oz*. Much of the gaiety, humor, and burlesque of that production came from their shenanigans. The enchantment came from some of the spectacular staging—a cyclone scene with which the play opened; a poppy field with chorus girls in large hats representing poppies; the lavish courtyard of the Wizard's palace.

Some of the best songs in this Sloane-Tietjens score were by Sloane: "Niccolo's Piccolo" and "The Medley of Nations." But the two biggest song hits to come from *The Wizard of Oz* were interpolated after the musical opened, and were by other composers. The first was "Sammy," by James O'Dea and Edward Hutchinson; the other was a comedy number, "Hurray for Baffin's Bay," by Vincent Bryan and Charles Zimmermann. Harold Arlen's popular Academy Award-winning song, "Over the Rainbow"—for which Judy Garland will always be remembered—was written for the motion-picture adaptation of Baum's novel, released by MGM in 1939. The entire score for this movie was done by Harold Arlen.

THE WIZARD OF THE NILE (1895), *a comic opera, with book and lyrics by Harry B. Smith. Music by Victor Herbert. Presented by Kirke La Shelle and Arthur F. Clark at the Casino Theater on November 4. Directed by Napier Lothian, Jr. Cast included Frank Daniels, Dorothy Morton, and Walter Allen (105 performances).*

Harry B. Smith, De Koven's librettist, wrote an Oriental text for a new operetta which he submitted to Kirke La Shelle, manager of the Bostonians (which had introduced De Koven's *Robin Hood*). La Shelle liked Smith's libretto and suggested that Victor Herbert be called on to write the music. Smith objected strongly, since at the time Herbert had written only a single operetta, and that had been a failure. But Smith finally permitted himself to be convinced of Herbert's potential gifts. Thus began a partnership between Smith and Herbert that was to yield a harvest of operetta productions, beginning with *The Wizard of the Nile*.

The setting was ancient Egypt, afflicted by a drought. Kibosh, a Persian magician (Frank Daniels), discovers that anybody capable of relieving the drought can win the hand of Cleopatra (Dorothy Morton), even though Cleopatra is in love with her music teacher, Ptarmigan. Since Kibosh knows he has an ally in the season of the year—a period in which the Nile overflows habitually—he performs an elaborate ritual calling upon the mighty river to relieve the distress. The Nile overflows—but, regrettably, much more generously than Kibosh had hoped for. Kibosh does not have the power to arrest the tide. The king (Walter Allen) condemns Kibosh to torture and death in a sealed tomb. Somehow the king and Kibosh are left in the tomb, but manage to escape. The king is so delighted with his freedom that he forgives Kibosh. As for Cleopatra and her music teacher, their romance comes to naught; for there are a Caesar and an Antony in *her* future.

The operetta and the role of Kibosh were conceived for the comedy gifts of Frank Daniels, here making his bow in comic opera. It was Daniels who was responsible for bringing to the play so much of its merriment. A favorite Kibosh phrase—"Am I a wiz?"—caught on outside the theater and entered the speech of the day. Daniels also helped make popular a witty topical song, "That's One Thing a Wizard Can Do."

*The Wizard of the Nile* proved so popular that it continued playing around America for over a decade, sometimes with a company headed by Daniels, sometimes with other troupes. It returned to New York several times; by May 1897, when *The Wizard of the Nile* was once again playing in New York, it had arrived at its five hundredth performance. In April and May of 1900 it enjoyed a six-week run at the Tivoli Theater at San Francisco. And it was still getting produced regularly in different parts of the country up to 1905.

Some of Herbert's music caught the Oriental spirit and atmosphere of the play, particularly the descriptive background music and the Oriental march. There was a fine choral number, "To the Pyramid," while one of the instrumental pieces, "Stonecutters' Song," boasted an unusual accompaniment—piano and xylophone. The most popular vocal numbers was the lilting waltz quintet, "Star Light, Star Bright," which became the most popular musical excerpt from the score, and the haunting ballad, "My Angeline."

> WONDERFUL TOWN (1953), *a musical comedy, with book by Joseph Fields and Jerome Chodorov, based on their play My Sister Eileen, in turn derived from stories by Ruth McKenney. Lyrics by Betty Comden and Adolph Green. Music by Leonard Bernstein. Presented by Robert Fryer at the Winter Garden on February 23. Directed by George Abbott. Dances by Donald Saddler. Cast included Rosalind Russell, Edith Adams, and George Gaynes (559 performances).*

It had not been the original intention of those involved in the writing and production of *Wonderful Town* to have Leonard Bernstein write the music. Another composer had been chosen for that assignment. But when George Abbott had *Wonderful Town* ready for rehearsal, he asked Bernstein to write one or two new musical numbers to spruce up a weak musical score. Bernstein refused to be partial collaborator but offered to write a new full score in five weeks. He went to work with his lyricists and completed his assignment on time, even though his ambitious score comprised fourteen numbers. Up to now, Bernstein had written only once for the popular musical stage—*On the Town,* in 1944.

The protagonist of *Wonderful Town* is Eileen (Edith Adams), an eager-eyed, baby-voiced innocent whose ingenuousness is a natural trap for the male animal. Her sister Ruth (Rosalind Russell) is more sophisticated and worldly wise, but less fortunate in winning the adulation of the opposite sex (as she laments in a hard-boiled satirical number, "One Hundred Easy Ways" —a surefire formula for losing a man). They both hail from Columbus, Ohio, and they come to New York in 1935 seeking success—Eileen as an actress, Ruth as a writer. They move into a basement apartment in Greenwich Village owned by a Greek whose hobby is painting modern pictures. Besides being decrepit and shabby, this apartment is noisy; underneath blasting is going on all day for the building of a subway. This is not quite the romantic setting Ruth and Eileen had dreamed about when they had decided to live in Greenwich Village. They cannot resist the temptation of yielding to sentimentality and nostalgia as they think of home, expressing their feelings in "O-H-I-O" ("Why, oh why, oh why oh, did we ever leave Ohio?"). But they have just scraped the surface of the discomforts of their new home. The place had formerly been occupied by an apparently successful *fille de joie;* at all hours of the night, poor Edith and Ruth are disturbed by menfolk trying to gain entrance into their place. Other picturesque characters seems to drift in and out of the apartment all day, as if it were the most natural thing for them to do. One of them is Wreck, a former football star (Jordan Bentley), who shares an apartment in the neighborhood with his girl friend. The girl's parents are due for a visit. Wreck has come to ask Ruth and Eileen to allow him to stay with them for a few days until his girl's parents leave— a favor Ruth and Eileen cannot find it in their heart to refuse. Then there is Valenti, the owner of a Greenwich Village nightclub, who gains Eileen's interest by promising her a chance in his nightspot if she can only succeed in getting her name known. Still another person who likes to drop in from time to time because he has taken quite a fancy to Eileen is Frank Lippencott, the manager of a drugstore.

Ruth leaves some of her manuscripts at the office of the *Manhatter,* which gives her a chance to meet its associate editor, Robert Baker (George Gaynes). To help promote Ruth's career, Wreck arranges a dinner at the girls' basement apartment, to which Robert Baker is invited; so is a young journalist cub, Chick, who vows to find Ruth a job on his paper. He succeeds in getting her an assignment to interview some Brazilian naval cadets who have just landed in Brooklyn. The Brazilians find Ruth irresistible, engage her in a Conga, then follow her meekly to her Greenwich Village home. Unfortunately, where men are concerned, Ruth is no match for Eileen. Our Brazilians proceed to forget Ruth in their effort to pursue Eileen. A riot develops that lands Eileen in jail. Even there Eileen is able to capture the male heart. One of the policemen serenades her with an Irish ballad, "Darlin' Eileen."

The news of Eileen's imprisonment brings her notoriety. Her name is now known, a fact that makes it possible for Valenti to book her into his nightclub. Ruth lands not only a newspaper job but at long last finds romantic fulfillment with Baker. All this calls for a huge celebration, which takes place at Valenti's nightclub with a frenetic, high-voltage dance number, "Wrong Note Rag."

The breathlessness of the overture, which leads to an electrifying ragtag dance by the Villagers, sets the hectic pace for the entire production (directed by George Abbott with his customary keen sense of perpetual movement and speed). The pace continues to accelerate in tempo and high-pitched nervousness until the devastating final curtain. "It roared into the Winter Garden," reported Robert Coleman about this musical, "like a hurricane."

The dynamo keeping these proceedings charged with electric energy was Rosalind Russell as Ruth. To her role she brought a seemingly inexhaustible vitality and lack of inhibitions that left audiences limp with exhaustion. She was the focal point for the play's searching caricatures of Broadway and Greenwich Village and for its stinging satires on sophisticates, sports, heroes, and college intellectuals in songs like "Story Vignettes" and "Pass the Football." She threw herself all over the stage without stopping to catch her breath. She was, in the words of Brooks Atkinson, "a full-fledged clown in a tumultuous musical show that is more literate than a lot of serious dramas."

Edith ("Edie") Adams, a graduate of television, provided a welcome and refreshing contrast as Eileen. She was the pianissimo giving greater impact to Ruth's fortissimo passages.

In writing "O-H-I-O," Bernstein really intended a tongue-in-cheek parody of hometown songs; but it was taken seriously by audiences and television and radio performers. There was, however, no mistaking the satirical intent in "My Darlin' Eileen," an obviously amusing takeoff on Irish ballads. Other Bernstein numbers were in a sentimental vein, the best being Baker's conception of his ideal soulmate in "A Quiet Girl" and Eileen's confession of her inmost feelings in "A Little Bit of Love."

*Wonderful Town* received the Drama Critics, Donaldson, Antoinette Perry, and Outer Circle awards as the best musical of the year. Besides its two-year stay on Broadway, the show was seen throughout the country in performances by a national company; was produced as a television special in 1959; and was mounted in several European cities. When *Wonderful Town* was revived by the City Center Light Opera Company in New York in 1967, it had lost none of its energy and appeal. Said the critic of *Variety:* "It's interesting to see how a show that seemed so timely fourteen years ago has stood up so well. . . . Some of the topical references remain pertinent, and the basic situation of a couple of guileless girls from Ohio trying to make careers in the big town, especially Greenwich Village, is a continuing phenomenon. . . . The weirdos of the 1930's didn't look too unlike the modern MacDougal Street creeps." This was not the first time *Wonderful Town* had been revived in New York, having been previously given at the City Center in 1957–58 and again in 1962–63. When *Wonderful Town* became a movie in 1955 it had none of Leonard Bernstein's music, but was fitted out with a completely new score by Jule Styne, with lyrics by Leo Robin. This was because Columbia Pictures had in 1942 made a picture out of the stage play, *My Sister Eileen* (also starring Rosalind Russell), and instead of buying out the expensive rights to *Wonderful Town,* decided to refilm *My Sister Eileen* with a cast headed by Betty Garrett and Janet Leigh, retaining the title of *My Sister Eileen.*

YIP, YIP, YAPHANK (1918), *an all-soldier revue with book, music, and lyrics by Irving Berlin. Presented by Irving Berlin at the Century Theater on September 20. Directed by William Smith. Cast was made up mostly of amateurs, the soldiers stationed at Camp Upton, New York (32 performances).*

Ancestor of the more ambitious and epoch-making all-soldier revue of World War II, *This Is the Army, Yip, Yip, Yaphank* was produced to raise $35,000 for a new Service Center at Camp Upton, where Irving Berlin was stationed during World War I. The cast of 350 was recruited from amateurs and professionals stationed at the camp. All the material was created by Berlin himself, and the scenery was improvised from whatever materials were available.

After the opening chorus, the captain appears before his men to order them to attack the enemy. The "enemy" in this case is the audience across the footlights, and the "attack" is made up of a relentless barrage of songs, skits, and dances. There followed a sometimes humorous, sometimes wistful, sometime poignant picture of rookie life in an Army camp—told in song, dance, comic routines, and large production numbers. Berlin, one of the stars, appeared in front of a pail of potatoes lamenting his fate as a KP. Another scene, "In the YMCA," brought up a picture of the loneliness of the average rookie as he writes a letter to his mother. One of the highlights was a song delivered by Berlin himself. Dragged from his cot by the bugler's morning blast, he scrambled to reveille and wailed, "Oh, How I Hate to Get Up in the Morning." This song became the hit of the show, and one of the song hits of World War I. (It was recalled in Berlin's World War II army show, *This Is the Army.*) Another song hit was "Mandy," although this did not become popular until it was interpolated into *The Ziegfeld Follies* of 1919.

*Yip, Yip, Yaphank* also included a boxing routine by then lightweight champion of the world, Benny Leonard, boxing director at Camp Upton. And there was stirring drama in the finale, in which soldiers, packs on their backs, board the ship for overseas duty, singing at the top of their voices as the ship moves slowly out of sight on the stage. (It was for this scene that Berlin wrote "God Bless America," but he deleted it from the production because, as he once explained, "it was painting the lily to have soldiers singing 'God Bless America' as they marched down the aisle of the theater, off to war. So I wrote a new song called 'We're on Our Way to France,' which was better for the purpose, and forgot all about 'God Bless America.'")

After the final curtain on opening night, Major General J. Franklin Bell, commanding officer of Camp Upton, rose to make a brief speech: "I have heard," he said, "that Berlin is among the foremost songwriters in the world, and now I believe it." *Variety* called *Yip, Yip, Yaphank* "one of the best and most novel entertainments Broadway has produced." It played to capacity houses for four weeks, earning $83,000 for the Service Center; and this sum grew to $150,000 after a brief tour in Boston, Philadelphia, and Washington.

YOU'RE A GOOD MAN, CHARLIE BROWN (1967), *a musical comedy, with book by John Gordon, based on the comic strip* Peanuts, *by Charles M. Schulz. Lyrics and music by Clark Gesner. Presented by Arthur Whitelaw and Gene Preston at the Theater 80 St. Marks on March 7. Directed by Joseph Hardy. Cast included Gary Burghoff as Charlie Brown.*

There was a large audience awaiting the offbeat musical *You're a Good Man, Charlie Brown,* which slipped into an intimate Off Broadway theater. The comic strip upon which it was based, *Peanuts,* had become something of a cult with a large army of sophisticates, intelligentsia, and those who delight in absurdity. The first attempt to lift that lovable failure, that born loser by the name of Charlie Brown from the comic strip to a more ambitious medium came about 1960 when a Princeton graduate adapted the characters, and their strange adventures, into a record album for MGM. Arthur Whitelaw, an adventurous producer, was convinced by that album that *Peanuts* could find a large market in the musical theater. He was not wrong. It has had an extraordinary run in New York. Other productions sprouted up in Chicago, Los Angeles, Washington, D.C., San Francisco, and London. A national company toured the major American cities. A special company in Boston played at the Wilbur Theater for fifty-two weeks. The original investment of $16,000 brought in over $400,000 by 1970, representing a payoff of well over one thousand percent to the investors.

It takes a true aficionado of *Peanuts* to know what is happening on the stage. The transition from the comic strip into a musical comedy was done with reverence, with faithful adherence to the spirit, the characters, and the situations of the comic strip. What followed in the musical was a long series of seemingly unrelated sequences—a procession of delicious (to *Peanuts* fans) or ridiculous (to those who do not relate to *Peanuts*) non-sequiturs.

The musical is more of a revue than a sustained plot show—for the first and basic law for anybody going to see *Peanuts* was not to try to find a story line or to seek out logic. The musical traces an average day in the life of Charlie Brown, with his hapless problems in school, with baseball, kites, redheads, Lucy, and so forth. One episode follows another like the parade of daily comic strips. Charlie Brown's world is his own; its inhabitants are *sui generis*. The curtain rises with his friends singing him a hymn of praise—the title song. Charlie Brown is in school. It is lunchtime. He comments on his food, on peanut butter, and a red-headed girl sitting nearby who he is sure is looking at him. Lunch over, things begin to happen. Lucy is fond of Schroeder's piano playing; Patty, a blond with a one-track mind, pledges allegiance to the flag; Charlie Brown and Linus discuss newspapers; Snoopy, the dog, remarks on "the curse of a fuzzy face"; and Patty and Linus comment that happiness is something ephemeral.

Lucy infuriates Schroeder by suggesting that someday his poverty might compel him to sell his piano. Patty makes a futile try at jumping rope. Lucy, having misbehaved, is punished by having her birthday party canceled. And when everybody begins playing with Snoopy, the dog sings with delight: "Faithful Friends Always Near Me."

Charlie is now pondering whether to speak to the red-headed girl or to fly to the moon.

Linus, who always carries with him his security blanket, reveals how much that blanket means to him in "My Blanket and Me." While he is watching television, Lucy enters and compels him to change to a different channel. She soon lapses into daydreaming: She is a queen. But Linus insists that this is impossible, since the position of queen is inherited, not acquired. This does not discourage Lucy, who insists she will become so rich she will be able to purchase a queendom. But the idea of becoming queen soon becomes a bore. Lucy concerns herself with cultivating her beauty ("Queen Lucy").

Charlie Brown arrives with a kite, and is overjoyed when he finally is able to make it fly successfully, expressing that delight in "The Kite Song."

And now Lucy is occupying a booth with the identifying sign: "The Doctor Is In." Charlie Brown comes for an examination. She convinces him that though he isn't much to boast about as a human being, nevertheless he is not altogether hopeless. This comforts Charlie no end, and he pays her her fee of five cents.

In class, the children are giving a book report on "Peter Rabbit." Some find it "stupid." Linus dissects "the more substantial fabric of its deeper implications." Charlie Brown's reaction is that his thinking might be upset. (The musical number "Book Report" is one of the best in the production.) The book report over, and the class dismissed, Charlie Brown is now outdoors, gazing at a leaf on a tree. He philosophizes that in spite of storms and winds, the leaf still clings to the tree. This convinces him that the greatest qualities a man can possess are courage and tenacity—with which the first act ends.

When the curtain rises on the second act, we discover Snoopy on top of the doghouse ruminating about the World War I flying ace seeking the Red Baron over the skies of France ("The Red Baron"). Snoopy is convinced that someday he himself will capture the Red Baron. Patty interrupts his musing by ordering him to chase rabbits, but Snoopy says this is impossible, since he would not know a rabbit if he saw one.

Suddenly, and for no apparent logical reason, Charlie Brown is the manager of a baseball team, giving his men a pep talk. They reply with a rousing song, "T.E.A.M." The game ended, Charlie reveals in a letter to his friend that he had been determined to win that game for the sake of the redhead. Now Lucy is making a survey about how popular she is, only to discover that she is a "super-crab" and to wonder why anybody bothers to talk to her. She bursts into tears, but is consoled by Linus, who reminds Lucy she has a brother who loves her. But the ungrateful Lucy gets involved in a quarrel with Linus, who has seized her pencil. During the heated to-do between them, Schroeder is organizing and leading a glee club in the singing of "Home on the Range." Then the singers leave. Only Snoopy remains. He throws Schroeder a kiss as gratitude for the song, then reveals that he not only hates cats but also fears them.

Lucy is also in a singing mood. She sings "Little Known Facts," a number about all the misinformation Linus has given her. This sends Charlie Brown into such a rage that he begins to bang his head against a tree, something which Lucy interprets as Charlie's attempt to loosen the tree's bark.

As Snoopy is waiting for Charlie to bring him supper, he dances about and sings "Suppertime" (another of the delectable musical episodes in the score). Snoopy's meal over, the dog begins to imitate the sounds of a coyote, explaining that this is the sound usually heard at night. Charlie returns in a happy mood. He has found a pencil dropped by his red-headed girl, with teeth marks over it. This is proof to Charlie that the red-headed girl is human. In "Happiness" he discloses that "happiness is finding a pencil."

Suddenly all of Charlie Brown's playmates join in singing what happiness is all about. To Linus, happiness is a sister; to Lucy, sharing a sandwich with somebody; to Lucy and Linus, getting along with each other; to Charlie Brown, anyone or anything you love; and to the entire group, singing together when day is done. Slowly, one after another of the characters begins to take leave. The last words heard are those spoken by Lucy to Charlie: "You're a good man, Charlie Brown."

*The wedding dance from*
FIDDLER ON THE ROOF *(1964)*

(*Friedman-Abeles*)

NO STRINGS *(1962)*,
*the first Richard Rodgers show*
*for which he wrote*
*both music and lyrics*

*Barbra Streisand as Fanny Brice*
*in* FUNNY GIRL *(1964)*

*Don Quixote with Sancho Panza espies
his Dulcinea in* MAN OF LA MANCHA *(1965)*

## SUCCESSES OF THE MIDDLE SIXTIES

*Angela Lansbury as* MAM
*sings her speakeasy number (1966*

*George Voskovec and Despo*
*in a quiet interlude in* CABARET *(1966)*

*Jerry Orbach hands over his keys*
*to Edward Winter in* PROMISES, PROMISES *(1968)*

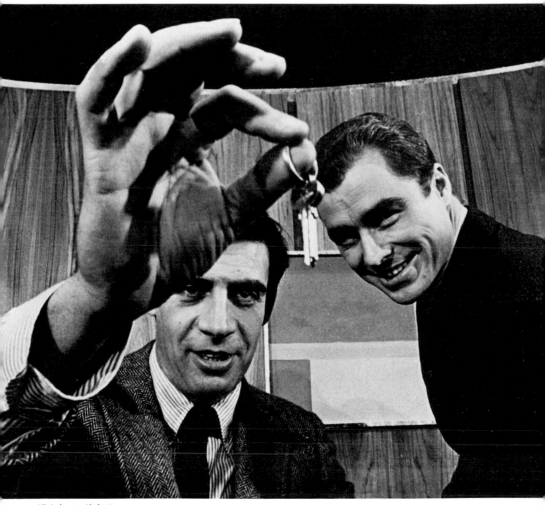

*Two ladies who made* HELLO DOLLY! *a resounding hit:*
*(left) Carol Channing in the original production (1964) and*
*Pearl Bailey (right) heading the Negro version (1967)*

*Katherine Hepburn g*
*the measure of events in* COCO *(196*

*Wild goings-on among the
cast of* HAIR *(1968),
the American tribal love-rock musical*

(Friedman-Abeles)

*Lauren Bacall leads the Village party in* APPLAUSE *(1970)*

YOUR OWN THING (1968), *a rock 'n' roll musical comedy, with book by Donald Driver, based on Shakespeare's* Twelfth Night. *Lyrics and music by Hal Hester and Danny Apolinar. Presented by Zev Bufman and Dorothy Love, in association with Walter Gidaly, at the Orpheum Theater on January 13. Directed by Donald Driver. Cast included Danny Apolinar, John Kubner, Tom Ligon, Leland Palmer, Rusty Thacker, and Marian Mercer.*

Long before *Your Own Thing* crept in so unobtrusively into a little Off Broadway theater on Second Avenue, Shakespeare had twice served musical comedy well. The first time was in the 1930's, with the Rodgers and Hart musical *The Boys from Syracuse,* from *The Comedy of Errors.* The second time was in the 1940's, with Cole Porter's *Kiss Me, Kate,* based on *The Taming of the Shrew. Your Own Thing* was a highly modernized, unconventional, uninhibited, and distorted version of *Twelfth Night.* (Strange to note, another musical based on *Twelfth Night* hit Off Broadway a week or so before *Your Own Thing* opened; that one, *Love and Let's Love,* was a failure.)

Though two of the songs are set to Shakespeare's lines ("Come Away, Death" and "She Never Told Her Love"), and though the two pairs of lovers are retained, any similarity between *Your Own Thing* and *Twelfth Night* is at best purely coincidental. *Your Own Thing* is as contemporary as hippies, LSD, and rock 'n' roll. Orson is no longer Orsino, Duke of Illyria, but a theatrical booking agent in charge of a rock 'n' roll group called the Apocalypse (appearing in the long hair and outlandish garb of rock 'n' roll singers). Olivia operates a discothèque. The musical score is in a rock 'n' roll idiom for the most part. Cinematic effects and trick sounds are effectively interpolated. Images of a polyglot group are from time to time flashed on a screen to make provocative, timely, comic comments; these include Humphrey Bogart, Queen Elizabeth, Shakespeare, God, John Wayne, the Pope, and Shirley Temple, among others. A fast and furious pace in keeping with the frenetic 1960's is maintained from opening to closing scene. The whole musical is charged with the electric dynamism—and the seemingly inexhaustible energy—of youth. All this may not be Shakespeare by any stretch of the imagination. But there could be little doubt that it was all solid theatrical fun, "cheerful, joyful, and blissfully irreverent to Shakespeare and everyone else," as Clive Barnes noted. For the first time in its history the New York Drama Critics Circle abandoned the Broadway scene to pick an Off Broadway production as the best musical of the season. *Your Own Thing* became a smash box-office success, both in its long New York run and in the tour of the national company.

Sebastian (Rusty Thacker) and Viola (Leland Palmer) a twin brother and sister, are the victims of a shipwreck and get separated. Viola arrives at Illyria convinced her brother has drowned. She does not know where to go until pictures of Manhattan are flashed on a screen. And it is to Manhattan she comes, even though it is "so much glass, so much steel."

In Manhattan, Orson (Tom Ligon), a member of the beat generation, is an agent handling the rock 'n' roll group the Apocalypse. Olivia (Marian Mercer), the owner of a discothèque who likes having men around her, listens to Orson's words of affection appreciatively, unaware that he is trying to win her interest in him so that he can book the Apocalypse in her place. Olivia is interested in making the booking until she discovers that one of the members has been drafted into the Army. Orson's problem, now, is to fill out the ranks of the rock 'n' roll group with a new singer.

The Apocalypse burst in upon the scene like a hurricane, and before long are heard in one of their typical numbers ("I'm Me"). When Viola arrives, seeking a job from Orson, the booking agent conceives the original idea of dressing her up as a male rock 'n' roller and using her as the fourth member of the group. As "Charlie," she becomes a member of the Apocalypse after they have performed for her another of their repertoire numbers, "Baby, Baby."

Viola's brother, Sebastian, has survived the wreck, recovered in a hospital, and is obsessed with the idea that his sister is dead. He, too, arrives in Manhattan; he, too, applies for the job with the Apocalypse, as a female singer. A comedy of amatory errors follows as Olivia makes a strong play for Viola (who Olivia thinks is a male), while Orson has become attracted to Sebastian (who Orson thinks is a girl). Each maintains a false sex identity for quite a while, as confusion is compounded upon confusion. When their true sex is revealed, Olivia and Sebastian become a loving pair, and so do Orson and Viola. Naturally, the play cannot end without a typical rock 'n' roll number. The Apocalypse is there to sing it—"Do Your Own Thing."

What Clive Barnes found most "refreshing" about the musical was its frequent indulgence in the unexpected. "Where else, for example, in *Twelfth Night* would you find Orson so disturbed by his feelings for Viola whom he thinks to be a boy, that he starts searching in psychology books for information on latent homosexuality? Where else would you get Olivia musing on the wisdom of falling in love with a boy ten years younger than herself?" Mr. Barnes adds: "The humor of the show is light-fingered and light-hearted, and its vitality and charm are terrific. The music is always engaging, and far from consistently strident. People who like *The Sound of Music* rather than the sound of music do not have to stay away—indeed one number has a ground bass taken from Beethoven's *Moonlight Sonata* and even the pop group on occasion plays Corelli on kazoos."

Refreshing, too, is the way in which the sexes get all mixed up without any suggestion of bad taste or vulgarity. "When the ponder comes about boys falling romantically for what seems to be another boy," wrote Whitney Bolton, "and Freud and others are invoked—the fun is excellent. The satire is sharp."

Two electrifying production numbers contribute additional zest to some highly zestful proceedings. They are "When You're Young and in Love" and "Hunca Munca."

A national company brought *Your Own Thing* throughout the United States. The musical was also produced in several European cities, and sold to the movies for $500,000 plus seven and a half percent of the gross. By early 1970, the original investment of $36,000 had brought in a profit of over 2,000 percent.

THE ZIEGFELD FOLLIES (1907), *a revue, with book and lyrics by Harry B. Smith and others. Music by various composers. Presented by Florenz Ziegfeld at the Jardin de Paris (roof of the New York Theater) on July 8. Directed by Herbert Gresham, Julian Mitchell, José Smith, and John O'Neil. Dances by Gus Sohlke and Jack Mason. Cast included Grace La Rue, Emma Carus, Harry Watson, Jr., and Helen Broderick (70 performances).*

(1908), *a revue, with book and lyrics mainly by Harry B. Smith. Music by Maurice Levi and others. Presented by Florenz Ziegfeld at the Jardin de Paris on June 15. Directed by Julian Mitchell and Herbert Gresham. Cast included Nora Bayes, Grace La Rue, Harry Watson, and Mlle. Dazie (120 performances).*

(1909), *a revue, with book and lyrics mainly by Harry B. Smith. Music by Maurice Levi and others. Presented by Florenz Ziegfeld at the Jardin de Paris on June 14. Directed by Julian Mitchell. Cast included Lillian Lorraine, Nora Bayes, Bessie Clayton, Jack Norworth, Mae Murray, and Eva Tanguay (64 performances).*

(1910), *a revue, with book and lyrics mainly by Harry B. Smith. Music by Gus Edwards and others. Presented by Florenz Ziegfeld at the Jardin de Paris on June 20. Directed by Julian Mitchell. Cast included Fanny Brice, Lillian Lorraine, and Bert Williams (88 performances).*

(1911), *a revue, with book and lyrics by George V. Hobart and others. Music by Maurice Levi, Raymond Hubbell, Irving Berlin, and others. Presented by*

*Florenz Ziegfeld at the Jardin de Paris on June 26. Directed by Julian Mitchell. Cast included Bessie McCoy, Leon Errol, the Dolly Sisters, Bert Williams, Lillian Lorraine, and Fanny Brice (80 performances).*

*(1912), a revue, with book and lyrics mainly by Harry B. Smith. Music by Raymond Hubbell and others. Presented by Florenz Ziegfeld at the Moulin Rouge on October 21. Directed by Julian Mitchell. Cast included Leon Errol, Harry Watson, Lillian Lorraine, Bert Williams, and Ray Samuels (88 performances).*

*(1913), a revue, with book and lyrics by George V. Hobart, Gene Buck, and others. Music by Raymond Hubbell, Dave Stamper, and others. Presented by Florenz Ziegfeld at the New Amsterdam Theater on June 16. Directed by Julian Mitchell. Cast included Ann Pennington, Leon Errol, and Frank Tinney (96 performances).*

*(1914), a revue, with book and lyrics by George V. Hobart, Gene Buck, and others. Music by Raymond Hubbell, Dave Stamper, and others. Presented by Florenz Ziegfeld at the New Amsterdam Theater on June 1. Directed by Florenz Ziegfeld and Leon Errol. Cast included Ed Wynn, Ann Pennington, Leon Errol, and Bert Williams (112 performances).*

*(1915), a revue, with book and lyrics by Channing Pollock, Rennold Wolf, and Gene Buck. Music by Louis A. Hirsch, Dave Stamper, and others. Presented by Florenz Ziegfeld at the New Amsterdam Theater on June 21. Directed by Julian Mitchell and Leon Errol. Cast included W. C. Fields, Ann Pennington, Mae Murray, Leon Errol, Bert Williams, George White, Ed Wynn, and Ina Claire (104 performances).*

*(1916), a revue, with book and lyrics by George V. Hobart and Gene Buck, among others. Music by Louis A. Hirsch, Dave Stamper, and others. Presented by Florenz Ziegfeld at the New Amsterdam Theater on June 12. Directed by Ned Wayburn. Cast included Ina Claire, Bert Williams, Marion Davies, Ann Pennington, Fanny Brice, and W. C. Fields (112 performances).*

*(1917), a revue, with book and lyrics by George V. Hobart, Gene Buck, and others. Music by Raymond Hubbell, Dave Stamper, Irving Berlin, and others. Patriotic finale by Victor Herbert. Presented by Florenz Ziegfeld at the New Amsterdam Theater on June 12. Directed by Ned Wayburn. Cast included Will Rogers, Eddie Cantor, W. C. Fields, Bert Williams, the Fairbanks Twins, and Fanny Brice (111 performances).*

*(1918), a revue, with book and lyrics by Rennold Wolf, Gene Buck, and others. Music by Louis A. Hirsch and others. Presented by Florenz Ziegfeld at the New Amsterdam Theater on June 18. Directed by Ned Wayburn. Cast*

*included W. C. Fields, Marilyn Miller, Eddie Cantor, Ann Pennington, the Fairbanks Twins, and Lillian Lorraine (151 performances).*

*(1919), a revue, with book, lyrics, and music by Irving Berlin, Gene Buck, Eddie Cantor, Rennold Wolf, Dave Stamper, and others. Ballet music by Victor Herbert. Presented by Florenz Ziegfeld at the New Amsterdam Theater on June 23. Directed by Ned Wayburn. Cast included Marilyn Miller, Eddie Dowling, Johnny and Ray Dooley, Eddie Cantor, Bert Williams, Van and Schenck, John Steel, and the Fairbanks Twins (171 performances).*

*(1920), a revue, with book, lyrics, and music by Irving Berlin, Gene Buck, Joseph McCarthy, Harry Tierney, Victor Herbert, and others. Presented by Florenz Ziegfeld at the New Amsterdam Theater on June 22. Directed by Edward Royce. Dances by Ray Dooley and Jack Donahue. Cast included Fanny Brice, W. C. Fields, Van and Schenck, Moran and Mack, Ray Dooley, and John Steel (123 performances).*

*(1921), a revue, with book and lyrics by Channing Pollock, Gene Buck, Willard Mack, Buddy de Sylva, and others. Music by Dave Stamper, Rudolf Friml, Victor Herbert, and others. Presented by Florenz Ziegfeld at the Globe Theater on June 21. Directed by Edward Royce. Cast included Raymond Hitchcock, Fanny Brice, W. C. Fields, and Van and Schenck (119 performances).*

*(1922), a revue, with book and lyrics by Ring Lardner, Ralph Spence, Gene Buck, and others. Music by Louis A. Hirsch, Dave Stamper, Victor Herbert, and others. Presented by Florenz Ziegfeld at the New Amsterdam Theater on June 5. Directed by Ned Wayburn. Cast included Will Rogers, Mary Eaton, Gallagher and Shean, and Olsen and Johnson (541 performances).*

*(1923), a revue, with book and lyrics by Gene Buck and others. Music by Dave Stamper, Rudolf Friml, Victor Herbert, and others. Presented by Florenz Ziegfeld at the New Amsterdam Theater on October 20. Directed by Ned Wayburn. Cast included Fanny Brice, Paul Whiteman and his orchestra, Bert and Betty Wheeler, and Brooke Johns (233 performances).*

*(1924–25), a revue, with book and lyrics by Gene Buck, Joseph M. McCarthy, and others. Music by Raymond Hubbell, Dave Stamper, Harry Tierney, Victor Herbert, and others. Presented by Florenz Ziegfeld at the New Amsterdam Theater on June 24. Directed by Julian Mitchell. Cast included Will Rogers, Ann Pennington, Vivienne Segal, George Olsen's Band. W. C. Fields and Ray Dooley joined the cast in the spring of 1925 (520 performances).*

*(1927), a revue, with book by Harold Atteridge, Eddie Cantor, and others. All the lyrics and music were by Irving Berlin. Presented by Florenz Ziegfeld*

*and A. L. Erlanger at the New Amsterdam Theater on August 16. Directed by Zeke Colvan. Dances by Sammy Lee. Cast included Eddie Cantor, Ruth Etting, the Brox Sisters, and Andrew Tombes (167 performances).*

(1931), *a revue, with book and lyrics by Gene Buck, Mark Hellinger, and others. Music by Dave Stamper, Gordon and Revel, Walter Donaldson, and others. Presented by Florenz Ziegfeld at the Ziegfeld Theater on July 1. Directed by Gene Buck. Dances by Bobby Connolly and Albertina Rasch. Cast included Harry Richman, Jack Pearl, Buck and Bubbles, Ruth Etting, and Helen Morgan (165 performances).*

(1934), *a revue, with book by H. I. Phillips, Fred Allen, David Freedman, and others. Lyrics by E. Y. Harburg and others. Music by Vernon Duke, Billy Hill, and others. Presented by Mrs. Florenz Ziegfeld (Billie Burke) at the Winter Garden on January 4. Directed by Edward C. Lilley and Bobby Connolly. Dances by Robert Alton. Cast included Fanny Brice, Jane Froman, Eugene and Willie Howard, Buddy Ebsen, and Everett Marshall (182 performances).*

(1936–37), *a revue, with book and lyrics by David Freedman, Ira Gershwin, and others. Music by Vernon Duke and others. Presented first by Mrs. Florenz Ziegfeld, then by Lee Shubert, at the Winter Garden on January 30. (Revue closed down after 115 performances, due to Fanny Brice's illness; it reopened at the Winter Garden on September 14, 1936.) Directed by John Murray Anderson and Edward C. Lilley. Dances by Robert Alton and George Balanchine. Cast included Fanny Brice, Josephine Baker, Harriet Hoctor, Bob Hope, Judy Canova, Gertrude Niesen, and Eve Arden (227 performances in all).*

(1943), *a revue, with book and lyrics by Lester Lee, Jerry Seelen, Ray Golden, William Wells, Harold Rome, and others. Lyrics by Jack Yellen, Buddy Burston, and others. Music by Ray Henderson, with an interpolation by Harold Rome. Presented by the Shuberts, in association with Alfred Bloomingdale and Lou Walters, at the Winter Garden on April 1. Directed by John Murray Anderson. Dances by Robert Alton. Cast included Milton Berle, Eric Blore, Ilona Massey, and Dean Murphy (553 performances).*

(1957), *a revue, with book by Arnie Rosen, Coleman Jacoby, David Rogers, and others. Lyrics by Howard Dietz, Carolyn Leigh, and others. Music by Sammy Fain, Jack Lawrence, Richard Myers, and others. Presented by Mark Kroll and Charles Conway at the Winter Garden on March 1. Directed by John Kennedy. Dances by Frank Wagner. Cast included Beatrice Lillie, Billie de Wolfe, and Jane Morgan (123 performances).*

*The Ziegfeld Follies* was the stage masterpiece of one of the greatest showmen America has known, Florenz Ziegfeld. The son of a serious musician (Florenz Ziegfeld, Sr., president of the Chicago Musical College), the younger Ziegfeld was born in Chicago in 1867. He entered show business in 1893 by managing Sandow the Strong Man at the Chicago World's Fair. Coming to New York, he focused his eye on the Broadway stage—and came up with a coup. Sans funds, sans influence, he was fired with the ambition of bringing to New York one of Paris' greatest stars—the petite Anna Held. Ziegfeld made the trip to Paris. Somehow he was able to persuade her to sign her name to a contract for a nonexistent show, with nonexistent backing. Once he had the contract, he came back to New York to scrounge for financial support. Helped by one or two influential Broadway friends, including Charles Dillingham, he created a truly lavish frame for his star of stars, a show called *A Parlor Match,* which opened at the Herald Square Theater on September 21, 1896. A year later, Anna Held became Mrs. Florenz Ziegfeld. He then starred her in a number of extravagantly mounted musicals (including *A Parisian Model, Miss Innocence,* and *The Little Duchess*), which made him a producer of consequence in the musical theater. It was in promoting Anna Held that Ziegfeld first proved his sure instincts in the art of promotion—a gift that would serve him well in making the *Follies* perhaps the most talked about, most imitated, and frequently the most publicized revue for almost two decades.

Anna Held was the one who gave Ziegfeld the idea to produce the *Follies.* Since female pulchritude and sex appeal were such sought-after attractions in the New York theater, why not—she inquired—create an American equivalent of the famed *Folies Bergères* of Paris: a spectacular revue featuring the most beautiful women that could be found?

The original plan was to make it a summer show. This is why for his first edition, in 1907, Ziegfeld selected the roof of the New York Theater, which he named the Jardin de Paris. This production was called simply *Follies of 1907* (not until 1911 was the name of Ziegfeld used in the title). The name "Follies" was derived by Harry B. Smith from a popular newspaper column of the day, "Follies of the Day."

That first edition cost $13,000 to produce and had a weekly expense of $3,800 in salaries and overhead (approximately one-tenth of the amount *The Ziegfeld Follies* would cost in another decade). The strong accent Ziegfeld would henceforth place on female beauty was already evident with the decorative presence of fifty so-called "Anna Held Girls"—with Annabelle Whitford, appearing in one scene as a Gibson Girl Bathing Beauty, becoming the first Ziegfeld beauty to get highly publicized. To give his audience a closer look at the kind of female beauty he was featuring, Ziegfeld had one number in which he had them march up and down the aisles beating on snare drums as they paraded.

Another of Ziegfeld's pet fetishes—elaborate sets, costumes, and production numbers, regardless of cost—was also already evident in the first edition. One of the spectacular attractions provided a kind of motion-picture effect showing girls swimming in water. Mlle. Dazie performed a provocative Salome dance, and with a Japanese partner an exotic jujitsu waltz. Helen Broderick revealed her flair for comedy in several amusing skits. One of the best comedy numbers was a satire on Sandow the Strong Man (in remembrance of Ziegfeld's beginnings as a showman) called "The Modern Sandow Girl." Other humorous spices included Dave Lewis' rendition of "I Think I Ought to Auto No More" and Nat Willis' song "If a Table at Rector's Could Talk" (the latter a provocative little number suggesting the kind of whispered talk that took place over the dinner table at Rector's famous restaurant). Grace La Rue sang "Miss Ginger from Jamaica"; Emma Carus delivered some dynamic numbers in her inimitable boisterous manner. Among the other songs were Jean Schwartz' "Handle Me with Care," Gus Edwards' "Bye, Bye, Dear Old Broadway," and E. Ray Goetz' "Come and Float Me, Freddie Dear." "Mr. Ziegfeld," reported one unidentified critic, "has given New York the best mélange of mirth, music, and pretty young girls that has been seen here in many summers."

With summer over, the production moved indoors to the Liberty Theater. Nora Bayes was a newcomer in the cast. She had already become famous in vaudeville as "The Wurzburger Girl" (by virtue of her inimitable rendition in vaudeville of Harry von Tilzer's "Down Where the Wurzburger Flows"); but her initial salary with Ziegfeld was only seventy-five dollars a week. She went over so big that her salary had to be boosted to several hundred dollars a week for the next edition of the *Follies*. When the New York run of the *Follies* ended, Ziegfeld brought his production to Washington and Baltimore. All in all, his first venture at producing a girlie revue netted him a profit of over $100,000.

From then on, for many years, Ziegfeld would continue to produce an annual edition of the *Follies,* which was the yardstick by which all other revues were measured. Nobody spent money with such a lavish hand as he in getting the best stars, the most ornate settings, the most stunning costumes that money could buy. But he also had a unique flair for uncovering new talent. Many a newcomer to the *Follies,* unknown and unheralded, would soar to the topmost peaks of theatrical fame in these productions.

A unifying theme provided the integration to the 1908 *Follies,* which once again opened at the Jardin de Paris. It was a history of civilization from the Garden of Eden to New York. The "Ziegfeld girl" was glorified in stunning spectacles, one of them "Merry Widows of All Nations," inspired by the then recent success in New York of Franz Lehár's *The Merry Widow,* and in a production number inspired by a popular cover girl of the time, "The Nell Brinkley Girl." Gertrude Vanderbilt sang "Take Me Around in a Taxicab," following which the Ziegfeld girls wore flimsy costumes, had headlights, red tin flags, and signs reading "For Hire." Nora Bayes proved the principal star of the production, singing "You Will Have to Sing an Irish Song" and a song she wrote with her husband, Jack Norworth, and which from then on would serve as her musical trademark, "Shine On, Harvest Moon." An English music-hall singer, Lucy Weston, was heard in "That's All" and "As You Walk down the Strand." Mlle. Dazie returned to do some more dancing, and a new Ziegfeld beauty was given the limelight—Mae Murray.

The *Follies* continued to be seen at the Jardin de Paris in 1909, 1910, 1911 (with the 1911 edition, as already has been noted, being named *Ziegfeld Follies* for the first time). Sophie Tucker was contracted as one of the stars of the 1909 edition, but her presence was virtually ephemeral. During tryouts in Atlantic City, New Jersey, she proved such a sensation that the envy of Nora Bayes was aroused. Miss Bayes allowed Sophie Tucker to remain in the jungle scene, "Moving Day in Jungle Town," but insisted she be stripped of all her songs. Soon after the *Follies* came to New York, Miss Tucker was deprived even of her jungle number, her place being assumed by the female hurricane Eva Tanguay, the "I Don't Care Girl" (a song that had previously made her famous in vaudeville). Sophie Tucker left the *Follies* then and there and never again appeared in a Ziegfeld production.

Lillian Lorraine made her *Follies* debut in 1909. She was seen in a sea of soap bubbles singing "Nothing but a Bubble," and then cruising about in a flying machine, scattering flowers on the audience while singing "Up, Up, in My Aeroplane." "By the Light of the Silvery Moon" (the Gus Edwards ballad, which had already been introduced in vaudeville in one of Gus Edwards' schoolroom revues) was a pleasing song interpolation after the show had opened. Harry Kelly provided the comedy highlight with a remarkable impersonation of Teddy Roosevelt; Nora Bayes caricatured a prima donna in "I'm After Mme. Tetrazzini's Job." A lavish spectacle costumed the girls as American states; they wore hats made to look like miniature battleships which lit up when the stage was darkened, and became an effective naval display in front of a huge background screen.

The 1910 edition was historic in that it marked the Broadway debut of Fanny Brice. She had just come out of burlesque, where she sang "coon" songs in blackface. Ziegfeld had discovered her in 1909 at the Columbia Theater, where, at a benefit, she did what for her was a new specialty. She appeared without burned cork and sang a Yiddish dialect song by Irving Berlin, "Sadie Salome, Go Home." Her costume had apparently been stiffly starched, and it kept clinging to and irritating a part of her anatomy. As she sang, she tried to extricate the dress from her body. Her physical contortions (which the audience interpreted to be a part of her act) went well with her comedy number, and she brought down the house. A great comedienne was born that night. Ziegfeld went backstage and signed her for the next edition of his *Follies* for seventy-five dollars a week. The first song she presented in her *Follies* debut was a ragtime number, "Lovely Joe," but her success came soon after that with another Yiddish dialect song by Irving Berlin, "Goodbye, Becky Cohen." The morning after her premiere, Ziegfeld generously tore up the contract she had signed, made a generous increase in her salary, and elevated her to the status of a star, from which she never descended.

That 1910 edition was historic for still another reason. It was the first time that a Negro performer was allowed to star with white performers in a major Broadway musical production. The Negro was the one and only Bert Williams—formerly a member of the vaudeville team of Williams and Walker. With a gift at pantomime equaled by few, and an ability to deliver a Negro dialect song with dignity and at times even poignancy, he became (as was noted in *Show Biz: From Vaude to Video*) one of the first Negroes "to break loose from the standard formula of colored acts—the chicken-stealing, crapshootin', gin-guzzlin', razor totin' no account." He made his *Follies* debut with songs like "Late Hours," "I'll Lend You Everything I've Got Except My Wife," and a number with which undoubtedly he will always be associated—"Nobody."

A swimming-tank act gave the Ziegfeld girls an opportunity to appear in bare legs, an important Ziegfeld gesture toward undressing his chorines. A novelty feature was a short movie in which Anna Held was shown as a comet descending from the skies toward Harry Watson, Jr., on the actual stage, throwing him a kiss, and then soaring back heavenward. Lillian Lorraine and a group of girls sang "Swing Me High, Swing Me Low" while soaring on swings—accompanied by bells attached to their toes. And one of the best comedy numbers was a cacophonous rehearsal of a band by Bickel and Watson.

Bessie McCoy, fresh from her triumphs as the "Yama-Yama Girl" in Hoschna's *The Three Twins,* made her *Follies* bow in the 1911 edition. She was irresistible, particularly in the dance "Tad Daffydilles" and the song "Take Care, Little Girl" by Hubbell. Among those whose hearts she won completely was that of a newspaperman, Richard Harding Davis, who habitually occupied a front-row seat to watch her, and then married her in 1912.

Another eventful *Follies* debut in 1911 was that of Leon Errol, whose rubbery legs and eccentric dancing were to be a feature of the *Follies* for several years to come. For his debut Errol appeared with Bert Williams in what has been described as one of the funniest skits to come out of the *Follies:* "Upper and Lower Level," in which Williams played the part of a redcap for Errol's Major Waterbrush. The entire skit, except for four opening lines, was done in pantomime. Another sketch starred Arline Boley as an outraged American traveler in trouble with a United States Customs officer. She haughtily insists she is innocent of smuggling, but then is found with yards and yards of fabric under the folds of her dress. Though travesty was never a *Follies* attraction, the 1911 edition had two, one on *Everyman* (called "Everywife," with seven chorines appearing as the Seven Deadly Sins), and another on the great operetta hit of that period, *The Pink Lady,* in which a bedraggled, unkempt Harry Watson, Jr., starred.

The Ziegfeld beauty singled out this year for special attention was Vera Maxwell, who appeared as "The Spirit of the Follies." Spectacle emerged in a beautiful poppy field, in which stacks of wheat soon turned out to be dancing girls; also in a scene called "New Year's Eve on the Barbary Coast," in which an apache dance was performed by Harry Watson, Jr., Leon Errol, and Lillian Lorraine.

Lillian Lorraine and Vera Maxwell took turns in singing "The Texas Tommy Song." Irving Berlin had two songs interpolated into the score: "Ephraham," sung by Fanny Brice, and "Woodman, Woodman, Spare That Tree," offered by Bert Williams. Jerome Kern also had a song interpolated— the already mentioned "Tad Daffydilles." Bert Williams had the spotlight to himself for the rendition of one of his famous numbers, "Dat's Harmony."

*The Ziegfeld Follies* remained atop the New York Theater in 1912, though the place was no longer called Jardin de Paris, but Moulin Rouge. Bert Williams was an even greater star than before; his numbers this time included "My Landlady" and "You're on the Right Road, but You're Going the Wrong Way." Leon Errol and Vera Maxwell introduced a dance soon to achieve something of a vogue—"The Seasick Dip," described as a "whirling maze." Leon Errol was also seen as a bounder in a sketch involving Bert Williams as a cab driver; without the aid of Williams, he impersonated a horse that had grown too sophisticated for Broadway. "A Palace of Beauty" was an outstanding spectacle number, an eye-filling tableau of Ziegfeld beauties who paraded around to the strains of "Beautiful, Beautiful Girls." Another gorgeous spectacle used the song "Daddy Has a Sweetheart and Mother Is Her Name," words by Gene Buck, music by Dave Stamper, both of whom would henceforth make significant song contributions to the *Follies.*

Ray Samuels, a graduate from vaudeville, gave a dynamic delivery of "Down in Dear Old New Orleans." Hubbell's best songs were "Romantic Girl" and "The Broadway Glide," but an interpolated number was far more popular— "Row, Row, Row," lyrics by William Jerome and music by Jimmie V. Monaco, sung by Lillian Lorraine. When the *Follies* visited Washington, D.C., this number was taken over by an Oriental beauty, Chee Toy, who also sang the now already famous ragtime number, "Waiting for the Robert E. Lee."

In 1913 *The Ziegfeld Follies* moved into the auditorium which would be its home for many an edition—the New Amsterdam Theater on 42nd Street. Ann Pennington here made both her *Follies* debut and her first important appearance in the Broadway theater. She was a sensation for her exciting dancing, and also for her role in a beautiful tableau, "September Morn." For the next few years she would be the dancing star of the *Follies,* before going over to George White's *Scandals.* This edition was also memorable for an eccentric dance by Leon Errol (in which he continually lost his pants) satirizing the Turkey Trot (called "Turkish Trottishness"); for a satire on the suffragette movement in the number "That Ragtime Suffragette"; for the debut of a new comic, Frank Tinney, who had a particular gift at ad-libbing; for the presence of Jose Collins, imported from England, singing such favorites as "Peg o' My Heart" and "Rebecca of the Sunnybrook Farm"; for Fanny Brice's impersonation of a telephone switchboard operator; and for a closing-scene spectacle with the Panama Canal as a setting, a warship seen entering one of the locks. A significant song interpolation was "Isle d'Amour," words by Earl Carroll and music by Leo Edwards, sung by Jose Collins.

For Florenz Ziegfeld the year of 1914 was significant in that this was when he married his second wife, Billie Burke (who survived him), after having divorced Anna Held in 1913. In his 1914 edition of the *Follies* Leon Errol did a dance travesty, this time of the tango. He also appeared in a sketch where, in a dancing school, he is mistaken for the teacher, and a group of girls follow his dance steps with hilarious consequences. The best spectacle was a Fifth Avenue scene immediately after a snowstorm, with a skyscraper in the process of construction. A first-act finale assumed a martial character with the Revolutionary Army marching downhill behind George Washington. Bert Williams did what is unquestionably his most famous pantomime routine, the poker pantomime in "Darktown Poker Club." But the greatest single element in the 1914 edition was Ed Wynn, making his *Follies* debut and his first appearance on Broadway after many years in vaudeville—his lisp, foolish hats, peculiar gestures of the hands, giggle, and gift for absurd monologues contributing an altogether new form of comedy for the *Follies*. Odette Myrtil, subsequently a star of musical comedy and operetta, also made her New York debut. Annette Kellerman was featured as "Neptune's Daughter" in a tight-fitting one-piece bathing suit, but what caused gasps was the flesh-colored tights revealing the luscious outlines and physical endowments of a beauty named Kay Laurell.

By 1915 *The Ziegfeld Follies* had become one of the most lavish and glamorous spectacles on Broadway (so much so that for the opening-night performance, Diamond Jim Brady paid $750 for a pair of tickets). The reason for the new extravagant visual opulence was the fact that Joseph Urban replaced Julian Mitchell as stage designer—and, encouraged by Ziegfeld, Urban went all out in the creation of spectacular effects, scenes, and breathtaking production numbers. One took place underwater, "Under the Sea." Another was a patriotic spectacle, "America," in which Mae Murray and Carl Randall represented the Army; Ann Pennington and George White (the latter in his *Follies* debut) the Navy; and Justine Johnstone, the Ziegfeld beauty of the year, featured as "Columbia." Urban also devised a scene at the gates of Elysium calling for elephants spouting water.

This edition was notable for other reasons. This was the first *Follies* in which W. C. Fields appeared; previously he had been a comparatively obscure comedian and juggler. He wore the high hat, spats, and cane which he would henceforth favor as his costume. His bulbous nose was aglow like a lit red bulb. His eyes looked always with suspicion at the world around him. His nasal vocal delivery, filled with pompous phrases, revealed his malice toward all.

Fields stopped the show in his *Follies* debut with one of his most famous acts—a game of billiards. He handled the cue as if it were rubberized; it slipped upward from his fingers when he aimed at a ball; it wriggled out of reach when he tried applying chalk to it. All the while he explained how he came to be known as "Honest John": He once found a glass eye and instead of keeping it, returned it to its owner. The New York *Mirror* described this act as a "screamingly funny exhibition." Fields was also seen in another hilarious act, a skit with Ann Pennington, Leon Errol, and Bert Williams, called "Hallway of the Bunkem Court Apartments."

Ed Wynn, now an established star, presented caricatures of a motion-picture director and of a cabaret impresario. But one of his funniest performances was an impromptu affair devised one evening. He hid under W. C. Fields' pool table and stole the laughs away from Fields with his pantomiming. Fields took one look under the table, tightened the slits of his eyes, and smashed his cue stick over Ed Wynn's head.

This was the first *Follies* for Ina Claire, who sang the most famous song in the production, "Hello, Frisco"—words by Gene Buck, music by Louis A. Hirsch, saluting the opening of transcontinental telephone service in the United States. Before coming to the *Follies,* Miss Claire had enjoyed an immense success in the Broadway play *Marie Odile.* Frances Starr did a delightful takeoff on Miss Claire in the song "Marie Odile."

The Ziegfeld girls were seen in a parade of months, one girl representing each month in appropriate costume. The submarine, then a comparatively recent invention, was shown in a sketch to be a highly desirable place for making love, while "Hold Me in Your Arms" provided the score with one of its best love songs.

In 1915 Ziegfeld inaugurated a midnight show, following the evening's performance of the *Follies,* atop the New Amsterdam Theater. He called it the *Midnight Frolic.* It lasted seven years. Important to the *Follies* was the fact that the *Midnight Frolic* became a kind of proving ground in which a good many unknown or little-known performers were given their opportunity to audition and perform for Ziegfeld. If they proved themselves then, Ziegfeld hired them for the *Follies.* This is what happened to Will Rogers and to Eddie Cantor, for example.

Will Rogers had made his debut in the first *Midnight Frolic* in 1915, featuring his lariat act. He had come straight from his success in Karl Hoschna's operetta *Wall Street Girl.* He graduated into *The Ziegfeld Follies* in the 1916 edition, adding a dry and penetrating monologue, filled with crisp, penetrating comments on the happenings of the day, to his lariat act— a practice he would continue thereafter. In 1916 W. C. Fields (now a *Follies* favorite) gave impersonations of Teddy Roosevelt and Secretary of the Navy Josephus Daniels. Fanny Brice was no less funny in her satire on the Russian ballet in Dave Stamper's "Nijinsky," while Ina Claire displayed an unusual gift at mimicry in her caricatures of Geraldine Farrar, Irene Castle, and Jane Cowl. The spectacular numbers included a travesty on Shakespeare's *Romeo and Juliet;* the new Ziegfeld beauties included Marion Davies and Lilyan Tashman; and specialty numbers were effectively presented by Frances White and William Rock. Hirsch's best songs were "Beautiful Island of Girls," "I Want That Star," and a number exploiting the craze at the time for things Hawaiian, "I Left Her on the Beach in Honolulu." Ragtime was represented by Dave Stamper's "There's Ragtime in the Air." Both Irving Berlin and Jerome Kern each had a song interpolated, but neither was of particular interest.

In 1917 the most significant event was the debut of Eddie Cantor. Ziegfeld had discovered Cantor in *Canary Cottage,* which played on the West

Coast in 1916; and in the same year Ziegfeld presented Cantor in the *Midnight Frolic,* where he brought down the house in Albert von Tilzer's "Oh, How She Could Yacki, Hacki, Wicki, Wacki, Woo." After that, the step downstairs to the stage of the New Amsterdam, and into the *Follies,* was inevitable—and immediate. Cantor once again was a triumph, this time with "That's the Kind of Baby for Me" (by Alfred Harrison and Jack Egan), in which he had to give a dozen encores each evening. (Victor had him make a recording of it only two days after his *Follies* premier.) Cantor also sang "A Modern Maiden's Prayer" (by Ballard MacDonald and James Hanley). He was a triumph—but for Cantor himself the event was one of heartbreak. His grandmother, who had raised him from childhood, and whom he had always regarded as mother and father in one, had died a few months earlier and therefore was not there to witness his first great stage triumph. Will Rogers found him on opening night in his dressing room weeping. Rogers asked Cantor: "What makes you think, Eddie, she *didn't* see you—and from a very good seat?"

Rogers continued twirling his lariat and making trenchant comments on the current scene. ("Congress is so strange," he said. "A man gets up to speak and says nothing. Nobody listens. Then everybody disagrees.") Fanny Brice did one of her famous routines, a takeoff on an Egyptian dancer, and was heard in the finale in "Ziegfeld Follies Rag." Bert Williams sang a number by Ring Lardner, "Home, Sweet Home." A dog stole the limelight with a drunk act. One of the sketches, "Velvet Lady," introduced a new performer, making his first appearance on the New York stage—Eddie Dowling. And a new Ziegfeld beauty came to the fore: Dolores, whose statuesque beauty dominated a stunning sequence entitled "Episode of the Chiffon."

Hubbell's songs included "Beautiful Garden of Girls," "Hello, Dearie," "Just You and Me," and "Chu Chin Chow," the last, in spite of its Chinese title, a ragtime number. Some of the interpolated numbers also proved popular—those sung by Eddie Cantor, for example. Victor Herbert contributed the music for a stirring patriotic finale, "Can't You Hear Your Country Calling?", which started out with Paul Revere's ride and ended with a parade of the United States forces before President Wilson (enacted by Walter Catlett).

An innovation in this edition was the "Ziegfeld Walk," which Robert Baral has described as a "combination of Irene Castle's flair for accenting the pelvis in her stance, the lifted shoulder, and a slow concentrated gait." Baral then described the walk as follows: "A girl would enter into the spotlight very quietly—no smile visible. As she proceeded downstage, a small glimmer would appear, then, as she reached the center stage, she'd turn her full allure on to the audience. With that walk the effect was exciting."

Stage history was made in 1918 through the first *Follies* appearance of Marilyn Miller. She walked down a flight of stairs—dressed in a minstrel costume emphasizing her exquisitely shaped legs—and became the very essence of feminine allure. She was also seen as a ballet dancer, while other dancing acts included the dynamic Ann Pennington, and Joe Frisco (derby askew over one eye) doing a jazz routine with Bee Palmer, "I Want to Learn to Jazz Dance."

W. C. Fields added a golf routine to his growing repertory, and appeared with Eddie Cantor in a sketch in which they became involved in a battle of half-wits in a patent attorney's office. Eddie Cantor, in still another skit, was an Air Corps recruit receiving a physical examination. In blackface, he was heard singing "But After the Ball Was Over."

This being the time of World War I, there were some timely martial songs and scenes. The former included two Irving Berlin songs: "I'm Gonna Pin a Medal on the Girl I Left Behind," introduced by Frank Carter, and "Blue Devils of France," sung by Lillian Lorraine (in her last appearances in the *Follies*); also "Would You Rather Be a Colonel with an Eagle on Your Shoulder or a Private with a Chicken on Your Knee?" (words by Sidney D. Mitchell, music by Archie Gottler). Among the spectacles was a wartime tableau devised by Ben Ali Haggin, "Forward Allies."

Other attractions included the female impersonations of Bert Savoy, and the madcap comic routines of Savoy when he was teamed with Brennan. One of the best songs in the score was "Garden of My Dreams," sung by Lillian Lorraine and Frank Carter in a Japanese setting.

Ziegfeld brought a greater wealth of setting and costuming to his 1919 edition than he had done up to now. His production cost hit a new high of $100,000 and had such a glittering array of stars that he had to meet a weekly payroll of $20,000, a figure unparalleled at the time. The lavishness of setting was particularly evident in a harem scene, which, in 1919, was considered the last word in garish display. Almost equally elaborate in sets, costuming, and beautiful girls were those provided by Ziegfeld for one of Irving Berlin's greatest songs, written expressly for this production, "A Pretty Girl Is like a Melody." It was sung by John Steel for a production number in which each of the girls was costumed to represent a classical piece of music. "A Pretty Girl Is like a Melody" henceforth became a kind of theme song for all subsequent *Ziegfeld Follies,* besides serving fashion shows and beauty contests everywhere.

For three of the greatest stars of the *Follies,* the 1919 edition marked their final appearances in this revue: Marilyn Miller, Eddie Cantor, and Bert Williams. Marilyn Miller brought the glamor and radiance which were uniquely hers to a song called "Sweet Sixteen," with a floral setting, and more significantly to Irving Berlin's "Mandy." The latter had been lifted from *Yip, Yip, Yaphank*—Berlin's all-Army show in World War I—for a minstrel-show routine serving as the first-act finale. Each of the performers was dressed as some famous minstrel of the past. Marilyn Miller appeared as George Primrose, and Ray Dooley was costumed as Mandy.

Eddie Cantor sang Berlin's slightly suggestive "You'd Be Surprised" and brought down the house. (His recording made at that time became Cantor's only one to sell a million discs.) His clowning was at its best in a skit entitled "At the Osteopath." Bert Williams made his *Follies* farewell with several characteristic numbers, one of which was "You Cannot Make Your Shimmy Shake on Tea," which mocked at the recently passed Volstead Act prohibiting the sale of liquor.

Jessie Reed represented the *Follies* girl of the year, while one of the chorines was a pert little performer, Mary Hay, whose talent was soon enough noticed by Ziegfeld, who gave her featured billing. Among the better songs, besides those already mentioned, were "Tulip Time" (words by Gene Buck, music by Dave Stamper), introduced by De Lyle Aida in a Dutch setting, and "My Baby's Arms," by Joseph McCarthy and Harry Tierney.

In 1920 Mary Eaton was called upon to replace the absent Marilyn Miller. Those were formidable shoes to fill—and apt toe dancer that Mary Eaton was, she did very well. Fanny Brice was heard in at least two numbers for which her personal delivery was so suited: "I'm a Vamp from East Broadway" and "I'm an Indian." Comedy was further enhanced by W. C. Fields in a sketch in which he and Fanny Brice were involved with a noisy automobile, and, in another, in which he was paired with a howling infant played by Ray Dooley. Jack Donahue, a newcomer, did some effective eccentric dancing. (Other newcomers, then unknown, included Charles Winninger and the blackfaced team of Moran and Mack.) Van and Schenck scored a major success with "All She'd Say Was Uh-Hum" (by King Zany and Van and Schenck). Irving Berlin wrote several songs for this edition, including "Girl of My Dreams," "Tell Me, Little Gypsy," and a novelty number, "Bells," which called for the girls to be costumed in bells which carried the tune when they started dancing. The score also profited from the presence of Victor Herbert's "The Love Boat," which used a Venetian setting crowded with Ziegfeld beauties. One of the novelties in this production was the presence of a name band, something to which Ziegfeld was not generally partial: that of Art Hickman, brought in from California.

In 1921, Fanny Brice, still a comedienne without equal in singing a song like "Second Hand Rose" (words by Grant Clark, music by James F. Hanley), turned for the first time from laughter to tears with her unforgettable rendition of "My Man." This, of course, was the famous French song *"Mon Homme,"* by Maurice Yvain, adapted by Channing Pollock. Ziegfeld had intended it for Mistinguette, the darling of Paris' Casino de Paris, whom he brought to America for the 1921 edition. But once he saw and heard her, Ziegfeld became convinced that—regardless of the exalted position Mistinguette held in Paris—she just was not *Follies* material. Ziegfeld turned over the ballad to Fanny Brice because, with his sure showman's instincts, he knew that the parallel between the subject matter of the song and Fanny Brice's then tragic marriage to the gangster Nick Arnstein, whom she loved deeply and on whom she had spent a fortune in an attempt to extricate him from the arms of the law, would affect audiences deeply. Attired as a gamin, and leaning against a lamppost, Fanny Brice sang her first torch song, her eyes welled up with tears. There were tears in the eyes of the audience as well. From then on, it is impossible to conceive of anybody else singing "My Man," unless it be Barbra Streisand, who did so in the motion picture *Funny Girl,* the screen adaptation of the stage-musical biography of Fanny Brice.

In that 1921 edition a sentimental tribute was paid to Marilyn Miller when Van and Schenck sang "Sally Won't You Please Come Back?" (Miss Miller having in the interim starred in the Jerome Kern musical *Sally*). One of the principal production numbers came at the beginning of the second act, "Birthday of the Dauphin," in which Raymond Hitchcock appeared as the king of France, and W. C. Fields as an old roué. W. C. Fields was at his comic best in a sketch, "The Professor"; and Raymond Hitchcock, Fanny Brice, and W. C. Fields did a satire on the three Barrymores. The score was enhanced with a Rudolf Friml number, "Bring Back My Blushing Rose," sung by Mary Eaton.

Jack Whiting, formerly a private secretary and an amateur actor, seized the limelight in the 1922 edition with his ingratiating singing and dancing. He would hold that limelight in the Broadway theater for many years more. This score was one of the best by Hirsch and Stamper (written in collaboration), with songs like " 'Neath the South Sea Moon," introduced by Gilda Gray, who stopped the show regularly by following its rendition with the performance of the shimmy; "My Rambler Rose," sung by Andrew Tombes, then danced to by Tombes and Evelyn Law; and "Some Sweet Day." But the song that caught on most quickly, then spread through the country like contagion, was a topical series of verses set to a humdrum tune, presented by Gallagher and Shean in a sprightly exchange of questions and humorous replies. The song was entitled "Mr. Gallagher and Mr. Shean." (Almost half a century later Arthur Miller used the 1922 recording of "Mr. Gallagher and Mr. Shean" in his play *The Price.*)

Gilda Gray once again proved to be a thunderbolt in a provocative number, "It's Getting Dark on Old Broadway," in which she was aided by a brown-tinted ensemble. "Lace Land"—for which Herbert wrote "Weaving My Dreams," sung by Mary Lewis before she became an opera prima donna— was a ravishing spectacle. Indeed, it proved so popular that it was carried over into the next edition. Ballet invaded the 1922 edition with "Farlanjandio" and "Frolicking Gods," both choreographed by Michel Fokine. The first had a gypsy theme, and the latter (set to Tchaikovsky's music) depicted statues in a museum come to life. Will Rogers was seen in two skits written by Ring Lardner, "Rip Van Winkle" and "The Bull Pen." An exciting specialty dance was performed by the Ziegfeld beauty of that year, Evelyn Law.

Though editions between 1923 and 1927 included some of the firmly established performers of the *Follies,* most of these productions were substandard. For a novelty, Ziegfeld introduced into the 1923 edition the boxer James J. Corbett, to appear with Jack Norton in a sketch, "The Society Breakfast." It cannot be said that the boxing champion was a stage asset. Ann Pennington (following her defection to *George White's Scandals*) was back in the *Follies* fold again; but her frenetic dancing, good though it still was, was no longer much of a novelty. She was at her best in "Take, Oh Take, Those Lips Away" (by Joseph McCarthy and Harry Tierney), after it had been sung by Brooke Johns. Some welcome new comedy was interjected by the team of Bert and Betty Wheeler, making their first musical-stage appearance after their long apprenticeship in vaudeville. A glamorous spectacle was devised by Ben Ali Haggin to the accompaniment of Rudolf Friml's piano composition *Chasonette* (which Friml would a decade later use for the song "The Donkey Serenade"). An exotic dance injected an element of excitement because its dancer, Muriel Stryker, gilded her entire body in "The Maid of Gold."

Both Will Rogers and Ann Pennington made their last *Follies* appearances in the 1924 edition. Ann Pennington danced to the strains of Dave Stamper's "Biminy," accompanied by George Olsen's band. Dorothy Knapp, lured from *The Earl Carroll Vanities,* was the Ziegfeld beauty of the year. Victor Herbert's "The Beauty Contest" (written in collaboration with Harry Tierney) was one of the last pieces of music he was destined to write, since Herbert died in 1924. One of the better songs to come out of this edition was "Adoring You," by Joseph McCarthy and Harry Tierney.

A good deal of the material from the 1924 edition was carried over into

1925, but there were some new interpolations. W. C. Fields here bid farewell to the *Follies,* an irreparable loss in the comedy department. For this edition J. P. McEvoy created the comic character of Gertie for Ray Dooley, which she would repeat in later sketches—but funny as she was, she was no substitute for the likes of Fanny Brice, Bert Williams, or W. C. Fields. The edition had a typical Ziegfeld spectacular—which by this time was beginning to become something of a bore: "I'd Like to Be a Gardener in the Garden of Girls," on a stage overcrowded with Ziegfeld beauties. And the then popular dance, the toddle, was well exploited by Peggy Fears in "Toddle Along" (by Gene Buck and Werner Janssen).

There was no *Ziegfeld Follies* in 1926, a gap that hinted strongly that the skein of annual *Follies* was soon drawing to an end.

*The Ziegfeld Follies* of 1927 was one of the costliest Ziegfeld ever mounted—costing almost $300,000. It had two particularly spectacular scenes. One of them required some ninety girls on the stage: after the Brox Sisters sang "It's Up to the Band," the curtains parted, revealing the girls either playing on white grand pianos or on kazoos. The other spectacle, "Jungle Jingle," had Claire Luce riding on a live ostrich decorated with a rhinestone collar.

That 1927 edition broke precedent on two counts. It was the first *Follies* produced by Ziegfeld in which the entire score was written by a single man; and it was the first *Follies* with a single star, Eddie Cantor. Cantor was on the stage most of the time. He impersonated Mayor James J. Walker distributing keys to the city to so many celebrities that before long there were more celebrities than keys; he appeared in a sketch as the proprietor of a dog shop who tries to sell a poor sad sack of a dog nobody wants to buy, and in another one in which he took the part of a harried taxi driver. He sang three fine Berlin numbers: "You Gotta Have It," "Learn to Sing a Love Song," and "It All Belongs to Me." Somewhere during the run of the show he managed to interpolate into the production a song not by Berlin, but one he helped catapult to success—"My Blue Heaven," by Walter Donaldson. (When Cantor's fifth child, Janet, was born, he announced it from the stage in the song by changing the lyric to "But five is a crowd/For crying out loud/We're crowded in my blue heaven.") Beyond all these strong elements, the 1927 edition was notable in that it was the springboard from which Ruth Etting first leaped to fame as a torch singer, particularly when she delivered "Shaking the Blues Away."

The 1931 *Follies* was the last produced by Ziegfeld. As if in memory of past glories—and almost as if aware that with this edition Ziegfeld had reached the end of the road—Ruth Etting revived the old Nora Bayes hit,

"Shine On, Harvest Moon." For the first time a master of ceremonies was used. He was Harry Richman, who had become successful in George White's *Scandals*. He sang a number of songs in his suave, sophisticated manner, including "Doin' the New York" (by J. P. Murray, Barry Trivers, and Ben Oakland) in the first-act finale. A South Sea Island dancer, Reri, had been imported for a jungle scene, while another scene offered three entries from the Miss Universe beauty contest. Helen Morgan shared with Harry Richman, the song "I'm with You," by Walter Donaldson, and without collaboration presented Noël Coward's "Half Caste Woman." But neither number was material suitable for Helen Morgan's plangent type of delivery. One of the best songs was "Broadway Reverie" (words by Gene Buck, music by Dave Stamper). Two outstanding production numbers were devised by Joseph Urban: "Illusion in White," featuring the Albertina Rasch dancers, and "Changing of the Guards," with the Ziegfeld girls marching in appropriate uniform in front of Buckingham Palace. The Ziegfeld beauty of the year, the last destined to be glorified by Ziegfeld, was Gladys Glad.

Ziegfeld died in 1932, but the *Follies* did not die with him. There was an edition in 1934, produced by his widow, Billie Burke, with the help of the Shuberts. Fanny Brice was back doing her inimitable satirical concepts of Aimee Semple McPherson, the then celebrated female evangelist, in "Soul Saving Sadie"; of a nudist in "Sunshine Sarah"; and as Countess Dubinsky, fan dancer from Minsky's burlesque. She also presented publicly for the first time a "Baby Snooks" sketch. Eugene and Willie Howard also returned—to ensure the strength of the comic element. The most important singer was Jane Froman; her best numbers were Vernon Duke's "What Is There to Say?" and "Moon About Town," by E. Y. Harburg and Dana Suess. Vilma and Buddy Ebsen did the hoofing, and Eve Arden made her Broadway debut. Two songs by Billy Hill, both sung by Everett Marshall, stood out prominently in the musical department: "Wagon Wheels" and "The Last Roundup."

Once again Billie Burke appeared as part producer of the *Follies* in 1936, with Lee Shubert. Fanny Brice was the star, singing as brilliantly as ever. She was a modern dancer in "Modernistic Moe" ("Rewolt, rewolt—oy, am I hungry!" she exclaimed while going through her grotesque dance postures). She did a new Baby Snooks number. She appeared in a sketch by David Freedman, "The Sweepstakes Ticket," She paired up with Bob Hope, sometimes in sketches, sometimes in song; together they introduced the best musical number in the score, Vernon Duke's "I Can't Get Started with You" (lyrics by Ira Gershwin). Added to the cast was Josephine Baker, the American Negro performer who had become a sensation in Paris. Her biggest numbers included a conga, "An Island in the West Indies," and "Maharanee"

—but, strange to say, in all three her performance fell flat. Gertrude Niesen was assigned a few innocuous songs hardly worthy of her talent. Robert Alton choreographed some striking dances, and Vincente Minnelli designed some imaginative scenes, including one in which the girls appeared in cellophane dresses.

Fanny Brice's illness compelled the show to close after 115 performances. When it reopened on September 14, 1936, Josephine Baker, Bob Hope, and Gertrude Niesen had all left. But Fanny Brice was back (in what was destined to be her last appearances in the Broadway theater), supplemented by Bobby Clark (seen on the stage for the first time without his partner McCullough, who had recently died). Clark, joining Fanny in "The Sweepstakes Ticket," made it even funnier than it had been before. Novelty entered with the appearance of Gypsy Rose Lee, a graduate from burlesque, not only doing her specialty (the strip-tease) but also appearing as mama in the Baby Snooks sketch and as a gray-haired performer on the kazoo and cymbals in a talent-scout show.

*The Ziegfeld Follies of 1943* had the longest run of any *Follies*—553 performances. It had a score by Jack Yellen and Ray Henderson and starred Milton Berle and Ilona Massey, the latter in her Broadway debut. Berle was all over the place most of the time. He appeared as the proprietor of a lunch counter arguing with his customer; as a butcher guarded by tommy guns as he deposits a steak in the safe (this was the war year of 1943, when meat was scarce); as Noël Coward in a parody of *Private Lives,* presented in the style of *Hellzapoppin'*. He was continually intruding into other acts and at times engaged in informal conversations with the audience. Berle's follies dominated the *Follies* that year, but there were other diversions nevertheless. Ilona Massey nostalgically recalled the first *Follies* of 1907 by singing "Thirty-five Summers Ago," and presented one of the production's best ballads, "Love Songs Are Made at Night." Jack Cole appeared in two outstanding dance sequences, "Hindu Serenade" and "The Wedding of the Solid Sender." Dean Murphy was a winner in his impersonations of Bette Davis, President and Mrs. Franklin D. Roosevelt, Katharine Hepburn, and Wendell Willkie.

The fiftieth anniversary of the birth of *The Ziegfeld Follies* was celebrated in 1957 with a new edition. Here Beatrice Lillie dominated the limelight (after absenting herself from the Broadway theater for four years), doing a pantomime in a restaurant in "Milady Dines Alone"; acting as an airline hostess in "High and Flighty"; performing as a favorite of an Indian rajah; and singing "Intoxication," by Dean Fuller and Marshall Barer. She also interpolated a piece of stage business she had previously performed in *The Show Is On:* swinging out into the audience and dropping garters. Billie de Wolfe did an impersonation of Elvis Presley, and joined Beatrice Lillie in a travesty on *My Fair Lady* in "My Late, Late, Lady." Seminudes descending stairs tried to bring back reminders of the days when the *Follies* was in its glory—but the female chorus line consisted merely of six girls, something which must have made Ziegfeld turn in his grave. All in all, except for Miss Lillie, the 1957 edition bore little resemblance to the genuine product when it was handled by the great Ziegfeld. As Louis Kronenberger remarked: "The spirit had all but vanished: the songs had no tunefulness, the lyrics no bounce, the sketches no crackle; and though the dances had moments of color, they quite lacked distinction."

Not until 1945 did the movies get around to producing a screen *Ziegfeld Follies*. This was an MGM production starring Fred Astaire, Judy Garland, Lena Horne, and Fanny Brice (the last repeating her sketch "The Sweepstakes Ticket"). The best songs included an old George and Ira Gershwin number, "The Babbitt and the Bromide," presented by Fred Astaire and Gene Kelly; "Limehouse Blues," lifted from the *Charlot's Revue* of 1924, an import from London; "Love," by Ralph Blane and Huge Martin, sung by Lena Horne; and "The Interview," by Kay Thompson, introduced by Judy Garland.

Before *The Ziegfeld Follies* was screened, Hollywood had used the name of Ziegfeld for two other movies: *The Great Ziegfeld,* an MGM production in 1936 in which William Powell played Ziegfeld and in which Luise Rainer received an Oscar for her performance as Anna Held; and *The Ziegfeld Girl,* an MGM production in 1941 starring Lana Turner and Judy Garland.

ZORBA (1968), *a musical play, with book by Joseph Stein, based on Nikos Kazantzakis' novel* Zorba the Greek. *Lyrics by Fred Ebb. Music by John Kander. Presented by Harold Prince at the Imperial Theater on November 17. Directed by Harold Prince. Dances by Ronald Field. Cast included Herschel Bernardi, Maria Karnilova, and John Cunningham (305 performances).*

Zorba—that huge, lovable, amusing, simple-minded Greek whose philosophy of life is to enjoy each experience and emotion as if it were the first and last of one's life—first came into being in a distinguished best-selling novel, Nikos Kazantzakis' *Zorba the Greek*. After that, Zorba (vitalized by a remarkable performance by Anthony Quinn) reappeared in a vibrant motion picture, also named *Zorba the Greek*. The musical play that followed—the title shortened to *Zorba*—was fully conscious of where lay the strength of both the novel and the motion picture. The same strength is found in the musical play. There is the depth of the characterizations, now vigorously, now subtly delineated by Herschel Bernardi as Zorba, Maria Karnilova as Hortense, and John Cunningham as Nikos. The underlying philosophy of novel and motion picture was emphasized—a healthy zest, even lust for life. The setting had exotic appeal, picturesquely suggested by Boris Aronson's scenic designs. The virile, athletic Greek dances choreographed by Ronald Field had a feeling of native authenticity. John Kander's music frequently captured a Greek sound, sometimes with virile songs, sometimes with bouzouki-like music. The text remained basically simple as the plot line moved swiftly and smoothly, while all the other elements of the production sprang as naturally from that text as flowers do from rich soil.

The Greek background and personality of the text leap forcefully to life in the opening scene, in a present-day café in Greece, gathering place of working people. They dance; they perform on their bouzoukis; they sing "Life Is," in which they express their personal philosophy. ("Life is what you do while waiting to die.") But what unfolds after that is a story that moves back to 1924—and to Crete. Nikos, a young studious man (John Cunningham), is in a café in Piraeus, where he soon shares a table and exchanges conversation with Zorba (Herschel Bernardi). Nikos discloses that he has inherited an abandoned mine in Crete, and that he is going there to restore it to operation. Zorba talks his way into getting a job with Nikos. They arrive in Crete, where they find lodgings at the home of a French woman, Hortense (Maria Karnilova). It does not take Zorba long to arouse Hortense's interest. They begin to dance to the music of a gramophone, and then sneak off for lovemaking.

The entire village is overjoyed at the prospect of having the mine repaired and reopened, for that would mean more jobs. An attractive widow (Carmen Alvarez) comes bringing the men lunch. Zorba tries to interest Nikos in her, but Nikos insists that where women are concerned he is highly cautious.

Nikos sends Zorba off to Piraeus to buy supplies for repairing the mine. Once he has come to Piraeus, the irresponsible Zorba proceeds to spend the supply money on a voluptuous belly dancer he had met in a local café. Hortense, now in love with Zorba, of course knows nothing of this; she is dreaming that Zorba will return to her, bringing her the gift of a wedding ring. Meanwhile, Nikos has come to think more and more about the widow, until he pays her a call. A young man, Pavli, in love with the widow, realizes what has happened and drowns himself.

The next day, the dancing of the villagers is suddenly interrupted with the arrival of Pavli's body. Zorba has come home—no money, no supplies. Nikos takes him severely to task for having squandered the funds on a woman.

At the same time, he informs Zorba that Hortense expects him to bring her a wedding ring. Zorba is too kindly a man to hurt Hortense. He agrees to be a partner to a mock wedding ceremony with her so as not to hurt her feelings.

Nikos confides to the widow how much she has come to mean to him, while she, in turn, reveals that something deep inside of her keeps her from giving voice to her inmost emotions. That evening the widow tries to enter the church, but is prevented by Pavli's family, which insists she is the cause of the boy's suicide. Zorba tries to protect her, but in vain. One member of Pavli's family stabs her fatally.

At last, the mine is about to be opened. There is celebration in the village. Zorba, however, changes the emotional climate radically by bringing the disconcerting news that the mine is in such a disreputable state it can never be used. This upsets Nikos. He is also deeply angered at the way in which Zorba is kind to those responsible for the widow's death. But Zorba is philosophic about it all: Death must be accepted just as life is. When something disastrous occurs, there is only one thing to do—to dance.

Nikos puts Zorba's philosophy to use when he hears that Hortense is mortally ill. Rushing to her side, he finds her radiant, for in a state of delusion she believes herself to be a young girl again. Grief-stricken, Nikos slowly begins a dance, in which he is soon joined by Zorba. The dance over, Nikos announces his intention to return to Athens. As for Zorba—he is a man who, having nothing, and without responsibilities, can do whatever he wishes and go wherever his heart leads him.

An ingenious method is achieved by Boris Aronson in his settings, and by Harold Prince in his direction, throughout the production. "This style," says Henry Hewes, "employs a device wherein some of the people in the opening number change costumes to enact roles in the story, and others become a chorus, which both evokes action and makes comment on it." Later on, "when Zorba and his young employer, Nikos, move from Athens to Crete, Aronson merely brings in a few stark abstractions, a banner of choppy white sky, a sculpture of sun-bleached rooftops in the distance, a few more realistic foreground elements, and a lovely stylized tree. Except for the faded green of its foliage, the scenery is all in black and white in order to challenge the story's main characters with the cruelty of nature and the bleakness of death."

Clive Barnes, in *The New York Times,* pointed to the "ethnic Greek element to the music and the cheerfully philosophical note struck by the lyrics—often Mr. Ebb is both witty and true," thus endowing the production with "fire and spirit." One of the most touching songs is the ballad "Why Can't I Speak?", in which the widow complains she is incapable of articulating her emotions. Particularly arresting, too, for its Greek identity, is Zorba's dance, "Grandpapa." Hortense's song, "Only Love"—nothing else exists for her—and two of Zorba's songs, "The First Time" and his closing number, "I Am Free," add further distinction to both a superior score and a superior musical play.

*Part Two*

# LIBRETTISTS, LYRICISTS, AND COMPOSERS

## ABBOTT, GEORGE, *librettist*

In addition to his fruitful career as director of stage comedies and musicals, George Abbott has also distinguished himself as librettist for musical comedies. He was born in Forestville, New York, on June 25, 1887. His education took place in New York, at the Kearney Military Academy and the Hamburg High School; at the University of Rochester, from which he received a Bachelor of Arts degree in 1911; at Harvard University, where in 1912 he attended the "47 Workshop," Professor George Pierce Baker's famous school of the drama.

His bow on the Broadway stage took place in 1913, when he appeared in *A Misleading Lady*. And it was as an actor that he first achieved success: in George S. Kaufman's *Dulcy* (1921); in the 1923 Pulitzer Prize drama by Hatcher Hughes, *Hell-Bent for Heaven;* and in John Howard Lawson's social-conscious expressionist play *Processional* (1925). Meanwhile, in 1919, Abbott branched out into stage direction, soon bringing to farces an infallible sense of timing—that breathless pace and exciting tempo which have since become his personal trademark. Among his earlier important productions were *Chicago* (1926), *Twentieth Century* (1932), *Boy Meets Girl* (1935), *Room Service* (1936) and *Brother Rat* (1936). This same kind of excitement, energy, and seemingly tireless motion he brought into plays of his own writing, sometimes with the collaborative assistance of other playwrights. Some of these are among the best stage comedies of the 1920's and 1930's: *Broadway,* written with Philip Dunning; *Love 'Em and Leave 'Em,* with John V. A. Weaver; and *Three Men on a Horse,* with John Cecil Holm.

His first association with musical comedy came about when Rodgers and Hart suggested that he get the "feel" of musical comedy by working with them on *Jumbo,* an extravaganza with Rodgers and Hart music which Billy Rose was planning for the Hippodrome. Abbott helped direct that production, which opened in 1935.

Rodgers and Hart then called upon Abbott to tighten the script they had written for the musical comedy about ballet and ballet dancers, *On Your Toes* (1936). "George straightened out the story line and kept it straight through the turmoil and upheaval of rehearsals and out-of-town tryouts," Rodgers recalls. Abbott's name appeared in the credits (with those of Rodgers and Hart) as a collaborator on the book of *On Your Toes.* After that, Abbott's association with Rodgers and Hart continued through several more musicals; in one instance he also worked with Rodgers and Hammerstein. After that he was connected with numerous other outstandingly successful musical productions, most of the time as director, but frequently as librettist as well. His autobiography, *Mister Abbott,* was published in 1963.

Only those musicals in which Mr. Abbott had a part as librettist are listed below.

PRINCIPAL WORKS: On Your Toes (1936); The Boys from Syracuse (1938); Where's Charley? (1948); A Tree Grows in Brooklyn (1951); The Pajama Game (1954); Damn Yankees (1955); New Girl in Town (1957); Fiorello! (1959), Tenderloin (1960).
*See:* THE BOYS FROM SYRACUSE; DAMN YANKEES; FIORELLO!; GIRL IN TOWN; ON YOUR TOES; THE PAJAMA GAME; TENDERLOIN; A TREE GROWS IN BROOKLYN; WHERE'S CHARLEY?


ADAMS, LEE, *lyricist. See* STROUSE, CHARLES, AND ADAMS, LEE.


ADAMSON, HAROLD, *lyricist*
He was born in Greenville, New Jersey, on December 10, 1906. He attended the New York public schools, the University of Kansas, and Harvard

University. While at school he interested himself in theatrical and literary matters. He wrote poetry for various school papers and sketches for school productions. While attending the University of Kansas he completed lyrics for several songs and won some prizes at Harvard, where he wrote some fraternity shows and contributed sketches and lyrics to a few Hasty Pudding Shows. During the summers he played in a stock company. He then entered upon a professional career as lyricist. In 1930 he provided some lyrics for the Broadway musical *Smiles,* music by Vincent Youmans, in which he realized his first hit song with "Time on My Hands." In 1933 he collaborated with Jimmy McHugh on three songs for the gala opening of the Radio City Music Hall in New York. That same year he went to Hollywood to work for the movies, his first motion picture being *Dancing Lady,* starring Fred Astaire, where he wrote lyrics to Burton Lane's music, one of whose songs was "Everything I Have Is Yours." He established his success in Hollywood with various motion pictures, including *An Affair to Remember, Around the World in Eighty Days,* and the *Las Vegas Story,* his words being set to music by such famous composers as Hoagy Carmichael, Jimmy McHugh, Vernon Duke, Walter Donaldson, and Victor Young. His title song to *Around the World in Eighty Days* (music by Victor Young) became one of the leading hit songs of 1956–57.

PRINCIPAL WORKS: The Earl Carroll Vanities of 1931; Banjo Eyes (1941); As the Girls Go (1948).
*See:* AS THE GIRLS GO; BANJO EYES; THE EARL CARROLL VANITIES OF 1931.

## ADE, GEORGE, *librettist*
He was a distinguished newspaperman, playwright, and writer of fables. He was born in Kentland, Indiana, on February 9, 1866. After experiences in journalism he achieved his first success with a book of stories, *Artie* (1896). In 1900 he published the first of several volumes of fables, *Fables in Slang.* His theatrical debut took place with a musical comedy, *The Sultan of Sulu* (1902). Nonmusical plays included *The Country Chairman* (1903); *The College Widow* (1904), which was the source of the Jerome Kern musical *Leave It to Jane;* and *Father and the Boys* (1908). He died in Brook, Newton County, Indiana, on May 16, 1944.

PRINCIPAL WORKS: The Sho-Gun (1904); The Fair Co-Ed (1909).
*See:* THE FAIR CO-ED; THE SHO-GUN.

## ADLER, RICHARD, and ROSS, JERRY, *lyricists-composers*
Richard Adler was born in New York City on August 23, 1923, the only son of Clarence Adler, a well-known pianist and teacher. Richard attended the

Columbia Grammar School in New York City and was graduated from the University of North Carolina, where he had studied playwriting with Paul Green. For three years during World War II he served with the Navy in the Pacific. Though he had no musical education, could neither read music nor play the piano by ear, Adler started writing songs while holding down various jobs. One day in June, 1950, he was introduced to another young man who, like himself, wrote songs and was incapable of getting them marketed, Jerry (Jerold) Ross. They decided to work together.

Jerry Ross was born in New York City on March 9, 1926. As a boy he combined attendance in the city public schools with appearances in singing roles in Yiddish stage productions and a Yiddish motion picture. While attending high school he wrote his first song. He kept up his songwriting activity during a four-year academic course at New York University, where he took courses in music. After graduation he wrote songs for productions for the so-called "Borscht Circuit" in the Catskill Mountains. There he met Eddie Fisher, who, in turn, introduced him to several publishers, none of whom showed any interest in Ross's songs. Nevertheless, Ross kept on composing while supporting himself with odd jobs. In 1950 he met Richard Adler and they became a team, theirs being a unique collaboration, since they worked together on both words and music.

For a while they produced material for several singers, acts, and for the radio give-away program "Stop the Music." They finally attracted Frank Loesser, the famous popular composer who headed his own publishing firm. Loesser placed the young pair under contract. It was not long before they justified his faith by producing their first song hit, "Rags to Riches" (1953), which sold a million copies of sheet music and records and reached the top of the Hit Parade. More hits, though of lesser stature, followed, including "Teasin'," "The Newspaper Song," "Now Hear This," "Even Now," and "You're So Much a Part of Me."

Their first assignment for Broadway came with four numbers in *John Murray Anderson's Almanac* in 1953. George Abbott now became convinced of their talent and engaged them to write the complete score for a musical comedy he was projecting, *The Pajama Game*. That musical was a triumph in 1954. So was its successor a year later, *Damn Yankees*. Two successive smashes on Broadway and five songs on the Hit Parade made the team of Adler and Ross one of the most important to appear in Tin Pan Alley in over a decade. Tragically, this fruitful partnership came to an abrupt end in 1955 with the death of Jerry Ross of chronic bronchiectasis.

After Ross's death, Adler wrote the words and music for a Broadway musical set in Africa, *Kwamina* (1961). It was a failure (thirty-two performances), but it boasted two fine songs in "Cocoa Bean Song" and "Another Time, Another Place." The female star of that production was Sally Ann Howes, whom Adler had married in 1958 and whom he has since divorced. For television, Adler wrote words and music for the songs to two CBS productions in 1957, *Little Woman* and *The Gift of the Magi*. In 1962 he produced at the White House the Press Correspondents and Photographers Show for President Kennedy and Prime Minister Macmillan of England; also an entertainment in New York commemorating President Kennedy's birthday. In 1963 he produced and directed the Inaugural Anniversary Salute to President Kennedy in Washington, D.C., and in 1964 was director and master of ceremonies for the first State Dinner entertainment at the White House of President Johnson's administration.

PRINCIPAL WORKS: The Pajama Game (1954); Damn Yankees (1955).
*See:* DAMN YANKEES; THE PAJAMA GAME.

## ANDERSON, MAXWELL, *librettist*
He was one of America's most distinguished dramatists. He was born in Atlantic, Pennsylvania, on December 15, 1888, and was graduated from the University of North Dakota in 1911. His first Broadway play was *White Desert* in 1923; his first huge success, *What Price Glory?*, a year later, was written in collaboration with Laurence Stallings. His later important plays included *Saturday's Children* (1927); *Elizabeth the Queen* (1930); *Both Your Houses,* which received the Pulitzer Prize (1933); *Winterset* (1935); and *Key Largo* (1939). He made his bow as librettist of musical comedies in 1938 with *Knickerbocker Holiday.* Anderson died in Stamford, Connecticut on February 28, 1959.

PRINCIPAL WORKS: Knickerbocker Holiday (1938); Lost in the Stars (1949).
*See:* KNICKERBOCKER HOLIDAY; LOST IN THE STARS.

## ARCHER, HARRY, *composer. See* Part I, LITTLE JESSE JAMES.

## ARLEN, HAROLD, *composer*
He was born Hyman Arluck in Buffalo, New York, on February 15, 1905. His father was a synagogue cantor, his mother a gifted pianist. The chants of the synagogue and the piano were significant in Harold's early musical development. As a boy he sang in the synagogue choir and was given formal piano instruction by his mother. (To this day when he performs his own songs, which he does most effectively, he brings to them the figurations and inflections of a cantorial hymn.)

His father hoped he would become a cantor; his mother wanted him to go on the concert stage. But the boy had a mind of his own. He hoped to make a place for himself in popular music. Soon after his fifteenth year he found odd jobs playing the piano in a little Buffalo nightclub and on lake steamers. He soon formed his own jazz ensembles, for which he sang the vocal choruses and wrote all the arrangements. The latter were so good that a New York booking agent brought the ensemble in 1927 to the Silver Slipper, a New York nightclub.

When Arlen first entered the Broadway theater professionally, it was as pianist and arranger rather than as composer. His first job was in the orchestra pit of one of the editions of *George White's Scandals*. After that he worked as rehearsal pianist for Vincent Youmans' musical *Great Day*. While playing the accompaniment for one of Youmans' songs, Arlen improvised an accompaniment that led the choral director of the show to advise him to put it down on paper. Ted Koehler wrote lyrics for this melody, and the number was published as "Get Happy." It was introduced in 1930 in the *9:15 Revue*, a show that ran only seven performances. But the song became popular and is still heard. George Gershwin, who saw an out-of-town tryout of the revue, came to Arlen after the performance to tell him he thought "Get Happy" one of the best production numbers he had heard.

Arlen now found a job as composer at the publishing house of J. H. Remick in Tin Pan Alley. For about three years, up to 1933, he supplied songs for shows produced at the Harlem nightspot, the Cotton Club. Among these songs were such outstanding successes as "Between the Devil and the Deep Blue Sea," "Minnie Moocher's Wedding Day," "I Love a Parade," and a classic, "Stormy Weather." The last was introduced at the Cotton Club by Ethel Waters. These songs are among the most successful numbers ever written directly for a nightclub.

Random numbers by Arlen appeard in the 1930 and 1932 editions of *The Earl Carroll Vanities*. Between these two years came Arlen's first complete score for a Broadway production—*You Said It,* a splash-dash musical starring Lou Holtz in which a newcomer named Lyda Roberti brought a piquant Hungarian accent and a dynamic personality to several pleasing Arlen songs, including "Sweet and Hot." In 1934 there was *Life Begins at 8:40. Hooray for What?,* three years later, was Arlen's first Broadway success.

Meanwhile, Arlen went out to Hollywood, where, in a few years' time, he wrote some of the songs by which he will always be remembered: "It's Only a Paper Moon," "Let's Fall in Love," "Blues in the Night," "That Old Black Magic," "Happiness Is a Thing Called Joe," "Accentuate the Positive," and "Over the Rainbow"—the last, a number which Judy Garland introduced in *The Wizard of Oz* and which henceforth became her theme song, and which brought Arlen an Academy Award in 1939.

Some of Arlen's most felicitous songwriting was done in collaboration with either E. Y. Harburg or Johnny Mercer as lyricists. Arlen and Harburg wrote their first song, "As Long as I Live," in 1934. In the same year they worked together on the musical numbers for *Life Begins at 8:40*. After that Harburg and Arlen collaborated on *Hooray for What?* and for such motion-picture songs as "It's Only a Paper Moon," "Over the Rainbow," and "Happiness Is a Thing Called Joe."

Arlen's first song to words by Mercer was "Satan's Li'l Lamb" (Mercer collaborating with Harburg), heard in the revue *Americana* in 1932. In Hollywood, Arlen's music to Mercer's lyrics included such classics as "Blues in the Night," "That Old Black Magic," "One for My Baby," and "Ac-cent-u-ate the Positive." In 1946 Arlen and Mercer produced the score for their first Broadway musical, *St. Louis Woman*.

When Arlen had returned to Broadway from Hollywood in 1944, after a seven-and-a-half-year absence, it was with his foremost stage box-office attraction, *Bloomer Girl* (lyrics by Harburg). After that Arlen alternated between Broadway and Hollywood. For Broadway he wrote the scores for *House of Flowers* and *Jamaica* as well as for the already mentioned *St. Louis Woman,* and a musical, *Saratoga,* based on Edna Ferber's novel *Saratoga Trunk,* which opened on December 7, 1959, and proved a dismal failure. In Hollywood Arlen wrote songs for *A Star Is Born,* starring Judy Garland—one of whose songs, "The Man That Got Away," was nominated for an Academy Award—and for *The Country Girl,* starring Bing Crosby. In both motion pictures his lyricist was Ira Gershwin.

PRINCIPAL WORKS: The Earl Carroll Vanities of 1930 and 1932; Life Begins at 8:40 (1934); Horray for What? (1937); Bloomer Girl (1944); St. Louis Woman (1946); House of Flowers (1954); Jamaica (1957).
*See:* BLOOMER GIRL; THE EARL CARROLL VANITIES of 1930 and 1932; HOORAY FOR WHAT?; HOUSE OF FLOWERS; JAMAICA; LIFE BEGINS AT 8:40; ST. LOUIS WOMAN.

## ATTERIDGE, HAROLD, *librettist and lyricist*

He was born in Lake Forest, Illinois, on July 9, 1886. He received his academic education in the public schools and at the University of Chicago, from which he was graduated in 1907 with a Phi Beta Kappa key. The ambition to become a professional writer brought him to New York, where he ultimately found a job as staff librettist and lyricist for the Shuberts, for whom he wrote texts and lyrics for numerous musicals, extravaganzas, and revues to music by Louis Hirsch, Al Jolson, Sigmund Romberg, and Jean Schwartz, among others. One of the earliest of these Shubertian productions was *Vera Violetta,* in 1912, Jolson's first starring vehicle. Atteridge subsequently provided many of the texts and lyrics which Jolson used in his Winter Garden extravaganzas, beginning with *The Honeymoon Express* in 1913. Meanwhile, in 1912, Atteridge became affiliated as a writer for *The Passing Show,* a revue in which he was involved for twelve editions. He continued writing for the Broadway musical stage up into the early 1930's. Among his last Broadway endeavors were *The Greenwich Village Follies* of 1928 and the revue *Everybody's Welcome* in 1931 (the last with music by Sammy Fain). Atteridge produced librettos and/or lyrics for over forty Broadway musicals, as well as scripts for radio. He died in Lynnbrook, New York, on January 15, 1938.

PRINCIPAL WORKS: Vera Violetta (1911). The Passing Show, 1912 through 1916; Robinson Crusoe, Jr. (1916); The Passing Show of 1917 and 1918; Sinbad (1918); The Passing Show of 1919 and 1921; Bombo (1921); The Passing Show of 1922 and 1923; Artists and Models of 1923; Innocent Eyes (1924); The Passing Show of 1924; Artists and Models of 1925; A Night in Paris (1926); Ziegfeld Follies of 1927; Greenwich Village Follies of 1928.

*See:* ARTISTS AND MODELS of 1923 and 1925; BOMBO; THE GREENWICH VILLAGE FOLLIES of 1928; INNOCENT EYES; A NIGHT IN PARIS; THE PASSING SHOW, 1912 through 1919, and 1921 through 1924; ROBINSON CRUSOE, JR.; SINBAD; VERA VIOLETTA; ZIEGFELD FOLLIES of 1927.

BACHARACH, BURT, *composer. See* Part I, PROMISES, PROMISES.

BERLIN, IRVING, *composer-lyricist*

Irving Berlin was born Israel Baline in Temun, Russia, on May 11, 1888. In 1892 a pogrom by the cossacks drove the Baline family to America, and they settled on New York City's East Side. When Irving was about nine, shortly after his father's death, he ran away from home to be on his own. For a while he earned pennies by leading a blind singer along the Bowery and into saloons, sometimes singing with him the sentimental ballads of the day. Irving soon found occasional employment as a singer in popular haunts near Chinatown, and after that as a song plugger for the publishing firm of Harry von Tilzer.

His first full-time job was as singing waiter at Pelham's Café in 1906. While holding this job he wrote his first song, "Marie from Sunny Italy"— but only the lyrics, the music being the work of the café pianist, Nick Michaelson. It was published in 1907 by Joseph W. Stern & Company, Berlin's total income in royalties being thirty cents. It was on this occasion that Irving Berlin assumed for the first time the name that he was to make famous.

While working as a singing waiter at Jimmy Kelly's restaurant in Union Square, Berlin kept on writing lyrics to other people's music. Accident transformed him into a composer. He had written words for a ballad about an Italian marathon runner then in the news, Dorando, and tried to peddle it to a firm headed by Ted Snyder. The manager assumed Berlin had a tune for it and offered twenty-five dollars for both words and music. Rather than lose the sale, Berlin hastily concocted a melody.

Success first came through his lyrics for "Sadie Salome, Go Home" (music by Edgar Leslie), which sold over 200,000 copies, and "My Wife's Gone to the Country" (music by Ted Snyder), which had a 300,000-copy sale. Now a staff lyricist for Ted Snyder's publishing house, Berlin was reaping a harvest in 1910 not only with his published songs but also with parodies that the New York *Journal* published, and with personal appearances with Ted Snyder in the Broadway musical *Up and Down Broadway* (1910).

He also was beginning to write the music for his own words. In 1909 he had a hit in "That Mesmerizing Mendelssohn Tune," a ragtime version of Mendelssohn's popular "Spring Song." And it was through ragtime that he first became famous as a composer. In 1911 he completed music and words (a practice he would henceforth follow) for a ragtime tune that put him as a leader in Tin Pan Alley. The song was "Alexander's Ragtime Band," which Emma Carus helped to make the rage in Chicago. In a short period it sold over a million copies of sheet music, and the whole country was rocking to its rhythm. "Alexander's Ragtime Band" made Berlin the king of ragtime, a position he maintained with several other outstanding ragtime numbers, including "That Mysterious Rag," and "Everybody's Doin' It."

Hardly had he solidified his position as a ragtime writer when he achieved popularity with the sentimental ballad. The sudden death of his bride, the former Dorothy Goetz, a victim of typhoid contracted in Cuba during their honeymoon, drove him to write "When I Lost You" in 1913. This ballad joined the select company of million-copy song hits. For the remainder of his career Berlin would pour forth some of his most beautiful and tender melodies—and some of his most personal sentiments—within the ballad.

He placed some of his songs in *The Ziegfeld Follies* of 1910 and 1911. Then, in 1914, he wrote his first complete score for the Broadway stage, a ragtime musical, *Watch Your Step,* out of which came "Play a Simple Melody." One year later, another Broadway revue, *Stop! Look! Listen!,* boasted fifteen Berlin numbers, including one that is a particular favorite with the composer, "I Love a Piano." In 1916 Berlin wrote six songs for the Victor Herbert operetta *The Century Girl,* and in 1918 he collaborated with George M. Cohan in writing the score for *The Cohan Revue of 1918.*

Soon after America's entry into World War I, Berlin was called into uniform and stationed at Camp Upton. His main contribution to the war effort was the producing and writing of an all-soldier show, *Yip, Yip, Yaphank,* the proceeds from which provided the funds for the building of a new Service Center for Camp Upton.

After the war Berlin extended his activities to the point where he became a one-man trust of popular music. He formed his own publishing firm (after having been associated for a dozen years with Waterson, Berlin, and Snyder). The opening of Irving Berlin, Inc., was celebrated throughout America with an "Irving Berlin Week," with theaters everywhere playing his songs. From the beginning this firm was one of the most powerful in Tin Pan Alley. But besides engaging in publishing, Berlin also toured the vaudeville circuit; in partnership with Sam H. Harris he built the Music Box, a new Broadway theater on 45th Street; and he kept on writing songs for Tin Pan Alley and scores for Broadway.

In 1925 Berlin met Ellin Mackay, daughter of the Postal Telegraph tycoon, and heiress to a fortune then estimated at thirty million dollars. They fell in love, but Ellin's father would not hear of marriage, and used every resource at his command to break up the affair. Nevertheless, Berlin and Ellin were secretly married on January 4, 1926. It was some years before her father became reconciled to the marriage. Out of this turbulent love affair came some of Berlin's most celebrated love ballads: "Always," "Remember," "All Alone," "What'll I Do?", and others.

Berlin became a victim of the economic crisis that ravaged the country in 1929. He lost most of his fortune. To make matters even worse, he suddenly lapsed into a period of creative sterility and frustration that lasted almost two years and convinced him he was through as a composer. But in 1931 he recovered his winning stride with his score for the Broadway revue *Face the Music.* In 1932 two old ballads—"Say It Isn't So" and "How Deep Is the Ocean?"—were successfully revived. In 1933 he enjoyed a major Broadway hit with the revue *As Thousands Cheeer.*

Once again at the top of his profession, Berlin stayed there, and his position in Tin Pan Alley and Broadway was never again threatened. His music was heard in a long succession of Broadway plays and revues, and in some of the best motion-picture musicals of the 1930's. One of his motion-picture songs, "Cheek to Cheek," won an Academy Award; another, "White Christmas," not only won an Academy Award but became a holiday classic which sold more records and sheet music than any other popular song in America.

During World War II Berlin became America's musical laureate. In 1938 he revived "God Bless America" for Kate Smith (originally written for *Yip, Yip, Yaphank* but never used). Just preceding and then during World War II it assumed almost the status of a second national anthem. (It was sung in both national conventions for President in 1940, and in 1954 it received from President Eisenhower a special gold medal.) After Pearl Harbor, Berlin enlisted his music in the war effort. He wrote songs for patriotic causes and war agencies, the sale of war bonds, the Red Cross, to spur arms production, for Navy Relief. His supreme war effort, however, came with the writing of his second all-soldier show, *This Is the Army*. Everything Berlin earned from "God Bless America" and from his war songs and soldier show went to various government agencies and charities.

After the war Berlin achieved the greatest box-office success of his career (and coincidentally producing his finest Broadway score) with *Annie Get Your Gun*, in 1946. Other musicals followed: *Miss Liberty, Call Me Madam*, and *Mr. President*.

His eightieth birthday was celebrated nationally. Ed Sullivan broke precedent by extending his TV Sunday-night program to an hour and a half, devoting the entire program as a tribute to Berlin. During the performance President Johnson was seen on film delivering birthday greetings, and Irving Berlin was heard introducing a new song.

PRINCIPAL WORKS: The Ziegfeld Follies of 1911; Watch Your Step (1914); Stop! Look! Listen! (1915); The Century Girl (1916); The Ziegfeld Follies of 1917; Yip, Yip, Yaphank (1918); The Ziegfeld Follies of 1919 and 1920; The Music Box Revue, 1921 through 1924; The Cocoanuts (1925); The Ziegfeld Follies of 1927; Face the Music (1932); As Thousands Cheer (1933); Louisiana Purchase (1940); Annie Get Your Gun (1946); Miss Liberty (1949); Call Me Madam (1950); Mr. President (1962).

See: ANNIE GET YOUR GUN; AS THOUSANDS CHEER; CALL ME MADAM; THE CENTURY GIRL; THE COCOANUTS; FACE THE MUSIC; LOUISIANA PURCHASE; MISS LIBERTY; MR. PRESIDENT; THE MUSIC BOX REVUE, 1921 through 1924; STOP! LOOK! LISTEN!; THIS IS THE ARMY; WATCH YOUR STEP; YIP, YIP, YAPHANK; THE ZIEGFELD FOLLIES of 1911, 1917, 1919, 1920, and 1927.

## BERNSTEIN, LEONARD, *composer*

Conductor, serious composer, pianist, teacher, lecturer, author—Bernstein has proved his incredible versatility further by writing popular music for the Broadway stage. Here, as elsewhere, he has proved resoundingly successful.

He was born in Lawrence, Massachusetts, on August 25, 1918. While attending public school, he studied piano with Helen Coates (in later years his secretary). Later on, as a student at Harvard College, he continued piano study with Heinrich Gebhard while taking music courses at college with Walter Piston and others. He revealed a most remarkable talent from his very beginnings. One of his fellow students at Harvard recalls: "His extraordinary memory and his flair for improvisation were almost legendary."

He was graduated from Harvard in 1939. He now entered the Curtis Institute as a conducting student of Fritz Reiner, and after that worked under Serge Koussevitzky at the Berkshire Music Center, where he soon became Koussevitzky's protégé. It was Koussevitzky who in 1943 convinced Artur Rodzinski (then appointed musical director of the New Philharmonic Orchestra) to take on Bernstein as assistant, even though Bernstein had never conducted a professional orchestra.

A dramatic incident brought him forcefully to the attention of the entire music world. When, in November of 1943, Bruno Walter, then guest conductor of the New York Philharmonic, fell suddenly ill, Bernstein was called on to conduct the Sunday-afternoon performance on November 13, with hardly more than a dozen hours' notice. He had to conduct without a single rehearsal, and he had to assume an exacting program that included a world premier. The concert went off brilliantly. The following morning *The New York Times* reported the performance on its front page and commented on it editorially. Overnight Bernstein was a celebrity.

Fortunately, his formidable talent was the insurance that subsequent conducting appearances with orchestras—soon frequent events—were not anticlimactic. He gathered triumph after triumph in Europe as well as in the United States. In 1953 he became the first American-born conductor to conduct at La Scala in Milan. In 1958 he succeeded Dimitri Mitropoulos as music director of the New York Philharmonic, the only American-born and the second-youngest conductor ever to hold this post. Bernstein resigned in 1969 to devote more time to composition, at which time the New York Philharmonic created for him the post of "conductor laureate."

While pursuing an extraordinarily varied program of activity in serious music, Bernstein was also scaling heights in the Broadway musical theater. *On the Town* (1944), his first musical comedy, immediately established him as one of the most successful new composers on Broadway. A decade later came *Wonderful Town,* an even greater stage hit. *West Side Story,* in 1957, found him achieving new altitudes of financial and artistic fulfillment in the theater.

PRINCIPAL WORKS: On the Town (1944); Wonderful Town (1953); Candide (1956); West Side Story (1957).
*See:* CANDIDE; ON THE TOWN; WEST SIDE STORY; WONDERFUL TOWN.

# BLITZSTEIN, MARC, *composer-librettist-lyricist*

Blitzstein, who first became popular in the 1930's with "social-conscious" musicals, was born in Philadelphia on March 2, 1905. His musical training was intensive from boyhood on. At the Curtis Institute he specialized in composition, while commuting regularly to New York to study piano with Alexander Siloti. In 1926 and for a number of years thereafter he studied composition with Nadia Boulanger and Arnold Schoenberg in Berlin.

Back in the United States, Blitzstein at first supported himself by lecturing on music and writing avant-garde compositions that were so dissonant that one critic described them as "full of Donner and Blitzstein." The impact of the Depression in the early 1930's removed him from his ivory tower. But even before this happened he revealed himself capable of a light touch by writing a satirical one-act opera, *Triple Sec,* which appeared in the 1930 edition of *The Garrick Gaieties.* After 1930 Blitzstein embraced the leftist movement in politics, and became motivated by the mission to make his music an instrument of propaganda. This new social viewpoint first became evident in 1932 with an oratorio, *The Condemned,* inspired by the trial of Sacco and Vanzetti, a political cause célèbre in the 1920's. For three years after that, Blitzstein wrote little. In 1932 he did a good deal of traveling in Europe, and in 1933 he married Eva Goldbeck, a writer. She died during the summer of 1936. As an escape from his grief Blitzstein plunged into the writing of text and music for a musical play that carried the social revolution to the musical stage—*The Cradle Will Rock* (1938). Politics continued to dominate his writing for several years thereafter. In 1937 he wrote *I've Got the Tune,* a musical for radio. A second stage musical, *No for an Answer,* was produced in New York on January 5, 1941, but soon had to close down because the commissioner of licenses considered the theater not equipped to handle stage musicals; it was no secret that the real reason for its closing was its radical viewpoint.

During World War II Blitzstein served in the Army Air Force, for which he completed several musical assignments. Out of uniform, he returned to professional commitments. In 1946 he completed a "social-conscious" ballet, *The Guests,* produced by the New York City Ballet in 1949. A few years later came his musical *Regina,* followed by a brilliant adaptation (text only) of Kurt Weill's *The Threepenny Opera.* The latter was a triumph in an Off Broadway production, where its sustained run, begun on March 10, 1954, was the longest of any Off Broadway presentation up to that time.

Blitzstein was completing an opera based on the Sacco-Vanzetti case when, on a vacation in Martinique, he was attacked and beaten by three sailors. He died in a hospital in Fort-de-France twenty-four hours later, on January 23, 1964.

PRINCIPAL WORKS: The Cradle Will Rock (1938); Regina (1949).
*See:* THE CRADLE WILL ROCK; REGINA.

## BLOSSOM, HENRY, *librettist-lyricist*

He was most famous as one of Victor Herbert's important collaborators. He was born in St. Louis, Missouri, on May 6, 1866, and was educated at the Stoddard School in St. Louis before entering the insurance business. He left insurance to pursue a writing career, launching it with several books and plays, the first one of the latter being *Checkers.* He then concentrated on writing librettos and lyrics for the musical theater, one of his earliest successes being *The Yankee Consul* in 1904, and Victor Herbert's *Mademoiselle (Mlle.) Modiste* in 1905 and *The Red Mill* in 1906. Other Herbert musicals in which he collaborated included *The Prima Donna* (1908), *The Only Girl* (1914), *The Princess Pat* (1915), *Eileen* (1917), and *The Velvet Lady* (1919). He also wrote texts and lyrics for other composers. His last musical was *The Velvet Lady.* He died in New York City on March 23, 1919.

PRINCIPAL WORKS: Madamoiselle (Mlle.) Modiste (1905); The Red Mill (1906); The Only Girl (1914); The Princess Pat (1915).
*See:* MADEMOISELLE (MLLE.) MODISTE; THE ONLY GIRL; THE PRINCESS PAT; THE RED MILL.

## BOCK, JERRY, *composer*

He was born in New Haven, Connecticut, on November 23, 1928, but became a resident of Queens, New York, when he was two. He began studying the piano in his ninth year, but detested practicing, and by the time he entered Flushing High School had given up formal musical training. At school his extracurricular activities included the editing of the school paper, contributing prose and verses to journals, and writing the text and music of a musical produced in Queens for charity. His music study was resumed at the Music School of the University of Wisconsin and was pursued with intensity. In his third year there he wrote the score for a musical produced by the college dramatic society.

After coming to New York he married Patti Faggen in 1950 (he had met and fallen in love with her in Wisconsin). With Larry Holofcener as his lyricist, Bock wrote songs for musical shows then being produced over television by Max Liebman. They also contributed continuity and sketches for other television programs, including the Kate Smith Hour. In 1954, four of their songs appeared in *Wonders of Manhattan,* a motion-picture documentary that received honorable mention at the Cannes Film Festival. On September 7, 1955, Bock and Holofcener made their Broadway debut with three songs in a revue, *Catch a Star*. Their next assignment for Broadway was the complete score for *Mr. Wonderful,* starring Sammy Davis, Jr. (1956), a box-office success.

*Mr. Wonderful* marked the end of the collaboration of Bock and Holofcener. Bock found a new lyricist in Sheldon Harnick, with whom he was destined to work so fruitfully in the years that followed.

Harnick was born in Chicago, Illinois, on April 30, 1924. He received a comprehensive musical training over a period of many years, specializing in the violin. After serving in the Army Signal Corps he was graduated in 1950 from Northwestern University with a degree of Bachelor of Music; at the university he contributed lyrics and music for a college production. The year of his graduation also marked his marriage to his first wife, Mary Boatner, an actress, which ended in divorce in 1957. (Harnick's second wife was Elaine May—the partner of Nichols and May in the presentation of improvisations—whom he married in 1962 and divorced about a year later.) Harnick's bow on Broadway took place in 1952 with one song in *New Faces of 1952* and another in *Two's Company*. During the next few years he continued contributing songs—words and music—to various revues.

Teaming up with Bock, Harnick decided to concentrate on words and leave the music to his partner. Their first Broadway venture was *The Body Beautiful* (1958), a failure. Fame, however, was not far off. They achieved renown with *Fiorello!* (1959), which received the Pulitzer Prize for drama. The musicals that followed during the next five years were modest successes. They included *Tenderloin* (1960) and *She Loves Me* (1963). But *Fiddler on the Roof* (1964) placed them solidly on the top of their profession, with one of the greatest stage successes Broadway has known. *Generation* in 1965 was a failure.

PRINCIPAL WORKS: Mister (Mr.) Wonderful (1956); Fiorello! (1959); Tenderloin (1960); She Loves Me (1963); Fiddler on the Roof (1964); The Apple Tree (1966).
*See:* THE APPLE TREE; FIDDLER ON THE ROOF; FIORELLO!; MISTER (MR.) WONDERFUL; SHE LOVES ME; TENDERLOIN.

## BOLTON, GUY, *librettist*

Bolton has been one of the most prolific writers of musical-comedy books and nonmusical plays Broadway has known. He was born in Broxbourne, Hertfordshire, England, on November 23, 1886, son of a famous engineer. After being trained in France as an architect, he pursued his profession in

New York, where he helped to design the Soldiers and Sailors Memorial on Riverside Drive. He turned to playwriting by collaborating with Douglas J. Wood on *The Drone* in 1912. He had two more plays produced after that, in 1914 and 1915, besides contributing sketches for *The Smart Set,* when, in 1915, he met Jerome Kern and they decided to work together. Their first collaboration was *Ninety in the Shade* (1915), in which Clare Kummer assisted Bolton in writing the text. The second Kern-Bolton musical was *Nobody Home,* again in 1915, which helped to initiate a new genre in musical comedy known as "The Princess Theater Shows" (*see* PRINCESS THEATER SHOWS). Bolton also collaborated with Kern in the writing of more formal musical comedies: *Leave It to Jane* and *Sally.* Bolton was the writer of the motion-picture script for Kern's screen biography, *Till the Clouds Roll By.*

Bolton has produced innumerable musical-comedy texts (sometimes in collaboration with others) for other famous Broadway composers besides Kern, among them being Ivan Caryll, George Gershwin, Cole Porter, Harry Ruby, and Harry Tierney. At the same time, he wrote many plays, the most famous of which, perhaps, was *Anastasia* (1954). With the collaboration of P. G. Wodehouse he wrote a book of reminiscences of his experiences in the musical theater—*Bring on the Girls* (1953). He also completed two novels: *The Olympians* (1961) and *The Enchantress* (1964).

PRINCIPAL WORKS: The Princess Theater Shows (Nobody Home, 1915; Very Good, Eddie, 1915; Oh, Boy!, 1917); Leave It to Jane (1917); The Princess Theater Shows (Oh, Lady! Lady!, 1918; Oh, My Dear!, 1919); Sally (1920); Tangerine (1921); Lady, Be Good! (1924); Tip-Toes (1925); Oh, Kay! (1926); Five O'Clock Girl (1927); Rio Rita (1927); Rosalie (1928); The Ramblers (1928); Simple Simon (1930); Girl Crazy (1930); Anything Goes (1934); Hold on to Your Hats (1940); Follow the Girls (1944).
See: ANYTHING GOES; FIVE O'CLOCK GIRL; FOLLOW THE GIRLS; GIRL CRAZY; HOLD ON TO YOUR HATS; LADY, BE GOOD!; LEAVE IT TO JANE; OH, KAY!; THE PRINCESS THEATER SHOWS (NOBODY HOME; VERY GOOD, EDDIE; OH, BOY!; OH, LADY! LADY!; OH, MY DEAR!); THE RAMBLERS; RIO RITA; ROSALIE; SALLY; SIMPLE SIMON; TANGERINE; TIP-TOES.

## BRAHAM, DAVID, *composer*

Though David Braham wrote many songs with lyricists other than Ed Harringan, he achieved his foremost successes as a composer for the burlesques of Harrigan and Hart. He is always identified as a "Harrigan and Hart" composer.

Braham was born in London in 1838, and he settled in the United States fifteen years later. While still in England he knew he wanted to become a professional musician and began to study the harp. The story goes that his failure to get his bulky instrument aboard an stagecoach was the motivation for his changing to violin, on which he became such an adept performer that he actually did some concert work.

Upon arriving in New York, Braham found a job as violinist in the orchestra accompanying the Pony Moore Minstrels. After that he led a military band, and played in the pit orchestras of most of the famous New York auditoriums. In the early 1870's he achieved some measure of fame with popular songs modeled after English music-hall tunes. These included special numbers for Annie Yeamans as a child star ("The Bootblack" and "The Sailing on the Lake"), for James McKee ("Over the Hill to the Poorhouse"), and for Major Tom Thumb when he appeared with P. T. Barnum.

Braham's first collaboration with Harrigan and Hart was on the song "The Mulligan Guard," lyrics by Harrigan, in 1873. Though Braham occasionally wrote melodies to the lyrics of other writers after that, both his personal and musical history from 1873 on was inextricably associated with Harrigan and Hart—his personal history because in November, 1876, Harrigan married Braham's sixteen-year-old daughter, Annie; his musical career because Braham's success in the Broadway theater came almost exclusively from his Harrigan and Hart scores. When Harrigan and Hart came to the parting of the ways in 1885, Braham wrote the music for Harrigan's burlesques. Braham died on April 11, 1905.

*See:* THE MULLIGAN GUARDS' BALL (which includes the other Harrigan and Hart burlesques).

BROWN, LEW, *lyricist. See* DE SYLVA, BROWN, AND HENDERSON.

## BUCK, GENE, *lyricist and librettist*

Gene (Edward Eugene, officially) Buck is perhaps best known through his long and rich association with Florenz Ziegfeld. He was born in Detroit on August 8, 1885, attended Detroit public schools, then in his eighteenth year found a job as bank messenger for two dollars a week. His ambition at that time lay in art rather than the theater. He took courses at the Detroit Art Academy, after which he found employment as a designer for a Detroit stationer and printer who produced all the sheet-music covers for Whitney and Warner, a major publisher in Tin Pan Alley. At that time covers were simple in design and done only in black and white. For his firm Buck originated colored posterlike covers, which soon became a rage in Tin Pan Alley. When Remick bought out Whitney and Warner, Buck was hired to design all its song covers. He created over five thousand, an occupation that proved so taxing to his sight that he lost it and had to suspend all work for eight months.

After recovering from a blindness that fortunately proved to be temporary, Buck came to New York with only thirteen dollars in his pocket and no job. He was, however, known in Tin Pan Alley, and before long he was back at his old occupation of designing song covers.

In 1911 he wrote his first song lyric, "Daddy Has a Sweetheart and Mother Is Her Name," music by Dave Stamper. This song and the one that followed it—"Some Boy," also to Stamper's melody—were introduced by Lillian Lorraine in her vaudeville act. She helped skyrocket both songs to a million-copy sheet-music sale.

Now a successful lyricist, Buck was sought out by Ziegfeld. In the 1912 edition of *The Ziegfeld Follies,* Buck's song "Daddy Has a Sweetheart" was interpolated, thus setting into motion an association between Buck and Ziegfeld that lasted seventeen years. In the 1913 edition of the *Follies,* Buck and Stamper had three numbers. After that, Buck provided songs and sketches for eighteen more *Follies* and for all the sixteen editions of *The Midnight Frolic,* a restaurant-nightclub atop the New Amsterdam Theater, which he helped to originate for Ziegfeld. Among Buck's best-known songs in the various *Follies* were: "Hello, Frisco, Hello" (Hirsch) in 1915, "Garden of My Dreams" (Hirsch) in 1918, "Tulip Time" (Stamper) in 1919, " 'Neath the South Sea Moon" (Hirsch and Stamper) in 1922, and "Lovely Little Melody" (Stamper) in 1924. As Ziegfeld's right-hand man, Buck also helped uncover many outstanding stars for the *Follies,* including Ed Wynn, Eddie Cantor, Will Rogers, and Joe Frisco.

Between 1927 and 1931 Buck became a producer of musical shows, one of them being *Take the Air* (1927). In 1931 he returned to work for Ziegfeld for the last of the *Follies* produced by Ziegfeld himself. After that Buck confined his activities to executive duties with ASCAP, serving as its president from 1924 to 1941.

Gene Buck died in a hospital in Manhasset, Long Island, on February 25, 1957.

PRINCIPAL WORKS: The Ziegfeld Follies, 1913 through 1927; Take the Air (1927).
*See:* TAKE THE AIR; THE ZIEGFELD FOLLIES, 1913 through 1927.

## BURROWS, ABE, *librettist*

Burrows has contributed to the musical stage as a writer of texts (in collaboration with others), director, and play doctor. Born in New York City on December 18, 1910, he attended public schools in Manhattan, Brooklyn, and the Bronx. After graduating from New Utrecht High School in 1928, he took a premedical course at the College of the City of New York, but the thought of attending sick people proved too morbid, and after two years he transferred to the New York University School of Finance to study accounting. In 1931 he found a job with a Wall Street brokerage firm, where he remained three years. Then for several years more he worked in his father's paint business and traveled as a salesman for a maple-syrup firm.

Several summers as an entertainer in the Catskill Mountains, on the Borscht Circuit, convinced him that humor was the commodity he could best sell. In 1938 he started selling sketches for radio, and in a few years' time became "top banana" in the industry through his writing chores for programs such as Ed Gardner's *Duffy's Tavern* (with which he remained four years), the *CBS Texaco Theater, The Joan Davis Show,* and *The Ford Program.*

While working in Hollywood on his radio programs, he became famous at swank, exclusive parties for his satirical songs and recitations. He startled and delighted audiences with zany songs like "The Girl with the Three Blue Eyes," "I Looked Under a Rock and I Found You," and "I'm Walking Down Memory Lane Without a Single Thing to Remember"; also with his wry commentaries on education, radio, and the Boulder Dam. He subsequently recorded two albums of his songs, published an *Abe Burrows Song Book,* appeared on many radio and television programs, and in 1948–49 was a nightclub star.

One of his bosses at CBS in Hollywood was Ernest Martin. When Martin joined with Cy Feuer to produce *Guys and Dolls,* he asked Burrows to work with Jo Swerling in making the stage adaptation of the Damon Runyon stories. Burrows' initiation into musical comedy, then, came with a production that ran for several years and became a classic. A year after *Guys and Dolls* had opened on Broadway, Burrows was asked to doctor the musical *Make a Wish* (1951), based on Ferenc Molnár's *The Good Fairy,* and to direct the revue *Two on the Aisle.* Both were comparative failures. But later assignments on Broadway—sometimes as director, sometimes as a collaborator in the writing of the texts, and sometimes in both capacities—proved him to be one of the most astute showmen of his time. With *How to Succeed in Business Without Really Trying* (1964) he received the Pulitzer Prize. Only those musicals in which Burrows was involved as a librettist are listed below.

PRINCIPAL WORKS: Guys and Dolls (1950); Can-Can (1953); Silk Stockings (1955); How to Succeed in Business Without Really Trying (1964).
*See:* CAN-CAN; GUYS AND DOLLS; HOW TO SUCCEED IN BUSINESS WITHOUT REALLY TRYING; SILK STOCKINGS.

## CAESAR, IRVING, *lyricist*

Irving Caesar (who has frequently written music as well as words, though he is best known as a lyricist) was born in New York City on July 4, 1895. He received his education at the Chatauqua Mountain Institute and at the College of the City of New York. In 1915 Henry Ford hired him as official stenographer for the Henry Ford Peace Ship, which Ford hoped would end World War I. After the war Caesar was employed in Ford's automobile plant. Caesar's free time was devoted to writing song lyrics. Among his first-published songs were several to music by the then still young and unknown George Gershwin, the most successful being "Swanee" in 1919. Caesar now abandoned factory work to concentrate on lyric writing, a field in which he proved extraordinarily prolific as well as successful. In 1922 he wrote the lyrics for *The Greenwich Village Follies,* a revue in which he was involved for three editions. He also contributed lyrics to numerous other Broadway musicals and revues, the most successful being *No, No, Nanette* (1925) and the *George White's Scandals of 1929.* Among his hit songs, besides "Swanee," have been "Tea for Two," "I Want to Be Happy," "Just a Gigolo," and "Is It True What They Say About Dixie?" He has also written words and music for children's songs promoting safety, friendship, and health which achieved national popularity in classrooms.

PRINCIPAL WORKS: The Greenwich Village Follies, 1922 through 1925; No, No, Nanette (1925).
*See:* THE GREENWICH VILLAGE FOLLIES, 1922 through 1925; NO, NO, NANETTE.

## CAHN, SAMMY, *lyricist*

As the lyricist for Jule Styne, the composer, Cahn had proved himself one of Hollywood's ace songwriters before he finally put a foot into the Broadway musical theater. Cahn was born on the East Side of New York on June 18, 1913. His academic education ended when he deserted Seward Park High School and supported himself by holding down various menial jobs while trying to fulfill himself as a songwriter, an already fully crystallized ambition. With Saul Chaplin as his composer, Cahn got his first break in 1935 when Jimmie Lunceford asked them to write "Rhythm Is Our Business" for his band, which Lunceford henceforth used as his signature music. Success came a year later with two songs, "Shoe Shine Boy," introduced by Louis Armstrong at the Cotton Club, and "Bei Mir bist du Schoen," which the Andrews Sisters made famous on records. This brought Cahn and Chaplin a contract to work for motion pictures. They did not do well in this new endeavor and broke up partnership. Cahn now became Jule Styne's lyricist, the first fruit being "I've Heard That Song Before" which became an enormous hit. Other hit songs for the screen followed. Then, having conquered Hollywood, Cahn and Styne invaded Broadway in 1947 with *High Button Shoes,* a smash box-office success. Not for two decades would Cahn write again for the Broadway musical stage. Meanwhile he was back in Hollywood—this time producing words to the music of James Van Heusen—and becoming one of the top lyricists in the movie capital, what with the winning of Oscars for "Three Coins in the Fountain" (1954), "All the Way" (1957), "High Hopes" (1959), and "Call Me Irresponsible" (1963). He also received an Emmy for "Love and Marriage," a song in the TV musical adaptation of Thornton Wilder's *Our Town.*

Still with Van Heusen as his composer, Cahn returned to the Broadway theater in 1966 with *Skyscraper,* following it one year later with a second musical comedy, *Walking Happy.* Neither of these productions was particularly successful, though the title number for *Walking Happy* and "Everybody Has a Right to Be Wrong" from *Skyscraper* were hits. He revived his partnership with Jule Styne for the Broadway musical, *Look to the Lilies,* a failure in 1970.

PRINCIPAL WORKS: High Button Shoes (1947); Skyscraper (1965).
*See:* HIGH BUTTON SHOES; SKYSCRAPER.

## CALDWELL, ANNE, *librettist-lyricist*

Besides being a successful musical-comedy librettist and lyricist, she was also a singer and actress. She was born in Boston, Massachusetts, on August 30, 1867. After attending local public schools and appearing as a singer with the Juvenile Opera Company, she pursued for several years a career as an actress. She collaborated on the texts of *Top o' the World* (1907), *Lady of the Slipper* (1912), and *Chin-Chin* (1914), also helping with the lyrics in the last-named production. For *Pom Pom* (1916) she wrote both libretto and lyrics without assistance. For the next two decades she collaborated with such significant composers as Hubbell, Kern, and Youmans. Among the musicals for which she wrote libretto and lyrics without collaborative assistance were *She's a Good Fellow* (1919), *The Night Boat* (1920), *The Sweetheart Shop* (1920), *Good Morning Dearie* (1921) and *Oh, Please!* (1926). She wrote the lyrics for *Criss Cross* (1926), the libretto for *Take the Air* (1927), and collaborated in the writing of book and lyrics for *Hitchy-Koo of 1920* and *Stepping Stones.* She died in Hollywood, California, on October 22, 1936.

PRINCIPAL WORKS: Chin-Chin (1914); Good Morning Dearie (1921); Stepping Stones (1923); Criss Cross (1926); Take the Air (1927).
*See:* CHIN-CHIN; CRISS CROSS; GOOD MORNING DEARIE; STEPPING STONES; TAKE THE AIR.

## CARYLL, IVAN, *composer*

Ivan Caryll, born Felix Tilken, was one of the most successful composers of operettas before 1920. He was born in Liège, Belgium, in 1860 and received a thorough musical training at the Liège Conservatory and in Paris with Eugene Ysaÿe and Saint-Saëns. After writing music for the French stage he came to London, where he conducted musicals, wrote functional music for the stage, and adapted French operettas for the English theater. *La Cigale,* starring Lillian Russell, was the first show to introduce his name to the American public (1891).

The first operetta with his own music was *Little Christopher Columbus,* a London success in 1893, and well received in New York a year later. For the next seventeen years Caryll kept on writing music for the London stage, some of his musicals being imported to America, occasionally with the original English casts, sometimes in American adaptations. The first to achieve success was *The Girl from Paris* (1897), with an English cast. *The Runaway Girl* was an even greater hit in 1898. Later Caryll musicals originating in London and achieving New York success were: *The Girl from Kay's* (1903), in which Sam Bernard portrayed the part of Mr. Hoggenheimer for the first time, and in which Mary Nash made her first professional stage appearance; *The Earl and the Girl* (1905), of special interest to American music since it was the showcase for Jerome Kern's first Broadway song hit, "How'd You Like to Spoon With Me?"; *The Orchid* (1907), in which Eddie Foy achieved his first success.

In 1911 Caryll settled in the United States, which then became his permanent home and where he became a citizen. His most important operettas now had their point of origin in New York and thus belong to the American rather than English repertory, beginning with *The Pink Lady* (1911). In *Jack O'Lantern* (1917), written for Fred Stone, "Rags" Ragland made one of his rare excursions out of burlesque into musical comedy. This score had two numbers that became popular: "Wait Till the Cows Come Home" and "Come and Have a Swing with Me." In 1918 two of Caryll's operettas boasted lyrics by P. G. Wodehouse: *The Girl Behind the Gun* and *The Canary.* In the former can be found two more popular Caryll songs: "There's a Light in Your Eyes" and "There's Life in the Old Dog." Caryll's last operetta, *Tip-Top,* was produced on October 5, 1920. He died in New York on November 28, 1921.

PRINCIPAL WORKS: The Pink Lady (1911); Oh! Oh! Delphine (1912); Chin-Chin (1914).
*See:* CHIN-CHIN; OH! OH! DELPHINE; THE PINK LADY.

## CHODOROV, JEROME, *librettist*

Chodorov is best known as a writer of nonmusical plays, director of stage productions, and screen writer. He was born in New York City on August 10, 1911, was educated in the New York City public schools, and during World War II served in the United States Air Force. His debut in the Broadway theater took place in 1938 with *Schoolhouse on the Lot,* written with Joseph Fields, with whom he would henceforth frequently collaborate. Success came the same year with *My Sister Eileen,* based on the Ruth McKenney stories that years later were the source of the musical *Wonderful Town.* Other successful nonmusical plays included *Junior Miss* (1941) and *The French Touch* (1945). Chodorov's first libretto for a musical was *Pretty Penny,* which was produced in Pennsylvania during the summer of 1940. *Wonderful Town,* his first highly successful musical, came in 1953. Among the motion pictures with which Chodorov was involved as writer were *Louisiana Purchase, My Sister Eileen, Junior Miss,* and *Happy Anniversary.*

PRINCIPAL WORKS: Wonderful Town (1953); The Girl in Pink Tights (1954). *See:* THE GIRL IN PINK TIGHTS; WONDERFUL TOWN.

## COHAN, GEORGE M., *composer-lyricist-librettist*

The son of veteran vaudevillians, George Michael Cohan was born in the city of Providence, Rhode Island, on July 3, 1878. He was only an infant when he made his first stage appearance, carried on as a human prop for his father's vaudeville sketch. When he was nine, George made a more official stage bow, billed as "Master Georgie" in a sketch starring his parents in Haverstraw, New York. In 1888 the act was further extended to include still another Cohan, George's sister, Josephine. "The Four Cohans" soon became headliners across the country, and as time passed it was George Michael who was its spark plug. He was not only the principal performer, but also business manager and the writer of most of the songs and dialogue. By the time the century closed, the act boasted still a fifth Cohan in the person of the singing comedienne, Ethel Levey, who became George M. Cohan's wife in the summer of 1899.

In 1901 Cohan expanded one of his vaudeville sketches into a musical comedy, *The Governor's Son,* produced at the Savoy Theater in New York on February 25, 1901, starring the five Cohans. Cohan's debut on the musical-comedy stage was not particularly auspicious, since the play lasted only thirty-two performances. In 1903 Cohan made a second attempt at expanding a vaudeville sketch into a Broadway musical comedy, and once again met failure. Then in 1904 Cohan entered into a producing partnership with Sam

H. Harris. Their first venture was a completely new George M. Cohan musical, *Little Johnny Jones*. As was often to be his practice in the future, Cohan not only helped produce the play and wrote book, lyrics, and music, but he also starred in it. At first *Little Johnny Jones* did not do well in New York, since the critics were hostile, but after a successful out-of-town tour it returned to New York to establish itself as a hit.

For the next decade the firm of Cohan and Harris—and sometimes other producers—put on musicals by Cohan in which he often starred. Generally they were the cream of the season's crop. In 1906 there were *Forty-five Minutes from Broadway* and *George Washington, Jr.,* two of Cohan's best musicals. After that came *The Talk of the Town* (1907), *The Yankee Princess* (1908), *The Man Who Owns Broadway* (1910), *The Little Millionaire* (1911), and *Hello, Broadway!* (1914).

As a writer of musical-comedy texts and songs he introduced a fresh, new manner. The plays, like their author, were jaunty, swiftly paced, vivacious. As Heywood Broun once wrote, Cohan became "a symbol of brash violence in theatrical entertainment, a disciple of perpetual motion." Cohan was not equally gifted in all the departments in which he functioned. He himself once confessed his limitations by saying: "As a composer I could never find use for over four or five notes in any musical number . . . and as a playwright, most of my plays have been presented in two acts for the simple reason that I couldn't think of an idea for the third act." He also once remarked, "I can write better plays than any living dancer, and dance better than any living playwright." He had his limitations, and for all his bravado and self-assurance he recognized them. But he knew the theater and his audience, and he was a superb showman. He might frequently be "a vulgar, cheap, blatant, ill-mannered, flashily dressed, insolent smart Alec," as James S. Metcalf described him in *Life* magazine at the time, but he did succeed in bringing into the musical theater a new exuberance, a healthy vitality, a contagious excitement.

Up to 1919 Cohan continued to dominate the Broadway theater as producer, writer, composer, and actor. Several of his nonmusical plays were also outstanding hits, particularly *Get-Rich-Quick Wallingford* (1910), *Broadway Jones* (1912), and *Seven Keys to Baldpate* (1913). In 1917 he wrote the song destined to become one of America's foremost war hymns, "Over There," inspired by America's entry into World War I. By 1919 he was at the height of his fame and power—one of the richest and most influential figures in the American theater.

But in 1920 he began to lose interest in the theater. One reason was his bitterness in losing a major battle with the Actors Equity Association, which in 1919 had called a strike to compel theater managers to recognize it as a bargaining representative for its members. Cohan lined up against Equity and expected all his actor-friends to do likewise. Their alliance with Equity appeared to him as personal betrayal. The complete victory of Actors Equity represented a personal defeat to Cohan, and he became a tired and bitter man. He withdrew his membership from both the Friars and Lambs Clubs; he refused to speak any longer to many who had been his lifelong friends; he dissolved the prosperous firm of Cohan and Harris.

But he did not withdraw completely from the stage, though at one point he threatened to do so. He continued writing and appearing in plays, both musicals and nonmuscials. Two nonmusicals were minor successes: *The Tavern* (1920) and *The Song and Dance Man* (1923). Most of the others were failures. "I guess people don't understand me no more," he remarked, "and I don't understand them."

What Cohan was suffering from was not merely the aftermath of his defeat by Equity, with its shattering blow to his ego. No less poignant to him was his discovery that the theater had been moving so rapidly forward that it was leaving him behind. Both on the musical and the nonmusical stage there had emerged writers with creative imagination, subtlety of wit, technical mastery, and inventiveness of ideas. Their best work was mature, slick, sophisticated. Cohan's plays and Cohan's songs—compared to theirs— seemed old-fashioned, and many of the audiences no longer responded to them. An unhappy episode in Hollywood in 1932, where Cohan went to star in the Rodgers and Hart screen musical *The Phantom President* and where he was continually ignored and slighted, accentuated for him his loss of caste in the theater.

Yet he was not forgotten, nor was he a man without honors. In the 1930's he was starred in two Broadway plays: Eugene O'Neill's homespun American comedy, *Ah, Wildnerness!*, and the Rodgers and Hart musical satire *I'd Rather Be Right*, in which he was cast as President Franklin D. Roosevelt. Both performances were acclaimed, and there were even some to consider him one of the foremost actors of the American stage. In May, 1940, by a special act of Congress, he received from President Roosevelt a special gold medal. And in 1942 his rich career in the theater was brilliantly dramatized on the screen in *Yankee Doodle Dandy,* with James Cagney playing Cohan.

Cohan was gradually recovering from an abdominal operation in 1942 when he insisted that his nurse allow him to tour Broadway in a taxi. Accompanied by the nurse, he cruised around Union Square, then up to Times

Square and through its side streets. He stopped off for a few minutes at the Hollywood Theater to catch a scene from *Yankee Doodle Dandy*. It was almost as if he were reviewing for the last time the highlights of his career.

A few months later—on October 5, 1942—he died. "A beloved figure is lost to our national life," wired President Roosevelt. Mayor La Guardia said: "He put the symbols of American life into American music." And Gene Buck hailed him as "the greatest single figure the American theater has produced."

PRINCIPAL WORKS: Little Johnny Jones (1904); Forty-five Minutes from Broadway (1906); George Washington, Jr. (1906); The Little Millionaire (1911); Hello, Broadway! (1914).
*See:* FORTY-FIVE MINUTES FROM BROADWAY; GEORGE WASHINGTON, JR.; HELLO, BROADWAY!; LITTLE JOHNNY JONES; THE LITTLE MILLIONAIRE. In addition, *see* GEORGE M!, Cohan's stage-musical biography.


## COLEMAN, CY, *composer*

He was born in New York City on June 14, 1929. A precocious child, he early revealed unusual talent for music by giving piano recitals at the age of six. Academic study took place at the High School of Music and Art; music was pursued at the New York College of Music, and piano lessons with Rudolf Gruen and Adele Marcus. Drifting from serious to popular music, Coleman formed a trio which played in nightclubs. Between 1950 and 1953 he wrote background music for the TV program *Date in Manhattan*. In 1953 he made his first contact with the Broadway musical theater by contributing a number to *John Murray Anderson's Almanac*. During this period he was also writing popular songs, with Joseph A. McCarthy as his lyricist, the best being "Why Try to Change Me Now?" (1952) and "I'm Gonna Laugh You Outa My Life" (1955).

Coleman worked for the Kate Smith TV show between 1955 and 1956, and for Art Ford's *Greenwich Village Party* radio program for a year after that. In 1957 he was also the musical director for a stage musical play, *Compulsion*.

Meeting Carolyn Leigh, also a writer for television, proved a decisive turning point in his career, for in her he found a lyricist who could stimulate him to surpass his previous efforts in the field of popular music. Together they produced a number of songs between 1957 and 1959 that became decisive hits, notably "Witchcraft," "I Walked a Little Faster," "A Doodlin' Song," "You Fascinate Me So," "Firefly," "It Amazes Me," and "The Best Is Yet to Come." They wrote their first Broadway musical-comedy score in 1960—*Wildcat*—following it with *Little Me* in 1962. In 1964 they wrote "Pass Me By," another solid hit song, for the motion picture *Father Goose*. Coleman wrote the background music for this movie as well as for *The Troublemaker* and *The Art of Love*. In the Broadway musical *Sweet Charity* (1966), Coleman's lyricist was Dorothy Fields.

PRINCIPAL WORKS: Wildcat (1960); Little Me (1962); Sweet Charity (1966). *See:* LITTLE ME; SWEET CHARITY; WILDCAT.

## COMDEN, BETTY, and GREEN, ADOLPH, *lyricist-librettists*

In the writing of musical-comedy books and song lyrics, Betty Comden and Adolph Green have functioned as a single creative organism. It consequently should afford little surprise to find that their biographies coincide in many details. They were both born in New York City, and in the same year, 1915 —Betty on May 3, Adolph on December 2. Both attended New York University; both were active as members of the Washington Square Players, a period in which their friendship ripened. In the 1930's Comden and Green appeared in a nightclub act, for which they wrote their own songs and dialogue. During this period they called themselves "The Revuers," and one of the members of this group was the actress Judy Holliday. But success did not come to Comden and Green until 1944, when they wrote book and lyrics for, and acted in, *On the Town,* music by Leonard Bernstein. The spontaneity and vitality of their writing was by no means the least of the factors in the substantial success of this musical. Now recognized as important new writers for the musical stage, Comden and Green found numerous assignments awaiting them both on Broadway and in Hollywood. For Broadway—above and beyond the productions listed below—they wrote the texts and lyrics for *Billion Dollar Baby* (1945), *Say, Darling* (1958), and *Subways Are for Sleeping* (1961). In 1958–59 they appeared on Broadway in an evening of entertainment devoted exclusively to their own songs and sketches, entitled *A Party with Comden and Green*. Among their screen credits are *Good News, The Barkleys of Broadway, On the Town, Singin' in the Rain, The Band Wagon, It's Always Fair Weather, Auntie Mame, Bells Are Ringing* and *What a Way to Go*.

PRINCIPAL WORKS: On the Town (1944); Two on the Aisle (1951); Wonderful Town (1953); Bells Are Ringing (1956); Do, Re, Mi (1960); Fade Out—Fade In (1964); Hallelujah, Baby; (1967); Applause (1970).
*See:* APPLAUSE; BELLS ARE RINGING; BILLION DOLLAR BABY; DO, RE, ME; FADE OUT—FADE IN; HALLELUJAH, BABY!; ON THE TOWN; TWO ON THE AISLE; WONDERFUL TOWN.

## COOTS, J. FRED, *composer*

He was born in Brooklyn, New York, on May 2, 1897. His mother, an excellent pianist, hoped he would become a concert artist, and Fred was given instruction early. But he had other ambitions. After his academic education ended when he was sixteen, he tried to emulate a successful uncle by making his way in the world of finance. His first job was in the banking house of the Farmers Loan and Trust Company in Wall Street. One year later Coots found a new goal. A song-plugger playing some Tin Pan Alley tunes in a music shop stimulated him to become a popular composer. He gave up his banking job and became a stock boy and pianist in the McKinley Music Company, a small Tin Pan Alley firm.

His first song came in 1917, inspired by the efforts of Henry Ford to send a peace ship to war-torn Europe and thus bring World War I to a conclusion. Called "Mister Ford You've Got the Right Idea," it was published and earned for its proud composer a royalty of five dollars. Encouraged by the sight of his name on printed sheet music, Coots now became prolific, completing a number of songs that were heard in vaudeville theaters.

At the Friars Club, of which he was a member, Coots gained access to Eddie Dowling, then planning a Broadway musical. Somehow Coots managed to convince Dowling to gamble on him as the composer of the score. The results were happy for both Dowling and Coots, for the show was *Sally, Irene and Mary* (1922), one of the biggest stage hits of the period.

Now an esteemed composer, Coots was contracted by the Shuberts as staff composer. For nine years he wrote songs for many important Shubert musicals and revues. During this period he also wrote special numbers for nightclubs and the movies, appeared as a headliner in vaudeville, and wrote a few independent songs that were outstanding successes, including "I Still Get a Thrill Thinking of You" (1930); "Love Letters in the Sand" (1931), which Pat Boone revived successfully in 1957 with a million-disc sale; "One Minute to One" (1933), a Harry Richman specialty; "Santa Claus Is Coming to Town (1934); "You Go to My Head (1938), popularized by Frank Sinatra; "Why Don't They Let Me Sing a Love Song?" (1942), introduced in the movie *This Time for Keeps;* and "Me and My Teddy Bear" (1953), Rosemary Clooney's first successful recording. However, long before 1953, Coots's career on the Broadway stage ended, and to round out the circle of his Broadway activity, it ended as it had begun, with a major hit, *Sons o' Guns* (1929).

PRINCIPAL WORKS: Sally, Irene and Mary (1922); Artists and Models, 1924 and 1925; A Night in Paris (1926); Sons o' Guns (1929).
*See:* ARTISTS AND MODELS, 1924 and 1925; A NIGHT IN PARIS; SALLY, IRENE AND MARY; SONS O' GUNS.

CROUSE, RUSSEL, and LINDSAY, HOWARD, *librettists*

The playwriting team of Crouse and Lindsay made stage history with their adaptation of *Life with Father,* which enjoyed the longest run of any Broadway play (3,224 performances). *Life with Father* was their first nonmusical play. Before that they had written a number of texts for musical comedies.

Russel Crouse was born in Findlay, Ohio, on February 20, 1893. After receiving his education in Toledo public schools, he found a job in his seventeenth year as reporter for the Cincinnati *Commercial Tribune.* Other newspaper jobs followed, including one as sports writer for the Kansas City, Missouri, *Star* for five years, and as political reporter for the Cincinnati *Post* for one year. During World War I he served in the Navy as yeoman second class. After the war he settled in New York, working successively in the newsrooms of the city's leading papers. The apex of his newspaper career was a daily humor column in the New York *Evening Post* between 1924 and 1929.

The theater soon became a new and broader avenue of activity. In 1928 he turned actor by playing the part of a newspaperman in Ward Morehouse's *Gentlemen of the Press.* In 1931, in collaboration with Morrie Ryskind and Oscar Hammerstein II, he wrote his first musical-comedy text, *The Gang's All Here,* music by Lewis Gensler. *The Gang's All Here* folded after only twenty-three performances. Two years after that, Crouse collaborated with Corey Ford on *Hold Your Horses,* a musical starring Joe Cook that accumulated only eighty-eight performances.

Between 1932 and 1937 Crouse was press agent for the New York Theater Guild. One year after assuming this post, he worked with Howard Lindsay for the first time. They adapted a text by Guy Bolton and P. G. Wodehouse into the Cole Porter musical *Anything Goes,* a smash box-office hit. Russel Crouse had won his first laurels in the theater, and at the same time he had found a writing partner in Lindsay.

Before becoming Crouse's collaborator, Howard Lindsay had achieved success in the theater as actor and director, besides being a writer. He was born in Waterford, New York, on March 29, 1889. When he was thirteen, his family moved to Boston, where Howard attended the Boston Latin School and Harvard College on a scholarship. He was heading toward a career as a minister when he came upon a catalog of the American Academy of Dramatic Arts. Interest in the theater thus awakened, Lindsay enrolled at the academy and stayed there six months. In 1909 he acted in a road show, *Polly of the Circus.* For a few years after that he performed in vaudeville, burlesque, and silent films; and for five years, from 1913 on, he was a member of the Margaret Anglin company. After a hiatus during World War I—when he served in France with the 76th Division and for a few months produced soldier shows—Lindsay acted in and helped direct a major Broadway hit, *Dulcy,* by George S. Kaufman and Marc Connelly (1921). After that he was active as actor and director, both on and off Broadway. He was director of the Skowhegan Playhouse when he met Dorothy Stickney, a young actress there; they were married on August 13, 1927. Lindsay also distinguished himself as a playwright by collaborating on several Broadway stage hits, including *She Loves Me Not, By Your Leave,* and *A Slight Case of Murder.*

In 1936 Crouse and Lindsay wrote two more musical-comedy texts, Cole Porter's *Red, Hot and Blue* (wth Ethel Merman and Jimmy Durante) and Harold Arlen's *Hooray for What?* In 1937 Crouse abandoned press-agenting and went out to Hollywood to work on the screenplays of several important motion-picture musicals, including *The Great Victor Herbert. Life with Father* brought Crouse back to Howard Lindsay and to Broadway. Subsequently, Crouse and Lindsay wrote the 1946 Pulitzer Prize play, *State of the Union,* together with several other successful stage plays and librettos for musical comedies.

Russel Crouse died in New York City on April 3, 1966; Howard Lindsay died on February 11, 1968.

PRINCIPAL WORKS: Anything Goes (1934); Hooray for What? (1937); Call Me Madam (1950); Happy Hunting (1956); The Sound of Music (1959); Mister (Mr.) President (1962).
*See:* ANYTHING GOES; CALL ME MADAM; HAPPY HUNTING; HOORAY FOR WHAT?; MISTER (MR.) PRESIDENT; THE SOUND OF MUSIC.


DARION, JOE, *lyricist. See* Part I, MAN OF LA MANCHA.


DE KOVEN, REGINALD, *composer*
The comic operas of De Koven may be strangers today, but in their time they were popular, and their composer was generally regarded as one of the leading writers of operetta music in the era immediately preceding Victor Herbert.

Reginald de Koven was born in Middletown, Connecticut, on April 3, 1859, the son of a clergyman. When he was thirteen the family moved to England, where Reginald received his academic training. In 1879 he received his degree from St. John's College at Oxford. By this time he had arrived at the decision to make serious music his life work. He consequently went to Germany for intensive training in piano, harmony, and counterpoint. His studies ended in Paris under Léo Delibes.

He returned to the United States in 1882, settling in Chicago. For a while he earned his living as a bank teller, and after that in the office of a stock-brokerage house. His marriage to Anna Farwell, daughter of a successful dry-goods merchant, brought him affluence. For a while he worked in his father-in-law's establishment. When an investment in Texas real estate, made for him by his father-in-law, brought him wealth, he abandoned business permanently and returned to music.

During a visit to Minneapolis, De Koven met Harry B. Smith, a young writer who had written librettos and lyrics for two unsuccessful operettas. They decided to collaborate. For De Koven this partnership was to carry him into the popular theater; for Smith it meant his first contact with success.

In their first comic opera, De Koven and Smith tried to imitate Gilbert and Sullivan's *The Mikado*. Their comic opera *The Begum* had for its setting India, where the reigning princess (the Begum) is permitted as many husbands as she desires; when she tires of one of them, a general, she creates a war to get rid of him. Starring De Wolf Hopper, Digby Bell, and Jefferson de Angelis, *The Begum* was introduced in Philadelphia on November 17, 1888; four days later it appeared at the Fifth Avenue Theater in New York, where it was a failure.

Their next effort, *Don Quixote* (1889), was also a failure. But then came their crowning success—*Robin Hood* (1890). After that a string of comic operas unfolded, some of them successes enjoying several revivals, but all now forgotten. Besides *Rob Roy* and *The Highwayman,* the team of De Koven and Smith wrote *The Knickerbockers* (1892), *The Little Duchess* (1901), *Maid Marian* (1902), and *The Golden Butterfly* (1908), among others.

While working for the popular theater, De Koven did not abandon serious music. He wrote two operas, both introduced by the Metropolitan Opera: *The Canterbury Pilgrims* (1917) and *Rip Van Winkle* (1920). Over a period of many years De Koven also served as music critic and symphony conductor.

De Koven died in New York City on January 16, 1920.

PRINCIPAL WORKS: Robin Hood (1890); Rob Roy (1894); The Highwayman (1896).
*See:* THE HIGHWAYMAN; ROBIN HOOD; ROB ROY.


DE SYLVA, BROWN, and HENDERSON, *librettist, lyricist, and composer*
The songwriting team of De Sylva, Brown, and Henderson introduced a welcome tonic into the musical theater of the 1920's. In contrast to the often escapist and often unreal world in which most of the musical comedies of that period moved, those of De Sylva, Brown, and Henderson were concerned

with comparatively everyday themes of everyday life—modern Americana generously spiced with the salt and pepper of comedy and satire.

Ray Henderson was the composer. Buddy de Sylva and Lew Brown collaborated on the lyrics. Buddy de Sylva also had a hand in the writing of the texts. But the three men worked together so intimately and harmoniously that they represented a single entity. The musician often contributed ideas and approaches to the lyricists, and vice versa. As long as they functioned as a single unity they were fruitful contributors to the theater.

Buddy de Sylva was the base of the triangle on which the other two rested. He was born George Gard de Sylva in New York City on January 27, 1895. His father had toured the vaudeville circuit until marriage, when he abandoned the stage for law. Buddy was only a child when he made his stage bow at the Los Angeles Grand Opera House; he was such a success in a song-and-dance routine that a vaudeville tour was planned for him on the Keith circuit. This attempt to exploit a child prodigy was frustrated by Buddy's grandfather, and a more normal development followed in California's public schools, and after that at the University of South California.

In his freshman year De Sylva helped produce a college show. During the same period he played a ukulele in a Hawaiian band and started writing song lyrics. A few of the last (beginning with " 'N Everything") came to the attention of Al Jolson, who set them to music and interpolated some of them in *Sinbad* at the Winter Garden. These De Sylva lyrics (often written with the aid of others), with which his Broadway debut as lyricist was made, included such substantial hits as "Avalon" and "I'll Say She Is." De Sylva's first royalty check from Tin Pan Alley—the sum of $16,000—lured him from New York City to pursue more actively a career as a songwriter. Engaged by the publishing house of J. H. Remick, he went to work with Arthur Jackson, also a lyricist, in writing the lyrics for George Gershwin's first musical comedy, *La, La, Lucille*. During the next few years De Sylva became an ace lyricist who (still often working hand in hand with other writers) produced the words for Jerome Kern, Victor Herbert, George Gershwin, and Jolson, among others, and was involved in such outstanding song hits as "Look for the Silver Lining" (Kern), "California Here I Come" (Joseph Meyer), "A Kiss in the Dark" (Herbert), "Somebody Loves Me" (Gershwin), and "April Showers" (Louis Silvers). Among the musicals in which De Sylva was represented during this period were *Sally, The Ziegfeld Follies of 1921, Bombo, Orange Blossoms,* and *George White's Scandals* from 1921 through 1924.

When George Gershwin withdrew as the composer of the *Scandals*, he was replaced by the songwriting team of De Sylva, Brown, and Henderson.

Lew Brown was also a lyricist. By the time he joined up with De Sylva and Henderson he had become successful for ballads like "I May Be Gone for a Long, Long Time" and "I Used to Love You." He was born in Odessa, Russia, as Louis Brownstein on December 10, 1893. At five, he came with his family to the United States, living at first in New Haven, and then settling in New York, where Brown attended elementary school and De Witt Clinton High School. While working as a lifeguard on Rockaway Beach he amused himself by writing parodies of popular songs. This activity stimulated a latent desire to write songs. He now abruptly terminated his academic education at the high-school level to invade Tin Pan Alley. His first published song, "Don't Take My Lovin' Man," earned him only seven dollars in royalties, even though it was sung by Belle Baker in vaudeville. But before long Brown found a place for himself with the veteran composer-publisher Albert von Tilzer. In 1912 Brown wrote lyrics for five Tilzer songs, one of which was popular, "I'm the Lonesomest Gal in Town." For the next two years he kept on writing words to Albert von Tilzer's music, collaborating on the popular World War I ballad "I May Be Gone for a Long, Long Time" (heard in *Hitchy Koo of 1917*), "Oh, by Jingo" (interpolated into the Broadway musical *Linger Longer Letty*), and "I Used to Love You." Then, in 1922, Lew Brown produced lyrics for "Georgette," a song heard in *The Greenwich Village Follies* of 1922, music by Ray Henderson. The same year he wrote with Henderson "Humming."

Ray Henderson had been trained as a serious musician. Born in Buffalo. New York, on December 1, 1896, he was the son of a mother who was an excellent pianist and who gave him his first music instruction before he could read or write. As a boy, Ray played the organ and sang in the choir of the local Episcopal church. He also started writing serious music. Showing unusual musical aptitude, he was then enrolled in the Chicago Conservatory of Music for intensive training. But even before he had entered the conservatory he began to drift toward popular music by playing the piano in jazz bands. While attending the conservatory he received a regular income by performing popular tunes on the piano at parties and by occasionally appearing in vaudeville in an act that included an Irish tenor and a Jewish comedian.

Once out of the conservatory, he abandoned serious music. His first job was as song plugger for the firm of Leo Feist in Tin Pan Alley. After a few weeks there he became arranger and staff pianist for Fred Fisher. His next job was with Shapiro-Bernstein, where his talent impressed Louis Bernstein, who found a post for Henderson with various vaudevillians. He was also instrumental in getting Ray Henderson to work with Lew Brown, a lyricist who had already proved himself. It was the firm of Shapiro-Bernstein that published the two first fruits of Brown and Henderson, "Georgette" and "Humming."

Now sometimes with Brown, now sometimes with other lyricists, Ray Henderson wrote songs that became leaders in Tin Pan Alley: "That Old Gang of Mine," "Alabamy Bound," and "Five Foot Two, Eyes of Blue," among others. Buddy de Sylva helped in writing the lyrics for "Alabamy Bound," the first time he worked with Henderson. When George White had to replace George Gershwin he called on Buddy de Sylva (who had previously worked so successfully in the *Scandals*) to join with Ray Henderson and Lew Brown in producing the songs for his annual revue. This trio of writers worked in the editions of 1925, 1926, and 1928; and it was there that their first song successes as a song triumvirate were born.

While working for George White, De Sylva, Brown, and Henderson were able to complete several musical comedies, some of them major box-office attractions. Their first musical was *Good News* (1927), a hit. *Manhattan Mary,* starring Ed Wynn, came three weeks after *Good News,* but it proved to be merely a hiatus between two triumphs. *Hold Everything* (1928) was another box-office bonanza, and was followed by *Follow Through* (1929) and *Flying High* (1930).

The closing decade also brought about the end of this fruitful collaboration. De Sylva went to Hollywood to work as a producer, first for Fox, then for 20th Century-Fox. (Before this, however, the team of De Sylva, Brown, and Henderson had contributed some excellent songs for the screen: "Sonny Boy" and "There's a Rainbow 'Round My Shoulder" for Al Jolson's *Sonny,* and the score for the Janet Gaynor-Charles Farrell musical, *Sunny Side Up.*) Somewhere and somehow, in the midst of his frenetic activities in Hollywood, De Sylva found time to return to Broadway to produce several musical shows and to write some musical-comedy texts. In 1932 he helped produce and write *Take A Chance.* After that he had three box-office triumphs in succession: *Du Barry Was a Lady, Panama Hattie,* and *Louisiana Purchase;* for the first two of these he also helped to write the books. De Sylva died in Hollywood on July 11, 1950, still a giant figure on Broadway and in Hollywood.

Divorced from De Sylva, the team of Brown and Henderson kept on writing songs for the Broadway stage. None of these productions had the vigor or originality that enlivened the shows they had previously written with De Sylva. Their failure to hit a winning stride led them to break up partnership temporarily. Lew Brown went out to Hollywood as a producer. He died in New York City on February 5, 1958. Henderson worked with other lyricists on songs for various Broadway and Hollywood productions. His Broadway plays included *George White's Scandals* of 1931 and 1935 and *The Ziegfeld Follies* of 1943, the last of which achieved the longest run of any edition of the *Follies*.

It was the screen that helped recall the heyday of De Sylva, Brown, and Henderson in 1956, when it presented *The Best Things in Life Are Free*, a biography of the songwriting trio and a cavalcade of their most popular songs.

The listing below includes not only those musicals in which the three men collaborated, but also those in which they individually made contributions.

PRINCIPAL WORKS: La, La, Lucille (1919); Bombo (1921); The Ziegfeld Follies of 1921; George White's Scandals, 1922 through 1926; Good News (1927); George White's Scandals of 1928; Hold Everything (1928); Follow Thru (1929); Flying High (1930); George White's Scandals of 1931; Take a Chance (1932); Du Barry Was a Lady (1939); Louisiana Purchase (1940); Panama Hattie (1940). *See:* BOMBO; DU BARRY WAS A LADY; FLYING HIGH; FOLLOW THRU; GEORGE WHITE'S SCANDALS, 1922 through 1926, 1928, 1931; GOOD NEWS; HOLD EVERYTHING; LA, LA, LUCILLE; LOUISIANA PURCHASE; PANAMA HATTIE; TAKE A CHANCE; THE ZIEGFELD FOLLIES of 1921.

## DIETZ, HOWARD, *lyricist*

Dietz achieved his greatest successes in the musical theater as lyricist for Arthur Schwartz, the composer. Dietz was born in New York City on September 8, 1896. He first attended Townsend Harris Hall, then Columbia College, where he was a fellow student of Lorenz Hart and Oscar Hammerstein II. He contributed verses and humorous pieces to college magazines and to the famous newspaper columns of F.P.A. (Franklin P. Adams) and Don Marquis while attending Columbia, and even won a prize of $500 for writing copy for an advertisement for Fatima cigarettes. Upon being graduated from Columbia, he entered the advertising field and—after a stint in the Navy during World War I—became a successful advertising executive. One of his accounts was Goldwyn Pictures Corporation, for whom he created the slogan *"ars gratia artis"* and the head of a roaring lion as a symbol. In 1924 he was made advertising director and promotion manager of Metro-Goldwyn-Mayer, a post he held for thirty years, eventually holding the office of vice-president.

Lyric writing remained a major interest, then an all-important and remunerative activity during all these years. Dietz' first published lyric was "Alibi Baby" (music by Arthur Samuel), and it was also his first lyric to get heard on the Broadway stage, in *Poppy* (1923). In 1924 he wrote lyrics for Kern's musical *Dear Sir,* and in 1927 he collaborated with Morrie Ryskind in writing book and lyrics for an intimate revue, *Merry-Go-Round*.

An ardent admirer of Dietz' talent, Arthur Schwartz had for some time tried to convince Dietz to become his lyricist. Dietz finally succumbed to

Schwartz' persuasion. Their first important collaboration also proved to be their first box-office triumph, *The Little Show,* in 1929. The collaboration of Schwartz and Dietz continued for many years after that, resulting in several outstanding Broadway successes, and a few failures. Among the failures was an interesting experiment in musical playwriting, *Revenge with Music* (1934), which contained such outstanding songs as "You and the Night and the Music" and "If There Is Someone Lovelier than You." Generally, Dietz and Schwartz proved successes in the field of revues, and failures in musical comedies.

In 1944 Dietz wrote the lyrics to Vernon Duke's music for the musical *Sadie Thompson* (based on Somerset Maugham's *Rain*), a failure. The Dietz and Schwartz combination was resumed with *Inside U.S.A.* in 1948, and after a long hiatus continued with two musical comedies that represented box-office deficits, *The Gay Life* (1961) and *Jennie* (1963), the latter starring Mary Martin. In addition to his work in the theater, Dietz wrote material for radio and television, and in 1950 collaborated with Garson Kanin in preparing an English text for the famous Johann Strauss operetta *Die Fledermaus,* which was produced by the Metropolitan Opera.

PRINCIPAL WORKS: The Little Show (1929); The Second Little Show (1930); Three's a Crowd (1930); The Band Wagon (1931); Flying Colors (1932); At Home Abroad (1935); Inside U.S.A. (1948); The Ziegfeld Follies of 1957.
*See:* AT HOME ABROAD; THE BAND WAGON; FLYING COLORS; INSIDE U.S.A.; THE LITTLE SHOW 1929 and 1930; THREE'S A CROWD; THE ZIEGFELD FOLLIES of 1957.

## DONNELLY, DOROTHY, *librettist-lyricist*

Before achieving fame as a musical-comedy librettist and lyricist, she was a successful actress. She was born in New York City on January 28, 1880, and raised in a convent. She received her theatrical apprenticeship with the Henry Donnelly Stock Company. Among the notable plays in which she later starred were *Candida* (where she created for the United States the title role) and *Madam X.* As a librettist she worked fruitfully with Sigmund Romberg, providing him with the books for *Blossom Time, The Student Prince in Heidelberg,* and *My Maryland,* the last of these (a failure) in 1927. She died in New York on January 3, 1928.

PRINCIPAL WORKS: Blossom Time (1921); Poppy (1923); The Student Prince in Heidelberg (1924).
*See:* BLOSSOM TIME; POPPY; THE STUDENT PRINCE IN HEIDELBERG.

## DRAKE, ERVIN, *composer-lyricist. See* Part I, WHAT MAKES SAMMY RUN?

## DUKE, VERNON, *composer*

He was born Vladimir Dukelsky on on October 10, 1903, in Pskov, Russia. He was seven when he started music study, eight when he completed the score for a ballet. Though his father wanted him to become a diplomat or find a career in the Russian Navy, Vladimir—or Vernon as we shall henceforth call him—entered the Kiev Conservatory at the age of fifteen, where his teacher was Glière. During the Revolution, Vernon fled with his mother and brother to Constantinople, where Duke supported himself by arranging concerts for a club for refugees run by the YMCA. There he came across several copies of sheet music of American popular songs, one of which was Gershwin's "Swanee." From that moment on he not only became a dedicated Gershwin fan but was stimulated to write popular songs of his own. After coming to the United States in 1921 he was introduced to Gershwin, for whom he played some of his esoteric piano sonatas. "There's no heart in it," Gershwin told him and urged him to try "writing real popular tunes, and don't be scared about going low-brow." Gershwin was generous with advice, help, and encouragement; he was also responsible for creating an American name for him, that of Vernon Duke, used by Duke for his popular productions and from 1955 on for all his music. In 1937 Duke repaid at least partly the debt he owed Gershwin by completing Gershwin's score for *The Goldwyn Follies,* left unfinished by Gershwin's last fatal illness.

While making tentative efforts at writing popular tunes, Duke supported himself by writing musical accompaniments for a magician's act, playing the piano in a 42nd Street restaurant, creating music for a nightclub show, and (for one week) conducting an orchestra in a 14th Street burlesque house. He finally decided to concentrate on serious music. In 1924 he returned to Paris, where he wrote a ballet, *Zephyr et Flore,* which was produced by the Ballet Russe de Monte Carlo in 1925, and was performed soon afterward in Paris, London, and Berlin.

In Paris he met Serge Koussevitzky, then recently appointed music director of the Boston Symphony Orchestra. Koussevitzky became an ardent champion of Duke's music. Over a period of years, beginning with 1929, Koussevitzky frequently introduced major works by Duke with the Boston Symphony, including a symphony, a violin concerto, and a cello concerto.

After his stay in Paris, in 1925 Duke proceeded to London, where he contributed six numbers to a musical, *Yvonne,* produced in 1926; Noël Coward described it as "Yvonne the terrible." Soon after that, Duke wrote his first complete stage score: it was for an Edgar Wallace thriller, *The Yellow Mask,* which had a London run of seven months.

Duke was back in the United States in 1929. For a while he worked in

Astoria, Long Island, for Paramount Pictures, writing background music for several motion pictures. During this time he first stormed the citadels of Broadway with songs. Two were heard in the third edition of *The Garrick Gaieties* in 1930: "I'm Only Human After All" (lyrics by Ira Gershwin and E. Y. Harburg) and "Too Too Divine" (lyrics by Harburg). Other songs appeared in various revues; of particular interest were "Talkative Toes" in *Three's a Crowd* (1930), "Muchacha" in *Shoot the Works* (1931), "Let Me Match My Private Life with Yours" in *Americana* (1932), and "Autumn in New York" in *Thumbs Up* (1935).

A modest success came in 1932 with his first full Broadway score, for the revue *Walk a Little Faster,* in which "April in Paris"—probably his most famous song—was introduced. In 1934 and 1935 he contributed some numbers for *The Ziegfeld Follies,* including such fine songs as "What Is There to Say?" and "I Can't Get Started with You." The revue *The Show Is On* (1936) had a good deal of Duke music in it. However, a musical comedy with a score entirely his own did not appear on Broadway until *Cabin in the Sky* (1940). In 1941 came *Banjo Eyes,* starring Eddie Cantor, a box-office success. After that came a string of failures, including *Sadie Thompson* (1944), an unhappy adaptation of Somerset Maugham's *Rain,* and two revues. The first of these revues was *Two's Company* (1952), in which Bette Davis made a heroic effort to sing and play comedy, an effort that never quite came off; the other was an unimpressive thing called *The Littlest Revue* (1956). In 1957 (the year in which he married Kay McCracken, a young singer) he wrote the background music for the Jean Anouilh play *Time Remembered,* starring Helen Hayes, on Broadway. In 1957 and again in 1961 he wrote scores for ballets. Two later musicals to which he contributed scores—*Zenda* and *The Pink Jungle*—never reached Broadway.

Duke translated the lyrics of numerous American popular songs into Russian, beamed to the Soviet Union by Radio Liberty. His autobiography, *Passport to Paris,* was published in 1955. Duke died in Santa Monica, California, on January 17, 1968.

PRINCIPAL WORKS: Walk a Little Faster (1932); The Ziegfeld Follies of 1934 and 1936–1937; Cabin in the Sky (1940); Banjo Eyes (1941).
See: BANJO EYES; CABIN IN THE SKY; WALK A LITTLE FASTER; THE ZIEGFELD FOLLIES of 1934 and 1936–1937.

EBB, FRED, *lyricist. See* KANDER, JOHN, AND EBB, FRED.

ENGLANDER, LUDWIG, *composer*
His fame has been so completely eclipsed that very little information about him

has survived. When he died, only a few lines of obituary reminded theatergoers that he had once written some lovable operetta scores. Since his death he has been forgotten so completely that not even the standard reference books mention him. The meager biographical facts are these: He was born in Vienna in 1859, received his academic education at the university there, and had some musical training from Jacques Offenbach. In 1882 he came to New York, where he became the conductor at the Thalia Theater. His first musical, *The Princess Consort,* was a failure. In 1894 he became known through *The Passing Show,* and in the next dozen years or so his reputation was established with several prominent productions, among them *The Rounders* (1899); *The Casino Girl* (1900); *Belle of Bohemia* (1900); *The Strollers* (1901); *A Madcap Princess,* based on Charles Major's novel *When Knighthood Was in Flower* (1904); and *Miss Innocence* (1908). By the time he died—at his home in Far Rockaway, New York, on September 13, 1914—he had written the music for thirty-five operettas. He was a skilled craftsman in writing facile melodies that had the lilt, pulse, and charm of Vienna. But his range was small, and his storehouse of melodic ideas not too well stocked. His last few operettas were failures; the last one, *Mlle. Moselle* (1914) ran only nine performances. And by the time he died there were not many to recall that a decade earlier he had been a prominent musical figure on Broadway.

PRINCIPAL WORKS: The Passing Show (1894); Belle of Bohemia (1900); The Casino Girl (1900); The Strollers (1901); The Rich Mr. Hoggenheimer (1906). *See:* BELLE OF BOHEMIA; THE CASINO GIRL; THE PASSING SHOW; THE RICH MR. HOGGENHEIMER; THE STROLLERS.

## FAIN, SAMMY, *composer*

He was born in New York City on June 17, 1902, the nephew of the famous comedians Eugene and Willie Howard. In his boyhood, Fain's family moved to the Sullivan County section of New York State, where Sammy attended public schools, taught himself to play the piano, and started writing popular songs, which he faithfully dispatched by mail to Tin Pan Alley, with discouraging results. After completing high school, Fain returned to New York City, where he found a job as staff pianist for the Jack Mills publishing house, then toured the vaudeville circuit with Artie Dunn, and finally made a name for himself as a radio entertainer.

His first professional song came in 1925, "Nobody Knows What a Red-Headed Mama Can Do." In 1927 Fain met and teamed up with Irving Kahal, lyricist, with whom he established a seventeen-year partnership. Kahal was born in Houtzdale, Pennsylvania, on March 5, 1903, was educated in public schools in Connecticut and New York City, and at sixteen attended Cooper

Union art school on a scholarship. By the time Fain met him, Kahal had already toured with the Gus Edwards Minstrels as a singer and had written some song lyrics.

The first song by Fain and Kahal was a winner, "Let a Smile Be Your Umbrella" (1927). This was followed in 1929 by another hit, "Wedding Bells Are Breaking Up That Old Gang of Mine." From then on—and up to the time of Kahal's death in New York on February 7, 1942—they produced a long string of song successes, some for the Broadway stage but most for Hollywood, where they had worked since 1930. Their best motion-picture songs were: "You Brought a New Kind of Love to Me" (made famous by Maurice Chevalier); "When I Take My Sugar to Tea"; "By a Waterfall"; and "I'll Be Seeing You," a popular World War II ballad. Other outstanding songs by Fain for the screen were to the words of other lyricists: the lyricist for "That Old Feeling" was Lew Brown; that for "Dear Hearts and Gentle People," Bob Hilliard; that for "The Dickey Bird Song," Howard Dietz; while with Paul Francis Webster, Fain wrote two songs that won Academy Awards: "Secret Love" in 1953 and "Love Is a Many-Splendored Thing" in 1955.

Fain's first endeavors for the Broadway stage were in collaboration with Kahal: a single song, "Satan's Holiday," in *Manhattan Mary* (1927); the entire score for a revue, *Everybody's Welcome* (1931).

Fain's greatest successes on Broadway came with two riot-filled extravaganzas of Olsen and Johnson: *Hellzapoppin'* (1938) and *Sons o' Fun* (1941). Other musicals and revues with Fain's songs included the following: *Right This Way* (1938), which had "I Can Dream, Can't I?"; *George White's Scandals of 1939,* where "Are You Having Any Fun?" was introduced; *Boys and Girls Together* (1939), a revue starring Ed Wynn; *Toplitsky of Notre Dame* (1946); *Flahooley* (1951); *Ankles Aweigh* (1955); and *The Ziegfeld Follies* of 1957.

PRINCIPAL WORKS: Hellzapoppin' (1938); George White's Scandals of 1939; Sons o' Fun (1941); The Ziegfeld Follies of 1957.
See: GEORGE WHITE'S SCANDALS of 1939; HELLZAPOPPIN'; SONS O' FUN; THE ZIEGFELD FOLLIES of 1957.


## FIELDS, DOROTHY, *librettist-lyricist*

She was born with theater blood in her veins. Her father was Lew Fields, erstwhile partner in the famous team of Weber and Fields, which for many years starred in Broadway extravaganzas (*see* WEBER AND FIELDS EXTRAVAGANZAS). After the breakup of this partnership, Lew Fields embarked on a new career—as producer, and sometimes star, of Broadway musicals. Dorothy's two brothers, Herbert and Joseph, also distinguished themselves in the musical theater as librettists. Dorothy Fields often worked collaboratively, now with one and now with the other of her two highly gifted brothers, whose biographies appear below.

She was born in Aldehurst, New Jersey, on July 15, 1905, and was educated in the Benjamin School for Girls in New York, where she participated in school productions (some written by the then still unknown and inexperienced Rodgers and Hart). Her schooling ended, she taught art in high school while submitting poems to magazines and trying her hand at song lyrics. Trying to market her lyrics brought an unexpected but rich dividend when, one day, at the publishing house of Mills Music, she met the composer Jimmy McHugh. They decided to form a partnership. Their maiden effort was the songs for the highly successful revue *Blackbirds of 1928,* from which came Dorothy Fields' first giant hit song, "I Can't Give You Anything but Love, Baby." This was followed by the musicals *Hello Daddy* (1928) and the *International Revue* (1930)—from the latter coming the hit songs "On the Sunny Side of the Street" and "Exactly like You." Dorothy Fields and McHugh then worked in Hollywood, contributing songs to numerous motion pictures. Between 1933 and 1935 their screen songs included "I Feel a Song Comin' On," "I'm in the Mood for Love," "Thank You for a Lovely Evening," and (in collaboration with Jerome Kern) "Lovely to Look At." In 1935 she began a hardly less fruitful words-and-music partnership with Jerome Kern in Hollywood, from one of whose pictures (*Swing Time*) came an Oscar-winning song in "The Way You Look Tonight" (1936).

Returning to Broadway, Dorothy worked with her brother Herbert in several notable musicals for which Cole Porter supplied the music, beginning with *Let's Face It* (1941). In subsequent Broadway musicals she worked (frequently in collaboration with one of her two brothers) with other composers, too—notably, with Sigmund Romberg in *Up in Central Park* (1945); Irving Berlin in *Annie Get Your Gun* (1946); Arthur Schwartz in *A Tree Grows in Brooklyn* (1951) and *By the Beautiful Sea* (1954); Albert Hague in *Redhead* (1959); and Cy Coleman in *Sweet Charity* (1966). In these and other productions she has proved herself one of the most skillful and versatile writers for the musical stage both in texts and in lyrics.

PRINCIPAL WORKS: Blackbirds of 1928; Hello Daddy (1928); Let's Face It (1941); Something for the Boys (1943); Mexican Hayride (1944); Up in Central Park (1945); Annie Get Your Gun (1946); A Tree Grows in Brooklyn (1951); By the Beautiful Sea (1954); Redhead (1959); Sweet Charity (1966).
*See:* ANNIE GET YOUR GUN; BLACKBIRDS OF 1928; BY THE BEAUTIFUL SEA; HELLO DADDY; LET'S FACE IT; MEXICAN HAYRIDE; REDHEAD; SOMETHING FOR THE BOYS; SWEET CHARITY; A TREE GROWS IN BROOKLYN; UP IN CENTRAL PARK.

# FIELDS, HERBERT, *librettist*

He was the son of Lew Fields (of Weber and Fields) and the brother of Joseph and Dorothy, the latter of whom he frequently collaborated with in the writing of musical-comedy texts. He was born in New York City on July 26, 1897, and educated in New York City schools and at Columbia College. When first he entered the theater, it was as an actor and not as a writer. He had a pleasing stage presence, a nice voice, and a gift for dialect; all these qualities led his father to cast him in minor roles.

The idea of his turning from actor to writer was born with his friends Lorenz Hart and Richard Rodgers. Hart and Fields had known each other from boyhood. They used to play on the city streets in Harlem, where both lived at the time; during the summer of 1910 they produced shows at a boys' camp. Fields's first meeting with Rodgers, however, did not take place until 1919, when the latter came to Lew Fields's summer place in Far Rockaway, New York, to play some of his songs. When Lew Fields accepted the Rodgers and Hart song "Any Old Place with You" for *A Lonely Romeo,* the paths of Rodgers and Herbert Fields crossed again, for Herbert played a small role in that show.

One evening, at Larry Hart's home on 119th Street, Rodgers and Hart suggested to Herbert Fields that he try writing musical-comedy texts. The three of them went to work on a musical, *Winkle Town,* which nobody wanted to produce. Under a pseudonym the three men then wrote a comedy about Tin Pan Alley (with several interpolated songs) called *The Melody Man.* Lew Fields produced and starred in it in 1924, but it was a failure. Rodgers, Hart, and Fields also worked together on some amateur musical productions.

They achieved their first musical-comedy success in 1925 with *Dearest Enemy,* for which Herbert Fields wrote the text, and Rodgers and Hart the songs. For the next half-dozen years, the team of Rodgers, Hart, and Fields wrote a succession of musicals, some of which were outstanding successes. Herbert Fields's courage in the selection of unusual subjects for musical-comedy treatment, his complete sympathy with the unusual approaches and procedures of his partners, made him one of the most important musical-comedy writers of the 1920's. But during this period he worked with other composers as well, notably Vincent Youmans and Cole Porter.

After Herbert Fields parted company with Rodgers and Hart, he continued to write musical-comedy texts for other composers, the most important of whom was Cole Porter. It was for the Cole Porter musical *Let's Face It* (1941) that the brother-and-sister writing partnership was launched; but by then Dorothy Fields, like Herbert, had already won acceptance as a writer for the musical stage.

Besides working with Cole Porter on Broadway, Dorothy and Herbert Fields also wrote texts (and Dorothy the lyrics as well) for such other celebrated composers as Irving Berlin, Sigmund Romberg, and Arthur Schwartz. Above and beyond his activity on Broadway, Herbert Fields wrote numerous film scenarios, besides helping to adapt some of his Broadway musicals for the screen. He died of a heart attack in New York City on March 24, 1958.

PRINCIPAL WORKS: Dearest Enemy (1925); The Girl Friend (1926); Peggy-Ann (1926); Hit the Deck (1927); Present Arms (1928); Hello Daddy (1928); Fifty Million Frenchmen (1929); Du Barry Was a Lady (1939); Panama Hattie (1940); Let's Face It (1941); Something for the Boys (1943); Mexican Hayride (1944); Up in Central Park (1945); Annie Get Your Gun (1946); By the Beautiful Sea (1954); Redhead (1959).

See: ANNIE GET YOUR GUN; BY THE BEAUTIFUL SEA; DEAREST ENEMY; DU BARRY WAS A LADY; FIFTY MILLION FRENCHMEN; THE GIRL FRIEND; HELLO DADDY; HIT THE DECK; LET'S FACE IT; MEXICAN HAYRIDE; PANAMA HATTIE; PEGGY-ANN; PRESENT ARMS; REDHEAD; SOMETHING FOR THE BOYS; UP IN CENTRAL PARK.

## FIELDS, JOSEPH, *librettist*

He was the oldest of the Fields children, the son of Lew Fields (of Weber and Fields), and the brother of Dorothy and Herbert Fields (*see* above). He was born in New York City on February 21, 1885, and received his education in the New York City public schools, Hamilton Institute in New York, and New York University. He is perhaps best known as a playwright in the non-musical field, his first Broadway opus being *Schoolhouse on the Lot,* written in collaboration with Jerome Chodorov (1938). This was followed by such redoubtable successes as *My Sister Eileen* (1940), *Junior Miss* (1941), and *The French Touch* (1945), all with Chodorov. His first significant musical-comedy book was *Gentlement Prefer Blondes* (1949). Many other successful musicals came after that, the scores by such distinguished composers as Leonard Bernstein, Romberg, and Richard Rodgers. Joseph Fields was also singularly active as a director of stage productions and as a scenario writer for (and sometimes producer of) motion pictures, musical as well as nonmusical.

PRINCIPAL WORKS: Gentlemen Prefer Blondes (1949); Wonderful Town (1953); The Girl in Pink Tights (1954); Flower Drum Song (1958).

See: FLOWER DRUM SONG; GENTLEMEN PREFER BLONDES; THE GIRL IN PINK TIGHTS; WONDERFUL TOWN.

## FORREST, GEORGE, *composer-lyricist. See* WRIGHT, ROBERT, AND FORREST, GEORGE.

## FRIML, RUDOLF, *composer*

Rudolf Friml was in his heyday before and during the 1920's, when the

American operetta was popular and subservient to European methods and styles. What he produced before 1930 has won for him the right to join the foremost composers of that period. The traditions in which he functioned best—the European-type operetta—might have died, but the music Friml wrote conforming to those traditions has survived.

He was born in Prague on December 7, 1879. He revealed unusual musical ability from childhood on. He was only ten when his "Barcarolle" for piano was published. Friends and relatives pooled contributions into a fund, sending him to the Prague Conservatory, then directed by Anton Dvořák. Friml, aged fourteen, took entrance examinations and was put into the third year, thus enabling him to complete a six-year course in three years.

After leaving the conservatory, Friml became the piano accompanist for Jan Kubelik, a young violin virtuoso. They toured Europe and America— their first tour of America taking place in 1901, and a second in 1906. Friml now decided to remain in the United States for good to further his own musical career, since he had already made a good impression in his debut as concert pianist in Carnegie Hall in 1904, and in a performance of his own Piano Concerto with the New York Symphony Society in 1906. After that he was heard in recitals and with orchestras. He also wrote a good deal of music—mostly songs which revealed a highly pleasing lyricism as well as a sound technique.

He was an industrious, competent, but not particularly brilliant composer when chance brought him into the Broadway theater. Victor Herbert had planned an operetta for Emma Trentini, to follow his own *Naughty Marietta.* During the run of *Naughty Marietta,* however, Herbert and Trentini became involved in a bitter feud and refused to communicate with each other. Herbert bowed out as composer for the singer's new operetta, and a new composer had to be found. Rudolph Schirmer and Max Dreyfus, two perceptive publishers, suggested the then unknown Rudolf Friml, both feeling that Friml had the talent to write well for voices and for the stage. Arthur Hammerstein, the producer, followed their advice and contracted Friml. Thus Friml put both feet into the theater for the first time with a triumphant production— for the play for which he was asked to write the music was *The Firefly* (1912).

With *The Firefly* outstandingly successful, Friml no longer had a dearth of assignments. When the book did not stand in the way of his gracious, charming lyricism, he created operettas that were acclaimed, among them some of the best-loved ones in the American theater. Among the lesser Friml successes, but those with attractive scores, were *Katinka* (1915), *You're in Love* (1917), and *Tumble Inn* (1919).

But by 1930 Friml's day as a successful stage composer was over. The musical theater had changed radically, and Friml's musicals had not changed with it. Like Victor Herbert before him, Friml found himself outdated. An operetta with a Hawaiian setting, *Luana* (1930), was a failure; so was *Anina* (1934). After 1934, Friml's main center of creative activity was Hollywood, but this was short-lived.

On December 7, 1969, a testimonial concert, sponsored by ASCAP, took place in New York to honor Rudolf Friml on his ninetieth birthday, and the forty-fifth anniversary of one of his most famous operettas, *Rose-Marie*.

PRINCIPAL WORKS: The Firefly (1912); High Jinks (1913); Sometime (1918); The Ziegfeld Follies of 1921 and 1923; Rose-Marie (1924); The Vagabond King (1925); The Three Musketeers (1928).

*See:* THE FIREFLY; HIGH JINKS; ROSE-MARIE; SOMETIME; THE THREE MUSKETEERS; THE VAGABOND KING; THE ZIEGFELD of 1921 and 1923.


## GERSHWIN, GEORGE, *composer*

George Gershwin wrote music for over twenty Broadway musicals and contributed songs to about another dozen. Only three of these productions sounded a new note for the American stage: *Strike Up the Band, Of Thee I Sing,* and the folk opera *Porgy and Bess.* All the other Gershwin musicals were traditional in aim and technique, faithful to the well-tried patterns of the period. The best of the Gershwin musicals were outstanding, however, because Gershwin was an outstanding composer.

He was born in Brooklyn, New York, on September 26, 1898. There was little in his boyhood to suggest that here were the makings of a musician. He liked to play the games of the streets with his friends, and showed little interest in books, music, or the theater.

A few scattered musical experiences stirred something deep within him. One was hearing Rubinstein's "Melody in F" in a penny arcade when he was six. Another was listening to some real jazz music outside a Harlem nightclub when he was seven. A third was a violin performance by a schoolmate at a public-school assembly. It was this schoolmate who first helped to introduce him to good music—a boy named Maxie Rosenzweig, who later in life became famous as a violin virtuoso under the name of Max Rosen.

When George was twelve, a piano entered his home, and he started taking lessons. A significant influence came into his life when he began studying with Charles Hambitzer in 1912. Hambitzer was a remarkable musician who had the capacity to excite in his pupils the wonder of great music. Through Hambitzer, Gershwin came to know for the first time the music of many classical composers, and even of such moderns as Debussy and Ravel.

Though Gershwin now came to cherish the classics, he knew even then that if he was to make his way in music it would have to be in the popular field. He loved ragtime, Irving Berlin, the songs of Tin Pan Alley. And, amazing to remark, he already felt strongly that American popular music could become an important art—if the composer brought to it the same background and equipment he did to the writing of a symphony or opera. Again and again Gershwin tried to convince Hambitzer of the validity of such convictions. "The boy is a genius without a doubt," Hambitzer wrote to his sister. "He wants to go in for this modern stuff, jazz and what not. But I'm not going to let him for a while. I'll see that he gets a firm foundation in the standard music first." To get that firm foundation, Hambitzer encouraged Gershwin to study theory, harmony, and instrumentation with Edward Kilenyi.

When Gershwin was fifteen, he found a job in Tin Pan Alley as song plugger and staff pianist for J. H. Remick. He now started writing popular song. "When You Want 'Em You Can't Get 'Em" was the first to be published. "Making of a Girl" became his first song sung on the Broadway stage, in *The Passing Show* of 1916, which opened at the Winter Garden on June 22, with a score by Sigmund Romberg.

Gershwin soon felt constricted by his work at Remick's and decided to find something else. Max Dreyfus, head of the powerful publishing house of Harms, became interested in him and offered him thirty-five dollars a week just to write songs and submit them to him. Gershwin had no other set duties and no set hours. The first Gershwin song published by Harms was "Some Wonderful Sort of Someone" in September, 1918.

Through Dreyfus' influence, Gershwin received an assignment in 1918 to write the score for a revue, *Half-Past Eight*. The revue opened and closed in Syracuse, New York, and Gershwin never received the fifteen hundred dollars promised him. But other associations with the musical stage proved happier. Nora Bayes sang his "Some Wonderful Sort of Someone" and "The Real American Folk Song" in *Ladies First* (1918); "You-oo Just You" was interpolated into *Hitchy-Koo of 1918;* three songs were heard in *Good Morning, Judge* (1919); and, also in 1919, Al Jolson brought "Swanee" into his Winter Garden production *Sinbad,* and made it such a hit that it sold two million phonograph records and a million copies of sheet music. Then, on May 26, 1919, came Gershwin's first score for a Broadway musical comedy, *La, La, Lucille.*

By 1920 Gershwin was sufficiently well known to write the music for *George White's Scandals.* He wrote all the music for the first editions, through

1924, and, with songs like "Stairway to Paradise" and "Somebody Loves Me," became one of Broadway's most highly esteemed composers.

Gershwin was also now destined to make musical history—with the *Rhapsody in Blue,* his first symponic work (though not his first attempt at writing serious music), which Paul Whiteman and his orchestra introduced at Aeolian Hall on February 19, 1924. This was the first of several large works for orchestra in the jazz idiom that made Gershwin one of the outstanding American composers of the time, including a piano concerto, a tone poem, a second rhapsody, and an overture.

Gershwin now became a Colossus bestriding the world of music (as Isaac Goldberg once described him), one foot in Carnegie Hall, the other in Tin Pan Alley or Broadway. After leaving the *Scandals,* Gershwin returned to the musical-comedy field with his first success, *Lady, Be Good!* (1924). *Lady, Be Good!* was the first musical for which George's older brother, Ira, provided all the lyrics. From this time on they would work together harmoniously, producing a long string of imperishable songs and successful musical comedies. (Ira Gershwin's biography appears below.)

After *Lady, Be Good!,* George and Ira Gershwin were often represented on Broadway with musical comedies that were excellent box-office attractions. The most important of these are discussed in this book. Others—failures in varying degrees—included *Tell Me More* (1925), *Treasure Girl* (1928), and *Pardon My English* (1933).

Gershwin's last production on Broadway was also his most ambitious, the opera *Porgy and Bess* (1935), in which he finally succeeded in elevating musical comedy to a folk art. After that he devoted himself to writing music for motion pictures. He had worked for Hollywood in 1931 when he wrote music for *Delicious,* starring Janet Gaynor and Charles Farrell. He returned to Hollywood in 1936, staying there permanently, and created music for two important musicals, *Shall We Dance* and *A Damsel in Distress,* both in 1937. *The Goldwyn Follies* was his last movie. He did not live to complete the score, a chore that was done for him by Vernon Duke.

George Gershwin died at the Cedars of Lebanon Hospital in Los Angeles on July 11, 1937, following an operation on the brain; he had been suffering from a cystic tumor on the right temporal lobe of the brain. Memorial concerts and radio broadcasts expressed the shocked reaction of the entire country to the sudden death of a beloved composer.

In 1945 Gershwin's screen biography, *Rhapsody in Blue* (with Robert Alda playing the composer), paid tribute to his genius with a presentation of his greatest songs and concert works. In 1951 another motion picture—inspired by and named after his tone poem, *An American in Paris*—was chosen as the Academy Award winner, the best picture of the year. And between 1952 and 1956 almost the entire world paid tribute to Gershwin's genius when *Porgy and Bess* toured Europe, the Near East, the Soviet Union, other countries behind the Iron Curtain, South America, Mexico, and other distant points. Since then, *Porgy and Bess* has been produced by local opera companies in Europe and the Near East, while all-Gershwin concerts in all parts of the civilized world have made his a legendary figure of twentieth-century music.

PRINCIPAL WORKS: La, La, Lucille (1919); George White's Scandals, 1921 through 1924; Lady, Be Good! (1924); Song of the Flame (1925); Tip-Toes (1925); Oh, Kay! (1926); Funny Face (1927); Rosalie (1928); Show Girl (1929); Strike Up the Band (1930); Girl Crazy (1930); Of Thee I Sing (1931); Let 'Em Eat Cake (1933); Porgy and Bess (1935).
*See:* FUNNY FACE; GEORGE WHITE'S SCANDALS, 1921 through 1924; GIRL CRAZY; LADY, BE GOOD!; LA, LA, LUCILLE; LET 'EM EAT CAKE; OF THEE I SING; OH, KAY!; PORGY AND BESS; ROSALIE; SHOW GIRL; SONG OF THE FLAME; STRIKE UP THE BAND; TIP-TOES.

## GERSHWIN, IRA, *lyricist*

Although Ira Gershwin wrote lyrics for his brother's music intermittently at an early stage in their careers, they did not establish a permanent words-and-music partnership until 1924 with *Lady, Be Good!* Ira Gershwin was born about two years before George—in New York City, on December 6, 1896. While attending Townsend Harris Hall he served as art editor and wrote a column for the school paper. At the College of the City of New York, where he remained only two years, he collaborated with Edwin Harburg (who later became a famous lyricist) in writing a column for the college weekly. Ira Gershwin also contributed pieces to the college monthly and had quips and verses printed in important columns in the New York City newspapers. Leaving the daytime session at the college, he transferred to night courses, and during the day worked as cashier for a Turkish bath partly owned by his father. While holding this job he sold a little humorous paragraph to *The Smart Set,* edited by H. L. Mencken and George Jean Nathan. This was in 1917. Later the same year he worked as vaudeville critic for *The Clipper,* a theatrical newspaper that paid him nothing for his services. By 1918 he was beginning to write lyrics, a few of which were set to music by his brother George. Their first song to get a public hearing was "The Real American Folk Song," which Nora Bayes introduced out-of-town in *Ladies First* in the fall of 1918. During this period, and for the next few years, Ira Gershwin assumed for his lyric-writing the pseudonym of Arthur Francis in order not to capitalize on his brother's growing fame. As Arthur Francis, Ira achieved his first success as lyricist for the stage with *Two Little Girls in Blue* (1921), music by Vincent Youmans and Herbert Stothart. Between 1921 and 1924 Ira Gershwin contributed lyrics for various Broadway productions, including *For Goodness Sake* (1922), *The Greenwich Village Follies* (1923), *Nifties of 1923,* and *Top Hole* (1924). In 1924 he wrote the lyrics for the musical comedy *Be Yourself,* music by Lewis Gensler and Milton Schwarzwald; it was on this occasion that he used his own name professionally for the first time. Later the same year, when he teamed up officially with his brother George for their first musical comedy, *Lady, Be Good!,* he used his own name again. The brothers remained collaborators, one of the major words-and-music teams in the musical theater of the 1920's and 1930's.

Occasionally, during the period that he worked with his brother, Ira Gershwin wrote lyrics for other composers: with Joseph Meyer and Phil Charig in *That's a Good Girl* (1928); with Harry Warren in the revue *Sweet and Low* (1930); with Harold Arlen in *Life Begins at 8:40* (1934); and with Vernon Duke in *The Ziegfeld Follies* of 1936. After George's death, Ira wrote the lyrics for three Broadway musicals: *Lady in the Dark* (1941) and *The Firebrand of Florence* (1945), both with music by Kurt Weill, and *Park Avenue* (1946), music by Arthur Schwartz. Gershwin's main activity, however, was concentrated on motion pictures, working with Aaron Copland (*North Star*), Jerome Kern (*Cover Girl*), Kurt Weill (*Where Do We Go from Here?*), Harry Warren (*The Barkleys of Broadway*), Burton Lane (*Give a Girl a Break*), and Harold Arlen (*A Star Is Born* and *The Country Girl*). His song "Long Ago and Far Away," to music by Jerome Kern (from *Cover Girl*), achieved the largest record and sheet-music sale of anything he had written during his entire career; "The Man That Got Away," to music by Harold Arlen, from *A Star Is Born,* was nominated for an Academy Award.

Ira Gershwin was married to Leonore Strunksy in New York on September 14, 1926.

PRINCIPAL WORKS: Two Little Girls in Blue (1921); Lady, Be Good! (1924); Tip-Toes (1925); Oh, Kay! (1926); Funny Face (1927); Strike Up the Band (1930); Girl Crazy (1930); Of Thee I Sing (1931); Let 'Em Eat Cake (1933); Life Begins at 8:40 (1934); Porgy and Bess (1935); The Ziegfeld Follies of 1936; Lady in the Dark (1941).

*See:* FUNNY FACE; GIRL CRAZY; LADY, BE GOOD!; LADY IN THE DARK; LET 'EM EAT CAKE; LIFE BEGINS AT 8:40; OF THEE I SING; OH, KAY!; PORGY AND BESS; STRIKE UP THE BAND; TIP-TOES; TWO LITTLE GIRLS IN BLUE; THE ZIEGFELD FOLLIES of 1936.

## GOETZ, E. RAY, *composer-librettist-lyricist*

He distinguished himself primarily as a producer and director of numerous successful musicals, though previously he had participated in the writing of lyrics and/or librettos. He was born in Buffalo, New York, on June 12, 1886. One of the earliest musicals to which he contributed lyrics was *A Matinee Idol* (1910), with his first success as lyricist following a year later with *The Hen Pecks*. Other musicals for which he wrote either librettos or the lyrics, or both, were *The Never Homes* (1911), *Hokey-Pokey* (1912), *Hanky Panky* (1912), *Roly Poly* (1913), *Hitchy-Koo of 1918,* and *George White's Scandals of 1922*. For *All Aboard* (1913), *The Pleasure Seekers* (1913), and *Hitchy-Koo of 1917* he wrote music as well as lyrics. Among the hit songs in which he collaborated were "For Me and My Gal" and "Yaka Hula Hickey Dula." Beginning with the late 1920's he became successful as a producer and director, among his most important musicals being *Paris, The French Doll, Fifty Million Frenchmen, Little Miss Bluebeard,* and *The New Yorkers*. His wife was the musical-comedy star Irene Bordoni. Goetz died in Greenwich, Connecticut, on June 12, 1954.

PRINCIPAL WORKS: The Hen Pecks (1911); Hokey Pokey (1912); George White's Scandals of 1922 and 1923.
*See:* GEORGE WHITE'S SCANDALS of 1922 and 1923; THE HEN PECKS; WEBER AND FIELDS EXTRAVAGANZAS (HOKEY POKEY).

## GORNEY, JAY, *composer*

He was born in Bialystok, Russia, on December 12, 1896. Like Irving Berlin's family, the Gorneys fled from Russia during a pogrom. They came to the United States in 1906 and made a home in Detroit. There Jay started studying the piano when he was ten, and at twelve he founded and led the Cass Technical High School Orchestra. Later on, while attending the University of Michigan, he created a student jazz band of his own, which performed at college dances.

Despite his activity in music, he did not plan a musical career. He attended law school, but the war in 1917 interrupted his studies. Gorney enlisted in the United States Navy, where, at one period, he led one of John Philip Sousa's bands at the Great Lakes Training Station. After the war he completed his law course, passed the bar exams, and started a practice in Detroit. He practiced law for only one year. In 1923 he landed one of his songs, "I've Been Wanting You," in a Broadway musical, *The Dancing Girl*. A year later his songs were placed in three other Broadway productions: *The Greenwich Village Follies* of 1924, *Top Hole,* and *Vogues of 1924*. In 1927 Gorney contributed several songs to the intimate revue *Merry Go 'Round,* and in 1929 to *The Sketch Book*.

In 1929 Gorney made a trip to Hollywood to write music for Paramount. He returned to Hollywood in 1933 to work at the Fox studios, where he remained several years; there he was credited with helping to discover Shirley Temple, for whom he found a starring role in her first major picture, *Stand Up and Cheer.* In Hollywood, Gorney wrote such successful songs as "Ah, But Is It Love?" "You're My Thrill," "Baby, Take a Bow," and "I Found a Dream."

His work in Hollywood did not keep him from contributing more songs to various Broadway musical productions in the 1930's—notably to *The Earl Carroll Vanities* in 1929 and 1930; the last of *The Ziegfeld Follies* produced by Ziegfield himself (1931); and such intimate revues as *Shoot the Works* (1931) and *Americana* (1932). For the last-named production he wrote a smash hit (lyrics by Harburg) to a song that became something of the leitmotiv, or lament, of the Great Depression: "Brother, Can You Spare a Dime?" His greatest success on the Broadway stage came with a topical revue, *Meet the People,* which originated in Hollywood in 1939, before coming to New York for a long run.

In 1942 and 1943 Gorney was a producer for Columbia Pictures. During World War II he was active with the Hollywood Writers Mobilization Committee, creating songs and sketches for radio programs sponsored by the armed forces. Two of his later Broadway musicals were failures: *Heaven on Earth* (1948) and *Touch and Go* (1949). Between 1948 and 1951 he was chairman of the musical-play department of the Dramatic Workshop at the New School for Social Research in New York, and in 1952 he was on the faculty of the American Theater Wing. He received an award from the American Theater Wing in 1962.

PRINCIPAL WORKS: The Greenwich Village Follies of 1924; The Earl Carroll Vanities of 1925; The Sketch Book of 1929; The Earl Carroll Vanities of 1930. *See:* THE EARL CARROLL VANITIES of 1925 and 1930; THE GREENWICH VILLAGE FOLLIES of 1924; MEET THE PEOPLE; THE SKETCH BOOK of 1929.

GOULD, MORTON, composer. *See* BILLION DOLLAR BABY.

GREEN, ADOLPH, *librettist-lyricist. See* COMDEN, BETTY, AND GREEN, ADOLPH.

GREY, CLIFFORD, *librettist-lyricist*
He was born in Birmingham, England, on January 5, 1887, and received his principal education at the King Edward School. After coming to the United States, and after having received his apprenticeship in the theater as an actor, he achieved his first major success as lyricist with Jerome Kern's *Sally* (1920).

He subsequently continued contributing lyrics to Broadway musicals, including, besides those listed below, *June Days* (1925), *Gay Paree* (1925), *Great Temptations* (1926), *The Merry World* (1926), and *The Madcap* (1928). He wrote the librettos as well as the lyrics for *Lady Butterfly* (1923), *Marjorie* (1924), *Mayflowers* (1925), *Sunny Days* (1928), and *Ups-a-Daisy* (1928). Among the composers with whom he worked, besides Kern, were J. Fred Coots, Romberg, Jean Schwartz, Friml, and Youmans. Clifford Grey died in Ipswich, England, on September 25, 1941.

PRINCIPAL WORKS: Sally (1920); Artists and Models of 1924 and 1925; A Night in Paris (1926); Hit the Deck (1927); The Three Musketeers (1928).
*See:* ARTISTS AND MODELS of 1924 and 1925; HIT THE DECK; A NIGHT IN PARIS; SALLY; THE THREE MUSKETEERS.


## HAGUE, ALBERT, *composer*

He was born in Berlin on October 13, 1920, and completed his music study at the College of Music of the University of Cincinnati in 1939. During World War II he served in the United States Air Force. After the war he came to New York to pursue a career as a popular composer. A musical comedy for which he provided the score—*Reluctant Lady*—was produced in Cleveland. Then in 1948 he wrote the background music for a Broadway play, *The Madwoman of Chaillot*. In 1950 a song, "One Is a Lonely Number," was interpolated into a Broadway musical, *Dance Me a Song*. After that Hague wrote the background music for a documentary film (*Coney Island, U.S.A.,* which won first prize at the Edinburgh and Venice Festivals) and for Robert Anderson's Broadway play *All Summer Long*. His first published song was "Wait for Me Darling," in 1954. Recognition came with his Broadway musical *Plain and Fancy* in 1955.

PRINCIPAL WORKS: Plain and Fancy (1955); Redhead (1959).
*See:* PLAIN AND FANCY; REDHEAD.


## HAMMERSTEIN, OSCAR II, *librettist-lyricist*

He was born in New York City on July 12, 1895, to a distinguished theatrical family. His grandfather (after whom he was named) was the opera impresario who built the Manhattan Opera House in 1906, for several years a formidable rival to the Metropolitan Opera. The lyricist's father, William, was the manager of the leading vaudeville theater in New York, the Victoria on 42nd Street. His uncle Arthur was a successful Broadway producer.

Though the youngest of the Hammersteins loved the theater and wanted to follow the family tradition by engaging in it professionally, he was directed to law. When he was seventeen he entered Columbia College, where his classmates included several later famous in the theater—Lorenz Hart, Howard Dietz, Morrie Ryskind, among others. At Columbia he appeared in and wrote several skits and lyrics for the annual Columbia Varsity Show. In 1917 he passed on to the law school and while attending there served as process server for a New York law firm. When he asked his employer for a raise and was turned down, he decided to abandon law for a job in the theater. His uncle Arthur hired him as assistant stage manager and general factotum for a Broadway musical, *You're in Love,* in 1917.

During the year he worked backstage for *You're in Love,* he wrote a song lyric that was interpolated into one of the shows put on by his uncle. His debut as lyricist passed unnoticed, and with good reason: this was no lion's roar. The lyric began: "Make yourself at home, 'neath our spacious dome, do just as you please." After that, Oscar Hammerstein completed a four-act tragedy of small-town girls, which opened and closed out of town. One year more, and he wrote book and lyrics for a musical comedy produced by his uncle on January 5, 1920—*Always You,* music by Herbert Stothart. *Always You* had a short run of sixty-six performances, but a critic for *The New York Times* did point out that the "lyrics are more clever than those of the average musical comedy." A few days after the road tour of *Always You* ended, Hammerstein was once again represented on Broadway—this time with *Tickle Me,* music by Stothart, and with Otto Harbach and Frank Mandel assisting Hammerstein in the writing of book and lyrics. *Tickle Me* was Hammerstein's first success. An even more substantial success followed in *Wildflower* (1923), music by Vincent Youmans and Stothart; and in 1924 came Rudolf Friml's *Rose-Marie,* a box-office triumph and now a stage classic.

In 1924 Hammerstein met Jerome Kern at Victor Herbert's funeral. They joined up as a words-and-music team, their first show, *Sunny,* coming in 1925 and starring Marilyn Miller. In 1927 they collaborated on *Show Boat,* to this day one of the proudest achievements of the American musical theater. After that followed *Music in the Air* and *Sweet Adeline.* During this period Hammerstein also wrote either book or lyrics (or both) for other important Broadway composers, including Sigmund Romberg, George Gershwin, and Vincent Youmans.

After enjoying major successes on Broadway and in Hollywood (including the winning of an Academy Award for the song "The Last Time I Saw Paris" in 1941, music by Kern), Hammerstein came upon a lean period in which failure followed failure. In Hollywood, on Broadway, in London, he seemed incapable of recovering a winning stride, and even his closest friends suspected that his career was over.

Then in 1943 he teamed up with Richard Rodgers, with whom he was henceforth to work exclusively. He had known Rodgers many years. More than twenty years earlier he had written one or two lyrics to Rodgers' melodies; and he was on the Columbia Varsity committee that selected a Rodgers and Hart musical for the Varsity Show. But not until Lorenz Hart bowed out as Rodgers' collaborator in 1942 did Rodgers and Hammerstein begin to work together professionally. And their first production made stage history—for it was *Oklahoma!* From then on—with Rodgers' music—Hammerstein scaled new heights as a writer for the theater, with a series of Broadway productions that contributed to the musical stage much of the grandeur it now possesses. In addition to their stage work, they wrote the songs for the motion picture *State Fair,* winning and Academy Award for the song "It Might As Well Be Spring," and for the television production *Cinderella.* A skillful and even significant writer when he had worked with Friml, Kern, and Youmans, Oscar Hammerstein was stimulated by Rodgers' music—and the inspiration of his friendship—to achieve new horizons as a sensitive poet and a humane dramatist.

His last collaboration with Rodgers was *The Sound of Music* in 1959, a triumph of the first magnitude both on the stage and even more particularly on the screen. Oscar Hammerstein II died of cancer at his home in Dolyestown, Pennsylvania—Highland Farms—on August 23, 1960. He was one of the giants to emerge from the American musical theater. As Howard Lindsay wrote: "All of us who work in the theater always walked more proudly because Oscar Hammerstein was of the theater."

PRINCIPAL WORKS: Tickle Me (1920); Wildflower (1924); Rose-Marie (1924); Song of the Flame (1925); Sunny (1925); The Desert Song (1926); Show Boat (1927); Good Boy (1928); Rainbow (1928); The New Moon (1928); Sweet Adeline (1929); Music in the Air (1932); May Wine (1935); Oklahoma! (1943); Carmen Jones (1943); Carousel (1945); Allegro (1947); South Pacific (1949); The King and I (1951); Me and Juliet (1953); Pipe Dream (1955); Flower Drum Song (1958); The Sound of Music (1959).
*See:* ALLEGRO; CARMEN JONES; CAROUSEL; THE DESERT SONG; FLOWER DRUM SONG; GOOD BOY; THE KING AND I; MAY WINE; ME AND JULIET; MUSIC IN THE AIR; THE NEW MOON; OKLAHOMA!; PIPE DREAM; RAINBOW; ROSE-MARIE; SHOW BOAT; SONG OF THE FLAME; THE SOUND OF MUSIC; SOUTH PACIFIC; SUNNY; SWEET ADELINE; TICKLE ME; WILDFLOWER.

## HARBACH, OTTO, *librettist-lyricist*
Few were so prolific as Harbach in writing texts and lyrics for musical comedies. He wrote for several hundred productions, which had an aggregate of over 12,000 performances. Few writers for the musical theater were more

distinguished. A skillful craftsman who knew both the stage and its audience, Harbach had a facile pen that dripped entertainment—and at times enchantment.

He was born Otto Hauerbach in Salt Lake City, Utah, on August 16, 1873, the fourth of eight children. His parents had migrated to America from Denmark, then had come to Salt Lake City by foot and ox cart during the Civil War era.

Otto received a comprehensive academic education, first at the Salt Lake College Institute (a Presbyterian grade school where he was a classmate of Maude Adams), later at Knox College, in Galesburg, Illinois. All the while he supported himself by delivering newspapers and groceries and shining shoes. In 1895 he won an interstate prize for oratory and soon after became a teacher of English and public speaking at Whitman College in Walla Walla, Washington.

He came to New York in 1901, intending to work toward a doctorate at Columbia University. But when both his money and his eyesight gave out, he abandoned his studies and went to work on various jobs: as an insurance agent, a reporter on the *Evening News,* an advertising copywriter for six years with George Batton.

In 1902 he collaborated with Karl Hoschna, the composer, on *The Daughter of the Desert.* For six years they tried marketing the play (on three occasions they actually received options), but without success. They were luckier with *The Three Twins* in 1907, which not only was produced but was a hit. Harbach did not make much money from his text (all he was paid was a flat fee of a hundred dollars and a royalty of one cent copy for the sale of sheet music), but he had finally won recognition.

For several years he continued doubling as an advertising copywriter and stage librettist. With Hoschna he wrote a few more successes, including the formidable *Madame Sherry* (1910), which finally convinced him that he could make a living entirely from his stage efforts.

He continued as Hoschna's collaborator until the composer's death in 1911. He then worked with Rudolf Friml, and after that with many other important Broadway composers, including Kern, Romberg, Gershwin, Tierney, and Youmans. In the meantime—while working with Friml after 1910—he had changed the spelling of his name from Hauerbach to Harbach, having become impatient with the many combinations and permutations of the way it was being misspelled.

Harbach's creative fertility was truly remarkable. Season after season he had two, three, and sometimes four musicals running simultaneously. In the season of 1925 he had five plays on Broadway at the same time.

Between 1950 and 1953 Harbach served as president of ASCAP. He died in New York City on January 24, 1963.

PRINCIPAL WORKS: The Three Twins (1908); Madame Sherry (1910); The Firefly (1912); High Jinks (1913); Going Up (1917); Mary (1920); Tickle Me (1920); Kid Boots (1923); Wildflower (1923); No, No, Nanette (1925); Sunny (1925); Song of the Flame (1925); Criss Cross (1926); The Desert Song (1926); Good Boy (1928); Rose-Marie); The Cat and the Fiddle (1931); Roberta (1933).
*See:* THE CAT AND THE FIDDLE; CRISS CROSS; THE DESERT SONG; THE FIREFLY; GOING UP; GOOD BOY; HIGH JINKS; KID BOOTS; MADAME SHERRY; MARY; NO, NO, NANETTE; ROBERTA; ROSE-MARIE; SONG OF THE FLAME; SUNNY; THE THREE TWINS; TICKLE ME; WILDFLOWER.

## HARBURG, E. Y., *lyricist*

E. Y. Harburg (better known as "Yip" Harburg) was born in New York City on April 8, 1898. He was a child of the New York City East Side slums who had to support himself through public and high school by selling newspapers and working for the city, lighting streetlamps. At Townsend Harris Hall he collaborated with a fellow student, Ira Gershwin, in writing a literary column for the school paper. Then, while attending the College of the City of New York, from which he was graduated in 1918, he not only contributed verses to school publications but also to the renowned newspaper column of F.P.A. (Franklin P. Adams). For three years he lived in South America, holding down various jobs. Back in New York, in 1921 he went into an electric business which was bankrupt in 1929. "I had my fill of this dreamy abstract thing called business," he later revealed to an interviewer, "and I decided to face reality by writing lyrics."

His first lyrics (to music by Jay Gorney) made an impression on Earl Carroll, who used six of his songs in the *The Sketch Book* (1929). This landed them a contract to write songs for Paramount in Hollywood, where they were represented in several motion pictures. At the same time, Harburg contributed lyrics to several Broadway revues, many of them of the intimate variety that came into vogue in the 1930's. Among these productions were the third edition of *The Garrick Gaieties* (1930), where, collaborating with Ira Gershwin, he wrote the words for Vernon Duke's first popular song to get a public hearing; *Shoot the Works* (1931), his composer once again being Gorney; *Americana* (1932), where his words were set to music by Vernon Duke, Burton Lane, and Harold Arlen; and, again collaborating with Ira Gershwin, *Life Begins at 8:40,* music by Harold Arlen. With Gorney he also wrote some songs for the more ambitious revues produced by Earl Carroll and

Florenz Ziegfeld. From these varied productions came some songs that established Harburg's reputation as an ace lyricist, among them the anthem of the Depression of the early 1930's, "Brother, Can You Spare a Dime?" (Gorney), and "April in Paris" (Duke)

Other song successes came to Harburg in Hollywood, where he worked mostly with Harold Arlen, producing such standards as "Only a Paper Moon" and "Over the Rainbow"; the latter was introduced by and became the theme song of Judy Garland, besides capturing the Academy Award.

When Harburg returned to Broadway, it was to be Arlen's collaborator first in *Hooray for What?* (1937) and then in *Bloomer Girl* (1944). Three years after that he reaped an even richer harvest—and revealed himself a master of his craft—in *Finian's Rainbow,* music by Burton Lane. Harburg's mastery at lyric writing was also forcefully evident in *Jamaica* (1957), music by Arlen.

PRINCIPAL WORKS: The Sketch Book of 1929; Walk a Little Faster (1932); The Ziegfeld Follies of 1934; Life Begins at 8:40 (1934); Hooray for What? (1937); Hold on to Your Hats (1940); Finian's Rainbow (1947); Jamaica (1957).

*See:* BLOOMER GIRL; FINIAN'S RAINBOW; HOORAY FOR WHAT?; HOLD ON TO YOUR HATS; JAMAICA; LIFE BEGINS AT 8:40; THE SKETCH BOOK of 1929; WALK A LITTLE FASTER; THE ZIEGFELD FOLLIES of 1934.

## HARNICK, SHELDON, *lyricist. See* BOCK, JERRY.

## HART, LORENZ, *librettist-lyricist. See* RODGERS, RICHARD.

## HART, MOSS, *librettist*

To his texts for musical comedies and revues, Moss Hart carried his incisive wit, trenchant intelligence, sparkling dialogue, and impertinence of spirit that made him one of Broadway's foremost writers of nonmusical stage comedies.

He was born in New York City on October 24, 1904, and was educated in the city public schools. In 1925, while working as office boy and typist for Augustus Pitou, Broadway producer and manager, he submitted anonymously a melodrama, *The Holdup Man.* Pitou liked it well enough to try it out in Chicago, where it died stillborn. Thus ended Hart's career as a writer of melodrama, but it was some time before he was reincarnated into a creator of comedy. Meanwhile he performed various chores as dramatic director for several Jewish organizations in New York City and Newark, and as social director in resort hotels in New York.

In 1930 he completed a play satirizing Hollywood, *Once in a Lifetime,* which was drastically revised by George S. Kaufman. Produced on Broadway, it was a smash hit. The Hart-Kaufman collaboration flourished during the next decade with other sparkling Broadway comedies, all of them nonmusical. The best were: *Merrily We Roll Along, You Can't Take It with You* (which won the Pulitzer Prize in 1937), *George Washington Slept Here,* and the incomparable caricature of Alexander Woollcott, *The Man Who Came to Dinner.*

Hart's first effort in writing for the musical stage came in 1932 with *Face the Music,* for which Irving Berlin provided music and lyrics. This was followed by a succession of impressive musicals, culminating with what is perhaps Hart's finest musical-comedy book, *Lady in the Dark* (1941), music by Kurt Weill, lyrics by Ira Gershwin. Of lesser interest were his adaptation for Broadway of *The Great Waltz* (1934) and his text for Cole Porter's *Jubilee* (1935). During World War II Hart wrote and helped produce the Air Force play *Winged Victory.*

Hart also won accolades for his highly skillful stage direction of several important musicals, including *Miss Liberty, My Fair Lady,* and *Camelot.* He wrote a best-selling autobiography, *Act One* (that was made into a motion picture), covering his life up to the time of *Once in a Lifetime* (1959). He died of a heart attack in Palm Springs, California, on December 20, 1961.

An impressive posthumous tribute to Moss Hart in six acts, produced by Collier Young, staged by William Harbach, and starring many of the "greats" of show business was given by the University of Southern California Friends of the Library Association in Los Angeles on April 12, 1970.

PRINCIPAL WORKS: Face the Music (1932); As Thousands Cheer (1933); The Great Waltz (1934); Jubilee (1935); I'd Rather Be Right (1937); Lady in the Dark (1941); Inside U.S.A. (1948).
*See:* AS THOUSANDS CHEER; FACE THE MUSIC; THE GREAT WALTZ; I'D RATHER BE RIGHT; INSIDE U.S.A.; JUBILEE; LADY IN THE DARK.

HENDERSON, RAY, *composer. See* DE SYLVA, BROWN, AND HENDERSON.

HERBERT, VICTOR, *composer*
A giant figure in American operetta, Victor Herbert was of Irish birth—Dublin, February 1, 1859. His father died when Victor was three, and the child and his mother went to live with her father, Samuel Lover, a novelist famous for *Handy Andy,* and a dilettante who cultivated the arts. His house, twenty miles from London, was a gathering place for artists, writers, and musicians. In such an atmosphere of culture Herbert spent five impressionable

years. It was his mother who first detected in him signs of musical talent. Herself a competent pianist, she began giving him lessons when he was only seven. After the mother married Dr. Carl Schmid, she settled with her new husband and her son, Victor, in Stuttgart, Germany, where Victor studied the cello at the conservatory. Six years later he went to Baden-Baden for an additional year or so of private study with Bernhardt Cossman. After this he spent four years playing the cello in small-town orchestras and in several led by world-renowned musicians. He finally accepted a permanent post as cellist with the Stuttgart Royal Orchestra, conducted by Max Seifritz. The conductor became Herbert's teacher in composition and orchestration, and under his guidance Herbert wrote several symphonic works, introduced by the Stuttgat Orchestra.

Now a man-about-town, tall and strikingly handsome, Herbert was adored by women, and he had a roving eye for them. But one woman above others attracted his interest. She was Theresa Förster, principal soprano of the Stuttgart Opera. He contrived to meet her and offered his services as voice coach. They fell in love and became engaged when Theresa Förster received a contract from the Metropolitan Opera in New York. Her acceptance was contingent on the engagement of her fiancé as cellist in the opera-house orchestra.

Herbert and Theresa Förster were married in Germany in the spring of 1886. Soon afterward they sailed for America, where she made her Metropolitan Opera debut on the opening night of the 1886–87 season in Karl Goldmark's *The Queen of Sheba*. The critics found much to praise in her performance. Nobody, of course, suspected that the big news that evening was the presence in the orchestra pit of a cellist named Victor Herbert. In the future the limelight would be his.

Herbert became an American and took out his papers for citizenship. He identified himself with American music in every way he could. He conducted and wrote for American festivals. He created American music—for example, the *American Fantasia,* a spirited medley of American patriotic tunes climaxed by a Wagnerian treatment of "The Star-Spangled Banner." In 1893 he became head of one of America's native musical outfits when he succeeded Patrick Gilmore as bandmaster of the renowned 22nd Regiment Band. From 1898 to 1904 he was principal conductor of the Pittsburgh Symphony, one of America's leading orchestras. In 1904 he organized a band of his own, and in 1910 he wrote an American opera (*Natoma*). In 1916 he became the first American composer to write an original score for a motion-picture presentation (*Birth of a Nation*). But his greatest contribution to American music and American culture came through the scores he wrote for operettas that enlivened the American theater for more than a quarter of a century, and the best of which are still loved.

His first attempt at writing music for the stage consisted of a few numbers for a pageant planned for the Chicago World's Fair. The pageant was never produced, but Herbert's appetite for writing stage music was whetted. "I *must* write for the theater," he told his wife with finality. Consequently, he was highly receptive to a suggestion by William MacDonald, director of the Boston Light Opera Company, which had introduced De Koven's *Robin Hood,* that he write an operetta. The proposed text was a satire on people of the theater by Francis Neilson (later a distinguished writer on politics). *Prince Ananias,* as the operetta was called, was introduced by the Bostonians at the Broadway Theater in New York on November 20, 1894, and was a failure.

Success came early—only one year and one operetta later—and it came with *The Wizard of the Nile.* This was the first of many operettas that brought Herbert to the pinnacle of his profession.

There was much to sadden Herbert in the last decade of his life. The war in 1917 put a stigma on all things German. There was never any question of Herbert's allegiance to America or of his disavowal of Prussian militarism. But the sudden vilification of all German culture and music was hard for him to accept. When the prejudice of the times compelled Herbert to re• move from his concert programs works by German composers, he complained bitterly: "What have Beethoven and Wagner to do with this war?" But he yielded to public pressure. The end of the war resolved his conflicts with his integrity, but it brought him a deprivation of another kind. Prohibition had become the law of the land, denying Herbert one of his greatest pleasures —alcohol. So keenly did Herbert miss wines and beer that for a period he seriously contemplated leaving America and reestablishing his home in Europe.

His own music also caused personal disturbances. His disappointment in the public and critical reaction to his two operas, both performed by the Metropolitan Opera, was immense; yet it is extremely doubtful if, deep within him, he was not aware of the serious shortcomings of his operas. Even his lighter music was giving him cause for concern. His greatest triumphs were behind him. He seemed incapable of recapturing the formula that had once made him unique. He felt, for example, that the finest score he wrote was for the Irish operetta *Eileen* (1917), set in rebellion-torn Ireland. Indeed, the score does contain one of Herbert's most beautiful songs, "Thine Alone," whose sale through the years has been rivaled only by "Ah, Sweet Mystery of Life." Yet *Eileen* lasted only sixty-four performances.

His operettas continued to appear on Broadway up to the end of his life. He also wrote special music for other productions, including *The Ziegfeld Follies* between 1918 and 1923. He was still in demand, still regarded with veneration by his associates. More important, he still had his rare gift of melody, as in "Thine Alone" and "A Kiss in the Dark," the latter heard in *Orange Blossoms* in 1922. Yet it was obvious that his heyday had passed. He had belonged to the era of the waltz, an era in which he was king, for he had the precious gift of wonderful melody, and the knowledge of harmony and orchestration to set off that melody to best advantage. His romantic, tender, sentimental music belonged to an epoch that died with World War I. In the newer, frenetic period of the fox-trot and the Charleston, of ragtime and jazz, his songs sounded almost like an anachronism. "My day is over," he told a friend. "They are forgetting poor old Herbert."

Yet in spite of lengthening shadows, the last years of his life were by no means somber. To the end he retained his extraordinary zest for living, working, eating, and drinking, and for the society of friends.

He was working on some special numbers for the 1924 edition of *The Ziegfeld Follies* when, on May 26, he suffered a heart attack at the Lambs Club. He died a few hours later in his physician's office.

Fifteen years after Herbert's death Paramount Pictures released *The Great Victor Herbert,* starring Allan Jones as the composer. The soundtrack boasted seventeen Herbert gems—only a fraction of his life's production—but enough to remind a later generation of how much Victor Herbert had once meant for so long a time and to so many people.

PRINCIPAL WORKS: The Wizard of the Nile (1895); The Serenade (1897); The Fortune Teller (1898); Babes in Toyland (1903); It Happened in Nordland (1904); Mademoiselle (Mlle.) Modiste (1905); The Red Mill (1906); Naughty Marietta (1910); Sweethearts (1913); The Only Girl (1914); The Princess Pat (1915); The Century Girl (1916).

*See:* BABES IN TOYLAND; THE CENTURY GIRL; THE FORTUNE TELLER; IT HAPPENED IN NORDLAND; MADEMOISELLE (MLLE.) MODISTE; NAUGHTY MARIETTA; THE ONLY GIRL; THE PRINCESS PAT; THE RED MILL; THE SERENADE; SWEETHEARTS; THE WIZARD OF THE NILE.

## HERMAN, JERRY, *composer-lyricist*

He was born Gerald Herman in New York City on July 10, 1933. His father owned a children's camp; his mother was a schoolteacher. As a child, Jerry began studying the piano. After attending schools in New York, he was graduated from the University of Miami in 1954. There he majored in drama, inaugurated an annual college show, and appeared in *The Madwoman of Chaillot.* Following his graduation he came to New York, where his first musical, *I Feel Wonderful,* was produced Off Broadway (1954). After a year in the armed forces, he returned to New York and began writing special material for various performers, including Garry Moore, Hermione Gingold, Jane Froman, and Tallulah Bankhead. A revue, *Nightcap,* given Off Broadway in 1958, had a run of over four hundred performances, while another, *Parade* (1960), was seen both Off Broadway and in California. One of his songs, "Best Gold," was introduced into a Broadway musical in 1960, *From A to Z.* It was in the same year that he became a full-fledged Broadway composer-lyricist, by contributing all the songs for the musical *Milk and Honey,* a success. This was followed by *Hello, Dolly!* (1964), whose title song became one of the most successful on records (thanks to Louis Armstrong's recording) and in sheet music in several years. In 1964 he received an Antoinette Perry Award and that of *Variety* as best composer and lyricist of the year. In 1965 he was selected by the United States Junior Chamber of Commerce as one the Ten Outstanding Young Men. *Mame* (1966) was his second big Broadway success. *Dear World,* a musical-stage version of *The Madwoman of Chaillot* produced on Broadway in 1969, for which he contributed the songs, was a failure.

PRINCIPAL WORKS: Milk and Honey (1961); Hello, Dolly! (1964); Mame (1966).
*See:* HELLO, DOLLY!; MAME; MILK AND HONEY.

## HIRSCH, LOUIS A., *composer*

Just how prolific Hirsch was in writing songs for the Broadway stage was forcefully underscored during World War I. There was one period when about a dozen plays running simultaneously had one or more of his songs. One of his songs, "The Love Nest," sold millions of copies of sheet music and records and for many years served Burns and Allen as their theme music on television.

Louis Achille Hirsch was born in New York City on November 28, 1887. A musical prodigy, he managed to teach himself the piano when he was an infant. While attending New York public and high schools he studied the piano with local teachers. During his senior year at the College of the City of New York, he was taken by his parents to Europe, where he attended the renowned Stern Conservatory in Berlin, a pupil of Rafael Joseffy. He was now fired with the ambition of becoming a concert pianist. But after his return to the United States, in 1906, he came to the conclusion that he had set a too distant goal for himself, and he compromised by engaging in popular-musical activity. He found a job as staff pianist in Tin Pan Alley—first with the firm of Gus Edwards, then with Shapiro-Bernstein. He also started writing songs and making arrangements. One of his assignments was writing the music for Lew Dockstader's Minstrels. Other Hirsch songs sprouted in various Broadway musicals, including *The Gay White Way* (1907), *Miss Innocence,* starring Anna Held (1908), and *The Girl and the Wizard* (1909). His first complete musical-comedy score was for *He Came from Milwaukee* (1910); the first revue with his complete score was the *Revue of Revues* (1911), in which Gaby Deslys, mistress of King Alfonso of Spain, made a sensational American stage debut.

Success came to Hirsch in 1911 with *Vera Violetta.* In 1912, as staff composer for the Shuberts, Hirsch wrote songs for the Winter Garden production *The Whirl of Society,* starring Al Jolson, and for the first edition of *The Passing Show.*

Toward the end of 1912 Hirsch and the Shuberts parted company, his job assumed by Sigmund Romberg. Hirsch went to England, where he wrote for the London stage. When World War I broke out in Europe, he managed to get boat passage home. Back in the United States, he was hired by Ziegfeld to write music for *The Ziegfeld Follies* of 1925. During the next decade Hirsch's music was heard in several editions of *The Ziegfeld Follies,* as well as in editions of *The Greenwich Village Follies,* and several musical comedies, the most successful being *Going Up* (1917) and *Mary* (1920).

Hirsch was at the height of his success when he died in New York City on May 13, 1924.

PRINCIPAL WORKS: Vera Violetta (1911); The Passing Show of 1912; The Ziegfeld Follies of 1915 and 1916; Going Up (1917); The Ziegfeld Follies of 1918; Oh, My Dear! (1918); Mary (1920); The Ziegfeld Follies of 1922; The Greenwich Village Follies of 1922 and 1923.
*See:* GOING UP; THE GREENWICH VILLAGE FOLLIES of 1922 and 1923; MARY; THE PASSING SHOW of 1912; THE PRINCESS THEATER SHOWS (*Oh, My Dear!*); VERA VIOLETTA; THE ZIEGFELD FOLLIES of 1915, 1916, 1918, and 1922.

## HOSCHNA, KARL, *composer*

He was Bohemian by birth—in Kuschwarda, on August 16, 1877. His musical education took place at the Vienna Conservatory on a scholarship. One of the requirements of that scholarship was the study of some band instrument, and Hoschna selected the oboe. Upon graduating with honors, Hoschna played the oboe in the Austrian Army band for several years. In 1896 he came to the United States, which from then on remained his permanent home. For two years after his arrival he played in one of Victor Herbert's orchestras.

An obsession that the vibration from the oboe's double reed might affect his mind led him to write an unusual letter to the publishing house of Witmark, asking for a job, no matter "how menial" and "at any salary you care to pay." Isidor Witmark later recalled that this letter was so pitiful and so original that he decided to give the signer a chance. Hoschna was at first engaged as a copyist. After that he served as an arranger, and finally as Isidor Witmark's personal adviser on manuscripts and other musical matters. During this period Hoschna also started writing popular songs.

In 1902 he met and became a friend of a young advertising man, Otto Hauerbach (later Otto Harbach), who had ambitions to write for the stage. They started a partnership and in short order completed *The Daughter of the Desert*. During the next few years they rewrote this operetta several times, and on three occasions even succeeded in getting options. But always some unforeseen development blocked a production. Between 1905 and 1908 Hoschna finally did manage to put a foot into the professional theater with music for three operettas. The first was *Belle of the West* (1905), book and lyrics by Harry B. Smith. It was a failure, and so were its two successors.

In 1908 Witmark engaged Hoschna to write music for a projected operetta adaptation of a play, *Incog*. Hoschna in turn interested Witmark in hiring Harbach for the lyrics. As *The Three Twins* it reached Broadway in 1908 and established the reputations of both Hoschna and Harbach.

During the next three years Hoschna and Harbach wrote eight operettas, the crowning success of which was *Madame Sherry* (1910). Hoschna also provided music for plays by other writers, the most prominent being *Wall Street Girl* (1911).

Hoschna was not fated to enjoy his successes for a long time. He died only a year or so after the premiere of *Madame Sherry*—on December 23, 1911. He was only thirty-four. *Wall Street Girl* was produced posthumously.

PRINCIPAL WORKS: The Three Twins (1908); Madame Sherry (1910); Wall Street Girl (1912).
*See:* MADAME SHERRY; THE THREE TWINS; WALL STREET GIRL.

## HUBBELL, RAYMOND, *composer*

While Hubbell's name is today probably remembered exclusively for a single song—"Poor Butterfly" (lyrics by John Golden)—he was one of Broadway's most successful composers in the early 1900's. His melodies flooded the stage of thirty-eight productions, including seven *Ziegfeld Follies* and several Hippodrome extravaganzas between 1915 and 1923.

He was born in Urbana, Ohio, on June 1, 1879, where he received his academic education in the public schools. In early manhood he came to Chicago, there to study harmony and counterpoint, to organize a dance orchestra, then to work as staff composer for the publishing house of Charles K. Harris. In 1902 he wrote the music for *Chow Chow,* an operetta success-fully produced in Chicago that year. Under the new title of *The Runaways,* it had a prosperous run at the Casino Theater in New York and a five-year tour on the road.

Hubbell then proved he was no flash-in-the-pan. Three box-office success followed: *Fantana* (1905), *Mexicana* (1906), and *A Knight for a Day* (1907). The last had two of his best songs in "Life is a See-Saw" and "Little Girl Blue." Now an established composer, Hubbell was eagerly sought after by major Broadway producers. His music was heard in musical comedies, revues, and extravaganzas. His last appearance on Broadway was in 1928 with *Three Cheers.* After 1928 Hubbell went into retirement in Miami, Florida, where he died on December 13, 1954.

PRINCIPAL WORKS: The Runaways (1903) ; Fantana (1905) ; The Ziegfeld Follies, 1911 through 1914; Hippodrome Extravaganzas, 1915 through 1917; The Zieg-feld Follies of 1917; Hippodrome Extravaganzas of 1919, 1920, and 1922; The Ziegfeld Follies of 1924–25.
*See:* FANTANA; HIPPODROME EXTRAVAGANZAS of 1915, 1916, 1917, 1919, 1920, and 1922; THE RUNAWAYS; THE ZIEGFELD FOLLIES, 1911 through 1914, 1917, and 1924–25.

JONES, TOM, *lyricist. See* SCHMIDT, HARVEY, AND JONES, TOM.

KAHAL, IRVING, *lyricist. See* FAIN, SAMMY.

KALMAR, BERT, *lyricist. See* RUBY, HARRY.

KANDER, JOHN, *composer,* and EBB, FRED, *lyricist*
John Kander was born in Kansas City, Missouri, on March 18, 1927, and re-ceived his Bachelor of Arts degree from Oberlin College in 1951 and his Masters from Columbia University in 1953. His earliest experiences in the musical theater came from conducting orchestras for stock companies and making dance arrangements for the musicals *Gypsy* and *Irma la Douce.* In 1962 he was one of the collaborators in the Broadway musical *The Family Affair* and contributed the incidental music to the Broadway play, *Never Too Late.* This was the year when he first formed a song partnership with Fred Ebb, lyricist, their first effort being an outstanding hit song, "My Coloring Book," which was soon followed by another hit song, "I Don't Care Much," both recorded by Barbra Streisand.

Fred Ebb, who was born in New York City on April 8, 1932, attended

New York University and Columbia University. His official introduction to the musical theater came in 1963 with *Morning Sun,* produced by the Phoenix Theater, for which he wrote both the book and lyrics. He followed this with contributions for lyrics to various revues and to the television show "This Was the Week That Was," before becoming Kander's lyricist.

Their first musical was a failure, *Flora, the Red Menace,* (1965). But one year later came *Cabaret,* and their position in the Broadway musical theater was solidified.

PRINCIPAL WORKS: Cabaret (1966) ; The Happy Time (1968) ; Zorba (1968). *See:* CABARET ; THE HAPPY TIME ; ZORBA.

## KAUFMAN, GEORGE S., *librettist*

One of Broadway's most brilliant writers of comedy, Kaufman left the strong impression of his wit and satire on the musical stage. He was born in Pittsburgh, Pennsylvania, on November 16, 1889, and was educated in the public schools. He held down various jobs—stenographer for a coal company, surveyor for the city of Pittsburgh, a traveling salesman for a concern manufacturing shoelaces—while contributing witty pieces to the celebrated newspaper column of F.P.A. (Franklin P. Adams). It was F.P.A. who arranged for Kaufman to run his own column, "This and That," for the Washington *Times.* Kaufman came to New York in 1914, where he wrote another humorous column—this time for the *Evening Mail*—and afterward served as reporter for the *Herald* and the *Times.*

In 1918 he made his stage debut with the play *Someone in the House,* of which he was co-author. During the next two decades all of his most successful plays (with the exception of *The Butter and Egg Man* in 1925) were written collaboratively with various writers—principally Moss Hart, Marc Connelly, Edna Ferber, and Ring Lardner. The best of these were smash box-office hits, including *To the Ladies, Dulcy, Merton of the Movies, Beggar on Horseback, The Royal Family, June Moon, Dinner at Eight, Merrily We Roll Along, You Can't Take It with You* (which won the Pulitzer Prize), *The Man Who Came to Dinner,* and *The Solid Gold Cadillac.*

In 1923 Kaufman, in collaboration with Marc Connelly, entered the musical theater for the first time with *Helen of Troy, New York,* music by Harry Ruby. A year later came *Be Yourself,* again with Connelly, but this time with music by Lewis Gensler and Milton Schwartwald and lyrics by Ira Gershwin. In 1925 Kaufman completed the book for the Four Marx Brothers' jamboree *The Cocoanuts,* music by Irving Berlin. The habit of success now assumed in the musical theater (as well as in the nonmusical theater), Kaufman became associated with some of the leading musical comedies and revues of the 1930's. With Gershwin's *Of Thee I Sing* he won the Pulitzer Prize. His last musical was *Silk Stockings,* in 1955.

In still another capacity, as stage director, his gift for timing and pace was profitably felt in the musical theater—in such major productions as Irving Berlin's *Face the Music* and Frank Loesser's *Guys and Dolls.* The list of outstandingly successful nonmusicals for which he served as director is as long as it is distinguished (including *The Front Page, Merrily We Roll Along, Stage Door, You Can't Take It with You, Of Mice and Men,* and *The Solid Gold Cadillac*).

In the late 1950's George S. Kaufman appeared on a regular weekly television program. He died on June 2, 1961.

PRINCIPAL WORKS: Helen of Troy, New York (1923); The Cocoanuts (1925); Strike Up the Band (1930); The Band Wagon (1931); Of Thee I Sing (1931); Let 'Em Eat Cake (1933); I'd Rather Be Right (1937); Silk Stockings (1955). *See:* THE BAND WAGON; THE COCOANUTS; HELEN OF TROY, NEW YORK; I'D RATHER BE RIGHT; LET 'EM EAT CAKE; OF THEE I SING; SILK STOCKINGS; STRIKE UP THE BAND.

## KERKER, GUSTAVE A., *composer*

A favorite on Broadway when operettas were popular, Gustave Kerker was born in Hereford, Germany, on February 28, 1857. As a child of seven he started to study the cello, and at ten he came to the United States, settling in Louisville, Kentucky. He conducted several theater orchestras there and when he was twenty-two wrote the music for his first operetta, *Cadets,* which made a four-month tour of the South. Edward E. Rice, the producer, was so impressed by this music that he arranged for Kerker to come to New York and become conductor at the Casino Theater, then the home of outstanding musical productions. Kerker's first Broadway operetta was *The Pearl of Pekin* (1888), and success came with *Castles in the Air* (1890). His operettas, many of them produced at the Casino Theater, placed him with the popular Broadway composers of his day. Even his less successful musicals yielded ingratiating songs, such as "In Gay New York" (in the operetta of the same name), "Baby, Baby" (in *The Lady Slavey*), and "The Good Old Days" (in *The Whirl of the Town*). Kerker died in New York City on June 29, 1923.

PRINCIPAL WORKS: Castles in the Air (1890); The Belle of New York (1897); A Chinese Honeymoon (1902); The Social Whirl (1908). *See:* THE BELLE OF NEW YORK; CASTLES IN THE AIR; A CHINESE HONEYMOON; THE SOCIAL WHIRL.

## KERN, JEROME, *composer*

The later musicals of Jerome Kern are so fresh in the mind as a result of revivals, screen adaptations, and even presentations over television that it is sometimes difficult to remember how early he first appeared on the Broadway scene. The year, as a matter of fact, was 1904; Victor Herbert and George M. Cohan were in their heyday—musical comedy in its infancy.

Kern was born in New York City on January 27, 1885. The Kerns were comparatively well off, the father being head of a water-sprinkling company that had the concession to water the city streets. His mother was an amateur pianist and a devoted music lover who gave Jerome his first piano lessons. When she sensed that the boy had talent she engaged a local piano teacher for more professional instruction.

When Jerome was ten, his father became head of a merchandising house in Newark, New Jersey; the family went there to live; and Jerome continued his piano lessons while completing his elementary and secondary schooling. At Newark High School he played the piano in assemblies, wrote music for the school shows. His teachers sometimes referred to him as "that musical genius" and were quietly tolerant of his comparative indifference to any subject in the curriculum outside of music.

After leaving high school Kern prevailed on his father to permit him to continue his music study. He entered the New York College of Music, where his teachers included Paolo Gallico and Alexander Lambert. He also took some private lessons in theory and harmony from Austin Pierce. Kern then wanted to go to Europe for instruction under some of its outstanding teachers, but his father preferred his going into business. It was the father's opinion that Kern had thus far not sufficiently proved himself in music to consider it a life career.

In 1902 Kern entered the father's merchandising house. One day the father sent him to the Bronx to buy two pianos. Hypnotized by the talk of a glib salesman, Kern bought not two but two hundred pianos, and with that single transaction almost ruined the merchandising business. This led the father to reconsider his earlier decision. He now gave his son his blessing to go off to Europe and continue his music study there.

Kern went to Europe in 1903. He did some studying in Germany, but mostly he traveled about absorbing musical experiences. He also tried writing some serious music, but abandoned these attempts when he recognized the sad truth that his ambition was greater than either his technique or talent. Finally he settled in London, there to find a job with Charles K. Frohman, an American producer then putting on musical shows in London. Kern was employed to write songs and musical pieces for the opening numbers of these productions, a poorly paid and insignificant assignment, since London theatergoers came habitually late and never saw the opening act. But this humble position accomplished one thing for Kern. It convinced him that if he was to make his way in music it would have to be through popular music—and probably in the popular music theater.

In London Kern wrote several songs, one of which was a topical number, "Mr. Chamberlain"—Mr. Chamberlain being an important statesman, and father of England's future prime minister, Neville. Kern's lyricist here was a young writer named P. G. Wodehouse, with whom he was working for the first time. In the future Wodehouse was to be not only famous as the author of humorous tales and whimsical novels, but he also would become Kern's collaborator in the writing of American musical comedies as well as of musical comedies by other composers. (*See* WODEHOUSE, P. G.)

By the time Kern returned to the United States in 1904 he knew that his ambition lay with popular music. Consequently he decided to work in Tin Pan Alley, and for two years filled several menial jobs there. He worked as a song plugger, adapted songs of other composers, wrote stock numbers of his own. One of his jobs was as salesman for the publishing house of Harms, Inc., headed by Max Dreyfus. Dreyfus, whose sensitive nostrils had an uncanny faculty for sniffing out potential talent, recognized Kern's gifts and did what he could to encourage and develop them. He published some of Kern's early songs, found for him a job as accompanist for the vaudevillian Marie Dressler, then helped him get some assignments for Broadway.

Kern's first step into the Broadway theater came in 1904, when he revised the George Darnley–George Everard score of, and interpolated four of his own songs in, *Mr. Wix of Wickham,* produced at the Bijou on September 19. "Who is this Jerome Kern," inquired Alan Dale in his review in the New York *American,* "whose music towers in an Eiffel-way above the average hurdy-gurdy accompaniment of the present-day musical comedy?" On November 4, 1905, Kern's first American hit song was published by Harms and introduced in *The Earl and the Girl.* It was "How'd You Like to Spoon with Me?", sung by Georgia Caine and a bevy of girls on swings. And in 1906 several other Kern songs were interpolated in *The Rich Mr. Hoggenheimer* (score by Englander) and in *The Little Cherub* (music by Caryll). From then on, for the next half-dozen years, many of his songs were interpolated in various Broadway musical comedies.

On October 25, 1910, Kern married Eva Leale. She was an English girl, and the ceremony took place in the girl's home town, Walton-on-Thames.

In 1911 the Shuberts engaged Kern to collaborate with Frank Tours in writing music for *La Belle Paree,* an extravaganza that was part of the bill opening the Winter Garden on March 20. One year later Kern wrote his first complete original score for Broadway, *The Red Petticoat,* a play about Nevada miners, a failure. *Oh I Say!*, the second Broadway musical with a complete Kern score, produced in 1913, was also a dud.

In 1914 Kern had several remarkable songs interpolated in *The Girl from Utah*, an English operetta adapted for the American stage. One of these numbers was "They Didn't Believe Me," which had a sheet-music sale of two million copies. When Victor Herbert heard Kern's song from *The Girl from Utah* at the office of Harms, he said: "This man will inherit my mantle."

Between 1915 and 1919 Kern collaborated first with Guy Bolton, and then with Bolton and P. G. Wodehouse, in a series of intimate musical comedies produced at the Princess Theater that came to be known as the Princess Theater Shows. This series was inaugurated with *Nobody Home* (1915), and its first outstanding hit was *Very Good, Eddie* (1915). For the next few years the Princess Theater Shows helped inject a new note of informality and charm and vivacity into the American musical theater. (*See* THE PRINCESS THEATER SHOWS.)

With lavish productions like *Sally* (1920), *Good Morning Dearie* (1920), *Stepping Stones* (1923), and *Sunny* (1925), Kern reverted to a more traditional kind of musical theater than the Princess Theater Shows, a theater dependent on stars, sets, costuming, routines, and songs. But in 1927 he once again departed from accepted procedures when, to Oscar Hammerstein's book and lyrics, he wrote the music for *Show Boat*, since then become a stage classic. From 1927 on Kern divided his energies and interests between musical productions that were new and fresh in their material and approach—musicals like *The Cat and the Fiddle* (1931) and *Music in the Air* (1932)—and the more routine and formal.kind of stage entertainment represented by *Sweet Adeline* (1929) and *Roberta* (1933). Kern's last musical comedy for the Broadway stage was *Very Warm for May* (1939), a failure. But *Very Warm for May* has not been forgotten, for it was the showcase for one of Kern's song masterpieces, "All the Things You Are."

After 1939 Kern wrote exclusively for motion pictures. A song written independent of any stage or screen production—but interpolated into the motion picture, *Lady, Be Good!*—won the Academy Award in 1941. It was "The Last Time I Saw Paris," lyrics by Oscar Hammerstein, and inspired by the then recent occupation of Paris by Nazi troops. This was the second time the Academy Award was won by Kern; the first time had been in 1936 for "The Way You Look Tonight," in *Swing Time*.

After completing the score for the motion picture *Centennial Summer* in 1945, Kern planned to return to the Broadway stage. Rodgers and Hammerstein, as producers, contracted him to write music for a new show to be put on the following season, and at the same time a new revival of *Show*

*Boat* was being projected. Kern consequently came East. On November 5— a half-hour after auditioning singers for *Show Boat*—he collapsed on Park Avenue in New York. He died six days later at Doctors Hospital. Irving Berlin, who came to visit Kern on November 11, was one of the first to learn that Kern had just died. (And it was Irving Berlin who took over the assignment of writing the score for the musical Kern had been engaged to do; and who achieved with that musical—*Annie Get Your Gun*—the greatest stage triumph of his career.)

Less than three years after Kern's death his life was told in the motion picture *Till the Clouds Roll By,* scenario by Kern's lifelong friend and collaborator, Guy Bolton. In 1949 came a second motion picture studded with Kern's songs, the biography of Marilyn Miller, *Look for the Silver Lining.*

PRINCIPAL WORKS: Mister (Mr.) Wix of Wickham (1904); La Belle Paree (1911); The Girl from Utah (1914); Nobody Home (1915); Oh, Boy; (1917); Leave It to Jane (1917); Oh, Lady! Lady! (1918); Sally (1920); Good Morning Dearie (1921); Stepping Stones (1923); Sunny (1925); Criss Cross (1926); Show Boat (1928); Sweet Adeline (1929); The Cat and the Fiddle (1931); Music in the Air (1932); Roberta (1933).

*See:* LA BELLE PAREE; THE CAT AND THE FIDDLE; CRISS CROSS; THE GIRL FROM UTAH; GOOD MORNING DEARIE; LEAVE IT TO JANE; MISTER (MR.) WIX OF WICKHAM; MUSIC IN THE AIR; THE PRINCESS THEATER SHOWS (*Nobody Home, Oh, Boy!, Oh, Lady! Lady!, Very Good, Eddie*); ROBERTA; SALLY; SHOW BOAT; STEPPING STONES; SUNNY; SWEET ADELINE.

## KLEIN, MANUEL, *composer*

Though Manuel Klein wrote scores for several Broadway musical comedies, his name is always associated with the spectacles, or extravaganzas, that made the Hippodrome an institution for many years. He was born in London on December 6, 1876, a member of a notable family in English culture. His brothers, Herman, Charles, and Alfred, were famous as music critic, playwright, and actor respectively. Manuel received his musical training in London. He came to the United States early in the 1900's, and in 1903 made his Broadway debut with *Mr. Pickwick,* the text by his brother Charles, with De Wolf Hopper as star. Through Gus Edwards, the songwriter, he managed to get the job of music director of the Hippodrome in 1905, soon after its sensational opening, and for the next decade he not only led the orchestra there but also wrote the music for the annual presentations.

A disagreement between J. J. Shubert, then managing the Hippodrome, and Manuel Klein brought about the latter's removal in 1915. Shubert needed some drums and trumpets for a Winter Garden show and asked Klein to send them over; Klein refused, needing those instruments for his own orchestra.

Klein was summarily dismissed; and Shubert, now having antagonized the Hippodrome company, relinquished his interest in the Hippodrome to Charles Dillingham.

Klein died in London on June 1, 1919.

*See:* HIPPODROME EXTRAVAGANZAS, 1905 through 1914.

## LANE, BURTON, *composer*

He was born in New York City on February 2, 1912, the son of a successful real-estate operator. The boy early showed his aptitude for music, but the family was opposed to his studying it, feeling that it imposed too much of a strain on him. Nevertheless, while attending elementary and secondary schools in New York, and the Dwight School, Burton Lane managed to take piano lessons and receive instruction in theory; while still a boy he began writing serious pieces for the piano.

In his fourteenth year Lane impressed the noted bandleader Harold Stern, then working for J. J. Shubert. Stern arranged fo Shubert to hear some of Lane's compositions. The result was that Shubert commissioned the boy to write music for a forthcoming edition of *The Greenwich Village Follies.* Stimulated by this assignment, Lane completed about forty numbers, asking Shubert to take his pick. Unfortunately, Lane's debut on Broadway had to be delayed, since the projected *Follies* was canceled due to the illness of one of its stars. However, Lane did manage to write some marches for the Dwight School, which were published.

From 1927 to 1929 Lane was employed as pianist at J. H. Remick's. Here he acquired his apprenticeship in writing popular songs, now his main interest. George Gershwin gave him valuable criticism and encouragement. Howard Dietz, the lyricist, arranged to have two of Lane's songs appear in the Broadway revue *Three's a Crowd* (1930): "Forget All Your Books" and "Out in the Open Air" (lyrics by Howard Dietz). In 1931 Lane's songs appeared in two more Broadway musicals: Beatrice Lillie sang "Say the Word" in the third *Little Show,* while four Lane songs were heard in *The Earl Carroll Vanities.*

For a while, victimized by the Depression, Lane was unable to place more songs in Broadway productions (though he did manage to publish two). Then, when the talkies became popular, Lane was hired by the MGM Studios in Hollywood. From 1934 to 1936 he worked for various other lots, and in 1936 he became an ace composer for Paramount Pictures.

Lane returned to Broadway in 1940 with his first complete stage score— *Hold on to Your Hats,* starring Al Jolson. That play was important in Lane's career by bringing him a working partner in E. Y. Harburg, the lyricist. Lane had previously written a few melodies to Harburg's lyrics, but in *Hold on to*

*Your Hats* he worked with Harburg on a Broadway musical for the first time. And it was with Harburg that Lane achieved his greatest Broadway success in 1947—*Finian's Rainbow*.

From 1957 on Lane served as president of the American Guild of Authors and Composers. He returned to the Broadway scene with the musical *On a Clear Day You Can See Forever* (1965), after doing considerable work in Hollywood for the movies during the preceding three decades.

PRINCIPAL WORKS: Hold on to Your Hats (1928); The Earl Carroll Vanities of 1930 and 1931; Laffing Room Only (1944); Finian's Rainbow (1947); On a Clear Day You Can See Forever (1965).
*See:* THE EARL CARROLL VANITIES of 1930 and 1931; FINIAN'S RAINBOW; HOLD ON TO YOUR HATS; LAFFING ROOM ONLY; ON A CLEAR DAY YOU CAN SEE FOREVER.

## LA TOUCHE, JOHN, *librettist-lyricist*

Born in Richmond, Virginia, on November 13, 1917, he attended the Richmond Academy of Arts and Sciences, where he won a prize in composition. When he was fifteen he came to New York and attended the Riverdale Preparatory School (on a scholarship) and Columbia College. At Columbia he became the first freshman to win the Columbia Award for both prose and poetry; and in his sophomore year he collaborated in the writing of music and lyrics for the annual Varsity Show.

His debut in the professional theater came in 1937 with *Pins and Needles,* to which he contributed two numbers. In 1939 *Sing for Your Supper* (a revue produced by the WPA) included a stirring cantata, "Ballad for Uncle Sam," lyrics by John La Touche, music by Earl Robinson. Renamed "Ballad for Americans," it proved outstandingly popular in the 1940's after having been used as an inaugural feature of the Republican National Convention in 1939.

La Touche first established his reputation as lyricist for the Broadway stage with *Cabin in the Sky* (1940), music by Vernon Duke. He subsequently wrote either the lyrics or book, or both, for several musicals, including Vernon Duke's *Banjo Eyes,* starring Eddie Cantor (1941), and *The Golden Apple* (1954), which received the New York Drama Critics Circle Award. His last associations with the popular musical stage came in 1955 with two failures, *The Vamp* and Leonard Bernstein's *Candide.* He also wrote the libretto for Douglas Moore's successful opera, *The Ballad of Baby Doe* (1956). John La Touche died in Calais, Vermont, on August 7, 1956.

PRINCIPAL WORKS: Cabin in the Sky (1940); Banjo Eyes (1941); The Golden Apple (1954); Candide (1956).
*See:* BANJO EYES; CABIN IN THE SKY; CANDIDE; THE GOLDEN APPLE.

## LAURENTS, ARTHUR, *librettist*

He is a highly successful Broadway playwright. He was born in Brooklyn, New York, on July 14, 1918. Among his Broadway nonmusical plays are *Home of the Brave* (1956); *The Time of the Cuckoo* (1952), which was the source of the Rodgers musical *Do I Hear a Waltz?; A Clearing in the Woods* (1957); and *Invitation to a March* (1960). He also wrote several notable screenplays (including *Anastasia, Anna Lucasta, The Snake Pit,* and *Bonjour Tristesse*). In addition to the musicals listed below, he wrote the book for *Anyone Can Whistle,* which he also directed (1964), and he directed the Harold Rome musical *I Can Get It for You Wholesale* (1962).

PRINCIPAL WORKS: West Side Story (1957); Gypsy (1959); Do I Hear a Waltz? (1965); Halleulujah, Baby! (1967).
*See:* DO I HEAR A WALTZ?; GYPSY; HALLELUJAH, BABY!; WEST SIDE STORY.

## LEIGH, CAROLYN, *lyricist*

She was born in New York City on August 21, 1926, and received her education at Queens College in New York and at New York University. Before achieving success as a lyricist she worked as a copywriter for an advertising firm and wrote texts for several TV specials. In 1954 she wrote the words for a hit song, "Young at Heart," music by Johnny Richards, and made her first entry into the Broadway musical theater with a few songs for *Peter Pan,* starring Mary Martin, for which Mark Charlap provided Miss Leigh with the music. Major success as a songwriter, however, came to her between 1957 and 1959, when she produced a string of hit songs, with lyrics set to music by Cy Coleman. These songs included "Witchcraft," "I Walked a Little Faster," "A Doodlin' Song," "Firefly," "You Fascinate Me So," and "It Amazes Me." Once again, with Coleman as her composer, she contributed all the lyrics for the Broadway musicals *Wildcat* (1960) and *Little Me* (1962), and for motion pictures the successful song "Pass Me By" for *Father Goose.* In 1963 she contributed a song to the motion picture *The Cardinal:* "Stay with Me," music by Jerome Moross. In 1967, with Elmer Bernstein as her composer, she wrote the lyrics for the unsuccessful Broadway musical *How Now, Dow Jones.*

PRINCIPAL WORKS: The Ziegfeld Follies of 1957; Wildcat (1960); Little Me (1962).
*See:* LITTLE ME; WILDCAT; THE ZIEGFELD FOLLIES of 1957.

## LEIGH, MITCH, *composer. See* Part I, MAN OF LA MANCHA.

## LERNER, ALAN JAY, *librettist-lyricist,* and LOEWE, FREDERICK, *composer*

Lerner was born to wealth, in New York, on August 31, 1918; his parents were proprietors of the prosperous Lerner Shops in New York. Alan received an intensive academic education at Bedales, in Hampshire, England, and in the United States at the Choate School and Harvard College, graduating from the latter with a degree of Bachelor of Science in 1940. While attending Harvard, Lerner wrote sketches and lyrics for two Hasty Pudding Shows.

His ambition was to write for the theater, but his first attempts to do so proved thoroughly discouraging and frustrating. While biding his time and waiting for opportunity to knock, Lerner wrote material for radio programs; in a period of two years he wrote over five hundred scripts.

Chance brought him into contact with Frederick Loewe, a frustrated composer, at the Lambs Club in 1942, and chance made them collaborators.

Frederick Loewe, composer, was the son of a famous tenor of Viennese operettas (creator of the role of Prince Danilo in *The Merry Widow*). Frederick was born in Vienna on June 10, 1904, and was a prodigy who started playing the piano when he was five and wrote music at seven when he contributed some numbers for his father's variety act; and at thirteen he became the youngest pianist ever to appear as soloist with the Berlin Symphony Orchestra. He received piano instruction from two of Europe's foremost keyboard masters and scholars—Ferruccio Busoni and Eugéne d'Albert —and in 1922 was the recipient of the Hollander medal. He then went through a period of study of composition with Nikolaus von Reznicek.

Both his talent and his training were calculated to bring him a career in serious music, but popular music interested him from the beginning. He was only five when he wrote his first popular tune. By the time he was fifteen, he was the proud author of an impressive hit, "Katrina," which sold over one million copies of sheet music.

He came to the United States in 1942 to begin his American career in music, but found he could make no headway with either serious or popular scores. He then decided to quit music for good. For several years he earned his living playing the piano in theaters and nightspots, working in a cafeteria as busboy, teaching horseback riding at a resort, and even engaging in professional boxing. He also worked out West as a gold prospector, mail carrier on horseback, and cowpuncher.

He was back East in the early 1930's, working as a pianist in a German beer hall. Still determined to make his way as a composer, preferably for Broadway, he joined the Lambs Club, a social gathering place for people of the theater. Through the actor Dennis King he had one of his songs, "Love Tiptoed Through My Heart," interpolated into a nonmusical production,

*Petticoat Fever,* in which Dennis King was starring. This was in 1934. Two years later another of Loewe's numbers, "A Waltz Was Born in Vienna," was used in the *Illustrators Show* on Broadway. In 1937, in collaboration with Earl Crooker, he contributed a complete score for a musical comedy, *Salute to Spring,* produced in St. Louis. Renamed *Great Lady,* it came to Broadway the same year but proved a dismal failure. In 1942, however, a Detroit producer suggested to Loewe a revival of this musical, but with extensive revisions, calling for the services of a new writer. At the Lambs Club Loewe asked Lerner to do that job, which the young writer eagerly accepted. They rewrote the old musical in about two weeks, and it was seen in Detroit in October of 1942.

Their first Broadway musical came soon after that. It was *What's Up?* (1943), starring Jimmy Savo, which Lerner has since described as a "disaster." Two years after that Lerner and Loewe reappeared on Broadway with *The Day Before Spring.*

Success came to Lerner and Loewe in 1947 with *Brigadoon,* since become a classic in the American musical theater. Less than a decade later they made stage history with *My Fair Lady* (1956), following this unprecedented triumph with *Camelot* (1960). In between these two stage productions they made an excursion to Hollywood to write the songs for the screen musical *Gigi* (1958), which received nine Academy Awards, including those for best picture of the year and for the title song.

While Lerner was still Loewe's collaborator, he occasionally worked with other composers. In 1948 he wrote book and lyrics for Kurt Weill's *Love Life.* And still without Loewe's partnership he worked with some outstanding screen musicals for Hollywood, including *An American in Paris,* which won the Academy Award in 1951.

The partnership of Lerner and Loewe collapsed after *Camelot.* Loewe went into temporary retirement. For a while, an attempt was made to establish a working arrangement between Lerner and Richard Rodgers, but their differences in approach and outlook compelled them to separate before the musical on which they were at work could be produced. As *On a Clear Day You Can See Forever*—with music by Burton Lane—it finally came both to Broadway in 1965 and to the Hollywood screen in 1970. André Previn was the next composer with whom Lerner worked, their efforts resulting in *Coco* in 1969.

PRINCIPAL WORKS: The Day Before Spring (1945); Brigadoon (1947); Paint Your Wagon (1951); My Fair Lady (1956); Camelot (1960).
*See:* BRIGADOON; CAMELOT; THE DAY BEFORE SPRING; MY FAIR LADY; PAINT YOUR WAGON.

LINDSAY, HOWARD, *librettist. See* CROUSE, RUSSEL, AND LINDSAY, HOWARD.

LOESSER, FRANK, *composer and librettist-lyricist*

Frank Loesser was born in New York City on June 29, 1910. His family was musical, his father being a piano teacher, and his brother Arthur a concert pianist and famous piano teacher. Nevertheless, Frank was never given musical instruction—the reason being that at the time, Frank, unlike the other members of a highly charged intellectual family, had little sympathy for serious music. When he tried playing the piano (at first only with one finger) it was to pick out popular tunes. Since his family regarded such music contemptuously, they preferred leaving Frank to his own devices. He learned to play the piano by ear; he also managed to acquire an ingratiating personal singing style; and he became adept with a harmonica. What he accomplished in music had to come without benefit of a teacher, and through a hit-and-miss process.

Recalling his youth, Loesser remarked: "In those days I had a rendezvous with failure." Nothing he did, or tried to do, seemed to turn out right. His academic schooling, never distingushed, took place at elementary public schools, the Speyer and Townsend Harris High Schools, and ended abruptly after a single year at the College of the City of New York. He then held one job after another in rapid succession: process server for some lawyers; inspector of a chain of restaurants, testing food; an office boy in a wholesale jewelry house; a waiter and pianist in a Catskill Mountains hotel; reporter for a small paper in New Rochelle; knit-goods editor of a small-town journal; press agent.

While thus floundering about in poorly paid jobs, he tried to write song lyrics. The initial impulse for writing verses came from a favor done for a certain gentleman who needed couplets for each of the guests attending a Lions Club dinner. Loesser wrote these couplets, and they were pretty awful. One of them ran: *"Secretary Albert Vincent, Read the minutes—right this instant."* But the guests at the dinner seemed delighted with his efforts, and the exhilaration of creation had touched Loesser. From then on he spent most of his time writing verses and song lyrics. One of these, a ballad called "Armful of You," was sold to a vaudevillian for fifteen dollars.

He was not yet twenty when he submitted a handful of lyrics to the publisher Leo Feist, who offered Loesser a job as staff lyricist for one hundred dollars a week. During that year Loesser wrote many lyrics to melodies by Joseph Brandfron, but none was considered good enough to publish. Only after Feist had dispensed with Loesser's services was one of his songs published: "I'm in Love with the Memory of You," in 1931. This song is significant because it was Loesser's first publication; also because its composer was a young hopeful named William Schuman, subsequently one of America's most significant serious composers and president of the Juilliard School of Music and later of the Lincoln Center for the Performing Arts.

Loesser's first hit—though only a minor one—came in 1934, "I Wish I Were Twins," music by Joseph Meyer. This success was instrumental in bringing him out to Hollywood to write songs for grade-B pictures on the Universal lot. When this contract expired, Loesser went to work for Paramount, for whom he completed his first important lyrics. They were "Says My Heart" (music by Burton Lane), "Small Fry" and "Two Sleepy People" (Hoagy Carmichael), "I Don't Want to Walk Without You, Baby" (Jule Styne), and "Jingle, Jangle, Jingle" (Joseph J. Lilley). Other Loesser lyrics were set to music by Arthur Schwartz, Frederick Hollander, and Jimmy McHugh.

Loesser wrote his first melody (as well as the lyrics) under the stimulation of World War II—"Praise the Lord and Pass the Ammunition" (1942), which had the formidable sale of two million records and over one million copies of sheet music. A second war song was equally distinguished and almost as successful, "Rodger Young," written at the request of the infantry. With these two war hymns Loesser immediately proved himself as gifted in writing melodies as in lyrics, and from then on he wrote both music and lyrics for most of his songs.

During World War II Loesser served as private first class in Special Services, when he wrote soldier shows packaged and distributed to Army camps. He wrote individual songs for various branches of the service, one of which became the official song of the infantry, "What Do You Do in the Infantry?" He also wrote songs for the WACS, Service Forces, Bombardiers, and so forth.

Loesser's first musical-comedy score came after he had become one of Hollywood's topflight lyricists and composers. In 1948 *Where's Charley?* started a Broadway run of 729 performances. While this musical was prospering on Broadway, Loesser kept on writing distinguished songs for the screen, winning an Academy Award in 1949 for "Baby, It's Cold Outside" from *Neptune's Daughter* and receiving critical accolades for his score to *Hans Christian Andersen* (1953), starring Danny Kaye.

Loesser's second musical on Broadway was an even greater triumph than his first one, for it was *Guys and Dolls* (1950). A half-dozen years later, with his third musical, *The Most Happy Fella,* Loesser wrote not only music and lyrics but also (for the first time) his own musical-comedy text. In *Green-*

*willow* (1960), also a musical play, he collaborated with Lesser Samuels on the book while also providing lyrics and music. *Greenwillow* was a failure, but with the musical comedy *How to Succeed in Business Without Really Trying* (1961) Loesser realized a production that not only had a run of almost fifteen hundred performances but also brought him the Pulitzer Prize. Frank Loesser died of lung cancer in New York City on July 28, 1969.

PRINCIPAL WORKS: Where's Charley? (1948); Guys and Dolls (1950); The Most Happy Fella (1956); How to Succeed in Business Without Really Trying (1961).
*See:* GUYS AND DOLLS; HOW TO SUCCEED IN BUSINESS WITHOUT REALLY TRYING; THE MOST HAPPY FELLA; WHERE'S CHARLEY?

LOEWE, FREDERICK, *composer. See* LERNER, ALAN JAY, AND LOEWE, FREDERICK.

LOGAN, JOSHUA, *librettist*
Joshua Logan has distinguished himself as one of the most significant directors of both the stage and the screen. He was born in Texarkana, Texas, on October 5, 1908, and attended Princeton University, where he wrote and acted in two Triangle shows, and was president of the club for one year. A scholarship then enabled him to study under Constantin Stanislavsky at the Moscow Art Theater. His entry into the Broadway theater came as an actor, when he appeared in *Carrie Nation* (1932); as director, his first effort was *Camille,* starring Jane Cowl, which toured the United States in 1933. Among the musicals which he directed were three by Rodgers and Hart (*I Married an Angel, Higher and Higher,* and *By Jupiter*), as well as *Knickerbocker Holiday, Annie Get Your Gun, Wish You Were Here,* and *South Pacific;* for the last of these he was also co-author and co-producer. His most successful nonmusical productions included *On Borrowed Time, Happy Birthday, Middle of the Night, Blue Denim, Kind Sir,* and *The World of Suzie Wong.* For Hollywood he directed, among other films, *South Pacific, Fanny, Bus Stop, Picnic, Sayonara,* and *Paint Your Wagon.*

PRINCIPAL WORKS: South Pacific (1949); Wish You Were Here (1952); Fanny (1954).
*See:* FANNY; SOUTH PACIFIC; WISH YOU WERE HERE.

LUDERS, GUSTAV, *composer*
Luders, composer of delightful operettas and operetta tunes in the early 1900's, was born in Bremen, Germany, on December 13, 1865. He studied music extensively in Europe before coming to the United States in 1888 and

settling in Milwaukee. There he conducted orchestras in theaters and beer gardens. Charles K. Harris, composer of "After the Ball," urged Luders to seek out the richer opportunities offered by a metropolis like Chicago. There Luders found employment as conductor in theaters and a permanent post as arranger for the local office of the music publisher Witmark. One of Luders' chores, in 1896, was an arrangement of one of the most popular ragtime tunes of that day, Barney Fagan's "My Gal's a Highborn Lady."

Luders' first score for the stage came in 1899. It was *Little Robinson Crusoe,* book and lyrics by Harry B. Smith, and starring Eddie Foy. Luders' musicianship led Henry W. Savage, the producer, to commission him to write music for *The Burgomaster,* a comic opera that Savage was planning for Raymond Hitchcock. *The Burgomaster,* produced in Chicago in 1900, was only moderately successful, but it did boast an outstanding song hit (Luders' first) in "The Tale of the Kangaroo." (From this time on, Luders was partial to songs using the word "Tale" in the title; among his best-known songs are "The Tale of the Bumble Bee" and "The Tale of the Turtle Dove.")

The text and lyrics of *The Burgomaster* were by Frank Pixley, editor of the Chicago *Times-Herald.* This play initiated a collaborative arrangement between Pixley and Luders that lasted many years and brought forth a few more operettas—including *The Prince of Pilsen* (1903), their greatest success. Among other Pixley-Luders operettas were: *King Dodo* (1902); *Woodland* (1904), a fantasy in which all the characters appeared as birds; *The Grand Mogul* (1907); *Marcelle* (1908); and *The Gypsy* (1912).

Pixley was not Luders' only collaborator. On other operettas Luders worked with George Ade, the celebrated columnist and humorist, their best musicals being *The Sho-Gun* (1904) and *The Fair Co-ed* (1909).

The number "13" proved the downfall of Luders. His thirteenth operetta was *Somewhere Else,* produced in 1913. After the opening-night performance Luders was convinced he had another hit, since his friends said the play was as good as *The Prince of Pilsen.* The morning after the opening the critics were annihilating, a fact that so discouraged the producer that he closed down the show after the third performance. Apparently Luders felt his defeat deeply. He died of a heart attack only one day after the show closed.

PRINCIPAL WORKS: King Dodo (1902); The Prince of Pilsen (1903); The Sho-Gun (1904); Hippodrome Extravaganzas (1905); The Fair Co-ed (1909).
*See:* THE FAIR CO-ED; HIPPODROME EXTRAVAGANZA, 1905; KING DODO; THE PRINCE OF PILSEN; THE SHO-GUN.

## McCARTHY, JOSEPH, *lyricist*
He was born in Somerville, Massachusetts, on September 27, 1885. He started

making his living by singing in cafés. After that he became a music publisher in Boston, and found employment in Tin Pan Alley. In 1918 he provided the lyrics for the Broadway musical *Oh, Look!*, music by Harry Carroll. *Irene,* a year later, was the first of his many major successes. Besides the musicals listed below, he wrote lyrics to music by Harry Tierney for *The Broadway Whirl* (1921), *Glory* (1922), and *Cross My Heart* (1928). He also provided lyrics to Sigmund Romberg's music for *Follow Me,* which starred Anna Held in 1916, and to George M. Cohan's musical *Royal Vagabond* (1919). McCarthy's hit songs included "You Made Me Love You," "What Do You Want to Make Those Eyes at Me For?", "They Go Wild, Simply Wild Over Me," "Ireland Must be Heaven, for My Mother Came from There," "I'm Always Chasing Rainbows," and "Alice Blue Gown." McCarthy died in New York City on December 18, 1943.

PRINCIPAL WORKS: Irene (1919); The Ziegfeld Follies of 1920; Up She Goes (1922); Kid Boots (1923).
*See:* IRENE; KID BOOTS; UP SHE GOES; THE ZIEGFELD FOLLIES of 1920.

## MacDONOUGH, GLEN, *librettist-lyricist*
He was born in Brooklyn, New York, on November 12, 1870. His education was completed at Manhattan College. In 1900 he wrote text and lyrics for a comic opera by John Philip Sousa, *Chris and the Wonderful Lamp,* and in 1903 he realized success with his text and lyrics for Victor Herbert's extravaganza *Babes in Toyland.* Besides working with Herbert, he also wrote librettos and lyrics for Hubbell's music in *The Midnight Sons* (1909), *The Jolly Bachelors* (1910), *The Never Homes* (1911) and *The Kiss Burglar* (1918). MacDonough was also a contributor to the revue *Hitchy-Koo,* editions of 1917, 1918, and 1920. He died in Stamford, Connecticut, on March 30, 1924.

PRINCIPAL WORKS: Babes in Toyland (1903); It Happened in Nordland (1904); The Summer Widowers (1910); The Hen Pecks (1911).
*See:* BABES IN TOYLAND; THE HEN PECKS; IT HAPPENED IN NORDLAND; THE SUMMER WIDOWERS.

## McEVOY, J. P., *librettist*
Joseph Patrick McEvoy was famous for a comic strip, "Dixie Dugan," which he created; for his magazine articles; and for a volume of sketches published in 1956. He was born in New York City on January 10, 1895, and began his literary career in 1919 with a book of light verse. In 1925 he contributed sketches to a revue, *The Comic Supplement.* He continued working for the Broadway musical theater by contributing sketches to revues and collaborating

on musical-comedy texts: for *Americana* (1926), *Allez Oop* (1927), *Show Girl* (1928), and *Stars in Your Eyes* (1939). He died on August 8, 1958.

PRINCIPAL WORKS: Americana, 1926; Show Girl (1929).
*See:* AMERICANA, 1926; SHOW GIRL.

McHUGH, JIMMY, *composer*
He was born in Boston on July 10, 1894. While attending St. John's Preparatory School he studied piano with his mother. For a while, after his academic schooling ended, he assisted his father, a plumber. Then, eager to get on with a career in music, he turned down a scholarship to the New England Conservatory to work as office boy and rehearsal pianist for the Boston Opera Company. When he reached the conclusion that his future lay in popular, and not serious, music, he found a job in the Boston branch of the Irving Berlin publishing house, serving as song plugger in local theaters and five-and-ten-cent stores. He then came to New York, where he wrote "Emaline," his first published song (1921). For seven years after that he wrote songs for revues produced in the Cotton Club, the Harlem nightspot; among these efforts was his first hit, "When My Sugar Walks Down the Street."

Meeting the young and still unpublished lyricist Dorothy Fields in 1928 at a publishing house, and deciding to write music for her words, was as much a turning point in his career as it was in hers—even though up to this time he had already written such song favorites as "What's Become of Hinky Dinky Parley Vous?", "The Lonesomest Girl in Town," and "I Can't Believe That You're in Love with Me." With Dorothy Fields as lyricist, McHugh completed his first Broadway score, and with it came his first success in the theater—*Blackbirds of 1928*. This all-Negro revue helped establish the fame of the songwriting team of McHugh and Fields. During the next two years they collaborated on numerous songs, interpolated in various musicals. Among their own musical comedies the most successful was *Hello Daddy* (1928). They also contributed songs to two revues that were box-office failures, *International Revue* (1930), which had two fine songs in "On the Sunny Side of the Street" and "Exactly like You," and *Vanderbilt Revue* (1930), which had "Blue Again."

After 1930 McHugh worked not only with Dorothy Fields but also with other lyricists. The most significant of these, as far as McHugh's career is concerned, was Harold Adamson. In 1933 they collaborated on three songs for the gala opening of the Radio City Music Hall in New York.

Meanwhile, in 1930, McHugh started writing songs for motion pictures. To Dorothy Fields's lyrics he contributed music to about a dozen films. In 1936 McHugh and Adamson wrote the songs for the motion picture *Banjo on*

*My Knee.* In later pictures McHugh collaborated most frequently with Adamson; but he also wrote music for several other lyricists, including Dorothy Fields, Frank Loesser, Gus Kahn, and Johnny Mercer. Among McHugh's most famous screen songs were "It's a Most Unusual Day," "I Feel a Song Coming On," "A Lovely Way to Spend the Evening," and "I'm in the Mood for Love."

Jimmy McHugh returned to Broadway with songs for *The Streets of Paris* (1939)—lyrics, this time, by Al Dubin—in which Carmen Miranda was lifted to Broadway fame with the help of McHugh's song "South American Way." A year after that came another Jimmy McHugh musical, *Keep Off the Grass.*

During World War II McHugh was awarded the Presidential Certificate of Merit for his activities selling war bonds; his War Bond Aquacade raised twenty-eight million dollars in a single evening. He also wrote effective war songs, the most popular of which was "Comin' in on a Wing and a Prayer" (1943).

McHugh's greatest Broadway success came in 1948 with *As the Girls Go.* His last Broadway musical, *Strip for Action* (1956), was a failure. Meanwhile, in 1953, President Eisenhower commissioned him to write the official "Crusade for Freedom" song for Radio Europe. In 1959 he was honored with a salute at the Hollywood Bowl for his "contributions to the music of our country," an event that was reported in the Congressional Record. After 1956 McHugh concentrated his creative efforts on writing scores for the movies. He died in Beverly Hills, California, of a heart attack on May 23, 1969. On November 11, 1969, a benefit performance sponsored by ASCAP was dedicated to his memory.

PRINCIPAL WORKS: Blackbirds of 1928; Hello Daddy (1928); The Streets of Paris (1939); As the Girls Go (1948).

*See:* AS THE GIRLS GO; BLACKBIRDS OF 1928; HELLO DADDY; THE STREETS OF PARIS.

## MARTIN, HUGH, *composer-lyricist*

He was born in Birmingham, Alabama, on August 11, 1914. His schooling took place at local public schools and for two years at the Birmingham-Southern College. During this period he studied the piano intensively. In 1937 he was a member of the cast in the Broadway musical *Hooray for What?* After that he formed a vocal quartet, and served as vocal director and arranger for several successful Broadway musicals by Rodgers and Hart, Cole Porter, Jule Styne, and Vernon Duke, among others. With the collaboration of Ralph Blane, he wrote his first score for a Broadway musical. It was *Best Foot Forward* (1941), a success. Before working again for the Broadway theater,

Martin and Blane went to Hollywood, where they contributed songs for *Meet Me in St. Louis,* starring Judy Garland, and *The Ziegfeld Follies,* with Lena Horne. Out of these emerged such hit numbers as "The Trolley Song," "The Boy Next Door," and "Love." In 1948 Martin returned to Broadway with songs for the musical *Look, Ma, I'm Dancing. Make a Wish* followed in 1951, and *High Spirits* in 1964. Martin also contributed scores for several musicals produced in London; served as vocal director and arranger for major television programs; and was vocal coach for a number of Hollywood stars, including Lena Horne, Judy Garland, Nanette Fabray, Rosalind Russell, and Ray Bolger.

PRINCIPAL WORKS: Best Foot Forward (1941); High Spirits (1964). *See:* BEST FOOT FORWARD; HIGH SPIRITS.


MERRILL, BOB, *composer-lyricist*
He was born in Atlantic City, New Jersey, on May 17, 1921. After attending high school he studied acting with Richard Bennett at the Bucks County Playhouse. During World War II he served in the armed forces. Then, settling in California, he was employed as dialogue director at Columbia Pictures from 1943 to 1948, and as casting director for CBS-TV from 1948 to 1949. He achieved his first hit song in 1950 with "If I Knew You Were Comin' I'd 'Ave Baked a Cake." Other hits followed rapidly, among them "Truly, Truly Fair," "Sparrow in the Tree Top," "Doggie in the Window," and "Honeycomb," for all of which he wrote both the words and the music. Eighteen of his songs were represented on the Hit Parade between 1950 and 1954.

After working as television production consultant for the firm of Liggett and Myers from 1951 to 1956, Merrill received the first contract ever given by MGM covering four capacities, as producer, composer, writer, and publisher. While thus employed, he wrote the songs for his first Broadway musical, *New Girl in Town* (1957), a minor success. Two greater Broadway box-office attractions followed with *Take Me Along* (1959) and *Carnival* (1961), as well as the songs for the motion picture *The Wonderful World of the Brothers Grimm* (1962). For *Funny Girl* (1964) he served merely as lyricist, with Jule Styne providing the music, but he once again appeared in the dual role of composer-lyricist in the Broadway musical *Henry, Sweet Henry* (1967), a failure.

PRINCIPAL WORKS: New Girl in Town (1957); Take Me Along (1959); Carnival (1961); Funny Girl (1964). *See:* CARNIVAL; FUNNY GIRL; NEW GIRL IN TOWN; TAKE ME ALONG.

## PORTER, COLE, *composer-lyricist*

He was born in Peru, Indiana, on June 9, 1892. His grandfather's speculations in West Virginia coal and timber had made him a millionaire, and the Porter family moved in a setting of luxury. Cole's mother, Kate, a cultured woman, saw to it that the boy begin his musical training early, both on the violin and the piano. He was precocious musically, having a piano piece published in Chicago by the time he was eleven.

The grandfather wanted Cole to become a lawyer. After graduating from the Worcester Academy in Massachusetts in 1909, Porter went to Yale. There his extracurricular activities included the writing of football songs, two of which became famous ("Bingo Eli Yale" and "Bulldog") and were published in 1911. He also sang in and directed the glee club, wrote and helped produce college shows, and was voted "the most entertaining man" of his class. In 1913 Porter entered Harvard Law School, where his stay was brief. Having by now decided that his future rested with music, he transferred to the School of Music at Harvard, where he remained for three years of intensive music study. During this period two of his songs were used in the Broadway musical *Miss Information* (1915).

Cole Porter's first complete score for a Broadway musical comedy was *See America First* (1916), a satire on patriotic musicals. It was a failure. During World War I he served in an artillery regiment, then in the Bureau of the Military Attaché of the United States in Paris. At this time he acquired a luxurious apartment in Paris and began laying the groundwork for his subsequent reputation as a wealthy playboy of Europe and one of Europe's most gracious hosts. Despite his military duties, he had time to entertain lavishly, and at these parties he always performed for his guests by singing his own sophisticated songs. The war over, he spent a period of music study at the Schola Cantorum—composition with Vincent d'Indy. On December 18, 1919, he married Linda Lee Thomas, divorced wife of the publisher of the *Morning Telegraph,* one of the most beautiful women and famous hostesses in Paris.

Just before that marriage Porter paid a brief visit home. While aboard ship he became acquainted with the musical-comedy star and producer Raymond Hitchcock, whose latest venture then was an annual revue, *Hitchy-Koo.* During the Atlantic crossing Porter sang some of his songs to Hitchcock, who commissioned him to write the score for the next edition of his revue. Porter fulfilled this assignment by contributing ten numbers to *Hitchy-Koo of 1919,* the best and most successful of which was "Old-Fashioned Garden."

After their marriage, the Porters set up house on Rue Monsieur in Paris.

The ornate, even garish, furnishings were matched only by the splendor of the parties given there. For one of these affairs the entire Monte Carlo Ballet performed; on another occasion, at the whim of a moment, all guests were transported by motorcade to the French Riviera. Parties were going on all the time; guests sometimes arrived for the evening but stayed on for a week.

Despite his frenetic social activity, Porter kept on writing songs, placing six songs in *Hitchy-Koo of 1922* (which opened and closed in Boston) and five in *The Greenwich Village Follies* of 1924. None of the songs made an impression. His friends insisted that the kind of numbers he was writing were not commercial, and that when he tried coming to terms with the commercial theater his vivacity and spontaneity were inhibited. Elsa Maxwell put it this way to him: "You are just too good, Cole. Your standards are too high. But one day you will haul the public up to your own level, and then the world will be yours."

Cole Porter's conquest of his public began with his fourth entry into the Broadway theater: with *Paris* (1928), starring Irene Bordoni. Three of the songs in this show were in the slightly risqué and delightfully sophisticated manner he would soon make so famous: "Let's Misbehave" (though this one was left out of the production by the time the musical reached Broadway), "Two Little Babes in the Wood," and "Let's Do It." In 1929 came an even greater Broadway success, *Fifty Million Frenchmen*. Two Cole Porter song classics appeared in 1929 and 1930: "Love for Sale" in *The New Yorkers* and "What Is This Thing Called Love?" in *Wake Up and Dream*.

By the time the Porters deserted Paris and set up their permanent home at the Waldorf-Astoria in New York in the early 1930's, his style, both as composer and lyricist, had crystallized. (Like Irving Berlin, Cole Porter always wrote his own lyrics.) In his lyrics, he combined the most skillful versification with a debonair manner, sprinkling through his verses sophisticated references to smart names and places, and all kinds of cultural allusions. He also established a definite individuality in his melodies—the best of them languorous tunes in the minor mode with broad sweeps of melody against pulsating background of at times dynamic rhythms.

In the 1930's Cole Porter became one of the most successful composers for the Broadway theater. Many of his musicals were tremendous box-office draws. Some were generously endowed with wonderful songs that will probably never be forgotten—"Night and Day" from *The Gay Divorce* (1932); "You're the Top" and "I Get a Kick Out of You" from *Anything Goes* (1934); "My Heart Belongs to Daddy" from *Leave It to Me* (1938). Even musicals that were failures boasted song gems. In *Jubilee* (1935) there was

"Begin the Beguine"; in *Red, Hot and Blue* (1936) there was "Its De-Lovely."

He was also proving productive in Hollywood, a rich crop of remarkable songs springing up from the soil of the motion-picture screen. Among these were "I've Got You Under My Skin," "Easy to Love," "In the Still of the Night," "You'd Be So Nice to Come Home To," "Don't Fence Me In," and "True Love." Porter's best songs of stage and screen (fourteen) formed the backbone of his screen biography, *Night and Day,* in 1946, with Cary Grant playing the composer.

Porter's capacity for sustained and concentrated work proved that this man had tough fiber—particularly since, being a wealthy man, he had no economic drive sending him to work. Just how tough a fiber he had was demonstrated after a tragic accident in 1937. While riding horseback on Long Island, his horse slipped in the mud and fell on top of him. Porter's legs were so badly crushed, and his nerve tissues so seriously damaged, that at first it was believed he would have to suffer amputation. He had to undergo thirty or more painful operations to save his legs as long as possible. Two of the seven years following this accident were spent continually in the hospital; the rest of those seven years he was a prisoner to a wheelchair. He had to take drugs continually to alleviate the pain. Despite his almost continuous suffering, his theatrical and social activities were pursued stubbornly; nor were his good humor, personal charm, and love of life destroyed. He continued to travel to far-off places, continued to entertain friends in the grand manner. Through all the operations and the mental and physical tortures attending them, he maintained a high standard in his songwriting for the theater, emerging with the greatest artistic and box-office success of his entire career with *Kiss Me, Kate* (1948)—and at a time when the belief prevailed on Broadway and in Hollywood that he was professionally "through."

The last years of Porter's life were tragic. His mother died in 1952, his wife, Linda, in 1956. In 1958 his right leg had to be amputated. After that he just went through the motions of living, abandoning both work and play, and keeping himself a total recluse. He refused to attend the mammoth "Salute to Cole Porter" at the Metropolitan Opera in 1960 and the celebration of his seventieth birthday at the Orpheum Theater in New York in 1962. When Yale University presented him with an honorary doctorate of humane letters in June of 1960 he would not make the trip to New Haven, but received the degree *in absentia*. Nevertheless, in 1964 he was able to summon enough energy to follow his long practice of going to California each June. There he underwent a minor operation for the removal of a kidney stone.

Complications set in, however. On October 15, 1964—two days after the operation—he died in the hospital.

PRINCIPAL WORKS: The Greenwich Village Follies of 1924; Fifty Million Frenchmen (1929); The Gay Divorce (1932); Anything Goes (1934); Jubilee (1935); Du Barry Was a Lady (1938); Leave It to Me (1938); Panama Hattie (1940); Let's Face It (1941); Something for the Boys (1943); Mexican Hayride (1944); Kiss Me, Kate (1948); Can-Can (1953); Silk Stockings (1955).
See: ANYTHING GOES; CAN-CAN; DU BARRY WAS A LADY; FIFTY MILLION FRENCHMEN; THE GAY DIVORCE; THE GREENWICH VILLAGE FOLLIES OF 1924; JUBILEE; KISS ME, KATE; LEAVE IT TO ME; LET'S FACE IT; MEXICAN HAYRIDE; PANAMA HATTIE; SILK STOCKINGS; SOMETHING FOR THE BOYS.

## ROBIN, LEO, *lyricist*

He was born in Pittsburgh, Pennsylvania, on April 6, 1900. Originally he planned to be a lawyer and attended Pittsburgh Law School. His interest in the theater made him abandon law study to enter the Drama School of the Carnegie Institute. For a while he earned his living as a newspaper reporter. In 1927 he wrote the lyrics for the Broadway musicals *Judy* and *Just Fancy* and for the revue *Allez Oop*, all three short-lived. But he also enjoyed a major success the same year with *Hit the Deck*. After *Hello Yourself* (1928) he went to Hollywood, where through the years he contributed lyrics to numerous motion pictures, including *Little Miss Marker; The Big Broadcast* of 1935, 1937, and 1938; *My Gal Sal; One Hour with You;* and *My Sister Eileen*. Among the composers who set his words to music were Kern, Harry Warren, Youmans, Arthur Schwartz, Jule Styne, and Romberg. One of Robin's screen songs was "Thanks for the Memory," recipient of the Academy Award in 1938, and it subsequently became Bob Hope's musical signature; another was "Louise," which Maurice Chevalier introduced in *Innocents of Paris* (1929).

PRINCIPAL WORKS: Hit the Deck (1927); Gentlemen Prefer Blondes (1949); The Girl in Pink Tights (1952).
See: GENTLEMEN PREFER BLONDES; THE GIRL IN PINK TIGHTS; HIT THE DECK.

## RODGERS, MARY, *composer*. See Part I, ONCE UPON A MATTRESS.

## RODGERS, RICHARD, and HART, LORENZ, *composers-lyricists*

He was born in Hammels Station, near Arverne, Long Island, on June 28, 1902. His father was a physician, his mother an amateur pianist. His first musical experiences came at home when he heard his father sing and his mother play songs from the famous operettas then popular on Broadway. Dick began playing the piano by ear when he was four, but he soon received formal instruction, which he abandoned because he detested exercises. Henceforth, and for some time to come, he learned music by trial and error, by continually improvising melodies of his own, or playing his favorite songs to his own formal accompaniments. He became an expert ear-executant, and eventually learned to put down his melodies on paper.

The piano was not his only passion; another was the theater. He saw his first musical when he was only six. Before long he was an inveterate theatergoer. At first he enjoyed the operettas of Victor Herbert and others. Then in 1916 he saw a Jerome Kern musical for the first time—it was *Very Good, Eddie*—and a new world seemed to open up for him. He now lost interest in foreign-made operettas and sought out American musical comedies, particularly those by Kern. He sometimes saw a Kern musical half a dozen times. The vitality and freshness of Kern's music was something of a revelation. "The influence of the hero on such a hero worshiper," he later wrote, "is not easy to calculate."

At the New York public schools he occasionally played the piano at assemblies. At his own graduation ceremonies, at P.S. 166, in 1916, he performed a potpourri of opera melodies that he himself prepared. He also engaged in musical activity at Weingart's summer camp, where he spent several summers from 1914 on. In 1916 he wrote his first two complete songs, "Campfire Days" and "The Auto Show Girl," the latter a bouncy one-step, which he multigraphed for private distribution.

While attending De Witt Clinton High School, Rodgers became a dedicated lover of good music by attending opera and concert performances. But his musical ambitions never rose above the popular field, and he kept on writing popular songs. In 1917, through his brother Mortimer (later a successful gynecologist), he was asked to write a complete score for an amateur production put on by a boys' club in New York. This show, *One Minute Please,* was presented at the Hotel Plaza on December 29, 1917—Rodgers' debut in writing for the stage. He kept on writing songs for other amateur productions after that.

Up to now he had been writing melodies to lyrics by various friends or relatives. In 1918 he acquired a permanent working partner in Lorenz Hart, who was to be his lyricist for the next quarter of a century. They met at Hart's house on 119th Street through a mutual friend. At the time Hart was twenty-three, Rodgers was only sixteen. During that first meeting Rodgers was impressed by the older man's wit, sophistication, cultural background, and skill at versification—most of all by his trenchant ideas of what a good song should be. Hart recognized Dick's musical gifts immediately. Before the afternoon was over they knew they would henceforth work together. "It was a case of love at first sight," Rodgers recalls. "I acquired in one afternoon a partner, a best friend—and a source of permanent irritation."

Lorenz Hart was born in New York City on May 2, 1895. Except for a brief period at De Witt Clinton High School, his entire elementary and secondary schooling took place in private schools: at Weingart's Institute and the Columbia Grammar School. In 1913, after a European holiday with his family, he entered Columbia College. There, after a single year, he transferred to the school of journalism. While he had always been a brilliant student in literature and languages, and while he did well in all his college subjects, his major interest was the Varsity Show. In 1915 and 1916 he appeared in the Columbia Varsity Shows as a female impersonator, besides writing skits and satirical lyrics.

He left Columbia in 1917 without a degree. For several summers he worked at Brant Lake Camp, a boys' summer camp, putting on shows. His aim was the theater, and for a while he worked for the Shuberts translating German operettas into English, saving his money to produce two plays, both failures. A brilliant intelligence, a fine cultural background that embraced music and opera as well as the theater, and an original and creative thinker, Hart was searching for some avenue of his own in the theater when he first met Richard Rodgers.

Rodgers and Hart began by writing a few songs that, one summer day in 1919, Rodgers brought to Rockaway Beach to play for Lew Fields. Fields liked one particularly, "Any Old Place with You," and placed it in his production of *A Lonely Romeo* on August 16, 1919, where it was sung by Eve Lynn and Alan Hale. This was the official entry of Rodgers and Hart into the professional theater; and this song was also their first to get published.

In the fall of 1919 Rodgers entered Columbia College. During his first year there he worked with Hart on the Varsity Show, *Fly with Me,* produced in the grand ballroom of the Hotel Astor on March 24, 1920, Rodgers conducting. This was the first time that the work of a freshman had been taken for one of the Varsity Shows. "Several of the tunes are capital," reported the columnist S. Jay Kaufman in the *Globe.* "They have a really finished touch. . . . We had not heard of Richard Rodgers before. We have a suspicion we shall hear of him again."

Lew Fields liked the Rodgers music of *Fly with Me* so well that he offered to use some of the numbers in a Broadway production he was projecting. Seven Rodgers and Hart songs appeared in *The Poor Little Ritz Girl,* which opened on July 2, 1920. (Eight other songs in this production were by the veteran Sigmund Romberg.) Since *The Poor Little Ritz Girl* had a run of 119 performances, the first of the Rodgers and Hart musicals on Broadway was a modest hit. Of Rodgers' music, H. T. Parker, the noted Boston drama and music critic, said: "He writes uniformly with a light hand; now and then with neat modulations or pretty turns of ornament; here and there with a clear sensibility to instrumental voices; and once again with a hint of grace and fancy."

It was some time before Rodgers and Hart reappeared successfully on Broadway. Meanwhile they took any assignment that came along, mostly for amateur productions. During this period they acquired a third collaborator— Herbert Fields, son of Lew—who sometimes was the stage director of their amateur shows and sometimes wrote the books for their musical comedies. With Herbert Fields, Rodgers and Hart completed *Winkle Town,* a musical that was never produced. Using the pen name of Herbert Richard Lorenz, they also wrote a Tin Pan Alley comedy, *The Melody Man,* in which Lew Fields starred, presented on May 13, 1924. This last production had only two Rodgers and Hart songs, both of them travesties on Tin Pan Alley. *The Melody Man* was a failure.

Discouragement in the slow progress he was making led Rodgers in 1922 to abandon his songwriting career and return to music study. He spent the next two years at the Institute of Musical Art, and during this period he wrote and helped to put on several shows for the school; and for a few months he served as conductor of Lew Fields's *Snapshots of 1922,* which was then touring the Shubert vaudeville circuit.

After leaving the Institute, Rodgers resumed collaboration with Hart in writing amateur shows. Once again he became discouraged, as neither producers nor publishers seemed interested in what he was doing. This time Rodgers decided to leave music for good and become a salesman for a children's underwear firm. He was about to accept this job when he and Hart were offered the assignment to write the music for *The Garrick Gaieties,* a production put on by several young people connected with the Theater Guild. The success of *The Garrick Gaieties* in 1925 established the reputation of Rodgers and Hart.

In the same year, 1925, Rodgers and Hart had another successful musical on Broadway—*Dearest Enemy,* for which Herbert Fields wrote the book. During the next half-dozen years Rodgers and Hart wrote the songs for musical comedies, with books by Fields, which not only were major box-office successes but also were responsible for introducing some new techniques and approaches to the writing of musical comedy and which continually tapped fresh and unorthodox materials. These musicals—from *Dearest Enemy* (1925) to *America's Sweetheart* (1931)—made the team of Rodgers, Hart, and Fields a triumvirate that ruled the musical stage for a decade. Several of their shows, however, were failures—but are remembered because they were the point of origin for some unforgettable songs by Rodgers and Hart: "With a Song in My Heart" in *Spring Is Here* (1929); "Ten Cents a Dance," made famous by Ruth Etting in the Ed Wynn extravaganza *Simple Simon* (1930); "A Ship Without a Sail" in *Heads Up* (1929).

In 1930 Rodgers and Hart went out to Hollywood, where for a few years they wrote songs for various motion pictures. They were back on Broadway in 1934, and made their reappearance on the Broadway stage with the Billy Rose circus extravaganza, *Jumbo*. Both Rodgers and Hart now became fired with the ambition of abandoning old formulas and clichés of musical comedy for good by realizing a musical play in which every element would be integral to the play and which would treat unusual themes. With a series of remarkable successes, beginning with *On Your Toes* (1937) and ending with *By Jupiter* (1942), they created a veritable revolution in the musical theater.

Hart had never been a disciplined worker, and collaborating with him had always been a serious problem to Rodgers. To his formerly irresponsible ways Hart added, after 1940, a deterioration of health and spirit brought on mostly by alcoholic excesses. After *By Jupiter* he lost the will to work, and eager for a long vacation in Mexico, asked Rodgers to seek out a new collaborator. A proposition from the Theater Guild—to set Lynn Riggs's folk play *Green Grow the Lilacs* to music—held little interest for Hart. He went off for his Mexican holiday, and Rodgers found a new collaborator in Oscar Hammerstein II.

After Hart's return from Mexico, Rodgers tried to revive Hart's interest in creation by bringing back to Broadway *A Connecticut Yankee*—their success of 1927—for which he and Hart wrote some new songs, including "To Keep My Love Alive." For a while it seemed that Hart was willing to settle down, but after the play tried out in Philadelphia he was off again on a binge that made it necessary to hospitalize him in New York. He disappeared from the theater at the New York premier of the revival on November 17, 1943, and was not seen for two days. When found, he was lying unconscious on his hotel bed. He died soon after that at Doctors Hospital, on November 22. Five years after his death the story of his collaboration with Rodgers was told in the motion picture *Words and Music,* in which Mickey Rooney played Hart, and Tom Drake, Rodgers.

The partnership of Rodgers and Hart was one of the most fruitful in the entire history of the American musical stage. They wrote twenty-seven musicals in twenty-five years, and for these productions they completed over five hundred songs. The impact of their work on the musical theater, on popular music, and on the song lyric can hardly be overestimated. They changed the destiny of the musical stage by carrying the musical comedy to full maturity. And they enriched popular music through the inventiveness and originality of Rodgers' music and Larry Hart's incomparably brilliant lyrics.

After almost a quarter of a century of working solely with lyricist Larry Hart, in 1942 Richard Rodgers had to seek out a new collaborator. He found him in Oscar Hammerstein II, a librettist and lyricist who had also enjoyed a rich and productive career in the theater. As collaborators, Rodgers and Hammerstein were destined to reach heights in their respective careers which would even tower above their previous formidable individual achievements. As collaborators they were to open new vistas for the musical theater, to transform musical comedy into a native art. As Cole Porter said, "The most profound change in forty years of musical comedy has been—Rodgers and Hammerstein."

Rodgers was only thirteen when first he met Oscar Hammerstein, then twenty years old. Rodgers' brother Mortimer—Hammerstein's classmate at Columbia College—took Dick to a performance of *On Your Way,* a Columbia Varsity Show in 1915, in which Hammerstein sang some songs and appeared in a few skits. "I noted with satisfaction," Hammerstein later recalled, "young Richard's respectful awe in the presence of a college junior."

In the fall of 1919, when Rodgers and Hart wrote their first Columbia Varsity Show, *Fly with Me,* the committee that passed favorably upon them included Hammerstein. In that show most of the lyrics were by Hart, but one was by Hammerstein himself, "Roof for One More," which Rodgers set to music. But even this was not the first time Rodgers and Hammerstein worked together. Rodgers had already written melodies for two Hammerstein lyrics—"Can It" and "Weaknesses"—used in an amateur show, *Up Stage and Down,* early in 1919.

But though their paths frequently crossed in the years that followed, Rodgers and Hammerstein did not begin a professional partnership until late in 1942 when Larry Hart decided to go off to Mexico.

With their very first collaboration, *Oklahoma!* (1943), Rodgers and Hammerstein ushered in a new era for the musical theater. This beautiful folk play realized fully that for which the earlier Rodgers and Hart musicals had been striving—a synchronization of all the elements of the musical theater into a single and indivisible entity. This concept was further enlarged, developed, and crystallized by succeeding Rodgers and Hammerstein shows, several of which are now classics of the Broadway stage. Brought into association with the poetry and lyricism of Hammerstein's dialogue and verse—and

Hammerstein's wisdom and humanity—Rodgers acquired new scope, depth, and dimension in his musical writing, so much so that many of his scores for Hammerstein have the breadth of music dramas.

Rodgers and Hammerstein made significant contributions outside the Broadway theater, too. They wrote the songs for the motion picture *State Fair* in 1945, one of which, "It Might as Well Be Spring," won the Academy Award. In 1957 they collaborated on their first original musical play for television, *Cinderella,* which was presented in London in a pantomime version in 1958, and then given over television in a completely new production in 1965. And without Hammerstein, Rodgers wrote ambitious and artistic background music for two documentary films presented on television: *Victory at Sea* (1952), recipient of numerous honors, and *Winston Churchill—the Valiant Years* (1960).

When Hammerstein died in 1960, Rodgers lost his second collaborator, with whom he had worked so fruitfully for half of his creative life. In *No Strings* (1962) Rodgers wrote his own lyrics, just as he did for several new songs interpolated in a remake of the motion-picture musical *State Fair* (1962). Though these lyrics were professional and skillful, Rodgers felt the need of the stimulation of a collaborator, and so, in *Do I Hear a Waltz?* (1965), he wrote music to the lyrics of Stephen Sondheim. Then Rodgers attempted to form a permanent partnership with Alan Jay Lerner, which collapsed before their first musical comedy was produced. That musical was finally seen on Broadway as *On a Clear Day You Can See Forever,* with music by Burton Lane.

As the first composer of the American musical theater, Richard Rodgers has himself been the recipient of more honors than have been accorded to any other stage composer. In 1949 he received the Columbia University Medal of Excellence; in 1950, the Award of the Hundred Year Association; in 1955, a life membership in the National Institute of Arts and Letters; in 1956, the Alexander Hamilton Award of Columbia College. In 1955 the Library of Congress in Washington, D.C., presented an exhibition of illustrations, photographs, programs, and manuscripts tracing his career in the theater; this was only the second time that a composer of nonclassical music was honored in this way, the first being Stephen Foster.

In 1962 Rodgers was named head of the New York State Music Theater at the Lincoln Center for the Performing Arts, where several of the more famous Rodgers and Hammerstein classics were revived. The spring of 1963 saw six productions near or on Broadway with Rodgers' music, including a successful Off Broadway revival of the Rodgers and Hart musical *The Boys from Syracuse.*

Rodgers' daughter, Mary, is the composer of the musical, *Once upon a Mattress*.

PRINCIPAL WORKS: The Garrick Gaieties of 1925 and 1926; Dearest Enemy (1925); The Girl Friend (1926); Peggy-Ann (1926); A Connecticut Yankee (1927); Present Arms (1928); Simple Simon (1930); America's Sweetheart (1931); Jumbo (1935); On Your Toes (1936); I'd Rather Be Right (1937); Babes in Arms (1937); I Married an Angel (1938); The Boys from Syracuse (1938); Pal Joey (1940); By Jupiter (1942); Oklahoma! (1943); Carousel (1945); Allegro (1947); South Pacific (1949); The King and I (1951); Me and Juliet (1953); Pipe Dream (1955); Flower Drum Song (1958); The Sound of Music (1959); No Strings (1962); Do I Hear a Waltz? (1965).

*See:* ALLEGRO; AMERICA'S SWEETHEART; BABES IN ARMS; THE BOYS FROM SYRACUSE; BY JUPITER; CAROUSEL; A CONNECTICUT YANKEE; DEAREST ENEMY; DO I HEAR A WALTZ?; FLOWER DRUM SONG; THE GARRICK GAIETIES of 1925 and 1926; THE GIRL FRIEND; I'D RATHER BE RIGHT; I MARRIED AN ANGEL; JUMBO; THE KING AND I; ME AND JULIET; NO STRINGS; OKLAHOMA!; ON YOUR TOES; PAL JOEY; PEGGY-ANN; PIPE DREAM; PRESENT ARMS; SIMPLE SIMON; THE SOUND OF MUSIC; SOUTH PACIFIC.

## ROMBERG, SIGMUND, *composer*

When Romberg died in 1951 a dynasty in the American musical theater came to an end. For Romberg was the last in the royal line of operetta composers that included Reginald de Koven, Victor Herbert, Gustave Kerker, Karl Hoschna, and Rudolf Friml, among others. He possessed a Continental charm, an old-world glamor, a touch of magic not often encountered on the American musical stage. Romberg's best scores retain a distinct European flavor, even when the setting of his play is American. Although he was an American citizen and lived in the United States for half a century, his musical roots lay deep in the soil of Vienna, where he had spent his most impressionable years.

He was born in the Hungarian border town of Nazy Kaniza on July 29, 1887. Soon after Sigmund's birth, the family moved to Belisce, where the boy's musical education began on the violin. He was, however, directed not to music but to engineering. He attended the Realschule in Oslek for five years as preparation for engineering studies. There his musical interest was kept alive by the director of the school orchestra. When he heard Sigmund play the violin he waived the rules forbidding students to join the orchestra before their fifth year.

While attending another school in Szeged, Romberg wrote his first piece of music, a march which he dedicated to the Grand Duchess. When she expressed interest in it, the town created an orchestra so that Romberg might conduct it in a public performance. This was his debut as a conductor.

Romberg's next move was to Vienna, to acquire an engineering degree at the Polytechnical High School. The greatest German-language operettas could then be seen at the historic Theater-an-der-Wien and other Viennese houses—classics like *Die Fledermaus, The Gypsy Baron,* and *The Merry Widow.* Through one of his friends, Romberg managed to gain access backstage to the Theater-an-der-Wien, where he could watch the operettas being rehearsed; for a brief period he even served there as assistant manager.

He now knew that he wanted to desert engineering for music, but his parents were not sympathetic to this plan and offered a compromise. Since military service was then required of all young men, they suggested that Romberg delay a final decision on his future until his military commitment had been met. Romberg joined the 19th Hungarian Infantry Regiment stationed in Vienna and stayed with it a year and a half. Once again he expressed his determination to engage in musical activity, and once again his parents suggested a compromise. They would agree to any decision Sigmund wished to make about his future if he delayed making that decision for a year and spent the intervening period traveling.

Romberg spent two weeks in London. Then, in his twenty-second year, he came to the United States. The year was 1909. He found a job in a pencil factory for seven dollars a week and spent his free time wandering around New York. Thus he came upon the Café Continental on Second Avenue, where he found employment as café pianist for fifteen dollars a week (plus a percentage of any tips). After a week he found a more desirable post at the Pabst-Harlem Restaurant on 125th Street. He then announced to his parents his intention of staying in America for good, becoming a citizen, and trying to make a success of music.

In 1912 he conducted his own orchestra at Bustanoby's Restaurant, playing salon music mostly of the Viennese variety and usually in his own arrangements. Before long he decided to include in his programs music for dancing— an innovation, since dancing at the time was unknown in restaurants. The novelty took hold. His dance music became such an integral part of Bustanoby's that he performed every day from noon to three A.M., earning $150 a week. He also extended his activity by writing music. The publishing house of Joseph W. Stern issued his first three songs: two were one-steps, "Leg of Mutton" and "Some Smoke"; a third was a waltz, "Le Poème." All three became popular with dance orchestras everywhere. Before long, J. J. Shubert came to him with an offer. He had just lost the services of his staff composer, Louis Hirsch, and he wanted Romberg to take over Hirsch's job of preparing the music for Shubert's varied productions.

Romberg's Broadway debut came with a Winter Garden extravaganza, *The*

*Whirl of the World,* starring Eugene and Willie Howard and the Dolly Sisters, opening on January 10, 1914. He soon became one of Broadway's most prolific composers. Between 1914 and 1917 he wrote 275 numbers for seventeen musicals; fifteen of these productions came within a twenty-two-month period. These shows included Winter Garden extravaganzas, revues, and Romberg's first attempt at writing for America a Continental-type operetta, *The Blue Paradise* (1915). With *Maytime* (1917), *Blossom Time* (1921), and *The Student Prince in Heidelberg* (1924), Romberg became one of America's outstanding composers of operettas.

In the early 1930's Romberg settled in Hollywood, where he worked for motion pictures, sometimes assisting in screen adaptations of his famous operettas, sometimes writing new music for original screenplays. From the latter came one of his most famous ballads, "When I Grow Too Old to Dream" from *The Night Is Young* (1934).

Soon after Pearl Harbor the William Morris Agency prevailed on him to form his own orchestra and tour the country in concerts of "middle-brow music." The first tour, in 1942, was a failure. But subsequent tours proved more favorable, and the fourth, beginning with a performance at Carnegie Hall on September 10, 1943, broke attendance records in several cities. Henceforth, "An Evening with Sigmund Romberg"—as these concerts were billed—was an assured success everywhere. Just before his death Romberg was planning an international tour with his orchestra.

Romberg never failed to recognize how strong were his ties to Vienna. Toward the end of his life he told his wife: "I'm two wars away from my time. My time was pre-World War I. . . . I've got to get away from Vienna. That's all passé."

In line with such thinking he wrote two new Broadway musicals, both thoroughly American. One was outstandingly successful, *Up in Central Park* (1945); the other, *The Girl in Pink Tights,* produced posthumously, was a failure.

But the truth was that he was not at his best in any vein but the Viennese. He knew it, and he confessed it to a Baltimore audience when he made his first appearance conducting an orchestra. "I have been told that the music I have lived with for many years," he said in part, "now belongs to the past. . . . Perhaps this is so. If so, they are right, and I am wrong."

Sigmund Romberg died in New York on November 10, 1951. His valedictory to the stage was *The Girl in Pink Tights,* which he did not live to see produced. In 1954 his screen biography, *Deep in My Heart,* was released, with José Ferrer playing the part of the composer.

PRINCIPAL WORKS: The Passing Show of 1914; The Blue Paradise (1915); The Passing Show of 1916; Robinson Crusoe, Jr. (1916); The Passing Show of 1917; Maytime (1917); The Passing Show of 1918; Sinbad (1918); The Passing Show of 1919; Bombo (1921); Blossom Time (1921); The Passing Show of 1923; Innocent Eyes (1924); Artists and Models of 1924; The Passing Show of 1924; The Student Prince in Heidelberg (1924); The Desert Song (1926); The New Moon (1928); Rosalie (1928); May Wine (1935); Up in Central Park (1945); The Girl in Pink Tights (1954).

*See:* ARTISTS AND MODELS of 1924; BLOSSOM TIME; THE BLUE PARADISE; BOMBO; THE DESERT SONG; THE GIRL IN PINK TIGHTS; INNOCENT EYES; MAYTIME; MAY WINE; THE NEW MOON; THE PASSING SHOW of 1914, 1916 through 1919, 1923, and 1924; ROBINSON CRUSOE, JR.; ROSALIE; SINBAD; THE STUDENT PRINCE IN HEIDELBERG; UP IN CENTRAL PARK.

## ROME, HAROLD, *composer-lyricist*

He was born in Hartford, Connecticut, on May 27, 1908. He received his education in local schools, at Trinity College in Hartford, and at Yale. After acquiring his Bachelor of Arts degree at Yale in 1929, he entered Yale Law School. A year later he transferred to the School of Architecture, from which he was graduated in 1934.

Music had always been a major interest. He had studied the piano in boyhood, and while attending college and postgraduate school earned his living by playing in jazz bands. He also wrote special numbers for ballet companies and other groups. At Yale he took courses in music and joined the college orchestra, which toured Europe.

He came to New York in 1934 to find a place for himself as an architect. The Depression, then at its peak, made such jobs scarce, particularly for novices. The necessity of earning a living led him to write songs, sometimes only the lyrics, at other times the melodies, occasionally both. Gypsy Rose Lee was effectual in getting one of his lyrics published; and the Ritz Brothers used another of his songs in one of their pictures. Since his income from these tentative efforts exceeded what he earned from architecture, he decided to abandon the latter profession to make his way as a songwriter.

He found a job in Green Mansions, an adult summer camp in the Adirondack Mountains in New York, where considerable emphasis was placed on entertainment. This was in the summer of 1935. Green Mansions put on original musical productions with a resident company, and Rome's assignment was to write some of the material and help with the production. He did this work for three summers, and during this period he wrote about a hundred songs, lyrics as well as music.

One of the members of the social staff was Charles Friedman, who had been invited by the International Ladies Garment Workers Union to stage an amateur show with union members. Since a revue was planned, Friedman asked Rome to write some of the songs. That amateur union show was *Pins and Needles,* which made stage history by becoming the most successful Broadway musical production up to that time. It also helped establish Rome as a songwriter.

Sponsored as it was by a trade union, *Pins and Needles* had a left-wing slant. Max Gordon now commissioned Rome to write lyrics and music for another political revue, *Sing out the News* (1938), in which there appeared one of Rome's best political songs, "Franklin D. Roosevelt Jones." *Let Freedom Ring* (1942) was another political and "social-conscious" revue engaging Rome's music, a box-office failure.

In 1942 Rome entered the Army. For a while he was stationed at the New York Port of Embarkation, in the Fort Hamilton section of Brooklyn, where he wrote Army shows and orientation songs. He also toured the Pacific combat zone. During this Army period he completed only a single commercial assignment, the song "Micromania," used in *The Ziegfeld Follies* of 1943.

Mustered out of the Army in 1945, Rome completed lyrics and music for a brilliant revue that stayed on Broadway for several years—*Call Me Mister* (1946). Though intended to reflect the experiences and emotions of Americans reverting to civilian life, *Call Me Mister* (like the revues with which Rome had previously been associated) had a pronounced social and political viewpoint. But the political climate was changing rapidly in America, and the left-wing theater was losing its audience. Rome's next revue, *Bless You All* (1950), sought out nonprovocative subjects for humor and sentiment: movie stars from the Deep South; miracle drugs; the Parent-Teacher Association. And the tender songs contributed by Rome—"When," for example, and "You'll Never Know"—were completely devoid of political implications.

Rome contributed songs to various revues, including *Alive and Kicking* and *Michael Todd's Peep Show,* both in 1950. His number "The Money Song" became a hit, even though it was interpolated in a musical, *That's the Ticket* (1947), that opened and closed in Philadelphia.

In passing from revue to musical comedy, Rome achieved three box-office triumphs with *Wish You Were Here* (1952), *Fanny* (1954), and *Destry Rides Again* (1959) with which he assumed a significant position among contemporary composers for the popular stage. Besides these, and the other musicals listed below, Rome contributed a dozen songs to *The Zulu and the Zayda,* a "play with music," starring Menasha Skulnik; opening on November 10, 1965, it was a failure. However, *Scarlett*—an American-made musical based on the motion picture *Gone With the Wind*—for which Rome wrote the complete score, proved a triumph when it was produced for the first time in Tokyo, Japan, on January 2, 1970. Rome writes his own lyrics to his music.

PRINCIPAL WORKS: Pins and Needles (1937); The Ziegfeld Follies of 1943; Call Me Mister (1946); Wish You Were Here (1952); Fanny (1954); Destry Rides Again (1959); I Can Get It for You Wholesale (1962).
See: CALL ME MISTER; DESTRY RIDES AGAIN; FANNY; I CAN GET IT FOR YOU WHOLESALE; PINS AND NEEDLES; WISH YOU WERE HERE; THE ZIEGFELD FOLLIES of 1943.

ROSS, JERRY, *composer-lyricist*. *See* ADLER, RICHARD, AND ROSS, JERRY.

RUBY, HARRY, *composer-lyricist*
A child of the New York City streets, Ruby was born on January 27, 1895. He attended the city public schools, commercial high school, then went into business. But music interested him more than business. Having learned to play the piano by himself (he received virtually no formal instruction in any department of music), he found a job as staff pianist with Gus Edwards' publishing company in Tin Pan Alley. He remained in Tin Pan Alley several years, working for various publishers as song plugger.

He also toured vaudeville as pianist for two acts, the Messenger Boys Trio and the Bootblack Trio. While touring the vaudeville circuit he met and befriended another vaudevillian whose extracurricular activities included part-ownership in a music-publishing firm, writing song lyrics and special material for Vaudevillians. He was Bert Kalmar, born in New York City on February 16, 1884, who made his stage debut as a magician in a tent show. Kalmar engaged Ruby as staff pianist and song plugger. Then when Kalmar, who was also a performer in vaudeville, had to abandon the stage because of a knee injury, he became Rudy's lyricist. Their first song was "He Sits Around," which they wrote for Belle Baker just before America's entry into World War I. In 1917 they wrote "When Those Hawaiian Babies Roll Their Eyes"; in 1920, "So Long, Oo Long" and "Timbuctoo"; and in 1921, "My Sunny Tennessee." All four songs were moderate successes. Besides, in 1920, Fanny Brice was bringing down the house at *The Ziegfeld Follies* with their song "The Vamp from East Broadway."

The year 1923 was decisive in their writing career, for it brought them not only their biggest song hit, "Who's Sorry Now?" (for which Ruby and Kalmar wrote merely the words, while Ted Snyder provided the music, and which Connie Francis revived with such phenomenal success in 1957 that it transformed her from an unknown performer into a major recording star), but also their first Broadway musical, *Helen of Troy, New York*.

For the next decade they continued writing both individual songs and Broadway scores. Between 1928 and 1941 they worked mainly in Hollywood, where they wrote for various screen productions such song hits as "Three Little Words," "Keep on Doin' What You're Doin'," and "A Kiss to Build a Dream On." They returned to the Broadway musical theater in 1941 with *The High Kickers,* a musical starring George Jessel and Sophie Tucker. After Kalmar's death in 1947, the songwriting career of Ruby and Kalmar—and some of their best songs—appeared in the motion picture *Three Little Words* (1950).

After 1950 Harry Ruby made many appearances as a guest on major television programs.

PRINCIPAL WORKS: Helen of Troy, New York (1923); Five O'Clock Girl (1927); Good Boy (1928); The Ramblers (1928).
*See:* FIVE O'CLOCK GIRL; GOOD BOY; HELEN OF TROY, NEW YORK; THE RAMBLERS.

## RYSKIND, MORRIE, *librettist*

He was born in New York City on October 20, 1895, educated in the city schools, and graduated from Columbia University School of Journalism in 1917. He first became known through verses published in the famous newspaper column of F.P.A. (Franklin P. Adams). His bow in the theater took place with several minor contributions to *The '49ers* (1922), in which George S. Kaufman helped him write the book. He collaborated with Kaufman on the texts for *The Cocoanuts* (1925) and *Animal Crackers* (1928), each starring the Four Marx Brothers. During this period Ryskind contributed material to the intimate revues *Americana* (1926) and *Merry-Go-Round* (1927). He then adapted Kaufman's text for the George and Ira Gershwin musical *Strike Up the Band* (1930), and was a collaborator in the Pulitzer Prize-winning Gershwin musical, *Of Thee I Sing* (1931). He wrote texts for several other musicals by the Gershwins, Irving Berlin, and Harry Ruby. After 1940 Ryskind worked for the motion pictures in Hollywood, where his screenplays included *The Cocoanuts, Animal Crackers, A Night at the Opera* (all three with the Marx Brothers), and *My Man Godfrey.* Ryskind established his permanent residence in Beverly Hills, where he has since lived in retirement, as far as the stage and screen are concerned, confining his literary activities to writing a newspaper column.

PRINCIPAL WORKS: Strike Up the Band (1930); Of Thee I Sing (1931); Let 'Em Eat Cake (1933); Louisiana Purchase (1940).
*See:* LET 'EM EAT CAKE; LOUISIANA PURCHASE; OF THEE I SING; STRIKE UP THE BAND.

## SAIDY, FRED, *librettist*

He was born Fareed Milhelm Saidy in Los Angeles, California, on February 11, 1907, but received his education in New York, including a degree from New York University, where he studied journalism. He engaged in journalistic endeavors and in the import business before becoming involved with the theater. In 1942 he contributed sketches to a revue produced in Hollywood, *Rally 'Round the Flag*. Two years later he was collaborator in his first Broadway stage musical, *Bloomer Girl,* a major success. He collaborated on texts for numerous other Broadway musicals, including two failures, *Flahooley* (1951) and *The Happiest Girl in the World* (1961). He also collaborated on screenplays.

PRINCIPAL WORKS: Bloomer Girl (1944); Finian's Rainbow (1947); Jamaica (1957).
*See:* BLOOMER GIRL; FINIAN'S RAINBOW; JAMAICA.

## SCHMIDT, HARVEY, *composer,* and JONES, TOM, *librettist-lyricist*

Harvey Schmidt was born in Dallas, Texas, on September 12, 1929, and was graduated from the University of Texas, where he became a friend of Tom Jones (born in Littlefield, Texas, on February 17, 1928). They began collaborating in 1951 while still attending the university. While both served in the armed forces (Schmidt in El Paso in the Field Artillery and Jones in Baltimore in the Counter Intelligence Corps) they continued their collaboration through the mails. In 1955 they came to New York, where they produced material for supper-club revues. Without Schmidt's collaboration, Jones contributed lyrics for two intimate Off Broadway revues, *Shoestring '57* (1956) and *Kaleidoscope* (1957). When Schmidt and Jones worked together for the stage for the first time they produced a blockbuster in *The Fantasticks* (1960), an Off Broadway production. They continued working together on subsequent musicals. Besides being a composer, Schmidt is a highly gifted artist whose work has appeared in *Life, Esquire, Fortune,* and other magazines.

PRINCIPAL WORKS: The Fantasticks (1960); 110 in the Shade (1963); I Do! I Do! (1966); Celebration (1969).
*See:* CELEBRATION; THE FANTASTICKS; I DO! I DO!; 110 IN THE SHADE.

## SCHWARTZ, ARTHUR, *composer*

He was born in Brooklyn, New York, on November 25, 1900. His father, a lawyer, allowed his oldest son to specialize in music; but for Arthur he had other plans. Though Arthur early revealed an unmistakable gift for music by playing the harmonica skillfully and by making up his own tunes, Father Schwartz wanted him to follow in his own footsteps by becoming a lawyer. A formal musical education, then, was denied Arthur; and all the musical instruction he ever received was a term in harmony at New York University.

His academic education took place in Brooklyn public schools, at Boys High School, also in Brooklyn, and at New York University and Columbia University. At NYU, from which he received his Bachelor of Arts degree in 1929, he was known for the marches and songs he wrote for the college football games. At the time his main interest was not music but books and the theater. He specialized in literature and the contemporary drama, continuing these and relevant studies at Columbia University, from which he received a Master's degree in 1921. For a while he contemplated a literary career, having done some writing for the college paper. But he bowed to parental guidance by taking up law at Columbia, supporting himself during this period by teaching English in a New York high school.

He was admitted to the bar in 1924. For four years he practiced law, and did well at it. But in 1928 he suddenly decided to abandon law for the theater —this decision reached after some minor successes with some of his songs. He applied himself to placing his songs in Broadway productions.

His debut in the Broadway theater took place in 1924 with the song "All Lanes Have a Turning" in a Jerome Kern musical, *Dear Sir*. Soon after that came "Baltimore, Md., You're the Only Doctor for Me" in the 1925 edition of *The Grand Street Follies,* and four numbers in the next edition of the same revue. In 1927 he wrote half the score for the unsuccessful revue *The New Yorkers*. Not until he was able to convince Howard Dietz to become his lyricist did Schwartz get a taste of success. Their first venture was *The Little Show* (1929), a box-office triumph. The collaboration of Schwartz and Dietz continued for many years after that, resulting in several outstanding Broadway successes (in the field of revues) and some failures (in musical comedy). Among the failures was an interesting experiment in musical-play writing, *Revenge with Music* (1934), which contained such remarkable Schwartz songs as "You and the Night and the Music" and "If There Is Someone Lovelier than You."

It was quite some time before Schwartz was able to achieve any measure of success in musical comedy. When he finally did so it was with a comparatively minor box-office attraction, *A Tree Grows in Brooklyn* (1951)—written without Dietz's collaboration. But on several occasions before that Schwartz had worked with collaborators other than Dietz: for example, *Stars in Your Eyes* (1939), book by J. P. McEvoy and lyrics by Dorothy Fields; *Park Avenue* (1946), book by George S. Kaufman and Nunnally Johnson and lyrics by Ira Gershwin.

From 1941 on Arthur Schwartz was for many years active in Hollywood, first as a composer for motion-picture musicals, then as a producer. He returned to the Broadway stage in 1951 with *A Tree Grows in Brooklyn,* mentioned above, and followed it with another minor success, *By the Beautiful Sea* (1954). Later musicals—*The Gay Life* (1961) and *Jennie* (1963), the latter starring Mary Martin, and in both of which the collaboration of Schwartz and Dietz was resumed—were failures.

PRINCIPAL WORKS: The Little Show (1929) ; Three's a Crowd (1930) ; The Second Little Show (1930) ; The Band Wagon (1931) ; Flying Colors (1932) ; At Home Abroad (1935) ; Inside U.S.A. (1948) ; A Tree Grows in Brooklyn (1951) ; By the Beautiful Sea (1954).
*See:* AT HOME ABROAD; THE BAND WAGON; BY THE BEAUTIFUL SEA; FLYING COLORS; INSIDE U.S.A.; THE LITTLE SHOW, 1929 and 1930; THREE'S A CROWD; A TREE GROWS IN BROOKLYN.


SCHWARTZ, JEAN, *composer*

He was born in Budapest, Hungary, on November 4, 1878. His sister (a pupil of Liszt) gave him his first piano lessons. When Jean was in his early teens, his family settled on New York's East Side. In the next few years he held various jobs: as office boy in a cigar factory; night cashier in a Turkish bath; pianist in a Coney Island band; pianist in the first sheet-music department installed in a department store, that of Siegal-Cooper; and pianist and song plugger for the Tin Pan Alley firm of Shapiro-Bernstein. Before the nineteenth century ended he published an instrumental number, *Dusky Dudes Cakewalk.*

In 1901 he was hired as an onstage pianist in the Weber and Fields burlesque *Hoity Toity.* One of his songs was interpolated into that production, "When Mr. Shakespeare Comes to Town," lyrics by William Jerome. A few more hits came from them after that: "Rip Van Winkle Was a Lucky Man" in 1901, "Mister Dooley" in 1902, and the sensational "Bedelia" in 1903, the last made famous by Blanche Ring. They also wrote special numbers for several important performers, including Eddie Foy. In 1904 they created all the words and music for their initial Broadway stage success, the musical *Piff, Paff, Pouff,* following it in 1905 with songs for *The Ham Tree,* starring McIntyre and Heath. After that came a few more song hits, including "Chinatown, My Chinatown," and appearances on the vaudeville circuits, singing and playing their songs.

Their partnership was over by 1914. Jerome went on to write lyrics for other composers, with no diminution in his popularity. With other lyricists Schwartz proved equally productive. He wrote scores for many Broadway musicals, including numerous editions of *The Passing Show,* and contributed songs to several editions of *Artists and Models*. Schwartz also became identified with Al Jolson, for whom he wrote the score for the Winter Garden extravaganza *The Honeymoon Express* in 1913. Two of his songs interpolated in *Sinbad* (1918) became Jolson favorites: "Rock-a-bye Your Baby" and "Hello, Central, Give Me No Man's Land." Among his later song hits was Ben Bernie's radio signature, "Au Revoir, Pleasant Dreams." Jean Schwartz died in Los Angeles, California, on November 30, 1956.

PRINCIPAL WORKS: Piff, Paff, Pouff (1904); The Passing Show of 1913, 1918, 1919, 1921, 1923, and 1924; Innocent Eyes (1924).
*See:* INNOCENT EYES; THE PASSING SHOWS of 1913, 1918, 1919, 1921, 1923, and 1924; PIFF, PAFF, POUFF.

## SIMON, NEIL, *librettist*

He is one of today's most brilliant and successful writers of stage nonmusical comedies who has also directed to musical-comedy texts his exceptional gift of creating unusual characterizations and situations, with scintillating lines of dialogue. He was born Marvin Neil Simon in New York City on July 4, 1927. After attending De Witt Clinton High School and New York University he served in the United States Air Force during World War II. Between 1948 and 1960 he provided material for major television productions starring Phil Silvers, Sid Caesar, Gary Moore, and Tallulah Bankhead, among others. During this period, in 1952–53, he was employed to write sketches for shows produced weekly at Camp Tamiment, a summer adult's camp in Pennsylvania. His entrance into the Broadway theater came in 1955 and 1956, when, collaborating with his brother Daniel, he contributed sketches for the revues *Catch a Star* and *New Faces of 1956*. Without his brother's assistance, he became a full-fledged playwright with his first Broadway nonmusical comedy, *Come Blow Your Horn* (1962), which was subsequently made into a movie starring Frank Sinatra. This was followed by one major Broadway success after another, including such comedy triumphs as *Barefoot in the Park* (1963), *The Odd Couple* (1964), *Plaza Suite* (1968), and *The Last of the Red Hot Lovers* (1969). His first musical-comedy text was *Little Me* (1962).

PRINCIPAL WORKS: Little Me (1962); Sweet Charity (1966); Promises, Promises (1968).
*See:* LITTLE ME; PROMISES, PROMISES; SWEET CHARITY.

## SLOANE, A. BALDWIN, *composer*

He was born in Baltimore, Maryland, on August 28, 1872, where he attended the public schools, received his musical training from private teachers, and helped found the Baltimore Paint and Powder Club, which produced some of his earliest operettas. He came to New York in the early 1890's, where he became a successful songwriter, his first hits including "While Strolling Down the Forest" and "When You Ain't Got No Money, Well You Needn't come Around," the latter made famous by May Irwin. Edward E. Rice, the producer, became interested in him and arranged for the first Broadway productions of Sloane's musicals. These early Sloane productions are forgotten, but a few of their songs have survived, such as "My Tiger Lily" in *Aunt Hannah* (1900), "There's a Little Street in Heaven Called Broadway" in *The Belle of Broadway* (1902), and "What's the Matter with the Moon Tonight?" in *The Mocking Bird* (1902).

Sloane's first Broadway success came with the sensational *The Wizard of Oz* (1903), in which he collaborated with Paul Tietjens in preparing the music. It was some time before Sloane realized another stage success of such magnitude. Meanwhile, in 1909, one of his biggest song hits appeared in a musical called *Tillie's Nightmare,* starring Marie Dressler; the hit was one of the leading sentimental ballads of the 1890's, "Heaven Will Protect the Working Girl." (In 1927 Herbert Fields adapted *Tillie's Nightmare* for the Rodgers and Hart musical *Peggy-Ann.*) *Tillie's Nightmare* had a secondary Sloane hit in "Life Is Only What You Make It, After All."

Sloane's first Broadway success after *The Wizard of Oz* was *The Summer Widowers* (1910). After that, and up to the time of his death, Sloane continued writing music for the Broadway stage. His last production was *China Rose* (1921), a failure. Sloane died in Red Bank, New Jersey, on February 21, 1926.

PRINCIPAL WORKS: The Wizard of Oz (1903); The Summer Widowers (1910); The Hen Pecks (1911); Ladies First (1918); The Greenwich Village Follies of 1919 and 1920.
*See:* THE GREENWICH VILLAGE FOLLIES of 1919 and 1920; THE HEN PECKS; LADIES FIRST; THE SUMMER WIDOWERS; THE WIZARD OF OZ.

## SMITH, EDGAR, *librettist*

He was born in Brooklyn, New York, on December 7, 1857, and was not related to either Harry B. or Robert Smith (see following pages). Before making his debut as an actor in 1878 he was educated at the Pennsylvania Military Academy. Between 1886 and 1892 he served as the librettist for the New York Casino Company. He helped prepare the librettos for the Weber and Fields shows. Among the other popular musicals for which he wrote librettos were *The Girl Behind the Counter* (1907), *Merry-Go Round* (1908), *The Mimic World* (1908), *Tillie's Nightmare* (1910), *The Kiss Waltz* (1911),

*The Pleasure Seekers* (1913), and *The Blue Paradise* (1915). He died in Bayside, Queens, New York, on March 8, 1938.

PRINCIPAL WORKS: Weber and Fields Extravaganzas, 1898 through 1907; La Belle Paree (1911); Weber and Fields Extravaganzas (*Hokey Pokey,* 1912); Robinson Crusoe, Jr. (1916).
*See:* LA BELLE PAREE; ROBINSON CRUSOE, JR.; WEBER AND FIELDS EXTRAVA-GANZAS, 1898 through 1907.

SMITH, HARRY B., *librettist-lyricist*
Harry Bache Smith, brother of Robert Smith (see next page), was one of the most prolific writers of operetta and musical-comedy texts the American stage has known. He is believed to have written books for over three hundred musicals; there were times when he had from six to ten shows running simultaneously.

He was born in Buffalo, New York, on December 28, 1860. Before turning to the theater he had been a newspaperman, working as a reporter and later music critic for the Chicago *Daily News,* then as drama critic for the Chicago *Tribune.* To both these newspapers he used to contribute a daily column made up of verses, quips, and humorous comments; and while holding down his newspaper jobs he also wrote articles on music and literature for outstanding magazines.

His initiation into musical comedy came with the texts for *Rosita* and *Amarylis,* two failures. In 1887 he entered into collaboration with Reginald de Koven, with whom he wrote *The Begum* (1887), an attempt to imitate *The Mikado* of Gilbert and Sullivan. This, too, was a failure, and so was *Don Quixote,* which followed in 1889. But with their third effort, the comic opera *Robin Hood* (1890), Smith and De Koven achieved a triumph. After that they produced a string of comic operas and musical comedies, many of which were successes.

Even more fruitful was Smith's collaboration with Victor Herbert, begun in 1895 with *The Wizard of the Nile* and continuing for two decades. They wrote about a dozen operettas, among them some of Herbert's most popular ones. Berlin, Englander, Hubbell, Kerker, Kern, Romberg, and Sloane were some other composers with whom Smith worked successfully. Smith died in Atlantic City, New Jersey, on January 2, 1936.

PRINCIPAL WORKS: Robin Hood (1890); Rob Roy (1894); The Wizard of the Nile (1895); The Highwayman (1897); The Serenade (1897); The Fortune Teller (1898); Weber and Fields Extravaganzas, 1898 through 1900; The Belle of Bohemia (1900); The Casino Girl (1900); Weber and Fields Extravaganzas

(*Hoity Toity,* 1901); The Strollers (1901); Weber and Fields Extravaganzas (*Twirly Whirly,* 1902); A Parisian Model (1906); The Rich Mr. Hoggenheimer (1906); The Ziegfeld Follies of 1910 and 1912; Sweethearts (1913); The Girl from Utah (1914); Watch Your Step (1914); Stop! Look! Listen! (1915); Ladies First (1918).

*See:* THE BELLE OF BOHEMIA; THE CASINO GIRL; THE FORTUNE TELLER; THE GIRL FROM UTAH; THE HIGHWAYMAN; LADIES FIRST; A PARISIAN MODEL; THE RICH MR. HOGGENHEIMER; ROBIN HOOD; ROB ROY; THE SERENADE; STOP! LOOK! LISTEN!; THE STROLLERS; SWEETHEARTS; WATCH YOUR STEP; WEBER AND FIELDS EXTRAVAGANZAS, 1898 through 1902; THE WIZARD OF THE NILE; THE ZIEGFELD FOLLIES, 1907 through 1910, and 1912.

## SMITH, ROBERT B., *librettist-lyricist*

Robert Bache Smith was the brother of Harry B. Smith (see preceding page). Robert Smith was born in Chicago, Illinois, on June 4, 1875. He was originally a reporter for the Brooklyn *Eagle* and a press agent for the Casino Theater, after which he wrote sketches for vaudeville and burlesque. In 1902 he collaborated with Edgar Smith (no relation) in writing the lyrics for the Weber and Fields burlesque *Twirly Whirly.* It was Robert Smith who wrote the words for "Come Down Ma Evenin' Star," from this production, introduced by Lillian Russell and with which she subsequently became continually identified. He then wrote the lyrics for numerous musicals, including *Mexicana* (1906), *The Girl and the Wizard* (1909), *Sweethearts* (1913), *The Lilac Domino* (1914), *The Debutante* (1914), *Follow Me* (1916), and *A Lonely Romeo* (119). He also either wrote or collaborated on the librettos for about half a dozen other musicals. Among the composers with whom he worked were Victor Herbert, Hubbell, and Romberg. He died in New York City on November 6, 1951.

PRINCIPAL WORKS: Weber and Fields Extravaganzas (Twirly Whirly, 1902); Fantana (1905); Sweethearts (1913).

*See:* FANTANA; SWEETHEARTS; WEBER AND FIELDS EXTRAVAGANZAS (*Twirly Whirly*).

## SONDHEIM, STEPHEN, *composer-lyricist*

He was born in New York City on March 22, 1930, and attended the George School in Newtown, Pennsylvania, and Williams College, where he majored in music. At college he wrote book, lyrics, and music for two school productions. Winning the Hutchinson Prize enabled him to devote two years of study in composition in New York with Milton Babbitt. In 1953 he was co-author of the scripts for the television series "Topper," and one year after that he completed music and lyrics for a musical, *A Saturday Night,* which never reached Broadway due to the death of its producer. While writing scripts for the Columbia Broadcasting System, and background music for the Broadway play *Girls of Summer,* he worked on the lyrics for *West Side Story,* with which he achieved renown. For *A Funny Thing Happened on the Way to the Forum* (1962), a major success, and *Anyone Can Whistle* (1964), a box-office failure, he wrote both the music and the lyrics. For two other musicals he wrote only the lyrics, while Jule Styne wrote the music for one (*Funny Girl*), and Richard Rodgers for another (*Do I Hear a Waltz?*). He reverted to the practice of writing both words and music for *Company,* in 1970.

PRINCIPAL WORKS: West Side Story (1957); Gypsy (1959); A Funny Thing Happened on the Way to the Forum (1962); Do I Hear a Waltz? (1965); Company.
*See:* COMPANY; DO I HEAR A WALTZ?; A FUNNY THING HAPPENED ON THE WAY TO THE FORUM; GYPSY; WEST SIDE STORY.

## SPEWACK, BELLA AND SAMUEL, *librettists*

The husband-and-wife team of Samuel and Bella Spewack were collaborators on numerous highly successful Broadway nonmusical comedies, including *Clear All Wires* (1932), which was the source of the Cole Porter musical *Leave It to Me; Boy Meets Girl* (1935); and *My Three Angels* (1953). They also wrote about twenty screenplays and several television scripts. Samuel Spewack wrote a number of plays without his wife's assistance. The collaboration was terminated with their divorce. Bella was born in Bucharest, Romania, on March 25, 1899; Samuel, in Bachmut, Russia, on September 16, 1899.

PRINCIPAL WORKS: Leave It to Me (1938); Kiss Me, Kate (1948).
*See:* KISS ME, KATE; LEAVE IT TO ME.

## STAMPER, DAVE, *composer*

The name of David (Dave) Stamper is inevitably associated with that of Florenz Ziegfeld. For almost twenty years he contributed songs to the *Follies* and the *Midnight Frolic.* Though occasionally other Broadway musicals used his music, Stamper will always be remembered as a "Ziegfeld composer." And it was perhaps no coincidence or accident that with Ziegfeld's death, Dave Stamper's career as a successful stage songwriter came to an end.

He was born in New York City on November 10, 1883, and attended the city public schools. He learned the piano by himself. When he was seventeen, he left school for good and found a job as a pianist in a Coney Island dance hall. From there he progressed to Tin Pan Alley to work as a song plugger and staff pianist for various publishers. When he was twenty, he toured the vaudeville circuits as a piano accompanist, working for four years with Nora Bayes.

While pursuing his own career as a popular pianist, Stamper was writing songs, his first effort being "In the Cool of the Evening." His first song to appear in a *Ziegfeld Follies* was "Daddy Has a Sweetheart and Mother Is Her Name," in the 1912 edition, lyrics by Gene Buck, henceforth Stamper's most frequent collaborator. From then on hardly a season of the *Follies* passed without at least one Stamper song in it. He had three in the 1913 edition; in 1914 he shared responsibility for most of the score with Raymond Hubbell, and in 1915 with Louis A. Hirsch. Among his most prominent songs in later editions of the *Follies* were "Sweet Sixteen" and "Tulip Time" (1919); "Plymouth Rock," "Come Back to Our Alley," and "Raggedy Ann" (1921); "My Rambler Rose" and " 'Neath the South Sea Moon," both written with Hirsch (1922); "It's Getting Dark on Old Broadway" (1922); "Some Sweet Day," again with Hirsch (1923). The last *Follies* produced by Ziegfeld was in 1931, and it was with this production—to which he contributed "Broadway Reverie" and "Bring on the Follies Girl"—that Stamper made his last major appearance on Broadway. Stamper died in New York City on September 18, 1963.

PRINCIPAL WORKS: The Ziegfeld Follies, 1913 through 1917, 1919, 1921 through 1927; Lovely Lady (1927); Take the Air (1927); The Ziegfeld Follies of 1931. *See:* THE LOVELY LADY; TAKE THE AIR; THE ZIEGFELD FOLLIES, 1913 through 1917, 1919, 1921 through 1927, 1931.

## STEIN, JOSEPH, *librettist*

He was born in New York City on May 30, 1912, was graduated from the College of the City of New York in 1934, then completed his academic education at Columbia University. For a while he was employed as a social worker, then wrote scripts for radio and television for numerous major productions, beginning in 1944. His first venture into the musical theater was in collaboration with Will Glickman, with sketches for the revues *Lend an Ear* (1948) and *Alive and Kicking* (1950). In 1955, he was the co-librettist of the highly successful Broadway musical *Plain and Fancy*. Besides the musicals listed below, he was also either librettist or co-librettist of *The Body Beautiful* (1958) and Marc Blitzstein's *Juno* (1959), based on Sean O'Casey's play *Juno and the Paycock*. Stein was also the author of the nonmusical Broadway play *Enter Laughing* (1963).

PRINCIPAL WORKS: Lend an Ear (1948); Plain and Fancy (1955); Mister (Mr.) Wonderful (1956); Take Me Along (1959); Fiddler on the Roof (1964).

*See:* FIDDLER ON THE ROOF; LEND AN EAR; MISTER (MR.) WONDERFUL; PLAIN AND FANCY; TAKE ME ALONG.

## STEWART, MICHAEL, *librettist*

He was born in New York City on August 1, 1929, and was graduated from Yale, where in 1953 he received the degree of Master of Arts. Before writing the book for *Bye Bye Birdie* (1960), his first major Broadway musical, he contributed some sketches to two editions of the *Shoestring Revue* (1955, 1956) and to *The Littlest Revue* (1956). Between 1955 and 1959 he wrote for Sid Caesar's television show.

PRINCIPAL WORKS: Bye Bye Birdie (1960); Carnival (1961); Hello, Dolly! (1964).
*See:* BYE BYE BIRDIE; CARNIVAL; HELLO, DOLLY!

## STOTHART, HERBERT, *composer*

He was a highly prolific and successful writer of music for the Broadway stage in the 1920's, though frequently with collaboration of other composers. He was born in Milwaukee, Wisconsin, on September 11, 1885, was trained as a teacher at the Milwaukee Teachers College, then taught in public schools. After attending the University of Wisconsin he became a member of its faculty, concentrating on choral and musical-dramatic activities, his study of music having previously taken place in both America and Europe. For a number of years after leaving the field of education—and activity in choral and church music—he directed orchestras for Broadway musicals. One of his earliest musicals was *Always You* (1920), the first Broadway show for which Oscar Hammerstein II wrote a book and lyrics. Other Stothart musicals, beyond those listed below, included *Jimmie* (1920); *Daffy Dill* (1922); *Mary Jane McKane* (1923), in collaboration with Vincent Youmans; and *Golden Dawn* (1927), in collaboration with Emmerich Kalman. In 1929 Stothart went to Hollywood, where he wrote songs for *The Cuban Love Song,* starring Lawrence Tibbett, and was the musical director for and collaborator on the screen versions of such famous stage musicals as *Maytime, The Firefly, Rose-Marie, Naughty Marietta, The Merry Widow,* and *The Wizard of Oz.* He wrote the background music for numerous other films, including *The Good Earth, Mutiny on the Bounty,* and *Mrs. Miniver.* Stothart died in Los Angeles, California, on February 1, 1949.

PRINCIPAL WORKS: Tickle Me (1920); Wildflower (1923); Rose-Marie (1924); Song of the Flame (1925); Good Boy (1928).
*See:* GOOD BOY; ROSE-MARIE; SONG OF THE FLAME; TICKLE ME; WILDFLOWER.

## STROMBERG, JOHN, *composer*

Though he wrote a popular-song hit before becoming the official conductor and composer of the Weber and Fields extravaganzas, Stromberg's six-year career as an important composer for the Broadway stage was devoted exclusively to his activity at the Weber and Fields Music Hall.

John ("Honey") Stromberg was born in 1853 and received his musical apprenticeship in Tin Pan Alley, where he worked as arranger for the publishing house of Witmark. The success of his song "My Best Girl's a Corker," in 1895, drew the interest of Weber and Fields. Since they were about to open their own theater in New York featuring their burlesques, they invited Stromberg to be their composer and conductor. Thus Stromberg wrote the score for *The Art of Maryland,* with which Weber and Fields opened their Music Hall in 1896. During the next six years he wrote the scores for ten Weber and Fields productions (conducting nine of them). He amassed a fortune and invested most of his money in a quixotic real-estate development in Freeport, Long Island—a residential community to be called Stromberg Park, with streets named after stars from the various Weber and Fields productions. This venture was a failure.

He was working on the score for the Weber and Fields production, *Twirly Whirly,* when he was found dead in his New York apartment in July, 1902. It was generally agreed that he had committed suicide. In his pocket was the manuscript of his last song, and probably his greatest hit, "Come Down, Ma Evenin' Star," written for Lillian Russell. When *Twirly Whirly* opened two months after Stromberg's death (a new conductor in the pit for the first time in six years), Lillian Russell introduced the song, breaking down before she could finish it. It has remained the one with which Lillian Russell has ever since been identified.

*See:* WEBER AND FIELDS EXTRAVAGANZAS, 1896–1902.

## STROUSE, CHARLES, *composer,* and ADAMS, LEE, *lyricist*

Charles Strouse was born in New York City on June 7, 1928. While attending the city public schools he studied the piano with Willie Sauber, but did not become genuinely interested in music until Abraham Sokolow became his teacher and taught him to play jazz chords. In 1947, Strouse was graduated from the University of Rochester where he had studied music seriously at the Eastman School. From 1947 to 1953 he studied composition and orchestration with Aaron Copland, and in 1951, composition with Nadia Boulanger in Paris. In 1950 he became a friend of Lee Adams, a young lyricist, with whom he soon formed a writing partnership for popular music. Lee Adams was born in Mansfield, Ohio, on August 14, 1924, was graduated from Ohio

State University, and studied journalism at Columbia University. In 1955, Strouse and Adams contributed one song to the Broadway revue *Catch a Star*. They also contributed songs to weekly revues mounted at Green Mansions, an adult camp in the Adirondack Mountains of New York, for two summers and, in 1956, to two editions of *The Shoestring Revue* and *The Littlest Revue,* all presented in New York, and all failures. For a while Strouse earned his living playing the piano for club dates and making vocal arrangements for Jane Morgan, Carol Burnett, and Dick Shawn. Success came to Strouse and Adams with the smash Broadway musical *Bye Bye Birdie* (1960). Their later musicals were *All American* (1962), *Golden Boy* (1964), *It's a Bird, It's a Plane, It's Superman* (1966), and *Applause* (1970). They wrote the title song for the motion picture *The Mating Game,* starring Debbie Reynolds. Strouse also wrote the title song and background music for *The Night They Raided Minsky* and *There Was a Crooked Man,* and the background music for *Bonnie and Clyde.*

PRINCIPAL WORKS: Bye Bye Birdie (1960); Golden Boy (1964); It's a Bird, It's a Plane, It's Superman (1966); Applause (1970).
*See:* APPLAUSE; BYE BYE BIRDIE; GOLDEN BOY; IT'S A BIRD, IT'S A PLANE, IT'S SUPERMAN.

## STYNE, JULE, *composer*

He was born in London, England, on December 31, 1905. When he was eight his family settled in Chicago. Since both parents were musical, they saw that he received a thorough training on the piano. Jule made great progress, appearing as a child prodigy with the Detroit and Chicago Symphony orchestras. A scholarship then brought him to the Chicago Musical College when he was thirteen. There he specialized in piano while receiving a thorough grounding in theory and composition.

Renouncing serious music, Styne organized his own dance band in 1931, which performed in various Chicago hotels and clubs. For this group he made up all the arrangements, and Chicago soon sat up and took notice of his original harmonizations and unusual tonal colorations. Even Hollywood was impressed. Styne was hired to do a job as vocal coach for Twentieth Century-Fox, where he worked with Alice Faye, Linda Darnell, and Shirley Temple, among others. He was also beginning to write songs for the movies, one of which became a decided hit—"I Don't Want to Walk Without You" —introduced in *Sweater Girl* (1942).

In 1942 he formed a permanent working partnership with the lyricist Sammy Cahn. Their first song was a winner, "I've Heard That Song Before," which Frank Sinatra introduced in a movie short before it was heard in the film *Youth on Parade* (1942). This partnership reaped a song harvest during the ensuing years. Their songs appeared in many important motion pictures, and some of them were successes of the first order. Only a few of these need be mentioned "It's Been a Long, Long Time," "Let It Snow! Let It Snow! Let It Snow!", "I'll Walk Alone" (one of the outstanding ballads of World War II), "There Goes That Song Again," "Give Me Five Minutes More," "I Love an Old-Fashioned Song," and the song with which they received an Academy Award in 1954, "Three Coins in the Fountain."

Still with Cahn as his lyricist, Styne first invaded the Broadway theater in 1947 with a smash success, *High Button Shoes*. In the early 1950's Cahn, who preferred writing songs for the movies, found a new musical partner in James Van Heusen. Styne pursued his career on Broadway with the cooperation of other lyricists, something which it was not difficult for him to do, because after *High Button Shoes,* and before his break with Cahn, he had written the score for *Gentlemen Prefer Blondes* (1949) with Leo Robin as his lyricist; in 1951, his lyricists for *Two on the Aisle* were Betty Comden and Adolph Green; and in 1953, Bob Hilliard wrote the words to his music for *Hazel Flagg*. Among the lyricists with whom Styne worked for his later musicals were Comden and Green, Stephen Sondheim, and E. Y. Harburg. Besides musicals listed below, Styne contributed songs to *Peter Pan* (1954), in which Mary Martin starred, and wrote the complete scores for *Say, Darling* (1958), *Subways Are for Sleeping* (1961), and *Darling of the Day* (1968). He revived his partnership with Sammy Cahn for the Broadway musical, *Look to the Lilies,* a failure in 1970.

PRINCIPAL WORKS: High Button Shoes (1947); Gentlemen Prefer Blondes (1949); Two on the Aisle (1951); Bells Are Ringing (1956); Gypsy (1959); Do, Re, Mi (1960); Fade Out—Fade In (1964); Funny Girl (1964); Hallelujah, Baby! (1967).
*See:* BELLS ARE RINGING; DO, RE, MI; FADE OUT—FADE IN; FUNNY GIRL; GENTLEMEN PREFER BLONDES; GYPSY; HALLELUJAH, BABY!; HIGH BUTTON SHOES; TWO ON THE AISLE.

## TIERNEY, HARRY, *composer*
Tierney was born in Perth Amboy, New Jersey, on May 21, 1890. He came from a musical household, his mother being an excellent pianist and his father a trumpet player in symphony orchestras. Harry received his first instruction in music from his mother. After being graduated from the Perth Amboy High School, he continued his musical education at the Virgil School of Music in New York, receiving training in piano and theory.

His preference was popular rather than serious music. He wrote popular songs even while engaged in the study of the more serious branches of music and while touring as concert pianist. When his studies ended, he went to England in 1915, where he worked as staff composer for a London music publisher, had three songs published, and received two commissions to write music for the stage.

He was back in the United States in 1916, when he found employment in Tin Pan Alley. His songs were now being interpolated into current Broadway productions, and several became hits. "M-i-s-s-i-s-s-i-p-p-i" was heard in Ziegfeld's *Midnight Frolics* in 1916; "It's a Cute Little Way of My Own" was sung by Anna Held in *Follow Me* (1917); "My Baby's Arms" appeared in *The Ziegfeld Follies* of 1919; and "Take, Oh Take, Those Lips Away" was in *The Ziegfeld Follies* of 1923.

The year 1919 marked Tierney's first complete stage score in New York. Since that production was *Irene,* it immediately gave him a high status among Broadway composers. He became one of Ziegfeld's favored composers. Ziegfeld not only interpolated his songs in some of the *Follies,* as mentioned above, but also assigned to him the writing of complete scores for some of his pet projects, including *Kid Boots* (1923) and *Rio Rita* (1927). Tierney also wrote musical scores for other Broadway producers. Among his musicals, above and beyond those listed below, were *The Broadway Whirl* (1921), *Glory* (1922), and *Cross My Heart* (1928).

In 1929 Tierney went out to Hollywood to help in the screen adaptation of *Rio Rita.* In 1931 he became a staff composer for Paramount Pictures. His stay in the movie capital, however, was not fruitful. He wrote music for only two screen musicals, neither of which was successful. Back on Broadway, he found himself haunted by the same bad luck that had oppressed him in California—and it spelled doom to his career. One of his musicals, an operetta about Omar Khayyam, never reached production. Another operetta (his last stage score), with Beau Brummel as hero, was played in St. Louis in 1933. Tierney died in New York City on March 22, 1965.

PRINCIPAL WORKS: Irene (1919); The Ziegfeld Follies of 1920; Up She Goes (1922) Kid Boots (1923); The Ziegfeld Follies, 1924–25; Rio Rita (1927). *See:* IRENE; KID BOOTS; RIO RITA; UP SHE GOES; THE ZIEGFELD FOLLIES of 1920 and 1924–25.

## WEIDMAN, JEROME, *librettist*

Weidman distinguished himself as a novelist and short-story writer before he became interested in the musical theater. He was born in New York City on April 4, 1913; was educated at New York University and at its Law School; and achieved recognition as a writer with the novel *I Can Get It For*

*You Wholesale* (1937), which later became a Broadway musical. Later novels included *What's In It for Me?* (1938), *The Price Is Right* (1949), *The Sound of Bow Bells* (1962), and *Word of Mouth* (1964). He also published several collections of short stories. He made his bow as musical-comedy librettist with *Fiorello!* (1959), for which he received the Pulitzer Prize. One of his musicals, *Cool Off!* (1964) was a failure.

PRINCIPAL WORKS: Fiorello! (1959); Tenderloin (1960); I Can Get It for You Wholesale (1962).
*See:* FIORELLO!; I CAN GET IT FOR YOU WHOLESALE; TENDERLOIN.

## WEILL, KURT, *composer*

Weill was born in Dessau, now East Germany, on March 2, 1900. As a child he received some music instruction from his parents. In 1918 he continued his musical education at the Berlin High School of Music, and in 1921 he studied privately with one of Europe's most scholarly musicians and esoteric musical thinkers, Ferruccio Busoni. Weill's training, then, was a comprehensive preparation for a career in serious music, a career launched early in the 1920's with several orchestral and chamber-music works and a concerto.

Though much of the music he wrote at the time made use of the advanced techniques and ideas of the avant garde in German music, Weill was no ivory-tower musician. While still a student he earned his living playing popular tunes in a German beer hall. Other jobs—coach and conductor in various small theaters—taught him something of the way a theater functions, and what appeals to the audiences.

In Germany in the 1920's there came into vogue a cultural movement called "contemporary art" (*Zeitkunst*). Composers marching under this banner produced "functional music" (*Gebrauchsmusik*) based on popular techniques and idioms. Since Weill had always been interested in popular music and since he was a devotee of the stage, he soon came to write operas that became outstanding examples of *Zeitkunst*. Within the formal framework of the opera Weill produced music-hall songs and ballads, current dances like the tango and the shimmy, and idioms like the "blues" and American jazz. Beginning with his first opera and continuing with each successive work, Weill used these popular ideas more and more boldly and made them more and more essential to his overall texture. "I want to reach the real people, a more representative public than any opera house attracts," he said at the time. "I want to write for today. I don't care about writing for posterity."

His first opera was *The Protagonist,* written in 1924 to a surrealistic text by Georg Kaiser, and produced in Dresden in 1926. Here Weill's interpolation of popular musical elements was still cautious; but the juxtaposition of popular and serious ideas created enough of a shock for one eminent critic, Oskar Bie, to remark that "all the philosophical theories of teacher Busoni have been swept aside by the reality of Kurt Weill's score."

Weill next wrote *The Royal Palace* (1927), a typically *Zeitkunst* work in its interpolation of actual motion pictures within the play, and in the free mixture of drama and pantomime. It was also *Zeitkunst* in the music's increasing interest in the grammar of American jazz.

Weill's third opera, *The Czar Himself Photographed* (1928), shows greater boldness in introducing jazz and popular songs within the operatic texture; in fact, one German critic did not hesitate to designate it a "jazz opera." The intelligentsia might lament that Weill had strayed from the classical fold and was "decadent"; but the rank and file in Germany liked the opera so well that the work played in eighty theaters to meet the tremendous box-office demand.

By the time Weill started writing his next opera—a one-act sketch, *Mahagonny*—he had a clear idea of the kind of work he wanted to produce. *Mahagonny* was his first work for the theater in a new form of his own invention, called "song-play." The formal arias and ensemble numbers of traditional opera were now entirely displaced by popular songs; and the operatic vocabulary made way for the argot of the people.

The text of *Mahagonny* was by Bertolt Brecht. When Weill and Brecht next collaborated, they created their most famous work, and one of the most provocative stage musicals of the twentieth century—*The Threepenny Opera* (*Die Dreigroschenoper*) in 1928. Brecht here revised and adapted the historical *Beggar's Opera* of John Gay and transformed it into a bitter, scathing indictment of life and manners in twentieth-century Germany. Weill's music was now completely in the style and ritual of the popular musical theater. It was filled with engaging airs, ballads, tunes, duets, trios. Each number was basic to the play, serving either as a character study or to point up some situation or provide a commentary on what was happening. *The Threepenny Opera* had about 4,000 performances in over 120 different theaters in Germany in a single year. It has since become a stage classic, frequently revived in all parts of the world, and on several occasions adapted for the screen. An Off Broadway revival at the Theater de Lys on March 10, 1954—with text modernized and revised by Marc Blitzstein, but with the Weill score left intact—resulted in the longest run achieved up to that time by an Off Broadway production before it went on an extensive national tour.

The star of the original Berlin production of *The Threepenny Opera* was a young singer and diseuse named Lotte Lenya Blaumauer, who appeared as Jenny. She would appear as Jenny in several later revivals of *The Three-*

*penny Opera,* including the sensational 1954 Off Broadway production. She also became Kurt Weill's wife.

The next opera by Weill and Brecht was *Happy Ending* (1929) from which came "The Bilbao Song," which, with new English lyrics by Johnny Mercer, became one of the leading hit songs of 1951 in the United States, popularized by Andy Williams. In 1930, Weill and Brecht expanded their one-act sketch, *Mahagonny,* into a three-act opera renamed *The Rise and Fall of the City of Mahagonny.* This was one of the most controversial musical stage works given in Germany between the two world wars. Weill's treatment was not only in the popular style of his earlier operas but even in the vein of Tin Pan Alley. Some of his lyrics were in English (at times gibberish English), and it is for this reason that the hit song had the English title of "Alabama Song," one of the biggest song successes in Germany in the early 1930's. When *The Rise and Fall of the City of Mahagonny* received its belated American premier—in an Off Broadway production on April 28, 1970 —it was not a success.

Weill's last opera in Germany was *The Lake of Silver.* It gave every promise of approximating the triumph of *The Threepenny Opera.* Eleven theaters in as many different cities arranged for a simultaneous premiere. on February 18, 1933. A long run seemed indicated. But on February 19 the Reichstag in Berlin was set aflame by the Nazis, Weill realized that *Der Tag* had come, and he fled with his wife to Paris.

In Paris, Weill wrote music for several productions that proved failures. Nursing his wounds, he welcomed an offer to come to America. Max Reinhardt had been engaged to stage and direct a pageant of Jewish history by Franz Werfel, *The Eternal Road.* In this production Reinhardt sought to make "a perfect fusion of speech and music," and envisioned the music as the unifying thread within the play. He wanted Weill to write that music. Weill arrived in the United States in 1935. Even then he knew he was coming here for good, for no sooner did he arrive than he began studying the English language, applied for citizenship, and did some research in American popular music and the American musical theater.

*The Eternal Road* hit one snag after another, suffering numerous delays and postponements; it was not produced until 1937. Consequently, when Weill made his bow in the American theater, it was with a play far different from a religious spectacle. That play was *Johnny Johnson,* a fable about World War I by Paul Green, produced by the Group Theater in 1936.

The two scores for *The Eternal Road* and *Johnny Johnson,* each so different from the other yet each so remarkably effective within its own context, gave proof of Weill's versatility and pronounced gift in writing for the stage. Though neither production was good box office, Weill became a composer greatly in demand. He was called to Hollywood to write music for several films; he was commissioned to write background music for a spectacle at the New York World's Fair; he was engaged to prepare the score for a Broadway musical that turned out to be his first American success, *Knickerbocker Holiday* (1938).

After *Knickerbocker Holiday,* Weill was invited to become a member of equal status in the newly formed Playwrights Company, which included Maxwell Anderson, Elmer Rice, and Robert E. Sherwood. Their first production requiring music was Moss Hart's *Lady in the Dark* (1941). This, and its immediate successor, *One Touch of Venus* (1943), placed Weill among the leaders of those writing music for the stage.

*Firebrand of Florence* (1945) was an unhappy attempt to dress Edwin Justus Mayer's risqué Broadway comedy about Benvenuto Cellini with music and dances. Weill's subsequent music for Broadway acquired operatic dimensions. He now collaborated in three productions whose artistic value has always been appreciated, but none of which enjoyed financial success: *Street Scene* (1947), *Love Life* (1948), and *Lost in the Stars* (1949). The circle of Weill's artistic career had now closed. He had begun his career in Germany by making opera into popular music; he now succeeded making popular music into opera. Indeed, Weill's last work for the stage actually was an opera, an American folk opera, *Down in the Valley,* introduced at Indiana University on July 15, 1948, and since then become a staple in the repertory of many amateur, semiprofessional, and professional opera companies. *Down in the Valley* was excellent theater, but it also made for excellent listening. To the end of his life Weill succeeded in being popular in the serious theater, and serious in the popular theater.

He died in New York City on April 3, 1950. A few years after his death, in commenting on the happy revival of *The Threepenny Opera,* Brooks Atkinson wrote: "Everyone agrees that Mr. Weill was one of the finest composers we have had in the last twenty-five years, and there is reason to think he was the best."

PRINCIPAL WORKS: Johnny Johnson (1936); Knickerbocker Holiday (1938); Lady in the Dark (1941); One Touch of Venus (1943); Street Scene (1947); Love Life (1948); Lost in the Stars (1949).
*See:* JOHNNY JOHNSON; KNICKERBOCKER HOLIDAY; LADY IN THE DARK; LOST IN THE STARS; LOVE LIFE; ONE TOUCH OF VENUS; STREET SCENE.

WHITE, GEORGE, *librettist-lyricist. See* GEORGE WHITE'S SCANDALS.

## WHITING, RICHARD A., *composer*

He was born in Peoria, Illinois, on November 12, 1891. Both parents were musical, but neither gave him formal instruction. What he learned about piano and harmony he acquired for himself. Even while attending Harvard Military School in Los Angeles he began writing popular songs. After his graduation he found employment as office manager of the Detroit branch of Remick. Remick published his first song in 1913. Two years later Whiting wrote "It's Tulip Time in Holland," which sold one and a half million copies of sheet music. "Mammy's Little Coal Black Rose" in 1916 and "Where the Black-Eyed Susans Grow" in 1917 were also hits, the latter interpolated by Al Jolson in *Robinson Crusoe, Jr.* In 1918 came one of the great ballads of World War I in Whiting's "Till We Meet Again," which amassed the formidable sale of five million copies.

In 1919 Whiting came to New York, where his first stage assignment was to write music for a postwar revue, *Toot Sweet.* In the same year he was also engaged by George White to produce a score for the first edition of the *Scandals.*

Between 1920 and 1931 Whiting did no writing for the Broadway theater, but in Tin Pan Alley his stature kept growing all the time by virtue of such resounding song hits as "Japanese Sandman," "Ain't We Got Fun," and "Sleepy Time Gal."

In 1929 he went out to Hollywood, where during the next decade his songs appeared in over two dozen screen musicals. Among his most popular screen songs were two written for and made famous by Maurice Chevalier, "Louise" and "One Hour With You." Others included "Beyond the Blue Horizon," "Too Marvelous for Words," and "When Did You Leave Heaven?"

When Whiting returned to Broadway in 1931 it was with a failure, *Free for All,* which lasted only fifteen performances. But one year later he had a major success in *Take a Chance* (a score he shared with Vincent Youmans), his valedictory to Broadway. From 1932 on Whiting's musical writing was confined to Hollywood, where he died on February 10, 1938.

PRINCIPAL WORKS: George White's Scandals of 1919; Take a Chance (1932).
*See:* GEORGE WHITE'S SCANDALS of 1919; TAKE A CHANCE.

## WILLSON, MEREDITH, *composer-lyricist-librettist*

By the time he wrote his first musical comedy, with which he gathered so many accolades as well as financial rewards—*The Music Man*—Meredith Willson had already long become recognized as a gifted flute player, symphony conductor, composer of serious music, composer of popular hit songs, and an outstanding radio personality.

He was born in Mason City, Iowa, on May 18, 1902, where, as a boy, he learned to play the flute and piccolo. In 1919 he came to New York, where he attended the Institute of Musical Art and completed the study of the flute with George Barrere. From 1921 to 1929 Willson played the flute with Sousa's band, with various theater orchestras, and with the New York Philharmonic. In 1929 he was made music director of a radio station in San Francisco, where, three years later, he was elevated to the post of music director of the Western Division of NBC. In this capacity, he directed the popular "Good News" program over radio for several years, a period in which he also was heard in public concerts as a symphony conductor and as a composer of serious orchestral compositions. In 1940 he began writing screen music, beginning with *The Great Dictator,* starring Charles Chaplin, and one year after that he was composer-lyricist of a song hit, "You and I." During World War II he served in the music division of the Armed Forces Radio Service. After the war, while resuming his radio activities, he continued writing popular songs. "May the Good Lord Bless and Keep You," one of his most successful numbers, was written in 1950 and used weekly on the famous Tallulah Bankhead radio program, of which Willson was music director. During the Korean War, another of his songs became popular, this time with American soldiers, "I See the Moon."

He was, then, not unknown when he initiated a new career for himself on the Broadway musical stage by writing the libretto, music, and lyrics for *The Music Man* (1957). He remained his own lyricist for all his subsequent musicals, and often also served as his own librettist. A musical in which Christopher Columbus was a principal character—*1491*—was produced in Los Angeles in 1969 and was a failure.

PRINCIPAL WORKS: The Music Man (1957); The Unsinkable Molly Brown (1960); Here's Love (1963).
*See:* HERE'S LOVE; THE MUSIC MAN; THE UNSINKABLE MOLLY BROWN.

## WODEHOUSE, P. G., *lyricist-librettist*

Though P. G. Wodehouse is most famous for his whimsical novels and stories—particularly those involving Psmith and Jeeves as characters—he has also been a significant writer for the popular Broadway musical stage. As a lyricist he has been a pioneer in bringing a skillful technique at versification and an adult sophistication to song verses, thereby setting the stage for mature lyricists like Lorenz Hart, Ira Gershwin, Oscar Hammerstein, and Cole Porter.

Pelham Grenville Wodehouse ("Plum" to his friends) was born in Guildford, Surrey, England, on October 15, 1881. He was educated at Dulwich College with the hope of becoming a banker. After completing his schooling he did make an attempt at banking, but after two years was firmly told by his employer that his talent lay elsewhere. Wodehouse agreed, for by then he was already earning money with his pen. Still a comparative unknown in 1903, he started writing lyrics to music by Jerome Kern for songs appearing on the London stage; their first song was a hit—a topical song, "Mr. Chamberlain" (Mr. Chamberlain being a noted politician of the time, the father of the prime minister, Neville).

From 1903 to 1909 Wodehouse filled a post as columnist for the London *Globe*. During this period he also started writing stories about a bright young fellow named Psmith, his first novel about him being *Psmith in the City* (1910), which made Wodehouse famous.

Wodehouse paid a number of visits to the United States, and had contributed stories to *The Saturday Evening Post* by the time he arrived in 1915 to stay in America, part of the year to serve as drama critic for *Vanity Fair*. In this capacity he attended the opening-night performance of the Kern musical *Very Good, Eddie,* where his onetime London friendship with the composer was revived. Kern introduced Wodehouse to Guy Bolton, his collaborator, and suggested that the three of them join forces in writing musicals. Thus it came about that Wodehouse, Bolton, and Kern became the writing triumvirate responsible for some of the best Princess Theater Shows.

After that Wodehouse wrote either libretto or lyrics (or both) for almost two dozen musicals by Kern, Gershwin, Caryll, Friml, and Hirsch, among others. After World War II Wodehouse established permanent residence in the United States, at Remsenburg, Long Island. Though he had ceased writing for the stage, he has remained prolific in the production of novels and nonfiction.

PRINCIPAL WORKS: The Princess Theater Show (*Oh, Boy!,* 1917); Leave It to Jane (1917); The Princess Theater Show (*Oh, Lady! Lady!,* 1918); The Princess Theater Show (*Oh, My Dear!,* 1918); *Oh, Kay!* (1926); *Rosalie* (1928); The Three Musketeers (1928); Anything Goes (1934).
See: ANYTHING GOES; LEAVE IT TO JANE; OH, KAY!; THE PRINCESS THEATER SHOWS (*Oh, Boy!, Oh, Lady! Lady!, Oh, My Dear!*); ROSALIE; THE THREE MUSKETEERS.

## WRIGHT, ROBERT, and FORREST, GEORGE ("CHET"), *composers-lyricists*

Robert Wright and George Forrest have collaborated in writing both lyrics and music. Their careers have followed parallel lines. Wright was born in Daytona Beach, Florida, on September 25, 1914; Forrest was born less than a year later, in Brooklyn, New York, July 31, 1915. Both attended the Miami (Florida) High School and the University of Miami. Both achieved their first successes in Hollywood, where, in a writing partnership, they produced special material for stage and nightclub revues, and contributed songs to several screen musicals, including *Maytime, The Firefly,* and *Sweethearts.* For *The Firefly* they wrote the lyrics of "Donkey Serenade" (music by Friml and Stothart); for *Sweethearts,* the lyrics and music for still another song hit, "Pretty as a Picture."

Their career in the American musical theater combines formidable successes and equally formidable failures. Success came first—with *Song of Norway* (1944)—which more than two decades after its Broadway success was made into a movie. *Gypsy Lady* (1946)—an operetta, whose score was made up of Victor Herbert favorites—was a dud. Then came another box-office smash in *Kismet* (1953), the score based on music by Borodin. But in 1957 *Carefree Heart* (text derived from the "Doctor" comedies of Molière) expired out of town, as did *Dumas, Father and Son,* an operetta, a decade later. *Kean,* produced on Broadway in 1961, was also a failure.

PRINCIPAL WORKS: Song of Norway (1944); Kismet (1953).
*See:* KISMET; SONG OF NORWAY.


## YELLEN, JACK, *librettist-lyricist*

He was born in Poland on July 6, 1892, and received a Bachelor of Arts degree from the University of Michigan. After working as a reporter for the Buffalo, New York, *Courier,* he came to New York, where he wrote songs and special material for prominent entertainers, including Sophie Tucker, who made his song "A Yiddisha Momme" (1925), which he wrote with Lew Pollack, one of her specialties. But before that, he worked with the composer Milton Ager, with whom he wrote the score for the Broadway musical *What's in a Name?* (1920) and the song hit "I Wonder What's Become of Sally?" (1924). Still with Ager, he wrote the songs for another Broadway musical, *Rain or Shine* (1928), as well as two outstanding song successes, "Ain't She Sweet?" (1927) and "Hard Hearted Hannah" (1929). Working with Sid Silvers, he wrote the libretto for the Broadway musical *You Said It* (1931), besides contributing the lyrics. Before returning to Broadway with *Sons o' Fun,* in 1941, he worked in Hollywood writing songs and screen plays for motion pictures. His major hit song to come out of Hollywood was "Happy Days Are Here Again," music by Milton Ager, introduced in *Chasing Rainbows* (1930). Besides Ager, Yellen worked successfully with such other composers as Harold Arlen, Sammy Fain, and Ray Henderson.

PRINCIPAL WORKS: Rain or Shine (1928) ; George White's Scandals of 1935 and 1939; Sons o' Fun (1941) ; The Ziegfeld Follies of 1943.
*See:* GEORGE WHITE'S SCANDALS of 1935 and 1939; RAIN OR SHINE; SONS O' FUN; THE ZIEGFELD FOLLIES of 1943.

## YOUMANS, VINCENT, *composer*

He was born in New York City on September 27, 1898. His father was a famous hatter, whose stores in the early 1900's helped dictate the prevailing hat fashions for men. Financially comfortable, the Youmans family moved from New York City to Larchmont, New York, when Vincent was a child. He started piano lessons in childhood with the local organist, Charles André Feller. His academic schooling took place at private schools in Mamaroneck and in Rye, New York. Engineering was selected by his parents for his profession; they enrolled him at Sheffield at Yale. But Youmans had ideas of his own. Without attending a single class there, he rejected engineeering for good and found a job as a runner in a Wall Street brokerage house.

He soon came to the decision that his future lay with music—popular music. He left the world of commerce to work as a song plugger and piano demonstrator in Tin Pan Alley. During World War I he enlisted in the Navy, where he was assigned to produce musicals, write songs, and play in the band at the Great Lakes Naval Station. The bandleader at the station, "Red" Carney, encouraged Youmans' attempts at composition. One of the songs Youmans wrote at this time became a favorite of Navy bands and was featured by John Philip Sousa at some of his concerts. Some years later this same piece became even more popular as "Hallelujah" in *Hit the Deck*.

The war ended, Youmans returned to Tin Pan Alley to work as a song plugger for the firm of Harms. His first piece published was "The Country Cousin," in 1920. The first Broadway musical for which he contributed music (though in collaboration with Paul Lannin) was *Two Little Girls in Blue*— the first show for which Ira Gershwin (hiding under the pen name of Arthur Francis) wrote all the lyrics.

During the next four years Youmans was associated with several highly successful stage productions, beginning with *Wildflower* (1923), written in collaboration with Oscar Hammerstein II, then still green at the business of writing lyrics or working with musical-comedy books. *No, No, Nanette,* a year later, was an even greater success and put Youmans with the foremost writers of stage music of his day. Youmans' third major musical came to Broadway two years after that, *Hit the Deck*.

Between 1927 and 1933 Youmans was represented on Broadway with a disconcerting succession of box-office failures, most of them disasters because Youmans frequently assumed the duties of producer, for which he had neither the temperament nor the capabilities. But he did not have to be ashamed of two of these failures, since each in its own way represented a courageous attempt on Youmans' part to bring a fresh, new approach to the musical theater: *Rainbow* (1928) and *Through the Years* (1932). The latter was Brian Hooker's adaptation of a sentimental play by Jane Cowl long popular on stage and screen, now acquiring new radiance through Youmans' songs. Two of them became particularly famous: the title song, the composer's own favorite among his brainchildren, and "Drums in My Heart."

Individual songs, rather than the productions for which they were intended, brought significance to several Youmans musicals. *Great Day* (1929) had "More than You Know" and "Without a Song"; *Smiles* (1930) might have had one of Youmans' classics, "Time on My Hands," if its star, Marilyn Miller, had not objected to it and forced its removal from that play (it was released as an independent song). *Take a Chance* (1932), where he shared the score with Whiting, had another Youmans delight in "Rise 'n Shine," in the style of a revival hymn.

Youmans' music for *Take a Chance* was his last contribution to Broadway. In 1933 he went to Hollywood to write an original score for the Fred Astaire-Ginger Rogers musical *Flying Down to Rio,* a score that boasted "Carioca" and "Orchids in the Moonlight."

A victim of tuberculosis from 1934 on, Youmans had to quit work and settle in Colorado, where he stayed sometimes in a sanatorium, and sometimes in hotels. An improvement in his health finally enabled him to indulge in some music study, and in 1943 to return to New York, where he began planning a new kind of musical production. He called it the *Vincent Youmans Ballet Revue* and conceived it as an artistic project embracing classic and modern dance, interludes for puppets, music derived partly from the classics, and the most beautiful costuming and scenery that could be devised. Financed by Dorothy Duke, this production opened in Toronto, Canada, on January 20, 1944, then a week later played in Baltimore, where it expired—collapsing under the dead weight of its overpretentious aims.

This was Youmans' farewell to the theater. His health broke down again. He had to return to Colorado, where, early in 1946, he stayed for a month in a sanatorium before defying doctors' orders and removing himself to the Park Lane Hotel in Denver. He died there on April 5, 1946.

PRINCIPAL WORKS: Two Little Girls in Blue (1921); Wildflower (1923); No, No, Nanette (1925); Hit the Deck (1927); Rainbow (1928); Take a Chance (1932). *See:* HIT THE DECK; NO, NO, NANETTE; RAINBOW; TAKE A CHANCE; TWO LITTLE GIRLS IN BLUE; WILDFLOWER.

## YOUNG, RIDA JOHNSON, *librettist-lyricist*

She was born in Baltimore, Maryland, on February 28, 1869. After completing her education at Wilson College, she entered the theater as an actress in productions with E. H. Sothern and those put on by the Viola Allen Company. Her first resounding success as librettist-lyricist came with Victor Herbert's *Naughty Marietta* (1910). She subsequently also worked with Romberg and Friml. Besides those listed below, Broadway musicals in which she was involved included: Jerome Kern's *The Red Petticoat* (1912), libretto only; *Lady Luxury* (1914); *Her Soldier Boy* (1916); *His Little Widows* (1917), lyrics only; *Little Simplicity* (1918); and *Dream Girl* (1924), in collaboration with Harold Atteridge. She died in Stamford, Connecticut, on May 8, 1926.

PRINCIPAL WORKS: Naughty Marietta (1910); Maytime (1917); Sometime (1918). *See:* MAYTIME; NAUGHTY MARIETTA; SOMETIME.

# APPENDICES

# CHRONOLOGY OF THE MUSICAL THEATER*

○○○○○○○○○○○○○○○○○○○○○○○○○○○○○○○○○○○○○○○○○○○○○○○○○○○○○○○○○○○○○○○

*1866*
The Black Crook

*1868*
Humpty Dumpty

*1874*
Evangeline

*1879*
The Brook; The Mulligan Guards' Ball (and other Harrigan and Hart burlesques)

*1884*
Adonis

*1887*
The Little Tycoon

*1890*
Castles in the Air; Robin Hood

*1891*
Wang

*1892*
The Isle of Champagne

*1893*
A Trip to Chinatown

*1894*
The Passing Show of 1894; Rob Roy

*1895*
Princess Bonnie; The Wizard of the Nile

* Only musicals discussed in this book listed here.

*1896*
The Art of Maryland (*see* WEBER AND FIELDS EXTRAVAGANZAS); El Capitan

*1897*
The Belle of New York; The Highwayman; The Serenade

*1898*
The Fortune Teller; Hurly Burly (*see* WEBER AND FIELDS EXTRAVAGANZAS)

*1899*
The Rogers Brothers in Wall Street (and other Rogers Brothers vaudeville-farces); Whirl-i-Gig (*see* WEBER AND FIELDS EXTRAVAGANZAS)

*1900*
The Belle of Bohemia; the Casino Girl; Fiddle-De-Dee (*see* WEBER AND FIELDS EXTRAVAGANZAS)

*1901*
Hoity Toity (*see* WEBER AND FIELDS EXTRAVAGANZAS); The Strollers

*1902*
A Chinese Honeymoon; King Dodo; Twirly Whirly (*see* WEBER AND FIELDS EXTRAVAGANZAS)

*1903*
Babes in Toyland; The Prince of Pilsen; The Runaways; Whoop-De-Doo (*see* WEBER AND FIELDS EXTRAVAGANZAS)

*1904*
Higgeldy Piggelgy (*see* WEBER AND FIELDS EXTRAVAGANZAS); It Happened in Nordland; Little Johnny Jones; Mr. Wix of Wickham; Piff, Paff, Pouf; The Sho-Gun

*1905*
Fantana; Mademoiselle (Mlle.) Modiste; A Society Circus (*see* HIPPODROME EXTRAVAGANZAS)

*1906*
Forty-five Minutes from Broadway; George Washington, Jr.; A Parisian Model; Pioneer Days (*see* HIPPODROME EXTRAVAGANZAS); The Red Mill; The Rich Mr. Hoggenheimer; Twiddle

Twaddle (*see* WEBER AND FIELDS EXTRAVAGANZAS)

*1907*
The Auto Race (*see* HIPPODROME EXTRAVAGANZAS); Hip! Hip! Hooray! (*see* WEBER AND FIELDS EXTRAVAGANZAS); The Ziegfeld Follies of 1907

*1908*
Sporting Days (*see* HIPPODROME EXTRAVAGANZAS); The Three Twins; The Ziegfeld Follies of 1908

*1909*
The Fair Co-ed; A Trip to Japan (*see* HIPPODROME EXTRAVAGANZAS); The Ziegfeld Follies of 1909

*1910*
The International Cup (*see* HIPPODROME EXTRAVAGANZAS); Madame Sherry; Naughty Marietta; The Social Whirl; The Summer Widowers; The Ziegfeld Follies of 1910

*1911*
Around the World (*see* HIPPODROME EXTRAVAGANZAS); La Belle Paree; The Hen Pecks; The Little Millionaire; The Pink Lady; Vera Violetta; The Ziegfeld Follies of 1911

*1912*
The Firefly; Hokey Pokey (*see* WEBER AND FIELDS EXTRAVAGANZAS); Oh! Oh! Delphine; The Passing Show of 1912; Under Many Flags (*see* HIPPODROME EXTRAVAGANZAS); Wall Street Girl; The Ziegfeld Follies of 1912

*1913*
America (*see* HIPPODROME EXTRAVAGANZAS); High Jinks; The Passing Show of 1913; Sweethearts; The Ziegfeld Follies of 1913

*1914*
Chin-Chin; The Girl from Utah; Hello, Broadway!; The Only Girl; The Passing Show of 1914; Wars of the World (*see* HIPPODROME EXTRAVAGANZAS); Watch Your Step; The Ziegfeld Follies of 1914

*1915*

The Blue Paradise; Hip, Hip, Hooray! (*see* HIPPODROME EXTRAVAGANZAS); Nobody Home (*see* THE PRINCESS THEATER SHOWS); The Passing Show of 1915; The Princess Pat; Stop! Look! Listen!; Very Good, Eddie (*see* THE PRINCESS THEATER SHOWS); The Ziegfeld Follies of 1915

*1916*

The Big Show (*see* HIPPODROME EXTRAVAGANZAS); The Century Girl; The Cohan Revue of 1916 (*see* Hello, Broadway!); The Passing Show of 1916; Robinson Crusoe, Jr.; The Ziegfeld Follies of 1916

*1917*

Cheer Up (*see* HIPPODROME EXTRAVAGANZAS); Going Up; Leave It to Jane; Maytime; Oh, Boy! (*see* THE PRINCESS THEATER SHOWS); The Passing Show of 1917; The Ziegfeld Follies of 1917

*1918*

The Cohan Revue of 1918 (*see* HELLO, BROADWAY!); Everything (*see* HIPPODROME EXTRAVAGANZAS); Ladies First; Listen Lester; Oh, Lady! Lady! (*see* THE PRINCESS THEATER SHOWS); Oh, My Dear! (*see* THE PRINCESS THEATER SHOWS); The Passing Show of 1918; Sinbad; Somebody's Sweetheart; Sometime; Yip, Yip, Yaphank; The Ziegfeld Follies of 1918

*1919*

Apple Blossoms; George White's Scandals of 1919; The Greenwich Village Follies of 1919; Happy Days (*see* HIPPODROME EXTRAVAGANZAS); Irene; La La, Lucille; The Ziegfeld Follies of 1919

*1920*

George White's Scandals of 1920; Good Times (*see* HIPPODROME EXTRAVAGANZAS); Honeydew; Mary; Sally; Tickle Me; The Ziegfeld Follies of 1920

*1921*

Blossom Time; Bombo; George White's Scandals of 1921; Get Together (*see* HIPPODROME EXTRAVAGANZAS); Good Morning Dearie; The Greenwich Village Follies of 1921; The Music Box Revue; The Passing Show of 1921; The Perfect Fool; Shuffle Along; Tangerine; Two Little Girls in Blue; The Ziegfeld Follies of 1921

*1922*

Better Times (*see* HIPPODROME EXTRAVAGANZAS); George White's Scandals of 1922; The Gingham Girl; The Grand Street Follies; The Greenwich Village Follies of 1922; Lady in Ermine; The Music Box Revue of 1922; The Passing Show of 1922; Sally, Irene and Mary; Up She Goes; The Ziegfeld Follies of 1922

*1923*

Artists and Models of 1923; The Earl Carroll Vanities of 1923; The Greenwich Village Follies of 1923; Helen of Troy, New York; Kid Boots; Little Jessie James; The Music Box Revue of 1923; The Passing Show of 1923; Poppy; Stepping Stones; Wildflower; The Ziegfeld Follies of 1923

*1924*

Artists and Models of 1924; The Earl Carroll Vanities of 1924; George White's Scandals of 1924; The Grand Street Follies of 1924; The Greenwich Village Follies of 1924; I'll Say She Is; Innocent Eyes; Lady, Be Good!; The Music Box Revue of 1924; The Passing Show of 1924; Rose-Marie; The Student Prince in Heidelberg; The Ziegfeld Follies of 1924-25

*1925*

Artists and Models of 1925; The Cocoanuts; Dearest Enemy; The Earl Carroll Vanities of 1925; The Garrick Gaieties; George White's Scandals of 1925; The Grand Street Follies of 1925;

The Greenwich Village Follies of 1925; No, No, Nanette; Song of the Flame; Sunny; Tip-Toes: The Vagabond King

**1926**
Americana; Criss Cross; The Desert Song; The Earl Carroll Vanities of 1926; The Garrick Gaieties of 1926; The Girl Friend; The Grand Street Follies of 1926; Honeymoon Lane; A Night in Paris; Oh, Kay!; Peggy-Ann; Queen High; The Ramblers

**1927**
A Connecticut Yankee; Five O'Clock Girl; Funny Face; Good News; The Grand Street Follies of 1927; Hit the Deck; Lovely Lady; Rio Rita; Show Boat; Take the Air; The Ziegfeld Follies of 1927

**1928**
Animal Crackers; Blackbirds of 1928; The Earl Carroll Vanities of 1928; George White's Scandals of 1928; Good Boy; The Grand Street Follies of 1928; The Greenwich Village Follies of 1928; Hello Daddy; Hold Everything; The New Moon; Present Arms; Rainbow; Rain or Shine; Rosalie; The Three Musketeers; Whoopee

**1929**
Fifty Million Frenchmen; Follow Thru; Hot Chocolates; The Little Show; Show Girl; The Sketch Book of 1929; Sons o' Guns; Sweet Adeline

**1930**
The Earl Carroll Vanities of 1930; Fine and Dandy; Flying High; The Garrick Gaieties of 1930; The Second Little Show; Simple Simon; Strike Up the Band; Three's a Crowd

**1931**
America's Sweetheart; The Band Wagon; The Earl Carroll Vanities of 1931; George White's Scandals of 1931; The Cat and the Fiddle; The Laugh Parade; Of Thee I Sing; The Ziegfeld Follies of 1931

**1932**
The Earl Carroll Vanities of 1932; Face the Music; Flying Colors; The Gay Divorce; Music in the Air; New Americana of 1932 (see AMERICANA); Take a Chance; Walk a Little Faster

**1933**
As Thousands Cheer; Let 'Em Eat Cake; Roberta

**1934**
Anything Goes; The Great Waltz; Life Begins at 8:40; New Faces of 1934

**1935**
At Home Abroad; George White's Scandals of 1935; Jubilee; Jumbo; May Wine; Porgy and Bess; The Sketch Book of 1935

**1936**
New Faces of 1936; Johnny Johnson; On Your Toes; The Show Is On; Thumbs Up; The Ziegfeld Follies of 1936–37

**1937**
Babes in Arms; Hooray for What?; I'd Rather Be Right; Pins and Needles

**1938**
The Boys from Syracuse; The Cradle Will Rock; Hellzapoppin'; I Married an Angel; Knickerbocker Holiday; Leave It to Me

**1939**
Du Barry Was a Lady; George White's Scandals of 1939; Streets of Paris

**1940**
Cabin in the Sky; The Earl Carroll Vanities of 1940; Hold on to Your Hats; Louisiana Purchase; Meet the People; Pal Joey; Panama Hattie

**1941**
Banjo Eyes; Best Foot Forward; Lady in the Dark; Let's Face It; Sons o' Fun

**1942**
By Jupiter; Star and Garter; This Is the Army

*1943*

Carmen Jones; Oklahoma!; One Touch of Venus; Something for the Boys; The Ziegfeld Follies of 1943

*1944*

Bloomer Girl; Follow the Girls; Laffing Room Only; Mexican Hayride; On the Town; Song of Norway

*1945*

Billion Dollar Baby; Carousel; The Day Before Spring; Up in Central Park

*1946*

Annie Get Your Gun; Call Me Mister; St. Louis Woman

*1947*

Allegro; Brigadoon; Finian's Rainbow; High Button Shoes; Street Scene

*1948*

As the Girls Go; Inside U.S.A.; Kiss Me, Kate; Lend an Ear; Love Life; Make Mine Manhattan; Where's Charley?

*1949*

Gentlemen Prefer Blondes; Lost in the Stars; Miss Liberty; Regina; South Pacific

*1950*

Call Me Madam; Guys and Dolls; Michael Todd's Peep Show

*1951*

The King and I; Paint Your Wagon; Top Banana; A Tree Grows in Brooklyn; Two on the Aisle

*1952*

New Faces of 1952; Wish You Were Here

*1953*

Can-Can; John Murray Anderson's Almanac; Kismet; Me and Juliet; Wonderful Town

*1954*

By the Beautiful Sea; Fanny; The Girl in Pink Tights; The Golden Apple; House of Flowers; The Pajama Game

*1955*

Damn Yankees; Pipe Dream; Plain and Fancy; Silk Stockings

*1956*

Bells Are Ringing; Candide; Happy Hunting; Li'l Abner; The Most Happy Fella; Mister (Mr.) Wonderful; My Fair Lady; New Faces of 1956

*1957*

Jamaica; The Music Man; New Girl in Town; West Side Story; The Ziegfeld Follies of 1957

*1958*

Flower Drum Song; Say, Darling (*see* THE PAJAMA GAME)

*1959*

Destry Rides Again; Fiorello!; Gypsy; Little Mary Sunshine; Once Upon a Mattress; The Sound of Music; Take Me Along

*1960*

Bye Bye Birdie; Camelot; The Fantasticks; Tenderloin; The Unsinkable Molly Brown; Wildcat

*1961*

Carnival; From the Second City; How to Succeed in Business Without Really Trying; Milk and Honey

*1962*

Alarums and Excursions (*see* FROM THE SECOND CITY); A Funny Thing Happened on the Way to the Forum; I Can Get It for You Wholesale; Little Me; Mister (Mr.) President; No Strings; Seacoast of Bohemia (*see* FROM THE SECOND CITY)

*1963*

Here's Love; 110 in the Shade; She Loves Me

*1964*

Fade Out—Fade In; Fiddler on the Roof; Funny Girl; Golden Boy; Hello, Dolly! (white cast); High Spirits; What Makes Sammy Run?

*1965*

Baker Street; Do I Hear a Waltz?; Man of La Mancha; On a Clear Day You Can See Forever; Skyscraper

*1966*

The Apple Tree; Cabaret; I Do! I Do!; It's a Bird, It's a Plane, It's Superman; Mame; Sweet Charity

*1967*

Hallelujah, Baby!; Ilya Darling; You're a Good Man, Charlie Brown

*1968*

Dames at Sea; George M!; Golden Rainbow; Hair; The Happy Time; Hello, Dolly! (Negro cast); Promises, Promises; Your Own Thing; Zorba

*1969*

Celebration; Coco; From the Second City; Promenade; Salvation; 1776

*1970*

Applause; Company; Joy; The Last Sweet Days of Isaac; Minnie's Boys; Purlie

*Appendix B*

# OUTSTANDING SONGS*

∘∘∘∘∘∘∘∘∘∘∘∘∘∘∘∘∘∘∘∘∘∘∘∘∘∘∘∘∘∘∘∘∘∘∘∘∘∘∘∘∘∘∘∘∘∘∘∘∘∘∘∘∘∘∘∘∘∘∘∘

AFTER THE BALL, by Charles K. Harris, introduced by J. Aldrich Libbey in *A Trip to Chinatown,* an interpolation.

AH! SWEET MYSTERY OF LIFE, introduced by Emma Trentini in *Naughty Marietta.*

AIN'T MISBEHAVIN', introduced by Louis Armstrong in *Hot Chocolates.*

ALICE BLUE GOWN, introduced by Adele Rowland in *Irene.*

ALL ALONE, introduced by Grace Moore and Oscar Shaw, interpolated into *The Music Box Revue* of 1924.

ALL ALONE MONDAY, introduced by Marie Saxon in *The Ramblers.*

ALL OF YOU, introduced by Don Ameche in *Silk Stockings.*

ALMOST LIKE BEING IN LOVE, introduced by David Brooks and Marion Bell in *Brigadoon.*

ALWAYS TRUE TO YOU IN MY FASHION, introduced by Lisa Kirk in *Kiss Me, Kate.*

AND THIS IS MY BELOVED, introduced by Doretta Morrow in *Kismet.*

* Outstanding songs introduced in productions not discussed in this book are not listed.

A song is identified by its author or authors only when the score of the production in which it was introduced is the work of several different people.

743

THE ANGELUS, introduced by Christine MacDonald in *Sweethearts.*

APRIL IN PARIS, introduced by Evelyn Hoey in *Walk a Little Faster.*

APRIL SHOWERS, by Louis Silvers, with lyrics by Buddy de Sylva, introduced by Al Jolson in *Bombo,* an interpolation.

AQUARIUS, introduced by Ronald Dyson in *Hair.*

AUF WIEDERSEHEN, introduced by Vivienne Segal and Cecil Lean in *The Blue Paradise.*

AUTUMN IN NEW YORK, by Vernon Duke, introduced by J. Harold Murray in *Thumbs Up.*

BAMBALINA, introduced by Edith Day in *Wildflower.*

THE BEST THINGS IN LIFE ARE FREE, introduced by Mary Lawlor and John Prince in *Good News.*

BEWITCHED, BOTHERED AND BEWILDERED, introduced by Vivienne Segal in *Pal Joey.*

BIG D, introduced by Susan Johnson and Shorty Long in *The Most Happy Fella.*

BILL, introduced by Helen Morgan in *Show Boat.*

THE BIRTH OF THE BLUES, production number in *George White's Scandals* of 1926.

BLACK BOTTOM, introduced by Ann Pennington in *George White's Scandals* of 1926.

BLOW, GABRIEL, BLOW, introduced by Ethel Merman in *Anything Goes.*

BLUE HEAVEN. *See* "The Desert Song."

BLUE ROOM, introduced by Eva Puck and Sam White in *The Girl Friend.*

BODY AND SOUL, by John Green, with lyrics by Edward Heyman, Robert Sour, and Frank Eyton, introduced by Libby Holman and Clifton Webb in "Three's a Crowd," an interpolation.

THE BOWERY, introduced by Harry Conor in *A Trip to Chinatown,* an interpolation.

BROTHER, CAN YOU SPARE A DIME? by Jay Gorney, with lyrics by E. Y. Harburg, introduced by Rex Weber in *New Americana.*

BUCKLE DOWN, WINSOCKI, introduced by Tommy Dix and Stuart Langley in *Best Foot Forward.*

A BUSHEL AND A PECK, introduced by Vivian Blaine in *Guys and Dolls.*

BUT NOT FOR ME, introduced by Ginger Rogers in *Girl Crazy.*

BUTTON UP YOUR OVERCOAT, introduced by Jack Haley and Zelma O'Neal in *Follow Thru.*

CABARET, introduced by Jill Haworth in *Cabaret.*

CALIFORNIA, HERE I COME, by Al Jolson, Buddy de Sylva, and Joseph Meyer, introduced by Al Jolson in *Bombo,* an interpolation.

CAMELOT, introduced by Richard Burton in *Camelot.*

CAN'T HELP LOVIN' DAT MAN, introduced by Norma Terris, Howard Marsh, and Helen Morgan in *Show Boat.*

CAROLINA IN THE MORNING, by Walter Donaldson, with lyrics by Gus Kahn, introduced by Eugene and Willie Howard in *The Passing Show* of 1922, an interpolation.

CAROUSEL IN THE PARK, introduced by Maureen Cannon in *Up in Central Park.*

C'EST MAGNIFIQUE, introduced by Lilo in *Can-Can.*

CHEERFUL LITTLE EARFUL, by Harry Warren, with lyrics by Ira Gershwin and Billy Rose, introduced by Hannah Williams and Jerry Norris in *Sweet and Low.*

CLAP YO' HANDS, introduced by Harland Dixon in *Oh, Kay!*

CLIMB EV'RY MOUNTAIN, introduced by Patricia Neway in *The Sound of Music.*

CLOSE AS PAGES IN A BOOK, introduced by Maureen Cannon and Wilbur Evans in *Up in Central Park.*

COCOANUT SWEET, introduced by Lena Horne in *Jamaica.*

COME DOWN MA' EVENIN' STAR, introduced by Lillian Russell in *Twirly Whirly.*

COME RAIN OR COME SHINE, introduced by Harold Nichols and Ruby Hill in *St. Louis Woman.*

COME TO ME, BEND TO ME, introduced by Lee Sullivan in *Brigadoon.*

CUDDLE UP A LITTLE CLOSER, introduced by Alice Yorke in *The Three Twins.*

DANCING IN THE DARK, introduced by John Barker in *The Band Wagon.*

THE DAWN OF LOVE, introduced by Emma Trentini in *The Firefly.*

DEEP IN MY HEART, introduced by Ilse Marvenga and Howard Marsh in *The Student Prince in Heidelberg.*

THE DESERT SONG ("Blue Heaven"), introduced by Vivienne Segal and Robert Halliday in *The Desert Song.*

DIAMONDS ARE A GIRL'S BEST FRIEND, introduced by Carol Channing in *Gentlemen Prefer Blondes.*

DIGA, DIGA, DOO, introduced by Adelaide Hall in *Blackbirds* of 1928.

DINAH, by Harry Akst, with lyrics by Sam M. Lewis and Joe Young, introduced by Eddie Cantor in *Kid Boots,* an interpolation.

DINAH (Stromberg). *See* "Kiss Me Honey, Do."

DO, DO, DO, introduced by Gertrude Lawrence in *Oh, Kay!*

DON'T RAIN ON MY PARADE, introduced by Barbra Streisand in *Funny Girl.*

THE DOOR OF MY DREAMS, introduced by Mary Ellis in *Rose-Marie.*

DO RE MI, introduced by Mary Martin and the children in *The Sound of Music.*

DRINKING SONG, introduced by chorus in *The Student Prince in Heidelberg.*

EADIE WAS A LADY, introduced by Ethel Merman in *Take a Chance.*

EASTER PARADE, introduced by Marilyn Miller and Clifton Webb in *As Thousands Cheer.*

EMBRACEABLE YOU, introduced by Ginger Rogers in *Girl Crazy.*

EVERYBODY'S GOT A RIGHT TO BE WRONG, introduced by Timothy Bushman in *Skyscraper.*

EVERYBODY STEP, introduced by the Brox Sisters in *The Music Box Revue* of 1921.

EVERY LITTLE MOVEMENT HAS A MEANING OF ITS OWN, introduced by Florence Mackie and Jack Reinhard in *Madame Sherry.*

EVERYTHING'S COMING UP ROSES, introduced by Ethel Merman in *Gypsy.*

EVERYBODY'S GOT A RIGHT TO BE WRONG, introduced by Timothy Bushman in *Sky-*

FALLING IN LOVE WITH LOVE, introduced by Muriel Angelus in *The Boys from Syracuse.*

FANNY, introduced by William Tabbert in *Fanny.*

A FELLOW NEEDS A GIRL, introduced by William Ching and Annamary Dickey in *Allegro.*

FEUDIN' AND FIGHTIN', introduced by Pat Brewster in *Laffing Room Only.*

FRIENDSHIP, introduced by Ethel Merman and Bert Lahr in *Du Barry Was a Lady.*

THE GABY GLIDE, introduced by Gaby Deslys and Harry Pilcer in *Vera Violetta.*

THE GENTLEMAN IS A DOPE, introduced by Lisa Kirk in *Allegro.*

GEORGETTE, by Ray Henderson, with lyrics by Lew Brown, introduced by Ted Lewis and his band in *The Greenwich Village Follies* of 1922, an interpolation.

GIANNINA MIA, introduced by Emma Trentini in *The Firefly*.

THE GIRL THAT I MARRY, introduced by Ray Middleton in *Annie Get Your Gun*.

GIVE MY REGARDS TO BROADWAY, introduced by George M. Cohan in *Little Johnny Jones*.

GOLDEN DAYS, introduced by Howard Marsh in *The Student Prince in Heidelberg*.

GOODBYE BROADWAY, HELLO FRANCE, by C. Francis Reisner, Benny Davis, and Billy Baskette, introduced in *The Passing Show* of 1917, an interpolation.

GOODBYE GIRLS, I'M THROUGH, introduced by Fred Stone in *Chin-Chin*.

GOOD NEWS, introduced by Zelma O'Neal in *Good News*.

GREEN-UP TIME, introduced by Nanette Fabray in *Love Life*.

GUYS AND DOLLS, introduced by Stubby Kaye and Johnny Silver in *Guys and Dolls*.

GYPSY LOVE SONG ("Slumber On, My Little Gypsy Sweetheart"), introduced by Eugene Cowles in *The Fortune Teller*.

HALLELUJAH, introduced by the ensemble in *Hit the Deck*.

HAUNTED HEART, introduced by John Tyers and Estelle Loring in *Inside U.S.A.*

HAVE YOU MET MISS JONES?, introduced by Joy Hodges and Austin Marshall in *I'd Rather Be Right*.

HEAT WAVE, introduced by Ethel Waters in *As Thousands Cheer*.

HELLO, DOLLY, introduced by Carol Channing in *Hello, Dolly!*

HELLO, FRISCO, introduced by Ina Claire in *The Ziegfeld Follies* of 1915.

HELLO, YOUNG LOVERS, introduced by Gertrude Lawrence in *The King and I*.

HERE AM I, introduced by Helen Morgan in *Sweet Adeline*.

HERE IN MY ARMS, introduced by Helen Ford and Charles Purcell in *Dearest Enemy*.

HERNANDO'S HIDEAWAY, introduced by Carol Haney and John Raitt in *The Pajama Game*.

HEY, LOOK ME OVER, introduced by Lucille Ball and Paula Stewart in *Wildcat*.

HOLD ME, HOLD ME, HOLD ME, introduced by Dolores Gray in *Two on the Aisle*.

HONEY IN THE HONEYCOMB, introduced by Katherine Dunham in *Cabin in the Sky*.

HOW ARE THINGS IN GLOCCA MORRA?, introduced by Ella Logan in *Finian's Rainbow*.

HOW LONG HAS THIS BEEN GOING ON?, introduced by Bobbe Arnst in *Rosalie*.

I AIN'T DOWN YET, introduced by Tammy Grimes in *The Unsinkable Molly Brown*.

I CAN'T GET STARTED WITH YOU, by Vernon Duke, with lyrics by Ira Gershwin, introduced by Bob Hope and Fanny Brice in *The Ziegfeld Follies* of 1936.

I COULD HAVE DANCED ALL NIGHT, introduced by Julie Andrews in *My Fair Lady*.

I COULD WRITE A BOOK, introduced by Gene Kelly and Leila Ernst in *Pal Joey*.

I ENJOY BEING A GIRL, introduced by Pat Suzuki in *Flower Drum Song*.

I FEEL PRETTY, introduced by Carol Lawrence in *West Side Story*.

IF EVER I WOULD LEAVE YOU, introduced by Robert Goulet in *Camelot*.

IF I LOVED YOU, introduced by Jan Clayton and John Raitt in *Carousel*.

I GET A KICK, OUT OF YOU, introduced by Ethel Merman in *Anything Goes*.

I GOT PLENTY O' NUTHIN', introduced by Todd Duncan in *Porgy and Bess*.

I GOT RHYTHM, introduced by Ethel Merman in *Girl Crazy*.

I GOTTA RIGHT TO SING THE BLUES, by Harold Arlen, with lyrics by Ted Koehler, introduced by Lillian Shade in *The Earl Carroll Vanities* of 1932.

I GUESS I'LL HAVE TO CHANGE MY PLAN, introduced by Clifton Webb in *The Little Show*.

I HAVE DREAMED, introduced by Doretta Morrow and Larry Douglas in *The King and I.*

I JUST CAN'T MAKE MY EYES BEHAVE, introduced by Anna Held in *A Parisian Model.*

I'LL BUILD A STAIRWAY TO PARADISE. *See* "Stairway to Paradise."

I'LL NEVER FALL IN LOVE AGAIN, introduced by Jill O'Hara and Jerry Orbach in *Promises, Promises.*

I'LL SAY SHE DOES, by Al Jolson, with lyrics by Buddy de Sylva and Gus Kahn, introduced by Al Jolson in *Sinbad,* an interpolation.

I LOVE PARIS, introduced by Lilo in *Can-Can.*

I LOVE YOU, introduced by Nan Halperin in *Little Jessie James.*

I LOVE YOU, introduced by Wilbur Evans in *Mexican Hayride.*

I MARRIED AN ANGEL, introduced by Dennis King in *I Married an Angel.*

I'M THE BELLE OF NEW YORK, introduced by Edna May in *The Belle of New York.*

I'M FALLING IN LOVE WITH SOMEONE, introduced by Orville Harrold in *Naughty Marietta.*

I'M FOREVER BLOWING BUBBLES, by Jean Kenbrovin and John La Kellette, introduced by June Caprice in *The Passing Show* of 1918, an interpolation.

I'M GOIN' SOUTH, by Harry Woods, with lyrics by Abner Smith, introduced by Al Jolson in *Bombo,* an interpolation.

I'M IN LOVE WITH A WONDERFUL GUY, introduced by Mary Martin in *South Pacific.*

I'M JUST WILD ABOUT HARRY, introduced by Florence Mills in *Shuffle Along.*

THE IMPOSSIBLE DREAM ("The Quest"), introduced by Richard Kiley in *Man of La Mancha.*

INDIAN LOVE CALL, introduced by Mary Ellis and Dennis King in *Rose-Marie.*

THE ISLE OF OUR DREAMS, introduced by Augusta Greenleaf and Joseph W. Ratliff in *The Red Mill.*

IT AIN'T NECESSARILY SO, introduced by John W. Bubbles in *Porgy and Bess.*

ITALIAN STREET SONG, introduced by Emma Trentini in *The Fortune Teller.*

IT'S ALL RIGHT WITH ME, introduced by Peter Cookson in *Can-Can.*

I'VE GOT A CRUSH ON YOU, introduced by Jack Whiting and Harriet Lake (Ann Sothern) in *America's Sweetheart.*

I'VE GOT TO BE ME, introduced by Steve Lawrence in *Golden Rainbow.*

I'VE NEVER BEEN IN LOVE BEFORE, introduced by Robert Alda and Isabel Bigley in *Guys and Dolls.*

I'VE TOLD EV'RY LITTLE STAR, introduced by Walter Slezak and Katherine Carrington in *Music in the Air.*

I WANNA BE LOVED BY YOU, introduced by Helen Kane in *Good Boy.*

I WANT TO BE HAPPY, introduced by Louise Groody and John Barker in *No, No, Nanette.*

JOEY, JOEY, JOEY, introduced by Art Lund in *The Most Happy Fella.*

JOHNNY ONE NOTE, introduced by Wynn Murray in *Babes in Arms.*

JUBILATION T. CORPONE, introduced by Stubby Kaye in *Li'l Abner.*

JUNE IS BUSTIN' OUT ALL OVER, introduced by Christine Johnson and Jean Darling with ensemble in *Carousel.*

JUST IN TIME, introduced by Sydney Chaplin and Judy Holliday in *Bells Are Ringing.*

JUST ONE OF THOSE THINGS, introduced by June Knight and Charles Walters in *Jubilee.*

KA-LU-A, introduced by Oscar Shaw in *Good Morning, Dearie.*

KATIE WENT TO HAITI, introduced by Ethel Merman in *Du Barry Was a Lady.*

KISS ME AGAIN, introduced by Fritzi Scheff in *Mademoiselle (Mlle.) Modiste.*

KISS ME HONEY, DO, introduced by Peter F. Dailey in *Hurly Burly.*

KISS WALTZ, introduced by Hazel Dawn in *The Pink Lady.*

THE LADY IS A TRAMP, introduced by Mitzi Green in *Babes in Arms.*

LADY OF THE EVENING, introduced by John Steel in *The Music Box Revue* of 1922.

THE LAST ROUNDUP, by Billy Hill, introduced by Everett Marshall in *The Ziegfeld Follies* of 1932, an interpolation.

LEAVE IT TO JANE, introduced by Edith Hallor *in Leave It to Jane.*

LEGALIZE MY NAME, introduced by Pearl Bailey *in St. Louis Woman.*

LET'S HAVE ANOTHER CUP O' COFFEE, introduced by Katherine Carrington and J. Harold Murray in *Face the Music.*

LET THE SUNSHINE IN, introduced by Melba Moore in *Hair.*

LIFE IS JUST A BOWL OF CHERRIES, introduced by Ethel Merman in *George White's Scandals* of 1931.

LITTLE GIRL BLUE, introduced by Gloria Grafton in *Jumbo.*

LIZA, introduced by Ruby Keeler in *Show Girl.*

LONG BEFORE I KNEW YOU, introduced by Sydney Chaplin in *Bells Are Ringing.*

LOOK FOR THE SILVER LINING, introduced by Marilyn Miller and Irving Fisher in *Sally.*

LOOKING FOR A BOY, introduced by Queenie Smith in *Tip-Toes.*

LOOK TO THE RAINBOW, introduced by Ella Logan in *Finian's Rainbow.*

A LOT OF LIVIN' TO DO, introduced by Dick Gautier and Susan Watson in *Bye Bye Birdie.*

LOUISIANA HAYRIDE, introduced by Clifton Webb and Tamara Geva in *Flying Colors.*

LOVE IS LIKE A FIREFLY, introduced by Emma Trentini in *The Firefly.*

LOVE IS SWEEPING THE COUNTRY, introduced by June O'Dea and George Murphy in *Of Thee I Sing.*

LOVE MAKES THE WORLD GO ROUND, introduced by Anna Maria Alberghetti in *Carnival.*

LOVE ME OR LEAVE ME, introduced by Ruth Etting in *Whoopee.*

LOVE NEST, introduced by Jack McGowan in *Mary.*

LOVER, COME BACK TO ME, introduced by Evelyn Herbert in *The New Moon.*

MA BLUSHIN' ROSIE, introduced by Fay Templeton in *Fiddle-De-Dee.*

MAGGIE MURPHY'S HOME, introduced by Emma Pollack in *Reilly and the 400s* (see THE MULLIGAN GUARDS' BALL).

THE MAGIC MELODY, introduced by Adele Rowland in *Nobody Home.*

MAKE BELIEVE, introduced by Howard Marsh and Norma Terris in *Show Boat.*

MAKE SOMEONE HAPPY, introduced by John Reardon in *Do, Re, Mi.*

MAME, introduced by Charles Braswell in *Mame.*

MANDY, introduced by the ensemble in *Yip, Yip, Yaphank,* but popularized by Marilyn Miller in *The Ziegfeld Follies* of 1919.

MANHATTAN, introduced by June Cochrane and Sterling Holloway in *The Garrick Gaieties* of 1925.

THE MARCH OF THE MUSKETEERS, episode in *The Three Musketeers.*

MARCH OF THE TOYS, episode in *Babes in Toyland.*

MARIA, introduced by Larry Kert in *West Side Story.*

MARY, introduced by Donald Brian in *Forty-five Minutes from Broadway.*

MAYBE, introduced by Gertrude Lawrence and Oscar Shaw in *Oh, Kay!*

MELODY IN 4-F, by Sylvia Fine and Max Liebman, introduced by Danny Kaye in *Let's Face It,* an interpolation.

THE MESSAGE OF THE VIOLET, introduced by Albert Paar and Anna Lichter in *The Prince of Pilsen.*

MINE, introduced by William Gaxton and ensemble in *Let 'Em Eat Cake.*

MISTER GALLAGHER AND MISTER SHEAN, introduced by Gallagher and Shean in *The Ziegfeld Follies* of 1922, an interpolation.

MISTER (MR.) WONDERFUL, introduced by Olga James in *Mister (Mr.) Wonderful.*

MOANIN' LOW, by Ralph Rainger, with lyrics by Howard Dietz, introduced by Libby Holman in *The Little Show,* an interpolation.

MONOTONOUS, introduced by Eartha Kitt in *New Faces* of 1952.

MOONBEAMS, introduced by Augusta Greenleaf in *The Red Mill.*

THE MOST BEAUTIFUL GIRL IN THE WORLD, introduced by Donald Novis and Gloria Grafton in *Jumbo.*

MOUNTAIN GREENERY, introduced by Bobbie Perkins and Sterling Holloway in *The Garrick Gaieties* of 1926.

MUTUAL ADMIRATION SOCIETY, introduced by Ethel Merman and Virginia Gibson in *Happy Hunting.*

MY BABY JUST CARES FOR ME, introduced by Eddie Cantor in *Whoopee.*

MY BEAUTIFUL LADY, introduced by Hazel Dawn in *The Pink Lady.*

MY DARLING, MY DARLING, introduced by Doretta Morrow and Byron Palmer in *Where's Charley?*

MY FAVORITE THINGS, introduced by Mary Martin in *The Sound of Music.*

MY FUNNY VALENTINE, introduced by Mitzi Green in *Babes in Arms.*

MY HEART BELONGS TO DADDY, introduced by Mary Martin in *Leave It to Me.*

MY HEART STOOD STILL, introduced by William Gaxton and Constance Carpenter in *A Connecticut Yankee* (originally heard in *One Dam Thing After Another* in London).

MY LUCKY STAR, introduced by John Barker in *Follow Thru.*

MY MAN, by Maurice Yvain, adapted by Channing Pollock, introduced by Fanny Brice in *The Ziegfeld Follies* of 1921, an interpolation.

MY ROMANCE, introduced by Donald Novis and Gloria Grafton in *Jumbo.*

MY SHIP, introduced by Gertrude Lawrence in *Lady in the Dark.*

NEAPOLITAN LOVE SONG, introduced by Joseph R. Letora in *The Princess Pat.*

NEVER ON SUNDAY, by Manos Hanijdakis, with Lyrics by Billy Towne, originally in the motion picture of the same name but interpolated for Melina Mercouri in *Ilya Darling.*

NEW SUN IN THE SKY, introduced by Fred Astaire in *The Band Wagon.*

NEW YORK, NEW YORK, introduced by John Battles, Cris Alexander, and Adolph Green in *On the Town.*

NIGHT AND DAY, introduced by Fred Astaire in *The Gay Divorce.*

THE NIGHT WAS MADE FOR LOVE, introduced by George Meader in *The Cat and the Fiddle.*

NOBODY, by Bert Williams, introduced by Bert Williams in *The Ziegfeld Follies* of 1910.

NO OTHER LOVE, introduced by Bill Hayes and Isabel Bigley in *Me and Juliet.*

OF THEE I SING, introduced by William Gaxton and Lois Moran in *Of Thee I Sing*.

OH, HOW I HATE TO GET UP IN THE MORNING, introduced by Irving Berlin in *Yip, Yip, Yaphank*.

OHIO, introduced by Rosalind Russell and Edith Adams in *Wonderful Town*.

OH, LADY BE GOOD!, introduced by Walter Carlett in *Lady, Be Good!*

OH, PROMISE ME, introduced by Jesse Bartlett Davis in *Robin Hood*.

OH, WHAT A BEAUTIFUL MORNIN', introduced by Alfred Drake in *Oklahoma!*

OL' MAN RIVER, introduced by Jules Bledsoe in *Show Boat*.

ON A CLEAR DAY YOU CAN SEE FOREVER, introduced by John Cullum in *On a Clear Day You Can See Forever*.

ONCE IN LOVE WITH AMY, introduced by Ray Bolger in *Where's Charley?*

ONE ALONE, introduced by Robert Halliday in *The Desert Song*.

ONE KISS, introduced by Evelyn Herbert in *The New Moon*.

ONLY A ROSE, introduced by Dennis King in *The Vagabond King*.

ON THE STREET WHERE YOU LIVE, introduced by Michael King in *My Fair Lady*.

PACK UP YOUR SINS, introduced by the McCarthy Sisters in *The Music Box Revue* of 1924.

PAPA, WON'T YOU DANCE WITH ME?, introduced by Jack McCauley and Nanette Fabray in *High Button Shoes*.

THE PARTY'S OVER, introduced by Judy Holliday in *Bells Are Ringing*.

PEOPLE, introduced by Barbra Streisand in *Funny Girl*.

PEOPLE WILL SAY WE'RE IN LOVE, introduced by Alfred Drake and Joan Roberts in *Oklahoma!*.

PLAY A SIMPLE MELODY, introduced by Sallie Fisher and Charles King in *Watch Your Step*.

POOR BUTTERFLY, introduced by Haru Onuki in *The Big Show*.

POVERTY'S TEARS EBB AND FLOW, introduced in *Old Lavender*.

PRETTY BABY, by Egbert van Alstyne, with lyrics by Gus Kahn and Tony Jackson, introduced by Dolly Hackett in *The Passing Show* of 1916, an interpolation.

A PRETTY GIRL IS LIKE A MELODY, introduced by John Steel in *The Ziegfeld Follies* of 1919.

A PUZZLEMENT, introduced by Yul Brynner in *The King and I*.

THE QUEST. *See* "The Impossible Dream."

REAL LIVE GIRL, introduced by Sid Caesar in *Little Me*.

REUBEN, REUBEN, introduced in *A Trip to Chinatown*.

RIO RITA, introduced by Ethelind Terry and J. Harold Murray in *Rio Rita*.

RISE 'N SHINE, by Vincent Youmans, with lyrics by Buddy de Sylva, introduced by Ethel Merman in *Take a Chance*.

ROCK-A-BYE YOUR BABY, by Jean Schwartz, with lyrics by Joe Young and Sam M. Lewis, introduced by Al Jolson in *Sinbad,* an interpolation.

A ROOM WITHOUT WINDOWS, introduced by Steve Lawrence and Sally Ann Howes in *What Makes Sammy Run?*

ROSE-MARIE, introduced by Dennis King and Arthur Deagon in *Rose-Marie*.

ROW, ROW, ROW, by Jimmie V. Monaco, with lyrics by William Jerome, introduced by Lillian Lorraine in *The Ziegfeld Follies* of 1912, an interpolation.

THE SAGA OF JENNY, introduced by Gertrude Lawrence in *Lady in the Dark*.

SAM AND DELILAH, introduced by Ethel Merman in *Girl Crazy*.

SAY IT WITH MUSIC, introduced by Wilda Bennett and Paul Frawley in *The Music Box Revue* of 1921.

SECOND HAND ROSE, by James F. Hanley, with lyrics by Grant Clarke, introduced by Fanny Brice in *The Ziegfeld Follies* of 1921, an interpolation.

SEPTEMBER SONG, introduced by Walter Huston in *Knickerbocker Holiday.*

SERENADE, introduced by Howard Marsh in *The Student Prince in Heidelberg.*

SEVENTY-SIX TROMBONES, introduced by Robert Preston and ensemble in *The Music Man.*

SHALL WE DANCE?, introduced by Gertrude Lawrence and Yul Brynner in *The King and I.*

SHALOM, introduced by Robert Weede and Mimi Benzell in *Milk and Honey.*

SHE DIDN'T SAY YES, introduced by Bettina Hall in *The Cat and the Fiddle.*

SHINE ON, HARVEST MOON, by Jack Norworth and Nora Bayes, introduced by Nora Bayes in *The Ziegfeld Follies* of 1908.

SHOW BUSINESS, introduced by William O'Neal, Ray Middleton, Marty May, and Ethel Merman in *Annie Get Your Gun.*

SING SOMETHING SIMPLE, by Herman Hupfeld, introduced by Ruth Tester in *The Second Little Show* (*see* THE LITTLE SHOW).

SIREN'S SONG, introduced by Edith Hallor in *Leave It to Jane.*

SLUMBER ON, MY LITTLE GYPSY SWEETHEART. *See* "Gypsy Love Song."

SMILES, by Lee M. Roberts, with lyrics by J. Will Callahan, introduced by Neil Carrington in *The Passing Show* of 1918, an interpolation.

SMOKE GETS IN YOUR EYES, introduced by Katherine Carrington and J. Harold Murray in *Face the Music.*

SOFTLY AS IN A MORNING SUNRISE, introduced by William O'Neal in *The New Moon.*

SO IN LOVE, introduced by Patricia Morison in *Kiss Me, Kate.*

SOLILOQUY, introduced by John Raitt in *Carousel.*

SO LONG, MARY, introduced by Donald Brian in *Forty-five Minutes from Broadway.*

SOMEBODY LOVES ME, introduced by Winnie Lightner in *George White's Scandals* of 1924.

SOME ENCHANTED EVENING, introduced by Ezio Pinza in *South Pacific.*

SOMEONE TO WATCH OVER ME, introduced by Gertrude Lawrence in *Oh, Kay!*

SOMETHING SEEMS TINGLE-INGLEING, introduced by Elaine Hammerstein in *High Jinks.*

SOMETHING TO REMEMBER YOU BY, introduced by Libby Holman in *Three's a Crowd.*

SOMETIMES I'M HAPPY, introduced by Louise Groody and Charles King in *Hit the Deck.*

THE SONG IS YOU, introduced by Tullio Carminati in *Music in the Air.*

SONG OF LOVE, introduced by Bertram Peacock and Olga Cook in *Blossom Time.*

SONG OF THE VAGABONDS, choral episode in *The Vagabond King.*

SONG OF THE WOODMAN, by Harold Arlen, with lyrics by E. Y. Harburg, introduced by Bert Lahr in *The Show Is On.*

SOON, introduced by Margaret Schilling in *Strike Up the Band.*

THE SOUND OF MUSIC, introduced by Mary Martin in *The Sound of Music.*

SOUTH AMERICAN WAY, introduced by Carmen Miranda in *The Streets of Paris.*

SOUTH AMERICA TAKE IT AWAY, introduced by Betty Garrett in *Call Me Mister.*

SPRING IS HERE, introduced by Vivienne Segal and Dennis King in *I Married an Angel.*

STAIRWAY TO PARADISE, introduced by Winnie Lightner in *George White's Scandals* of 1922.

STANDING ON THE CORNER, introduced by Shorty Long, Alan Gilbert, John Henson, and Roy Lazarus in *The Most Happy Fella.*

STAR LIGHT, STAR BRIGHT, introduced by a vocal quintet in *The Wizard of the Nile.*

STOUT-HEARTED MEN, introduced by Robert Halliday in *The New Moon.*

STRANGE MUSIC, introduced by Lawrence Brooks and Helena Bliss in *Song of Norway.*

STRANGER IN PARADISE, introduced by Doretta Morrow and Richard Kiley in *Kismet.*

STRIKE UP THE BAND, choral episode in *Strike Up the Band.*

SUMMERTIME, introduced by Abbe Mitchell in *Porgy and Bess.*

SUNDAY IN THE PARK, introduced in *Pins and Needles.*

SUNRISE, SUNSET, introduced by Zero Mostel and Maria Karnilova in *Fiddler on the Roof.*

SUNSHINE GIRL, introduced by Del Anderson, Eddie Phillips, and Mike Dawson in *New Girl in Town.*

SWANEE, by George Gershwin, with lyrics by Irving Caesar, introduced by Al Jolson in *Sinbad,* an interpolation.

SWEET AND LOW-DOWN, introduced by Al Kaye and Gertrude MacDonald in *Tip-Toes.*

THE SWEETEST SOUNDS, introduced by Diahann Carroll and Richard Kiley in *No Strings.*

SWEETHEARTS, introduced by Christine McDonald in *Sweethearts.*

SWEET LADY, by Howard Johnson, Frank Crumit, and David Zoob, introduced by Julia Sanderson and Frank Crumit in *Tangerine.*

TAKE IT SLOW, JOE, introduced by Lena Horne in *Jamaica.*

TAKE ME ALONG, introduced by Jackie Gleason and Walter Pidgeon in *Take Me Along.*

TAKING A CHANCE ON LOVE, introduced by Ethel Waters and Dooley Wilson in *Cabin in the Sky.*

TAMMANY, by Gus Edwards, with lyrics by Vincent Bryan, introduced by Lee Harrison in *Fantana.*

TEA FOR TWO, introduced by Louise Groody and John Barker in *No, No, Nanette.*

THAT CERTAIN FEELING, introduced by Queenie Smith and Allen Kearns in *Tip-Toes.*

THAT'S THE KIND OF A BABY FOR ME, by Alfred Harrison and Jack Egan, introduced by Eddie Cantor in *The Ziegfeld Follies* of 1917, an interpolation.

THERE'S A SMALL HOTEL, introduced by Ray Bolger and Doris Carson in *On Your Toes.*

THERE'S NO BUSINESS LIKE SHOW BUSINESS. *See* "Show Business."

THEY CALL THE WIND MARIA, introduced by Rufus Smith in *Paint Your Wagon.*

THEY DIDN'T BELIEVE ME, introduced by Julia Sanderson in *The Girl from Utah.*

THEY SAY IT'S WONDERFUL, introduced by Ethel Merman and Ray Middleton in *Annie Get Your Gun.*

THIS CAN'T BE LOVE, introduced by Eddie Albert and Mary Wescott in *The Boys from Syracuse.*

THREE O'CLOCK IN THE MORNING, by Julian Robledo, with lyrics by Dorothy Terris, introduced in *The Greenwich Village Follies* of 1921, an interpolation.

TICKLE TOE, introduced by Edith Day in *Going Up.*

TILL THE CLOUDS ROLL BY, introduced by Anna Wheaton and Lynn Overman in *Oh, Boy!*

TOGETHER, introduced by Ethel Merman, Sandra Church, and Jack Klugman in *Gypsy.*

TO KEEP MY LOVE ALIVE, introduced by Vivienne Segal in *A Connecticut Yankee,* 1943 revival.

TONIGHT, introduced by Carol Lawrence and Larry Kert in *West Side Story.*

TOO CLOSE FOR COMFORT, introduced by Sammy Davis in *Mister (Mr.) Wonderful.*

TOOT, TOOT, TOOTSIE, by Gus Kahn, Ernie Erdman, and Dan Russo, introduced by Al Jolson in *Bombo,* an interpolation.

THE TOUCH OF YOUR HAND, introduced by Tamara and William Hain in *Roberta.*

TOYLAND, choral episode in *Babes in Toyland.*

TRY TO REMEMBER, introduced by Jerry Orbach in *The Fantasticks.*

TSCHAIKOWSKY, introduced by Danny Kaye in *Lady in the Dark.*

THE VARSITY DRAG, introduced by Zelma O'Neal in *Good News.*

WAGON WHEELS, by Billy Hill, introduced by Everett Marshall in *The Ziegfeld Follies* of 1932.

WALTZ HUGUETTE, introduced by Jane Carroll in *The Vagabond King.*

WANTING YOU, introduced by Robert Halliday in *The Desert Song.*

WERE THINE THAT SPECIAL FACE, introduced by Alfred Drake in *Kiss Me, Kate.*

WHATEVER LOLA WANTS, introduced by Gwen Verdon in *Damn Yankees.*

WHAT'LL I DO?, introduced by Grace Moore in *The Music Box Revue* of 1923, an interpolation.

WHEN CHLOE SINGS A SONG, introduced by Lillian Russell in *Whirl-i-Gig.*

WHEN HEARTS ARE YOUNG, by Sigmund Romberg, with lyrics by Cyrus Wood, introduced by Wilda Bennett in *The Lady in Ermine,* an interpolation.

WHEN A MAID COMES KNOCKING AT YOUR HEART, introduced by Emma Trentini in *The Firefly.*

WHEN MY BABY SMILES AT ME, by Bill Munro, with lyrics by Andrew B. Sterling and Ted Lewis, introduced by Ted Lewis and his band in *The Greenwich Village Follies* of 1919, an interpolation.

WHERE OR WHEN, introduced by Mitzi Green and Ray Heatherton in *Babes in Arms.*

WHO, introduced by Marilyn Miller and Paul Frawley in *Sunny.*

WHY DO I LOVE YOU?, introduced by Norma Terris and Howard Marsh in *Show Boat.*

WHY WAS I BORN?, introduced by Helen Morgan in *Sweet Adeline.*

WILDFLOWER, introduced by Guy Robertson in *Wildflower.*

WILL YOU REMEMBER?, introduced by Peggy Wood and Charles Purcell in *Maytime.*

WISH YOU WERE HERE, introduced by Jack Cassidy in *Wish You Were Here.*

A WOMAN IS A SOMETIME THING, introduced by Edward Matthews in *Porgy and Bess.*

YACKA HULA, HICKEY DOOLA, by E. Ray Goetz, Jose Young, and Pete Wendling, introduced by Al Jolson in *Robinson Crusoe, Jr.,* an interpolation.

THE YANKEE DOODLE BOY, introduced by George M. Cohan in *Little Johnny Jones.*

YAMA-YAMA MAN, introduced by Bessie McCoy in *The Three Twins.*

YESTERDAYS, introduced by Fay Templeton in *Roberta.*

YOU ARE LOVE, introduced by Norma Terris and Howard Marsh in *Show Boat.*

YOU'D BE SURPRISED, by Irving Berlin, introduced by Eddie Cantor in *The Ziegfeld Follies* of 1919.

YOU DO SOMETHING TO ME, introduced by William Gaxton in *Fifty Million Frenchmen.*

YOU'LL NEVER WALK ALONE, introduced by Christine Johnson in *Carousel.*

YOU NAUGHTY, NAUGHTY MEN, by T. Kennick and G. Bicknell, introduced by Milly Cavendish in *The Black Crook.*

YOUNG AND FOOLISH, introduced by Gloria Marlowe and David Daniels in *Plain and Fancy.*

YOUNGER THAN SPRINGTIME, introduced by William Tabbert in *South Pacific*.

YOU'RE THE CREAM IN MY COFFEE, introduced by Jack Whiting in *Hold Everything*.

YOU'RE A GRAND OLD FLAG, introduced by George M. Cohan in *George Washington, Jr.*

YOU'RE HERE AND I'M HERE, introduced by Julia Sanderson in *The Girl from Utah*.

YOU'RE JUST IN LOVE, introduced by Ethel Merman and Russell Nype in *Call Me Madam*.

YOU'RE MY EVERYTHING, by Harry Warren, with lyrics by Mort Dixon and Joe Young, introduced by Jeanne Aubert and Lawrence Gray in *The Laugh Parade*, an interpolation.

YOU'RE AN OLD SMOOTHIE, by Richard Whiting with lyrics by Buddy de Sylva and Nacio Herb Brown, introduced by Ethel Merman and Jack Haley in *Take a Chance*.

YOU'RE THE TOP, introduced by Ethel Merman and William Gaxton in *Anything Goes*.

YOU TOOK ADVANTAGE OF ME, introduced by Alison Smith and Busby Berkeley in *Present Arms*.

YOU'VE GOT THAT THING, introduced by William Gaxton in *Fifty Million Frenchmen*.

ZING WENT THE STRINGS OF MY HEART, by James Hanley, introduced by Hal Le Roy and Eunice Healy in *Thumbs Up*.

# INDEX

*Note: Only those works not treated alphabetically in Part One are listed below. Persons listed include all performers, producers, and directors, but only those librettists, lyricists, and composers not listed alphabetically in Part Two.*